HANDBOOK ON ELECTRICITY MARKETS

Handbook on Electricity Markets

Edited by

Jean-Michel Glachant

Director, Florence School of Regulation, European University Institute, Italy

Paul L. Joskow

Elizabeth and James Killiam Professor of Economics and Management, Massachusetts Institute of Technology, USA

Michael G. Pollitt

Professor of Business Economics, Judge Business School, University of Cambridge, UK

Edward Elgar
PUBLISHING

Cheltenham, UK • Northampton, MA, USA

Published by
Edward Elgar Publishing Limited
The Lypiatts
15 Lansdown Road
Cheltenham
Glos GL50 2JA
UK

Edward Elgar Publishing, Inc.
William Pratt House
9 Dewey Court
Northampton
Massachusetts 01060
USA

Paperback edition 2023

A catalogue record for this book
is available from the British Library

Library of Congress Control Number: 2021946150

This book is available electronically in the **Elgar**online
Economics subject collection
http://dx.doi.org/10.4337/9781788979955

ISBN 978 1 78897 994 8 (cased)
ISBN 978 1 78897 995 5 (eBook)
ISBN 978 1 0353 1241 2 (paperback)

Typeset by Cheshire Typesetting Ltd, Cuddington, Cheshire
Printed and bound by CPI Group (UK) Ltd, Croydon, CR0 4YY

Contents

Contributors

Kenneth Anderson, appointed by Texas Governor Rick Perry in 2008, served over nine years on the three-member Public Utility Commission of Texas (PUCT), USA. Before his service on the PUCT, he worked on the senior staffs of two Texas governors, and for almost 20 years practised federal and state corporate and securities law, as well as federal and Texas political law. He received a bachelor's degree in international affairs from Georgetown University and a law degree from Southern Methodist University, USA.

Ross Baldick is Professor Emeritus in the Department of Electrical and Computer Engineering at the University of Texas at Austin, USA. He has undergraduate degrees from the University of Sydney, Australia, and graduate degrees from the University of California, Berkeley, USA. His current research involves optimization, economic theory and statistical analysis applied to electric power systems, particularly in the context of increased renewables and transmission. Dr Baldick is a Fellow of the Institute of Electrical and Electronics Engineers (IEEE) and the recipient of the 2015 IEEE PES Outstanding Power Engineering Educator Award.

Kathryne Cleary is a Senior Research Associate at Resources for the Future (RFF), Washington, DC, USA, and works on RFF's Future of Power Initiative. Her work focuses on wholesale market reform, electrification and decarbonization of the power sector. Kathryne graduated from the Yale School of Forestry and Environmental Studies, USA in May 2018 with a Master of Environmental Management focussing on energy policy. Her earlier experience includes private and public sector work in solar energy project development in Massachusetts and at the US Department of Energy.

Bentley C. Clinton is a Postdoctoral Associate with the MIT Energy Initiative, USA. His primary research focus is understanding the role that policy plays in driving the adoption of new energy technologies. Prior to his current role at MIT, Dr Clinton was a researcher with the National Renewable Energy Laboratory and a senior analyst at Analysis Group, specializing in issues of energy, environment and antitrust economics. He holds an MA and a PhD in Economics from the University of Colorado Boulder, USA.

Gabrielle Dyson is Energy Transition Consultant at Power Futures Lab at the University of Cape Town, South Africa, and an independent research specialist in energy and ecological economics. Gabrielle advises development organizations and writes on renewable energy, electrification, agro-food systems and inclusive development, with publications including titles such as 'What is the impact of investing in power? Practical thinking on investing for development', *Insight* (2020). Gabrielle holds a Master's in Nature, Society and Environmental Policy from the University of Oxford.

Anton Eberhard, Professor Emeritus at the University of Cape Town, South Africa, directs the Power Futures Lab at the Graduate School of Business. His work focuses on governance and regulatory incentives to improve utility performance, the political economy of power sector reform, power investment challenges, and linkages to electricity access and sustainable development. Anton has co-authored over 100 peer-reviewed publications, including three recent books: *Independent Power Projects in Sub-Saharan Africa*; *Power Sector Reform and Regulation in Africa*; and *Africa's Power Infrastructure: Investment, Integration and Efficiency*.

Mathilde Fajardy is a Research Associate in the Energy Policy Research Group at the University of Cambridge, UK, exploring decarbonization pathways for the heat sector in the UK. Mathilde holds a PhD in Environmental Policy and Process Systems Engineering from Imperial College London, where she studied the role of bioenergy with carbon capture and storage (BECCS) in mitigating climate change, and the implications of BECCS deployment on the water–land–energy nexus.

Carolyn Fischer holds joint appointments as Professor of Environmental Economics at the Vrije Universiteit Amsterdam, the Netherlands, and as holder of the Canada 150 Research Chair in Climate Economics, Innovation and Policy at the University of Ottawa. She is also a Senior Fellow with Resources for the Future (RFF), Washington, DC, USA, and with the European Institute on Economics and the Environment (EIEE), a Tinbergen Institute affiliate, a fellow of the CESifo Research Network and a member of Environment Canada's Economics and Environmental Policy Research Network.

Vivien Foster is Chief Economist for the Infrastructure Vice-Presidency of the World Bank, Washington, DC, USA where over the last 20 years she has been advising governments of more than 30 countries across the developing world. Vivien's policy-oriented research has been extensively published, including titles such as *Water, Electricity and the Poor*; *Africa's Infrastructure*; *Building Bridges*; and *Rethinking Power Sector Reform in the Developing World*. She is a graduate of Oxford University, holds a master's from Stanford University and a doctorate from University College London, all three in economics.

Jean-Michel Glachant is the Director of the Florence School of Regulation, European University Institute, Italy, and the Holder of the Loyola de Palacio Chair. He took his PhD in Economics at La Sorbonne in France, where he later became professor. He has been advisor to the European Commission and the French Energy Regulatory Commission (CRE). He has been coordinator and scientific advisor for several European research projects and editor-in-chief of *Economics of Energy & Environmental Policy* (EEEP). He is currently President-elect of the International Association for Energy Economics.

Richard Green is Professor of Sustainable Energy Business at Imperial College Business School, London. He was previously Professor of Energy Economics at the University of Birmingham and Professor of Economics at the University of Hull, having started his career at the Department of Applied Economics, University of Cambridge, UK. He has been working on the economics and regulation of electricity markets for over 30 years.

William W. Hogan is the Raymond Plank Research Professor of Global Energy Policy at the John F. Kennedy School of Government, Harvard University, USA. He is research director of the Harvard Electricity Policy Group (HEPG), which examines alternative strategies for a more competitive electricity market.

Grégoire Jacquot holds an MS in General Engineering from the Ecole des Mines de Paris, France, and an MS in Technology & Policy from MIT, USA. He is a graduate researcher at the MIT Energy Initiative and Institute for Data, Systems, and Society. He is also technical advisor to the French government on international development since 2018, and member of the executive board of off-grid solar companies since 2017. He held previous positions in academia and government in France and Sub-Saharan Africa.

Paul L. Joskow is Elizabeth and James Killian Professor of Economics at the Massachusetts Institute of Technology (MIT), USA, where he has been on the faculty since 1972. He was the head of the MIT Department of Economics from 1994 to 1998 and the Director of the MIT Center for Energy and Environmental Policy Research from 1999 to 2007. Professor Joskow was the president of the Alfred P. Sloan Foundation from 2008 to 2017. His recent research has focused on electricity sector restructuring, wholesale and retail pricing, energy storage and deep decarbonization.

Christopher R. Knittel is the George P. Shultz Professor of Applied Economics at the Sloan School of Management, Director of the Center for Energy and Environmental Policy Research, and Co-Director of the MITEI Low-Carbon Energy Center for Electric Power Systems Research at the Massachusetts Institute of Technology, USA. Professor Knittel received his MA in Economics from University of California, Davis and a PhD in Economics from University of California, Berkeley, USA. His research focuses on environmental economics, industrial organization and applied econometrics.

Chloé Le Coq is Professor of Economics at the University of Paris II (CRED), France, and Research Fellow at the Stockholm School of Economics (SITE), Sweden. Her research investigates issues related to antitrust policy, industrial organization. and experimental economics, with a particular focus on the energy markets and their regulation. She held visiting positions at the University of Purdue, University of California Energy Institute at Berkeley, USA, and National Singapore University.

Thomas-Olivier Léautier is Chief Economist and Director of the EDF Corporate University for Management and Associate Researcher at the Toulouse School of Economics, France. He has accumulated more than 20 years of experience in the electric industry, both as an academic (MIT and Toulouse School of Economics) and a practitioner (McKinsey & Company, Alcan Inc. and EDF).

Stephen Littlechild is Emeritus Professor (formerly Professor of Commerce) at the University of Birmingham, UK. He was UK Director General of Electricity Supply 1990–1998. He is also a Fellow of the Cambridge Judge Business School and Associate of the Energy Policy Research Group, University of Cambridge, UK.

Nils May was a Senior Researcher in DIW Berlin's Climate Policy Department, Germany and recently moved to the German Finance Ministry. He analyses renewable energy investments, inferring how policies and industry sourcing renewables can work together to enable investments and help firms to lower emissions. Both at a European and a global level, Nils looks at how international climate finance can support climate change mitigation action. He holds a PhD from the DIW Graduate Center and TU Berlin, studied in Norway, the USA, Germany and China and worked at IT company SAP.

Konstantinos Metaxoglou is Associate Professor in the Economics Department at Carleton University, Canada. He joined the faculty at Carleton as Assistant Professor in 2013, having previously worked as a senior consultant and manager with the antitrust practice of Bates White LLC. His research focuses on econometrics, applied industrial organization, energy economics, environmental economics and empirical finance. Metaxoglou earned his PhD in Economics from the University of California, Davis, USA.

Divyam Nagpal holds an MSc in Sustainable Energy Futures (Imperial College London) and is a Doctor of Public Administration candidate (University College London), in the UK. He is a Programme Officer for Energy Access with the International Renewable Energy Agency (IRENA). Previously, he was a member of the research team at the MIT Energy Initiative, supporting the Global Commission to End Energy Poverty, and worked as energy access consultant with the International Renewable Energy Agency, GIZ, ICIMOD (Nepal) and REN21. Previous positions include in intergovernmental agencies and the private sector in the UAE, the UK and India.

Karsten Neuhoff leads the Climate Policy Department at the German Institute for Economic Research (DIW Berlin) and is Professor at the TU Berlin. He holds a PhD in Economics from Cambridge University, UK. His research focuses on how policies and markets can be designed to achieve carbon neutrality in the power, industry and building sectors. He (co-) authored dozens of research articles, policy briefs and, *inter alia*, the book *Planetary Economics: Energy, Climate Change and the Three Domains of Sustainable Development*.

David Newbery, CBE, FBA, Director of the Energy Policy Research Group and Emeritus Professor, University of Cambridge, UK, was educated at Cambridge in mathematics and economics, research projects on utility privatization and regulation, road pricing, transition in Central Europe, electricity restructuring and market design, transmission pricing, market integration, climate policies, and the economics of zero-carbon electricity. He is currently an independent member of the Single Electricity Market Committee of the Republic of Ireland. His books include *Privatization, Restructuring and Regulation of Network Utilities*.

Shmuel S. Oren is Professor of the Graduate School and the Earl J. Isaac Chair Professor in Industrial Engineering and Operations Research at UC Berkeley, USA. He is a co-founder and the Berkeley site director of PSerc, a multi-university Power Systems Research Center. He was a Senior Adviser to the Market Oversight Division of the Public

Utility Commission of Texas (PUCT) and served as a member of the California Independent System Operator (CAISO) Market Surveillance Committee. He holds a PhD from Stanford University, is an Institute of Electrical and Electronics Engineers (IEEE) Life Fellow, Institute for Operations Research and the Management Sciences (INFORMS) Fellow and member of the US National Academy of Engineering.

Karen Palmer is a Senior Fellow and Director of the Electric Power Program at Resources for the Future, Washington, DC, USA. Dr Palmer specializes in the economics of environmental regulation and public utility regulation, particularly on issues at the intersection of climate policy and electricity. In the 1990s, Dr Palmer was a visiting economist in the Office of Economic Policy at the Federal Energy Regulatory Commission. She was elected as a Fellow of the Association of Environmental and Resource Economists in 2018.

Ignacio J. Pérez-Arriaga holds an MS and PhD in Electrical Engineering from MIT, USA and an electrical engineering degree from Comillas University, Spain. He is a visiting professor at MIT since 2008, professor at the Institute for Research in Technology (IIT, Comillas) since 1981 and training director at the Florence School of Regulation, Italy since 2004. Former commissioner in Spain and Ireland and former member of the Board of Appeal of the European Union Agency for the Cooperation of Energy Regulators (ACER), he is a life member of the Spanish Engineering Royal Academy and an Institute of Electrical and Electronics Engineers (IEEE) Fellow. He has been advisor to institutions and governments in about 40 countries. He currently works on planning, and design of business models and regulatory frameworks for electrification in developing countries.

Michael G. Pollitt is Professor of Business Economics and Assistant Director of the Energy Policy Research Group (EPRG) at Judge Business School, University of Cambridge, UK. Michael is a Fellow in Economics and Management at Sidney Sussex College, Cambridge, and has particular research interests in the future of electricity markets and electricity networks under deep decarbonization. He has published 12 books and over 90 refereed journal articles on efficiency analysis, energy policy and business ethics. He is currently a vice-president of the International Association for Energy Economics (IAEE).

David M. Reiner is University Senior Lecturer in Technology Policy at Judge Business School, University of Cambridge and Assistant Director of the Energy Policy Research Group (EPRG) at Cambridge, UK. His research focuses on energy and climate change politics, policy, economics, regulation and public attitudes, with a focus on social licence to operate for energy technologies. He is currently leading projects on reducing emissions from energy-intensive industries, decarbonizing the heat and electricity sectors and on greenhouse gas removal technologies.

Fabien Roques is Associate Professor at University Paris Dauphine, France and the Florence School of Regulation, Italy and Executive Vice-President with the economics consultancy Compass Lexecon. Fabien is a regular contributor to academic and professional journals on economic issues related to the energy industry. His research focusses on the evolution of electricity, gas and emissions trading market design and regulation in Europe and globally.

Richard Schmalensee is Howard W. Johnson Professor of Management Emeritus and Professor of Economics Emeritus at MIT, USA. He has served as Dean of the MIT Sloan School of Management, and from 1989 to 1991 he was the member of the President's Council of Economic Advisers with responsibility for energy and environmental policy. Professor Schmalensee is a Fellow of the Econometric Society, a Member of the American Academy of Arts and Sciences, and a Director of the National Bureau of Economic Research.

Eric S. Schubert covered policy and regulatory issues in US power markets for BP for more than a decade. Before working at BP, Dr Schubert spent eight years at the Public Utility Commission of Texas (PUCT) where he was project leader in PUCT rulemakings on wholesale (nodal) market design, resource adequacy and renewables. Dr Schubert also worked at the Chicago Board of Trade and Bankers Trust Company earlier in his career. He earned his PhD in Economics at the University of Illinois at Urbana-Champaign.

Sebastian Schwenen is Assistant Professor at the Technical University of Munich, School of Management, and Research Fellow at the German Institute for Economic Research (DIW) Berlin and at the Mannheim Institute for Sustainable Energy Studies (MISES), Germany. His research fields are energy economics, industrial organization and applied econometrics, with a focus on market design and regulation.

Paul Simshauser, AM, is a Professor of Economics at the Centre for Applied Energy Economics & Policy Research, Griffith University, and the Chief Executive Officer of Powerlink Queensland, one of Australia's largest electricity utilities. He is also a Research Associate at the Energy Policy Research Group, University of Cambridge, UK. Paul has a PhD in Economics from the University of Queensland and a Master of Commerce from Griffith University. In 2019, he was awarded a Member of the Order of Australia for significant contribution to the energy industry through executive roles and applied economics and policy research.

Fereidoon Sioshansi is President of Menlo Energy Economics, a consulting firm based in San Francisco, California, USA, advising clients on strategies in the transformation of the electric power business. He is the editor and publisher of *EEnergy Informer*, a monthly newsletter. His professional experience includes working at Southern California Edison Co., Electric Power Research Institute, National Economics Research Associates (NERA) and Global Energy Decisions. Since 2006, he has edited 13 books including *Behind and Beyond the Meter* (2020) and *Consumer, Prosumer, Prosumager* (2019).

Robert Stoner is the Deputy Director for Science and Technology of the MIT Energy Initiative, Founding Director of the MIT Tata Center for Technology and Design, and Faculty Co-Director of the MIT Electric Power Systems Center, USA. He is currently a member of the MIT Energy Council and the Science and Technology Committee of the

US National Renewable Energy Laboratory (NREL). He earned his bachelor's degree in engineering physics from Queen's University, Canada and PhD from Brown University, USA in condensed matter physics.

Frank A. Wolak is the Holbrook Working Professor of Commodity Price Studies in the Department of Economics and the Director of the Program on Energy and Sustainable Development at Stanford University, USA. His current research and teaching focus on design, performance and monitoring of energy and environmental markets. He served as Chair of the Market Surveillance Committee (MSC) of the California Independent System Operator and was a member of the Emissions Market Advisory Committee (EMAC) for California's Market for Greenhouse Gas Emissions allowances.

Xu Yi-chong is Fellow of the Academy of the Social Sciences of Australia (FASSA), and Professor of Government and International Relations at Griffith University, Australia. Xu is author of several books, including *Powering China*; *Electricity Reform in China, India and Russia*; *The Politics of Nuclear Energy in China*; and *Sinews of Power: The Politics of the State Grid Corporation of China*.

Acknowledgements

The editors owe several substantial debts of gratitude in the bringing together of this handbook. First, we are very grateful to the International Association for Energy Economics (IAEE) for first bringing us together as founding editors of their *Economics of Energy & Environmental Policy* (EEEP) journal. This was a wonderful experience setting up a new journal in 2012, on which we worked for five years.

Second, the editors wish to thank the many distinguished authors who contributed to the 21 original chapters of this handbook. Their chapters showcase the vast amount of global learning that has occurred on electricity markets since electricity markets become a reality in the 1980s. The willingness with which they participated in this handbook and their good nature in revising their chapters is a testament to the lively and well-connected community of scholars who work on electricity market reforms.

Third, we wish to acknowledge the generous support given towards this volume by the Florence School of Regulation (FSR) at the European University Institute, who funded the editorial assistance we have received.

Finally, the editors of the handbook wish to acknowledge the wonderful support that they have received from several young scholars and research assistants at the Florence School of Regulation. Nicolò Rossetto, Golnoush Soroush, Mara Radulescu and Elena Iorio did a tremendous job keeping in touch with our authors and copy-editing their contributions. Thank you all.

Jean-Michel Glachant
Paul L. Joskow
Michael G. Pollitt

1. Introduction to the *Handbook on Electricity Markets*

Jean-Michel Glachant, Paul L. Joskow and Michael G. Pollitt

The electric power industries in all countries have changed enormously over the roughly 140-year history of central station generation/transmission/distribution systems supplying electricity to the public. The evolution has reflected technological change on both the supply and demand sides, exploitation of economies of scale, environmental and other policy constraints, organizational and regulatory innovation, interest group politics and ideology.[1] This handbook focuses on the latest set of institutional changes to electric power sectors around the world that are generally captured by the phrases restructuring, competition, decarbonization and regulatory reform.

The contemporary restructuring of the electric power industry has involved: (1) the separation or unbundling of the previously (typically) vertically integrated – through common ownership or regulated long-term contracts – generation, transmission, distribution and retail supply segments of the industry; (2) the deconcentration of and free entry into the generation segment; (3) the reorganization of the transmission/system operations segment; and (4) the separation of the physical distribution (delivery) segment from the financial arrangements for retail supply of energy. These restructuring initiatives have been designed to enable competition between generators to supply energy, ancillary services and capacity in wholesale markets and to open retail supply to competition. Regulatory reform has been focused on actions to facilitate the efficient evolution of competition, to improve the performance of the remaining regulated monopoly segments of the industry and, most recently, to integrate efficiently intermittent wind and solar generation along with electricity storage, as electric power systems respond to constraints on greenhouse gas emissions.

Government policies and regulation have been particularly important in directing the design of wholesale markets, defining the obligations and behaviour of transmission owners and system operators, improving the performance of regulatory mechanisms that specify how transmission and distribution system owners and system operators are compensated, and guarding against anti-competitive behaviour in the newly competitive wholesale markets and retail supply segments. Policies designed to decarbonize the electricity sector by replacing fossil-fuel generation with zero carbon resources, primarily adding intermittent wind and solar generation along with storage, have created a new set of issues for system operation, wholesale market design, retail rate design, the investment framework for wind, solar and storage, reliability and other considerations. Electric power systems built around dispatchable, primarily thermal generation with capacity constraints are now evolving to manage systems with intermittent wind and solar generation at scale, energy storage and high levels of spot market price volatility as zero marginal operating cost intermittent resources penetrate these systems. Deep

1

decarbonization is transforming electric power systems from capacity-constrained systems to energy-constrained systems. This transition requires aggressive carbon emissions constraints with network reliability criteria.

Different countries, and even states and provinces within countries, have approached this basic restructuring programme in different ways. The first major initiative occurred in England and Wales starting in 1989.[2] Restructuring and competition initiatives in the US, Canada, Australia, the EU and other countries proceeded in the late 1990s and early 2000s. In most cases, early reforms have been followed with additional design and regulatory changes in response to problems that emerged during the reform process, lessons learned, new environmental policies, especially policies to respond to climate change, and the evolution of generation supply and storage technologies compatible with these environmental goals – wind, solar, storage, system operations and computing capabilities, energy efficiency and demand response. While the basic architecture of restructuring is similar across countries, states and provinces, there are significant differences in the details. And there are some countries and regions that have not restructured at all and continue to rely on traditional arrangements – for instance, large parts of the US and Canada.

This handbook brings together a wealth of expertise to look at both the current legacy state of power markets around the world (in Part I) and how those power markets can and should adapt to new low and zero carbon generation technologies, energy storage and the policy priorities that are driving their adoption (in Part II). In the rest of this introduction, we briefly summarize some of the key issues covered in the 21 chapters that follow this one.

PART I   TAKING STOCK: THE LEGACY

Chapter 2 by Richard Schmalensee discusses the strengths and weaknesses of the traditional institutional arrangements, outlined above, as they emerged following the First World War. The chapter also identifies some of the challenges to wholesale and retail markets and retail pricing associated with deep decarbonization of electricity supply and the associated reliance on intermittent wind and solar generation and energy storage as dispatchable fossil-fuel generation is replaced.

The handbook then turns to wholesale and retail market design, strengths and weaknesses of different approaches, and adaptations over time in several different countries and regions. There are many similarities between these market models, but also some important differences. The market models have all evolved in response to lessons learned from experience and to changes in public policies. While Part I of the handbook does not cover the market models adopted in all countries and regions, the range of wholesale and retail market design differences and adaptations to imperfections and public policy changes capture most of the variations that we see around the world.

Chapter 3 by Paul Joskow and Thomas-Olivier Léautier presents the basic theory of optimal investment and pricing at the bulk power or wholesale level for systems comprised primarily of dispatchable fossil-fuelled and nuclear thermal generating capacity. This theory can be traced back to the work of Marcel Boiteux, Ralph Turvey and others in the 1950s and 1960s. That work focused on optimal investment and optimal pricing for a centrally planned monopoly with dispatchable thermal generation at what we would now call the wholesale level.[3] However, this basic theory formed the basis for the initial design of competitive wholesale markets, essentially assuming a duality between optimal investment and pricing in a centrally planned system with price formation and investment in competitive wholesale markets. Whether and how this basic theory and its application to wholesale market design must be revised to account for deep decarbonization of the electricity sector with high levels of intermittent wind and solar generation and storage is the focus of Part II of this handbook.

Chapter 4 by Frank Wolak discusses the key design features of successful wholesale electricity markets in general. These include: (1) matching the wholesale market design and resulting generator dispatch and congestion management to the physical attributes of electric power systems; (2) market and regulatory mechanisms to govern the incentives for entry and exit of generators consistent with achieving long-term generation resource adequacy criteria; (3) horizontal market power concerns and mitigation mechanisms; and (4) mechanisms to integrate demand response into wholesale markets. The chapter also discusses issues that arise in small markets and developing country contexts. It concludes with a brief discussion of market design issues associated with the integration of grid-scale and distributed renewables – mainly wind and solar.

Chapter 5 by Stephen Littlechild discusses the development of competitive retail supply markets. The unbundling of physical delivery services (distribution) from the contractual arrangements defining how independent intermediaries can compete to arrange for and are compensated for the electricity consumed by retail customers is truly an innovation that departs from the historical responsibilities of local distribution companies both to deliver electricity and arrange for its supply (and be paid for them in return). Retail competition has been especially valuable for larger customers with interval meters, demand management capabilities and some on-site generation. Competitive electricity retail suppliers can offer contracts that give these customers better price signals and can integrate retail consumption and load management decisions with wholesale markets. Retail competition for residential and small commercial customers has been more controversial, though this may change as smart meters, real-time pricing, smart grid enhancements and individual customer utilization settlements protocols (rather than load profiles) are more widely deployed. The chapter starts by discussing early thinking about restructuring and competition during the 1980s. It goes on to analyse the creation of retail markets around the world during the 1990s and early 2000s. The concerns about and interventions in retail supply markets during the 2010s are presented next. Finally, Littlechild questions whether the concerns are justified and asks what might happen in the future.

The handbook then moves on to in-depth discussions of the details of wholesale market designs in specific countries or sub-regions of countries, their strengths and weaknesses, and their evolution in response to weaknesses and changes in public policies. Chapter 6 by David Newbery discusses the market model initially adopted in England and Wales and how it has changed over time. The chapter provides background information on the pre-restructuring (post-First World War) electricity sector in England and Wales and the motivations for privatization and restructuring for competition. The chapter then turns to a discussion of the post-restructuring ownership structure of generation, the design of the new wholesale market and the horizontal market power problems that emerged.

Dissatisfaction with the performance of the initial industry structure and market design led to deconcentration of generation ownership and major changes in wholesale market design, transforming the initial market into an energy-only market without capacity payments (NETA). We then learn why and how capacity markets and government-mandated procurement of carbon-free resources pursuant to long-term purchased power agreements were reintroduced to support resource adequacy goals and, more importantly, decarbonization goals. The chapter concludes with thoughts on the integration of carbon-free generation resources and potential future reforms.

Chapter 7 by William Hogan discusses the market model adopted by PJM Interconnection in the US. PJM covers all or portions of 13 US states located east of the Mississippi River. PJM is a regional transmission organization (RTO), though in the US context it makes sense to use RTO and ISO (independent system operator) interchangeably. PJM manages wholesale energy, ancillary services and capacity markets for most of the investor-owned utilities, generators and transmission owners in this region. Unlike in most European countries, the day-ahead markets are fully integrated with day-of markets and real-time operations. These markets are also fully integrated with the management of transmission constraints by relying on a security-constrained bid-based economic dispatch auction market design for energy and ancillary services dispatch and prices. This mechanism yields locational (nodal) prices that vary from location to location when transmission constraints are binding. The chapter starts with a history of PJM (originally just New Jersey and Pennsylvania), going back to its roots in the 1920s as a centrally dispatched power pool, to the reforms during the 1990s and the ultimate creation of the basic wholesale market framework that defines PJM today. The chapter goes on to discuss many of the details of the PJM market model, whose basic version has largely been adopted by the other ISOs/RTOs in the US. Interestingly, PJM includes states that have fully restructured to rely on competitive wholesale and retail competition as well as those that continue to rely on vertically integrated monopolies.

Chapter 8 by Ross Baldick, Shmuel Oren, Eric Schubert and Kenneth Anderson discusses the market model in the Electric Reliability Council of Texas (ERCOT) (covering most of Texas). The chapter places the restructuring programme in ERCOT in a fascinating historical, political and ideological context. Unlike PJM, ERCOT is a single-state ISO. Nor is ERCOT subject to Federal Energy Regulatory Commission (FERC) jurisdiction but rather to the jurisdiction of the Public Utility Commission of Texas (PUCT). As a result, state policies, ISO policies and market design features can be harmonized more easily than in multi-state ISOs, where each state is a stakeholder and federal and state policies, especially regarding efforts to decarbonize the electricity sector, often differ. ERCOT model also reflects a deep commitment to competition in the electricity sector by Texas policy makers. The chapter reviews the restructuring process in ERCOT, the goals for wholesale and retail markets, the evolution of the design of both and brings us up to date on current issues. Today, ERCOT wholesale markets have many similarities to the other ISO/RTO markets in the US. However, there is an important difference regarding how ERCOT handles resource adequacy. Unlike the other ISO/RTO markets, ERCOT does not have a capacity market or use a centralized market to allocate capacity obligations.[4] It does not establish forward capacity reserve requirements. Rather, ERCOT is an 'energy-only' market, though this simple phrase can be misleading. ERCOT model recognizes that for an electricity market to achieve an efficient long-run equilibrium and to achieve associated resource adequacy goals, energy prices must be allowed to rise to very high levels to reflect the value of lost load as capacity constraints begin to bind and the market must ration scarce capacity. To do that, ERCOT introduced an administratively determined operating reserve demand curve (ORDC) and associated protocols to manage generating capacity scarcity with a price mechanism. The ORDC is in turn based on assumptions about the value of lost load, loss of load probabilities and other variables. In ERCOT, energy prices can rise to 9000 $/MWh, the presumptive value of lost load. On the contrary, the other ISOs define capacity needs and use a capacity market to allocate responsibilities for paying for the needed generating capacity or demand response. These markets have price caps in response to concerns about market power in energy and ancillary services supply markets. The price caps are in the range of 1000–2500 $/MWh. The chapter describes nicely how these market design features evolved and how they work today. Texas also has abundant wind and solar resources and wind generation in particular grew early and rapidly. The chapter illuminates how ERCOT has managed the influx of intermittent generation, as well as a pragmatic application of central planning combined with competitive tenders to choose and select transmission projects to relieve congestion between the major wind generation region and load regions.

Chapter 9 by Paul Simshauser discusses the Australian market model. The chapter considers the design features of the National Electricity Market (NEM), retail competition, incentive regulation for transmission and distribution, the regulatory framework and adaptations to the rapid expansion of intermittent renewable energy. Unlike the markets that have been discussed so far, the NEM has no organized day-ahead market, though over-the-counter trades can be arranged day ahead and futures contracts can be bought and sold as well. There are no formal capacity obligations and no capacity market. Accordingly, the NEM is a real-time energy-only market with a high price cap (AU$15000/MWh 2020). The chapter goes on to discuss the challenges to efficiently integrate intermittent renewable energy supplies and, more generally, to align electricity markets with climate change policies. Recent reforms, their strengths and weaknesses are analysed.

Chapter 10 by Chloé Le Coq and Sebastian Schwenen discusses the Nordic power market that comprises the national markets of the Scandinavian countries. This market also includes trading arrangements with other countries with interconnections (Germany, the UK, the Netherlands and the Baltic countries). The chapter discusses the evolution and design features of Nord Pool, focusing on trading arrangements between the countries that are part of the Nordic market and the harmonization of differences between national markets. The chapter concludes with discussions of the adaptation of the Nordic market to decarbonization goals and security of supply issues.

Chapter 11 by Fabien Roques discusses the market models adopted in EU countries. There is no single market model that covers all the countries in the EU or, more precisely, the European internal market for electricity. Rather, there are a set of national markets with varying design features that follow EU guidance on certain attributes. The chapter explains that the European model for electricity markets has been shaped by successive laws and policy reforms. These have driven a degree of convergence in the designs of the various national (and regional) markets based on EU competition principles for the electricity sector. Beginning in the 1990s, the focus has been on creating an integrated

European market that supports efficient cross-border trade and competition. Unlike the US, where the RTO/ISO markets have 'centralized' day-ahead markets, day-of markets and integrated congestion management yielding locational price differences, EU markets typically have decentralized day-ahead markets and transmission congestion management. The chapter then emphasizes how policy priorities changed in the 2000s with the emergence of climate change and security of supply concerns. These changing policy priorities have led national markets to adopt their own rules, reversing the coordination trend. European electricity markets have evolved toward hybrid markets with a number of new features, including: (1) support mechanisms for clean technologies; (2) capacity mechanisms to address security of supply concerns; and (3) new planning processes to coordinate generation and grid development.

PART II   ADAPTING TO NEW TECHNOLOGIES AND NEW POLICY PRIORITIES

Part II shifts the focus from the current organization of the electricity supply sector to potential future developments. It does this by discussing the promising new technologies that are emerging and indeed scaling up on the supply and demand side (Chapters 12 and 13), the near- and further-term impacts of renewables and decarbonization on the design of the electricity market and its companies (Chapters 14–17), the potential for electrification of transport and heating (Chapters 18 and 19) and the issues facing the electricity sector beyond the Organisation for Economic Co-operation and Development (OECD) countries (Chapters 20–22).

The electricity system has been undergoing a remarkable technology transition since 2000. Large subsidies to both research and development, and to strategic roll-out, have resulted in more than half of all new capacity additions globally by MW[5] and by value being in renewable electricity in recent years. This is beginning to change the nature of electricity generation from being characterized by synchronous fossil-fuel generation (from coal, oil and natural gas) to one where both dispatchable renewable (for instance, biomass) and increasingly intermittent renewable (for instance, wind and solar) generation dominate additions of generation in OECD countries.

The nature of these generation technologies is discussed in Chapter 12 by Nils May and Karsten Neuhoff. They discuss the remarkable decline in the cost of both wind and solar generating capacity, which has seen these technologies reach cost parity with fossil fuels (especially with carbon pricing) in many jurisdictions, including in the developing world. May and Neuhoff analyse the prospects for onshore and offshore wind, solar photovoltaics (PV) and concentrating solar power, biomass, geothermal technologies and wave and tidal power within the electricity system. They note that challenges remain if these technologies are to rise to dominate the electricity system. These include local opposition to the siting of facilities, their intermittency (across the day and the season) and their high upfront financing costs. However, there is good reason to be optimistic of continuing technological progress and successful roll-out, especially where this is combined with market expansion, demand flexibility and storage.

Since the oil crisis of the 1970s, energy conservation and efficiency have been a policy priority in many jurisdictions. Recent developments with renewables on the supply side has refocused attention on demand side technologies to not only reduce demand (relative to business as usual) but also to make it more flexible. This is the focus of Chapter 13 by Fereidoon Sioshansi. Annual and peak electricity demand are now below peak levels in many OECD countries, partly because of slower industrial demand growth, the impact of more energy-efficient appliances, low-energy lighting and more recently the diffusion of prosumers – that is, consumers that self-generate (part of) of the electricity they consume by typically installing roof-top solar. Sioshansi discusses how self-generation, rising numbers of electric vehicles (EVs) and distributed batteries could add further – often behind-the-meter – flexibility to the electricity system and allow it to better match demand to intermittent electricity supply. He documents several nascent technologies such as ground source heat pumps and remote digital control technologies, which offer promising sources of local energy and supply and demand matching. While the timing of any mass take-up of demand-side technologies remains highly uncertain, it is clear that in densely populated cities, such technologies seem much less likely to be significant than in more sparsely populated regions where prosumagers – that is, prosumers with their own storage – might make economic sense.

Next, the attention turns to future changes to the market context in which electricity systems will be operating. A major driver of new technologies in electricity are policies that explicitly or implicitly promote decarbonization of the sector. This is the subject of Chapter 14 by Kathryne Cleary, Carolyn Fischer and Karen Palmer. The authors introduce and compare a range of policies that governments have been using to promote decarbonization. These include carbon taxation and trading mechanisms, renewables subsidies and portfolio standards, energy efficiency measures and policies targeting nuclear and coal. As the authors point out, these policies have very different levels of efficacy if the ultimate goal is decarbonization (early phase-out of existing nuclear power plants by pro-renewables governments, for instance, is a pro-carbon policy). Often, governments enact a range of policies simultaneously that conflict with one another and would benefit from policy rationalization (cap-and-trade plus renewables subsidy can result, for example, in more expensive decarbonization than is necessary). The authors conclude that putting a price on CO_2 emissions remains the most efficacious policy for decarbonization, while recognizing that other market failures such as those arising from myopia may justify policies to help investments in capital-intensive renewables and energy efficiency.

What impact will renewables have on the operation of electricity markets? The nearer-term effects of this are discussed in Chapter 15 by Richard Green. Green analyses how the rise in renewable energy supply (RES) will affect electricity market design. First, context is important. While some jurisdictions have seen large rises in their RES share in total production, globally low carbon electricity supply is dominated by hydro and nuclear. Biomass is also significant. However, it is the rise of intermittent RES that poses new challenges for the electricity system by shifting supply to when the wind and the sun are available. Rising intermittent supply will impact prices that will encourage demand to be more flexible. In turn, this will provide incentives for electrical energy storage investments and further investments in transmission interconnection capacity. Green suggests that in the medium term there is plenty of scope for the existing market design to accommodate rising RES shares in many jurisdictions.

Market design for electricity markets is not just about matching aggregate electrical energy supply and demand, it is about maintaining power quality at every node in real time as well. Thus, power markets must also procure voltage and constraint management services. This is the focus of Chapter 16 by Michael Pollitt, who discusses the extent to which increasingly distributed electricity generation from intermittent RES and locally flexible electricity demand (in the presence of storage and EVs) can be accommodated within the two benchmark market designs that we currently see in Europe and in the US (as exemplified by PJM). He discusses two contrasting visions of the future (drawing on ideas from Fred Schweppe and Ronald Coase, respectively): one where more use is made of spot granular power prices at the nodal or device level; and one where the system operator makes more use of longer-term flexible control contracts. Reflecting on the experience of the pricing and rationing of the Internet, he suggests that at very high levels of intermittent RES, a new future market design that combines price signals with non-price rationing of intermittent renewables that match device demand in priority order would seem to be more acceptable within many regulatory systems than pure price-based rationing.

The future of the electricity supply industry is not just a function of technology or market design but is also importantly determined by the success of the business models that the companies within it adopt. The future of various electricity business models is the focus of Chapter 17 by Jean-Michel Glachant. Glachant unpacks and distinguishes a range of different business models within both the competitive and regulated parts of the electricity supply sector. These include the business models being pursued by generators in onshore and offshore wind (for the many and for the few), solar PV at utility scale and on rooftops. These new business models also involve aggregators moving from retail into wholesale markets, peer-to-peer bypassing of conventional utilities and the emergence of behind-the-meter territories. In this changing environment, grid companies are facing regulatory pressures to adapt their business models. These include the need to focus on the cost-effectiveness/competitiveness of grid capacity additions and strong revenue incentives for quality of service. The author argues that this fundamentally changes their business model from 'fit-and-forget' asset owners to companies engaged in seeking asset-light innovations.

What are the prospects for the electrification of transport? This subject is addressed in Chapter 18 by Bentley Clinton, Christopher Knittel and Konstantinos Metaxoglou. Transport consumes a considerable amount of the world's fossil fuels and much of surface transport could in theory be electrified. The authors focus on the prospects for electric vehicles. Passenger cars consume 50 per cent of surface transport vehicle energy demand and recent technological developments have seen a take-off in sales of battery electric vehicles (BEVs) and plug-in hybrid electric vehicles (PHEVs). EVs have substantial challenges to overcome such as the current price of the batteries (around $200 per kWh storage in 2019), their range and the time taken to charge them. The authors show that many electricity systems could likely cope with 100 per cent penetration of BEVs in the time frame over which such a rise in penetration is likely (to 2040) but that EV life cycle economics remains challenging over the next ten years. Beyond passenger cars, electrification of buses and trucks remains at least as difficult in part due to the much higher battery capacity required. A key issue raised by transport electrification is the need to replace the lost transport fuel tax revenue.

What are the prospects for the electrification of residential and commercial heating and cooling? This is the issue discussed in Chapter 19 by Mathilde Fajardy and David Reiner.

The authors outline the scale of the heating challenge. Current global non-electrified heating demand is twice as much as current electricity demand: thus, the electrification of heating would significantly increase the demand for electricity. Worse than this, peak heating demand can be five times higher than peak electricity demand. Technologies do exist to decarbonize heating and cooling, including electric heat pumps, district heating, PV, green hydrogen from renewables via electrolysis or with blue hydrogen from natural gas with carbon capture and sequestration, and the use of biomass and biomethane. On the demand side, building energy efficiency and heating and cooling appliance efficiency can be increased. However, none of these routes to decarbonization are cheap or quick to implement. The authors conclude by showing that all major possible opportunities come with associated challenges (for example, more use of peak load pricing to encourage energy consumption shifting and storage poses challenges in public acceptability given energy poverty concerns).

We go on to examine the issues facing the electricity sector beyond OECD countries. Chapter 20 by Ignacio Pérez-Arriaga, Divyam Nagpal, Grégoire Jacquot and Robert Stoner focuses attention on the problem of how to achieve universal access to electricity. Despite extensive efforts to improve electricity access, 840 million of the world's population lacked access to electricity in 2017. The authors argue that the key to promoting electricity access is to empower local distribution grids, via what they call an integrated distribution framework (IDF). The chapter notes that traditional grid extension, mini-grids and stand-alone electricity systems can all play a role in providing access. The IDF approach is all about ensuring that the appropriate mix of access provision (and associated revenue recovery mechanisms) is employed within a local distribution company area to achieve near total electricity access, especially when the unserved are in increasingly difficult-to-reach areas. Countries such as Sierra Leone and Uganda are successfully extending access in this way. The authors conclude by suggesting that the IDF approach can improve on the current projection (in 2019) that 650 million people will still be without access to electricity in 2030.

China has emerged as the world's electricity super-power. In 2019, more than 27 per cent of the world's electricity was produced in China, only slightly less than the US and Europe combined. China's electricity sector has grown spectacularly since 2004, but it remains a state-owned and heavily regulated sector. Chapter 21 by Xu Yi-chong discusses the recent history of the Chinese electricity industry and its prospects for reform. The short-lived State Power Corporation (SPC) was broken up in 2002 to form two grid companies – State Grid Company of China (SGCC) and China Southern Grid (CSG) – five generation companies and four power service companies. While both final prices and generator prices remained heavily regulated following the 2002 reform, there were strong incentives to build new assets for both generators and grid companies. This underpinned the rapid growth of the sector. By 2015, this system had given rise to high costs and high prices, causing the government to embark on a new round of reform, introducing pilot provincial wholesale electricity markets and large reductions in the regulated prices. Recently, China has also sought to internationalize its electricity sector by buying up overseas electric utilities and by building power plants abroad, in line with its 'One Belt, One Road' initiative. The author concludes that the current contradiction between China's desire to participate in global electricity markets and its slowness in creating a domestic electricity market, is a function of China's unique history and the considerable influence of the Chinese Communist Party within the state-owned electricity system.

The final chapter focuses on Africa, where over half the population lacks access to electricity and consumption per capita is very low (although electricity production and consumption vary enormously between countries). Chapter 22 by Vivien Foster, Anton Eberhard and Gabrielle Dyson discusses the prospects for the electricity sector across Africa. The chapter begins by noting that things have been changing in the final years of the decade to 2020: Chinese investment in the power sector has been significant (in line with the previous chapter) and the prospects for solar power have improved enormously. Nonetheless, there are still great opportunities to improve regional power pools via more extensive transmission interconnection, in part to exploit the huge regional RES potential; in addition, access to electricity is on average still rather low – it was around 60 per cent in 2017 – because many choose not to connect to the grid due to cost, unreliability and lack of demand. Although some countries have shown notable improvements – Kenya went from an access rate of 22 per cent to 75 per cent between 2010 and 2018 – the lack of effective power sector reform often represents a key barrier to development. A lack of competition, private ownership and industry restructuring persists in many countries, leading to low prices (for those lucky enough to receive on-grid electricity), underinvestment and poor quality of service. The authors suggest that low-cost renewable technologies combined with innovative business models might allow poorly served African countries to avoid the need for expensive centralized grid expansions, spurring electrification despite (or indeed, because of) a lack of reform.

* * *

Together, the chapters of the handbook offer a global tour of an industry on which much of the world's hopes for decarbonizing the global energy system depend. We are very grateful to our authors for writing their chapters specifically for this book and hope their efforts provide food for thought and inspiration for what might be possible by way of power market developments in the coming years.

NOTES

1. For good histories of early developments in electricity supply, demand, organization and regulation for several countries, see Caron and Cardot (1991), Hughes (1983) and Klein (2008).
2. Chile, which unbundled generation, transmission and distribution in 1982, is sometimes identified as the first system to adopt these reforms. However, while Chile restructured and unbundled generation, transmission and distribution, its system remained highly regulated with relatively little real competition. The Electricity Act of 1982 has been amended three times (1999, 2004 and 2005) after major electricity shortages.
3. Optimal scheduling and the derivation of shadow prices for water stored behind dams in hydroelectric stations were developed in parallel.
4. California Independent System Operator (CAISO) is another exception since it has relied on a murky resource adequacy requirement protocol that requires load-serving entities to meet resource adequacy criteria specified by the California Public Utilities Commission.
5. See REN21 (2019, p. 33).

REFERENCES

Caron, F. and F. Cardot (1991), *Histoire de l'électricité en France: 1881–1918*, Paris: Fayard.

Hughes, T. P. (1983), *Networks of Power: Electrification in Western Society 1880–1930*, Baltimore, MD: Johns Hopkins University Press.

Klein, M. (2008), *The Power Makers: Steam, Electricity and the Men Who Invented Modern America*, New York: Bloomsbury Press.

REN21 (2019), *Renewables Global Status Report 2019*, Paris: REN21 Secretariat.

PART I

TAKING STOCK: THE LEGACY

2. Strengths and weaknesses of traditional arrangements for electricity supply

*Richard Schmalensee**

1. INTRODUCTION

Prior to the worldwide wave of restructuring that began in the 1990s,[1] electricity supply industries (ESIs) differed substantially between nations and even within them. As Section 2 of this chapter describes, the extent of ownership by various levels of governments and cooperative institutions varied widely, as did the regulatory regimes faced by investor-owned enterprises. A common feature of these traditional arrangements, though, was the lack of reliance on markets, and a central focus of restructuring was to increase the role of markets and decrease the role of administrative decision-making.

To assess strengths and weaknesses of traditional arrangements, a benchmark is required. Prior to restructuring, studies of the performance of ESIs often implicitly used various ideals as benchmarks, and the focus was on how far ESI performance fell short of the ideal. Restructuring has enabled a more operationally relevant set of comparisons, and Section 3 of this chapter describes a generic post-restructured ESI that will serve here as such a benchmark.

Section 3 also introduces the distinction between the *historical* regime, in which, to a first approximation, all generation technologies are dispatchable and government policy is technology-neutral, and the *emerging* regime, in which variable energy resources (VERs), primarily wind and solar generation, and the policies that support them play an increasingly important role.

The historical regime is the focus of Part I of this handbook. That regime describes the pre-restructuring world everywhere, and it still describes some regions well. It is the regime for which restructured institutions were initially designed. Chapter 3 considers optimal pricing and investment in electricity generation in this regime, Chapter 4 describes what is required in practice for post-restructuring wholesale power markets to work well, Chapter 5 examines retail competition in this regime, while Chapters 6 to 11 provide country studies of restructured ESIs. Section 4 of this chapter provides a broad-brush assessment of the relative strengths and weaknesses of traditional arrangements for electricity supply in the historical regime.

Part II of this handbook focuses on the emerging regime, in which VERs and the policies that support them have become important enough to have material effects on energy market operations and investment decisions. Chapter 12 describes the new electricity supply technologies involved in that regime and Chapter 15 examines operational problems posed by high penetration of VER technologies. Chapter 16 considers implications for market design in restructured ESIs. Section 5, below, attempts to shed some light on the relative strengths and weaknesses of traditional arrangements for electricity supply in the emerging regime.

13

Because, as Section 3 discusses, some areas in the US have been restructured and some have not, and some areas in the country are well described by the historical regime and others are not, comparisons within the US hold a range of institutional and economic factors roughly constant. Consequently, I emphasize evidence from the US in both Section 4 and Section 5. Since there is no US experience with systems in which VERs are dominant, however, the discussion in Section 5 is necessarily more speculative than that in Section 4. It draws on informal comparisons between two US states in which VERs are already important and there are statutory commitments to carbon-free ESIs by 2045: Hawaii, where traditional arrangements persist, and California, one of the earliest states to restructure. Section 6 provides a brief summary of the main conclusions and some of their apparent implications.

2.   TRADITIONAL ARRANGEMENTS

The first institutions supplying electricity in the late nineteenth century were generally private, vertically integrated firms serving a single city or part thereof.[2] These enterprises were subject to supervision of various sorts by city governments as a condition for the right to use public rights-of-way for the poles and wires of their distribution systems. After the very early years, enterprises engaged in electricity supply generally became larger, and their geographic scope expanded in response to economies of scale in generation, the development of high-voltage transmission and growth in electricity demand.

By the early 1950s, the basic technology of electricity supply had diffused broadly, but a wide variety of institutional structures had emerged, with mixtures of private ownership and government ownership at national, regional and local levels. In many countries, the institutional structures of ESIs endured until the early 1990s, on the eve of restructuring.[3] At that time, some countries, including France, Italy, the Republic of Ireland and Greece, were served by a single, integrated utility owned by the national government. In the UK, by contrast, when the Electricity Act of 1947 nationalized over 500 ESI organizations, it consolidated them into what became the Central Electricity Generating Board (CEGB), responsible for generation and long-distance transmission, and 14 area electricity boards, which acquired bulk supplies of electricity from the CEGB and distributed it in their areas. In Germany, a small number of integrated regional generation and transmission companies co-existed with many municipal distributors. The Japanese system was dominated by ten private firms with regional monopolies, while municipalities played a central role in Norway. Vertical integration was the rule rather than the exception everywhere, organized wholesale power markets did not exist and retail customers had only a single source of supply.

The ESI in US in the early 1990s involved a complicated mixture of private ownership and public ownership at various levels of government that had remained fairly stable since the early 1950s.[4] State regulation of investor-owned utilities spread after 1910 as firms' service areas grew. In the 1920s and 1930s, the issue of public versus private ownership of distribution utilities was put to a vote in many municipalities, but by the 1960s few elections were being held on this issue (Schap 1986). The federal role in regulation and generation expanded substantially in the 1930s, and federal policies were enacted that favoured municipal and cooperative utilities.

In the US by 1994, 250 investor-owned utilities, generally vertically integrated into generation, transmission and distribution, accounted for 76.2 per cent of kilowatt-hour (kWh) sales to ultimate customers, 2015 utilities owned by federal, state and local governments accounted for 16 per cent and 939 cooperatives accounted for the remaining 7.8 per cent (US Energy Information Administration [US EIA] 1995). One state, Hawaii, had only investor-owned utilities, while another one, Nebraska, had no investor-owned utilities. Most cooperative and publicly owned enterprises were relatively small distribution-only utilities, but the federally owned Tennessee Valley Authority (TVA) has long been the largest utility in the nation as measured by generation,[5] while the city-owned Los Angeles Department of Water and Power provided electricity to around 3.5 million people.

Trading electric energy seems to have been more important in the US than in most other countries around the world, probably in part because the number and diversity of industry participants made potential gains from trade unusually large. There were two sorts of wholesale transactions (lightly) regulated at the federal level. Large utilities entered into requirements contracts that obliged them to meet the demands of publicly owned (typically municipal) or cooperative utilities that had little or no generation capacity. In addition, vertically integrated firms made so-called coordination sales to each other to reduce costs, in some regions through organized power pools. Some 'tight' power pools engaged in central dispatch, running the generating units of all member companies and attempting to minimize total pool cost. In these cases, cost savings were allocated to pool participants by formula; there were no market prices.

The Public Utilities Regulatory Policies Act (PURPA) of 1978 and the Energy Policy Act of 1992 opened the door to wholesale sales by non-utility generators in the US. But by 1996, when restructuring began, such independent power producers accounted for less than 2 per cent of total net generation (US EIA 2003). Thus, in the US, as elsewhere, vertical integration was the rule rather than the exception and, while there was some inter-utility coordination and the beginnings of wholesale competition, organized wholesale markets did not exist.

Traditionally, regulated and publicly owned electric utilities charged retail prices that were constant over time and thus did not reflect changes in system marginal cost. Prices were generally the same throughout each utility's service area for customers in each of a few classes and thus did not reflect locational differences in the cost of service. Finally, retail tariffs typically had only nominal fixed charges and thus recovered almost all fixed costs though volumetric prices. Most customers had no choice of retail supplier and most had meters that were read infrequently – typically once a month in the US.

3.   RESTRUCTURED ALTERNATIVES

The post-1990 restructuring of ESIs around the world had a variety of motivations, including raising revenue by selling government-owned assets, started from a variety of traditional institutional structures and, as this handbook indicates, produced a variety of institutional arrangements and market designs.[6] In the US, ESI restructuring followed on the heels of a remarkable period of deregulation and regulatory reform in several important industries.[7] Globally, ESI restructuring had two main dimensions.

First, in many nations, much or all of the generation segment of the industry was privatized. This was not the case in the US, where most of the ESI was already investor owned, interest in privatizing municipal electric utilities had waned, and Republican resistance to privatization of the federal utilities from which their constituents disproportionately benefitted was fierce (Schmalensee 2016b). Globally, privatization emerged in the 1990s as a broadly applicable policy tool within and beyond the electric power sector. Privatization has been well studied and it has generally been found to improve enterprise efficiency, particularly where a truly hard budget constraint has been imposed by effective competition (Megginson and Netter 2001, Vickers and Yarrow 1988). Because privatization has been well studied and because its effects on ESI structure have varied substantially among nations, I will not consider it further.

Second, ESI restructuring greatly increased the roles of competition and organized markets. It is generally recognized that transmission is a natural monopoly, so transmission systems must be planned and managed as unitary systems by non-profit or regulated entities – independent system operators (ISOs) and regional transmission organizations (RTOs) in the US and transmission system operators (TSOs) in the EU – though ownership of transmission assets may be centralized or distributed.[8] This change has created opportunities, recognized by the US Federal Energy Regulatory Commission (US FERC) in its Order 1000 in 2011, for competition of various sorts in transmission investment. Distribution systems are also generally treated as natural monopolies, and the wires and associated equipment are either government owned or managed by regulated investor-owned utilities. Restructuring in the US has not made significant changes in the role of competition in transmission procurement or in the physical delivery of electricity to ultimate customers in most of the country (Joskow 2019b).[9]

The major change in the role of markets in restructured ESIs has been in generation. All have adopted one form or another of an organized wholesale market for electric energy.[10] Such markets meet about two-thirds of demand in the US and serve all EU Member States and some other nations. To ensure that firms that own both generation and transmission assets are not advantaged in competition in these markets, most (and perhaps all) restructured ESIs have imposed some sort of separation between the ownership of generation plants and the operation of transmission facilities. In some cases, divestiture and separate ownership have been required; in others, administrative separation with some supervision of behaviour has been deemed to be sufficient. Ownership of generating plants was often restructured horizontally as well to reduce concentration in the interest of effective wholesale market competition.

Wholesale markets for electric energy were expected to play a key role, analogous to the role played by central dispatch in tight power pools in the US, in ensuring the efficient supply of energy from existing assets. The good news is that competitive markets provide higher-powered incentives for efficiency than either regulation or government ownership. Before restructuring, regulation generally adjusted retail prices to keep profits within bounds, though often with lags (Joskow 1974), while government enterprises rarely had absolutely hard budget constraints. In both cases, slack in the budget constraint reflected in part the fact that utility managers had better information than those who were charged with supervising them. The bad news is that unregulated or lightly regulated bulk power suppliers may have market power and have every incentive to exercise what power they have (see Chapter 4). Energy markets were also generally expected to play a central role in ensuring efficient investment in generating capacity, just as competition in output markets is assumed to induce efficient investment in most other sectors.

In distribution, the *delivery* function – that is, the construction and operation of the physical network – is universally performed either by a regulated investor-owned utility or a public enterprise, while the *supply* of electricity has been unbundled from delivery and opened to alternative vendors, mainly in regions with competitive bulk power markets (see Chapter 4).[11] Retail competition was introduced in New Zealand in 1999 and has been the stated goal in the EU since 2003, though the pace of implementation has varied among Member States (Council of European Energy Regulators [CEER] 2018, Morey and Kirsch 2016). In the US, 23 states allowed competition in electricity supply at one time or another, but ten states had repealed or suspended these programmes by late 2018 (Morey and Kirsch 2016, US EIA 2018). These structural changes represented shifts in the boundaries between public and investor-owned firms on the one hand and markets on the other, giving different answers to the questions originally posed by Coase (1937).

Particularly in the early days, economies of scale in generation and inelastic demand meant that reliance on markets instead of vertical integration would have carried a substantial risk of market power in the provision of an essential service. By the mid-1980s, however, the evidence on scale economies in generation suggested that competitive wholesale power markets were possible, at least in some regions.[12] The experience of power pools seems to have persuaded designers of restructured systems that competitive wholesale power markets could induce efficient supply from existing assets. Moreover, the designers of restructured systems, perhaps influenced by the pioneering work of Boiteux (1960, 1964) and Turvey (1968), seem generally to have assumed that competition in wholesale power markets could induce the efficient supply of long-lived generation assets.[13] Since generation traditionally accounted for 60–65 per cent of total ESI cost, more efficient generation could be expected to have a significant impact on the total cost of electricity and, presumably, on retail rates.

Competition in electricity *supply* at the retail level essentially involves only a financial relationship between the retail supplier and the customer. There are no changes in physical power flows and there do not appear to be substantial economies of scale, so the case for continued integration between supply and delivery was even weaker than the case for continued integration of generation and transmission. On the other hand, while distribution traditionally accounted for around 25 per cent of total ESI cost, most of distribution cost was attributable to delivery, not supply, and competing suppliers would all buy electricity, a commodity, in the same wholesale market. Thus, the scope for reductions in overall system cost from competition in supply would seem to be modest at best. Competition in supply would create some opportunities for innovation and differentiation, of course. In principle it could also lead to retail prices that varied over time with system marginal cost, but most residential meters at the time of restructuring were only read infrequently.

The following two sections compare in broad terms the strengths and weaknesses of traditional vertically integrated utilities with restructured ESIs in which markets, particularly wholesale power markets, play an important role. As noted above, I rely heavily on comparisons in the US, where both traditional and restructured arrangements have existed side by side.

Section 4 considers performance in the historical regime, in which VERs are unimportant. This regime existed everywhere before restructuring and still describes ESIs well in some regions in the US and elsewhere. Even though significant federal tax incentives favouring VERs have generally been in effect in the US since the early 1990s (Schmalensee 2010, 2012), as recently as 2014, wind and solar accounted for only 5.1 per cent of net generation in the US as a whole and only 4.6 per cent if California and Hawaii are excluded (US EIA 2016).[14] Policies favouring wind and solar generation had little impact on energy markets or generation investment in much of the US until quite recently.

In contrast, under the emerging regime, considered in Section 5 (and in detail in Part II of this handbook), VERs play a significant and growing role in electricity supply. In Germany, where government support for VERs via feed-in tariffs has been very important, wind and solar accounted for 28.8 per cent of generation in 2018 (Burger 2019). Some US states have provided strong support for VER generation, mainly through so-called renewable portfolio standards (RPS).[15] In California, one of the first US states to restructure, wind and solar accounted for 24.4 per cent of generation in 2018, of which 6.2 per cent was contributed by small-scale solar.[16] Wind and solar accounted for 16.2 per cent of 2018 generation in Hawaii, also a sunny state but one that has not restructured, of which 9.3 per cent was contributed by small-scale solar. Legislation commits both states to have carbon-free ESIs (by some definition) by 2045.

In these and some other US states, wind and solar now play important roles in generation, and government policies favouring these technologies thus have had important impacts on both energy markets and patterns of generation investment. While the original round of restructuring can be viewed as attempts to improve the performance of well-understood systems, under the emerging regime both traditional and restructured institutions have been tasked with transforming historical-regime ESIs into VER-dominated systems for which there is no operating experience.

4.   COMPARISONS IN THE HISTORICAL REGIME[17]

At the outset of the restructuring movement, participants seemed to expect that devising workable wholesale markets to guide operations of generation facilities would not be much more complex than simply replacing short-run system marginal cost with the spot market price.[18] After all, there had been many decades of experience building and operating vertically integrated ESIs under the traditional regime, and power engineering had ceased to be an exciting academic field. Restructuring in the traditional regime basically involved attempting to use competition rather than regulation or public ownership to improve performance of well-understood systems.

In the event, restructuring in the historical regime turned out to be much more complex than many expected. Elaborate rules for wholesale energy markets had to be developed over time. Markets had to be created for so-called ancillary services, including frequency regulation and various categories of reserves. In many areas, capacity markets or capacity requirements were added later to encourage adequate levels of investment in generation. Market power was a significant concern, particularly early on. The California electricity crisis of 2000–2001 provided a vivid example of the potential costs of a flawed market design (Borenstein 2002, Hogan 2002). It also stopped market-oriented ESI reform in the US in its tracks.

In the US and the EU, wholesale energy markets in ESIs are complex and evolving. For instance, the RTO PJM's website contains links to 34 manuals that describe the structure, operations and processes of its energy market,[19] while the most recent report of its independent market monitor makes 15 recommendations for changes in markets for energy, capacity and ancillary services (Monitoring Analytics 2019). Ahlqvist et al. (2018) and Chapters 6 to 11 in this handbook discuss the strengths and weaknesses of a number of complex energy market designs in restructured ESIs. In contrast, retail market regimes in the EU and various US states appear relatively simple and do not seem to have changed materially over time.

To assess the strengths and weaknesses of traditional arrangements in the historical regime, the remainder of this section considers evidence, mainly from the US, on the impacts of restructuring on (1) the cost and price of supply from existing generating facilities; (2) the level of generation capacity; and (3) the efficiency of prices charged to ultimate customers. For economic efficiency, the wholesale price should equal the minimized marginal cost of generation except during periods of shortage,[20] the stock of generation assets should minimize expected cost and provide an optimal level of reliability, and retail prices at the margin should equal the corresponding wholesale prices adjusted for any marginal transmission and distribution losses, with fixed costs and profits covered by fixed charges.

In principle, an overall assessment of the strengths and weaknesses of traditional arrangements should also consider the effects of restructuring on power quality (for example, departures from ideal voltages and frequency), reliability (for example, frequency and duration of outages), and the development and use of innovative technologies and practices. Data on power quality are not readily available, however. Outages at the bulk power level are too rare in modern systems to permit informative statistical analysis, and outages at the distribution level are mainly shaped by investment decisions (in particular, tree-trimming and undergrounding of lines) made by entities not generally affected by restructuring. Finally, data on the relative rates of adoption of new technologies (generally developed by vendors to ESIs) do not seem to be available. There is a brief discussion of the impact of retail competition on innovation in Section 4.3.

4.1 Generation Operations

In the US, direct comparisons of generating plants that were deregulated with those that were not has provided strong evidence that deregulation plus competition served to reduce generators' operating costs.[21] Davis and Wolfram (2012) found greater improvement in the performance of deregulated nuclear generating plants than in those that remained subject to conventional rate-of-return regulation. Fabrizio, Rose and Wolfram (2007) provided similar evidence for a broader set of plants. Cicala (2015) has shown that deregulated coal-fired generators reduced the cost of coal that they burn more than plants that were not deregulated. He does not find the same result for gas-fired plants, which he plausibly attributes to the fact that gas is a homogeneous commodity traded in relatively well-organized markets, making it easier for generators (and regulators) to identify the best price.

In an influential theoretical analysis of rate-of-return regulation, Averch and Johnson (1962) predicted that regulated utilities' costs would be higher than optimal because they had incentives to overuse capital relative to other inputs.[22] This article has been cited more than 3500 times, but most of the literature it spawned has been theoretical: before the deregulation of some US generating plants, it was hard to perform a clean test of the core Averch and Johnson prediction. Fowlie (2010) and Cicala (2015) were able to perform such tests and to confirm that prediction by showing that deregulated generating plants used less capital-intensive strategies than regulated or publicly owned plants to comply with environmental regulations that permitted alternative compliance strategies.

While, as noted above, there was trading between firms in the US ESI before restructuring, the development of organized ISO/RTO wholesale power markets seems to have dramatically increased both the volume of and gains from trade. Mansur and White (2012) showed that when a region in the Midwestern US joined the organized PJM market to the east, trade across the boundary that had separated these regions literally tripled overnight, with substantial efficiency gains. Cicala (2019) used the staggered introduction of wholesale markets across the US to identify the impacts of those markets on the allocation of generation among plants and found substantial cost savings at the system level from more efficient use of generation facilities.

All US wholesale markets have moved over time to pricing systems with considerable spatial granularity, following the nodal pricing scheme first proposed by Fred Schweppe and colleagues (1988).[23] Wolak (2011) analysed the transition to nodal pricing in California and found that it yielded substantial benefits.

The evidence in the preceding paragraphs seems to establish that restructuring and the introduction of formal bulk power markets reduced the cost of generating electricity from existing facilities. That is, traditional arrangements entailed costs that were higher than was feasible.

A concern early on in discussions of restructuring was that with privatization and deregulation, weak competition in bulk power markets might enable generators to capture any efficiency gains – and perhaps more – as monopoly rents (Joskow and Schmalensee 1983, Chapter 13). Because the demand for electricity at the wholesale level has generally been almost perfectly inelastic, when demand is high and available capacity is fully utilized, even relatively small strategic reductions in supply have the potential to produce large increases in price. Such exercises of market power have in fact been significant in some markets at some times, particularly in the early days of restructuring (see Chapter 4 in this handbook). The wholesale power market in England and Wales was initially set up as a duopoly and market prices were significantly above costs, though by less than traditional oligopoly models predicted (Wolfram 1999).[24] Structural changes made that market more competitive over time (Newbery 2005b), and market power seems no longer to be a major concern, at least in official circles (Ofgem 2018).

Market power was significant in the early days of restructuring (Mansur 2008) in the US, particularly in California (Borenstein, Bushnell and Wolak 2002, Joskow and Kahn 2002), and it played a role in the California energy crisis of 2000–2001 (Borenstein 2002, Hogan 2002). Some market power still exists in US bulk power markets, at least in some hours: Woerman (2018), for instance, finds that when the Electric Reliability Council of Texas (ERCOT) market is fragmented by transmission congestion, mark-ups over marginal cost rise, as predicted by oligopoly theory. All US wholesale power markets are now monitored for significant competitive problems (California Independent System Operator [CAISO] 2019a, Monitoring Analytics 2019, US FERC 2014), and most observers seem satisfied that departures from the competitive ideal are not more dramatic than those in most other real, imperfectly competitive markets.

Thus, while it seems clear that restructuring generally reduced the costs of electricity generation, it also seems plausible that departures of wholesale electricity prices from costs became somewhat larger than under traditional arrangements, which focused more on limiting profits than on controlling costs. Taking into account Oliver Williamson's (1968) observation that cost reductions produce welfare gains that dominate the losses produced by comparable departures of price from cost, and considering the available evidence, including efficiency gains from increased trading, it seems at least plausible that restructuring of ESIs has lowered wholesale electricity prices for fixed portfolios of generation assets, at least in the US and the UK, bringing them closer to minimized marginal cost on average.[25]

4.2 Generation Capacity

Restructured markets in the US generally had excess generating capacity at the time of restructuring (Borenstein and Bushnell 2015), so the provision of adequate investment incentives was not a pressing concern. Moreover, the existence of excess capacity seemed to some to confirm either the Averch and Johnson (1962) prediction that regulation would lead to excessive investment or the simpler notion that regulators were not very good at cost control. The designers of early post-restructuring bulk power markets, at least in the US and UK, seemed to believe that, as in other industries, profits from selling generators' outputs would provide efficient incentives for the supply of generation capacity.

In addition to creating internal or external market monitoring units to deal with the problem of market power, all US markets imposed caps on wholesale prices.[26] Price caps created another problem, however. Price caps that are below the value of lost load – that is, what customers would be willing to pay on the margin to avoid having their electricity consumption curtailed – create the so-called 'missing money' problem (Joskow 2007). It follows from the classic Boiteux (1960, 1964)/Turvey (1968) models that if price is capped below the value of lost load, competitive energy market revenues will be insufficient to cover the fixed costs of an efficient mix of generating assets.[27] Restructuring thus shifted the capacity risk from over-investment driving up rates to under-investment driving down reliability.

With the exception of Texas,[28] US electricity markets established price caps below most estimates of the value of lost load and over time put in place centralized or bilateral markets for capacity to supplement generators' energy market revenues.[29] Additional supplements include out-of-merit-order dispatch for reliability reasons and payments to generating units designated as 'reliability must run' to prevent their retirement (see, for instance, CAISO 2019a, pp. 207–16 and 264–5). These supplements to energy markets have become a very important source of revenue for generators. In the PJM market in 2018, for instance, capacity market revenue would have accounted for 47 per cent of total revenues for a new combustion turbine and 36 per cent for a new combined-cycle unit (Monitoring Analytics 2019, p. 329).

System operators outside the US were slower to add capacity markets or related mechanisms. After the UK committed in 2013 to adding a capacity market (Grubb and Newbery 2018), however, other EU Member States followed, and by mid-2015 nine of them had capacity mechanisms in place to supplement energy market revenues (European Commission 2016, p. 55). Chapter 11 in this handbook provides a more detailed discussion of the evolution of capacity mechanisms in the EU. There, Figure 11.6 is particularly informative.

Under traditional regulation, utilities' integrated resource plans, which took into account load forecasts, planned retirements and administratively determined reliability standards, would contain capacity requirements. If the new investments called for by these requirements were approved by regulators, utilities were (in principle at least) guaranteed to recover the costs involved, including a reasonable rate of return on investment. Post-restructuring capacity markets rest on similar administrative determinations of capacity requirements. In the US, the design of markets to procure the required capacity has not been straightforward and design changes have been common.[30] A particularly difficult issue has been determining appropriate penalties for non-availability during shortage conditions. These markets seem generally to have procured adequate capacity, at least in a period of relatively slow load growth, and to have encouraged the development of demand response aggregators, which provide demand reduction services to the wholesale market. Given the continued heavy role of administrative decision-making in this process, however, it is hard to argue that restructuring improved the efficiency of investment in generation capacity substantially or, indeed, at all, relative to traditional arrangements.

4.3   Retail Pricing

As one would predict, locational difference in competitive retail rates in the US reflect persistent locational differences in the wholesale prices that retail suppliers pay. There is also some evidence that retail competition is associated with greater (though not very great) penetration of pricing to all customer types that also reflects differences over time in marginal cost (Morey and Kirsch 2016).

In the US, large commercial and industrial consumers pushed hard for retail competition, and it is not surprising that they have generally been enthusiastic participants in active programmes (Morey and Kirsch 2016, US EIA 2012). When electricity is a substantial cost, firms can afford to monitor their electricity consumption and to shift their demand over time to reduce cost. If they can, in effect, buy at wholesale, perhaps with hedges against very high spot prices, they can benefit by shifting load to low-price periods. Large retailers, for instance, can cool their stores at night when wholesale rates are low, shut off air conditioning when prices rise in the morning and turn it on again when prices fall.

Even without retail choice, it seems that most commercial and industrial customers in the US have obtained increased access to time-of-use pricing over time. Wee and Coffman (2018) report that 260 utilities in 47 states offered such pricing in 2016, sometimes on a mandatory basis. Real-time pricing of some sort was offered by 36 utilities in 24 states, typically on an optional basis. Whether this pricing appropriately reflects changes in wholesale spot prices is, of course, another question.[31]

In the US residential sector, there is some evidence that retail competition has been associated with lower average rates, all else equal (Ros 2017). Nonetheless, there have been recent calls to abolish residential retail choice in several US states (Baldwin and Felder 2019). And, as noted above, ten states had already repealed or suspended these programmes by late 2018.

One of the reasons for this opposition may be that whatever the average benefit to households from retail competition, it is clear that there is a substantial variance. Electricity is a small fraction of most households' spending, and it would often not be worth much effort to save a small fraction of that small fraction by finding and switching to a supplier with lower rates, particularly when suppliers' offerings change over time. Not surprisingly, then, while some households find and enjoy good deals, many households are not active in retail markets and pay prices above the lowest on offer.

In most areas with retail choice in the US, the incumbent distribution utility is required to offer a default tariff, and consumers are required to take positive action if they wish to switch to another supplier.[32] One author has found that households in Massachusetts who had switched away from the default supplier were more likely to have lower incomes than non-switchers and paid higher prices on average (Baldwin 2018, 2019).[33]

In contrast, Hortaçsu, Madanizadeh and Puller (2017) found that in the early years of retail competition in ERCOT, households switching away from the default supplier were *less* likely to be low-income and paid lower prices, while the New Zealand Government similarly found that 'Lower-income households are especially likely to be among non-moving customers who unwittingly pay too much' (New Zealand Government 2019, p. 31). In the UK in 2018, as in several previous years, Ofgem found that 'More than half of currently non-price protected energy customer accounts are still on expensive default tariffs' (Ofgem 2018, p. 17). Ofgem went on to conclude that, 'For the least engaged, prices and quality outcomes are a source of concern' (ibid., p. 18). In September 2018, the UK Parliament put a cap on default tariffs to protect 'less active' consumers.[34]

In some areas in the US, households have had the option of paying a premium to buy from suppliers that purchase their power from 'green' generators, but these programmes have had only limited appeal (Morey and Kirsch 2016, pp. 29–30). Otherwise, apart from some vendors offering time-varying prices, there seems to have been only modest product differentiation in residential markets.

5.   THOUGHTS ON THE EMERGING REGIME FOR RENEWABLES

In the emerging regime, VERs, particularly wind and solar, account for a large and growing fraction of generation as public policy moves to decarbonize ESIs and support schemes for these technologies tilt the level playing field that prevailed for the most part in the traditional regime. The maximum output of a wind or solar generator is intermittent – variable and only imperfectly predictable in advance – and actual output can only be dispatched downward from its maximum. This intermittency and the fact that these generators have zero short-run marginal cost means that systems dominated by VERs will necessarily look different from systems in the historical regime (see Chapter 15 in this handbook for more on this). ESIs with traditional arrangements will have to solve those technical problems along with their regulators. Restructured ESIs will face another set of problems: how to modify market designs created for the historical regime to induce the adoption of efficient solutions to the new problems of the emerging regime.[35] As in the preceding section, I consider in turn (1) generation operations; (2) generation capacity; and (3) pricing at retail.

There is not much experience with the behaviour of traditional arrangements in the emerging regime and no formal studies of which I am aware that compare the performance of traditional and restructured ESIs in that regime. In the absence of more comprehensive evidence, I provide anecdotal evidence on similarities and differences between experience under traditional public utility regulation in Hawaii and a restructured system in California.[36] As noted above, both states are currently leaders in the US in reliance on wind and solar generation, and both are committed to carbon-free ESIs by 2045.

Both Hawaii and California have better solar resources than most US states, but they are very different from each other on other dimensions. Hawaii has a population of about 1.4 million, living on seven electrically isolated islands. One island is privately owned, has fewer than 100 residents and no power lines; five are served by a single investor-owned, regulated utility, the Hawaiian Electric Company (HECO); and one, with 4.7 per cent of the state's population, is served by a cooperative. Since 2006, new utility-scale generation capacity has been procured via competitive bidding, and a good deal of VER generation is now sold to HECO under power purchase agreements. Hawaii's push toward carbon-free electricity began in 2008, when 90 per cent of the state's electricity was generated with oil (National Renewable Energy Laboratory [NREL] 2018). California's population is much larger, about 39.7 million, and it has substantial transmission linkages to neighbouring states. California is mainly served by three investor-owned utilities and one municipal utility, the Los Angeles Department of Light and Power. California's first RPS legislation was passed in 2002, so it began the transformation of its much more complex ESI earlier than Hawaii.

5.1   Generation Operations

A very visible difference between energy markets in the historical and emerging regimes is the occasional appearance of zero and negative prices in the latter.[37] These reflect the incentives provided by the most common subsidy schemes and power purchase agreements, which reward VER generation whenever it occurs.[38] Under such schemes, renewable generators have a negative private marginal cost and bid accordingly, though their social marginal cost is zero. Baseload generators often operate during negative price periods, choosing to lose money on their production rather than to incur start-up and shutdown costs.[39] Of course, a vertically integrated firm would have the same incentive to run its renewables if it could receive per-kWh subsidies. And inflexible baseload generators would come under the same economic pressure in either structure because they have a much reduced role in VER-dominated power systems.

It is a happy coincidence that as public policies have increased intermittent VER penetration, battery storage that can help manage that intermittency has become cheaper, largely because of scale and learning economies induced by growth of electric vehicles. Storage in ESIs is nothing new, of course: vertically integrated utilities have used pumped hydro storage facilities for decades. However, it seems unlikely that pumped hydro capacity can be expanded sufficiently in most regions to cope with the increased supply-side volatility that follows increased VER penetration, and attention now centres on the use of batteries to help dampen price fluctuations.

In California, legislation passed in 2010 (Assembly Bill 2514) required large utilities to procure specified quantities of storage by 2022, while legislation passed in 2016 (Assembly Bill 2868) required procurement of distributed storage. California utilities have in fact acquired more than the required 1.3 GW of storage, but it appears that it has mainly been used in distribution systems and to supply ancillary services, not to manage VER-induced volatility. In February 2018, US FERC for the first time ordered RTOs and ISOs to adopt 'market rules that, recognizing the physical and operational characteristics of electric storage resources, facilitate their participation in the RTO/ISO markets' (US FERC 2018, p. 2).[40]

In contrast, the Hawaiian utility, HECO, has not been required to acquire battery storage, and its regulator has not had to develop the general rules for the use of storage that would be necessary in a restructured system. Instead, HECO has been able to gain its regulator's approval for a number of (relatively) large solar-plus-storage facilities. The developers of these projects are selected by competitive bidding and HECO generally procures their output under a power purchase agreement (HECO 2019a).[41] It seems to be much easier to get relatively novel facilities approved on a case-by-case basis to help satisfy a statutory requirement than to have multi-party agreement on general rules applicable to all such facilities – though this may just reflect the utility's greater information advantage in unfamiliar situations. Moreover, HECO will almost certainly continue to face lower-powered incentives for efficient use of storage than California market participants.

5.2 Generation Capacity

If most generation is wind or solar, with zero short-run marginal cost, the subsidy-free spot market energy price will often also be zero. Nonetheless, if wholesale prices are capped at the value of lost load, capacity markets are not necessary to provide incentives for efficient investment. The classic Boiteux/Turvey analysis of the economics of wholesale competition is still valid.[42] The Appendix provides a simple demonstration assuming a smooth demand curve; see Joskow and Tirole (2007) for a more general discussion. System operators have been extremely averse to high spot prices in the historical regime, however, and it is hard to imagine any being willing to live with the more severe high-price periods necessary to provide adequate investment incentives in a market in which the price is often zero.

Thus, it is almost certain that in the emerging regime, restructured ESIs will continue to rely on capacity mechanisms of one sort or another to supplement generators' energy market revenues and encourage investment. Unfortunately, the capacity market designs put in place under the historical regime are not well suited to meet the challenges of high, subsidized VER penetration.[43] When all generators are dispatchable, a market design that rewards promised availability in periods of system stress and imposes a penalty on units that are not available ex post makes perfect sense. Extending that design to intermittent generators is not straightforward, however (see Chapters 15 and 16 in this handbook for more on this). It seems reasonable to pay less for 1 megawatt (MW) of solar or wind nameplate capacity than for 1 MW of dispatchable capacity, but there is no obviously best way to determine how much less is appropriate in general or for units at specific sites. Moreover, since the actual capacity of wind and solar generators is heavily weather dependent, any formula will be wrong at some times. Similarly, it seems sensible to penalize an intermittent VER unit less for non-availability than a fossil unit, but it is not clear how to determine how much less is appropriate. Serious penalties for non-availability can cause VER developers to avoid capacity markets entirely and to rely exclusively on power purchase agreements with load-serving entities that have RPS obligations.[44]

US generators, VER based or not, that receive state subsidies are naturally advantaged in capacity markets. The US FERC has ordered ISOs and RTOs with capacity markets to redesign those markets to eliminate subsidy-driven advantages (GreenbergTraurig 2020). For markets covering a single state, this should pose no technical challenge, though some have objected that state subsidies may be legitimate attempts to mitigate externalities, and FERC's authority to overrule state policies is not clear. When markets cover multiple states, however, both technical and political complexities mount.

Finally, classic capacity markets reward baseload capacity as much as flexible capacity, but under high VER penetration flexible capacity is much more valuable. California has come to recognize this: since at least 2014, the California ISO has calculated annual requirements for levels of three types of flexible capacity and passed those requirements on to state regulators (CAISO 2019b). Of course, if gas combustion turbines are the cheapest way to provide such flexibility, this approach is inconsistent with California's goal of 100 per cent renewable generation. Going forward, it may be better to use variants of the technology-neutral 'operating reserve demand curve' pioneered in ERCOT (2014), perhaps with a tilt toward renewable generation, or some other innovative mechanism.

Under traditional institutional arrangements, when regulators have approved an investment, that investment normally earns a guaranteed rate of return. There is no need for formal rules distinguishing among different types of generating capacity or other investment; ultimate decisions are taken project by project. Per Averch and Johnson (1962) and the confirming evidence provided by Fowlie (2010) and Cicala (2015), this gives regulated utilities incentives to err in the direction of capital intensity. In 2016, HECO filed a 1972-page 'Power Improvement Plan', which had been revised at the regulator's request, which presented HECO's plans through 2021 and alternative pathways to become 100 per cent carbon free by 2045 (HECO 2016). This long-run system-level planning exercise was clearly informative and it is hard to believe that it could have been duplicated in a market-driven system. On the other hand, this plan moves into uncharted territory where the utility's information advantage over the Public Utility Commission (PUC) must be substantial. Accordingly, the PUC did not give up its project-by-project approval process. Unlike California, Hawaii has no formal flexible capacity requirement, but it is worth noting that its newest non-solar plant is designed for flexibility and to run on biodiesel (HECO 2018).

HECO's novel solution of a problem on the island of Molokai (population 7345) provides an interesting example of the behaviour of traditional institutions faced with unfamiliar problems. In 2015, HECO found that if it granted all pending applications for rooftop solar facilities on Molokai, the difference between demand and solar output would occasionally fall below the minimum output level of the diesel generator used to follow load on the island, causing the generator to trip off and the island to black out.

The novel solution, approved by the PUC, was to install a 'load bank', a dispatchable resistive load that transforms electric power into waste heat (Hawai'i Natural Energy Institute 2020). With the load bank in place, the moratorium on rooftop solar could be lifted. This seems a particularly capital-intensive solution and competition might have produced a lower-cost alternative. But setting the rules of the competition for solving such a novel problem might have delayed the outcome for several years.

5.3 Retail Pricing

Imelda, Fripp and Roberts (2018) argue that real-time pricing would not add much social value to Hawaii's current ESI but that it could substantially reduce the cost of moving to 100 per cent renewables by inducing load-shifting. The clearest example of what is possible there with existing technology for commercial and industrial customers is making ice when power is cheap on the margin and using that ice for cooling when power is expensive. While the quantitative results in this study are clearly specific to Hawaii, it seems apparent that regions in the emerging regime, including both California and Hawaii, would benefit substantially by transitioning toward rates that vary with system marginal cost.

It seems reasonable to hope that retail competition using smart meters and other new technologies that enable automatic response to price changes will significantly advance such a transition, but neither California nor Hawaii have retail choice at the individual customer level.[45] All non-residential customers in California are on time-of-use rates, but only Southern California Edison (SCE) offers a form of optional real-time pricing.[46] Time-of-use pricing will be the default for residential customers in California beginning in 2021, but some observers have argued that concerns that customers might opt for time-invariant rates has led to suppression of within-day rate differences in these tariffs, so that less load shifting will be induced than would be optimal. Time-of-use pricing is optional for all customers in Hawaii, but in 2019 HECO proposed an Advanced Rate Design Strategy involving transition to default time-of-use pricing by 2024, with dynamic pricing to follow (HECO 2019b).

California has moved more aggressively than Hawaii toward dynamic pricing, but neither have moved as aggressively as economists would prescribe. Regulators in both states seem similarly reluctant to impose major changes on consumers. It will be interesting to see whether this general resistance persists as system marginal costs and wholesale prices become more volatile in coming decades.

6. SOME TENTATIVE CONCLUSIONS

The available evidence suggests that in the historical regime, restructuring generally produced positive net benefits, at least after the difficult process of market design was largely worked through. The overall gap between the performance of traditional arrangements and feasible restructured alternatives does not seem to have been dramatic, however.

Restructuring reduced generation costs relative to traditional arrangements by providing stronger incentives and reduced transactions costs, and it seems unlikely that those gains have been erased by greater exercise of market power. While capacity risks seem to have shifted from excessive capacity under regulation to insufficient investment with reliance on markets, capacity markets and related devices seem to have reduced the risk of insufficient investment to tolerable levels, at least during a period of low load growth. As VER penetration has increased, administrative supervision has come to play a greater role in the provision of generation capacity in restructured systems, as under traditional arrangements. Efficient pricing at the wholesale level has not led to more efficient retail pricing for most US residential customers despite widespread deployment of smart meters, though large commercial and industrial customers seem to have had increasing access to tariffs that vary with marginal cost.

Today's restructured and traditional systems were both designed in and thus for the historical regime and are facing new challenges in the emerging regime in which VERs and the policies that support them are of substantial and growing importance. The designs of markets, particularly capacity markets, in restructured systems will need fundamental change. A comparison of California and Hawaii suggests that traditional systems have more flexibility, at least in principle, to meet the new challenges of the emerging regime in a timely fashion, since utilities and their regulators can engage in classic integrated resource planning and project-by-project decision-making without needing to devise, adopt and modify complex new market designs. On the other hand, in the new terrain of the emerging regime, the information advantage of utilities over regulators is likely to be substantial, regulatory processes are rarely speedy, and the flip side of greater flexibility may be higher costs and rates than could be attained under competition.

NOTES

* I am indebted to Severin Borenstein, Stephen Littlechild, Michael Roberts and the editors, especially Paul Joskow, for useful comments.

1. The law mandating Chile's restructuring was passed in 1986 under Pinochet, while restructuring in England and Wales began in 1989. Though it has received relatively little international attention, Norway's restructuring was both early (1991) and thorough; see International Energy Agency (IEA) (1994, pp. 259–68).

2. Before the London Power Company was established in 1925, the city was served by ten companies that used a variety of voltages and frequencies (see https://en.wikipedia.org/wiki/London_Power_Company, accessed 4 July 2021).

3. IEA (1994), on which this paragraph is based, provides a useful overview of the electric power sectors in OECD member countries circa 1992 as well as a good deal of historical information.

4. Schmalensee (2016b) discusses the institutional evolution of the US ESI. For a fairly detailed picture of the US ESI and its regulation in 1980, the essential features of which persisted through most of the 1990s, see Joskow and Schmalensee (1983, Chapter 2).

5. Like the other federal electric utilities, TVA sold (and sells) mainly to other utilities (primarily municipal utilities and cooperatives) rather than to ultimate customers.

6. On rent-seeking and other motivations for restructuring in the US, see Borenstein and Bushnell (2015) and Hogan (2002) and the references they cite. On the EU, see Newbery (2005a) and the references he cites. On the scope of ESI restructuring outside the US and the EU, see Jamasb et al. (2004) and for an illuminating example of restructuring in a developing nation, see Pollitt (2008).

7. See MacAvoy and Schmalensee (2014) for an overview of this period of deregulation and set of readings.

8. In the US, ISOs and RTOs manage but do not own the transmission systems in their regions. Similarly, they manage wholesale markets for electrical energy and various related ancillary services but do not own any generators. Both ISOs and RTOs – there is little difference between them – engage in regional planning of transmission systems, but individual US states must approve any new construction within their borders.

9. The main exception has been competitive selection of providers for the massive Competitive Renewable Energy Zones (CREZ) transmission project that connected wind-rich regions in west Texas with load centres in the east. Three non-incumbents were among those selected (Joskow 2019b). Competitive procurement of transmission has been the rule in Argentina since the 1990s (Pollitt 2008) and it has also been employed in Brazil and elsewhere in Latin America.

10. Ahlqvist, Holmberg and Tangerås (2018) provide a summary of the main differences between wholesale power markets in the US and the EU.

11. In the US, six states that did not have competition at the wholesale level (Arizona, Arkansas, Montana, Nevada, New Mexico and Oregon), nonetheless allowed retail competition for some customers for some periods.

12. See, for instance, Schmalensee and Golub (1984).

13. Joskow and Schmalensee (1983) seem to have implicitly accepted the view that the transition from power pools to competitive power markets would be straightforward, but argued that getting the right capital stock in place would require a regime built on long-term contracts.

14. These statistics include EIA estimates of generation from small-scale solar facilities.

15. Renewable portfolio standards (RPS) oblige load-serving entities to obtain specified fractions of the energy they sell via contract with generators in specified locations employing specified technologies; for a discussion, see Schmalensee (2012). It turns out that states that belong to organized bulk power markets are considerably more likely than others to have RPS.

16. Except as noted, the statistics in this paragraph are from US EIA (2019). Statistics for small-scale solar are EIA estimates.

17. Borenstein and Bushnell (2015) provide an overall assessment for the US, while Joskow (2008a) provides a more international discussion.

18. Joskow and Schmalensee (1983) devoted essentially no attention to the design of short-term markets for power, implicitly assuming that it would not be difficult to design them. The initial market design in England and Wales simply used dispatch software that had been employed by the vertically integrated CEGB (Newbery 2005b).

19. PJM Manuals, accessed 4 July 2021 at https://www.pjm.com/library/manuals.aspx.

20. On the need for electricity prices in periods of shortage to exceed the marginal cost of the highest cost generator dispatched to provide adequate incentives for generation investment, see Joskow and Tirole (2007) and Joskow (2019a).

21. Similarly, Newbery (2005b) found more substantial efficiency gains in England and Wales than in Scotland, where competition was less intense.

22. They assumed that regulators hold the regulated firm's rate of return on assets constant at all times. While this is clearly not descriptive of real US regulation (Joskow 1974), it was certainly plausible that because regulation was concerned with allowing an adequate return on assets, regulated firms would overuse capital relative to other inputs.

23. Hogan (2002) discusses this movement, which was far from smooth. Markets outside the US have been less receptive to nodal pricing; see Ahlqvist et al. (2018).

24. Wolfram (1999) suggested that long-term fixed-price commitments to distribution entities was one factor that served to moderate wholesale energy prices in the early days of UK restructuring. Mansur (2007), Bushnell, Mansur and Saravia (2008) and MacKay and Mercadal (2019) find evidence that vertical commitments had similar effects in US markets in the early years of restructuring.

25. This assessment is consistent with Joskow (2007) for the US and the cost–benefit study of Newbery and Pollitt (1997) for England and Wales. Borenstein and Bushnell (2015) provide a less positive assessment of US restructuring.

26. In addition, the US FERC (2016) has imposed caps on bids in wholesale energy markets that mainly focus on the recovery of short-run marginal cost.

27. For important generalizations of these classic models, see Joskow and Tirole (2007).

28. The reference here is to the Electric Reliability Council of Texas (ERCOT), the ISO that serves most of the state of Texas. It continues to operate an 'energy only' market with no payments for capacity, but since 2014 it has increased payments for generation above the market-clearing price as its reserve margin shrinks, following a so-called operating reserve demand curve (ERCOT 2014).

29. Since 2004, the California Public Utilities Commission (CPUC) has required all load-serving entities to have contracted for specified levels of capacity, thus establishing a set of bilateral capacity markets (CPUC n.d.). In the absence of transmission congestions, a single state-wide market would be more efficient (and transparent), but California is a large state and congestions do occur.

30. Joskow (2008b) discusses early capacity market designs; Spees, Newell and Pfeifenberger (2013) provide a more recent assessment.

31. For instance, Southern California Edison offers to large customers an optional real-time tariff in which energy prices are not directly linked to wholesale spot prices. Rather, this tariff offers time-of-use pricing

with six possible prices in each time interval, depending on system conditions. These prices are presumably more predictable than prices under classic real-time pricing, but they are, of course, less closely correlated with spot prices.

32. Texas is an exception: all customers served by investor-owned utilities in the ERCOT region are required to make a positive choice of supplier (Morey and Kirsch 2016, p. 4; see also Chapter 5 in this handbook).

33. Intelometry (n.d.) provides a critique of these studies but concludes that 'the issues raised by [Baldwin 2018] are serious enough that a more comprehensive review of this market may be warranted' (Intelometry n.d., p. 4).

34. Ofgem (n.d.), 'Check if the energy price cap affects you', accessed 4 July 2021 at https://www.ofgem.gov.uk/energy-price-caps/about-energy-price-caps.

35. Newbery et al. (2018) and Joskow (2019a) address these problems in the context of the EU and the US, respectively; see also IEA (2016) and Chapters 15 and 16 in this handbook. Pollitt and Anaya (2016) discuss market modifications under way in Germany, the UK and New York State.

36. Joskow (2019a) provides a very useful discussion of the California experience.

37. For the Belgian, French and German markets, see De Vos (2015). Schmalensee (2016a) finds negative prices for all the US markets except New England, which barred negative bids during his study period. For more recent experience in New England, see ISO New England (ISO-NE) (2019, pp. 68–70) and for California see CAISO (2019a, pp. 86–8).

38. Such schemes include feed-in tariffs, production tax credits and RPS that simply require fixed amounts of generation, with no restrictions on timing. Negative prices also reflect congestion in the transmission system, since at any time there is always some place on earth where incremental electricity would have positive value.

39. On the negative impact of subsidized renewables on the economic viability of baseload generators in California, see Bushnell and Novan (2018) and Joskow (2019a).

40. Writing about the EU, Newbery et al. (2018, p. 696) contend that the likely value of battery storage is relatively modest, but they note that 'The surrounding incentives and business models that will allow batteries to capture this value still need to be clarified'.

41. In contrast to most of the battery storage facilities built in California with three-hour batteries, HECO's generally include four-hour or five-hour batteries designed to operate during the entire evening peak. Storage that can be charged only by a solar facility, rather than from the grid, is treated as part of the facility and receives a 30 per cent federal tax credit. There is also a technical benefit from combining a battery and a solar generator: they can share a single inverter.

42. Under similar assumptions, competition also induces the optimal supply of storage under perfect foresight (Brown and Reichenberg 2020) or, in some cases, under risk neutrality (Schmalensee 2019).

43. Bushnell, Flagg and Mansur (2017) and Joskow (2019a) provide thoughtful discussions.

44. Some version of the operating reserve demand curve used in ERCOT, using actual, instantaneous capacities instead of nameplate capacities to determine reserves, may be workable.

45. In California and six other states, community choice aggregation (CCA) can provide a form of competition (US Environmental Protection Agency [US EPA] n.d.). Under CCA, municipalities may seek competitive bids from retail suppliers to serve *all* eligible customers in the municipality (subject to a customer opt-out option) at a price determined through a competitive bidding process.

46. See Note 31 above. These offerings appear to have been stimulated in part by the so-called 'duck curve' time-shape of hourly net-system load that has resulted from increased small-scale solar generation. See, for instance, CAISO (2016).

REFERENCES

Ahlqvist, V., P. Holmberg and T. Tangerås (2018), 'Central- versus self-dispatch in electricity markets', *Cambridge Working Papers in Economics 1902*, accessed 29 July 2019 at http://www.econ.cam.ac.uk/research-files/repec/cam/pdf/cwpe1902.pdf.

Averch, H. and L. L. Johnson (1962), 'Behavior of the firm under regulatory constraint', *American Economic Review*, **52** (5), 1052–69.

Baldwin, S. M. (2018), *Are Consumers Benefiting from Competition? An Analysis of the Individual Residential Electric Supply Market in Massachusetts*, Commonwealth of Massachusetts, Attorney General's Office, March, accessed 29 July 2019 at https://www.mass.gov/files/documents/2018/03/29/Comp%20Supply%20Report%20Final%20032918.pdf.

Baldwin, S. M. (2019), *Are Consumers Benefiting from Competition? An Analysis of the Individual Residential Electric Supply Market in Massachusetts: 2019 Update*, Commonwealth of Massachusetts, Attorney General's Office, August, accessed 17 January 2020 at https://www.mass.gov/doc/2019-ago-competitive-electric-supply-report/download.

Baldwin, S. M. and F. A. Felder (2019), 'Residential energy supply market: unmet promises and needed reforms', *The Electricity Journal*, **32** (3), 31–8.

Boiteux, M. (1960), 'Peak load pricing', *Journal of Business*, **33** (2), 157–79.

Boiteux, M. (1964), 'The choice of plant and equipment for the production of electric energy', in J. R. Nelson (ed.), *Marginal Cost Pricing in Practice*, Englewood Cliffs, NJ: Prentice-Hall.

Borenstein, S. (2002), 'The trouble with electricity markets', *Journal of Economic Perspectives*, **16** (1), 191–211.

Borenstein, S. and J. Bushnell (2015), 'The U.S. electricity industry after 20 years of restructuring', *Annual Review of Economics*, **7**, 437–63.

Borenstein, S., J. Bushnell and F. A. Wolak (2002), 'Measuring market inefficiencies in California's restructured wholesale electricity market', *American Economic Review*, **92** (5), 1376–405.

Brown, T. W. and L. Reichenberg (2020), 'Decreasing market value of variable renewables is a result of policy, not variability', working paper, Karlsruhe Institute of Technology, accessed 4 July 2021 at https://arxiv.org/pdf/2002.05209.pdf.

Burger, B. (2019), *Net Public Electricity Generation in Germany in 2018*, Fraunhofer Institute for Solar Energy Systems, 5 January, accessed 29 July 2019 at https://www.ise.fraunhofer.de/content/dam/ise/en/documents/News/Stromerzeugung_2018_2_en.pdf.

Bushnell, J. and K. Novan (2018), 'Setting with the sun: the impacts of renewable energy on wholesale power markets', *Energy Institute at Haas Working Paper 292*, August, accessed 27 July 2019 at https://ei.haas.berkeley.edu/research/papers/WP292.pdf.

Bushnell, J., M. Flagg and E. Mansur (2017), 'Electricity capacity markets at a crossroads', *Energy Institute at Haas Working Paper 278*, April, accessed 29 July 2019 at https://ei.haas.berkeley.edu/research/papers/WP278Updated.pdf.

Bushnell, J., E. Mansur and C. Saravia (2008), 'Vertical arrangements, market structure, and competition: an analysis of restructured U.S. electricity markets', *American Economic Review*, **98** (1), 237–66.

California Independent System Operator (CAISO) (2016), 'What the duck curve tells us about managing a green grid', accessed 17 January 2020 at https://www.caiso.com/Documents/FlexibleResourcesHelpRenewables_FastFacts.pdf.

California Independent System Operator (CAISO) (2019a), *2018 Annual Report on Market Issues and Performance*, Department of Market Monitoring, May, accessed 29 July 2019 at http://www.caiso.com/Documents/2018AnnualReportonMarketIssuesandPerformance.pdf#search=annual%20report%20on%20market%20issues%20and%20performance.

California Independent System Operator (CAISO) (2019b), *Flexible Capacity Needs Assessment for 2020*, May, accessed 28 July 2019 at http://www.caiso.com/Documents/Final2020FlexibleCapacityNeedsAssessment.pdf.

California Public Utilities Commission (CPUC) (n.d.), 'Resource adequacy', accessed 29 July 2019 at https://www.cpuc.ca.gov/ra/.

Cicala, S. (2015), 'When does regulation distort costs? Lessons from fuel procurement in US electricity generation', *American Economic Review*, **105** (1), 411–44.

Cicala, S. (2019), 'Imperfect markets versus imperfect regulation in US electricity generation', University of Chicago, working paper, May, accessed 29 July 2019 at https://epic.uchicago.edu/wp-content/uploads/2019/07/UCH-ElectricityDistribute.Final_.pdf.

Coase, R. (1937), 'The nature of the firm', *Economica*, **4** (16), 386–405.

Council of European Energy Regulators (CEER) (2018), *Performance of European Retail Markets in 2017: CEER Monitoring Report*, C18-MRM-93-03, December, accessed 17 January 2020 at https://www.ceer.eu/documents/104400/-/-/31863077-08ab-d166-b611-2d862b039d79.

Davis, L. W. and C. D. Wolfram (2012), 'Deregulation, consolidation, and efficiency: evidence from US nuclear power', *American Economic Journal: Applied Economics*, **4** (4), 194–225.

De Vos, K. (2015), 'Negative wholesale electricity prices in the German, French, and Belgian day-ahead, intraday and real-time markets', *The Electricity Journal*, **28** (4), 36–50.

Electric Reliability Council of Texas (ERCOT) (2014), *About the Operating Reserve Demand Curve and Wholesale Prices*, accessed 29 July 2019 at http://www.ercot.com/content/news/presentations/2014/ORDCUpdate_FINAL1.pdf.

European Commission (2016), *Commission Staff Working Document: Final Report of the Sector Inquiry on Capacity Mechanisms*, 30 November, SWD (2016) 752 final, accessed 29 July 2019 at http://ec.europa.eu/competition/sectors/energy/capacity_mechanism_swd_en.pdf.

Fabrizio, K. R., N. L. Rose and C. D. Wolfram (2007), 'Do markets reduce costs? Assessing the impact of regulatory restructuring on US electric generation efficiency', *American Economic Review*, **97** (4), 1250–77.

Fowlie, M. (2010), 'Emissions trading, electricity restructuring, and investment in pollution abatement', *American Economic Review*, **100** (3), 837–69.

Greenberg Traurig (2020), 'FERC upholds June 2020 PJM Minimum Offer Price Rule Order thwarting state subsidies', 24 April, accessed 1 July 2021 at https://www.gtlaw.com/en/insights/2020/4/ferc-upholds-june-2018-pjm-minimum-offer-price-rule-order-thwarting-state-subsidies.

Grubb, M. and D. Newbery (2018), 'UK electricity market reform and the energy transition: emerging lessons', *The Energy Journal*, **39** (6), 1–15.

Hawaiian Electric Company (HECO) (2016), *Power Supply Improvement Plan*, accessed 28 July 2019 at https://www.hawaiianelectric.com/clean-energy-hawaii/integrated-grid-planning/power-supply-improvement-plan.

Hawaiian Electric Company (HECO) (2018), 'Hawaiian Electric, U.S. Army announce completion of Schofield Generating Station', press release, 31 May, accessed 28 July 2019 at https://www.hawaiianelectric.com/documents/about_us/news/2018/20180531_schofield_generating_station.pdf.

Hawaiian Electric Company (HECO) (2019a), 'New solar-plus-storage projects set low-price benchmark for renewable energy in Hawai'i', press release, 3 January, accessed 29 July 2019 at https://www.hawaiianelectric.com/documents/about_us/news/2019/20190103_hawaiian_electrics_new_solar_plus_storage_projects_set_low_price_benchmark.pdf.

Hawaiian Electric Company (HECO) (2019b), *Grid Modernization Strategy Phase 1*, Docket No. 2018-0141 – 25, September, accessed 23 January 2020 at https://www.hawaiianelectric.com/documents/clean_energy_hawaii/grid_modernization/dkt_2018_0141_20190925_cos_ARDS.pdf.

Hawaii Natural Energy Institute (2020), 'Dynamic load bank for islanded grid solutions', press release, University of Hawaii, October, accessed 1 July 2021 at https://www.hnei.hawaii.edu/wp-content/uploads/DLB-for-Islanded-Grid-Solutions.pdf.

Hogan, W. W. (2002), 'Electricity market restructuring: reforms of reforms', *Journal of Regulatory Economics*, **21** (1), 103–32.

Hortaçsu, A., S. A. Madanizadeh and S. L. Puller (2017), 'Power to choose? An analysis of consumer inertia in the residential electricity market', *American Economic Journal: Economic Policy*, **9** (4), 192–226.

Imelda, M. Fripp and M. J. Roberts (2018), 'Variable pricing and the cost of renewable energy', *NBER Working Paper No. 24712*, National Bureau of Economic Research, June.

Intelometry, Inc. (n.d.), 'Comments on the Massachusetts Attorney General's Office report titled Are Consumers Benefitting from Competition?', accessed 17 January 2020 at https://www.resausa.org/sites/default/files/Comments-on-MA-AGO-Report.pdf.

International Energy Agency (IEA) (1994), *Electricity Supply Industry: Structure, Ownership and Regulation in OECD Countries*, Paris: OECD Publishing.

International Energy Agency (IEA) (2016), *Repowering Markets: Market Design and Regulation During the Transition to Low-carbon Power Systems*, Paris: OECD Publishing.

ISO New England (ISO NE) (2019), *2018 Annual Markets Report, Internal Market Monitor*, 23 May, accessed 29 July 2019 at https://www.iso-ne.com/static-assets/documents/2019/05/2018-annual-markets-report.pdf.

Jamasb, T., R. Mota, D. Newbury and M. G. Pollitt (2004), 'Electricity reform in developing countries: a survey of empirical evidence on determinants and performance', *Cambridge Working Papers in Economics 0439*, accessed 29 July 2019 at https://www.repository.cam.ac.uk/bitstream/handle/1810/456/ep47.pdf?sequence=1.

Joskow, P. L. (1974), 'Inflation and environmental concern: structural change in the process of public utility rate regulation', *Journal of Law and Economics*, **17** (2), 291–327.

Joskow, P. L. (2007), 'Markets for power in the United States: an interim assessment', *The Energy Journal*, **27** (1), 1–36.

Joskow, P. L. (2008a), 'Lessons learned from electricity market liberalization', *The Energy Journal*, **34** (Special Issue), 9–42.

Joskow, P. L. (2008b), 'Capacity payments in imperfect electricity markets: need and design', *Utilities Policy*, **16** (3), 159–70.

Joskow, P. L. (2019a), 'Challenges for wholesale electricity markets with intermittent renewable generation at scale: the US experience', *Oxford Review of Economic Policy*, **35** (2), 291–331.

Joskow, P. L. (2019b), 'Competition for electric transmission projects in the US: FERC Order 1000', MIT Center for Energy and Environmental Policy Research, *Working Paper 2019-004*, revised 9 November 2019.

Joskow, P. L. and E. Kahn (2002), 'A quantitative analysis of pricing behavior in California's wholesale electricity market during summer 2000', *The Energy Journal*, **23** (4), 1–35.

Joskow, P. L. and R. Schmalensee (1983), *Markets for Power: An Analysis of Electrical Utility Deregulation*, Cambridge, MA: MIT Press.

Joskow, P. L. and J. Tirole (2007), 'Reliability in competitive electricity markets', *Rand Journal of Economics*, **38** (1), 60–84.

MacAvoy, P. W. and R. Schmalensee (eds) (2014), *The Causes and Effects of Deregulation* (2 vols), Cheltenham, UK and Northampton, MA, USA: Edward Elgar Publishing.

MacKay, A. and I. Mercadal (2019), 'Shades of integration: the restructuring of US electricity markets', *Harvard Business School Working Paper 18*.

Mansur, E. T. (2007), 'Upstream competition and vertical integration in electricity markets', *Journal of Law and Economics*, **50** (1), 125–56.

Mansur, E. T. (2008), 'Measuring welfare in restructured electricity markets', *Review of Economics and Statistics*, **90** (2), 369–86.

Mansur, E. T. and M. W. White (2012), 'Market organization and efficiency in electricity markets', working paper, Dartmouth College, accessed 29 July 2019 at https://mansur.host.dartmouth.edu/papers/mansur_white_pjmaep.pdf.

Megginson, W. L. and J. M. Netter (2001), 'From state to market: a survey of empirical studies on privatization', *Journal of Economic Literature*, **39** (2), 321–89.

Monitoring Analytics, LLC (2019), *PJM State of the Market – 2019: Volumes I and II*, 14 March, accessed 29 July 2019 at https://www.monitoringanalytics.com/reports/PJM_State_of_the_Market/2018.shtml.

Morey, M. J. and L. D. Kirsch (2016), *Retail Choice in Electricity: What Have We Learned in 20 Years?*, Christensen Associates Energy Consulting, 16 February, accessed 29 July 2019 at https://hepg.hks.harvard.edu/files/hepg/files/retail_choice_in_electricity_for_emrf_final.pdf.

National Renewable Energy Laboratory (NREL) (2018), *Celebrating 10 Years of Success: Hawaii Clean Energy Initiative: 2008–2018*, DOE/GO-102018-5063, January, accessed 29 July 2019 at https://www.nrel.gov/docs/fy18osti/70709.pdf.

Newbery, D. (2005a), 'Introduction', *The Energy Journal*, **26** (Special Issue), 1–10.

Newbery, D. (2005b), 'Electricity liberalisation in Britain: the quest for a satisfactory wholesale market design', *The Energy Journal*, **26** (Special Issue), 43–70.

Newbery, D. and M. G. Pollitt (1997), 'The restructuring and privatization of the CEGB: was it worth it?', *Journal of Industrial Economics*, **45** (3), 269–303.

Newbery, D., M. G. Pollitt, R. A. Ritz and W. Strielkowski (2018), 'Market design for a high-renewables European electricity system', *Renewable and Sustainable Energy Reviews*, **91**, 695–707.

New Zealand Government (2019), *Electricity Price Review: Final Report*, accessed 19 January 2020 at https://www.mbie.govt.nz/assets/electricity-price-review-final-report.pdf.

Ofgem (2018), *State of the Energy Market 2018*, 11 October, accessed 29 July 2019 at https://www.ofgem.gov.uk/system/files/docs/2018/10/state_of_the_energy_market_report_2018.pdf.

Pollitt, M. G. (2008), 'Electricity reform in Argentina: lessons for developing countries', *Energy Economics*, **30** (4), 1436–567.

Pollitt, M. G. and K. L. Anaya (2016), 'Can current electricity markets cope with high shares of renewables? A comparison of approaches in Germany, the UK, and the State of New York', *The Energy Journal*, **37** (SI2), 69–88.

Ros, A. J. (2017), 'An econometric assessment of electricity demand in the United States using utility-specific panel data and the impact of retail competition on prices', *The Energy Journal*, **38** (4), 73–99.

Schap, D. (1986), *Municipal Ownership in the Electric Utility Industry*, New York: Praeger.

Schmalensee, R. (2010), 'Renewable electricity generation in the United States', in B. Moselle, J. Padilla and R. Schmalensee (eds), *Harnessing Renewable Energy in Electric Power Systems*, Abingdon, UK: Routledge, pp. 209–32.

Schmalensee, R. (2012), 'Evaluating policies to increase the generation of electricity from renewable energy', *Review of Environmental Economics and Policy*, **6** (1), 45–64.

Schmalensee, R. (2016a), 'The performance of U.S. wind and solar generating units', *The Energy Journal*, **37** (1), 123–51.

Schmalensee, R. (2016b), 'Socialism for red states in the electric utility industry', *Journal of Competition Law and Economics*, **12** (3), 477–94.

Schmalensee, R. (2019), 'On the efficiency of competitive energy storage', MIT Center for Energy and Environmental Policy Research', *Working Paper WP-2019-009*, accessed 27 July 2019 at http://ceepr.mit.edu/publications/working-papers.

Schmalensee, R. and B. W. Golub (1984), 'Estimating effective concentration in deregulated wholesale electricity markets', *RAND Journal of Economics*, **15** (1), 12–26.

Schweppe, F., M. Caramanis, R. Tabors and R. Bohn (1988), *Spot Pricing of Electricity*, Boston, MA: Kluwer Academic Press.

Spees, K., S. A. Newell and J. P. Pfeifenberger (2013), 'Capacity markets – lessons learned from the first decade', *Economics of Energy & Environmental Policy*, **2** (2), 1–26.

Turvey, R. (1968), *Optimal Pricing and Investment in Electricity Supply: An Essay in Applied Welfare Economics*, Cambridge, MA: MIT Press.

US Energy Information Administration (US EIA) (1995), *Electric Sales and Revenue: 1994*, DOE/EIA-0540(94), accessed 28 July 2019 at https://www.eia.gov/electricity/sales_revenue_price/archive/054094.pdf.

US Energy Information Administration (US EIA) (2003), *Electric Power Annual 2001*, DOE/EIA-0348(2001), accessed 29 July 2019 at https://www.eia.gov/electricity/annual/archive/03482001.pdf.

US Energy Information Administration (US EIA) (2012), 'State electric retail choice programs are popular with commercial and industrial customers', *Today in Energy*, 14 May, accessed 29 July 2019 at https://www.eia.gov/todayinenergy/detail.php?id=6250.

US Energy Information Administration (US EIA) (2016), *Electric Power Annual 2015*, November, accessed 12 September 2019 at https://www.eia.gov/electricity/annual/archive/03482015.pdf.

US Energy Information Administration (US EIA) (2018), 'Electricity residential retail choice participation has declined since 2014 peak', *Today in Energy*, 8 November, accessed 29 July 2019 at https://www.eia.gov/todayinenergy/detail.php?id=37452.

US Energy Information Administration (US EIA) (2019), *Electric Power Monthly with Data for December 2018*, revised 15 March 2019, accessed 29 July 2019 at https://www.eia.gov/electricity/monthly/archive/february2019.pdf.

US Environmental Protection Agency (US EPA) (n.d.), 'Community choice aggregation', accessed 9 September 2019 at https://www.epa.gov/greenpower/community-choice-aggregation.

US Federal Energy Regulatory Commission (US FERC) (2014), *Staff Analysis of Energy Offer Mitigation in RTO and ISO Markets*, Docket No. AD14-14-000, October, accessed 29 July 2019 at https://ferc.gov/legal/staff-reports/2014/AD14-14-mitigation-rto-iso-markets.pdf.

US Federal Energy Regulatory Commission (US FERC) (2016), *Order No. 831: Offer Caps in Markets Operated by Regional Transmission Organizations and Independent System Operators*, Docket No. RM16-5-000, 17 November, accessed 9 September 2019 at https://www.ferc.gov/sites/default/files/2020-06/RM16-5-000.pdf.

US Federal Energy Regulatory Commission (US FERC) (2018), *Order No. 841: Electric Storage Participation in Markets Operated by Regional Transmission Organizations and Independent System Operators*, Docket Nos. RM16-23-000; AD16-20-000, 15 February, accessed 29 July 2019 at https://www.ferc.gov/sites/default/files/2020-12/Order-No-841.pdf.

Vickers, J. and G. Yarrow (1988), *Privatization: An Economic Analysis*, Cambridge, MA: MIT Press.

Wee, S. and M. Coffman (2018), 'Integrating renewable energy: a commercial sector perspective on price-responsive load shifting', UNHERO, University of Hawaii, 23 July, accessed 27 July 2019 at https://uhero.hawaii.edu/wp-content/uploads/2020/05/IntegratingRenewableEnergy_PriceResponsiveLoadShifting.pdf.

Williamson, O. E. (1968), 'Economics as an antitrust defense: the welfare tradeoffs', *American Economic Review*, **58** (1), 18–36.

Woerman, M. (2018), 'Market size and market power: evidence from the Texas electricity market', *Energy Institute at Haas Working Paper 298*, 3 December, accessed 29 July 2019 at https://haas.berkeley.edu/wp-content/uploads/WP298.pdf.

Wolak, F. A. (2011), 'Measuring the benefits of greater spatial granularity in short-term pricing in wholesale electricity markets', *American Economic Review: Papers & Proceedings*, **101** (3), 247–52.

Wolfram, C. D. (1999), 'Measuring duopoly power in the British electricity spot market', *American Economic Review*, **89** (4), 805–26.

APPENDIX

Consider a simple power market with 100 per cent renewables and price-responsive demand. Renewable capacity is R and the maximum renewable generation in short periods (hours, days) is αR, where α is a random variable on $[0,1]$ with distribution function F and density f. Assume for notational simplicity that the smooth market inverse demand function is non-stochastic, $P = d(Q)$, with $0 = d(M)$. Note that if the market demand curve were stochastic, the first two terms in equation (A2.1) would be replaced by the expectation over M of those terms. I assume that if $\alpha > M/R$, so that maximum renewable generation exceeds maximum consumption, the excess generation can be curtailed without costs and the market price of energy is zero. Let the unit per-period cost of renewable capacity be γ.

A social planner wants to maximize expected consumer surplus minus capital cost:

$$E(U) = [1 - F(M/R)] \int_0^M d(t)dt + \int_0^{M/R} \left[\int_0^{\alpha R} d(t)dt \right] f(\alpha)d\alpha - \gamma R. \qquad (A2.1)$$

The first term reflects the assumption that when $\alpha > M/R$ and there is surplus generation, $Q = M$ and consumer surplus is the integral under the inverse demand curve from zero to M. The second term is the probability-weighted sum of surpluses for values of α less than M/R.

Differentiation yields the first-order condition for a social optimum:

$$dE(U)/dR = \int_0^{M/R} [\alpha d(\alpha R)] f(\alpha)d\alpha - \gamma = 0. \qquad (A2.2)$$

For any value of α less than M/R, the market price of energy is $d(\alpha R)$ and the output from a unit of renewable capacity is just α. Condition (A2.2) is thus a break-even condition for competitive equilibrium: it equates the expected revenue per unit of renewable capacity to the corresponding marginal cost, γ. It is easy to show that the second-order condition for a maximum of $E(U)$ is satisfied as long as demand is downward-sloping.

Thus, with no caps on energy prices and price-responsive demand, the classic Boiteux/Turvey result holds in this pure VER case: competitive equilibrium in the energy market corresponds to the socially optimal level of capacity.

3. Optimal wholesale pricing and investment in generation: the basics[1]

Paul L. Joskow and Thomas-Olivier Léautier

1. INTRODUCTION

This chapter presents the basic microeconomic theory underlying the formation and the structure of efficient wholesale power prices and optimal investment in dispatchable generating capacity.[2] The presentation in the chapter is designed to be accessible to non-economists interested in understanding the basic economics of electricity supply and demand. We use examples and graphics rather than mathematics to articulate the relevant microeconomic principles. The chapter also provides a theoretical link between the 'old world' of vertically integrated regulated electricity monopolies and the 'new world' based on vertical and horizontal restructuring to support competitive wholesale markets.

Over the last two decades, many countries have moved to restructure their electric power sectors to replace investment, operation and pricing of electric generation services through internal often non-transparent regulated monopoly 'hierarchies' with transparent unregulated competitive wholesale market mechanisms (Joskow 1996). The conceptual basis for the design of organized wholesale electricity markets during the late 1990s and early 2000s can be traced directly to the mid-twentieth century economic-engineering literature on optimal dispatch of and optimal investment in dispatchable generating facilities and the associated development of marginal cost pricing principles for generation services. While these models were developed to apply to pre-restructuring vertically integrated electric utility monopolies subject to some kind of regulation, including government ownership, these models of generation dispatch, marginal cost pricing and investment have also guided the design of decentralized wholesale markets. That is, the basic microeconomic principles developed to facilitate efficient decisions regarding investment, generator dispatch and optimal pricing of generation services have not changed. Rather, they must now be applied to the design of wholesale markets rather than serving as guides to electric utility management and regulators governing the behaviour of vertically integrated electric power monopolies.

One of the key insights from the microeconomics of electricity production is that the structure of wholesale power prices is similar to that of other non-storable goods for which demand varies significantly across time – for example, hotels rooms or plane tickets: the price is set close to the variable cost of production when capacity exceeds demand, while it is set by the value for the marginal consumer when demand is exactly equal to capacity. For example, the price for a room at the beach on Cape Cod is close to the cost of clean-up in the winter and rises much higher in the summer. This particular price structure is called 'peak-load pricing' in the power industry. The main difference between electric power and other non-storable goods is the magnitude of the peak price:

the summer price may be three to four times the winter price for a room at the beach, while the peak price for power may exceed 50 or even 100 times the off-peak price.[3] Thus, while electricity supply and demand have a number of unique attributes, we can find analogies in markets for many other goods and services.

This chapter begins with a very simple set-up in Section 2 to illustrate the peak-load pricing results. The model developed in this section has price-responsive demand and one generating technology. Despite its simplicity, the model yields important insights into optimal short-run and long-run pricing, optimal generator dispatch and optimal investment in long-run equilibrium. Section 3 then introduces a number of more realistic features that also play an important role in the design of wholesale markets. These include the introduction of non-price-responsive demand, an important consideration if consumers are not faced with wholesale spot prices due to metering or political constraints, demand uncertainty, customer curtailments and the value of lost load (VoLL), multiple generating technologies, transmission congestion and security of supply considerations. Section 4 concludes.

2.   THE SIMPLEST PEAK-LOAD PRICING STORY

2.1   Set-up

The simplest situation is characterized by a fully price-responsive electricity demand and a single production technology. These two assumptions make peak-load pricing results easy to derive and to understand. As discussed in Section 3, they are not essential: the economic intuition is unchanged when they are relaxed.

2.1.1   Demand

Units   First, a word on units. The main unit of measure for electric energy used in this text is the megawatt-hour (MWh). Kilowatt-hours (kWh) and terawatt-hours (TWh) are sometimes used. A megawatt-hour is 1000 kWh, a terawatt-hour a million MWh. To provide orders of magnitude, average annual consumption for residential customers worldwide is about 5 MWh per year. In aggregate, France consumes about 500 TWh per year and the US, a much larger country, consumes about 3700 TWh per year. Wholesale electricity prices are usually expressed in €/MWh,[4] while retail prices are expressed in euro cents/kWh. One cent/kWh is equal to 10 €/MWh.

The rate at which energy is produced or consumed is called power. Throughout this text, we consider the hourly rate; hence it is measured in megawatts (MW) – that is, megawatt-hours per hour. This is the appropriate unit for wholesale market transactions. Kilowatts (kW) and gigawatts (GW) are sometimes used. A gigawatt is 1000 MW, while 1000 kilowatts is a megawatt. For example, peak demand for a country like France is about 92 400 MW or 92.4 GW. The peak demand in California is about 50 000 MW or 50 GW, while the (non-coincident)[5] peak demand for the entire US is about 800 GW. Kilowatts are used to measure the average residential customer's maximum demand, which is typically lower than 10 kW in OECD countries.

Load duration curve   Electricity demand varies greatly across hours within a year and across years. Electricity demand is higher during the day than at night and higher on weekdays than on weekends. In Northern Europe and Canada, electric heating leads to higher demand in the winter than in the summer. In most of the United States, air conditioning leads to higher demand in the summer than in the winter.

Power engineers represent this variation using a 'load duration curve', which displays demand for every hour or half-hour, ordered from the highest to the lowest. As an example, the load duration curve for France in 2009 is presented in Figure 3.1.[6] The peak demand was reached for only one half-hour on 8 February at 7:00 pm and it was equal to 92 400 MW. The minimum demand that year was 31 526 MW.

Load duration curves are used to determine the number of hours or half-hours in which demand exceeds a given level. By construction, demand exceeds the minimum of 31 526 MW for all half-hours of the year. The curve shows that demand exceeds 60 000 MW for 5676 half-hours of the year. These are not consecutive half-hours – some might be February evening; others might be January mid-day. This non-chronological representation of electricity demand is extremely powerful, as will be shown throughout this chapter.

Demand exceeds 90 000 MW for a very small number of the hours in the year. This means that due to the large variations in demand from hour to hour and a very limited

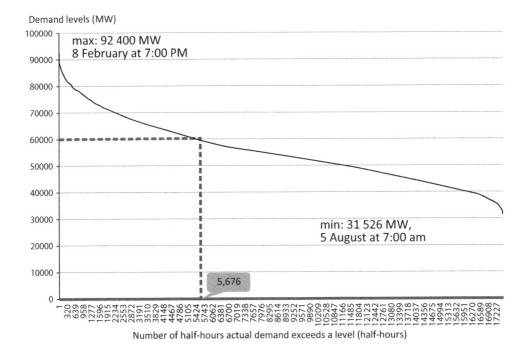

Note: All half-hours of a given year are represented on the horizontal axis; demand is represented on the vertical axis. The load duration curve represents demand for every half-hour, ordered from the highest to the lowest.

Source: Léautier (2019), Figure 2.1, p. 18.

Figure 3.1   Load duration curve for France in 2009

ability to store electricity economically, a large fraction of the generating capacity installed to meet demand operates for a very small fraction of the year.

Inverse demand curves   In this introductory section, we assume that all consumers can adjust their consumption to respond to variations in spot prices (that is, variations in the real-time price) of electric power. When the spot price increases, consumers reduce their demand. The natural representation of demand would be to have the price on the horizontal axis and the quantity demanded at that price on the vertical axis. However, for reasons that will soon become clear, economists prefer to represent inverse demand – that is, a diagram with the quantity on the horizontal axis and the price on the vertical axis. For a given price (on the vertical axis), the quantity consumed is measured on the horizontal axis. Demand decreases as the price increases; hence, inverse demand curves are sloping downwards, as seen in Figure 3.2.

Since demand varies across hours of the year, we have numerous downward-sloping inverse demand curves, one for each hour, as illustrated in Figure 3.2. For France, the left-most curve in Figure 3.2 corresponds to a summer morning, the right-most to a winter evening.

The basic model also assumes all customers are identical. Thus, they all have the same load duration curve and the same sensitivity to prices.

2.1.2   Supply

Variable and fixed cost of production   The second assumption that we make initially is that only one generating technology is available.[7] This technology is characterized by a variable cost of production per unit, expressed in €/MWh, and an hourly (amortized) fixed cost of production per unit, also expressed in €/MWh. The variable cost is essentially the cost of the fuel burned to generate electricity. It is assumed constant and denoted by c. It depends on the technology used and on fuel prices and usually

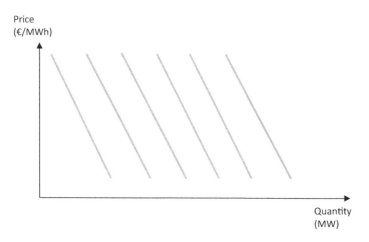

Source: Léautier (2019), Figure 2.2, p. 19.

Figure 3.2   Inverse demand curves for different half-hours of the year

ranges between 20 and 100 €/MWh for nuclear and fossil fuel-fired thermal plants. The variable cost is essentially zero for plants using intermittent renewable energy sources (RES) such as wind turbines and solar panels. Stored hydro is more complicated as the quantity of stored energy is limited and its utilization (dispatch) is controlled by the system operator. While there is no direct cost to release the stored energy behind a dam, the relevant marginal cost is the opportunity cost of releasing water at a particular point in time rather than holding it to be released at other points in time. Calculating this shadow value of water is a complex stochastic dynamic programming problem.

The annual fixed cost of production includes the amortized capital cost for the technology (depreciation, return on investment, taxes and so on) plus fixed operations and maintenance costs (O&M). The annual fixed cost is also assumed to be constant per unit of capacity, hence is sometimes called capacity cost, and is denoted by r. The fixed cost used in this discussion is the hourly fixed cost – that is, the annual fixed cost is divided by 8760 hours per year.[8] The magnitude of the fixed cost varies from one technology to another. As we will see later, a particularly relevant fixed cost for the models presented here is the fixed cost of an open cycle gas turbine (a peaking turbine).

In the example presented in this section, we use variable cost $c = 50$ €/MWh and annual fixed cost equal to 60 000 €/MW per year, hence $r = \dfrac{60\ 000\ €/MW}{8760\ h} = 6.85$ €/MWh.[9]

Constant returns to scale in power generation Consider a power plant of capacity K MW, which means it is impossible to produce output $Q > K$. As discussed above, the hourly capacity cost is assumed to be proportional to installed capacity and equal to rK. It must be paid every hour of the year. If the plant produces $Q \le K$ MWh during a given hour, the total cost of production for this hour is $rk + cQ$.

This representation of the cost of producing electricity is, of course, an approximation. In reality, the variable cost increases as production gets closer to the maximum feasible capacity and the capacity cost per unit often decreases as capacity increases, as it includes a portion that is independent of capacity. For example, a power plant developer needs to pay lawyers to write up the contracts with the building contractors and equipment manufacturers. Planning, engineering, siting, regulatory and other legal fees are not proportional to the size of the asset; hence, the power plant developer will pay an amount independent of the size of the asset. However, this approximation is close enough to reality that we can safely use it.

Under this approximation, electric power generation *for a given technology* exhibits constant returns to scale: producing 200 MWh using a 200 MW power plant costs exactly the same as producing them using two 100 MW plants *of the same technology*.

2.2 The Problem

Inverse demand is downward sloping and time dependent. Furthermore, electricity cannot be stored economically on a large scale. This raises two questions: (1) how should we price electricity; and (2) how much capacity should we build?

The term 'should' is ambiguous. The problem is first solved from the perspective of a benevolent central planner; hence, the questions can be rephrased as: 'What are the optimal electricity prices and generating capacity?' As is often in economics, if

competition is perfect, which is assumed in this chapter, the equilibrium reached by industry participants decentralizes the optimum; hence, the questions can be rephrased as:
'What electricity prices and capacity arise in equilibrium?'

Electrical engineers and economists have attempted to find a rigorous answer to these
questions since the early days of the power industry in the 1890s. The formal answer was
provided in 1949 by a young French economist, Marcel Boiteux on his return from the
Second World War (Boiteux 1949 [1960], 1951, Drèze 1964, Turvey 1968).

Before describing the solution, observe that other goods share these two features – for
example, hotel rooms and plane tickets. Neither can be stored: a seat on the 8 pm flight
from New York to Paris must be 'consumed' at 8 pm. Demand for both varies over time:
more seaside hotel rooms are requested in the summer than in the winter. The solution
to the electricity pricing problem has been applied to these other industries, albeit with a
major difference: retail price discrimination among consumers is added to peak-load
pricing.

2.3   The Solution

2.3.1   Optimal prices

A general result in economics is that to maximize the net surplus from consumption, price
should be equal to the marginal cost of production and the marginal surplus from consumption. Understanding this result requires a few definitions.

Consumer surplus   The consumer surplus, sometimes called the gross surplus or the
surplus from consumption, is the surplus (or the utility, or the pleasure, or the benefit)
that a representative consumer derives from consuming a given quantity of a good. To
compute the gross surplus, economists estimate the surplus that a representative consumer derives from consuming each unit of the good, then add these surpluses.

Suppose that, for a given hour in a winter evening, a family consumes 5 kWh of electricity. One kWh goes to heating and is valued at 30 cents – that is, it generates a surplus of
30 cents. Another kWh goes to lighting, which matters slightly less, yielding a surplus of
15 cents. Another kWh goes to the various screens (television, computers and so on), and
is valued at 10 cents. Finally, another 2 kWh each go to domestic appliances (dishwasher
and washer-drier) that could run later and are valued at 5 cents. The gross surplus from
these 5 kWh is the sum of the surplus from each kWh: 30 + 15 + 10 + 2 × 5 = 65 cents.

Suppose now many infinitesimally small units of electricity are consumed. They can be
ordered by decreasing per unit surplus: the first unit generates the highest per unit surplus,
the next very slightly less and so on. If we plot the surplus per unit as a function of the
number of units consumed, we obtain a downward-sloping curve. This is the inverse
demand curve, as presented in Figure 3.2.

The gross surplus derived from consuming quantity Q is represented by the hatched
surface under the inverse demand curve on the left panel of Figure 3.3: it is the surface
under the inverse demand curve up to the vertical line at quantity Q.

Short-term net surplus   The net surplus from consumption is the surplus from consuming a given quantity minus the cost of producing this quantity. It measures the economic
value generated by production and consumption. In the short term, the net surplus is

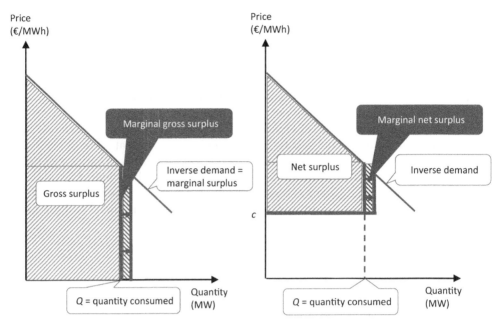

Source: Léautier (2019), Figure 2.3, p. 22.

Figure 3.3   Gross consumer surplus and marginal gross consumer surplus (left panel) and net surplus and marginal net surplus (right panel)

the consumers' surplus minus the variable production cost. For example, if the variable cost of producing electricity is 3 cents/kWh, the short-term net surplus is $65 - 3 \times 5 = 50$ cents.

The net surplus from producing and consuming quantity Q is represented on the right panel of Figure 3.3 as the area under the inverse demand curve and above the production cost c, up to the vertical line at Q.

Marginal surplus   The word 'marginal' is often used in this chapter. It refers to the last unit produced or consumed, called the marginal unit, or to an attribute of the marginal unit. For example, the marginal surplus (sometimes called the marginal value) is the surplus of the last unit consumed. In the above example, the marginal surplus is equal to 5 cents/kWh. Similarly, the marginal cost is the cost of producing the last unit produced. The marginal gross surplus is represented on the left panel of Figure 3.3, the marginal net surplus on the right panel. For every infinitesimally small quantity, the inverse demand is the marginal surplus.

Optimal production and consumption   The objective of a benevolent central planner is to maximize the net surplus. Production and consumption are short-term decisions; hence, the short-term optimum is to maximize the short-term net surplus. The optimal production and consumption plan is that every unit that generates a positive short-term net surplus is produced and consumed, while no unit that generates negative short-term net surplus is produced. The optimal quantity produced and consumed therefore sets the marginal short-term net surplus to zero. Under reasonable conditions, this optimal quantity exists and is unique.

Equilibrium price Which price leads to the optimum? Consider it first from the perspective of the consumers. If the marginal surplus were higher than the price, consumers would consume more since this would increase their surplus. Thus, they consume exactly all units whose surplus is higher than the price they pay. Consumption for any given price is such that the marginal surplus is equal to the price.

Consider now producers. If the price were higher than the cost, producers would produce more to capture positive profits. Production for any given price is such that the cost of the last unit produced (also called the marginal cost) is equal to the price.

Under reasonable conditions, there exists a unique equilibrium price such that supply is exactly equal to demand – that is, the quantity produced is exactly equal to the quantity consumed. At this price, the marginal surplus is equal to the price, which is also equal to the marginal cost. The marginal net surplus is equal to zero: the equilibrium leads to the optimum.

Off-peak and on-peak prices How does that insight apply to peak-load pricing? The key is to separate two different configurations: off-peak – that is, when production is lower than installed capacity, producing a marginal megawatt-hour requires essentially only incremental fuel costs. Thus, the off-peak price is equal to the variable cost, which we have denoted as c. Consumption then adjusts to this variable cost – that is, consumption is such that the marginal surplus is exactly equal to the variable cost of production c. This situation is observed on the left of Figure 3.4.

On-peak – that is, when production and consumption are precisely equal to installed capacity – the price is equal to the value of the last unit consumed, the value of the marginal megawatt-hour that fully utilizes the available capacity. This situation is observed at the right of Figure 3.4.

Observe the duality between off- and on-peak. Off-peak, price is set by the variable generation cost and determines consumption. On the contrary, on-peak price is set by the value of the marginal megawatt-hour, that is, the megawatt-hour such that cumulative consumption equals capacity.

Supply curve A useful concept to examine markets and price is the supply curve that traces the short-run marginal cost, that is, the cost of producing a marginal unit of a good for various quantities of this good when capacity is already built. In our example, the supply curve is L-shaped.

Off-peak, the cost of producing one additional megawatt-hour is the variable production cost (essentially the fuel cost), denoted as c. The off-peak supply curve is the horizontal segment at the left of Figure 3.4. On-peak, when production equals installed capacity, the cost of producing one additional megawatt-hour exceeds the variable production cost, since this would require the deployment of additional capacity. The on-peak supply curve is then the vertical segment at the right of Figure 3.4.

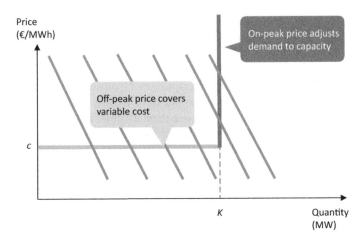

Figure 3.4   Demand and supply curves for a single generation technology

2.3.2 Optimal and long-term equilibrium capacity

Optimal capacity   The capacity choice is a long-term investment decision; hence, the long-term optimum is to maximize the average hourly long-term net surplus, which is the average hourly short-term net surplus minus the hourly capacity cost.

Consider adding a (marginal) megawatt of generation capacity. Installed capacity has no impact on surplus off-peak; hence, the analysis is limited to on-peak hours. For every on-peak hour, since consumption is exactly equal to installed capacity, adding a megawatt of generation capacity leads to the consumption of one additional megawatt-hour, which generates an hourly net surplus equal to the marginal surplus minus the variable cost of production c. For any on-peak hour, the left panel of Figure 3.5 presents the *short-term* net surplus, which is the area below the inverse demand curve and above the variable production cost c, and the marginal short-term net surplus from a marginal increment in generation capacity, which is a rectangle of base the capacity increment and of height the marginal net surplus minus the variable production cost c.

The average hourly net surplus generated by a marginal megawatt of generation capacity is thus the average overall on-peak hours of these hourly net surpluses. It is represented by the hatched triangle in Figure 3.5.

On the other hand, adding 1 MW of generation capacity costs the hourly capacity cost r. Under reasonable conditions, there exists a unique optimal capacity that precisely equates the average hourly marginal net surplus and the hourly capacity cost.

Long-term equilibrium capacity   The equality between the average hourly marginal net surplus and the hourly capacity cost is both an optimality condition – that is, it maximizes the net surplus – and also an equilibrium condition. Consider a producer adding a (marginal) MW of generating capacity. They realize no operating profit off-peak since they sell at a price equal to their variable cost of production c; hence, their analysis is limited to on-peak hours. For any on-peak hour, the right panel of

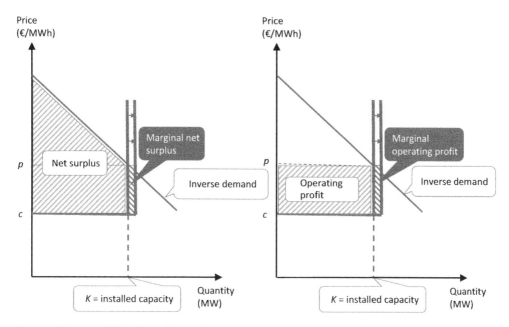

Source: Léautier (2019), Figure 2.5, p. 25.

Figure 3.5   *Short-term net surplus and marginal short-term net surplus (left panel), and operating profit and marginal operating profit (right panel) for any on-peak hour*

Figure 3.5 presents their operating profit, which is a rectangle of base the generating capacity and of height the price p minus the variable production cost c, and the marginal operating profit from a marginal increment in generating capacity, which is a rectangle of base the capacity increment and of height the price p minus the variable production cost c. A comparison of the left and right panels of Figure 3.5 shows that the marginal operating profit is exactly equal to the marginal net surplus, since the price is equal to the marginal surplus, even though the net surplus exceeds the operating profit.

If competition is perfect, producers build capacity until the last unit precisely breaks even – that is, until the average hourly marginal operating profit is precisely equal to the hourly fixed cost r. Otherwise, if the average hourly marginal operating profit exceeds (resp. was lower than) the hourly fixed cost, producers would increase (resp. decrease) installed capacity. This is known as a 'free entry condition'.

Since marginal operating profit is equal to the marginal net surplus, the long-term equilibrium is also the optimum.

Resulting price structure   The above story seems simple enough. However, it has profound implications. The price in off-peak hours is the variable cost, which we assumed here to be around 50 €/MWh. Meanwhile, the on-peak margin must cover the capacity cost, which we have assumed to be 60 000 €/MW/year. The price structure is illustrated in Figure 3.6.

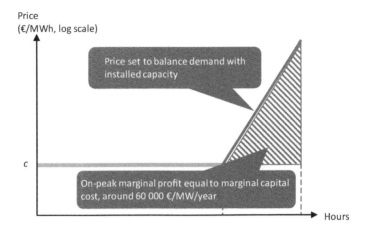

Price
(€/MWh, log scale)

Price set to balance demand with installed capacity

c

On-peak marginal profit equal to marginal capital cost, around 60 000 €/MW/year

Hours

Note: Hours are represented on the horizontal axis, prices on the vertical axis. For most hours, price is equal to the variable cost *c*. On-peak, price rises above the variable cost. The operating margin is equal to the fixed cost.

Source: Léautier (2019), Figure 2.6, p. 26.

Figure 3.6   Price structure

Different combinations of on-peak hours and on-peak prices could yield the same on-peak margin: many on-peak hours at low on-peak prices, or few on-peak hours at high on-peak prices. Which combination occurs depends on the sensitivity of power demand to prices. If electric power demand is not very sensitive to prices, which is currently the case, the on-peak price will rise very high; hence, on-peak hours will be few. On the other hand, if electric power demand were very sensitive to power prices, the equilibrium price would not rise very high; hence, the number of on-peak hours would be large.

Demand sensitivity to price is determined by two factors: (1) the share of consumers adapting their consumption in response to spot wholesale prices; and (2) each consumer's sensitivity to spot wholesale price. Suppose first that all consumers are identical and respond to wholesale spot prices. Léautier (2019, pp. 82–3) estimates that, if individual customers' sensitivity is at the high end of empirical estimates, on-peak would last around 600 hours per year and price would rise to around 350 €/MWh, seven times greater than the off-peak price. On the other hand, if all customers respond to price, but their individual sensitivity is at the low end of empirical estimates, the on-peak period would last less than 150 hours per year and price would rise to around 1200 €/MWh, more than 20 times the off-peak price.

In reality, not all customers respond to prices, nor are they identical in other dimensions. Suppose, for example, 20 per cent of demand responds to wholesale prices, which is higher than in most markets today, but a reasonable target in a few years once demand response policies are implemented (advanced or 'smart' meters that can measure consumption over very short periods of time and spot prices that vary accordingly).[10] Léautier (2019) estimates that, if individual customers' sensitivity is high, on-peak would last around 200 hours per year and price would rise to around 800 €/MWh, more than 15 times the off-peak price. If individual customers' sensitivity is low, on-peak would last around 50 hours per year and price would rise to around 3300 €/MWh, more than 60 times the off-peak price. Basic microeconomics suggests that, due to low demand sensitivity to prices, on-peak prices 20 or 60 times higher than the off-peak prices are to be expected and are perfectly legitimate.

Long-run marginal cost   In the long run, before capacity is built, producing one megawatt-hour requires building one megawatt of capacity and burning fuel for one hour. The hourly long-run marginal cost is thus $(c + r)$. The free entry condition implies that the *average* hourly price is equal to the hourly long-run marginal cost. An additional megawatt of capacity produces electricity in every hour; hence, its average hourly revenue is the average hourly price. If the latter exceeded (resp. was below) the hourly long-run marginal cost, producers would profitably increase (resp. decrease) installed capacity.

3.   A MORE REALISTIC STORY

Reality appears to be much more complex than the above example. Surely, the economics of large and complex power systems cannot boil down to such a simple story. Well, in fact, it (almost) can, even though multiple new elements must be added: (1) demand does not fully respond to spot wholesale prices; (2) there exists more than one technology to produce power; (3) electric power is transported across continents over transmission networks that have capacity constraints that may limit transfers of power from one location (node) on the network to another, thereby causing congestion and yielding optimal wholesale prices that vary from one location to another on the network; and (4) running a power system requires energy, but also operating reserves and other ancillary services to accommodate uncertain variations in demand and generating plant outages. This section examines each consideration in turn and concludes that adding them does not significantly alter the basic peak-load pricing story. Finally, this section discusses 'security of supply', a term loosely used in policy debates, which covers, in fact, three distinct time horizons.

   The main message of this section is that the standard model does surprisingly well at explaining the main economic intuitions about the attributes of competitive wholesale power markets. It misses key ingredients, such as inter-temporal linkages and geographical differentiation, hence some numbers may not be completely accurate, but its logic is robust.

3.1   Non-price-responsive Demand

The standard model assumes that all consumers are (1) identical; and (2) they adjust their consumption to respond to variations in the spot price of electric power. The first assumption is clearly not realistic: customers have different uses for power, hence different needs and valuations. At best, we can group customers by classes (for example, industrial, commercial, residential). However, this richness in usage across customers does not modify the structure of the analysis: all we need is a downward-sloping aggregate demand curve, which can be built by the aggregation of different customers' demand curves.

3.1.1   Retail and wholesale prices

The second assumption is not met in reality either. Most customers purchase electricity from a 'retailer' (or 'distributor' or 'supplier' or more generally a 'load-serving entity'), usually through contracts of varying durations, while retailers purchase power from producers on wholesale markets also pursuant to contracts of varying durations.[11]

This general description covers multiple situations. In Europe, wholesale markets are decentralized – that is, buyers and sellers enter into bilateral transactions that the market operator aggregates and ultimately adjusts to meet network feasibility constraints. In North America, wholesale markets are centralized – that is, the market operator runs an auction to collect all offers from producers and demand from retailers and consumers, and determines the equilibrium production and price. This distinction is ignored in this text since both market organizations should lead to the same outcome under perfect competition.

Wholesale markets exist for multiple dates. The most important is the spot market since the hourly wholesale spot price defines the value of energy at every hour. In most markets, the spot market is, in fact, a day-ahead market, not a true real-time market. Since technological constraints imply that (most) power plants must decide today whether to be online tomorrow, buyers and sellers agree today on the quantities each will buy and sell, and on the price for electricity for tomorrow between, for example, 4 pm and 5 pm. Since demand and supply conditions may vary between 4 pm today and tomor-row, adjustment markets also exist, which also produce prices for electricity for tomor-row between 4 pm and 5 pm. Thus, most electric power markets are 'two-settlement' markets, in which the price for electricity for a given hour is settled twice, once day-ahead and then in the day-of adjustment market. This introductory chapter does not open the 'black box' of complexities associated with wholesale price formation in practice and assumes a single wholesale spot price exists for a particular hour. For discussions of the details of wholesale power market designs in several different countries see Chapters 4 and 6–11 in this handbook.

Forward wholesale markets also exist, where producers and buyers can exchange power for the next weeks, months and years. In addition, financial instruments are avail-able to hedge future prices. For example, a producer can sell a future's contract, which pays the difference between the spot price at a given date and the forward price.

The structure described above applies to most commodities – for example, oil, metals, agricultural products and so on. In most of these industries, customers face wholesale spot prices, sometimes with a lag. For example, drivers pay the wholesale spot price for gasoline at the pump (plus a retail margin and a variety of taxes) and wheat retail prices follow the wholesale spot prices. In the power industry, by contrast, most customers pay a constant retail price, sometimes called a 'flat rate', that does not vary from hour to hour. Historically, meters could only record consumption between two readings separated by 30 to 90 days; hence, customers were paying the same price for every megawatt-hour they consumed, irrespective of the true value of energy at the hour of consumption or the marginal cost of supplying it.

If all customers face a constant retail price, the inverse demand is a vertical line. This may have been a reasonable representation of demand 20 or 30 years ago but is now unrealistic in most markets. Today, most electro-intensive customers purchase directly from wholesale markets or from intermediaries that convey them variable wholesale market prices.[12] Smart meters and enhanced communications technology enable retailers to record hourly demand and to charge a different price for every hour, even for residential customers, although most retail contracts, in particular for residential customers, still offer a flat rate.

As long as a positive fraction of customers responds to the spot price, the aggregate demand remains downward sloping.

3.1.2   System operator and power exchange

At this juncture, it is useful to briefly discuss the primary organizational attributes of wholesale power markets in more detail. Power markets require a system operator (SO) to physically control supply and demand in real time. More detailed discussions of these organizational arrangements and their variations across wholesale markets can be found in Chapters 4 and 6–11 of this handbook. This feature is unique to the power industry. In most other markets, physical delivery of the underlying commodity is decentralized: no single central entity controls the production of all oil fields, the consumption of all oil refineries and the movement of all oil tankers; rather, every market participant optimizes the physical movements of its own assets.

In the power industry, the SOs have their fingers on the switch(es): in real time, they are allowed to turn power plants on or off and to curtail customers. This function is conceptually different from the power exchange (PX), which organizes the wholesale market(s) in Europe – that is, provides a platform for producers and consumers to sell and buy energy. In the US, the functions of the PX and the SO are integrated, as discussed below.

A simple example illustrates the articulation between PX and SO. Consider a producer who sells 100 MW for the next day from 4 pm to 5 pm into the PX. The next day at 4:30 pm, the producer's plant suddenly trips and cannot produce at all. To balance the system – that is, to ensure that supply meets demand – the SO must turn on another plant. They then request the defaulting producer to pay for this additional energy.

In most markets in the United States, the SO is also the PX. The underlying argument for this choice is that engineering constraints perfectly understood and mastered by the SO also structure the work of the PX. On the contrary, in most European markets, the SO and the PX are different and, in fact, multiple PXs exist for a single SO and vice versa. This structure reflects the implicit choice of power markets' designers to place less weight on engineering and physical constraints. In the end, it is not clear whether the results of these two institutional designs are very different. In a world that satisfies all the assumptions of perfect competition, the results should be the same.

3.1.3   Administrative curtailment and the value of lost load

When demand is vertical, the peak-load pricing logic applies differently: demand can no longer be adjusted to capacity through an increase in price. When demand (at any price) exceeds capacity, administrative curtailment is required. The SO implements rolling blackouts to balance supply and demand – that is, selectively shut down parts of the power system for a few hours. The government usually approves the curtailment plan.[13]

When demand is curtailed, the SO should value electricity at the value of lost load (VoLL) to define an efficient curtailment plan (Schröder and Kuckshinrichs 2015). Unless rationing is efficient, the (marginal) VoLL – that is, the value a user is willing to pay for a (marginal) megawatt-hour when rationing occurs – is higher than the (marginal) value of power when it does not. An example illustrates the argument.

Consider two customers: customer A uses electricity for heating with value 200 €/MWh, while customer B uses electricity for lighting with value 100 €/MWh. When there is no rationing, each consumes 1 kWh and the marginal value for the system is 100 €/MWh.

Suppose now rationing must be implemented and only 1.9 kWh is available. If rationing is efficient, the lowest value usage is curtailed: customer A uses 1 kWh to heat their house, and customer B is rationed and uses 0.9 kWh to light their house. How much would the SO value the marginal 0.1 kWh? They would deliver it to user B, hence value it at 100 €/MWh. Thus, the marginal values with and without rationing are equal.

In practice, however, rationing is often inefficient – that is, the SO cannot curtail consumer B alone and instead must curtail both. Each will have 0.95 kWh available for heating and 0.95 kWh available for lighting. A marginal 0.1 kWh would be used for heating and lighting, hence would be valued at 150 €/MWh, which is higher than without rationing.

There are many reasons for inefficient rationing. In many cases, the SO cannot curtail individual consumers, but only groups of consumers on a controllable distribution circuit (although in the not-too-distant future, smart meters with two-way communications and advanced monitoring and control of distribution circuits will facilitate rationing of individual consumers). Furthermore, the VoLL is uncertain both in the aggregate and across individual consumers. We turn to this issue next.

3.1.4   What is the VoLL?

In the above two-usage example, the SO is able to compute the VoLL for each customer. This is not the case in reality since a customer's VoLL depends on a number of factors. First, it depends on usage. Students in a classroom hit by a power outage are probably not willing to pay much to get the light back and resume the course. In fact, most would be willing to pay (at least a small sum) to enjoy a break in the sunny courtyard. On the other hand, a patient receiving open-heart surgery would be willing to pay a significant sum to avoid curtailment.

Second, the VoLL depends on the duration of the outage. Supermarkets have deep-frost fridges, which keep perishable products at extremely low temperatures. They are not willing to pay much to avoid an outage that lasts only a few minutes. In fact, in some instances, they are willing to reduce their fridge's consumption of electricity and resell part of their energy into the market for a short duration. On the other hand, they would be willing to pay a large amount to avoid an outage lasting a few hours, which would destroy all their stocks.

Third, the VoLL depends on the information given to customers. If you know you will be curtailed tomorrow at 10 am, you do not step in an elevator at 9:59 am. On the other hand, if the curtailment catches you unaware and you end up stuck in a cramped elevator with foul-smelling colleagues, you will be willing to pay a significant sum to get power back and terminate your ordeal.

It is therefore not surprising that estimates of the VoLL vary in an extremely wide range, from 2000 £/MWh in the British Pool in the 1990s to 200 000 $/MWh (Cramton and Lien 2000). Schröder and Kuckshinrichs (2015) provide a recent survey. As an illustration, we use in this chapter 20 000 €/MWh as an estimate of the VoLL, which is consistent with the security of supply standard used in France.

3.1.5   Resulting demand curves
When all customers face a constant retail price, the inverse demand curve is vertical for prices up until the VoLL and horizontal afterwards, unless there are administrative price caps below VoLL (Figure 3.7).[14] When only a small fraction of customers respond to spot prices, there may also be instances when administrative curtailment is required. In that case, inverse demand is a steeply sloping line up until the price equals VoLL, and then a horizontal line when the price is equal to the VoLL (Figure 3.8).

3.1.6   Resulting price structure
The peak-load pricing logic still applies to that inverse demand curve. The only difference is that the visible hand of an administrative intervention replaces the invisible hand of market forces to adjust demand to available capacity through curtailment and to set the wholesale price at VoLL.

When demand does not respond to price, the latter is equal to the variable cost (around 50 €/MWh in our illustrative example) for almost all hours and is set by the SO at the VoLL for the remaining hours, during which power is curtailed. This is illustrated in Figure 3.9.

When demand partially responds to price, the latter is equal to the variable cost for most of the hours. When demand (for price equals variable cost) is equal to installed capacity, price increases and price-responsive customers reduce their demand

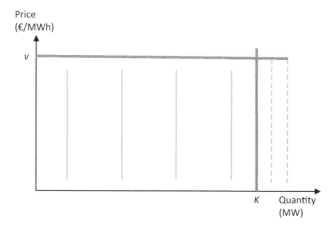

Note: When demand is lower than installed capacity *K*, be entirely served. When demand exceeds installed capacity *K*, it must be reduced through involuntary curtailment. The price is then set at the VoLL: inverse demand is a horizontal line at the VoLL.

Source: Léautier (2019), Figure 2.7, p. 33.

Figure 3.7   *Demand curves if demand is perfectly inelastic: in every hour, demand does not vary with price*

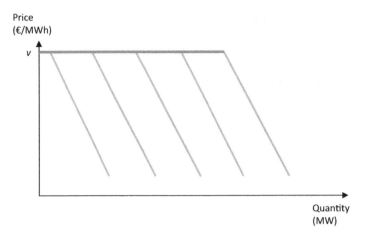

Source: Léautier (2019), Figure 2.7, p. 33.

Figure 3.8   Demand curves if demand is partially elastic: demand is slightly reduced as price increases, up to the VoLL

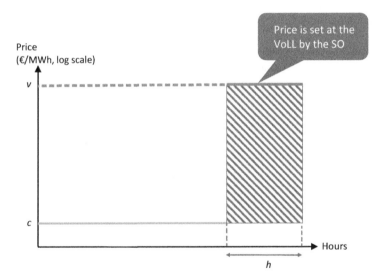

Note: The SO starts curtailing customers when demand (at the variable cost of production) is equal to installed capacity and sets the price to VoLL.

Source: Léautier (2019), Figure 2.8, p. 36.

Figure 3.9   Price structure when no customer is price responsive

accordingly. As was the case in Section 2, this is voluntary demand reduction and not involuntary curtailment. As long as the price is lower than the VoLL, the SO does not curtail any customers administratively: responsive demand balances supply and demand as prices rise.

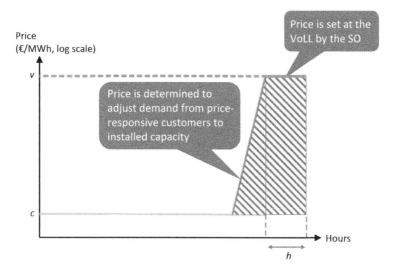

Note: The price rises on-peak as in Section 2. If the price rises to the VoLL, the SO starts curtailing constant price customers and sets the price at VoLL.

Source: Léautier (2019), Figure 2.8, p. 36.

Figure 3.10   *Price structure when a fraction of customers are price responsive and curtailment occurs*

If the price rises up to the VoLL, the SO starts curtailing non-price-responsive customers and sets the price at the VoLL, which represents the value of an additional megawatt-hour. Price-responsive customers adapt their demand to this price. This price structure is illustrated in Figure 3.10.

3.1.7   When is administrative curtailment not required?

Figure 3.9 represents the pricing structure of the past when no customer was price responsive. Figure 3.10 represents the evolving pricing structure when a small – but growing – fraction of customers is price responsive. In a few years, the fraction of price responsive customers will be large enough that the pricing structure is that of Section 2. This naturally raises the question: 'How much demand response is required for curtailment never to be necessary?'

Intuitively, the higher the share of demand responding to the wholesale spot price, the lower the probability that administrative curtailment is required. Numerical simulations presented in Léautier (2019) put a number on this intuition. Rationing is not required for the optimal generation mix when more than 3.9 per cent of demand is price responsive if the price elasticity of demand is low. If demand elasticity is high, rationing is no longer required when more than 13.9 per cent of demand is price responsive. *This result may seem counter-intuitive*: a less elastic demand results in less curtailment. The intuition is that, for a given share of price responsive customers, optimal capacity is *higher* when demand is less elastic: since customers reduce their demand less when price raises, it is optimal to increase installed capacity. Since capacity is higher, curtailment is less frequent.

These results are obtained under specific assumptions on the shape of the demand function and the nature of the uncertainty. Further research is required to refine these values. Still, they are good news. If less than 20 per cent of demand responding to price is indeed sufficient for curtailment never to occur at the optimal capacity, rationing will soon be a practice of the past.

3.1.8   Optimal capacity

As in Section 2, the optimal capacity is such that the average hourly marginal operating profit of a megawatt of capacity is equal to its hourly fixed cost (Boiteux 1956, Turvey 1968).

If no customer responds to price, the marginal operating profit is VoLL minus production cost, usually approximated by VoLL, times the number of curtailment hours. This corresponds to the hatched rectangle in Figure 3.9. Suppose for example the system operator sets the VoLL 20 000 €/MWh. Thus, if the marginal fixed cost of capacity is assumed to be 60 000 €/MW/year, the optimal capacity is such that power is curtailed three hours per year on average since 60 000 €/MW/year = 20 000 €/MW/hour times three hours/year.

If a fraction of customers responds to price, the marginal operating profit is the price minus the production cost, where the price is set to balance demand from price responsive customers with installed capacity (hatched triangle in Figure 3.10) then set at the VoLL by the SO (hatched rectangle in Figure 3.10).

3.1.9   Engineering generation adequacy criterion

Power engineers do not design power systems using the VoLL. Rather, they use a physical generation adequacy criterion – for example, 'available generation should exceed demand for all but three hours per year on average'. The criterion is determined administratively and may or may not coincide with the economic optimum.

To meet the criterion specified in the above example, engineers and statisticians first compute the distribution of possible future peak demands, considering different scenarios for weather and economic growth (and other relevant variables), and determine the $(8760 – 3)/8760 = 99.066$ percentile of the distribution. Suppose, for example, it is 108 GW. The probability that demand exceeds 108 GW is only 0.034 per cent, which is equivalent to say that, on average, demand will be lower than 108 GW for 99.966 per cent of the time or all but three hours per year.

Then, system planners decide how much generation capacity should be built, so that, on average, generation assets can produce 108 GW for a few peak hours. To do so, planners take into account unplanned outages in power generation units (sometimes called forced outages). For example, let us suppose they assume a forced outage rate of 7 per cent, which implies that, on average, generation units produce 93 per cent of their nominal capacity during peak hours. Therefore, the adequate generation capacity, which guarantees that, on average, demand is met for all but three hours per year, is $108/0.93 = 116$ GW.

This does not mean that three hours of rolling blackouts will occur every single year. If the weather is mild and plants' operating conditions are good, no rolling blackout may occur for one or more years. On the other hand, if the weather is unfavourable (a winter colder than average in Europe or a summer hotter than average in the United States), and if plants' operating conditions are weak, three or more hours of rolling blackouts may occur. On average, however, if the engineers and statisticians' computations are correct, rolling blackouts should occur about three hours per year.

The outcome of the generation adequacy computation is often expressed as a capacity or reserve margin – that is, the generation capacity minus the expected peak demand, as a fraction of expected peak demand. In the previous example, suppose, for example, that the expected peak demand is 100 GW. The capacity margin is $\frac{116 - 100}{100} = 16\%$. Adequate generation capacity is 16 per cent higher than expected peak demand: 8 per cent is due to demand being higher than expected and another 8 per cent is due to forced outages in production. This number is actually representative of capacity margins used by engineers up until RES were introduced. If the capacity margin exceeds 20 per cent, too few on-peak hours occur, wholesale spot price remains close to marginal cost and capital cost cannot be recovered. If the capacity margin falls below 10 per cent, rolling blackouts are likely to exceed three hours per year on average.

The capacity margin loses its meaning as RES enter electricity markets since they produce on average 15–50 per cent of the time (solar at the low end and offshore wind in good locations at the high end of this range) and their production cannot be controlled – that is, production is intermittent and responds to variations in sun and wind availability; unlike conventional dispatchable generation it cannot be dispatched economically by the system operator.[15]

While still widely in use today, traditional generation adequacy criteria should become almost irrelevant in the future as demand becomes fully price responsive. As demand becomes progressively more price responsive, it will adjust to available supply through an increase in price, not through administrative curtailment as long as investment in generating capacity reflects this reality as well. Anticipating this trend, some countries such as New Zealand have abolished the engineering reliability criterion altogether.[16] Other countries are holding on to the criterion. In the US, most regions continue to rely on traditional resource adequacy criteria. However, the Electric Reliability Council of Texas (ERCOT) does not officially have a resource adequacy criterion either. The ERCOT has an 'energy-only' market. It has constructed an operating reserve demand curve (ORDC) that allows for 'scarcity pricing' when generation supplies get tight. The ORDC reflects an estimate of VoLL, demand variation and associated uncertainty, generating unit outage rates and loss of load probabilities. See Chapter 8 of this handbook for a detailed discussion of the ERCOT market.

3.1.10 Formal equivalence between the VoLL and the generation adequacy criterion

Both approaches are formally equivalent. Since the product of the (expected) number of hours of curtailment multiplied by the VoLL is equal to the marginal fixed cost of capacity, choosing a generation adequacy criterion is mathematically equivalent to choosing a VoLL and vice versa. In our example, if the capital cost of a peaking turbine is 60 000 €/MW/year, a VoLL set at 20 000 €/MWh is mathematically equivalent to a generation adequacy criterion that 'available generation should exceed demand for all but three hours per year on average'. The higher the generation adequacy criterion (that is, the lower the expected number of curtailment hours), the higher the VoLL.

However, setting a VoLL or setting a generation adequacy criterion leads to dramatically different market designs. In the first approach, known as the 'energy-only' market design, regulatory intervention is in theory limited to setting the price for electricity when rolling blackouts are required and designing a plan for curtailments under extreme conditions.[17] In the second approach, policymakers require the SO to set up an additional 'capacity mechanism' to guarantee the generation adequacy criterion is met, which is a much more complex market design.

3.1.11 The no rationing puzzle

The economic analysis presented above suggests that, if demand is not very elastic, rationing should occur for a few hours per year to cover the fixed cost of generation. Suppose, for example, demand is perfectly inelastic. As seen previously, if rationing never occurs, the wholesale spot price is always equal to the variable cost of production and no fixed cost recovery occurs.

In practice, in developed countries with robust electric power systems, there are very few hours when curtailments take place due to inadequate supplies of generation, if any. Multiple reasons explain this. First, in the US, as previously mentioned, there is a set of 'emergency responses' – for example, allowing operating reserves to fall below targets, voltage reductions, emergency payments to customers and on-site emergency generators to reduce demand or provide energy to the network and so on. While economic analysis suggests that the price should rise to VoLL (or towards VoLL) during these conditions, it is not always so. Second, the mandated 'reserve margins' are probably too high. In other words, policymakers and system operators attempt to limit price increases and customer rationing, while economists argue they are necessary (when demand is inelastic) to cover fixed costs of generation.

Policymakers and system operators must choose between either (1) rationing customers for a few hours; or (2) failing to cover fixed generation costs from energy market revenues. This difficult choice arose with the restructuring of the power industry. When generation was a regulated regional monopoly, policymakers and the utility could agree on a sufficiently high generation adequacy criterion that rationing never occurred under reasonable scenarios or equivalently that rationing occurred only under scenarios so severe they were politically acceptable (for example, the worst blizzard of the century). The resulting excess generation capacity was then included in the regulated asset base.

This practice was one of the first casualties of the restructuring of the power industry. By construction, unregulated generating assets cannot be included in the regulated asset base. Interestingly enough, this was not a concern at the onset of restructuring, since most restructured power systems had excess generation capacity (which partially explains why they were restructured in the first place).

This choice stands at the heart of market design. On the one hand, policymakers may opt to recreate the previous situation by mandating a high generation adequacy criterion and paying quasi-regulated payments to the owners of generating assets to invest and maintain the required generating capacity. These are called 'capacity mechanisms' and are reviewed in Chapters 6–11 in the context of the individual market designs discussed there. On the other hand, policymakers may recognize that one of the main objectives of the restructuring of the power industry was to have market participants and not bureaucrats make investment decisions and take the accompanying risks. They will then accept that the price rises to the VoLL (hence a fraction of customers are rationed) for a few hours, in the hope that these high prices will spur enough demand response that rationing is no longer required.

Policymakers in the US, with the notable exception of ERCOT – that is, most of Texas – have chosen the 'capacity mechanism' route.[18] In Europe, as of writing, most countries have a capacity mechanism or are designing one.

Further discussion of capacity mechanisms applied in different markets is offered in Chapters 6–11 of this handbook. See also Cramton and Stoft (2005), Joskow and Tirole (2007), Joskow (2008), Léautier (2016), Léautier (2019, Chapter 9) and Keppler (2017). From this chapter, readers should simply take away that setting up a capacity mechanism is really a legitimate political choice, not an economic imperative.

3.2 Multiple Technologies

These price and investment concepts extend naturally to the more realistic case of multiple generating technologies. When only one technology is present, we have seen that the supply curve is L-shaped: horizontal at the variable production cost until capacity, then vertical when capacity is reached. When multiple technologies are present, the supply curve is a staircase – that is, a succession of Ls (Boiteux 1956, Turvey 1968).

3.2.1 Characteristics of multiple technologies
To make things concrete, suppose three technologies are available: nuclear, combined cycle gas turbine (CCGT) and open cycle gas turbine (OCGT). Table 3.1 presents illustrative estimates of the variable and fixed costs of each technology.

As shown in Table 3.1, the technologies are ordered by increasing operating cost: nuclear is cheaper than CCGT, which is cheaper than OCGT. The technologies are also ordered by decreasing fixed costs: if a technology has lower short-term marginal cost than another, it has higher fixed costs. This makes sense: if a technology were cheaper to build and to run than all others, it would be the only one installed. Similarly, no one would install a technology more expensive to run and build than the others.

3.2.2 Screening curves and optimal usage of different technologies
The trade-off fixed versus variable cost of generation is illustrated on the screening curves, presented in Figure 3.11. Hours are represented on the horizontal axis and the vertical axis presents the total annual cost of producing one megawatt during a strip of any

Table 3.1 Illustrative fixed and variable cost of different production technologies

	Fixed Cost (€/MW/year)	Fixed Cost (€/MWh)	Variable Cost (€/MWh)
Nuclear	299 000	34	10
Combined cycle (CCGT)	72 000	8	90
Gas turbine (OCGT)	53 000	7	130

Source: International Energy Agency and Nuclear Energy Agency (IEA/NEA) (2010), projected costs of generating electricity – median case with two modifications: gas price 40 €/MWh and CO_2 price 50 €/ton.

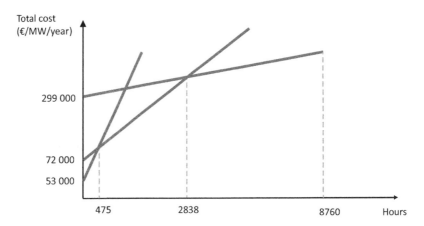

Source: Léautier (2019), Figure 2.9, p. 41.

Figure 3.11   Screening curves for three generation technologies: nuclear, CCGT and OCGT

number of hours. For example, producing one megawatt for one hour using nuclear technology costs €299 000 of fixed cost, plus €10 per hour of production. The total cost of serving a strip of hours using a nuclear power plant is, therefore, a straight line of intercept €299 000 and slope €10 per hour. Similarly, the total cost of serving a strip of hours using a CCGT is a straight line of intercept €72 000 and slope €90 per hour.

Figure 3.11 illustrates that hourly long-run marginal costs are decreasing along with operating costs. Consider the OCGT. Its fixed cost is lower than that of the CCGT. Its variable cost has to be high enough so that the sum of fixed and variable costs crosses the total cost of the CCGT; otherwise, the CCGT would never be installed. The same argument shows that the long-run marginal cost of the nuclear technology is lower than that of the CCGT.

This particular cost structure translates into a differentiated usage pattern. Remember that demand varies significantly across months, weeks, days and hours of the day. The issue is: under which circumstances should a specific technology be turned on? Since nuclear is the most expensive to build and the cheapest to run, it should run all the time. It is the 'baseload' technology. In markets where nuclear is not present, coal is often the baseload technology.

At the other extreme, since the OCGT is cheap to build and expensive to run, it should be turned on for high demand situations (winter evenings in Europe, summer afternoon in the United States). This corresponds to a peaking usage. Finally, CCGT being the intermediary technology (sometimes called semi-base or mid-merit or load-following), it starts running for intermediary demands – for example, 2000–5000 hours per year.

These results can be illustrated using the screening curves presented in Figure 3.12 and Figure 3.13. The three lines cross: the total cost of CCGT crosses the total cost of OCGT at 475 hours of utilization and crosses the total cost of nuclear at 2838 hours of utilization. As presented in Figure 3.12, to produce a strip of hours lasting more than 2838 hours, nuclear is the cheapest technology, measured in € per MW per year. Figure 3.13 shows that to produce a strip of hours lasting less than 475 hours, OCGT is the cheapest

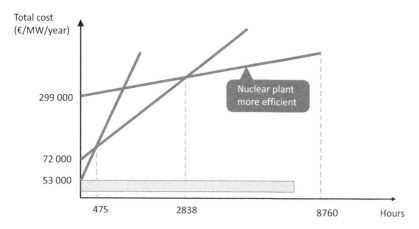

Source: Léautier (2019), Figure 2.10, p. 42.

Figure 3.12   Optimal usage of a nuclear power plant

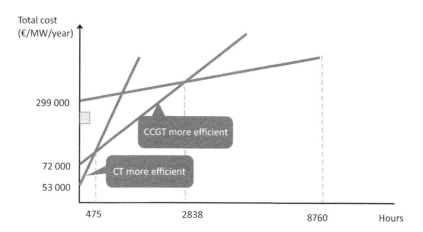

Source: Léautier (2019), Figure 2.10, p. 42.

Figure 3.13   Optimal usage of an open cycle gas turbine (OCGT or combustion turbine – CT)

technology. For an intermediate number of hours, CCGT is the cheapest technology. This analysis constitutes an excellent and highly illustrative 'first approximation'. It is rigorously exact if and only if no customer responds to prices.

3.2.3   Resulting supply or dispatch curve

Let us now turn to the generation supply curve (or dispatch curve), presented in Figure 3.14. The first flat portion corresponds to the hours when nuclear is the only technology producing. The price is thus equal to the variable production cost of nuclear, which determines demand. Then comes the first vertical portion of the supply curve: demand is equal

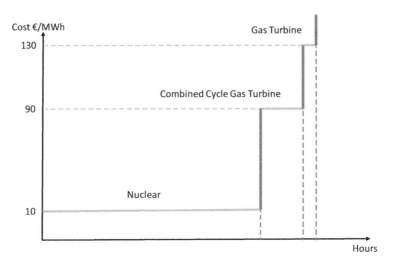

Source: Léautier (2019), Figure 2.11, p. 42.

Figure 3.14   Supply curve for three generation technologies

to nuclear production, which is equal to nuclear capacity and the price rises to precisely balance demand and nuclear capacity. If nuclear was the only technology present, this would be the end of the story.

However, since another technology is present, the story continues. The CCGT is turned on as soon as demand is high enough that the price exceeds its variable production cost – that is, when users are willing to pay more for a megawatt-hour than the cost of gas to produce it. Then, we travel the second flat portion of the supply curve: the price is equal to the variable production cost of CCGT, which determines demand. Then comes the second vertical portion of the demand curve: price increases so that demand is equal to the cumulative nuclear plus CCGT capacity. Finally, we travel the third L of the supply curve: a flat portion where the price is the variable production cost of OCGT, then a vertical portion where the price is such that demand is equal to the cumulative nuclear plus CCGT plus OCGT capacity.

3.2.4   Optimal cumulative capacity and generation mix

If demand responds to price, the logic presented in Section 2 also applies here to determine the optimal capacity and generation mix. The OCGT captures positive operating margin only when it produces at capacity – that is, when demand is equal to the cumulative capacity of all three technologies. In Figure 3.15, this is the last vertical segment of the supply curve, starting from point A_3 on the right (all technologies produce at capacity).

The cumulative capacity K_3 (on the right of the horizontal axis on Figure 3.15) installed in the long-term equilibrium is, therefore, such that the OCGT's average hourly operating margin is exactly equal to its hourly fixed cost. It is solely determined by (1) the cost of the marginal technology, in this case the OCGT; and (2) the demand function. Thus, the long-term equilibrium cumulative installed capacity

K_3 does not depend on the entire generation mix, but only on the marginal (peaking) technology.

Once the cumulative capacity has been determined, we need to define the long-term equilibrium generation mix. By construction, each technology produces if and only if its operating margin is non-negative. In Figure 3.15, the CCGT, for example, captures positive operating margin on the segments $[A_2, B_2]$ (CCGT produces at capacity, OCGT not yet turned on), $[B_2, A_3]$ (CCGT produces at capacity, OCGT produces partially) and the last vertical segment of the supply curve, starting from point A_3.

The free entry condition for each technology is that: average hourly operating margin, generated during the fraction of hours it produces at capacity, is exactly equal to hourly fixed cost. For example, the long-term equilibrium cumulative nuclear plus CCGT capacity K_2 is such that the CCGT operating margin (from point A_2 onwards) is equal to the hourly CCGT fixed cost. It does not depend on the cost of the nuclear capacity. The same argument applies to the nuclear technology, which produces at every hour. The long-term equilibrium nuclear capacity K_1 is such that the average nuclear operating margin when nuclear produces at capacity is equal to the hourly nuclear fixed cost.

An essential feature of the long-term equilibrium is that the free entry condition applies to all technologies – that is, the three technologies precisely break even. Suppose the generation mix is at the long-term optimum and the system operator decides to impose a price cap, higher than 130 €/MWh (otherwise the OCGT would never be turned on), but low enough to be binding in some states of the world. The operating margin of the OCGT will be reduced and will be lower than the fixed hourly cost of OCGT. The operating margins of all technologies will also be reduced by the same amount and fall below the hourly fixed costs. This property is very important for market design: if the peaking technology is 'missing money' at the long-term equilibrium, then all technologies are also 'missing money' by the same amount.

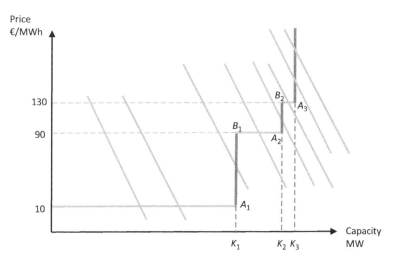

Source: Authors' elaboration.

Figure 3.15   Supply and demand curves for three generation technologies

Finally, the free entry condition for inframarginal technologies can be interpreted as: the equilibrium mix is such that substituting one megawatt of one technology by one unit megawatt of the next technology generates no gain nor loss in total generating cost on the margin.

3.2.5   Optimal cumulative capacity and generation mix if no customers respond to price

Power engineers, who historically assumed demand does not respond to prices, determined the optimal capacity and generation mix by combining the load duration curve (Figure 3.1) and the screening curves (Figure 3.11). This analysis is presented in Figure 3.16.

First, cumulative capacity is determined to meet peak demand, up to the generation adequacy criterion – for example, 116 per cent of expected peak demand.[19] Second, analysis of the screening curves in this example shows that nuclear is the most efficient technology to serve a strip of demand lasting more than 2838 hours. As discussed in Section 2, the load duration curve shows that demand exceeds 60 000 MW for 5676 half-hours of the year, which is exactly 2838 hours. An equivalent formulation is that the size of demand strips lasting more than 2838 hours is 60 000 MW. Therefore, optimal nuclear capacity is 60 000 MW or 64 per cent of installed capacity. Similarly, the load duration curve shows that demand exceeds 77 000 MW for 475 hours per year or equivalently the size of demand strips lasting more than 77 000 MW is 475 hours. Therefore, the optimal CCGT capacity is 77 000 – 60 000 = 17 000 MW or 19 per cent of peak demand. Finally, OCGT constitutes the remaining generation capacity, 17 per cent of peak demand.

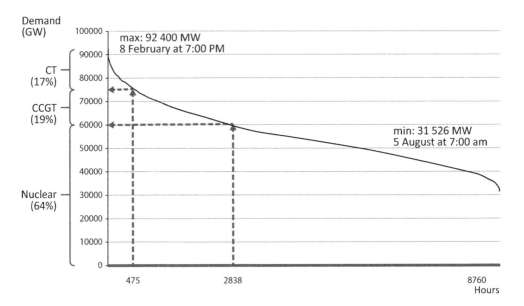

Source: Léautier (2019), Figure 2.12, p. 43.

Figure 3.16   Determination of the optimal generation mix combining (a) the screening curves and (b) the load duration curve

Figure 3.16 illustrates that nuclear capacity (for example) exceeds nuclear generation 5676 non-consecutive half-hours per year. During these hours, nuclear produces at less than full capacity.[20] These hours correspond to the first flat portion of the supply curve (Figure 3.15).

3.2.6 Invariance of the long-run average price

We have seen that the baseload technology runs all the hours. Thus, a baseload producer receives the (time-weighted) average price over the year. If this average is higher than the hourly long-run marginal cost, an additional unit is added into the market; hence, the average price is reduced. This process is repeated until the average price is exactly equal to the hourly long-run marginal cost. Conversely, if the average price is lower than the hourly long-run marginal cost, baseload installed capacity is retired until the time-weighted average price is exactly equal to the hourly long-run marginal cost. This is the free entry condition. The average price is entirely determined by the hourly long-run marginal cost of the baseload technology.

This property holds exactly for the long-run optimum. Industry equilibrium at any time differs from this long-run optimum. Still, this property is directionally correct: if the time-weighted average price is today and is expected to remain for the next few years below the hourly long-run marginal cost of the baseload technology, investors in base-load assets will tend to retire them.

This property is very important and produces counter-intuitive results. For example, increasing the share of price responsive customers, while increasing the net surplus, does not modify the time-weighted average price in the long term.

Similarly, since the mid-2000s, RES producers (for example, wind and solar) have been subsidized, hence have massively entered into electricity markets. Since their marginal operating cost is essentially zero (wind and sun are free) and their fixed cost is subsidized, one would expect the average price to be significantly reduced. And indeed, this is what we observe in Europe. However, this average price reduction is a short-term effect. Since the operating margin is lower than the fixed cost and expected to remain so for the foreseeable future, a fraction of the installed capacity is being retired, hence the average price will increase.[21] This process will stop precisely when the average price equals the hourly long-run marginal cost of the baseload technology, in this case nuclear. Thus, renewables entry has no impact on the average time-weighted wholesale price in the long-term equilibrium, which is determined by the cost of the baseload technology. This property holds until baseload technology is pushed entirely out of the market by intermittent generation.

3.2.7 Long-run marginal costs

We have seen that long-run marginal costs are higher for a CCGT and an OCGT than for the baseload nuclear plant. We have also seen that the time-weighted average price is exactly equal to the long-run marginal cost of the baseload technology for an optimal system in long-run equilibrium. Therefore, the time-weighted average price is strictly lower than the long-run marginal costs of a CCGT and an OCGT. If they were producing all the time, a CCGT and an OCGT would not cover their fixed cost at an average price equal to the long-run marginal cost of baseload generating capacity. How can they cover their cost by operating less than full time? The answer is that these technologies operate for fewer hours than the baseload technology, but these hours have higher than average prices. The number of hours a plant is operating is not sufficient to determine its profitability. What matters is the number of hours a plant is producing at capacity, which are the only hours when it captures positive operating profit and the price during these hours.

3.2.8 Is the generation mix ever optimal?

The analysis above appears simple enough. In reality, the generation mix is, of course, never optimal, for three main reasons, which are not specific to the power industry.

First, generation assets last more than 20 years. Investment is decided today based on assumptions of future screening curves (that is, fixed and variable costs of generation technologies) and future load duration curves. These assumptions are almost always wrong: fuel prices change, taxes or subsidies are decided that impact costs, demand grows more or less than expected and so on.

Second, adjustment is not easy. When excess capacity has been installed, it is not immediately shut down, as has been observed in the northeast of the United States in the early 2000s and in Europe since 2010. Investors may keep assets running even if they do not fully recover their cost of capital, as long as they cover their variable costs. This decision is consistent with economic theory, which suggests that, since sunk costs are sunk, investors prefer to run an asset (as opposed to shutting it down) as long as its operating margin is positive (more precisely, as long as it generates a positive free cash flow). Thus, as long as an existing generating unit expects to cover its going-forward costs (fuel, O&M, including incremental capital costs), it is rational to continue operating rather than retiring it. When expected future revenues fall below expected future operating costs, it is rational to retire the generating plant. In reality, assets are financed by debt and equity. When the free cash flow falls below the level required to service the debt (interest payment and principal repayment), the company files for bankruptcy and assets are restructured. During the restructuring process, a fraction of the profitable assets may be retired. Also, decisions could be less rational – for example, attributable to regulatory or political considerations.

Third, we have assumed throughout this chapter that industry equilibrium is optimal. In reality, this is not true. Investors do not necessarily coordinate to reach the optimal generation mix. They have a tendency to over-invest when prices are high and under-invest when prices are low. This is known as the 'boom–bust' investment cycle.

3.3 Congestion on the Transmission Grid

So far we have ignored the spatial dimension of power markets: we have considered only one location, where production and consumption both occur. In reality, power markets are spread geographically. Production often occurs far away from consumption centres. These different locations are connected to a high voltage transmission grid that transmits electric power over hundreds and sometimes thousands of miles. For example, a single transmission grid connects all of continental Europe – that is, all generation units and consumption centres in continental Europe are connected to the same grid and synchronized. In North America, three grids exist: the Western and Eastern grids and a separate grid for most of Texas (ERCOT). All generation units and consumption centres in the Eastern United States and Canada (roughly west of the Rocky Mountain states and Canadian provinces) are connected to the same synchronized grid. Similarly in the West, with British Columbia and Alberta connected to the Western network.[22]

This section discusses briefly how the peak-load pricing logic presented in Section 2 applies to an interconnected grid. Readers are referred to Chapters 4 and 7 in this handbook, Léautier (2019, Chapter 6), Schweppe et al. (1988) and Hogan (1992) for more detailed discussions of transmission networks, congestion and locational pricing.

The main issue considered here is congestion on the transmission grid.[23] Power flows on transmission lines are limited. These limits arise for two reasons. First, there are thermal limits: if power flowing on a line is too high, the line will heat up and may break. Alternatively, the line will sag and may touch nearby trees, which would produce a short-circuit. Second, there are operating limits. If a power plant or another line on the network fails, power flows are instantaneously rearranged, following the laws of physics. The operating limit on each line is such that, in the event of one (or more) failure on the system, the resulting flow on this line does not exceed the physical limit. This is called the N-1 criterion or the single contingency rule: the system typically is operated to withstand the loss of one major component. Some system operators use an N-2 criterion and operate their system to withstand the loss of two major components. For this reason, operating limits are often much lower than thermal limits.

Thus, a power market can be viewed as a series of 'power islands' linked by bridges of limited capacity. When the traffic is low, it flows freely, the islands are all connected; hence, a single market exists, and the analysis presented in Section 2 applies.

When traffic is high, congestion sets in, the islands are separated, and different markets exist. The analysis presented in Section 2 applies within each market: the local price is determined by the intersection of supply and demand (including import and export). When a technology is marginal, the local price is the variable cost of this technology. When a technology produces at capacity, the local price is the value of the marginal megawatt-hour consumed, up until the next technology starts producing.

The peak-load pricing logic applies to interconnected markets in another, more subtle, way. When there is no congestion between two markets, prices in each market are equal; hence, the price for transmitting one megawatt-hour from one market to the other is zero, which is the marginal cost of transmission.[24]

When congestion is present between two markets, prices differ. To transmit one megawatt-hour from the low price to the high price market, a market participant injects one megawatt-hour in the low price market and withdraws it in the other. Thus, they receive the low price and pay the high price.

This leads to two observations. First, the price of transmission services is defined implicitly and is equal to the difference in local electricity prices. Second, the peak-load pricing logic presented in Section 2 applies to the pricing of transmission capacity: when the grid is not congested, the price of transmission service is equal to the variable cost of transmission, in this case, zero. When the grid is congested, the price of transmission service increases above the variable cost of transmission and is determined by the users' marginal valuation, which is the difference in locational prices.

3.4   Inter-temporal Linkages and Operating Reserves

The previous story does not specify how the system adjusts in real time to supply or demand shocks. We have simply said, 'in each hour demand is equal to supply, since limited storage is available today'. We have therefore implicitly assumed that production can adjust perfectly to changes in demand.

In practice, it is not that simple. Most production facilities have limited abilities to adjust. For example, the ramp-up rate determines the speed at which a power plant can increase its production and the ramp-down rate the speed at which it can decrease its production. Ramp-up and ramp-down capabilities vary by technologies, some being more flexible than others. In addition, starting up and/or shutting down a power plant is costly.

Furthermore, supply and demand are subject to sudden random shocks. For example, a power plant may 'trip' and suddenly stop production, the wind may exceed the acceptable speed and wind turbines may suddenly shut down, a large user may unexpectedly stop their production process, hence their electricity consumption. This would not be a problem if production facilities had unlimited ability to adjust, but adjustment is limited.

How do power systems cope with the presence of random shocks and limited ramp-up and ramp-down flexibility? First, system operators and power producers do not make production decisions based on a single hour, rather based on a stream of hours: production at an hour $(t + 1)$ is partially determined by production at hour t. For most power plants, the dispatch decision can be decomposed in two related decisions: (1) decide today whether to turn the plant on tomorrow, a decision known as unit commitment; then (2) decide how much to produce for every hour tomorrow, taking into account the ramp-up and ramp-down rates, as well as the minimum production level required by the machine. This two-stage unit commitment problem is significantly harder to resolve analytically. Fortunately, a branch of applied mathematics, called operations research, is dedicated to solving these kinds of problems. The economic intuition is basically unchanged, although the analysis is much richer.

Second, system operators create operating reserves as a 'cushion' to respond to these kinds of shocks. Operating reserves are extremely important operationally, as the lights would go out otherwise. From an economic perspective, they can be treated as additional demand, that is, the system operator demands operating reserves in the same way a user demands electric power. Thus, operating reserves do not modify the standard peak-load pricing story.

3.5   Three Time Horizons of 'Security of Supply'

Policymakers and practitioners often mention 'security of supply' when discussing the electricity industry, usually in sentences such as 'the Government will guarantee security of supply'. This term is confusing, since it mixes three different time horizons, hence three different notions. It is essential to disentangle them.

3.5.1   Energy security of supply
Energy security of supply is the ability of a region (for example, a country, a group of countries or a state in a federal country) to secure its long-term supply of primary energy.

It can be crudely measured in units of energy: terawatt-hours (TWh), tons of oil equivalent (TOEs), or gigajoules (GJ).

The simplest form of security of supply is to own the primary energy required to fuel the economy for the foreseeable future. A more sophisticated approach is to have long-term contracts or agreements with 'friendly' foreign governments.

For example, when the US President Franklin Roosevelt met King Abdulaziz of Saudi Arabia on board the US Navy cruiser *Quincy* on 14 February 1945, he entered into a security of supply agreement: the US would protect Saudi Arabia and, in return, Saudi Arabia would continue to export its oil to the US. This agreement was particularly important during the 1970s when Saudi Arabia was a force stabilizing Organization of the Petroleum Exporting Countries (OPEC) supply and prices (Yergin 1990).

In 1973, faced with the oil crisis and the risk of oil supply constraints and price spikes, the French government launched the nuclear electricity programme to guarantee the security of its power supply by replacing electricity produced with petroleum with nuclear electricity and displacing oil used by consumers with electricity (so-called electrification of end uses). The primary fuel, uranium, was procured from current or former French colonies (New Caledonia in the Pacific Ocean and Niger in Africa).

Can competitive firms guarantee energy security of supply? Theoretically yes. In practice, however, probably no. While private firms sign long-term commercial contracts, these contracts are often linked to broader alliances between countries. Energy security of supply falls squarely within the government's purview.

3.5.2 Generation adequacy

As we have seen above, when electricity demand does not respond to short-run price variations, which was the case for most of the twentieth century, generating capacity is determined to meet demand for the next year, the next five years or the next ten years to achieve in expectation an agreed-upon reliability criterion. The capacity that satisfies the generation adequacy standard is measured in units of electric power (usually GW). It is routinely estimated and reported by (transmission) system operators.

Generation adequacy is often confused with security of supply in the public discourse. This is misleading. The former is ensuring that, on average, rolling blackouts do not exceed an agreed-upon level – for example, three hours per year. If the generation adequacy standard is not met, rolling blackouts may reach ten hours during a very cold winter in Europe (or a very warm summer in the United States) or brownouts may occur. This is, of course, unpleasant. No one likes to be deprived of electric heating precisely when the temperature drops. But it is much less dramatic than having to ration all users for the entire winter because the gas reserves in the country are insufficient.

3.5.3 System reliability

System reliability is the ability for the system to react in real time to unforeseen circumstances – for example, a sudden loss of generation, a sudden demand increase, or any event that materially and suddenly affects power flows. Remember that power injected in the grid must equal power taken out of the grid (either for consumption or dissipated through losses or stored) at all times. Excess demand causes a frequency drop and, reciprocally, excess supply causes a frequency increase. If this deviation exceeds a certain very tight level, parts of the power system automatically shut down. This would yield an uncontrolled blackout or system collapse. In August 2019, Great Britain experienced an uncontrolled blackout due to two power plants shutting off simultaneously; hence, the frequency dropped below 48.8 Hertz. This triggered the National Grid's (the system operator in Great Britain) automated system to cut off supply to around 5 per cent of demand. One million customers, including train stations and hospitals, lost power for a few hours.

This must be distinguished from an organized rolling blackout reflecting an ex-ante plan to respond to inadequate generating capacity to balance supply and demand. In the latter, the underlying economics is that it is more efficient (ex ante) to curtail customers for a few hours than to build an additional power plant. An uncontrolled blackout, on the other hand, is uneconomic. Buyers and sellers are prevented from executing economic transactions. One attribute of uncontrolled system blackouts is that it takes time (and effort) to recover. A power grid that has collapsed is not simply switched back on with the flip of a switch. The 2003 blackout in the Northeastern United States is a good example of a system collapse and recovery, though the cause of the system collapse was a transmission outage rather than a generation shortage.[25]

To guarantee the reliability of the power grid, system operators have put in place protocols and practices. As previously discussed, SOs procure operating reserves to guarantee system reliability. Another example: the maximum power allowed to flow on transmission lines is lower than the physical capacity of the line so that the system is able to operate even if one large component (for example, a large power plant or another transmission line – the largest contingency) suddenly fails – the N-1 criterion. What matters for reliability is the ramp rate (up or down) at which generators can adjust their output. It is expressed in megawatts per minute.

The economics of reliability constitutes an area for fertile future joint work by economists and engineers. First, most reliability protocols and practices are very static, which were designed before the condition of system components could be measured and analysed in real time. As sensors and remote control devices are installed on the power grid, these reliability protocols and practices will become dynamic, hence more efficient. Second, in the (near) future, demand response and batteries will become a non-negligible reality in power markets and will contribute to system reliability. Robust rules to include them will have to be designed.

3.5.4   Additional thoughts

The link between the three time horizons   The three time horizons are not as separate as the previous discussion may suggest. They feed continuously into one another. For example, generation adequacy can be estimated the day before or even two hours before actual dispatch, hence resembles system reliability. However, they are different notions, expressed in different units. Poor security of supply leads to long episodes of shortages, usually administered through rolling blackouts. Inadequate generation adequacy leads to more rolling blackouts than is efficient. Inadequate reliability leads to unmanaged system blackouts.

Comparison with other industries   Observers sometimes argue that reliability is unique to the power industry: 'if there is a shortage of planes in Chicago, it does not affect travellers on the East Coast'. The distinction between capacity adequacy and system reliability helps clarify this point.

Adequacy is having sufficient infrastructure to accommodate the next anticipated spike in demand – for example, having sufficient planes in Chicago next summer. If planes are short next summer in Chicago, prices will go up, some travellers will not be able to fly on their preferred date and some may find themselves on the wrong end of overbooking. This is indeed unlikely to affect passengers on the East Coast.

On the other hand, as all US air travellers know, if thunderstorms hit Chicago in the summer, as they often do, flights in and out of Chicago will be delayed, possibly cancelled, which will most definitely affect travellers on the East Coast (and on the West Coast also). The consequences of a local reliability issue are less severe for the air travel system than for the power grid. In particular, total blackouts are extremely infrequent. The difference, however, is a matter of degree, not principle.

4. CONCLUDING REMARKS

This chapter has shown that the structure of wholesale power prices is relatively straight-forward: prices are close to the variable cost of production during off-peak hours, when capacity exceeds demand, and are set by the valuation of the marginal consumer when demand is exactly equal to capacity. On-peak prices can be 20 to 50 times higher than off-peak ones. We have developed this basic result and other important results that it implies by introducing increasingly realistic models.

There are several relevant economic considerations that we do not address in this chapter. We assume implicitly that there is no market power in wholesale markets: suppliers are price takers. Market power considerations are introduced in Chapter 4, and Chapters 6–11 discuss, among other things, how market power has been addressed by these different market designs. Nor do we discuss the variations in the mechanisms that individual wholesale market designs have employed to implement these basic principles. Chapters 6–11 of this handbook do so.

The discussion in this chapter also embodies the assumption that generating plants are dispatchable by the system operator – that is, the system operator can effectively control the economic dispatch of generators that have been scheduled to supply through the prevailing wholesale market mechanisms. However, in response to policies to decarbonize the electric power sector, traditional dispatchable generation is being replaced by wind and solar (primarily PV) technologies. The supply of electricity from these technologies is 'intermittent', depending on uncontrollable variations in wind and sun. Furthermore, distributed generation (DG) on the customer side of the meter, primarily rooftop PV, rather than on the transmission grid, is also expanding quickly in many countries. The large-scale diffusion of these intermittent technologies, combined with government policies that are replacing market mechanisms with administrative obligations, is creating new challenges for the design of efficient wholesale markets (Joskow 2019). How these challenges can be addressed is discussed in Chapters 15 and 16 in Part II of this handbook. One technological response to intermittency is investments in energy storage technologies that can essentially shift electricity supplied when it is cheap to periods when it is dear, subject to a variety of storage capacity, cycle time, charge and discharge constraints. Storage technologies are sometimes consumers of energy and sometimes producers of energy. Efficient integration of storage opportunities into wholesale markets is another challenge. Finally, new metering and remote sensing and control technologies are creating new opportunities to create a much more active demand side that allows consumers to respond more quickly and effectively to price changes and to express their willingness to pay for reliability. These opportunities are discussed in Chapter 13 of this handbook.

Whether it is the relatively simple models considered in this chapter or enhancements to accommodate the changes noted above, there is one fundamental pricing principle that continues to prevail. This is the role of prices that vary widely with variations in supply and demand. Producers capture their highest profits when consumers desperately need electric power to heat (or freshen) their houses. This is likely to be even more important for producing market revenues sufficient to cover the total costs of new generating technologies, as the short-run marginal costs of wind and solar are essentially zero. If the market price is zero, no net revenues are produced to cover generators' capital costs. Thus, scarcity pricing – that is, incidents of very high prices necessary to clear the market – must play a more important role in the future to satisfy generators balanced budget constraints. Economists argue that this outcome is perfectly acceptable; in fact, it is optimal. Consumers and their elected representatives have a different opinion. They argue that profiteering from consumers' need is amoral, hence unacceptable.

Resolving this tension is essential to the future of the power industry. Consumers (some at least) and policymakers are looking forward to the decentralization of the power industry: consumers equipped with green and decentralized generation and storage (for example, a Tesla car in their garage) will be active participants in the power markets. How do we coordinate the decisions of millions of economic agents? Prices reflecting the value of power at every instant and every location seems the most natural approach. This requires policymakers and consumers to reconcile themselves with possibly extremely high prices at some instants in some locations. Otherwise, the decentralization of the electricity system will prove an elusive goal.

NOTES

1. This chapter draws heavily on Chapter 2 of Léautier (2019). Mathematical derivations of the primary results discussed here can be found there as well.
2. Extensions of these models to integrate intermittent or non-controllable generating capacity and electricity storage are discussed in Chapter 2, Chapter 15 and Chapter 16 of this handbook. See also Léautier (2019, Chapter 8), Joskow (2019), Newbery et al. (2018) and the references they cite.
3. An additional difference between the wholesale spot price for power and the retail price for hotel rooms or plane seats is that hotels and airlines also are able to price discriminate among users: two passengers seated next to one another may have paid vastly different prices for their seat. This type of price discrimination does not exist in wholesale spot markets where 'the law of one price' holds at any point in time. A more precise formulation of the above statements would be 'the minimum price for a room in the winter is close to the cost of clean-up'.
4. We use euros as the currency in most of the chapter, but we sometimes use $/MWh and £/MWh when referencing data or studies that use US dollars or British pounds. Given current exchange rates, all three units are roughly equivalent.
5. The United States has a large number of system operators, sometimes vertically integrated utilities and sometimes independent system operators (ISOs), spread over a country with four time zones, variations in customer composition and variations in weather. The time of peak demand for each system operator varies. Thus, the peak demands of the system operators are 'non-coincident' and adding them all up yields the non-coincident peak demand. This is how the aggregate data for the United States are reported.

6. The load duration curve is still representative as it has not changed significantly in the last ten years.
7. Multiple generating technologies are introduced into the model below.
8. Numbers are expressed according to the following convention: a thin space separates the tens of thousands and a dot separates the integer from the decimal parts.
9. Fixed and variable costs of producing electricity vary over time, since technologies, interest rates and commodity price evolve. The costs used here are purely illustrative. For example, the variable cost in the US is currently lower than 50 $/MWh because natural gas and coal are less expensive than in Europe and Asia. The US Energy Information Administration (US EIA) reports a levelized capital cost of about $75 000 per MW (2018 figures) for a conventional combustion turbine. See US EIA (2019, Table 1b). Levelized fixed O&M costs add another $18 000 per MW (2018 figures).
10. The efficiency of real-time prices that reflect the marginal cost of supplying electricity, including scarcity prices (more below), is well established in the literature – for example, Borenstein (2005) and Wolak (2018).
11. Many residential and small commercial consumers in some countries are still faced with a bundled price that includes both wholesale energy costs and delivery (transmission and distribution) charges. We will ignore this complication in this discussion.
12. In the US, industrial customers typically avoid buying directly in the wholesale market for a variety of legal, regulatory and practical reasons. They rely on wholesale market intermediaries that compete to be their electricity supplier.
13. Actual curtailment plans are more complex than this. Typically, the SO or a government agency will first issue a public call for conservation by consumers in light of a pending emergency. Next, the SO may allow operating reserves to decline below their target level. Then, the SO may reduce the voltage on the system ('brownout'). Finally, the SO will turn to rolling blackouts or curtailments to reduce demand on the system.
14. Regulators may require system operators to apply price caps below VoLL to wholesale market realizations to mitigate real or imagined market power problems in wholesale markets. However, when *competitive* market clearing prices exceed the price cap, non-price rationing of supply is necessary to balance supply and demand. Binding price caps in competitive wholesale markets can have significant effects on short-run and long-run (investment) market efficiency. The rules for price caps (or offer caps) for system operations in the US are specified in Federal Energy Regulatory Commission (FERC) Order 831 – (2016), accessed 29 June 2012 at https://www.ferc.gov/sites/default/files/2020-06/RM16-5-000.pdf.
15. The short-run marginal cost of generating electricity from a wind and solar plant is roughly zero. If wind and solar facilities with specific generating capacities were dispatchable, an economic dispatch would lead the system operator to call on this capacity whenever the aggregate specified wind and solar capacity is greater than or equal to demand. However, wind and solar generation is intermittent, and its availability depends on variations in the wind and sun. Thus, its effective generating capacity varies based on the intensity of the wind and the sun at any particular time.
16. New Zealand is largely hydro based. The main supply risk is represented by a dry year during which rolling blackouts would occur for a few winter days.
17. In practice, ERCOT and other energy-only markets also design a schedule of administrative procedures and out-of-market actions they employ before initiating rolling blackouts.
18. California is also an exception. Since 2001, the California Public Utilities Commission has placed resource adequacy requirements on load-serving entities, until recently primarily distribution utilities, whether covered by the California ISO or not, rather than on a centralized capacity market administered by the ISO. This is a rather bizarre system that leads to all kinds of problems, especially as retail competition is introduced. California has been considering moving to a centralized capacity market mechanism. More information is available at https://www.cpuc.ca.gov/RA/, accessed 29 June 2021.
19. To simplify the example, we choose installed capacity equal to peak demand and round up the numbers.
20. In real power markets, nuclear plants schedule their maintenance during these hours so that the active cumulative capacity follows the load curve. In addition, they may export to neighbouring markets.
21. The dynamics here are complex, as discussed later.
22. However, the Eastern and Western Interconnections have several balancing authorities with operating responsibilities for portions of each of these grids. ERCOT has one balancing authority. See https://www.eia.gov/todayinenergy/detail.php?id=27152, accessed 29 June 2021.
23. To simplify this introductory discussion, we ignore transmission losses, which does not alter the basic economic analysis.
24. Since transmission losses are ignored.
25. Wikipedia (n.d.), 'Northeast blackout of 2003', accessed 29 June 2021 at https://en.wikipedia.org/wiki/Northeast_blackout_of_2003.

REFERENCES

Boiteux, M. ([1949] 1960), 'Peak load pricing', *Journal of Business*, April, **XXXIII** (2), 157–79.

Boiteux, M. (1951), 'La tarification au coût marginal et les demandes aléatoires', *Cahiers Seminaire d'Econométrie*, **1**, 56–69.

Boiteux, M. (1956), 'Le choix des équipements de production d'énergie électric', *Review de Recherche Opérationelle*, **1** (1), 45–60.

Borenstein, S. (2005), 'The long run efficiency of real-time electricity prices', *The Energy Journal*, **26** (3), 93–116.

Cramton, P. and J. Lien (2000), 'Value of lost load', mimeo, University of Maryland.

Cramton, P. and S. Stoft (2005), 'A capacity market that makes sense', *The Electricity Journal*, **18** (7), 43–54.

Drèze, J. (1964), 'Some post-war contributions of French economists to theory and public policy: with special emphasis on problems of resource allocation', *American Economic Review*, **54** (4), Part 2, Supplement, 2–64.

Hogan, W. (1992), 'Contract networks for electric power transmission', *Journal of Regulatory Economics*, **4** (3), 211–42.

International Energy Agency and Nuclear Energy Agency (IEA/NEA) (2010), *Projected Costs of Generating Electricity – 2010 Edition*, Paris: OECD Publications.

Joskow, P. L. (1996), 'Introducing competition into regulated network industries: from hierarchies to markets in electricity', *Industrial and Corporate Change*, **5** (2), 341–82.

Joskow, P. L. (2008), 'Capacity payments in imperfectly competitive electricity markets', *Utilities Policy*, **16** (3), 159–70.

Joskow, P. L. (2019), 'Challenges for wholesale electricity markets with intermittent renewable generation at scale: the U.S. experience', *Oxford Review of Economic Policy*, **35** (2), 291–331.

Joskow, P. L. and J. Tirole (2007), 'Reliability in competitive electricity markets', *Rand Journal of Economics*, **38** (1), 60–84.

Keppler, J. H. (2017), 'Rationales for capacity remuneration mechanisms: security of supply, externalities and asymmetric investment incentives', *Energy Policy*, **105**, 562–70.

Léautier, T.-O. (2016), 'The visible hand: insuring optimal investment in electric generation', *The Energy Journal*, **37** (2), 89–109.

Léautier, T.-O. (2019), *Imperfect Markets and Imperfect Regulation*, Cambridge, MA: MIT Press.

Newbery, D., M. G. Pollitt, R. A. Ritz and W. Strielkowski (2018), 'Market design for a high-renewables European electricity system', *Renewable and Sustainable Energy Reviews*, **91**, 695–707.

Schröder, T. and W. Kuckshinrichs (2015), 'Value of lost load: an efficient economic indicator for power supply security? A literature review', *Frontiers in Energy Research*, **3**, 1–12.

Schweppe, F., M. Caramanis, R. Tabors and R. Bohn (1988), *Spot Pricing of Electricity*, Boston, MA: Kluwer Academic Press.

Turvey, R. (1968), *Optimal Pricing and Investment in Electricity Supply*, London: George Allen & Unwin.

US Energy Information Administration (US EIA) (2019), 'Levelized cost and levelized avoided cost in the *Annual Energy Outlook 2019*', February 2020, accessed 9 September 2020 at https://www.eia.gov/outlooks/archive/aeo19/pdf/electricity_generation.pdf.

Wolak, F. (2018), 'Efficient pricing: the key to unlocking radical innovation in the electricity sector', manuscript, 22 July.

Yergin, D. (1990), *The Prize: The Epic Quest for Oil, Money and Power*, New York: Simon & Schuster.

4. Wholesale electricity market design
Frank A. Wolak

1. INTRODUCTION

Although different jurisdictions around the world had different motivations for restructuring their electricity supply industries and introducing wholesale electricity markets, all had the goal of improving industry performance. Because electricity market design requires an explicit regulatory process to set market rules, initial conditions in the industry and political factors can drive the choice of a jurisdiction's initial market design. This choice can interfere with the ability of the subsequent regulatory process to improve industry performance and ultimately benefit electricity consumers.

Particularly in the United States (US) and Europe, there has been a convergence of market designs, although the standard market design in the US is quite different from the standard market design in Europe. This difference can be largely explained by differences in initial conditions and the political forces driving the restructuring process in each region. However, the desire of many jurisdictions to scale the amount of intermittent wind and solar generation resources is creating new market design challenges that are likely to lead to greater convergence between the market designs in the US and Europe.

International experience with more than 25 years of wholesale electricity market design has revealed several factors that are crucial to achieving lasting improvements in industry performance and tangible economic benefits to electricity consumers. These factors are: (1) the match between the short-term market used to set prices and dispatch generation units and how the actual electricity network is operated; (2) effective market and regulatory mechanisms to ensure long-term generation and transmission resource adequacy; (3) appropriate mechanisms to mitigate system-wide and local market power; and (4) mechanisms to allow active involvement of final demand in the short-term market.

As we discuss below, these factors must be addressed in any successful restructuring process because wholesale and retail market mechanisms decentralize many of the activities that formerly took place within the vertically integrated monopoly. In addition, at least during the initial stages of the restructured industry, there is a small number of wholesale and retail market participants, which implies that wholesale and retail market rules can significantly affect the behaviour of market participants, often to the detriment of electricity consumers.

Consequently, designing wholesale and retail market rules requires accounting for the impact each market rule has on the behaviour of individual market participants. These market rules must create economic incentives for actions by individual wholesale and retail market participants that enhance, or at least do not detract from, real-time system reliability or long-term supply adequacy.

The market designer must recognize that any wholesale or retail market rule will be exploited by all market participants to enhance their ability to maximize profits from selling wholesale or retail electricity or minimizing retail electricity procurement costs. The most successful restructured markets are those with market rules that account for the self-interested behaviour of all market participants. Much of this chapter is devoted to analysing each of the above-mentioned four factors determining the performance of a restructured electricity supply industry from this perspective and using the lessons learned from international experience to provide recommendations for the design of a successful wholesale electricity market.

The remainder of this chapter proceeds as follows. Section 2 first describes why electricity requires an explicit market design process. Section 3 summarizes the factors leading to the different experiences with and outcomes of the wholesale market design process in the US versus Europe and other industrialized countries. Sections 4 to 7 present the four major lessons from international experience with wholesale market design. Section 4 outlines the importance of the match between the network model used to operate the forward market that sets prices and dispatch levels and the physical network used to operate the electricity supply industry in real time. This section argues that a multi-settlement locational marginal pricing (LMP) wholesale market is likely to achieve the best possible match between how the transmission network operates and how the wholesale market determines prices and dispatch levels for any feasible configuration of the transmission network. Section 5 explains why a liquid forward market for energy is likely to be the most efficient way to ensure both short-term and long-term resource adequacy. This section also discusses the properties of a capacity payment mechanism, an alternative approach to long-term resource adequacy. Section 6 describes why fixed-price long-term contracts are an effective mechanism for limiting the incentive of suppliers to exercise system-wide unilateral market power in the short-term market. This section also discusses local market power mitigation mechanisms that exist in all US markets and most international markets, although the details of these mechanisms differ across markets. Section 7 emphasizes the benefits of active involvement of final demand in the wholesale market, particularly in regions that have deployed hourly meters.[1] A multi-settlement LMP market is shown to provide the ideal platform for active participation of final demand.

Section 8 builds on the discussion in Sections 4 to 7 to propose a market design for developing countries that is likely to capture the major source of economic benefits possible from electricity industry restructuring, while recognizing the regulatory and institutional challenges facing developing countries. This market design avoids many of the more costly features of formal wholesale electricity markets in the industrialized world with a significantly reduced regulatory burden. This section also describes how this market design can be implemented in a small market with a vertically integrated utility that purchases a portion of its electricity from independent power producers.

Section 9 considers the question of what market design can successfully integrate a significant amount of intermittent renewable resources at both the transmission and distribution grid levels. A number of countries have policies to increase the amount of renewable energy they consume. I describe how a multi-settlement LMP market with a forward energy contracting-based long-term resource adequacy mechanism can support the efficient deployment of intermittent renewable resources in both the transmission and distribution grids.

2.   WHY ELECTRICITY IS DIFFERENT

It is difficult to conceive of an industry where introducing market mechanisms at the wholesale and retail level is more challenging for a policymaker. Virtually every aspect of the technology of electricity delivery and how it has been historically priced to final electricity consumers enhances the ability of suppliers to raise the prices they are paid through their unilateral actions – what is typically referred to as exercising unilateral market power. Supply must equal demand at every instant in time and at each location in the transmission and distribution networks. If this does not occur then, these networks can become unstable, and brownouts and blackouts can happen. It is also very costly to store electricity. Constructing storage facilities typically requires substantial up-front investments and basic physics implies significantly more than 1 megawatt-hour (MWh) of energy must be produced to store 1 MWh of energy. Production of electricity is subject to extreme capacity constraints in the sense that it is physically impossible to get more than a pre-specified amount of energy from a generation unit in an hour. These capacity constraints limit the size of the supply response by competitors to the attempts of a generation unit owner to raise the price it is paid for electricity. Finally, delivery of the product consumed must take place through a potentially congested, looped transmission network, and how transmission capacity is allocated to different market participants exerts an enormous influence on their behaviour.

Historically, how electricity has been priced to final consumers makes wholesale demand extremely inelastic, if not perfectly inelastic, with respect to the hourly wholesale price. Customers are usually charged a single fixed price or according to a fixed non-linear price schedule for each kilowatt-hour (KWh) they consume during the billing cycle, regardless of the value of the wholesale price when each KWh is consumed. Paying according to a fixed-retail price schedule implies that these customers have hourly demands with zero price elasticity with respect to the hourly wholesale price, which significantly enhances the ability of suppliers to exercise unilateral market power in the short-term market.

The requirement to deliver electricity to final electricity consumers through a specialized transmission and distribution network that is too expensive to duplicate for a given geographic area precludes the usual approach to finding a market design that best meets the needs of consumers and producers. For most products, the market design process involves consumers deciding which products and locations to patronize and producers deciding which products and locations to serve. Some locations and products favour producers and others favour consumers. However, the existence of willing buyers and sellers of the same product at the same location is a necessary condition for trade to take place.

Coffee retailing is a recent example of the typical market design process. Historically, a customer interested in purchasing a cup of coffee would go to a diner or convenience store. However, specialized coffee retailers such as Starbucks entered and attracted customers, and, as a result, many traditional coffee outlets lost customers. The customers lost by traditional coffee shops and diners and gained by specialized coffee retailers reduced the profitability and increased the likelihood of exit by the former and increased the financial viability of the latter. This dynamic is continually taking place in all markets where consumers and producers can vote with their feet for their preferred market design.

This process of consumers and producers voting with their feet is not available to the electricity supply industry because the product must be injected and delivered to final consumers through the same transmission and distribution network, and even in developing countries customers have limited tolerance for an interruption of their supply of electricity. Moreover, reliable delivery of the electricity requires maintaining supply and demand balance at all locations in the grid at every instant in time. Consequently, any new supplier still delivers its electricity through this network and all customers still receive grid-supplied electricity from this network. As a consequence, the market design process must take place through explicit regulatory actions that set the rules for how market participants connect to the network and how they are paid for the electricity they inject and how they pay for the electricity they withdraw, rather than through the unilateral actions of producers and consumers of electricity.

3.   WHOLESALE MARKET DESIGN IN THE US AND EUROPE

The electricity supply industries in the US and Europe and other industrialized countries started from different initial conditions that also led to different political motivations for electricity industry restructuring. Europe and other industrialized countries typically started with state-owned national or regional vertically integrated monopolies. The primary public policy concern was that these state-owned entities were over-capitalized and inefficiently operated. The political motivation was that privatizing them and introducing competition would create stronger incentives for efficient operation. For example, in England and Wales, the Central Electricity Generating Board (CEGB), a state-owned entity, was broken up and sold off by the Margaret Thatcher government to create three wholesale electricity suppliers – National Power, PowerGen and Nuclear Electric – and the National Grid Company that operated the transmission grid. The 12 regional electricity companies (RECs) that sold retail electricity and operated local distribution networks in their service territory were also privatized.[2] The Nordic countries, having both state-owned companies and local public authority-owned companies, did not choose to privatize them, but instead let them all compete in the same wholesale market (as Le Coq and Schwenen explain in Chapter 10 of this handbook). Australia and New Zealand pursued a similar strategy in restructuring their electricity supply industries, with both privately owned and government-owned companies competing to supply wholesale electricity.[3]

In the US, very few of the vertically integrated utilities in the regions that introduced a wholesale electricity market were state owned. The vast majority were shareholder owned, with their output prices set by state public utilities commissions for almost 100 years. Although far from perfect, this state-level regulatory process was significantly more effective at squeezing out productive inefficiencies than the state-owned utility model in Europe and in other industrialized countries.[4] As Joskow (1997) notes, the major motivation for restructuring in the US was that competition for wholesale electricity would cause more efficient new capacity investment decisions than the vertically integrated regulated monopoly regime. According to Fabrizio, Rose and Wolfram (2007), there is also evidence that restructuring reduced plant labour and non-fuel expenses.

In contrast to the US, countries in Europe and other parts of the world had little experience with monopoly regulation given their history of state ownership of the electricity supply industry. Consequently, when the restructuring process began, these jurisdictions found their electricity supply industries with significantly different initial conditions relative to their privately owned, state-regulated counterparts in the US. Specifically, all US regions that restructured their electricity supply industries started with significantly less modern delivery infrastructure than many of their European counterparts. The efforts of state regulators in the US to limit retail price increases in response to the run-up in fossil fuel prices in the late 1970s led to very little investment in new transmission capacity until the early 2000s. Load growth over this time period in most parts of the country was met through generation capacity additions near major load centres rather than through large new capacity investments distant from the load centre served by new transmission capacity. Consequently, the wholesale markets in the US began operations with significantly less modern transmission networks and less transmission capacity than their counterparts in Europe and other industrialized countries, where the state-owned electricity supply industry was able to make significant investments in transmission capacity over this same time period.

This difference in initial conditions eventually led to a different evolution of wholesale market designs, despite the fact that most wholesale market designs in the US were initially very similar to those in Europe. The United Kingdom was the first European country to restructure in the early 1990s and it chose a market design that assumed a transmission network where all generation units were equally effective at meeting demand at any location in England and Wales. Specifically, this market set a single national price for electricity each half-hour of the day. The other early wholesale market in Europe, the Nord Pool, set potentially different prices in a small number of geographic zones in Norway and Sweden, the two initial members of the Nord Pool, which later expanded to include Denmark and Finland and now allows energy trading in 13 European countries.[5]

All the European markets have evolved to zonal or single-zone pricing models where the day-ahead forward market clears at this level of spatial granularity. These markets determine market-wide or zonal generation and load schedules and market prices. This is followed by a redispatch process where intra-zonal transmission constraints and other real-time operating constraints are managed by the system operator for that region or country.

Virtually all the US wholesale electricity markets began as either a single pricing zone market, as was the case in the New England ISO, or a zonal market, as was the case in the PJM Interconnection, New York ISO, California ISO and Electricity Reliability Council of Texas (ERCOT), which followed a similar design to the standard European market. These markets had a day-ahead forward market where generation and load schedules and prices were determined at the zonal or single-pricing zone level. This was followed by a congestion management or redispatch process run by the system operator to produce final schedules that were physically feasible given the configuration of the transmission network.

Starting with the PJM Interconnection in the Eastern US, market operators found that the incidence and magnitude of transmission congestion was so large and the cost of managing it increasingly expensive that a market design with a more spatially granular pricing was adopted. This process led the PJM Interconnection to adopt an LMP market design with a day-ahead forward market and a real-time market – what is referred to as a multi-settlement LMP market design. All the other regions of the US had similar experiences with the operational challenges and cost of managing transmission congestion within the pricing zones in their single or multiple zone pricing markets. Each eventually implemented a multi-settlement LMP market design, with ERCOT being the last to do so in December of 2010.

Because of their history of state-owned utilities and significantly greater investments in transmission capacity from the 1970s up to the start of the restructuring process, wholesale markets in Europe and most other industrialized countries have managed to maintain their zonal market designs. However, the costs of making final schedules physically feasible has grown significantly as the share of intermittent renewable energy in many European countries has increased. In 2017, these costs were over 1 billion euros in Germany, more than 400 million euros in Great Britain, over 80 million euros in Spain and approximately 50 million euros in Italy.[6] These costs have led a number of European countries to consider adopting more granular approaches to electricity pricing.

4.   MATCH BETWEEN MARKET MECHANISM AND ACTUAL SYSTEM OPERATION

An important lesson from electricity market design processes around the world is the extent to which the market mechanism used to dispatch and operate generation units is consistent with how the grid is actually operated. As noted in the previous section, in the early stages of wholesale market design in the US, all the regions attempted to operate wholesale markets that used simplified versions of the transmission network. The single zone or zonal markets assumed infinite transmission capacity between locations in the transmission grid or only recognized transmission constraints across large geographic regions. These simplifications of the transmission network configuration and other relevant operating constraints can create opportunities for market participants to increase their profits by taking advantage of the fact that in real time the actual configuration of the transmission network and other operating constraints must be respected.

These markets set a single market-clearing price for a half-hour or hour for an entire country or large geographic region, despite the fact that there were generation units with offer prices below the market-clearing price not producing electricity, and units with offer prices above the market-clearing price producing electricity. This outcome occurs because of the location of demand and available generation units within the region and the configuration of the transmission network prevents some of these low offer-price units from producing electricity and requires some of the high offer-price units to supply electricity. The former units are typically called 'constrained-off' units and the latter are called 'constrained-on' or 'must-run' units.

A market design challenge arises because how generation units are compensated for being constrained-on or constrained-off impacts the offer prices they submit into wholesale energy market. For example, if generation units are paid their offer price for electricity when they are constrained-on and a unit's owner knows that it will be constrained-on, a profit-maximizing unit owner will submit an offer price far in excess of the variable cost of the unit and be paid that price for the incremental energy it supplies, which raises the total cost of electricity supplied to final consumers.

A similar set of circumstances can arise for constrained-off generation units. Constrained-off generation units are usually paid the difference between the market-clearing price and their offer price for not supplying electricity that the units would have supplied if not for the configuration of the transmission network. This market rule creates an incentive for a profit-maximizing supplier that knows its unit will be constrained-off to submit the lowest possible offer price to receive the highest possible payment for being constrained-off and raise the total cost of electricity supplied to final consumers. Bushnell et al. (2008a) discuss this problem and the market efficiency consequences in the context of the initial zonal-pricing market in California. Graf, Quaglia and Wolak (2020) document the incentives for generation unit owner offer behaviour created by the divergence between the day-ahead zonal market model and the full network model used to operate the Italian market in real time. However, this outcome is not unique to markets in industrialized countries. Wolak (2009) discusses these same issues in the context of the Colombian single price market with its negative and positive reconciliations payment mechanism.

A zonal or single zone pricing market design can address the requirement that the market model used to set prices and dispatch levels and the model used to operate network in real time match if there is sufficient investment in transmission capacity to make the actual network match for as many hours of the year as possible the network assumed in the forward markets used to set schedules and prices. For example, a single zone pricing model can be a viable market design if the transmission planning process commits to transmission investments that make transmission congestion and the need for redispatch of generation units sufficiently infrequent and unpredictable as to not impact the behaviour of generation unit owners. As noted in Wolak (2015a), the wholesale electricity market for the province of Alberta in Canada sets a single price for the entire province and has adopted a transmission policy that ensures sufficient transmission capacity to make this energy market assumption a reality for actual system operation for the vast majority of hours of the year. The wholesale market in Australia operates a zonal market based on state boundaries. Because most of the major load centres are on the east coast of the country and the major generation units tend to be further inland near the coal and natural gas resources, historically there was a limited amount of intrazonal congestion. However, this situation is changing with the increasing amount of intermittent renewable generation capacity installed in the Australian electricity market.

4.1 Locational Marginal Pricing

Almost any difference between the market model used to set dispatch levels and market prices and the actual operation of the generation units needed to serve demand creates an opportunity for market participants to take actions that raise their profits at the expense of overall market efficiency. Multi-settlement wholesale electricity markets that use LMP, also referred to as nodal pricing, largely avoid these constrained-on and constrained-off problems, because all transmission constraints and other relevant operating constraints are respected in the process of determining dispatch levels and locational prices in the wholesale market.

All LMP markets in the US co-optimize the procurement of energy and ancillary services.[7] This means that all suppliers submit to the wholesale market operator their generation unit-specific willingness-to-supply schedules for energy and any ancillary service the generation unit is capable of providing. Likewise, large loads and load-serving entities submit their willingness-to-purchase energy schedules. Locational prices for energy and ancillary services and dispatch levels and ancillary services commitments for generation units at each location in the transmission network are determined by minimizing the as-offered costs of meeting the demand for energy and ancillary services at all locations in the transmission network, subject to all transmission network and other relevant operating constraints. No generation unit will be accepted to supply energy or an ancillary service if doing so would violate a transmission or other operating constraint.

An important distinction between an LMP market design and the standard European market design is the centralized commitment of generation units to provide energy and ancillary services. European markets do not typically require all generation units to submit energy offer curves into the day-ahead market and instead allow individual producers to make the commitment decisions for their generation units. A self-commitment market can result in higher cost generation units operating because of the differences among producers in their assessment of the likely market price. Self-commitment markets also do not allow the simultaneous procurement of energy and ancillary services and instead rely on sequential procurement of ancillary services after energy schedules have been determined. As Oren (2001) demonstrates, sequential clearing of energy and ancillary services markets increases the opportunities for generation unit owners to exercise unilateral market power in the ancillary services market, because they know that units committed to supply energy cannot compete in the subsequent ancillary services market.

In contrast, LMP markets that co-optimize the procurement of energy and ancillary services ensure that each generation unit is used in the most cost-effective manner based on the energy and ancillary services offers of all generation units, not just those owned by a single market participant. Specifically, the opportunity cost of supplying any ancillary service a unit is capable of providing will be explicitly taken into account in deciding whether to use the unit for that ancillary service. For example, if the market-clearing price of energy at that generation unit's location is 40 $/MWh, the unit's offer price for energy is 30 $/MWh, and the price for the only ancillary service the unit can supply is 5 $/MW, then the unit will not be accepted to supply the ancillary service. At a $0/MW offer price, it would be accepted to supply the ancillary service only if the price was greater than or equal to 10 $/MW because of the 10 $/MWh opportunity cost of energy for that unit. In contrast, self-commitment markets such as those that exist in Europe and other industrialized countries must rely on individual market participants to make the choice between supplying energy or ancillary services from each generation unit.

The LMP process sets potentially different prices at all locations in the transmission network, depending on the configuration of the transmission network and geographic location of demand and the availability of generation units. Because the configuration of the transmission network and the location of generation units and demand is taken into account in operating the market, only generation unit dispatch levels that are expected to be feasible in real time given the expected configuration of the transmission network will be accepted to serve demand and they will be paid a higher or lower LMP than other units, depending on whether the generation unit is in a generation-deficient or a generation-rich region of the transmission network.

The nodal price at each location is the increase in the minimized value of the 'as-offered costs' objective function as a result of a one unit increase in the amount of energy withdrawn at that location in the transmission network. The price of each ancillary service is defined as the increase in the optimized value of the objective function as a result of a one unit increase in the demand for that ancillary service. In most LMP markets, ancillary services are procured at a coarser level of spatial granularity than energy. For example, energy is typically priced at the nodal level and ancillary services are priced over larger geographic regions. Bohn, Caramanis and Schweppe (1984) provide an accessible discussion of the properties of the LMP market mechanism.

Another strength of the LMP market design is the fact that other constraints that the system operator takes into account in operating the transmission network can also be accounted for in setting dispatch levels and locational prices. For example, suppose that reliability studies have shown that a minimum amount of energy must be produced by a group of generation units located in a small region of the grid. This operating constraint can be built into the LMP market mechanism and reflected in the resulting locational prices. This property of LMP markets is particularly relevant to the cost-effective integration of a significant amount of intermittent renewable generation capacity in the transmission network, because additional reliability constraints may need to be formulated and incorporated into the LMP market to account for the fact that this energy can quickly disappear and reappear.

An important lesson from the US experience with LMP markets is that explicitly accounting for the configuration of the transmission network in determining dispatch levels both within and across regions can significantly increase the amount of trade that takes place between the regions. Mansur and White (2012) dramatically demonstrate this point by comparing the volume of trade between two regions of the Eastern US – what the authors call the Midwest and East of PJM – before and after these regions were integrated into a single LMP market that accounts for the configuration of the transmission network throughout the entire integrated region. Average daily energy flows from the Midwest to East of PJM almost tripled immediately following the integration of the two regions into an LMP market. There was no change in the physical configuration of the transmission network for the two regions. This increase in energy flows was purely the result of incorporating the two regions into a single LMP market that recognizes the configuration of the transmission network for the two regions in dispatching generation units.

4.2 Multi-settlement Markets

Multi-settlement nodal pricing markets have been adopted by all US jurisdictions with a formal short-term wholesale electricity market. A multi-settlement market has a day-ahead forward market that is run in advance of real-time system operation. Generation unit owners submit unit-level offer curves for each hour of the following day and electricity retailers submit demand curves for each hour of the following day. The system operator then minimizes the as-offered cost to meet these demands simultaneously for all 24 hours of the following day subject to the anticipated configuration of the transmission network and other relevant operating constraints. This gives rise to locational marginal prices (LMPs) and firm financial commitments to buy and sell electricity each hour of the following day for all generation unit and load locations.

The day-ahead market typically allows generation unit owners to submit their start-up and no-load cost offers as well as energy offer curves, and both of these costs enter the objective function used to compute hourly generation schedules and LMPs for all 24 hours of the following day. This logic implies that a generation unit will not be dispatched in the day-ahead market unless the combination of its start-up and no-load costs and energy costs are part of the least-cost solution to serving hourly demands for all 24 hours of the following day. As noted earlier, to the extent that generation unit owners submit start-up, no-load and energy offer curves that are representative of their actual costs, the total cost of committing and dispatching the generation units that arises from this centralized unit commitment process is likely to be less than the total commitment and dispatch costs that result from a self-commitment market, such as those that exist in Europe and other industrialized countries.

The energy schedules that arise from the day-ahead market do not require a generation unit to supply the amount sold or a load to consume the amount purchased in the day-ahead market. The only requirement is that any shortfall in a day-ahead commitment to supply energy must be purchased from the real-time market at that same location or any production greater than the day-ahead commitment is sold at the real-time price at that same location. For loads, the same logic applies. Additional consumption beyond the load's day-ahead purchase is paid for at the real-time price at that location and the surplus of a day-ahead purchase relative to actual consumption is sold at the real-time price at that location.

In all US wholesale markets, real-time LMPs are determined from the real-time offer curves from all available generation units and dispatchable loads by minimizing the as-offered cost to meet real-time demand at all locations in the geographic region that contains the LMP market, taking into account the current configuration of the transmission network and other relevant operating constraints. This process gives rise to LMPs at all locations in the transmission network and actual hourly operating levels for all generation units. Real-time imbalances relative to day-ahead schedules are cleared at these real-time prices.

To understand how a two-settlement market works, suppose that a generation unit owner sells 50 MWh in the day-ahead market at 60 $/MWh. It receives a guaranteed $3000 in revenues from this sale. However, if the generation unit owner fails to inject 50 MWh of energy into the grid during the specified delivery hour of the following day, it must purchase the energy it fails to inject at the real-time price at that location. Suppose that the real-time price at that location is 70 $/MWh and the generator only injects 40 MWh of energy during the hour in question. In this case, the unit owner must purchase the 10 MWh shortfall relative to its day-ahead schedule at 70 $/MWh. Consequently, the net revenues the generation unit owner earns from selling 50 MWh in the day-ahead market and only injecting 40 MWh is $2300, the $3000 of revenues earned in the day-ahead market less the $700 paid for the 10 MWh real-time deviation from the unit's day-ahead schedule.

If a generation unit produces more output than its day-ahead schedule, then this incremental output is sold in the real-time market. For example, if the unit produced 55 MWh, then the additional 5 MWh beyond the unit owner's day-ahead schedule is sold at the real-time price. By the same logic, a load-serving entity (what Europeans call a supplier) that buys 100 MWh in the day-ahead market but only withdraws 90 MWh in real time, sells the 10 MWh not consumed at the real-time price. Alternatively, if the load-serving entity consumes 110 MWh, then the additional 10 MWh not purchased in the day-ahead market must be purchased at the real-time price.

By this same logic, a multi-settlement nodal pricing market is well-suited to countries that do not have an extensive transmission network because it explicitly accounts for the configuration on the actual transmission network in setting both day-ahead energy schedules and prices and real-time output levels and prices. This market design eliminates much of the need for ad hoc adjustments to generation unit output levels that can increase the total cost of wholesale electricity to final consumers because of differences between the prices and schedules that the market mechanism sets and how the actual electricity network operates.

Wolak (2011b) quantifies the magnitude of the economic benefits associated with the transition to nodal pricing from a zonal-pricing market that was very similar to the standard market design in Europe and other industrialized countries. On 1 April 2009, the California market transitioned to a multi-settlement nodal pricing market design from a multi-settlement zonal-pricing market. Wolak (2011b) compares the hourly conditional means of the total amount of input fossil fuel energy in millions of British thermal units (BTUs), the total hourly variable cost of production from fossil fuel generation units, and the total hourly number of starts from fossil fuel units before versus after the implementation of nodal pricing, controlling non-parametrically for the total hourly output of the fossil fuel units in California and the daily prices of the major input fossil fuels. Total hourly BTUs of fossil fuel energy consumed to produce electricity is 2.5 per cent lower, the total hourly variable cost of production for fossil fuels units is 2.1 per cent lower, and the total number of hourly starts is 0.17 higher after the implementation of nodal pricing. This 2.1 per cent cost reduction implies a roughly $105 million reduction in the total annual variable cost of producing electricity from fossil fuels in California associated with the introduction of nodal pricing.

A multi-settlement LMP market design is also particularly well suited to managing a generation mix with a significant share of intermittent renewable resources. The additional operating constraints necessary for reliable system operation with an increased amount of renewable resources can easily be incorporated into the day-ahead and real-time market models. Therefore, the economic benefits from implementing a multi-settlement LMP market relative to market designs that do not model transmission and other operating constraints are likely to be greater the larger is the share of intermittent renewable resources. Consequently, any region with significant renewable energy goals is likely to realize significant economic benefits from implementing a multi-settlement LMP market.

A multi-settlement LMP market also values the dispatchability of generation units even though it pays all resources at the same location in the grid the same price in the day-ahead and real-time markets. Suppose that a wind unit sells 50 MWh and a thermal resource sells 40 MWh in the day-ahead market at 30 $/MWh. If in real time not as much wind energy is produced, the dispatchable thermal unit must make up the difference. Suppose that the wind unit produces only 30 MWh, so that the thermal unit must produce an additional 20 MWh. Because of this wind generation shortfall, the real-time price is now 60 $/MWh. Under this scenario, the wind unit is paid an average price of 10 $/MWh = (50 MWh × 30 $/MWh – 20 MWh × 60 $/MWh)/30 MWh for the 30 MWh it produces, while the dispatchable thermal unit is paid an average price of 40 $/MWh = (40 MWh × 30 $/MWh + 20 MWh × 60 $/MWh)/60 MWh for the 60 MWh it produces.

A similar logic applies to the case that the wind resource produces more than expected and the thermal resource reduces its output because the real-time price is lower than the day-ahead price due to the unexpectedly large amount of wind energy produced. For example, suppose the wind unit sells 30 MWh and the thermal resource sells 60 MWh in the day-ahead market at 30 $/MWh. However, in real time there is significantly more wind, so that the wind unit produces 50 MWh at a real-time price of 10 $/MWh. Because of this low real-time price, the thermal resource decides to produce 40 MWh and purchases the additional 20 MWh from its day-ahead energy schedule from the real-time market. The average price received by the wind unit is 22 $/MWh = (30 MWh × 30 $/MWh + 20 MWh × 10 $/MWh)/50 MWh and the average price received by the thermal unit is 40 $/MWh = (60 MWh × 30 $/MWh – 20 MWh × 10 $/MWh)/40 MWh. Despite paying the same price to all energy in the day-ahead and real-time markets, a multi-settlement market pays a higher average price to the dispatchable generation unit for the energy it provides during the same hour as the wind unit.

One complaint often levelled against LMP markets is that they increase the likelihood of political backlash from consumers because prices paid for wholesale electricity can differ significantly across locations within the same geographic region. For example, customers in urban areas that primarily import electricity over congested transmission lines will pay more than customers located in generation-rich rural regions that export electricity to those regions. Because more customers live in urban areas than in rural regions, charging final consumers in urban areas a higher retail price to recover the LMPs at their location may be politically challenging for the regulator to implement.

Most regions with LMP markets have addressed this issue by charging all customers in a state, region or utility service territory a weighted average of the LMPs at all load withdrawal points in the geographic region. In the above example, this implies charging the urban and rural customers the weighted average of the LMPs in urban and rural areas, where the weight assigned to each price is the share of system load that is withdrawn at that location. Under this scheme, generation units continue to be paid the LMPs at their location, but all loads pay a geographically aggregated hourly price. For example, in Singapore all generation units are paid the LMPs at their location, but all loads are charged the Uniform Singapore Electricity Price (USEP), which is the quantity-weighted average of the half-hourly LMPs for all generation nodes in Singapore. This approach to pricing captures the reliability and operating efficiency benefits of an LMP market while addressing the equity concerns regulators often face with charging customers at different locations prices that reflect the configuration of the transmission network. Tangerås and Wolak (2018) present evidence that this market rule can result in more competitive behaviour in the wholesale market by vertically integrated suppliers with the ability to exercise unilateral market power.

5.   MECHANISMS TO ENSURE LONG-TERM RESOURCE ADEQUACY

Why do wholesale electricity markets require a regulatory intervention to ensure long-term resource adequacy? Consumers want to be able to withdraw electricity from the network when they need it, just like other goods and services. But it is unclear why electricity is so fundamentally different from other products that it requires paying suppliers for production capacity to exist. For example, consumers want cars, but they do not pay for automobile assembly plants. They want point-to-point air travel, but they do not pay for airplanes. They want a loaf of bread, but do not pay for the existence of a bakery. All these industries are high fixed cost, relatively low marginal cost production processes, similar to electricity supply. Nevertheless, all these firms earn their return on capital invested by selling the good that consumers want at a price above the variable cost of producing it. Clearly, cars, air travel and bread are in many ways essential commodities, yet there is no regulatory intervention that ensures there is sufficient production capacity for these products to meet demand.

So, what is different about electricity markets that necessitates the need for a long-term resource adequacy mechanism? The answer lies in how short-term markets for these products operate relative to that for wholesale electricity. This difference is the result of the regulatory history of the electricity supply industry and the technology historically used to meter electricity. The limitation on the level of short-term prices and the way that supply shortfalls are dealt with in wholesale electricity markets creates what has been termed a 'reliability externality' that requires a regulatory intervention to internalize (Wolak 2013).

In the market for automobiles, air travel and even bread, there is no explicit prohibition on the short-term price of the good rising to the level necessary to clear the market. Take the example of air travel. Airlines adjust the prices for seats on a flight over time in an attempt to ensure that the number of customers travelling on that flight equals the number of seats flying. This can result in very different prices for a seat on the same flight, depending on when the customer purchases the seat. A customer that waits too long to purchase a seat faces the risk of an infinite price in the sense that all of the seats on the flight are sold out. This ability to use prices to allocate the available seats is also what allows the airline the flexibility to recover its total production costs. Airlines can set low prices to fill flights with low demand and extremely high prices on other flights, or at other times for the same flight, when demand is high.

The ability to use the short-term price to manage the supply and demand balance in the electricity supply industry is limited first by the fact that many wholesale electricity markets have offer caps that limit a supplier's offer price into the wholesale market and/ or a price cap that limits the magnitude of the eventual market-clearing price. In addition, historically virtually all electricity supply industries did not have hourly meters that could record a customer's consumption during each hour of the month. Even today, most regions only have mechanical meters that compute the customer's consumption for the entire month as the difference between two consecutive meter readings. With monthly or bi-monthly reading of mechanical meters, it is impossible for the utility to know how much electricity a customer consumed within a given hour of the month.[8]

Although these offer caps and price caps can limit the ability of suppliers to exercise unilateral market power in the short-term energy market, they also reduce the revenues suppliers can receive during scarcity conditions. This is often referred to as the *missing money* problem for generation unit owners. However, this missing money problem is only a symptom of the existence of a reliability externality, it is not the cause.

This externality exists because offer caps limit the potential downside to electricity retailers and large consumers (able to purchase from the short-term market) delaying their purchases of electricity until real-time operation. Specifically, if a retailer or large consumer knows the price cap on the short-term market is 250 $/MWh, then it is unlikely to be willing to pay more than that for electricity in any earlier forward market. This creates the possibility that real-time system conditions can occur where the amount of electricity demanded at or below the offer cap is more than the amount suppliers are willing to offer at or below the offer cap. This outcome implies that the system operator must be forced to either abandon the market mechanism or curtail load until the available supply offered at or below the offer cap equals the reduced level of demand, as was the case a number of times during the period January 2001 to March 2001, and more recently in August 2020, in California.

Because random curtailments of supply – also known as rolling blackouts – are used to make demand equal to the available supply at or below the bid cap under these system conditions, this mechanism creates an 'externality' because no retailer or large consumer bears the full cost of failing to procure adequate amounts of energy in advance of delivery. A retailer that has purchased sufficient supply in the forward market to meet its real-time energy demand is equally likely to be randomly curtailed as the same size retailer that has not procured adequate amounts of energy in the forward market. For this reason, all retailers and large loads have an incentive to under-procure their expected energy needs in the forward market.

Particularly for markets with very low offer caps, retailers have little incentive to engage in sufficient fixed-price forward contracting with generation unit owners to ensure a reliable supply of electricity for all possible realizations of future real-time demand. For example, a 200 MW generation unit owner that expects to run 100 hours during the year with a variable cost of 80 $/MWh would be willing to sign a fixed-price forward contract to provide up to 200 MWh of energy for up to 100 hours of the year to a retailer. Because this generation unit owner is essentially selling its expected annual output to the retailer, it would want a $/MWh price that at least exceeds its average total cost of supplying energy during that year. This price can be significantly above the average price in the short-term wholesale market during the hours in which this generation unit operates because of the offer cap on the short-term market and other market power mitigation mechanisms. This fact implies that the retailer with the option purchase energy from a short-term market with a low price cap would find it profit-maximizing not to sign a forward contract that allows the generation unit owner full cost recovery but instead wait until the short-term market to purchase the necessary energy at prices that are limited by the offer cap.

Although this incentive for retailers to rely on a price-capped short-term market is most likely to impact generation units that run infrequently, if the level of demand relative to the amount of available supply is sufficiently large, it can even impact intermediate and baseload units. Because of the expectation of very low prices in the short-term market and the limited prospect of very high prices because of offer caps, retailers may decide not to sign fixed-price forward contracts with these generation unit owners and purchase their energy in the short-term market. By this logic, a short-term energy market with an offer cap always creates an incentive for retailers to delay purchasing some of their energy needs until real time, when these caps can be used to obtain the energy at a lower price than the supplier would be willing to sell it in the forward market.

The lower the offer cap, the greater is the likelihood that the retailer will delay its electricity purchases to the short-term market. Delaying more purchases to the short-term market increases the likelihood of the event that insufficient supply will offer into the short-term market at or below the offer cap to meet demand. If a retailer knows that part of the cost of its failure to purchase sufficient fixed-price forward contracts will be borne by other retailers and large consumers because of random curtailment, then it has an incentive to engage in less fixed-price forward contracts than it would in a world where all customers had hourly meters and all customers could be charged hourly prices high enough to cause them to reduce their demand to equal the amount of supply available at that price.

Because externalities are generally caused by a missing market, another way of characterizing this reliability externality is as a missing market for long-term contracts for energy. In this case, because retailers do not bear the full cost of failing to procure sufficient energy to meet their real-time needs in the future, there is a missing market for long-term contracts for long enough delivery horizons into the future to allow new generation units to be financed and constructed to serve demand under all possible future conditions in the short-term market.

The above discussion implies that unless the regulator is willing to eliminate the offer cap on the short-term market so that the short-term price can be used to equate available supply to demand under all possible future short-term market conditions, some form of regulatory intervention is necessary to internalize the resulting reliability externality. However, if customers do not have hourly meters that can record their consumption during each hour of the billing cycle, they have a limited ability to benefit from shifting their consumption away from high-priced hours, so having no offer cap on the short-term market would not be advisable.

As the above discussion makes clear, relying on a capped short-term energy market price to ensure long-term resource adequacy does not address the reliability externality and leaves both a 'missing money' and a 'missing market' problem. Capacity mechanisms are one approach to addressing this reliability externality designed primarily for thermal generation-dominated markets, where the major concern is insufficient generation capacity to meet future demand peaks. In intermittent renewable-dominated markets the major reliability concern is more likely to be insufficient renewable energy (that is, not enough water, wind or sunshine) to meet a sustained demand for energy, which implies that other approaches to addressing the reliability externality may dominate a capacity-based approach for these electricity markets.

As the share of intermittent renewable generation in a wholesale electricity market increases, the magnitude of the reliability externality is also likely to increase. The uncertain availability of wind and solar resources increases the magnitude and duration of potential future energy supply shortfalls that must be managed, which implies many more instances when a capped short-term energy market may not yield a sufficient energy supply increase or demand decrease to maintain real-time supply and demand balance.

Two general approaches have been developed to address this reliability externality. The first is based on fixed-price and fixed-quantity long-term contracts for energy signed between generation unit owners and load-serving entities at various horizons to delivery. The second approach is a regulator-mandated capacity mechanism. Typically, the regulator requires that load-serving entities purchase sufficient firm generation capacity, a magnitude defined by the regulator, to cover their annual peak demand. Generation unit owners receive a regulator-determined payment for the capacity they provide to the load-serving entity. Differing degrees of regulatory invention are used to determine this $/KW per year payment across the existing capacity mechanisms.

5.1   Fixed-price Forward Contract Approach to Long-term Resource Adequacy

The fixed-price forward contract solution is the standard approach used to ensure a real-time supply and demand balance in markets for products with high fixed costs of production. The prospect of a high real-time price for the product provides incentives for customers to hedge this real-time price risk through a fixed-price forward contract. A supplier benefits from signing such a contract because it has greater quantity and revenue certainty as result.

The airline industry is a familiar example of this phenomenon. There is a substantial fixed cost associated with operating a flight between a given origin and destination pair. Regardless of how many passengers board the flight, the airplane, pilot and co-pilot, flight attendants and fuel must be paid for. Moreover, there is a finite number of seats on the flight, so passengers wanting to travel face the risk that if they show up at the airport one hour before the flight and attempt to purchase a ticket, they may find that it is sold out or tickets are extremely expensive because of the high real-time demand for seats. Customers hedge this short-term price risk by purchasing their tickets in advance, which is a fixed-price, fixed-quantity (one seat) forward contract for travel on the flight. These forward market purchases allow the airline to better plan the types of aircraft and flight staff it will use to serve each route and how much fuel is needed for each flight.

Similar arguments apply to wholesale electricity markets to the extent that real-time prices can rise to very high levels. For example, in Australia the offer cap on the short-term market is currently A$15 000 per MWh, yet annual average wholesale prices are less than 100 A$/MWh. The potential for short-term prices at or near the price cap provides a very strong incentive for electricity retailers and large customers to purchase their electricity through fixed-price forward contracts, rather than face the risk of these extreme short-term prices. However, even at this level of the offer cap on the short-term market in Australia there have been a small number of half-hour periods when supply shortfalls occur, consistent with the reliability externality argument.

Purchasing fixed-price and fixed-quantity forward contracts far enough in advance of delivery for new entrants to compete to provide this energy ensures that retailers will receive a competitive forward market price for their purchases. These forward market purchases far in advance of delivery also ensure that the seller of the contract has sufficient time to construct the new generation capacity needed to meet the demand secured through the fixed-price forward contracts. Consequently, in the same sense that fixed-price forward contracts for air travel allow an airline to better match airplanes and flight staff to routes, fixed-price forward contracts for electricity allow generation unit owners to choose the least-cost mix of capacity to serve the demand that has purchased the fixed-price forward contracts for energy.

Key to the success of this strategy for obtaining sufficient generation capacity to meet future demand is the threat of very high short-term prices, which provides the incentive for load-serving entities to sign fixed-price forward contracts for their expected future demand far enough in advance of delivery to allow new entrants to compete with existing generation unit owners in the provision of these forward contracts for energy. However, most regions with restructured electricity markets are unwilling to allow short-term prices to rise to the level allowed in Australia. Until 17 November 2016, all wholesale markets in the US that were under the oversight of the Federal Energy Regulatory Commission (US FERC) had offer caps equal to 1000 $/MWh. FERC Order 831 revised that policy, allowing suppliers to submit, after that date, the higher of 1000 $/MWh or the unit's verified cost-based incremental energy offer. This order also capped verified cost-based incremental energy offers at 2000 $/MWh.[9] The ERCOT, the only non-FERC jurisdictional wholesale market in the US, currently caps the offer price that suppliers can submit at 9000 $/MWh, which in US dollars is very close to Australia's offer cap. Again, this level of the offer cap significantly limits but does not eliminate the likelihood of supply shortfalls in the real-time market due to the reliability externality.

Many wholesale electricity markets outside the US, particularly those in the developing countries, have offer caps far below 1000 $/MWh. Low offer caps do not create a strong enough incentive for load-serving entities to purchase enough fixed-price forward contracts far enough in advance of delivery to ensure sufficient generation capacity to meet future demand. Consequently, in a number of Latin American countries, there are regulator-mandated requirements for load-serving entities to purchase certain percentages of their final demand in fixed-price forward contracts in advance of delivery. For example, it could be 90 per cent of forecast demand one year in advance, 85 per cent two years in advance and so forth. This regulatory mandate provides sufficient demand for long-term contracts far enough in advance of delivery to ensure enough generation capacity to meet future demand.

It is important to emphasize that mandating these contracting levels is unlikely to impose a financial hardship on retailers that lose customers to competing retailers. If a retailer purchased more fixed-price forward contract coverage than it ultimately needs because it lost customers to a competitor, it can sell this obligation in the secondary market. Unless the market demand for energy in the future is unexpectedly low, this retailer is just as likely to make a profit on this sale as it is to make a loss, because one of the retailers that gained customers needs forward contracts to meet its regulatory requirements for coverage of its final demand. Only in the unlikely case that the aggregate amount of forward contracts purchased is greater than the realized final demand for the entire market will there be a potential for stranded forward contracts held by retailers that lose customers.

Fixed-price forward contract obligations also significantly limit the incentive of generation unit owners to exercise unilateral market power in the short-term market. To understand this logic, let PC equal the fixed price at which the generation unit owner agrees to sell energy to an electricity retailer in a forward contract and QC equal the agreed upon quantity of energy sold. This contract is negotiated in advance of the date in which the generation unit owner will supply the energy, so the value of *PC* and *QC* are predetermined from the perspective of the supplier's behaviour in the short-term wholesale market.

Wolak (2000) demonstrates that the quantity of fixed-price forward contract obligations held by the generation unit owner determines what short-term market price the firm finds ex post profit-maximizing given its marginal cost of producing energy, the supply offers of its competitors and the level of aggregate demand. Incorporating the payment stream a generation unit owner receives from its forward contract obligations, its variable profit function for a given hour of the day is:

$$\pi(PS) = (PC - C)QC + (QS - QC)(PS - C) \tag{4.1}$$

where *QS* is the quantity of energy sold in the short-term market and produced by the generation unit owner, *PS* is the price of energy sold in the short-term market and *C* is the supplier's marginal cost of producing electricity, which for simplicity is assumed to be constant.

The first term in (4.1) is the variable profit from the forward contract sales and the second term is the additional profit or loss from selling more or less energy in the short-term market than the generation unit owner's forward contract quantity. Because the forward contract price and quantity are negotiated in advance of the delivery date, the first term, $(PC - C)QC$, is a fixed profit stream to the generation unit owner before it offers into the short-term market. The second term depends on the price in the short-term market, but in a way that can significantly limit the incentive for the generation unit owner to raise prices in the short-term market.

For example, if the generation unit owner attempts to raise prices by withholding output, it could end up selling less in the short-term market than its forward contract quantity ($QC > QS$), and if the resulting market-clearing price is greater than the firm's marginal cost ($PS > C$), the second term in (4.1) will be negative. Consequently, only in the case that the generation unit owner is confident that it will produce more than its forward contract quantity in the short-term market does it have an incentive to withhold output to raise short-term prices.

The quantity of forward contract obligations held by a firm's competitors also limits its incentive to exercise unilateral market power in the short-term market. If a producer knows that all of its competitors have substantial fixed-price forward contract obligations, then this producer knows these firms will submit offer curves into the short-term market close to their marginal cost curves. Therefore, attempts by this generation unit owner to raise prices in the short-term market by withholding output are likely to be unsuccessful because the aggressiveness of the offers into the short-term market by its competitors with substantial fixed-price forward contract obligations limits the price increase a producer can expect from these actions.

This dynamic creates the following virtuous cycle of forward contracting. If a producer knows all its competitors have a substantial amount of their expected energy sales covered by fixed-price forward contracts, then it has an incentive to sign fixed-price forward contracts for a substantial fraction of its expected energy sales. When all generation unit owners have a substantial fraction of their expected energy sales covered by fixed-price forward contracts, then all of them have a common interest in reducing the cost of meeting these fixed-price forward contract obligations.

The resulting reductions in the short-term prices creates another virtuous cycle from fixed-price forward contracts. Generation unit owners that have sold forward contracts have a strong incentive to make the cost of supplying these contracts as low as possible. This should result in low short-term prices for energy, which will then be factored into subsequent negotiations for the next round of fixed-price forward contracts. This dynamic for reducing short-term wholesale prices results from a persistent high level of coverage of final demand by fixed-price forward contracts that creates the incentive for all generation unit owners to reduce the cost of meeting their forward contract obligations.

5.2 Capacity Mechanism Approach to Long-term Resource Adequacy

Particularly in the US, capacity mechanisms appear to be a holdover from the vertically integrated regulated regime with regional power pools where capacity payments compensated generation units for their capital costs, because the regulated power pool typically only paid unit owners their variable operating costs for the electricity they produced. Therefore, all fixed costs had to be recovered through other mechanisms besides the sale of wholesale electricity.

Capacity payments typically involve a dollar per kilowatt per year ($/kW/year) payment to individual generation units based on some measure of the amount of their capacity that is available to produce electricity during stressed system conditions, what is often referred to as the unit's 'firm capacity'. This value depends, among other things, on the technology of the generating unit. For example, a baseload coal-fired unit would have a firm capacity value very close to its nameplate capacity. Indeed, the firm capacity of a thermal unit is usually equal to the unit's capacity in megawatts times its availability factor.[10]

In hydroelectric-dominated markets, determining the firm capacity of a generation unit is an extremely challenging task. The firm capacity of a hydroelectric generation unit is typically based on the amount of energy the unit is capable of providing under the worst possible hydrological conditions. However, it is difficult, if not impossible, to determine the maximum amount of capacity or energy a hydroelectric unit can provide under these conditions, so there is a significant degree of arbitrariness in setting the firm capacity of a hydroelectric unit. Second, because every hydroelectric unit owner would like a larger capacity value for its generation unit, to avoid accusations of arbitrary firm capacity values for individual generation units, the entity making this decision typically bases the figure on the amount of energy the unit produced during the historically worst hydrological conditions even though the system operator may have sound reasons for believing that this firm capacity value is set too high. As consequence, particularly in Latin America, there are numerous examples of capacity mechanisms that failed to ensure an adequate supply of energy and rationing conditions have been declared. Virtually all the restructured markets in Latin America that have capacity mechanisms – specifically, Brazil, Chile and Colombia – have experienced supply shortfalls that have required rationing. McRae and Wolak (2019) present an analysis of the most recent supply shortfall period in Colombia and conclude that the perverse incentives created by the capacity payment mechanism there was a major contributing factor to this outcome.

Wind and solar generation units have a firm capacity value significantly below their nameplate capacity but substantially higher than the amount of energy these units are able to produce during stressed system conditions, which suggests that the capacity market construct is poorly suited to an electricity supply industry with significant intermittent renewable generation capacity. For example, on an extremely hot night solar generation units are not likely to produce any energy, while on a hot sunny day very little wind energy will be produced. Consequently, the process of computing the firm capacity values for wind and solar units involves a significant number of unverifiable assumptions often aimed at increasing the resulting firm capacity values.

Capacity mechanisms differ along a number of dimensions. In some regions, the payment is made to all generation unit owners regardless of how much total generation capacity is needed to operate the system. In other regions, the independent system operator (ISO) specifies a system-wide demand for capacity equal to peak system demand plus some planning reserve, typically between 15 to 20 per cent, and only makes capacity payments to enough generation units to meet this demand.

There have been attempts to use market mechanisms to set the value of the $/kW/year payment to the generation units needed to meet the total demand for capacity. However, these capacity markets have been subject to almost continuous revision because they are extremely susceptible to the exercise of unilateral market power. The nature of the product sold – installed generation capacity – and a publicly disclosed perfectly inelastic demand for the product creates extreme opportunities for suppliers to exercise unilateral market power.

In early versions of Eastern US capacity markets, there were instances of the exercise of enormous amounts of unilateral market power. During the off-peak months of the year when no single supplier is pivotal in the capacity market, the price paid for capacity was very close to zero, which is the marginal cost of a supplier providing an additional megawatt of available capacity from existing generation capacity.[11] During the peak and shoulder months when one or more suppliers are pivotal in the capacity market, there was no limit on the price a supplier could charge.

This market power problem leaves open the question of how to set the value of the $/kW/year price cap on the capacity payment. In all regions of the US with capacity payment mechanisms, there is an administratively set process for determining this price. The value of the maximum capacity payment is based on the regulator's estimate of the annual $/kW fixed cost of a peaking generation unit. This maximum price is typically backed by the argument that because of the offer cap on the short-term market and other market power mitigation mechanisms this peaking unit could only set an energy price slightly higher than its variable operating costs. Because this generation unit and all other generation units are missing the hours when the market price would rise above their variable operating costs, the annual $/kW cost of the peaking unit is needed to compensate all generation units for the revenues they do not receive because of the offer cap and market power mitigation mechanisms.[12]

This logic for setting the value of the $/kW/year capacity payment explicitly assumes that the real-time demand for electricity is completely price inelastic and that suppliers are unable to exercise significant amounts of unilateral market power in the short-term market for energy. Both of these assumptions are clearly false. An increasing number of jurisdictions around the world are installing hourly meters that allow dynamic pricing plans to be implemented. Wolak (2013) discusses these technologies and the pricing plans they enable.

A number of studies document the exercise of unilateral market power in wholesale electricity markets. Wolfram (1999) applies a structural model of imperfect competition to measure the extent of unilateral market power exercised in the early England and Wales electricity market. Wolak and Patrick (2001) document the strategic use of market rules to raise prices by two large generation unit owners in this same electricity market. Wolak (2003a) documents changes in the unilateral ability of the five largest generation unit owners in the California electricity market to exercise unilateral market power from 1998 to 2000. Borenstein, Bushnell and Wolak (2002) document the magnitude of the rent transfers and economic inefficiencies caused by these actions. McRae and Wolak (2012) demonstrate that the four largest generation unit owners in New Zealand have both a substantial ability and incentive to exercise unilateral market power.

Capacity mechanisms make it extremely difficult for consumers to benefit from electricity industry restructuring relative to the case of a market without a capacity payment mechanism and active demand-side participation in the wholesale market. Recall that the capacity payment is made to either all generation units in the system or all generation units needed to meet the ISO's demand for capacity. On top of this, all generation unit owners typically receive the same market-clearing price for capacity. Thus, to the extent that producers are able to exercise unilateral market power in the short-term energy market, they can raise market-clearing energy prices significantly above the variable cost of the highest cost unit operating within the hour for all hours of the year, on top of receiving a market-clearing capacity price set by the highest offer price needed to meet the system demand for capacity.

As noted above, capacity payment mechanisms are typically accompanied by offer caps on the short-term energy market that significantly limit the incentive for final consumers to become active participants in the short-term wholesale market. For example, if the maximum wholesale price in an hour is 250 $/MWh because of an offer cap at this level, then a 1 KWh reduction in demand for a residential customer (a very large demand reduction) during an hour only saves the customer 25 cents, which is likely to be insufficient to cause that consumer to reduce its demand. This lack of an active demand-side in the wholesale market impacts how generation unit owners offer their units into the market, because all producers know that system demand will be the same regardless of the hourly wholesale price.

Active participation by final demand substantially increases the competitiveness of the short-term wholesale market because all producers know that higher offer prices will result in less of their generation capacity being called upon to produce because the offers of final consumers to reduce their demand are accepted instead. Without an active demand-side of the wholesale market, generation unit owners know that they can submit offers that are further above their variable cost of supplying electricity and not have these offers rejected. Consequently, a market with a capacity payment mechanism can charge consumers for the $/kW/year fixed cost of a peaker unit for their entire capacity needs and then give producers greater opportunities to exercise unilateral market power in the short-term market, which clearly reduces the likelihood that consumers will realize economic benefits from the restructuring of the electricity sector.

Another argument given for capacity payments is that they reduce the likelihood of long-term capacity inadequacy problems because the promise of a capacity payment provides incentives for new generation units to enter the market. However, until very recently, in most markets around the world, capacity payments were only promised for at most a single year and only paid to existing generation units. Both of these features substantially dulled the incentive for new generation units to enter the market, because a generation unit that entered the market only had a guarantee of receiving the capacity payment for one year and no guarantee that if it received the payment the first year the unit owner would continue to receive it later. This led the Eastern US wholesale markets to develop a long-term capacity product that is sold two to three years in advance of delivery to provide a sufficient lead time for new generation units to participate and capacity payments beyond a single year. This is a positive development for capacity markets, but it also raises the question of why not simply transition to a forward energy purchase requirement rather than a forward capacity requirement, given that most consumers do not want more generation capacity built but they do want their future energy needs met.

Capacity markets are also poorly suited to regions with a significant share of intermittent renewables. In these markets it is rarely, if ever, the case that there is a capacity shortfall in the sense that there is insufficient installed generation capacity to meet peak demand. The more common problem is insufficient energy, typically in the form of water stored behind a dam, to meet anticipated demand. With wind and solar photovoltaic generation units, capacity shortfalls are also extremely unlikely. It is more likely that the sun does not shine or the wind does not blow for a sustained period of time. In both these cases, the problem is not a capacity shortfall but an energy shortfall. Consequently, a capacity payment mechanism that focuses on ensuring adequate installed capacity is unlikely to deliver the most cost-effective solution for consumers to the problem of long-term energy adequacy in regions with a significant amount of intermittent renewable resources.

The argument for a capacity market is strongest in a region with all dispatchable thermal generation units and no potential for active participation of final consumers in the wholesale market, particularly if the capacity procurement decision is made far enough in advance of delivery and for a long enough period of time to support new investment. The similarity between this forward capacity market solution and the long-term energy contracting solution argues in favour of the latter solution to the long-term resource adequacy problem. Galetovic, Muñoz and Wolak (2015) use the example of the Chilean market design to demonstrate the market efficiency improvements from transitioning from a capacity payment-based market to an energy contracting-based market.

5.3   The Role of a Liquid Forward Market for Energy

The previous two subsections emphasize that short-term energy and capacity markets are extremely susceptible to the exercise of unilateral market power and the key to long-term resource adequacy at a reasonable price is the purchase of sufficient energy or capacity far enough in advance of delivery by electricity retailers and large customers for new entrants to compete with existing generation unit owners to provide the product.

Signing a fixed-price forward contract for energy or capacity a day, month, or even a year ahead of delivery limits the number of firms and technologies that are able to provide this energy or capacity. For example, a contract negotiated one day in advance limits the sources of supply to existing generation units able to produce energy the following day. Even a year in advance limits the sources that can compete to the generation units already in place because it takes longer than 18 months to site and build a substantial new generation unit in virtually all wholesale electricity markets. Therefore, to obtain the most competitive prices, at a minimum, the vast majority of the fixed-price forward contracts should be negotiated far enough in advance of delivery to allow new entrants to compete with existing generation unit owners.

This logic argues for regulatory intervention to internalize the reliability externality through a long-term resource adequacy process that ensures a liquid forward market for energy for delivery two to three years into the future. If a liquid forward market for energy exists at this time horizon and there is adequate demand for energy at this delivery horizon, a restructured market will achieve long-term resource adequacy. A liquid forward market at the two- to three-year delivery horizon implies less need for regulatory intervention into shorter-term forward markets. The regulator can raise the offer cap on the short-term market and this will stimulate the demand for retailers and large consumers to hedge their wholesale energy purchases at delivery horizons less than two years into the future. By purchasing a hedge against the short-term price risk at the locations in the network where it is going to withdraw energy, the buyer can rely on the financial incentives that the seller of the contracts faces to procure or produce this energy at the lowest possible cost.

Focusing the long-term resource adequacy process on the construction of new generation units misses the important point that there is an increasing number of ways for markets to achieve long-term resource adequacy besides building additional capacity. For example, by the appropriate choice of the mix of generation units, the same pattern of hourly demand throughout the year can be met with less total generation capacity and that can also cost electricity consumers less on an annual basis. Investment in distributed generation and storage, and active participation of demand in the wholesale market can also allow the same number of customers to be served with less grid-connected generation capacity.

It is important to emphasize that most capacity mechanisms do little to limit the ability or incentive of generation unit owners to exercise unilateral market power in the short-term energy market. Capacity mechanisms typically have the requirement that the generation unit owner must offer their capacity into the short-term market at or below the offer cap on the short-term energy market. This requirement does little to limit the ability or incentive of generation unit owners to raise short-term prices by exploiting the distribution of residual demand curves they face, as long as the resulting short-term prices are below the offer cap. Even in capacity markets with a scarcity of payment refunds, the capacity payment mechanism does not limit the ability or incentive of producers to exercise unilateral market power below the scarcity price.[13] This is different from the case that a producer has a fixed-price forward contract obligation to supply energy, which endows the producer with a strong incentive to reduce the cost of meeting this forward contract obligation for energy.

Another advantage of focusing on the development of a liquid forward market for energy instead of capacity is that an active forward market for energy has other hedging instruments besides so-called 'swap contracts', where a generation unit owner and a retailer agree to a fixed price at a location in the transmission network for a fixed quantity of energy. Cap contracts are also very effective instruments for guarding against price spikes in the short-term market and for funding peaking generation capacity. For example, a generation unit owner might sell a retailer a cap contract that says that if the short-term price at a specific location exceeds the cap contract exercise price, the seller of the contract pays the buyer of the contract the difference between the spot price and the cap exercise price times the number of MWh of the cap contract sold. For example, suppose the cap exercise price is 300 $/MWh and market price is 400 $/MWh, then the payoff to the buyer from the cap contract is 100 $/MWh = 400 $/MWh – 300 $/MWh × the number of MWh sold. If the spot price is less than 300 $/MWh, then the buyer of the cap contract does not receive any payment.

Because the seller of a cap contract is providing insurance against price spikes, it must make payments when the price exceeds the cap exercise price. This price spike insurance obligation implies that the buyer must make a fixed up-front payment to the seller for the seller to be willing to take on this obligation. This up-front payment can then be used by the seller of the cap contract to pay for a peaking generation unit that provides a physical hedge against price spikes at this location. The Australian electricity market has an active financial forward market where these types of cap contracts are traded and these contracts have been used to fund peaking generation capacity to provide the seller of the cap contract with a physical hedge against this insurance obligation.

Cross-hedging between generation resource owners is likely to become even more important in ensuring long-term resource adequacy in energy systems with significant amounts of wind and solar resources. A wind or solar resource owner that sells a fixed-price and fixed-quantity forward contract for energy to a retailer is going to need to reinsure the quantity risk associated with such a contract. The wind or solar resource owner can sign a contract with a thermal resource owner that provides insurance against the quantity risk it faces from selling a fixed-price and fixed-quantity contract. For example, the wind resource owner could purchase a cap contract for the quantity of energy sold in the fixed-price, fixed-quantity contract to the retailer at a certain strike price and in this way have insurance against having to purchase energy from the short-term market at an extremely high price when the wind or solar resource is not producing energy. The up-front payment to the thermal resource for the price spike insurance would help to finance the fixed costs of the thermal resource that operates significantly less frequently because of the large amount of intermittent renewable generation capacity. The wind or solar resource owner would then factor in the cost of this quantity risk insurance in the price it is willing to sell any fixed-price, fixed-quantity forward contract for energy.

One question often asked about an approach that focuses on the development of an active forward market for energy is whether sufficient generation resources will be built to meet demand if consumers only buy forward financial hedges against the spot price at their location in the network. On this point, it is important to bear in mind the incentives faced by a seller of the forward financial contract once this contract has been sold. The generation unit owner maximizes its expected profits by ensuring that the forward contract quantity of energy can be purchased at the agreed-upon location in the spot market (or whatever market the forward contract clears against) at the lowest possible short-term price. The seller of the contract bears all the risk associated with higher spot prices at that location. To prudently hedge this risk, the seller has a very strong incentive to ensure that sufficient generation capacity is available to set the lowest possible price in the short-term market at that location in the network for the quantity of energy sold in the fixed-price forward contract.

This logic implies that if a generation unit owner signs a forward contract guaranteeing the price for 500 MWh of energy for 24 hours a day and seven days per week at a specific location in the network, it will construct or contract for more than 500 MW of generation capacity to hedge short-term price risk. Building only a 500 MW facility to hedge this risk would be extremely imprudent and expose the producer to significant risk, because if this 500 MW facility is unavailable to provide electricity, the producer must purchase the energy from the short-term market at the price that prevails at the time. Moreover, if this generation unit is unavailable, then the short-term price is likely to be extremely high.

An additional source of economic benefits from the energy-based resource adequacy process is that the energy contract adequacy approach does not require the regulator to set the total amount of firm capacity needed to meet system demand. Instead, the regulator only ensures that retailers and large customers have adequate fixed-price forward contract coverage of their demand at various delivery horizons into the future and then relies on the incentives that the sellers of these contracts face to construct sufficient generation capacity or procure other resources to meet these forward contract obligations for energy. The sellers of these forward contracts for energy have a strong incentive to find the least-cost mix of generation and demand-side resources necessary to meet their contractual obligations.

6.   MANAGING AND MITIGATING SYSTEM-WIDE AND LOCAL MARKET POWER

The configuration of the transmission network, the level and location of demand, as well as the level of output of other generation units can endow certain generation units with a significant ability to exercise unilateral market power in a wholesale market. A prime example of this phenomenon is the constrained-on generation problem described earlier. The owner of a constrained-on generation unit knows that regardless of the unit's offer price, it must be accepted to supply energy. Without a local market power mitigation (LMPM) mechanism, there is no limit to what offer price that generation unit owner could submit and be accepted to provide energy.

The system-wide market power problem is typically addressed through sufficient fixed-price and fixed-quantity long-term contracts between electricity producers and retailers and large consumers. The logic of Wolak (2000) described in Section 5.1 demonstrates how fixed-price, fixed-quantity forward contracts limit the incentives of generation unit owners to exercise system-wide unilateral market power in the short-term market.

6.1   Solutions to the Local Market Power Problem

In an offer-based market, the regulator must design and implement an automatic LMPM mechanism that is built into the market-clearing software. In general, the regulator must determine when any type of market outcome causes enough harm to some market participants to merit explicit regulatory intervention. Finally, if the market outcomes become too harmful, the regulator must have the ability to temporarily suspend market operations. All these tasks require a substantial amount of subjective judgment on the part of the regulatory process, which can be extremely challenging for countries and regions with limited regulatory experience.

In all offer-based electricity markets, an LMPM mechanism is necessary to limit the offers a generation unit owner submits when it faces insufficient competition to serve a local energy need because of a combination of the configuration of the transmission network, the levels and geographic distribution of demands, and the concentration of ownership of generation units. One lesson from the experience of US markets (in particular) is that system conditions can arise when virtually any generation unit owner has a substantial ability and incentive to exercise unilateral market power. That is why prospective market power mitigation mechanisms where certain units are designated in advance as having the ability to exercise unilateral market power, a practice typically used in Europe and other industrialized countries and initially employed in the US as well, are likely to miss many instances where the exercise of substantial unilateral market power is possible.

An LMPM mechanism built into the market software that relies on actual system conditions to determine whether a generation unit has a substantial ability and incentive to exercise unilateral market power is likely to be significantly more effective than the prospective approaches used in Europe and initially in the US. This logic explains why all US markets currently have such a mechanism built into their market software and running automatically during each pricing interval.

An LMPM mechanism is a pre-specified administrative procedure (written into the market rules) that determines: (1) when a producer has local market power worthy of mitigation; (2) what the mitigated producer will be paid; and (3) how the amount the producer is paid will impact the payments received by other market participants. Without a prospective market power mitigation mechanism system, conditions are likely to arise in all wholesale markets when almost any generation unit owner can exercise substantial unilateral market power. It is increasingly clear to regulators around the world, particularly those that operate markets with limited amounts of transmission capacity, that these automatic regulatory interventions are necessary to deal with the problem of insufficient competition to serve certain local energy needs.

An important component of any local and system-wide market power mitigation mechanism is the provision of information to market participants and the public at large. This is often termed 'smart sunshine regulation' and implies that the regulatory process gathers a comprehensive set of information about market outcomes, analyses it and makes it available to the public in a manner and form that increases the likelihood of market participants' compliance with all market rules and allows the regulatory and political process to detect and correct market design flaws in a timely manner. Smart sunshine regulation is the foundation for all the tasks the regulatory process must undertake in the wholesale market regime. Wolak (2014) discusses the benefits of smart sunshine regulation and public data release on wholesale market performance.

Another tool a regulator has in managing local and system-wide market power in an offer-based market is determining the configuration of the transmission network. Because the configuration of the transmission network can often determine the extent of competition that individual generation unit owners face, the regulator must take a more active role in the transmission planning and expansion process to ensure that competition-enhancing upgrades that improve market efficiency are built. Welsh (2020) describes the distinctly different roles of transmission network planning in the vertically integrated monopoly regime versus the wholesale market regime. Wolak (2015a) presents a framework for measuring the competitiveness benefits of transmission expansions in an offer-based wholesale market and applies it to the wholesale electricity market of the province of Alberta in Canada.

6.2 Cost-based Short-term Market

An alternative approach to market power mitigation is used in a number of Latin American markets is a cost-based market. Under this mechanism, generation unit owners do not submit offers to the market operator. Instead, the market operator takes the technical characteristics of generation units and input fuel prices to compute the variable cost of operating each generation unit. These variable cost estimates are used by the market operator to dispatch generation units and set market prices.

This mechanism avoids the need for an LMPM mechanism but is not without its challenges. For example, it does not completely close off opportunities for generation unit owners to exercise unilateral market power because they can still withhold their output from the cost-based dispatch as a way to increase short-term prices. They can also take actions to raise their regulated variable cost that enters the cost-based dispatch process. Wolak (2014) discusses the market efficiency trade-offs between offer-based versus cost-based markets.

6.3 Solutions to System-wide Market Power

As discussed in Section 5 and in detail in Wolak (2000), fixed-price forward contract commitments sold by generation unit owners reduce their incentive to exercise unilateral market power in the short-term energy market because the generation unit owner only earns the short-term price on any energy it sells in excess of its forward contract commitment and pays the short-term price for any production shortfall relative to these forward contract commitments.

This logic argues in favour of the regulator monitoring the forward contract positions of retailers as part of its regulatory oversight process to ensure that there is adequate fixed-price forward contract coverage of final demand. As discussed in Wolak (2003b) and reinforced by the simulation results of Bushnell et al. (2008b), the California electricity crisis is very unlikely to have occurred if there had been adequate coverage of California's retail electricity demand with fixed-price and fixed-quantity forward contracts. Consequently, to protect against periods when one or more generation unit owners have a strong incentive to exercise unilateral market power, the regulator should, at a minimum, monitor the forward contracting levels of the retailers they oversee as the primary mechanism to protect against the exercise of system-wide unilateral market power.

7.   ACTIVE INVOLVEMENT OF FINAL DEMAND IN THE WHOLESALE MARKET

The active involvement of final consumers in the wholesale market can reduce the amount of installed generation capacity needed to serve them and can reduce the cost of integrating an increasing amount of intermittent renewable generation. An important market design feature that facilitates active participation by final demand is a multi-settlement market with a day-ahead forward market and a real-time market. This mechanism allows loads to purchase energy in the day-ahead market that they can subsequently sell in the real-time market. Without the ability to purchase demand in the day-ahead market that is not consumed in real-time, demand reduction programmes require the regulator to set an administrative baseline relative to which demand reductions are measured, which can significantly reduce the system-wide benefits of active demand-side participation. This issue is discussed in Bushnell, Hobbs and Wolak (2009).

7.1   Customers Can Respond to Dynamic Retail Prices

There are three necessary conditions for active involvement of final consumers. First, customers must have the necessary technology to record their consumption on time granularity/time scale similar to that of the wholesale market products. Second, they must receive actionable information that tells them when to alter their consumption.[14] Third, they must pay according to a price that provides an economic incentive consistent with the actionable information to alter their consumption.

Mechanical meters that record a customer's consumption during a monthly or bi-monthly billing cycle as the difference of two consecutive meter readings cannot be used in a dynamic pricing plan because the retailer has no way of knowing when during the billing cycle the customer consumed electricity. Even if the customer is billed for wholesale electricity using a standardized load shape, a customer's monthly bill falls by the same amount regardless of when the customer reduces its consumption within the month. For example, if $w(h)$ is the load shape weight for hour h in the month ($\sum_{h=1}^{H} w(h) = 1$), $p(h)$ is the hourly wholesale price, and $Q(m)$ the household's monthly consumption, the wholesale electricity cost for the monthly billing cycle is $\sum_{h=1}^{H} p(h) w(h) Q(m)$, where H is the total number of hours in the billing cycle.

The above equation makes it clear that with mechanical meters read on a monthly or bi-monthly basis, dynamic pricing is impossible to implement because the customer's monthly bill falls by the same amount regardless of when consumption is reduced within the month. Therefore, a household faced with a higher average monthly price would reduce consumption when it is least costly for it to do so, not when the hourly price of electricity is the highest.

There is growing empirical evidence that all classes of customers can respond to short-term wholesale price signals if they have the metering technology to do so. Patrick and Wolak (1999) estimate the price responsiveness of large industrial and commercial customers in the United Kingdom to half-hourly wholesale prices and find significant differences in the average half-hourly demand elasticities across types of customers and half-hours of the day. Wolak (2006) estimates the price responsiveness of residential customers to a form of real-time pricing that shares the risk of responding to hourly prices between the retailer and the final customer. The California Statewide Pricing Pilot (SPP) selected samples of residential, commercial and industrial customers and subjected them to various forms of real-time pricing plans to estimate their price responsiveness. Charles River Associates (2004) analysed the results of the SPP experiments and found precisely estimated price responses for all three types of customers. More recently, Wolak (2011a) reports on the results of a field experiment comparing the price responsiveness of households on a variety of dynamic pricing plans. For all the pricing plans, Wolak found large demand reductions in response to increases in hourly retail electricity prices across all income classes.

Although all these studies find statistically significant demand reductions in response to various forms of short-term price signals, none are able to assess the long-run impacts of requiring customers to manage short-term wholesale price risk. Wolak (2013) describes the increasing range of technologies available to increase the responsiveness of a customer to short-term price signals. However, customers have little incentive to adopt these technologies unless regulators are willing to install hourly meters and require customers to manage short-term price risk. Although most dynamic pricing experiments and programmes have relied on day-ahead price signals, recent work by Andersen et al. (2019) has shown that customers can respond to within-day price signals.

7.2   Managing Bill Risk with Dynamic Pricing

Politicians and policymakers often express the concern that subjecting consumers to real-time price risk will introduce too much volatility into their monthly bill. These concerns are, for the most part, unfounded as well as misplaced. Wolak (2013) suggests a scheme (described below) for facing a consumer with the hourly wholesale price for its consumption above or below a pre-determined load shape so that the consumer faces a monthly average price risk similar to a peak/off-peak time-of-use tariff.

If a state regulatory commission sets a fixed retail price or fixed pattern of retail prices throughout the day (time-of-use prices), it must still ensure that over the course of the month or year, the retailer's total revenues less its transmission, distribution and retailing costs, cover its total wholesale energy costs. If the regulator sets this fixed price too low relative to the current wholesale price, then either the retailer or the government must pay the difference.

Charging final consumers the same hourly default price as generation units owners provides strong incentive for them to become active participants in the wholesale market or purchase the appropriate short-term price hedging instruments from retailers to eliminate their exposure to short-term price risk. These purchases of short-term price hedging instruments by final consumers increase a retailer's demand for fixed-price forward contracts from generation unit owners, which reduces the amount of energy that is actually sold at the short-term wholesale price.

7.3   Fostering Investments in Automated Response Technologies

Perhaps the most important, but most often ignored, lesson from electricity restructuring processes in industrialized countries is the necessity of treating load and generation symmetrically. Symmetric treatment of load and generation means that unless a retail consumer signs a forward contract with an electricity retailer, the default wholesale price the consumer pays is the hourly wholesale price. This is precisely the same risk that a generation unit owner faces unless it has signed a fixed-price forward contract with a load-serving entity or some other market participant. The default price a generation unit owner receives for any short-term energy sales is the hourly short-term price. Just as very few generation unit owners are willing to risk selling all of their output in the short-term market, consumers are likely to have similar preferences against too much reliance on the short-term market and would therefore be willing to sign long-term contracts for a large fraction of their expected hourly consumption during each hour of the month. Consistent with the above logic, a residential consumer might purchase a right to buy a fixed load shape for each day at a fixed price for the next 12 months. This consumer would then be able to sell energy it does not consume during any hour at the hourly wholesale price or purchase any power it needs beyond this baseline level at that same price.[15]

This type of pricing arrangement would result in a significantly less volatile monthly electricity bill than if the consumer made all of its purchases at the hourly wholesale price. If all customers purchased according to this sort of pricing plan, then there would be no residual short-term price risk that the government needs to manage using tax revenues. All consumers manage the risk of high wholesale prices and supply shortfalls according to their preferences for taking on short-term price risk. Moreover, because all consumers have an incentive to reduce their consumption during high-priced periods, wholesale prices are likely to be less volatile. Symmetric treatment of load and generation does not mean that a consumer is prohibited from purchasing a fixed-price full requirement contract for all the electricity it might consume in a month, only that the consumer must pay the full cost of the retailer supplying this product.

Customers facing the risk of paying the real-time price for their electricity consumption is what creates the business case for investments in automated demand-response and storage technologies. If a customer can avoid consumption when the real-time price is high and consume more when this price is low through an investment in one of these devices, the customer is very likely to do so if the avoided wholesale energy purchase costs that this technology avoids more than covers the investment cost. A single fixed retail price or single fixed price schedule regardless of real-time system conditions cannot provide the revenue stream needed to finance investments in these technologies. Consequently, without exposing customers to the real-time price risk, investments in these technologies will not occur, unless some explicit support mechanism is introduced. Wolak and Hardman (2021) provide a comprehensive analysis of these issues and others related to the future of electricity retailing.

8.　MARKET DESIGN LESSONS FOR DEVELOPING COUNTRIES

Electricity market design in developing countries and small control areas has the additional challenge of delivering significant economic benefits with a low implementation cost and limited regulatory burden. This section proposes such a market design using the insights from Sections 4 to 7.

8.1 A Simplified Market Design for Developing and Small Countries

The transition to formal market mechanisms in a number of developing and small countries has been slow. A number of regions in Africa, Latin America and Asia proposed wholesale markets in the early 2000s, but these regions have yet to begin operating a formal market mechanism. These regions frequently face significant challenges because of limited transmission capacity between and within their member countries. Consequently, any attempt to operate an offer-based market for most developing countries is likely to run into severe local and system-wide market power problems. In addition, the almost complete absence of hourly meters in these regions limits the opportunities for active demand-side participation, which makes implementing an offer-based wholesale market even more challenging.

Building on the experience of Latin American countries discussed in Wolak (2014), a viable market design for these regions is a cost-based short-term market that uses LMP. This market design is straightforward to implement because it simply involves solving for the optimal dispatch of generation units in the region based on the market operator's estimate of each unit's variable cost subject to the operating constraints implied by the actual regional transmission network and other reliability constraints.

Because it is cost based rather than offer based, this market design also eliminates the need for a local or system-wide market power mitigation mechanism, which typically involves a significant regulatory burden. Because it uses the LMP market-clearing mechanism to set locational prices and generation unit dispatch levels, the resulting market outcomes optimize the use of the limited transmission network within and across regions. This cost-based market could be run as a multi-settlement market with day-ahead prices and schedules and real-time pricing and settlement or with a single real-time market and settlement.

All generation unit owners would submit the characteristics – for instance, the heat rate and the amount of fuel required to start up the unit – of their generation units to the market operator, which then determines the variable cost for each generation unit using a publicly available price index for the unit's input fossil fuel. For example, for a coal-fired generation unit, the market operator could use a globally traded price for coal and a benchmark delivery cost to the generation unit to determine the fuel cost of the unit. This would be multiplied by the unit's heat rate to compute its variable fuel cost. An estimate of the variable operating and maintenance cost for the unit could be added to this variable fuel cost to arrive at the total variable cost of the unit. To provide incentives to minimize their actual total variable cost of producing electricity, the values of the components of the total variable cost could be based on benchmark values for the technology used by the generation unit owner, rather than an estimate of that unit owner's variable cost.

The variable cost computed by the market operator along with the configuration of the transmission network would be used to set day-ahead schedules and prices for each location in a multi-settlement version of this market design. In real time, the dispatch and LMP process would be completed using the actual system demand and actual configuration of the transmission network with these same generation unit-level variable cost figures.

To ensure long-term resource adequacy in this market, retailers would be required to purchase forward contracts for energy at various delivery horizons equal to pre-specified fractions of their actual realized demand or face a financial penalty for under-procurement. For example, retailers could be required to purchase 100 per cent of their actual demand in a forward contract purchased before the short-term market operates for that day, 95 per cent of their demand one year in advance, 92 per cent two years in advance and 90 per cent three years in advance. The financial penalty for under-compliance should be sufficiently high to ensure compliance with the mandated level of contracting.

These contracting mandates for all retailers are necessary to establish a liquid forward market for energy in a region with a cost-based short-term market. As discussed in Section 5, without the risk of high short-term prices, retailers have a financial incentive to purchase all their energy from the short-term market, which could quickly lead to inadequate generation resources to serve demand. The contracting mandate on retailers described above ensures that adequate generation capacity will always be available to serve demand because there is a generation unit owner that has sold each MWh of energy the retailer's customers consumes in a fixed-price forward contract.

The role of the short-term cost-based market is simply to provide a transparent mechanism for buyers and sellers of these forward contracts to clear their imbalances, because a generation unit owner rarely produces the exact quantity sold in a fixed-price forward contract during any given hour of the day. Retailers also rarely consume exactly their hourly fixed-price forward contract quantity. The cost-based short-term market provides a transparent mechanism for differences between forward energy sales and actual production and forward energy purchases and actual consumption to be settled. For example, if the generation unit owner sold 400 MWh each hour of the day in a forward contract and its unit failed to operate during certain hours of the day, it needs a mechanism for purchasing replacement energy during these hours. The cost-based short-term market provides that mechanism. The seller knows it can purchase the replacement energy at the price set in the cost-based short-term market during those hours. It is likely that the seller would pay a high price for this replacement energy because units with higher costs than its own units would be required to operate. This provides an incentive for the unit owner to maximize the availability of its own units to avoid this set of circumstances.

It is important to emphasize that this short-term market is only for settling imbalances. That is the purpose of the requirement for retailers to procure 100 per cent of their realized demand as of the actual delivery date in a fixed-price forward contract. Because of these contracting mandates on retailers and large consumers, retailers are purchasing no net energy from the short-term market.

Joskow (1997) argues that the majority of the economic benefits from the electricity industry restructuring are likely to come from more efficient investment decisions in new generation capacity. The combination of a cost-based short-term market and fixed-price forward contract mandates on electricity retailers is a low-cost and low-regulatory burden approach to realizing more efficient investments in new generation capacity.

The counterparties to the fixed-price forward contracts sold to the electricity retailers have a strong financial incentive to find the least-cost mix of new generation capacity to supply the energy they have sold in these forward contracts. The cost-based short-term market tells them what they will be paid or pay for differences between the hourly production of their generation units and the amount of energy they have sold for that hour in a fixed-price forward contract. Electricity retailers can use this short-term market to clear hourly imbalances between the amount of energy they withdraw from the transmission network and their fixed-price forward contract purchases.

This market design also has the advantage that it can easily transition to an offer-based market once the transmission network in the region is expanded, hourly meters are deployed, and the regulator is able to design an effective LMPM mechanism. The LMP market is already in place and generation unit owners' costs as computed by the market operator can easily be replaced by the offers of these producers. Starting from a cost-based market and transitioning to an offer-based market is a low-risk approach to introducing an offer-based market. The PJM Interconnection in the Eastern US followed this strategy during the early stages of its development. It ran one year as a cost-based market before transitioning to an offer-based market.

To address concerns that different consumers purchase their imbalances at different locational prices, all consumers in the region could be charged the quantity-weighted average of all LMPs at all load withdrawal nodes in the region. This would allow all fixed-price forward contracts to clear against this quantity-weighted average price, which enhances liquidity in the forward market for energy.

8.2 Improving Performance in Small Markets

Even in regions that have a vertically integrated monopoly industry structure but have or would like to have independent power producers sell energy to this monopoly, the cost-based market has the potential to reduce the cost of serving demand. The cost-based short-term market is used to dispatch all generation units in the region – those owned by the vertically integrated monopoly and those owned by independent power producers. The vertically integrated firm can still be subject to cost-of-service regulation for the retail price it is allowed to charge and the independent power producers can continue to be compensated according to their power purchase agreements. During the periods when an independent power producer's generation unit does not operate because it is not dispatched in the cost-based market, the unit owner can purchase the energy required under its power purchase agreement from the cost-based short-term market.

This cost-based market mechanism ensures that all of the resources in the control area are used in the least-cost manner to serve demand, rather than allowing certain generation units to be dispatched in preference to lower variable cost units because of pre-existing contractual requirements. This mechanism should also reduce the cost to the vertically integrated utility of purchasing long-term contracts for wholesale energy because all independent power producers that sell energy to the vertically integrated monopoly know that they have the option to purchase energy from the cost-based market and sell additional energy from their generation units when it is economic to do so.

9. INTEGRATING RENEWABLES

An increasingly important consideration in formulating any wholesale market mechanism is the extent to which it can accommodate a significant amount of intermittent renewable generation in both the transmission and distribution networks. A growing number of jurisdictions in the developing world have significant renewable energy targets in place. A number of small control areas also have significant renewable energy goals.[16] Consequently, any market design adopted by these regions should support cost-effective integration of renewable resources. As we discuss below, the cost-based LMP market design is well-suited for integrating any amount of intermittent renewables into a national or regional electricity market. However, as we also discuss, the integration of an increasing share of renewables is likely to require incorporating additional constraints into the region's LMP market and the introduction of additional products to deal with the increasing share of intermittent renewable resources.[17]

9.1 Cost-based Market and Renewables Integration

The strength of a cost-based LMP market design is that all of the resources in the control area, including intermittent renewable resources, will be dispatched in a least-cost manner using the variable costs determined by the market operator. How these resources are compensated for the energy sold in the forward market will not depend on how the resource is used to produce energy. The existence of a cost-based LMP market will allow renewable resource owners to sell fixed-price and fixed-quantity contracts for energy because they have the short-term market to purchase energy from when their renewable units do not produce sufficient energy to meet their forward market obligation and can sell excess energy beyond their forward market obligation when their units produce more than the forward contract quantity.

The renewable resource owner can factor in how these imbalances will be settled in making offers to supply fixed-price and fixed-quantity long-term contracts for energy. Shifting renewable resource owners to fixed-price and fixed-quantity forward contract from fixed-price and quantity-produced contracts will also provide financial incentives for renewable resource owners to manage the intermittency of their production through storage investments and financial contracts that support investments in fast-ramping dispatchable generation resources to provide insurance against renewable energy shortfalls. Transitioning forward contracts for renewable energy to require the seller to manage the quantity risk associated with the energy it sells is an important step in the process of increasing the amount intermittent renewable energy is produced in a region.

In all LMP markets operating around the world there is an ongoing process of updating the set of constraints incorporated into the market mechanism to ensure that the match between how the market sets prices and dispatch levels agrees as closely as possible with how the grid is actually operated. This logic implies that as the share of intermittent renewable resources increases, the LMP market can be easily adapted to deal with the new reliability challenges this creates.

A multi-settlement LMP market can efficiently manage the sudden generation unit starts and stops that arise with a significant amount of intermittent renewable generation units and the need to configure combined cycle natural gas units to operate as either individual combustion turbines or as an integrated pair of combustion turbines and a steam turbine. A formal day-ahead market allows these generation units to obtain day-ahead schedules that are consistent with their physical operating constraints. The real-time market can then be used to account for unexpected changes in these day-ahead schedules because of changes in the operating characteristics of generation units such as a forced outage or limitations in the amount of available input fossil fuel, as well as changes in demand between the day-ahead and real-time markets. As discussed in Section 4, this multi-settlement market also rewards dispatchable resources for their ability to supply more or less energy, depending on the instructions of the market operator.

Markets with significant intermittent renewables such as California and Australia have seen significant investments in battery storage, mostly driven by regulatory mandates. Battery storage systems can be connected to either the high-voltage transmission system or the local distribution network, but decisions about where to install battery systems are currently driven by regulatory mandates or inefficient distribution network pricing, as discussed in Wolak (2018).[18] An energy-contracting approach to long-term resource adequacy and the increase in short-term price volatility that it allows should bring about more market-based investments in battery storage.

10. CONCLUSIONS AND DIRECTIONS FOR FUTURE RESEARCH

The experience of the past 25 years identifies the following fundamental ingredients for a successful market design. First, a multi-settlement LMP wholesale market is most likely to achieve the best possible match between how the transmission network operates and how the wholesale market determines prices and dispatch levels. Second, a liquid forward market for energy appears to be the most efficient way to ensure both short-term and long-term resource adequacy, although capacity payment mechanisms continue to be employed in many regions of the world. Capacity mechanisms have also begun to emphasize the development of a liquid forward market for capacity, which would make it easier to transition to a forward market for energy. Third, fixed-price long-term contracts are an effective mechanism for limiting the incentive of generation unit owners to exercise system-wide unilateral market power in the short-term market. All US markets and most international markets have LMPM mechanisms, although the details of these mechanisms differ across markets. Fourth, there is increasing recognition of the need for active involvement of final demand in the wholesale market, particularly in regions that have deployed interval meters. A multi-settlement LMP market provides the ideal wholesale market platform for this to occur. The need for active involvement of final demand is even greater in regions with significant intermittent renewable energy.

Nonetheless, there are several issues that still deserve additional research. The two major drivers of future research on electricity market design are: (1) outstanding issues in markets with conventional generation resources; and (2) new issues created by the increasing penetration of renewables both at the transmission and distribution level. On the first topic, the chapter identifies challenges for future research. A regulatory mechanism for developing an active forward market for energy to ensure long-term resource adequacy is perhaps the most important topic for future research. There are many different regulatory mechanisms for developing an active forward market to ensure long-term resource adequacy that exist around the world. A comparative quantitative analysis of the performance of these mechanisms could be extremely informative. There are also many different approaches to LMPM that exist around the world. A comparative quantitative study of the performance of these mechanisms could help all regions improve their mechanisms. An understanding of the advantages and disadvantages of cost-based versus offer-based markets as a function of the initial conditions in the country and the electricity industry could provide important guidance to developing countries and small regions that are considering reforming their electricity industries. A number of economic experiments with information provision and dynamic pricing programmes could inform how to achieve the greatest amount of customer acceptance and participation in active load management.

On the second topic, the engineering studies of how demand for ancillary services is likely to scale with different scenarios for renewables deployment in the transmission and distribution grids could be extremely helpful for developing countries wanting to expand the contribution of renewable resources to their electricity mix. Another important area for economic and engineering studies is on the design of new wholesale market products to reward fast-ramping and fast-starting dispatchable generation resources. It is also likely that new paradigms for transmission and distribution system operation will need to be developed to deal with increasing intermittency at the customer level because of investments in distributed generation and at the transmission level because of investments in grid-scale renewables.

NOTES

1. In this chapter, I use the term hourly meter to refer to any meter than can record consumption in a fixed time interval such as every 15 minutes, half-hour or hour.
2. Vickers and Yarrow (1988) provide a comprehensive treatment of this process. In Chapter 6 of this handbook, Newbery discusses more recent experience with the British electricity supply industry.
3. In Chapter 9 of this handbook, Simshauser describes recent experience with the Australian electricity market.
4. Different from government-owned utility oversight, US state public utilities commissions are explicitly tasked with protecting consumers from excessive prices and only allowing the utilities they regulate to recover prudently incurred costs.
5. Wolak (1999) provides a description of the wholesale market design and regulatory oversight processes in England and Wales, Norway and Sweden, Australia, and New Zealand as of 1 January 1998.
6. See Figure 90 in European Network of Transmission System Operators – Electricity (ENTSO-E) (2018).
7. Ancillary services are composed of different operating reserves required by the system operator to maintain real-time supply and demand balance. For the California ISO market, these are composed of regulation up and regulation down automatic generation control (AGC) reserves, spinning reserves and non-spinning reserves.
8. Many regions have eliminated or are eliminating this technological barrier to allow price to manage the real-time supply and demand balance by installing interval meters for all customers and offering real-time meter reading as a regulated service.
9. A copy of FERC Order 831 is available at https://www.ferc.gov/sites/default/files/2020-06/RM16-5-000. pdf, accessed 26 September 2020.
10. Thermal generation units convert heat energy into electricity. These include coal-fired, natural gas-fired, oil-fired, nuclear and geothermal power plants. The availability factor of a generation unit is equal to the fraction of hours of the year such unit is available to produce electricity.
11. A supplier is said to be pivotal in a market with an inelastic demand if some of its supply is needed to meet this demand regardless of the offers of other market participants.
12. In Section 2 of Chapter 3 of this handbook, Joskow and Léautier discuss this process in detail.
13. A scarcity price refund requires the seller of firm capacity to pay $\max(0, P(market) - P(scarcity)) \times QFirm$, where $P(market)$ is the market price, $P(scarcity)$ is an administratively set scarcity price, and $QFirm$ is the firm energy sold by the supplier. The function $g = \max(0, y)$ means that $g = y$ is $y > 0$ and zero otherwise.
14. McRae and Meeks (2016) present the results of a field experiment in Central Asia that demonstrates the importance of actionable information for facilitating active demand-side participation. Kahn and Wolak (2013) find that once customers understand non-linear pricing, they subsequently make energy-consuming

decisions consistent with responding to the marginal price. Wolak (2015b) presents evidence consistent with real-time consumption feedback producing energy conservation efforts by households in Singapore.

15. This pricing plan requires the customer to have an interval meter. Wolak (2013) draws analogy between this pricing plan for electricity and how cell phone minutes are typically sold. Consumers purchase a fixed number of minutes per month and typically companies allow customers to rollover unused minutes to the next month or purchase additional minutes beyond the minutes purchased in advance at some penalty price. In the case of electricity, the price for unused KWh and additional KWh during a given hour is the real-time wholesale price during that hour.

16. The state of Hawaii has a 100 per cent renewable energy target by 2045 and already has the largest share of distributed solar capacity as a percentage of peak demand of any control area in the world: more than 400 MW out of a peak demand of 1200 MW.

17. Interested readers may also look at Chapter 15 by Richard Green for a general introduction to the economics of wholesale electricity markets with significant intermittent renewables.

18. Relations between the central power system and off-grid or mini grid systems are addressed by Pérez-Arriaga et al. in Chapter 20 and by Foster et al. in Chapter 22 of this handbook.

REFERENCES

Andersen, L. M., L. G. Hansen, C. L. Jensen and F. A. Wolak (2019), 'Can incentives to increase electricity use reduce the cost of integrating renewable resources?', accessed 26 September 2020 at http://web.stanford.edu/group/fwolak/cgi-bin/sites/default/files/Into_versus_Away_January_2019.pdf.

Bohn, R. E., M. C. Caramanis and F. C. Schweppe (1984), 'Optimal pricing in electrical networks over space and time', *RAND Journal of Economics*, **15** (5), 360–76.

Borenstein, S., J. B. Bushnell and F. A. Wolak (2002), 'Measuring market inefficiencies in California's restructured wholesale electricity market', *American Economic Review*, **92** (5), 1367–405.

Bushnell, J. B., B. F. Hobbs and F. A. Wolak (2008a), 'Final opinion on "The DEC Bidding Activity Rule under MRTU"', accessed 26 September 2020 at https://www.caiso.com/Documents/MSCFinalOpinionon DECBiddingActivityRuleunderMRTU.pdf.

Bushnell, J. B., B. F. Hobbs and F. A. Wolak (2009), 'When it comes to demand response, is FERC its own worst enemy?', *The Electricity Journal*, **22** (8), 9–18.

Bushnell, J. B., E. T. Mansur and C. Saravia (2008b), 'Vertical arrangements, market structure, and competition: an analysis of restructured US electricity markets', *American Economic Review*, **98** (1), 237–66.

Charles River Associates (2004), *Statewide Pricing Pilot Summer 2003 Impact Analysis*, Oakland, CA: Charles River Associates.

European Network of Transmission System Operators – Electricity (ENTSO-E) (2018), *Bidding Zone Configuration Technical Report 2018*, October, accessed 26 September 2020 at https://docstore.entsoe.eu/Documents/Events/2018/BZ_report/20181015_BZ_TR_FINAL.pdf.

Fabrizio, K. R., N. L. Rose and C. D. Wolfram (2007), 'Do markets reduce costs? Assessing the impact of regulatory restructuring on US electric generation efficiency', *American Economic Review*, **97** (4), 1250–77.

Galetovic, A., C. M. Muñoz and F. A. Wolak (2015), 'Capacity payments in a cost-based wholesale electricity market: the case of Chile', *The Electricity Journal*, **28** (10), 80–96.

Graf, C., F. Quaglia and F. A. Wolak (2020), 'Simplified electricity market models with significant intermittent renewable capacity: evidence from Italy', accessed 26 September 2020 at http://web.stanford.edu/group/fwolak/cgi-bin/sites/default/files/GrafQuagliaWolak_SimplifiedElectricityMarketModelsRenewables.pdf.

Joskow, P. L. (1997), 'Restructuring, competition and regulatory reform in the U.S. electricity sector', *The Journal of Economic Perspectives*, **11** (3), 119–38.

Kahn, M. E. and F. A. Wolak (2013), 'Using information to improve the effectiveness of non-linear pricing: evidence from a field experiment', accessed 26 September 2020 at http://web.stanford.edu/group/fwolak/cgi-bin/sites/default/files/files/kahn_wolak_July_2_2013.pdf.

Mansur, E. T. and M. W. White (2012), 'Market organization and efficiency in electricity markets', accessed 26 September 2020 at https://mansur.host.dartmouth.edu/papers/mansur_white_pjmaep.pdf.

McRae, S. D. and R. Meeks (2016), 'Price perceptions and electricity demand with non-linear prices', accessed 26 September 2020 at https://www.sdmcrae.com/publication/price-perception-and-electricity-demand/.

McRae, S. D. and F. A. Wolak (2012), 'How do firms exercise unilateral market power? Evidence from a bid-based wholesale electricity market', in J.-M. Glachant and E. Brousseau (eds), *Manufacturing Markets: Legal, Political and Economic Dynamics*, Cambridge, UK: Cambridge University Press.

McRae, S. D. and F. A. Wolak (2019), 'Market power and incentive-based capacity payment mechanisms', accessed 26 September 2020 at web.stanford.edu/group/fwolak/cgi-bin/sites/default/files/2019-03-mcrae-wolak-capacity.pdf.

Oren, S. S. (2001), 'Design of ancillary service markets', in *Proceedings of the 34th Annual Hawaii International Conference on System Sciences*, https://doi.org/10.1109/HICSS.2001.926283.

Patrick, R. H. and F. A. Wolak (1999), 'Customer response to real-time prices in the England and Wales electricity market: implications for demand-side bidding and pricing options design under competition', in M. A. Crew (ed.), *Regulation Under Increasing Competition*, Boston, MA: Kluwer Academic Publishers, pp. 155–82.

Tangerås, T. P. and F. A. Wolak (2018), 'The competitive effects of linking electricity markets across space and time', accessed 26 September 2020 at http://web.stanford.edu/group/fwolak/cgi-bin/sites/default/files/The_Competitive_Effects_of_Linking_Electricity_Markets_Across_Space_April_2021.pdf.

Vickers, J. and G. K. Yarrow (1988), *Privatization: An Economic Analysis*, Cambridge, MA: MIT Press.

Wolak, F. A. (1999), 'Market design and price behavior in restructured electricity markets: an international comparison', in T. Ito and A. Krueger (eds), *Competition Policy in the Asia Pacific Region*, Chicago, IL: The University of Chicago Press, pp. 79–134.

Wolak, F. A. (2000), 'An empirical analysis of the impact of hedge contracts on bidding behavior in a competitive electricity market', *International Economic Journal*, **14** (2), 1–40.

Wolak, F. A. (2003a), 'Measuring unilateral market power in wholesale electricity markets: the California market, 1998–2000', *American Economic Review*, **93** (2), 425–30.

Wolak, F. A. (2003b), 'Diagnosing the California electricity crisis', *The Electricity Journal*, **16** (7), 11–37.

Wolak, F. A. (2006), 'Residential customer response to real-time pricing: the Anaheim critical-peak pricing experiment', *CSEM WP 151*, Center for the Study of Energy Markets, accessed 26 September 2020 at https://haas.berkeley.edu/wp-content/uploads/csemwp151.pdfk.

Wolak, F. A. (2009), *Report on Market Performance and Market Monitoring in the Colombian Electricity Supply Industry*, accessed 26 September 2020 at http://web.stanford.edu/group/fwolak/cgi-bin/sites/default/files/files/sspd_report_wolak_july_30.pdf.

Wolak, F. A. (2011a), 'Do residential customers respond to hourly prices? Evidence from a dynamic pricing experiment', *American Economic Review*, **101** (3), 83–7.

Wolak, F. A. (2011b), 'Measuring the benefits of greater spatial granularity in short-term pricing in wholesale electricity markets', *American Economic Review*, **101** (3), 247–52.

Wolak, F. A. (2013), 'Economic and political constraints on the demand-side of electricity industry restructuring processes', *Review of Economics and Institutions*, **4** (1), 1–42.

Wolak, F. A. (2014), 'Regulating competition in wholesale electricity supply', in N. L. Rose (ed.), *Economic Regulation and Its Reform: What Have We Learned?*, Chicago, IL: University of Chicago Press, pp. 195–289.

Wolak, F. A. (2015a), 'Measuring the competitiveness benefits of a transmission investment policy: the case of the Alberta electricity market', *Energy Policy*, **85**, 426–44.

Wolak, F. A. (2015b), 'Do customers respond to real-time usage feedback? Evidence from Singapore', accessed 26 September 2020 at http://web.stanford.edu/group/fwolak/cgi-bin/sites/default/files/Singapore%20residential_nov_2015.pdf.

Wolak, F. A. (2018), 'The evidence from California on the economic impact of inefficient distribution network pricing', *NBER Working Paper 25087*, National Bureau of Economic Research.

Wolak, F. A. (2020), 'Transmission planning and operation in the wholesale market regime', *Transmission Network Investment in Liberalized Power Markets*, pp. 101–33. Springer, Cham.

Wolak, F. A. and Hardman, I. (2021) *The Future of Electricity Retailing and How We Get There, Lecture Notes in Energy Volume 41*, Springer International Publishing.

Wolak, F. A. and R. H. Patrick (2001), 'The impact of market rules and market structure on the price determination process in the England and Wales electricity market', *NBER Working Paper 8248*, National Bureau of Economic Research.

Wolfram, C. D. (1999), 'Measuring duopoly power in the British electricity spot market', *American Economic Review*, **89** (4), 805–26.

5. The evolution of competitive retail electricity markets

*Stephen Littlechild**

1. INTRODUCTION

Competitive retail electricity markets are barely 30 years old. As Schmalensee explains in Chapter 2 of this handbook, the 'traditional' arrangements for the electricity industry involved a mixture of numerous privately owned, government-owned or cooperative entities, regulated in various different ways. In the UK[1] and some other countries, nationalization replaced this initial variety by one or several government organizations. At the wholesale level, in some systems there were 'pools' or internal bidding processes to determine which plants should run. But there was no concept of customer choice between different electricity retailers.

In the 1980s, these traditional arrangements were questioned: were they conducive to efficiency and innovation? In the US, following the 1978–82 deregulation of airlines, railroads, trucking and bus services, the challenge was to deregulate the privately owned electricity sector. Electricity generation could be deregulated, and wholesale markets for electricity created, but it was initially assumed that retail prices, as well as network investment, would continue to be regulated. In the UK, following the 1979–87 privatizations of some 20 major companies in other industries, the challenge was to replace public ownership of the electricity industry by private ownership. With appropriate restructuring, this would enable competition in generation, although privatization would mean the introduction, rather than reduction, of regulation in the sector.

During the 1990s, these ideas began to be implemented. Electricity sectors were restructured and privatized, competition was allowed and encouraged in generation, wholesale markets were introduced, national transmission and local distribution grids were regulated. But what about retail? Could there and should there be competitive retail markets for electricity? Gradually, it was accepted that retail competition was possible and indeed desirable for large industrial and commercial customers. Often, this was extended to small businesses. But as to retail competition for residential customers, with which this chapter is mainly concerned, proponents of reform differed, as did national and state policies, and many of these differences continue.

The first part of this chapter (Sections 2–3) describes early developments. Section 2 describes initial thinking during the 1980s and the creation of retail markets around the world during the 1990s and early 2000s. The Nordic countries, Australia, New Zealand and some other European countries followed the UK in restructuring, encouraging competition in generation, and introducing full retail competition for all customers, often with a transitional price cap that was eventually phased out. Other European countries followed to a lesser extent and more reluctantly. Section 3 explains that, in the US, there was great variety in approach: California introduced then rescinded retail competition; Texas adopted the UK approach; 12 other US states plus Washington DC introduced and maintained retail competition but hedged their bets by obliging incumbent network utilities to provide a 'default supply tariff'; a half-dozen states allowed retail competition only for large industrial customers; and the remaining 30 or so states either did not introduce or did not persevere with retail competition for residential customers.

The second part of this chapter (Sections 4–6) describes subsequent experience during the 2010s in the US (Section 4), Australia and New Zealand (Section 5) and the UK (Section 6). As these retail electricity markets developed, there was increasing evidence of new entry, lower prices and new kinds of tariffs.[2] Varying numbers of customers switched to the new suppliers. But critics began to interpret price differentials as evidence, not of competition, but of a lack of it. There was increasing concern for vulnerable customers. Some regulators and governments have taken more interventionist steps, including by reintroducing limits on the prices or tariffs that suppliers can offer. In parallel, economists have increasingly shed light on how suppliers and customers act, how retail markets work, and the effects of regulatory interventions. However, the arguments and evidence used in these policy discussions have been much disputed.

The likely direction of future policy is as yet unclear, but the context is changing. Later chapters in this handbook explain how radically different electricity systems and markets are now envisaged, including 'prosumers' engaged in behind the meter generation, storage and peer-to-peer trading in a decarbonizing world. Governments have also committed to a zero-carbon world. Section 7 of this chapter suggests that full retail competition will be more, not less, important in such a world, because customers and retailers will need to be more actively involved, and retail competition seems a more effective way of involving them than government exhortations or regulatory restrictions.

2.   EARLY THINKING AND MARKET OPENING IN THE UK AND OTHER NON-US MARKETS

2.1   Early Thinking About the Possibility of Competitive Retail Electricity Markets

In the US, the 1980s' focus was on extending the deregulation policy that had been applied to airlines, natural gas and trucking. Joskow and Schmalensee (1983) provided particularly informed, thoughtful, imaginative and influential economic analysis of electricity deregulation. They emphasized that there was no one single solution and that deregulation would need to be accompanied by restructuring of the sector and other regulatory reforms. To increase efficiency, the priority was to get competition into the generation of electricity.

Their book was particularly timely for the UK, where nationalization was increasingly associated with inefficiency. Shortly after Margaret Thatcher's election in 1979, Energy Acts in 1982 and 1983 made provision for common carriage in gas pipelines and electricity networks to facilitate new entry and wholesale competition and give Area Boards and large industrial customers a choice of supplier. This paralleled the concept of 'wheeling' in the US electricity sector.[3] With the interest in privatization of nationalized industries, Beesley and Littlechild (1983a) assessed the candidate industries and concluded that the priority was electricity because of its size and potential for competition. They advised the Treasury that the electricity industry could be privatized by restructuring and introducing incentive regulation and competition (Beesley and Littlechild 1983b). But how could the expected benefits of wholesale competition best be conveyed to customers? Regulation might require each existing Area Board, effectively a regional network utility, to purchase generation economically on behalf of its captive customers and to pass on the costs to them. But in the US, regulation had proved part of the problem because of its costs, delays, restrictions, distortions, cross-subsidies and disincentive effects. So, regulated purchasing and pricing would be solving one UK problem by introducing another. A few US towns had competing electric utilities and Primeaux (1975, 1985a, 1985b) had argued that these utilities were more efficient. But it seemed costly and disproportionate to string two (or more) sets of electricity wires down each street.

The author's proposed method of bringing the benefits of wholesale competition to customers was complete retail competition (Beesley and Littlechild 1983b, paras 77–78, also Littlechild 2009, 2014). It was inspired by then-recent developments in the US and UK telecommunications sectors, whereby incumbent telecoms companies were required to provide access to their local networks to new entrant long-distance carriers, who then signed up not only businesses but also household customers. Why not do the same for electricity? That is, require the national transmission grid and the regional Area Boards (the distribution utilities) to make available their wires to potential entrants into retail supply (in effect, universal 'wheeling'). Then, existing and new generators, or network utilities that developed their own generation, could sell in the areas of other network utilities without having to install, or even threaten to install, new sets of wires. In fact, business and household customers themselves, or wholly new-entrant retailers acting on their behalf, with no existing generation or network assets, could buy electricity from generators located anywhere in the country and have it delivered to themselves, or to other business and household customers located anywhere else in the country. Transmission and distribution grids would remain natural monopolies and their charges would need regulating. But with freedom of entry into retail, there seemed no need for regulation of retail prices.

2.2   Phased Introduction of Retail Competition in the UK

Was retail competition the solution? Some were sceptical. The author explained his idea to Hogan and Joskow in Boston around 1983. 'No', they said, 'the big electricity customers already have good deals and the small customers won't be interested'. But the UK Secretary of State for Energy was more receptive.[4] There would be retail competition for all customers, although this was phased in (larger industrial customers first) over the eight years 1990–98. (The government's purpose in this was to enable the Area Boards to sign contracts with the high-cost British coal industry without threat of being undercut by competing retailers buying from generators using lower cost imported coal, which in turn would assist in privatizing the coal industry.) But would a customer actually buy electricity from anyone but their local Area Board? For large customers, at least, the answer turned out to be yes. In fact, so many large industrial customers asked to sign up with competing suppliers that the government had to put a temporary limit on the number of customers that could leave each Area Board, otherwise it feared not being able to privatize the Area Boards.

Retail competition (between rival generators and Area Boards increasingly developing their own generation) was immediately successful for large industrial customers (maximum demand over 1 megawatt [MW]) and, after 1994, for medium commercial and industrial customers (maximum demand over 100 kilowatts [kW]). There were some metering hiccups for the latter (Green 2005, pp. 117–18, Green and Newbery 1997), in the light of which the Office of Electricity Regulation (OFFER) appointed project management consultants to oversee the opening of the market for residential customers, and phased the opening over a period of nine months. With competition in generation, prices for such customers now reflected the lower cost of new-build gas plant and, to a lesser extent, the increased use of imported coal displacing the more expensive British coal. Newbery provides further context on the England and Wales market model in Chapter 6 of this book.

Conceptually, retail electricity competition was simple. But on a thoroughgoing basis it had never been done before. Other countries soon followed suit: in the 1990s, Norway, Sweden and Finland, Australia and New Zealand, California and a few other US states, and a few other European Union countries; in the 2000s, Texas, some other US states, Alberta and Ontario, Japan, Singapore and eventually most of the European Union. Other countries such as Malaysia are contemplating it. Retail competition is now more or less uncontroversial for large customers, but for residential customers it is still the subject of debate and evolving policy.

2.3   Opening the UK Retail Market for Residential Customers

In the UK in 1998, OFFER was faced with several questions. When the residential market is opened, will retail suppliers find it worthwhile to market to such customers? Will they be able to offer discounts sufficient to incentivize residential customers to switch supplier? Or is it possible that competition will be so weak that incumbent suppliers will simply raise their prices and other suppliers and/or customers will not respond? Would the various costs of market opening exceed the benefits?

Some had voiced such doubts. Henney (1987, also 1994) had supported retail competition for large and medium-sized customers, but not for residential (domestic) customers, on the grounds that it would not be worthwhile at such low consumption levels. Green and McDaniel (1998) pointed out that even with lower prices there would need to be substantial efficiency savings to cover the £500 million to £1 billion cost of modified systems (this amount included the cost of load profiling systems to avoid the need for half-hourly metering for smaller customers).

During the eight-year so-called franchise period (1990–98) before retail competition was introduced for all customers in the UK, there had been a retail price control essentially passing through the actual network charges, wholesale generation costs and retail supply business costs incurred by the incumbent utilities. Rather than remove this entirely in 1998, OFFER introduced a temporary transitional fixed-price cap for the next two years to reassure customers (and the media and politicians). If the newly privatized Area Boards had increased prices because of negligible initial retail competition, or perhaps even because wholesale costs increased, that could have compromised the whole concept of retail competition. Admittedly, it might be difficult to remove the price cap later, but given that this was a step into the unknown, it seemed a prudent measure.

The level of the transitional cap was set equal to the previous price-controlled level, adjusted downwards to reflect the (reducing) levels of regulated network costs over the next two years, just as the previous price control would have been adjusted downwards. To prevent the price cap imposing a risk on the incumbents or limiting competition, OFFER checked that, within this level of cap, it was possible to buy power forward for the next two years, if the incumbent suppliers chose to do so. It was up to each supplier whether to take or hedge the risk of wholesale price fluctuations. The aim was not to estimate the 'competitive level' of prices, or to benefit entrants or incumbent utilities. Rather, it was to enable retail competition, rather than regulation, to determine the price level, to bring the benefits of wholesale competition to customers, and to be seen to be doing so.

So, the level of the price cap meant that there was scope for new entrants to compete by setting prices below it. However, there was more to competition than just offering a lower price for an assumed homogeneous product. Indeed, some potential competitors began by reimagining the supposedly homogeneous product, tailoring or differentiating their products to meet different customer needs. Thus, one executive told the author: 'We started by asking what discount customers would need to persuade them to switch from the incumbent, then we redesigned the product to enable us to sell at that price. Later, we realized that no suppliers wanted customers with poor payment records, so we decided to aim at that part of the market with a prepayment meter product that would be attractive to these customers and make them profitable to supply'. (Before the deployment of smart meters, competition included finding the most convenient ways for customers to top up prepayment meters by tokens, keys or cards, and later by mobile phone apps. Prepayment products became, and remain, popular with retailers and with about 16 per cent of all residential customers, and have meant that disconnections for non-payment of energy bills are now virtually non-existent in the UK.)

Would retail competition work at residential level? In the author's then-view as regulator (head of OFFER), if only about 5 per cent of residential customers switched supplier it would have been difficult to justify the policy and the costs incurred in enabling switching, but if 10 per cent of customers switched supplier then the policy could be defended. In the event, this was not a problem. Switching supplier soon caught on, as it had a year or two earlier in natural gas and in Norway. Retail competition was seen to be working. In 2002, after once renewing and reducing the scope of the price cap, Ofgem (the Office of Gas and Electricity Markets, successor body to OFFER) fully removed the cap, with the chairman commenting that 'evidence is overwhelming that competition is effective over all social groups and methods of payment' (Littlechild, 2016, fn 58).

2.4   The First Decade of Retail Competition in the UK

Competition developed strongly between previously incumbent retail suppliers, all now offering 'dual-fuel' supply. The previous incumbent residential gas supplier (British Gas/Centrica) soon took over 20 per cent of the electricity market. After numerous mergers and takeovers, the 14 former electricity companies consolidated into five and soon took in aggregate over 50 per cent of the retail gas market. From 2000 to 2007, there were nine new entrants into the UK residential retail market, but most soon went out of business or were taken over. As of 2005, entrants instanced a number of problems associated with complexity and cost of the entry qualification process, cost of credit cover, lack of whole-sale market liquidity, consumption data quality (on change of supplier), lack of competition for metering services and regulatory restrictions and burdens (Littlechild 2005). Entrants supplied a negligible proportion of residential customers until about 2009, and in the next few years 1 per cent at most.

Littlechild (2002), referencing Austrian economists Schumpeter, Hayek and Kirzner (1985, 1997), argued that the development of retail competition illustrated the nature of competition as a process over time, the entrepreneurial and learning nature of this process, the role of marketing in alerting customers, the role of competition in establishing price and in discovering the services and suppliers that customers prefer, and the advantages of competition over regulation.

Others were less convinced. Otero and Waddams Price (2001) found price discrimination with respect to payment methods and also area, and Salies and Waddams Price (2004) concluded that the overall net social benefits of liberalization were negative. Giulietti, Waddams Price and Waterson (2005) deduced that British Gas/Centrica retained considerable market power. Green (2005) questioned whether retail competition adequately protected loyal customers. Newbery (2006, p. 140) conjectured that 'most domestic customers would probably be better off with a regulated supply margin and benchmarked contract costs passed through under regulatory supervision', and the only case for retail competition was 'the reasonable assumption in some jurisdictions that regulators would be less effective at protecting consumer interests than competition'. (This regulatory ability was about to be tested.)

Nonetheless, Ofgem (2007a) remained positive, noting vigorous price competition for all customers, innovation by suppliers in terms of fixed and capped price deals, cheaper online deals and green tariffs, improving customer service, and customer switching rates at their highest in four years. It explained that competition in the market was increasing and beneficial. It also noted that suppliers engaged in various 'voluntary measures to help vulnerable and fuel poor customers and in particular . . . social tariffs, rebates and trust fund arrangements' (Ofgem 2007b, p. i).

2.5 Opening Other Non-US Retail Markets

The Nordic countries (Norway, Sweden, Denmark and Finland) were early and success-ful adopters of wholesale and retail competition (Amundsen, Bergman and Von der Fehr 2006, Littlechild 2006b). A transitional price cap was not deemed necessary there, perhaps because of the prevalence of state-owned and municipally owned utilities. In Chapter 10 of this book, LeCoq and Schwenen report that retail competition is 'a strength of the Nordic market, conditional, however, on typical drawbacks regarding limited consumer response in power markets'. The relative success of the retail market opening is 'attributed to light regulation. In particular, the absence of price controls contributed to relatively high switching rates of consumers'. Amundsen et al. (2006) found that retail prices were more variable and more related to wholesale prices in Norway than in Sweden and attributed this to higher meter-related switching costs in Sweden. They also suggested that integrated generation retailers might have an advantage over independent retailers, possibly via the exercise of market power. Bergman (2009) characterized the design and functioning of the Norwegian retail market as 'best practice'.

In Europe generally, the 1996 Electricity Directive 96/92/EC set out basic rules to bring about a single European market in electricity. It provided for all member states to open their retail markets for large users and distribution companies by 2003. Many countries went further than required. To put pressure on slowly reforming countries, the 2003 Directive 2003/54/EC required that all non-residential electricity and gas consumers be allowed to choose their retail suppliers by 2004 and that residential consumers should be allowed retail competition by 2007. Haas et al. (2006) found it unlikely that the conditions for vibrant competition would be fulfilled in Continental Europe, and opined that, without competition in the wholesale market, there was little prospect of successful competition in retail. (This has indeed been true internationally.)

An inquiry by the European Commission (2007) had little to say about retail but commented: 'Regulated retail tariffs can have highly distortive effects and in certain cases pre-empt the creation of liberalized markets. It is of crucial importance to assess the impact of remaining regulated supply tariffs on the development of competition, and remove distortions' (European Commission 2007, p. 14, para. 66). The European Regulators Group for Electricity and Gas (ERGEG 2008, pp. 6–7) found 'a very heterogeneous picture', price increases, high concentration, low switching rates (in many countries 0–2 per cent per year) and (in 16 member states) regulated end-user prices that were distorting and restricting competition. ERGEG (2009, summary) reported 'no major progress . . . competition in retail electricity and gas markets is almost non-existent . . . regulated prices (distorting competition) persist in several countries; and there is often a "fuzzy" separation of the distribution system operator (DSO) from the supply arm of vertically-integrated firms'. The EU's 'Third Energy Package', effective 2009, made only minimal reference to retail issues (European Commission, 2009), and ERGEG observed in 2010 that evolution towards a real competitive market was still slow. It is clear that some national governments were not enthusiastic and opened their markets only under pressure from the EU.

Several states in Australia began reform in the early 1990s, phasing the opening of their markets: Victoria 1994–2002, New South Wales 1996–2002, Queensland 1998–2007 and South Australia 1998–2003. All retained transitional price caps until 2009. Moran (2006, p. 182) noted the increased importance of retail 'as the interface with the consumer', and the 'quite considerable churn rate' of customers changing suppliers, despite 'maximum prices that make it less attractive for retailers to poach customers'. He also complained that 'On top of price safety nets, the Labor state governments have all imposed their social and green policy objectives via retail regulations for domestic customers. This has resulted in a considerable mish-mash of compliance requirements for retailers selling to small customers and reduced the potential for competition'. Nevertheless, in the sector as a whole, 'a successful outcome has been observed' (p. 200).

New Zealand had an electricity system similar to the UK, with a state-owned monopoly generator and transmission grid (the New Zealand Electricity Division NZED) that was corporatized in 1987, and many local government electrical supply authorities responsible for distribution and retail in each geographical area. A 1989 task force recommended restructuring, privatization, wholesale and retail competition, no regulation of retail prices, and 'light-handed regulation' of distribution charges. This policy was implemented to the extent of not setting up an industry regulator, but relying instead on industry self-regulation and general competition law. Transmission was separated off in 1994, the larger generation plant was split among four successor companies by 1999, only one of which was subsequently privatized. The retail market was opened to competition in 1993–94 but competitors took only 5 per cent of customers from incumbents. In 1998, ownership separation of distribution and retailing was enforced. Most local supply authorities divested their retail operations, which were bought by the five main generators, who became vertically integrated so-called 'gentailers'. Four of them accounted for 90 per cent of generation capacity and the fifth for a further 5 per cent. Independent retailers entered the market but soon left: in 2003, the five 'gentailers' supplied 98 per cent of residential customers (Electricity Authority NZ, 2020b). In 2003, the government decided to establish an Electricity Commission but confined its price-regulating power to transmission pricing.

Bertram (2006), from which the above summary is taken, was critical of these 'light-handed' regulatory arrangements. He argued that the initial restructuring was insufficient to achieve competitive outcomes, and that the vertical integration constituted a barrier to entry for independent retailers. After various industry disputes, the Electricity Commission was replaced by a new Electricity Authority in 2010, which explicitly had no responsibility for considering fairness or equity issues. One of its functions was 'to promote to consumers the benefits of comparing and switching retailers'. Bertram (2013, p. 659) was critical of regulatory action here too, arguing that a new Powerswitch website, diversified 'gentailer' brand names and an intensive advertising campaign 'succeeded in raising the rate of customer churn amongst retailers, at the cost of a very large deadweight burden of information-gathering, calculation and anxiety borne by individual consumers and voluntary budget advisory services; the [Electricity] Authority nevertheless judged its efforts a success'. (But it must be said that the Authority's present Electricity Market Information (EMI) website is extremely impressive.)

Japan, and Ontario and Alberta in Canada, also restructured their electricity sectors and opened their retail markets to competition. The proportion of 88 developing countries that had adopted any kind of electricity sector reform increased from one-third in 1995 to two-thirds in 2010, while the proportion adopting retail competition increased from 1 per cent to 7 per cent (Foster et al. 2017, Figure 5.2). The latter countries and their opening dates are listed (Foster et al. 2017, Annex 1B) as Argentina 1995, Turkey 2001, Philippines 2006, Romania 2007 and Ukraine 2010.

3.   OPENING RETAIL MARKETS IN THE US

3.1   The Debate Over How to Provide Retail Competition

A distinctive characteristic of US experience was the debate about whether, and if so, how best to provide retail competition in the restructured electricity markets. Although some (for instance, Brennan 1991) had urged caution about allowing new entry in the hitherto-regulated sectors, practitioners in Faruqui and Malko (1999) surveyed 'the dynamics of this brave new world of customer choice' (p. 3) and sought to identify strategies that could create lasting value. Using evidence from other sectors, Goulding, Ruffin and Swinand (1999) argued that the absence of vibrant retail markets would fail to provide the products that customers really want, raise the barriers to new retail entry, reduce innovation, accentuate monopoly power and make entry more difficult in wholesale generation markets.

Yet others envisaged a different approach. Hogan (1994) had argued that charging residential customers a time-of-use tariff based on the wholesale market spot price would give them what he called 'efficient direct access' to the competitive wholesale market. If they wished, customers could then enter contracts for differences with generators or retailers to provide whatever security, price stability or flexibility they preferred. Hogan saw this as an easy way to provide retail access. Ruff (1999) explained that he had made similar proposals for spot price pass-through at the time of UK restructuring. Some US states began to offer a hedged default service (see below), although Flaim (2000) was concerned that this was leading to too few customers switching to competitive suppliers, and argued that 'default supply should clearly be based on the unhedged price of the commodity' (p. 46).

Joskow (2000) suggested that many of the traditional 'convenience services' provided by retailers in other industries were irrelevant in electricity, which was essentially a homogeneous good. Suppose incumbent electricity distribution companies were required to provide what he called a 'Basic Electricity Service' that simply passed through the (unhedged) wholesale spot market price of electricity. Retail consumers would thereby receive the benefits of competitive generation markets without suppliers incurring large increases in advertising, promotion and customer service costs. Retailers could compete with this basic service by offering value-added products such as hedges against price fluctuations, if customers were willing to pay for them. The basic service would provide a competitive benchmark against which consumers could compare the value added associated with offers from competing retailers, so it would help to protect residential and small commercial customers from exploitation by these other retailers. And it would mitigate wasteful expenditures on marketing and promotion by rent-seeking retailers that would increase prices.

Littlechild (2000, 2003) replied that this perspective did not fully acknowledge the importance of retail price competition, which, *inter alia*, could incentivize efficiency improvements to offset the costs of marketing. It neglected the role of contract markets and hence the importance of retail competitors in strengthening wholesale competition. And it underestimated the costs and disadvantages of imposing this proposed obligation on distribution companies.

3.2   Opening the Retail Market in California

Within the US, California was at the forefront of moving to wholesale and particularly retail competition. Members of the California Public Utilities Commission came to the UK to see how policy and competition were developing. Between 1992 and 1995 the Commission developed its initial thinking. The original plan was to restructure the three main utilities by divesting all their generation plants, and to open the retail market to large customers in 1996, extending this to all customers by 2002.

At the time, the California Commission seems to have taken the Hogan-Ruff-Joskow view that the incumbent utilities should pass through the unhedged wholesale price to customers. Customers could be left to decide whether to hedge these prices by buying from another retail supplier. In 1996, California state legislation AB1890 legalized the restructuring proposed by the California commission, including the creation of a power exchange where the utilities would purchase all their power. However, the legislation went further, changing the Commission's proposed cap on the Competition Transition Charge (a surcharge introduced to recover stranded costs incurred by incumbent utilities) to a cap on retail prices, mandating a 10 per cent retail rate cut, and shortening the transition period. These modifications increased the difficulty of recovering stranded costs, and the mandated price reductions turned out not to be sustainable in the face of wholesale gas and electricity price increases in early 2000 (since the Commission had discouraged the utilities from hedging). In San Diego, where the utility's price cap had expired because it had recovered its stranded costs, retail prices increased sharply. The California legislature stepped in with its own price cap, one utility filed for bankruptcy, and there were arguments between the California and Federal Commissions. In January 2001, the power exchange operations were suspended and a state of emergency declared. In March and May, the California Commission announced rate increases, and in September it suspended retail choice. These misfortunes have been much studied (for instance, Joskow 2001, Sweeney 2006).

The California experience led Joskow to modify his view that incumbent utilities should simply pass on wholesale costs: although 'the default service option for larger commercial and industrial consumers should be to purchase their electricity at real-time prices', for other (residential and small commercial) customers, '[a] good retail procurement framework . . . must assure that a large fraction of retail demand is being met with longer-term fixed price contracts and only a small fraction fully exposed to the spot market' (Joskow 2001, p. 387). As will be evident shortly, there has been continued discussion and dispute about how best to hedge this default service in most US retail markets.

3.3   Opening the Retail Market in Texas

Texas was keen to introduce competition, but proceeded more carefully, especially in the light of California's experience. Since the Electric Reliability Council of Texas (ERCOT) grid was essentially not interconnected with the networks in other US states, Texas was not subject to the Federal Energy Regulatory Commission (FERC), which regulates interstate transmission and wholesale markets. So, Texas could pursue its own course, responsible for transmission, wholesale and retail. Baldick et al. tell the story in Chapter 8 of this book.

Texas introduced wholesale competition in 1995, and in 1999 provided for retail competition, but deferred its introduction until 2002, by which time wholesale competition was expected to be effective. Incumbent utilities were required to unbundle network and competitive activities, but not necessarily to dispose of them into separate ownership, hence the reference in places to 'utility-affiliated retailers'. In contrast to most other US jurisdictions, retailers rather than network utilities were made responsible for billing customers.

The Public Utility Commission of Texas (PUCT, 2001 p. 39) set a temporary 'price to beat' for each utility-affiliated retailer, which 'will freeze the incumbent retailers' rates at a level that the new competitors should be able to undercut. New competitors should be able to enter the market, gain customers, and make a profit'. The price to beat was essentially a marker for competitors to aim at, and the affiliated retailer was not allowed to charge a lower price. In the event, the price to beat embodied a 6 per cent reduction on previous prices but there was provision for wholesale price adjustments. The price to beat was to remain in place, for each utility's affiliated retailer, for five years or until 40 per cent of the utility's load had switched to another supplier. It would be removed for commercial customers in 2004 and at the latest for residential customers in 2007.

The PUCT estimated that residential customers saved about $900 million in the first year, although Joskow (2005, pp. 67–8) and Baldick and Niu (2005) expressed some reservations about that number. Zarnikau and Whitworth (2006) found that average residential prices in retail choice areas increased faster than in other parts of Texas, but this seems to have reflected increases in the price to beat (which was indexed to the natural gas price). Kang and Zarnikau (2009) found that expiration of the price to beat led to a reduction in prices by competitive retailers.

Adib and Zarnikau (2006, p. 406) referred to 'an extremely difficult transition period' to retail competition, instancing early problems with switches, billing data and computer systems. They emphasized that creation of a central registration agent function can be an overwhelming task and needed a longer transition time. Adequate resources were needed for market monitoring. The Commission was given a $36 million budget for customer education, which increased customer awareness considerably, although more than 70 per cent of residential customers still remained with the incumbent utility-affiliate retailers, and the authors recommended additional customer education. Nonetheless, they were already dubbed Texas 'the most robust competitive market in North America' (ibid.).

3.4 The Retail Markets in Other US Jurisdictions

After California opened its retail electricity market in 1996, a number of bills were put forward in Congress, proposing that all states should open their retail markets to competition or explain why not. In the US generally, some two-thirds of the states had little or no interest in retail competition or in electricity reform generally. The remaining third – notably, those with higher electricity prices (Joskow 2005, p. 36) – were keen to implement reform, especially access by large users to alternative retail suppliers. Some states initially planned to copy the UK and Texas, in the sense of transitioning to a competitive market with no retail price controls. But all were conscious of what happened in California, and perceived that some further protection, perhaps transitional, was required, particularly for those customers that did not wish to become actively involved purchasing hedges in the competitive market. Flaim (2000), Joskow (2005) and Tschamler (2006) provide early discussion of these US approaches and experience.

In the event, 14 US jurisdictions (Texas and 12 other states plus Washington DC) made provision for retail competition down to residential level, and have maintained this policy to date.[5] These jurisdictions have required the incumbent network utility in each area to divest itself of generation assets in the rate base and to offer a default supply tariff that passes through market-based and/or wholesale prices in a way defined by the state regulatory commission. Customers have the option of choosing an alternative retail supplier if they wish.

The precise basis on which utilities purchase power and set the default tariff differs across states, and has evolved over time (Kim 2013, Littlechild 2018a). Purchasing of power usually occurs through a mixture of auctions, hedging contracts and spot price purchases. In all these states except New York, the default rates are set ex ante for periods of a few months, sometimes varying on a seasonal basis to reflect wholesale price movements. In New York, the default rates are set ex post.

These arrangements reflect the spirit of Joskow's 'Basic Electricity Service' to the extent that residential customers that do not wish to move from the incumbent utility are provided with electricity at essentially wholesale cost plus (unlike his original proposal) the cost of smoothing or hedging this over a few months to reduce or average out unexpected fluctuations in wholesale cost. Customers that want additional services, like a fixed price for a year or two ahead, can get such contracts from competing retailers.

In addition, all these states require the incumbent network utility to provide metering, billing, revenue collection and purchase of receivables services for competing retail suppliers, on a regulated basis. (In the non-US competitive markets discussed in this chapter, most of these functions except metering generally fall to each retail supplier.) Supply from a competing retailer is thus largely undistinguishable from supply from the incumbent network utility, insofar as the utility continues to send the bill and collect the revenues, so the only difference that the customer sees is a different supplier name in one small section of the utility's bill. However, although the stated aim of this may have been to facilitate retail competition and minimize total costs, the actual effect seems to have been to limit the scope for competition and to cross-subsidize the default tariff at the expense of the distribution business, as explained below.

3.5   Interim Evaluation of Retail Competition as of Late 2000s

How then did residential retail competition work out in practice over the first decade or so? Joskow (2005) provided an initial evaluation of US experience, based on half a dozen states that were early adopters of the policy. Switching levels varied, being lower than in Texas and the UK, and negligible in New Jersey where the default price was initially held below the wholesale price. Switching was high in particular parts of Ohio where the default price was high and there was an active policy of municipal aggregation, whereby local communities that voted for that policy would switch all residents to a preferred supplier unless the resident actively opted to choose another supplier (Littlechild 2008). But claimed savings in many states reflected the level at which the default price was set rather than benefits from retail competition alone.

Joskow (2005) concluded that, while retail competition could bring benefits in terms of lower prices and/or improved services or innovation, it was 'still a work in progress' and had been a disappointment in many states that implemented it. He doubted whether residential customers would benefit much if at all from retail competition. However, if retail competition were to be pursued then the UK/Texas approach was likely to be most successful, hence default prices should be deregulated when the market was sufficiently competitive. Tschamler (2006) shared this view. Littlechild (2006a, p. xxvii) argued that 'the market will offer better value in the longer term when one considers how regulation will actually operate'. Pollitt (2008) compared the cases for liberalization and for regulation, noting the importance of institutional capability, and commenting on the 'pale version of [retail] competition' (p. xx) in some US states.

Looking beyond the US, Joskow (2006, 2008) provided extensive and valuable assessments of the lessons learned internationally. The brief account above indicates that experience was very positive in the Nordic countries; the subject of different views in the UK (with the regulator more impressed than some commentators); 'very heterogeneous' in the EU generally, with retail competition 'best practice' in Norway and 'almost non-existent' in some other EU countries; and generally positive in Australia and New Zealand, with some commentators critical of too little restructuring and too much regulatory intervention. So, by no means generally 'a disappointment', but 'a work in progress' seems a valid description internationally.

4.   THE LAST DECADE: CONCERNS AND POLICIES IN US RETAIL ELECTRICITY MARKETS

4.1   Increasing Concerns About US Retail Markets Except Texas

What is the more recent experience of retail competition in the last decade, what views have been expressed on it and what regulatory policies have been enacted? This section considers the situation in the US, Section 5 considers Australia and New Zealand and Section 6 the EU and UK.

Kim (2013) referred to 'admirable progress' in US retail markets, noting that the proportion of customers with competitive suppliers was then 54 per cent compared with 19 per cent in 2003. He agreed that 'The most durable choice model is Texas, in which there is no default service' (p. 360) and suggested that 'the primary barrier' to more competitive markets was 'long-term default service procurement contracts' (p. 361).

In Texas, confidence in both wholesale and retail markets remains high (Baldick et al., Chapter 8 in this handbook). Adib, Zarnikau and Baldick (2013) had described this already successful market as 'getting better' but noted 'slow progress by Retail Electricity Providers in offering new and innovative products and services, which is anticipated to be addressed by full implementation of smart meters by 2013' (p. 294). Smart meters have now been installed for almost all residential customers, with consequent reductions in operating costs and improvements in customer service. Switching is possible within a day. As in the UK, there are auto-switching or 'concierge services' that will choose and switch suppliers on a customer's behalf. There are now prepay tariffs, many green tariffs (77 out of 315 tariffs being from 100 per cent renewable sources per PUCT 2019, p. 2), various time-of-day tariffs and access to real-time wholesale prices for $9.99 per month with new entrant Griddy. The market is responding to customer preferences, although customers as yet seem less convinced about time-of-day pricing than proponents are. There have been minor issues with retail suppliers gaming the Texas Commission's Power to Choose comparison and switching site (which to some extent reflected the limitations of the site), but there has been no challenge to the central role of retail competition.[6]

Surprisingly, given the widespread support by commentators for the Texas model with no default tariffs, there appears to be no interest, among the other retail choice jurisdictions, in moving in that direction. There is ongoing debate about the appropriate specification of the default supply tariff, particularly as to how frequently it should be changed and on what basis it should be defined (Littlechild 2018a). But there are no proposals for removing it. Rather, there has been increased examination of whether competing retailers charge higher or lower prices than the default supply tariff, and what prices vulnerable customers in particular are paying. This has led to questioning whether retail competition adds value and on what terms competing retailers should be allowed to operate, but also to counterarguments about the default supply tariff specification.

Thus, Morey and Kirsch (2016) find 'little evidence that retail choice has yielded significant benefits' (pp. v, 65), and conclude that 'less-educated or low-income consumers are more likely than other consumers to make poor retail supply choices' (pp. vii, 62, 67). Some customer groups and state offices argue that default tariffs offer better value than tariffs offered on the competitive market. Baldwin (2019) calculates that 'Massachusetts consumers in the competitive supply market paid $176.8 million more than they would have paid if they had received electric supply from their [default] electric company during the two-year period from July 2015 to June 2017' (p. vii). Moreover, 'low-income households participate in the competitive supply market at twice the rate as non-low-income households' (ibid.), hence pay especially high prices. Baldwin has made similar claims in several retail choice states. Some regulatory commissions have made similar calculations: Bosco (2018, pp. 2–3) instances overpayments of $67 million in Connecticut in 2016/17, $152 million in Illinois in 2016/17, and $817 million in New York January 2014–June 2016.

Bosco (2018, p. 8) further claims that '[d]eceptive and aggressive door-to-door marketing appears to be disproportionately directed towards older consumers, people with limited English proficiency, and low-income communities'. This leads her to call for Massachusetts to follow Connecticut, New York and Illinois and put in place stronger consumer protections, starting with 'Reconsider the sale of competitive energy supply to individual residential customers' (p. 3), and instead limit it to commercial and industrial markets and municipal aggregation. She also made ten further recommendations.[7]

In 2015, the Connecticut legislature banned variable rate products. This was essentially a reaction to the 'polar vortex' wholesale price increases of 2013–14, and the Connecticut regulatory authority subsequently invited the legislature to relax the ban. Subsequently, however, the Connecticut Public Utilities Regulatory Authority (2019) found that hardship customers paid more with competitive suppliers and took steps to transfer them back to default service and to prevent them contracting with competitive suppliers. Illinois, Pennsylvania and New York too now have low-income customer restrictions – for example, providing that competing suppliers can only offer low-income customers rates that are at or below the utility's default supply rate.

4.2   Regulatory Restrictions in New York State

The restrictions in New York were among the earliest, most far-reaching (for example, going beyond hardship or low-income customers) and most challenged. This is perhaps surprising, since only a few years earlier Kim (2013, p. 341) found New York to be 'one of the most vibrant competitive retail markets as measured by the number of competitors, switching levels, and competitive market size', and 'second best' to Texas, with a 'strong default service model'.

Staff at the New York Public Service Commission (NYPSC) had expressed concerns about many customers paying higher prices than the default tariff. In 2014, the

Commission decided that competing retailers (there called Energy Services Companies, or ESCOs) must guarantee savings (over the default supply tariff) to low-income customers. In December 2019, after surviving several appeals through the courts, the Commission extended this requirement to all customers (NYPSC 2019). This requirement is more onerous in New York than elsewhere because the New York default supply tariff is set ex post, reflecting some fixed price hedges that the utilities put in place plus the remainder at wholesale spot price, so the rate that needs to be beaten is not known until after the event and cannot be hedged. Furthermore, there are six different utilities in New York, each with its own unique hedging strategy for default supply service, and all the data is kept confidential and not publicly available.

Consumer groups, New York State and Commission staff argued that the current retail market does not benefit customers; some argued for shutting it down, others for substantial reforms to limit suppliers' products and/or prices. Staff calculated that ESCO customers paid $1.2 billion more than utility customers would have paid over the three years to December 2016, and one party calculated that fewer than 25 per cent of ESCO customers saved money. ESCOs disputed these calculations and one retailer calculated that actually a small majority (52 per cent) of customers saved money. The Commission held that 'there is no demonstrated customer benefit to allowing ESCOs to offer this service [variable rate products] to mass-market customers' (NYPSC 2019, p. 37), and that the 20 per cent of ESCO customers that received a fixed price product paid a substantial premium. Moreover, any value-added products and services were not energy-related, but marketing devices, of relatively little value, which 'serve none of the goals of the retail energy market' (p. 11). And the complaint rate was unacceptably high: over 11 000 complaints from 2014 to 2016, about half of which alleged deceptive marketing tactics. (Interestingly, this complaint rate, which works out at about 2 per 1000 customer accounts, is roughly the recent UK average, but UK retail suppliers are responsible for a wider range of functions than ESCOs in New York, and sales and marketing feature hardly at all in the top five causes of UK complaints.)

The NYPSC announced several new measures, including enhanced ESCO eligibility criteria and more transparent pricing information (whereby utilities and ESCOs should include in bills a calculation of what an ESCO customer would have paid the previous month and previous year on the utility's default supply rate). Most significantly, an ESCO cannot take on or renew a customer except with: (1) a variable tariff incorporating a guaranteed savings over the utility price, as reconciled on an annual basis; or (2) a fixed-rate product priced no more than 5 per cent above the last 12-month average utility supply rate; or (3) a product with significantly higher renewable content than the present required minimum. The Commission decided against further marketing restrictions because of the difficulty and cost of enforcement. It also decided not to move from utility billing to ESCO billing because not all ESCOs could be trusted with the authority to terminate customer service, and if ESCOs did the billing then the Commission would no longer have access to important information about customer usage and pricing that the ESCOs presently transmit to utilities. (Neither of these issues seem to have been a problem elsewhere.)

What impact will such regulatory policies have? Are such restrictions on retail suppliers consistent with their continued existence, and in particular with the envisaged role of competing retail suppliers in taking forward New York Governor Cuomo's Reforming the Energy Vision (REV)? This project was to 'create a stronger and healthier economy by stimulating a vibrant private sector market to provide clean energy solutions to communities and individual customers throughout New York' (Cassell 2015). The expectation was that competing ESCOs would have an important role in sculpting combinations of purchases in the market, energy efficiency, demand response, storage and behind-the-meter generation (including combined heat and power). Or is it now the case, as Huntoon (2019) suggests, that 'REV as a customer-empowerment revolution that reduces customer costs is dead'?

4.3   Counterarguments and Further Evidence

Competing retailers in the default tariff jurisdictions (such as the Retail Energy Supply Association RESA, and Intelometry 2018) make two main counterarguments to those of the customer groups and Commission staff. First, the calculations mentioned above typically do not value other aspects of the competitive market (for example, lower-risk fixed-price products, green products, miscellaneous rewards and incentives), as acknowledged by Illinois Commerce Commission (2019, p. 30). Moreover, given search costs, all competitive markets are characterized by price dispersion, so this is not a sign of the markets malfunctioning. And active customers, at least, can do better with the competitive tariffs than with the default tariff: RESA (2019) claims that Connecticut customers could have saved over $14 million in just the first month of 2019.

Second, the market is distorted because default service is under-priced and cross-subsidized by the utility's regulated network operations. 'The indirect costs not allocated include billing, customer care, enrolments, metering, and other overhead and add up to billions of dollars annually', and in two recent cases the claimed subsidy amounted to 1 or 1.25 cents/kWh ($10–12.50/MWh), or more than 10 per cent of the default rate (Lacey 2019, p. 4, see also Gramlich and Lacey, 2020). In addition, default service is required to be provided at cost, without provision for even a reasonable rate of return.

Regulation in other countries has been alert to such distortions. Pollitt (2008, p. xxiii) notes that in 2000, Ofgem reallocated 18 per cent of the controllable costs of the UK distribution companies from their wires businesses to their retail businesses to correct the previous misallocation. It may seem surprising that more regulatory attention has not been given to resolving this issue in the US, given that the suggested magnitude of the distortion is of the same order as the presently claimed average excess of market prices above the default tariffs. So, if the default service had been correctly costed and priced, there would be no significant issue about the level of competitive retail rates. Presumably, the present distortion is another example of regulation responding to political pressures.

There has been some published empirical work on whether, and to what extent, different US customers benefit from retail choice. Swadley and Yücel (2011) find that 'retail competition makes the market more efficient by lowering the markup of retail prices over wholesale costs' (p. 7702). Although effects are mixed across states, competition generally appears to reduce prices in states with high participation rates. Using 1990–2011 data, Su (2015) found that residential customers benefited during the transitional period of restructuring, when rate freezes and reductions were often in place, but commercial and industrial customers did not benefit. Moreover, the reduction was significant in the short term (say five years) but not later.

Some studies argue that customers as a whole are better off with a competitive retail market because of the stimulus it provides to more efficient wholesale markets, and more efficient purchasing, compared to the previous policy of vertically integrated monopoly utilities. Comparisons are difficult in the early years because of differing transitional arrangements, but by 2008 most of these were complete, including generation separation and recovery of stranded costs. In contrast to findings mentioned earlier, O'Connor (2017, p. 5) finds 'compelling evidence of superior economic performance since 2008' in the 14 competitive states compared to those states that do not have retail competition. An update on that study calculates that residential customers in the 35 monopoly states are paying 21.6 per cent more than in 2008, while residential customers in the 14 competitive states are paying only 3.1 per cent more (O'Connor and Khan 2018; see also RESA 2020). Ros (2017, p. 1) finds that 'retail electricity competition is associated with lower deflated electricity prices'.

Dormady et al. (2019) argue that many studies ignore regulatory intervention via, for instance, riders and surcharges on consumer bills. In Ohio, they 'identify two main sources of cross-subsidization [between customer classes, and between utility-owned generators and others] that have generally cancelled out the favourable effects of restructuring. Both types of cross-subsidies result in substantial burden shifts to residential consumers' (p. 161). There is also evidence of the default service distorting the market: in Connecticut, Tsai and Tsai (2018, p. 275) found that from January 2015 to December 2016, 'competitive suppliers on average were aligning their rates with the changes in regulated Standard Service rates rather than the movement of wholesale electricity prices'. Similarly, Galetovic and Muñoz (2011, p. 6454) found that in Chile, 'the regulated price system has significant and costly deficiencies, which regulators have been either slow or incapable to correct'.

There are mixed results regarding market participation by low-income customers. Kleit, Shcherbakova and Chen (2012, p. 443) found that, in Pennsylvania, 'customers with higher usage levels (especially around the time of the program's introduction), electric heating, and those living in more urban and more educated communities with lower unemployment rates and higher median household incomes were both more likely to switch, and more likely to do so faster'. But this did not mean that competition disadvantages poor and elderly ratepayers. 'Customers living in communities with higher poverty rates were actually more likely to switch (and do so faster) than middle-income consumers. Communities with higher shares of senior population were not found to have lower switching rates from [sic] younger communities' (ibid.). Hortaçsu, Madanizadeh and Puller (2017) find that, in Texas, customer inertia is larger for neighbourhoods with lower income, although this difference declines over time, suggesting learning from experience. And customers are not irrational or characterized by weak response: Ros (2020, p. 1) finds that 'residential electricity customers in Illinois are acting in a manner consistent with standard consumer theory, with price elasticity of demand estimates that are generally in line with estimates in the economics literature . . . customers served by REPs [retail electricity providers] are sensitive to the default service price . . . a 1% decrease in the default service price will lead to approximately 0.5% REP customers switching to the default service'.

Hartley, Medlock and Jankovska (2019, p. 2) compare the experiences of competitive and non-competitive market areas within Texas (the latter areas are served by municipalities or cooperatives). They find that 'residential rates in competitive market areas reflect wholesale rates with a declining gap between them, which is consistent with competition driving cost reductions. By contrast, residential rates in non-competitive areas generally do not reflect wholesale rates, and the gap between them generally has not been shrinking'. Also, 'commercial electricity consumers in non-competitive areas face prices above costs and thus are called upon to cross subsidize residential customers' (ibid.). This is consistent with early UK experience, where at market opening in the 1990s the largest price reductions were for commercial and small industrial customers, suggesting that they had previously been cross-subsidizing the large industrial users and the residential customers, both of whom previously had more political influence. Moran (2006, p. 174, fn 3) reports the same in Australia, where commercial users 'were previously subject to Ramsey-type price gouging'.

4.4   Community Choice Aggregation in the US

One distinctive type of US retail market activity – namely, municipal aggregation (Littlechild 2008) – is beginning to re-emerge in a different form, as Community Choice Aggregation (CCA). In some US default tariff states, such as New York, Illinois, New Jersey and Ohio and particularly Massachusetts, there has been an increasingly strong push towards opt-out CCA in recent years, aimed particularly at increasing the use of green energy. This has also been especially the case in California, even though (or perhaps because) the competitive retail market remains suspended there.

CCA is similar to municipal aggregation insofar as the community organization chooses a retail supplier and a tariff for residents, perhaps giving them some choice among green options. The resident can opt out: to stay with the incumbent utility or, where allowed, to move to a competing retail supplier. However, a significant difference from municipal aggregation is that (in Ohio and Illinois) this policy required a prior affirmative vote by electors, while in California a city council or county board of supervisors can itself simply decide to create a CCA. By end-2019, 170 communities (cities, towns, counties) in California were providing CCA service to more than 10 million customers and had long-term power purchase agreements for over 3000 megawatts of new renewable energy (California Community Choice Association [CALCCA] 2019).

CCA means that 'local governments can control local electricity portfolios' (O'Shaughnessy et al. 2019, p. 1110). Incumbent California utilities are allowed to charge exit fees, the level of which seems to have fluctuated, but the full implications for the investor-owned utilities, and for the electricity system as a whole, and for customers, are unclear. In 2018, the California Commission raised concerns about the implications of splintering decision-making and started a process to plan for the future. 'In the last deregulation, we had a plan, however flawed. Now, we are deregulating electric markets through dozens of different decisions and legislative actions, but we do not have a plan. If we are not careful, we can drift into another crisis' (California Public Utilities Commission, 2018, p. iii).

In 2019, the major investor-owned utility PG&E filed for bankruptcy, and in February 2020 a bill was introduced in the California Senate whereby taxpayers would buy the company, give it a 'safety-first mission ahead of shareholder profits', and 'Local governments would have a chance to buy pieces of the network to start their own municipal power districts' (Fox Business, 2020). Interesting.

5.   THE LAST DECADE: DEVELOPMENTS IN NEW ZEALAND AND AUSTRALIA

5.1   New Zealand

Retail competition is under scrutiny not only in those US states that retained default supply tariffs, but also in many competitive retail markets that removed price controls. Perhaps not in the Nordic countries and Texas, but in New Zealand, Australia and the UK there have been questions of whether customers are adequately protected by competition or whether retail suppliers, particularly incumbents, are exploiting the most vulnerable of them. Until recently, regulators and governments have not intervened, but this policy has now changed. Consider these countries in turn.

In March 2018, the New Zealand Government commissioned an Electricity Price Review. As elsewhere, it was prompted by retail price increases: 'Residential electricity prices have risen by around 50 per cent since 2000 but the price for business remained flat. We want to find out why that is', said the Energy and Resources Minister (New Zealand Government 2018a). The Review would consider the entire supply chain including the regulatory framework, and had a wide compass: the terms of reference explained that 'The objective of the review is to ensure that the New Zealand electricity market delivers efficient, fair and equitable prices as technology evolves and we transition to a lower emissions future, taking into consideration the requirements of environmental sustainability and the need to maintain security and reliability of supply – the energy trilemma' (New Zealand Government, n.d.).

The *Electricity Price Review First Report* in August 2018 found that new entry was no longer a problem: 28 of the 36 retailers were new since 2005. But the 'Big Five' vertically integrated retailers still had 90 per cent of the residential market, and five new entrants had almost all the rest. (By international standards, customer numbers are small in absolute terms: in May 2019 the five largest suppliers had between 222 000 and 450 000 customers each, the five largest entrants had between 19 000 and 73 000 customers each.) The first report did not find excessive profits, but it noted the possible emergence of a 'two-tier market', as in Australia and the UK, contrasting 'well-off, internet savvy households that are able to seek out the best deals; and poorer, vulnerable households that lack the motivation or means to make informed choices' (New Zealand Government 2018b, p. 37).

The *Electricity Price Review Options Paper* favoured measures to make it easier for customers to shop around and also a collective switching approach trialled by Ofgem in the UK (see Section 6.5 below). It held that 'retail competition is working more effectively here than in Australia and Britain. We consider introducing retail price caps would do more harm than good, and there are better ways to tackle the problems of the two-tier retail market' (New Zealand Government 2019a, p. 17). Furthermore, it was not clear that lower-income customers were unduly disadvantaged: 'a 2017 survey for the Authority suggested that switching rates were similar across households with different incomes' and draft results from a recent Authority analysis 'suggest average switching rates among the most deprived consumers are similar to, or higher than, other consumers' (New Zealand Government 2018b, pp. 38–9).

Nonetheless, the *Electricity Price Review Final Report* in May 2019, published with the government's endorsement (New Zealand Government 2019b), made over 30 recommendations for policy. Eight recommendations addressed energy hardship. The short-term (three months) recommendations included to prohibit prompt payment discounts but to allow reasonable late payment fees, and to prohibit 'saves and win-backs' (see following paragraphs). The medium term (12 months) recommendations included to improve consumer awareness of industry-funded bodies Powerswitch (a price comparison website) and Utilities Disputes. The longer-term (18 months) recommendations included to establish a pilot scheme to help non-switching consumers find better deals, and to make generator-retailers release information about the profitability of their retailing activities.

An issue of particular concern was 'saves' and 'win-backs', which is intriguing because it has not been an issue in other competitive retail markets. The small (entrant) retailers had argued that it was difficult to expand because incumbent retailers offered discounts to existing customers to cancel a switch (known as a 'save') or to return a customer after the switch had happened (a 'win-back'). As from January 2015, a retailer could 'opt in' to 'save protection', whereby a losing retailer could not initiate contact to 'save' a customer departing to a 'protected' retailer. A 'protected' retailer was also prohibited from itself carrying out 'saves'. An initial review in 2017 found that the number of 'saves' fell and the number of 'win-backs' increased, and there was no evidence that the scheme improved or harmed retail competition. In a thoughtful evidence-based paper, the Electricity Authority's Market Development Advisory Group advised in March 2019 that 'saves' and 'win-backs' increased competitive pressure and there was 'no strong evidence of regulatory problems'.[8]

However, the *Electricity Price Review Final Report* took the view that extending the ban from 'saves' to 'win-backs' would 'help counter the development of a two-tier market', which was 'inherently unfair'. It placed 'significant weight' on submissions from consumers and new retailers (ibid., pp. 36–7) – evidently mainly new retailers since many of the consumer submissions failed to comment on, or expressed ignorance of, 'win-backs'. It noted that the Australian Competition and Consumer Commission (ACCC) in Australia had recommended price caps 'to limit the loyalty tax that is levied on disengaged customers' and declared 'We prefer to address the causes of this competition problem directly by banning win-backs, rather than interfere with retail prices' (ibid., p. 38). In February 2020, the Electricity Authority, citing a remarkably extensive and confident list of benefits –'The amendment is expected to increase retail competition, reduce retail margins, increase innovation, increase customer acquisition by retailers and price-search by consumers, reduce information asymmetries between losing and gaining retailers about the consumers they are seeking to serve' (Electricity Authority NZ 2020a, p. 4, para 3.11) – prohibited 'win-backs' for 180 days after a switch, with a review of the policy after three years. The world awaits confirmation of this prediction.

5.2   Australia

In the four Australian states, the transitional retail price caps were removed between 2009 and 2016. Retail prices rose, and Simshauser (Chapter 9 in this handbook) explains that retail markets were forced to deliver the bad news of rising wholesale and network costs. Nevertheless, the Commonwealth Government directed the ACCC to investigate the supply of retail electricity and the competitiveness of retail electricity prices. It found (ACCC 2018) that wholesale and retail markets were too concentrated; regulation and poorly designed policy had added significant costs to electricity bills; retailers' marketing of discounts was inconsistent and confusing to consumers and had left many consumers on excessively high 'standing' offers; and lower-income customers were disadvantaged. (But note rather slightly: 9 per cent of households with an income of under A\$25 000 were on (higher) standing tariffs, compared to an average of 7 per cent for all households; ACCC 2018, p. 245.)

The ACCC made 56 recommendations detailing ways to fix the National Electricity Market. The main proposals on the retail side were price caps and simpler tariffs – despite warnings from the ACCC's consultants on overseas experience, advising that 'We are not aware of any clear example where widely-available regulated prices coexist with successful retail competition . . . we have not found any examples of a regulated default tariff that successfully provides protections for a targeted group of customers without unintended adverse consequences' (Ros et al. 2018, p. x). Specifically, the ACCC proposals included abolishing the then-current retail 'standing' offers (which were not the same between retailers) and replacing them with a new Default Market Offer (DMO) consistent across all retailers and set at a price determined by the Australian Energy Regulator. Retailers would have to reference any discounts to the Default Market Offer, making it easier for consumers to compare offers. Any conditional discounts offered by retailers should be limited to a reasonable estimate of the retailer's expected savings should the customer meet the conditions specified in the discount. These recommendations were accepted by the Commonwealth Government and soon implemented.

An independent and apparently similar (but in fact more severe) approach was taken in the state of Victoria – traditionally the most pro-competitive of the Australian states (but no longer). There, the Independent Review of Electricity and Gas Retail Markets (Thwaites, Faulkner and Mulder, 2017) found that consumers were not gaining the benefits of a competitive retail market. Problems included price increases, customer acquisition costs, incumbent advantages and complex tariffs (although price discrimination was not mentioned). The proposed remedy was for all retailers to provide a basic default service offer not more expensive than a regulated price. Retailers could also offer other tariffs not subject to price regulation, although many new 'simple tariff' type restrictions were proposed (as introduced earlier in the UK, and later abandoned as counterproductive, as explained below). This was not envisaged as a temporary transition until the market was working more effectively, and there was no plan to remove this obligation at a later stage.

The Victorian Government asked the Essential Services Commission (the state energy regulator) to advise on calculating a Victorian Default Offer (VDO) for residential and small business electricity customers, to apply from 1 July 2019. This was to be a 'simple, trusted and reasonably priced electricity option that safeguards consumers unable or unwilling to engage in the retail electricity market without impeding the consumer benefits experienced by those who are active in the market' (Victorian Government, 2018, p. 1). The Commission's proposed methodology implied that 'Residential customers on standing offers and using 4,000 kWh may see their annual electricity bills reduce by between $390 and $520 Australian dollars, [about US$275–365], when compared with the median standing offer in their distribution zone' (Essential Services Commission, 2019, p. 7). In addition, there were some 'new entitlements for energy customers' (p. 9), including an obligation on retailers to advise customers of their best offer and the savings that customers might make if they switched plan.

On 1 July 2019, the Default Market Offer (DMO) came into effect in three competitive states (New South Wales, South Australia and South East Queensland) and the Victorian Default Offer (VDO) came into effect in Victoria. A significant difference was the level at which these default offers were set. The DMO was intended to limit the 'loyalty tax', whereby disengaged customers tended to pay higher prices, but explicitly not to undermine retail competition. The initial level for 2019–20 was set using a 'top-down approach': equal to the mid-point between the median standing offer and the median market offer by distribution zone. In contrast, the aim of the VDO was in effect to provide an alternative to retail competition, and the VDO was set much lower. It used a 'bottom-up approach': taking the estimated efficient level of each cost component plus a maximum profit margin, but not including customer acquisition and retention costs or 'headroom' to encourage competition.

After four months, both schemes had led to reductions in higher priced market offers, reductions in the number of available offers, significant reductions in price dispersion particularly for the largest (tier 1) retailers, and an across-the-board shift away from conditional discounting (where customers must take particular actions, such as paying on time, in order to receive discounts). 'Where the two schemes have differed, at least in their initial impacts, are: the magnitude of savings to standing offer customers has been significantly greater in Victoria, reflecting the lower default price setting, and the ACCC has observed that the reduction in the spread of prices in DMO jurisdictions (New South Wales, South-east Queensland and South Australia) has generally been driven by an increase in the cheapest market offers, while in Victoria this has been largely due to a decrease in the highest market offers' (Thomas, Funston and Lowe, 2019, p. 18).

Esplin et al. (2020) estimate that the squeezing of rate differentials reduced the saving over the median price by A$37 per year on average. This disadvantaged those customers (including vulnerable customers) on the lowest rates, and also reduced the incentive on customers to search for better rates. Mountain and Burns (2020) calculate that, in Victoria, the differential between the 10th and 90th percentile offer narrowed by about A$600 a year and the median increased by nearly A$200.

Is the Australian retail electricity market as problematic as some critics and the ACCC report suggest? Economists have explained why the emergence of price dispersion or discrimination there is an indication of competition, and welfare enhancing (Nelson et al. 2018, Simshauser 2018, Simshauser and Whish-Wilson 2017 and Chapter 9 herein). Nelson et al. (2018, p. 158) explain that 'Climate change policy and the emergence of new technologies such as household solar PV, battery storage and home energy management systems will create further price dispersion in Australian electricity markets due to even greater product heterogeneity. We contend that policy makers will need to facilitate, rather than prevent, both price and tariff structure dispersion with the objective of improving consumer outcomes'.

Simshauser (Chapter 9 in this handbook) concludes that the deregulated retail electricity market is 'on balance' performing well, although a couple of issues needed to be addressed: 'vulnerable rusted-on customers [those who have never switched] represent a misallocation problem (that is, low-income households are on a tariff designed for an inelastic segment), and discounts are no longer anchored to a common price'. Confusing discounts have perhaps been addressed by the DMO. Some retailers earlier sought to protect vulnerable customers: in 2017, major supplier AGL introduced an automatic 15 per cent discount for concession card (low-income) customers (Simshauser and Whish-Wilson 2017). UK suppliers too used to offer various voluntary price reductions to vulnerable customers until the government replaced them by its own compulsory Warm Home Discount scheme. Perhaps voluntary arrangements for vulnerable customers, with some regulatory facilitation, could once again replace the present Australian and UK price caps, and maybe address US concerns too.

Governments, regulators and customer groups in Australia and elsewhere have urged customers to switch retailers to get better deals in the 'two-tier market' and not 'leave money on the table'. Mountain and Rizio (2019) analyse the electricity bills that some 48 000 Victorian households uploaded to the state comparison site. They do not find that poorer and less educated customers are less engaged in the market. And they find that the typical non-switcher left $281 per year (about 20 per cent of their bill) on the table and that switchers left $187, a difference of only $45. So, there is no simple 'two-tier market' in which higher income switchers get all the benefits and lower income non-switchers get none. Rather, even those customers who do switch do not seem to be selecting the lowest price offers. The authors conjecture that this might reflect '[d]iscounts that are not as they seem and poor advice from price comparison service providers' (Mountain and Rizio, p. 1). Might it not also reflect a preference for familiar 'brands' and a reluctance to choose unknown suppliers (as in the UK too, see below)?

Extending this research, Mountain and Burns (2021) find the third tier of retailers (the smallest new entrants with market shares of less than 3 per cent) impose higher 'loyalty taxes' than the other two tiers (incumbents and mid-sized retailers). For many consumers, the mid-sized retailers may indeed reward loyalty. Again, this seems consistent with a recent finding in the UK (below).

6.   THE LAST DECADE: RETAIL COMPETITION POLICY IN THE EU AND UK

6.1   Developments in the EU

At EU level, and in the Council of European Energy Regulators (CEER), there continued to be support for retail competition and concern about national policies that restricted it. In 2012, the newly created EU Agency for the Cooperation of European Regulators (ACER) expressed concern about regulated prices that were too low to allow competition, also noting the importance of non-price competition and the expected roll out of smart meters. In 2013, it advised that non-quantifiable aspects of consumer behaviour (consumer loyalty, inertia and risk aversion) might act as a barrier to retail entry. Regulated prices remained an important feature of retail energy markets, with two-thirds (18 out of 27) member states still regulating prices to household consumers. In 2014, ACER found, with few exceptions, a vicious circle where competition was still weak with often little product and price differentiation, giving little incentive to consumers to participate actively in the market, which in turn was used as a justification for maintaining retail price regulation, which itself hampered competition. 'This vicious circle needs urgently to be broken by, on the one hand, facilitating consumer switching behaviour and awareness and improving the comparability and comparison of different suppliers' offers; on the other hand, by removing the barriers to entry into retail markets and phasing out price regulation as soon as possible' (ACER 2014, pp. 6–7). ACER also found that 'In a number of Member States, public authorities set energy retail prices with greater attention to political considerations than to underlying supply costs. In some Member States, regulated prices are set below cost levels, which hampers the development of a competitive retail market' (pp. 11–12).

IPA Advisory (2015), in a report to ACER, ranked 29 EU countries in terms of competitiveness of retail electricity markets, based on assessments of structure (e.g., market concentration), conduct (e.g., entry, switching) and performance (e.g., price dispersion, mark-up). Top countries were Finland at 8.3 out of 10, Norway at 7.1 and Netherlands at 7.0, above Italy, UK, Austria and Sweden. France at 3.4 was seventh from bottom, just below Hungary and Romania.

Looking at a few individual countries, Amelung (2019) and Mulder and Willems (2019) give largely favourable reports on experience in Germany and the Netherlands, respectively. Portugal is removing price controls and has high switching rates, but there too the market is still highly concentrated and Fotouhi Ghazvini et al. (2019) find that retail rates are not following changes in wholesale prices. France is perhaps an extreme case of a market that allowed the possibility of switching to a different supplier but retained traditional price regulation. The (85 per cent state-owned) French incumbent still has a 78 per cent retail market share.

In Italy, the nationalized incumbent Enel was privatized, although the state retains control and has the largest shareholding. Enel's market share in generation was successfully reduced below 20 per cent, but (contrary to the high rating just mentioned) Italy was much less effective in promoting retail competition, where Enel retains 70 per cent residential retail market share (Stagnaro 2017). Residential customers have been formally free to switch tariff or supplier since 2007, but customers who have not done so are supplied by an associated company of the local distribution utility and the price is set by the regulator based on the wholesale costs incurred by Acquirente Unico, a state-owned company in charge of buying for these customers. This mechanism has been conducive to a highly concentrated market. Enel's 70 per cent share comprises about 42 per cent supplied under the regulated tariff plus 28 per cent having chosen a tariff offered by Enel in the competitive market. Of the remaining 30 per cent of customers, about 7 per cent are on the regulated tariff and the remaining 23 per cent are in the competitive market. So, about half of all customers are on the regulated tariff and half in the competitive market. In 2017, Italy decided to phase out the single buyer system by 2019, but this deadline has since been postponed to 2022. Stagnaro et al. (2020) propose a new phase-out mechanism.

CEER continued to argue for improved regulation, particularly the phasing out of price controls. By 2017, it was able to report that, as a result of unbundling and other liberalization measures, many new companies entered the retail markets, there had been a very mild increase in average annual switching rate (from 5 per cent in 2011 to 6.4 per cent in 2016) and now just over one-third of EU countries still had price regulation. In 2019, it found encouraging signs of increased retail competition. EU Directive 944/2019 (para. 10) says that '[h]ealthy competition in retail markets is essential' and Article 5 therein envisages the possibility of legislation in 2025 to set an end date for any remaining price regulation.

6.2   Market Developments in the UK and Ofgem Regulation 2008–14

In real terms, UK household energy prices steadily declined from the early 1980s to the early 2000s, but from then to the late 2000s they doubled. (Deller and Waddams 2018 examine the impact on energy affordability and associated support schemes.) There was public and political pressure, and a new Secretary of State for Energy was not averse to intervention. Ofgem's Energy Supply Probe in 2008 briefly noted the causes of price increases ('unprecedented increases in world fuel prices') but focused instead on relative rather than absolute prices and on customer behaviour. Thus, there were 'unfair price differentials' because 'relatively few customers are proactively and confidently engaged', and less active customers were paying £1 billion per year more than they need have done. In particular, those five of the 'Big Six' retailers that were former incumbent electricity utilities were charging a higher price to 'sticky' customers in their former incumbent areas, while charging a lower price to attract out-of-area customers from other incumbent suppliers. They were also charging higher prices in areas where natural gas was not available as a rival fuel.

Ofgem's remedies put into effect during 2009–12 began with a non-discrimination condition, requiring that price differentials should not differ by more than cost differentials (the differential in cost, between supplying in and out of area, net of network charges, was regarded as small). The former incumbent retailers responded by increasing their lower out-of-area prices rather than reducing their in-area prices (Hviid and Waddams Price 2012, Waddams Price and Zhu 2016). Customer switching, which had increased from about 15 per cent per year in 2004 to 20 per cent in 2008, now fell back to about 17 per cent. Retail profits increased, though from a previously low level as retail prices had failed to keep up with wholesale cost increases during the mid-2000s. In 2010, Ofgem imposed restrictions on doorstep selling, which was attracting public criticism because of mis-selling. The decline in switching accelerated.

Ofgem's Retail Market Review in 2010 attributed the fall in switching to 'complex pricing structures' and an 'increase in the number of tariffs available' (not acknowledging that its own non-discrimination condition had likely reduced the willingness of customers to switch and encouraged suppliers to create different tariffs). To remedy this perceived problem Ofgem proposed Simple Tariffs rules to encourage switching. Suppliers were allowed a maximum of four tariffs per fuel. Most discounts were banned, including introductory discounts, cash-back schemes, loyalty discounts and prompt payment discounts. This meant that several much-valued and distinctive tariffs were discontinued. For example, supplier E.ON discontinued its StayWarm tariff that fixed the monthly bill to the over 60s, regardless of usage. Ofgem (2001, p. 2) had described this tariff as one of 'a number of major initiatives by energy companies to address the needs of the fuel poor'. Innovation was restricted – for example, wholesale tracker tariffs were banned. Ofgem's restrictions were gradually implemented during 2012 and 2013, by which time the annual switching rate had fallen to 10 per cent.

Behavioural explanations of customer behaviour, as opposed to conventional economic assumptions, began to be invoked. Defeuilley (2009, p. 377) argued that retail competition had failed to meet initial expectations because the Austrian concept of competition as an entrepreneurial process 'lacks behavioural and technical depth' because it neglected cognitive bias affecting consumers' decisions to switch and because opportunities for innovation were limited by technology. The cognitive bias explained why there were two distinct retail markets: an active one involving customers who benefit from vibrant competition and an inactive one involving loyal customers paying prices above cost. (See Littlechild 2009 for a rejoinder on initial expectations and on the characterization of the Austrian concept of competition.) Ofgem (2011) explained that its 2008 Probe and 2010 Review had been informed by behavioural economics. It identified four particular biases that hampered consumer engagement: limited consumer capacity, status quo bias, loss aversion and time inconsistency, and said that this categorization influenced its regulatory policy – for example, in trying to reduce the complexity of tariffs. There are numerous critical reviews of Ofgem's retail regulation during this period (Littlechild 2018b, 2019b, Pollitt and Haney 2014, Smith 2015, Waddams Price 2018). As explained below, the Competition and Markets Authority (CMA, 2016) also took a behavioural view, finding that reluctance to switch to lower-price suppliers constituted 'weak customer response', but the CMA also rejected Ofgem's remedies as having made things worse.

He and Reiner (2017, 2018) look at the effect of individual attitudes, commenting that household participation in energy markets is a complex social issue affected by multiple factors including cognitive, environmental and psychological constraints. They examine how external information (for example, retailer messaging) and internal information (for example, consumer knowledge) can affect consumer engagement in markets. Ofgem (2018b) has explored the thinking of six 'customer segments' with different attitudes and motivations.

Others sought to understand better the search and switching costs. Wilson and Waddams Price (2010, p. 647) showed that 'the ability of consumers to choose the best alternative supplier is limited . . . those consumers switching exclusively for price reasons appropriate less than a half the gains available . . . at least 17% of consumers actually reduced their surplus as a result of switching'. Giulietti, Waterson and Wildenbeest (2014, p. 555) developed a sequential search model, which indicated that 'consumer search costs must be relatively high in order to rationalize observed pricing patterns'. Flores and Waddams Price (2018) examined characteristics (that is, consumer attitudes) associated with engagement and disengagement in the UK residential electricity market. They found that recollection of direct marketing had little effect on searching and switching, recall of advertising had a negative effect on switching, and advice from family and friends was associated with greater searching but not switching. While low-income customers were thought to be less active market participants, Deller et al. (2021) found that, although switchers live in a somewhat higher median income area, this does not appear to influence the decision to switch once a wide range of other variables are controlled for. (Note, however, that the sample itself was self-selecting, had higher than average income and was already a very active subset of consumers.) Interestingly, Hyland, Leahy and Tol (2013) found that in Ireland, gross retail margin was highest for the richest households (not for the poor or vulnerable). There are also studies of differential customer response in other European retail electricity markets.[9]

6.3 The CMA Investigation 2014–16 and Customer Engagement Remedies

Several developments in the early to mid-2010s alleviated the concerns discussed in Section 2.4 above that had limited new entry before that. In particular:

- Independent facilitators developed 'supplier in a box' products so that potential entrants could purchase a retail supply company that had already passed the Ofgem entrance requirements, they also offered IT systems on a pay-as-you-go basis that minimized the up-front cost, and they provided technical support and facility for contracting out various activities.
- Major players stepped in to offer collateral-free trading, and management of small suppliers' trading positions.
- Government and/or Ofgem exempted new entrants from significant social and environmental costs, amounting on one view to over £100 on an average dual-fuel bill of about £1000.
- A period of falling wholesale prices (2013–15) allowed entrants to offer fixed-price products (then relatively new) at below the incumbents' hedged standard variable tariffs.
- Many price comparison websites emerged to inform, assist and encourage potential switchers (following OFFER's policy not to provide or sponsor a website itself).

These developments led to a rapid increase in new entry: over 20 new suppliers between 2009 and 2014, then 17 new suppliers in 2015 alone. Entrants increased their aggregate market share from under 1 per cent of the residential market in 2009 to 7 per cent in mid-2014 to over 12 per cent by end 2015.

Nonetheless, retail pricing and Ofgem's regulatory policy were still controversial. In 2014, Ofgem (with a new chairperson looking to re-evaluate this policy) referred the energy sector for investigation by the Competition and Markets Authority (CMA). Although Ofgem had been concerned about vertical integration, the CMA's Final Report (CMA 2016) found no significant problems with this or with the wholesale market.

The CMA shared Ofgem's concern that residential customers were not responding to large price differentials, and noted that a higher proportion of these non-engaged customers were low income, less educated, renting rather than home owning, and older. The CMA called this 'weak customer response' and held that it gave incumbent suppliers market power, which they exploited via higher prices and price discrimination. The CMA estimated that the resulting customer detriment averaged £1.4 billion per year over the period studied, increasing to £2 billion in 2015.

However, the CMA also shared economists' concerns about Ofgem's non-discrimination policy and found, rather damningly, that Ofgem's Simple Tariffs policy had no tangible benefit but actually had an adverse effect on competition and should be abandoned. The CMA instead proposed two main remedies to promote greater customer engagement. First, Ofgem should carry out a programme of testing, including through randomized controlled trials, and should implement measures to provide customers with additional information. Second, it should create a disengaged customer database, to give customer details to other potential suppliers. Because of certain technical limitations with respect to available prepayment meters, and because prepayment meter customers (about 16 per cent of all residential customers) were on average more vulnerable, the CMA also recommended a temporary price cap on prepayment meter tariffs.

The CMA was quite explicit that more extensive price caps on tariffs would generally undermine competition such that customers would be worse off in the longer term. However, a dissenting view by one CMA panel member argued that the customer detriment was very severe (the £2 billion annual detriment amounted to about £100 per household) and the proposed remedies were untested and would take time to implement. He recommended extending the new prepayment price cap to all default tariffs and standard variable tariffs, which served about 70 per cent of all customers. As explained below, this view proved more appealing to politicians than did the CMA's view.

6.4   Critique of the CMA Analysis

The tariff caps introduced in the UK took the interventions in competitive retail markets to a new level. The CMA investigation that led to them is surely the most thorough and extensive official analysis of such markets, especially in terms of gathering evidence, and its non-retail analyses and recommendations have been well regarded. Given the public concern about high and differential retail prices, it is understandable that the CMA was sensitive to this issue. Unfortunately (in the author's view), its retail market analysis had significant flaws (Littlechild 2020).

The CMA's central thesis was that the retail market was characterized by 'weak customer response', which the large suppliers exploited via price discrimination and/or prices in excess of efficient cost, and that this detriment was very severe. Consider each of these elements in turn.

As regards 'weak customer response', there was no evidence that customers were less engaged in the energy sector than in other sectors: to the contrary, switching was higher for energy than for most consumer products (as in Australia, per Simshauser in Chapter 9 of this handbook, Table 9.5). Nor were customers less engaged in the UK than elsewhere: switching was higher in the UK than in most countries. Moreover, the 'savings left on the table' by disengaged customers depended greatly on what range of options were assumed available and acceptable to customers. For example, if customers were able and willing to change supplier, tariff type and payment method, the average annual available saving was £164. But for those customers that did not have bank accounts and could not use the direct debit payment method, the average available saving was only £65 (CMA 2016, para. 8.249).

The explicit or implicit assumption was that customers that have not switched supplier or are not 'engaged' in the market are dissatisfied and/or not well served, while in reality many customers may not search around for another supplier because they are satisfied with their present one. Normally, customer loyalty is regarded as desirable rather than as an indication that the market is not working, and a market where customers had to change supplier every few years would be regarded as unsatisfactory.

Price differentials and price discrimination are not per se evidence that competition is not working. There are many possible reasons for different prices. For example, small suppliers were exempt from certain costs. Many new suppliers were deliberately pricing low and loss-leading to attract customers and grow. Other suppliers simply miscalculated: in 2018 and 2019, some 20 small suppliers went out of business. Several low-price suppliers were run by municipal governments as a social service, did not plan to make a profit and had considerable borrowings from these governments – in the event they made serious losses and have since withdrawn from the market. Price differentials are also to be expected where customers have different tastes or values of time spent engaging in the market. Price discrimination to cover overhead costs is normal in competitive markets, may serve to extend the market to customers that could otherwise not afford to consume as much, or at all, may intensify competition, and may indeed be necessary for firms to survive (for instance, Baumol 2006, Borenstein 1985, Borts 1998, Brennan 1991, 2007, Cooper et al. 2005, Klemperer 1987a, 1987b, 1995, Levine 2002 and for recent discussion in the electricity context Simshauser 2018, Waddams Price, 2018 and Chapter 9 in this handbook).

The CMA calculated an average annual customer detriment of £1.4 billion (£2 billion in 2015). It acknowledged that this detriment mostly comprised a hypothetical inefficiency rather than actual excess profit. The CMA compared the actual standard variable tariff prices of the large suppliers against what the CMA assumed would be an efficient price, calculated by taking the costs and prices of the two most efficient mid-tier suppliers and conjecturing what prices these suppliers would have charged if they had not been exempt from social and environmental policy costs, if they had similar customer profiles, if they had made reasonable returns on capital, if they had not been growing but had been in a steady state, and so on. This approach was at variance with previous practice by UK competition authorities and inconsistent with the CMA's own guidelines that explicitly disavowed the use of a perfect competition benchmark. It is also implausible that the whole sector would have transformed to display the hypothesized efficiency had customers simply been 'more engaged'.

Finally, using the more conventional benchmark of excess profit, the CMA calculated that the detriment averaged £303 million per year, far lower than its much-cited detriment figures of £1.4 or £2 billion per year. Even this is arguably high: if the return in the large industrial market – a market agreed to be so competitive as not to require investigation – is taken as the benchmark, and if an adjustment is made to reflect the CMA's view that there is higher risk in the residential market because residential tariffs involve less direct pass-through of changing wholesale costs, then the excess profit reduces to only £170 million (Littlechild 2020). So, arguably, any excess profit was rather low: £170 million corresponds to under £6 per customer per year.

For these various reasons, the CMA's analysis and calculations are unpersuasive. Unfortunately, its unprecedented and unjustifiably high headline figures for estimated customer detriment gave one CMA panel member, politicians and the media tangible reason to argue that there was a need for an equally unprecedented and unjustifiable remedial action.

6.5   Implementation of CMA Customer Engagement Remedies

To implement the CMA recommendations, Ofgem promptly withdrew its Simple Tariffs restrictions. It planned that the disengaged customer database would go live in April 2018, although there were concerns about data privacy, including on the part of the Information Commissioner's Office. Later, Ofgem (2019a) decided not to pursue the disengaged customer database because of data privacy issues and opined that 'there may be more effective ways of enabling the necessary data to be shared'.

Ofgem focused instead on other customer engagement initiatives. In the light of background research (for example, Deller et al. 2017, ESP Consulting and vaasaETT 2018), Ofgem carried out several randomized control trials, notably three collective switch trials.[10] In the first trial, some 22.4 per cent of trial participants opted to change their dual-fuel energy tariff; this was a switching rate over eight times higher than in a trial control group (2.6 per cent). The savings were significant: around £300 on a dual fuel bill of about £1000.[11] There were interesting findings with respect to age, communication methods and size/familiarity of alternative supplier. For example, over a quarter of the participants using Energy Helpline were aged over 75, and around 70 per cent of them used the phone rather than online 'as it made customers feel secure and reassured . . . and it felt like less effort' (Ofgem 2019a, p. 49). A later trial, where the exclusive tariff was provided by a small or medium supplier rather than a large one, had a lower take-up (26 per cent compared to the 44 per cent, 70 per cent and 66 per cent observed in those three collective switch trials), although the average saving was relatively low at about £200 compared to £250, £150 and £300, respectively (Ofgem 2019, Fig. 9 on p. 48 and Fig. 11 on p. 51). Ofgem (ibid., p. 48) commented that 'We know from wider survey evidence that disengaged customers can feel uncertain of less well-known brands'. The significance of this plausible explanatory factor was not appreciated in the allegations of 'weak customer response'.

Ofgem (2019a, p. 55) concluded that these trials 'proved beyond doubt that simple prompts and a behaviourally informed intervention can increase consumer engagement'. Note, however, that there was considerable customer contact before there was an opportunity to opt out, and that the customer was provided with a personalized indicative estimate of saving that could not easily have been provided at scale or outside a regulatory context: 'The following processes occurred without any involvement from customers: data was securely transferred from customers' suppliers to the service provider and data cleaned. Projected savings calculations are made "behind the scenes" and included on the letters. Energy Helpline conducted an auction where suppliers bid to provide the exclusive tariff listed on the collective switch letter. This tariff was not available on the open market' (Ofgem 2019a, slidepack slide 5).

Moreover, in one case, nearly one-fifth of the customers approached were transferred from one supplier to its competitors, which the supplier estimated cost it £30 million in lost revenues. Regulatory intervention and redistribution of income on this scale needs careful consideration. There was in fact a legal challenge to one of the trials. But perhaps such intervention is no longer an issue. Ofgem (2020, p. 1) referred back to its work on understanding the barriers to consumer engagement and stated: 'With the increasing importance and emphasis on decarbonization, our focus has now shifted to understanding the role consumers can play as we transition to a net zero energy system'. However, a subsequent statement from BEIS (August 2021) suggests that opt-in and opt-out switching are still very much under consideration.

6.6   Tariff Caps Since 2017

The CMA's price cap for customers with prepayment meters (PPMs) came into force in April 2017 and covered approximately 4 million households. Ofgem extended this cap, with effect from February 2018, to include almost a million additional vulnerable consumers. The initial impact on competition for prepayment customers was considerable and adverse. Ofgem (2017, p. 32) indicated the consequent severe clustering of prices: before the cap, eight electricity PPM tariffs ranged about equally from £500 to £570 per year; after the cap three-quarters of them were at the £550 cap level. (For gas PPM tariffs, the range from highest to lowest reduced from nearly £140 to £10.) Although some subsequent prices were apparently significantly below the price cap, many of these were problematic. Thus, Littlechild (2018d) found that, with one exception, prepayment tariffs offered by all large and medium suppliers, and some small suppliers, clustered at the level of the cap. Other small suppliers offered savings in the range £50 to £80, but a good proportion of this saving reflected the value of their exemption from social and environmental policy costs. Some 21 tariffs offered on price comparison sites appeared to offer savings in the range £80 to £165, but on closer inspection only one tariff offering a saving of £112 was actually widely available and the status of a second, possibly saving £92, was unclear. Both these last two suppliers had poor reputations for customer service. Within a couple of months both suppliers had failed financially and left the market.

One supplier reported that switching had fallen by a third. The CMA later accepted that the initial prepayment cap was unduly severe with respect to government policy costs and smart metering costs, so the extent of the 'problem' and the customer benefits of the price cap were less than first appeared. From October 2019 the CMA adjusted the methodology to bring it in line with the subsequent default tariff price cap. But PPM competition had already been damaged (for example, with respect to customer service).

During the 2017 UK General Election there was much reference to 'rip-off energy tariffs', 'the broken energy market' and the CMA's calculated £1.4 billion or £2 billion detriment. All political parties proposed more intervention. Some politicians and suppliers argued for a relative price cap instead of an absolute cap, but Waddams Price (2018, p. 153) counter-argued that 'while relative price caps may seem intuitively attractive, they are likely to damage competition more than absolute price caps through tying the competitive and "unresponsive" sides of the market. They would eliminate some of the best deals in the market and provide no guarantee of lowering prices paid by loyal consumers'.

The Domestic Gas and Electricity (Tariff Cap) Act of July 2018,[12] which required Ofgem to set a cap on default tariffs and standard variable tariffs, had all-party support. The level of the cap should have regard to '(a) the need to create incentives for holders of supply licences to improve their efficiency; (b) the need to set the cap at a level that enables holders of supply licences to compete effectively for domestic supply contracts; (c) the need to maintain incentives for domestic customers to switch to different domestic supply contracts; (d) the need to ensure that holders of supply licences who operate efficiently are able to finance activities authorised by the licence'. Ofgem is required to review the level of the cap at least once every six months. Each year it must 'carry out a review into whether conditions are in place for effective competition for domestic supply contracts' and recommend whether the tariff cap should be extended for another year. The tariff cap would cease in 2020 unless the Secretary of State decided, in light of Ofgem's report, that it should be extended for another year, in which case the process would be repeated, until 2023 at the latest. Even then, regulatory intervention might not cease, insofar as, before and after the Act ceases to have effect, Ofgem must review suppliers' pricing practices and consider whether some customers need protection against excessive charges or excessive tariff differentials if they move from fixed rates to variable tariffs or default rates. Ofgem must also review whether vulnerable customers need protection; if so, it must take appropriate action.

Ofgem introduced the default tariff cap on 1 January 2019, at £1137 for an average dual-fuel customer, commenting that the cap would save 11 million people an average of £76 per year (and as much as £120 on the most expensive tariffs). But Ofgem soon announced a cap increase of £117 after three months, to reflect higher wholesale and other costs. Later, British Gas won a judicial review case against Ofgem, to the effect that that the original cap had understated wholesale costs (by implication, to deliver a politically promised level of price reduction).

The cap methodology means that the level of the cap of default tariffs lags the level of wholesale prices. Since wholesale prices have generally been declining since April 2019, this has enabled competitors to offer fixed prices undercutting the (hedged) default tariffs, so the adverse impact on the range of tariff prices and on customer switching has so far been less than expected. But this will reverse as and when wholesale prices start increasing. (Unfortunately, by the same token, evidence of the adverse effects of the cap on competition will be most apparent when removing the cap would likely lead to increases in the default tariffs.)

Supplier profits have been heavily affected by the cap: as of February 2021, all suppliers subject to the cap were reporting negative net profit margins. Financial results partly reflect, too, increasingly costly regulatory obligations (smart meter rollout, faster switching, the move to half-hourly settlement), the reduced scope of exemptions from social and environmental obligations, the strength of competition and the willingness of many smaller and medium suppliers to operate at a loss to buy or retain market share. Also, the cap was imposed during a period when competition was growing more strongly than was apparent at the time of the CMA report. For example, after the report, the number of retail suppliers increased from about 30 to over 70 when the Tariff Cap Act passed: the number is now down to under 50. About 20 suppliers that were unable to survive in the market exited or were taken over, and in 2019–20 Ofgem tightened the financial conditions both on new entrants and on existing retailers (with, e.g., emphasis on ongoing risk management, and 'milestone assessments' at 50 000 and 200 000 customers). The switching rate rose to over 20 per cent per year. The proportion of residential electricity customers with non-incumbent medium and small suppliers more than doubled from 12 per cent to 30 per cent. So, there are many factors involved.

In considering 'whether conditions are in place for effective competition', Ofgem (2019b) said it would consider structural changes (especially smart meter rollout and faster switching), competitive process (no barriers to market participation and 'consumers must be able to choose confidently and well'; Ofgem 2019b, p. 16), and 'fair outcomes' (ibid.). Ofgem (2020) argued, rather unconvincingly, that conditions were not in place for effective competition because progress was slower than expected on the smart meter rollout and faster switching programmes, Ofgem was still concerned about the number of disengaged customers, and it was not clear that customers on default tariffs would continue to pay a fair price if the cap were lifted. It recommended that the tariff cap not be removed. In October, the government decided to extend it until the end of 2021 (at the earliest).

Throughout this disruption, the competitive market is continuing to innovate. For example, Octopus Energy has developed a better and lower-cost cloud-based digital energy service platform (Kraken) that is now being leased to other suppliers, including in Australia and the US, with a target of 100 million customers worldwide. The market is responding to and stimulating evolving customer preferences, not least with respect to renewable energy. The proportion of UK customers with 100 per cent renewable suppliers increased from 0 per cent in 2002 to 5 per cent in 2018, then shot up to 37 per cent at the beginning of 2020 (Cornwall Insight 2020, Figure 1, p. 2). Eight suppliers presently offer special tariffs for EV drivers. In addition to its fixed and variable tariffs, Octopus Energy offers Tracker (daily prices), Agile (half-hourly), Go (four hours cheap at night) and Outgoing (paying for energy supplied to the grid). Oil major Shell has purchased the medium retail supplier First Utility, invested in projects to develop electric vehicle charging stations and signed contracts for solar power in the UK and elsewhere. Britton et al. (2019, Table 6) show 58 'traditional' energy-only UK suppliers and 34 suppliers offering between one and nine of 15 different non-traditional value propositions relating to local energy, electric vehicles, prosumers (including storage and smart home), time of use, bundled with other products, additional services, and segmentation (specific consumer groups including prepayment). See also Hall and Roelich (2016) and Poudineh (2019, Section 2) on new business models, and Deloitte (2019), which concludes: 'A rapidly evolving retail power market is forcing companies to either disrupt or be disrupted'.

But will the future regulatory framework be appropriate? Ofgem (2018a) noted the 'need to make sure that any future retail market design can unlock the full potential for innovation and competition, over the longer term' (p. 4), and concluded that 'fundamental reforms to the supplier hub model need to be explored' (p. 5). Poudineh (2019, p. ii) argues that 'retail market design and regulations need to be rethought to enable innovation and deliver the decarbonized, resilient, and affordable electricity that all consumers need'. Harris (2019) is concerned about the 'death spiral', where suppliers lose customers and must increase prices to remaining customers to cover overhead costs. He argues that tariff dispersion (the alleged two-tier market) is normal and a way of coping with the actual cost structures. So that 'continuation of the series of substantial [regulatory and government] interventions will achieve no more than it has for the last 20 years . . . The realpolitik of interventions means that they will continue, but we must, whilst this happens, turn our attention together to the bigger picture of the zero net carbon society, and how to emerge together from the death spiral we are heading into' (p. 11).

7.   CONCLUDING REMARKS

7.1   What is the Verdict?

Nearly 40 years after it was proposed, 30 years after it was first implemented, and over 20 years since it was available to residential customers, what is the verdict on retail competition in the electricity sector? Are large industrial customers supportive? Unequivocally yes, because they can get consistently better deals by negotiating with competing retail suppliers and/or by using the suppliers' facilities to hedge in the wholesale market, than from time spent lobbying governments.

Are residential customers interested? Some are, some are not. The difference has been striking and has led to a significant learning process for economists and regulators as well as retailers and customers. This process has been immense and is ongoing. Evidently, there are personality differences between customers, but there are also more familiar economic explanations of price differentials, including product differentials, differential costs of search and switching, and higher risks associated with new suppliers. And there is learning over time: today's customers and retailers are more experienced and active than those of ten and 20 years ago.

Is wholesale spot price pass-through or something similar a convenient way to give customers access to the wholesale market? It has not proved popular to date, and the Texas legislature was divided on whether to make hedging mandatory for such products or simply to prohibit direct wholesale pass-through.

Should the incumbent utility be required to offer regulatory-specified default supply tariffs that hedge the wholesale price? Unfortunately, by thus intervening in the market, US regulators seem to have under-priced and cross-subsidized the default supply tariffs, thereby distorting the market against competing suppliers. They have also opened themselves up to continuing political pressures and consumer group complaints, leading in turn to further regulatory intervention.

Are markets with no default supply tariffs the answer? In the Nordic countries, UK, Texas, Australia and New Zealand, such markets have worked well. But regulators and governments misinterpreted increases in retail prices reflecting increases in wholesale prices as the exercise of market power by incumbent retailers. Embarrassingly, the worst analyses by regulatory and competition authorities were in the UK, where it all began, and in Victoria, the then-leading competitive state in Australia. As a result, retail competition is now impaired by politically inspired price caps in both jurisdictions.

To date, the price caps have been convenient for politicians and regulators, an easy way of claiming that customers are protected. Will such price caps ever be removed? In the UK, the 'conditions for effective competition' are dangled in front of retailers like carrots in front of a donkey's nose, intended to incentivize behaviour in line with regulatory preferences, but destined never to be quite met. Alternative arrangements need consideration, perhaps with voluntary arrangements to reassure consumer groups about vulnerable customers. If a competitive market without a price cap really is inconceivable to politicians, perhaps a practicable solution is a price cap limited to vulnerable customers but set at a realistic competitive level (such as the upper-quartile price used by the ACCC) rather than an unrealistic level (everyone equal to the most efficient cost or excluding certain costs) as used by the CMA and in Victoria.

7.2   Comparing Alternative Markets

Surprisingly (to the author), despite the many studies of competitive retail electricity markets, there does not seem to have been a systematic empirical comparison of such markets with and without default tariffs or tariff caps. Of course, this is not easy given the many differences between electricity systems and their customers, and perhaps default tariffs and tariff caps are more likely to have been adopted in markets that were more problematic anyway. But we do need to know more about the impact of such interventions on costs and prices, efficiency, innovation, choice and customer satisfaction. Recent policy introducing tariff caps in the UK and default tariffs in Australia should not be interpreted as an acknowledgement that markets without such intervention do not work.

Whatever the other characteristics of the various markets, the extent of customer engagement is evidently inversely related to the extent of regulatory intervention. Thus, in retail markets without (until recently) default tariffs or price caps, the proportion of residential customers that have moved to other retail suppliers rather than stayed with their incumbent utility is now around or over 70 per cent, while for the US default tariff markets and other restricted or price-capped markets that proportion is around 20 per cent. Similarly, for the 'unconstrained' competitive markets, the median percentage of customers that switch retail supplier in any year is around 16 per cent, while for 12 European countries with price caps it is 3 per cent (CEER 2019, Figure 16). It is not believed to be higher than 3 per cent for the default tariff US markets where this statistic is apparently not considered relevant enough to calculate.

More customer engagement does not necessarily make the former markets 'better' – indeed, one of the original purposes of a default tariff was to save customers the need to shop around. It means, however, that a significantly greater proportion of pricing, product and output decisions are made or influenced by hundreds of retailers and millions of customers themselves, as opposed to being made by a regulator specifying what products should be offered and how a utility should pass on costs incurred. This is surely of relevance to the evolving electricity markets of the future, as now indicated.

7.3   What of the Future?

In Chapter 2 of this handbook, Schmalensee concludes by asking what kinds of systems will be most appropriate in the future. Sioshansi (Chapter 13 in this handbook) explains that all consumers, including residential ones, increasingly have choices that did not previously exist, such as the ability to become 'prosumers' or 'prosumagers' that 'consume, produce and store energy depending on the circumstances'. They will be able to trade, share, join 'energy communities', or allow a smart aggregator to turn them into a virtual power plant (VPP) through smart aggregation. Elsewhere, Faruqui, Hledik and Lam (2020) seek 'to identify rate design options that could better accommodate customer adoption of emerging energy technologies such as smart thermostats, digitally-communicative appliances, rooftop solar panels, battery storage, other forms of on-site generation, and battery-powered electric vehicles' (p. ii). Much of the digital infrastructure and other investment will fall to retail suppliers and customers rather than to established transmission and distribution networks. Glachant (Chapter 17 in this handbook) describes new business models in the electricity sector, which have many variants, including aggregators as new intermediaries, digital platforms bypassing intermediaries, peer-to-peer direct exchange as blockchains, fleets of consumption, generation and storage devices managed 'behind the meter', as mini-grids or off-grid.

All this will revolutionize retail markets. Indeed, it raises the question: what are retailers and retail markets? This in turn suggests the need for a broader approach. Insofar as the new world depends not only on innovation but also on customers taking various more active roles, experience to date poses the question whether customers will be interested in participating. It also suggests a way ahead. Would customer participation not be easier to achieve in a market where more consumers have been used to being actively engaged in the retail market, exploring which products and suppliers suit them best? And where retail suppliers are accustomed to the process of discovering which products, services and marketing approaches appeal to consumers and which do not?

Hayek (1979, p. 68) argued that '[c]ompetition must be seen as a process in which people acquire and communicate knowledge'. Will not more knowledge be acquired and communicated if hundreds or thousands of retailers and millions of customers are actively involved in the discovery process, rather than if a few retailers are taking orders from a handful of regulators?

It might be argued that it would be easier and quicker for regulators to require incumbent utilities to undertake various kinds of specified activities necessary to achieve the desired policy goals, and then to specify products and default tariffs accordingly, than to rely on innovations by retailers and responses by customers in a market with unrestricted retail competition. But that seems to assume a set of active, efficient, imaginative and enlightened regulatory authorities. That is not easy to reconcile with the pre-reform experience that led to calls for deregulation in the US and privatization elsewhere, or with some of the retail market regulation mentioned in this chapter, or with the recent stance of the California Commission as vividly portrayed by its former Chairman Peevey: 'Institutionally at the Commission, there was a tendency to proceed slowly and on top of that there was a fear that going too far, too fast with rate reform would create a consumer backlash . . . Institutions largely move slowly, particularly when facing controversial or likely controversial issues' (Faruqui and Peevey 2020, pp. 59, 60). Faruqui (2020) gives two dozen more examples of regulatory inertia and calls for 'new ways to engage with customers' (p. 26).

There are, of course, yet more issues to consider. For example, how to reconcile the tension between customer choice and a pre-defined policy endpoint of decarbonization? But there is a more fundamental question: can the answer be to remove retail choice rather than to build upon it? Perhaps another meeting in Boston in about 2023, some 40 years after the first conversation about introducing retail competition in electricity, will answer all these questions. But don't count on it.

7.4   Evolution of the Species

Can a biological analogy shed light on the outstanding questions? The electricity industry as a species (*Res electrica*) has gradually evolved over more than a century, but in the 1980s, following a series of mutations, there emerged a new variant, the retail electricity market (*Mercatus electricus venditionis*, or *Mercatus* for short). Two main species have survived. One (*Mercatus liber*), generally held to be the fittest, spread internationally, principally from the UK to the Nordic countries, Australia, New Zealand, Texas, Alberta and parts of Western Europe. A slightly more cumbersome species (*Mercatus timidus*) established itself in north-eastern and central parts of the US (with somewhat similar versions in France and Italy). One initially prominent species (*Mercatus californiensis*) did not survive. In large areas of the US, Africa and Asia, conditions were evidently not favourable for this type of *Mercatus* to emerge at all.

A strong symbiotic relationship soon developed with the larger of the customer species (*Emptor industrialis*) and with some of the smaller customer species (*Emptor domesticus*). However, unexpectedly, it seemed that the latter comprised various different sub-species, one of which (*Emptor domesticus industrius*) was manifestly thriving with the *Mercatus*, while others (*Emptor domesticus negligens* and *Emptor domesticus indefensus*) appeared not to do so. Indeed, there were reports of rogue *Mercatus* variants such as the two-tier market (*Mercatus duo verso*) preying on the latter emptor sub-species.

In Texas and the Nordic countries, the *Mercatus liber* still thrives. But in many other areas, tensions between the *Mercatus* and representatives of the *Emptor domesticus* agitated a hitherto supportive regulatory species (*Tribuni praescriptorum*), which began to skirmish with the *Mercatus* species. In the UK and Australia, the even more powerful governmental species (*Imperium*) has also been attacking and restricting the *Mercatus*. In the short term, this may have protected the *Emptor domesticus negligens* but harmed the *Emptor domesticus industrius*.

Observing all this was the economist species (*Discipulus oeconomica doctrinae*). The different perceptions and recommendations of the various economist sub-species (such as *Discipulus fervidus* and *Discipulus haesitans*) make it difficult to predict the future of the *Mercatus* species. It seems unlikely that the *Imperium* will have the incentive or even ability to drive the *Mercatus liber* to extinction, given its increasing acceptance by the *Emptor domesticus* and the propensity of the *Mercatus* to mutate. Indeed, as environmental conditions themselves change, might the *Mercatus* begin to interbreed with the *Emptor domesticus*, facilitating the mutual survival of all the species involved?

NOTES

*   The author is grateful for comments and suggestions from Ross Baldick, Tim Brennan, David Deller, Ryan Esplin, Ahmad Faruqui, Richard Green, Alex Henney, Eileen Marshall, Alan Moran, Bruce Mountain, Tim Nelson, David Newbery, Robert Ritz, Agustin Ros, Paul Simshauser, Fereidoon Sioshansi, Carlo Stagnaro, Tim Tutton, Catherine Waddams, editor Jean-Michel Glachant and assistant editor Nicolò Rossetto, and numerous colleagues from the industry. He hopes to have appeased at least some of them.
1.   In this chapter, the familiar term UK is used, although, strictly speaking, the issues, policies and evidence discussed are those of Great Britain (that is, England, Wales and Scotland) and not Northern Ireland, which followed a later and different reform path.
2.   In this chapter, the term 'tariff' is not limited (as in some US jurisdictions) to the regulated prices of the utilities, but includes the unregulated prices and other terms offered by retailers in the competitive market.
3.   Some US utilities, and large industrial and municipal customers, had bought power from a second utility and paid that second utility to transmit or 'wheel' the power to the first. Although the Public Utility Regulatory Policies Act (PURPA) in 1988 gave the Federal Energy Regulatory Commission (FERC) some power to order wheeling, this was in very limited circumstances. In practice, wheeling was somewhat ad hoc rather than systematic and widespread, often resisted, and had not been considered for application on a large scale or for the purpose now envisaged in the UK.
4.   The author was an adviser on electricity privatization to the UK Secretary of State for Energy 1987–89, then first Director General of Electricity Supply, Head of the Office of Electricity Regulation (OFFER) 1989–98.
5.   In addition to Texas, the other 12 states that have introduced and maintained retail competition for residential customers are Connecticut, Delaware, Illinois, Maine, Maryland, Massachusetts, New Hampshire, New Jersey, New York, Ohio, Pennsylvania and Rhode Island, plus the jurisdiction of Washington DC. Some states introduced limited retail competition – for example, Georgia, Montana, Nevada, Virginia and Oregon for industrial customers, and Michigan for a limited proportion of customers. Florida, Arizona and Nevada recently considered introducing or extending retail competition.
6.   Does the Texas blackout of February 2021 provide reason to qualify this judgement? The analyses of economists (e.g., Cramton 2021) and former Texas regulators (Wood et al. 2021) suggest that the main issues are not in the retail market. Littlechild and Kiesling (2021) have expressed concern about the regulatory implementation of the scarcity pricing mechanism during the blackout. Unfortunately, the resulting

    continued high prices led to the Texas legislature prohibiting retail electricity providers from offering a wholesale indexed product to residential customers (as Griddy had done), rather than allowing such a product with an appropriate hedging provision.

7.   These are to: (1) limit the ability of energy supply companies to sell to low-income customers; (2) prohibit contracts that lock customers into variable rates; (3) prohibit automatic re-enrolment; (4) limit cancellation fees; (5) provide better information on the utility bill, including details of the default tariff; (6) prohibit deceptive and aggressive marketing; (7) give consumers an easy and binding way to opt out of marketing; (8) report actual prices paid (as opposed to initial offers and as compared to the default tariff); (9) make data about consumer problems and complaints involving competitive energy supply companies easily accessible to the public; and (10) step up enforcement.

8.   'We find, nationally, almost all retailers use saves and win-backs; win-back rates are highest between retailers with high market shares (average win-back rate between the 5 largest retailers is 25%, average win-back rate of the 5 largest retailers against the next 5 largest retailers is 15%); the largest retailers have the highest rates of failed acquisitions (28%) (i.e. acquisitions lost through win-backs) . . . There is no strong evidence of regulatory problems or market failures related to customer acquisition and switching processes, including saves and win-backs practices. Patterns of win-back activity are consistent with increasing competitive pressure as retailers need to pay attention to costs and to price levels to avoid losing customers to counter-offers. The fact that win-backs are most prevalent between larger retailers is significant evidence of this . . . there is no strong rationale for regulating customer acquisition processes, particularly saves and win-backs, in order to promote greater transparency of retail pricing' (Market Development Advisory Group 2019, pp. 6–7).

9.   For example, Ek and Söderholm (2008) found that households in Sweden anticipating significant gains were more likely to engage, and households expecting high search and information costs were less likely to engage, but also that 'constraints on time, attention, and the ability to process information, may lead to optimizing analyses being replaced by imprecise routines and rules of thumb, and the benefits of the status quo appear to represent one of those simplifying rules' (p. 254). Frondel and Kussel (2019, p. 1) find that in Germany 'only those households that are informed about prices are sensitive to price changes, whereas the electricity demand of uninformed households is entirely price-inelastic'. They recommend 'low-cost information measures on a large scale, such as improving the transparency of tariffs, thereby increasing the saliency of prices' (ibid.). Schleich, Faure and Gassmann (2018) study 13 000 households from eight EU countries and find (*inter alia*) that internal switching (between tariffs of the existing supplier) and external switching (between suppliers) are not driven by the same factors.

10. For the first trial, in March/April 2018, 50 000 'passive' customers of one large supplier (that is, customers that had not switched supplier in the previous three years) were sent details of an exclusive tariff negotiated by Ofgem-appointed agent Energy Helpline. Ofgem had required the supplier to give Energy Helpline the customers' details so it was able to tell each customer what its annual savings would be compared to its present tariff (assuming usage at the previous year's level) and was also able to give customers personal advice and assistance. Ofgem (2019a) has further details.

11. Participants who did switch their energy tariff did so in one of four different ways. In the first trial, 44 per cent of the switchers chose the exclusive tariff, saving on average £261 a year. Twenty-three per cent of the switchers used Energy Helpline and saved on average £352 a year. Twenty-two per cent of switchers undertook an open market tariff search, switched supplier themselves and saved on average £300. The remaining 11 per cent of switchers stayed with their present supplier but switched to a different (fixed) tariff, saving on average £239 per year. Cave (2018) and Littlechild (2018c, 2019a) discuss Ofgem's early trials and their possible implications for the UK and New Zealand.

12. See https://bills.parliament.uk/bills/2213, accessed 25 June 2021.

REFERENCES

Adib, P. and J. Zarnikau (2006), 'Texas: the most robust competitive market in North America', in F. Sioshansi and W. Pfaffenberger (eds), *Electricity Market Reform: An International Perspective*, Amsterdam: Elsevier, pp. 383–417.

Adib, P., J. Zarnikau and R. Baldick (2013), 'Texas electricity market: getting better', in F. Sioshansi (ed.), *Evolution of Global Electricity Markets: New Paradigms, New Challenges, New Approaches*, Waltham, MA: Elsevier/Academic Press, pp. 265–96.

Agency for the Cooperation of Energy Regulators (ACER) (2014), *Market Monitoring Report 2014*, 22 October.

Amelung, T. (2019), 'Competition in the German electricity retail business: innovation and growth strategies', ZBW-Leibniz Information Centre for Economics, Kiel, Hamburg.

Amundsen, E. S., L. Bergman and N.-H. M. von der Fehr (2006), 'The Nordic electricity market: robust by design?', in F. Sioshansi and W. Pfaffenberger (eds), *Electricity Market Reform: An International Perspective*, Amsterdam: Elsevier, pp. 145–70.

Australian Competition and Consumer Commission ACCC (2018), *Restoring Electricity Affordability and Australia's Competitive Advantage: Retail Electricity Pricing Inquiry – Final Report*, June.

Baldick, R. and H. Niu (2005), 'Lessons learned: the Texas experience', in J. M. Griffin and S. L. Puller (eds), *Electricity Deregulation: Choices and Challenges*, Chicago, IL: University of Chicago Press, pp. 182–224.

Baldwin, S. (2019), *Are Consumers Benefiting from Competition? An Analysis of the Individual Residential Electric Supply Market in Massachusetts*, Massachusetts Attorney General's Office, Commonwealth of Massachusetts, August 2019 update.

Baumol, W. J. (2006), *Regulation Misled by Misread Theory: Perfect Competition and Competition-Imposed Price Discrimination*, Washington, DC: AEI-Brookings Joint Center for Regulatory Studies.

Beesley, M. and S. Littlechild (1983a), 'Privatization: principles, problems and priorities', *Lloyds Bank Review*, **149**, 1–20.

Beesley, M. and S. Littlechild (1983b), 'Privatisation and monopoly power', paper for H.M. Treasury, Energy Policy Research Group, University of Cambridge, November accessed 12 July 2021 at https://www.eprg.group.cam.ac.uk/wp-content/uploads/2021/01/S.-Littlechild_Nov1983.pdf.

Bergman, L. (2009), 'Addressing market power and industry restructuring', in J.-M. Glachant and F. Leveque (eds), *Electricity Reform in Europe*, Cheltenham, UK and Northampton, MA, USA: Edward Elgar Publishing, pp. 65–8.

Bertram, G. (2006), 'Restructuring the New Zealand electricity sector 1984–2005', in F. Sioshansi and W. Pfaffenberger (eds), *Electricity Market Reform: An International Perspective*, Amsterdam: Elsevier, pp. 203–34.

Bertram, G. (2013), 'Weak regulation, rising margins, and asset revaluations: New Zealand's failing experiment in electricity reform', in F. Sioshansi (ed.), *Evolution of Global Electricity Markets: New Paradigms, New Challenges, New Approaches*, Waltham, MA: Elsevier/Academic Press, pp. 645–77.

Borenstein, S. (1985), 'Price discrimination in free-entry markets', *Rand Journal of Economics*, **16** (3), 380–97.

Borts, K. (1998), 'Third-degree price discrimination in oligopoly: all-out competition and strategic commitment', *Rand Journal of Economics*, **29** (2), 306–23.

Bosco, J. (2018), *Competing to Overcharge Consumers: The Competitive Electric Supplier Market in Massachusetts*, Boston, MA: National Consumer Law Center, April.

Brennan, T. J. (1991), 'Entry and welfare loss in regulated industries', in M. A. Crew (ed.), *Competition and the Regulation of Utilities*, Boston, MA: Kluwer Academic Publishers, pp. 141–56.

Brennan, T. J. (2007), 'Consumer preference not to choose: methodological and policy implications', *Energy Policy*, **35** (3), 1616–27.

Britton, J., J. Hardy, C. Mitchell and R. Hoggett (2019), *Changing Actor Dynamics and Emerging Value Propositions in the UK Electricity Retail Market*, IGov New Thinking for Energy, accessed 12 July 2021 at http://projects.exeter.ac.uk/igov/wp-content/uploads/2019/01/IGov-BM-Analysis-report.pdf.

California Community Choice Association (CALCCA) (2019), *California Aggregator – The Quarterly Report of the California Community Choice Association, Q4 2019*, accessed 12 July 2021 at https://cal-cca.org/wp-content/uploads/2020/02/CalCCA-Q4-2019-Report-FINAL-1.pdf.

California Public Utilities Commission (2018), *California Customer Choice: An Evaluation of Regulatory Framework Options for an Evolving Electricity Market*, accessed 12 July 2021 at https://www.cpuc.ca.gov/uploadedFiles/CPUC_Public_Website/Content/Utilities_and_Industries/Energy_-_Electricity_and_Natural_Gas/Cal%20Customer%20Choice%20Report%208-7-18%20rm.pdf.

Cassell, B. (2015), 'New York unveils latest plan for a cleaner energy future', *Transmission Hub*, 26 June.

Cave, M. (2018), 'Retail lessons for New Zealand from the UK energy market investigation', 18 May, accessed 12 July 2021 at https://blob-static.vector.co.nz/blob/vector/media/articles/vector180518_cave-report_clean-final.pdf.

Competition and Markets Authority (CMA) (2016), *Energy Market Investigation, Final Report*, 24 June.

Connecticut Public Utilities Regulatory Authority (2019), *Review of Feasibility, Costs and Benefits of Placing Certain Customers on Standard Service*, Docket 18-06-02, 18 December.

Cooper, J., L. Froeb, D. O'Brien and S. Tschantz (2005), 'Does price discrimination intensify competition? Implications for antitrust', *Antitrust Law Journal*, **72** (2), 327–73.

Cornwall Insight (2020), *Energy Spectrum*, Issue 705, 9 March.

Council of European Energy Regulators (CEER) (2019), *Monitoring Report on the Performance of European Retail Markets in 2018*, Ref. C19-MRM-99-02, 21 November.

Cramton, P. (2021), 'Lessons from the 2021 Texas electricity crisis', working paper, University of Cologne, 17 May, accessed 12 July 2021 at http://www.cramton.umd.edu/papers2020-2024/cramton-lessons-from-the-2021-texas-electricity-crisis.pdf.

Defeuilley, C. (2009), 'Retail competition in electricity markets', *Energy Policy*, **37** (2), 377–86, and 'Reply', 764–5.

Deller, D., P. Bernal, M. Hviid and C. Waddams Price (2017), *Collective Switching and Possible Uses of a Disengaged Customer Database*, Ofgem-commissioned report by the University of East Anglia Centre for Competition Policy, 10 August.

Deller, D., M. Giulietti and G. Loomes et al. (2021), 'Switching energy suppliers: it's not all about the money', *The Energy Journal*, **42** (3), 95–120.

Deller, D. and C. Waddams Price (2018), 'Energy affordability in the UK: corrected energy expenditure shares 1992–2014', *CCP Working Paper 18-8*, University of East Anglia Centre for Competition Policy, accessed 12 July 2021 at http://competitionpolicy.ac.uk/documents/8158338/24898393/CCP+WP+18-8+complete.pdf/4960a073-a343-53c8-9aa2-d5017f78651e.

Deloitte (2019), 'Widening the lens: big-picture thinking on disruptive innovation in the retail power sector', *Deloitte Insights*, 16 January.

Dormady, N., M. Holt, A. Roa-Henriquez and W. Welch (2019), 'Who pays for retail electric deregulation? Evidence of cross-subsidization from complete bill data', *The Energy Journal*, **40** (2), 161–94.

Ek, K. and P. Söderholm (2008), 'Households' switching behavior between electricity suppliers in Sweden', *Utilities Policy*, **16** (4), 254–61.

Electricity Authority NZ (2020a), *Saves and Win-backs Codes Amendment, Decision Paper and Summary of Submissions*, 18 February.

Electricity Authority NZ (2020b), 'Retail reports', accessed 12 July 2021 at https://www.emi.ea.govt.nz/Retail/Reports.

ESP Consulting and vaasaETT (2018), *Customer Switching and Disengaged Customers: Detailed Case Studies*, prepared for Ofgem, July.

Esplin, R., B. Davis, A. Rai and T. Nelson (2020), 'The impacts of price regulation on price dispersion in Australia's retail electricity markets', *Energy Policy*, **147**, Article 111829.

Essential Services Commission (2019), *Victorian Energy Market Update: March 2019*, 28 March.

European Commission (2007), *Communication from the Commission: Inquiry Pursuant to Article 17 of Regulation (EC) No. 1/2003 into the European Gas and Electricity Sectors (Final Report)*, Brussels, 10.1.2007 COM (2006) 851 final.

European Commission (2009), *Third Energy Package, Energy Directive 2009/72/ED*, 13 July.

European Regulators Group for Electricity and Gas (ERGEG) (2008), *2008 Status Review of the Liberalisation and Implementation of the Energy Regulatory Framework*, C08-URB-15-04, 10 December.

European Regulators Group for Electricity and Gas (ERGEG) (2009), *2009 Status Review of the Liberalisation and Implementation of the Regulatory Framework*, C09-URB-24-03, 10 December. Summary accessed 25 June 2021 at https://www.ceer.eu/eer_publications/national_reports/national_reporting_2009.

Faruqui, A. (2020), 'Refocusing on the consumer', *Regulation*, **43** (1), 20–26.

Faruqui, A. and J. R. Malko (1999), *Customer Choice: Finding Value in Retail Electricity Markets*, Vienna, VA: Public Utilities Reports Inc.

Faruqui, A. and M. Peevey (2020), 'Why dynamic pricing gets back seat in California', *Public Utilities Fortnightly*, March, 58–61.

Faruqui, A., R. Hledik and L. Lam (2020), *Modernising Distribution Rate Design*, Brattle Group report prepared for ATCO, 13 March.

Flaim, T. (2000), 'The big retail "bust": what will it take to get true competition?', *The Electricity Journal*, **13** (2), 41–54.

Flores, M. and C. Waddams Price (2018), 'The role of attitudes and marketing in consumer behaviours in the British retail electricity market', *The Energy Journal*, **39** (4), 153–79.

Foster, V., S. Witte, S. G. Banerjee and A. Moreno (2017), 'Charting the diffusion of power sector reforms across the developing world', *World Bank Policy Research Paper No. 8235*, November.

Fotouhi Ghazvini, M. A., S. Ramos and J. Soares et al. (2019), 'Liberalization and customer behaviour in the Portuguese residential retail electricity market', *Utilities Policy*, **59**, Article 100919.

Fox Business (2020), 'California lawmaker introduces PG&E bill to make publicly owned utility', 3 February, accessed 12 July 2021 at https://www.foxbusiness.com/markets/california-lawmaker-introduces-pge-bill-to-make-publicly-owned-utility.

Frondel, M. and G. Kussel (2019), 'Switching on electricity demand response: evidence for German households', *The Energy Journal*, **40** (5), 1–16.

Galetovic, A. and C. Muñoz (2011), 'Regulated electricity retailing in Chile', *Energy Policy*, **39** (10), 6453–65.

Giulietti, M., C. Waddams Price and M. Waterson (2005), 'Consumer choice and competition policy: a study of UK energy markets', *The Economic Journal*, **115** (506), 949–68.

Giulietti, M., M. Waterson and M. Wildenbeest (2014), 'Estimation of search frictions in the British electricity market', *Journal of Industrial Economics*, **62** (4), 555–90.

Goulding, A.J., C. Ruffin and G. Swinand (1999), 'The role of vibrant retail electricity markets in assuring that wholesale electricity markets operate effectively', *The Electricity Journal*, **12** (10), 61–73.

Gramlich, R. and F. Lacey (2020), *Who's the Buyer? Retail Electric Market Structure Reforms in Support of Resource Adequacy and Clean Energy Deployment*, prepared for Wind Solar Alliance, March.

Green, R. (2005), 'Restructuring the electricity industry in England and Wales', in J. M. Griffin and S. L. Puller (eds), *Electricity Deregulation: Choices and Challenges*, Chicago, IL: University of Chicago Press, pp. 98–144.

Green, R. and T. McDaniel (1998), 'Competition in electricity supply: will 1998 be worth it?', *Fiscal Studies*, **19** (3), 273–93.

Green, R. and D. M. Newbery (1997), 'Competition in the electricity industry in England and Wales', *Oxford Review of Economic* Policy, **13** (1), 27–46.

Haas, R., J.-M. Glachant, N. Keseric and Y. Perez (2006), 'Competition in the continental European electricity market: despair or work in progress?' in F. Sioshansi and W. Pfaffenberger (eds), *Electricity Market Reform. An International Perspective*, Amsterdam: Elsevier, pp. 265–315.

Hall, S. and K. Roelich (2016), 'Business, model innovation in electricity supply markets: the role of complex value in the United Kingdom', *Energy Policy*, **92**, 286–98.

Harris, C. (2019), 'Concluding the 40-year utilities experiment – death spiral or rebirth?', Beesley Lecture, London, 23 October.

Hartley, P. R., K. B. Medlock III and O. Jankovska (2019), 'Electricity reform and retail pricing in Texas', *Energy Economics*, **80**, 1–11.

Hayek, F. A. (1979), *Law, Legislation and Liberty, Vol. 3: The Political Order of a Free People*, Chicago, IL: University of Chicago Press.

He, X. and D. Reiner (2017), 'Why do more British consumers not switch energy suppliers? The role of individual attitudes', *The Energy Journal*, **38** (6), 25–53.

He, X. and D. Reiner (2018), 'Consumer engagement in energy markets: the role of information and knowledge', *EPRG Working Paper No. 1835*, Energy Policy Research Group, University of Cambridge.

Henney, A. (1987), *Policy Study No. 83. Privatise Power: Restructuring the ESI*, London: Centre for Policy Studies.

Henney, A. (1994), *A Study of the Privatisation of the Electricity Supply Industry in England and Wales*, London: EEE Limited.

Hogan, W. W. (1994), 'Efficient direct access: comments on the California blue book proposals', *The Electricity Journal*, **7** (7), 30–41.

Hortaçsu, A., S. A. Madanizadeh and S. Puller (2017), 'Power to choose? An analysis of consumer inertia in the residential electricity market', *American Economic Review*, **9** (4), 192–226.

Huntoon, S. (2019), 'New York's surreal new deal', *Counterflow*, 1 October, accessed 12 July 2021 at http://www.energy-counsel.com/docs/New-Yorks-Surreal-New-Deal.pdf.

Hviid, M. and C. Waddams Price (2012), 'Non-discrimination clauses in the retail energy sector', *The Economic Journal*, **122**, F236–F252.

Hyland, M., E. Leahy and R. S. J. Tol (2013), 'The potential for segmentation of the retail market for electricity in Ireland', *Energy Policy*, **61**, 349–59.

Illinois Commerce Commission (2019), *Office of Retail Market Development, 2019 Annual Report*, June.

Intelometry (2018), 'Comments on the Massachusetts Attorney General's Office Report titled Are Consumers Benefiting from Competition?', prepared on behalf of the Retail Energy Supply Association (RESA), accessed 12 July 2021 at https://www.resausa.org/sites/default/files/Comments-on-MA-AGO-Report.pdf.

IPA Advisory (2015), *Ranking the Competitiveness of Retail Electricity and Gas Markets: A Proposed Methodology, Final Report to Agency for the Cooperation of Energy Regulators*, 4 September, accessed 12 July 2021 at http://www.acer.europa.eu/en/Electricity/Market%20monitoring/Documents_Public/IPA%20Final%20Report.pdf.

Joskow, P. L. (2000), 'Why do we need electricity retailers? Or can you get it cheaper wholesale?', Center for Energy and Environmental Policy Research, MIT, 13 February, accessed 12 July 2021 at https://economics.mit.edu/files/1127.

Joskow, P. L. (2001), 'California's electricity crisis', *Oxford Review of Economic Policy*, **17** (3), 365–88.

Joskow, P. L. (2005), 'The difficult transition to competitive electricity markets in the United States', in J. M. Griffin and S. L. Puller (eds), *Electricity Deregulation: Choices and Challenges*, Chicago, IL: University of Chicago Press, pp. 31–97.

Joskow, P. L. (2006), 'Introduction to electricity sector liberalization: lessons learned from cross-country studies', in F. Sioshansi and W. Pfaffenberger (eds), *Electricity Market Reform: An International Perspective*, Amsterdam: Elsevier, pp. 1–32.

Joskow, P. L. (2008), 'Lessons learned from electricity market liberalization', *The Energy Journal*, **29** (2) (Special Issue), 9–42.

Joskow, P. L. and R. Schmalensee (1983), *Markets for Power: An Analysis of Electrical Utility Deregulation*, Cambridge, MA: MIT Press.

Kang, L. and J. Zarnikau (2009), 'Did the expiration of price caps affect prices in the restructured Texas electricity market?', *Energy Policy*, **37** (5), 1713–17.

Kim, Y. (2013), 'Unfinished business: the evolution of US competitive retail electricity markets', in P. Sioshansi (ed.), *Evolution of Global Electricity Markets: New Paradigms, New Challenges, New Approaches*, Waltham, MA Elsevier/Academic Press, pp. 331–61.

Kirzner, I. M. (1985), 'The perils of regulation: a market process approach', in I. M. Kirzner, *Discovery and the Capitalist Process*, Chicago, IL: University of Chicago Press, pp. 119–49.

Kirzner, I. M. (1997), 'Entrepreneurial discovery and the competitive market process: an Austrian approach', *Journal of Economic Literature*, **35** (1), 60–85.

Kleit, A. N., A. V. Shcherbakova and X. Chen (2012), 'Restructuring and the retail residential market for power in Pennsylvania', *Energy Policy*, **46**, 443–51.

Klemperer, P. (1987a), 'Markets with consumer switching costs', *Quarterly Journal of Economics*, **102**, 375–94.

Klemperer, P. (1987b), 'The competitiveness of markets with switching costs', *Rand Journal of Economics*, **18**, 138–50.

Klemperer, P. (1995), 'Competition when consumers have switching costs: an overview with applications to industrial organization, macroeconomics, and international trade', *Review of Economic Studies*, **62**, 515–39.

Lacey, F. (2019), 'Default service pricing – the flaw and the fix: current pricing practices allow utilities to maintain market dominance in deregulated markets', *The Electricity Journal*, **32** (3), 4–10.

Levine, M. E. (2002), 'Price discrimination without market power', *Yale Journal on Regulation*, **19**, 1–36.

Littlechild, S. C. (2000), 'Why we need electricity retailers: a reply to Joskow on wholesale spot price pass-through', *Cambridge Working Paper in Economics, WP21/2000*, 22 August, revised and extended in Littlechild (2003).

Littlechild, S.C. (2002), 'Competition in retail electricity supply', *Journal des Économistes et des Études Humaines*, **12** (2), 353–76.

Littlechild, S. C. (2003), 'Wholesale spot price pass-through', *Journal of Regulatory Economics*, **23** (1), 61–91.

Littlechild, S. C. (2005), 'Smaller suppliers in the UK domestic electricity market: experience, concerns and policy recommendations', 29 June, Energy Policy Research Group, University of Cambridge, accessed 12 July 2021 at https://www.eprg.group.cam.ac.uk/wp-content/uploads/2014/01/smallersuppliersintheuk.pdf.

Littlechild, S. C. (2006a), 'Foreword: the market versus regulation', in F. Sioshansi and W. Pfaffenberger (eds), *Electricity Market Reform: An International Perspective*, Amsterdam: Elsevier, pp. xvii–xxix.

Littlechild, S. C. (2006b), 'Competition and contracts in the Nordic residential electricity markets', *Utilities Policy*, **14** (3), 135–47.

Littlechild, S. C. (2008), 'Municipal aggregation and retail competition in the Ohio energy sector', *Journal of Regulatory Economics*, **34** (2), 164–94.

Littlechild, S. C. (2009), 'Retail competition in electricity markets – expectations, outcomes and economics', *Energy Policy*, **37** (2), 759–63.

Littlechild, S. C. (2014), 'The creation of a market for retail electricity supply', in E. Brousseau and J.-M. Glachant (eds), *The Manufacturing of Markets: Legal, Political and Economic Dynamics*, Cambridge, UK: Cambridge University Press, pp. 166–98.

Littlechild, S. (2016), 'The CMA energy market investigation, the well-functioning market, Ofgem, Government and behavioural economics', *European Competition Journal*, **11** (2–3), 574–636.

Littlechild, S. C. (2018a), 'Retail competition and regulation in US electricity markets', Energy Policy Research Group, University of Cambridge, 28 February, accessed 12 July 2021 at https://www.eprg.group.cam.ac.uk/report-the-regulation-of-retail-competition-in-us-residential-electricity-markets-by-s-littlechild/.

Littlechild, S. C. (2018b), 'Competition, regulation and price controls in the GB retail energy market', *Utilities Policy*, **52**, 59–69.

Littlechild, S. C. (2018c), 'Retail lessons for New Zealand from UK regulation and the CMA's energy market investigation, including a critique of Professor Cave's analysis', paper submitted by Meridian Energy to the New Zealand Electricity Price Review, 8 October, accessed 12 July 2021 at https://www.mbie.govt.nz/dmsdocument/4195-meridian-energy-electricity-price-review-first-report-submission.

Littlechild, S. C. (2018d), 'Is there competition below the PPM tariff cap? What are the implications for policy?', Energy Policy Research Group, University of Cambridge, 16 October, accessed 12 July 2021 at https://www.

eprg.group.cam.ac.uk/report-is-there-competition-below-the-ppm-tariff-cap-what-are-the-implications-for-policy-by-s-littlechild/.

Littlechild, S. C. (2019a), 'Ofgem's collective switching trial and possible application in New Zealand', Energy Policy Research Group, University of Cambridge, 19 March, accessed 12 July 2021 at https://www.eprg.group.cam.ac.uk/wp-content/uploads/2019/03/S.-Littlechild_Ofgems-collective-switching-trial-NZ_Mar19.pdf.

Littlechild, S. C. (2019b), 'Promoting competition and protecting customers? Regulation of the GB retail energy market 2008–2016', *Journal of Regulatory Economics*, **55**, 107–39.

Littlechild, S. C. (2020), 'The CMA's assessment of consumer detriment in the UK retail energy market', *Journal of Regulatory Economics*, **57**, 203–30.

Littlechild, S. and L. Kiesling (2021), 'Hayek and the Texas blackout', *The Electricity Journal*, **34** (6), July.

Market Development Advisory Group (2019), *Saves and Win-backs – Recommendations Paper*, 11 March.

Moran, A. (2006), 'The electricity industry in Australia: problems along the way to a national electricity market', in F. Sioshansi and W. Pfaffenberger (eds), *Electricity Market Reform: An International Perspective*, Amsterdam: Elsevier, pp. 173–202.

Morey, M. and L. Kirsch (2016), *Retail Choice in Electricity: What Have We Learned in 20 Years?*, Christensen Associates Energy Consulting LLC for Electric Markets Research Foundation, 2 February.

Mountain, B. and K. Burns (2020), 'Retail electricity market monitoring of diverse consumers and market offers', *Working Paper WP2008*, Victoria Energy Policy Centre, October.

Mountain, B. and K. Burns (2021), 'Loyalty taxes and search costs in retail electricity markets: not as they seem?', *Journal of Regulatory Economics*, **59**, 1–24.

Mountain, B. and S. Rizio (2019), 'Do Victoria's households leave less money on the table when they switch electricity retailers?' *Working Paper WP1909*, Victoria Energy Policy Centre, September, accessed 12 July 2021 at https://docs.wixstatic.com/ugd/cb01c4_8babedb580d44ca080fefea8b2ae8b0b.pdf.

Mulder, M. and B. Willems (2019), 'The Dutch retail electricity market', *Energy Policy*, **127**, 228–39.

Nelson, T., E. McCracken-Hewson, P. Whish-Wilson and S. Bashir (2018), 'Price dispersion in Australian retail electricity markets', *Energy Economics*, **70** (1), 158–69.

Newbery, D. (2006), 'Electricity liberalization in Britain and the evolution of market design', in F. Sioshansi and W. Pfaffenberger (eds), *Electricity Market Reform: An International Perspective*, Amsterdam: Elsevier, pp. 109–44.

New York Public Service Commission (NYPSC) (2019), *Order Adopting Changes to the Retail Access Energy Market and Establishing Further Process*, 12 December.

New Zealand Government (2018a), 'Details of retail power price review released', press release, 27 March.

New Zealand Government (2018b), *Electricity Price Review, First Report*, 30 August.

New Zealand Government (2019a), *Electricity Price Review, Options Paper*, 18 February.

New Zealand Government (2019b), *Electricity Price Review, Final Report*, 21 May.

New Zealand Government (n.d.), 'Terms of reference', Expert Advisory Panel.

O'Connor, P. (2017), *Restructuring Recharged: The Superior Performance of Competitive Electricity Markets 2008–2016*, Retail Energy Supply Association, April.

O'Connor, P. and M. A. Khan (2018), The Great Divergence in Competitive and Monopoly Electricity Price Trends, Retail Energy Supply Association, September.

Ofgem (2001), *Report on the Social Action Plan*, 14 September, accessed 8 July 2021 at https://www.ofgem.gov.uk/publications/report-social-action-plan.

Ofgem (2007a), *Domestic Retail Market Report – June 2007*, Ref. 169/07, 4 July.

Ofgem (2007b), *Ofgem's Review of Suppliers' Voluntary Initiatives to Help Vulnerable Customers*, Ref. 203/07, 7 August.

Ofgem (2011), 'What can behavioural economics say about GB energy consumers?', 21 March.

Ofgem (2017), *State of the Energy Market 2017*, 31 October.

Ofgem (2018a), 'Future supply market arrangements – response to our call for evidence', 31 July.

Ofgem (2018b), *Consumer Engagement in the Energy Market 2018: Report on a Survey of Energy Consumers*, 10 October.

Ofgem (2019a), *Ofgem's Collective Switch Trials*, 27 September.

Ofgem (2019b), *Decision – Framework for Assessing Whether Conditions Are in Place for Effective Competition in Domestic Supply Contracts*, 3 October.

Ofgem (2020), 'Open letter on evolving our customer engagement work', 30 September.

O'Shaughnessy, E., J. Heeter and J. Gattaciecca et al. (2019), 'Empowered communities: the rise of community choice aggregation in the United States', *Energy Policy*, **132**, 1110–19.

Otero, J. and C. Waddams Price (2001), 'Price discrimination in a regulated market with entry: the residential UK electricity market', *Bulletin of Economic Research*, **53** (3), 161–75.

Pollitt, M. G. (2008), 'Forward: liberalization and regulation in electricity systems – how can we get the balance right?', in F. Sioshansi (ed.), *Competitive Electricity Markets: Design, Implementation, Performance*, Amsterdam: Elsevier, pp. xvii–xxxiv.

Pollitt, M. G. and A. Haney (2014), 'Dismantling a competitive retail electricity market: residential market reforms in Great Britain', *The Electricity Journal*, **27** (1), 66–73.

Poudineh, R. (2019), 'Liberalized retail electricity markets: what we have learned after two decades of experience?', *Oxford Institute for Energy Studies Paper EL 38*, December.

Primeaux, W. J. (1975), 'A re-examination of the monopoly market structure for electric utilities', in A. Phillips (ed.), *Promoting Competition in Regulated Markets*, Washington, DC: Brookings Institution Press, pp. 175–200.

Primeaux, W. J. (1985a), 'An end to natural monopoly', *Economic Affairs*, **5** (2), 15–16.

Primeaux, W. J. (1985b), *Direct Electricity Utility Competition: The Natural Monopoly Myth*, New York: Praeger Publishers.

Public Utility Commission of Texas (PUCT) (2001), *Report to the 77th Legislature: Scope of Competition in Electric Markets in Texas*, January.

Public Utility Commission of Texas (PUCT) (2019), *Report to the 86th Legislature: Scope of Competition in Electric Markets in Texas*, January.

Retail Energy Supply Association (RESA) (2019), 'Analysis reveals retail electric suppliers could have saved Connecticut consumers more than $14 million in the first month of 2019', 4 February, accessed 12 July 2021 at https://www.resausa.org/news-events/analysis-reveals-retail-electric-suppliers-could-have-saved-connecticut-consumers-more.

Retail Energy Supply Association (RESA) (2020), 'Phil O'Connor thought leadership', accessed 12 July 2021 at https://www.resausa.org/phil-oconnor-thought-leadership.

Ros, A. J. (2017), 'An econometric assessment of electricity demand in the United States using utility-specific panel data and the impact of retail competition on prices', *The Energy Journal*, **38** (4), 73–99.

Ros, A. J. (2020), 'Does electricity competition work for residential consumers? Evidence from demand models for default service and competitive residential electricity services', *Journal of Regulatory Economics*, **58** (1), 1–32.

Ros, A. J., T. Brown and N. Lessen et al. (2018), *International Experiences in Retail Electricity Market: Consumer Issues*, Brattle Group, prepared for the Australian Competition and Consumer Commission (ACCC), accessed 12 July 2021 at https://brattlefiles.blob.core.windows.net/files/14257_appendix_11_-_the_brattle_group_-_international_experiences_in_retail_el.pdf.

Ruff, L. E. (1999), 'Competitive electricity markets: one size should fit all', *The Electricity Journal*, **12** (9), 20–35.

Salies, E. and C. Waddams Price (2004), 'Charges, costs and market power: the deregulated UK electricity retail market', *The Energy Journal*, **25** (3), 19–37.

Schleich, J., C. Faure and X. Gassmann (2018), 'Household internal and external electricity contract switching in EU countries', *Applied Economics*, **51** (6), 1–14.

Simshauser, P. (2018), 'Price discrimination and the modes of failure in deregulated electricity markets', *Energy Economics*, **75**, 54–70.

Simshauser, P. and P. Whish-Wilson (2017), 'Price discrimination in Australia's retail electricity markets: an analysis of Victoria and Southeast Queensland', *Energy Economics*, **62**, 92–103.

Smith, S. (2015), 'The use and abuse of the notion of effective competition: Carroll, Orwell and McCarthy revisited', Zeeman Lecture, Regulatory Policy Institute Annual Conference, Oxford, 8 September.

Stagnaro, C. (2017), 'Competition and innovation in retail electricity markets: evidence from Italy', *Economic Affairs*, **37** (1), 85–101.

Stagnaro, C., C. Amental, G. Di Croce and L. Libecchio (2020), 'Managing the liberalization of Italy's retail electricity market: a policy proposal', *Energy Policy*, **137**, Article 111150.

Su, X. (2015), 'Have customers benefited from electricity retail competition?', *Journal of Regulatory Economics*, **47** (2), 146–82.

Swadley, A. and M. Yücel (2011), 'Did residential electricity rates fall after retail competition? A dynamic panel analysis', *Energy Policy*, **39** (12), 7702–11.

Sweeney, J. L. (2006), 'California's electricity restructuring, the crisis and its aftermath', in F. Sioshansi and W. Pfaffenberger (eds) (2006), *Electricity Market Reform: An International Perspective*, Amsterdam: Elsevier, pp. 319–81.

Thomas, C., K. Funston and C. Lowe (2019), *Victorian Default Offer Expert Panel Report on the Initial Market Outcomes Since the Introduction of the Victorian Default Offer*, November.

Thwaites, J., P. Faulkner and T. Mulder (2017), *Independent Review into the Electricity and Gas Retail Markets in Victoria*, August.

Tsai, C.-H. and Y.-L. Tsai (2018), 'Competitive retail electricity market under continuous price regulation', *Energy Policy*, **114** (12), 274–87.

Tschamler, T. (2006), 'Competitive retail power markets and default service: the U.S. experience', in F. Sioshansi and W. Pfaffenberger (eds) (2006), *Electricity Market Reform: An International Perspective*, Amsterdam: Elsevier, pp. 529–62.

Victorian Government (2018), 'Fair pricing in the energy market: terms of reference for the Essential Services Commission'.

Waddams Price, C. (2018), 'Back to the future? Regulating residential energy markets', *International Journal of the Economics of Business*, **25** (1), 147–55.

Waddams Price, C. and M. Zhu (2016), 'Non-discrimination clauses: their effect on GB retail energy prices', *The Energy Journal*, **37** (2), 111–32.

Wilson, C. and C. Waddams Price (2010), 'Do consumers choose the best suppliers?', *Oxford Economic Papers*, **62**, 647–68.

Wood III, P., R.W. Gee and J. Walsh et al. (2021), 'Never again: how to prevent another major Texas electricity failure', *CGMF.org*, June, accessed 8 July 2021 at https://www.cgmf.org/blog-entry/435/REPORT-%7C-Never-Again-How-to-prevent-another-major-Texas-electricity-failure.html.

Zarnikau, J. and D. Whitworth (2006), 'Has electric utility restructuring led to lower electricity prices for residential consumers in Texas?', *Energy Policy*, **34** (15), 2191–200.

6. Strengths and weaknesses of the British market model

*David Newbery**

1. INTRODUCTION

The British model has evolved to cover the island of Great Britain (England, Wales and Scotland), while Northern Ireland, part of the UK, has evolved into a quite different market model covering the island of Ireland in its Single Electricity Market (SEM). This chapter discusses the British market – its relationship to the SEM is discussed in Newbery (2017). The main emphasis here is on England and Wales, which experienced the main restructuring. Scotland had two vertically integrated regional state-owned utilities that retained their unbundled structure after privatization.

2. THE BRITISH ELECTRICITY MARKET 1947–89

Before restructuring and privatization in 1989–90, the state-owned Central Electricity Generating Board (CEGB) was responsible for generation and transmission in England and Wales. Transmission and site location of new generation was coordinated by the CEGB, although the main high-tension (275 and 400 kilovolts [kV]) grid had been largely completed by the 1960s with substantial spare capacity. Similarly, the intense period of building large power stations (with 500 and 660 megawatt [MW] turbines) was predicated on continued growth in demand of 8 per cent per annum, which had come to an abrupt halt with the first oil shock. The stations under construction would deliver substantial excess capacity once completed. Twelve Area Boards, who paid the CEGB the Bulk Supply Tariff (BST) and set tariffs for their captive retail customers, managed distribution and supply (retailing).

The BST evolved into a two-part fixed charge (base and peak) per kilowatt (kW), allocated on the basis of the Area Boards' use of base and peak capacity of both transmission and generation. A variable energy charge was set equal to the marginal energy cost, varying between night-time, shoulder and peak periods. With a growing nuclear share and large coal stations that cannot be rapidly stopped and started, the problem was excess capacity at night and excess demand at the peak. The solution was to build very costly pumped storage schemes and to introduce cheap rates for night-time electrical storage units, both storing either power or heat for later use. Meek (1968) compares this tariff structure with the theoretical ideal more closely followed in France, where Boiteux was both the theorist behind such tariffs and the head of EDF (Boiteux 1949), foreshadowing the tariff problems created by high renewables penetration with similarly high fixed and very low variable costs. Trade with France was through balanced bilateral swaps designed to benefit from the one-hour difference in timing of peak demand.

The CEGB's performance had been strongly criticized for its inefficiency, particularly in delivering timely and cost-effective investment, and under-pricing its output (Henney 1994, Newbery and Green 1996). After the success and lessons learned from earlier UK utility privatizations, the electricity supply industry was ripe for restructuring to create competitive wholesale and retail markets, and regulated transmission and distribution networks (Newbery 2000).

3.   PRIVATIZATION, RESTRUCTURING AND MARKET POWER

The CEGB was restructured in 1989 to separate transmission and generation. The 12 Area Boards became Regional Electricity Companies (RECs) with temporary ownership of the National Grid. The networks were subject to price-cap regulation by the Office of Electricity Regulation (OFFER). All were privatized in 1990 with the exception of Nuclear Electric, which was finally sold in 1995. The vertically integrated Scottish companies were privatized unrestructured in 1991.

Figure 6.1 shows the evolution of the fuel mix from 1970 (after the shift from coal to oil in the 1960s). By 1989, just before restructuring for privatization, around 90 per cent of the conventional thermal generation was from coal, 7 per cent from oil and the remainder largely from industrial by-product gases. The share of oil rapidly fell to 1 per cent in 2002. After privatization, the coal share declined as imported electricity and nuclear power increased. It declined more rapidly with the 'dash for gas' – a period in which there was massive investment in new build gas-fired combined cycle gas turbines (CCGTs) despite the considerable spare existing capacity.

The market structure of generation in England and Wales was initially highly concentrated in two price-setting fossil companies, National Power (NP) and PowerGen (PG). The state-owned Nuclear Electric (whose eight modern stations were privatized in 1995 and restructured in 1996 to become British Energy, leaving the old Magnox stations in British Nuclear Fuels Ltd, BNFL in Figure 6.2) was a price-taking baseload company. NP was structured (as 'Big G') to be large enough to carry the risks of owning the nuclear power stations, whose performance had been poor and whose accounts were opaque. PG ('Little G') was two-thirds as large to provide a sufficient counterweight to NP. The City of London financiers baulked at underwriting the unknown risks of the nuclear stations, so they were pulled out of NP and kept in state ownership. By then it was too late to choose a better market structure. Henney (1987) had argued for breaking the CEGB into ten companies (there were ten large coal stations), while Green and Newbery (1992) argued that five companies would have created a workably competitive structure, a conclusion endorsed by the Competition and Markets Authority (CMA 2016) in their study of the six large energy companies selling electricity and gas.

Figure 6.2 shows the evolution of the market structure in England and Wales from a de-facto price-setting duopoly to a competitive structure just before the 2001 New Electricity Trading Arrangements (NETA) were imposed.

Before 2001, all generators (above 50 MW) offered their generating units into the Electricity Pool day-ahead market, specifying the prices and quantities for each unit, which the system operator (National Grid) used to determine the unconstrained system

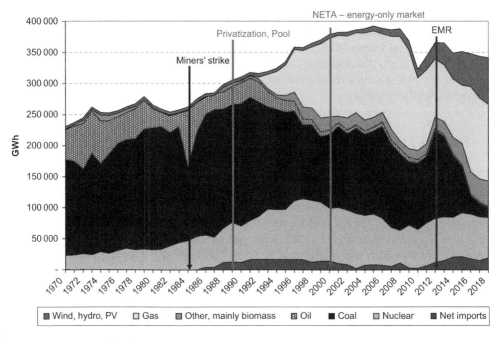

Note: 'Other' = all thermal generation from other generators (that is, not the public supply companies), non-CCGT gas and thermal renewables. Pumped storage (net negative) is not shown, nor are (small) amounts of annual average exports. NETA = the New Electricity Trading Arrangements, EMR = the Electricity Market Reform, both discussed below.

Sources: Department for Business, Energy & Industrial Strategy (2020), Digest of UK Energy Statistics (DUKES) (2019).

Figure 6.1   UK electricity generation by fuel, 1970–2018

marginal price (SMP, the price of the last plant accepted). Market power allowed the two companies, NP and PG, to game the Pool and exploit capacity constraints that had been efficiently managed under the CEGB's central dispatch. Constraint costs rose rapidly, until National Grid convinced OFFER to provide incentives for their better management.

Newbery and Pollitt (1997) concluded that the way the CEGB had been privatized to unbundle generation and transmission combined with an open-access wholesale market (the Electricity Pool) created substantial value (equal to a permanent cost reduction of 6 per cent) but that the benefits were more than appropriated by the new owners of the generation assets. In Scotland, vertical integration appeared to obstruct any efficiency gains, and consumers (and taxpayers) lost to the owners of the new companies (Domah and Pollitt 2001, Pollitt 1998). The lesson was clear, privatization without restructuring to introduce competition was not necessarily beneficial, and an imperfectly competitive structure prevented efficiency gains being passed through to consumers. It would have been better to introduce competition before privatization and avoid the lengthy regulatory struggles and the fortunate arrival of cheap gas-fired stations to slowly rectify that mistake.

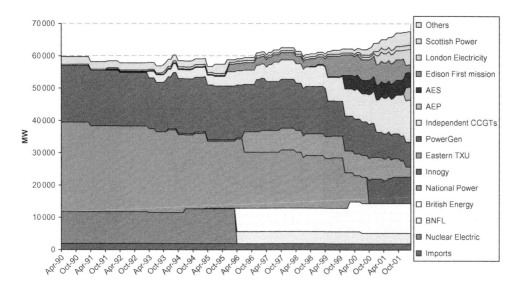

Source: National Grid, *Seven Year Statements*, various years.[1]

Figure 6.2   Output by company in England and Wales, 1990–2002

The consequences of market structure on electricity prices have been elegantly teased out by Sweeting (2007) and illustrated in Figure 6.3.

The Herfindahl–Hirschman Index (HHI) is shown for the then price-setting coal stations in Figure 6.3.[2] The first period 1990–94 was one in which NP and PG were privatized with sales contracts with the RECs and purchase contracts for coal from the state-owned National Coal Board, giving revenue and cost certainty needed for their sale prospectuses. Contract cover mitigated market power (Allaz and Vila 1993, Newbery 1995), but as the contracts fell away, the price–cost margin rose, restrained only by the threat of a monopoly inquiry. In 1994, to avoid a reference to the Monopolies and Mergers Commission, NP and PG agreed a price control with OFFER, to last until they had divested 6 gigawatts (GW) of their 27 GW of coal plant, as shown in Figure 6.2. The sale to Eastern TXU came with an 'earn-out' charge of 6 £/megawatt-hour (MWh), ostensibly to cover the cost of the sulphur permits that went with the stations sold (Newbery 2005a) but raising costs to Eastern TXU, causing it to set the wholesale price much of the time. This allowed the three companies to maximize their profits as the original duopolists could hide behind Eastern.

Before 1998, the duopolists were blocked from buying the supply businesses from the distribution companies. In 1998, the government allowed vertical integration to take place in exchange for further divestment and ending the 'earn-out' clause (ibid.). Sweeting (2007) characterizes this period as one of tacit collusion, in which NP and PG aimed to sustain the wholesale price as market concentration rapidly fell with divestment. Arguably, NP, which became Innogy in October 2000, and PG played a long game in which the original quasi-referral by OFFER with a price cap and divestment demonstrated their ability to

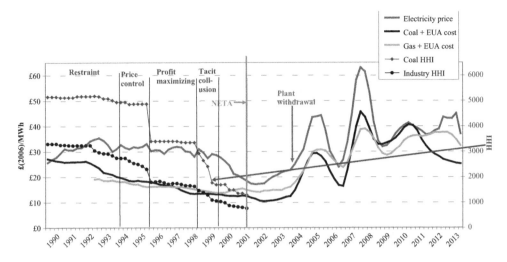

Note: EUA = European Allowance; HHI = Herfindahl–Hirschman Index.

Sources: National Grid, *Seven Year Statements*, various years, and data from J. Bower and C. Humphries (Bower 2002).

Figure 6.3   Wholesale electricity and fuel costs, 1990–2014 and market concentration

sustain market power, followed by a demonstration that divesting plants if anything increased their price–cost margin. This encouraged new entrants to buy old coal stations to diversify their plant mix. Even British Energy, the nuclear power company, having failed to buy a supply company, a more sensible hedge, bought a coal station instead (Taylor 2007). High price–cost margins convinced potential buyers of their profitability, ensuring a high price for such plant. Buying retail businesses allowed generating companies to hedge internally against wholesale price movements, a strategy that British Energy tried and failed to follow, with subsequent disastrous results as it subsequently went into administration (ibid.).[3] Internal hedges reduce wholesale market liquidity that deters entry of competitive retailers, leading Ofgem[4] (eventually) to encourage all sales to be transacted through a (moderately) transparent wholesale market.

4.   COMPETITION AND THE SWITCH TO AN ENERGY-ONLY MARKET

As divestment created lower concentration, the structure evolved towards the current 'Big Six' generation plus retailing companies.[5] As the new buyers started competing, believing somewhat naively that they could raise their plant load factors from 20–40 per cent without impacting price, so Figure 6.3 shows that the wholesale price collapsed and the market finally became workably competitive, albeit in the face of quite wildly fluctuating fuel prices.

Before that price collapse, however, OFFER remained concerned about the persistence of market power in the wholesale market, despite all the divestment. To address that, it pressed to abolish the Pool and replace it by a bilateral energy-only market (that is, one without an explicit capacity payment), termed the New Electricity Trading Arrangements (NETA). Generators would have to contract with buyers to submit a balanced physical position to the system operator by gate closure (initially four hours, then one hour before dispatch). The argument, noted above, was that fully contracting removes the incentive to manipulate the spot market. To encourage full contracting, imbalances were settled through the balancing mechanism (not a market) at penal buy-or-sell prices (depending whether the agent was short or long). This was enthusiastically accepted by the Big Six who were now vertically integrated. They were effectively already hedged internally with little need to trade bilaterally, while the illiquidity of such trading over the counter and the penal balancing mechanism helpfully deterred entry. Newbery (1998) criticized the proposed reforms then under discussion, while Bower (2002), Evans and Green (2003) and Newbery (2005a) argued that by 2001 they were redundant because of the pre-existing development of competition. Ofgem estimated that market participants could incur total costs of up to £580 million in implementing NETA over the first five years.[6] In a careful econometric study, Giulietti, Grossi and Waterson (2010) examined the impact of NETA on final consumer prices, which include retail margins and other (unchanged) costs in addition to wholesale prices. They find a sharp increase in the retail margins in England and Wales compared to Scotland, where NETA was not introduced until later, strongly suggesting that NETA raised retail margins. The new market design made entry by retailers lacking generation much riskier as they now had no Pool reference price on which to contract.

It has taken nearly 400 modifications to make the balancing mechanism fit for purpose and closer to a single price balancing market.[7] It took a further major reform of the electricity market in the Energy Act 2013 (House of Commons [HoC] 2013) to restore a capacity market and address other market failures (Newbery 2012, 2016a). The resulting Electricity Market Reform (EMR in Figure 6.1) made the market reasonably efficient in the eyes of the CMA (2016). After over a decade, some of the virtues of the original Pool, with its single price, liquidity for contracting, ease of entry and a scarcity element in the form of a capacity payment, were once again realized (Grubb and Newbery 2018).

5. POOLS, CENTRAL DISPATCH, CAPACITY PAYMENTS OR ENERGY-ONLY MARKETS?

The CEGB was centrally dispatched and the newly restructured market design in England and Wales retained central dispatch (using the CEGB's dispatch algorithm) but created a Pool with a capacity payment. The logic of this structure was sound for a competitive market. The Pool set the total price in a half-hour as:

$$Price = (1 - LoLP) \times SMC + LoLP \times VoLL \qquad (6.1)$$

where LoLP is the loss of load probability in that half-hour and VoLL is the value of lost load.[8] The first term in equation (6.1) is the energy price assuming adequate capacity, which applies a fraction $(1 - LoLP)$ of the time, while the second part is the rationing value to consumers when there is inadequate capacity, occurring a fraction LoLP of the time. The efficient wholesale price can also be written as the sum of the system marginal cost (SMC) plus a capacity payment, CP, which, from equation (6.1), is:

$$CP = LoLP \times (VoLL - SMC) \tag{6.2}$$

The wholesale price would be efficient if, as in the Single Electricity Market of the island of Ireland, generators were required to bid their marginal cost, but not in the duopoly market of the early Pool. Instead, the price in equation (6.2) is determined by the SMP, possibly considerably above SMC.

The capacity payment was paid to all power plants declared available the day ahead but the duopoly gamed this by withdrawing some of the plants day ahead to increase scarcity and hence the LoLP and capacity payment, then declaring them available to collect the manipulated capacity payment (Newbery 2005a). OFFER responded to this blatant manipulation by not excluding any unavailable plant in the calculation of LoLP for the first eight days (even if the plants were genuinely unavailable and caused scarcity). This market manipulation strengthened OFFER's resolve to abolish capacity payments, which it did in the 2001 move to the energy-only market of NETA. Under NETA, owners decided whether to make plant available, were responsible for finding buyers and, if operating, were required to make offers and bids into the balancing mechanism that the system operator would use to balance the system after gate closure.

Figure 6.1 shows the massive entry of gas-fired CCGTs and the improved availability of nuclear power. As a result, the market had a large reserve margin. This is further exemplified in Figure 6.4, which gives plant load (capacity) factors from 1989/90. Nuclear availability increased after privatization but fell soon after it went into administration in 2002 before an eventual resale to EDF in 2009. Both coal and CCGT were well below their auction de-rating factors of 88 per cent.[9] The balance between coal and gas output was driven by relative fuel and, later, carbon prices. Later declines also reflect growing renewables penetration.

Capacity payments would have been redundant in an oversupplied market, as the LoLP would remain close to zero all the time, but as the decade after NETA wore on, concerns over the life expectancy of ageing coal and nuclear plants emerged, strengthened by tightening emissions controls under first the EU Large Combustion Plant Directive and then the Industrial Emissions Directive, and the perceived difficulty of life extensions for the nuclear fleet. It was expected that some 12 GW of the older coal-fired plant (about 20 per cent of peak demand) would close by 2015 and an additional 6.3 GW of nuclear plant by 2016. In the event, nuclear plant was granted life extensions so that at the end of 2017 nuclear capacity was 9.36 GW compared to 9.91 GW at the end of 2013 (DUKES 2018, Table 5.7).

An energy-only market might address this looming scarcity if everyone were confident that future generators would be allowed to extract scarcity value in tight periods, and that all investment in new capacity were based on the same expectations and relied on the same wholesale price. Without futures markets to lock in such scarcity prices, and knowing the political pressures to restrain high prices, it must be doubtful that an energy-only market would deliver adequate reliability.

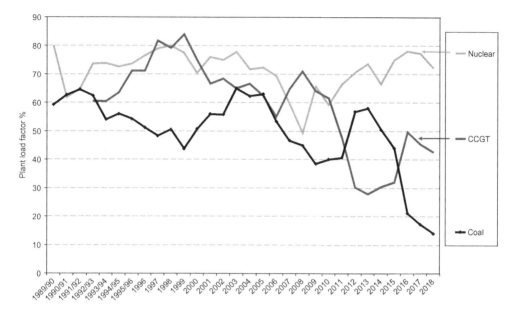

Source: DUKES, various years.

Figure 6.4 Plant load factors by fuel type 1989–2018

In addition, the UK had signed up to a challenging share of renewable energy under the EU's Renewables Directive (2009/28/EC).[10] Variable energy sources such as wind and solar photovoltaic (PV) require considerably more flexible and controllable (effectively fossil-fuel-fired) plants to maintain security of supply. The ageing stock of large coal plants and first-generation CCGTs would be inadequate, requiring new investment. However, the British electricity market was not attractive – prices would not cover fixed costs, futures markets to signal future higher scarcity prices were lacking and government energy policy was in disarray, with three energy white papers published between 2003 and 2007. In 2008, the UK Climate Change Act 2008[11] was passed to provide the legal framework for ensuring that government meets its climate change commitments. The electricity sector would bear the brunt of decarbonization, mostly through renewables (nuclear power was lagging and seen as excessively expensive). Renewables support policy oscillated between auctioned contracts in the 1990s, to a premium payment under the Renewables Obligation Scheme and small-scale feed-in tariffs (FiTs). All, except the overly generous FiTs, under-delivered relative to the target. Investors, looking at the price-depressing effects of massive renewables in Germany (Hirth 2018), and concerned that the UK government would need to accelerate its renewables programme, were increasingly worried about the profitability of any conventional generation investment.

The wide range of criticisms, notably from Ofgem (2010), that the market was not likely to deliver secure, sustainable and affordable electricity, finally provoked the government to publish a white paper (Department of Energy and Climate Change [DECC] 2011). That set out an intellectually coherent basis for electricity market reform. After extensive consultation and parliamentary debate, this package was finally enacted as the Energy Act 2013 (HoC 2013).

The lack of a credible carbon price would be addressed by a Carbon Price Floor, enacted by HM Treasury in the Budget in March 2011 (HM Treasury 2011). Fossil fuels used to generate electricity would be taxed through the Carbon Price Support (CPS) to bring the minimum price of CO_2 up to 16 £/tonne (t) in 2013, rising linearly to 30 £/t in 2020, and projected to rise to 70 £/t by 2030 (all at 2009 prices).[12] As any tax (such as the CPS) could be changed at each Budget, the commitment to decarbonizing was under-pinned by an Emissions Performance Standard of 450 grams of CO_2 per kilowatt-hour (g/kWh) 'at base load' (that is, averaged over the year and effectively a cap per kW of capacity), for any new plant, set to rule out any new coal stations without carbon capture and storage (CCS) capability. This is discussed below in Section 5.2.

To accelerate renewables investment and to lower its cost by de-risking revenue streams, the Renewables Obligation (RO) scheme would be phased out and replaced by a contract-for-differences support (described as a CfD with FiT). A CfD offers a guaran-teed (and price-indexed) strike price for 15 years, with the holder receiving (or paying) the difference between a reference day-ahead market price and the strike price. In con-trast to a standard CfD that specifies the volume on which the payments are made, this would apply to the actual delivery to the grid (hence, it had FiT-like characteristics). The question of how best to support renewables will be addressed in Section 6.

The final element was a capacity payment, marking an end to the energy-only market that the EU had contemporaneously set out in the EU Third Package. The Target Electricity Model (European Parliament 2009) came into effect in 2014. A capacity auction for unsupported plant (that is, existing and new fossil-fuel generation) would determine the payment required to make new investment financeable, or to keep existing plant operating. New entry would have 15-year contracts, while existing plant a one-year contract (major refurbishments could claim a three-year contract). The case for a capac-ity payment is that it addresses both a 'missing money' and a 'missing market' problem (Newbery 2016a). The lack of sufficiently far forward futures markets to sell electricity puts revenue streams at the mercy of unstable energy policies that can undermine the market (for example, renewables targets and support). Without adequate remuneration for the new flexibility services needed by massive renewable penetration, there can be a missing money problem as well, although this terminology has normally pointed to the problems of price-capped markets.

5.1   The GB Capacity Market

The GB Capacity Market offers 15-year capacity agreements for new plant provided they have connected their plant by the start of the electricity year (April–March), four years after the four-year-ahead T-4 auction held in December. The successful plant must be available for dispatch in 'stress' periods announced four hours ahead, with penalties for failures to connect or deliver. Existing plants could also bid into the same auction and receive the same clearing price but only for the first year, or they could wait until the auction held one year ahead of delivery (T-1). The auction was designed after careful study of the US experience and was a pay-as-clear descending clock auction with a single price for the whole of GB (despite the presence of a potentially significant constraint on the Scottish border). The issue of the interaction of transmission constraints and capacity payments will be considered further below.

The auction was expected to clear at the net cost of new entry (CoNE) of 49 £/kilowatt year (kWyr) (based on a new CCGT and net of all the other revenue earned in energy and ancillary service markets). The auction demand schedule has a kink at the target capacity to procure at this level and a cap of 1.5 times net CoNE, reaching zero 1.5 GW above target. Existing plants cannot bid higher than 0.5 times net CoNE without obtaining an exemption. National Grid as system operator was charged with determining the amount of capacity to procure needed to meet the government's reliability standard of three hours loss of load expectation (LoLE, averaged over many years),[13] and to advise the minister who makes the final decision (see, for example, National Grid 2014).

The relationship between the security standard and the VoLL is symmetric in that if capacity investment decisions are based on revenues determined by equation (6.2) and the VoLL is pre-determined, then the resulting capacity will give rise to a LoLE. Zachary and Wilson ([2015] 2019) show that the optimal capacity to procure is such that *LoLE = netCoNE/VoLL*. As National Grid estimated net CoNE at 49 £/kWyr and LoLE was required to be 3 hrs/yr, the required VoLL is 17 £/kWh. The government also commissioned a study of the VoLL from London Economics (2013), which rather undermined the required VoLL of 17 £/kWh. A more plausible and lower value of VoLL would argue for a less reliable standard. The Single Electricity Market of the island of Ireland has an LoLE of 8 hrs/yr and a VoLL of about 12 €/kWh, although a higher net CoNE of 74.12 €/kWyr in 2017, again roughly internally consistent.[14]

The Department of Energy and Climate Change (DECC) responsible for managing the EMR and the capacity auction appointed an independent Panel of Technical Experts (PTE) to comment on the system operator's analysis of the amount of capacity to procure.[15] They noted (DECC 2014) that there is a bias towards over-procurement in that the system operator stands accountable if 'the lights go out' but does not pay for the capacity, while the minister wishes to avoid newspaper headlines predicting blackouts resulting from his decision. Newbery and Grubb (2015) set out the argument in more detail.

The first auction appeared to be highly successful in that it cleared at 19.40 £/kWyr (40 per cent of the estimated net CoNE). However, the success was short-lived as the major entrant was a firm offering two large CCGTs (total 1.6 GW) that failed to secure funding and shortly thereafter withdrew, leading to DECC increasing the penalty for failure to build. The PTE had also criticized the analysis for assuming no contribution from interconnectors, despite many reports commissioned by the government claiming that interconnectors contributed to security of supply. Arguably, the failure to include their contribution more or less balanced out the exit of the CCGTs. Shortly thereafter, the Directorate-General for Competition of the European Commission required interconnectors to be allowed to bid into the capacity auction. Interconnectors were successful in the early 2018/19 auction held to remedy the exit of the CCGTs. Grubb and Newbery (2018) describe the results of the first six capacity auctions in more detail.

The other entrants were small gas or diesel reciprocating engines (average size 10 MW) connecting to the distribution networks, rather than the high-tension grid. They depressed the auction clearing price as they received a distorted 'embedded benefit' as the avoided payment to the transmission grid of local connections. Almost all this payment was to recover the fixed costs of the transmission grid, rather than the avoided cost of actually using the network. This avoided payment of about 50 £/kWyr gives distribution-connected generation an effective capacity payment of 70 £/kWyr rather than 20 £/kWyr for a transmission-connected plant. It took the regulator, Ofgem, three years to remove this 'embedded benefit' payment.[16]

Just as the capacity auctions appeared to be bedding down as an efficient and credible way of procuring the right kind of capacity to deliver reliability and flexibility, the EU's General Court annulled the earlier decision of the European Commission to approve the GB Capacity Market on 15 November 2018.[17] In 2014, Tempus Energy complained that the auctions failed to give equal treatment to new investment to deliver demand-side response (DSR) by denying Tempus Energy the 15-year indexed contract offered to generation. The UK government had little choice but to suspend all capacity payments and the 2018 December auction. Fortunately, on 28 October 2019, the European Commission found the GB Capacity Market to be in line with EU state aid rules, restoring the status quo. The island of Ireland had avoided this asymmetry and to date has been allowed to continue its capacity auctions.

5.2   Climate Change Policy: Budgets and the Carbon Price Support

The UK has taken a lead on climate change mitigation, driven in part by dissatisfaction with the EU Emissions Trading System (ETS). The ETS seemed systemically unable to deliver an adequate, credible and durable carbon price to guide the required low-carbon and very long-lasting power sector investments needed to meet the EU's 2050 carbon targets. In 2008, the UK Parliament passed the Climate Change Act 2008 (HoC 2008), which sets legally binding carbon targets, the latest of which, the Fifth Carbon Budget for 2028–32, commits the UK to reduce emissions by 57 per cent from 1990 (Committee on Climate Change [CCC], 2015). In the electricity sector, the main instrument for delivering the target has been the Carbon Price Floor (CPF) described above, which is implemented by announcing the Carbon Price Support (CPS) in autumn budgets – an additional carbon tax on fuels burned in power stations that is added to the EU ETS Allowance (EUA) price. Figure 6.5 shows the CPF, the EUA price, the CPS, and their sum, shown as the GB price, all in nominal terms.[18]

Figure 6.5 also illustrates the dramatic effect of the implementation of the EU Market Stability Reserve (MSR) in November 2017 (European Council 2017). The MSR cancels surplus allowances from 2023 and makes carbon reductions more attractive, driving up the EUA price (Newbery, Reiner and Ritz 2019). The GB carbon price for electricity is now at or above the original CPF, although how long the CPS will remain at its current, now quite high level, will depend both on the evolution of the EUA price and Britain's future role in EU climate change policy.

The effect of the CPS has been dramatic, moving coal plants from being the cheapest and hence running on baseload, to more costly than all but the oldest CCGTs. Figure 6.1 shows the resulting decline in coal, which fell from 41 per cent in 2013 to 8 per cent in 2018. The CPS also raises the price of electricity in GB, by roughly 15.7 £/MWh when coal is setting the price and by 6 £/MWh if CCGTs set the price, making imports more attractive. Thus, if coal were at the margin 60 per cent of the time and gas 30 per cent of the time, the price might rise by 11 £/MWh, although competition from abroad might reduce that somewhat.

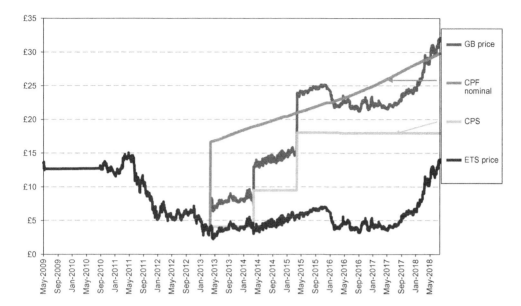

Source: European Energy Exchange.

Figure 6.5   Evolution of the European Allowance (EUA) price for 1 tonne of CO_2 and CPF

As GB was already mostly importing electricity over its interconnectors to the Netherlands and France, the CPS merely made this even more attractive. However, Figure 6.6 shows that before the CPS reached its current level of 18 £/t CO_2, GB was mainly exporting to the Single Electricity Market of the island of Ireland, as its fuel prices were higher than in GB. After the March 2015 rise in the CPS, prices in GB normally exceeded those in the SEM, reducing exports and increasing imports from their previous very low level.

Chyong, Guo and Newbery (2019) have studied the implications of the GB CPS in depth, looking at its impact in reducing emissions in the short run, as well as the emission reductions from wind in the short and long run. They find that an extra MWh of wind output resulting from a long-run increase in wind capacity reduces coal output by 0.63 MWh and gas (CCGT) output by 0.37 MWh, leading to a saving of 0.68 t CO_2 when the CPS is 18 £/t CO_2 and fuel prices were those of 2016. If instead there had been no CPS and just the EUA price of 6 £/t CO_2, coal would fall by 0.32 MWh, gas by 0.67 MWh and emissions by 0.51 t CO_2 in response to 1 MWh of wind output.

6.   SUPPORTING RENEWABLES: SUCCESSES AND REMAINING PROBLEMS[19]

Newbery (2016b) sets out a brief history of UK renewable electricity policy, which has come almost full circle since 1989 when the industry was privatized. At that date, the

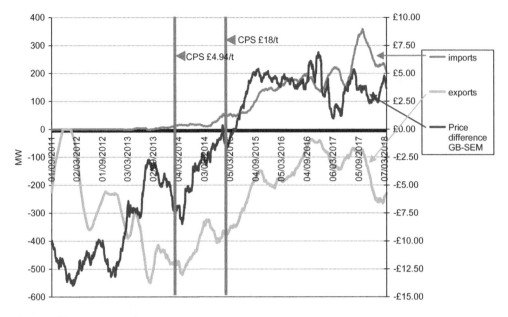

Source: Elexon.

Figure 6.6   GB exports and imports with SEM (both Moyle and East West Interconnectors), 2011–18

government imposed a Fossil Fuel Levy on fossil generation to finance nuclear decommissioning. The European Commission insisted that this support be made available to all zero-carbon generation, including renewables. A Non-Fossil Fuel Obligation (NFFO) was placed on electricity supply companies in the Electricity Act 1989, requiring them to buy a certain amount of nuclear or renewable electricity at a premium price. Support for renewables was provided through NFFO auctions for effectively FiTs (Mitchell 2000).

The early NFFO auctions demonstrated their power of price discovery and competition in driving down costs and prices, although later the winner's curse (combined with the absence of any penalty for failure to deliver) led to under-procurement and disillusionment. The auctioned FiT contracts were replaced in the Utilities Act 2000, which changed the NFFO price obligation into a quantity obligation. Renewables would be given a form of premium FiTs, called Renewables Obligation Certificates (ROCs). The amount suppliers had to procure was set annually and shortfalls were charged at a penalty rate, the revenue from which was recycled to augment the value of ROCs. The value of ROCs varied somewhat with supply and demand, although they can be banked, reducing their variability. The main problem in financing renewables is that the future price of electricity, on top of which the ROC value is added, is itself highly volatile, and hard to hedge more than a year or two ahead. In contrast to gas-fired generation, which by setting the price has a natural hedge, renewables are exposed to the full price volatility.

As noted above, the Energy Act 2013 phased out ROCs for new generation from 2017 (although previously accredited generators will continue to receive support for 20 years until the scheme closes in 2037). ROCs were replaced by CfDs, which required all but small-scale renewables to be marketed at the wholesale price. They receive a top-up equal to the excess of their contracted strike price over a reference market price (or, if the market price is above the strike price, the developer must pay back the excess). This exposes renewables to imbalance risk, although they can avoid that by contracting with other utilities at a discount on the contract price.

Initially, the strike price was set administratively, but the PTE in their first report (DECC 2013) criticized the high strike prices for the 15-year renewables contracts. That, amplified by pressure from the EU Commission's concerns over state aids, led to periodic auctions. Newbery (2016b) used the clearing prices to estimate that the fixed-price contracts for onshore wind lowered the cost of financing investments (their weighted average cost of capital or WACC) by 3 per cent real compared to the previous ROCs.

In the meantime, the government had won an election with a promise to remove support for the now remarkably competitive onshore wind (Grubb and Newbery 2018). Subsequent auctions have excluded onshore wind and solar PV, but auctions for offshore wind resulted in even more dramatic cost reductions. Prices fell from an administered price of 155 £/MWh for the first offshore wind farm, to 120 £/MWh in the Round 1 auction (East Anglia One, 714 MW, delivery 2020), and then to 57.50 £/MWh in Round 2 (Hornsea II, 1386 MW, delivery 2022). Figure 6.7 shows the EU countries that have added the largest amounts of renewable generation by output since 2006, where the UK is second behind Germany.

While the auctions for all technologies, and the commitment to offshore wind in particular, have delivered remarkable cost reductions, the form of support that raises output prices has distorted location decisions. A better solution would be to run an auction for the premium to be paid for the first 20 000 (or 30 000) full operating hours (MWh/MW installed capacity). This would provide an investment subsidy (as required by the EU Clean Energy Package)[20] for the purchase and installation of the renewable generation. It would direct support to the source of the learning spillovers that arise from the development, manufacture and installation, and not from subsequent operation. The subsidy design requires the plant to operate successfully to secure the full subsidy but pays for the electricity generated at its value (which might require adjustment if the carbon price is below its correct level). The present payment per MWh amplifies the apparent advantage of locating in windy (or sunny) locations, even where these incur higher transmission costs. Locating wind farms in Scotland has resulted in a huge increase in costly offshore grid investments. These offshore 'bootstrap' connections might, under the original incremental cost formula for determining transmission charges, have doubled the charges for North Scotland generation (including wind) but the published tariffs have hardly changed from 2017/18 (before the Western Bootstrap transmission cable was commissioned in March 2018) to 2019/20.

Another criticism is that each EU Member State supports renewables within its territory, rather than where it could be delivered most cost-effectively (Booz et al. 2013; Green et al. 2016). A more efficient use of resources would be for each Member State to contribute an agreed sum (for example, as a percentage of GDP, per MWh consumed, or per tonne of CO_2 released) to a fund. This would hold EU-wide competitive auctions (perhaps with a share designated for R&D) to deliver the learning benefits at least cost.

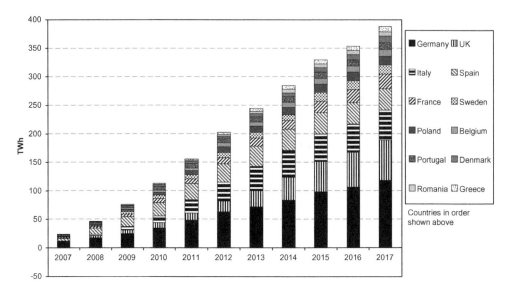

Note: RES-E refers to the electricity generated from clean energy sources such as PV, hydro, tidal/wave, wind, geothermal and renewable biomass.

Source: Eurostat.

Figure 6.7   EU renewable generation added since 2006

It would be hard to secure political consent for this, as it touches on tax and finance, always sensitive issues. The out-turn in which Germany has led the way and made major contributions to cost reductions could also be defended, although the cost to German consumers has been considerable. A more efficient support system might have resulted in less capacity built to meet the output target, which would have created less learning spillover, but if these spillovers had been recognized, it might have led to more ambitious targets and support.

7.   REGULATION: SUCCESSES AND PROBLEMS

Transmission and distribution networks are natural monopolies and as such need regulation if they are to be owned by profit-maximizing private utilities (Newbery 2000). The UK pioneered price-cap regulation with the privatization of BT, the state-owned telephone monopoly. The regulator sets a base-weighted price index for the various goods and services offered, indexed to the Retail Price Index, P_t, but subject to a productivity improvement at rate X – hence the short-hand RPI-X. Armstrong, Cowan and Vickers (1994) describe this in more detail and provide the rationale for the price basket. Thus, for product j the price p_{jt} and the resulting quantity sold, q_{jt}, at date t years after the price control at date 0 must satisfy:

$$\Sigma p_{jt}q_{j0} \leq \Sigma p_{j0}q_{j0} \left(P_t/(P_0(1 + X)^t)\right) \tag{6.3}$$

In addition, and especially important for capital-intensive network utilities, the regulator has a duty to ensure that efficiently incurred investment is properly remunerated, so that banks and shareholders are willing to finance the planned investment. This is done by starting with an initial regulatory asset base or value (RAB_0) to which is added the approved investment, I_t at date t, and deducting the depreciation, D_t, to give the updated RAB:

$$RAB_t = RAB_0 + I_t - D_t \qquad (6.4)$$

The regulator then determines the WACC to apply to the RAB and includes this in the revenue that the utility can recover (capital expenditure – Capex) in addition to operating costs (operating expenditure – Opex).

Price controls are normally for five years (a recent experiment to set an eight-year term was considered too long). The utility submits its business plan setting out its evolution of Opex and its investment plan, I_t. The regulator can (and does) benchmark the Opex against comparable utilities (easy when there are 14 distribution network companies, hard when there is a single transmission company) and sets two critical parameters, P_0 and X. The initial level of the price control, P_0, will be set based on the revised business plan that the regulator finally accepts after inviting consultants to pore over it. X is set to gradually catch up with the frontier (most efficient) comparator.

With a price cap, all the cost reductions relative to expectations accrue to the utility until clawed back at the next price control, providing strong incentives to cut costs. This incentive to cut costs must not be at the expense of reduced quality or reliability, so a large part of this form of incentive regulation has become to set and monitor service standards with penalties for breaches, such as interruptions to service.

This form of regulation has worked reasonably well in driving down costs and has improved reliability and quality, although utilities have earned more than the WACC and typically invested less than their business plans. Ajayi, Anaya and Pollitt (2018) look at 27 years of regulatory experience of the electricity networks since privatization in 1990–91. They find a total factor productivity growth in distribution networks of about 1 per cent per annum (higher before the financial crisis of 2008, negative after) and a worse performance for transmission (in both cases ignoring the value of the quality improvement). They suspect that low productivity reflects government objectives of increased renewables that will have raised investment needs without increasing conventional measure of network outputs.

Figure 6.8 shows the early experience of the distribution network utilities, where they submitted forecasts of their planned investment (Pollitt and Dale, 2018 give more up-to-date investment data). The regulator revised these down and then the utilities outperformed (or succeeded in misleading the regulator). The problem is that the main cost of networks lies in enhancing and maintaining its capital, but there is no obvious benchmark for efficient investment. It is difficult to measure the current state of the assets and what upgrades, replacements or extensions are justified in each different region. Various attempts have been made to reduce the information asymmetry between utility and regulator, and to subject investment to similar incentives as Opex. In 2010, 20 years after RPI-X in the energy sector, Ofgem introduced RIIO, short for Revenue = Incentives + Innovation + Outputs. Opex and Capex are combined into Totex, and subject to

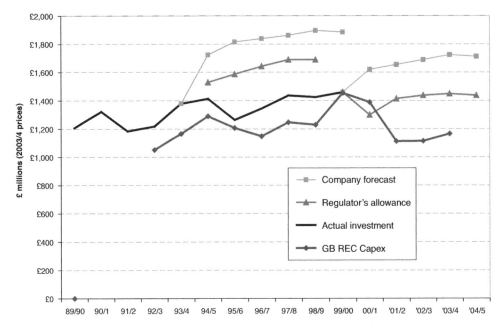

Source: Newbery (2005b).

Figure 6.8   The game between the utility and regulator in submitting business plans

incentive regulation, with innovation now playing an important role as explained in the next section.

7.1   Ofgem's Network Innovation Competitions

A regulated utility has little incentive to innovate as, if it succeeds in reducing cost, the regulator will likely reduce prices at the next price control, while if it fails, the cost of the innovation will be deemed unjustified and hence not compensated. To counter this, Ofgem originally had a modest Innovation Funding Incentive (IFI), replaced by a Network Innovation Allowance in 2013,[21] but the major change in scale came in 2010 when Ofgem introduced its Low Carbon Network Fund (LCNF) for electricity network companies, and then extended this to Gas and Electricity Network Innovation Competitions. In contrast to the earlier schemes, the LCNF was a competition, with potentially losers as well as winners. The original LCNF sum of up to £500 million for the period 1 April 2010 to 31 March 2015 was financed by a levy on consumers and had to offer the prospect of reducing future consumer bills by more than this sum. Ofgem commissioned Pöyry (2016) to evaluate the programme.[22] Pöyry concluded that 'the potential future net-benefit from the LCNF projects is significant and is estimated to range from 4.5 to 6.5 times the cost of funding the scheme' (p. 2). The benefits are passed on to consumers by setting future price controls for network utilities on the assumption that they will adopt proven better value solutions identified by these competitions. One of the main benefits has been to embed an innovative culture in the management of these utilities, whose professional pride depends on winning projects in the annual competition.

7.2 Tariff Setting

Tariffs are important in guiding efficient location and use decisions, as transmission and distribution tariffs make up 25 per cent of the domestic bill, compared to just 33 per cent for the wholesale electricity cost.[23] Ideally, they should be fair, efficient and cost-reflective – aims that can conflict. The variable or short-run marginal cost (SRMC) of using a network is either almost zero or a scarcity price if the network is fully used (which is rarely the case). The efficient price is as in equation (6.1), the sum of the SRMC and a capacity or scarcity payment that will be zero most of the time. The private owners of the grid need to receive the average cost, far above the SRMC. The shortfall in revenue is akin to a tax, for which public economics lays out good design principles. Ramsey/ Boiteux pricing argues that this shortfall in revenue or tax should be concentrated on the least elastic demands – for example, through a fixed charge for access. More exactly, the mark-up on SRMC should lead to equal proportionate reductions in all uses. Peak demand pricing if there is scarcity is the first element, then charging for access or capacity rather than use follows next. The tension is that the results may not be considered fair or equitable, but this can be addressed with multi-part tariffs. For low demands, a mark-up on the energy cost can be added, which, once it reaches a level that covers a suitable fixed cost, can be replaced by a two-part tariff with a fixed and variable (energy) charge.[24]

Domestic energy bills have a very low fixed charge and quite a high energy mark-up, which over-encourages self-production (and efficiency, which, if misperceived, may correct a behavioural bias). Industrial and large customers pay a triad charge, levied on the three system peak half-hours (separated by ten days), an apparently closer approximation to an efficient charge. The main distortion is that distribution companies pay this to the transmission company at their off-take point, and until recently compensated those who supplied electricity to the distribution network at the avoided Transmission Network Use of System Charge. This massively distorted location decisions for new capacity bidding into the capacity auction, as described above. Ofgem finally reformed this 'embedded benefit' in 2017.[25]

8. NEW NUCLEAR – THE FINANCING PROBLEM

Taylor (2016) charts the sorry development of British Energy under private ownership. The collapse of electricity prices precipitated by an outbreak of competition in an over-supplied market pushed the company into insolvency in December 2002 when it failed to renegotiate its reprocessing contracts with the state-owned BNFL. The then Labour government had members actively hostile to nuclear power, but others recognized that to address climate change post-Kyoto would require active decarbonization of electricity. Replacing ageing nuclear stations with gas would raise emissions, exactly the wrong direction to decarbonization. After a series of reports on nuclear power from 2003 to 2008 (documented in Taylor, 2016), the Labour government published a white paper (Department for Business Enterprise & Regulatory Reform 2008). Combined with the

Climate Change Act 2008 (HoC 2008), this paved the way for active government support for new nuclear plants. At the same time, the government was trying to sell British Energy, a sale finally completed in early 2009 to EDF, the (largely) state-owned French nuclear power company.

The first new nuclear project to be considered under this new regime was Hinkley Point C (HPC), which had been actively considered as the second pressurized water reactor (PWR) station under the CEGB in the 1980s – the first, Sizewell B, was finally commissioned after privatization in 1995. EDF started public consultations in 2008 and finally signed a contract with the UK government in October 2013 for a stated cost of £16 billion, or 5 million £/MW – a record. The final investment decision was taken in 2016 for planned completion in 2025.

Taylor (2016, p. 167) notes that the state aid approval document by the European Commission estimated the maximum full cost with financing and contingencies as £24 billion, or 50 per cent more. The cost was high partly as none of the same European pressurized reactor (EPR) design under construction were anywhere near completion and had huge cost over-runs, and partly as the government insisted that all the construction risk lay with the private company. That is about the most expensive form of risk sharing imaginable (as the National Audit Office then made clear; NAO 2017). The project was to be financed by a CfD lasting 35 years at a strike price of 92.50 £/MWh in 2013 pound purchasing power. That might have seemed reasonable compared to renewables at the time, but is more than twice the cost of the auctioned offshore wind in Round Two in 2017.

It gradually became clearer to everyone that this was not the right way to finance new nuclear power. Many took the view that it was an argument against financing any new nuclear power. No private company has ever successfully completed a nuclear power station without substantial government or regulatory financial guarantees. HPC is no exception, only unusual in the amount of risk placed on the private utility. The most recent assessment by the National Infrastructure Commission in 2018 was to not 'agree support for more than one nuclear power station beyond Hinkley Point C, before 2025'.[26] The argument is that by 2025 the cost of a second (and possibly subsequent) stations should be clearer. There was no reason to rush ahead until the cheapest (full system) cost of zero carbon electricity had been more robustly identified. Since that report, Toshiba has scrapped its plans for a new nuclear station in Cumbria after spending £125 million,[27] while Hitachi pulled out of its new nuclear power plant at Wylfa Newydd (North Wales) in September 2020, although the BBC News on 30 September 2020 reported that 'developer Horizon Nuclear Power has sent two letters to ministers stating talks with other "third parties" are continuing'.[28]

EDF has proposed that the next station should be an almost exact replica of HPC at Sizewell, and that it should be financed by the RAB model described above. This is standard for utilities like water and transmission companies, in which the RAB is rolled forward by adding an agreed flow of investments (and decreased by depreciation of the assets). The finance is made available in line with investment expenditure and a return on the RAB is paid to investors. This allows access to low-cost finance from pension funds. It avoids the uncertainty about when returns will be paid, given the uncertain date of future commissioning, as with HPC. As with other utilities, the allowed investment would be agreed in advance with an oversight authority (for example, the Low Carbon

Contracts Company that acts as counterparty to renewable CfDs).[29] As with other utility investments, incentives in the form of cost or profit sharing with consumers of any cost over- or under-runs would reduce risk and hence lower the cost of capital. Sharing risk over a large number of consumers rather than concentrating it on one company where the asset would be a very large fraction of its market worth would reduce the cost of that risk.

The other model would be for the government to take the construction risk on balance sheet (as with large transport projects like CrossRail or High Speed 2) and finance it at low-cost public sector interest rates, as was standard for the previously nationalized energy companies. The choice between the two models depends on a balance between the public sector's lower cost of finance compared with the remarkably low rates now achieved for RAB financing of other infrastructure projects like the Thames Tideway Tunnel, and the possibility that project management and financial control are better handled by a private company with current experience of building an all but identical project. The objection that it would add to public debt is spurious, as the International Monetary Fund (2018) argues that it is the net wealth (assets less liabilities) that matter, not just one side of the balance sheet. Good investments strengthen, not weaken, net wealth.

9. CONCLUDING REFLECTIONS

The British privatized electricity system is now 30 years old and a good moment to take stock of its successes and weaknesses.[30] The premise of privatization was that private owners would invest and operate more efficiently than state-owned enterprises, and that by escaping the dead hand of ministries of finance (the Treasury in the UK case) they would have access to more investment funds, would choose more cost-effective investments, and would, through board-level and shareholder scrutiny, cease unprofitable activities sooner and respond to new opportunities more quickly. These potential benefits would have to be weighed against the increased cost of private capital and a possible loss of concern over distributional issues and environmental impacts, unless incentivized to take them into account.

Avner Offer (2018) has pointed out that the private sector is well placed to invest where the credit time horizon, defined as the time to pay back the loan, is attractive to private lenders. Roughly speaking, private finance is twice the cost of public finance, so the private payback period (simply computed) is half that of the government. Government guarantees or their regulatory equivalent (such as the US model of rate-of-return regulation underpinned by a constitutionally backed rule of law) can offer reassurances, lower the cost of capital and extend this credit horizon. Offer points out that as telecoms landlines may last a century, they required state-ownership or regulated monopolies to undertake the investment. Mobile telephony has equipment that may be replaced in less than a decade, lending itself to private ownership.

The British electricity supply industry in 1989 was well placed to reap many of the benefits of private ownership and to avoid initially many of the downside costs.[31] Spare capacity avoided the need for costly durable generating capacity and the risk of an inappropriate credit time horizon. The arrival of cheap CCGTs of modest scale, rapid delivery and high efficiency, at a time of falling gas prices, made any such investments lower risk. Even then, such investments needed long-term power purchase agreements and a captive franchise market. The more capital-intensive and durable networks were assured of financeability through licence conditions, obligations on the regulator and a credible dispute resolution process. The RAB form of asset regulation arguably improved on the US model of utility regulation (Gilbert and Newbery 1994). Distributional concerns emerged, and were, with varying degrees of success, met with licence conditions on utilities, low (and distorting) rates of value-added tax on energy, political pressure on the regulator, Competition and Market Authority inquiries (CMA 2016) and price caps. Environmental concerns were met with increasingly stringent emissions standards on pollutants, the ETS, various EU Directives, and in GB the CPS.

Problems emerged when new capital-intensive generation investment was needed, both to meet carbon and renewables targets and to maintain reliability. The ideology of the market initially led to auctions for renewables that were remarkably effective at driving down costs, less so at delivering adequate volumes. The shift to the RO pulled through more delivery but at a high cost of finance. It took over 20 years to learn from experience elsewhere that long-term contracts at assured off-take prices would lower the cost of capital and with it the delivered cost of renewable electricity.

Nuclear power and CCS demonstrated the force of Offer's credit time horizon. No nuclear power station has ever been constructed without strong and credible underwriting from either the government or a utility empowered to pass the cost through to final consumers. Even that model came off the rails in the US after the oil shocks of the 1970s raised inflation and electricity costs. Rate reviews are needed when utility rates need raising. That requires utility commissions to scrutinize costs and investment plans to ensure they are 'just and reasonable'. The Washington Public Power Supply System (WPPSS), aptly nicknamed Whoops, had started on one nuclear plant and had plans for four more, with two units starting in 1977. WPPSS had the right to issue tax-favoured municipal bonds to finance investments without voter approval but a voter initiative in 1981 denied WPPSS the right to issue more bonds. Construction was suspended and eventually only the first reactor was ever completed.[32]

In Britain, as described above, Hinkley Point C has staggered on since before privatization, and only (just) secured its final investment decision after one of the costliest financing arrangements with government guarantees was struck. Given a possible construction period of ten years and a subsequent life of 60 years, followed by possibly centuries of waste management, nuclear power busts Offer's credit time horizon comprehensively. CCS has had an even worse experience, with over a decade of unfulfilled promises to deliver a commercial-scale plant. Even conventional CCGTs now need 15-year capacity payments to encourage investment, so that to a greater or lesser extent all new generation now receives underwritten guarantees by the government.

Critics (for example, Darwell 2015) argue that this reflects a betrayal of the original aims of privatization, while realists (and very belatedly and to a limited extent, the government) argue that durable essential infrastructure like electricity needs access to low-cost finance that only government-backed or guaranteed finance can assure.[33] Perhaps the most useful lesson from privatizing utilities is that the UK has evolved a system of regulating at least part of the infrastructure (the natural monopoly pipes and wires) that works reasonably well and has delivered high levels of investment at modest rates of interest. It would be encouraging to think that the UK can continue to learn how better to finance the necessary capital-intensive zero carbon energy to meet our climate goals in a timely fashion.

NOTES

*   I am indebted to anonymous referees and Mike Waterson and Richard Green for helpful comments.

1. These have been superseded by National Grid, *Electricity Ten Year Statements*, accessed 4 July 2021 at https://www.nationalgrid.com/uk/publications/electricity-ten-year-statement-etys.

2. The HHI is the sum of the squared market shares in percentages, with 10 000 a perfect monopoly, 5000 a symmetric duopoly and above 1800 indicating significant market power.

3. British Energy also imprudently bought one of the divested coal stations and along with other buyers suffered a 50 per cent loss in value after a few months when wholesale prices collapsed.

4. OFFER became Ofgem, the Office of Gas and Electricity Markets, in 1999.

5. The 'Big Six' are Centrica (originally a gas monopolist), SSE plc, RWE npower, E.ON, Scottish Power and EDF Energy (who bought the nuclear stations from the bankrupt British Energy).

6. National Audit Office (2003), 'The new electricity trading arrangements in England and Wales', 9 May, accessed 4 July 2021 at https://www.nao.org.uk/report/the-new-electricity-trading-arrangements-in-eng land-and-wales/.

7. Elexon BCS (2021), 'List of all BSC [Balancing and Settlement Code] modifications', accessed 4 July 2021 at https://www.elexon.co.uk/change/modifications/?show=all.

8. LoLP is roughly negative exponential, $\exp(-am)$, in the margin, m, of available supply less demand; VoLL was reset in 2014 at 17 £/kWh.

9. Plant offering into the capacity auction (discussed below) is de-rated to reflect its expected availability in stress periods. Actual availability will be lower to allow for scheduled maintenance.

10. Directive 2009/28/EC, accessed 4 July 2021 at http://eur-lex.europa.eu/LexUriServ/LexUriServ.do? uri=CELEX:32009L0028:EN:NOT.

11. Climate Change Act 2008, accessed 4 July 2021 at https://www.legislation.gov.uk/ukpga/2008/27/con tents.

12. HM Treasury (2011). The intention was to move towards a carbon price that would make it possible to claim that new nuclear power would not be subsidized.

13. Compare the former CEGB's standard of disconnecting some consumers in three winters over 100 years, decided in 1962 (Bates and Fraser 1974, p. 122). The annual LoLE is the sum of the LoLPs in each hour over the year.

14. See https://www.semcommittee.com/sites/semc/files/media-files/SEM-20-034%20CRM%202024-25%20 T-4%20Capacity%20Auction%20Parameters%20decision%20paper.pdf, accessed 4 July 2021.

15. The author was then a member of the PTE but writes here in his personal capacity, drawing only on published material.

16. See https://www.ofgem.gov.uk/publications/embedded-benefits-impact-assessment-and-decision-indus try-proposals-cmp264-and-cmp265-change-electricity-transmission-charging-arrangements-embedded-generators, accessed 30 June 2021.

17. General Court of the European Union (2018), 'General Court annuls the Commission's decision not to raise objections to the aid scheme establishing a capacity market in the UK', 15 November, accessed 4 July 2021 at https://curia.europa.eu/jcms/jcms/p1_1442288/en/.

18. The CPF only applies to GB, as Northern Ireland was granted an exemption to avoid distorting the Single Electricity Market of the island of Ireland.

19. See also Chapter 15 by Richard Green in this handbook.

20. COM/2016/0860 final, accessed 4 July 2021 at http://eur-lex.europa.eu/legal-content/EN/TXT/?qid=1481 278671064&uri=CELEX:52016DC0860.

21. Ofgem (n.d.), 'RIIO-1 network innovation funding', accessed 4 July 2021 at https://www.ofgem.gov.uk/ electricity/distribution-networks/network-innovation/innovation-funding-incentive.

22. Ofgem (2016) reviews the results of, and learnings from, the supported projects in detail.

23. See https://www.ofgem.gov.uk/energy-data-and-research/data-portal/all-available-charts?keyword=bre akdown%20electricity%20bill&sort=relevance, accessed 13 July 2021. In addition, 23 per cent of the bill is 'environmental and social costs' (that is, effectively taxes to fund renewables, energy efficiency programmes and the like), and 17 per cent is 'operating costs' of the supply companies, including their profit margin and all the costly advertising to persuade customers to switch to and not away from them.

24. See also Chapter 3 in this handbook by Paul Joskow and Thomas-Olivier Léautier.
25. See Ofgem (2018), *Impact Assessment and Decision on Industry Proposals (CMP264 and CMP265) to Change Electricity Transmission Charging Arrangements for Embedded Generators*, accessed 4 July 2021 at https://www.ofgem.gov.uk/publications-and-updates/embedded-benefits-impact-assessment-and-deci sion-industry-proposals-cmp264-and-cmp265-change-electricity-transmission-charging-arrangements-em bedded-generators. Ofgem launched a Targeted Charging Review in August 2017 to examine a wider range of tariff design issues (see Ofgem, 'Targeted Charging Review', accessed 4 July 2021 at https://www. ofgem.gov.uk/publications-and-updates/targeted-charging-review-significant-code-review-launch).
26. See Chapter 2 at https://nic.org.uk/studies-reports/national-infrastructure-assessment/, accessed 30 June 2021.
27. See Vaughan, A. (2018), 'UK nuclear power station plans scrapped as Toshiba pulls out', *The Guardian*, 8 November, accessed 4 July 2021 at https://www.theguardian.com/environment/2018/nov/08/toshiba-uk-nuclear-power-plant-project-nu-gen-cumbria.
28. See World Nuclear News Horizon secures more time for Wylfa planning decision, 01 October 2020, accessed 21 September 2021 at https://world-nuclear-news.org/Articles/Horizon-secures-more-time-for-Wylfa-planning-decis.
29. See Department for Business, Energy & Industrial Energy Policy Paper on Contracts for Difference, accessed 4 July 2021 at https://www.gov.uk/government/publications/contracts-for-difference.
30. See also Chapter 2 by Richard Schmalensee and Chapter 15 by Richard Green in this handbook.
31. Pollitt (2012) discusses the wider lessons from electricity liberalization.
32. See Wikipedia (2020), 'WNP-3 and WNO-5', 18 December, accessed 4 July 2021 at https://en.wikipedia. org/wiki/WNP-3_and_WNP-5.
33. One of the major failings of the post-Thatcher civil service is its declining ability to attract and retain the brightest and best, coupled with excessive rates of staff turnover that makes learning from the past and reaching informed financial decisions increasingly difficult (Sasse and Norris 2019).

REFERENCES

Ajayi, V., K. Anaya and M. Pollitt (2018), *Productivity Growth in Electricity and Gas Networks Since 1990*, report prepared for the Office of Gas and Electricity Markets (OFGEM), revised 21 December, accessed 4 July 2021 at https://www.ofgem.gov.uk/system/files/docs/2019/01/ofgem_productivity_report_dec_2018_1.pdf.
Allaz, B. and J.-L. Vila (1993), 'Cournot competition, forward markets and efficiency', *Journal of Economic Theory*, **59** (1), 1–16.
Armstrong, M., S. Cowan and J. Vickers (1994), *Regulatory Reform – Economic Analysis and British Experience* (Vol. I), Cambridge, MA: MIT Press.
Bates, R. and N. Fraser (1974), *Investment Decisions in the Nationalised Fuel Industries*, Cambridge: Cambridge University Press.
Boiteux, M. (1949), 'La tarification des demandes en pointe: application de la théorie de la vente au coût marginal', *Revue Générale de l'Electricité*, **58**, 321–40.
Booz & Company, D. Newbery and G. Strbac et al. (2013), *Final Report: Benefits of an Integrated European Energy Market*, prepared for Directorate-General Energy, European Commission, accessed 4 July 2021 at https://ec.europa.eu/energy/sites/default/files/documents/20130902_energy_integration_benefits.pdf.
Bower, J. (2002), 'Why did electricity prices fall in England and Wales? Market mechanism or market structure?', Oxford Institute for Energy Studies, EL 02, accessed 4 July 2021 at https://www.oxforden ergy.org/publications/why-did-electricity-prices-fall-in-england-and-wales-market-mechanism-or-market-structure/.
Chyong, K., B. Guo and D. M. Newbery (2019), 'The impact of a carbon tax on the CO_2 emissions reduction of wind', *EPRG Working Paper 1904*, Energy Policy Research Group, University of Cambridge, accessed 4 July 2021 at https://www.eprg.group.cam.ac.uk/category/working-papers-2019/.
Committee on Climate Change CCC (2015), *Fifth Carbon Budget – The Next Step Towards a Low-carbon Economy*, November 2015, accessed 4 July 2021 at https://d423d1558e1d71897434.b-cdn.net/wp-content/ uploads/2015/11/Committee-on-Climate-Change-Fifth-Carbon-Budget-Report.pdf.
Competition and Markets Authority CMA (2016), *Energy Market Investigation: Final Report*, 24 June, accessed 4 July 2021 at https://assets.publishing.service.gov.uk/media/5773de34e5274a0da3000113/final-report-en ergy-market-investigation.pdf.
Darwell, R. (2015), *Central Planning with Market Features: How Renewable Subsidies Destroyed the UK Electricity Market*, Centre for Policy Studies, accessed 4 July 2021 at http://euanmearns.com/renewable-energy-the-most-expensive-policy-disaster-in-modern-british-history/.

Department for Business, Energy & Industrial Strategy (2020), 'Historical electricity data: 1920 to 2019', accessed 9 November 2020 at https://www.gov.uk/government/statistical-data-sets/historical-electricity-data.

Department for Business Enterprise & Regulatory Reform (2008), *Meeting the Energy Challenge: A White Paper on Nuclear Power*, CM 7296, accessed 4 July 2021 at https://www.gov.uk/government/uploads/system/uploads/attachment_data/file/228944/7296.pdf.

Department of Energy and Climate Change (DECC) (2011), *Planning Our Electric Future: A White Paper for Secure, Affordable and Low-carbon Electricity*, July 2011, accessed 4 July 2021 at https://assets.publishing.service.gov.uk/government/uploads/system/uploads/attachment_data/file/48129/2176-emr-white-paper.pdf.

Department of Energy and Climate Change (DECC) (2013), *Annex F: EMR Panel of Technical Experts Final Report for DECC*, July 2013, accessed 9 November 2020 at https://www.gov.uk/government/uploads/system/uploads/attachment_data/file/223656/emr_consultation_annex_f.pdf.

Department of Energy and Climate Change (DECC) (2014), *EMR Panel of Technical Experts Final Report on National Grid's Electricity Capacity Report*, June, accessed 9 November 2020 at https://assets.publishing.service.gov.uk/government/uploads/system/uploads/attachment_data/file/324976/EMR_Panel_s_Final_Report_on_National_Grid_s_ECR.pdf.

Digest of UK Energy Statistics (DUKES) (various years), accessed 9 November 2020 at https://www.gov.uk/government/collections/digest-of-uk-energy-statistics-dukes.

Domah, P. and M. G. Pollitt (2001), 'Restructuring and privatisation of electricity distribution and supply businesses in England and Wales: a social cost–benefit analysis', *Fiscal Studies*, **22** (1), 107–46.

European Council (2017), 'Reform of the EU Emissions Trading System – Council endorses deal with Parliament', press release, 22 November, accessed 9 November at https://www.consilium.europa.eu/ro/press/press-releases/2017/11/22/reform-of-the-eu-emissions-trading-system-council-endorses-deal-with-european-parliament/?Page=1.

European Parliament (2009), *Directive 2009/72/EC of the European Parliament and of the Council of 13 July 2009 Concerning Common Rules for the Internal Market in Electricity and Repealing Directive 2003/54/EC*, accessed 4 July 2021 at https://eur-lex.europa.eu/legal-content/EN/ALL/?uri=CELEX%3A32009L0072.

Evans, J. and R. J. Green (2003), 'Why did electricity prices fall after 1998?', *Cambridge Working Papers in Economics CWPE0326*, accessed 4 July 2021 at https://www.repository.cam.ac.uk/bitstream/handle/1810/358/EP26.pdf?sequence=1&isAllowed=y.

Gilbert, R. J. and D. M. Newbery (1994), 'The dynamic efficiency of regulatory constitutions', *Rand Journal of Economics*, **25** (4), 538–54.

Giulietti, M., L. Grossi and M. Waterson (2010), 'Price transmission in the UK electricity market: was NETA beneficial?', *Energy Economics*, **32** (4), 1165–74.

Green, R. J. and D. M. Newbery (1992), 'Competition in the British electricity spot market', *Journal of Political Economy*, **100** (5), 929–53.

Green, R. J., D. Pudjianto, I. Staffell and G. Strbac (2016), 'Market design for long-distance trade in renewable electricity', *The Energy Journal*, **37** (Special Issue), 5–22.

Grubb, M. and D. M. Newbery (2018), 'UK Electricity Market Reform and the energy transition: emerging lessons', *The Energy Journal*, **39** (6), 1–25.

Henney, A. (1987), *Policy Study No. 83: Privatise Power: How to Restructure the Electricity Supply Industry*, London: Centre for Policy Studies.

Henney, A. (1994), *A Study of the Privatisation of the Electricity Supply Industry in England and Wales*, London: EEE Ltd.

Hirth, L. (2018), 'What caused the drop in European electricity prices? A factor decomposition analysis', *The Energy Journal*, **19** (1), 132–57.

HM Treasury (2011), *Budget 2011*, HC 836, March 2011, accessed 4 July 2021 at http://webarchive.national archives.gov.uk/20130105112918/http://cdn.hm-treasury.gov.uk/2011budget_complete.pdf.

House of Commons (HoC) (2008), *Climate Change Act 2008*, accessed 9 November 2020 at http://www.legislation.gov.uk/ukpga/2008/27/contents.

House of Commons (HoC) (2013), *Energy Act 2013*, accessed 9 November 2020 at http://www.legislation.gov.uk/ukpga/2013/32/contents/enacted/data.htm.

International Monetary Fund (IMF) (2018), *Fiscal Monitor: Managing Public Wealth*, October, accessed 9 November 2020 at https://www.imf.org/en/Publications/FM/Issues/2018/10/04/fiscal-monitor-october-2018.

London Economics (2013), *The Value of Lost Load (VoLL) for Electricity in Great Britain*, final report for OFGEM and DECC, July, accessed 4 July 2021 at https://www.gov.uk/government/uploads/system/uploads/attachment_data/file/224028/value_lost_load_electricty_gb.pdf.

Meek, R. L. (1968), 'The new bulk supply tariff for electricity', *The Economic Journal*, **78** (309), 43–66.

Mitchell, C. (2000), 'The England and Wales Non-Fossil Fuel Obligation: history and lessons', *Annual Review of Energy and the Environment*, **25**, 285–312.

National Audit Office (NAO) (2017), *Hinkley Point C*, HC 40, Session 2017-18, 23 June, accessed 9 November 2020 at https://www.nao.org.uk/report/hinkley-point-c/.

National Grid (various years), *GB Seven Year Statements*, accessed 9 November 2020 at https://web.arch ive.org/web/20110606045512/http://www.nationalgrid.com/uk/sys_08/default.asp?sNode=SYS&action=& Exp=Y.

National Grid (various years), *Electricity Ten Year Statements*, accessed 9 November 2020 at https://www. nationalgrid.com/uk/publications/electricity-ten-year-statement-etys.

National Grid (2014), *Electricity Capacity Report*, accessed 9 November 2020 at https://www.endsreport.com/ article/1536244/national-grid-report-national-grid-emr-%E2%80%93-electricity-capacity-report-june-2014.

Newbery, D. M. (1995), 'Power markets and market power', *The Energy Journal*, **16** (3), 41–66.

Newbery, D. M. (1998), 'The regulator's review of the English electricity pool', *Utilities Policy*, **7** (3), 129–41.

Newbery, D. M. (2000), *Privatization, Restructuring and Regulation of Network Utilities*, Cambridge, MA: MIT Press.

Newbery, D. M. (2005a), 'Electricity liberalisation in Britain: the quest for a satisfactory wholesale market design', *The Energy Journal*, **26** (Special Issue), 43–70.

Newbery, D. M. (2005b), 'The regulatory framework for access pricing', in P. Vass (ed.), *Access Pricing, Investment and Efficient Use of Capacity in Network Industries – A Comparative Review of Charging Principles and Structure*, Bath, UK: Centre for the Study of Regulated Industries, pp. 1–46.

Newbery, D. M. (2012), 'Reforming competitive electricity markets to meet environmental targets', *Economics of Energy & Environmental Policy*, **1** (1), 69–82.

Newbery, D. M. (2016a), 'Missing money and missing markets: reliability, capacity auctions and interconnectors', *Energy Policy*, **94**, 401–10.

Newbery, D. M. (2016b), 'Towards a green energy economy? The EU Energy Union's transition to a low-carbon zero subsidy electricity system – lessons from the UK's Electricity Market Reform', *Applied Energy*, **179**, 1321–30.

Newbery, D. M. (2017), 'Tales of two islands – lessons for EU energy policy from electricity market reforms in Britain and Ireland', *Energy Policy*, **105**, 597–607.

Newbery, D. M. and R. J. Green (1996), 'Regulation, public ownership and privatisation of the English electricity industry', in R. J. Gilbert and E. P. Kahn (eds), *International Comparisons of Electricity Regulation*, New York: Cambridge University Press, pp. 25–81.

Newbery, D. M. and M. Grubb (2015), 'Security of supply, the role of interconnectors and option values: insights from the GB Capacity Auction', *Economics of Energy & Environmental Policy*, **4** (2), 65–81.

Newbery, D. M. and M. G. Pollitt (1997), 'The restructuring and privatisation of the CEGB – was it worth it?', *Journal of Industrial Economics*, **XLV** (3), 269–303.

Newbery, D. M., D. Reiner and R. Ritz (2019), 'The political economy of a Carbon Price Floor for power generation', *The Energy Journal*, **40** (1) 1–24.

Offer, A. (2018), 'Patient and impatient capital: time horizons as market boundaries', *Oxford Discussion Papers in Economic and Social History*, **165**, August.

Ofgem (2010), *Project Discovery: Options for Delivering Secure and Sustainable Energy Supplies*, February, accessed 4 July 2021 at https://www.ofgem.gov.uk/ofgem-publications/40354/projectdiscoveryfebcondocfi nal.pdf.

Ofgem (2016), *Summary of the Low Carbon Network Fund Learning*, April, accessed 9 November 2020 at https://www.ofgem.gov.uk/system/files/docs/2016/04/summary_of_low_carbon_networks_fund_learning_1.0. pdf.

Pollitt, M. G. (1998), 'The restructuring and privatization of the electricity supply industry in Scotland', mimeo, June.

Pollitt, M. G. (2012), 'The role of policy in energy transitions: lessons from the energy liberalisation era', *Energy Policy*, **50**, 128–37.

Pollitt, M. G. and L. Dale (2018), 'Restructuring the Chinese electricity supply sector – how industrial electricity prices are determined in a liberalized power market: lessons from Great Britain', *EPRG Working Paper 1839*, Energy Policy Research Group, University of Cambridge, accessed 4 July 2021 at https://www.eprg. group.cam.ac.uk/wp-content/uploads/2018/11/1839-Text.pdf.

Pöyry (2016), *An Independent Evaluation of the LCNF: A Report to Ofgem*, October, accessed 4 July 2021 at https://www.ofgem.gov.uk/system/files/docs/2016/11/evaluation_of_the_lcnf_0.pdf.

Sasse, T. and Norris, E. (2019), *Moving On – The Costs of High Staff Turnover in the Civil Service*, Institute for Government, accessed 4 July 2021 at https://www.instituteforgovernment.org.uk/sites/default/files/publica tions/IfG_staff_turnover_WEB.pdf.

Sweeting, A. (2007), 'Market power in the England and Wales wholesale electricity market 1995–2000', *The Economic Journal*, **117**, 654–85.

Taylor, S. (2007), *Privatization and Financial Collapse in the Nuclear Industry – The Origins and Causes of The British Energy Crisis of 2002*, Abingdon, UK: Routledge.

Taylor, S. (2016), *The Fall and Rise of Nuclear Power in Britain; A History*, Cambridge, UK: UIT Cambridge Ltd.

Zachary, S. and A. Wilson ([2015] 2019), 'Robustness of reliability measures, mimeo', Durham University, subsequently published as Zachary, S., A. Wilson and C. Dent (2019), 'The integration of variable generation and storage into electricity capacity markets', accessed 9 November 2020 at https://arxiv.org/abs/1907.05973.

7. Strengths and weaknesses of the PJM market model

*William W. Hogan**

1. INTRODUCTION

PJM Interconnection, a regional transmission organization in the United States, enjoys iconic status as a major innovator in electricity restructuring. Building on its long history as a major power pool, PJM demonstrated the capability to provide the necessary coordination for competition in electricity markets. The core of the PJM market design, a bid-based-security-constrained-economic-dispatch-with-locational-marginal-prices (BBSCE DLMP) model, works in theory and in practice. It is the only electricity market design that integrates engineering and economics to support efficient markets under the principles of transmission open access and non-discrimination. This market design was eventually adopted in every organized wholesale electricity market in the United States. Development of this market followed a process combining analysis, experimentation and learning. The evolutionary process continues to meet new challenges.

2. BRIEF HISTORY OF THE PJM WHOLESALE POWER POOL

Electric utilities started out local, typically in a single city, and grew. Given the variability of electric load and the diversity of generating plants, it became the norm for interconnection arrangements to share generating, transmission and other resources. The power pool called the Pennsylvania-New Jersey Interconnection began in 1927 when Public Service Electric and Gas Company, Philadelphia Electric Company and Pennsylvania Power & Light Company agreed to pool their resources in what would become the wholesale bulk power market, and dispatch electric generating plants on a lowest-cost basis, thereby producing shared savings.[1] Subsequently, Baltimore Gas and Electric Company and General Public Utilities joined in 1956, and the name was changed to the Pennsylvania-New Jersey-Maryland Interconnection, and later the PJM Interconnection.

The slow pace of expansion continued with the addition of other utilities in New Jersey, Maryland, the District of Columbia and Delaware, eventually reaching a relatively stable configuration in 1981. The pace of development accelerated after passage of the US Energy Policy Act of 1992 (EPAct92). This seminal legislation broadened the scope of wholesale market competition and presented new challenges that strongly favoured expansion and reform of regional power pools. The Federal Energy Regulatory Commission (FERC) encouraged these efforts to build on power pool operations and in 1997 approved PJM as the first fully functioning independent system operator (ISO) in the United States. PJM later transformed into the first regional transmission organization (RTO) in 2002.

The events and key decisions that accompanied reformulation of the functions of the RTO in PJM are important, as discussed below. One of the major impacts was the move to expand the footprint of PJM and the coordinated wholesale market. Allegheny Power and Rockland Electric joined in 2002. A major expansion of the coordinated footprint went live in 2004 with integration of large utilities such as American Electric Power, Commonwealth Edison and Dayton Power and Light. Expansion continued apace with seven more utility service areas, with the most recent being Ohio Valley Electric Corporation (OVEC) in 2018. By then, the affected region included 13 states and ranged from Illinois in the west to the District of Columbia in the east, with over 1000 market entities, 180 086 megawatts (MW) in generating capacity and 65 million ultimate customers. The energy generation mix was roughly balanced across nuclear, coal and natural gas, with about 5 per cent coming from renewable sources (PJM Interconnection 2018a).

The centrepiece of power pool operation was economic dispatch of the generating fleet, subject to the security constraints dictated by reliability needs. The security constraints included the industry standard of N-1 contingency conditions. With an identified list of credible major contingencies, such as the loss of a transmission line or a large power plant, system operation is constrained to ensure that the system will remain stable immediately after any one of these contingency events. The system operator accomplished this feat by maintaining adequate reserves of generation and headroom on transmission, along with various voltage support and frequency response capabilities under the general heading of ancillary services. This is a complicated operational problem, and one of the advantages that facilitated electricity restructuring was the long history and familiar practice in PJM. In principle, all these well-developed operating structures could be maintained, and the major change induced by the expansion of wholesale competition would be in the pricing regime and further efficiencies in coordinated operation.

In the event, PJM launched the first reformed wholesale market in 1997. This followed the long tradition based on exploiting engineering cost estimates, a cost-based market. Economic dispatch with cost-based generation produces market clearing prices analogous to the textbook economics of competitive markets equilibrating supply and demand. These real-time prices would in principle differ by location. The initial PJM model called for a single market clearing price (MCP) across the entire pool. This does not work in theory and it did not work in practice (Hogan 2002). In 1998, after a year of operations under this flawed single MCP design, PJM converted to a cost-based economic dispatch with locational marginal prices (LMPs) that applied to load and generation at each location. In 1999, FERC approved a revised 'market-based' pricing approach where generator engineering cost estimates would be replaced by market bids and offers for most market participants (FERC 1999). The exceptions to market-based offers would be cases that raised issues of market power, where generators would face offer caps derived from the engineering cost estimates plus a small premium. The new LMP market was accompanied by the introduction of Financial Transmission Rights (FTRs) and an early installed reserve capacity market. A PJM Market Monitoring Unit began in 1999 to provide market-efficiency and market power analysis. In 2000, PJM introduced a day-ahead market and a regulation ancillary services market. Then followed an early version of an initial spinning reserve ancillary service market in 2002, and annual FTR auctions in 2003, for FTR obligations and options. A reform of the capacity market came in 2007 with the Reliability Pricing Model (RPM). An important supplement to the energy markets is the Regional Transmission Expansion Plan (RTEP) coordinating transmission investments and the associated transmission cost allocation.

3.   TRANSITION TO OPEN ACCESS AND NON-DISCRIMINATION

In the last decade of the twentieth century, electricity reform was in the air, especially after the decision to create a wholesale power pool in England and Wales in 1990. The first penetration of competitive supply in the United States came via the Public Utility Regulatory Policies Act of 1978, which mandated purchases from generator types designated as qualifying facilities. The ensuing debate in the United States regarding competition in the electric utility sector contributed to the passage of EPAct92 that covered many issues beyond electricity restructuring. However, an important component of EPAct92 established a national policy that would open the wholesale market to competition with many new entrants outside the club of the traditional utilities. The process continued over the next two decades: 'competition in wholesale power markets is national policy. The Energy Policy Act of 2005 embraced wholesale competition as national policy for this country. It represented the third major federal law enacted in the last 25 years to embrace wholesale competition'.[2]

A key feature of this policy in support of wholesale competition included access to the high-voltage transmission system. As FERC recognized, competition for electricity transactions would depend on access to the essential facility of the grid. This principle was not controversial, and the national regulator embraced the broad notions of 'open access' and 'no undue discrimination'. The resulting Order 888 set out principles and examined the challenges of giving content to a workable implementation that would meet these objectives (FERC 1996).

The long and costly debate surrounding Order 888 revealed a central difficulty that had major implications for competitive electricity market design. The discussion began with the assumption that generators and loads would be able to make bilateral arrangements for contracts of various durations and then arrange for transmission rights, much as had already been done under the open access regime for interstate natural gas pipelines that were also under the jurisdiction of FERC. The term of art was the 'contract path', whereby the market participants would identify a path through the grid and make arrangements to utilize the available transmission capacity (ATC). However, unlike natural gas flowing along a specific pipeline, the movement of electric power is completely different.

The essential problem is that power injected at one location and removed at another would travel along every parallel path, distributing itself according to the laws of physics to (roughly) equate the marginal losses on every path (Hogan 1992). The issue was discussed at length and Order 888 laid out the arguments as explained by the industry. The implications were severe. For example, a fully decentralized market was not possible. There must be a system operator to coordinate the use of the grid. Furthermore, implementation of the contract path model was intended to determine how the transmission system would be used, and this required an ex ante determination of the ATC with the assumption of a meaningful relationship between the contract path and physical reality. However, as FERC itself summarized (FERC 1996, p. 95):

> A contract path is simply a path that can be designated to form a single continuous electrical path between the parties to an agreement. Because of the laws of physics, it is unlikely that the actual power flow will follow that contract path . . . Flow-based pricing or contracting would be designed to account for the actual power flows on a transmission system. It would take into account the 'unscheduled flows' that occur under a contract path regime.

In other words, we need to know how the system is used to identify the ATC. The same contradiction arose in European market design discussions: 'in order to compute the maximal use of the network, one needs to make assumptions on the use of the network!' (Boucher and Smeers 2002, pp. 401–2). The circularity of the argument is inherent in the physics of power systems where the configuration of generation and load fully determines the power flows on the transmission system.

However, asserting a lack of a better approach, FERC adopted the contract path model as the centrepiece of its initial open access policy (FERC 1996, p. 96):

> We will not, at this time, require that flow-based pricing and contracting be used in the electric industry. In reaching this conclusion, we recognize that there may be difficulties in using a traditional contract path approach in a non-discriminatory open access transmission environment, as described by Hogan and others. At the same time, however, contract path pricing and contracting is the longstanding approach used in the electric industry and it is the approach familiar to all participants in the industry. To require now a dramatic overhaul of the traditional approach such as a shift to some form of flow-based pricing and contracting could severely slow, if not derail for some time, the move to open access and more competitive wholesale bulk power markets. In addition, we believe it is premature for the Commission to impose generically a new pricing regime without the benefit of any experience with such pricing. We welcome new and innovative proposals, but we will not impose them in this Rule.

From an economic perspective, the defect of the 'contract path' created material market externalities. Individual bilateral transactions would interfere with all other transactions. The contract path model might have been a convenient fiction when there were only a few members of the club of cooperating utilities, but the open access market would be overwhelmed when new entrants responded to the perverse incentives created by the externality. Thus followed the quick imposition of administrative Transmission Loading Relief to undo what the contract path schedules and the associated market design had done (Hogan 2002).

Although PJM complied with the pro forma requirements of Order 888, the contract path model was not the focus of its developing market design. Instead, PJM called upon its tradition and experience and pursued an alternative approach based on a power pool and economic dispatch.[3]

4.   ELECTRICITY MARKETS AND ECONOMIC DISPATCH

The initial focus of market participants and the system operator was on the real-time wholesale market in PJM. The background and motivating example of competitive market equilibrium came from the textbook example shown in Figure 7.1.

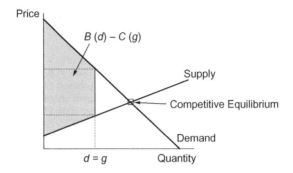

Figure 7.1   Benefits, costs, welfare maximization and market equilibrium

The partial equilibrium framework applies for a single good at a single location. The supply curve is upward sloping and the demand curve is downward sloping. Let $B(d)$ define the benefits of bid-in load (d) and $C(g)$ the cost of generation (g) offers, which are equal to the areas under the respective curves. The net benefit is $B(d) - C(g)$, as shown in the shaded area of Figure 7.1. The welfare-maximizing goal is to choose a quantity where demand and supply balance and that maximizes the net benefit. Inspection of the figure indicates that this maximum is achieved at the quantity where the supply and demand curves intersect. This is also the point of the competitive equilibrium and the associated price is the MCP that supports the equilibrium welfare-maximizing solution. With this MCP, the best (that is, surplus-maximizing) choice for the buyer is the quantity at the competitive equilibrium; similarly, the best (that is, profit-maximizing) choice for the supplier is at same competitive equilibrium point. The prices support the dispatch.

4.1   Electricity Market Coordination

This competitive equilibrium and welfare-maximizing property stands behind the 'invisible hand' arguments for the efficiency of decentralized markets that operate without formal coordination. By the same logic, it follows that the visible hand of coordination for competition can achieve the same outcome as the idealized competitive equilibrium. This is important in the electricity system where explicit coordination is required and is always present. Because of the physics, there is always a system operator. The only question at issue is the form of the coordination and the associated pricing.

This observation lies at the heart of the use of economic dispatch for an open access market without undue discrimination. Since PJM already was the system operator and coordinated the dispatch, the main challenge was to complete the pricing regime.

The basic framework for the electricity market takes the real power load and generation, (d, g), but redefines these as the column vector of values across each location (node or bus) in the network where load, generation and transmission lines connect.[4] The net load is defined as the vector $y = d - g$. Aggregate losses balance the sum of the differences between load and generation, $L(y) + 1'y = 0$. Finally, the many transmission and other security constraints defined over the power flows appear in the vector function $K(y)$. With these definitions, we treat the underlying security-constrained economic dispatch problem as:

$$\underset{d \in D,\, g \in G,\, y}{Max} \quad B(d) - C(g)$$

$$s.t. \quad \begin{aligned} d - g &= y, & &: p \\ L(y) + 1^t y &= 0, & &: \lambda \\ K(y) &\leq 0 & &: \mu. \end{aligned} \qquad (7.1)$$

For this generic model, everything is assumed to be well-behaved enough to yield an optimal solution for the dispatch and associated prices. This is a complicated problem with many variables and constraints. With thousands of locations and thousands of transmission lines, the complete statement of the contingency-constrained problem can run into millions of variables and millions of constraints. Fortunately, system operators are familiar with this model and have workable methods using a blend of optimization tools and operator judgement to approximate an economic dispatch solution.

The formulation in equation (7.1) allows for a great deal of flexibility. Fixed supplies and fix loads can enter directly, in addition to explicit benefit and cost functions. A bilateral transaction between generation and load appears as a matched injection at one location and a withdrawal at another.

Following Schweppe et al. (1988), the dual variables are the locational MCPs. In particular, the prices in the vector p obtain as a natural by-product of producing the optimal dispatch in equation (7.1). See also Liu, Tesfatsion and Chowdhury (2009).

The prices lend themselves to a natural decomposition:

$$p = 1\lambda + \nabla L \lambda + \nabla K^t \mu. \qquad (7.2)$$

The components have the interpretations as the cost of energy at the system reference bus (λ), plus the marginal cost of losses ($\nabla L \lambda$) and the cost of congestion ($\nabla K^t \mu$), both relative to the reference bus. The decomposition is not unique given the dependence on the choice of the reference bus (Rivier and Pérez-Arriaga 1993), but with a given reference bus the decomposition is useful and widely applied.

With optimal dispatch of $y^* = d^* - g^*$, the market settlement with the system operator is:

$$p^t y^* = p^t (d^* - g^*) \geq 0. \qquad (7.3)$$

This is the market surplus of the payments from load minus the payments to generators that has the interpretation as a loss surplus ($[\lambda 1^t + \lambda \nabla L^t] y^*$), because marginal losses are greater than average losses, plus a congestion surplus ($\mu^t \nabla K y^*$) arising from the price differences due to transmission constraints. Aggregate energy payments by load at locational prices will always exceed payments to generators.

The system operator long had this information available, but the prices had not entered into the traditional cost-based economic dispatch with administrative shared savings. In the competitive market, the prices p, known as the locational marginal prices (LMPs), become a centre of attention.

First, just as in Figure 7.1, the LMP was market clearing in the sense that it supported the competitive equilibrium at the welfare maximizing solution. In particular, we have:

$$p = \nabla B = \nabla C. \qquad (7.4)$$

Taking the prices as given, each market participant would find the value of its best solution as that produced by the economic dispatch. System operators would soon report that this pricing model makes it much easier to operate the system because of the implied cooperation of the market participants.

Perhaps the most important insight from Schweppe et al. (1988) deals with the marginal cost of transmission. Transmission of 1 MW from location i to location j is physically equivalent to simultaneously selling 1 MW at i and purchasing 1 MW at j. Hence, by a simple no-arbitrage argument, at equilibrium the marginal cost of transmission must be the same as the value of the purchase minus the sale. Therefore, the marginal cost of transmission must be $p_j - p_i$.

The complexity of the calculation that stands behind this simple rule had defied a workable solution for decades. The 'contract path' did not resolve the issue and the industry had struggled to track all the flows in the system, such as through the failed efforts of the General Agreement on Parallel Paths (GAPP), the 'megawatt-mile' morass, and other related efforts (Ruff 2001). All the complexity is there in the economic dispatch in equation (7.1), but the complexity is already internalized by the system operator. Simple application of the resulting LMPs and differences in LMPs cut through the clutter.

This formulation allows treatment of bid-in load with $B(d)$, generation offers with $C(g)$, and point-to-point bilateral schedules of injections and withdrawals to be settled at the difference in the respective LMPs. This is a different approach to market design, with coordination for competition, but it is a feasible market model that does not depend on the unworkable tracking of participant power flows through the grid.

By definition, the efficient outcome is the solution to the economic dispatch in equation (7.1). In any system under open access and non-discrimination principles, market participants will have the freedom and discretion to buy and sell power according to their own interests. If market prices support the economic dispatch solution, then the private interests will operate as with the 'invisible hand' to follow the efficient outcome. The LMP prices are precisely the market prices that support the economic dispatch. Any other pricing approach would, necessarily, create incentives to deviate from the efficient outcome. It is in this sense that the BBSCEDLMP model is the only electricity market design that can support efficient markets under the principles of transmission open access and non-discrimination.

4.2 Single Market Clearing Price Settlements

Following the discussion of Order 888, PJM launched its own market reform. The emphasis on flexibility for bilateral transactions was constant, but the reliance on contract path scheduling was recognized as unworkable and destabilizing. Market participants and the system operator agreed on the necessity of continuing the practice of economic dispatch along the lines of equation (7.1). But there was sharp disagreement about the use of the corresponding LMPs as in equation (7.2).

The debate centred around the importance of transmission congestion and the apparent complexity of having a different price at each location. In the event, the decision of a majority of the market participants, but not a majority of the utilities, was to adopt a single MCP that would be based on a hypothetical dispatch without transmission constraints. Hence, in the continuing zonal-versus-nodal debate (Hogan 1998), the initial decision by FERC was to accept a PJM market design with a single zone. Since the actual dispatch would have to respect the transmission constraints, the cost of extra out-of-merit dispatch would be paid as an 'uplift' cost to be socialized across all loads.

Using engineering costs to define the generation offers, this system was put in effect on 1 April 1997. Initially, there was no system congestion and everything worked well because the nodal prices would be about the same as the single MCP, except for marginal losses. However, on the first hot day, with high demand in the east and transmission congestion from west to east, the MCP model quickly fell apart. For details, see Hogan (2002). The essential problem was that the prices did not support the least-cost dispatch solution and the option to self-schedule through bilateral transactions provided the avenue to follow the incentives to deviate from the economic dispatch. Parties soon engaged in numerous bilateral agreements to circumvent the single clearing price signal. Sellers who were constrained-off due to congestion were able to offer their generation bilaterally at a price lower than the single clearing price. The system operator was required to honour these bilateral agreements until system reliability was jeopardized, at which point the market would be suspended. These experiences made clear the flawed assumption underlying uniform non-locational pricing in a constrained network.

4.3   Locational Marginal Price Settlements

PJM's response to the failure of the single MCP model was to turn to implementation of the LMP model for market settlements. PJM had continued with the conceptual and software work for a nodal market during the single clearing price experiment. One year after the start of the single MCP model, PJM made the conversion to LMP. During the year, while PJM ran both systems in parallel prior to full conversion, there were a litany of problems with the lingering MCP model and these required increasingly intrusive interventions by the system operator.

The introduction of the LMP model, publishing the so-far implicit marginal costs and using the prices for the settlement system, produced many surprises. It takes time and analysis to develop an intuitive understanding of the implications of grid interactions and the impact on prices. For instance, it is easy to construct examples where the lowest LMP is lower than the lowest generator offer and, simultaneously, the highest LMP is higher than the highest generator offer. This occurs because the parallel path flows in the network may require increasing generation by x MW at one location and decreasing generation by $x - 1$ MW at another location to meet a marginal increase of system load of 1 MW. It is even possible to construct examples where all the generator offers are positive but some of the LMPs are negative. These conditions, which cannot occur in the single MCP model, are routine in the real transmission system.

The initial implementation of the LMP model in PJM utilized the principles of dispatch-based pricing. The actual dispatch involves both formal modelling such as in equation (7.1) and manual operator interventions to handle reliability concerns not otherwise reflected in the dispatch software. Hence, the actual dispatch is only approximately optimal. The dispatch-based pricing approach takes the actual metered dispatch as the optimal solution, with a given set of binding constraints, and computes prices that are approximately consistent with that dispatch. For further details, see Ott (2003).

The switch to market-based generation offers in 1999 provided other advantages (Munoz et al. 2018), but did not change anything fundamental about the market model. PJM has now used the LMP model for two decades, eventually updating the real-time spot prices every five minutes for over 12 000 locations. The price differences caused by congestion are sometimes dramatic, reflecting the reality of the transmission grid. But the experience demonstrates both the feasibility and advantages of linking prices to the actual dispatch conditions.

The BBSCEDLMP dispatch model for the real-time spot market provides flexibility for market participants. For example, generators at a location can enter into long-term energy contracts of a great variety of forms with different profiles and options for delivery. The contracts can be structured as financial contracts for differences (CfDs), a standard form of financial derivative. The actual delivery and receipt will take place in the spot market at the locational price. The contract parties then have a financial obligation between themselves to settle the contracts consistent with whatever provisions they have set. For example, if the contract calls for delivery of 100 MW over the relevant interval, the parties pay to and receive from each other the difference between the spot price at the point of withdrawal and the contract price.

The financial approach of marrying a spot market and CfDs has the major advantage that the system operator does not need to know anything about the financial arrangements, or even if a long-term contract exists. The connection to the market is simply handled through the bids, offers or physical schedules of the parties in the real-time market. Everything else is a separate settlement process that does not affect the dispatch or the spot prices.

This use of long-term CfDs would be all that would be required if prices at all locations were the same at the same time, which was part of the motivation for the single MCP. In the LMP model, CfDs can be part of the solution at each location. The added requirement to deal with the differences across locations is addressed through Financial Transmission Rights (FTRs).

4.4   Financial Transmission Rights

Part of the motivation for the failed 'contract path' model was to provide a means of determining the real-time dispatch and use of the transmission grid without requiring a coordinated economic dispatch. However, the other part of the story was the need for long-term transmission rights that would allow a generator at one location to arrange a long-term contract with a customer at another location. The strong emphasis on having a long-term contracting capability made this a high-priority issue.

The search for physical transmission rights failed because the physics of the electric transmission system made any flow-based definitions of transmission rights unworkable. By contrast, FTRs would provide the critical economic and business requirement for linking CfDs at distinct locations.

The real-time transmission charge from location i to location j is $p_j - p_i$. The locational prices are volatile and this price difference is even more volatile. Hence, parties who wished to enter into CfDs, but were at different locations, would be exposed to changes in the spot price of transmission.

Market participants needed a hedge for the locational price difference. And there needed to be some consistent way to account for the capacity of the transmission grid to support power transactions and long-term contracts. The direct solution was to create a financial contract that would be administered by the system operator (Hogan 1992). The new contract would include a MW amount and a direction of flow between two points on the grid. The contract, an FTR, provides payment of the price difference $p_j - p_i$ for the designated MW amount. If a party scheduled 100 MW between the two points, it would pay the price differential between the point of withdrawal and the point of injection. If the same party also held an FTR for 100 MW between these two locations, it would receive the same payment. Hence, the spot price is perfectly hedged. When coupled with a CfD at either end, the market participants would be able to have a long-term fixed price for the contract transaction. And when the actual schedules deviated from the contract, the market participants would see the efficient incentives of balancing through the real-time spot market.

The initial implementation of FTRs in PJM only addressed the congestion component of the locational price, ignoring the marginal losses that were not included in the LMPs until later. Under the standard DC load model that ignores losses, the FTRs administered by the system operator have a natural internal correlation. Although it is impossible to define ATC for physical flows in the dynamically changing system, FTRs have an aggregate property that limits the exposure of the system operator. In particular, if the MW injections and withdrawals of the collection of all extant FTRs would be simultaneously feasible given the configuration of the grid in the spot market, then the revenues collected from the spot market locational prices would always be sufficient to make the required payments for the FTRs (ibid.). With the simultaneous feasibility condition, there would be no revenue exposure for the system operator.

In principle, anyone in or outside of the market could provide the financial equivalent of FTRs on a bilateral basis, but they would not enjoy this same feature of revenue adequacy. Furthermore, absent the provision of the FTRs, the market participants would not be able to obtain the functional equivalent of the benefit of the grid. The multiple owners of a complex grid would not be able to internalize all the congestion costs. Only a monopoly owner or a monopoly operator of the grid would provide this service. In the PJM system, with multiple owners of the grid, but a system operator as a monopoly, FTRs provide the missing economic piece to support a long-term contracting market.

Under the FTR model, the exposure of the system operator, grid owners or market participants is to collective allocation of FTRs that exceeds the capacity of the grid in the spot market. This has been a problem in the past in PJM, confounded by various cost socializations, especially during the period from 2009/10 to 2013/14 when FTR funding fell to 67 per cent of the FTR obligation. PJM eventually made a number of corrections and the pay-out ratio returned to 100 per cent in 2014/15 through 2018/19 (Monitoring Analytics 2019).

PJM provides both FTR options and obligations. The obligations require payment of the price difference even when the price differential $p_j - p_i$ is negative. The FTR options do not require payment when the differential is negative. In effect, FTR options are more valuable, but they also reduce the transmission capacity for the simultaneous feasibility test.

In addition, PJM uses Auction Revenue Rights (ARRs) to distribute the value of the FTRs to the owners of the grid. In essence, the ARR is formally the same as the FTR, but the ARR is allocated through an administrative process to reflect rough justice about the historic investment and utilization in the grid. The logic was to enable parties to replicate their traditional supply paths via ARRs/FTRs as a proxy for their historic entitlements. As load grew, the footprint expanded and retail access enlarged, and this proxy has proved to be more problematic. In each annual auction for FTRs, the auction prices set the market value of the ARRs and these funds are distributed proportionally across the ARR holders. ARR holders are given the option to 'self-schedule' these rights in the annual FTR auction, converting the right to the auction revenues into the actual FTR.

Investment in expansion of the grid creates incremental transmission capacity and therefore incremental FTRs. If the combination of the incremental FTRs and the existing long-term FTRs meet the simultaneous feasibility test, then the award of these incremental rights and the associated congestion collections preserves FTR revenue adequacy going forward, indefinitely.

PJM pioneered the use of FTR auctions. The details, with long-term auctions and short-term updates are more complicated, along with various rules about allocating other system uplift costs. In addition, there is a continuing controversy about the deviations of the actual payments under FTRs and the implied value as revealed in the forward auctions (ibid.).

FTRs are forward contracts and holders of FTRs must comply with various credit requirements. Designing good credit risk protocols is a standard business issue that extends beyond the main focus of electricity market design. In 2018, PJM faced a significant problem of default on the large FTR position held by GreenHat, LLC. For further details, see Monitoring Analytics (2019).

4.5   Day-ahead Market

Soon after the second launch of the real-time market in April 1999, market participants began a discussion about the development of a day-ahead market. The real-time market took the availability of (most) of the generation as given and solved for the energy dispatch in equation (7.1). There were a few related actions to ensure enough capacity was started and online, but this was a relatively minor part of operations as initially the majority of supply was self-scheduled.

When looking ahead over a longer period like a day, however, there would be many more decisions required about commitment of generating units that had longer lead times. The change in horizon and the ability to commit units, results in the economic dispatch problem expanding into an economic unit commitment and dispatch problem. This would open the door to more formal consideration of multi-part generation offers to include start-up costs, minimum run times and related complications that arise in the management of real systems.

For market participants, a day is a long time and real-time prices can be quite volatile. A popular demand emerged for a mechanism that operated one day ahead to create hedges for the real-time operations to help manage this volatility. Although these hedges could be arranged in the open market, the system operator again had a special role to play in coordinating day-ahead schedules and dispatch to respect the capabilities of the transmission system. For the same reason as found for FTRs, only the system operator can determine a consistent set of day-ahead contracts that could be converted to physical delivery within the limits of reliability.

The essence of the problem was to create a new model that included unit commitment and related control variables, $u \in U$, and expanded the optimization to include these control variables as follows:

$$
\begin{aligned}
&\underset{d \in D,\, g \in G,\, u \in U,\, y}{Max} \quad B(d) - C(g,u) \\
&\qquad\qquad\quad d - g = y, \qquad : p \\
&\text{s.t.} \quad L(y) + 1^t y = 0, \quad : \lambda \\
&\qquad\qquad\quad K(y) \le 0 \qquad\quad : \mu.
\end{aligned}
\tag{7.5}
$$

Typically formulated as a dynamic model with an hourly interval, load bids and generator offers are for day-ahead forward contracts that will be settled against the relevant intervals for the real-time dispatch in equation (7.1). Multi-part offers with start-up, no-load and multiple steps with incremental energy offers that make up a generator cost are incorporated in equation (7.5), and the resulting schedules provide the hedges for real-time markets. To the extent one's real-time generation or load matches the day-ahead schedules, the party is fully insulated from real-time price volatility.

The day-ahead model includes a reliability unit commitment (RUC) for supplemental units if needed to ensure real-time reliability. In effect, this can be included as part of the constraints in equation (7.5). For further details, see Cadwalader et al. (1998).

One problem with the day-ahead unit commitment model is that the unit commitment variables are integers, and thus the model in equation (7.5) may not have prices that fully support the solution. The broader topic is discussed under the name of extended LMP (ELMP). Essentially, the initial PJM implementation accepted the optimal day-ahead unit commitment as given, which reduces equation (7.5) to a dynamic version of equation (7.1), and took the results as the day-ahead prices. This gives rise to cases where generators could be committed but losing money at the day-ahead prices. In essence, PJM's practice is to pay an added uplift to cover the difference and ensure support of the commitment and dispatch. The extra uplift costs are spread across the loads.

The day-ahead market includes explicit and implicit transmission schedules. Since it was not intended to sell transmission capacity twice, introduction of the day-ahead market required a change to redefine the settlement for FTRs as at the day-ahead prices. In effect, the day-ahead market purchases all the outstanding FTRs and reconfigures the rights to match the transmission dispatch in the day-ahead, which will then be settled at the real-time prices. A market participant that wishes to carry through an FTR to the real-time market can achieve this end by submitting a matching point-to-point schedule in the day-ahead market.

Very few of the decisions in the day-ahead energy dispatch and commitment have an immediate physical effect. Commitment decisions are the principal example, but the related energy dispatch schedules are the functional equivalent of financial forward contracts. This recognition stimulated the rise of so-called 'virtual' transactions where the bids and offers in the day-ahead market are not directly connected to any load or generation, and the market participant simply unwinds the contract through the real-time settlements. Hence, a virtual award for 100 megawatt-hours (MWh) of generation in the day-ahead will lead to a payment at the day-ahead price and a corresponding obligation at the real-time price. In other words, the virtual bidder is arbitraging the difference between the day-ahead bid and the expected real-time price.

To a material extent, virtual bidding is impossible to avoid as long as generators and loads have any discretion for offers and bids in the day-ahead market. In PJM, capacity resources have a must-offer obligation in the day-ahead market but flexibility in offers when not constrained-on. Load has much more flexibility with respect to the amount it can purchase in the day-ahead market. Further, the entry of additional financial market participants without explicit physical assets substantially expands the number of possible participants in the day-ahead market. The resulting increase in liquidity from financial participants is important for removing conditions that would otherwise allow an exercise of market power by either generation or load. The limited empirical estimates support the view that allowed explicit virtual bidding provides material benefits and enhances convergence between day-ahead and expected real-time prices (Hogan 2016). For PJM, difference between 'the average real-time price and the average day-ahead price was –$0.06 per MWh in 2017, and $0.06 per MWh in 2018' (Monitoring Analytics 2019, p. 24).

4.6 Capacity Markets and Resource Adequacy

From the beginning of the PJM restructuring process, regulators were concerned about the ability of markets to support resource adequacy. The objective was to ensure that installed generation capacity was maintained with a reserve margin large enough to limit events leading to involuntary load curtailment with a probability of an event occurring no more than the one-day-in-ten-years standard. PJM's various state regulators were not convinced that the energy market alone would provide revenue sufficient to support investment in new generation to meet this standard. The call was for a capacity market that would provide forward-looking support for generation asset investment to meet the resource adequacy standard.

Designing forward capacity markets is much harder than designing real-time or even day-ahead energy markets. The difficulties are fundamental. Forward capacity purchased for availability many years ahead is not an observable quantity. There must be some connection, eventually, to measurable quantities such as energy delivered. While these assumptions were made in planning models, translating this into market design consistently has been challenging. Defining this connection without simply creating a forward energy market is difficult and contentious. The original definition of capacity reflected the traditional dispatchable thermal generation plants. But capacity markets soon had to take on definitions of the contribution to capacity of intermittent resources, energy demand response, and later short-term storage devices.

Perhaps most complicated is the task of dealing with transmission constraints years in the future. If we knew how to do this well, the contract path model might have worked. However, identifying the ability of capacity resources to be delivered to meet load requirements under stressed conditions is not a simple modelling task. The practice in PJM is to make some engineering judgements and construct a zonal model for capacity with a simplified transportation model that does not explicitly account for the actual power flows and transmission constraints.

In this context, there are two classes of generators in PJM. Energy-only resources are connected to provide energy in the real-time market and have only minimal interconnection requirements – for example, they must be able to operate without causing operating problems – but their interconnection upgrades are not designed to assure the resource is deliverable to the system on an integrated basis. Capacity resources have more stringent interconnection requirements and are connected to the grid and allowed to participate in the capacity market only after meeting an engineering deliverability test. To be certified as 'deliverable', a new resource may be required to make investments in upgrading the grid. In exchange for such upgrades they receive a Capacity Interconnection Right (CIR). However, once certified, such capacity resources only retain their CIRs and ability to participate in the capacity market if they continue to offer into the capacity market. They lose their CIRs after three years if they do not participate in the capacity market auctions.

A major revision of the PJM capacity market, referred to as the Reliability Pricing Model (RPM), was implemented effective 1 June 2007. In this model, there are local deliverability areas (LDAs) for capacity. For each LDA, PJM produces a forward estimate of the peak energy demand, the capability to accept transfers from the rest of the footprint, and a target level of reserves needed within the LDA. The interface capacity for the zones is set according to a one-day-in-twenty-five-year standard for transmission flow capacity. This conservative planning requirement is used to approximate the infinite internal transmission that PJM assumed when determining the one-day-in-ten-year requirement for generation reserves for PJM as a whole.

Given the target level of internal requirements for each LDA, PJM utilizes a cost of new entry (known as CoNE) for a typical combustion turbine and the net CoNE (that is, CoNE adjusted for energy and ancillary services income) to establish a demand curve for each represented LDA. The CoNE represents the levelized capacity cost that would have to be earned on average to support investment in the turbine. This estimate is reduced to the net CoNE by subtracting an estimate of the energy and ancillary services (E&AS) revenues that will be earned, based on a backward-looking average on-peak dispatch of the turbine plant. A significantly positive net CoNE is an indicator of the 'missing money' in the energy market (Joskow 2008). In PJM, revenue adequacy from the E&AS market alone has not been sufficient to support investment (Monitoring Analytics 2019). The RPM capacity revenues have been a significant and growing part of the PJM market. Capacity revenues represent almost 100 per cent of the income for demand response capability that is sold as capacity.

Net CoNE and an installed reserve requirement set an anchor point for the variable resource requirements (VRR) curve, an administratively set demand curve. The VRR is a piecewise linear function similar in appearance to a demand curve, although there is no connection to demand other than to meet the resource adequacy requirement. The original intent of the shape of the VRR was to create a control type mechanism that would result in prices over time oscillating around the net CoNE with a frequency/cycle satisfactory to meeting the one-day-in-ten-year reliability requirement. This objective has been less visible over the 12 years of regulatory adjustments to the capacity construct.

With this VRR and zonal model, the RPM three-year-ahead forward auction and interim adjustment auctions combine offers from approved resources to determine capacity resource awards and capacity prices. A forward auction must-offer obligation (with limited exception) applies to all resources with CIRs. The winning capacity resources have an obligation to offer into the subsequent day-ahead and real-time energy markets.

The polar vortex cold snap in the winter of 2014 revealed a problem in non-performance of generating capacity. At the peak, PJM reported that 22 per cent of total generating capacity was unavailable (PJM Interconnection 2018b). This was problematic as the underlying reliability models used by PJM assumed that forced outages of generators were random and independent. Clearly this was not the case, as cold weather froze operating equipment, stopped fuel convoys and made gas supplies unobtainable in certain areas. This precipitated a process to strengthen the capacity performance incentives and non-performance penalties. A modified paradigm referred to as Capacity Performance was put in place with stiffer penalties for unavailability during specified periods. The full effect of the new model will not be in place until the delivery year 2020/21, illustrating the lag time for contentious market reforms and the fundamental forward nature of the capacity market design. Under the Capacity Performance requirement reform, capacity resources that are called upon but do not deliver energy will be charged at the hourly rate of 150 per cent of the annualized net CoNE allocated over the estimated 30 hours when the resources would be needed. PJM calculates this value for the RTO resources as just over 3300 $/MWh for 2020/21, with a cumulative stop/loss of 150 per cent of net CoNE. This compares with the 2018 annual load weighted average LMP of 38 $/MWh. With the exception of the exemptions for solar and wind, this capacity performance penalty structure provides a significant incentive to meet the capacity obligation.

A feature of the Capacity Performance penalty is the revenue collected from the underperforming assets shared among the over-performing assets, including those that are not capacity resources. Therefore, the marginal incentive for generators is similar to real-time scarcity pricing. However, the prices are not translated into the market prices, as seen by the loads. This will create situations where the same product, energy at a specific location, has more than one implied spot price. Deficient generators will see the price as LMP + 3300 $/MWh, and they could take actions incurring large costs to capture the market price and avoid the 3300 $/MWh penalty. But loads at the same location would be paying only the market LMP. Given experience, it would not be surprising if the inconsistent incentives create unintended consequences for market efficiency.

4.7   Transmission Expansion and Cost Allocation

The Regional Transmission Expansion Plan (RTEP) sets out investments in the transmission grid to meet several different 'drivers': (1) reliability; (2) market efficiency; and (3) public policy objectives. In this context, reliability refers to various operating standards to meet dispatch security constraints and reliability standards. Market efficiency refers to improved economic performance through reduced congestion in the forecast economic dispatch. Public policy projects are those that do not arise under the first two categories but are needed to meet public policy objectives, such as interconnection of distant renewables resources. Transmission investments typically affect all three of these benefits and thus the RTEP also includes procedures for evaluating multi-driver projects.

In the background of all this planning there are also transmission projects known as Supplemental Projects that can be built by the various transmission owners outside of the RTEP, with the requirement being that the Supplement Project does not diminish the system capability. In recent years, Supplemental Project spending has far exceeded RTEP central transmission planning investments.

Although there are provisions for merchant investments, where the costs and transmission benefits (for example, incremental FTRs) are assigned to the merchant provider, the main outlines of the RTEP are essentially the same as found in traditional monopoly utility planning practices. PJM organizes stakeholders in two related processes for five-year and 15-year planning horizons. Using forecast of load, costs and related infrastructure changes, PJM conducts production simulation analysis across a range of scenarios.

The choice among reliability projects broadly follows the standard of the least-cost means to meet the constraint. Market-efficiency projects are evaluated according to changes in the simulated production cost and subject to a benefit–cost ratio of 1.25 as a minimum threshold. Public policy projects would be proposed by other government entities requesting the transmission investment. PJM has introduced limited competition and open seasons for various RTEP transmission projects. This new element, linked to FERC Order 1000 mandates, has proven contentious, with the introduction of competition in an area previously the exclusive domain of regulated monopolist transmission owners (FERC 2011).

Cost allocation for the initial existing transmission assets follows a 'licence plate' method that, in effect, recovers historical costs as a zonal connection charge, with different charges in each zone. Cost allocation for transmission expansion investment follows a series of rules that are a mixture of proportional allocation based on load-ratio shares and a distribution factor (DFAX) based on a hypothetical power flow analysis. Notably, these load-ratio and DFAX methodologies are not derived from the cost–benefit analysis performed with the production simulations (Hogan 2018). The result can be a sharp divergence between the cost allocation and the anticipated benefits. PJM members have continually disputed the resulting allocations, particularly those in recent years where the allocation criterion has changed from violation-based DFAX to beneficiary-based DFAX. The allocation disputes have also spilled over into the merchant transmission arena where owners of controllable DC lines between PJM and New York ISO have engaged in litigation regarding criteria for the application of costs responsibility and eligibility for certain services as they modify the basic service taken to avoid certain cost allocations.

4.8 Market Power Mitigation

Mitigating a possible exercise of market power has been a continuing thread of electricity market restructuring. An early focus was on generator market power. The concern derived from theoretical arguments and experience in other markets, such as the power pool in England and Wales, according to which concentrated ownership of generators would create incentives to withhold some supply to raise market prices and increase profits on the remaining generation (Wolfram 1999).

The central tool to mitigate generator market power in PJM is through the must-offer requirement for capacity resources with various associated offer caps. In a simplest case with an increasing incremental energy offer, an offer cap sets an upper limit on the generator's offer price. For generators deemed to have market power, either in general or under constrained transmission conditions, the cap is set based on an agreed-upon measure of a 10 per cent premium over an audited cost on file with PJM. The capped offer remains as part of the dispatch in equation (7.1), which produces the associated market clearing LMP. The generator is paid according to the LMP at its location. Since the perfect competitive incentive, without market power, would be to offer at true marginal cost, the outcome of mitigation will be a close approximation of what would occur in a competitive market if the cost estimate used for mitigation were reasonably accurate.

In the presence of virtual bidding, easy market entry makes the day-ahead market highly competitive, and it would be difficult to exercise market power on a sustained basis. In any event, a primary function of the market monitor is to track market performance and identify any evidence of market manipulation. The reports of the market monitor consistently find results of the energy market as competitive. For the various ancillary services, such as regulation and reserves, the market monitor finds the structure as not competitive, indicating a potential problem, but finds the actual market behaviour as competitive.

The capacity market is the principal exception to this broadly competitive finding. Here the market monitor finds both the structure and performance as consistently non-competitive (Monitoring Analytics 2019). The problems affect supply offers that are deemed too high as being non-competitive, as well as the associated challenges of accommodating subsidized generation where the supply offers are too low.

5.   PRICE FORMATION AND MARKET DESIGN CHALLENGES

The substantial progress of the PJM market after more than two decades of operation as an open access, non-discriminatory power pool must be counted as a successful market design (SMD) (Cramton 2017). The main features of BBSCEDLMP should be the starting point for any future successful market design. The remaining challenges are not as significant as those of the first days of the market opening in 1997. However, PJM will likely maintain its process to prioritize and improve on a number of electricity market design challenges.

5.1   Scarcity Pricing and Operating Reserve Demand Curves

Scarcity pricing refers to conditions when load is close to using all available generating capacity, including capacity reserved to meet contingency constraints. In textbook theory, prices should rise to reduce demand and ration the available supply. In addition to supporting reliability, scarcity prices would provide a major element in supporting returns on generation investment. For a variety of reasons, electricity market implementations have embedded rules and procedures that tend to suppress market prices, particularly under scarcity conditions (Joskow 2008).

PJM implemented a limited form of scarcity pricing in 2012 through penalty factors that would apply to operating reserve shortages during scarcity conditions. However, the penalty factors were set more based on cost principles than on the value of the reserves. The impact on scarcity pricing was insufficient and PJM found that the relative share of energy prices in the total contribution to generator revenues was declining significantly.

An operating reserve demand curve (ORDC), based on valuing the impacts of outages and reserve shortages, provides a practical way to address scarcity pricing within the framework of current economic dispatch models (Hogan 2013). To address its scarcity pricing problem, PJM proposed a major reform that would significantly revise the prior penalty factors and implement a version of an ORDC. Under this proposal, the scarcity price within a constrained zone could rise as high as 12 000 $/MWh (PJM Interconnection 2019).

The proposed PJM ORDC reform targets in part the expected need for and greater use of flexible operating reserves. PJM does not have the same potential for renewable resources as found in other regions. However, policies to support renewable generation are likely to produce a similar trend of an increasing penetration of intermittent resources.

5.2   Market Design and the Green Agenda

Although PJM has been behind other regions in the arrival of renewable energy resources, the future could be quite different. The challenges include dealing with the intermittent supplies that can increase stress on the system. The balanced mix of generation resources in PJM provided a substantial capability that helped accommodate the needs of efficient and reliable economic dispatch. Future increases in intermittent resources will require emphasis on flexible resources, better look-ahead dispatch practices, and related operating procedures that should develop as part of the natural evolution of the RTO.

A closely related issue will address modifications in the basic market design needed to accommodate a different cost structure, the implications for MCPs, and the associated long-term incentives. In particular, the arrival of increasing volumes of zero marginal-cost renewable resources prompts a concern that this will drive down energy prices and make the fundamental market design unravel (Joskow 2019, Lopes and Coelho 2018).

A notable feature of the formulation in equation (7.1) is the lack of any specification of the details of the underlying cost functions. The model is quite general and the basic analysis from first principles is unaffected by the arrival of low- or zero-variable cost resources. The prices, values and incentives all change, but the basic efficiency arguments all lead to the same market design and pricing prescriptions. The principal conclusion of a closer analysis is that the importance of scarcity pricing increases with the increasing penetration of zero-variable cost resources. In a hypothetical limiting case of only such resources with an energy-only market, scarcity prices would supply all the revenues in the energy market and all the incentives for investment. Hence, the direction of the future for PJM is to emphasize the scarcity pricing reforms it has already proposed (Hogan 2019, PJM Interconnection 2019).

5.3   Disconnect Between Economic and Reliability Standards

Resource adequacy and reliability standards in PJM and elsewhere typically invoke the one-day-in-ten-years standard for system failures that lead to involuntary load curtailments. This standard takes slightly different forms, but all the implementations have the characteristic that the standard continues because it has always been the standard.

The logic behind the rule has been challenged repeatedly by showing that the implied value of lost load is orders of magnitude above the levels that actual loads would be willing to pay (Telson 1973, Wilson 2010). The analysis of the economic level of installed capacity compared to the historical reliability standard has been quite detailed in work for the Texas system operator (Newell et al., 2018). The implied economically efficient reserve margin for installed capacity is materially lower than that required by the traditional reliability standard.

The gap between these installed reserve requirement estimates implies that energy-only markets with efficient scarcity pricing require either revising the reliability standard or providing some other means to support pricing and investment. A capacity market, as in PJM, is one approach. An ORDC constructed with conservative assumptions, as ordered by the Public Utility Commission of Texas, is another.

5.4   Beneficiary Pays and Transmission Cost Allocation

In its landmark Order 1000 on transmission expansion and cost allocation, FERC set out the fundamental requirement for transmission expansion criteria and the 'beneficiary pays' principle for cost allocation (FERC 2011). The cost-allocation principle is important for maintaining compatibility among the investment incentives for load, generation and transmission. The broad principle, reinforced by a series of Federal court decisions, required that cost-allocation rules be 'roughly commensurate' with the investment benefits.

Almost immediately, implementation of the rule revealed either an unwillingness or an inability to follow the logical precepts of the 'beneficiary pays' principle (Radford 2013). PJM is not alone in facing a challenge to make the transmission expansion process, cost–benefit analyses and cost-allocation rules conform to the basic principles.

5.5   Buyer Market Power and Minimum Offer Price Rules

The RPM capacity auctions are vulnerable to manipulation by the functional equivalent of market power exercised by loads. Although individual loads are generally not large enough to influence capacity market prices, state governments can act on behalf of loads to manipulate capacity prices. The process first appeared with New Jersey proposing subsidies for a new natural gas plant that customers would be required to subsidize, but where a major objective was to lower capacity market prices to the greater benefit of those same customers.

The same effect happens through any subsidies for competing generation, such as through policies to support renewables or maintain existing fleets of generating plants in the name of improved resiliency. The impact of subsidies in the energy market is ubiquitous and material (Nordhaus 2013). According to the PJM market monitor, 'Subsidies are contagious. Competition in the markets could be replaced by competition to receive subsidies' (Monitoring Analytics 2017, p. 2). The main response in PJM has been through RPM Minimum Offer Price Rule (MOPR) intended to remove the effects of various subsidies and determine a forward capacity price that is not subject to manipulation. This continuing discussion prompted then FERC Chairman Norman Bay to argue that regulators of electricity markets cannot solve this problem (FERC 2017).

5.6   Multi-period Dispatch and Price Consistency

In the real-time spot market, PJM utilizes a look-ahead for various commitment and dispatch decisions. The dispatch updates every five minutes, with a rolling look-ahead period set by system conditions and that varies from 15 minutes for generators to up to two hours ahead for various ancillary services. The real-time LMP pricing model applies for each five-minute dispatch interval without a look-ahead feature.

Dispatch intervals are not separable. For example, ramping limits can constrain the dispatch and affect both cost of operations and intertemporal prices to reflect these limits. In principle, the formulation in equation (7.1) can include intertemporal constraints and the associated prices. The LMP prices estimated separately for each period may not be the same and might not support the solution with binding ramping constraints. Calculating the prices for each interval with a look-ahead with related constraints, and then updating prices after every five-minute interval, is feasible, would provide consistent intertemporal prices when the forecast and actual load and operating conditions are the same, and is the practice in other organized markets. In the system with constantly changing forecasts, the deterministic models cannot ensure that the forecast prices and actual prices would be the same. Hence, there is another application of uplift payments to support the dispatch. However, simulations for the ISO New England system found test cases where the deviations produced for the rolling calculations were relatively small (Hua et al. 2019).

5.7   Day-ahead and Real-time Market Design Interaction

The PJM real-time and day-ahead market models in equation (7.1) and (7.5) are deterministic. The models are based on bids and offers and expected system conditions. The real dispatch faces uncertain conditions over the near future in real time, and over the day in the day-ahead problem. Full formulation of a stochastic optimization and the accompanying market equilibrium is a research topic but not yet a workable possibility for large-scale power systems with security-constrained dispatch (Bjørndal et al. 2018). However, the treatment of operating reserves in real time and day-ahead in PJM is an example of building in approximations that serve to proxy for some of the major effects of uncertainty while maintaining a simplified representation in a deterministic model. The problem becomes even more interesting in the presence of virtual bidding and assumptions of perfect arbitrage between day-ahead and expected real-time prices (Hogan and Pope 2019).

5.8   Extended Locational Marginal Pricing and Energy Uplift

The market model with unit commitment, as in equation (7.5), includes binary on-off decisions for generators and other facilities that violate the conditions that guarantee that the LMPs support the efficient solution. In this more general model with endogenous unit commitment decisions, there may be no set of market prices that supports the efficient solution. Recognized early in the development of electricity markets, the general practice is to pay generators an additional 'uplift' whenever the energy revenues at the market prices are not sufficient to support the efficient outcome.

Under these conditions, different choices for the locational prices lead to different uplift amounts. Setting the prices to minimize the total uplift payments is possible in principle (Gribik, Hogan and Pope 2007). However, the theoretical ideal can be computationally intractable for a real system such as PJM.

The alternative approach, sometimes described as extended locational marginal pricing (ELMP), would choose the market prices according to a separate pricing model that approximates equation (7.5) by relaxing the integer restrictions to treat commitment decisions as continuous rather than binary. Although the associated dispatch in the pricing model need not be the same as the actual dispatch, the resulting prices are a good workable approximation to the exact minimization of uplift (PJM Interconnection 2017). This would be a generalization of the similar treatment of 'fast start' resources already approved by FERC (FERC 2019).

6. CONCLUSION

The physics of power transmission systems make existing electricity markets unlike markets for other commodities. Markets cannot solve the problem of electricity market design and simple analogies to other markets can lead design astray. PJM has been at the forefront of applying first principles of engineering and economics in the context of providing coordination for competition as needed to support efficient markets. Perfection is elusive, both in theory and in practice. PJM strives for the best approximation of a successful market design organized around BBSCEDLMP. The evolution of market design, to accommodate the changing mix of load and generation resources, should avoid mistakes of the past and continue to emphasize the fundamentals while improving the characterization of scarcity pricing, dynamic dispatch and the close connection between physical and financial markets.

NOTES

*   This chapter draws on research for the Harvard Electricity Policy Group and for the Harvard-Japan Project on Energy and the Environment. Thanks to Scott Harvey, Adam Keech, Susan Pope and Roy Shanker. The views presented here are not necessarily attributable to any of those mentioned, and any remaining errors are solely the responsibility of the author.
1.   Unless otherwise noted, the historical information is from 'PJM History' at https://www.pjm.com/about-pjm/who-we-are/pjm-history, accessed 28 June 2021.
2.   Joseph T. Kelliher, 'Statement of Chairman Joseph T. Kelliher', Federal Energy Regulatory Commission, Conference on Competition on Wholesale Power Markets AD07-7-000, 27 February 2007.
3.   The PJM market design and operating rules include more detail than can be included in this conceptual overview. PJM maintains detailed operating manuals that are continuously revised and available with the revision history on https://www.pjm.com/library/manuals (accessed 28 June 2021). Key market design manuals include M06: Financial Transmission Rights; M11: Energy & Ancillary Services Market Operations; M14B: PJM Region Transmission Planning Process; M18: PJM Capacity Market; M20: PJM Resource Adequacy Analysis.
4.   As is common practice, reactive power flows and voltage magnitudes are treated here as separable following the assumptions of a DC load model modified to include losses. For simplicity, we assume all the functions are differentiable.

REFERENCES

Bjørndal, E., M. Bjørndal, K. Midthun and A. Tomasgard (2018), 'Stochastic electricity dispatch: a challenge for market design', *Energy*, **150**, 992–1005.

Boucher, J. and Y. Smeers (2002), 'Towards a common European electricity market', *Competition and Regulation in Network Industries*, **3** (4), 375–24.

Cadwalader, M. D., S. M. Harvey, S. L. Pope and W. W. Hogan (1998), 'Reliability, scheduling markets, and electricity pricing', accessed 16 July 2021 at https://scholar.harvard.edu/whogan/files/schd0598.pdf.

Cramton, P. (2017), 'Electricity market design', *Oxford Review of Economic Policy*, **33** (4), 589–612.

Federal Energy Regulatory Commission (FERC) (1996), *Order 888: Promoting Wholesale Competition Through Open Access Non-Discriminatory Transmission Services by Public Utilities, Recovery of Stranded Costs by Public Utilities and Transmitting Utilities*, Dockets No. RM95-8-000, No. RM94-7-001, accessed 16 July 2021 at https://www.ferc.gov/sites/default/files/2020-05/rm95-8-00w.txt.

Federal Energy Regulatory Commission (FERC) (1999), *Order Approving PJM Supporting Companies' Request for Market-based Pricing Authority*, Docket No. ER97-3739-000, accessed 16 July 2021 at https://elibrary.ferc.gov/eLibrary/#.

Federal Energy Regulatory Commission (FERC) (2011), *Order 1000: Transmission Planning and Cost Allocation by Transmission Owning and Operating Public Utilities*, Docket No. RM10-23-000, accessed 28 June 2021 at https://www.ferc.gov/sites/default/files/2020-04/OrderNo.1000.pdf.

Federal Energy Regulatory Commission (FERC) (2017), *Order Granting Complaint in Part and Denying in Part Re New York State Public Service Commission et al vs. New York Independent System Operator, Inc. under EL16-92*, Docket No. EL16-92-000, accessed 19 July 2021 at https://elibrary.ferc.gov/IDMWS/common/opennat.asp?fileID=14483864.

Federal Energy Regulatory Commission (FERC) (2019), *Order on Paper Hearing*, Docket No. EL18-34-000, accessed 19 July 2021 at https://elibrary.ferc.gov/idmws/common/opennat.asp?fileID=15221762.

Gribik, P. R., W. W. Hogan and S. L. Pope. 2007, 'Market-clearing electricity prices and energy uplift', *Harvard Electricity Policy Group Working Paper*, accessed 19 July 2021 at https://scholar.harvard.edu/whogan/files/gribik_hogan_pope_price_uplift_123107.pdf.

Hogan, W. W. (1992), 'Contract networks for electric power transmission', *Journal of Regulatory Economics*, **4** (3), 211–42.

Hogan, W. W. (1998), 'Nodes and zones in electricity markets: seeking simplified congestion pricing', in H.-P. Chao and H. G. Huntington (eds), *Designing Competitive Electricity Markets*, New York: Springer, pp. 33–62.

Hogan, W. W. (2002), 'Electricity market restructuring: reforms of reforms', *Journal of Regulatory Economics*, **21** (1), 103–32.

Hogan, W. W. (2013), 'Electricity scarcity pricing through operating reserves', *Economics of Energy & Environmental Policy*, **2** (2), 65–86.

Hogan, W. W. (2016), 'Virtual bidding and electricity market design', *The Electricity Journal*, **29** (5), 33–47.

Hogan, W. W. (2018), 'A primer on transmission benefits and cost allocation', *Economics of Energy & Environmental Policy*, **7** (1), 25–45.

Hogan, W. W. (2019), 'Market design practices: which ones are best?', *IEEE PES Magazine*, **17** (1), 100–104.

Hogan, W. W. and S. L. Pope (2019), *PJM Reserve Markets: Operating Reserve Demand Curve Enhancements*, FTI Consulting Inc. report, 21 March, accessed 19 July 2021 at https://scholar.harvard.edu/whogan/files/hogan_pope_pjm_report_032119.pdf.

Hua, B., D. A. Schiro and T. Zheng et al. (2019), 'Pricing in multi-interval real-time markets', *IEEE Transactions on Power Systems*, **34** (4), 2696–705.

Joskow, P. L. (2008), 'Capacity payments in imperfect electricity markets: need and design', *Utilities Policy*, **16** (3), 159–70.

Joskow, P. L. (2019), 'Challenges for wholesale generation at scale: intermittent renewable electricity markets with the U.S. experience', *Oxford Review of Economic Policy*, **35** (2), 291–331.

Liu, H., L. Tesfatsion and A. A. Chowdhury (2009), 'Locational marginal pricing basics for restructured wholesale power markets', paper presented at the 2009 IEEE Power and Energy Society General Meeting, PES '09.

Lopes, F. and H. Coelho (eds) (2018), *Electricity Markets with Increasing Levels of Renewable Generation: Structure, Operation, Agent-Based Simulation, and Emerging Designs*, Cham, Switzerland: Springer International Publishing.

Monitoring Analytics (2017), *2016 State of the Market Report for PJM. Volume 2: Detailed Analysis*, accessed 28 June 2021 at http://www.monitoringanalytics.com/reports/PJM_State_of_the_Market/2016/2016-som-pjm-volume2.pdf.

Monitoring Analytics (2019), *2018 State of the Market Report for PJM. Volume 2: Detailed Analysis*, accessed 28 June 2021 at https://www.monitoringanalytics.com/reports/PJM_State_of_the_Market/2018/2018-som-pjm-volume2.pdf.

Munoz, F. D., S. Wogrin, S. S. Oren and B. F. Hobbs (2018), 'Economic inefficiencies of cost-based electricity market designs', *The Energy Journal*, **39** (3), 51–68.

Newell, S., R. Carroll and A. Kaluzhny et al. (2018), *Estimation of the Market Equilibrium and Economically Optimal Reserve Margins for the ERCOT Region: 2018 Update*, report prepared for Electric Reliability Council of Texas, December, accessed 28 June 2021 at https://brattlefiles.blob.core.windows.net/files/15258_estimation_of_the_market_equilibrium_and_economically_optimal_reserve_margins_for_the_ercot_region.pdf.

Nordhaus, W. D. (2013), *The Climate Casino: Risk, Uncertainty, and Economics for a Warming World*, New Haven, CT: Yale University Press.

Ott, A. L. (2003), 'Experience with PJM market operation, system design, and implementation', *IEEE Transactions on Power Systems*, **18** (2), 528–34.

PJM Interconnection (2017), *Proposed Enhancements to Energy Price Formation*, 15 November, accessed 19 July 2021 at http://www.pjm.com/-/media/library/reports-notices/special-reports/20171115-proposed-enhancements-to-energy-price-formation.ashx.

PJM Interconnection (2018a), *Leading Through the Transition: 2018 PJM Annual Report*, accessed 19 July 2021 at https://www.pjm.com/-/media/about-pjm/newsroom/annual-reports/2018-annual-report.ashx?la=en.

PJM Interconnection (2018b), *Strengthening Reliability: An Analysis of Capacity Performance*, accessed 19 July 2021 at https://www.pjm.com/-/media/library/reports-notices/capacity-performance/20180620-capacity-performance-analysis.ashx.

PJM Interconnection (2019), *Enhanced Price Formation in Reserve Markets of PIM Interconnection, L.L.C.*, Docket Nos ER19-1486-000, EL19-58-000, accessed 19 July 2021 at https://pjm.com/directory/etariff/FercDockets/4036/20190329-el19-58-000.pdf.

Radford, B. (2013), 'Very roughly commensurate: analyzing the Order 1000 comply filings from non-RTO regions', *Public Utilities Fortnightly*, January, 16–29.

Rivier, M. and I. J. Pérez-Arriaga (1993), 'Computation and decomposition of spot prices for transmission pricing', paper presented at the 11th PSC Conference, Avignon, France, August, accessed 19 July 2021 at https://www.researchgate.net/profile/IJ_Perez-Arriaga/publication/245739246_Computation_and_decomposition_of_spot_prices_for_transmission_pricing/links/54ae64020cf2828b29fce214/Computation-and-decomposition-of-spot-prices-for-transmission-pricing.pdf.

Ruff, L. E. (2001), 'Flowgates, contingency-constrained dispatch, and transmission rights', *The Electricity Journal*, **14** (1), 34–55.

Schweppe, F. C., M. C. Caramanis, R. D. Tabors and R. E. Bohn (1988), *Spot Pricing of Electricity*, Boston, MA: Kluwer Academic Publishers.

Telson, M. L. (1973), *The Economics of Reliability for Electric Generation Systems: MIT Energy Laboratory, Report No. MIT-EL 73-016*, May, accessed 19 July 2021 at http://dspace.mit.edu/handle/1721.1/27285.

Wilson, J. (2010), 'Reconsidering resource adequacy: part 1', *Public Utilities Fortnightly*, April, 33–9.

Wolfram, C. D. (1999), 'Measuring duopoly power in the British electricity spot market', *American Economic Review*, **89** (4), 805–26.

8.   ERCOT: success (so far) and lessons learned
Ross Baldick, Shmuel S. Oren, Eric S. Schubert* and Kenneth Anderson

1.   INTRODUCTION

This chapter describes the evolution of the restructured electricity market in the Electric Reliability Council of Texas (ERCOT) region, which covers most of Texas. It highlights the successes to date and the lessons learned and is divided into three main sections. Section 2 will provide an historical and legal introduction to ERCOT, particularly highlighting its unique geographical and jurisdictional aspects. After that, Section 3 will describe the challenges of creating a self-sustaining power market, while Section 4 will consider how ERCOT has met those challenges. Finally, Section 5 will conclude by summarizing the main points presented in the chapter.

2.   OVERVIEW OF ERCOT

Electric Reliability Council of Texas, Inc. (ERCOT) is a non-profit corporation that manages the flow of electric power to more than 26 million Texas customers who are located within the Texas Interconnection, which along with the Eastern and Western Interconnections, comprise the three synchronously connected electric grids in the continental United States.[1] These three interconnections are not connected synchronously, but do have the ability to transfer relatively small amounts of power over direct current (DC) ties. The Texas Interconnection is located entirely within the State of Texas and covers over 75 per cent of the state's geography and represents about 90 per cent of the state's total electric consumption. The region does not include the El Paso area in far West Texas, which is within the Western Interconnection, nor the northern Panhandle area in the Eastern Interconnection (except for some transmission facilities built to move renewable generation from that region into the population centres of Texas located in the ERCOT region), nor does it include some relatively small areas around Northeast and Southeast Texas, which are also located in the Eastern Interconnection. Figure 8.1 shows an exploded map of the Western Interconnection, ERCOT and Eastern Interconnection. Figure 8.2 shows a map of Texas with the footprint of ERCOT in more detail.

The origins of the Texas Interconnection lay in the Second World War when, in 1941, a group of Texas electric utilities joined together as the Texas Interconnected System (TIS) to support the war effort. TIS sent excess power supplies to industrial manufacturing companies on the Texas Gulf Coast to provide power for energy-intensive production processes. Recognizing the reliability advantages of remaining interconnected, the TIS members continued to use and develop the interconnected Texas grid, including agreeing not to interconnect or sell power outside the interconnection to avoid becoming subject

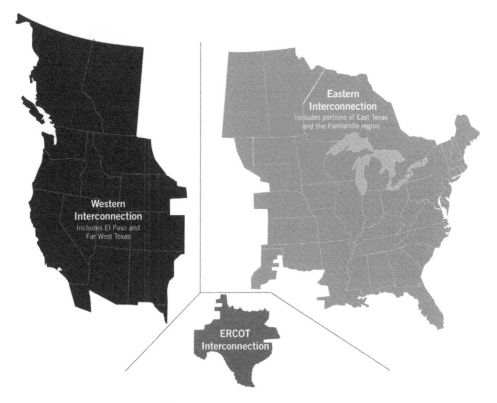

Source: ERCOT, www.ercot.com.[2]

Figure 8.1 *Map of the Western Interconnection, ERCOT and Eastern Interconnection*

to the Federal Power Act, and to avoid the jurisdiction of the Federal Power Commission, the predecessor of the Federal Energy Regulatory Commission (FERC).[3] For this reason ERCOT and the Texas Interconnection are not subject to FERC jurisdiction under the Federal Power Act except for certain reliability matters arising from the Energy Policy Act of 2005 and for wholesale sales to and from ERCOT over its asynchronous ties with the Eastern Interconnection.[4] TIS members adopted official operating guides for their interconnected power system and established two monitoring centres within the control centres of two utilities, one in North Texas and one in South Texas.[5] TIS formed ERCOT in 1970 to participate with the North American Reliability Council, predecessor of the North American Reliability Corporation, as utilities nationally increased coordination following the Northeast Blackout of 1965. ERCOT continued to evolve over the ensuing decades to take on more responsibilities and roles.[6]

In 1995, the Texas Legislature acted to deregulate the wholesale generation market within the Texas Interconnection and the Public Utility Commission of Texas (PUCT) began the process of expanding ERCOT's responsibilities and capabilities to enable wholesale competition and facilitate efficient use of the power grid by all market participants.[7] In August of the following year, the PUCT adopted an electric utility joint task force recommendation that ERCOT become an independent system operator (ISO) to

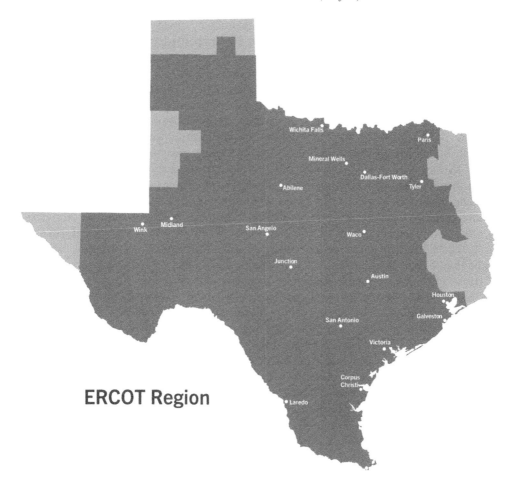

Wichita Falls

Paris

Mineral Wells

Dallas-Fort Worth

Tyler

Abilene

Wink   Midland   San Angelo   Waco

Junction   Austin

Houston

San Antonio   Galveston

Victoria

ERCOT Region

Corpus Christi

Laredo

Source: ERCOT, www.ercot.com.

Figure 8.2   Map of Texas showing ERCOT region

ensure that an impartial, third-party organization was overseeing equitable access to the power grid by competitive market participants. About a month later, this change was implemented officially, when the ERCOT Board of Directors restructured its organization and initiated operations as a not-for-profit ISO, making it one of the first electric ISOs in the United States. Three years later, the Texas Legislature completed its restructuring of the Texas Interconnection by enacting Senate Bill 7, which required investor-owned utilities (IOUs) to unbundle their functions (generation, delivery and retail sales of electricity) and required by 1 January 2002 the creation of a competitive retail electricity market to give customers the ability to choose their retail electric providers. Senate Bill 7 also gave the PUCT authority to oversee ERCOT and to develop rules to protect competition in the wholesale market and consumers in the retail market. Over time, the Texas legislature has continued to give the PUCT increased authority over ERCOT and its operations, including the ability to confirm ERCOT's independent directors and approve its budget.

From 1999 to 2000, ERCOT sponsored a stakeholder process to address how ERCOT would administer its responsibilities to support the competitive retail and wholesale electricity markets while maintaining the reliability of electric services. In thousands of hours of meetings and mark-up sessions, the market participants worked together to develop new ERCOT protocols, which, when approved by the PUCT, are enforceable rules and standards for implementing market functions regarding energy scheduling and dispatch, ancillary services, congestion management, outage coordination, settlement and billing, metering, data acquisition and aggregation, market information systems, transmission and distribution losses, renewable energy credit trading, registration and qualification, market data collection, load profiling and alternative dispute resolution.

Historically, there had been ten interconnected control areas in ERCOT. Each corresponding control area operator had been responsible for balancing supply and demand within its area in cooperation with the other operators. At the end of July 2001, the existing ten control areas in the ERCOT region were consolidated into a single control area (now called a 'balancing area' under North American Reliability Corporation – NERC – terminology). Wholesale power sales among parties began to operate under the new electric industry restructuring guidelines, including centralization of power scheduling and procurement of ancillary services to ensure reliability. Commercial functions were centralized to facilitate efficient market operations, including meter data acquisition and aggregation, load profiling and state-wide registration of retail premises to facilitate switching by customers between competitive retail electricity providers (REPs). On 1 January 2002, ERCOT and its market participants launched the competitive retail electric market under the auspices of the PUCT, allowing individuals and businesses in areas previously served by incumbent IOUs to choose their retailer. The 1999 restructuring law applied to IOUs, but allowed public power entities, municipally owned utilities and electric cooperatives, then approximately 24 per cent of the ERCOT load, to decide if they wanted to participate in retail competition.

A day-ahead 'scheduling' process was established in 2001 where market participants provided matched generation and consumption information for each 15-minute interval in the following day and made offers to provide ancillary services. After initial operation of the ERCOT wholesale market without any representation of transmission limits, ERCOT was divided in 2002 into four zones for the purposes of dispatching and pricing power purchases from generators and sales to retail customers. Supply was specified based on portfolios of generation in each zone and demand was also specified zonally. A 'balancing market' then sought bids and offers to deviate from the day-ahead schedules.

It soon became evident that such a system of zonal portfolio dispatch was inefficient in maintaining grid reliability and expensive for wholesale market participants (Baldick 2003). As a result, in September 2003, the PUCT ordered ERCOT to develop a nodal wholesale market design, with the goal of improving market and operating efficiencies through more granular pricing and scheduling of energy services (PUCT 2003). The ERCOT stakeholder process worked from 2003 through the middle of 2005 on developing nodal protocols and in September of that year ERCOT submitted draft nodal protocols to the PUCT. In April 2006, the PUCT issued an order approving the stakeholder-developed protocols for the nodal market, with an implementation date of 1 January 2009. After an almost two-year delay because of implementation difficulties, on 1 December 2010 ERCOT launched the nodal market, which included locational marginal prices (LMPs) for generation, a day-ahead energy and ancillary services co-optimized market, day-ahead and hourly reliability-unit commitment, and congestion revenue rights. In this new framework, the real-time market prices and dispatches generation in five-minute periods and settled in 15-minute increments. Instead of zonal portfolio offers and bids as in the previous market, the nodal market required offers specifically from each generating unit.

As ISO for the region since 1996, ERCOT has managed the open-access regime and today schedules power on an electric grid that connects more than 46 500 miles of transmission lines owned by transmission-only service providers, transmission and distribution-only IOUs, municipally owned utilities, and electric cooperatives with over 680 generation units[8] to deliver electricity to multiple public entities and private companies for distribution to their retail customers. In addition, ERCOT performs financial settlement for the competitive wholesale bulk-power market and administers retail switching for nearly 8 million premises in competitive choice areas of Texas, which represents approximately 75 per cent of ERCOT's electric load. As of the end of June 2021, ERCOT had over 100 000 MW of resources available to serve electric consumers, including 26 728 MW of installed wind capacity, and 4648 MW of installed utility-scale solar capacity (ERCOT, 2021a).

ERCOT is a membership-based 501(c)(4) non-profit corporation,[9] governed by a Board of Directors and is subject to regulatory oversight by the PUCT. Its members include groups representing consumers, electric cooperatives, independent generators, independent power marketers, REPs, IOUs that build, own, operate and maintain transmission and distribution lines, and municipally owned electric utilities. The ERCOT Board of Directors is a 16-member 'hybrid' group that includes six market participants, one from each of the six electric utility market groups, three consumer representatives, five independent and unaffiliated members, the ERCOT chief executive officer, and the chair of the PUCT, who does not have a vote. Directors representing market groups are nominated and elected by members from that group. The five independent and unaffiliated directors are nominated by a nominating committee and, subject to confirmation by the PUCT, elected by the ERCOT members at an annual meeting of members.

ERCOT's stakeholder process for adopting new or revised protocols, operating guides and other documents is conducted through the Technical Advisory Committee (TAC), which is made up of members selected from and by each of the market segments. TAC has five standing subcommittees as well as numerous workgroups and task forces, where proposed new and revised protocols, operating guides and other policy matters are first discussed and debated. The staff of the PUCT observe and occasionally participate in the process at TAC. After a thorough review process as described below, TAC, by majority vote, makes policy recommendations, including minority views, to ERCOT's Board of Directors, who must approve any new or changed protocol, operating guide or other policy before it becomes effective. Any decision by the ERCOT's Board of Directors in these or other substantive matters may be appealed to the PUCT.

TAC also makes recommendations to the ERCOT's Board regarding the need for new transmission lines or major upgrades to existing facilities, whether for reliability reasons or improved economic benefits to consumers. A recommendation by ERCOT's Board is sufficient to satisfy the PUCT criterion of the need for investment in the subsequent proceeding. In 2020, over $2.3 billion of transmission projects were energized in the ERCOT region (ERCOT 2021b).

ERCOT has evolved and changed over recent decades, with principal events involving the establishment of the ERCOT ISO itself, the development of a governance structure, and the restructuring of the wholesale and retail markets. With this general historical setting established, the rest of this chapter will focus in detail on the challenges posed in creating a viable power market and how ERCOT has met those challenges.

3.   CHALLENGES OF CREATING A SELF-SUSTAINING POWER MARKET

Power markets and market design need to evolve to meet changing conditions associated with more consumer-driven behaviour and the widespread deployment of intermittent renewables. As a result, the designs of organized power markets in North America, Europe and Australia have been forced to continuously change over the past 20 years. Arguably, ERCOT has converged, through a series of trials and errors, on a workable solution for addressing that evolution.

The following two sections discuss the policy goals of customer choice in the ERCOT market (Section 3.1) and the specific challenges in meeting these goals (Section 3.2).

3.1   Policy Goals of Customer Choice in the ERCOT Market

This section details two main policy goals related to customer choice in ERCOT – namely, implementing retail choice in Section 3.1.1, and facilitating the integration of new technologies in Section 3.1.2.[10] This will set the stage for the discussion in Section 3.2 of the challenges overcome in meeting these goals.

3.1.1   Implement retail choice[11]
In the law that restructured the power industry in ERCOT in 1999,[12] the Texas Legislature explicitly wanted to facilitate full competition across all retail customer classes: large commercial and industrial (C&I), small commercial and residential.

Full retail choice was to begin for large C&I customers on 1 January 2002, as it was believed that this segment had the financial and technical skills to manage the commercial risks of negotiating with a competitive retailer without a transition. In contrast, the Texas Legislature decided that the market for residential and small commercial customers, also known as mass market customers, should have a five-year transition before full retail choice was implemented. Nevertheless, it was intended that the benefits of restructuring would accrue eventually to all market segments and not just to large customers.

The Texas retail market design had some uncommon or unique features compared to restructuring in other parts of the United States. For instance, as is more common internationally under retail restructuring, competitive retailers were given responsibility for customer billing rather than giving responsibility to the wires companies that remained rate and service regulated, so customers would more readily see who their retail agents were. Also, residential and small commercial customers were not given the easy fall-back of 'basic or standard offer' or 'default service' from regulated wires companies, which also encouraged mass market customers to actively shop for retail electric service rather rely on a regulated default service provider.

As well as not emphasizing a default service, the Texas Legislature chose to use a 'price-to-beat' mechanism, which froze the offerings to mass market customers from the retail affiliate of the incumbent unbundled utility, allowing competing REPs to undercut the incumbent. At the start of the retail market in 2002, the previously regulated prices had been high enough to permit all eligible customers to immediately benefit from the price to beat, while the price to beat was nevertheless at a high enough level to enable profitable entry by new REPs. The price to beat was also indexed to the cost of natural gas to maintain headroom for competitive retailers if wholesale power prices rose as a result of increases in the cost of natural gas (a fuel for a significant portion of the ERCOT generation fleet). It should be mentioned in this context that some of the financial difficulties of utilities in California in 2000 stemmed from increases in natural gas prices that could not be passed on to retail customers, so the issue of gas price volatility had already provided painful lessons in retail restructuring elsewhere.

Another ongoing goal of the Texas Legislature was to have a set of policies to maintain the ease of entry into both wholesale and retail markets, which provided consumers with an ample choice of REPs and REPs with an ample choice of wholesale suppliers. Among the policies that facilitated entry of independent REPs, there were (1) the use of ERCOT as a centralized switching registration agent; and (2) having simple, straightforward registration requirements for power generation companies (PGCs) at the PUCT. Furthermore, to help spur supply competition and ensure that prices were reasonably fair and not the product of an abuse of market power, the restructuring law limited any one PGC or their affiliates from owning and controlling more than 20 per cent of the installed generation capacity within ERCOT.[13]

Municipally owned utilities and electric cooperatives (collectively 'non-opt-in entities', or NOIEs) were exempted as a compromise in the original restructuring laws, with an underlying premise that, over time, competitive retail competition in other parts of Texas would pressure NOIEs to either allow retail competition or keep their rates comparable to areas with retail choice.

After restructuring, the Texas Legislature encouraged the deployment and use of smart meters and the PUCT adopted rules to facilitate their installation by the regulated wires companies. Currently, ERCOT has achieved nearly system-wide installation of smart meters (over 98 per cent of all energy settled in areas with retail choice). As a result, customers can switch retailers faster (often within a day) and more easily than in many other jurisdictions. As part of the system-wide deployment of smart meters, PUCT required ERCOT to settle smart meters in 15-minute increments, which facilitated new products and services for residential and small commercial customers, among which are voluntary aggregated load reduction programmes administered by REPs. The smart meter deployment has also enabled REPs to offer these customer classes more varied and flexible products to manage their energy use based upon the time of consumption, such as 'free nights or weekends' (with a related increase in the price during other hours of the day) and even products that provide for the real-time wholesale settlement price to be passed through to the retail customer with no mark-up other than a small monthly charge together with the transmission and distribution charge.

Strong political mandates by state legislators, who are responsive to voters who are also consumers, ensured that prices were as fair (not the product of market power abuse) and as uniform across the relevant geographic footprints as reasonably possible. The

PUCT has responded by making it a consistent policy to remove import constraints into large load centres and to make the transmission network more robust in the South and West load zones.[14]

3.1.2   Integrate new, rapidly evolving technologies

Behind the deregulation law of 1999 was, among other things, the hope that by unbundling the vertically integrated IOUs, and thereby taking generation out of the rate base regulated and approved by the PUCT, competition would be harnessed between generation asset owners and among competitive retailers. Unleashing competition in other previously regulated industries had resulted in them adapting more quickly to changes in technologies and market conditions and allowing consumer preferences, rather than the preferences of regulators and their regulated industries, to guide the introduction of new technologies, products and services.

In the initial legislation in 1999, the Texas Legislature also decided to slowly introduce renewable technologies into the ERCOT grid through a renewable portfolio standard (RPS). The RPS was modest by today's standard – a requirement of 2000 MW of installed renewable facilities by 2009, without specifying the technology. The market's choice for renewables soon became wind generation, which benefitted from both federal production tax credits (PTCs) and rapidly improving technology, as well as relatively cheap land and abundant wind resources in West Texas. Also often mentioned by wind developers was the relative ease, speed and low expense of ERCOT's interconnection process. The result was that ERCOT reached the 2000 MW goal in 2006 and had an installed wind capacity of nearly 9000 MW by the end of 2009, greatly exceeding the modest expectations of the Texas Legislature. Utility-scale solar did not see the same growth during this period because of the nature of its federal subsidy (investment tax credit), the higher cost of the technology, and the relatively constrained transmission system in West Texas that existed at that time. However, more recently, ERCOT has experienced and expects to continue to see rapid growth in utility-scale solar investment as the cost of solar has continued to decline and incremental transmission has been built. Between 2015 and the end of 2019, utility-scale solar grew from 288 MW to nearly 2300 MW in ERCOT.

The Texas Legislature made three key policy decisions in the second quarter of 2005 to facilitate the integration of new technologies on the ERCOT grid. The first policy decision was to increase the RPS to 5880 MW by 2015 with an additional target of 10 000 MW by 2025. The second policy choice was granting the PUCT the authority to order the construction of new transmission capacity in what were called Competitive Renewable Energy Zones (CREZs). The purpose was to enable the construction of a substantial network of new transmission lines in areas with a strong potential for wind and solar development in West Texas and the Texas Panhandle, thereby facilitating renewable investment in those regions, without the transmission developers having to first demonstrate actual need in a PUCT contested administrative proceeding, as would otherwise have been required by the Texas Public Utility Regulatory Act (PURA). Last, the Texas Legislature granted the PUCT the authority to order wires companies in areas with retail choice to install smart meters to help improve retail competition for residential and small commercial customers by enabling customers to switch REPs much more quickly[15] and also facilitating the adoption of new technologies and the offering of new products and services by REPs.

There were many drivers of these policy directions, including several unrelated to wind energy itself.[16] Moreover, in the period 2002–05, the PUCT also ordered the ERCOT market to improve locational pricing (the move from zonal portfolio offer/bidding to a nodal unit-specific model) and create a crude proxy for scarcity pricing (high offer caps in an explicit 'energy-only' market design with loosened constraints on exercise of market power by generation fleets that had 5 per cent or less of installed capacity).

While the move to locational pricing had also become standard in other restructured wholesale markets in the US, the energy-only market arrangement in ERCOT is unique. In those other organized markets, there remain either obligations on load-serving entities (LSEs) to procure capacity or an ISO-administered forward capacity market to meet a specific mandatory minimum reserve margin of installed generation capacity above the peak demand forecasted by the ISO, or both in combination. (See Chapters 4 and 7 in this handbook for a discussion of capacity markets in other regions of the US.) ERCOT has no mandatory minimum reserve margin of installed generation capacity above its forecasted peak demand. The PUCT and the ERCOT stakeholders made a conscious decision to allow market forces to determine the system's reserve margin of installed capacity. ERCOT reserve margin is merely a target reference for stakeholders to guide investment decisions by both generation owners and consumers.

Since the ERCOT market is, in several respects, including its energy-only character, unlike other US markets, it is important to understand various aspects of its design. An effective energy-only market requires several characteristics. First, it needs 'shock absorbers' in the face of external shocks and sometimes rapid, unexpected changes, as described in more detail in the next section. Second, an energy-only market also needs a means to provide scarcity price signals despite the presence of mechanisms that are designed to mitigate and consequently mask such scarcity – for example, through operating reserves deployment or as part of market power mitigation. Improved locational and enhanced scarcity pricing have accomplished this second task so far by creating financial incentives for buyers and sellers of power to reinforce reliability in real time and resource adequacy in the long run.

3.2 Challenges in Meeting Those Goals

This section details several challenges in meeting the goals described in the previous section, including the implications of unpredictability, adaptability to rapid changes, engineering challenges, policy challenges and commercial challenges.

3.2.1 Coping with the unpredictability of evolving markets[17]

The Texas Legislature had a policy goal of making ERCOT as open to market forces as reasonably possible.[18] As a result, ERCOT wholesale and retail markets at any given moment reflect investor psychology, market enthusiasms (for instance, the rush to build combined-cycle plants or wind farms and, more recently, utility-scale solar facilities), changing consumer tastes (for example, the desire for clean energy), and other emerging new technologies such as energy storage and customer-driven demand response. The ERCOT market has long been open to new opportunities that have not been fully understood or planned for by market participants or regulators.

In this uncertain world, markets continue to see waves of investment, shakeouts and consolidations, with market participants having differing risk profiles and motives for investing in new capacity or services. Some will make smart investments, some will make prudent investments, and some will make foolish investments. Arguably, this process, which involved rapid evolution of both wholesale and retail markets, was facilitated by the fact that the Texas Legislature had an overriding goal that the 'market' – not the ERCOT stakeholder process or even the PUCT – was to be the leading force in determining winners and losers.

3.2.2 Adaptability to rapid deployment of new technologies

The technological dynamics of today's electric market are very different from the old world of regulation. Electric generation options will include increasingly smaller-scale units. Consumers have a variety of technologies at their disposal to manage the timing, fuel source and amount of electricity they consume. Older utility-scale generation will be displaced through direct competition from various resources, including the demand side, particularly during demand peaks, not by explicit regulator's edict.

Changing technology, changing relative prices and changing consumer preferences lead to everyone having the same 'great idea' at the same time, so adoption of new or improved technologies often takes place in waves by investors with a very different risk profile than the typical regulator.[19] As mentioned above, combined-cycle generators were the dominant new construction from the early years of wholesale restructuring, giving way to significant new wind in recent years, and more recently solar.

These waves are the result of a combination of factors such as (1) the uncertainty about the size and scope of the new market opportunity; (2) the uncertain profitability of the investments in the new technology; (3) the uncertain extent to which the new technology will affect current business practices; (4) the fight for market shares among investors in the new technology; (5) loose monetary policy or low interest rates that increase the potential for loans for investors; (6) the response to a government subsidy with a fixed expiration date; and (7) the willingness of many market participants to make high risk/high reward bets on developing the new technology.

In this new world of power generation and energy management technologies, deployment of resources is faster and fraught with greater uncertainty, and new capacity is installed in a fraction of the time historically taken for large-scale coal or nuclear plants. Combined-cycle gas plants can be built within a couple of years, while wind farms can be sited and built within a year; capacity can be expanded in even less time. A wind developer might obtain a site for 150 wind turbines, build 100 initially, and add 50 at an undetermined future date. Distributed generation (DG) and market-based demand response has been growing into this quick-response model as well, but in the first decade of the twenty-first century required the PUCT to order improved locational and scarcity pricing to ensure that customers realize the greatest efficiency gains with the least amount of risk. Arguably, significant further increases in DG may require further improved locational signals, including having net injections into the grid from behind-the-meter generation settled nodally instead of zonally.

3.2.3 Engineering challenges in a policy context

One of the key questions that has been debated in the US and all over the world in the process of restructuring electricity markets has been the extent to which technical considerations and constraints should be reflected in the commercial model underlying the wholesale trading of electricity. This consideration is the primary aspect differentiating the prevailing wholesale market design in Europe from the real-time and day-ahead markets with unit commitment and locational pricing adopted in the United States and differentiating the early market designs in California and Texas from the eventual market designs adopted in these systems, which now both embody the principles implemented throughout restructured regions of the US. The European systems and the initial designs in California and ERCOT attempted to simplify the commercial models by treating electricity as a homogeneous commodity and suppressing technical constraints such as transmission constraints, reliability considerations, prevailing system operating norms and unit-specific characteristics. This approach works quite well in systems with ample hydro storage such as Nord Pool, where technical infeasibilities of a schedule resulting from day-ahead and further forward trading can be rectified easily through intraday markets and a balancing phase. However, in systems dominated by thermal resources and with significant transmission constraints, the pure homogeneous commodity view of electricity and the economic paradigm associated with that view is challenged by the physical and economic realities of electric power systems. Additionally, although not a concern at the time that the US and European market designs were being developed, the recent significant increase in intermittent renewable resources is also beginning to present further challenges to market paradigms.

Features that are unique to electricity, and that hinder the use of a simplistic commodity-based commercial model, include: (1) the lack of cost-effective utility-scale storage (when hydro capacity is limited); (2) pervasive externalities due to congestion and potential cascading failures; (3) the need for energy balancing at the seconds timescale; (4) transportation being governed by complicated physical laws (Kirchhoff's laws) on constrained networks; and (5) increasing amounts of production by intermittent resources.

Of these features, the first four were relevant at the time of initial restructuring of the industry in the US. For instance, the initial market designs in California and Texas ignored transmission constraints and allowed portfolio bidding in the day-ahead market that did not specify the location and generation unit that would provide the awarded electricity offer. This approach, which still prevails in European markets, typically results in infeasible dispatch that must be rectified by the system operator in real time using counter-flows provided by incremental and decremental offers procured as part of a balancing mechanisms (using the European parlance) or in a real-time market (using the US term).

In California and Texas, this approach of ignoring transmission constraints in the commercial model resulted in pervasive gaming (for example, the infamous inc-dec game)[20] through overscheduling by entities that deliberately created congestion and were then paid to relieve the fictitious congestion they caused.[21] Similarly, some generators adversely chose supply units for portfolio awards that led to infeasible dispatch and had to be replaced by other units at a premium. Even if asset owners do not take deliberate advantage of this gaming opportunity, the dispatch incentives provided by a crude zonal model as in the initial market designs in California and Texas then necessitate a subsequent step that involves unit-specific dispatch to handle intra-zonal transmission constraints. The eventual reforms implementing nodal prices in the commercial model, both in California and ERCOT, rectified these problems by recognizing transmission constraints and power flow laws and by implementing unit-specific offers in the day-ahead market clearing and pricing. These changes internalize the effect of congestion into the economic decisions of market participants.

Some technical challenges to the implementation of a market-based system are the result of traditional operating norms that have evolved to maintain high reliability standards in an environment with limited demand response capability. While modern metering and control technology is gradually changing this reality, system operation practices are still ingrained in treating demand as inelastic.[22] One aspect of such practice is the procurement and deployment of operating reserves to avoid load shedding. In the absence of scarcity pricing when reserves are lower than desired, deployment of reserves has the effect of muting price signals that would have otherwise led to high scarcity prices that stimulate investment. In some cases, if the deployed reserves have relatively low marginal offer prices for energy, the wholesale energy price can even decrease when the reserves are deployed, despite the apparent scarcity of capacity. Suppression of scarcity signals through reserves deployment or price caps results in missing money that may lead to under-investment in (1) new generation; and (2) maintenance of existing machines. The latter leads to unnecessarily high forced outages rates during times of heaviest electricity demand when grid reliability is at greatest risk.[23]

Capacity markets have been adopted in some systems as an attempt to correct for the missing money phenomenon. However, a more direct approach to provide incentives to bring new generation to market and have that generation available during times of grid stress is the implementation of an operating reserve demand curve (ORDC). An ORDC develops a proxy to the demand for reserves based on the value of lost load (VoLL) and a probabilistic assessment of the likelihood of demand curtailment versus the level of reserves. As will be discussed in Section 4.3.2, a simplified implementation of an ORDC currently used in ERCOT augments the prices resulting from the day-ahead and real-time market clearing auctions with an adder reflecting operating reserves use and grid stress.

In general, grid reliability – that is, the ability of 'keeping the lights on' – has been a major challenge in the evolution of restructured electricity markets. The unpopularity of new transmission construction and the decisions by state regulators to allow significant import constraints to certain areas to persist complicates the management of the power grid in some US regional transmission organization (RTOs) such as the California Independent System Operator (CAISO). The growing effect of intermittent renewable resources placed on the grid by state and federal policies has further complicated real-time operations. As a result, the reliability 'value' of the resources in the real-time market has become far more important as the grid moved from a mix of cost-of-service utilities with very slow entry and exit of resources to a system with retail choice or policy-driven new entry of resources with a rapid shift in the resource mix, and its location, compared to historical norms.

For purposes of the grid operator, the value of generation availability became a combination of the locational and operational characteristics of the unit in the face of real-time pricing throughout the year. The grid operator had to consider the key factors such as (1) lower minimum loading vs higher minimum loading; (2) faster start-up time vs slower start-up time; (3) faster ramping vs slower ramping units; (4) unit readily dispatchable vs intermittently available; and (5) highly reliable vs somewhat reliable resources.

Concurrently, the need for congestion and scarcity pricing to send generation owners the right reliability signals rose substantially. As mentioned in Section 3.1.2, scarcity pricing in ERCOT initially relied on limited exercise of market power. In particular, during the early part of this century, the PUCT objected to proposals for the administrative imposition of scarcity rents based on an estimate of the VoLL, an estimate that was necessary for scarcity pricing in the absence of meaningful demand response. The PUCT instead insisted that (a proxy to) scarcity prices should result from high offers by suppliers.

There are clear economic drawbacks of relying on such exercise of market power through withholding of supply to provide investment signals; however, a countervailing issue is that such withholding also risked the use of command-and-control procedures by ERCOT to commit generating units near real time. Since such commitment was remunerated on the basis of verified operating costs, it would significantly limit returns for the owners of any unit so committed. Arguably, the net result was relatively strong incentives for self-commitment of resources in ERCOT, mitigating the potential exercise of market power. ERCOT increasingly relied on such pricing to support decentralized self-commitment of generation and coordination with near real-time decisions. It was also argued that a secondary feature of this pricing approach was to reward units that were more reliable, had lower minimum loads overnight, and had better operating characteristics (such as smaller start-up time and faster ramping).

In addition to the physical challenges, power systems are also plagued by economic aspects that violate the basic assumptions underlying the theoretical foundation of competitive markets. The long construction time for transmission and generation assets, for instance, challenges the premise that the market will respond to scarcity in a timely fashion and raises the policy question of how to mitigate wealth transfers between consumers and producers while the market adjusts. Market concentration is a prevailing phenomenon in electricity systems in large part because ownership of generation prior to restructuring was typically by utilities with geographical monopolies. Even when the geographical scope of a restructured system is much larger than the footprint of individual utilities, the geographical concentration remains. For example, Luminant, the generation arm of Vistra Energy Corporation, is the current owner of the remaining portion of the generation portfolio of its regulated Dallas-based predecessor, Texas Utilities. Luminant owned essentially all generation capacity in the region in and around Dallas. This issue is exacerbated by congestion, since local market power can be a problem even when, from a system-wide perspective, market concentration is acceptable.

Market power mitigation procedures, to be discussed later, attempt to correct for such market imperfections. However, unlike a typical commodity market, where Department of Justice antitrust procedures allow for gradual market corrections to take place, market power mitigation procedures in electricity markets are complex and must typically be implemented proactively as part of the market clearing process. The principle of 'small fish swim free' adopted at ERCOT initially, which relieves firms with small market share from market power mitigation, was too simplistic since a small fish in the ocean may still be relatively big in the lagoon when the geographic scope of the market is restricted by congestion. Indeed, there have been instances where units owned by small 'fish' with capability to produce limited but essential amounts of counter-flow on transmission lines between south and north of Texas caused a dramatic increase in the Dallas area LMPs. Due to the dynamic nature of electricity markets, exercising market power even for short time intervals and limited geographic scope can result in large wealth transfers from consumers to producers, as demonstrated during the California energy crisis. Local market power mitigation procedures in these contexts are heuristic screens that are either based on structural tests or on conduct and impact of market participants. ERCOT's 'Texas two-step' typifies structure-based screens that invoke default energy offers when the local market for congestion relief fails a competitiveness test. Similar mitigation procedures are employed at CAISO and PJM, while the New York ISO (NYISO), ISO New England (ISO-NE) and Midcontinent ISO (MISO) use conduct and impact screens.

Another critical assumption underlying the economic theory supporting the invisible hand principle of competitive markets is convexity. The fundamental theorems of welfare economics set out conditions under which competitive markets are efficient. With convex operating cost functions then, under competitive conditions, market prices would equate marginal costs and marginal benefits, ensuring that each consumer's surplus and each producer's surplus is maximized, and that the maximum social welfare is attained at market equilibrium.

For commodities that can be stockpiled, there is, in principle, time for decentralized adjustment of prices to result in close to optimal social welfare despite variations in supply and demand conditions, and without calamitous shortages or gluts, assuming production cost functions are convex. That is, the invisible hand is effective in such commodities to allocate market production and consumption decisions. The advantages of decentralized decision-making, including its encouragement of innovation, typically mean that such markets may not only achieve close to static welfare optimality but can also be expected to improve dynamically over time through technological development.

However, there is a requirement in electricity for balancing of supply and demand at the seconds timescale due to the lack of ability to stock-pile. There is, therefore, a need for a system operator to match supply and demand, most typically by dispatching generation. Given the need for a system operator to match supply and demand, the key question is what criteria should be adopted in choosing the generation to be dispatched. A natural answer is to emulate the favourable outcome of welfare optimality.

Duality theory for convex programming indicates that welfare optimal market allocations and efficient prices can be jointly determined from, respectively, the primal and dual solutions for one convex optimization model. The system operator could therefore emulate the favourable outcome of welfare optimality, at least in the short term, through solving an optimization problem. Such central optimization is premised on the assumption that the real-time market is incentive compatible and sufficiently competitive so that the cost information used in the optimization reflects true production costs. In certain real-time markets such as ERCOT currently, where there are no commitment decisions considered, the short-term decision-making at the scale of minutes is indeed reasonably well approximated by a convex optimization problem.

Unfortunately, the cost functions of generators are non-convex when considering their full operating range, including being out of service, and considering the characteristics of their operating costs (including start-up and no-load costs). Furthermore, even in the real-time context, operating cost functions may not be convex over their full operating range. When there are unit commitment decisions, non-zero start-up and minimum- or no-load costs and minimum production limits, there is non-convexity in operating costs. The prevailing approach to this issue in European markets is to allow for a sequence of forward markets – day-ahead and intraday – that allow for generator owners to trade in and out of financial positions until the position matches a feasible trajectory of commitment and dispatch for the asset. Commitment decisions are therefore decentralized in European markets.

In contrast, there are no intraday markets in the US run by ISOs. Moreover, US day-ahead markets and some real-time markets allow decentralized commitment and allow for the ISO to make unit commitment decisions in the day-ahead market and in some real-time markets (Sioshansi, O'Neill and Oren, 2008). The prevailing three-part offer format in US markets includes start-up cost, no-load cost and what is typically described in discussions at RTO stakeholder meetings as an 'upward sloping offer curve'. This representation provides useful information to the system operator for making efficient allocation decisions for economic commitment and dispatch in pool-based markets, assuming offers reflect actual marginal costs. However, it should be recognized that this three-part offer is an approximate representation of generation cost chosen so that for any given commitment it will result in a convex energy cost curve and hence yield a unique global solution to the economic dispatch problem, given the commitment decisions. The aggregate supply function for the unit commitment problem is non-convex as it includes jumps due to start-up and no-load cost as well as lumpiness of the minimum production blocks.

The prevailing LMP-based pricing mechanism was adopted in the US as a simple and reasonable approximation for efficient pricing. In a convex market environment, a system operator would dispatch generation smoothly, starting with the cheapest resource and including more expensive resources until demand is fully met (after considering constraints imposed by the transmission system and generator constraints such as minimum run times), with all generation paid at the price of the marginal cost of the most expensive resource dispatched. Without market power, generators cannot gain by deviating their offer price from marginal costs and the system operator would be able to dispatch at the lowest possible cost. Each price-taking unit would receive the greatest possible profit by offering in a way that reflects its true costs and operating constraints, while consumers would benefit. In practice, with a workably competitive market, the offers could be close enough to reflecting marginal costs so that close to efficient dispatch prevailed.

However, with non-convexities, there have always been circumstances where the prices could not reflect everything relevant to sending the right market signals that will support the optimal dispatch and provide the correct incentives to generators for not deviating from the centrally optimized dispatch instructions. The potential for such problems has been known since the beginning of the wholesale electricity markets. Under convex conditions, the dispatch and pricing solutions are simply obtained from the primal and dual solutions of the same security-constrained unit commitment and economic dispatch (SCUC/SCED) model run. LMP provides efficient signals that reflect the marginal costs of resources needed to serve demand in supporting efficient security-constrained commitment and dispatch. The conventional remedy to the non-convexity has been an uplifted make-whole payment that guarantees non-negative net revenue over each 24-hour period to generators submitting economic day-ahead offers. This correction has been reasonable, with a total uplift cost around 3 per cent of total energy sales. This may be changing, however, with a flattening supply curve, rapid penetration of renewable energy and other changes, so that the effects of ignoring non-convexity are becoming increasingly pronounced, and proposals to address these challenges are under consideration at various ISOs (PJM Interconnection 2017).

Although the ERCOT ISO market clearing process considers start-up and minimum-load costs as part of three-part offers, ERCOT is in practice largely a self-commitment market, with commitment decisions decentralized and most commitment costs covered through private contracts. There are multiple incentives (high VoLL,[24] ORDC and power balance penalty curve – PBPC) and penalties (capped earnings based on verified operating costs in the reliability unit commitment – RUC – and direct assignment of RUC costs to retailers whose customers consume more in real time than cleared in day ahead) to encourage self-commitment.[25]

In addition, recently, there are firms in Texas deploying small-scale reciprocating engines at grocery stores and gas stations. These distributed energy resources have primarily been installed to provide back-up against failures on distribution feeders and to mitigate peak demand charges for transmission and distribution. However, in addition to these roles, these generators can also respond to real-time prices at thresholds that are below $100 per MWh and can ramp to full production in a few minutes. This technology is filling some of the gaps in self-commitment of larger gas-fired generators, providing a smoother transition between the marginal costs of conventional generators and the willingness-to-pay of conventional demand response, and at clearing prices well below estimates of VoLL. There may be as much as 3 gigawatts (GW) of demand response in ERCOT today and a growing amount of distributed energy resources. It is likely that energy storage will also play a larger role in filling the non-convexities over time.[26]

Real-time markets have evolved from clearing at 15-minute intervals to clearing at five-minute intervals. However, as discussed above, the requirement of system operators is for balancing supply and demand at the seconds timescale. In this context, real-time markets should be viewed as a surrogate to balancing essentially continuously. Additional mechanisms are therefore needed to achieve the requirement of essentially continuous balancing, and fundamental questions revolve around the design of such mechanisms and whether a market process is suitable. At significantly sub-five-minute timescales, it is difficult to imagine a process converging fast enough to provide reliable matching of supply to demand, while satisfying transmission constraints and all the other technical constraints. Moreover, while sub-five-minute timeframes may not be terribly important for economic decisions of market participants, they continue to be critically important to matching supply and demand, suggesting that a 'satisficing' solution involving command and control may be reasonable in this case (Simon 1955).

The standard approach in electricity markets to ensure matching of supply and demand at sub-five-minute timescales has been to define additional 'ancillary' services (AS) – that is, agreements by market participants to sell a certain amount of their generation capacity to the grid operator to use as back-up power under command and control to address real-time reliability issues that cannot be resolved by five-minute dispatch. The norm in ERCOT and other US markets is to procure commitments for these services in the day-ahead market (and in some cases the real-time market). In contrast, several European markets procure ancillary services well in advance of day ahead.

The provision of ancillary services typically requires reserving some amount of generation capacity that could otherwise be used to generate energy in five-minute dispatch. There are important implications of this observation. For example, the initial market design in ERCOT combined a day-ahead ancillary services market and a real-time balancing market, but no day-ahead market for energy. The competing use of generation capacity for ancillary services and energy implies that there is an opportunity cost for selling ancillary services day ahead that is due to the (uncertain) profitability of selling energy in the balancing market. The type of design originally used in ERCOT that separates ancillary services from energy then requires market participants to estimate real-time energy prices and use that information in shaping offers for ancillary services. Because the price estimates have errors, the procurement of ancillary services and dispatch of remaining capacity for energy will typically be inefficient. The practice in some European markets to procure ancillary services even further in advance implies an even greater uncertainty in the estimation of opportunity costs in the relevant energy market.

All US day-ahead markets, including ERCOT, now consider energy and ancillary services together in so-called 'co-optimized' markets, so that opportunity costs are automatically incorporated into the price of ancillary services without any need for estimation by market participants. To summarize, the procurement of these services is integrated into the market process, but the services themselves are deployed under command and control by the ISO without an attempt to economically dispatch these resources at the sub-five-minute timescale. Nevertheless, it is likely that this co-optimization has improved the efficiency of dispatch compared to separated procurement of energy and ancillary services. Most US markets, but not yet ERCOT, also consider both energy and ancillary services in real time as well.[27] In contrast, most European markets still appear to have separated energy and ancillary services markets. Going forward, the challenge of integrating increasing amounts of renewables will dictate the need to modify the definitions of existing ancillary services and define new ones. As mentioned above, the relative cost of procurement of ancillary services suggest that 'satisficing' solutions may be appropriate for dealing with such challenges; however, the procurement of such services should continue to be co-optimized with energy.

3.2.4   Commercial challenges: decentralized commodity markets and integrating new technologies[28]

As stated above, the PUCT wanted to ensure that the right market structure and price signals were developed to integrate intermittent renewables and smart technologies most effectively, including smart meters, into the ERCOT market.[29] There is no clear path or one single way to integrate such technologies. Every buyer and seller of power using these technologies will be participating in, and benefitting from, a process of experimentation to determine which approaches work best, and this can most efficiently occur in a free-market environment.

In a properly functioning market, new technologies and business strategies enter an open, dynamic, non-linear system with buyers and sellers that have limited information. Market participants use a range of approaches, from intuition and rules of thumb to sophisticated data mining and optimization tools, to make decisions based on incomplete information, and are sometimes subject to miscalculations and biases, but learn and adapt over time.[30] The continuous interaction among market participants creates new market niches and services by uncovering previously unknown opportunities to buy, sell and manage risk and reward with offers of products and services. Not only do consumers get an increasing array of useful choices, but the relationships among market participants change over time, as some enter the market, others thrive, and some exit the marketplace.[31]

Healthy market ecosystems spontaneously emerge, as has happened over the centuries for the array of traditional commodities markets. For the best market outcomes, legislators and regulators must allow the market to provide real price signals, with their positive and negative incentives, for buyers and sellers to innovate, test those innovations, and adopt the fittest business plans for deploying and using new technologies for the broadest use within the electricity market.[32] The fittest adaptations would be replicated and dispersed throughout the electricity market, with the costs of unsuccessful approaches being absorbed by the shareholders of experimenting companies, not by electricity consumers.

Legislators and regulators have an important role in facilitating the evolution of competitive power market ecosystems through: (1) planning and approving new transmission facilities; (2) ensuring the most efficient and reliable commitment, dispatch and pricing of generation through centralized RTO operations in day ahead and real time; (3) deploying smart meters to provide retail energy consumers with the gateway tool that enables a greater range of energy management choices (as well as significantly expediting power restoration times after distribution outages due to weather and equipment failure); and (4) addressing the potential for fraud and abuse by participants in wholesale and retail markets.

Given the continuing reliability challenges and the potential for market power abuse associated with power grids, however, there has been a strong temptation for legislators and regulators to intervene between buyers and sellers in retail and wholesale markets in other ways that can hinder the natural evolution of competitive power markets. This continuing policy intervention by legislators and regulators who are not in complete control of the allocation of resources, as they are in jurisdictions with regulated cost-of-service procurement of electricity, leads to a continuous cascade of unintended consequences that are difficult to resolve in a timely and efficient manner to the satisfaction of energy consumers.[33] Fortunately, Texas, so far, has largely avoided this problem.

It should be recognized, however, that matching of supply and demand does require some sort of centralized process for balancing at the seconds timescale. That is, the supply–demand matching process cannot be purely decentralized at its lowest level. As alluded to above, the key question then is how far to continue 'up' with centralization. For example, FERC has approved the plans by other US organized power markets to operate centralized capacity procurement mechanisms such as centralized forward capacity markets to manage the entry and exit of new resources over multiple years, in the name of both local and system-wide reliability. This represents a 'top-down' view that centralized planning is needed at even the capacity procurement stage to ensure that capacity is available and can be delivered when needed 'to keep the lights on'; however, it is exceedingly difficult to define the reliability product of 'deliverable capacity' in a manageable auction. Moreover, the demand to be met is inevitably an estimate made by the ISO that is imposed on all LSEs, since the procurement auction uses an ISO estimate of demand growth over several years into the future. The increasing deployment of intermittent renewables has complicated this centralized procurement process further, leading to a never-ending game of 'whack-a-mole' to maintain grid reliability because the unintended consequences of a centralized, forward auction have arisen at the speed of markets but has required corrections delivered at the speed of administrative law, which is much slower. The issue of ISO forecasts becomes even more problematic at high penetrations of renewables, since the relevant forecast is of peak net demand, which is even more uncertain than the forecast of peak demand. An emerging issue is the increased magnitude and uncertainty of net demand ramps, such as embodied in the neck of the California 'duck curve'.

Another complication is that having regulators in charge of integrating twenty-first-century technologies would prevent consumers, retailers and other market participants from using their local knowledge and ingenuity to find the next killer app or great idea that would provide all of us with cleaner, more efficient and thoughtful use of energy. Or put another way, would we even have smartphones today if regulators had never broken up the Bell Telephone Company? More prosaically, it is unclear that regulators and ISOs have a better view of multi-year demand growth, as required for centralized procurement auctions, than do LSEs. The issue is even more salient in the context of predicting net demand.

With the proper price signals, buyers and sellers in ERCOT's energy-only market have and should continue to be able to procure and manage enough resources to meet their individual needs and preferences while keeping the market resource adequate (despite the need to plan new generation a year to several years in advance) and the grid reliable. The challenge of this path, however, is keeping the lights on during the transition; none of us can fully understand at this moment how the integration of the new technologies will happen, and what new ways of doing business and managing electricity use will spontaneously emerge over time.

4. HOW TEXAS ADDRESSED THE CHALLENGES

This part describes how Texas, and, specifically, ERCOT, has addressed the challenges described in Section 3. Section 4.1 first provides some background on how Texas culture and geography assisted the development of the ERCOT market. Section 4.2 explains how complex phenomena have been managed and then Section 4.3 provides five examples of such management. Previous sections have already described some of the particular features that have enabled ERCOT to respond to these challenges. However, this section seeks to put those features into what could be considered either a more general philosophical or broader social science context.

4.1 How Texas Culture and Geography Assisted the Development of the ERCOT Power Market

Texas culture and geography have played an important role in the development of the ERCOT power market by providing policymakers with abundant degrees of freedom to make choices that facilitate good market outcomes for Texas energy producers and consumers.

Self-governance has been a force driving the policies of the Texas Legislature and the PUCT across the retail, wholesale and wires parts of the ERCOT market. This approach is part of a long tradition dating back to the early days of the Texas Interconnection when the evolving Texas grid became a separate interconnection based on the desire for Texans to manage their own electric power system issues without Federal Power Commission/ FERC jurisdiction. This was enabled by the historical pattern of interconnections, which were driven largely by Texas geography, which allowed interpretations of the Federal Power Act to limit FERC jurisdiction.[34] As a result, Texas policymakers did not have the added complication of working with FERC during the evolution of the ERCOT market, with the risk that FERC might have second-guessed or hindered the policy choices Texans preferred.

Being a single state power market with a single state regulator has allowed the Texas Legislature and the PUCT to institute policies that addressed market power (20 per cent limit on generation ownership and 'Texas two-step') and allocation of costs of building new transmission (four-coincident peak allocation across the entire ERCOT footprint) in ways that complement retail choice in ERCOT. The straightforward, simple market power screens and cost allocation mechanisms reduce potential regulatory bottlenecks associated with a growing generation fleet and transmission footprint, albeit at the cost of not representing technical details of transmission coherently in the market power analysis and not considering the implications of demand response on transmission cost allocation.

On the other hand, in 2019, ERCOT began increasing its efforts to track the growth of market-based demand response but has found the task difficult because that side of the market is rapidly evolving and the information is often deemed commercially sensitive by market participants who question ERCOT's authority to require it. At the time of writing, ERCOT stakeholders are negotiating with ERCOT staff on the exact terms and conditions this information is provided.[35]

As the oil and gas industry has experienced in recent years, technology and experience make the boundary between a resource (where hydrocarbon deposits have been identified but are too expensive to develop) and a reserve (where hydrocarbon deposits can be developed at a profit) fluid over time. Similarly, the boundary between potential demand response and economically viable demand response is shifting faster than the timescale of transmission infrastructure development. As a result, at some point in the future, when technological advances and commercial expertise makes market-based demand response commonplace across all customer classes, ERCOT may have a period of excess capacity of one type or another.

Recent trends in the development of intermittent renewables, storage, distributed generation and market-based demand response have been weakening system-wide market power. The large thermal fleets can still be influential on forward transactions, but overall, market power is diminished compared to a decade ago. Some of the same trends are happening in local market power, but ERCOT and the PUCT continue to address this issue through aggressive transmission construction. The transmission construction is not without its critics who have questioned the cost and the methodology of transmission cost allocation, and its effect on ERCOT's wholesale market (Hogan and Pope 2017).

The ERCOT market has also benefited from continuity of market-friendly political leadership in Texas Government relative to other US states, Canadian provinces and foreign countries with retail choice, especially during the painful teething periods in the first decade of the market. Republicans George W. Bush and Rick Perry were governors of Texas from 1995 through 2015, appointing all the commissioners involved in deciding PUCT regulatory policy for the ERCOT market from 1999 until 2017. During this time, Republicans also dominated the Texas Legislature. Without commenting on the specifics of their policy directions, this consistency between legislative actions and executive appointments did enable a relatively uninterrupted sequence of market-friendly adjustments to the market design. Given the long life of electricity system assets, such extended continuity of consistent leadership has arguably facilitated investment.

The Texas energy culture has also fostered innovation and risk taking, bolstered by the strong belief that interaction of supply and demand, not government decisions, lead to the best price outcomes. Market participants are also viewed as the best judges on what new products and services should be developed. Such an approach, combined with the robust infrastructure of wires and smart meters, has allowed even small commercial and residential customers to have a wide range of innovative, energy management products, and time-of-use options offered by competitive retailers, such as 'free nights and weekends'. Remote disconnect capability of meters has enabled pre-paid electricity plans that are analogous to similar offerings in the telecommunications space.

The Texas energy culture and the wide, open spaces that most people associate with Texas also led to the development of a robust regulatory, legal and physical infrastructure that encouraged the development of new generation and transmission infrastructure where needed to support good market outcomes. The low cost of land outside urban areas, relatively small opposition to transmission construction and other infrastructure and the extensive network of gas pipelines has facilitated ERCOT's relatively quick and inexpensive generation interconnection access process that allowed easy entry and exit of thermal and renewable generation resources. Abundant land also facilitated transmission policies that allowed for quick, efficient siting and construction of new transmission that helped the widest range of buyers and sellers to transact through the ERCOT footprint in the face of robust economic growth during the last two decades. The astonishing pace of the CREZ transmission development, as compared to the development of large-scale transmission projects in other states, regions and countries, is a particularly vivid example of this phenomenon.

4.2 Overseeing the Simultaneous Evolution of Two Complex Phenomena in Organized Power Markets[36]

The PUCT has had a long-standing focus on ensuring that ERCOT's real-time operations software and market design permit good market outcomes consistent with competitive retail choice (PUCT 2002, pp. 6–13). A 'good market outcome' in this context is defined as real-time prices that reinforce both real-time grid reliability and operational efficiency and long-term resource adequacy for ERCOT. Good market outcomes, in turn, are vital to the continued success of the restructuring of the electricity market in ERCOT that the Texas Legislature enacted 20 years ago.

The current decentralized, energy-only resource adequacy design in ERCOT relies on the response of buyers and sellers to the potential for enhanced real-time scarcity pricing. This potential for high prices under scarcity provides incentives to be both reliable in real time and resource adequate in the long run. As a result, competitive retailers must constantly seek the best procurement practices at lowest cost for consumers, including forecasting needs that require new construction. A competitive retailer, through contracts with resource owners, provides ERCOT with a range of resources that are committed and dispatched to meet its customers' need for electricity in a given hour or day. If a competitive retailer uses more expensive and inefficient means to contract resources to meet the need of its customers for electricity, then the retailer will become a costlier provider and can be expected to lose market share to its competitors. If the retailer contracts for too few resources to meet the reliability needs of its customers in the real-time market, then the ERCOT real-time market could assess substantial amounts of scarcity pricing on the retailer's short position, forcing the retailer to potentially go out of business. In the long run, the discipline of the market combined with the appropriate reliability signals – that is, the potential for scarcity pricing – will lead to good market outcomes. A key reason for this outcome is that in the middle of the last decade, the PUCT required ERCOT to make substantial changes to the operational software/market design moving from portfolio zonal to a unit-specific nodal dispatch, and to an explicit energy-only market design with the potential of very high scarcity pricing.

These improvements, along with other smaller modifications have enabled ERCOT to embrace new generation technologies in a way that was compatible with commercial energy markets and best practices for maintaining grid reliability. ERCOT prices both congestion and scarcity in ways that provide strong incentives for new generation technologies to be procured, committed and dispatched when needed, and has a successful retail choice regime for residential and small commercial customers. This evolutionary process has been ongoing for nearly 20 years, as ERCOT, the PUCT and stakeholders have engaged in continuous review and debate over ways to ensure that ERCOT meet the reliability needs of the grid while simultaneously meeting the needs of the changing commercial energy marketplace.

Against this background of evolution, new technologies are rapidly changing the resource mix. Consequently, a key question for regulators overseeing any electricity market in the United States increasingly will be 'Where should market solutions stop and mathematical software solutions begin?' For decades, bilateral over-the-counter markets, electronic bulletin boards and futures exchanges have allowed market participants to manage risk in commodities such as oil, grains and metals from near real time to years in the future. As mentioned above, the engineering requirements of electricity generation, transmission and use, however, require that electricity markets such as ERCOT use a centralized engineering solution – a constrained optimization model – in real time to determine prices and quantities because a traditional commodities market cannot clear quickly enough 'to keep the lights on'.

While duality theory, the basis for electricity market modelling, suggests that a constrained optimization can mimic a centralized market, the duality theory itself does not provide any reason a constrained optimization should be used to determine prices outside the necessities of real time. The duality theory relies on the 'all other things being equal' assumption, which, in real time, is a very close approximation that works for both grid reliability and commercial energy markets. However, the further one moves from the real-time interface of the market and the model in an organized power market, the greater the complications that arise both in grid reliability and commercial energy markets. For example, as described earlier, commitment decisions for thermal generation units are non-convex and forecasts of both electricity demand and intermittent renewable output become increasingly less accurate the further from real time one moves.

As a result, the PUCT and other regulators considering and overseeing the potential evolution to new energy management, distributed generation technologies and intermittent renewable resources need to consider how can decentralized market solutions be enabled, encouraged, enhanced and expanded with this new technology while maintaining grid reliability. As mentioned previously, they must also determine where centralized optimization software solutions needed for grid reliability begin and decentralized market solutions end.

A key driver behind the emphasis on optimization models at the expense of traditional market mechanisms by regulators and legislators has been the historic paradigms of the electricity industry that existed at the time many of the current market designs first arose. The main assumptions underlying these market designs included: (1) dispatchable, large-scale generation meeting most of the daily electricity demand; (2) a passive or inelastic load with respect to its energy use; (3) load that is largely unaware of, or unexposed to, and therefore unresponsive to both spot market prices and real-time reliability conditions; and (4) a load that if left unprotected is subject to both potential market-power abuse and unstable reliability conditions.

However, in ERCOT, these underlying assumptions are being challenged by both the heavy penetration of intermittent renewables and the desire by consumers to use distributed generation and real-time energy management technologies. As a result, the optimal market design across the United States will need to evolve over time, somewhat decreasing reliance on centrally dispatched engineering control mechanisms such as security-constrained economic dispatch (SCED) and expanding the decentralized decision-making by consumers and other market participants that is the hallmark of more traditional commodity markets.[37] As will be discussed in the next paragraphs, underlying this transformation is the greatly expanded participation of price-based demand response.

Having grid operators include individual metered residences and small businesses in the centralized optimization software routines that are used for large-scale generation is neither feasible nor desirable. Including thousands or tens of thousands of market participants in the centralized optimization models would likely make centralized unit commitment and dispatch decisions far too complicated to run in a cost-effective manner. Such an approach would also expose certain customers to PUCT penalties for non-performance if dispatched directly by ERCOT in real time rather than voluntarily in response to real-time price signals. For that reason, ERCOT market participants have repeatedly avoided enrolling in programmes where demand response was dispatched directly as part of the SCED process in real time.

In short, when the system crosses a complexity threshold, the electricity market design needs to move away from a centralized co-ordination regime relying almost exclusively on SCED and increasingly work with the decentralized commercial market that responds to price signals, with the appropriate types of energy and ancillary service products to bridge the gap between model outputs and the decentralized commercial market.

Of course, such a move from centralized decision-making to decentralized decision-making is not a binary step but is a movement along a continuum. Aggregated, estimated price response of multiple market participants could, in principle, be incorporated explicitly into centralized decision-making. In addition, given the increased variability in the levels of net load based on increased deployment and use of wind and solar resources, procurement and deployment of ancillary services will play an even greater role. Essentially, ancillary services would act as call options on gas-fired generation, load resources and energy storage; they are all resources that would complement the level of volatility in net demand at any given date and time. There may also be a need for a more explicit option-based procurement of energy, and not just ancillary services, from thermal resources.

A key prerequisite for developing competitive retail and wholesale power markets in the United States has been the creation of organized power markets operated by ISOs or RTOs. In several cases, these power markets evolved from existing balancing authorities or power pools. The real-time market of organized power markets, by necessity, is the interface between grid reliability conditions and commercial energy markets. However, the two sides of the interface are also rapidly evolving in ways that are not fully predictable because of deploying new technologies that are increasingly preferred by legislators, regulators and energy consumers.

The simultaneous and fast-paced evolution of these two complex phenomena – reliability and commerce – associated with organized power markets, have challenged regulators and legislators across the globe. Arguably, the governance needed to nurture evolving power market ecosystems while maintaining grid reliability is radically different from traditional regulation of the power industry. Traditional regulation has the tools and structure to address complicated, static matters well, such as determining and allocating costs of new generation and transmission construction in cost-of-service proceedings and managing incremental power trades across balancing authorities from dispatchable, utility-scale generation. Arguably, however, traditional regulation has not developed the tools and structure to address complex issues, such as assessing static optimal capital investment or managing evolving dynamic market ecosystems and grid reliability of power pool resources associated with the deployment and use of intermittent renewables, distributed generation and active energy management, in a timely and effective way.

What are the definitions of 'complicated' and 'complex' in this context? Quoting from Berge and Van Laerhoven (2011, p. 164):

> A complex system is different from a complicated one. In a complicated system, there are many and diverse elements that may be isolated and studied without concern for other system components. In a complex system, however, the elements are interrelated, and one element cannot be studied without accounting for the others. Complexity is seen as lying between order and chaos, but it is not a fixed point.

Meeting these two challenges simultaneously is why organized power markets need governance that addresses phenomena that are complex (an emergent order such as a market ecosystem) as well as complicated (a planned order such as integrated resource planning, or cost-of-service regulation, or an SCED implementation).

FERC-jurisdictional markets in the US and power markets in Canada, Europe, New Zealand and Australia are well-suited for a complicated phenomenon but not a complex phenomenon. The governance of these other power systems arose from the legacy of governance of regulated power systems with utility-scale, dispatchable generation providing electricity to passive electricity customers at rates determined by regulators in administrative law hearings, public consultations, or by public power boards. This governance is better suited to manage change or variability in complicated systems, such as integrated resource plans, new transmission construction, operating an SCED model and implementing its results, or trading between balancing authorities, rather than complex systems based on competitive retail and wholesale power markets integrating new distributed and intermittent technologies in a fully integrated geographically large power grid.

In contrast, in part by intent, in part by good fortune, the three-tier governance that has emerged in Texas to oversee the ERCOT market is exceptionally well-suited for governing a complex phenomenon, especially given the rapid technological changes that are occurring in the power industry. This unique governance has addressed the uncertainties and challenges associated with two evolving, complex systems (grid reliability and commercial power markets) over the past 20 years.

In his review of complex systems in biology and society, Holling (2001) highlighted the adaptive significance of hierarchical structures in governing complex phenomena.[38] Semi-autonomous levels are formed from interactions among a set of variables that share similar speeds of change and other attributes. Each level communicates a small set of information to the next level. While the transfer from one level to the other is maintained, the interactions within levels can be transformed or the variables changed, without the whole system losing its integrity. As a result, this structure allows wide latitude for experimentation within levels, thereby greatly increasing the speed of evolution of the complex system in question. This phenomenon serves two functions: (1) conserving and stabilizing conditions that are presented to faster and lower levels; and (2) generating and testing innovations by experiments, occurring within a level.

Holling calls the second point 'an adaptive cycle which contributes to the understanding of the dynamics of complex systems' (p. 393). Over the past two decades, Texans have managed the evolution of the ERCOT market design and grid operations using this governance model based on a thorough, continuing and stakeholder-focused review process located in Austin, Texas. ERCOT evolved a 'constitution' (that is, a Texas statute – PURA), rules and regulations (PUCT rules), and operational protocols (ERCOT nodal protocols), each of which are developed simultaneously and sequentially, with the nodal protocols needing to be consistent with PUCT rules and the PUCT rules needing to be consistent with its 'constitution' (PURA, as amended from time to time), with stakeholder involvement in all three venues. This three-tier arrangement is consistent with adaptive governance of complex systems (Figure 8.3).[39] Under this system of governance, the ability to modify the nodal protocols is easier than the ability to modify the laws that govern ERCOT (the regulations adopted by the PUCT), which in turn are easier than modifying the 'constitution' (PURA). Challenges are addressed at the appropriate level.

The following section provides five key examples of how this structure has met the various challenges.

4.3 Meeting Current Challenges: Five Key Examples

4.3.1 Changes in ERCOT nodal protocols to facilitate wind integration

As mentioned in Section 3.2.3, at the time of initial restructuring of the electricity industry there was only a small amount of renewable generation in ERCOT and there was no explicit consideration given to the implications of integrating renewables. However, all else equal, with increasing amounts of renewable generation there is a growing need for ancillary services (AS). In matching demand and supply at the short timescales between dispatch intervals, variability of renewables requires larger frequency regulation reserves. Consistent with this observation, by the time of introduction of the nodal market, there was a monthly adjustment process for the required amount of frequency regulation reserves based on the historical use ('deployment') of those reserves and of the anticipated changes in needs due to changes in renewable capacity.

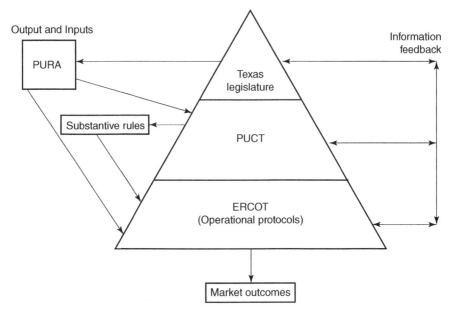

Source: Adapted from Ostrom (2005, p. 59).

Figure 8.3   Three-tiered arrangement of governance of ERCOT market

With the significant increase in wind production from essentially none at the time of initial restructuring to almost 27 GW today, it could have been anticipated that the need for frequency regulation reserves would have increased considerably. However, as described in Andrade, Baldick and Dong (2017) several changes in the ERCOT nodal protocols resulted in no overall increase in the need for frequency regulation reserves over this period. The principal change in this regard was the shift from 15-minute clearing intervals in the zonal market to five-minute clearing intervals in the nodal market. Although not made with wind as the sole driver, this change had a significant effect in reducing the amount of frequency regulation services, because the reduced time between dispatch updates implies that there is less uncertainty that must be handled outside the dispatch process. The change to the nodal system was ordered by the PUCT as a major change in the operation of the system, as reflected in the middle tier of Figure 8.3.

Many subsequent changes in the nodal protocols have been proposed, discussed and passed through action at the bottom tier of Figure 8.3. As described in detail in Andrade et al. (2017), these include many changes explicitly related to regulation reserve that have enabled the offered frequency reserve capacity to better compensate for the fundamentally increasing short-term variability due to increased wind production in ERCOT. The changes have been so substantive that required regulation reserve in ERCOT is now no more than it was at the time of initial restructuring. This is a key example of the process of responding to challenges at the appropriate level.

4.3.2 Operating reserve demand curve

Following the start of the nodal market on 1 December 2010, the most significant enhancement to price formation in ERCOT's energy-only market has been the adoption of an ORDC. The ORDC arose out of an extensive, prolonged and exhausting debate that occurred at the PUCT over whether to replace the then non-binding target reserve margin with a mandatory minimum reserve margin. This debate began in the fall of 2011 following a year of extreme weather and drought and continued until early 2014. On 2 February 2011, Texas experienced below-freezing weather across the entire state, the likes of which had not been experienced in 22 years, which resulted in 146 generator forced outages that required ERCOT to implement involuntary rotating outages for more than four hours across ERCOT to maintain grid stability despite ERCOT's having an actual installed capacity reserve margin of over 16 per cent that year. At the peak of the rolling outages, up to 4000 MW were required to be curtailed. This experience was quickly followed by a record hot summer that began in early spring and continued through most of September. By August of that year, Texas had experienced a record number of days with temperatures in excess of 100°F (around 38°C) and record temperatures across the state, coupled with a very severe drought. As a result, ERCOT came very close on several days to having to implement system-wide load curtailments because of generator forced outages and de-rates coupled with record peak loads, again despite having what was then an otherwise healthy installed capacity reserve margin.

Later that year, the then chair of the PUCT called for the establishment of a mandatory minimum reserve margin because of ERCOT's forecasts of declining target reserve margins. Taking this action would have resulted in the Commission having to abandon ERCOT's energy-only market design by adopting some mandatory mechanism to maintain that required reserve margin. The PUCT's chair was unable to move the proposal forward because the PUCT only had two members and was deadlocked over the issue. The Commission did agree to request ERCOT to have a study done to determine alternatives to its energy-only market design.[40] In the interim, the Commission took a number of steps to improve the performance of the existing energy market including establishing a timetable to raise ERCOT's offer cap from 3000 $/MWh to 9000 $/MWh. These actions helped relieve some of the pressure to 'do something'.[41]

While these and other enhancements to the energy market were being discussed and considered, the use of an ORDC in ERCOT was first brought to the attention of the PUCT commissioners individually through an original paper on ORDC authored by Hogan (2012). The commissioners decided to pursue the idea as a possible enhancement or even solution to the resource adequacy debate and requested input from ERCOT and other interested parties as to whether and how such an ORDC mechanism could or should be implemented in ERCOT. Ultimately, a preliminary consensus was reached around a modified version that was entitled 'Interim Solution B+', so named because Hogan's original paper assumed that ERCOT's real-time energy market was fully co-optimized, which was not the case.[42] Consequently, the proposed ORDC went through several iterations to reflect the ERCOT settlement systems and processes. 'Interim' reflects that further changes and enhancements to the ORDC to gain additional market efficiency can be made when ERCOT's real-time market is fully co-optimized. The PUCT requested that ERCOT do a back-cast study that estimated the proposed ORDC effect on the Brattle Group's previously estimated ERCOT equilibrium reserve margin. The

Commission also received staff and other studies from market participants regarding three key determinants of the equilibrium reserve margin:

- the value of lost load (VoLL);
- various options around what the minimum contingency requirement should be for purposes of the ORDC;[43] and
- the calculation of the loss of load probability (LOLP) – that is, the probability that at any given time the operating reserves would fall below ERCOT's minimum contingency requirement.

The minimum contingency requirement is the minimum amount of operating reserves maintained before implementing involuntary rotating load outages to preserve grid stability. This requirement was historically set at 1375 MW, which is equal to the largest single contingency in ERCOT.

Finally, on 12 September 2013, the Commission decided that the ORDC would produce a system-wide adjustment to the price of operating reserves utilizing a price adder to the real-time clearing price in each five-minute dispatch and pricing interval equal to the product of the VoLL multiplied by the LOLP. The VoLL was set at 9000 $/MWh because that was where the offer cap was going to be set by 2015 under the PUCT's prior order. The minimum contingency was set at 2000 MW under the rationale that when operating reserves fell below that figure, ERCOT's operators had historically ceased relying upon the market and began taking out-of-market actions to maintain the stability of the grid, although it should be recognized that this level of 2000 MW matches neither the largest single nor the largest double contingency in ERCOT. Consequently, the ORDC's LOLP reaches 100 per cent at a reserve level of 2000 MW and the ORDC adder would be 9000 $/MWh at this reserve level. Last, it was decided that ERCOT would use a continuous function advocated by the Independent Market Monitor (IMM), rather than the piecewise constant approximation used by ERCOT, and that when the ORDC was implemented, the energy offer price floors for deployment of ancillary services would be removed. These offer floors were intended to mitigate the price reversals that would otherwise occur when such services were deployed but became superfluous once the ORDC was implemented. The estimated LOLP was based on an ERCOT calculation that does not literally calculate the LOLP in the relevant dispatch interval, but rather is a proxy to the LOLP based on variation in net load over a longer time interval.

The PUCT then instructed ERCOT to draft the revisions to the nodal protocols necessary to implement the Commission's decisions and to push them through the stakeholder process. ERCOT subsequently filed a draft copy of the revisions for Commission review.[44] As an interesting note to the relationship between the PUCT and ERCOT (and the other stakeholders) no formal Commission order was thought necessary to implement the ORDC. ERCOT and the stakeholders simply moved forward to implement the Commission's decisions because each of the decisions made by the PUCT commissioners was unanimous.

However, the resource adequacy debate over implementing a mandatory reserve margin remained unresolved until February 2014, when a combination of previously requested reports were filed at the PUCT around the same time in January 2014. The first was the long-awaited ERCOT *Review of Preliminary Load Forecast*, dated 27 January

2014, which was a joint report from ERCOT staff and Itron Consulting. In the report, Itron supported ERCOT's new forecasting methodology, which broke from the methodology used by most of the other RTOs and ISOs. ERCOT's new forecast now showed reserve margins forecasted to be 16.7 per cent, 16.7 per cent, 17.2 per cent, 17.9 per cent and 16.4 per cent in years 2014 through 2018, versus 13.8 per cent, 11.6 per cent, 10.4 per cent, 10.5 per cent, and 9.4 per cent under the old peak load methodology. The second was the Brattle Group's report *Estimating the Economically Optimal Reserve Margin in ERCOT*.[45] In its base case, Brattle estimated ERCOT's economically optimal reserve margin to be 10.2 per cent and its then equilibrium reserve margin to be 11.5 per cent, which included the ORDC that was requested to be implemented later that year. Those two reports taken together, combined with overwhelming support for the energy-only market design by commercial and industrial customers, effectively ended the debate about the need for a mandatory reserve margin that had begun more than two years earlier.[46]

In the time since implementation, the ORDC has been operating to occasionally increase prices significantly. Some of the parameters defining the curve have been adjusted and the eventual implementation of real-time co-optimization will alter the implementation further (see next section for further details).

4.3.3 Market performance and tight reserve margins in summer 2019

In December 2018, ERCOT posted its semi-annual report on capacity, demand and reserves (CDR) with a projected reserve margin for summer 2019 of 8.1 per cent, a historic low. After the report was issued, the owners of Gibbons Creek coal-fired plant announced the retirement of the plant, which subsequently lowered the projected reserve margin to 7.4 per cent. Texas regulators and legislators for the last decade or so have been comfortable with a reserve margin of 10 to 12 per cent, having, before that, aimed for a reserve margin of 13.75 per cent based on a traditional one-in-ten-year loss of load expectation standard that the PUCT has abandoned in recent years.[47] A recent study sponsored by ERCOT suggests that the market, as currently designed, naturally would settle at the low end of that range – that is, 10.25 per cent (Newell et al. 2018).

In response to concerns about meeting demand in the summers of 2019 and 2020 with a smaller reserve margin and increased reliance on wind farms to meet summer peak demand, the PUCT ordered for 2019 a shift in the parameters of scarcity pricing embedded in the ORDC to increase the level of administrative pricing under reserve scarcity. The change was further increased for 2020.

The ERCOT market experienced two days of high levels of scarcity pricing in the summer of 2019, consistent with the energy-only market design and a cyclically low reserve margin in 2019. On the afternoons of 13 August and 15 August, real-time market prices repeatedly hit the cap of $9000 per MWh. The grid suffered no reliability problems on either day.

At an open meeting of the PUCT at the end of August 2019, the commissioners commended ERCOT for managing the grid effectively and noted that the market worked as it was supposed to do. At the meeting, the PUCT announced that it would hold an open meeting workshop on 11 October 2019 to review the performance of the ERCOT market in summer 2019.[48] A key part of that workshop was a detailed review of demand response during times of scarcity. Following this workshop, the PUCT directed ERCOT to perform a more comprehensive assessment of the demand response/price response that occurred during the summer of 2019, particularly focused in August of that year to supplement and expand upon ERCOT's preliminary observations presented at the workshop. On 6 February 2020, ERCOT filed the results of its study with the PUCT, which indicate that at least 2604 MW of demand response/price responsive loads existed within the system in August 2019.[49] As of 2020, there may be over 3 GW of such resources.

With more than 7 million smart meters installed and settled in 15-minute intervals and both buyers and sellers of power that have strong incentives to use these resources based on scarcity and ORDC pricing that can and has allowed prices to rise to 9000 $/MWh, the ERCOT market is now certainly more capable of operating with lower reserve margins, as traditionally measured. Demand response and behind-the-meter generation will likely respond to scarcity pricing in ways that were simply not possible with 'profiled' retail customers, where retailers purchased energy for their customers based on the average load share of customer classes. Whether such demand response is adequate for thin generation margins will continue to be tested in upcoming summer seasons that routinely experience high air-conditioning loads.

These distributed demand-side resources can be activated in four ways: (1) having large commercial and industrial customers provide additional capacity for the ancillary services market during super-peak hours by participating as a designated load resource in the ancillary service stack (whether by curtailing load, by serving load with behind-the-meter generation, or both); (2) relying on bilateral contracts through the commercial market to deploy utility-scale energy management resources on specific days or weeks stated in the contract; (3) activating load-reduction technologies that allow LSEs to curtail aggregated residential and small commercial customers in response to actual or expected high real-time prices; and (4) market design features that allow C&I loads to reduce usage the next day in response to high clearing prices over a number of hours in the ERCOT day-ahead market.

What concerns state regulators and legislators in Texas is that the size and effectiveness of such options are not as transparent as the installation and performance of utility-scale generation dispatched directly by the ERCOT in real time. Such approaches, however, are likely to continue to grow in importance as competitive retailers and other market participants have powerful incentives to take advantage of decentralized technologies that directly empower consumers at lower costs during times of grid stress and scarcity rather than contracting for utility-scale generation for a limited number of hours each year. A key observation is that 3 GW of demand response/price responsive load is larger than the typical increment of new utility-scale generation in ERCOT, allowing for the cyclic changes in supply due to lumpiness to be compensated for by demand response.

4.3.4   Integrating distributed energy resources

ERCOT divides distributed generation (DG) resources into two buckets. In the first are DG resources greater than 1 MW but less than 10 MW. They must register with ERCOT and are referred to as Settlement-Only Distributed Generation (SODG). Between 2010 and the end of 2019, SODG grew from less than 100 MW to 849 MW.[50] In a recent proposed revision of ERCOT protocols, ERCOT staff suggested that self-dispatched distributed generation that injects power into the grid should be settled at nodal prices rather than zonal prices to improve grid reliability by having generators alter their output to resolve local constraints on the transmission and distribution networks.[51] However, while there may be a theoretical argument that loads could be settled nodally as well, in 2003 the PUCT made a decisive policy call by placing in PUCT rules that LSEs would be required to settle on a zonal, not nodal, basis.[52]

In discussing the reasons to make the change to settlement for DG, ERCOT staff used the same arguments for pricing for utility-scale generation that prevailed at the PUCT during the zonal vs nodal market design debate in the early part of the last decade. The ERCOT staff advocated for nodal settlement for DG.

A challenge in getting ERCOT stakeholder approval for nodal settlement of DG was the desire of some of the existing 'behind-the-meter' generation to continue to be settled zonally rather than nodally. Ultimately, a compromise was reached that allows all distributed generation units to apply to ERCOT to continue to receive energy pricing at the relevant load zone price when injecting energy into the ERCOT grid until such time as they proactively opt in for nodal pricing, or 1 January 2030, whichever is earlier.

Distributed generation units of 1 MW or less are referred to as unregistered distributed generation because they are not required to register with ERCOT but they are required to register with the distribution utility in whose service territory they are connected. As of the end of 2019, ERCOT believes that there are 637.89 MW of this type of DG (484.38 MW of units under 50 kW and 153.51 MW of units equal or above 50 kW). As previously mentioned, advanced meters have been deployed throughout almost all the competitive regions within ERCOT and have or will be deployed in most of the NOIE service territories as well. PUCT rules specified that in competitive areas, the advanced meter's functionality had to include the ability to meter separately inflows of electricity from net output, if any, from a location in which a DG system was located. If a retail customer has a DG system capable of producing power in excess of that location's requirements, that customer must find an REP willing to buy the power at a rate offered by the REP (if a residential or small commercial retail customer) or at a negotiated rate (if a larger commercial customer), otherwise that customer's excess power production is not compensated. There are, however, a number of retail providers that do offer solar and other DG programmes because it helps the REP retain customers and the REP can be credited by ERCOT at the zonal price for that purchased power against what the REP would have otherwise been required to purchase to service its load. Effectively, it gives REPs an additional tool to hedge their load obligation physically.

ERCOT operators will continue to face the challenge that behind-the-meter generation and market-based demand response will not be directly dispatched in real time, because they are not visible to ERCOT and cannot be controlled by ERCOT. As a result, ERCOT operators will increasingly need to gather the most accurate and up-to-date information on the location, size and likely behaviour of self-dispatched resources to keep the grid reliable.

4.3.5 ERCOT vs multi-state RTO

In ERCOT, there is a single regulator (PUCT) that reports to a single legislative body (Texas Legislature). Subject to that legislative oversight, the PUCT oversees the grid operator, the wholesale and retail market designs, as well as the construction and cost allocation of new transmission lines. This combination has given Texas the ability to address the challenges of integrating low-carbon resources such as almost 27 GW of wind farms in an integrated, logical way and to maintain a consistent market-oriented approach over time without the complexity of multiple jurisdictions that occurs in other states and regions of the US.

Given the multiple jurisdictions, the regulatory and governance process has been far more challenging in the multi-state ISOs/RTOs and, moreover, across the Eastern and Western Interconnections that span multiple states and multiple market models. Grid reliability in an ISO/RTO in real time is commonly shared across the ISO/RTO footprint and more broadly across the interconnection, so all resources in the pool affect the dispatch and pricing of other resources throughout the ISO/RTO footprint and more widely. As a result, the procurement, commitment and dispatch of resources in multi-state ISOs/RTOs pose challenges to integrating disparate and at times contradictory environmental policies.

There are at least three distinct challenges that are evident when state policies clash (and when federal and state policies clash) within a multi-state ISO/RTO. First, there are challenges with transmission expansion. When some states enact policies where low-carbon resources such as intermittent renewables replace thermal generation for the energy consumers, transmission upgrades and expansions are necessary. As a result, ISO/RTO staff and stakeholders find challenges in agreeing to cost allocation methodologies for new transmission lines that satisfy all the regulatory and legislative bodies in the ISO/RTO footprint. Proposing and ordering new transmission lines to accommodate new generation located in windy, sunny or otherwise generation rich areas and to reduce associated transmission congestion can also be a subject of disagreement when the generation resources or new transmission corridors are not located in the states that are purchasing the energy. The long-standing difficulty in expanding transmission capacity from Arizona to California is an example. Historically, such expansion from Arizona to California would have accommodated export of nuclear power from Arizona, while more recently it would allow for expanded solar resources.

Second, there are dispatch issues with carbon price embedded in the offers of generators. Explicitly embedding a carbon price into the generator dispatch complicates the dispatch if different jurisdictions have different policies. Some states will see load zone prices rise despite not charging a carbon price. For instance, CAISO in California and its energy imbalance market (CAISO's out-of-state footprint) are struggling to develop multi-pass dispatch and pricing algorithms that address this policy conflict. It is axiomatic that a national carbon tax would solve the issue; however, US federal policy does not currently support a nation-wide carbon tax, again highlighting the problems associated with multiple jurisdictions.

Third, RPS goals in some states clash with the desire to maintain coal and nuclear power fleets in others. During times of low electricity demand, high output from new wind farms often clashes with the operation of long-standing nuclear and coal power plants. This clash has resulted in adverse outcomes. First, the resulting low locational prices force the nuclear and coal plants to endure low, and at times even negative, prices, creating insufficient revenues to recover fixed and sometimes even operating costs. Second, capacity constructs have had challenges providing stable capacity prices for coal and nuclear power plants that allow them to continue operating in the face of low energy prices. This result has increased uncertainty and state intervention (such as zero emission credits, or ZECs, for nuclear power plants). Third, there may be insufficient ramping capability from nuclear and coal power plants in the RTO to address the intermittency of increasing renewables penetration.

5. CONCLUSION

As of the time of writing, ERCOT appears to have been successful in meeting challenges of creating a self-sustaining power market as well as the policy goals envisioned in the restructuring legislation passed by Texas in 1999. Challenges remain, especially for ERCOT planning and operations, as they face the rapid development of new utility-scale wind and solar resources and the subsequent retirement of thermal generation over the next years.

While this positive result can tentatively be described as a success story with lessons learned that can be shared with policymakers worldwide, a review of the ERCOT experience cautions that the evolution of the ERCOT market design resulted in good part from a combination of factors that are Texas-specific, including the following variables:

- *Supportive political and economic climate.* Texas government and stakeholders were strongly supportive of (1) retail choice for all customer classes; (2) bilateral contracting to manage commercial and reliability risk; and (3) relative ease in building energy infrastructure, which facilitates the rapid development of the energy resources within Texas (based in part on the long history of Texas being a prominent producer of oil and natural gas).
- *Texas geography.* As discussed at the beginning of Section 4, the physical landscape of Texas allowed the rapid and thorough development of natural gas pipelines to support new gas-fired generation and power transmission lines that could easily reduce import constraints into load centres and integrate areas of Texas with plentiful wind and solar resources with its rapidly growing load centres.
- *Booming local economy.* The rapid population and industrial growth within the ERCOT footprint in the past decades reduced tensions between renewables growth and existing baseload resources over time.
- *Style of governance.* The Texas Legislature and the PUCT nurtured adaptive governance of the ERCOT market that allowed thoughtful and extensive review and debate of a wide range of market design alternatives within the confines of overriding policy goals set by the Texas Legislature, and allowed this to happen reasonably quickly without the delays that all too often inhibit the decision-making process in other regions of the United States.
- *Prominent role of business community in influencing the market debate.* There was a strong voice of the large commercial and industrial community in the stakeholder process, which opposed both capacity markets for resource adequacy and advocated for transmission expansion to eliminate persistent load pockets within ERCOT (which would otherwise balkanize the ERCOT power grid).
- *Clear and consistent policy directives.* The Texas Legislature and the PUCT provided ERCOT with a clear, consistent direction to take steps to integrate new technologies into the prevailing market design, to the benefit of retail choice for residential and small commercial consumers, which have increasingly been using real-time energy management systems and back-up distributed generation to respond to real-time price spikes associated with the ORDC and the prevailing energy-only market design.

In mid-February 2021, Texas endured a 1-in-30-year cold weather event where a large swath of electricity customers in ERCOT were without power for 48–96 hours. The Texas Legislature subsequently passed legislation ordering the PUCT to make certain changes to the ERCOT market to correct problems that were identified during the event.

NOTES

*   The opinions expressed in this chapter are those of the author in his individual capacity and are not being made on behalf of BP Energy Company.

1.   The states of Alaska and Hawaii have separate grids that remain completely isolated because of their geography as well.

2.   Several of the citations include links to webpages on www.ercot.com. However, this website is often not accessible from outside the US, although it can typically be accessed using a VPN. The authors can provide the documents upon request for those outside the US.

3.   Federal Power Act, 16 U.S.C. §§791–828c. For more information on this topic, see Fleisher (2008) and Cudahy (1995).

4.   Energy Policy Act of 1992, Pub. L. No. 102-486, 106 Stat. 2776 (codified as amended in scattered sections of 2, 11, 15, 16, 25, 26, 30, 31, 33, 38, 40 and 42 U.S.C.).

5.   The discussion regarding ERCOT's history relies heavily on the timeline set out on ERCOT's webpage. See www.ercot.com/about/profile/history, accessed 8 July 2021.

6.   Ibid.

7.   Ibid.; Act of 27 May 1995, 74th Legislature, R.S., ch. 765 (SB 373), 1995 Texas General Laws 3972, repealed by Act of 8 May 1997, 75th Legislature, R.S., ch. 166 (SB 1751), § 9, 1997 Texas General Laws 713, 1018 (PURA95).

8.   Excluding private use networks that are associated with larger industrial customers.

9.   Section 501(c)(4) refers to the section of the United States Internal Revenue Code that provides that certain non-profit social welfare organizations are exempt from federal income taxes. See 26 U.S.C. §501(c)(4) and the rules and regulations promulgated thereunder by the United States Internal Revenue Service.

10.   The interested reader may look at Chapter 2 by Schmalensee in this handbook for additional context for this chapter's discussions on the introduction of retail choice in Texas, and Chapter 15 by Green for additional context for this chapter's discussions on the integration of new technologies on the ERCOT grid.

11.   For a more detailed discussion of the early development of the ERCOT retail market, please see Kiesling (2009) and Tierney (2008).

12.   Senate Bill 7, 'An ACT relating to electric utility restructuring and to the powers and duties of the Public Utility Commission of Texas, Office of Public Utility Counsel, and Texas Natural Resource Conservation Commission; providing penalties'.

13.   Public Utility Regulatory Act (PURA) §§39, 154.

14.   As part of the PUCT order to move from portfolio zonal to a unit-specific nodal dispatch as described in the introduction, the PUCT stated its intent to remove various congested transmission bottlenecks to reduce the disparities in zonal pricing for load-serving entities (LSEs) that might otherwise happen. The PUCT also ordered that LSEs would be settled at regional load zones, rather than at nodes, to avoid 'cherry picking' (Schubert and Adib 2009).

15.   Before the deployment of smart meters within a particular wires company's distribution service territory it could take up to 45 days for a customer's switch to become effective unless that customer paid for an 'out-of-cycle' meter read.

16.   See Littlechild and Baldick (n.d.), which describe the role of ostensibly unrelated issues in the CREZ legislation. It should also be understood that climate change concerns played no publicly stated role as a rationale for the legislation.

17.   This section is adapted from PUC Project No. 26376, *Transmission Congestion Issues in the Electric Reliability Council of Texas*, 'Comments on issues related to the Transmission Congestion Workshop on September 18, 2002', Market Oversight Division, 9 September 2002, pp. 6–13. Dr Schubert was the primary author of the paper, accessed 14 July 2021 at http://interchange.puc.texas.gov/Documents/26376_20_364764.PDF.

18.   'The legislature finds that the production and sale of electricity is not a monopoly warranting regulation of rates, operations, and services and that the public interest in competitive electric markets requires

that . . . electric services and their prices should be determined by customer choices and the normal forces of competition'. See PURA §39.001(a).

19. A more detailed discussion on the dynamics of some of these waves and their impacts on financial and commodity markets over the centuries can be found in Kindleberger (2000).

20. The inc-dec game refers to the practice of over-scheduling fictitious transactions on congested paths and profiting from selling incremental and decremental transactions in the real-time balancing market to relieve the congestion due to the over scheduling.

21. For the case of Texas, see, for example, Baldick and Niu (2005).

22. At least in ERCOT, however, since the summer of 2011 grid operators seem to have gained more confidence in the elasticity of electric demand under scarcity conditions and have been a bit slower in implementing non-market operations too early.

23. In contrast, in recent years, ERCOT and others have noted that generation owners have scheduled the timing and duration of planned outages of their units in a way to increase the availability of those units during summer super-peak hours, in response to the potential that high levels of scarcity pricing have been possible since the offer cap in ERCOT was raised to $9000 per megawatt-hour (MWh).

24. Since June 2015 the VoLL has been 9000 $/MWh.

25. The PBPC often provides a shadow price for the value of ramping in the ERCOT system in any given dispatch interval.

26. As of the end of November 2019, there are 104 MW of installed battery capacity in ERCOT and an additional 200 MW of capacity from developers with signed interconnection agreements and who have posted financial security with transmission owners. 'Capacity changes by fuel type', posted 8 January 2020, accessed 8 July 2021 at http://www.ercot.com/content/wcm/lists/197386/Capacity_Changes_by_Fuel_Type_Charts_December_2019.xlsx.

27. In 2019, the PUCT ordered ERCOT to implement real-time co-optimization of energy and ancillary services. At the time of writing, ERCOT staff estimated that the implementation will be finished in 2024.

28. This section has been drawn from the following BP Energy Company (BPEC) filing on ERCOT market design in the PUCT market design reviews. Dr Schubert was the primary author of the document. Public Utility Commission of Texas, Project No. 40480, *Commission Proceeding Regarding Policy Options on Resource Adequacy*, 'Comments of BP Energy Company in response to questions asked by the Public Utility Commission of Texas', 12 July 2012, accessed 8 July 2021 at http://interchange.puc.texas.gov/Documents/40480_5_730732.PDF.

29. This theme also can be found in the 'Scarcity Pricing' white paper by PUCT staff. Project No. 24255, *Rulemaking Concerning Planning Reserve Margin Requirements*, 'An energy-only resource adequacy mechanism', E. S. Schubert, Wholesale Market Oversight, 14 April 2005, pp. 10–11, accessed 14 July 2021 at http://interchange.puc.texas.gov/Documents/24255_98_475491.PDF.

30. A more detailed exposition of the economic framework embedded in this discussion can be found in Smith (2008), specifically Chapter 2, 'The two forms of rationality', and Chapter 3, 'Relating the two concepts of a rational order'.

31. This concept also was implicit in the 'Locational Pricing' white paper by PUCT staff. (PUCT Project No. 26376, *Transmission Congestion Issues in the Electric Reliability Council of Texas*, 'Comments on issues related to the Transmission Congestion Workshop on 18 September 2002', Market Oversight Division (9 September 2002), pp. 10–12, accessed 14 July 2021 at http://interchange.puc.texas.gov/Documents/26376_20_364764.PDF.

32. For another exposition of this process, called 'complexity economics', see Beinhocker (2006), especially pp. 96–7.

33. These dynamics result from what is known as the 'knowledge problem' (Hayek 1945).

34. To a technical reader, the interpretations, not detailed here, may seem tortured and contrived; however, they have enabled a unique, single jurisdiction that has arguably been instrumental in achieving unified and coordinated restructuring of both wholesale and retail markets.

35. Nodal Protocol Revision Request Number 933, 'Reporting of demand response by retail electric providers and non-opt-in entities', accessed 8 July 2021 at http://www.ercot.com/mktrules/issues/NPRR933#keydocs.

36. This section has been drawn from four BPEC filings on market design in the PUCT market design reviews. Dr Schubert was the primary author of each document. For a discussion on the impact of decentralization on unit commitment, see Public Utility Commission of Texas, Project No. 31600, *Transition to an ERCOT Nodal Market Design*, 'Comments of BP Energy Company on the update cost–benefit analysis of the ERCOT Nodal Market design', 9 January 2009, accessed 14 July 2021 at http://interchange.puc.texas.gov/Documents/31600_15_607588.PDF. For a discussion on the impact of decentralization on real-time dispatch, see Public Utility Commission of Texas, Project No. 37897, *PUC Proceeding Related to Resource and Reserve Adequacy and Scarcity Pricing*, 'Comments of BP Energy Company in response to questions asked by the Public Utility Commission of Texas', 24 June 2011, accessed 14 July 2021 at http://interchange.puc.texas.gov/Documents/37897_26_701388.PDF; Public Utility Commission of Texas, Project

No. 40480, *Commission Proceeding Regarding Policy Options on Resource Adequacy*, 'Comments of BP Energy Company in response to questions asked by the Public Utility Commission of Texas', 12 July 2012, accessed 14 July 2021 at http://interchange.puc.texas.gov/Documents/40480_5_730732.PDF; Public Utility Commission of Texas, Project No. 48540, *Review of Real-time Co-optimization in the Real-time Market*, 'Comments of BP Energy Company in response to questions asked by the Public Utility Commission of Texas', 18 October 2018, accessed 14 July 2021 at http://interchange.puc.texas.gov/Documents/48540_9_995457.PDF.

37. See the discussion below on self-dispatched generation.
38. In part of his discussion, Holling highlights the framework developed in Simon (1973).
39. Holling (2001), p. 392; another example of this type of 'adaptive governance' is discussed in Ostrom (2009).
40. ERCOT selected the Brattle Group to perform the study, which was filed with the PUCT on 1 June 2012. See *Submission of the Brattle Group's 'ERCOT Investment Incentives and Resource Adequacy' Report*; Project 37897, *PUC Proceeding Relating to Resource and Reserve Adequacy and Shortage Pricing*; and *PUC Rulemaking to Amend PUC SUBST.R §25.505, Relating to Resource Adequacy in the Electric Reliability Council of Texas Power Region*, Project 40258, Item 178, 1 June 2012.
41. See 'The state of things: resource adequacy in ERCOT', Commissioner K. W. Anderson, Jr., Gulf Coast Power Association, 2 October 2012. Also, during this time, ERCOT was strongly encouraged by the commissioners to re-evaluate the methodology it used to forecast load growth, which historically had over-forecasted its growth.
42. ERCOT's 'Response to the Commission's request for additional analysis of the "Interim Solution B" scarcity pricing proposal discussed at the 24 January 2013 workshop in Project 40000', W. W. Hogan & ERCOT Staff, *Back Cast of Interim Solution B+ to Improve Real-Time Scarcity Pricing – White Paper*; *Commission Proceeding to Ensure Resource Adequacy in Texas*, Project No. 40000, Item 392, 21 March 2013; William W. Hogan, 'ERCOT electricity scarcity pricing with an operating reserve demand curve "interim B+"', *Commission Proceeding to Ensure Resource Adequacy in Texas*, Project No. 40000, Item 421, 27 June 2013.
43. London Economics International LLC, 'Estimating the value of lost load', *Commission Proceeding to Ensure Resource Adequacy in Texas*, Project No. 40000, Item 427, 17 June 2013. See also, 'Memorandums of Commissioner K. W. Anderson, Jr.', Project No. 40000, Item 435, 18 July 2013 and Item 451, 28 August 2013.
44. 'ERCOT'S proposed protocol revisions for ORDC B+ implementation', *Commission Proceeding to Ensure Resource Adequacy in Texas*, Project No. 40000, Item 454, 19 September 2013.
45. *Review of Preliminary Load Forecast*, 27 January 2014; *ERCOT Reserve Margin Comparison*, 30 January 2014, accessed at http://www.ercot.com/calendar/2014/1/27/325; Newell et al. (the Brattle Group) (2014), 'Estimating the economically optimal reserve margin in ERCOT', *Commission Proceeding to Ensure Resource Adequacy in Texas*, Project No. 40000, Item 649, 31 January 2014.
46. See 'Memorandum of Commissioner Kenneth W. Anderson, Jr.', *Commission Proceeding to Ensure Resource Adequacy in Texas*, Project No. 40000, Item 650, 5 February 2014.
47. ERCOT's reserve margin has always only been a 'target'. Neither the PUCT nor ERCOT has required a minimum mandatory reserve margin because it is deemed inconsistent with the energy-only market.
48. See materials filed in *Review of Summer 2019 ERCOT Market Performance*, Project No. 49852.
49. *Updated Total System Demand Response/Price Response Results for Summer 2019 Peak Week August 12–August 16, 2019, Review of Summer 2019 ERCOT Market Performance*, Project No. 49852, 6 February 2020.
50. ERCOT, 'Settlement-Only Distributed Generation in ERCOT 2010–2019' [used with permission of ERCOT]. An estimated 345 MW of the SODG comprises renewable and storage resources.
51. See NPRR 917, 'Nodal pricing for Settlement Only Distribution Generators (SODGs) and Settlement Only Transmission Generators (SOTGs)', initially filed on 2 January 2019, and adopted on 13 August 2019, accessed 8 July 2021 at http://www.ercot.com/mktrules/issues/NPRR917.
52. See PUCT Substantive Rule 25.501 (h), accessed 8 July 2021 at http://www.puc.texas.gov/agency/rulesn laws/subrules/electric/25.501/25.501.pdf.

REFERENCES

Andrade, J., R. Baldick and Y. Dong (2017), 'Analysis of ERCOT regulation-up and regulation-down operational reserves', *Proceedings of the IEEE Texas Power and Engineering Conference*, College Station, Texas, 9–10 February.

Baldick, R. (2003), 'Shift factors in ERCOT congestion pricing, paper presented to the Texas Public Utility Commission on 14 January 2003, 5 March, accessed 8 July 2021 at http://users.ece.utexas.edu/~baldick/papers/shiftfactors.pdf.

Baldick, R. and H. Niu (2005), 'Lessons learned: the Texas experience', in J. Griffin and S. Puller (eds), *Electricity Deregulation: Where To From Here?*, Chicago, IL: University of Chicago Press, pp. 182–224.

Beinhocker, E. (2006), *The Origin of Wealth*, Oxford: Oxford University Press.

Berge, E. and F. van Laerhoven (2011), 'Editorial: governing the commons for two decades: a complex story', *International Journal of the Commons*, **5** (2), 160–87.

Cudahy, R. D. (1995), 'The second Battle of the Alamo: the midnight connection', *Natural Resources & Environment*, **10** (1), 56–61 and 85–7.

ERCOT (2021a), 'ERCOT wind additions by year (as of June 30, 2021)', accessed 14 July 2021 at http://www.ercot.com/content/wcm/lists/219848/Capacity_Changes_by_Fuel_Type_Charts_June_2021_monthly.xlsx.

ERCOT (2021b), 'Project cost by service year', accessed 14 July 2021 at http://www.ercot.com/content/wcm/key_documents_lists/89026/ERCOT_June_TPIT_No_Cost_060121.xlsx.

Fleisher, J. M. (2008), 'ERCOT's jurisdictional status: a legal history and contemporary appraisal', *Texas Journal of Oil, Gas, and Energy Law*, **3**, 5–21.

Hayek, F. A. (1945), 'The use of knowledge in society', *American Economic Review*, **35** (4), 519–30.

Hogan, W. W. (2012), 'Electricity scarcity pricing through operating reserves: an ERCOT window of opportunity', 1 November, accessed 8 July 2021 at https://scholar.harvard.edu/whogan/files/hogan_ordc_110112r.pdf.

Hogan, W. W. and S. Pope (2017), *Priorities for the Evolution of an Energy-only Electricity Market Design in ERCOT*, FTI Consulting, filed in PUCT Project No. 47199, 9 May, accessed 8 July 2021 at https://hepg.hks.harvard.edu/files/hepg/files/hogan_pope_ercot_050917.pdf?m=1523367673.

Holling, C. S. (2001), 'Understanding the complexity of economic, ecological, and social systems', *Ecosystems*, **4** (5), 390–405.

Kiesling, L. L. (2009), 'Retail restructuring and market design in Texas', in L. L. Kiesling and A. N. Kleit (eds), *Electricity Restructuring: The Texas Story*, Washington, DC: American Enterprise Institute, pp. 154–73.

Kindleberger, C. P. (2000), *Manias, Panics and Crashes: A History of Financial Crises*, Basingstoke, UK: Palgrave Macmillan.

Littlechild, S. and R. Baldick (n.d.), 'The Texas Competitive Renewable Energy Zone (CREZ) transmission expansion project. Part I: the legislative framework', unpublished working paper.

Newell, S., R. Carroll and A. Kaluzhny et al. (2018), *Estimation of the Market Equilibrium and Economically Optimal Reserve Margins for the ERCOT Region: 2018 Update*, report prepared for Electric Reliability Council of Texas, December, accessed 8 July 2021 at https://brattlefiles.blob.core.windows.net/files/15258_estimation_of_the_market_equilibrium_and_economically_optimal_reserve_margins_for_the_ercot_region.pdf.

Ostrom, E. (2005), *Understanding Institutional Diversity*, Princeton, NJ: Princeton University Press.

Ostrom, E. (2009), 'The challenge of common pool resources', *Environment*, **50** (4), 17–18.

PJM Interconnection (2017), *Proposed Enhancements to Energy Price Formation*, 15 November, accessed 8 July 2021 at https://www.pjm.com/-/media/library/reports-notices/special-reports/20171115-proposed-enhancements-to-energy-price-formation.ashx.

Public Utility Commission of Texas (PUCT) (2002), 'Comments on issues related to the Transmission Congestion Workshop on 18 September 2002', Project No. 26376, *Transmission Congestion Issues in the Electric Reliability Council of Texas*, PUCT Market Oversight Division, accessed 8 July 2021 at http://interchange.puc.texas.gov/Documents/26376_20_364764.PDF.

Public Utility Commission of Texas (PUCT) (2003), *Rulemaking Proceeding on Wholesale Market Design Issues in the Electric Reliability Council of Texas*, Project No. 26376, Order Adopting New §25.501, 21 August.

Schubert, E. S. and P. Adib (2009), 'Evolution of wholesale market design in ERCOT', in L. L. Kiesling and A. N. Kleit (eds), *Electricity Restructuring: The Texas Story*, Washington, DC: American Enterprise Institute, pp. 65–7.

Simon, H. A. (1955), 'A behavioral model of rational choice', *Quarterly Journal of Economics*, **69** (1), 174–83.

Simon, H. A. (1973), 'The organization of complex systems', in H. H. Pattee (ed.), *Hierarchy Theory: The Challenge of Complex Systems*, New York: George Braziller, pp. 3–27.

Sioshansi, R., R. O'Neill and S. Oren (2008), 'Economic consequences of alternative solution methods for centralized unit commitment in day-ahead electricity markets', *IEEE Transactions on Power Systems*, **23** (2), 344–52.

Smith, V. L. (2008), *Rationality in Economics*, New York: Cambridge University Press.

Tierney, S. F. (2008), *ERCOT Texas's Competitive Power Experience: A View from the Outside Looking In*, white paper, Analysis Group accessed 8 July 2021 at http://citeseerx.ist.psu.edu/viewdoc/download?doi=10.1.1.554.3015&rep=rep1&type=pdf.

9. Lessons from Australia's National Electricity Market 1998–2018: strengths and weaknesses of the reform experience

Paul Simshauser

1. INTRODUCTION

Australia's National Electricity Market (NEM) formed part of a world-wide electricity industry microeconomic reform experiment which, as Pollitt (2004) and Schmalensee (see Chapter 2 in this handbook) note, began in Chile in 1982. The NEM, which covers the Eastern and South Eastern states of Australia,[1] reached its 20th birthday in December 2018. The centrepiece of the NEM reform is the wholesale market, a five-region energy-only gross pool with a real-time spot market and forward derivatives market – the former coordinating scheduling and dispatch, the latter tying the economics of the physical power system to resource adequacy and new capacity. By virtually any metric, for most of the past two decades, the wholesale market has been 'a marvel of microeconomic reform'.[2] A vast oversupply of generation capacity was cleared, unit costs plunged, plant availability rates reached world-class levels, new investment flowed when required, investment risks were borne by capital markets rather than captive consumers and reliability of supply – in spite of an energy-only market design – has been maintained with few exceptions thanks to a very high market price cap. At 15 000 Australian dollars per megawatt-hour (A\$/MWh) it is amongst the highest in the world.[3]

However, over the period 2016–19, the wholesale market struggled to maintain wholesale prices within politically tolerable limits, and one region, South Australia, experienced a black system event. Causes can be traced to (1) adverse effects of climate change policy discontinuity, which punctured new plant investment continuity; (2) sudden and uncoordinated exit of coal plants at scale, driven by climate change policy discontinuity; and (3) turmoil in the adjacent market for natural gas, which would otherwise provide the transitional fuel and shock absorbers required for coal plant exit at scale (Simshauser 2019a).

As Green notes in Chapter 15 of this handbook, decarbonization and the rise of variable renewable energy generation raises serious challenges for power system stability. The NEM's wholesale market is attempting to make this transition without the transitional fuel, and without a united and synchronized climate change and energy policy architecture. Indeed, the climate change policies that have existed were poorly designed in that they tended to collide with the NEM design by breaking essential links between investment requirements and system operations via certificate side-markets and more recently via off-market government intermediations (Simshauser 2019b).

Transmission and distribution networks across NEM regions are subject to economic regulation based on Littlechild's (1983) incentive-based 'RPI-X' approach. While considerable variation exists amongst NEM regions, network performance has been marked by (somewhat ironically) 'policy-based' Averch and Johnson (1962) gold plating. The regulatory asset base of combined networks servicing NEM customers surged from A\$32 billion in 2004 to A\$93 billion in 2018, while aggregate demand tracked sideways (Simshauser and Akimov 2019). Underlying policy problems were cauterized by 2012, but business inertia and time lags between regulatory determinations meant network tariffs did not alter from sharply rising trajectories until 2015.

Retail markets have been forced to deliver this bad news to customers through sharply rising retail prices. Retail markets followed the British approach to full retail contestability as set out in Chapter 5, albeit with each of the NEM regions (that is, jurisdictions) adopting contestability and price deregulation at different timeframes, which in turn were driven by local political constraints. As with the wholesale market, the NEM's contestable retail markets have, by and large, been successful, although, as with Great Britain, more recently consumer groups and politicians have conflated the problem of rising electricity prices with price discrimination – a largely unhelpful development. The term 'loyalty tax' for sticky customers made its media cameo in 2018 and the policy of reintroducing regulated tariff caps soon followed. Unfortunately for the market, the Commonwealth Government (and Victorian state government) had implemented legislation re-regulating retail prices.

One of the more interesting aspects of the Australian market model, if not a dry aspect, are the governance arrangements. First and foremost, although the 'N' in NEM stands for National, energy and energy policy are the domain of state governments, not the Commonwealth Government. Historically, vertical monopolies, called Electricity Commissions, were developed, owned and operated by the respective state governments. Given that the power system was built up around state borders, the fact that Australia has a centrally coordinated competitive 'national' market at all is remarkable. From an institutional design perspective, the functions of rulemaking, regulation and market operations are strictly separated amongst three entities: the Australian Energy Market Commission (AEMC), the Australian Energy Regulator (AER) and the Australian Energy Market Operator (AEMO), respectively. Policymaking and ultimate oversight of the energy industry occurs through a body known as 'COAG Energy Council' (Council of Australian Governments – Energy Council), comprising the energy ministers from each state government and the Commonwealth Minister.

In contrast to energy policy, climate change policy is the domain of the Commonwealth Government. Unfortunately, the democratic Labor and conservative Liberal Parties have been unable to identify common ground for decarbonizing Australia's CO_2-intensive power system for almost two decades, with the core of disagreement occurring within the Liberal Party itself. As with the USA and Canada, whenever the Commonwealth has misaligned climate change policies with Australia's international commitments (for example, most recently, the Paris Agreement), piecemeal state government policy activity emerges to fill the void demanded by business and stakeholders, but the design of these policies has frequently been incompatible with the NEM's wholesale market design.

The purpose of this chapter is to review the NEM's performance over the past two decades and to highlight the strengths and weaknesses of the Australian reform experiment. This chapter is structured as follows. Section 2 provides a brief background to Australian energy market reform. Section 3 examines industrial organization in the NEM and Section 4 reviews the governance structure. Sections 5 to 7 then analyse the performance of the wholesale market, regulated networks and retail markets, respectively. Section 8 presents strengths and weaknesses of the Australian approach to energy market reform. Conclusions follow.

2.   BACKGROUND TO AUSTRALIAN ELECTRICITY MARKET REFORMS

Prior to the reforms in the 1990s, vertically integrated monopoly electricity utilities were public assets built up within state boundaries. State Electricity Commissions were non-taxpaying entities, responsible to their state government owners with regard to system planning, investment, system operations, reliability of supply and tariffs. As with many vertical utilities around the world, during the 1980s and early 1990s, the status of the monopoly power generation industry in South Eastern Australia was bordering on critical.[4] New South Wales had invested in so much baseload capacity that it would take more than 20 years to clear, while Victoria's excess baseload plant investments adversely affected that state's credit rating.[5] Electricity tariffs were substantially above competitive levels and, consequently, the requirement for and objectives of microeconomic reform were clear and consistent with those outlined in Chapter 2 of this handbook.

Microeconomic reform of Australia's power industry can be traced back to 1991 when the Commonwealth Government initiated a national inquiry via one of its economics agencies, the Productivity Commission.[6] What evolved was a recommendation to restructure, deregulate and establish a four-state interconnected grid covering East and South Eastern Australia – that is, Queensland (QLD), New South Wales (NSW), Victoria (VIC) and South Australia (SA).[7] An undersea high-voltage direct current (HVDC) cable would later interconnect the island state of Tasmania (TAS). Western Australia and the Northern Territory could not be connected economically due to geographical distances.

This reform would create Australia's NEM. Cooperation amongst participating state governments was essential and was successfully achieved. Australian reforms were largely inspired by the British electricity market template. There were four key steps to reform:

1. State-owned monopoly Electricity Commissions were 'corporatized' (that is, commercialized). These entities became businesses incorporated under Australian corporations law, were given a commercial mandate and profit motive, and subsequently exposed to a taxation equivalence regime.
2. Corporatized monopoly utilities were then vertically restructured into three segments: generation, transmission and distribution/retail supply, within existing state boundaries. The credit standing of each business was also simulated 'as if' the firm was non-government owned, which removed any perceived benefit that may otherwise arise in transacting and raising capital. This corporatization process proved to be a critical step in levelling the playing field and removing any residual unfair advantage that would otherwise exist.
3. Competitive segments of generation and retail supply were horizontally restructured into a number of rival entities within each region.

4. Businesses were privatized but the timing of this final stage varied considerably across NEM due to regional political agendas. VIC privatized its electricity businesses in the late 1990s, SA followed in the early 2000s, QLD privatized its retail supply businesses (in the southeast corner) in 2007 and, after a number of failed attempts, has since resolved to retain the balance of the industry in public ownership (including transmission, distribution and two rival generation businesses with ~60 per cent market share). NSW privatized its merchant generation and retail supply businesses in the early 2010s and sold half of the regulated network businesses in the mid-2010s despite a bitter partisan campaign between the two major political parties, Labor and Liberal. In TAS, the industry remains publicly owned.[8]

It is notable that the NEM inherited a high-quality and oversupplied stock of monopoly-built utility-scale plant at inception, and thus gains from exchange via a competitive energy-only gross pool and associated forward derivatives market would be material – a common characteristic across many jurisdictions as explained in Chapter 2 of this handbook. Table 9.1 contrasts the NEM's starting generation fleet with a modelled 'optimal plant mix'. Note that the NEM was substantially 'overweight' baseload plant, with around 4100 MW of excess supply – located mainly in the states of VIC and NSW. Intermediate plant was roughly even, while peaking plant was 'underweight' by 1600 MW. The system was oversupplied in aggregate by around 2600 MW against a then optimal plant stock of ~30 600 MW and a coincident system maximum demand of about 25 000 MW. The market value of the structural faults at the time were ~A$5 billion or 13 per cent of the (then) A$44 billion NEM generating portfolio.

3. INDUSTRIAL ORGANIZATION

Before the wholesale market commenced, it was necessary to restructure state-owned monopoly Electricity Commissions. Accordingly, during the 1990s, the four vertical utilities in QLD, NSW, VIC and SA[9] were restructured into 16 portfolio generators,[10] five transmission entities and 15 distribution/retail supply entities[11] around state/NEM region boundaries. Over time, industrial organization would depart from this original NEM blueprint through three dimensions: vertical boundaries, horizontal boundaries and geographic lines.

Initially, the 15 incumbent (that is, franchise) retailers were stapled to a host monopoly distribution network. This 'retailer-distributor model' was common to Great Britain and

Table 9.1 NEM generating plant portfolio balance in 1998

NEM 1997/98	Optimal (MW)	Actual (MW)	Portfolio Balance
Baseload	20 400	24 500	4 100 overweight
Intermediate	2 000	2 100	100 overweight
Peaking	8 200	6 600	−1 600 underweight
Total	30 600	33 200	2 600 oversupplied

Source: Simshauser (2008).

Australia at reform onset, which, as Helm (2014, p. 2) explains, was 'the best that could be done at the time' due to the difficulty of splitting such complex business interfaces, and it ensured retail supply businesses had substantial asset backing.

However, horizontal boundaries would be altered: the lack of scope economies and vastly different risk profiles meant that all distribution networks in the NEM (and in Great Britain) would divest their retail supply businesses. These downstream structural separations were 'value-driven' investor events.[12] While a seemingly benign development, being stapled to a distribution network meant a retail business was credit-wrapped by the investment-grade rating of very substantial regulated 'poles & wires' businesses. Separation of retail from networks meant that the presence of investment-grade credit had been withdrawn from the merchant market in a two-step process. First, through the withdrawal of government ownership, and second through the separation of retailers from investment-grade monopoly distribution networks. This would later have profound implications for industrial organization.

Electricity supply is among the most capital-intensive industries in the world and understanding capital flows is therefore very important. Why is the presence of investment-grade credit important for the merchant/deregulated market for generation plant? Credit metrics applied to project financings, an historically dominant source of capital for capital-intensive new power-generating equipment in the reform era, were tightened by project banks from ca. 2004 in direct response to prolonged periods of low prices, generator economic losses and episodes of 'missing money' (see Section 5) in various energy markets around the world.[13] As a result, timely investment in new plant would require the involvement of an investment-grade credit-rated entity, either as principal investor or as the underwriter of long-dated power purchase agreements (PPAs). This was an entry hurdle not envisaged by policymakers or academics during the market design phase. Changes in credit parameters by risk-averse project banks were not unique to Australia – they were a characteristic of energy markets around the world (Finon 2008, 2011). Accordingly, changes to industrial organization would follow.

First, the 15 incumbent retailers lacked scale[14] and progressively consolidated horizontally to remain competitive – and this occurred amongst both privatized retailers and amongst government-owned retailers. Indeed, the states of QLD and NSW consolidated their own retail supply businesses from nine down to just four prior to, or during, privatization processes in 2007 and 2011 respectively.[15] By 2011, three 'incumbent' retailers emerged in the NEM from a long line of government privatizations, merger and acquisition (M&A) events. Curiously, state governments, the Commonwealth Government and Australia's competition regulator waved these horizontal mergers and privatizations through – prioritizing proceeds and private ownership over concentration and competition.

Second, reintegration became a visible trend as the three incumbent retailers pursued reverse vertical integration with merchant generation, thus becoming known as 'the gentailers'. Furthermore, forward integration became a dominant strategy amongst incumbent merchant generators – many of which now form large vertical businesses in their own right. A further 15–20 new entrant retailers formed the competitive fringe. Somewhat ironically, most policymakers view vertical reintegration, not horizontal consolidation, as the unwelcome development (Simshauser, Tian and Whish-Wilson 2015).

Opposition to vertical boundary changes appears amongst a majority of regulators and policymakers in the NEM. Their a priori reasoning is that vertical acquisitions collide with the NEM blueprint, may reduce forward market liquidity, and in turn adversely impact 'balances of competition'. By this logic, vertical integration was presumed to be anti-competitive. However, and to be perfectly clear on this, with the exception of bottleneck infrastructure[16] the weight of theoretical and empirical evidence on vertical integration overwhelmingly concludes the opposite (Bushnell, Mansur and Saravia 2008, Cooper et al. 2005, Joskow 2010, Lafontaine and Slade 2007, Mansur 2007).[17] To the extent that market power issues occasionally arise in the NEM, their common underpinnings are horizontal power, not vertical power – something that seems to have bedevilled the Australian Competition and Consumer Commission (ACCC).

4.   GOVERNANCE OF AUSTRALIA'S NEM

The NEM officially began in December 1998, but from 2006, governance arrangements underwent a structural change of their own with policy, rulemaking, regulation and system and market operations segregated, as follows:

1.   Policy – Energy Ministers from each NEM state and the Commonwealth form the members of the Council of Australian Governments Energy Council – that is, the COAG Energy Council.
2.   Rulemaking – the Australian Energy Market Commission (AEMC) operates on behalf of the COAG Energy Council as the market rulemaking entity and policy advisor, and has established an open-source platform for doing so.
3.   Regulation – the AER enforces wholesale and retail supply rules, and is the economic regulator of the NEM's regulated networks.
4.   Market operations – the Australian Energy Market Operator (AEMO) is the independent system and market operator – that is, the entity responsible for central dispatch, power system operations and wholesale market operations, including the spot electricity market and the eight frequency control ancillary markets.
5.   More recently, an Energy Security Board (ESB) was inserted above the three market institutions – that is, AEMC, AER and AEMO – for a time-limited period in an attempt to assist policy coordination following the black system event in SA.[18] The ESB comprises the heads of the AEMC, AER and AEMO, plus an independent chair and deputy chair.

A defining characteristic of Australia's NEM is its 'open source' approach to rulemaking, in which the AEMC consistently attempts to capture the wisdom of the crowd – that is, from market participants, capital markets, consumer groups and industry stakeholders. Under Australia's NEM rules, the system operator, the regulator, any market participant, investor, consumer group, interested entity or individual can originate a rule change. The AEMC is the institution charged with running a politically independent rule change process in a manner consistent with the National Electricity Objective[19] and does so using a conventional policy development cycle incorporating: (1) an initial issues paper; (2) a formal public consultation process; (3) a draft determination subject to a further round of consultation; and (4) a final determination. There are four channels to originate a rule change:

- Normal Rule Change: the AEMC initiates its policy development cycle within four months of receiving a Rule Change Request and must complete its process within six months (that is, ten months in total).
- Expedited Rule Change: it can be made within just eight weeks. However, a prerequisite to this channel is the existence of a (typically prior) formal consultation process either by a proponent or by the AEMC.
- Fast Track Rule Change: where no prior consultation exists, a rule change can be originated and policy development cycle completed within three months, but with the prerequisite that a genuine threat to power system security or reliability exists.
- Market Development Rule Change: the AEMC can propose a rule change to the COAG Energy Council, which in turn would have the effect of originating a rule change. For clarity, the AEMC cannot propose a rule change to itself.

The AEMC assesses any rule change against 'statutory objectives' (that is, the five AEMC commissioners are bound by these statutory objectives, including, above all, 'the long-term interests of consumers'). A common criticism that I hear – including from energy ministers, senior officials, consumer groups, lobby groups and (non-market facing) renewable project developers/investors – is the slow speed of change with regard to the NEM rules. Conversely, I rarely hear such complaints from the capital-intensive, market-facing participants who have made large investment commitments in plant and retail systems based on their understanding of market rules, nor from sophisticated debt and equity-capital market participants who ultimately fund these market-facing participants. These latter groups may not like the outcome of various rule changes, but they value the politically independent rulemaking process and the stability of the NEM rules (noting that the problem of climate change policy is *not* the domain of the AEMC or the rules).

In fact, most rule processes are completed within 9–12 months. And while there is considerable evidence of NEM rule change processes of urgency being the subject of delay, what virtually all stakeholders do not observe is the cause of delays. In almost every case, delays can be traced to the COAG Energy Council – when the form of an AEMC rule change is materially altered in the legal drafting stage (viz. over-reach by a jurisdiction trying to achieve some 'additional policy objective'), all prior consultation processes previously undertaken by the AEMC are no longer relevant. Consequently, under its statutory responsibilities, AEMC Commissioners are obliged to re-initiate the policy development cycle once again. Observable rulemaking process delays have an uncanny correlation with the level of interest and decision-making authority by the COAG Energy Council and their senior officials – of which I have first-hand experience.[20] In an outlier example, a Fast Track Rule Change, which should have taken three months to complete, took three and a half years to implement because of 'over-reach' by a particular state government attempting to deliver tangential policy outcomes.

5.   WHOLESALE MARKET

As noted at the outset, for most of the past two decades, the economic and technical performance of the NEM's wholesale market has been exceptional in that following reform, costs reduced, prices fell to competitive levels, plant oversupply was cleared and the NEM's reliability criteria of 'no more than 0.002% lost load' was met (Simshauser 2005, 2014a). One could conclude with considerable justification that the reform objectives of enhancing productive, allocative and dynamic efficiency were achieved.[21]

However, recent performance of Australia's wholesale market has been tarnished by a black system event in SA (Australia's first system collapse since 1964), with spot and forward electricity prices surging outside of politically tolerable levels. To be clear, the NEM market design remained faithful, with prices reflecting resource costs. Key problems have been sequential supply-side shocks: (1) a poor design and discontinuity of climate change policies; (2) shortages in the market for natural gas; and (3) an uncoordinated exit of coal power plants at scale without adequate notification periods, because of problem (1) mentioned above. As this section explains, the NEM is attempting to transition without the transitional fuel – that is, natural gas, and without the climate change policies that should guide any transition (Simshauser and Tiernan 2019).

5.1 Institutional Design

The NEM's electricity spot market is a real-time gross pool (that is there is no day-ahead market),[22] with five-minute zonal spot prices across the NEM's five regions formed under a conventional uniform first-price auction mechanism. There are also eight co-optimized frequency control ancillary service spot markets (MacGill 2010). The NEM's gross pool is an energy-only market – that is, there is no formal capacity mechanism.

AEMO has sole responsibility for real-time system security and is not responsible for resource adequacy per se. System reliability in the sense of resource adequacy is driven by future price expectations and underpinned by an extremely high market price cap of 15 000 A$/MWh – the level of the cap having a tight nexus with the reliability objective function: to ensure 'no more than 0.002% lost load' (Riesz, Gilmore and MacGill 2015). Investment in future plant capacity is thus guided by the NEM's forward markets; derivative contracts are traded both on-exchange and over-the-counter (OTC) and have historically exhibited turnover of 300+ per cent of physical trade, albeit with considerable variation between seasons and regions.

In real time, generators self-commit units for dispatch through their offers, with AEMO centrally coordinating the market to ensure that aggregate supply and demand are matched in the electricity and frequency control ancillary services spot markets, subject to real-time transmission system and system stability constraints. In the near term, AEMO can initiate emergency trader provisions if short-term resource adequacy is likely to compromise system security.[23]

From a transmission perspective, the NEM is a zonal market with five imperfectly interconnected regions and is an open access regime whereby generators are free to connect, pay only shallow connection costs but face the risk of congestion. Transmission planning is undertaken by the (five regional) regulated transmission network service providers.[24] Transmission investment approval, however, is vested with the AER.[25]

5.2   Historic Market Prices

For most of the past two decades, annual average spot prices spanned a relatively tight range. From 1998 to 2015, annual spot prices averaged 40 A$/MWh (that is, ~28 US$/MWh)[26] with a P90–P10 range of 27–57 A$/MWh (that is, 18.90–39.90 US$/MWh). These spot prices were underpinned by Australia's low cost coal-fired generation fleet. Figures 9.1 and 9.2 present historic average spot prices in nominal and real 2020 dollars, and contrast these with the estimated new entrant cost relevant at the time. There are four things worth noting in Figures 9.1 and 9.2:

- Spot prices experienced two major excursions. The first (2007–08) coincided with Australia's East Coast millennial drought. Apart from adverse effects on hydro plant, drought conditions were so severe that some coal-fired generators were forced to mothball units due to cooling water shortages (urban drinking water being prioritized from affected dams). The second (2017–19) was due to coal plant exit at scale (see Section 5.4) and turmoil in the adjacent market for natural gas (see Section 5.5).
- The new entrant cost series in Figures 9.1 and 9.2 exhibits a steep incline from 2005 to 2012, which coincides with a shift in the benchmark entrant technology, from coal to gas, and in line with expectations of a carbon constraint. Domestic gas

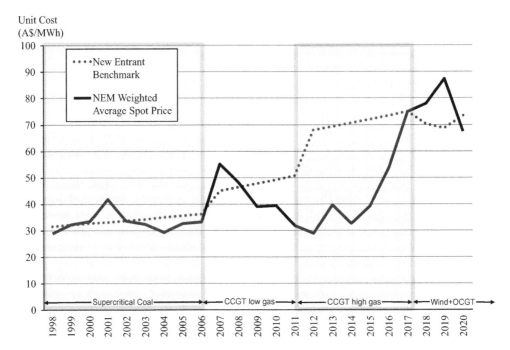

Note: CCGT = combined cycle gas turbine; OCGT = open cycle gas turbine.

Source: Simshauser and Gilmore (2020).

Figure 9.1   20-year NEM spot prices vs new entrant cost: 1998–2020 (nominal values)

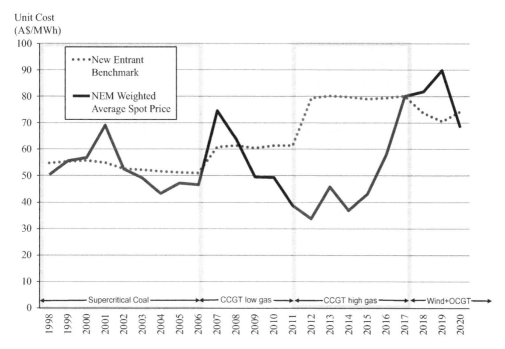

Note: CCGT = combined cycle gas turbine; OCGT = open cycle gas turbine.

Source: Simshauser and Gilmore (2020).

Figure 9.2   NEM spot prices vs new entrant cost: 1998–2020 (constant 2020 A$)

prices rose sharply following a series of liquified natural gas (LNG) export commitments, which had the effect of linking domestic gas prices with the seaborne market,
increasing them from 3 A$/gigajoule (GJ) to 9 A$/GJ (~2.21–6.85 US$/metric
million British thermal units – MMbtu) over the period 2005–12. By 2016, the cost
of renewables had fallen considerably even after accounting for intermittency (by
way of an open cycle gas turbine – OCGT) and consequently now forms the new
benchmark entrant.

- While not captured in Figures 9.1 and 9.2, the marginal running cost of the NEM's
coal-fired fleet is now beginning to rise; legacy coal supply agreements at a number
of marginal coal plants across QLD and NSW have been progressively expiring,
and replacement contracts are now based on the 5500 kilocalorie (kcal) coal futures
contract (export price ex-Newcastle, north of Sydney). International thermal coal
prices are materially higher (currently ~90 US$/tonne [t]) than legacy contract
prices (historically ~30–40 A$/t).
- Australia had a carbon tax from 2012 to 2014, but the (democratic) Labor government's policy was short-lived following a bitter general election campaign in which
the carbon tax (labelled the 'great big tax on electricity' by the conservative Liberal
opposition) formed centre stage. A core election commitment, the incoming Liberal
government dismantled the policy within nine months.

5.3   Reliability and Reserve Plant

From a resource adequacy perspective, the NEM's Reliability Panel sets the criteria and reviews overall power system performance. The reliability criteria has been achieved with few exceptions. NEM outage analysis covering the period 2009–19 identified that only 0.1 per cent of system minutes lost were related to generation capacity shortfalls – the balance arising from a black system event in SA[27] (1.6 per cent), transmission network outages (0.7 per cent) and distribution network outages (97.7 per cent) (Simshauser and Gilmore 2020, Wood, Dundas and Percival 2019).

Figure 9.3 presents NEM reserve plant based on nameplate capacity (which has the effect of overstating the apparent reserve capacity comparing thermal de-rating during summer peak periods). More important, however, are year-on-year changes in reserve capacity. During the transition from monopoly to competitive market, QLD (1998), SA (2000) and VIC (2001) experienced supply disruptions but these were legacy issues not market design issues (noting the NEM began in 1998). In response, market-based supply-side additions commissioned in 2002–04 were swift, as Figure 9.3 illustrates.

In 2009, VIC experienced supply disruptions following a very material jump in maximum demand and coincident lags to peaking plant capacity additions. These events coupled with the 2007–08 price cycle and the (then) looming expectation of a CO_2 Emissions Trading Scheme led to a large number of gas-fired capacity additions from 2009 to 2012, as Figures 9.6 and 9.7 later reveal. However, as this capacity was commissioned, NEM aggregate demand contracted (for the first time in history) throughout

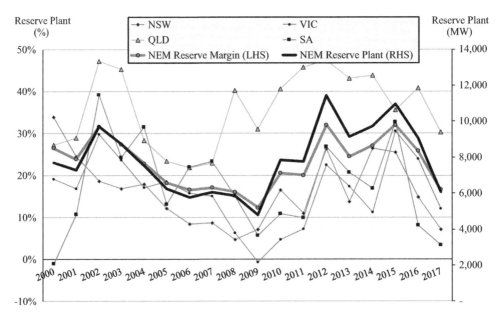

Source: AER (2018).

Figure 9.3   NEM reserve capacity (2000–17) nameplate vs maximum demand

2010–15. Australia's 20 per cent renewable energy target would also force more plant into the market (through an adjacent certificate 'side-market') and combined, this led to reserve capacity margins increasing materially. These conditions would eventually weigh heavily on spot electricity prices and culminate in aged coal capacity exit at scale (see Section 5.4). This coal capacity exit procession produced a sharp run-down in reserve capacity, which is visibly noticeable from 2015 onwards.

5.4   The NEM's Episode of Economic Losses and Exit at Scale

A known theoretical characteristic of energy-only markets is 'missing money' and risks of timely capacity entry (see Cramton and Stoft, 2006, amongst several others).[28] While the NEM's very high market price cap and associated contract markets has generally ensured resource adequacy, the energy-only market design has meant the economic consequences of supply imbalances are amplified. These have been further compounded by the presence of a poorly designed 20 per cent renewable energy target (that is, use of 'certificate' side-markets).

By combining underlying annual cost and price data from Figure 9.1 with thermal generation output, an estimate of economic losses (including the missing money subcomponent) over time can be established, presented in Table 9.2. To be clear, Table 9.2 excludes ancillary services revenues (typically smaller than 0.5 per cent of system

Table 9.2   Generator economic losses

Year	Average Total Cost (A$/MWh)	NEM Price (A$/MWh)	Shortfall (A$/MWh)	Generation (TWh)	Economic Losses (A$ Billions)
2000	35.75	33.36	−2.40	162.9	−0.3
2001	36.52	41.79	5.27	168.8	0.8
2002	37.31	33.63	−3.67	171.9	−0.6
2003	38.11	32.49	−5.62	175.8	−0.9
2004	38.93	29.29	−9.63	182.8	−1.6
2005	39.76	32.71	−7.06	186.0	−1.2
2006	40.62	33.17	−7.45	188.9	−1.2
2007	41.49	55.22	13.73	194.7	2.4
2008	42.39	48.26	5.88	197.8	1.0
2009	43.30	39.11	−4.19	197.4	−0.7
2010	44.23	39.46	−4.76	192.8	−0.8
2011	45.18	31.96	−13.22	187.4	−2.2
2012	46.15	28.83	−17.32	184.9	−2.8
2013	47.14	39.61	−7.53	174.0	−1.2
2014	48.16	33.71	−14.44	168.2	−2.1
2015	49.19	39.36	−9.83	173.4	−1.5
2016	50.25	54.81	4.56	172.9	0.7
2017	51.33	78.87	27.55	169.8	4.1
2018	52.43	82.47	30.04	166.5	4.4
Total	46.09	36.02	−10.07	1278.1	−3.7

Source: Simshauser (2018).

revenues) and hedge contract premiums (nominally ~3–7 per cent above spot prices). These are important caveats but these limitations aside, the estimated economic loss is A\$4 billion over the period 1999/00–2017/18 against the current capital stock of 46 000 MW with an estimated value of ~A\$49.7 billion.[29]

While the aggregate result in Table 9.2 is an economic loss of A\$4 billion, it is important to note that between 2009 and 2015 (shaded area) the result was approximately – A\$11.3 billion – a direct result of plant oversupply.[30] This period induced uncoordinated coal capacity exit at scale over the period 2012–17, as outlined in Table 9.3. Initial closure events (that is, between 2012 and 2015) were benign as NEM spot prices and Table 9.2 tend to indicate; they were warranted on economic grounds (that is, oversupply) and consistent with climate change policy objectives (that is, lower emission entrants causing the oversupply).

However, the exit of the last two power plants reported in Table 9.3 was material, uncoordinated and occurred with little warning. The 540 MW Northern Power Station, the last coal-fired plant in the NEM's SA region, announced it would close in mid-2016. With spot revenues declining and plant costs rising (that is, falling availability and utilization), closure became the dominant strategy. Two months later, unexpectedly, the 1600 MW Hazelwood Power Station in the adjacent VIC region (20 per cent VIC market share) announced it would close in April 2017, giving less than five months' notice. Closure was driven by mounting capital reinvestment requirements (A\$400 million) relating to plant safety. The Northern Power Station exit is an example of first-mover disadvantage. While Northern Power Station would eventually close due to declining coal resources, it is not obvious that April 2016 was the optimal closure date given Hazelwood's imminent, but unknown, exit timing. These uncoordinated exits in 2016–17 pushed spot electricity prices to multi-year highs and contributed to (but were not the cause of) supply

Table 9.3   NEM coal plant exit

Coal Plant	Capacity (MW)	NEM Region	Exit (Year)	Enter (Year)	Age at Exit (Years)	Warning (Months)	Notice Date	Closure Date
Swanbank B	500	Qld	2012	1972	40	23.6	26-Mar-10	27-Mar-12
Playford[a,b]	240	SA	2012	1960	52	6.9	7-Oct-15	8-May-16
Collinsville	180	Qld	2013	1972	41	5.9	1-Jun-12	1-Dec-12
Munmorah[c]	600	NSW	2013	1969	44	0.0	3-Jul-12	3-Jul-12
Morwell	195	Vic	2014	1958	56	1.0	29-Jul-14	30-Aug-14
Wallerawang[c]	1000	NSW	2014	1978	36	0.0	1-Nov-14	1-Nov-14
Redbank	151	NSW	2015	2001	14	0.0	31-Oct-14	31-Oct-14
Anglesea	150	Vic	2016	1969	47	3.6	12-May-15	31-Aug-15
Northern[b]	540	SA	2016	1985	31	6.9	7-Oct-15	8-May-16
Hazelwood	1600	Vic	2017	1967	50	4.8	3-Nov-16	1-Apr-17
Total/Average	5156			1972	42.5	5.2		

Notes:
a. Mothballed in 2012.
b. Original notice 11 June 2015 with planned closure date of March 2018.
c. Mothballed, notice was therefore immediate.

Source: Simshauser (2018).

disruptions in SA (2016, 2019) and VIC (2019). The NEM was about to begin its transition in earnest, but would be forced to do so without its historically cheap and abundant transitional fuel – natural gas.

5.5   Transitioning Without the Transitional Fuel: Gas Market Shortfalls

Central to current market conditions in the NEM is the dire state of the Australian East Coast market for natural gas. Following very large coal seam gas discoveries in QLD (that is, 40 000+ petajoules [PJ], or 6500+ million barrels of oil equivalent [Mboe] of proven and probable reserves), three large LNG export plants were commissioned in 2014–16, resulting in a three-fold increase in final Australian East Coast gas demand (Quentin Grafton, Shi and Cronshaw 2018, Simshauser and Nelson 2015a, 2015b). This change in aggregate final demand is illustrated in Figure 9.4 (daily resolution) over the period 2009–18. Note that there are three market segments identified: gas-fired power generation; final consumer demand (that is, domestic residential, commercial and industrial); and LNG exports, which begin from late 2014.

What Figure 9.4 does not capture is the under-utilization of new LNG export plant capacity and the consequential pressure this has placed on the domestic gas market. Domestic gas prices had historically cleared at 3–4 A\$/GJ (that is, ~2.21–2.96 US\$/MMbtu) under both short- and long-dated contracts. However, the advent of LNG export

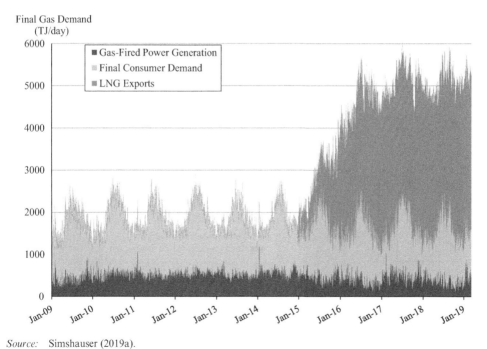

Source: Simshauser (2019a).

Figure 9.4   Expansion in aggregate demand for natural gas (terajoules [TJ] per day 2009–19)

terminals linked the 3–4 A$/GJ domestic market to a highly volatile 8–12 A$/GJ netback (~5.91–8.87 US$/MMbtu) seaborne market. And because excess LNG capacity had been built, marginal supplies in the domestic consumer market are forced to compete with sunk LNG export capacity – with domestic prices now clearing at (or above) the seaborne market range. Figure 9.5 presents the ramp-up and ongoing LNG plant capacity (from late 2014, daily resolution) and contrasts this with actual production. The extent of the visible market shortfall in Figure 9.5 (that is, at least one full LNG train, or about 250–300 PJ/yr) is very material – noting that aggregate domestic market demand is only 600PJ/yr.

With gas prices surging, legacy long-dated gas supply agreements held by generators (and struck at the pre-LNG prices of 3–4 A$/GJ or 2.21–2.96 US$/MMbtu) became more valuable as an export feedstock during the low spot price period of 2009–15. As Figure 9.6 illustrates, spark spreads (that is, the difference between the spot price of electricity and the marginal running cost of a gas turbine) from 2012 to 2014 were generally negative and well below that which could be sustainably achieved by mothballing a combined cycle gas turbine (CCGT) plant and on-selling the gas to LNG exporters under medium-term agreements. Consequently, many gas generators forward-sold their gas to LNG producers and temporarily exited the spot electricity market – unaware of looming coal plant exit at scale from 2016–17 onwards. When these power plants returned to market, their marginal costs were based on export-linked short-term gas prices. This would also have crucial implications for new capacity entry, as Section 5.6 explains.

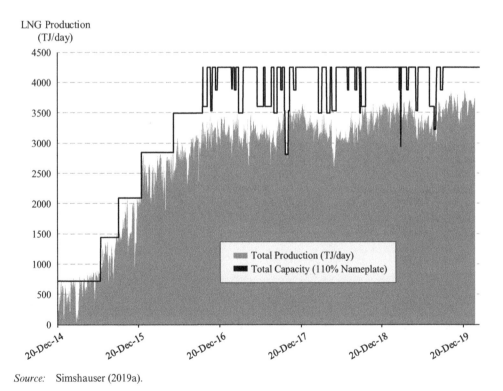

Source: Simshauser (2019a).

Figure 9.5   Australian East Coast LNG export capacity vs LNG production

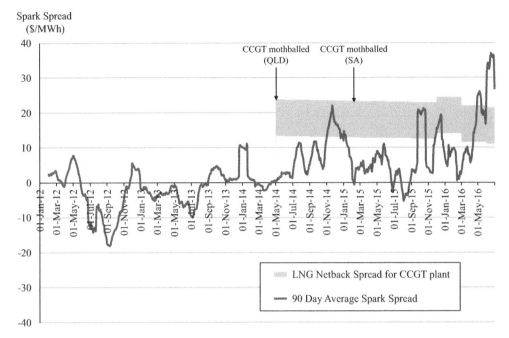

Source: Simshauser (2019a).

Figure 9.6 NEM spark spread (2012–16)

5.6 Entry and Investment Commitments: 1999–2018

Recall from Figures 9.1 and 9.2 that spot prices spiked above the cost of entry during 2017–18. A striking feature of the electricity price cycle over this period was the absence of gas turbine proposals, let alone gas plant entry. Gas plant entry was subject to critical hold-up for reasons outlined in Section 5.5.

During previous electricity price cycles (for example, 2007–08, driven by East Coast Australia's millennium drought), more than 5000 MW of gas-fired generation plant entered the coal-dominated NEM, as Figure 9.7 illustrates. In the 2017–19 cycle, there was no gas plant entry and, as noted above, many gas-fired generators forward-sold their long-term, low-cost gas supplies to the chronically short LNG export industry during the 'electricity price lull period', unaware that multiple, uncoordinated coal plant exit was imminent.

The entrant of choice in the Australian market has therefore switched to variable renewable energy (VRE), principally wind and solar photovoltaic (PV). Their material and timely reduction in entry costs along with an undersupplied 20 per cent renewable energy target helped drive a cyclical investment boom, as Figure 9.8 shows. Figure 9.8 builds on Figure 9.7 by adding in commissioned new entrant VRE plant and irreversible VRE investment commitments – that is, projects that have reached financial close and are now under construction.

While VRE capacity has seen record levels of investment, the majority of new plants are under construction at the time of writing. As Figure 9.21 later reveals, there appears

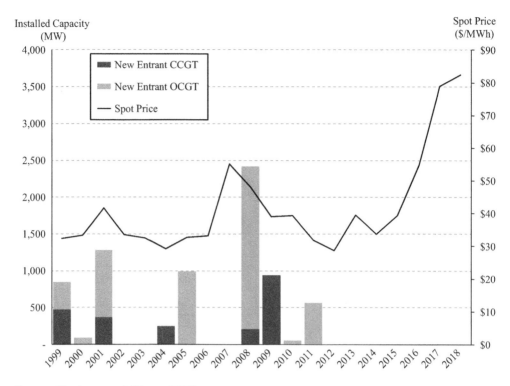

Source: Simshauser and Gilmore (2020).

Figure 9.7   *New entrant gas-fired plant (1999–2018)*

to be a tightening link between quarterly average spot electricity and quarterly average spot gas prices.

5.7   Market Power in the NEM

Central to the literature on energy-only markets is the matter of generator market power. Because there are no capacity payments, for an energy-only market to reach equilibrium it must have a high market price cap. In real time, participants are unable to optimize the number of price cap events. Actions by regulatory authorities and system operators compound matters by frequently suppressing legitimate price signals (Finon and Pignon 2008, Hogan 2013; Joskow 2008; Léautier 2016, Neuhoff and De Vries 2004, Spees, Newell and Pfeifenberger 2013, Wen, Wu and Ni 2004). Energy-only markets are therefore rarely in equilibrium and this creates risks for the continuity of timely investment to ensure the administratively determined reliability criteria are met (Bidwell and Henney 2004, Cramton and Stoft 2006, De Vries and Heijnen 2008, Hirth, Ueckerdt and Edenhofer 2016). In the circular calibration of reliability standards and a high market price cap, the risks and ability to distinguish market power events are compounded (Besser, Farr and Tierney 2002, Cramton and Stoft 2006, Joskow 2008, Oren 2003, Roques 2008, Roques, Newbery and Nuttall 2005, Simshauser 2008).

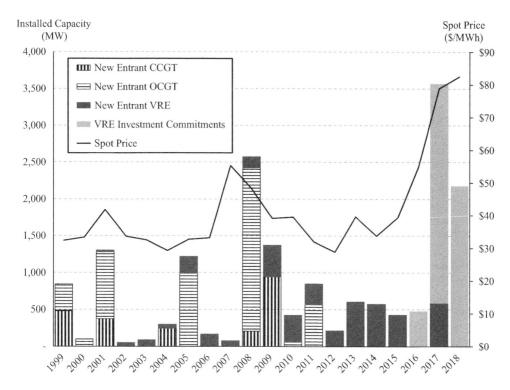

Source: Simshauser and Gilmore (2020).

Figure 9.8   New entrant plant (1999–2017) and investment commitments (2017–18)

In the NEM, the AER routinely investigates all price spikes above 5000 A$/MWh with the intent of monitoring competitive behaviour and compliance with the market rules. Because there are no capacity payments, NEM generators are free to bid their output at prices up to the market price cap, with competitive forces regulating the extent of economic withholding of capacity. As outlined in Table 9.2, the NEM has generally been characterized by intensely competitive prices – especially over the periods 1999–2006 and 2009–15.

Across the NEM's four major regions of QLD, NSW, VIC and SA from 1999 to 2018 (that is, '80 region years'), there have been eight notable episodes of economic withholding of capacity (and no doubt countless other minor episodes). However, half of these events merely reduced the economic losses outlined in Table 9.2. Table 9.4 provides the year, participant, portfolio size (MW), region and the (regional) average spot price relevant to the year in which the economic withholding of generating capacity occurred. Axiomatically, each case involved a large horizontal market participant.

From a policy perspective, each 'withholding event' triggered a response. Responses came in the form of: (1) competition via new entry; (2) regulation via rule change (for example, bidding in good faith rule, five-minute settlement rule); (3) intervention by government owners in the case of government trading enterprises; (4) litigation by the AER for a rule breach; or (5) longer-term changes in policymakers' attitudes and therefore subsequent policy adjustment.

Table 9.4   NEM market power events (1999–2018)

Year	Participant	MW	Region	Spot Price (Nominal A$)	Est. Average Total Cost (Regional) (A$)	Spot – Average Total Cost (A$)
1999	Tarong Energy[a]	1900	QLD	53.17	35.00	18.17
2000	TXU	1280	SA	59.27	40.75	$18.52
2001	Loy Yang Power	2000	VIC	44.57	38.52	6.05
2003	Enertrade[a]	2610	QLD	37.79	38.11	–0.32
2008	Macquarie Generation[a]	4600	NSW	41.66	42.39	–0.73
2008–10	AGL Energy	1280	SA	59.93	48.30	11.63
2013–14[b]	CS Energy[a]	4440	QLD	41.21	47.14	–5.93
2013–14[b]	Stanwell[a]	3854	QLD	41.21	47.14	–5.93
2017	Stanwell[a]	3854	QLD	95.41	51.33	44.08

Notes:
a.   Government owned.
b.   Incl. carbon price A$23/t.

There are two further points worth noting with respect to transient market power events in the NEM. First, in all but one case, participants were *not* vertically integrated. And in the vertical case, the source of market power was horizontal scale of the generator (privatized by the SA government), not vertical boundaries. Second is the prevalence of market power events involving government-owned generators.[31] As Wood and Blowers (2018) explain in their analysis of market power events covering the coal plant exit period, the NEM is 'mostly working'.

5.8   VRE and South Australia

A chapter on the NEM would be incomplete without reference to the special case of SA and the market implications of a sharply rising VRE market share, which is now above 50 per cent. By way of brief background, in 1997 Australia established the world's first renewable portfolio standard. Beginning at '2% renewables by 2010', the target market share was lifted to '20% renewables by 2020' following a general election in 2007. The national renewable energy policy required all liable retailers to submit sufficient 'Renewable Energy Certificates' each year to meet progressively higher targets. As an aside, the 20 per cent target will be comfortably met by 2020.

Inadequate thought went into how the certificated scheme design might be refined and improved[32] when it was expanded from 2 per cent to 20 per cent: in the event, the existing 2 per cent legislation was largely expanded and rolled over intact. The scheme collided with the NEM's wholesale market design – disconnecting entry decisions from the NEM's forward markets. One direct consequence of this was the world-class wind resources in SA attracting a disproportionate amount of investment because of the existence of the certificate side-market, and further compounded by off-market investments. Off-market investment came via subnational governments underwriting entry to acquit their own intra-state renewable aspirations. The Australian Capital Territory, for example, wrote a series of contracts for difference (CfDs) in the SA region, yet their own load is located within the NSW region – a region dominated by scheduled capacity, thus leaving SA with even more VRE plants than the side-markets would have otherwise delivered. As Figure 9.9 explains, between 2006 and 2018, VRE plant market share in the 'loosely interconnected' SA NEM region would rise from zero to 51 per cent (wind dominating at 42 percentage points). By comparison, the large and more strongly inter-connected regions of QLD, NSW and VIC would be greatly 'under-weight renewables', each with less than 8 per cent VRE market share in 2018.

Compounding matters for SA were its small system size (3100 MW peak demand and 12.5 terrawatt-hours [TWh] yearly energy consumption) and very poor load factor (0.45 – a very peaky power system). Indeed, SA is by far the smallest of the NEM's four main regions with an underlying baseload of just ~1100 MW and, as indicated above, limited interconnection to the adjacent VIC region.

With an influx of wind generation, the SA region experienced so-called 'merit order effects' from as early as 2011 (Bell et al. 2017, Cludius, Forrest and MacGill 2014, Forrest and MacGill 2013). Consistent with literature in the field, merit order effects eventually reverse (Nelson, Simshauser and Nelson 2012). With coal plants forced to withdraw, SA lost all coal-fired generating units over the period 2012–16, as Figure 9.9 illustrates (see also Table 9.3).

Once VRE annual market share rose above ~25 per cent,[33] coal plant operations became increasingly uneconomic. By the time VRE exceeded ~35 per cent (in 2016), the

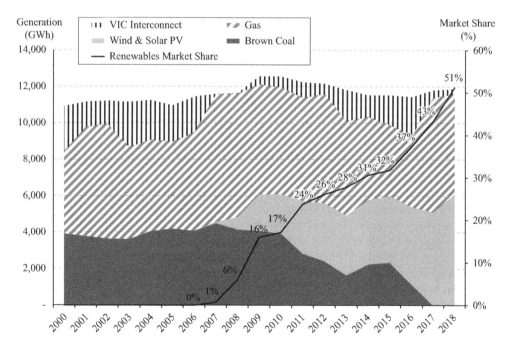

Source: AEMO.

Figure 9.9   South Australian generation (GWh) and VRE market share (%) from 2000 to 2018

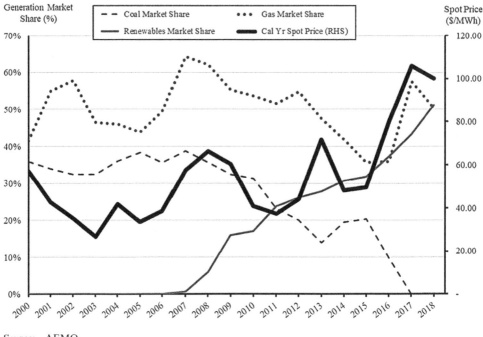

Generation Market Share (%)

Spot Price ($/MWh)

- – Coal Market Share   • • • Gas Market Share
— Renewables Market Share   ▬ Cal Yr Spot Price (RHS)

Source: AEMO.

Figure 9.10   SA generation market share vs spot price (calendar years 2000–18)[34]

coal fleet exited and gas-fired generation plant provided an expensive 'shock absorber', given the gas price dynamics outlined in Section 5.5. The sharp rise in spot prices is illustrated in Figure 9.10.

Although SA was visibly changing from a synchronous, dispatchable coal and gas resource-based system to one comprising an increasing and dominant level of asynchronous, stochastic VRE wind and solar PV resources, AEMO maintained the same levels of frequency contingency services (that is, six-second, 60-second and five-minute spinning reserves). In prior periods it had reduced the levels of frequency regulation and black start services.[35] Furthermore, AEMO maintained a practice of global procurement of frequency control ancillary services (FCAS) across NEM regions rather than localizing some minimum level of FCAS in the SA region – noting that SA is imperfectly interconnected to the adjacent VIC region.[36] These practices, coupled with a changing generation mix and how AEMO chooses to define what constitutes a credible contingency, were crucial elements that would exacerbate any supply-side shock.

At 4:18 pm on 28 September 2016, SA experienced a black system event. A severe storm cell with wind speeds of 190–250 kilometres per hour (km/h) moved through the state and damaged two transmission lines, causing a series of voltage dips over a two-minute window. In real time, SA system demand was 1826 MW and system dispatch configuration comprised 330 MW gas-fired generation, 883 MW wind generation and 613 MW imports through the VIC-SA Interconnector – the latter notably operating at close to its rated capacity during the storm event.

As a result of the voltage dips, a group of wind turbines operating at ~450 MW disconnected from the grid (note: an unknown fault ride-through issue).[37] In response, power imported across the main VIC-SA Interconnector, already operating at close to full load, surged from 613 MW to 890 MW (that is, 250 MW above the line's rated capacity) and within 0.6 of a second, protection systems tripped the interconnector offline. At this point SA was islanded from the balance of the NEM. Following the combined loss of ~450 MW wind generation and ~600 MW imports via VIC Interconnector, contingent capacity from indigenous dispatchable power plants (330 MW) and under frequency load shedding resources (UFLS) were simply inadequate to arrest the decline in frequency – noting that the time lapse of the events spanned two seconds, as Figure 9.11 illustrates. When combined with FCAS (frequency regulation and six-second frequency contingency), UFLS can generally arrest a rate of change of frequency (RoCoF) of ~3.5 hertz (Hz) per second. However, as Figure 9.11 shows, the estimated RoCoF in the black system event was closer to 6.25 Hz per second.

How AEMO had configured the SA power system just prior to the black system event was intriguing and can perhaps only reflect a rapid and unexpected deterioration in weather conditions. Noting the existence of Section 4.3.1 of the NEM Rules (see Section 4 in this chapter), power system operations immediately prior to material weather events in the NEM's northern region of QLD are always configured differently.

QLD has a long, skinny network spanning several thousands of kilometres, and the far north of the state will typically experience two or three cyclones per annum – some of which can be expected to cross the network. The long-standing coordinating and operating practices of Powerlink – the utility that owns and operates the transmission system in QLD – and AEMO – the NEM's independent system and market operator – in periods

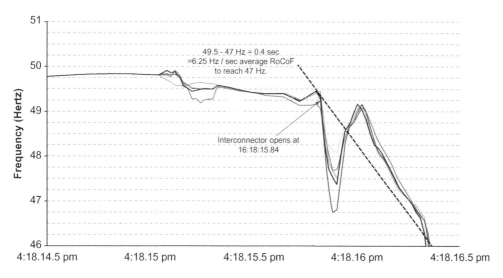

Source: AEMO (2017).

Figure 9.11 Frequency and rate of change of frequency (various measurement points)

prior to cyclones crossing land are to invoke a greater reliance on local dispatchable generation either side of the weather event (that is, dispatchable generation capacity in the north is constrained-on, out of merit order), thus reducing reliance on intra-connector flows from the south in the event of a contingency. Why SA was not similarly configured by AEMO during this one-in-50-year storm event (for example, by constraining-on local generation, reducing the load on the VIC-SA interconnector, and so on) is unclear. To be clear, the black system event was a system security event, not a resource adequacy event. That is, there was more than adequate available generating capacity within the SA region.

As a result of the blackout, AEMO undertook a review and made a series of changes. At the same time, the SA government stepped into the market and contracted a 100 MW Tesla battery to provide fast frequency response. So far, the battery has proven to be highly effective in supplying (and moderating the cost of) frequency control ancillary services. In addition to this and in anticipation of the potential impact of the combined exit of the Northern and the Hazelwood power stations, the latter located in the adjacent VIC region, the government added ~300 MW of fast-starting gas turbine capacity ahead of the looming 2018 and 2019 summer periods.

5.9   Ongoing Challenges for NEM Frequency

The normal operating frequency band in the NEM is 50 Hz +/–0.015 Hz and system frequency is to be maintained within that band for more than 99 per cent of time. With

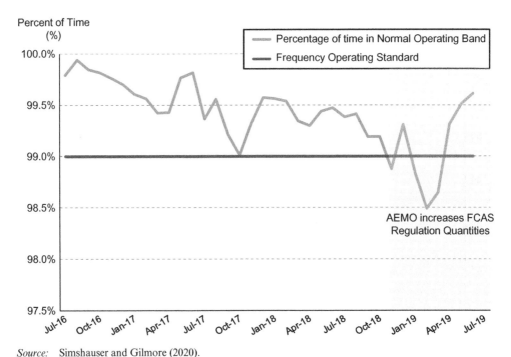

Source: Simshauser and Gilmore (2020).

Figure 9.12   System operations inside normal frequency band (% of time)

more VRE plants entering the electricity system (per Figure 9.8), NEM frequency has become increasingly volatile. From the mid-2000s to 2019, AEMO held FCAS quantities constant, at ~130 MW of frequency regulation and ~990 MW of combined regulation and contingent resources. AEMO's position on FCAS finally changed in early 2019 when frequency fell outside the normal operating band's '99% threshold' (Figure 9.12). Frequency regulation has now been increased to ~220 MW and remains under active review along with the quantity of frequency contingency services. The direction of FCAS volumes was, in my view, predictable and long overdue.

6. NETWORKS AND NETWORK REGULATION

The transmission and distribution (T&D) networks servicing the NEM's 10 million business and residential customers are regulated by the AER in rate cases of five years' duration. The form of regulation is based on Littlechild's (1983) incentive-based 'RPI-X', with annual regulated revenue caps derived by a traditional building block approach. Within the revenue cap, there is an ability to rebalance tariffs amongst consumer segments within limits, beyond which specific regulatory approval is required.

The form of tariffs for end users varies considerably. For households and small businesses, a conventional two-part tariff applies (that is, a fixed rate plus a variable rate) with the fixed rate representing ~20 per cent and the variable rate ~80 per cent of revenue. For large commercial and industrial (C&I) customers, conventional three-part tariffs (that is, fixed, variable and demand charge) are generally used.

Capital deployed by distribution networks tends to be dominated by residential segment peak loads. Conversely, adoption of rooftop solar PV has been prolific in the residential sector; with more than 2 million households having installed a rooftop PV system (that is, more than one-in-four households), Australia has among the highest take-up rates in the world. And this matters because solar PV systems greatly reduce energy (kWh) demand, but in certain regions only marginally impact peak (kW) demand (for example, see Simshauser 2016). Consequently, two-part tariffs dominated by a volumetric variable charge are not well suited with regard to rate stability. But while the economic justification for reforming residential tariff structures is (in my opinion) compelling, the political economy of doing so has proven almost impossible thus far. The inevitability of losers from tariff reform requires expending considerable political capital – and only policymakers in the Australian Capital Territory (ACT) have been prepared to take on such political risks.[38]

6.1 Network Performance

Network policy, network regulation and overall network performance have been amongst the most contentious aspects of Australia's energy market reforms – especially during 2007–15. This period coincided with an enormous increase in the combined T&D regulatory asset base (RAB), as Figure 9.13 illustrates. Key policy and regulatory decisions underpin this, including (1) erroneous policy decisions by the state governments of QLD and NSW to tighten reliability standards in 2004, following severe network-related blackouts in the capital cities of Brisbane and Sydney; (2) the decision to revalue network

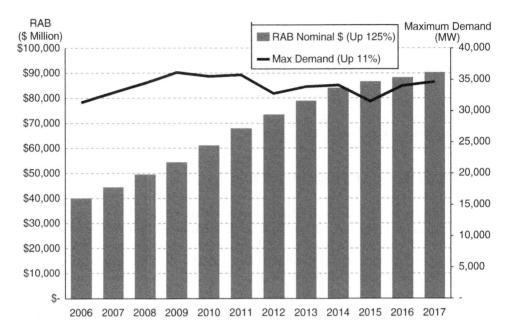

Source: Simshauser and Akimov (2019).

Figure 9.13 *Combined T&D RAB (in nominal dollars) vs maximum demand 2006–17*

assets in the mid-1990s before market start; and (3) a policy decision by all state governments in 2006 that had the effect of making network regulation formulaic, which amongst other things eliminated the ability of AER from pursuing RAB write-downs, the absence of any regulatory threat being a clear deficiency with regard to incentives of the firm.

By way of brief background, until 2006 distribution networks were regulated by state government regulatory authorities.[39] From 2006, the AER took over network regulation from the state-based regulators. Evidently lacking trust in the new regulator, state government senior officials attempted to minimize the risk of regulatory error by hard wiring a surprising number of variables that otherwise require considerable professional judgement. This had the consequence of constraining the AER when undertaking regulatory determinations. By way of specific examples, first, regulated returns are determined by estimating a fair weighted average cost of capital (WACC) using the capital asset pricing model (for equity returns) and BBB-rated ten-year corporate bonds (for debt returns). When the regulator attempted to make determinations in 2007–08 during the Global Financial Crisis, Australian credit markets had largely closed and the market for Australian ten-year corporate bonds literally disappeared.[40] The regulator was then forced to use thin market and proxy estimates, which in the event set excessively high allowances for debt returns.[41] Second, any capital invested by a network over and above the five-year regulatory allowance could be automatically rolled into the RAB at the next regulatory reset without any prudency or efficiency review.

What followed was predictable, and was predicted – Averch and Johnson (1962) gold plating, which when combined with excessive returns produced sharply rising network tariffs. Figure 9.13 presents the combined RAB of T&D networks servicing NEM customers (bar chart, LHS axis) and contrasts this with non-coincident NEM maximum demand (line chart, RHS axis) over the period 2006–17. Notice the combined T&D RAB increased from ~A$40 billion to A$90 billion (+125 per cent), while maximum demand had increased by only 11 per cent. Network utilization rates have consequently plunged. The aggregate distribution network utilization rate in particular has fallen from 0.59 to 0.45, with networks in NSW and QLD exhibiting large falls of 0.51 to 0.34, and 0.60 to 0.48, respectively.

Figure 9.14 presents a simplified average T&D network tariff for each region (line series) and in aggregate (bar series). Note the nominal average network tariff has increased by 91 per cent, from 4.5 c/kWh (cents per kWh) to 8.5 c/kWh with considerable variation amongst regions. This data series has been constructed by dividing aggregate T&D revenues by T&D energy delivered, and as a result masks the rich variation of tariffs by consumer segment.

Figure 9.15 presents RAB (A$) per customer connection by region (line series) and in aggregate (bar series – in both nominal and constant 2017 dollars). Notice the sharp increase in QLD (up 96 per cent) and NSW (up 120 per cent).

6.2   Regulatory and Policy Response

Once the effects of a tightened reliability standard became clear to regulators and policy-makers, along with the fact that demand growth had stalled, a series of material policy

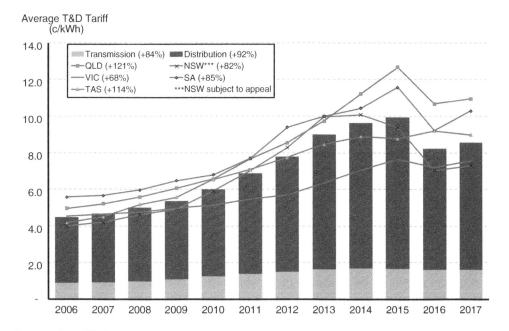

Source: AER (2018).

Figure 9.14   Average network tariff 2006–17 (nominal dollars)

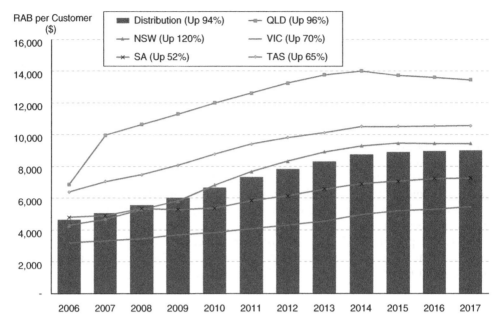

Source: AER (2018).

Figure 9.15   RAB per customer connection 2006–17 (nominal dollars)

and regulatory changes followed. Both QLD and NSW abandoned their tightened reliability criteria – essentially reverting back to a probabilistic approach (rather than a deterministic one). The AER maximized the low interest rate environment and pushed allowable WACCs in each determination down from 2015 – with returns falling from ~10 per cent to ~6 per cent, and more recent one determination in the mid-5 per cent range, as illustrated in Figure 9.16.

The AER also adopted a hard line on capital expenditure (Capex) and operating expenditure (Opex) allowances, routinely rejecting as much as 30 per cent of that proposed by network companies. Figure 9.17 illustrates the sharp reductions in total expenditure or Totex (that is, Capex and Opex together).

Two outstanding network policy issues that remain are (1) given dramatic falls in network utilization, how this excess capacity should be treated;[42] and (2) the efficiency of network tariff design – especially at the household level given sharply rising levels of distributed energy resources (DERs).[43] On the latter, the politics of rising prices and the nature of the current regulatory system means that policymakers and the regulator, respectively, have tended to focus on minimizing regulated revenues rather than tackle the requisite reform of the efficiency of network tariff structures.[44] Prevailing two-part residential tariff structures, which are dominated by variable charges, are known to be suboptimal given sharply rising levels of solar PV. Such tariffs over-value energy (that is, kWh) and undervalue network capacity (that is, kW), with a consequential risk of investment in grid bypass (that is, DERs) above the efficient level – and the costs of doing so redistributed in an inequitable manner (Simshauser 2016).

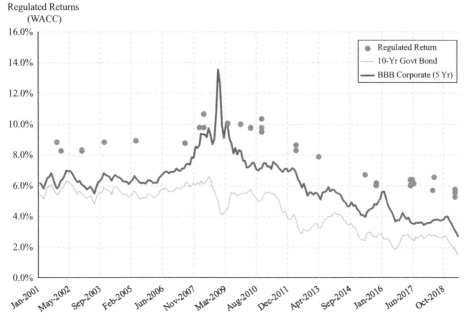

Source: AER (2018).

Figure 9.16   Regulated returns (five-year determinations made over the period 2002–18)

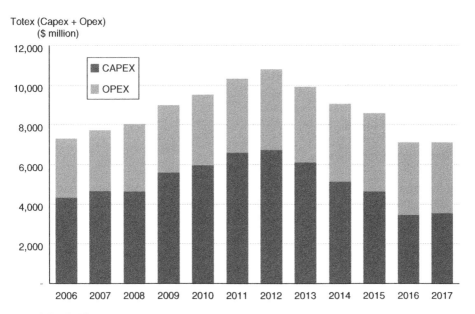

Source: AER (2018).

Figure 9.17   Allowable Totex in constant 2017 dollars

7. RETAIL MARKET

Competition in the retail segment formed a key component of Australia's energy market reforms and was based largely on Great Britain's approach to contestability (Littlechild 2016). Specifically, in the period leading up to market start, incumbent distribution/retail supply companies held a monopoly franchise over their customer base, but this franchise would diminish gradually. To ensure an orderly transition to a competitive market, retail electricity market contestability was phased in over a timetable comprising between four and six tranches of consumers (starting with the largest customers) and spanning a four- to eight-year window. The final tranche of customers (that is, residential) had added policy scaffolding in the transition to a fully contestable market – a 'regulated tariff cap' – retained as a transitional measure until the so-called mass market was deemed to be 'workably competitive'. The mass market would be deemed workably competitive by reference to measures such as (1) consumer awareness of their ability to switch supplier; (2) number of rival retailers; (3) array of products and the depth of discounting; (4) customer switching rates; (5) market share of incumbent retailers; (6) number of customers remaining on the default tariff, and so on.

In Great Britain, retail competition began in the C&I segment in the early 1990s, while the residential/household segment was made fully contestable in 1999, with full retail price deregulation in 2002. NEM contestability varied by region: VIC 1994–2002, NSW 1996–2002, QLD 1998–2007 and SA 1998–2003. Residential segment price deregulation occurred in 2009, 2014, 2016 and 2013, respectively (Simshauser 2018).

As Section 7.1 reveals, the experience of consumers over the period 2007–15 has been characterized by sharply rising electricity tariffs after a period of price stability. Rising prices, driven by network and wholesale prices (per Sections 5 and 6 above) have tended to mask the successes of retail competition in the NEM: the number of competitors, the array of products, discounts available, competitor rivalry, customer switching rates and reductions in the number of default tariff customers have all progressively intensified over time. But as with Great Britain, the evolution of price discrimination has become a political target – conflating the problem of rising prices (and some poor practices by certain retailers) with price dispersion.

7.1 Retail Tariff Increases

To understand the problem of rising final consumer prices in Australia, Figure 9.18 presents average retail tariffs from 1955 to 2019 in nominal and real terms using QLD data as the reference. As with all NEM data, there is variation by region, but the trend is largely consistent.

It took 45 years of technological advancement, scale economies and microeconomic reform from 1962 to 2007 to drive real tariffs from 30 c/kWh down to 16 c/kWh. Policy errors would unwind those gains in eight years (2007–15). Three distinct drivers were responsible for tariff increases, viz. network policy failure[45] (2007–15; see Section 6), environmental schemes (2011–17) and wholesale prices (2017–19; see Section 5). These pricing effects were sequential and cumulative. On the environmental costs, four schemes impacted tariffs over the period 2011–17. To be clear, each scheme was trivial, but

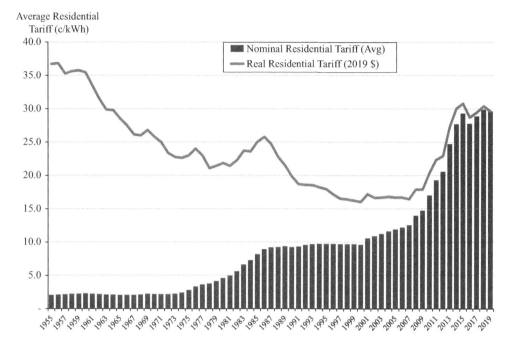

Average Residential
Tariff (c/kWh)

Figure 9.18   *QLD average residential electricity tariff (1955–2019)*

combined they aggravated network-driven tariff increases. Schemes included (1) solar feed-in tariffs (Nelson et al. 2012); the 20 per cent renewable energy target which was separated into two, viz. (2) small scale and (3) utility scale (MacGill 2010); and (4) the carbon tax from 2012 to 2014. At their peak, environmental schemes added 15 per cent to already sharply rising tariffs.

Compounding matters were the timing: the sharp run-up in household electricity tariffs occurred in the post-Global Financial Crisis era of low consumer price inflation, low productivity, low wage growth and in some jurisdictions coincident record-high house prices. Unsurprisingly (and understandably), and as with Great Britain, electricity prices and retail electricity markets became a cost of living 'focus event' for consumer groups and politicians (He and Reiner 2017, Littlechild 2014, Price and Zhu 2016, Simshauser and Tiernan 2019).

7.2   Price Discrimination the Target

As with Great Britain, there has been nothing politically contentious about the overall performance, and success, of the C&I retail market segment. However, as with Great Britain, recent performance of the NEM's residential retail market has been the subject of a highly charged and politicized debate that deteriorated badly over the period 2016–19. For the first time in a generation, an Australian prime minister became involved in what has traditionally been a state government responsibility. And unfortunately, two separate issues were conflated: rising prices and price discrimination (see Littlechild 2018 on Great Britain, and Simshauser 2018 on Australia). Rising prices are indeed a problem, including rising network charges (2010–15) and wholesale price dynamics (2017–19). But price discrimination is not, and the difficulty for policymakers is that misdiagnosing price discrimination for policy treatment may make some households considerably worse off and leave residential consumers as a class no better off (Simshauser 2018).

When contestability begins in the residential segment, prices begin a natural drift from a regulated uniform (two-part) tariff to discriminatory prices. A regulated price cap is initially retained as a proxy safety net for inactive household consumers as the market shifts from single monopoly provider to competitive market. This regulated default tariff forms a 'price to beat'. Rival and new entrant retailers entering a franchise service area will offer discounts off the incumbent's default tariff to poach customers. Incumbent retailers are forced to construct their own discounted matching products in response. Discounts off a default tariff are thus a central design feature of a contestable retail electricity market.

The success of full retail contestability (that is, household segment) is inextricably linked to expected gains from switching. Gains to household consumers are expressed as a 'percentage discount off'[46] an existing default tariff. When the mass market is deemed workably competitive, the requirement for an independent regulator to set a regulated default tariff cap no longer exists. Incumbent retailers – who retain an obligation to supply[47] in their former franchise area – must ensure that their default tariff (and associated levels of service) is available at all times.

When retail prices are deregulated, the number of rival suppliers will expand rapidly because a key business risk (that is, regulatory risk) has in theory been removed.[48] In addition, retailers segment the residential market into multiple sub-segments[49] and product bundles are then constructed to target those discrete sub-segments. Consequently, with the number of rival retailers expanding and consumer sub-segments multiplying, the number of products – and discounts –proliferates.

Certain 'reviews' of residential retail market practices and performance in Australia and in Great Britain have pointed to price discrimination as a key policy problem (see Chapter 5 in this handbook), suggesting that the practice produces unfair prices and 'loyalty taxes' for disengaged customers who do not switch supplier regularly (Littlechild 2016, Simshauser 2018). But price discrimination is unremarkable in economics, is a predictable outcome of rising competition where the products of consumer preferences are not perfectly homogeneous, and is frequently welfare enhancing. Price discrimination is pervasive throughout the economy and forms a vital means by which non-trivial joint fixed and sunk costs are efficiently recovered by firms, especially in capital-intensive or 'heavy' industries (Dana 1998, Elegido 2011, Levine 2002, Littlechild 2018).

Nonetheless, perceptions of fairness inevitably arise when a menu of tariffs emerge and deviate from an historic uniform price (Dana 1998). Deeply discounted tariffs are popular, while high default tariffs are derided by consumer groups (and in a rising price environment, with some justification). Regardless, their existence produces adverse media and political focusing events in which ill-advised claims of forcing retailers to shift all customers en masse to the cheapest tariff can be expected (He and Reiner 2017,

Littlechild 2017, Simshauser 2018). Implementation of such a policy would, of course, see cheap tariffs disappear overnight. As an aside, the business segment of electricity markets exhibits extensive second- and third-degree practices yet are never questioned by policymakers.

It is worth briefly reviewing some of the NEM retail market metrics to highlight the overall performance of the market (despite the network and wholesale market cost pressures).

7.3   Competitive Health of the Retail Market

Customer switching is frequently used as a headline measure of the health of contestable residential electricity markets. Switching rates in NEM regions have typically averaged 16–22 per cent per annum, which compares favourably to other Australian industry switching rates (Table 9.5).

Detailed historic data for the main NEM regions is presented in Table 9.6.

Another residential market metric that requires continual monitoring by policymakers is so-called 'rusted-on' customer numbers – that is, customers who have never switched and remain rusted on to incumbent retailer default tariffs. Table 9.7 presents rusted-on customer results for the primary NEM regions as at 2017.

Table 9.7 shows that Victoria is the oldest of the deregulated markets (2009) with the lowest number of rusted-on customers (10 per cent). After deregulating in 2016, 17 per cent of South East QLD customers are rusted on. These results compare favourably to the British market, which has about 33 per cent of rusted-on customers after full retail contestability in 1999 and price deregulation in 2002 (He and Reiner 2017, Littlechild 2016).

The final matter of interest is the extent of price dispersion, and for this Figure 9.19 presents data from the QLD region – ideally suited for such analysis because Regional QLD is a regulated monopoly (and is still subject to a regulated price based on the South East QLD cost inputs), while South East QLD is a fully contestable and deregulated market (thus enabling a direct comparison of a competitive and regulated

Table 9.5   Industry comparison of customer switching rates[50]

Industry	Switching Rate (%)
NEM electricity	23.5
NEM gas	15.9
Broadband	15.0
Mobile phones	13.0
Pay television	12.0
Insurance	12.0
Airlines	10.0
Banking	8.0
Health	4.0
Superannuation	4.0

Source: Simshauser (2014b).

Table 9.6   NEM electricity customer switching by region (2007/08–2017/18)

Financial Year	SE QLD	VIC	NSW	SA
2007/08	20.3	22.4	10.2	18.3
2008/09	20.7	25.4	10.9	15.0
2009/10	23.3	25.9	12.8	13.9
2010/11	25.3	27.1	14.9	18.6
2011/12	21.2	26.8	17.3	22.1
2012/13	18.1	28.7	20.1	22.0
2013/14	17.0	27.3	15.2	18.3
2014/15	16.7	26.6	15.9	16.0
2015/16	16.8	24.6	16.9	16.3
2016/17	22.1	27.4	18.6	16.5
2017/18	32.2	29.0	20.0	20.4
Five-year average	21.0	27.0	17.3	20.4

Source: AEMO.

Table 9.7   Year of reform and market customers vs 'rusted-on' customers in 2017

Region	Full Retail Contestability (Year)	Price Deregulation (Year)	Total Customers	Default Customers	'Rusted-on' Customers (%)
SE QLD	2007	2016	1 317 957	226 018	17.0
NSW	2002	2014	3 534 894	813 000	23.0
SA	2003	2013	864 876	121 000	14.0
VIC	2002	2009	2 807 280	281 000	10.0
		Total NEM	8 525 006	1 441 018	16.9

Source: Simshauser (2018).

market, which is unique by global standards). Figure 9.19 presents four discrete data series:

- the 2018 regulated tariff (applied to Regional QLD customers and based on the common QLD region wholesale price, and South East QLD network charges, and a suitable retail supply cost allowance);
- South East QLD competitive offers in 2015 *prior* to deregulation – that is, when QLD's regulated tariff acted as a tariff cap in the contestable South East QLD corner (as well as the regulated price to regional QLD customers) inflated to 2018 dollars;
- South East QLD competitive offers in 2018 *after* deregulation; and
- South East QLD competitive offers in 2019 (note: the 2019 regulated tariff was 29.6 c/kWh, ~0.8 per cent lower than the 2018 regulated tariff rate of 29.9 c/kWh – see Figure 9.18).

Figure 9.19 and the data behind it provide important insights for the competitive retail market. First, following deregulation of South East QLD in 2016, the number of rival

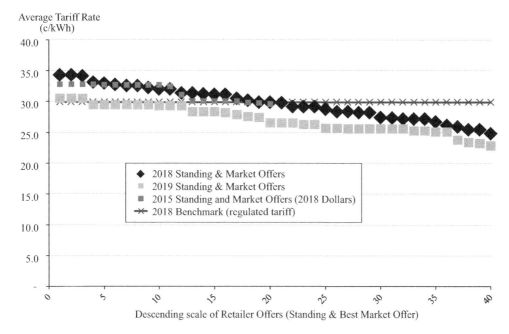

Source: Simshauser (2018).

Figure 9.19   Tariff dispersion: pre- and post-deregulation tariffs vs benchmark

retailers expanded from 12 to 20 by 2018, and the number of default tariffs and routine discounts offered by rival retailers expanded from 24 to 40+. Second, the dispersion of tariffs increased in line with general findings of the literature – that is, falling either side of the regulated rate. But to be clear, about 1.1 million out of 1.3 million South East QLD households were on a lower tariff than the regulated tariff, as Figure 9.20 shows (and as a class, South East QLD households in aggregate were paying 7 per cent less than the regulated rate, albeit with ~200 000 households paying more than the regulated rate – see Simshauser 2018). Third, by 2019, competition had forced high-end default tariffs closer to the counterfactual regulated rate, with deeper discounts also being exhibited.

On balance, one can conclude that the deregulated retail electricity market is performing well. The default tariffs of retailers is limited to a relatively small percentage of customers, has received a disproportionate level of political attention, and policy solutions of re-regulating prices through a price cap is unlikely to end well for those consumers active in the market (in the medium term) as retailers progressively readjust their market segmentations and profit strategies.

This is not to suggest the retail market is operating without fault – vulnerable rusted-on customers represent a misallocation problem (that is, low-income households are on a tariff designed for an inelastic segment), and discounts are no longer anchored to a common price. Both of these matters are serious policy problems that require further work by retailers and policymakers, respectively.

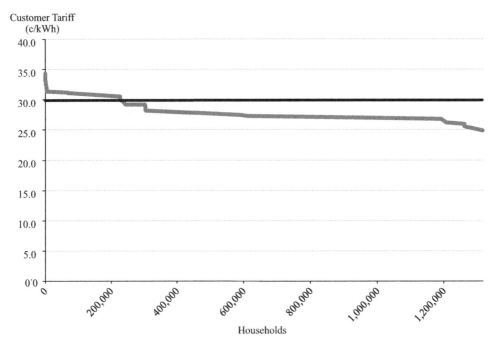

Source: Simshauser (2018).

Figure 9.20   2018 distribution of South East QLD households by tariff

8.   THE STRENGTHS AND WEAKNESSES OF AUSTRALIA'S ENERGY MARKET REFORMS

In light of the recent problems emerging in Australia's NEM, it is easiest to start with a review of weaknesses. There have been a series of reform weaknesses that stem from policy failures. With the benefit of hindsight, these include the following:

1.   The SA black system event in September 2016 was a crisis, and every energy industry crisis regardless of country invokes a formal government inquiry, and every formal inquiry provides a helpful platform for necessary reforms, but in addition, invariably unleashes a wave of unhelpful interventions as well (Helm 2014). In this instance, an additional layer of market governance was added (that is, the Energy Security Board – which has had the effect of blurring strict segregation between market operations, regulation and rulemaking – see Section 4). The Energy Security Board has also pursued propositions to investigate strategic generation plant reserves, day-ahead markets and other issues more suited to concerns with regard to resource adequacy when the prime issue associated with the SA black system event was one of system security and system operations. Rising levels of VRE requires greater thought on what constitutes a credible contingency and potential new modes of failure. This in turn requires a focus on the FCAS volumes procured, whether FCAS enablement should be globally or zonally procured across a vast, imperfectly interconnected

system, management of VRE-related voltage oscillations and system strength, and how a system with world-record levels of VRE should be configured in real time when confronted with a severe weather event. To be clear once again, the black system was a security event, not a resource adequacy problem – aggregate supply was more than adequate.

2. The lack of a clear gas market and LNG export capacity policy architecture prior to LNG investment commitments in 2010–12. Emphasizing the benefit of hindsight, LNG export licensing should have been restricted to the availability of 'booked' proven and probable (2P) reserves above that required to service the domestic market for natural gas. This 'missing policy' needed to be coordinated at the national level because no individual jurisdiction is able to reasonably assess, on a cost–benefit basis, adequacy of East Coast reserves. Gas shortages (Figure 9.5) on Australia's East Coast remain an unresolved problem and the impact on electricity price is evident, as the 34 quarterly data points in Figure 9.21 illustrate (note: correlation of 0.88). Forward resolution needs to turn to prospective measures on new supply, rather than retrospective policy intervention that may inflame perceptions of sovereign risk.

3. Policy discontinuity and design errors with regard to climate change policy, and a general lack of a united climate and energy policy architecture. At least four Australian prime ministers have lost their leadership through a two-decade-long 'climate change policy war', with both sides of politics suffering equally. This missing policy has adversely affected investment continuity in the NEM and remains a live

Source: AEMO.

Figure 9.21   Quarterly average: NEM spot price vs NEM gas price

problem at the time of writing. Furthermore, the policies that do exist, such as the expanded 20 per cent Renewable Energy Target amongst an array of others (Simshauser and Tiernan 2019), were incompatible with the NEM design in that investment was largely disconnected from forward markets – instead, investment was being driven by side-markets. This problem risks being further compounded by the rising use of government-initiated CfDs: while highly effective at encouraging new capacity to meet various policy objectives (for example, navigate missing policies relating to climate change), government-initiated CfDs are incompatible with the NEM design (Simshauser 2019b). Whether the NEM's wholesale market design needs to change to suit CfDs, or alternate mechanisms need to be found to suit the NEM design, is an open question.

4.   Plant exit policy, and coal plant exit in particular, could have been better managed in the NEM if the gas market had been functioning properly. But regardless of this, or perhaps because of it, transparency around exit timing needed to be greatly improved. This missing policy has been semi-resolved by way of a rule change that requires continuous disclosure of a plant exit timing (referred to as the three-year closure rule). This is a necessary, but not sufficient, policy adjustment. Looking forward, each state government should have a well-rehearsed plant exit policy – the closure of the 1600 MW Hazelwood Power Station (20 per cent VIC market share) with five months' notice did not represent an orderly exit. In the event, annual whole-sale spot market turnover rose from A$7.7 billion to A$17.2 billion either side of the Hazelwood exit. In hindsight, some component of Hazelwood's required A$400 million capital expenditure programme could have been taxpayer (or electricity consumer) funded on a cost-plus basis to ensure an orderly exit and provide the market with more time to adjust given predictable entry lags. Such a policy should not be interpreted nor designed to prevent an exit decision per se, and above all, should avoid outcomes that lead to costs being socialized and profits being privatized. It should be a contingent policy, used judiciously to facilitate orderly exit and only applied in critical circumstances.

5.   Competition policy. With the benefit of hindsight, the Commonwealth Government, state governments and the ACCC allowed an excess of horizontal M&A events. State governments sought to maximize privatization sale proceeds and in my view the ACCC over-diagnosed *vertical* integration and under-diagnosed more adverse *horizontal* aggregations.

6.   The over-diagnosis of price discrimination by various agencies and governments is likely to adversely impact a component of NEM reforms that has generally performed well. This is not to suggest the retail market is without fault; clear weaknesses include the lack of jurisdictional coordination over the timing of deregulation events across NEM regions (that is, lack of synchronization), how retailers deal with vulnerable customers on default tariffs, and the lack of a common anchor for advertised product discounts. But a policy of reinstating a regulated price cap will not solve the underlying problem of affordability, a point in economics that the AEMC has also recently noted.

7.   While NEM governance has certain unique advantages (for example, a strict segregation amongst market institutions), in the absence of a formal binding agreement to meet certain policy objectives the COAG Energy Council ultimately becomes a weakness of NEM governance in that it requires multiple state and territory

governments (and multiple political parties), and the Commonwealth, to agree to material policy change. Furthermore, state governments have de-skilled their energy departments over time (notably, there are virtually no specialist energy departments remaining. In most jurisdictions, the former Department of Energy now forms part of a broader mega-departmental structure, with the departmental secretary or director-general spread thinly across the long list of line responsibilities). It is worth noting that during the 1990s, 'competition payments' from Commonwealth to state governments were used to encourage a united approach to policy and reform objectives.

8. Network regulation in the NEM proved to be a weakness throughout the period 2004–15. Critical errors were made by certain state governments with regard to reliability standards and the rules from 2006–12 were too 'formulaic' to respond to the unique conditions of the Global Financial Crisis. These two conditions proved to be devastating for network prices, as the figures in Section 6 illustrate.

9. Network tariff reform in the NEM has been identified as crucial by the AEMC as early as 2012. World-record solar PV uptake rates makes this more, not less, important from the perspective of tariff efficiency, tariff stability and fairness of the burden of fixed cost recovery. By 2020, only one network utility (in the ACT) has thus far managed to establish a residential demand tariff on an 'opt-out basis' where consumers have a smart meter installed. This has thus far been more of a political constraint than a general policy failure, but network utilities have also spent too much time second-guessing political responses rather than defining solutions and implementation glide paths.

The strengths of the Australian reform experience could be summarized as follows:

1. The NEM's energy-only, gross pool market design with a very high VoLL and associated market for forward derivatives has delivered resource adequacy and withstood a wide array of economic and technical conditions. Market failures can generally be attributed to 'missing policies' of LNG export capacity, climate change and plant exit, design errors of renewable schemes, and the application (or lack thereof) of competition policy with regard to initial privatization events.

2. The NEM's core governance structure and approach to open source rulemaking has had the beneficial effect of minimizing misguided political interference, and ensured rule changes have *purposefully* thought through economic trade-offs. For example, the strict segregation between AEMC (rulemaking body) and AEMO (market operator) means that rule changes that enhance market operations and spot prices efficiency can be weighed against any efficiency losses that might arise in forward markets and, in turn, how capital markets interact with the energy market. Moreover, the segregation between the AEMC and AER has the effect of separating policy advice and rulemaking that follow such advice (AEMC functions) from the entity that enforces compliance with rules and acts as industry economic regulator (AER functions). The evidence on these separations is that capital markets have had confidence in the market and market institutions to back required investment. It is, however, noteworthy that interference by the Commonwealth Government has been rising, ironically due to market failures associated with the missing policies and the

misdiagnosis of price discrimination (that is, weaknesses number one, two, three and five identified above).

3. While I have argued that state governments and the ACCC have allowed too much horizontal aggregation, the same institutions have allowed (or been forced by courts to allow) capital markets to determine vertical business boundaries. Specifically, it was the capital markets that initiated the disaggregation of retail businesses from distribution network businesses, and also the reintegration of generation with retail. This has reduced the cost of capital in both the regulated and merchant segments.

4. Competition in the NEM's retail markets has generally performed well, especially in the industrial segment. Rising electricity prices and associated affordability for certain household segments are indeed a problem, but to be clear, these relate to sequential rises in network prices (weakness seven above) and wholesale prices (caused by the missing polices, weaknesses one, two and three above).

9. CONCLUSION

This chapter has provided a background to the Australian energy market reform experience and explained the critical importance of reform sequencing. The review of industrial organization in the NEM highlighted that the reform blueprint was eventually altered by the capital markets, which preferred aligning (and mitigating) the risk characteristics of merchant businesses through vertical integration and isolating regulated business units from merchant business units. The performance of the wholesale market revealed an institutional design that remained largely true to its objective function of enhancing productive, allocative and dynamic efficiency. But this high-performing energy-only market design with its high market price cap and associated forward markets could not navigate market failures associated with what I have described as the 'missing policies', relating to LNG export capacity, climate change policy discontinuity and disorderly coal plant exit at scale. Rising levels of VRE have presented Australia's NEM with operational challenges – the very challenges that Green outlines in Chapter 15 of this handbook. This requires the definition of what constitutes a power system credible contingency to be redefined, and a rethink of FCAS volumes in order to deal with rising intermittency and declining inertia and system strength as marginal (synchronous) coal-fired power plants exit.

The review of the NEM's regulated networks revealed major historic policy failures, specifically coincident (and coincidental) misguided changes to reliability standards in QLD and NSW along with an initial 'formulaic' approach to network regulation when professional judgement was required. Notably, both policy changes were instituted without a formal policy development cycle and the unintended consequences have severely damaged the network sector.

The review of the retail market revealed, on balance, a reform that has performed well and delivered prices that are more efficient than an alternate regulated result. With deregulation comes a rise in the number of rival retailers, greater customer switching, and marginal offers that meet the definition of efficient prices with regard to the marginal cost facing retailers. Vulnerable 'rusted-on' customers do, however, require persistent monitoring.

The review of Australia's NEM strengths centred on the overall success of the energy-only wholesale market design, underlying governance structures, and the fact that such structures allowed capital markets to dictate industrial organization away from the original market blueprint. The review of weaknesses included significant policy failures relating to climate change, gas markets, coal plant closures, network regulation and network tariff reform (viz. lack thereof).

NOTES

1. Queensland, New South Wales, Victoria, South Australia, Australian Capital Territory and Tasmania.
2. I should acknowledge Danny Price (founder and managing director of Frontier Economics) for this description, which was contained in one of his recent speeches.
3. $A15 000 is the market price cap in financial year 2020/21. Estimates of the value of lost load (VoLL) are considerably higher. Note all financial results are expressed in Australian dollars unless otherwise stated.
4. The exception to this was the Queensland Electricity Commission, which at that time had the fifth lowest electricity prices in the world. See Booth (2000).
5. Following a serious downgrading, a Labor Victorian state government was virtually forced to privatize its newest power station as a result.
6. The Productivity Commission was actually then known as the Industry Commission.
7. In 1992, the Commonwealth Government established a committee to investigate a national competition policy framework. The committee handed down its blueprint for the implementation of a formal competition policy in August of 1993, with the report becoming known as 'The Hilmer Report', after the committee chair, Professor Fred Hilmer.
8. As an aside, privatization of the industry (historic decisions and future possibilities) remains highly politically contentious in all jurisdictions.
9. TAS is somewhat complicated by the fact that it only joined the NEM in 2006, and for a range of reasons including scale, remained a largely monopoly/monopsony regional market.
10. This included four portfolio generators in QLD, four in NSW (including Snowy Hydro), five in VIC, three in SA and one in TAS.
11. This included two in QLD, six in NSW, one in the Australian Capital Territory (ACT), five in VIC and one in SA (and from 2005, one in TAS).
12. That is, stock markets were consistently undervaluing the combined distributor-retail businesses. In all cases, sum-of-the-parts valuations revealed that structural separation would result in better total shareholder returns.
13. Especially the USA, UK and Australia (Finon 2008, Joskow 2006, Nelson and Simshauser 2013, Simshauser 2010).
14. In the Australian utilities sector, investment-grade credit notionally begins with firm earnings of A$100 million or greater. Hence, scale is not unimportant from a credit rating perspective.
15. There were originally three franchise retailers in QLD and six in NSW. In QLD, Origin Energy and AGL Energy purchased the retail businesses. In NSW, Origin Energy and Energy Australia purchased the retail businesses.
16. An electricity transmission line linking generation and retail load is an example of bottleneck infrastructure.
17. Vertical integration is an organizational form of last resort that occurs in response to non-trivial market frictions and in most circumstances is welfare enhancing – even when horizontal issues take on considerable importance. Once the long list of explicit and implicit assumptions underpinning standard economic models are relaxed, boundary changes are likely when firms face hazards associated with asset specificity, incomplete markets, bounded rationality, asymmetric information and regulatory and policy uncertainty. When non-trivial hazards exist in relation to ex ante investment commitment and the ex post performance of highly specific assets, vertical integration will invariably achieve more 'adaptive, sequential decision-making procedures' than anonymous spot and forward market transactions, especially as market conditions change (Williamson, 1973, p. 318).
18. In an earlier market review by Australia's chief scientist on behalf of the COAG Energy Council, one recommendation was to add an Energy Security Board. In my view, it grinded against the structural separation, but given the black system event in SA, the COAG Energy Council had little choice but to endorse the recommendation. Of course, the black system event had nothing to do with policy coordination – it was strictly a matter of system operations.

19. That is, to promote efficient investment in, and efficient operation and use of, electricity services for the long-term interests of consumers of electricity with respect to price, quality, safety and reliability and security of supply of electricity.

20. The author was the director-general of the Queensland Department of Energy and Water Supply and the Queensland government's senior official for the COAG Energy Council from 2015 to 2017.

21. Performance improvements included average cost, price, plant availability and reserve margins (Simshauser 2005). In more recent research, the wholesale market was one of the few areas of the electricity market that was performing well (see, for example, Nelson and Orton 2016, Simshauser 2014a). From mid-2016, however, market performance deteriorated significantly.

22. Although as MacGill (2010) points out, the market operator does produce a very transparent 40 hour pre-dispatch forecast which is continuously updated.

23. AEMO also benefits from NEM Rule 4.3.1, which states amongst other things that the system operator should 'initiate action plans to manage abnormal situations or significant deficiencies which could reasonably threaten power system security'. Deficiencies are noted without limitation – that is, (1) power system frequency and/or voltage operating outside the definition of a satisfactory operating state; and (2) actual or potential power system instability.

24. In VIC, transmission planning is undertaken by AEMO. This is unique to VIC.

25. The approval of transmission investments is subject to a net benefits test, known as the RIT-T, the 'Regulatory Investment Test – Transmission'.

26. I use an AUD to USD exchange rate of 0.70.

27. The SA black system event was not a resource adequacy/reliability problem but a system security issue (that is, an unstable system in which a voltage collapse led to plant disconnecting, with the rate of change of frequency falling faster than supply and demand resources could respond to).

28. The interested reader may also see De Vries and Heijnen (2008), Finon (2008), Green and Staffell (2016), Joskow (2008), Keay (2016), Nelson and Simshauser (2013), Neuhoff and De Vries (2004), Roques, Newbery and Nuttall (2005) and Simshauser (2008).

29. Depreciated optimized valuation estimates are based on hydro plant at 1500 A$/kW, coal plant at 1000 A$/kilowatt (kW), combined cycle gas turbine (CCGT) and solar plant at 1500 A$/kW, wind at 2000 A$/kW and open cycle gas turbine (OCGT) plant at 500 A$/kW. Applying these statistics to the NEM's existing plant equates to A$49.7 billion.

30. Untangling missing money from within the economic loss is a difficult task, but my own prior estimates of VoLL were considerably higher than 14 500 A$/MWh. In Simshauser (2008) the estimate was 24 500 A$/MWh vs the then VoLL of 10 000 A$/MWh.

31. That transient market power has been exercised more frequently in QLD can be explained by the fact that it is the region with (1) the least vertical integration (that is, a market dominated by generators with long positions); and (2) the highest reserve margins (Figure 9.3) and consequently economic losses and the missing money subset tends to be amplified (Table 9.2). For most of the NEM's history, QLD has been a major net exporter of power to the south and this has produced large reserve margins. With a surplus of low-cost generating plants, economic losses and missing money are likely to be more prevalent. Conversely, because the supply-side is dominated by a small number of large (state-owned) portfolio generators, economic withdrawal of capacity is plausible, profitable and to avoid extended periods of economic losses, somewhat necessary – noting that not all episodes have actually produced an economic rent. Importantly, however, from a policymaker perspective, market power events have never been sustained without a response. That is, economic withholding on the supply side has invariably been met by new entrants, policymaker intervention or a NEM rule change.

32. A national target was thought to deliver the target at least cost, but this ignored other system integration costs from high concentrations in certain geographical areas.

33. This occurred in 2012 when the average VRE market share was 26 per cent, maximum VRE share in a single day was 68 per cent and more than 20 days were characterized by a higher than 50 per cent market share.

34. Spot prices in 2013 and 2014 have been adjusted downwards by 23 A$/t × 0.6t per MWh to remove the effects of the CO_2 tax. The actual spot prices were 69.75 A$/MWh and 61.71 A$/MWh, respectively.

35. In my prior role as a director-general of the Queensland Department of Energy and senior official to the COAG Energy Council, I had argued for a review of frequency control ancillary services (FCAS) quantities (viz. an increase in regulated FCAS demand, and a localization of some component of that demand) from April 2017. It appears that AEMO did not anticipate impacts of the changing generation mix. In a note to stakeholders on 3 October 2018, AEMO advised that 'Regulation FCAS volumes have not been revised for many years, over which time significant system changes have occurred; less governor-based frequency support and increased penetration of intermittent generation are most notable'. Regulated FCAS quantities were set in 2004 when the NEM had no intermittent renewable resources.

36. In the NEM, FCAS is determined dynamically in each five-minute interval. FCAS is also procured 'globally' across regions subject to no network congestion. In periods of higher variability, FCAS Regulation procurement automatically rises from the typical set point of 130 MW to as much as 230 MW (in 60 MW increments) to maintain frequency. Threshold quantities of FCAS Contingency (six-second, 60-second and five-minute spinning reserves) are based on the single largest contingency event – the potential loss of the largest generating unit and when combined with FCAS Regulation typically add to about 900–1000 MW.

37. The fault related to control systems configurations, which triggered disconnection after two minutes of continuous voltage dips – which in hindsight, the wind farms should have been able to ride through.

38. The ACT is pursuing a household demand tariff, under an opt-out regime. From a wholesale market perspective, the ACT is a small sub-region of the NSW region. However, it has its own distribution network and retail market.

39. The Queensland Competition Authority (QCA), the New South Wales Independent Pricing and Regulatory Tribunal (IPART), the Essential Services Commission of South Australia (ESCOSA), and so on.

40. See, for example, the SP AusNet transmission determination (January 2008) at p. 98 or the Electranet transmission determination (April 2018) at p. 66, accessed February 2019 at https://www.aer.gov.au/system/files/AER%20Final%20decision.pdf and https://www.aer.gov.au/system/files/Final%20decision%20%2811%20April%202008%29.pdf, respectively.

41. I specifically recall the then chief executives of Energex and Ergon in the early 2010s being embarrassed by the return levels in WACC determinations applying to their businesses. They were also at pains to point out that any future determination will be ~250 basis points (bps) lower. By the time the AER completed their determinations in 2015, they were 400bps lower.

42. See Simshauser (2017) and Simshauser and Akimov (2019).

43. See Simshauser (2016).

44. A series of 2012 rule changes removed the formulaic approach to network regulation, replaced them with descriptions of the factors the AER needed to take into account, and placed obligations on the AER to explain how they had done so. In retrospect, while this was sensible from an economic regulatory perspective, the replacement of formulas with words laid the groundwork for (excessive) legal challenges. The tendency of (or some would argue, abuse by) network businesses to do so ultimately led to a COAG Energy Council decision to abolish the limited merits review.

45. In relation to network policy failure, in the summer of 2004, South East QLD experienced a series of extreme weather events that produced three severe episodes of distribution network-related load-shedding. These were a political disaster because Energex, a government-owned distribution network company, had aggressively reduced operating and capital expenditures in prior periods to raise productivity and returns (as requested by shareholding departments). An inquiry into the blackouts recommended a change in planning standards, from stochastic to deterministic, which produced a form of Averch and Johnson (1962) gold plating. The huge expansion in the capital base began soon after, with network tariffs more than doubling from 2007 to 2013 (Simshauser 2017).

46. British research revealed that only 19 per cent of consumers wanted to stop discounts being expressed in percentage terms (compared with monetary savings). In addition, the strongest driver of customer activity is the size of anticipated gains from switching – not the simplicity of the offers available. See, for example, Flores and Waddams Price (2018), He and Reiner (2017), Littlechild (2016), Simshauser (2018), Waddams Price and Zhu (2016).

47. This is usually a condition of their retail licence.

48. In the NEM there are now thought to be three tiers of retailers: first-tier incumbents (that is, the Big Three), second-tier retailers, which are highly successful new entrants (most of which are also vertically integrated), and a third tier, which are boutique, sub-scale new entrants.

49. For example, affluent urban professionals, budget conscious families, pensioners, socially conscious households, time-poor families and tech-savvy households.

50. Note that 'superannuation' is Australia's mandatory pension retirement scheme. Superannuation funds under management are almost double Australia's GDP.

REFERENCES

Australian Energy Market Operator (AEMO) (2017), *Black System South Australia 28 September 2016*, accessed February 2019 at https://www.aemo.com.au/-/media/Files/Electricity/NEM/Market_Notices_and_Events/Power_System_Incident_Reports/2017/Integrated-Final-Report-SA-Black-System-28-September-2016.pdf.

Australian Energy Regulator (AER) (2018), *State of the Energy Market 2018*, Melbourne, VIC: AER.

Averch, H. and J. Johnson (1962), 'Behavior of the firm under regulatory constraint', *American Economic Review*, **52** (5), 1052–69.

Bell, W. P., P. Wild, J. Foster and M. Hewson (2017), 'Revitalising the wind power induced merit order effect to reduce wholesale and retail electricity prices in Australia', *Energy Economics*, **67**, 224–41.

Besser, J. G., J. G. Farr and S. F. Tierney (2002), 'The political economy of long-term generation adequacy: why an ICAP mechanism is needed as part of standard market design', *Electricity Journal*, **15** (7), 53–62.

Bidwell, M. and A. Henney (2004), 'Will the New Electricity Trading Arrangements ensure generation adequacy?', *Power UK*, **122**, 10–26.

Booth, R. (2000), *Warring Tribes: The Story of Power Development in Australia*, Perth: Bardak Group.

Bushnell, J. B., E. T. Mansur and C. Saravia (2008), 'Vertical arrangements, market structure, and competition: an analysis of restructured US electricity markets', *American Economic Review*, **98** (1), 237–66.

Cludius, J., S. Forrest and I. MacGill (2014), 'Distributional effects of the Australian Renewable Energy Target (RET) through wholesale and retail electricity price impacts', *Energy Policy*, **71**, 40–51.

Cooper, J. C., L. Froeb, D. O'Brien and M. G. Vita (2005), 'Vertical antitrust policy as a problem of inference', *International Journal of Industrial Organization*, **23**, 639–64.

Cramton, P. and S. Stoft (2006), *The Convergence of Market Designs for Adequate Generating Capacity with Special Attention to the CAISO's Resource Adequacy Problem*, white paper for the Electricity Oversight Board, Center for Energy and Environmental Policy Research, April.

Dana, J. D. (1998), 'Advance-purchase discounts and price discrimination in competitive markets', *Journal of Political Economy*, **106** (2), 395–422.

De Vries, L. and P. Heijnen (2008), 'The impact of electricity market design upon investment under uncertainty: the effectiveness of capacity mechanisms', *Utilities Policy*, **16** (3), 215–27.

Elegido, J. M. (2011), 'The ethics of price discrimination', *Business Ethics Quarterly*, **21** (4), 633–60.

Finon, D. (2008), 'Investment risk allocation in decentralised electricity markets: the need of long-term contracts and vertical integration', *OPEC Energy Review*, **32** (2), 150–83.

Finon, D. (2011), 'Investment and competition in decentralized electricity markets: how to overcome market failure by market imperfections?', in J.-M. Glachant, D. Finon and A. de Hauteclocque (eds), *Competition, Contracts and Electricity Markets: A New Perspective*, Cheltenham, UK and Northampton, MA, USA: Edward Elgar Publishing, pp. 55–74.

Finon, D. and V. Pignon (2008), 'Capacity mechanisms in imperfect electricity markets', *Utilities Policy*, **16** (3), 141–2.

Flores, M. and C. Waddams Price (2018), 'The role of attitudes and marketing in consumer behaviours in the British retail electricity market', *The Energy Journal*, **39** (4), 153–79.

Forrest, S. and I. MacGill (2013), 'Assessing the impact of wind generation on wholesale prices and generator dispatch in the Australian National Electricity Market', *Energy Policy*, **59**, 120–32.

Green, R. and I. Staffell (2016), 'Electricity in Europe: exiting fossil fuels?', *Oxford Review of Economic Policy*, **32** (2), 282–303.

He, X. and D. Reiner (2017), 'Why consumers switch energy suppliers: the role of individual attitudes', *Energy Journal*, **38** (1), 25–53.

Helm, D. (2014), 'The return of the CEGB? Britain's central buyer model', *Energy Futures Network Paper No. 4*.

Hirth, L., F. Ueckerdt and O. Edenhofer (2016), 'Why wind is not coal: on the economics of electricity generation', *Energy Journal*, **37** (3), 1–27.

Hogan, W. W. (2013), 'Electricity scarcity pricing through operating reserves', *Economics of Energy and Environmental Policy*, **2** (2), 65–86.

Joskow, P. L. (2006), 'Competitive electricity markets and investment in new generating capacity', MIT Center for Energy and Environmental Research.

Joskow, P. L. (2008), 'Capacity payments in imperfect electricity markets: need and design', *Utilities Policy*, **16** (3), 159–70.

Joskow, P. L. (2010), 'Vertical integration', *The Antitrust Bulletin*, **55** (3), 545–86.

Keay, M. (2016), 'Electricity markets are broken – can they be fixed?', *OIES Paper EL 17*, Oxford Institute of Energy Studies.

Lafontaine, F. and M. Slade (2007), 'Vertical integration and firm boundaries: the evidence', *Journal of Economic Literature*, **45** (3), 629–85.

Léautier, T.-O. (2016), 'The visible hand: ensuring optimal investment in electric power generation', *Energy Journal*, **37** (2), 89–109.

Levine, M. E. (2002), 'Price discrimination without market power', *Yale Journal on Regulation*, **19** (1), 1–36.

Littlechild, S. (1983), *Regulating Profits of British Telecom – Report to the Secretary of State*, February.

Littlechild, S. (2014), 'Promoting or restricting competition? Regulation of the UK retail residential energy market since 2008', *EPRG Working Paper 1415*, Energy Policy Research Group, University of Cambridge.

Littlechild, S. (2016), 'Contrasting developments in UK energy regulation: retail policy and consumer engagement', *Economic Affairs*, **36** (2), 118–32.

Littlechild, S. (2017), 'Competition and price controls in the UK retail energy market', *Network*, Issue 63, 1–11.

Littlechild, S. (2018), 'Competition, regulation and price controls in the GB retail energy market', *Utilities Policy*, **52** (63), 59–69.

MacGill, I. (2010),'Electricity market design for facilitating the integration of wind energy: experience and prospects with the Australian National Electricity Market', *Energy Policy*, **38** (7), 3180–91.

Mansur, E. T. (2007), 'Upstream competition and vertical integration in electricity markets', *Journal of Law and Economics*, **50** (1), 125–56.

Nelson, T. and F. Orton (2016), 'Climate and electricity policy integration: is the South Australian electricity market the canary in the coalmine?', *The Electricity Journal*, **29**, 1–7.

Nelson, J. and P. Simshauser (2013), 'Is the Merchant Power Producer a broken model?', *Energy Policy*, **53**, 298–310.

Nelson, T., P. Simshauser and J. Nelson (2012), 'Queensland solar feed-in tariffs and the merit-order effect: economic benefit, or regressive taxation and wealth transfers?', *Economic Analysis and Policy*, **42** (3), 277–301.

Neuhoff, K. and L. De Vries (2004), 'Insufficient incentives for investment in electricity generations', *Utilities Policy*, **12** (4), 253–67.

Oren, S. (2003), 'Ensuring generation adequacy in competitive electricity markets', paper prepared for the Electric Power Research Institute.

Pollitt, M. G. (2004), 'Electricity reform in Chile: lessons for developing countries', *Journal of Network Industries*, **5** (3–4), 221–62.

Price, C. W. and M. Zhu (2016), 'Non-discrimination clauses: their effect on British retail energy prices', *Energy Journal*, **37** (2), 111–32.

Quentin Grafton, R., X. R. Shi and I. Cronshaw (2018), '"Making cents" of the Eastern Australian gas market', *Economic Papers*, **37** (1), 42–54.

Riesz, J., J. Gilmore and I. MacGill (2015), 'Frequency control ancillary service market design: insights from the Australian national electricity market', *Electricity Journal*, **28** (3), 86–99.

Roques, F. A. (2008), 'Market design for generation adequacy: healing causes rather than symptoms', *Utilities Policy*, **16** (3), 171–83.

Roques, F. A., D. M. Newbery and W. J. Nuttall (2005), 'Investment incentives and electricity market design: the British experience', *Review of Network Economics*, **4** (2), 93–128.

Simshauser, P. (2005), 'The gains from the microeconomic reform of the power generation industry in East-Coast Australia', *Economic Analysis and Policy*, **35** (1–2), 23–43.

Simshauser, P. (2008), 'The dynamic efficiency gains from introducing capacity payments in the national electricity market', *Australian Economic Review*, **41** (4), 349–70.

Simshauser, P. (2010), 'Resource adequacy, capital adequacy and investment uncertainty in the Australian power market', *Electricity Journal*, **23** (1), 67–84.

Simshauser, P. (2014a), 'From first place to last: the National Electricity Market's policy-induced "energy market death spiral"', *Australian Economic Review*, **47** (4), 540–62.

Simshauser, P. (2014b), 'When does electricity price cap regulation become distortionary?', *Australian Economic Review*, **47** (3), 304–23.

Simshauser, P. (2016), 'Distribution network prices and solar PV: resolving rate instability and wealth transfers through demand tariffs', *Energy Economics*, **54** (C), 108–22.

Simshauser, P. (2017), 'Monopoly regulation, discontinuity & stranded assets', *Energy Economics*, **66**, 384–98.

Simshauser, P. (2018), 'Price discrimination and the modes of failure in deregulated retail electricity markets', *Energy Economics*, **75**, 54–70.

Simshauser, P. (2019a), 'Missing money, missing policy and resource adequacy in Australia's National Electricity Market', *Utilities Policy*, **60**, Article 100936.

Simshauser, P. (2019b) 'On the stability of energy-only markets with government-initiated contracts-for-differences', *Energies*, **12** (13), 2566.

Simshauser, P. and A. Akimov (2019), 'Regulated electricity networks, investment mistakes in retrospect and stranded assets under uncertainty', *Energy Economics*, **81**, 117–33.

Simshauser, P. and J. Gilmore (2020), 'Is the NEM broken? Policy discontinuity and the 2017–2020 investment megacycle', *Energy Policy Research Group Working Paper No. 2014*, University of Cambridge.

Simshauser, P. and T. Nelson (2015a), 'Australia's coal seam gas boom and the LNG entry result', *Australian Journal of Agricultural and Resource Economics*, **59** (4), 602–23.

Simshauser, P. and T. Nelson (2015b), 'The Australian East Coast gas supply cliff', *Economic Analysis and Policy*, **45**, 69–88.

Simshauser, P. and A. Tiernan (2019), 'Climate change policy discontinuity and its effects on Australia's national electricity market', *Australian Journal of Public Administration*, **78** (1), 17–36.

Simshauser, P., Y. Tian and P. Whish-Wilson (2015), 'Vertical integration in energy-only electricity markets', *Economic Analysis and Policy*, **48**, 35–56.

Spees, K., S. A. Newell and J. P. Pfeifenberger (2013), 'Capacity markets – lessons learned from the first decade', *Economics of Energy and Environmental Policy*, **2** (2), 1–26.

Waddams Price, C. and M. Zhu (2016), 'Non-discrimination clauses: their effect on British retail energy prices', *Energy Journal*, **37** (2), 111–32.

Wen, F. S., F. F. Wu and Y. X. Ni (2004), 'Generation capacity adequacy in the competitive electricity market environment', *International Journal of Electrical Power and Energy System*, **26** (5), 365–72.

Williamson, O. E. (1973), 'Organizational forms and internal efficiency', *The American Economic Review*, **63** (2), 316–25.

Wood, T. and D. Blowers (2018), *Mostly Working: Australia's Wholesale Electricity Market*, accessed February 2019 at https://grattan.edu.au/report/mostly-working/.

Wood, T., G. Dundas and L. Percival (2019), 'Keep calm and carry on: managing electricity reliability' [podcast], Grattan Institute, Melbourne, accessed March 2019 at https://grattan.edu.au/podcast/keep-calm-and-carry-on-managing-electricity-reliability.

10. Strengths and weaknesses of the Nordic market model
*Chloé Le Coq and Sebastian Schwenen**

1. INTRODUCTION

The so-called 'Nordic power market' comprises the national electricity markets of Norway, Sweden, Finland, Denmark and, more recently, the Baltic States. The different national markets have been liberalized and integrated successively, mainly by adapting and aligning national regulations. Trading arrangements and interconnections also exist with Germany, the Netherlands, Poland and the UK. Indeed, since its establishment, the Nordic market has become a leading example of an integrated cross-border electricity market.

In this chapter, we revisit the Nordic market model with a focus on its unique multi-national architecture and multi-partner governance. We discuss cross-border trading arrangements, benefits from pooling technologies across borders, the Nordic wholesale pricing system and congestion management, as well as regulations pertaining to decarbonization and security of supply. In addition, we review the existing literature on the functioning of the Nordic market and, based on the extant findings, highlight the Nordic market model's strengths and weaknesses.

2. THE NORDIC POWER EXCHANGE: NORD POOL

One of the main features of the Nordic market model is that it constitutes a 'common market' for several neighbouring countries, with a joint set of rules and product definitions. As the participating countries have adopted these rules at different points in time, the market design constantly evolved while integrating each country's national regulation.

2.1 The Creation of the First Institutionalized Multinational Electricity Market

The first step towards a common market was the liberalization of the power market in Norway.[1] Norway's reform was initialized and motivated by inefficiencies resulting from a fragmented industry structure, over-investment and lasting over-supply of electricity. With the Energy Act of 1991, the formerly regulated monopoly Statkraftsverkene was divided into Statkraft (generation) and Statnett (transmission and system operation). In addition, the Energy Act introduced free choice of suppliers for customers at the retail level and laid the foundation for the newly set-up electricity pool.

Sweden followed Norway closely in this process, implementing a similar Energy Act that included laws to deregulate and facilitate the cross-border trade between Sweden and

Norway. The vertical separation between the transmission system operator (TSO) and the incumbent generation and retail company Vattenfall took place in 1992.[2]

A first joint power exchange between Sweden and Norway was then established in 1996 with the creation of a day-ahead market and was named Nord Pool ASA. At that time, this entity was equally owned by the Norwegian TSO Statnett and the Swedish TSO Svenska Kraftnät. Since the beginning, Nord Pool has operated under a licence for cross-border trading issued by the Norwegian Directorate for Energy and Water Resources (NVE). Finland changed the structure of its electricity supply before joining this day-ahead electricity market in 1998. In 1996, the country decided on the unbundling of transmission and generation assets.[3] For Finnish policymakers, joining Nord Pool was a way to reduce the country's dependency on Russian electricity as well as to align the country's regulations with European energy policy. Denmark integrated in two steps: first the western region (often referred to as 'DK1' and including the regions of Jutland and Funen) became part of the Nordic day-ahead spot market in 1999, while the eastern region (referred to as 'DK2' and including the Zealand region) joined in 2000. This sequential integration was mostly due to the physical division of the Danish energy market and the lack of one joint regulatory body governing the two networks. Interestingly, this incremental integration of Denmark into Nord Pool ASA was actually driven by the industry itself and not by the government, as was the case in the other Nordic countries. Until 2005, the Danish grid was separately owned and operated by the two transmission companies, Eltra and Elkraft System, that were vertically separated from generating companies. Yet, no physical link existed between these two parts of the country before 2010.

Nord Pool continued to expand, most notably with the integration of the Baltic States.[4] Finland and Estonia were already connected since 2007 via the transmission cable Estlink 1, but a Nord Pool bidding area was only opened in Estonia in 2010.[5] The power trading between Lithuania and the four Nordic countries started in 2012. Cross-border trading has further developed with the submarine power cable NordBalt between southern Sweden and Lithuania. Finally, the Latvian integration with Nord Pool Spot was implemented in 2013 with an agreement with the Latvian independent system operator (ISO) Augstsprieguma tīkls.[6]

During this process, Nord Pool has pushed for further market coupling with the EU internal market. Nord Pool opened a separate marketplace in the UK in 2010, with its own futures, day-ahead and intraday market arrangements (Nord Pool 2011). More recently, Nord Pool has also been appointed as Nominated Energy Market Operator (NEMO) in many continental European markets (for example, Austria, Denmark, Estonia, Finland, France), giving Nord Pool the mandate to organize a day-ahead or intraday coupling in these countries. On its home ground, however, Nord Pool has recently lost its monopoly, as the Norwegian regulator NVE granted its competitor, EPEX Spot, permission to operate in the Nordic market (EPEX SPOT SE, 2018). Table 10.1 summarizes the main steps in the evolution of the Nordic power market.

2.2   Market Architecture

The Nordic market has a hybrid architecture where electricity trade is organized via bilateral contracts between generators and consumers, as well as via a centralized power

Table 10.1   Historical steps of Nord Pool

		General	Day-ahead Market	Intraday Market
Phase 1: Establishment of the Nordic Electricity Market		1991: Liberalization of the Norwegian power market		
		1992: Liberalization of the Swedish power market		
		1993: Statnett Market AS is founded		
			1996: Creation of the Norwegian-Swedish power exchange Nord Pool ASA	
			1998: Finland is integrated into the Nord Pool market area	1999: Cross-border intraday market Elbas between Finland and Sweden
			1999: Western Denmark joins	
			2000: Eastern Denmark joins	2004: Western Denmark joins
			2002: Nord Pool Spot (NPS) exchange	2007: Eastern Denmark joins
Phase 2: International Expansion				2006–09: Nord Pool covers the Kontek area in Germany
			2010: NPS opens N2EX-market in the UK	2009: Intraday market trading extends to Norway
			2010: NPS expands to Estonia	
			2012: NPS expands to Lithuania	
			2013: NPS expands to Latvia	2013: Latvia and Lithuania join Elbas
Phase 3: New European Regulations and Business Models		2015: Nord Pool is named NEMO in ten countries (incl. Sweden, Baltics and Denmark)	2014: NPS fully acquires N2EX	
		2016: Nord Pool is named NEMO in ten countries (incl. Germany and Belgium)	2016: NPS becomes service provider for the Croatian and Bulgarian markets	
		2017: Nord Pool is named NEMO in Ireland		2018: Further expansion of Nord Pool intraday market (France, Austria, Benelux) and European intraday market system (XBID) goes live
		2019: Nord Pool loses its monopoly on the Nordic power market		
		2020: Euronext buys 66% of the Nord Pool group		

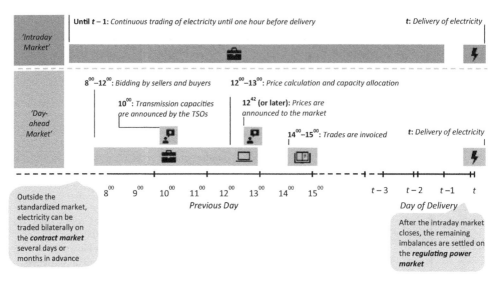

Source: Authors.

Figure 10.1   Market arrangements at Nord Pool

exchange. Trading on the Nordic wholesale electricity market takes place in a sequence of cross-border markets, followed by a set of national real-time markets. Figure 10.1 summarizes the organization of the sequential markets.

Producers, retailers and large energy-intensive consumers can gradually adjust production and delivery plans by trading on day-ahead and intraday markets. Historically, the day-ahead product was the first and most harmonized cross-border product for the Nordic market.[7] As a result, the largest volume of electricity in the Scandinavian and Baltic countries (about 95 per cent of the produced electricity) is traded on the day-ahead market, even though the intraday market is increasing in volume. Typically, hourly clearing prices are determined by a double auction with a uniform clearing price. Prices are determined for each hour of the following day. Since 2014, the day-ahead prices are determined jointly with a majority of EU power markets using the common price coupling algorithm, called EUPHEMIA. Hence, the day-ahead market clearing is, by design, for the EU, although the clearing algorithm allows for market-specific products in the different EU markets (see Chapter 11 in this handbook for an overview of the evolution of the EU electricity market model). For instance, some national markets have introduced products with different duration, while in other markets the price for demand is different from the price for supply of electricity.

The day-ahead market determines a system price, which is the price that would prevail if there were no transmission constraints within the Nordic market. Importantly, this system price typically serves as the reference price for the settlement of financial contracts by which market participants hedge their income risk. The system price is determined at noon prior to the delivery day.

The intraday market, originally named Elbas, offers 15-minute, 30-minute, hourly and block products. It opens on the afternoon prior to the delivery day and closes shortly before delivery. In contrast to the day-ahead auctions, the intraday market is structured as a market for continuous trading. Market participants can adjust their plans for each trading hour by buying and selling electricity on the intraday market – for example, with respect to incoming weather forecasts. Market players may also hedge against Nord Pool prices on the forward market. As standard, forward contracts can be agreed on bilaterally ('over the counter') or follow standardized futures products that are traded on financial markets. All Nord Pool financial products are traded on NASDAQ OMX.

Finally, to ensure continuous balancing between actual production and consumption, there is also a common 'regulating power market' managed by the TSOs. Each market participant is required to attain balance between available power resources, owned or contracted, and hourly delivery obligations. Each producer or consumer must either assume the role of a 'balance responsible party' (BRP) or transfer that obligation to another market participant by means of a contractual arrangement. There are penalties to be paid by a BRP in case of imbalances between expected and actual generation (or consumption) during 'the hour'. The BRPs, in response to calls by the system operator, make offers, in terms of price and quantity, to increase or reduce consumption or production.

The hybrid Nordic electricity model is rather complex to implement and requires many adjustments. However, the weaknesses of a 'pool-only market' (which does not allow negotiation between buyers and sellers and limits the flexibility of the market) or of 'bilateral contracts only' (where market participants might bear high negotiation costs and risks) are more limited with a hybrid structure (Ahlqvist, Holmberg and Tangerås 2019). Additionally, to limit complexity of cross-border trades, much policy effort has been spent to harmonize trading and clearing guidelines across the Nordic and the EU markets, especially with respect to balancing and grid operation. These so-called network codes are legally binding European regulations and govern cross-border transactions.[8]

2.3 Zonal Prices and Congestion Management

The Nordic market has a zonal pricing structure. The allocation of cross-zonal capacities (that is, transmission capacities between different zones) is calculated at the Nordic level in accordance with European capacity allocation rules. The local price of each specified zone takes into account potential transmission constraints. To organize market clearing for each zone, system operators must provide the capacities for the different lines that connect the zone. Based on the bid schedules submitted to the wholesale auction and the underlying network constraints, the clearing algorithm then determines a clearing price for each zone, along with corresponding hourly production and delivery plans for the next day.[9]

The Nordic market currently exhibits 15 price zones. The configuration of zones follows national borders but also includes zones within countries. For instance, Denmark is currently divided into two price areas, Norway into five and Sweden into four zones. However, the configuration of pricing zones is subject to change. Sweden initially had one price zone, which was split into four areas in 2011. It is up to the national TSO to propose and decide upon the number of bidding areas within each country.

By construction, the zonal approach implies some degree of approximation – that is, specific nodes are aggregated to create a zone with uniform pricing. The price differences that naturally occur between different zones should, in theory, stimulate investment in generation and transmission assets in import-constrained zones, and lead to more efficient energy trading as compared to large uniform price markets that do not account for the spatial distribution of load and generation. However, the day-ahead dispatch schedules with zonal prices are likely less efficient than those with nodal pricing. Also, the zonal pricing approach is more complex, as the system price is first calculated on a day-ahead market and then adjusted closer to the delivery time to consider the transmission constraints. Furthermore, as already mentioned in Harvey and Hogan (2000) and Holmberg and Lazarczyk (2015), a zonal system provides some opportunities to exercise market power due to arbitrage opportunities that facilitate non-competitive bidding behaviour. Additionally, under the current design, zonal prices cannot be perfectly hedged against and, thus, increase the risk for market participants. This is because futures contracts are often referenced against the system price rather than the zonal prices. Products to hedge the difference between the system price and the zonal price exist, but so far have shown a lack of liquidity.

After Elbas's gate closure, all deviations from the equilibrium schedules are handled by the national TSOs, who also manage congestion. This set-up is in stark contrast to most liberalized markets in the United States where the organization of the power exchange and system operation both fall within the domain of ISOs. However, in this case, there is a clear separation between transmission ownership and system operation to avoid any conflict of interests such as that stemming from the management of congestion rents (Ahlqvist et al. 2019).

2.4   Ownership and Governance

Since January 2020, the European stock market operator Euronext has owned 66 per cent of the Nord Pool group (including Nord Pool AS, Nord Pool Consulting AS and European Market Coupling Operator AS).[10] The TSOs own the remaining 34 per cent. Until this date, the physical power exchange Nord Pool was an independent entity and owned by a consortium of Nordic and Baltic power system operators. The Norwegian and the Swedish TSOs had the largest shares.[11] The differences in ownership reflected the cost of buying a share at the time of joining the power exchange. When Finland and Denmark joined, Nord Pool's market value had increased over the years. To reduce the share price for late-joining TSOs, Nord Pool was split into two entities: the physical markets (owned by all TSOs) and the financial market (owned only by the Norwegian and Swedish TSOs). Later, in 2010, the financial (or derivatives) market was sold to NASDAQ OMX.

Despite this multi-partner ownership, the Norwegian regulatory bodies continue to play an important role. Because Nord Pool operates under a licence from the Norwegian ministry of finance, the market surveillance is also ensured by the Norwegian regulatory body NVE. The principles of the exchange, such as efficient price formation, duty to disclose information, obligation to handle information confidentially and market surveillance are stated in the Nord Pool Spot licence that was approved by the Norwegian government. The market rules are indeed not fully detailed in the licence. Bredesen (2016) argues that this makes the Nordic market design flexible, as trading rules (for example, bidding format, security requirements and settlement calculations) can easily be changed and implemented in the market.

To further strengthen Nordic cooperation at the regulatory level, NordREG was formed and works a platform for Nordic energy regulators. Next to retail markets and network regulation, NordREG also facilitates the efficient operation of the Nordic wholesale market and its alignment within the European market – for example, with respect to balancing procedures and system operation.

The multinational governance of the Nordic market has led to some disputes – for instance, when national, Nordic and European regulations were not fully aligned. The decision to introduce four bidding areas in Sweden in 2011 is a good case in point. This decision was motivated by an antitrust dispute between the Swedish SO Svenska Kraftnät and Dansk Energi, a commercial organization of Danish energy companies. The EU Commission's Directorate General for Competition concluded that Svenska Kraftnät had abused its dominant position as a monopolist on the Swedish electricity transmission market by preventing the export of cheap hydropower to Denmark. It was argued that the prices in Sweden were artificially reduced and this negatively impacted the Danish consumers. The practice of curtailing international transmission capacities as a means of maintaining the single Swedish price zone was presented as a case of discriminatory behaviour, because Svenska Kraftnät treated domestic and international demand for transmission services differently. Soon after the decision, Svenska Kraftnät decided to split the market into four zones (European Commission 2010). Sadowska and Willems (2013) argue that without this antitrust settlement between the European Commission and the Swedish network operator, this drastic change would have been difficult to implement.

The above case also highlights that while market clearing at Nord Pool is multinational, the transmission system operation remains largely national.[12] Each Nordic transmission operator is state owned and regulated, either by a revenue cap regulation as for Statnett (Norway), Svenska Kraftnät (Sweden) and Fingrid (Finland), or by a cost-plus regulation as for Energinet.dk (Denmark).

3. MARKET PARTICIPANTS

The participants on the supply and demand side in the Nordic market are quite different in terms of size and production and consumption assets. Supply is diversified in technologies but is relatively concentrated in terms of generating companies. The demand side is traditionally characterized by relatively strong retail competition but limited consumer response.

3.1 Supply Side: Multiple Technologies and Competition Between Dominant Players

There is a clear dominance of hydropower (around 50 per cent of the total production) and to a lesser extent nuclear power (about 20 per cent) in the Nordic region. Wind, fossil fuels and biomass contribute with around 10 per cent, 8 per cent and 4 per cent of electricity production, respectively. There are some significant technological differences across the Nordic countries, as illustrated in Figure 10.2. Norway's supply stems almost entirely from hydropower. Nuclear power is only used in Sweden and Finland, where it represents a significant share of power generation (~43 per cent and ~35 per cent, respectively). Wind power has a large and increasing share in Denmark (~47 per cent), but also in Lithuania (~35 per cent) and to some extent in Sweden (~11 per cent). Fossil fuels

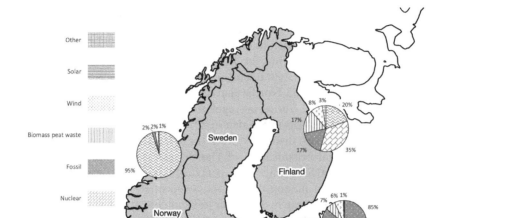

Source: Own map, data from European Network of Transmission System Operators for Electricity (ENTSO-E), https://www.entsoe.eu/data/ (2018).

Figure 10.2   Generation technologies per country

significantly contribute to the power generation of Estonia (~85 per cent), Latvia (~41 per cent) and Denmark (~32 per cent). Biomass, peat and waste mostly play a role in Denmark (~17 per cent), Finland (~17 per cent) and Lithuania (~16 per cent).

Hydropower resources are so vast that they have considerable price impact – that is, the market price depends on the hydrological conditions or the reservoirs' inflows. Peak inflows, mainly from precipitation and melted snow flow, are usually between April and June, and often lead to lower prices as hydro producers are forced to generate to avoid overflowing. Simultaneously, consumption is relatively low during this period, so that prices are usually relatively low. Figure 10.3 illustrates the clear link between dry and wet periods and market prices.

While supply is diversified in technologies, its ownership is relatively concentrated. Despite the liberalization of the Nordic power market, most incumbent power companies still hold significant market shares in their domestic market. Yet, while their market shares are large on the domestic market, they are relatively small when considering the Nordic market region, as illustrated in Table 10.2.

As large national firms become less dominant at the Nordic level, there is also relatively limited evidence of abuse of market power – that is, when transmission constraints are

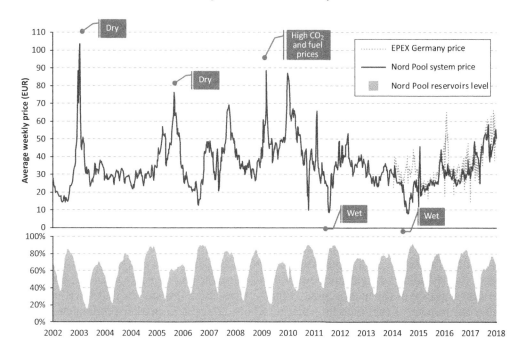

Figure 10.3   Historical prices and hydro reservoir levels in the Nordic market[13]

Table 10.2   Generation capacity by Nordic producers, 2013

Country	Largest Companies	Capacity (MW)	Share (%) Nordic Market
Denmark	Dong Energy[a]	5445	5.4
	Vattenfall	1578	1.6
Finland	Fortum	4528	4.5
	PVO	3197	3.2
	Helsingin Energia	1567	1.6
Norway	Statkraft	13 399	13.4
	E-CO Energi	2800	2.8
	Hydro	2000	2.0
Sweden	Vattenfall	13 879	13.8
	E.ON Sweden	6736	6.7
	Fortum	5825	5.8
Other generators		38 306	38.2
Total Nordic region		100 313	100.0

Note: a. The company changed its name to Ørsted in 2017.

Source: NordREG (2014), Table 9, p. 35.

non-binding and large firms compete across borders. For instance, Bask, Lundgren and Rudholm (2011) show that while there was a small but statistically significant market power in the period 1996–2004, the exercise of market power became very limited with the expansion of the Nord Pool area. However, there is still a potential for exercise of market power (see the detailed market performance assessment by Fridolfsson and Tangerås, 2009). This is partly due to the existence of temporal local monopolies with large shares in hydro generation. Tangerås and Mauritzen (2018) note that only a small number of firms own large reservoir capacities and that 30 per cent of Norwegian hydropower cannot be stored as it comes from run-of-the-river plants. This can lead to exercise of market power from the dominant hydro firms.

Despite the limited abuse of market power at the Nordic level, minor changes in ownership and relative size could favour anti-competitive behaviour. For instance, Amundsen and Bergman (2006) show that even a small increase in cross-ownership between the dominant Nordic companies will have anti-competitive effects. Lundin (2016) finds evidence that Swedish power companies coordinate maintenance schedules for co-owned nuclear power plants. As a result, they are able to obtain higher market prices. He estimates that avoiding concentrated ownership of nuclear power plants would lead to a 5 per cent decrease in the market price. Finally, there are a few studies that have investigated the impact of real-time information about changes to market fundamentals on electricity prices (Lazarczyk and Le Coq 2019) and on the potential misuse of real-time information about changes to market fundamentals leading to market abuse (Lazarczyk 2016), or that have discussed the potential for manipulative use of information (Fogelberg and Lazarczyk 2019). Mirza and Bergland (2015) argue that Norwegian generators are using information on transmission capacities to create congestion and exercise market power.

3.2   Demand, Retail Competition and the Role of Local Distribution

One of the arguments for establishing the common market was to pool demand risk. Pooling load patterns from different countries that do not always coincide offers gains from trade. As such, the common Nordic markets offer a natural hedge with respect to prices and adequate supply during extreme peak hours.[14] At the wholesale level, demand is typically represented by retail companies, which eventually deliver power to final consumers.

Retail market competition in the Nordic countries effectively started around 1998, when newly installed metering technologies allowed for a better measurement of consumption at the household level. Retail market competition has since been regarded as a strength of the Nordic market, conditional, however, on typical drawbacks with regard to limited consumer response in power markets.

The relative success of the retail market opening has been attributed by many scholars to light regulation. In particular, the absence of price controls contributed to relatively high switching rates of consumers. Depending on the country, between 11 per cent (Finland) and 29 per cent (Sweden) of households switched their supplier in the aftermath of the retail market opening (Littlechild 2006). Consumers actively pursued either better suppliers or alternative contract types, especially in Norway and Sweden, and to a lesser extent in Denmark and Finland (Olsen, Johnsen and Lewis 2006).[15]

Interestingly, in Norway, where retail market competition and switching rates were relatively high, many households had been on contracts with variable prices. These variable-price contracts were linked to Nord Pool prices and often subject to weekly changes at the discretion of the supplier (Von der Fehr, Amundsen and Bergman 2005). High price spikes in the early years of the market in 2002 and 2003 then led consumers to switch to fixed contract types (Amundsen and Bergman 2006), in many cases with new suppliers. In contrast, in Denmark and Finland, where fixed-price contracts dominated the market early on, initial switching rates during the first years of the market liberalization were low.

Despite the emergence of large retailing firms in most Nordic countries and their control of significant shares of the retail market, the level of competition and supplier switching remains relatively high as compared to other markets. The group of Nordic energy regulators reports continuous annual switching rates for recent years of about 10 per cent, along with a large variety of retail suppliers and contract types (NordREG 2017).

Retail supply and the operation of distribution systems have been unbundled in the Nordic market. As a consequence, many local distribution grids are still owned by local municipalities. The regulation of distribution system operators (DSOs) is typically designed as a revenue cap system.

In the Nordic countries, DSO regulation also allows for designing peak-load pricing schemes for network usage to steer local consumption patterns. However, time-varying network tariffs are not yet common in the Nordic market. This suggests that balancing consumption patterns over time might not be feasible so far. With an increasing number of electric vehicles in the Nordic markets, however, the need for time-varying tariffs may emerge in the years to come.

The recent regulatory developments at the retail level therefore aim to remove barriers to trade for distributed energy resources, such as electric vehicles. To facilitate trade and market entrance of aggregators, the Nordic market model foresees the use of data hubs (NordREG 2018). Data hubs allow consumers as well as potential entrants to access consumption data, thereby further easing supplier switching and contractual arrangements with aggregation service providers (Ruester et al. 2014). In Denmark, data hubs have been implemented since 2013. NordREG (2018) envisages a full implementation across the Nordic market by 2021.

4.   THE 'GREEN TRANSITION' AND THE NORDIC MARKET MODEL

The Nordic countries share ambitious climate policy targets, with the common goal to reduce energy usage from fossil fuels to close to zero by 2050. Sweden committed to no net emissions by 2045. Denmark aims at being independent from fossil fuels by 2050, when Norway envisages to become entirely carbon neutral. Figure 10.4 illustrates the changes that these goals imply for the power system. It displays the shares of selected low-carbon technologies in relation to total supply in Norway, Sweden and Denmark.

As can be seen, while Norway and Sweden traditionally exhibited large shares of low-carbon generation, the Danish system used to rely on fossil-fuelled plants, with an

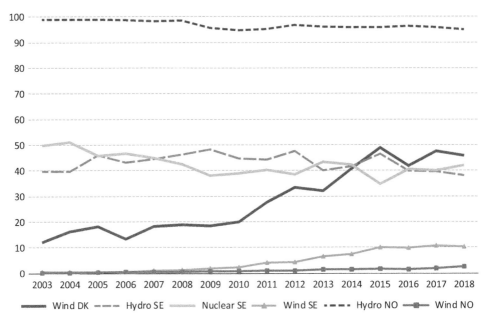

Source: Authors; data from the EU statistical pocketbook (https://ec.europa.eu/energy/data-analysis/
energy-statistical-pocketbook_en) and Norway Statistics (https://www.ssb.no/en), accessed 13 July 2021.

Figure 10.4   Shares of carbon-free generation in Nordic countries

increasing contribution of wind power. Given these different starting points for decarbonization, Denmark has made the greatest effort among these countries to increase wind
generation. In part, this is a direct consequence of the absence of hydropower as well as
nuclear plants in the Danish generation portfolio as well as the feasibility of installing
wind power in Denmark.

Consequently, support policies and shares of renewable generation differ between
Denmark and the remaining Nordic countries. Denmark already implemented a feed-in
tariff for renewable generation in 1993. In 2001, the Danish support scheme changed,
and the remuneration became a function of the spot market price for electricity plus a
predefined premium (Lipp 2007). From 1993 until the introduction of the premium
scheme in 2001, wind power capacity increased from about 0.5 gigawatts (GW) to just
below 3 GW (Gavard 2016). The share of about 44 per cent of wind generation in
Denmark in 2017, as shown in Figure 10.4, corresponds to an installed capacity of about
5 GW.

Norway and Sweden, with their large hydro and nuclear assets, instead opted for a
green certificate market. Sweden had implemented its national scheme already in 2003
and Norway joined in 2012. This market is planned to exist until 2035. Producers of
renewable sources can sell certificates according to the amount of renewable electricity
that they inject into the grid. Retailers and large industrial consumers are buyers of certificates. The government steers the demand for certificates by placing obligations on
consumers to hold certificates for a certain share of their consumption. As a result, producers of green electricity receive the power price plus the price for certificates for each

megawatt-hour (MWh) generated. This support system was mainly targeted at increasing generation from wind power and bio-fuel sources.[16]

At the time when the tradable electricity certificate system was introduced, none of the renewable electricity-producing technologies were competitive in terms of levelized costs of energy. Thus, support was a necessary condition for realizing the targeted increase in renewable electricity production. In Sweden, installed capacity of wind power has since grown from close to zero in 2003 to around 7 GW in 2017. Although the corresponding numbers for solar power are much smaller, the development of wind power since 2003 suggests that the renewable energy support system in Sweden has worked very well, at least in terms of adding generation capacity.[17]

Despite its effectiveness, the green certificate market has been viewed with scepticism. Von der Fehr and Ropenus (2017) have argued that green certificate markets give incumbents the possibility to squeeze the margins of renewable producers. By undersupplying conventional power and oversupplying renewable generation, the price for certificates decreases, alongside the supply from small renewable producers. In addition, the incumbent firm can increase the price for the conventional capacity for which it holds a dominant position.

Yet, the Nordic market so far performed well in the decarbonization of the power sector. As Figure 10.5 shows, Sweden, Finland and Denmark have already achieved their

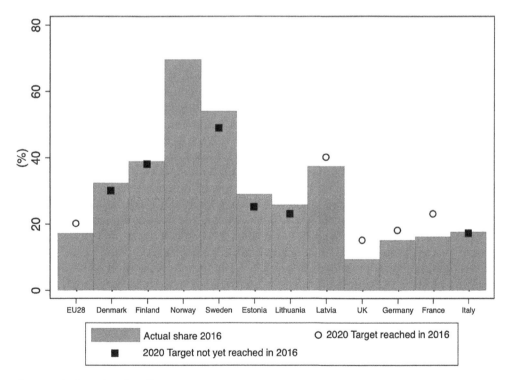

Source: Authors; data from Eurostat.

Figure 10.5 Targeted and actual renewable energy share

2020 renewable energy targets, in contrast to a range of other EU countries. Crucial to the future low-carbon portfolio will be the phase-out of nuclear generation in Sweden by 2040. As such, the renewable support policies will continue to play an important role.

5. SECURITY OF SUPPLY AND RISK MANAGEMENT

The security of supply in the Nordic market depends, like in any other power market, on the reliability of transmission and distribution networks but also on generalism capacity adequacy.[18]

5.1 Market Integration and Energy-only Approach

Until today there have been no major problems with respect to supply security in the generation segment of the Nordic electricity market. There are primarily three reasons for this. The first is the significant expansion of nuclear power in the 1980s, which to a large extent relieved the hydropower plants from the task of providing baseload power. The second is the significant amount of hydropower capacity in the region, combined with its inherent flexibility. The third is the existence of significant interconnection capacity that allows for a well-integrated market within the Nordic region but also with neighbouring EU markets. From 2014 to 2018, the differences across average monthly area prices in the Nordic and Baltic countries have shrunk, as illustrated in Figure 10.6. This price convergence is often considered to be exemplary for the high level of market integration in the Nordic region.

Moreover, the integration of the Nordic market with the neighbouring European markets is likely to improve, as the capacity from interconnectors between the Nordic power system and other systems is planned to increase significantly until 2025 (Statnett et al. 2015). Nevertheless, Grigoryeva, Hesamzadeh and Tangerås (2018) point out that there are still significant hourly price differences between areas that may persist even as the Nordic market is increasingly integrated. Market integration can only ensure security of supply if there is a strong cooperation between Nordic countries regarding transmission issues – in particular, with regard to cross-border investments. Network investments are decided at the national level, by each TSO separately. Such a situation may create free-rider problems if TSOs maximize domestic welfare and disregard the network externalities on the neighbouring countries (Tangerås 2018). While there are regional transmission organizations (RTOs) to manage a multi-state electric grid in the United States, there is nothing similar in the Nordic market.[19] The future cooperation of TSOs across the Scandinavian and Baltic countries may, however, be crucial for secure supply amidst further renewable integration into the Nordic market.

Finally, the Nordic electricity market is an energy-only market. Producers are paid for the energy they deliver, but not for the capacities they keep available. In the Nordic countries, there is no regulation of (minimum) available capacity, neither at the level of individual generators nor at the level of the system. Instead, the market design relies on scarcity prices in peak periods, together with penalties for not being in balance in peak hours, to provide incentives for generators to keep sufficient capacity available. In Finland and Sweden, TSOs also procure some reserve capacity to be used in the case of

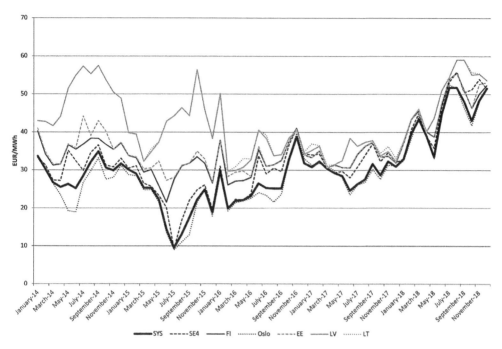

Source: Nord Pool data.

Figure 10.6   *Monthly average day-ahead prices in the Nordic market*

immediate risk of capacity shortage. This strategic reserve is defined through a volume-based mechanism where a certain capacity is set aside and only activated if there is a significant risk of power supply failure.[20] To avoid any competitive distortion, capacity in strategic reserves does not participate in the commercial part of the market. Denmark and Norway solely rely on the market for settling imbalances.

5.2   Capacity Mechanisms

With increasing shares of wind and solar power, future electricity price volatility is likely to be higher and less predictable than it currently is. The full decommission of Swedish nuclear power plants planned for 2040 may spur additional deployment of wind power. At the same time, Finland is investing in nuclear power plants, constructing new nuclear capacity and an additional 2800 MW should be available in 2024 (Statnett et al. 2015).[21] It is currently unclear whether the existing economic incentives to build and maintain the desired peak capacity will be enough. Without sufficient incentives, peak capacity may not be enough to safeguard security of supply in the long term. This last point raises the question of whether these incentives continue to be sufficient to guarantee security of supply in the new reality of the Nordic market. One feature of energy-only markets, as Nord Pool could be characterized, is that financial incentives rather than regulations are assumed to induce market participants to keep enough peak capacity available. Some analysts have argued that the increasing shares of wind and solar power amplify a missing money problem. Indeed, an increase in zero short-run marginal cost generation is likely to reduce the yearly number of operating hours of thermal power plants. Moreover, it is unlikely that price levels will allow fixed cost recovery for thermal power plants (see Chapter 3 in this handbook for a discussion of the basic economic principle). The missing money problem is the key argument for adding a capacity mechanism – that is, a mechanism for paying generators to keep capacity available during peak demand periods. The mechanism may also include operators of storage facilities and major consumers that are prepared to reduce their consumption when capacity shortage is imminent. There is some discussion whether the previously described changes would make it necessary to establish a capacity mechanism in some Nordic countries.

During the last few years, several European countries have introduced capacity mechanisms. However, compared to the rest of Europe, the Nordics are in a unique situation due to the significant amount of hydropower. The flexibility of hydropower makes it ideal for balancing the short-term variations of wind and solar power production (Mauritzen 2013). This means that the cost–benefit analysis of capacity mechanisms looks different in the Nordics than in the rest of Europe. Thus, a market solution seems more viable in the Nordics than in the rest of Europe. However, the optimal solution is unclear and still debated.

5.3 Demand Response

The issue of security of supply may also be addressed on the demand side. Demand response programmes in the Nordic countries are currently not well developed, despite the access to smart meters and the deregulation of the retail market. There are some flexibility potentials across the seven Nordic and Baltic countries. Söder et al. (2018) estimate a total flexibility of 15–29 per cent of the peak (that is, 12–23 GW) but this rate varies across countries (Table 10.3). This variation reflects the national differences in large industrial consumers (for example, forestry and metal processing industry).

Moreover, there are very few prosumers and limited adoption of new technologies (for example, rooftop photovoltaic, pumped storage or other storage technologies) across the Nordics. It is an open question whether the trade of 'flexibility' – will become attractive in countries like Norway and Sweden with a significant share of flexible supply of hydropower. Moreover, the regulatory framework differs across countries and technologies, making it difficult to ensure the right incentives for demand flexibility. A fully integrated market would require responsive and energy-efficient consumers but also common grid planning and renewable support mechanisms.

6. DISCUSSION AND CONCLUSION

The Nordic power market has been among the first liberalized markets in Europe. Since then, the Nordic market model has shown clear signs of strength, especially relative to other markets that have suffered from extensive market power or a lack of investment.[22] Price levels in the Nordic market have to a large extent been competitive in the decades after deregulation, while investment and generation capacities remained adequate to cover a growing demand. The relative success of introducing wholesale market

Table 10.3   The flexibility potential in the Nordic market

Country	Sweden	Denmark	Norway	Finland	Estonia	Latvia	Lithuania	Total
Utilization time (h)	5 037	5 053	5 250	5 462	5 161	5 482	5 273	5 204
Peak (M)	27 000	6 100	24 000	15 105	1 550	1 368	2 200	77 323
Industry energy (%)	36.8	33.1	43.7	47.0	32.0	28.0	40.0	40.6
Industry flexibility, share of peak (%)	7.0–8.5	0.3–3.5	1.1–6.3	9.0	4.2	0.5–1.0	0.2–0.8	4.7–7.1
Household heating energy (%)	22.1	6.1	36.1	15.8	10.0	2.0	2.8	22.8
Household heating, share of peak (%)	7.4–20.4	1.4–2.8	4.2–11.4	7.6–9.6	3.6–14.7	0.0	0.0	5.6–13.1
Other flexibility, share of peak (%)	0.7–0.8	9.9–23.1	3.2–7.2	12.5	7.2	4.6–5.1	3.3–3.7	5.1–9.4
Total share of peak (%)	15.2–29.7	11.5–29.4	8.5–24.9	29.1–31.1	15.0–26.1	5.1–6.1	3.5–4.6	15.3–29.5

Source: Söder et al. (2018), p. 663.

competition has been attributed by many to the vast hydropower resources and the various interconnectors across the Nordic states as well as with its neighbouring power systems.

The governance of Nord Pool is unique due to its bottom-up multinational approach. As outlined in this chapter, Nord Pool is an international power pool with national TSOs as owners and under the supervision of the Norwegian regulatory authority NVE. Nevertheless, even if NVE is the regulatory body, the market rules are enforced by the respective national regulatory authorities and congestion management is the task of national TSOs.

The Nordic market has been a frontrunner with regard to decarbonization. Although this market has historically exhibited relatively low-carbon generation due to its vast hydro resources, the Nordic countries (and to a lesser extent the Baltic States) have actively pushed for the construction of further low-carbon assets, mostly from wind energy. Especially in Denmark, which in contrast to its Nordic neighbours had to replace a significant share of conventional generation assets, the share of wind energy drastically increased due to aggressive support policies. While the Nordic markets are well endowed with a portfolio of carbon-free technologies, the major challenge with regard to their generation capacity will be to replace the nuclear generation in Sweden (about 43 per cent of the national production) that is to be phased out in 2040.

Safeguarding secure supply is dealt with foremost at the Nordic rather than the European level. To counteract outages, the Nordic model has so far relied on a strategic reserve as well as market mechanisms and can therefore be viewed as an energy-only market. Whether that mechanism will ensure capacity adequacy when the shares of wind and solar power are higher is a much-debated issue (see Chapters 15 and 16 of this book). Therefore, whether the Nordic arrangements to guarantee secure supply constitute a strength or a weakness remains to be seen.

The relative success of the Nordic market is also reflected by the geographical extension of Nord Pool, which increased its trading activities and products across Europe. At the same time, however, the European power exchange EPEX has been making steps to enter the Nordic market (EPEX SPOT SE, 2018). Thus, the Nordic and European markets might soon see the competition of different market operators within the same geographical zones, further strengthening the Nordic and EU market integration.

NOTES

*   We would like to thank Mats Kröger and Rebecca Ly for excellent research support, and Lars Bergman for providing valuable inputs. We are very grateful for detailed comments from Jean-Michel Glachant, Ewa Lazarczyk, Rickard Nilsson, Nicolò Rossetto and Klaus Skytte. All mistakes remain ours. Financial support from the Wallenberg Foundation and from Energiforsk EFORIS is gratefully acknowledged. Most of our analysis is based on characteristics and data as of 2018.
1.   Even before the liberalization, there had been a long-standing history of cooperation between the Nordic countries. The first official body for cooperation between the Nordic energy regulators (Nordel) was formed in 1963 (Nord Pool 2002). For a detailed historical account of the Nord Pool market, see Bredesen (2016).
2.   By creating a regional market, Sweden avoided splitting the historic incumbent Vattenfall into multiple entities. Without enlarging the market region, this split would otherwise have been necessary due to Vattenfall's dominant market position.
3.   At that time, the market was dominated by the state-owned firm Imatran Voima Oy with a 30 per cent market share and the private firm Pohjolan Voima; see Pineau and Hämäläinen (2000).

4. Note that the terms 'Nordic market' and 'Nord Pool' are used interchangeably through the text and both refer to the electricity trading exchange and its regulatory environment that today organizes trade between Norway, Sweden, Finland, Denmark and the three Baltic States.
5. In 2014, Fingrid (the Finnish TSO) and Elering (the Estonian TSO) built another cable, Estlink 2, between the two countries.
6. Lithuania and Poland have been connected via LitPol link since 2015.
7. One of the reasons for the maturity of the day-ahead market is that, until recently, all dispatchable generation as well as demand were very predictable (despite the seasonal fluctuation of the water reservoirs) and all electricity traded on the day-ahead market required only minor adjustments.
8. See also the EU Regulation 714/2009.
9. The Baltic region is not yet part of the Nordic system price. Furthermore, the Baltic and the Scandinavian market are legally considered separate regions for network capacity allocation. Hence the capacity calculation for the transmission network is not yet harmonized and is separated between the Scandinavian and the Baltic States.
10. The Nord Pool group's activities include power trading, clearing, settlement and associated services in both day-ahead and intraday physical energy markets.
11. The current ownership is divided between state-owned TSOs as follows: Statnett (Norway): 28.2 per cent; Svenska Kraftnät (Sweden): 28.2 per cent; Fingrid (Finland): 18.8 per cent; Energinet.dk (Denmark): 18.8 per cent; Elering (Estonia): 2.0 per cent; Litgrid (Lithuania): 2.0 per cent; Latvenergo (Latvia): 2.0 per cent.
12. TSOs, however, also coordinate at the international level. Recently, EU policy has established a mandate for international TSO cooperation via the 'Clean Energy Package'. For example, this regulatory package introduced 'regional coordination centres' and 'system operations regions'.
13. Figure 10.3 is reproduced from the IEA and Norden (2016) report, extending the dataset to include three more years using ENTSO-E data.
14. When listing the 200 hours of highest load for each country in 2018, coincident peak in all four countries occurs only in about 25 per cent of the cases.
15. Von der Fehr and Hansen (2010), however, find evidence of market power in Norwegian retail market segments where demand is relatively inelastic.
16. One of the reasons for Norway to join was the lack of sites to build new large hydropower plants (Von der Fehr et al. 2005).
17. Schusser and Jaraitė (2018) provide evidence that there is no conflict between the European Union's Emissions Trading System (EU ETS) and the Swedish-Norwegian tradable green certificate scheme.
18. This section draws extensively on Sections 3.4 and 7.4 in Bergman and Le Coq (2019).
19. Since May 2017, Fingrid, Svenska Kraftnät and Statnett no longer perform imbalance settlement in their country. The company eSett, owned by these three TSOs, performs services on their behalf (for example, imbalance settlement, invoicing or even some market monitoring). Ultimately, however, each TSO is responsible for balancing operations and imbalance settlement for its national market (eSett 2019).
20. The capacity of the strategic reserves is determined at the national level but there are some common activation rules. Indeed, Swedish and Finish TSOs decide together which source to activate in case of market failure risk.
21. Crosara, Tómasson and Söder (2019) investigated the issue of generation adequacy in Nord Pool considering different transmission capacity and regulatory barriers. They found some capacity deficit in the power system, especially after 2040.
22. Note that this chapter has discussed the Nordic market as compared to other deregulated markets in the EU or the US. As Schmalensee states in Chapter 2 of this handbook, pre-restructuring electricity supply regimes still exist in other regions.

REFERENCES

Ahlqvist, V., P. Holmberg and T. Tangerås (2019), 'Central- versus self-dispatch in electricity markets', *EPRG Working Paper No. 1902*, Energy Policy Research Group, University of Cambridge.
Amundsen, E. and L. Bergman (2006), 'Why has the Nordic electricity market worked so well?', *Utilities Policy*, **14** (3), 148–57.
Bask, M., J. Lundgren and N. Rudholm (2011), 'Market power in the expanding Nordic power market', *Applied Economics*, **43** (9), 1035–43.
Bergman, L. and C. Le Coq (2019), *Blowing in the Wind? On the Future Design of the Nordic Electricity Market: Report 2019:587*, Energieforsk/EFORIS.

Bredesen, H.-A. (2016), 'The Nord Pool market model', forum paper, Nord Pool Consulting AS, February 2016.

Crosara, A., E. Tómasson and L. Söder (2019), 'Generation adequacy in the Nordic and Baltic area: the potential of flexible residential electric heating', in *2019 IEEE PES Innovative Smart Grid Technologies Europe* (ISGT-Europe), Bucharest, Romania, pp. 1–5.

EPEX SPOT SE (2018), *Application for a Market Place License to Organize and Operate a Market Place for the Trading of Electricity for Physical Delivery in the Kingdom of Norway*, accessed 30 April 2019 at https://www. nve.no/media/7721/epex-spot-application-public-version.pdf.

eSett (2019), *Nordic Imbalance Settlement Handbook: Instructions and Rules for Market Participants*, accessed 13 January 2020 at https://www.esett.com/handbook/.

European Commission (2010), *Case 39351 – Swedish Interconnectors. Commission Decision of 14.4.2010*.

Fogelberg, S. and E. Lazarczyk (2019), 'Strategic withholding through production failures', *The Energy Journal*, **40** (5), 247–66.

Fridolfsson, S.-O. and T. Tangerås (2009), 'Market power in the Nordic electricity wholesale market: a survey of the empirical evidence', *Energy Policy*, **37** (9), 3681–92.

Gavard, C. (2016), 'Carbon price and wind power support in Denmark', *Energy Policy*, **92**, 455–67.

Grigoryeva, A., M. R. Hesamzadeh and T. Tangerås (2018), 'Energy system transition in the Nordic market: challenges for transmission regulation and governance', *Economics of Energy & Environmental Policy*, **7** (1), 127–46.

Harvey, S. M. and W. W. Hogan (2000), 'Nodal and zonal congestion management and the exercise of market power', Harvard University, accessed 10 November 2020 at https://scholar.harvard.edu/whogan/files/ zonal_jan10.pdf.

Holmberg, P. and E. Lazarczyk (2015), 'Comparison of congestion management techniques: nodal, zonal and discriminatory pricing', *The Energy Journal*, **36** (2), 145–66.

IEA and Norden (2016), *Nordic Energy Technology Perspectives 2016: Cities, Flexibility and Pathways to Carbon Neutrality*, International Energy Agency/Nordic Energy Research.

Lazarczyk, E. (2016), 'Market-specific news and its impact on forward premia on electricity markets', *Energy Economics*, **54**, 326–36.

Lazarczyk, E. and C. Le Coq (2019), 'Information disclosure rules and auction mechanism: how much information on electricity auctions?', *IAEE Energy Forum*, Third Quarter, 33–5.

Lipp, J. (2007), 'Lessons for effective renewable electricity policy from Denmark, Germany and the United Kingdom', *Energy Policy*, **35** (11), 5481–95.

Littlechild, S. (2006), 'Competition and contracts in the Nordic residential electricity markets', *Utilities Policy*, **14** (3), 135–47.

Lundin, E. (2016), 'Market power and joint ownership: evidence from nuclear plants in Sweden', *IFN Working Paper No. 1113*.

Mauritzen, J. (2013), 'Dead battery? Wind power, the spot market, and hydropower interaction in the Nordic electricity market', *The Energy Journal*, **34** (1), 103–23.

Mirza, O. and F. M. Bergland (2015), 'Market power in the Norwegian electricity market: are the transmission bottlenecks truly exogenous?', *The Energy Journal*, **36** (4), 313–30.

Nord Pool (2002), *Annual Report*.

Nord Pool (2011), *Annual Report*.

NordREG (2014), *Nordic Market Report: Development in the Nordic Electricity Market: Report 4/2014*.

NordREG (2017), *Electricity Customer in the Nordic Countries*, Status Report Retail Markets, March.

NordREG (2018), *Implementation of Data Hubs in the Nordic Countries: Status Report*, June.

Olsen, O. J., T. A. Johnsen and P. Lewis (2006), 'A mixed Nordic experience: implementing competitive retail electricity markets for household customers', *The Electricity Journal*, **19** (9), 37–44.

Pineau, P.-O. and R. P. Hämäläinen (2000), 'A perspective on the restructuring of the Finnish electricity market', *Energy Policy*, **8** (3), 181–92.

Ruester, S., S. Schwenen, C. Batlle and I. Pérez-Arriaga (2014), 'From distribution networks to smart distribution systems: rethinking the regulation of European electricity DSOs', *Utilities Policy*, **31**, 229–37.

Sadowska, M. and B. Willems (2013), 'Market integration and economic efficiency at conflict? Commitments in the Swedish interconnectors case', *World Competition: Law and Economics Review*, **36** (1), 99–132.

Schusser, S. and J. Jaraitė (2018), 'Explaining the interplay of three markets: green certificates, carbon emissions and electricity', *Energy Economics*, **71**, 1–13.

Söder, L., P. D. Lund and H. Koduvere et al. (2018), 'A review of demand side flexibility potential in Northern Europe', *Renewable and Sustainable Energy Reviews*, **91**, 654–64.

Statnett, Fingrid, Energinet.dk and Svenska Kraftnät (2015), *Challenges and Opportunities for the Nordic Power System*, accessed 10 November 2020 at https://www.fingrid.fi/globalassets/dokumentit/fi/yhtio/tki-toiminta/ report-challenges-and-opportunities-for-the-nordic-power-system.pdf.

Tangerås, T. (2018), 'Equilibrium supply security in a multinational electricity market with renewable generation', *Energy Economics*, **72**, 416–35.

Tangerås, T. and J. Mauritzen (2018), 'Real-time versus day-ahead market power in a hydro-based electricity
market', *The Journal of Industrial Economics*, **66** (4), 904–41.

Von der Fehr, N.-H. M., E. S. Amundsen and L. Bergman (2005), 'The Nordic market: signs of stress?', *The
Energy Journal*, **26** (Special Issue), 71–98.

Von der Fehr, N.-H. M. and P. V. Hansen (2010), 'Electricity retailing in Norway', *The Energy Journal*, **31** (1),
25–46.

Von der Fehr, N.-H. M. and S. Ropenus (2017), 'Renewable energy policy instruments and market power', *The
Scandinavian Journal of Economics*, **119** (2), 312–45.

11. The evolution of the European model for electricity markets
Fabien Roques*

1. INTRODUCTION

Part I of this handbook focuses on the initial arrangements and market model for electricity sector liberalization. Chapter 3 considers optimal pricing and investment in electricity generation in this regime, while Chapter 4 describes what is required in practice for post-restructuring wholesale power markets to work well. In this chapter, I review in Sections 2 and 3 the historical model for electricity market liberalization and integration followed in Europe and the key achievements reached three decades after the start of this process.

The creation of the European Coal and Steel Community (ECSC) in 1951 was a stepping-stone in the European integration project – an organization of six European countries aiming at regulating their industrial production under a centralized authority. But the real start of European energy policy integration dates to the 1980s, as part of the 1986 Single Act objective to integrate and liberalize some of the key sectors of the European economy. Most electricity and natural gas industries in Europe were historically national and organized around geographic monopolies. In the 1990s, the European Union and its member states gradually opened these markets to competition. The first liberalization directives, the so-called First Energy Package, were adopted in 1996 (electricity) and 1998 (gas), to be transposed into member states' legal systems by 1998 (electricity) and 2000 (gas).

More than 20 years after the start of liberalization of national electricity industries, the integration process remains incomplete in Europe. There have been significant achievements in removing barriers to cross-border trade, and liberalization has delivered benefits in a range of countries to consumers. However, the progress has been slowed by the technical challenges associated with integrating markets that have different designs and governance approaches. This partly results from the choice that was made not to impose a standard market design at the beginning, but instead to try to ensure gradual convergence of different market designs by progressively tightening the rules to drive further convergence through the harmonization of some of the technical rules affecting cross-border trade.

Part II of this handbook focuses on the emerging regime, in which variable renewable energy sources and the policies that support them have become important enough to have material effects on energy market operations and investment decisions. Chapter 12 describes the new electricity supply technologies involved in that regime and Chapter 15 examines operational problems posed by high penetration of variable renewable energy (VRE) technologies. Chapter 16 considers implications for market design in restructured electricity supply industries (ESIs). In Sections 4 and 5, I review the ways in which

European electricity markets are evolving and argue that a new model is emerging, despite the differences across countries.

In Europe, in the past decade, the emergence of concerns related to security of supply and the growing political commitment to fight climate change have led to a change in policy objectives, posing new challenges for the integration of power markets. National policies have not been coordinated. A number of new market design features have been introduced in a non-coordinated way, such as support mechanisms to foster the development of clean technologies and capacity mechanisms to ensure security of supply. This created the challenge of driving further market integration, while some of the underlying policies and the governance remain largely shaped at a national level. The 2019 Clean Energy Package[1] marks another step toward technical convergence but also shows the limits of further market integration absent further coordination and convergence of energy and climate policies (European Commission 2019, European Parliament and Council 2019).

This chapter aims to contribute to the existing literature by providing a review of the drivers and tensions that have been shaping the difficult progress towards liberalization and integration of European power markets. The chapter is organized in three main sections.

I first describe the initial drivers and approach for market liberalization and integration across Europe that was implemented in the 1990s and early 2000s. I show how the process has been driven by successive European legislations, promoting further coordination on a set of technical market rules despite the diverging starting points in terms of market organization across countries, which culminated with the adoption of the European network codes[2] and the 2019 Clean Energy Package. I also provide a brief overview of the literature that has evaluated the benefits of this integration, based on indicators such as wholesale price convergence.

I then argue that the changing policy focus in the late 2000s has created new challenges for European power market integration. A revival of national uncoordinated policy interventions has got in the way of further market integration and led to a range of new approaches being explored for market design across Europe. I also show how the changes in the dominant renewable technologies' cost structure and generation patterns have led to a shift in focus toward the improvement of the design of markets close to real time. I explain that the European power market model is now characterized by a patchwork of hybrid market approaches, mixing liberalized markets with state interventions introducing a number of new 'market modules' to drive investment choices, ensure security of supply (capacity mechanisms) and support clean technologies. I argue that these hybrid market approaches take different forms across Europe and are largely shaped by the differences in the national policies and governance, although common features can be identified across countries.

I conclude by exploring the challenges that must be confronted in the future to preserve and deepen the benefits of integrated electricity markets in Europe given these diverging forces. I put forward that the coordination of the new emerging hybrid market model across Europe will require a more integrated approach towards planning and deployment of key infrastructures, at different geographic levels, from the local to the regional and European levels. I also highlight that unleashing further market integration benefits for consumers will require coordination of some of the underlying policies and governance processes and put forward the key principles of a new market model that could emerge based on these developments.

2.   THE GRADUAL INTEGRATION OF EU ELECTRICITY MARKETS AND SINGLE MARKET BENEFITS

In this section, I provide an overview of the initial drivers and approach of the liberalization and market integration process in Europe that started in the 1990s. I then provide a brief overview of the literature that has evaluated the benefits of this integration, based on indicators such as wholesale price convergence.

2.1   The Initial Steps of EU Electricity Market Liberalization

Prior to 1996, EU electricity sectors were dominated by incumbent domestic utilities often vertically integrated from generation, transmission, distribution to retail.[3] Customers of these utilities had no possibility to switch suppliers and cross-border trade was controlled by the bilateral monopolists setting cross-border tariffs and allocating cross-border transfer capacity. The only example of zonal cross-border trading was the Nord Pool market between Norway, Sweden and later Finland (see Chapter 10 in this handbook for further information about the evolution of Nord Pool).

Three European legislative packages, in 1996, 2003 and 2009, have been adopted to achieve a liberalized internal energy market, from national electricity systems to an integrated European electricity market (European Parliament and Council 1996, 2003, 2009). The successive legislative packages opened markets to competition through the unbundling of supply, generation and networks, and through the market access to third parties. The directives also promoted cross-border markets. As Schmalensee points out in Chapter 2 of this handbook, restructuring in the historical regime turned out to be much more complex than many expected.

The 1996 Directive initiated the opening up to competition of generation, retail, as well as transmission and distribution systems (European Parliament and Council 1996). By the end of 1999, all generation would be either subject to free entry into a wholesale market arrangement or competitively procured by a single buyer under a tendering procedure. Access to transmission and distribution systems would be subject to negotiated or regulated third-party access. Finally, competition was introduced in the retail sector, with customers representing one-third of demand allowed to choose their retail supplier. Accounting unbundling was introduced with transmission and distribution businesses having to produce separate accounts.

The EU member states liberalized their industries without much coordination on the initial market design. As a result, a patchwork of approaches emerged. Table 11.1 identifies the key differences in approaches for the key building blocks shaping the electricity market design across Europe, including the forward, day-ahead and intraday market design. This lack of harmonization of the underlying key buildings blocks contributed to making the cross-border integration of these different markets challenging. In hindsight, one may wonder why there was not greater focus on ensuring some harmonization of the different market building blocks as a prerequisite to market integration.

Table 11.1   Key differences in the building blocks of the electricity market design across EU countries in the mid-2000s

Market Design	Ireland	ES, PT, IT	Nordic, CWE	GB
Forward market	No meaningful forward market	Financial forward market	Financial and physical forward market	Mainly physical forward market
Day-ahead	Central dispatch Traded volumes/ prices not firm Locational bidding	Quasi-mandatory day-ahead auction Locational bidding	Day-ahead auction with strong market support Portfolio bidding	No particular significance of day-ahead Portfolio bidding
Intraday	D-1 gate closure No intraday market	Intraday auction slots H-4 gate closure or more	Continuous trading H-1 gate closure (or less being considered)	Continuous trading H-1 gate closure

The 2003 Directive went further in the wholesale and retail competition and forced slowly reforming countries to catch up with leading countries (European Parliament and Council 2003, Jamasb and Pollitt 2005). By the end of 2007, all generation would be subject to wholesale market arrangements, all access to transmission and distribution systems would take the form of regulated open third-party access, and all retail customers could choose their retail supplier, competing with one another to acquire customers. Unbundling of vertically integrated transmission and distribution businesses was legally required. All cross-border trade would be subject to regulated open third-party access.

2.2   The Attempt to Define a European 'Target Model'

Whilst national electricity markets were reformed and became more competitive (though with significant differences across countries), the integration of markets into a single electricity market had made little progress by the late 1990s. In 1998, the European electricity regulatory forum, the so-called Florence Forum, was set up to discuss the creation of the internal electricity market. In 2004, the European Commission developed a set of proposals to support what became the 'target model' with the aim of gradually integrating markets through a system of market coupling allowing energy traders to implicitly bid for grid capacity through their energy bids instead of bidding in two separate auctions (European Commission 2011, Moffatt Associates 2007). Under market coupling, available transmission transfer capacity between each market is declared and conveyed to the markets, and power can be traded between both markets, with flows going from low-priced market to high-priced market when transmission constraints arise (Pollitt 2019).

In 2005, the European Commission Competition Directorate launched an energy sector competition inquiry following concerns about inefficient cross-border transfer capacity and more broadly of lack of market integration (European Commission 2007). The inquiry concluded that the slow progress in the single electricity market was the result of insufficient interconnecting infrastructures, inefficient allocation of existing capacities as well as incompatible market design between transmission system operators (TSOs) and spot market operators (Meeus and Belmans 2008).

As a result of the energy sector competition inquiry in 2005, the third electricity single market directive was introduced. The 2009 Directive enforced greater competition within the electricity sector, strengthening the unbundling requirements on transmission businesses, and also established a body for the cooperation of national regulators. In this context, the Agency for the Cooperation of Energy Regulators (ACER) helps ensure that the single European market in gas and electricity functions properly (European Parliament and Council 2009). ACER helps national regulatory authorities to perform their regulatory function at European level and, where necessary, coordinates their work.

In parallel, the Third Energy Package fostered the development of a more bottom-up market integration process through the creation of the Regional Initiatives (Figure 11.1) and other independent regional integration projects, such as the trilateral market coupling. These Regional Initiatives have had mixed success in driving regional market integration. One key achievement has been the implementation of market coupling on a regional basis, which is further developed in the next section.[4]

2.3   The Latest Developments to Drive Further Technical Convergence: The Network Codes and the Energy Market Regulation

The development of network codes and guidelines has been a key element in the achievement of an internal energy market in the Third Energy Package. A European market

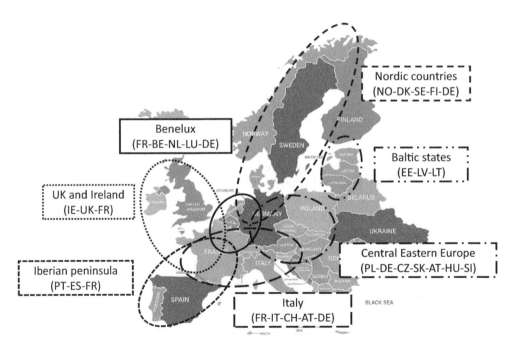

Figure 11.1   The seven Regional Initiatives

design grew out of the drafting of the first EU grid codes co-developed by the European Network of Transmission System Operators (ENTSO-E), ACER and the Commission through the EU regulation approval process named the 'comitology process'. These codes are a detailed set of rules pushing for the harmonization of previously more nationally oriented electricity markets and regulations. A total of eight network codes and guidelines entered into force by the end of 2017:

- Grid connection-related network codes that provide a set of connection requirements for all parties connecting to transmission networks (including generators, demand customers and high-voltage direct-current – HVDC – connections). There are three network codes from the grid connection area: Network Code on Requirements for Generators (NC RfG), Network Code on Demand Connection (NC DCC) and Network Code on HVDC connections (NC HVDC).
- System operation-related network codes that define common pan-European operation standards for the existing and future European electricity system in response to an increasing penetration of renewable energy generation and a greater interconnection between transmission systems in Europe. There are two codes covering this: the System Operation Guideline (SO GL) and the Network Code on Emergency and Restoration (NC ER).
- Market-related codes that outline the main features of a pan-European electricity market to promote effective competition, minimize risks for all parties and give incentives for market players to act in a way that supports an efficient operation of the system. They provide rules for calculating cross-border capacity and operating the markets in different timeframes. Three network codes from the market area focus on the Guideline on Capacity Allocation and Congestion Management (GL CACM), Guideline on Forward Capacity Allocation (GL FCA) and Guideline on Electricity Balancing (GL EB). The network code GL CACM plays a fundamental role in setting transparent conditions for fair access to cross-zonal capacity. This code is at the centre of Europe's market coupling development and progress towards a single market for electricity.

The Clean Energy Package made up of four directives and four regulations was adopted in June 2019 with the underlying objectives of promoting energy efficiency, achieving global leadership in renewable energies and providing a 'fair deal' for consumers. The new directive on common rules for the internal market for electricity (EU) 2019/944, and the new regulation on the internal market for electricity (EU) 2019/943 amend existing energy legislation in a number of areas with the objective of removing some of the barriers to efficient market functioning and cross-border trade (European Commission 2019).

The Clean Energy Package also introduced a new set of legislations and regulations, providing further specific guidance on key issues for market design that have emerged in recent years such as demand response including aggregation, energy storage and demand curtailment rules. The package also empowers the Commission to facilitate the adoption of certain network codes as delegated acts depending on their area of focus (third-party access rules and network connection rules, for example).

The Clean Energy Package therefore represents an important stepping-stone in ensuring further coordination of European electricity markets and adapting the market rules and governance to the changing policy and technology context. In the next section, I explain how both the changes in policy priorities and in the dominant technologies' cost structure have led a number of countries to revisit the electricity market arrangements and policy makers to intervene in electricity markets via a set of national uncoordinated policy interventions, which set new challenges for the integration of European electricity markets.

2.4   The Benefits of Market Integration

Assessing the economic effects of the liberalization and integration of European power markets is challenging, as some of the effects will only be felt in the long term. Pollitt (2019) provides a thorough literature review that shows strong evidence of positive benefits. Moreover, as Schmalensee points out in Chapter 2 of this handbook, an overall assessment of the benefits of liberalization and market integration should also consider the impact on power quality and reliability (frequency and duration of outages), and the development and use of innovative technologies and practices. The scope of this chapter does not allow a comprehensive assessment, and I concentrate in what follows on some of the key indicators of market integration – namely, wholesale price convergence.

2.4.1   Market coupling and the efficiency of cross-border trade
The successive legislative packages have contributed to the gradual integration of national markets. Trading of electricity across national borders went from 6 per cent in 1976 to nearly 14 per cent of electricity produced in the ENTSO-E area in 2015 (ENTSO-E 2017). This has been driven by further market integration and the development of interconnections.

The main success story of the European push for electricity market integration is the implementation of day-ahead market coupling. At the end of 2019, market coupling had risen to cover most of Europe. Figure 11.2 illustrates the progress with day-ahead market coupling implementation across Europe.

Day-ahead market coupling has made significant progress, with 27 countries representing 90 per cent of European electricity consumption involved in market coupling. Intraday coupling has witnessed a slower progression due to complexities linked to technical issues, as well as market design and governance. However, recent progress has been made with the signing of the intraday operational agreement by 26 countries (ENTSO-E 2019).

Progress on the day-ahead market coupling has resulted in an improvement of the efficiency of interconnector operation – that is, available commercial capacity used from low- to high-price areas – from 60 per cent in 2010 to 86 per cent in 2017. Intraday efficiency is lower at 50 per cent, although this is expected to improve with the new single intraday coupling platform introduced in 2018 (ibid.).

However, analysis from ACER and the Council of European Energy Regulators (CEER) (2017) shows that further gains could be realized if market coupling was extended to remaining borders (€203 million per year of potential gains).

2.4.2   Wholesale market price convergence
Wholesale price convergence is an indicator of the progress of market integration achieved through market coupling and interconnection. After implementation of market

Source: Own analysis.

Figure 11.2   Progress with market coupling in Europe (2012 and 2019)

315

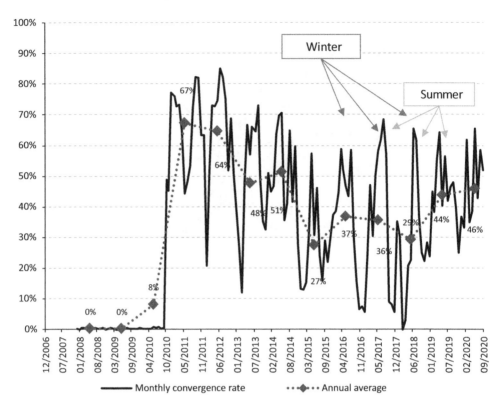

Note: Convergence rate is the percentage of hours where price difference is lower than 0.01 €/MWh (megawatt-hours).

Source: Own analysis based on data from the European Power Exchange (EPEX).

Figure 11.3   Convergence rate between French and German day-ahead prices (2008–20)

coupling, regional price convergence started to increase, with levels reaching 60 per cent in 2011 in the Central Western Europe (CWE) area, whilst other areas such as the Baltics or South Western Europe (SWE) still experienced very low levels of price convergence (ENTSO-E 2019).

However, whilst the historical trends show that price convergence has been increasing overall across Europe, there remain significant variations in the levels of price convergence across those regions. In the Baltics, price convergence reached 80 per cent in 2017, thanks to an increase in the interconnection capacity, while the CWE region showed a decrease of price convergence toward around 40 per cent. The growing penetration of renewables has indeed led to a decrease in price convergence in some of the regions (Annan-Phan and Roques 2018). Figure 11.3 illustrates the decrease in price convergence in the CWE region compared to earlier years, with large price differentials during winter seasons when there are significant amounts of wind power generated in Germany. This decrease of price convergence in the CWE region is a result of the bottlenecks created by insufficient interconnection that leads to more frequent price divergences.

3. NEW CHALLENGES AND POTENTIAL FURTHER GAINS OF MARKET INTEGRATION

In the late 2000s, the greater focus of EU energy policy on security of supply and climate change mitigation has created new challenges for European power market integration. This, combined with the growth of renewables dominated by fixed costs and with variable generation patterns, has led to a range of national reforms to support clean technologies and ensure security of supply. I explain in this chapter that the European power market model is now characterized by a patchwork of hybrid market approaches mixing liberalized markets with state interventions and that, although these hybrid markets take different forms across Europe and are largely shaped by the differences in the national policies and governance, a number of common features can be identified across countries.

3.1 The Changes in Policy Priorities that Affected the Electricity Liberalization

Whilst in the late 1990s and early 2000s, European policy efforts focused on creating the regulatory framework and common rules for the internal market in electricity, European energy policy in the mid-2000s began to focus on climate change mitigation – that is, on the decarbonization of the electricity sector and the electrification of transport and other sectors of the economy. In March 2007, EU leaders set targets for a low-carbon economy. Implementation policies were defined through a set of directives in 2009 often referred to as the 'Climate and Energy Package'. These targets, known as the '20-20-20' targets, set three key objectives for 2020: (1) a 20 per cent reduction in EU greenhouse gas emissions from 1990 levels; (2) raising the share of EU energy consumption produced from renewable resources to 20 per cent; (3) a 20 per cent improvement in the EU's energy efficiency. As part of the 2011 discussions on a 2050 Roadmap, EU leaders committed to reducing Europe's greenhouse gas emissions by 80–95 per cent by 2050 compared to 1990 levels.

In the late 2000s, security of supply also came back to the forefront of the European energy policy agenda. The Russia–Ukraine gas crisis of January 2009 that led to supply disruptions in several member states reminded Europeans of their dependence on imported gas and revived discussions on both a common approach toward energy supplies from external countries and a strengthened set of criteria for ensuring security of energy supplies within the internal market. More recently, the 2014 Russia–Ukraine dispute and the discussions on gas supplies have revived concerns about security of imported gas supplies in Europe. In response to the political crisis in Ukraine, in May 2014, the European Commission released a communication defining a new EU energy security strategy (European Commission 2014).

Finally, the 2008–09 economic crisis also brought a new dimension into the European energy policy objectives: policy scrutiny about the cost of some of the climate and green policies intensified, and concerns have grown that the uncontrolled deployment of low-carbon technologies could both undermine Europe's economic competitiveness and raise concerns about security of supply. The Green Paper, *A 2030 Framework for Climate and Energy Policies* (European Commission 2013) represents an inflexion point in European energy policy that clearly heralds competitiveness and affordability as one of the key issues for the years to come.

The emergence or re-emergence of decarbonization objectives, security of supply and competitiveness concerns led to a new context for the liberalization and further integration of European power markets. These trends indeed marked a profound shift, as creating a competitive liberalized and integrated internal market was not an end objective in and of itself anymore but would instead serve the other policy objectives – namely, ensuring the safe and affordable supply of energy to European citizens and working towards the long-term decarbonization objective.

In concrete terms, these new policy objectives have led policy makers to intervene in electricity markets via a set of uncoordinated national policy interventions that got in the way of further market integration and led to a range of new approaches being explored for market design across Europe. These approaches are further explored in Section 4.

3.2   The Rise of Clean Technologies Characterized by Fixed Costs and Variable Output

Another fundamental change in context that affected the European market liberalization process in recent years is the emergence and policy support for low-carbon technologies, which have both a different cost structure and different production patterns compared to the dispatchable thermal plants that historically shaped the dynamics of European power markets. The issue of the interaction of the support mechanisms and policies of these clean technologies with the wholesale markets is discussed in the next section.

The theory for electricity market liberalization was indeed developed in the early 1980s in a different technology context from today, when thermal plants (either coal, gas, fuel oil or nuclear) were dominant. These dominant technologies presented significant variable costs and were dependable. In contrast, most low-carbon technologies – renewables, nuclear, batteries, carbon capture and storage – are essentially fixed-cost technologies, as the investment costs represent a large fraction of the total generation costs. That is, these technologies are costly to build but have low short-run marginal costs of generation (an exception being biomass-based generation). In addition, some of these technologies have intermittent production profiles – for example, dependent on variable wind and solar irradiation patterns. That is, unlike the traditional generating technologies, the system operator cannot rely on a generation fleet that could be dispatched to meet demand based on bid-based economic dispatch principles.

The theory underpinning competitive power markets is based on the fundamental principles of the peak-load pricing approach (Boiteux 1949, 1951). Market participants bid their short-run marginal costs (SRMCs), and fixed costs are recovered through: (1) inframarginal rents as technologies with higher SRMCs clear the market and set the power price; and (2) scarcity rents when the market is tight and prices go beyond the SRMCs of the technology clearing the market. Whilst in theory, marginal cost pricing can still work with a part of the generation mix having zero or very low SRMCs, prices have become more volatile as the share of renewables increases. This has led, for instance, in some European countries to the emergence of negative or zero power prices in some periods, triggering a debate on the need for further market reforms.

This old market paradigm worked well to induce competition between technologies with significant variable costs, but the growing shares of renewables with a cost structure dominated by fixed costs in European markets led to adaptations of the market design to reflect the changes in the technology cost structure and production patterns associated with the growth of clean technologies. In particular, the development of variable renewables reinforces the need to reward operational flexibility as well as dependability on short timeframes, both for flexible power plants and demand-side response. The value of short-term operating flexibility is typically captured through intraday and ancillary services, and there has been growing focus in the past years and in the Clean Energy Package on addressing the market design issues that distort short-term price signals in real time.

Indeed, concerns have emerged in recent years that European power markets do not convey the proper scarcity value of operating flexibility in many countries, calling for revisiting the current arrangements for intraday trading and ancillary service procurement. Indeed, intraday exchanges remain limited in most member states. In addition, there are also concerns with the current arrangements for balancing and reserve procurement, which in many countries are not always procured by system operators on a competitive and transparent basis; and even where competitive auctions for the procurement of these products are in place, these are often based on long-term contracts and the lack of contestability and/or liquidity of such short-term products makes it difficult to reflect the fast-evolving value of these short-term balancing services to the system.

This recent focus of market reforms across Europe on ensuring that markets reflect the system constraints close to real time represents a significant shift, as European power market integration efforts had historically focused in the 2000s on ensuring efficient cross-border trade via day-ahead markets, which culminated with the European-wide roll-out of day-ahead market coupling. Most countries are indeed exploring ways to improve their balancing and ancillary service mechanisms, driven both by the network code harmonization process and the need to improve the market design to integrate growing shares of renewables.

In parallel, a number of countries have taken steps to introduce new mechanisms or 'market building blocks' to support investment in clean technologies, via tenders of long-term contracts, and to secure supplies via the introduction of capacity mechanisms. This has led to the emergence of 'hybrid markets' combining roles in public planning and interventions taking various shapes across countries, which are further explained in Section 4. In the next subsection, I turn to an assessment of the benefits of the European integration efforts for electricity markets and the key priorities to ensure further economic benefits from electricity market integration.

3.3 Key Priorities for Further Market Integration and Delivering Benefits to EU Consumers

The impacts of the single market have been estimated in a study by Booz & Company conducted for the European Commission in 2013 (Booz & Company et al. 2013), which was later published by Newbery, Strbac and Viehoff (2016). Booz & Company's study found that the benefits of integration due to market coupling could be up to €4 billion per year if markets were fully coupled. The study suggests that much larger benefits could be expected if market coupling of interconnectors were extended to intraday trading of electricity, balancing services and financial transmission rights.

Newbery et al. (2016) estimate a similar range of long-term potential benefits coming from short-term trading and balancing benefits, which would represent a 100 per cent increase of the current gains from trade over the interconnectors. The paper stresses the

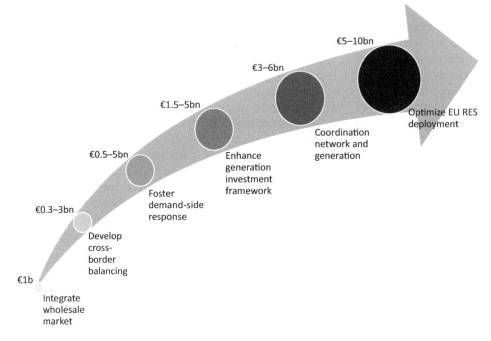

€5–10bn

€3–6bn

€1.5–5bn

€0.5–5bn

Optimize EU RES
deployment

Coordination
network and
generation

Enhance
generation
investment
framework

€0.3–3bn

Foster
demand-side
response

Develop
cross-
border
balancing

€1b

Integrate
wholesale
market

Source: Roques (2015), p. 43.

Figure 11.4   Orders of magnitude of the potential gains associated with different types of reforms (EU-wide, billion €/year)

policy implications of those estimated benefits, which should be used to compensate interconnector owners to incentivize them to make the necessary investments to increase interconnection capacity.

In addition, there are significant potential economic gains associated with a more coordinated approach toward the planning of investment in key energy infrastructures. Figure 11.4 is based on a large survey of the academic literature and shows the expected financial gains associated with different types of coordination measures at the European level. Figure 11.4 demonstrates that greater economic gains could be achieved via European coordination of the deployment of network infrastructure, as well as greater coordination of investments in generation – including renewable energy source (RES) development across Europe, instead of having national policies and targets.

4.   TOWARD A NEW HYBRID MARKET MODEL: KEY PRINCIPLES AND PREREQUISITES

In the previous section, I described how the changes in policy objectives and in the dominant technologies cost structure have led to a revival of uncoordinated policy interventions in European electricity markets. I highlighted that the potential larger economic gains that could be achieved through further integration of European electricity markets would require more coordination of these public interventions that aim to plan the deployment of clean technologies and key infrastructures that would support the power sector decarbonization across Europe. I also argued that although the current set of hybrid markets take different forms across Europe and are largely shaped by the differences in the national policies and governance, a number of common features can be identified across countries.

In this section, I explore how this current patchwork of hybrid markets could be better coordinated across Europe and could eventually evolve toward a new market model. I outline the common principles of this market model that emerge across the various national approaches and that feature competition in two-steps with competition 'for the market' (that is, for the investment) followed by competition 'in the market' (that is, for efficient system operation and dispatch). In particular, I highlight the key underlying policy and governance challenges that are necessary prerequisites to the emergence of such new market model.

4.1 Common Features of 'Hybrid Markets' with State and Regulatory Interventions

As discussed in the previous section, the initial market model has evolved to take into account the changes in policy objectives and European electricity markets are today 'hybridized' with various forms of regulatory intervention. Roques and Finon (2017) have studied how the revival of public interventions in electricity markets is driving a transformation of the standard historical approach of competitive market design towards a hybrid regime that combines planning and long-term arrangements established with public or regulated entities on one side and short-term 'organized markets' on the other.

The primary motivations for public intervention comprise three drivers that have recently attracted attention in most European countries:

- the need to overcome the perceived market failures that undermine investment in sufficient generation capacity to satisfy growing load needs and maintain security of supply;
- the determination of part of the generation mix through support for the clean or low-carbon technologies; and
- the need for greater coordination and system planning to optimize generation and transmission system development given the rise of decentralized resources and the need for greater coordination of infrastructures investment across sectors in the new regime.

Following from the seminal analysis of Glachant and Perez (2009) that provides an institutional framework to analyse the different modules in the electricity value chain, Roques and Finon (2017) analyse the 'reforms of the reforms' of electricity industries that aim to correct the market and regulatory imperfections stemming from the initial market architectures and address the new policy objectives by introducing some new market modules.

Roques and Finon (2017) explain that three different types of new market modules are typically implemented to resolve these issues. The 'long-term contracts module' to support risk transfers and facilitate investment, the 'capacity mechanism module' to guarantee security of supply and the 'RES-decarbonization module' to drive the decarbonization of the energy mix, as shown in Figure 11.5. These new market building blocks are designed

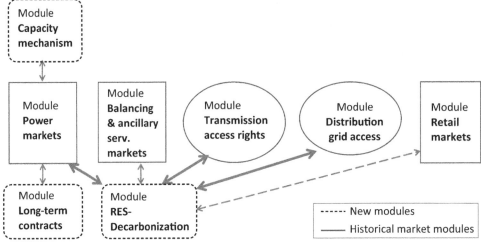

Source: Roques and Finon (2017).

Figure 11.5   *The initial electricity market modules and the three additional long-term*
modules in the hybrid market model

to complement the revenues from the energy markets, to guarantee the recovery of fixed costs and to de-risk investment via some risk-sharing arrangements between producers and consumers, and to support the deployment of the chosen clean technologies.

However, the implementation of these additional modules raises the issue of the consistency of these new modules with the initial wholesale market building blocks and their subsequent evolution. These policy and regulatory interventions have indeed often been national and uncoordinated across Europe, and therefore had significant impacts on electricity European markets and further undermined the ability of energy market prices to provide adequate coordination signals to market participants. Across Europe, policy interventions have created a number of inconsistencies with the market arrangements, leading to merit-order distortions, system balancing challenges, insufficient valuation of the flexibility of resources, or the lack of coordination of generation and transmission system development.

This marks a significant shift away from the initial theoretical textbook electricity market design that underpinned the liberalization process in the 1980s and 1990s, in which investment decisions are made by market participants based on price expectations. In other words, the initial reforms were based on the belief that the electricity sector could be freed up from policy interventions to influence the generation mix, and that market signals could ensure both an efficient short-term coordination between market players for system operation and plant dispatch as well as provide long-term coordination signals for investment in generation so that an optimal mix and capacity adequacy can be achieved in a timely way.

As discussed in Section 3 and in the previous paragraphs, the change in policy objectives and in the dominant technologies' cost structure has in fact led to a revival of national policy interventions and to the implementation of new market modules. In the next paragraphs, we describe in a more concrete way two sets of interventions for

(1) security of supply; and (2) support for clean technologies in European electricity markets, and the way in which these are affecting the market integration process and raise new market integration challenges. We review these in turn in the next paragraphs.

4.4.1 Security of supply: the capacity mechanism module

There is growing belief across Europe that the current markets cannot guarantee reliability of supply in every situation in the long term for various reasons, including: (1) price caps and barriers to scarcity pricing (the so-called 'missing money' issue); (2) aversion to risk associated with investing on the basis of uncertain revenues; and (3) the difficulty related to hedging or transferring risk on a long-term basis (Cramton, Ockenfel and Stoft 2013, Joskow 2008, Roques 2008, Roques and Finon 2008). This issue is exacerbated by the development of variable renewables that amplifies price volatility in peak hours and creates greater uncertainty for annual sales by peaking units (Cramton et al. 2013).

Fundamentally, the origin of the resource adequacy problem lies in two issues: (1) a market imperfection, which entails the absence of price-reactive demand – at least for the time being for a large number of consumers until smart meters are deployed and time-varying tariffs become widespread; and (2) the willingness of policymakers to intervene and define an administrative security of supply criterion that may differ from the socially optimal one.

In parallel to the reforms addressing market imperfections, most European countries have also introduced a capacity remuneration mechanism (CRM). There is a wide range of options – strategic reserves focused on some existing or specific new units, regulated capacity payments, capacity obligations on suppliers, forward capacity auctioning and reliability options auctioning – with different attributes in terms of effectiveness, market power mitigation, cost efficiency and risk management. The scope of this chapter does not allow a comparison of these mechanisms, which are well covered in the literature – for example, Roques (2008, 2019), Finon and Pignon (2008) and Roques and Verhaeghe (2015).

Figure 11.6 shows that most countries in the EU have taken steps to introduce or reform a capacity mechanism, using different approaches. The result is a patchwork of different national capacity mechanisms that could undermine the further integration of European electricity markets.

I have explained in previous publications – see, for example, Roques and Verhaeghe (2015) and Roques (2019) – that the drivers of capacity mechanisms across Europe are different depending on the country considered, such that it is unlikely that a common approach at the European level will be practical or even suitable. But I explained that there would be merits in working toward some degree of coordination to minimize the potential distortions associated with different capacity mechanism approaches.

A framework for cross-border participation in capacity mechanisms has started to emerge as part of the Clean Energy Package but will need to be developed further in the coming years. I list below a number of preliminary steps that would be necessary prerequisites for the coordination of capacity mechanisms across borders (see Glachant, Rossetto and Vasconcelos, 2017, Roques 2019, Roques and Verhaeghe 2015):

1. A critical first step for a coordinated approach across European countries consists in defining explicit reliability standard criteria in each country and ensuring their consistency (for example, loss of load expectation or target reserve margin).

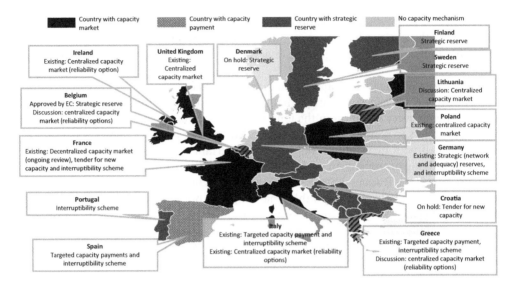

| Country with capacity market | Country with capacity payment | Country with strategic reserve | No capacity mechanism |

Finland
Strategic reserve

Ireland
Existing: Centralized capacity market (reliability option)

United Kingdom
Existing: Centralized capacity market

Denmark
On hold: Strategic reserve

Sweden
Strategic reserve

Lithuania
Discussion: Centralized capacity market

Belgium
Approved by EC: Strategic reserve
Discussion: centralized capacity market (reliability options)

Poland
Existing: centralized capacity market

France
Existing: Decentralized capacity market (ongoing review), tender for new capacity and interruptibility scheme

Germany
Existing: Strategic (network and adequacy) reserves, and interruptibility scheme

Portugal
Interruptibility scheme

Croatia
On hold: Tender for new capacity

Italy
Existing: Targeted capacity payment and interruptibility scheme
Existing: Centralized capacity market (reliability options)

Greece
Existing: Targeted capacity payment, interruptibility scheme
Discussion: centralized capacity market (reliability options)

Spain
Targeted capacity payments and interruptibility scheme

Source: Updated from Roques (2019).

Figure 11.6   Implementation of capacity mechanisms in Europe as of 2019

2. Regional coordination of TSOs is necessary to define a common methodological framework for resource adequacy assessment, as well as to define common certification and verification procedures for plants and demand response that will participate in capacity mechanisms across borders.

3. Most importantly, TSOs will need to develop on a regional basis a common coordination framework, including operational rules, to deal with situations of joint system stress across borders. At times of capacity shortage in one or two countries, there need to be clear rules and corresponding operational practices in place to ensure the physical delivery of energy according to the commercial contracts that have been signed.

4.4.2   The green agenda – mechanisms to support investment in clean technologies

There is a large literature that investigates the need for out-of-market support mechanisms to promote investment in clean technologies, in addition to the implementation of a carbon price (Grubb and Newbery 2008, Newbery 2011, Roques and Finon 2008, 2013, or Chapter 14 in this handbook). These mechanisms can have a double function to both subsidize the deployment of immature technologies in their infant phase and to support de-risking for the more mature ones to facilitate investment. The scope of this chapter does not allow us to revisit this literature in detail and I focus instead on the latter issue – that is, the role of some form of long-term arrangements to de-risk investment in clean technologies.

As the clean technologies mature and become competitive, the role of the support mechanisms that took the form of long-term arrangements changes, and concentrates mainly on the de-risking necessary to facilitate financing of capital-intensive technologies rather than providing a higher revenue level than these technologies would earn in the market. Across Europe, different countries have in the past years revisited the first generation of support mechanisms for renewables by, for example, phasing out feed-in tariffs and green certificate schemes and replacing these with a range of alternative arrangements. Although quite diverse, these arrangements typically share the same objectives of facilitating investment by securing revenues in the long term, whilst introducing competitive pressure, often via the auctioning of long-term contracts.

4.2 Key Principles Underlying the Emergence of a New Hybrid Market Model

Despite the diversity across European countries of market reforms and state interventions, a new market model based on the same fundamental principles seems to emerge in most European countries. This model is based on the fundamental premise that policymakers will continue to intervene and dictate the generation mix to decarbonize the power sector.

This model features competition in two steps, with 'competition for the market' (that is, for the investment in new generating capacity) in the form of tenders for longer-term contracts followed by 'competition in the market' (that is, to organize an efficient system operation) based on the set of short-term markets, as described in Figure 11.7. The reader interested in the international experience and lessons on such markets' organized competition in two steps are referred to Roques (2015) and Roques and Finon (2017). Schmalensee points out in Chapter 2 the advantages of the traditional utilities in the US

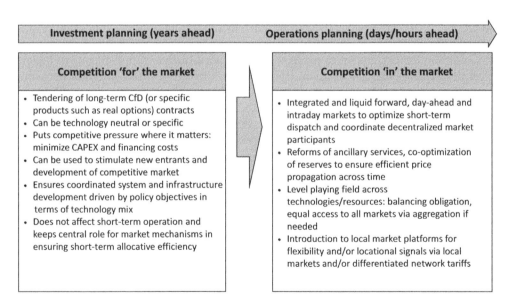

Note: CfD = contracts for differences.

Source: Adapted from Roques (2015), p. 6.

Figure 11.7   Two-step market with competition 'for the market' and competition 'in the market'

that can rely on the 'classic integrated resource planning' to deal with some of the coordination and planning challenges associated with the new changes that characterize the new regime.

The first step 'competition for the market' typically involves the tendering of long-term contracts based on the technology and infrastructure indicative planning processes at national or, ideally in the future, regional and European levels. Long-term commitments help facilitate investment and financing of low-carbon as well as storage and other flexibility resources (Roques and Finon 2008, 2013). The tendering of long-term contracts concentrates competition on the investment decision, which is the most important cost-minimization driver for capital-intensive technologies. Such long-term contracts and auctioning processes involve different products depending on the local electricity system needs, and there is currently a great diversity of approaches across Europe. One key issue is to ensure that these contracts are designed in a way that minimizes any potential distortions of the markets (Roques 2015).

The second step 'competition in the market' comprises the current set of trading arrangements for energy across different timeframes, as well as the common platforms for the procurement of balancing reserves cross-border by the TSOs, which are being implemented as part of the network codes (the platforms PICASSO and MARI). Further progress will be needed on several fronts in the next years, as highlighted by the Clean Energy Package, to ensure a better functioning of these energy markets that will remain the cornerstone of the EU market model. In particular, some significant gains are achievable by improving the interface between system operations and market operations, which will require tackling the difficult issue of cross-border capacity made available to the market, as well as the broader issue of the current suboptimal bidding zones that result in significant congestion in a number of countries.

In addition, the current set of markets will also need further improvements to better reflect the value of scarcity in prices (for example, through a better interface between reserves procurement and energy markets). In Chapter 8 of this handbook, Baldick et al. provide a thorough description of the benefits associated with their implementation across the US states that have liberalized their power industry of 'co-optimization' of energy and ancillary services, so that opportunity costs are automatically incorporated into the price of ancillary services without any need for estimation by market participants. This co-optimization has improved the efficiency of dispatch compared with separate procurement of energy and ancillary services. They also describe the implementation of scarcity pricing via operating reserve demand curves (ORDCs) in Texas.

The development of local flexibility platforms could also be useful to provide locational price signals and allow the management of the growing congestion at the distribution level, which will create new coordination challenges with the existing trading platforms and balancing reserve procurement platforms managed by TSOs.

This new European market model organized in two steps would create a set of new challenges to define the products to be contracted in the long term, to identify the needs for the resources to be contracted, and to coordinate and harmonize the types of contracts and their interface with the existing trading arrangements. Whilst the scope of this chapter does not allow for an extensive discussion of the challenges associated with the implementation and coordination across countries of such a new market model, the interested reader is referred to Roques (2015), in which I provide further discussions of the necessary implementation steps and conditions for the emergence of such a new market model.

The coordination of such a two-step market approach and of some of the underlying planning and processes and deployment of clean technologies and key infrastructures could yield potential significant economic benefits for consumers, as discussed in Section 3. However, this would require as a prerequisite further coordination across European countries (or at least among policy regions grouping neighbouring countries) of the key policy decisions affecting the first step (the competition for the market) – that is, further coordination of the planning and tendering processes for the deployment of clean technologies and the supporting critical infrastructures. For the reader interested in the concrete measures that could be taken to foster a stronger cooperation for policy and regulation on a regional basis, in a recent study I have put forward the concept of 'policy regions', based on a three-layer coordination forum involving TSOs, national regulatory authorities and a range of stakeholders at a regional and European level (Roques 2015, Roques and Verhaege 2016).

5.   CONCLUSION

Twenty-five years after the start of liberalization of electricity markets in Europe, the European project to integrate electricity markets has reached a crossroads. On the one hand, there have been significant achievements in removing barriers to cross-border trade, and the successive legislations and regulations have driven some degree of convergence in market design and improved trade efficiency – notably, through the implementation of day-ahead market coupling. However, progress has been slowed by the technical challenges associated with integrating markets with different designs and governance approaches. This originates in the initial choice not to impose a standard market design, but instead to try to focus on the harmonization of some of the technical rules affecting cross-border trade.

On the other hand, I argued in this chapter that the changes in policy objectives in the past decade – with the emergence of concerns related to security of supply and policy commitments to fight climate change – have led to a resurgence of policy interventions and created new challenges for European power market integration. National policies have not been coordinated and have led to a patchwork of new market and regulatory mechanisms to support the development of clean technologies and ensure security of supply (capacity mechanisms). I also showed how the changes in the dominant technologies (that is, variable renewables) cost structure and generation patterns have led to a shift in focus toward the improvement of the design of markets close to real time as well as the emergence of tendering processes for long-term contracts to reduce the risks associated with the financing of these technologies.

The last section of the chapter then explored how the mechanisms implemented at a national level to support investment in clean technologies and maintain security of supply are leading to the emergence of a new 'hybrid market' model, mixing liberalized markets with state intervention and long-term contracts. I showed that such hybrid approach takes different forms across Europe but presents some common features such as an organization in two steps with 'competition for the market' via tenders of long-term contracts followed by 'competition in the market' via short-term power exchanges coupled at the continental level.

I put forward that the coordination of a two-step market approach and of some of the underlying planning and processes and deployment of clean technologies could yield potential significant economic benefits for consumers. However, this would require as a prerequisite further coordination across European countries (or at least among policy regions grouping neighbouring countries) of the planning and tendering processes for the deployment of clean technologies and the deployment of critical infrastructures. In conclusion, the main challenge in the next years to preserve and deepen the benefits of integrated markets in Europe therefore lies primarily in the coordination of the national policies driving interventions in markets as well as the associated governance issues.

NOTES

*   The author would like to thank Jean-Michel Glachant, Paul Joskow, Jan Horst Keppler, as well as anonymous referees for their useful suggestions to improve the chapter. The views expressed and any remaining mistakes or inaccuracy remain the sole responsibility of the author. This chapter has benefited from the support of the Chaire European Electricity Markets (CEEM) of the Université Paris-Dauphine under the aegis of the Foundation Paris-Dauphine, supported by RTE, EDF, EPEX Spot and Total Direct Energie. The views and opinions expressed in this chapter are those of the author and do not necessarily reflect those of the partners of the CEEM.
1.   The 'Clean energy for all Europeans package' is a set of new legislations and rules completed on 22 May 2019. For a description, see, for instance, https://ec.europa.eu/info/news/clean-energy-all-europeans-package-completed-good-consumers-good-growth-and-jobs-and-good-planet-2019-may-22_en, accessed 11 July 2021.
2.   Network codes are a set of rules drafted by the European Network of Transmission System Operators (ENTSO-E), with guidance from the Agency for the Cooperation of Energy Regulators (ACER), to facilitate the harmonization, integration and efficiency of the European electricity market. See https://www.entsoe.eu/network_codes/ for a description of these network codes (accessed 11 July 2021). In addition, for further details please consider Schittekatte, Reif and Meeus (2020).
3.   There were significant differences across countries as numerous local utilities dominated in some countries (for example, Germany or the Netherlands), whilst national monopolies existed in other countries.
4.   Market coupling in wholesale power markets uses implicit auctions in which players do not receive allocations of cross-border capacity themselves but bid for energy on their exchange. The exchanges then use the available transmission capacity (ATC) to minimize the price differences between two or more areas. In so doing, market coupling optimizes the allocation of interconnection capacity and maximizes social welfare. This process increases price convergence between market areas and eliminates counterflows. Price differentials send a price signal for investments in cross-border transmission capacities.

REFERENCES

Agency for the Cooperation of Energy Regulators and Council of European Energy Regulators (ACER/CEER) (2017), *Annual Report on the Results of Monitoring the Internal Electricity and Gas Markets in 2016*, October.
Annan-Phan, S. and F. Roques (2018), 'Market integration and wind generation: an empirical analysis of the impact of wind generation on cross-border power prices', *The Energy Journal*, **39** (3), 1–23.
Boiteux, M. (1949), 'La tarification des demandes en point: application de la théorie de la vente au coût marginal', *Revue Générale de l'Electricité*, **58**, 321–40.
Boiteux, M. (1951), 'La tarification au coût marginal et les demandes aléatoires', *Cahiers du Séminaire d'Econométrie*, **1**, 56–69.

Booz & Company, D. Newbery and G. Strbac et al. (2013), *Benefits of an Integrated European Energy Market*, report prepared for Directorate-General Energy European Commission, July.

Cramton, P., A. Ockenfel and S. Stoft (2013), 'Capacity market fundamentals', *Economics of Energy & Environmental Policy*, **2** (2), 27–45.

European Commission (2007), *Communication from the Commission: Inquiry Pursuant to Article 17 of Regulation (EC) No 1/2003 into the European Gas and Electricity Sectors*, final report, 10 January, COM(2006) 851 final, accessed 11 July 2021 at https://eur-lex.europa.eu/LexUriServ/LexUriServ.do?uri=C OM:2006:0851:FIN:EN:PDF.

European Commission (2011), *Public Consultation on the Governance Framework for the European Day-ahead Market Coupling*, 28 November, D(2011) 1176339, accessed 11 July 2021 at https://ec.europa.eu/energy/sites/ener/files/documents/20120229_market_coupling.pdf.

European Commission (2013), *A 2030 Framework for Climate and Energy Policies*, Green Paper, COM(2013) 169, 27 March.

European Commission (2014), *Communication from the Commission to the European Parliament and the Council: European Energy Security Strategy*, COM(2014) 330 final, 28 May.

European Commission (2019), Chapter IV on Resource Adequacy, Article 21 on Cross-border participation in capacity mechanisms in *Regulation (EU) 2019/943 of the European Parliament and of the Council of 5 June 2019 on the internal market for electricity*, accessed 11 July 2021 at https://eur-lex.europa.eu/legal-content/EN/TXT/PDF/?uri=CELEX:32019R0943&from=en.

European Network of Transmission System Operators for Electricity (ENTSO-E) (2017), *Annual Report 2016*.

European Network of Transmission System Operators for Electricity (ENTSO-E) (2019), *Power Facts Europe 2019*.

European Parliament and Council (1996), *Directive (96/92/EC) of the European Parliament and of the Council of 19 December 1996 Concerning Common Rules for the Internal Market in Electricity*, accessed 11 July 2021 at https://op.europa.eu/en/publication-detail/-/publication/b9d99092-0a5f-4513-8073-74109730b1ad/langu age-en.

European Parliament and Council (2003), *Directive 2003/54/EC of the European Parliament and of the Council of 26 June 2003 Concerning Common Rules for the Internal Market in Electricity*, accessed 11 July 2021 at https://eur-lex.europa.eu/legal-content/EN/TXT/?uri=CELEX per cent3A32003L0054.

European Parliament and Council (2009), *Directive 2009/72/EC of the European Parliament and of the Council of 13 July 2009 Concerning Common Rules for the Internal Market in Electricity*, accessed 11 July 2021 at https://eur-lex.europa.eu/legal-content/EN/ALL/?uri=CELEX per cent3A32009L0072.

European Parliament and Council (2019), *Proposal for a Regulation of the European Parliament and of the Council on the Internal Market for Electricity (recast)*, ST 5070 2019 INIT, accessed 11 July 2021 at https://eur-lex.europa.eu/legal-content/EN/TXT/PDF/?uri=CONSIL:ST_5070_2019_INIT&from=EN.

Finon D. and V. Pignon (2008), 'Electricity and long-term capacity adequacy: the quest for regulatory mechanism compatible with electricity market', *Utilities Policy*, **16** (3), 143–58.

Glachant J.-M. and Y. Perez (2009), 'The achievement of electricity competitive reforms: a governance structure problem?', in C. Ménard and M. Ghertman (eds), *Regulation, Deregulation, Reregulation – Institutional Perspectives*, Cheltenham, UK and Northampton, MA, USA: Edward Elgar Publishing, pp. 196–215.

Glachant, J.-M., N. Rossetto and J. Vasconcelos (2017), *Moving the Electricity Transmission System Towards a Decarbonised and Integrated Europe: Missing Pillars and Roadblocks*, technical report, Florence School of Regulation, April, accessed 11 July 2021 at https://cadmus.eui.eu/handle/1814/46624.

Grubb, M. and D. Newbery (2008), 'Pricing carbon for electricity generation: national and international dimensions', in M. Grubb, T. Jamasb and M. G. Pollitt (eds), *Delivering a Low Carbon Electricity System: Technologies, Economies and Policy*, Cambridge, UK: Cambridge University Press, pp. 278–313.

Jamasb, T. and M. G. Pollitt (2005), 'Electricity market reform in the European Union: review of progress toward liberalization and integration', *The Energy Journal*, **26** (Special Issue), 11–41.

Joskow, P. L. (2008), 'Capacity payments in imperfect electricity markets: need and design', *Utilities Policy*, **16** (3), 159–70.

Meeus, L. and R. Belmans (2008), 'Electricity market integration in Europe', in *Proceedings of the 16th Power Systems Computation Conference*, Glasgow, 14–18 July, pp. 1505–9.

Moffatt Associates (2007), 'Market coupling: key to EU power market integration', *APX Energy Viewpoints*, Autumn, 5–9.

Newbery, D. (2011), 'Reforming competitive electricity markets to meet environmental targets', *Economics of Energy & Environmental Policy*, **1** (1), 69–82.

Newbery, D., G. Strbac and I. Viehoff (2016), 'The benefits of integrating European electricity markets', *Energy Policy*, **94**, 253–63.

Pollitt, M. (2019), 'The single market in electricity: an economic assessment', *Review of Industrial Organization*, **55** (1), 63–87.

Roques, F. (2008), 'Capacity mechanisms and institutional context: healing symptoms or causes?', *Utilities Policy*, **16** (3), 171–83.
Roques, F. (2015), 'Toward the Target Model 2.0 – policy recommendations for a sustainable EU power market design', *FTI-CL Energy*, June, accessed 11 July 2021 at https://www.fticonsulting-emea.com/~/media/Files/us-files/intelligence/intelligence-research/toward-the-target-model-20--executive-summary.pdf.
Roques, F. (2019), 'Counting on the neighbours: challenges and practical approaches for cross-border participation in capacity mechanisms', *Oxford Review of Economic Policy*, **35** (2), 332–49.
Roques, F. and D. Finon (2008), 'Financing arrangements and industrial organisation for new nuclear build in electricity markets', *Competition and Regulation in Network Industries*, **9** (3), 247–82.
Roques, F. and D. Finon (2013), 'European electricity market reforms: the "visible hand" of public coordination', *Economics of Energy & Environmental Policy*, **2** (2), 107–24.
Roques, F. and D. Finon (2017), 'Adapting electricity markets to decarbonisation and security of supply objectives: toward a hybrid regime', *Energy Policy*, **105**, 584–96.
Roques, F. and C. Verhaeghe (2015), 'Different approaches for capacity mechanisms in Europe: rationale and potential for coordination?', in L. Hancher, A. de Hauteclocque and M. Sadowska (eds.), *Capacity Mechanisms in the EU Energy Market: Law, Politics and Economics*, Oxford: Oxford University Press, pp. 79–94.
Roques, F. and C. Verhaeghe (2016), *Options for the Future of Power System Regional Coordination – Report for ENTSO-E*, 8 December, accessed 11 July 2021 at https://docstore.entsoe.eu/Documents/Publications/Position% per cent20papers% per cent20and% per cent20reports/entsoe_fti_161207.pdf.
Schittekatte, T., V. Reif and L. Meeus (2020), *The EU Electricity Network Codes (2020 edition)*, technical report, Florence School of Regulation, June, accessed 11 July 2021 at https://cadmus.eui.eu/handle/1814/67610.

PART II

ADAPTING TO NEW TECHNOLOGIES AND NEW POLICY PRIORITIES

12. New technologies on the supply side
Nils May and Karsten Neuhoff

1. INTRODUCTION TO NEW RENEWABLE TECHNOLOGIES ON THE SUPPLY SIDE

New renewable technologies are revolutionizing the electricity supply side. They increasingly substitute for thermal power plants emitting greenhouse gases that drive climate change and can reduce dependency on fossil fuel imports. Their different production and ownership characteristics require adjustments of the electricity market design and induce changes to the market structure. A portfolio of new technologies determined by their current and projected costs, their resource and energy potential and their positive and negative externalities will produce the majority of electricity in the future.

Based on these criteria, wind and solar power are the most promising of this class of new renewable energies. Globally, conventional renewable energies such as hydro power, traditional biomass and waste incineration continue to play large roles but have limited growth potential, such that they lose in relevance compared to newer renewable energy technologies. Wind and solar power have huge potential for generation growth (Deng et al. 2015) and have seen tremendous cost reductions over the last decades (BSW Solar 2016, Fraunhofer ISE 2019b, International Renewable Energy Agency [IRENA] 2018b, Statista 2019), leading to their strongly increasing global deployment (IRENA 2018a). Figure 12.1 shows how the global average costs of onshore wind power almost halved between 2000 and 2017. The development is even more dramatic for solar photovoltaics, where costs fell by more than 80 per cent. Paired with higher efficiencies and reductions in financing costs (Egli, Steffen and Schmidt 2018), this makes wind power and solar photovoltaics the central technologies for decarbonizing electricity systems. For example, the International Energy Agency's *World Energy Outlook 2018* (IEA 2018) foresees a more than five-fold increase in generation from wind and solar power between 2017 and 2040 in its Stated Policies Scenario (formerly, the New Policies Scenario), and a nine-fold increase in the Sustainable Development Scenario parameterized to achieve the goals of the Paris Agreement.

Biomass also has favourable attributes, particularly dispatchability, which makes integration into electricity systems built around thermal power plants easier. In countries where cheap feedstock is abundant, generating electricity from modern biomass can be a central component of decarbonizing the electricity supply. Yet, the higher value of its use in aviation and freight transportation, as well as easy storability for decentralized and seasonal energy needs like heating, suggest that there is limited potential for deployment in the electricity sector given that the potential for sustainable biomass is limited. Additionally, biomass combustion can emit significant quantities of particulate matter, leading to local air pollution (Sigsgaard et al. 2015).

Other technologies have interesting characteristics but are more limited by their resource potential or stages of technological and economic development. Geothermal energy holds more promise for heating purposes than for generating electricity. Electricity

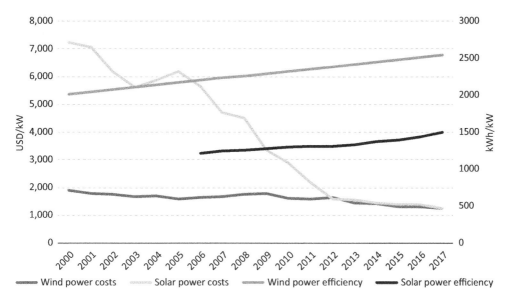

Sources: Based on IRENA (2018a and 2018b) and Fraunhofer ISE (2019b). The costs of solar photovoltaics are for Germany, based on BSW Solar (2016) and Statista (2019).

*Figure 12.1   Global development of costs and efficiencies of wind and solar power,
2000–2017*

generation from geothermal energy is constrained to specific locations where it can rep-resent an economically and technically viable part of the portfolio. Tidal energy, while potentially generating electricity reliably, depends on specific local topology and involves large engineering-type investments that have limited cost reduction potential, and thus does not have the resource potential to cover a significant share of global electricity demand. Last, wave energy, with, in principle, a large resource potential, is at an early technological stage and has yet to overcome these challenges and demonstrate potential for economic viability.

The decreased costs of renewables have strongly improved their competitiveness against conventional technologies and have been changing the role of remuneration mechanisms. Initially, policy support was granted because renewable energies produce electricity free of greenhouse gas emissions, because of active industry policy (building up a solar and wind power industry) and to support learning (Newbery 2018). However, renewable energies were not competitive with thermal power plants based on traditional cost assessments as the negative externalities of coal, gas and nuclear power plants such as greenhouse gas emissions, import dependency and nuclear waste were not reflected in their respective prices (Newbery 2018, Roth and Lawrence 2004). Currently, investments in wind and solar power cost less than new investments in thermal capacity (Fraunhofer ISE 2018b; Kruger, Eberhard and Swartz 2018). Further, even a second threshold is being reached more frequently: the levelized cost of electricity (LCOE) of new wind and solar power is lower than the operating costs of gas and hard coal plants that depend on fuel cost and carbon prices. With cheaper renewable energies and increasing carbon prices, this indicates the competitiveness of wind and solar energy and questions the economic sustainability of investments in and, increasingly, the operation of thermal power plants. Low financing costs and local acceptance underpin the competitiveness of renewables. Moreover, to facilitate the integration of high shares of intermittent renewables, various approaches to deal with their intermittency must be applied and developed.

2.   ONSHORE WIND POWER

Onshore wind power has been a mature technology for a relatively long time. Already in 2000, around 17 gigawatts (GW) were installed globally, almost exclusively in Germany, Denmark, the US and Spain. Deployment grew exponentially until around 2009 and growth has stabilized since then, as depicted in Figure 12.2. For example, net additions were only a third higher in 2017 than in 2009. Over time, the regional balance shifted from a European and US focus to a more balanced global distribution. By 2017, globally, almost 500 GW of wind power had been deployed, of which 33 per cent was in China, followed by 31 per cent in the EU and 18 per cent in the US. Installation volumes in individual countries are volatile. Adding installation volumes at the maximum historic level for each country would have resulted in a global installation volume of 87 GW. However, in any one year, global installations never exceeded the 2017 level of 42 GW. Producers likely benefited from the stabilization of the pooled global demand compared with more volatile national demand patterns. The comparison also suggests that, in principle, it would be possible to create a project pipeline to double the global installation volume if projects were developed in all countries in parallel at the higher end of historic rates.

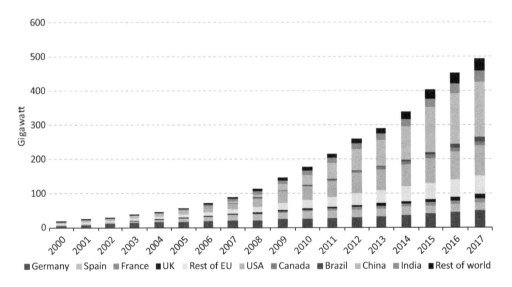

Source: Based on IRENA (2018a).

Figure 12.2   Cumulative onshore wind power capacity, 2000–2017

Onshore wind power has great global potential. Output hinges on wind speeds, as wind speed affects potential output in cubic form – a doubling of wind speeds increases output by a factor of eight. Jacobson and Delucchi (2011) estimate that if 5 megawatt (MW) wind turbines were to serve half of all global energy demand by 2030, wind parks would require about 1.2 per cent of all global land area. Lu, McElroy and Kiviluoma (2009) estimate that disregarding all land covered by permanent ice, forested or urban areas, using 20 per cent of the land suitable for wind power deployment by 2.5 MW wind turbines is sufficient to cover current global energy demand.

The cost of a wind turbine is the main cost component of wind power, responsible for around two-thirds of all costs (Stehly et al. 2018). Half of this is for the components contained in the nacelle, which sits atop the tower and connects to the rotor blades, and includes, for example, the generator and the gearbox, and the rest is approximately equally split between rotor and tower. The remaining third of the cost is linked to electrical infrastructure and installation, and for insurance and financing during the construction period. For offshore wind power, the turbine makes up only a third of the cost, despite its common larger dimensioning for offshore use. Installation, electricity connections and financing-related costs during installation represent half the cost due to considerably higher costs for the electrical infrastructure (a quarter of the cost) and for the substructure and foundation (another 14 per cent).

Operation and maintenance constitute a growing share of overall costs of wind power projects. For onshore wind power, IRENA (2018b) estimates a cost share in the LCOE of around a quarter, and thus well above the frequent notion that wind power has no variable costs. However, most of these costs are quasi-fixed – that is, not linked to output per se but reflect annual maintenance works (Wiser and Bolinger 2018). Unlike capital expenditures, costs for operation and maintenance have not been falling but remained roughly constant in the last decade (ibid.), reflecting labour intensity with limited technological learning.

Onshore wind power has experienced considerable learning effects since its commercial beginnings in the 1980s. Prices per generated kilowatt-hour (kWh) fell, towers grew taller, capacities increased and rotor blades became longer. For example, the average nameplate capacity for new installations in Germany in 2000 was 1.1 MW, the hubs were at 71 metres (m) and the rotor diameter was 58 m. In contrast, the average new installation in 2018 saw a threefold increase in capacity to 3.3 MW, a doubling of hub height to 133 m and rotor blades of 118 m (Fraunhofer IEE 2019a). New and more diverse wind turbines allow project developers to match the turbines to site characteristics.

Modern turbines are commonly considered more 'system friendly' than previous generations as their power production is less concentrated around periods of high wind speeds. They have lower specific powers – that is, less generator capacity relative to the area swept by the rotor blades. The power output at times of higher wind speeds is thus 'capped' at a lower level. Falling specific powers can be observed – for example, in the 2010s in the US (Wiser and Bolinger 2018), in Denmark (Dalla Riva, Hethey and Vītiņa 2017) and in Germany (Fraunhofer IEE 2018a). With relatively longer rotor blades in comparison to generator capacity, at any time the turbines can capture more kinetic energy from the wind and thus generate more electricity at low and medium wind speeds. This is considered beneficial for power systems based on variable renewable energies: power supply is relatively scarce when the wind is weak, such that the value and price of the output of system-friendly turbines is relatively high (Hirth and Müller 2016, May 2017). Moreover, their capacity factors are higher and produce electricity more constantly. Across countries, capacity factors have been increasing since 2010, reaching almost 30 per cent for new installations (IRENA 2018b) on average.

Turbine costs depend on larger commodity market developments, since much of the costs are for materials like steel, cement, copper and iron. Increasing material costs were the reason costs did not decrease despite some learning in the early 2000s in most countries, and why, for example, German feed-in tariffs for wind power barely declined in the 2000s (IWR 2019a, 2019b). Since peak prices for commodities in 2008, wind turbine costs per capacity have fallen strongly by around a third (Bloomberg New Energy Finance [BNEF] 2018). However, this ignores the fact that, per installed MW, turbines have been undergoing a trend towards longer rotor blades and higher hub heights, enabling higher capacity factors (i.e., output per installed capacity), such that LCOEs have actually decreased even more strongly in many countries (IRENA 2018b) (see Figure 12.1).

Future cost reductions are most likely to emerge from higher capacity factors based on higher efficiencies and improved turbine designs. IRENA (2016) estimates that about half of all cost reductions until 2025 will be due to higher capacity factors and another third from lower costs for towers, turbines and project development. Improvements in operations and maintenance such as higher reliability, use of best practices and improved anticipating maintenance are expected to lower costs by another sixth (ibid.). Further cost reductions can, for example, result from increasing automation in rotor blade manufacturing, a so far mostly manual task. Manual production results in high tolerances and requires high security margins on other parts as well, which could be reduced were production more automated (Rosemann et al. 2014).

3.　OFFSHORE WIND POWER

Offshore wind power developed later than onshore wind power due to more complex technology, infrastructure requirements and resulting initially higher costs. Towards significant investments in offshore wind power, onshore wind power paved the way by increasing the size of turbines to make proper use of the high and stable winds at sea. Thus, planning barriers due to land restrictions on land can be overcome, leading countries with large offshore potential like the UK to focus on offshore deployment over onshore.

Offshore wind power has developed heterogeneously around the world and is still in its infancy in most countries. In 2014, the UK had installed half of global capacity and Denmark was the only other country that had installed more than 1 GW. Until 2018, only Belgium, Germany and China followed to install more than 1 GW (IRENA 2019), making China the only non-EU country to have installed larger volumes of offshore wind power, as can be seen in Figure 12.3. With learning effects and falling costs, deployment has been picking up rapidly, moving offshore wind power from being a niche technology to becoming an increasingly important element of some countries' energy transitions.

Offshore wind power benefits from higher and more constant wind speeds and a limited correlation of wind patterns with onshore locations. Turbine designs reflect this, and

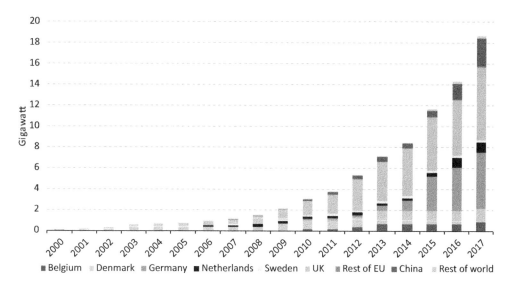

Source: Based on IRENA (2018a).

Figure 12.3 Cumulative offshore wind power capacity, 2000–2017

wind turbines have higher specific powers and lower hub heights than onshore turbines. With high wind speeds at sea, a high output at low and medium wind speed matters less than making use of the frequent high wind speeds, facilitated by a large generator capacity. While standard turbines on land have capacities between 3 and 5 MW, new developments for using offshore can easily double that. Wind speeds offshore suffice to enable global average capacity factors of more than 40 per cent (IRENA 2018b). The global potential for offshore wind power deployment is uncertain, as technologies like floating turbines are still emerging, opening up vast areas to deployment in deep waters, but might well exceed the potential of wind power on land in many parts of the world (Deng et al. 2015).

The costs of connecting offshore wind parks to land depend on the distance from shore and the depth of water. The grid connection can be either planned and paid for by grid operators, which shields offshore developers from risk and thus increases competition in the project development phase, or by the offshore project developers themselves to introduce competition for the connection (Girard et al. 2019). Near-shore turbines benefit from less costly transmission and, usually, from lower water depths, such that less steel is needed for the towers. To reduce connection costs, clusters of wind parks can be connected to land together. To reduce costs in deep waters, floating foundations are being developed to access deep locations where the steel for the towers would cost too much.

While connecting them costs more, far-shore turbines produce more electricity and are less visible, thus reducing issues of public acceptance, including concerns about impacts on tourism. In general, the further out the turbines, the stronger the wind, increasing capacity factors to up to 50 per cent and reducing the cost per MWh.

4. SOLAR PHOTOVOLTAICS

The direct conversion of sunlight into usable electricity with photovoltaics (PV) has experienced rapid growth. PA expanded mostly in Germany and Japan in the early 2000s. Notably, neither country has particularly abundant solar resources. Yet, both countries supported PV through stable policy frameworks that drove down financing costs and enabled households and project developers to invest under reliable conditions so that domestic industries and supply chains could emerge (Quitzow, Roehrkasten and Jaenicke 2016). By 2005, more than three-quarters of all PV was installed in these two countries (IRENA 2018a).

The regional balance shifted over time, as depicted in Figure 12.4. China installed its first GW only in 2011 but deployed the technology much faster than any other country, becoming the global leader in 2014 and with a third of all installed capacity in 2017. Many other countries have seen increasing deployment with the rapid expansion of solar panels. India, for example, set a target of 100 GW of capacity by 2022, although it had installed a mere 5 GW when the target was published in 2015. In contrast, several European countries have scaled back their annual installation volumes since around 2012, and PV expansion in individual countries varies widely over time. If all countries were to install as much capacity as they did in their maximum year, new installations would add up to 133 GW, considerably more than 2017's 92 GW (IRENA 2018b).

Three main technologies dominate global deployment: multicrystalline silicon, monocrystalline silicon and thin film. Crystalline technologies dominate global deployment, with more of 90 per cent of all historic and current installations. Multicrystalline modules have taken increasing market shares, such that they are used in about two-thirds of all new installations in 2017 (Fraunhofer ISE 2019b). The global potential for the deployment of PV is vast and exceeds the potential of other renewable energy

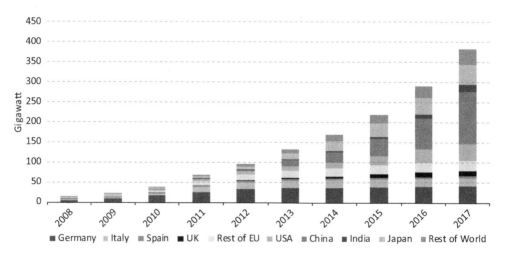

Source: Based on IRENA (2018a).

Figure 12.4 Cumulative PV capacity, 2000–2017

technologies, with the potential to generate many times the current global energy consumption (Deng et al. 2015).

Total installation costs per kW have dropped more than 70 per cent in most countries between 2010 and 2017 (IRENA 2018b), despite higher module efficiencies – that is, a higher output per installed capacity, such that LCOEs have decreased by more than 90 per cent since the beginning of PV in the early 2000s from several hundred €/mWh to new record lows of less than 30 $/MWh (IRENA 2018b). Inverters, hardware for racking and mounting and the mechanical installation constitute significant shares of cost in addition to the modules.

The largest contribution to the 70 per cent reduction of costs per installed kW can be attributed to a more than 90 per cent reduction in PV module costs since the early 2000s. While initially dominating overall investment costs, module costs now only constitute between a third and half of installation costs (ibid.). These cost reductions reflect both large-scale learning by doing and the effects of economies of scale. Crystalline silicon modules are used almost exclusively nowadays and have outcompeted thin-film modules. The efficiency of crystalline, silicon wafer-based commercial modules increased from about 12 per cent to around 17 per cent between 2007 and 2017 (ibid.).

With falling investment costs of solar PV, the operation and maintenance costs constitute a larger share of costs. Even though solar PV has no marginal costs directly linked to output, operation and maintenance costs, land lease, taxes and insurance are substantial and are responsible for 20–25 per cent of LCOEs (ibid.).

Large-scale ground-mounted PV projects provide solar power at the lowest costs. They benefit from scale effects both for sourcing modules and especially for costs of planning and installation (Fu, Feldman and Margolis 2018). However, they take up significant space, with for very large projects millions of modules filling many square kilometres of land (Ong et al. 2013). Therefore, some countries have introduced restrictions on land use for new PV projects.

Placing solar panels on rooftops opens up space for renewable energy deployment that would otherwise lie idle, which can increase PV potential by up to 50 per cent (Deng et al. 2015). House-owners (and industry) can generate electricity in a decentralized way, increasing the number of owners of power plants from a number of companies to thousands and millions of actors (IEA 2014). In the past, households usually optimized the returns of their investments by maximizing the size of their solar panels to fit their entire roofs with favourable orientation, and thus large areas were available for renewable energy deployment. However, this has been changing, and in many markets the size of rooftop PV projects is declining as renewable remuneration mechanisms that previously supported every MWh produced are being scaled back – households are dimensioning PV installations to meet their private electricity demand rather than contributing to overall electricity needs (Fares and Webber 2017, Schill, Zerrahn and Kunz 2017).

Installing small batteries can increase the share of self-consumption. However, this raises new debates around the financing of grids, where grids are refinanced through consumption-based levies. More self-consumption means fewer payments of grid fees. This raises questions about the sustainability of these grid fees when self-consumption increases, even though absolute volumes of self-consumption are still very low, particularly in comparison to other common exemptions of levies – for example, for industrial self-consumption from thermal power plants (IEA 2014).

5.   CONCENTRATED SOLAR POWER

Concentrated solar power (CSP) uses mirrors to concentrate sunlight, heat a liquid and drive a turbine to generate electricity. There are two main technologies under CSP today: parabolic troughs have traditionally been the norm, but power towers have been making up an increasing share of new installations. Both rely on direct radiation and are thus almost exclusively found in very sun-rich regions with clear skies. Parabolic troughs concentrate sunlight within mirrors shaped like parabolas to heat a synthetic oil that passes through a pipe in front of the mirrors. To increase output, the mirrors track the sun throughout the day. The heated liquids from the individual troughs then run together to power a conventional steam engine. Power towers capture the concentrated sunlight from large numbers of flat mirrors, the heliostats, to heat either water to directly power a steam engine or a liquid that can keep the heat for a while before it is used for powering a steam engine.

CSP deployment has lagged behind expectations but has recently gathered pace. Beyond some initial projects in the US, deployment only started around 2009 in Spain, which installed 2 GW over the following years, sparking hopes that CSP would grow comparably to wind and photovoltaic solar power. For example, Viebahn, Lechon and Trieb (2011) foresaw even in their most pessimistic scenario that 20 GW would be installed by 2020, which appears unlikely given 2018's total of only about 6 GW. Cost reductions and deployment volumes have lagged behind expectations, with costs remaining at around 140–200 \$/MWh (IRENA 2016), considerably above the costs of wind and solar PV. Yet, deployment has been picking up in more countries, with South Africa, India, Morocco and, in 2018, also China, installing several hundred MW. Further growth in these markets appears likely, given that recent tender bids in the UAE and Australia of 73 and 60 \$/MWh, respectively, massively undercut IRENA's (2016) cost estimates for 2025, even when taking into account the favourable locations and financing conditions offered in the tenders.

Concentrated solar power plants can be used to heat liquids with high heat capacities – for example, molten salt – and thus can store the energy for typically between four and 12 hours. Thus, CSP plants can 'delay' electricity generation to meet evening peak hours. Capacity factors vary widely, from 30 per cent to up to 50 per cent for projects with large storage capabilities (IRENA 2018b). Global potential is very large, equal to several times current energy consumption levels but limited to areas close to the Equator where direct solar radiation abounds (Deng et al. 2015).

Concentrated solar power requires water and, depending on the cooling approach, more water than conventional thermal power plants. The water is used mostly for cooling, depending on technology, steam-cycle processes and cleaning. Wet-cooling techniques can use up to 1000 gallons per MWh, which can be challenging and costly considering that the plants require plenty of space and undistorted solar radiation, which can readily be found in deserts, raising questions about the sustainability of production. Dry-cooling techniques increase generation costs by a few per cent but reduce water consumption greatly, down to less than 100 gallons per MWh (Bracken et al. 2015).

However, comparing the higher LCOE from CSP to solar PV and wind power does not yield a fair comparison, given CSP's benefit of dispatchability and thus the potentially higher value of its output (Joskow 2011) during evening peaks. This lowers required support payments and can also render profitable those projects with somewhat higher LCOEs.

6.   BIOMASS-BASED ELECTRICITY GENERATION

Modern biomass provides energy by converting a feedstock like oil crops, sugar and starch crops, organic waste or lingo-cellulosic biomass into a solid, liquid or gaseous state from which it can be used as biofuel for transport, combusted for heat and/or electricity generation, or turned into other kinds of products (IEA 2017). The technologies and feedstock used depend on countries' resource availability – for example, while emerging economies often use seasonal residue from agriculture, Northern European and American countries primarily use forestry residues (ibid.), but increasingly also harvested crops due to limited availability of the former (VITO et al. 2017).

Combined heat and power (CHP) plants provide both heat and power. Conventional coal power plants can use some biomass as feedstock, potentially reducing emissions. Bioenergy-based plants coupled with carbon capture and storage (CCS) have the potential to decarbonize the energy supply if the technological and economic issues of CCS are solved (IEA 2017).

Despite absolute growth in capacity, biomass has been losing generation shares in comparison to other modern renewables: while bioenergy made up more than half of all non-hydro renewable energy generation in 2006, ten years later it is only a quarter, ousted by solar and in particular by wind power (IRENA 2018a). This decrease occurred even though the capacity for biomass-based electricity generation increased by more than half between 2007 and 2017. Brazil, China, India, the EU (esp. Germany) and the US were leading deployment (ibid.), yet installations are quite dispersed, reflecting the availability of (some) biomass in many countries.

The main reason for the slower deployment of biomass-based electricity generation is its relatively high cost (IEA 2017). Up-front investment costs for planning, construction and equipment form the largest share of overall costs (IRENA 2018b) but usually a smaller share than for wind and solar power. The technology is relatively mature, such that the IEA (2017) expects no major cost reductions. Costs for feedstock account for 20–50 per cent of the LCOE (IRENA 2018b). Agricultural residues have very low costs but are often only available in harvesting seasons, such that, for example, plants in India that use bagasse run at relatively low full-load hours (ibid.). In contrast, European and North American plants have access to forestry residue, energy crops and residual waste all year long so that they reach very high full-load hours close to constant generation (ibid.).

In the long term, biomass is expected to play an important role in decarbonizing other sectors where few alternative technologies exist to provide seasonal storage (heating), high energy density (aviation) or chemical composition (bio-based chemicals). Thus, the combination of overall limited availability of sustainable biomass and the strong competition from other sectors with higher-value applications of biomass imply that in longer-term scenarios biomass-based power generation does not capture a higher share of electricity generation, even though its electricity generation is dispatchable. On the contrary, IEA (2017) expects a ten-fold growth in biojet fuel, ethanol, biodiesel and biomethane for transport. Similarly, IRENA (2019) sees a large role for biomass by 2050, yet the share in electricity generation remains well below 10 per cent, while wind power and solar PV produce more than two-thirds of electricity. To avoid deforestation, energy crops provide biomass with relatively low space requirements, but trade-offs with growing food can occur, such that the growth of energy crops is somewhat limited, and a very strong drop in feedstock prices seems unlikely. Another issue is local air pollution stemming from the combustion of biomass, which has adverse health effects not only in developing but also in developed countries, especially in the case of small-scale and inefficient equipment (Sigsgaard et al. 2015).

7.   GEOTHERMAL ELECTRICITY GENERATION

The vast heat stored in the Earth's crust can be tapped to directly provide heat and to generate electricity. On the one hand, for heating purposes, a heat-conveying fluid (for example, water) is pumped underground and circulated in a system consisting of a heat pump and buried pipes, for which moderately hot temperatures suffice, so that the resource potential is large. On the other hand, existing mature technologies like flash plants and direct dry steam plants rely on steam that is brought to the surface and used to run turbines in the plants. This requires high temperatures exceeding 150°C, meaning that deployment is limited to regions where the ground is permeable enough to access the heat sources – for example, close to volcanic activity (IRENA 2017) where plants commonly reach capacity factors of more than 80 per cent (IRENA 2018b). Binary plants can also use somewhat lower temperatures (ibid.).

Between 2000 and 2017, geothermal electricity capacity grew by about 50 per cent from around 8 GW to more than 12 GW, with installations picking up in the last years. The US, the Philippines, Indonesia, Turkey, New Zealand, Mexico, Italy and Iceland were at the forefront of this development, indicating that resource availability has limited deployment in other countries (IRENA 2018a).

The costs of geothermal electricity generation have been rather stable over the last decades. They increased between the late 1990s and 2009 due to higher costs for engineering, commodities and drilling (Goldstein et al. 2011). Since then, they have stabilized at between 2000 and 5000 $/kW, very much depending on the resource quality and exploitation status (IRENA 2018b). For a standard flash power plant, the most common plant type, the plant and surface installation constitute slightly more than half of all investment costs, another fifth is for activities around drilling, and there are further costs for planning, interconnection and insurance (Sigfusson and Uihlein 2015).

Inducing seismic activity can be a concern for new technologies that aim to enhance the resource potential of geothermal electricity generation. Goldstein et al. (2011) conclude that while existing technologies can cause some seismic activity, serious damage does not occur. Yet, to enhance the resource potential of geothermal electricity generation, enhanced geothermal systems (EGS) are being explored, where fluid is pressed into underground rock formations to open them up and make underlying heat reservoirs accessible. In South Korea, such a test site is likely to have induced seismic activity, leading to the strongest earthquake ever measured in the country (Kim et al. 2018). Therefore, expansion of geothermal electricity generation beyond areas with resource potential for existing technologies seems questionable.

8.   TIDAL AND WAVE ENERGY

Tidal and wave energy have great deployment potential as reliable and renewable energy sources, yet commercial applications have been limited so far. In 2010, EU countries projected almost 2 GW of total capacity by 2020 in their national renewable energy action plans, yet, globally, only a few hundred MW were in operation by 2017, with no strong increasing uptake either (IRENA 2018a). The most mature tidal technologies are tidal range technologies that work based on differences in altitude between low and high tide, and therefore generate electricity very reliably. Structures like dams hold the water, filling it up and releasing it with the low and high tides and generating electricity with hydro turbines. Two projects represent more than 90 per cent of total installed tidal energy capacity, indicating that commercial deployment at scale has so far been the exception. The first 240 MW plant was constructed in the 1960s in France, while the next large plant of 254 MW only came online in 2011 in South Korea. Its rather low costs, however, were only possible as the plant was installed on an existing dam and helped alleviate water quality issues as the dam had previously been closed off from the sea (IRENA 2014a). Further, tidal stream (or tidal current) technology harnesses the tides' incoming and outgoing flows of water, comparable to wind turbines harnessing energy from wind. Yet, apart from small demonstration projects, no large-scale projects have been implemented to date.

High costs have prevented tidal plants from greater deployment, driven by a high share of upfront costs for installation, the structure and turbines (SI Ocean 2013), and capacity factors of around 25 per cent. IRENA (2014c) notes that while projections from several European studies anticipated costs to fall to around 200 €/MWh, actual demonstration projects have high costs that are twice as high and are highly site-specific. SI Ocean (2013) estimates that costs lie between 240 and 470 €/MWh. Since construction requires large engineering-type projects, scope for drastic cost reductions is limited.

Wave energy technology is less mature than tidal energy and only small-scale projects of up to a few MW exist. The basic principle is that the energy contained in waves is converted to electricity through power take-off (PTO) systems. Due to the industry's early development stage, many different PTOs are tested – for example, hydraulic systems, direct-drive systems, hydraulic turbines and pneumatic systems (IRENA 2014b). The costs are considered higher than those of tidal energy. SI Ocean (2013) calculates costs between around 330 and 630 €/MWh, of which more than half is for the structure and the PTO system.

Tidal and wave energy have great potential to help decarbonize power systems in the long run since they are globally available and potentially have very few negative externalities and even environmental benefits besides their electricity production. Yet, the sector's immaturity and high costs mean that hopes to tap these potentials in the medium term remain doubtful. Tidal energy's potential is largely unexploited but somewhat limited – for example, Ecorys and Fraunhofer (2017) identify a maximum of less than 20 GW for Europe. On the contrary, wave energy has abundant potential, of around 170 GW in Europe (ibid.) and 500 GW globally (IRENA 2014b). The European Ocean Energy Association (2010) claims that almost 190 GW of ocean energy (also including osmotic energy) could be implemented in Europe by 2050 and Ocean Energy Systems (2012) envisions 337 GW globally by 2050.

9. DETERMINANTS OF ECONOMIC VIABILITY OF RENEWABLE ENERGY INVESTMENTS AND INTEGRATION

In addition to the costs of technology, several factors affect the costs of wind and solar power and how far long-term expansion is feasible. First, wind and solar power are capital intensive and improvements in financing costs have contributed to reductions in LCOE (Egli et al. 2018). Second, local acceptance can impact costs, as it shapes where and what land is available for installations and how far long-term expansion targets are attainable. Third, dealing with weather-dependent production requires a more flexible power system that can balance supply and demand.

9.1 Financing Costs Define Costs of Renewable Energies

Wind and solar power are capital-intensive investments, in contrast to fuel-intensive coal and gas power plants. Project developers finance these upfront costs over the lifetime of the projects commonly through project finance (Steffen 2018). This capital intensity means that the financing costs matter more for wind and solar power projects than for conventional thermal power plants (Hirth and Steckel 2016). Moreover, renewable energies with very low marginal costs do not have a natural hedge, as, for example, do gas power plants: when gas prices increase, costs increase, but the wholesale electricity price generally moves in the same direction, shielding gas power plant operators from part of the power price risk correlated with their fuel costs (Roques, Newbery and Nuttall 2008).

Cost of financing is a key driver of costs and are frequently one that regulators have the most control over. On the one hand, technology costs are to a large extent defined by global markets. Moreover, how much the wind blows or sun shines in a region or country is also out of the hands of regulators. On the other hand, regulators affect financing costs through policy design – for example, by the choice of remuneration mechanism and by creating either policy risk or attractive investment environments free from retrospective adjustments to previously agreed support (Haas et al. 2011, Kitzing 2014). Energy policies lower financing costs when they reduce inefficient regulatory risks – for example, through market designs that prevent retrospective changes to previously announced policies – and address market failures – for example, when project developers and electricity consumers, in principle, would like to sign private long-term offtake contracts, but market failures prevent them from doing so. Furthermore, concessional loans from public banks can provide debt at favourable rates.

Exposure to power prices can guide investments but provides only limited incentives during operation. Wind and solar power have marginal costs close to zero, unlike their quasi-fixed annual operation and maintenance costs. Therefore, they tend to produce whenever the wind blows or the sun shines. Only in the case of negative power prices can it lead to voluntary curtailment. At the investment stage, exposure to expected market prices can influence investment choices about locations and technologies in favour of options that allow the capture of higher expected market prices (Schmidt et al. 2013). When project developers are shielded from too many risks – for example, through fixed capacity payments made independent of output – inefficient incentives can arise, with negative consequences for maintenance and operation.

The role of remuneration mechanisms is changing. In the past, their focus was on providing additional remuneration to fill the gap between electricity prices and costs. With declining costs of renewable technology and expectations that electricity prices will increase with carbon prices, the focus of remuneration mechanisms has shifted from covering incremental costs towards securing revenue streams for investors to facilitate low-cost financing and to providing power price stability for electricity consumers. Without remuneration mechanisms, private hedging contracts are necessary – for example, based on long-term power purchase agreements (PPAs) with private counterparties – usually utility companies or energy-intensive industries. However, these counterparties then take over the market and regulatory risks. With durations of up to 20 years to reflect the financing structure, the value of this exposure can grow substantially, leading to higher gearing and, in consequence, deteriorating credit ratings and thus increasing financing costs of the utilities or electricity-intensive counterparties of the long-term PPAs (Baringa 2013). This introduces additional costs and limits the potential scale for private PPAs. This is because in liberalized electricity markets retail companies struggle to sign PPAs at a scale exceeding the contractual relationships with their customers as they would otherwise be exposed to long-term price developments (May, Jürgens and Neuhoff 2017).

Renewable energy projects are more competitive when financing costs are low. Hirth and Steckel (2016) compare how three exemplary projects, one coal-fired plant, one gas-fired plant and one wind power project, react to changes in the financing costs. On the one hand, leaving everything else aside, wind power reacts the strongest to an increase in the weighted average cost of capital costs from zero per cent to 20 per cent, roughly tripling its total costs. Coal power, considerably less capital-intensive, a little more than doubles its costs. Gas power, on the other hand, only becomes 50 per cent more expensive. Therefore, low financing costs are key to enabling investments in renewables and improving their competitiveness against investments in conventional, fuel-intensive technologies.

9.2 Local Acceptance Supports or Prevents New Projects

Wind power and solar power projects are usually smaller than conventional thermal plants and there are various ways they can have impacts on the local communities where they are built. Projects have the potential to benefit communities financially but can also meet local opposition. The effects naturally differ between the technologies, but also between policies and in how far they engage local citizens financially. While rooftop solar panels engage and benefit large numbers of households and thus have the potential to secure overall support for renewable technologies, such participation needs to be more explicitly introduced for other projects – for example, with financial participation in onshore wind farms. Local communities benefit when taxes are (also) paid where the plants stand, outside workers spend money locally during construction or maintenance work, the local workforce constructs or maintains the plants and infrastructure, or infrastructure is developed for the projects (Brown et al. 2012).

Local acceptance is valuable especially in densely populated countries. The long-term expansion of renewable energies depends on the availability of sufficient land for the installations. On the one hand, professional investors and owners from elsewhere can possibly bid lower prices in tenders due to economies of scale. On the other hand, routinely preferring such outside investors can harm local acceptance in the long run, reducing the land available for new installations and driving up the price of the remaining land, eventually rendering new renewable energy investments more costly. Therefore, considering local acceptance and local participation is crucial for sustained, long-term expansion of renewable energies (Ioga et al. 2016).

Local ownership is one way to foster acceptance and overcome deployment barriers. For example, when the owners of onshore wind farms live near the turbines, this increases their acceptance of the turbines. Living in the affected communities, local owners can engage their communities in the planning processes, increasing acceptance of the projects (ibid.). Regulation can support local ownership and co-investment. While large utility companies' risk-return profile makes them particularly suited for large-scale, relatively high-risk and high-return investments – that is, investments in thermal power plants – wind and solar power investments are commonly smaller and are made under policy remuneration mechanisms, decreasing risks and returns, generally making them suitable for smaller-scale developers (Helms, Salm and Wüstenhagen 2015).

Various examples exist on how to foster local ownership and acceptance. First, policymakers influence local ownership through the direct or indirect technology choice: while large-scale offshore wind parks are usually implemented by large firms, roof-top solar projects can be implemented at household level or by small and medium-sized companies. Second, regulators can set explicit requirements for projects that want to benefit from regulatory remuneration mechanisms. Denmark, for example, explicitly requires that project developers offer stakes in projects to affected communities. Third, the implicit design of remuneration mechanisms defines what group of project developers can submit lower bids than others in today's common bidding for access to remuneration mechanisms. Regulators can remove regulatory risks and help overcome market failures – for instance, design remuneration mechanisms that avoid the need for signing private long-term offtake contracts – such that project developers can finance their investments with little equity, enabling smaller companies to compete against those with plenty of equity.

9.3   Dealing with Intermittency for Integrating Renewable Energies

The power output from wind and solar power is intermittent, such that power prices in power systems with limited flexibility and significant shares of wind and solar power exhibit relatively low power prices when it is windy or sunny and relatively high prices when it is not (Hirth 2013, Joskow 2011). In regions with strong growth of solar PV, the daytime peak in power prices around noon is first flattened and eventually turns into a period of lower power prices. Consequently, market values of solar power decrease. In regions like California, it is expected that rapid ramps of other generation is required to fill the evening demand when a reduction of sunshine coincides with an increase of power demand for private air-conditioning (CAISO 2016). To decrease correlation with the output of other solar panels, alternative orientations west and east instead of south (in the Northern Hemisphere) are discussed, which sacrifice some output in terms of MWh achievable for higher market values of the produced power (Hartner and Ortner 2015). Engineering structures that track the sun are another similar common approach – for example, in the US.

In the Northern Hemisphere, wind and solar power are often complementary. For example, in Europe, wind power generates mostly in autumn and winter, while PV solar produces mostly in spring and summer. On a daily level, the wind blows strongest at night, while the sun shines exclusively by day. This complementarity is one reason a technology mix of both technologies prevents an all too drastic decline of renewable energy market values: usually, wind and solar power do not produce at full capacity at the same time. In addition, portfolios of several technologies can pay off long term when any individual technology's potential is limited (Neuhoff, May and Richstein 2017).

Besides portfolios of renewable energy technologies, there are many other approaches to dealing with intermittency. System-friendly wind and solar power plant designs and locations shift their production to hours with lower supply. The market design can support the flexible ramping of conventional plants and facilitate the exchange between regions and countries. Demand-side management can adjust demand to electricity prices and reduce or shift demand at high prices. Storing electricity – for example, in batteries or in pumped hydro stations – shifts supply of electricity from hours where supply is relatively low to hours where it is relatively high. Storage can be implemented in central, large-scale applications that make use of economies of scale – as implemented, for example, in Australia – or extremely decentralized together with demand at the household and company level, or with the renewable energy plants – that is, directly with wind and solar power farms. Zerrahn, Schill and Kemfert (2018) show that, at least in Germany, the necessary storage levels will not limit the expansion of renewable energies. Required storage levels are not extremely high when allowing for small amounts of spilled renewable energy. This is anchored in the market design in many countries and usually wind projects are compensated to limit the exposure of project developers to risks to maintain low-cost financing and thus keep total costs low.

At the system level, different groups propose two fundamentally different strategies for wind and solar power integration. First, it is suggested that project developers co-locate some form of storage with the renewable energy plants (Braff, Mueller and Trancik 2016). For example, the electricity can be stored in batteries, as hydrogen, or used directly as hydrogen, directly in industry or as methane in existing gas grids. Installing batteries with household PV panels is another existing example of this approach. This renders wind and solar power dispatchable, such that they can be fed into the grid with little extra requirements for the rest of the electricity system.

Second, it is suggested that renewable energy plants are distributed on a continental scale, making use of lower correlation of wind and solar radiation patterns while leveraging sites with the most favourable weather conditions. High voltage direct current (HVDC) transmission lines, which exhibit low losses even over very long distances, can transport the electricity from the far-flung plants to where the electricity is demanded (MacDonald et al. 2016). For example, the DESERTEC project envisions installing massive amounts of renewable energies in the deserts and coasts of North Africa and transporting this electricity to Europe. Another example is China's increasing electricity transmission across the country to its load centres in the east. Naturally, such an approach requires the coordination between many different actors and countries and the political coordination, trust and market design to enable such mega projects. Also with this approach, renewable energies' intermittency would be kept in check and electricity supply would resemble traditional baseload.

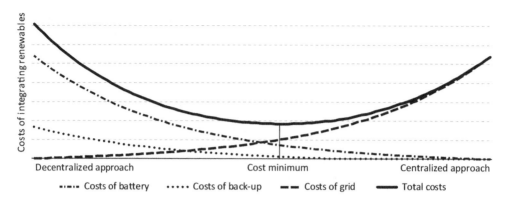

Source: Authors' own work.

*Figure 12.5   Illustrative integration costs when integrating renewables through different
approaches: purely decentralized vs centralized vs a combination of both*

From an economic perspective, Figure 12.5 illustrates the very much simplified approach,
focusing only on costs for balancing the electricity supply from renewable energies, following either a decentralized approach where all electricity is stored in batteries co-
located with the renewable energy plants, or a centralized approach where long
transmission lines connect supply and demand. In between, combinations of the two –
that is, some investments in batteries, some investments in interconnectors – are indicated. Additional costs for back-up capacity occur because even when being capable of
storing all renewable energy output, back-up capacity might be required if there is no or
very little investment in transmission grids. The total costs represent the sum of these
three cost components.

Costs for batteries, grid expansion and back-up capacity are assumed to be exponential. First, when aiming to store all electricity generated by renewables, storage also needs
to be installed at small and old installations at relatively high costs, and costs increase
exponentially when not allowing for small amounts of wind spill (Zerrahn et al. 2018).
Second, grid expansion costs are assumed to grow exponentially with the grid size, since
with larger interconnection rates more difficult topography must be traversed. Third,
back-up capacity costs are exponential. as more expensive plants need to be kept available. Given these effects, the cost minimum is reached when both some local storage and
some interconnection are combined. In the real world, large, central storage or conversion to hydrogen can prove more efficient due to economies of scale than balancing out
every individual plant's output on-site. Interconnection plays a role, yet is complicated
by the sheer scale and duration of the investments. Therefore, a combination of
approaches that render the energy system more flexible is required to facilitate the transition towards carbon-neutral electricity systems.

Energy transitions towards very high shares of wind and solar power must address the
need for frequency stabilization. When conventional, synchronous generation is reduced,
the grid frequency needs to be stabilized by other means. This shift is most challenging in
isolated systems with little hydro power capacity like Ireland (O'Sullivan et al. 2014).
Consequently, Ireland established a maximum share of non-synchronous generation of

50 per cent in 2011. However, this limit has since been increased to 65 per cent (Holttinen et al. 2019) due to successful integration and handling of frequency control. To this end, there are various approaches to stabilize grid frequency in systems with high shares of solar and wind power – for example, through synthetic inertia measures (Holttinen et al. 2019, O'Sullivan et al. 2014). While experiences with very high shares of variable renewables increase (individual hours with more than 100 per cent of electricity demand covered by renewable energy in Denmark and Portugal, and overall shares of wind power alone of 25–43 per cent in several countries and states of the US; Holttinen et al. 2019), further research will be needed to operate energy systems with very high shares of variable renewable energies.

10. CONCLUSION

New technologies on the supply side are changing power systems. The costs of wind power and especially of solar PV have fallen rapidly, bringing their LCOE commonly below those of thermal power plants and increasingly even below the marginal costs of thermal power plants. Their resource potential is widespread around the globe, making them accessible to most countries and regions.

Other renewable energy technologies can play important roles in the electricity sector as well, but will be limited to specific use, cases or regions. Concentrated solar power relies on direct solar radiation and has been lagging behind PV deployment, yet recent developments indicate that declining technology costs and short-term heat storage options allow for some dispatchability and may offer opportunities for their use. Biomass will most likely be used for reducing greenhouse gases in the heating and transport sectors as fewer low-carbon alternatives exist in those sectors. Geothermal energy is limited to specific regions with good resource potential, where it can play an important role not only in the heating but also the electricity sector. Tidal energy has overall limited resource potential and – dependent on site – large infrastructure costs that may offer limited cost reduction potential. Wave energy, while having great global potential, is at early stage of development and future pilot projects will show whether they can address engineering challenges and benefit sufficiently from technological learning to bring costs down.

Deployment of renewable energies hinges on their economic viability. They replace fossil-fuel-based thermal plants with capital-intensive renewable energy plants. Besides lowered technology costs, renewables have been benefitting from favourable investment environments that shielded project developers from regulatory and market risks, and thus enabled them to take up low-cost financing and provide electricity at low costs. Furthermore, failing to gain local acceptance of projects can constrain the space available for renewable energies, particularly in densely populated countries. Moreover, renewable energy output is intermittent, such that the investment incentives for renewables, the electricity grid, the demand side and the coupled sectors need to be able to facilitate the integration of vast amounts of renewable energies.

Regulation and market design need to take the characteristics, ownership structures, financing cost intensity, questions of local acceptance, and intermittency into account. Remuneration mechanisms can address regulatory risks and overcome market barriers for long-term bilateral contracting and thus enable investments at low financing costs, while retaining incentives to invest in technologies that provide high value and in locations where supply is otherwise scarce. Running power systems on very high shares of wind and solar power is unchartered territory and is easier to reach in systems well connected to neighbours or with large shares of hydro power. The electricity system as a whole must be adjusted to unlock flexibilities from supply and demand and to incorporate elements both from decentralized solutions with storage and use of electricity near its production and from centralized solutions where electricity is transported and traded over long distances. Then, project developers and the energy system as a whole can invest in the large quantities of renewable energies and storage, sector coupling and grids that are necessary to decarbonize electricity systems and provide clean and low-cost electricity to decarbonize other sectors.

REFERENCES

Baringa (2013), *Power Purchase Agreements for Independent Renewable Generators – An Assessment of Existing and Future Market Liquidity*, commissioned by the Department of Energy and Climate Change.

Bloomberg New Energy Finance (BNEF) (2018), '2H 2017 Wind Turbine Price Index', accessed 5 March 2019 at https://about.bnef.com/blog/2h-2017-wind-turbine-price-index/.

Bracken, N., J. Macknick and A. Tovar-Hastin et al. (2015), *Concentrating Solar Power and Water Issues in the U.S. Southwest*, Golden, CO: Joint Institute for Strategic Energy Analysis.

Braff, W. A., J. M. Mueller and J. E. Trancik (2016), 'Value of storage technologies for wind and solar energy', *Nature Climate Change*, **6**, 964–9.

Brown, J. P., J. Pender and R. Wiser et al. (2012), 'Ex post analysis of economic impacts from wind power development in U.S. counties', *Energy Economics*, **34**, 1743–54.

BSW Solar (2016), *Photovoltaik-Preisindex Deutschland 2016*.

CAISO (2016), 'What the duck curve tells us about managing a green grid', *Fast Facts*.

Dalla Riva, A., J. Hethey and A. Vītiņa (2017), *IEA Wind TCP Task 26: Impacts of Wind Turbine Technology on the System Value of Wind in Europe*, Ea Energy Analyses, NREL/TP-6A20-70337, November.

Deng, Y.Y., M. Haigh and W. Pouwels et al. (2015), 'Quantifying a realistic, worldwide wind and solar electricity supply', *Global Environmental Change*, **31**, 239–52.

Ecorys and Fraunhofer (2017), *Study on Lessons for Ocean Energy Development: Final Report*, commissioned by the European Commission.

Egli, F., B. Steffen and T. S. Schmidt (2018), 'A dynamic analysis of financing conditions for renewable energy technologies', *Nature Energy*, **3**, 1084–92.

European Ocean Energy Association (2010), *Oceans of Energy: European Ocean Energy Roadmap 2010–2050*, Brussels: EU-OEA.

Fares, R. L. and M. E. Webber (2017), 'The impacts of storing solar energy in the home to reduce reliance on the utility', *Nature Energy*, **2**, Article 17001.

Fraunhofer IEE (2018a), *Windenergie Report Deutschland 2017*, Stuttgart: Fraunhofer Verlag.

Fraunhofer ISE (2018b), *Levelized Cost of Electricity: Renewable Energy Technologies*, accessed 5 December 2019 at https://www.ise.fraunhofer.de/content/dam/ise/en/documents/publications/studies/EN2018_Fraunhofer-ISE_LCOE_Renewable_Energy_Technologies.pdf.

Fraunhofer IEE (2019a), 'Windmonitor', accessed 15 March 2019 at http://www.windmonitor.de/windmonitor_de/bilder_javascript.html?db_communicate=%27Windenergieeinspeisung.daten%27&p_lang=ger&img_id=427.

Fraunhofer ISE (2019b), *Photovoltaics Report*, accessed 20 March 2019 at https://www.ise.fraunhofer.de/content/dam/ise/de/documents/publications/studies/Photovoltaics-Report.pdf.

Fu, R., D. Feldman and R. Margolis (2018), *U.S. Solar Photovoltaic System Cost Benchmark: Q1 2018*, NREL/TP-6A20-72399, Golden, CO: National Renewable Energy Laboratory.

Girard, Y., C. Kemfert, A. Neumann and J. Stoll (2019), 'Marktdesign für eine effiziente Netzanbindung von Offshore-Windenergie: eine Studie im Auftrag von Ørsted Offshore Wind', *DIW Berlin: Politikberatung kompakt*, **127**(136).

Goldstein, B., G. Hiriart and R. Bertani et al. (2011), 'Geothermal energy', in O. Edenhofer, R. Pichs-Madruga and Y. Sokona et al. (eds), *Renewable Energy Sources and Climate Change Mitigation – Special Report of the International Panel on Climate Change*, Cambridge, UK: Cambridge University Press, pp. 401–36.

Haas, R., G. Resch and C. Panzer et al. (2011), 'Efficiency and effectiveness of promotion systems for electricity generation from renewable energy sources – lessons from EU countries', *Energy*, **36** (4), 2186–93.

Hartner, M. and A. Ortner (2015), 'East to west – the optimal tilt angle and orientation of photovoltaic panels from an electricity system perspective', *Applied Energy*, **160**, 94–107.

Helms, T., S. Salm and R. Wüstenhagen (2015), 'Investor-specific cost of capital and renewable energy investment decisions', in C. W. Donovan (ed.), *Renewable Energy Finance – Powering the Future*, London: Imperial College Press, pp. 77–101.

Hirth, L. (2013), 'The market value of variable renewables: the effect of solar wind power variability on their relative price', *Energy Economics*, **38**, 218–36.

Hirth, L. and S. Müller (2016), 'System-friendly wind power: how advanced wind turbine design can increase the economic value of electricity generated through wind power', *Energy Economics*, **56**, 51–63.

Hirth, L. and J. C. Steckel (2016), 'The role of capital costs in decarbonizing the electricity sector', *Environmental Research Letters*, **11**, Article 114010.

Holttinen, H., J. Kiviluoma and L. Jun et al. (2019), *Design and Operation of Power Systems with Large Amounts of Wind Power – Final Summary Report*, IEA WIND Task 25.

International Energy Agency (IEA) (2014), 'Residential prosumers – drivers and policy options (RE-PROSUMERS)', IEA Renewable Energy Technology Deployment (IEA-REDT).

International Energy Agency (IEA) (2017), *Technology Roadmap – Delivering Sustainable Bioenergy*, Paris: IEA.

International Energy Agency (IEA) (2018), *World Energy Outlook 2018*, Paris: IEA.

International Renewable Energy Agency (IRENA) (2014a), *Tidal Energy Technology Brief*, Abu Dhabi: IRENA.

International Renewable Energy Agency (IRENA) (2014b), *Wave Energy Technology Brief*, Abu Dhabi: IRENA.

International Renewable Energy Agency (IRENA) (2014c), *Ocean Energy – Technology Readiness, Patents, Deployment Status and Outlook*, Abu Dhabi: IRENA.

International Renewable Energy Agency (IRENA) (2016), *The Power to Change: Solar and Wind Cost Reduction Potential to 2025*, Abu Dhabi: IRENA.

International Renewable Energy Agency (IRENA) (2017), *Geothermal Power Technology Brief*, Abu Dhabi: IRENA.

International Renewable Energy Agency (IRENA) (2018a), *Renewable Energy Statistics 2018*, Abu Dhabi: IRENA.

International Renewable Energy Agency (IRENA) (2018b), *Renewable Power Generation Costs in 2017*, Abu Dhabi: IRENA.

International Renewable Energy Agency (IRENA) (2019), *Global Energy Transformation: A Roadmap to 2050*, Abu Dhabi: IRENA.

Ioga, D., M. Dragan and B. Claesens et al. (2016), *WISE Power Result-oriented Report – Fostering Social Acceptance for Wind Power*, October.

IWR (2019a), 'EEG-Vergütungssätze (2000–2004)', accessed 5 March 2019 at http://www.iwr.de/re/wf/e_preis.html.

IWR (2019b), 'EEG-Vergütungssätze für Strom aus erneuerbaren Energien – Windkraft', accessed 5 March 2019 at http://www.iwr.de/re/wf/eeg%20windkraft.htm.

Jacobson, M. Z. and M. A. Delucchi (2011), 'Providing all global energy with wind, water, and solar power. Part I: Technologies, energy resources, quantities and areas of infrastructure, and materials', *Energy Policy*, **39** (3), 1154–69.

Joskow, P. (2011), 'Comparing the costs of intermittent and dispatchable electricity generating technologies', *American Economic Review*, **101** (3), 238–41.

Kim, K.-H., J.-H. Ree and Y. Kim et al. (2018), 'Assessing whether the 2017 Mw 5.4 Pohang earthquake in South Korea was an induced event', *Science*, **360** (6392), 1007–9.

Kitzing, L. (2014), 'Risk implications of renewable support instruments: comparative analysis of feed-in tariffs and premiums using a mean-variance approach', *Energy*, **64**, 495–505.

Kruger, W., A. Eberhard and K. Swartz (2018), *Renewable Energy Auctions: A Global Overview*, Report 1: Energy and Economic Growth Research Programme (W01 and W05), Graduate School of Business, University of Cape Town, accessed 11 July 2021 at http://www.gsb.uct.ac.za/files/EEG_GlobalAuctionsReport.pdf.

Lu, X., M. B. McElroy and J. Kiviluoma, J. (2009), 'Global potential for wind-generated electricity', *Proceedings of the National Academy of Sciences*, **106** (27), 10933–8.

MacDonald, A. E., C. T.M. Clack and A. Alexander et al. (2016), 'Future cost-competitive electricity systems and their impact on US CO$_2$ emissions', *Nature Climate Change*, **6**, 526–31.

May, N. (2017), 'The impact of wind power support schemes on technology choices', *Energy Economics*, **65**, 343–54.

May, N., I. Jürgens and K. Neuhoff (2017), 'Renewable energy policy: risk hedging is taking center stage', *DIW Economic Bulletin*, No. 39/40, 389–96.

Neuhoff, K., N. May and J. Richstein (2017), 'Incentives for the long-term integration of renewable energies: a plea for a market value model', *DIW Economic Bulletin*, No. 46/47, 929–38.

Newbery, D. (2018), 'Evaluating the case for supporting renewable electricity', *Energy Policy*, **120**, 684–96.

Ocean Energy Systems (2012), *An International Vision for Ocean Energy*, Paris: IEA.

Ong, S., C. Campbell and P. Denholm et al. (2013), *Land-use Requirements for Solar Power Plants in the United States*, Golden, CO: National Renewable Energy Laboratory.

O'Sullivan, J., A. Rogers and D. Flynn et al. (2014), 'Studying the maximum instantaneous non-synchronous generation in an island system – frequency stability challenges in Ireland', *IEEE Transactions on Power Systems*, **29** (6), 2943–51.

Quitzow, R., S. Roehrkasten and M. Jaenicke (2016), 'The German energy transition in international perspective', Institute for Advanced Sustainability Studies (IASS).

Roques, F. A., D. Newbery and W. J. Nuttall (2008), 'Fuel-mix diversification incentives in liberalized electricity markets: a mean-variance portfolio theory approach', *Energy Economics*, **30**, 1831–49.

Rosemann, H., H. Braun and P. Malhotra et al. (2014), 'BladeMaker – advancing and demonstrating automated manufacturing of rotor blades, in *Proceedings of Europe's Premier Wind Energy Event, EWEA 2014*, 10–13 March 2014, Barcelona, Spain, pp. 135–40.

Roth, I. F. and L. A. Lawrence (2004), 'Incorporating externalities into a full cost approach to electric power generation life-cycle costing', *Energy*, **29**, 12–15.

Schill, W., A. Zerrahn and F. Kunz (2017), 'Prosumage of solar electricity: pros, cons, and the system perspective', *Economics of Energy and Environmental Policy*, **6** (1), 7–31.

Schmidt, J., G. Lehecka, V. Gass and E. Schmid (2013), 'Where the wind blows: assessing the effect of fixed and premium based feed-in tariffs on the spatial diversification of wind turbines', *Energy Economics*, **40**, 269–76.

SI Ocean (2013), *Ocean Energy: Cost of Energy and Cost Reduction Opportunities*, Edinburgh, UK: SI Ocean.

Sigfusson, B. and A. Uihlein (2015), *JRC Geothermal Energy Status Report – Technology, Market and Economic Aspects of Geothermal Energy in Europe*, Joint Research Centre for the European Commission.

Sigsgaard, T., B. Forsberg and I. Annesi-Maesano et al. (2015), 'Health impacts of anthropogenic biomass burning in the developed world', *European Respiratory Journal*, **46** (6), 1577–88.

Statista (2019), *Preise für Solaranlagen in Deutschland bis 2017*.

Steffen, B. (2018), 'The importance of project finance for renewable energy projects', *Energy Economics*, **69**, 280–94.

Stehly, T., P. Beiter, D. Heimiller and G. Scott (2018), *2017 Cost of Wind Energy Review*, NREL/TP-6A20-72167, Golden, CO: National Renewable Energy Laboratory.

Viebahn, P., Y. Lechon and F. Trieb (2011), 'The potential role of concentrated solar power (CSP) in Africa and Europe – a dynamic assessment of technology development, cost development and life cycle inventories until 2050', *Energy Policy*, **39** (8), 4420–30.

VITO, Utrecht University and TU Wien et al. (2017), *Sustainable and Optimal Use of Biomass for Energy in the EU Beyond 2020 – Final Report*, commissioned by the European Commission.

Wiser, R. H. and M. Bolinger (2018), *2017 Wind Technologies Market Report*, commissioned by the US Department of Energy.

Zerrahn, A., W. Schill and C. Kemfert (2018), 'On the economics of electrical storage for variable renewable energy sources', *European Economic Review*, **108**, 259–79.

13. New technologies on the demand side
Fereidoon Sioshansi

1. INTRODUCTION

Any discussion on the topic of new technologies on the demand side, or for that matter on the future of electricity demand, must begin with the context in which to consider the subject matter. If the aim is to have a global perspective, one must begin with an approach that recognizes that different countries at different stages of maturity and development are likely to face different patterns of electricity demand growth and different demand-side technologies.

This chapter starts with a brief overview of the current status of global electricity demand (Petit 2019), followed by an examination of new demand-side technologies and how they are likely to alter not only how much but also how electricity may be utilized at customers' premises in the future.

As time goes on, and depending on which region of the world we are talking about, customers will have increased options not only in how much, when and how they consume electricity but also to potentially generate some of the electricity they consume on-site – the most common is by investing in rooftop solar photovoltaics (PVs). These consumers are referred to as *prosumers* since they are producing and consuming electricity depending on the output of the solar PVs and demand (Sioshansi 2019a). As the cost of storage continues to decline – prosumers will have additional options such as storing some of the excess distributed generation for use at later times. These *prosumagers* consume, produce and store energy depending on the circumstances (Sioshansi 2020a). Technological innovations on the demand side become even more interesting, potentially leading to more *exotic* types of consumers who may trade some of their generated or stored energy with their peers, in what is called peer-to-peer (P2P) trading, usually enabled by third-party aggregators (Shipworth et al. 2019).

Moreover, advances in remote sensing and artificial intelligence (AI) allow the aggregation of large portfolios of load, distributed generation and storage – which can be remotely monitored, managed and optimized (Brown, Woodhouse and Sioshansi, 2019). Taken together, these advances allow transactions among and between customers on open platforms, creating additional opportunities for innovative companies to offer a myriad of new services and new business models (Fox-Penner 2020).

One particular demand-side technology worth examining is charging of electric vehicles (EVs) and other types of electrified transport, including electric buses, bikes and scooters. The International Energy Agency (IEA) in its *World Energy Outlook* released in November 2018 predicted that there may be as many as 1 billion EVs (or hybrids) by 2040, or roughly half the global fleet of light duty vehicles (IEA 2018). How and when these future EVs will be charged – and potentially discharged – are among the challenging issues facing generators, distribution companies and suppliers (Sioshansi 2020i).

As the preceding outline suggests, the emerging demand-side technologies and how they permeate the customers' homes, offices, factories and the potential uptake of EVs will determine how much electricity may be utilized and how it will be generated, distributed and supplied (Baak and Sioshansi 2019). The answer depends on where the customers are, in what state of economic and infrastructure maturity – topics further explored in the subsequent sections.

The chapter's main insight, however, is to suggest that the traditional view of 'customers' as consumers of electricity at the end of a one-way flow from upstream infrastructure – generation, transmission and distribution (T&D) – may be outdated (Sioshansi, 2016). The future is likely to be more decentralized, distributed and digitalized with more intelligence and connectivity behind the meter and more complex flows and transactions among the traditional and new players (Bauknecht et al. 2019). In such a future, consumption, generation, storage and other forms of transaction among and between consumers, prosumers and prosumagers will have to be re-examined from the perspective of the customers and what's best for them given a myriad of new options and possibilities at their disposal (Swanston 2020a). And as will be argued, many of these options will be enabled by new aggregators, orchestrators and intermediaries who, in turn, will be enabled by intelligent software and AI (Bashir, Smits and Nelson 2019). The future of demand, demand-side technologies – even the basic definition of electricity service – is likely to undergo radical change, at least for some customers as they migrate away from total reliance on receiving all services from traditional suppliers (Burger et al. 2019).

The balance of this chapter is organized as follows. Section 2 provides a primer on demand for electricity in different countries based on their current state of economic development. Section 3 examines the prime drivers of electricity demand – namely, major appliances and devices that use electricity and how the technologies embedded in these devices are changing (Sioshansi 2020c). This section also briefly examines the expected growth of EVs and their potential impact on electricity consumption and – more importantly – peak demand. Section 4 examines technologies that allow growing numbers of consumers to become prosumers and potentially prosumagers, including the fundamental reasons and implications for this 'stratification'. Section 5 examines the impact of digitalization on demand, including the proliferation of technologies that can remotely monitor and adjust load, distributed generation and storage and/or facilitate P2P trading (Löbbe et al. 2020). This section also examines new business models that allow intelligent aggregators to optimize a *portfolio* of loads, distributed generation and storage while enabling P2P trading and/or other forms of transaction. Section 6 asks what will ultimately matter and provides the chapter's conclusions.

2.   ECONOMIC DEVELOPMENT AND ELECTRICITY DEMAND

For the purposes of this chapter, countries may be grouped into four categories:

- the rich and advanced economies – the World Bank refers to these as 'high-income economies', including most Organisation for Economic Co-operation (OECD) member countries;[1]

- the developing economies that are nearing or aspiring to join the OECD economies – the World Bank refers to these as 'upper-income economies';
- the less-developed economies that are not advanced – the World Bank defines these as 'middle-income economies'; and
- those currently with little infrastructure and resources to provide basic electricity services to some or the bulk of their population – the 'low-income economies'.

As illustrated in Table 13.1, the wide disparities among the four categories means that demand-side technologies and trends further described in this chapter may not be equally applicable or relevant to all four groups.

The first category may be characterized by high per capita income levels, small to negligible economic and population growths, extensive and reliable generation, T&D infrastructure already in place and typically high per capita electricity consumption levels. These economies are at or near saturation levels in terms of per capita electricity demand. Typical citizens already own most of the appliances they need or desire – say a second TV – and use them more or less as much as needed – say for lighting, cooling or heating. With continued improvements in energy efficiency of buildings and appliances, electricity demand growth in these countries is low to nil. The only exceptions come from a few applications such as the electrification of transport and the rise of data centre demand.[2]

The second category may be characterized by modest but growing per capita income levels, higher levels of economic and population growth and reasonably reliable infrastructure. These economies are experiencing rising levels of per capita electricity demand. Typical citizens – given a chance – will acquire new electricity-using devices and use them more.

The third category may be characterized by relatively low per capita income levels, typically high population growth rates but not necessarily high levels of economic growth. These economies would be experiencing rising levels of per capita electricity demand only if they could deliver more electricity, as illustrated in the middle and lower parts of Table 13.2.

The last category may be characterized by countries with extremely low per capita income levels, typically high population growth rates but not necessarily high levels of economic growth, and inadequate, unreliable – or in some extreme cases – non-existent infrastructure. Moreover, many countries in this category may not have the resources or,

Table 13.1   Income and development status

Status	Per Capita Income ($)	Annual Per Capita Electricity Consumption (kWh)
High-income economies	41 000 +/–	8 800
Upper-income economies	8 600 +/–	3 500
Middle-income economies	5 100–2 200	2 000
Low-income economies	780 +/–	770

Note: Both the income levels and per capita consumption cover a range.

Source: Compiled by the author from various sources from the World Bank.

Table 13.2   Selected countries and per capita electricity consumption

Country	Annual Per Capita Electricity Consumption (kWh/person/year)
High-income/consumption economies	
Iceland	54 000
Norway	23 000
Bahrain	20 000
Canada, Qatar, Kuwait	15 000–16 000
Sweden, US	13 000–14 000
UAE, Korea, Australia	10 000–11 000
Saudi Arabia, NZ, Singapore	9 000
Japan, Germany, France, Russia	6 000–8 000
Spain, UK, Greece, Italy	5 000
Upper-income/consumption economies	
China, Argentina, Turkey, Brazil	3 000–4 000
Middle-income/consumption economies	
Mexico, Egypt	2 000
Iraq, Colombia	1 000
Indonesia, India, Philippines	under 1 000
Low-income/consumption economies	
Pakistan, Ghana, Sudan, Kenya	under 500
Tanzania, Ethiopia, Niger	under 100

Source: The World Bank.

in some cases, even the necessary institutions that would allow them to invest in infrastructure beyond select urban areas. It is estimated that globally as many as 1 billion people have limited or no access to reliable electricity supply.[3]

Any discussion on demand or demand-side technologies must start with an acknowledgment that these four groups are likely to follow rather different paths over time – with divergence among the various countries.

Figure 13.1 schematically shows a select number of countries falling into these four categories. The disparities among the four groups are stunning, underscoring the fact that the adoption of new demand-side technologies is likely to follow different trajectories in different parts of the world.

The top 20 electricity consumers account for the lion's share of global consumption, with the top ten highlighted in Table 13.3. The top four, China, the US, India and the European Union (as a group) account for a predominant portion of the total.

The balance of the chapter is mostly – but not exclusively – focused on the impact of new demand-side technologies in the more advanced economies. It should be obvious that while future trends in Afghanistan or Zimbabwe critically matter to the people living there, on a global scale, a handful of the populous countries with large economies will determine the future of global electricity demand growth.

However, as the costs of the new technologies continue to decline, many of the same patterns will apply to the developing economies. In fact, in some cases these countries may leapfrog, skipping the trajectory of the more advanced economies (Couture

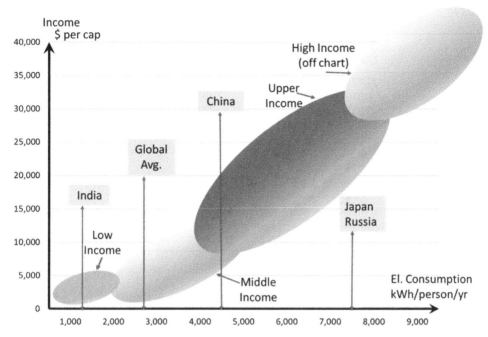

Note: There is considerable overlap among the four groups as shown. The high-income category falls out of the boundaries of the figure.

Source: Stylized graph compiled by the author from sources listed in endnote 3.

Figure 13.1   Income and per capita electricity consumption show wide divergence[4]

et al. 2019).[5] Other chapters in this handbook cover major and rapidly developing economies, including Southeast Asia and India in Chapter 20, China in Chapter 21 and Sub-Saharan Africa in Chapter 22.

3.   PRIME DRIVERS OF ELECTRICITY DEMAND AND TRENDS IN DEMAND-SIDE TECHNOLOGIES

This section provides a cursory look at:

- the main drivers of electricity demand (Jamasb and Pollitt 2011);
- how advances in demand-side technology are likely to impact future trends; and
- why in the future electricity consumption may diverge from electricity sales or purchases from the network (Sioshansi 2020b).

The latter phenomenon, which is currently evident in a few places, is expected to become more common as more consumers are able to generate some of the kilowatt-hours (kWh) they need and, as further described, may be able to store and/or trade their excess generation with others using the existing distribution network.

Table 13.3   Top ten electricity consuming nations

	Overall Electricity Consumption (TWh)	Population (millions)	Per Capita Electricity Consumption (kW)
World	21 776	7 323	2 678
China	6 310	1 403	4 475
USA	3 911	323	12 000
India	1 408	1 266	1 122
Russia	1 065	142	7 481
Japan	934	126	7 371
Germany	533	82	6 602
Canada	528	35	14 930
Brazil	518	206	2 516
South Korea	495	51	9 720
France	431	67	6 448
UK	309	64	4 795

Note: Dates and the sources for various countries varies.

Source: Wikipedia (2021), 'List of countries by electricity consumption', accessed 13 July 2021 at https://en.wikipedia.org/wiki/List_of_countries_by_electricity_consumption.

Fundamentally, electricity demand is driven by economic activity, income level, building codes, appliance energy efficiency standards, climate, cultural norms and demography. Aside from the transport sector and uses such as street and outdoor lighting, nearly all electricity is used within buildings, be they homes, offices, shopping centres, hospitals, warehouses, data centres, factories or farm barns (Duncan and Webber 2020). Not surprisingly, any study or forecast of electricity demand usually begins with an inventory of existing buildings and major energy-using devices within them, typically broken into major categories such as residential, commercial, industrial, agricultural and other categories[6] (street lighting and so on), and more recently electric transport.

Historically, the transport sector – with the exception of urban mass transit and electrified rail – was nearly totally dependent on liquid fuels. This, however, is rapidly changing, as further described in Chapter 18 of this handbook, as countries such as the UK are banning the sale of internal combustion engines (ICEs) as early as 2030.

An example of how demand forecasting is done may be found in the work of the IEA on global level, by the California Energy Commission (CEC) for the state of California or by independent system operators (ISOs) such as the New England ISO and others. In all cases, the demand forecast takes into account expected changes in demand-side technologies, including self-generation and the impact of energy efficiency improvements over time.

In the case of the state of California, the agency responsible for forecasting demand, the CEC, also happens to be the agency that sets building codes and appliance energy efficiency standards – which directly influence demand growth. And this being California, the CEC is doing its utmost to keep the demand growth to bare minimum while steering the state's economy towards carbon neutrality by 2045 as required by the Senate Bill 100 (California Legislative Information, 2018) further described in Box 13.1.[7]

BOX 13.1 CALIFORNIA ADOPTS ZERO NET ENERGY BUILDING CODE TO CURTAIL DEMAND GROWTH[8]

In May 2018, the CEC adopted a new building code that requires virtually all *new* residential buildings built in California beginning in 2020 to be zero net energy (Figure 13.2). In practice, this means that all new residential buildings not only have to be super energy efficient but come with solar panels on the roof – with a few exceptions.[9] In announcing the new building codes, CEC Commissioner Andrew McAllister said, 'The marketplace is ready', adding that the new standards are cost-effective and the technologies widely available and already required under many local building ordinances. The CEC expects to see some 80 000 new solar homes a year beginning in 2020.

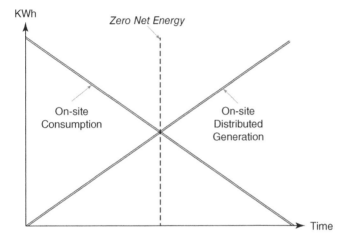

Source: Author.

Figure 13.2 Illustration of how a building can fulfil a zero net energy requirement

Based on its analysis, the CEC says typical homeowner would realize savings of over $19 000 in reduced energy bills over 30 years while adding only $9500 in costs, leaving them better off in net costs. The analysis depends on assumptions about costs and expected savings, both of which are likely to change over time.

The policy makers in California are under intense pressure to meet the state's ambitious 2006 climate bill, which aims to reduce state-wide greenhouse gas emissions to 1990 level by 2020 (already achieved) and further reducing them by 40 per cent by 2030.

As Box 13.1 makes clear, in some places, regulators and policy makers are actively engaged in managing demand growth through building codes and appliance efficiency standards. Such regulatory interventions impact future demand. Moreover, in some cases, retail prices are also used to encourage energy conservation – say by having tiered pricing schemes where the retail prices rise at higher consumption levels.[10]

Moving forward, it is becoming apparent that continuous energy efficiency improvements plus the rise of behind-the-meter self-generation will impact demand growth as well as peak demand, as illustrated in Box 13.2.

BOX 13.2   DISTRIBUTED GENERATION IS LOWERING CONSUMPTION AND PEAK DEMAND[11]

It must be self-evident that if you aggregate the collective actions of millions of customers who invest in distributed energy resources (DERs) – which include energy efficiency (EE) improvements and distributed generation (DG), primarily in the form of solar PVs – the result is lower electricity demand from the network (Asmus 2020). With the rising retail tariffs and falling costs of distributed generation, energy efficiency and distributed storage, generating more of the energy you need and using it more efficiently are both practical and profitable (Sioshansi 2014).

Confirmation of this phenomenon is appearing in more places, including a ten-year forecast of demand and peak load released by ISO New England (ISO NE) in March 2018. Similar impacts are beginning to be felt on many networks across the globe. DERs are real and are impacting both demand and peak loads on networks.

In the case of ISO NE, the gross forecast, *excluding* the effects of EE and PVs, projects a compound annual growth rate (CAGR) of about 0.9 per cent in total energy usage from 142 488 gigawatt-hours (GWh) in 2018 to 154 364 GWh in 2027. When the impact of EE and PVs is taken into account, however, *net* energy usage is expected to drop by a CAGR of –0.9 per cent, from 124 252 GWh to 114 981 GWh during the same period. In the case of the six-state New England region served by ISO NE, energy efficiency is projected to save on average about 2059 GWh each year through 2027.

Likewise, peak gross demand in New England is projected to rise by a CAGR of 0.8 per cent, from 29 060 megawatts (MW) in 2018 to an estimated 31 192 MW in 2027 under normal summer weather conditions. However, when the demand-reducing effects of PVs and EE are taken into account, net peak forecast *falls* slightly over the ten-year period, by about –0.4 per cent annually, from 25 729 MW to 24 912 MW. ISO NE projects that about 3442 MW of cumulative PV capacity will be added to its network over the next ten years – and New England is not the sunniest part of the US.

Looking at 2017, annual energy usage *declined* by 2.6 per cent, to 120 668 GWh, compared to a 2016 weather-normalized value of 123 953 GWh. System demand peaked at 23 968 MW between 4 pm and 5 pm on 13 June 2017. Without the demand reductions from the region's active demand-side resources, EE measures and behind-the-meter solar PVs, the peak would have been 27 014 MW.

On the west side of the US, the impact of energy efficiency and behind-the-meter distributed generation is also noticeable and growing. California Independent System Operator (CAISO) reported that energy efficiency and DERs saved $2.6 billion in avoided transmission costs.

Likewise, the National Grid in the UK reported that overall transmission system demand was anticipated to be *lower* in summer of 2018 than in 2017, with minimum transmission demand at 17 GW, and peak demand forecast at 33.7 GW between June and August. The reduced projected peak demand is due to the rising distributed generation, primarily from solar installations. 2017 marked the first time that National Grid observed a day-time minimum fall below the overnight minimum. This was caused by the high solar PV and wind output and is expected to become more pronounced over time as Britain experiences high PV output days, robust wind and high temperatures. Solar PV and wind generation connected to the distribution network has risen to 12.9 GW and 5.7 GW, respectively, and is changing the country's demand profile while adding challenges to the operability of the network for National Grid.

The preceding discussion illustrates that in forecasting future demand one must capture major departures from the historical patterns. Moreover, it is clear that anybody looking at the future of demand must focus on how demand-side technologies are changing and their long-term impact – including the following:

- accelerated conversion to electricity from other fuels – natural gas[12] and oil – notably in the transport sector but also in the commercial and industrial sectors;

- rapid advances in energy efficiency making virtually all electricity using devices, appliances and motors more efficient (Sioshansi 2013);
- improvements in building energy use from more stringent codes and standards;
- technological advances that include devices becoming *smarter* and increasingly *connected*, enabling improved monitoring and management of how much electricity is used as well as the pattern of use (Sioshansi 2020c); and
- increased interest in more granular tariffs that vary by time of use (Faruqui and Bourbonnais 2020) and potentially location – providing signals to consumers on when to use electricity, where to locate on the network, and how to take advantage of variable and locational prices – say by shifting or adjusting flexible loads, self-generation, storage or trading.

It is generally agreed that continued advances in energy efficiency will make all buildings and devices more electricity frugal over time – with wide variations across the globe. The evidence for this is further explained in Box 13.3.

It must, of course, be noted that the phenomenon of falling demand described in Box 13.3 is mostly applicable to the more advanced economies whose demand is already saturated, as explained in Section 2. In much of the rest of the world, demand for electricity is growing, only limited by the network's ability to meet it.

Against this background of broadly falling demand in OECD countries comes a development that may reverse the trend due to the rapid expected rise of EVs. EVs are among the most important demand-side technologies with potentially significant impact on electricity consumption and – more important – on peak demand depending on how and when they are charged (Sioshansi 2020i).

There is little disagreement that the number of EVs will rise over time (Box 13.4). It follows that more EVs will require more charging stations and that will increase electricity consumption as the global light-duty car fleet gradually converts to electric over time. There is, however, considerable debate on how fast this transition is likely to be.

BOX 13.3   WHY HAS ELECTRICITY DEMAND GROWTH BEEN FALLING WITHIN OECD ECONOMIES?[13]

While global electricity demand has grown every year in the past 50 years, except in 2009 (and 2020 due to the global pandemic), its rate of growth has declined relative to the level of economic activity. This phenomenon has been documented for the US by comparing real gross domestic product (GDP) growth with electricity demand growth between 1950 and the present. In nearly all OECD countries, the same is true: electricity demand is growing less than the rate of growth of GDP.

The differential between the two flipped in the 1980s in the US (Gruter and Moore 2018). While during the electric power industry's golden period of the 1950s–80s, US electricity demand grew at 5.6 per cent per annum *above* real GDP growth in subsequent decades, this spread declined and reversed in the 1980s. Since 2000, US electricity demand has been growing at 1.3 per cent per annum *below* real GDP growth. For the period 2016–17, it was 2.1 per cent below. Mature economies tend to be service economies, which means that the economic output can grow while using less energy (Rifkin 2014).

BOX 13.4 RAPID GROWTH OF EVs

For some time, there has been speculation about the expected growth of EVs with continuously rising projections of how many may be on the roads in the future. In its *World Energy Outlook*, the IEA, for example, projected that by 2040 half of all global light duty vehicles will be electric – roughly 1 billion of them (IEA 2018). Volkswagen, the world's biggest automaker, for example, expects to offer as many as 70 new electric models by 2028 and produce as many as 22 million EVs over the next decade.

Not surprisingly, both the automakers and oil companies are changing gear. For the former, the message is rather unambiguous: phase out ICEs while increasing production of EVs with new models to fit the needs of diverse global consumers. It will be an expensive changeover, but it is inevitable.

In some countries, generous government subsidies are leading to the virtual phase out of ICEs within the next decade, as in the case of Norway (Box 13.5). Sweden recently joined Denmark and Norway in proposing a total ban of ICE sales starting in 2030, the same as in the UK. California has announced that it would ban the sale of ICEs starting in 2035. Other countries and a number of cities have also proposed similar bans in the same time frame. This is yet another example of policy intervention impacting future demand for electricity, as was pointed out in case of building codes and appliance energy efficiency standards. What will ultimately matter, however, is not what Norway or Denmark decide but what policies are adopted in populous countries like China, the US or India.[14]

How much of an additional load will EVs become and how soon depends on how fast they replace the existing ICE fleet as well as other developments such as whether the future EVs will be autonomous and/or shared with the rising popularity of car hailing

---

BOX 13.5 WHY NORWAY LEADS IN EV ADOPTION[15]

In the race to substitute EVs for ICEs, no country currently matches Norway in penetration rates. By the end of 2018, Norway was approaching the 300 000 mark for all electric and plug-in hybrids (PHEVs). While China and California have more EVs, they are no way near the Norwegian levels when adjusted for the country's population of 5.2 million. Starting in 2019, more EVs are expected to be sold in Norway than ICEs.

Why is Norway promoting EVs? Because they can be charged from a nearly 100 per cent hydro-based system. Every ICE replaced by an EV in Norway results in a significant drop in greenhouse gas emissions. This is not necessarily true in China or say in Kentucky, where the bulk of generation is coming from coal.

The rapid conversion to EVs is such that if any Norwegian were to buy an ICE today, they may have a hard time selling it in a few years. Who would want to buy an ICE in a few years' time? Which explains why Norway plans to ban the sale of all ICEs starting in 2025. The way things are heading, by the time 2025 arrives, the ban may be a moot point.

By 2030, Norway expects to have 1.5 million EVs on the road, consuming an estimated 4 terawatt-hours (TWh) of hydro-generated electricity. The Norwegian Electric Vehicle Association says the existing grid should be able to handle the extra load with minor challenges. California, with a much bigger population, is planning to have as many as 5 million EVs within a decade, while China is likely to be the biggest EV market by a wide margin.

services and the emergence of transport-as-a service (TaaS) replacing the current car ownership model, especially in urban areas (Sperling 2018).

With the growth of renewable generation, many experts believe that much of the EV demand may be met by variable wind and solar generation resources, which tend to fluctuate from hour to hour, day to day and seasonally. EVs, the thinking goes, can help grid operators by soaking up the excess renewable generation when available for use at other times – the so-called grid-to-vehicle (G2V) mode (Sioshansi 2020i). Moreover, EVs can potentially discharge some of their stored energy back to the grid when and if needed, in the so-called vehicle-to-grid (V2G) mode.[16]

In this context, it is fair to say that the growing numbers of EVs can be a boom or a bust for the electricity sector depending on how and when they are charged, or potentially discharged. As described in Box 13.6, if charging is properly managed, EVs can be network friendly, and not necessarily adding a lot to the peak demand.

BOX 13.6   ELECTRIC VEHICLE CHARGING: FRIEND OR FOE?[17]

There is little doubt that electric transport is coming and soon. The only debate is how fast. This explains why in September 2018, ChargePoint, a US EV charging company, announced that it was installing 2.5 million EV charging spots worldwide by 2025. And this is just one among many.

The announcement represents significant growth for the company, which currently has just 50 000 charging spots. Pasquale Romano, ChargePoint's CEO said, 'The time for transformative change is now, and broadly distributed, substantial and immediate investments in charging infrastructure are necessary to usher in the future of e-mobility'. He is not alone in his enthusiasm for the rapidly growing EV charging business.

That is good news for those with range anxiety. But what are all those EVs going to do to the distribution network, especially if the drivers decide to plug in at the same time and on already congested networks? The answer is that EV charging, if cleverly managed, can help rather than hurt the grid operator (Sioshansi 2020i). A clue on how this may happen came from eMotorWerks, another EV charging provider, who said it was offering CAISO, the California's grid operator, additional flexibility by introducing 30 MW of demand response (DR) through a smart EV charging scheme.

eMotorWerks, acquired by Italy's Enel, is rolling out its smart grid EV charger as a virtual battery that can participate as a DR resource in the California's wholesale market. The company is in the midst of installing some 6000 smart EV chargers in California with 30 MW of capacity and 70 MWh of storage using eMotorWerks' JuiceNet cloud-based software platform to manage charging loads to balance grid demand, reducing wholesale energy costs while mitigating the intermittency of renewables.

EV charging companies have long touted the potential for electric vehicles to provide grid services, while utilities have been concerned about the impact the EV charging load could have on local distribution circuits. eMotorWerks says it is addressing both issues with one solution by relying on a sophisticated software that appears to the grid operator as a virtual battery. According to Preston Roper, chief operating officer of eMotorWerks, the proprietary software predicts when load will be high and can shift charging times at its connected EV chargers to reduce load without affecting drivers. The software only makes small reductions in charging for any individual EV for a short amount of time, but in aggregate is enough to have an impact on the grid. He said, 'We don't want the driver left high and dry', adding, 'We are reducing charging rather than taking energy out of the car'.

eMotorWerks says it developed the capability to track the status of all generation resources on the grid in real time. This allows EVs to charge when ample wind and solar resources are available, thus enabling greater integration of renewable energy. The software can also be used by commercial and industrial customers who can reduce load at times of peak demand to minimize demand charges, a valuable service.[18]

EVs, in other words, are not necessarily the grid or network operator's nemesis. On the contrary, they can serve as virtual batteries, shift load, absorb excess generation and relieve congestion on the network if the charging is properly managed.

Since the topic is covered in Chapter 18 of this handbook, this section does not dwell on forecasts of electricity demand growth from EVs. It suffices to say that government policies, mandatory targets as well as subsidies can have significant impact, as in the case of Norway or California. Other developments such as autonomous EVs, ride hailing and sharing are major factors, as are studies that suggest that high penetration of EVs and PVs – if cleverly matched and coordinated – can result in a situation where a large fleet of EVs can essentially be charged from the 'free' mid-day sunshine from solar rooftop panels without putting too much stress on the local distribution network – or in some cases potentially *relieving* congestion (Webb, Whitehead and Wilson 2019).

The key question, of course, is whether the decline in the rate of demand growth described in Box 13.3 – which is pronounced among the OECD economies – continues, or will the expected electrification of the transport sector increase electricity consumption over time – which effect in aggregate will prevail? The conventional wisdom is that the latter will outpace the former. But there are those who believe that the continued improvements in energy efficiency, especially in motors and lighting – two major consumers of electricity – may cancel much of the expected growth in EV demand as, further explained in Box 13.7.

Aside from EVs, there is speculation about the impact of digitalization, cloud services and data centre demand, demand for crypto currency mining and new data-intensive

---

BOX 13.7   WILL EVs BOOST ELECTRICITY CONSUMPTION?[19]

What can we expect for demand growth moving forward? Will new uses for electricity – most notably to charge increasing numbers of electric vehicles as well as the electrification of heating, industrial processes and other energy-intensive applications – lead to increased demand, and if so by how much and how soon?

Executives in the electric power sector are naturally excited at the prospects of EV demand growth and, more broadly, the electrification of the transport sector to boost electricity demand in the same way that the commercialization of air conditioning did in the 1950s–70s – a trend that is still strong in many developing economies.

That, however, may be wishful thinking. According to James Moore, partner in Capital Goods Research at Redburn in London, the electrification of the cars will *not* necessarily dent the established trends towards *reduced* electricity consumption (Gruter and Moore 2018). The reason? Ever more energy-efficient lighting and motors will offset most of the gains in increased EV electricity consumption. This, of course, is not what people in the power sector would like to hear.

According to Redburn's analysis, in the case of the US, roughly 60 per cent of electricity consumption comes from just four end uses, with similar numbers for many OECD countries. They are lighting, heating, ventilation and air conditioning (HVAC), machine drive and appliances.

A closer look at these four categories reveals that the electricity-consuming component of HVAC, machine drive and some appliances – notably, washing machines, tumble dryers and vacuum cleaners – is the motor. In fact, Redburn's research concludes that motors are the world's single biggest electricity-using device, ahead of lighting, accounting for an astonishing 30–35 per cent of world's electricity consumption. Not surprisingly, as motors get more efficient, demand for electricity can be expected to fall, all else being equal. A handful of big and hundreds of smaller suppliers dominate in manufacturing of electrical motors and all are confronted by ever more efficient standards forcing them to make their motors, particularly the big ones, more efficient.[20]

A similar scenario applies to lighting – currently accounting for roughly 22 per cent of the global electricity demand. Here again, significant reductions in consumption can be achieved by switching to more efficient types of lighting, such as the light emitting diodes (LEDs), which represented 10 per cent of new global lighting unit sales in 2016 but were projected to account for 36 per cent by 2020. The savings in the lighting sector can be equally significant – for example – 90 per cent saving by replacing incandescent light bulbs by LEDs and 75 per cent by replacing compact fluorescent lights (CFLs) by LEDs.

With incandescent light bulbs expected to fall from the current 80 per cent of the installed base to 20 per cent by 2023, Redburn expects the global lighting electricity consumption to halve in the next five years.[21] This alone should reduce global electricity demand by 2.3 per cent per annum. The pattern is already obvious in falling electricity sales in many parts of the world. Combined, these two end uses alone can *reduce* global annual electricity demand growth to roughly 3 per cent below global real GDP growth in the coming five years.

Will the expected rise of demand from EVs not more than offset the gains from energy efficiency? The short answer, according to Redburn is, not necessarily. Redburn expects average global electricity consumption from EVs to grow from around 8 TWh in 2017 to 1800 TWh by 2040. While this is a massive increase, it represents only 5 per cent of projected global electricity consumption in 2040. Why so little? The simple answer is that EVs are incredibly efficient in converting energy to mobility, certainly compared to ICEs (Sioshansi 2020i). According to Redburn, 'filling a vehicle with oil is one of the most expensive ways to purchase a usable unit of mobility: by a factor of 4–5x. This is because internal combustion engine (ICE) vehicles are inefficient and fuel taxes are high, especially in Europe'.

Moreover, driving 100 km in a conventional vehicle requires roughly 80 kWh of energy, because ICEs waste some 75–80% of their fuel generating heat rather than mechanical energy – the clue is in the word 'combustion'. Moreover, a typical ICE has as many as 1000 moving parts as opposed to 70–80 or fewer for an EV. This means that the average EV needs as little as 25 kWh to travel 100 km, even after accounting for the energy lost during charging and 'vampire losses' as the battery mildly depletes over time. Divide 80 kWh/100 km by 25 kWh/100 km and the result shows that EVs are 3.3x more efficient if not better.

Notwithstanding the 2020 global pandemic, Redburn expects EV sales to take off after 2023 as battery costs continue to decline, range continues to improve and charging infrastructure becomes ubiquitous, including more fast-charging stations. By 2023, Redburn expects 61 per cent of new car sales to be EVs with a fast rate of turnover given that the global fleet of ICEs, on average, reaches retirement age in 18 years. Not everyone, of course, agrees with these predictions given that EV sales are currently in low single digits globally.

According to Redburn, 'while the "peakiness" of fast-charging load profiles of EVs will need to be managed by utilities, we only expect EVs to add 3 per cent to global electricity demand by 2035, the equivalent of 0.2 per cent per annum demand growth. As such, while many players in the power industry talk about EVs as the next big thing, we do *not* expect the electrification of the car to in any way dent the electricity consumption reduction caused by more energy-efficient lighting and motors'.

applications in speech/facial recognition, AI and machine learning (Sioshansi 2017). Some analysts expect these applications to boost electricity consumption significantly, while others argue that data centres and other data-centric businesses will increasingly use customized chips and processors that use a fraction of the energy currently used to collect, crunch, store and transfer data, and these advances will result in total electricity consumption of the IT or the ICT sector to remain virtually flat.[22] Another important debate is how the more efficient and smarter future devices be controlled and managed, further described in Section 5.

Another interesting form of demand-side technology is the off-grid and pay-as-you-go or PAYGO model, where a self-contained, stand-alone system provides limited services in isolated locations with no infrastructure. A typical installation may consist of solar PV panels, a battery and few lights and high-value appliances such as mobile phone chargers (Couture et al. 2019). But similar examples of self-contained systems are increasingly seen across the globe where a stand-alone device produces, stores and consumes electricity without necessarily being connected to the network. For example, a number of bus stops in Zaragoza, Spain, have PV panels on the top of the canopy generating power, which can be stored in batteries under the seats, powering the screens and providing lighting for the canopy.[23]

Similarly, other self-contained, stand-alone applications are appearing in large numbers all over the world, including parking meters, outdoor lights, traffic signals, wireless relay signals, to mention a few. At the same time, many mobile and/or outdoor applications are emerging with a combination of distributed solar and storage, providing basic if limited services, such as for a houseboat. The advances in technology allowing self-contained generation, storage and consumption could play an increasing role as the costs of such devices continue to fall. The same pattern is observed with isolated PAYGO solar micro-grids and self-contained energy communities that are increasingly able to provide services with little reliance on the traditional networks (Robinson 2020b). In most cases, these stand-alone devices and/or semi-independent energy communities do not add to the demand on the network. In places with little existing infrastructure, they are a substitute for non-existing grids, and regulators are beginning to recognize their value in such applications (Rai et al. 2020).

Regardless of how these applications may be classified, self-generation plus storage and stand-alone systems are interesting new forms of demand-side technologies. Moreover, self-generation is expected to reduce the number of kWH bought from the network in places such as Australia with its 2 million solar roofs (Swanston 2020a). Utilities in Australia are encouraging remote, expensive-to-serve customers to switch to stand-alone power system or SAPS[24] with cost savings to the rest of the customers (ibid.). Over time, such developments may result in the divergence of kWh consumption of electricity from sales or purchases from the network, a phenomenon already projected for California (Box 13.8). While it is premature to say how widespread this trend may be, it is fair to say

---

BOX 13.8   CALIFORNIA'S ELECTRICITY CONSUMPTION DIVERGES FROM SALES

Historically, electricity sales – that is, number of kWh sold to customers – equalled consumption – that is, kWh consumed by customers. Not anymore.

In its projections released in early 2019, the CEC says electricity sales will rise from about 260 000 GWh to 290 000 GWh in 2030 (CEC 2019). With the rise of distributed self-generation – mostly from rooftop solar PVs – consumption is no longer the same as sales – that is, kWh bought from the grid. According to the CEC, consumption, which includes self-generated power, is expected to rise to about 340 000 GWh by 2030 under the commission's mid-case scenario. This suggests a significant and growing deviation – in this case 50 000 GWh – as more consumers self-generate more of what they consume and increasingly have the option to store some of the generated power for later use.

California's ambitious energy efficiency standards, including the recently adopted zero net energy building code, are likely to trim the growth of sales figures even further.

that at least in some places some consumers can conceivably turn into *nonsumers* – that is, consumers who self-generate most of the kWh they use – but not necessarily all the time. The term nonsumer, used in a different context was first coined by Ben David in the preface to Sioshansi (2019a).

4. CONSUMER STRATIFICATION

One of the most important developments in the electricity business is the stratification of traditional consumers – defined as those who buy all their kWH from the network, typically under a bundled regulated tariff – to prosumers, prosumagers and more exotic varieties, further described in Sioshansi (2019a).

Customers who invest in distributed generation, usually in the form of rooftop solar PV panels, can easily generate as much as they consume, becoming prosumers – that is, become net producers of power during sunny hours of the day (Figure 13.3), which they can generally feed into the distribution network. The details, of course, vary from place to place based on the prevailing regulations.[25]

Some prosumers may go a step further by investing in distributed storage, allowing them to store some of the excess generation for use at later times. EVs, of course, are a form of distributed storage, as are batteries or other devices that can store energy. As the price of storage continues to fall, more prosumers will become prosumagers. The key question is how likely or widespread might such *stratification* be? The answer depends on the confluence of three important factors, which vary from one place to another.

The first and most important variable is retail electricity prices, taxes and levies therein. The higher they are, the more incentive consumers have to become prosumers by generating more of their own and/or using less through energy efficiency investments. The second is the prevailing policy and regulations affecting the relative economics of DERs vs full reliance on bundled services from the distribution network. In places with generous feed-in tariffs (FiTs) or net energy metering (NEM) schemes, more consumers are likely to become prosumers. Conversely, in places where there are restrictions on how much of the excess solar PV generation can be fed into the network and/or if little is paid for it, then more of the self-generated power is used for self-consumption.

The third factor is the continuous innovation and technological advancements that makes alternative service options feasible and commercially viable (Sioshansi 2017).

Over time, and depending on these three variables, consumers will self-select, and in the process may be, broadly speaking, stratified into four more-or-less distinct groups:

- Consumer refers to those who continue to buy *all* kWH from the distribution network and pay more-or-less the current regulated bundled rates. These consumers, while not entirely thrilled with their current supplier, may nevertheless not be sufficiently motivated and/or have attractive options to move away from the status quo.[26]
- Prosumer refers to those who invest in energy efficiency and/or self-generation, thereby reducing or virtually eliminating their net electricity purchase from the network.[27] Most prosumers, however, will remain connected to the distribution network and be dependent on the grid for balancing their variable generation and load.

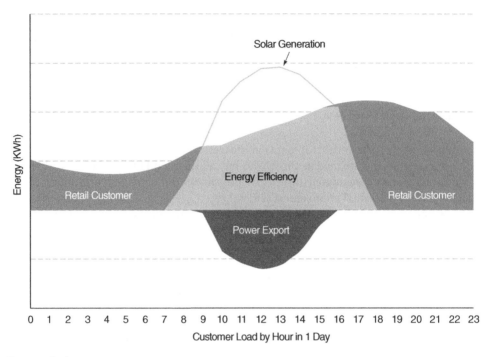

Source: Author.

Figure 13.3   The first step to consumer stratification: consumers become prosumers

- Prosumager refers to those who may go a step beyond prosumer by investing in distributed storage, making them even less dependent on the distribution network because they can store some of the excess generation for use at later times.
- More exotic versions of prosumagers, including consumers who may trade or share their energy generation and consumption imbalance with others. Such P2P schemes may become feasible through intermediaries and/or aggregators offering platforms where trading and sharing can take place (Glachant 2020). These more exotic options are currently in their infancy but are beginning to be introduced on pilot scale.

While there are those who speculate rising numbers of prosumers, prosumagers, aggregators and so on, others are sceptical, pointing out that their numbers will remain relatively small and their overall impact on demand minimal to negligible (Richter and Pollitt 2018). To what extent, how soon, and where such consumer stratification may take place is a matter of debate (Stagnaro and Benedettini 2020). In Australia, for example, over 2.4 million households (more than 20 per cent of the total) have already become prosumers by investing in solar roofs, primarily motivated to reduce their electric bills (Swanston 2020a). Whether and when they migrate further away from the status quo remains to be seen (Figure 13.4). In some places, a day may arrive where the bulk of the consumers may no longer be the traditional type (De Clerq et al. 2020). This is what happened to telephone customers who cut the cord by going wireless (Smith and MacGill 2020). In other

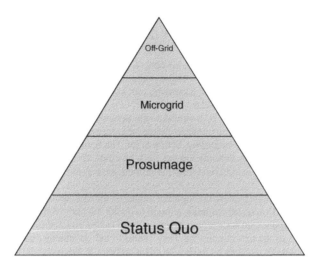

Note: The pyramid illustrates the potential migration of traditional customers (the status quo on bottom) to other forms, progressively less reliant on the traditional grid services (top).

Source: Author.

Figure 13.4   Consumer stratification pyramid

places, the bulk of customers may remain as traditional consumers, on the bottom of the pyramid (Mountain 2020).

If consumer stratification takes place it will have important implications, including:

- challenges for the traditional business model of distributor system operators and energy suppliers (Meeus and Glachant 2018);
- cost shifting among different customer groups (Schittekatte 2020);
- raising questions about who is subsidizing whom (Davis 2018);
- what regulators will do in response to such developments (Burger et al. 2019); and
- how this game will play out as new business models emerge (Mountain 2019).

Should the number of non-traditional consumers multiply – as in Australia – the interface and the relationship between each consumer category and their service providers will diverge. What is becoming obvious is that the technology is currently available – at a modest cost premium – to build homes and buildings that require little or no net kWH from the grid on an annual basis, and this cost premium is rapidly shrinking (Schlesinger 2020). This is not to say that such buildings can operate on their own or go off-grid, but they can easily generate as many kWH as they consume, as described in Box 13.9. The key question is how widespread will the adoption of such buildings be in the coming decades and if their numbers become pronounced, how will the costs of maintaining the grid be redistributed?

Box 13.9, however, raises a number of fairness and equity questions for the regulators as well as business issues for the distribution and retailing companies (Schittekatte,

---

BOX 13.9 GOING ZERO NET ENERGY (ZNE)[28]

The ZNE phenomenon is spreading in the US, Europe, Australia and elsewhere – even in the absence of a regulatory mandate. While still a narrow niche market appealing to the environmentally minded and upper end of the new housing market, it is taking root as more homebuyers demand it and more architects and builders learn how to build it.

A case in point is a new home built by Ben and Joyce Schlesinger in St. Michaels, Maryland, USA (Schlesinger 2020). In building the customized house, the couple had three main goals – beauty, functionality and environmental compatibility, in that order. The Schlesingers' home has a number of design features few homeowners or homebuilders have heard of. To start off, they drilled eight geo-thermal wells 220 feet deep to extract heat from the ground, even in the winter, using ground-source heat pump.[29]

The house has 50 SunPower high-efficiency solar panels on the roof, providing 18 kW of generation capacity plus three Tesla Powerwall batteries, enough to power the home through short outages. Not surprisingly, the Schlesingers are early EV adopters, with two Teslas, which they intend to charge from their own solar panels to the extent possible. They intend to rely as little as possible on the grid or fossil fuels. Posting periodic updates on the house on his website, in November 2018 Ben said, 'Rains have severely reduced solar energy production, but on even partly sunny days, energy use has been balancing out this fall – and that's with HVAC and hot water systems, the kitchen, and lighting all up and running!'

Pointing out that the house is *not* off-grid, Ben said, 'This house is on-grid . . . but . . . we've sized our battery storage large enough to let us use all excess solar energy during evening peak periods and at night. Also, together with the solar panels, the Powerwalls will serve as our emergency back-up generator in case the house loses power'. Ben explains that his intention is to run the EVs on solar-generated power and if possible 'will charge them during daylight hours so they'll be running on solar energy, versus the regional transmission organization PJM's coal-dominated daytime energy mix. Then, on evenings after charging the cars, what happens depends on the season – on winter nights, the house will probably need to use electricity from the grid, which at that point relies mostly on high-efficiency natural gas turbines; on summer nights after charging the EVs, we expect the Powerwalls will hold enough solar-generated electricity to make it till dawn without buying electricity'.

In December 2018, Ben reported that his monthly electric bill was $11 – many of his neighbours pay $400–500 or more per month for houses of equal size.[30] One can argue that Ben is being subsi-dized by his non-solar neighbours, who use many kWh and pay big bills that go to support the grid on which Ben continues to rely, not all the time but on occasions when his batteries are empty, say after a few cloudy days. This, however, is not Ben's fault. He dutifully pays his utility bills. They just happen to be extremely low since the prevailing regulation has not caught up with the type of pro-sumagers like Ben, of whom there may be more.

Ben has set up his house as a laboratory. On the website he asks: 'What did all this cost, and will it ever pay back? How much carbon are we preventing from entering the atmosphere, and what's our per-unit avoided cost of carbon? Will we actually be carbon neutral? Stay tuned. We'll know once we've gotten a full year of operations under our belt'.

What Ben has done is not for everyone. And not everyone has his knowledge or the financial resources. But there are probably many Schlesingers elsewhere in the world who would like to accomplish similar feats once the technologies move mainstream and prices fall over time. Moreover, if more states and countries adopt strict building codes such as the one already in place in California, the concept of ZNE may become the norm for new buildings.

Momber and Meeus 2018). The current bundled regulated tariffs were designed in an environment where customer defection and stratification did not exist (Sioshansi 2019b). As more consumers move away from total reliance on buying all kWH from the grid, they shift more of the fixed costs of maintaining the grid to the remaining consumers. Since prosumers and prosumagers pay little or nothing under current volumetric tariffs, this becomes a thorny regulatory issue especially in places with generous net energy metering laws or FiTs (Davis 2018).

The prevailing flat volumetric tariffs, currently the norm in the US and many parts of the world, plus very low or non-existent demand or fixed charges – also prevalent in much of the US for residential consumers – explain part of the appeal of distributed generation and storage. But even with adjustments in tariffs and increased fixed charges, the motivation to avoid paying high retail rates in many parts of the world will persist.[31]

5. IMPACT OF DIGITALIZATION ON DEMAND AND THE EMERGENCE OF NEW BUSINESS MODELS

As further described in Chapter 17 by Glachant in this handbook, it is widely expected that over time virtually all devices, as well as EVs, will get smarter, more efficient and increasingly connected to the Internet as well other devices and/or gateways to the house. This process, sometimes referred to as digitalization, will allow electricity consumption of individual devices to be remotely monitored and managed, greatly increasing both the utilization and efficiency of energy use. As more consumers opt to self-generate, store and potentially share or trade with their peers, the opportunities to better manage these behind-the-meter assets becomes overwhelming.

While it is not clear who will own or manage the gateway to homes and buildings and how soon the smart home concept may materialize, there are indications that existing Big Data-centric companies such as Amazon, Google, Apple, Microsoft and their counterparts in China and elsewhere are keen to enter the business, with significant implications, as further explained in Box 13.10.

BOX 13.10   AMAZON ENTERS THE SMART HOME[32]

For years, the biggest puzzle for those who follow Big Data-centric companies such as Apple, Google, Amazon, Facebook and others was, what is stopping them from entering the smart home and behind-the-meter (BTM) space? Why was, for example, Google not expanding the capabilities and the reach of its Nest wireless thermostat to do other, more interesting, and more useful things?

One answer may be that the smart home and BTM business is highly fragmented, with millions of gadgets, appliances and devices manufactured by thousands of vendors across the globe. Moreover, it is not easy to get the smart wireless thermostat to communicate with the lights, the garage door opener, the microwave or the TV – unless all these devices are manufactured by the same vendor with compatible built-in communication capabilities (Shaw-Williams 2020). While a few techno-freaks may enjoy the challenge of getting various devices to talk to one another, most homeowners do not. Another big obstacle is mounting concerns about privacy, cyber security and existing or pending regulations that may make it difficult for companies to gain access to potentially sensitive consumer or device data.

Despite the obstacles, Amazon has announced its intention to enter the smart home business[33] with Alexa, its voice activated personal assistant – which is already treated as a trusted family member in some households.[34] The aim is to reach a point where the homeowner can simply say, 'Alexa, dim the kitchen lights' and it is done. Even more useful would be to say, 'Alexa, goodnight' and have all the lights turned off, the doors locked, and the thermostat set on lower level until you wake up the next day and say, 'Alexa, good morning', when the coffee machine starts brewing, Alexa tunes in to your favourite radio station, gives you the day's news and weather forecast while adjusting the thermostat to whatever you are comfortable with.

But how could Amazon deliver on what has eluded others up to now? The answer may be Amazon's reach and its economies of scale. Since it sells a multitude of gadgets, it can make them all compatible with Alexa, turning it into a connected platform within the house and beyond.[35] Amazon already offers Alexa-enabled chips, which can be imbedded in all kinds of devices. Amazon believes that voice activated commands, for which Alexa is well-suited, is the easiest way to communicate with in-house devices.[36]

Not everyone is convinced that Amazon will succeed, but the company has deep pockets and is known to persevere in pursuing grand strategies to successful fruition even when others abandon them prematurely.

The proliferation of technologies that can remotely monitor and adjust load, distributed generation and storage and/or facilitate P2P trading are other areas where exciting developments can be expected in the near term. The evolution of smart and connected devices, of course, is not limited to stationary devices in buildings, but also expands to EVs. In this context, who manages and optimizes the charging of the EVs, when and where, and potentially also manages their discharging depending on prices and congestion on the distribution network, becomes critical, as further described in Box 13.11.

BOX 13.11   MY EV, YOUR PV – OR THE OTHER WAY AROUND?[37]

With so many solar homes and an increasing number of EVs, it is easy to imagine new and potentially profitable business models. One such idea was recently outlined by Vincent Schachter, senior vice-president of Energy Services of eMotorWerks in an interview with *Microgrid Knowledge*. The basic concept is that EVs, buildings with rooftop solar PVs and/or distributed storage and smallish microgrids will be key market actors in a future where consumers produce, store, share or trade energy.

It is not hard to imagine a future where an EV driver could pull up to a small microgrid consisting of one or more connected solar homes, plug in and 'trade' with the energy sellers within. Conversely, the EV could conceivably discharge some of its excess electricity to homeowners (or the grid) on a cloudy day. As described in the *Microgrid Knowledge* article, eMotorWerks and LO3 Energy have joined forces to demonstrate that such a future is feasible. The two companies announced in December 2018 that they were testing systems and software that will let consumers buy and sell electricity within microgrids using their solar homes and EVs without an intermediary or a central clearinghouse. The partners want to test the feasibility of an energy ecosystem where EVs do not just charge, but also discharge, and where future prosumers can better control their energy generation, consumption and storage.[38] The idea is not without merit. By 2025, there are likely to be an estimated 3 million EVs on the US roads – if not more – representing 26 GW of mobile storage capacity by one estimate.

However, while the basics are simple, many complicated transactions have to be managed. For example, the scheme has to allow participants to bid prices for buying or selling electricity similar to how traders currently do in competitive wholesale power markets but on a miniscule scale, with solar households and EV owners as traders. Crucially, the idea is to make this possible without a central clearinghouse or an intermediary using a blockchain ledger (Trbovich et al. 2020).

In practice, an EV driver could transact with the small-scale microgrid in a variety of ways. The EV owner can leverage the flexibility inherent in storage capacity of its battery, while the PV households can gain an additional source of revenue for the rooftop solar, especially during sunny days when there is generation exceeding demand on the distribution network.

Who buys or sells what will depend on circumstances, timing, price, location and congestion on the distribution network. On a cloudy day, for example, the homeowners in the microgrid may be willing to buy energy from the EV. On a sunny day, when the households have excess solar energy, they may offer the EV owner low-cost electricity for charging the batteries.

The buyers and sellers could agree on the price for such transactions (Barrager and Cazalet 2016, 2020). For example, a household might offer to buy energy if it falls below a threshold price. Or the EV owner may say you can use my battery all night so long as it is fully charged by 8 am when I leave for work and need the EV's full range for the morning commute. In practice, of course, the communication and the transactions will be automated, algorithm-driven and/or the parameters pre-set by buyers and sellers. In other words, the traders would hardly, if ever, be manually bidding in real time (Cazalet, Kohanim and Hasidim 2020). AI and machine learning will figure out when to buy or sell and at what price based on behaviour patterns, service needs and other parameters set by the traders in the scheme, observed, learned and improved over time.

Such automated schemes help with another major EV challenge – namely, managing the stress on the distribution network. Charging an EV, depending on the speed, can be equivalent to the capacity requirements of two or three typical homes on the distribution network. With millions of EVs added over time, how can the existing grid handle the extra load? The answer depends on the timing and location of EVs, when they are charged, or potentially discharged (see Box 13.6).

There are, of course, many anecdotal examples of other start-ups who are entering similar BTM applications, using remote monitoring and AI to better manage electricity consumption, distributed generation and storage. Many start-ups and established companies are trying to develop practical and profitable business models. Only time will tell how many will succeed and in what form (Sioshansi 2019a).

Among the exciting developments is the emergence of intelligent aggregators who are trying to manage and optimize a portfolio of loads, distributed generation and storage. Additionally, others are exploring opportunities to enable P2P trading and/or other forms of transactions. One particular opportunity with near-term potential is the so-called virtual power plants (VPPs), further described in Box 13.12.

BOX 13.12   VIRTUAL POWER PLANTS[39]

Over the past few years, a number of players have entered the virtual power plant or VPP business. They include well-known names such as Siemens, GE and Schneider Electric as well as companies traditionally in the energy management business such as Honeywell and others like Engie, Sonnen (now part of Shell) and Direct Energie, to name a few.

Increasingly, everyone is trying to manage and optimize an aggregation of both behind- and upfront-of-the-meter assets as a virtual power plant. By doing so, more value can be created as various devices make use of their inherent flexibility, consume at lower cost periods while relieving stress on the network. The most important gain, however, is that excess generation from variable solar and wind resources can effectively be harnessed and put into good use (Sioshansi 2020d). Otherwise wasted energy, be it low-priced solar or negative-priced wind – which is often curtailed when in excess of load – can be profitably utilized. This, in a nutshell is the emerging business model, assuming it can be profitably managed and scaled.

The fact that there is not enough storage and demand flexibility can be partly addressed by integrating a myriad of devices in existing buildings including air conditioners, heaters, water heaters, pool pumps, and so on.

At its heart, a VPP-based business model is about aggregation and smart intermediation (Lehmbruck et al. 2020). First, you gain scale by acquiring a large portfolio of assets – both in front and behind the meter – some generating power, others utilizing it and others storing and shifting usage. Any energy-using or -generating device, electric or otherwise, will do, including water heaters, air conditioners, chillers, batteries, EVs and/or EV charging stations, heat pumps, pool pumps, water pumps, back-up generators, you name it.

The larger the portfolio and the more varied the mix the better because the aggregate will contain more flexibility due to the fact that the various devices have little correlation in terms of when they use, generate, store or shift energy. This means that by combining the differing capacity profiles of a large number of connected devices the operator of the VPP can exercise maximum flexibility without impacting individual customers' usage or service experience.

The key enabling technology, of course, is the software and the AI that allows thousands or potentially millions of devices to be remotely monitored and controlled. As the AI learns more about each customer or participant's usage profile – for example, a baker's load profile vs an EV charging station – the better it can manage the services required while minimizing the costs.

VPPs gain additional revenue streams by extending their reach upstream of the meter, by providing desirable services to the distribution companies and/or the grid operator. Fluence, a joint venture of Siemens and AES, for example, recently acquired AMS (formerly Advanced Microgrid Solutions) to enhance its service offerings by using AMS's AI-enabled software. Others, including Sonnen, Sunrun, Tesla, Stem among others, are all essentially chasing the rapidly evolving VPP business model in one form or another (Sioshansi 2020d).

Next Kraftwerke (NK), based in Cologne, Germany, for example, has over 8.5 GW of flexible load/generation under management from over 10 000 participants on its network. By sending signals to its participating members, it can save them money by lowering their energy costs while getting paid by the grid operator for providing much needed capacity, ancillary services, flexibility, voltage support and other tangible services. Recently, NK, one of Europe's earliest and largest VPPs, announced that it was adding storage to its portfolio of assets to be able to provide enhanced frequency control as it expands beyond its German home base into new markets, including South Korea and Japan.

In the meantime, new businesses and business models are emerging that offer products and services that add value (Fox-Penner 2020). The challenge is to master the art of not only creating but monetizing that value to scale. As it happens, there is a powerful networking effect in running a VPP, a platform or data-driven business. The big players keep getting bigger and better, which attracts more business to their site at the expense of others (Löbbe et al. 2020). In the end, only a few will dominate the space, as has happened with Facebook, Uber, Airbnb and others, each dominating their respective space.

Additionally, many players are focusing on developing platforms, which have proven profitable in other industries. The surge of interest in platforms can be traced to the fact that they can bring large numbers of buyers and sellers together to trade in an open, transparent and efficient electronic marketplace while minimizing transaction costs – which can be significant given the complicated trades that are typically involved and the sheer volume of transactions, as further described in Box 13.13.

BOX 13.13   TRADING PLATFORMS FIND PROFITABLE NICHES

As the electricity sector is digitalized over time, it will make sense for all sorts of trading to take place among and between consumers, prosumers and prosumagers. Platforms, which are basically electronic marketplaces that bring buyers and sellers together, will make this possible and provide the means for such transactions to take place cheaply and with relative ease. For those who succeed, the profits could be enormous.

If the experience of other platforms in the restaurant food or flower delivery business is anything to go by, successful platform operators who can amass sizeable scale can enjoy profit margins in the

20–25 per cent range. Not bad, especially considering how little investment is required. And once successful, they can be scaled up quickly.

The promise of double-digit profit margins are attracting many start-ups who are beginning to make inroads into platforms in the electricity sector. Piclo, a UK start-up, for example, has developed a platform, Piclo Flex, for auctioning flexibility services on congested distribution networks – say those with heavy concentrations of EVs and/or PVs in particular neighbourhoods (Johnston and Sioshansi 2020).

Piclo has developed an online marketplace in the UK for distribution network operators (DNOs) who wish to procure demand-side flexibility to reduce congestion on the electricity grid. According to research by Imperial College, a smart and flexible grid could save UK customers £17–40 billion ($22–53 billion) by 2050 (Evans 2017). Electricity North West, one of the UK's DNOs, is posting areas on their network with flexibility needs in Piclo Flex to highlight where they are looking for flexibility services to better manage the network. Following the decision to test the Piclo Flex platform, Cara Blockley, Central Services Manager at Electricity North West, said: 'We are delighted to join the Piclo Flex consortium. An online platform could lower barriers and increase participation in this important new service needed by the industry'.

Electricity North West has joined other UK DNOs to trial the platform. Once a platform succeeds in delivering as promised, others are likely to join, making it more difficult for newcomers to enter the occupied space. First-mover advantage is of enormous value in electronic platforms.

James Johnston, CEO and co-founder of Piclo said: 'We hope to demonstrate how better visibility of flexible assets and streamlining of procurement processes through our platform can lead to better outcomes and more efficient operation of the grid'.

Other innovative developments are also taking place. For example, in a future where many consumers own EVs, solar roofs, distributed storage and intelligent BTM devices, they may choose to buy, sell or trade electricity in rather unorthodox ways. There is no longer a compelling reason a customer should buy (or sell) all its kWH from (to) a single supplier. These ideas are increasingly examined and accepted by regulators who do not wish to get in the way of new innovations and services, as further described in Box 13.14.

BOX 13.14 SINGLE CUSTOMER BUYING FROM MULTIPLE SUPPLIERS?

With the attention focused on BTM space and the innovations that promise to deliver new services – not just to individual customers but to aggregations of customers – the frontiers of what can and cannot be done are being extended to previously unchartered territory. One promising concept getting traction in some circles is the idea of allowing customers to get services not from one but multiple suppliers.

Traditionally, customers got electricity service from a single supplier, even when they have retail choice. In fact, in many places, they are obligated by regulation to buy from a single supplier – typically the local regulated monopoly distribution company serving their area. However, the electricity retailing market – particularly the BTM portion – is changing and there is a growing belief that customers should have the option to buy – or sell, or trade – their energy from/to multiple suppliers if they wish to do so, say because this lowers costs or has other benefits. The UK's energy regulator, Ofgem, has expressed interest in exploring such possibilities (Elexon 2018).

If this were allowed, customers may decide to buy energy to charge their EVs from one supplier, say under a special time-of-use tariff while buying the rest from a different supplier. Having the option to buy or sell from/to multiple suppliers would enable a range of innovations in the electricity supply business that is currently difficult if not impossible to realize. Imagine, for example, a customer buying:

- some of its supply from a renewable supplier only when prices are low – say below a pre-set point;
- the electricity to charge the EV from an alternative supplier – perhaps an auto company leasing the vehicle and its electricity usage; and
- the residual from another supplier at a fixed regulated price.

It is not difficult to imagine customers wanting to take advantage of such options as they become available. In a white paper titled *Enabling Customers to Buy from Multiple Suppliers*, Elexon outlines its vision for a new market structure that could allow multiple suppliers to deliver energy through a single meter or multiple meters. For this to happen, not only do regulations have to change, but there need to new metering and settlement arrangements to keep track of who bought what from whom, when and at what price.

6. WHAT WILL ULTIMATELY MATTER?

This chapter started by explaining why electricity demand will grow at different rates in different parts of the world and pointed out that what happens in a few populous countries will ultimately dwarf what happens in many smallish ones.

It noted that forecasting electricity demand growth – always a challenging exercise – is likely to become even more daunting because many new developments make historical extrapolation useless. The most important variables, all driven by the desire to move towards a lower carbon-emissions future, include the following:

- the impact of the electrification of the transport sector;
- trends towards more efficient buildings, appliances, motors and lighting; and
- the gradual conversion of heating and many industrial processes to green electricity.

The added complexities of demand forecasting were raised during recent debate at the CEC, where it was noted that the state will need to have 7.8 million zero emission vehicles by 2030 to achieve its emission reduction goal. At the same time, CEC believes that it can achieve a 40 per cent emission reduction in residential and commercial buildings by displacement of 3.8 million therms of natural gas – a therm is the energy content of 2.74 cubic metres of natural gas – which will require the additional generation of 32 852 GWh of electricity from renewable resources. Future demand is increasingly influenced by regulations and standards just as the future generation is mandated by government policies.

In this context, one might ask what will ultimately matter, given the many trends and opportunities that will prevail? The short answer is that it will depend on where and in what time frame. In Australia, for example, where a significant number of households have invested in solar roofs, the distributed future has already arrived. As more customers go solar, and some invest in storage and/or EVs, the transition from consumer to prosumager will accelerate. On the other hand, in densely populated places such as Hong Kong, Tokyo or Seoul where most people live in high-rise apartments with little opportunity to invest in distributed generation or storage, it will be a different story. In places where the delivery network is inadequate, unreliable or non-existent, the potential for stand-alone systems that generate, store and provide electricity service may be considerable. In such places, isolated mini-networks or micro-grids may provide more reliable service at lower cost. In all cases, the longer-term demand trends will depend on the relative costs, on regulatory policies and – perhaps most important – on the rapidly improved technologies and equally rapidly fall in costs.

What about some of the other topics and associated products and services described in this chapter? Will energy-using devices become digitalized and connected? Will demand aggregation and optimization or P2P trading platforms become widespread and profitable? The evidence is mixed, and it is too early to know the winners and losers based on the limited experience to date. Among a few start-ups featured in this chapter and elsewhere (Sioshansi 2020a, 2020d), only NK has grown to size and is profitable, although major incumbents such as Fluence, Enel X and others are capitalizing on the emerging opportunities. For some of the others, one has to do a five-year sanity test: wait five years or more to see how well they are doing. Many ideas or products launched with great fanfare – think of Segway or 3-D printing – have not delivered as promised. Electric scooters, by contrast, have made more of a dent than Segway, which appeals to a narrow niche. Similarly, the jury is still out on whether major players such as Amazon will eventually succeed in home energy management systems where others have not (Shaw-Williams 2020).

What about transactive energy where individuals or groups of individuals can trade and share electricity using blockchain and other means that obviates the need for intermediaries or a central clearinghouse? Much excitement exists in future potential of distributed ledgers. Only time will tell how soon and how profitable applications will emerge.

One thing, however, is universally agreed and that is the fact that consumers have more choices in more places, and they are likely to exercise their new-found freedom to move away from the traditional reliance on a single provider for all their needed services. This is a welcome development, encouraging service and product innovation in an industry not known for either.

But even here, the evidence is mixed. The research to date suggests that the average consumer is not necessarily well informed or sufficiently motivated to find the best available options or make the best investments (Burns and Mountain 2020). The retailers and vendors sometimes make matters worse by false or misleading claims, making it even more difficult for the average consumer to make rational, informed decisions (Swanston 2020b). Chapter 5 in this handbook provides an excellent discussion of the many complexities of retail electricity markets – which are intrinsically linked to the future of demand-side technologies and retail service.

However, most experts agree that demand must increasingly play a bigger role in balancing of supply and demand because much of the future generation in many regions will be variable renewable energy (Sioshansi 2020e, 2020f, 2020g, 2020h). Aggregation and management of BTM assets will have to be a part of the solution, one way or another, most likely enabled by aggregators.

Should this be a concern to the regulators? Yes and no. Yes, because a lot is at stake and regulatory clarity is needed to pave the way for service and business model innovations in the electricity sector. No because in most economic sectors consumers are free to make bad decisions – for instance, in buying insurance they don't need or risking their retirement savings. Why worry about poor decisions when it comes to electricity? Many regulators believe that aggregators, intermediaries or orchestrators may be able to provide useful services, not only unbiased advice but actually managing the customers' portfolio of assets, minimizing their bills while enhancing the quality and value of services received (Poplavskaya and de Vries 2020). How and how fast such intermediaries may emerge, and how useful they may be, remains to be seen – another reason for providing regulatory clarity (Robinson 2020a).

The good news is that many regulators are not only aware of these complexities but are also actively engaged in shaping regulations and policy in ways that will deliver better value and more service options for future prosumers and prosumagers, while protecting the traditional consumers who may be perfectly content with the status quo: bundled regulated tariffs (Hochstetler 2020).

Given a chance, emerging technologies promise to reduce the transactions costs as more consumers, prosumers, prosumagers and nonsumers begin to trade on open platforms, participate in VPP schemes or form semi-independent energy communities enabled by intelligent intermediaries.

It is not clear to what extent these new developments will impact electricity demand – which is likely to vary depending on where one is. With so much interest and effort devoted to developing new applications and business models, it is fair to say that the age of enabled, intelligent and connected demand-side devices is upon us, offering new opportunities and challenges for the incumbents and new entrants alike.

NOTES

1. Refer to the World Bank for international statistics at https://data.worldbank.org/indicator/EG.USE. ELEC.KH.PC, accessed 13 July 2021.
2. In some cases, advanced economies are actively engaged to encourage reduced consumption through energy efficiency standards, building codes, and so on, such as in California, where stringent building codes went into effect for all new residential buildings in 2020.
3. See https://data.worldbank.org/indicator/eg.elc.accs.zs, accessed 13 July 2021.
4. Data for Figure 13.1 has been compiled from several sources. Data on per capita electricity consumption are taken from https://data.worldbank.org/indicator/EG.USE.ELEC.KH.PC?year_high_desc=true and https://figure.nz/chart/77YxhDEyAtcVDZmJ. Data on total electricity consumption are taken from http://energyatlas.iea.org/#!/tellmap/-1118783123. GDP per capita is taken from https://knoema.com/ sijweyg/world-gdp-per-capita-ranking-2017-data-and-charts-forecast, while per capita income levels derive from https://data.worldbank.org/indicator/NY.GDP.PCAP.CD and from https://www.nation-master.com/country-info/stats/Economy/GDP-per-capita, accessed 13 July 2021.
5. For example, in many low-income economies, the only light bulbs available may be the more efficient LEDs. And since consumers' disposable income is limited, they can be persuaded to buy the most efficient and compact necessities – such as small refrigerators, efficient TVs and only selected appliances.
6. Climate variations result in significant anomalies, such as vast amounts of electricity used for water desalination in the Persian Gulf region – not an issue in the Scandinavian countries.
7. Further details at https://www.insideenergyandenvironment.com/2018/09/governor-jerry-brown-signs-sb-100-and-executive-order-to-achieve-carbon-neutrality-by-2045/, accessed 13 July 2021.
8. Further details at https://www.greentechmedia.com/articles/read/solar-mandate-all-new-california-homes#gs.3578b5 and at https://www.cpuc.ca.gov/ZNE/, accessed 13 July 2021.
9. Under the new code, builders must meet stringent energy efficiency standards such as high-efficiency heating and air conditioning systems, tighter windows, more insulated attics and doors to minimize the need for heating and cooling, while being encouraged but not obligated to install energy storage systems or heat pump water heating.
10. Until recently, California, for example, had five tiers for residential consumers, progressively rising with higher volumes with the intention of encouraging energy conservation, among other aims.
11. Refer to https://www.iso-ne.com/static-assets/documents/2018/02/2018_reo.pdf and https://www.iso-ne. com/static-assets/documents/2018/06/clg_meeting_george_iso_update_presentation_june_14_2018_final. pdf, accessed 13 July 2021.

12. The City of Berkeley, for example, passed a resolution that essentially bans natural gas hookup to new residential units beginning in 2020 to reduce emissions of greenhouse gases. Details at https://www.berke leyside.com/2019/07/17/natural-gas-pipes-now-banned-in-new-berkeley-buildings-with-some-exceptions, accessed 13 July 2021.
13. Refer to https://www.raponline.org/wp-content/uploads/2018/11/rap_hildermeier_esade_madrid_2018_nov_13.pdf, accessed 13 July 2021.
14. For example, refer to https://rmi.org/press-release/rocky-mountain-institute-launches-new-analysis-of-electric-autonomous-mobility-in-china-india-and-usa/, accessed 13 July 2021.
15. Refer to https://elbil.no/english/norwegian-ev-policy/ and https://www.greencarreports.com/news/1123160_why-norway-leads-the-world-in-electric-vehicle-adoption, accessed 13 July 2021.
16. There are a number of complicating issues with this model, including potentially negative impact on the life of batteries and battery warranty restrictions.
17. Refer to https://www.treehugger.com/cars/chargepoint-pledges-25-million-ev-charging-spots-2025.html and https://www.utilitydive.com/news/emotorwerks-provides-caiso-with-30-mw-of-dr-through-smart-ev-charging/532110/, accessed 13 July 2021.
18. Initially, eMotorWerks focused on working with CAISO on its demand response scheme but has the ability for other types of grid services, such as frequency response.
19. Refer to Gruter and Moore (2018), as reported at https://energypost.eu/the-impact-of-electric-vehicles-on-electricity-demand/, accessed 13 July 2021.
20. According to Redburn, the prevailing IE1 motors are being banned, and IE3 motors will become mandatory around the world – saving as much as 13 per cent depending on the size of the motor. It will take roughly 15 years for the entire installed motor base to be replaced with the new standard, reducing global electricity demand by 0.7 per cent per annum.
21. In Europe the sale of inefficient incandescent light bulbs has already been banned.
22. For example, refer to https://newscenter.lbl.gov/2016/06/27/data-centers-continue-proliferate-energy-use-plateaus/, accessed 13 July 2021.
23. For example, see products of Onyx Solar at https://www.onyxsolar.com/about-onyx/company, accessed 13 July 2021.
24. For example, refer to Ausgrid and Western Power at https://reneweconomy.com.au/ausgrid-prepares-to-take-customers-off-the-grid-with-solar-and-batteries-66528/, accessed 13 July 2021.
25. How much consumers can get by selling or exporting their excess generation into the network varies from one state to another in the US and similarly in other parts of the world. In California, for example, overly generous net energy metering laws allowed consumers to significantly reduce or eliminate their electricity bills.
26. For many consumers with small monthly bills, the motivation to move away may not be worth the effort. Moreover, many who live in apartments in city centres do not have options to install solar panels and/or may not have a garage for a battery or an EV.
27. A variation of this may be prosumers who may collectively share the rooftop solar, say on the roof of an apartment building, which may be community owned or owned by a third party.
28. Further details at http://bsaenergy.com/wordpress1/, accessed 13 July 2021.
29. The house incorporates ground-source heat pumps, SEER 45 – as efficient as you can buy on the market today.
30. 'We've moved into our new home . . . just paid an $11 electric bill . . . very low because we're . . . roughly matching solar and geothermal production to demand – this includes all HVAC, lighting, refrigeration and 3 EV car chargers. Could rise, however, with more intensive use and colder outdoor temperatures'.
31. In Australia, for example, the FiTs have been significantly reduced to the level of prevailing wholesale generation costs – rather than much higher retail tariffs – yet the prosumager exodus continues particularly in sunny suburban areas. The motivation is to avoid high retail tariffs.
32. For example, see https://www.geekwire.com/2018/amazon-set-unveil-new-line-alexa-powered-devices-seattle-event/ and https://www.nytimes.com/2019/03/03/business/amazon-alexa-david-limp.html, accessed 13 July 2021.
33. At a news conference at its headquarters in Seattle in September 2018 Dave Limp, an Amazon executive made the announcement, as referred to in https://www.thurrott.com/smart-home/175683/amazon-announces-a-smart-home-tsunami, accessed 13 July 2021.
34. Refer to https://www.fastcompany.com/40474833/amazons-alexa-is-a-real-smart-home-platform-now and https://www.androidcentral.com/amazon-just-declared-war-every-smart-home-device-company, accessed 13 July 2021.
35. To make sure its strategy succeeds, Amazon is pricing its new Amazon Smart Plug, new Echo Input and the Echo Wall Clock at give-away prices – and these are useful devices to have.
36. As it happens, the new Echo Plus speaker has a built-in temperature sensor. Amazon already has more than 100 devices that seamlessly work together from the outset. To connect them, all you have to do is to simply say, 'Alexa, discover devices'.

37.   Refer to https://microgridknowledge.com/emotorwerks-lo3-microgrids/ and https://cleantechnica.com/2019/02/02/my-ev-your-pv-or-the-other-way-around/, accessed 13 July 2021.
38.   The companies plan to test their ideas in New York's Brooklyn Microgrid project, where LO3 Energy has already successfully demonstrated a community blockchain scheme.
39.   Many examples of VPPs have emerged in the recent years, including Next Kraftwerke at https://www.next-kraftwerke.com/vpp/virtual-power-plant, accessed 13 July 2021.

REFERENCES

Asmus, P. H. (2020), 'Integrating DER: orchestrating the grid's last mile', *Guidehouse*, 29 October, accessed 13 July 2021 at https://energycentral.com/o/Guidehouse/integrated-der-orchestrating-grid's-last-mile.

Baak, J. and F. Sioshansi (2019), 'Integrated energy services, load aggregation and intelligent storage', in F. Sioshansi (ed.), *Consumer, Prosumer, Prosumager: How Service Innovations Will Disrupt the Utility Business Model*, London: Academic Press/Elsevier, pp. 53–73.

Barrager, S. and E. Cazalet (2016), *Transactive Energy: A Sustainable Business and Regulatory Model for Electricity*, Reading, UK: Baker Street Publishing.

Barrager, S. and E. Cazalet (2020), *Transactive Energy in California: A Platform for 100 Percent Clean Energy and Electrification*, Reading, UK: Baker Street Publishing.

Bashir, S., A. Smits and T. Nelson (2019), 'Service innovation and disruption in the Australian contestable retail market', in F. Sioshansi (ed.), *Consumer, Prosumer, Prosumager: How Service Innovations Will Disrupt the Utility Business Model*, London: Academic Press/Elsevier, pp. 75–95.

Bauknecht, D., J. Bracke and F. Flachshbarth et al. (2019), 'Customer stratification and different concept of decentralization', in F. Sioshansi (ed.), *Consumer, Prosumer, Prosumager: How Service Innovations Will Disrupt the Utility Business Model*, London: Academic Press/Elsevier, pp. 331–53.

Brown, M., S. Woodhouse and F. Sioshansi (2019), 'Digitalization of energy', in F. Sioshansi (ed.), *Consumer, Prosumer, Prosumager: How Service Innovations Will Disrupt the Utility Business Model*, London: Academic Press/Elsevier, pp. 3–25.

Burger, S., I. Schneider, A. Botterud and I. Pérez-Arriaga (2019), 'Fair, equitable and efficient tariffs in the presence of distributed energy resources', in F. Sioshansi (ed.), *Consumer, Prosumer, Prosumager: How Service Innovations Will Disrupt the Utility Business Model*, London: Academic Press/Elsevier, pp. 155–88.

Burns, K. and B. Mountain (2020), 'Do time-of-use tariffs make residential demand more flexible? Evidence from Victoria, Australia', in F. Sioshansi (ed.), *Variable Generation, Flexible Demand*, London: Academic Press/Elsevier, pp. 411–24.

California Energy Commission (CEC) (2019), *Energy Demand Forecast*, accessed 13 July 2021 at https://www.energy.ca.gov/data-reports/planning-and-forecasting.

California Legislative Information (2018), *Senate Bill 100: California Renewables Portfolio Standard Program: Emissions of Greenhouse Gases*, accessed 13 July 2021 at https://leginfo.legislature.ca.gov/faces/billNavClient.xhtml?bill_id=201720180SB100.

Cazalet, E., M. Kohanim and O. Hasidim (2020), *Complete and Low-Cost Retail Automated Transactive Energy System (RATES)*, final project report prepared for California Energy Commission, June, accessed 13 July 2021 at https://ww2.energy.ca.gov/2020publications/CEC-500-2020-038/CEC-500-2020-038.pdf.

Couture, T., S. Pelz, C. Cader and P. Blechinger (2019), 'Off-grid prosumers: electrifying the next billion with PAYGO solar', in F. Sioshansi (ed.), *Consumer, Prosumer, Prosumager: How Service Innovations Will Disrupt the Utility Business Model*, London: Academic Press/Elsevier, pp. 311–29.

Davis, L. (2018), 'Why am I paying $65/year for your solar panels?', *Energy Institute Blog*, 26 March, accessed 13 July 2021 at https://energyathaas.wordpress.com/2018/03/26/why-am-i-paying-65-year-for-your-solar-panels/.

De Clerq, S., D. Schwabender, C. Corinaldesi and A. Fleischhacker (2020), 'Emerging aggregator business models in European electricity markets', in F. Sioshansi (ed.), *Behind and Beyond the Meter: Digitalization, Aggregation, Optimization, Monetization*, London: Academic Press/Elsevier, pp. 285–303.

Duncan, R. and M. E. Webber (2020), *The Future of Buildings, Transportation and Power*, Austin, TX: DW Books.

Elexon (2018), *Elexon White Paper: Enabling Customers to Buy Power from Multiple Providers*, 16 April, accessed 13 July 2021 at https://www.elexon.co.uk/wp-content/uploads/2018/04/ELEXON-White-Paper-Enabling-customers-to-buy-power-from-multiple-providers.pdf.

Evans, S. (2017), 'In-depth: how a smart flexible grid could save the UK £40bn', *CarbonBrief*, 25 July, accessed 13 July 2021 at https://www.carbonbrief.org/in-depth-how-smart-flexible-grid-could-save-uk-40-billion.

Faruqui, A. and C. Bourbonnais (2020), 'Time of use rates: an international perspective', *Energy Regulation Quarterly*, **8** (2), accessed 13 July 2021 at https://www.energyregulationquarterly.ca/articles/time-of-use-rates-an-international-perspectives#sthash.N4vV759R.dpbs.

Fox-Penner, P. (2020), *Power after Carbon: Building a Clean, Resilient Grid*, Cambridge, MA: Harvard University Press.

Glachant, J.-M. (2020), 'Peer-2-peer in the electricity sector: an academic compass in the making', *RSCAS Policy Briefs, 2020/36*, European University Institute, October.

Gruter, S. and J. Moore (2018), *Capital Goods: Exit, Pursued by a Bear*, Capital Goods Research, Redburn, London, July.

Hochstetler, R. (2020), 'Markets for flexibility: product definition, market design and regulation', in F. Sioshansi (ed.), *Variable Generation, Flexible Demand*, London: Academic Press/Elsevier, pp. 451–76.

International Energy Agency (IEA) (2018), *World Energy Outlook 2018*, Paris: IEA.

Jamasb, T. and M. G. Pollitt (eds) (2011), *The Future of Electricity Demand: Customers, Citizens, and Loads*, Cambridge, UK: Cambridge University Press.

Johnston, J. and F. Sioshansi (2020), 'Platform for trading flexibility on the distribution network: a UK case study', in F. Sioshansi (ed.), *Behind and Beyond the Meter: Digitalization, Aggregation, Optimization, Monetization*, London: Academic Press/Elsevier, pp. 233–49.

Lehmbruck, L., J. Kretz, J. Aengenvoort and F. Sioshansi (2020), 'Aggregation of front- and behind-the meter: the evolving VPP business model', in F. Sioshansi (ed.), *Behind and Beyond the Meter: Digitalization, Aggregation, Optimization, Monetization*, London: Academic Press/Elsevier, pp. 211–32.

Löbbe, S., A. Hackbarth and T. Stillahn et al. (2020), 'Customer participation in P2P trading: a German energy community case study', in F. Sioshansi (ed.), *Behind and Beyond the Meter: Digitalization, Aggregation, Optimization, Monetization*, London: Academic Press/Elsevier, pp. 83–104.

Meeus, L. and J.-M. Glachant (2018), *Electricity Network Regulation in the EU: The Challenges Ahead for Transmission and Distribution*, Cheltenham, UK and Northampton, MA, USA: Edward Elgar Publishing.

Mountain, B. (2019), 'Do I have a deal for you? Buying well in Australia's contestable retail electricity markets', in F. Sioshansi (ed.), *Consumer, Prosumer, Prosumager: How Service Innovations Will Disrupt the Utility Business Model*, London: Academic Press/Elsevier, pp. 97–109.

Mountain, B. (2020), 'Behind-the-meter prospects: what do household customers' response to prices tell us?', in F. Sioshansi (ed.), *Behind and Beyond the Meter: Digitalization, Aggregation, Optimization, Monetization*, London: Academic Press/Elsevier, pp. 307–16.

Petit, V. (2019), *The New World of Utilities: A Historical Transition Towards a New Energy System*, Cham, Switzerland: Springer.

Poplavskaya, K. and L. de Vries (2020), 'Aggregators today and tomorrow: from intermediaries to local orchestrators?', in F. Sioshansi (ed.), *Behind and Beyond the Meter: Digitalization, Aggregation, Optimization, Monetization*, London: Academic Press/Elsevier, pp. 105–35.

Rai, A., C. Rozyn, A. Truswell and T. Nelson (2020), 'Regulating off-the-grid: stand-alone power systems in Australia', in F. Sioshansi (ed.), *Behind and Beyond the Meter: Digitalization, Aggregation, Optimization, Monetization*, London: Academic Press/Elsevier, pp. 317–40.

Richter, L. L. and M. G. Pollitt (2018), 'Which smart electricity service contracts will consumers accept? The demand for compensation in a platform market', *Energy Economics*, **72**, 436–50.

Rifkin, J. (2014), *The Zero Marginal Cost Society*, New York: St. Martin's Press.

Robinson, D. (2020a), 'What market design, fiscal policy and network regulation are compatible with efficient behind-the-meter investments?', in F. Sioshansi (ed.), *Behind and Beyond the Meter: Digitalization, Aggregation, Optimization, Monetization*, London: Academic Press/Elsevier, pp. 361–80.

Robinson, D. (2020b), 'Energy communities and flexible demand', in F. Sioshansi (ed.), *Variable Generation, Flexible Demand*, London: Academic Press/Elsevier, pp. 477–500.

Schittekatte, T. (2020), 'Distribution network tariff design for behind-the-meter: balancing efficiency and fairness', in F. Sioshansi (ed.), *Behind and Beyond the Meter: Digitalization, Aggregation, Optimization, Monetization*, London: Academic Press/Elsevier, pp. 341–60.

Schittekatte, T., I. Momber and L. Meeus (2018), 'Future-proof tariff design: recovering sunk grid costs in a world where consumers are pushing back', *Energy Economics*, **70**, 484–98.

Schlesinger, B. (2020), 'It is not science fiction: going zero net energy and loving it', in F. Sioshansi (ed.), *Behind and Beyond the Meter: Digitalization, Aggregation, Optimization, Monetization*, London: Academic Press/Elsevier, pp. 31–46.

Shaw-Williams, D. (2020), 'The expanding role of home management ecosystem: an Australian case study', in F. Sioshansi (ed.), *Behind and Beyond the Meter: Digitalization, Aggregation, Optimization, Monetization*, London: Academic Press/Elsevier, pp. 157–75.

Shipworth, D., C. Burger, J. Weinmann and F. Sioshansi (2019), 'Peer-to-peer trading and blockchains: enabling regional energy markets and platforms for energy transactions', in F. Sioshansi (ed.), *Consumer,*

Prosumer, Prosumager: How Service Innovations Will Disrupt the Utility Business Model, London: Academic Press/Elsevier, pp. 27–52.

Sioshansi, F. (ed.) (2013), *Energy Efficiency: Towards the End of Demand Growth*, Oxford: Academic Press.

Sioshansi, F. (ed.) (2014), *Distributed Generation and Its Implications for the Utility Industry*, Oxford: Academic Press/Elsevier.

Sioshansi, F. (ed.) (2016), *Future of Utilities – Utilities of the Future: How Technological Innovations in Distributed Energy Resources Will Reshape the Electric Power Sector*, London: Academic Press/Elsevier.

Sioshansi, F. (ed.) (2017), *Innovation and Disruption at the Grid's Edge: How Distributed Energy Resources Are Disrupting the Utility Business Model*, London: Academic Press/Elsevier.

Sioshansi, F. (ed.) (2019a), *Consumer, Prosumer, Prosumager: How Service Innovations Will Disrupt the Utility Business Model*, London: Academic Press/Elsevier.

Sioshansi, F. (2019b), 'The future of electricity distribution: a California case study', in F. Sioshansi (ed.), *Consumer, Prosumer, Prosumager: How Service Innovations Will Disrupt the Utility Business Model*, London: Academic Press/Elsevier, pp. 261–85.

Sioshansi, F. (ed.) (2020a), *Behind and Beyond the Meter: Digitalization, Aggregation, Optimization, Monetization*, London: Academic Press/Elsevier.

Sioshansi, F. (2020b), 'What lies behind-the-meter and why it matters?', in F. Sioshansi (ed.) (2020a), *Behind and Beyond the Meter: Digitalization, Aggregation, Optimization, Monetization*, London: Academic Press/Elsevier, pp. 3–29.

Sioshansi, F. (2020c), 'Creating value behind-the-meter: digitalization, aggregation and optimization of behind-the-meter assets', in F. Sioshansi (ed.) (2020a), *Behind and Beyond the Meter: Digitalization, Aggregation, Optimization, Monetization*, London: Academic Press/Elsevier, pp. 47–82.

Sioshansi, F. (ed.) (2020d), *Variable Generation, Flexible Demand*, London: Academic Press/Elsevier.

Sioshansi, F. (2020e), 'Introduction', in F. Sioshansi (ed.), *Variable Generation, Flexible Demand*, London: Academic Press/Elsevier, pp. xxxvii–liv.

Sioshansi, F. (2020f), 'The evolution of California's variable renewable generation', in F. Sioshansi (ed.), *Variable Generation, Flexible Demand*, London: Academic Press/Elsevier, pp. 3–24.

Sioshansi, F. (2020g), 'What is flexible demand; what demand is flexible?', in F. Sioshansi (ed.), *Variable Generation, Flexible Demand*, London: Academic Press/Elsevier, pp. 107–24.

Sioshansi, F. (2020h), 'How can flexible demand be delivered to scale?', in F. Sioshansi (ed.), *Variable Generation, Flexible Demand*, London: Academic Press/Elsevier, pp. 147–64.

Sioshansi, F. (2020i), 'Electric vehicles: the ultimate flexible demand', in F. Sioshansi (ed.), *Variable Generation, Flexible Demand*, London: Academic Press/Elsevier, pp. 165–94.

Smith, R. and I. MacGill (2020), 'Working backward from behind the meter: what consumer value, behavior and uncertainty mean for distributed energy technologies', in F. Sioshansi (ed.), *Behind and Beyond the Meter: Digitalization, Aggregation, Optimization, Monetization*, London: Academic Press/Elsevier, pp. 193–210.

Sperling, D. (2018), *Three Revolutions: Steering Automated, Shared, and Electric Vehicles to a Better Future*, Washington, DC: Island Press.

Stagnaro, C. and S. Benedettini (2020), 'Smart meters: the gate to behind-the-meter?', in F. Sioshansi (ed.), *Behind and Beyond the Meter: Digitalization, Aggregation, Optimization, Monetization*, London: Academic Press/Elsevier, pp. 251–66.

Swanston, M. (2020a), 'Two million solar roofs: what's in it for the consumer?', in F. Sioshansi (ed.), *Behind and Beyond the Meter: Digitalization, Aggregation, Optimization, Monetization*, London: Academic Press/Elsevier, pp. 381–406.

Swanston, M. (2020b), 'Flexible demand: what's in it for the customer?', in F. Sioshansi (ed.), *Variable Generation, Flexible Demand*, London: Academic Press/Elsevier, pp. 501–26.

Trbovich, A., S. Hambridge, E. Hesse and F. Sioshansi (2020), 'D3A energy exchange for transactive grid', in F. Sioshansi (ed.), *Behind and Beyond the Meter: Digitalization, Aggregation, Optimization, Monetization*, London: Academic Press/Elsevier, pp. 267–84.

Webb, J., J. Whitehead and C. Wilson (2019), 'Who will fuel your electric vehicle in the future? You or your utility?', in F. Sioshansi (ed.), *Consumer, Prosumer, Prosumager: How Service Innovations Will Disrupt the Utility Business Model*, London: Academic Press/Elsevier, pp. 407–29.

14. Tools and policies to promote decarbonization of the electricity sector
Kathryne Cleary, Carolyn Fischer and Karen Palmer

1. INTRODUCTION

Most nations have historically relied heavily on the burning of fossil fuels to generate electricity. As concerns about the impact of these resources on climate change escalate, governments around the world are exploring and using a variety of policies to transition toward and sustain a decarbonized electricity system.

Promoting decarbonization is largely motivated by climate change concerns, but there are also numerous other benefits associated with moving away from the use of fossil fuels. In particular, burning fossil fuels also contributes to local air pollution that can have numerous health consequences, especially for vulnerable populations. Moving toward a clean energy economy can also create local jobs, reduce dependence on foreign resources and promote technological innovation that can spill over into other sectors of the economy.

This chapter reviews the primary policy methods in use or under consideration to promote decarbonization. First, we discuss the more technology-inclusive and market-oriented tools like carbon pricing and tradable standards. Next, we consider common policies targeting specific supply technologies, like renewable energy, coal or nuclear power. Finally, we address demand-side programmes for encouraging energy efficiency. While some of these policies are substitutes, many can be complementary and work together to accelerate the transition to a cleaner electricity system.

2. TECHNOLOGY-INCLUSIVE AND MARKET-BASED MECHANISMS FOR DECARBONIZATION

2.1 Carbon Pricing

Electricity generation from the combustion of fossil fuels produces carbon dioxide (CO_2), a greenhouse gas (GHG) that contributes to climate change. GHG emissions from electricity and heat production are equal to 25 per cent of global emissions (Intergovernmental Panel on Climate Change [IPCC] 2014). Climate-related damages from electricity generation impose costs on society but are not factored into the privatized cost of providing electricity. For the market to reach the efficient outcome for the quantity and price of electricity consumption, it must internalize these societal costs by including the costs of carbon-related damages in the price of electricity. Instituting a price for carbon damages can be implemented either through a price policy, like a carbon tax, or through a quantity-based policy, like a cap-and-trade policy. These methods do not pick clean technology winners but rather allow the market to decide, which reduces cost and encourages innovation (Stewart and Weiner 2003).

As of 2019, 46 national and 28 subnational jurisdictions are implementing a form of carbon pricing, with policies fairly evenly split between carbon taxes and tradable emissions quotas (World Bank Group 2019). Roughly 20 per cent of global CO_2 emissions are covered by these schemes. Invariably, the electricity sector is the first to be covered by these schemes, as it represents the largest point-source emitters of GHGs, as well as those least exposed to foreign competition.

2.1.1 Carbon tax

A carbon tax is a tax per ton of carbon dioxide emitted from the burning of fossil fuels. It can be applied uniformly across many sectors of the economy, although the carbon tax discussed here is applied specifically to the electricity sector. For electricity, the tax is typically applied at the point of generation but is passed on to consumers through electricity rates. To achieve an economically efficient market outcome, the tax rate should reflect the cost to society of emitting one ton of carbon dioxide.

The tax reduces damages from carbon dioxide pollution from the electricity sector by increasing the cost of providing fossil-based electricity, which incentivizes switching to cleaner fuels or other non-emitting technologies to avoid the tax. Even if applied upstream, a carbon tax will also raise retail electricity prices, which reduces demand for electricity overall and thus lowers carbon emissions. Additionally, it lays the groundwork for a low-carbon future by providing investment signals that discourage investment in fossil plants while encouraging the deployment and use of cleaner generation.

A carbon tax can be a favourable policy for several reasons. First, relative to other policies, it can be simpler for policymakers to understand and implement since it does not require much programme administration relative to a cap-and-trade or renewable portfolio standard. Second, it is inherently flexible and can be altered by adjusting the tax rate or base. Last, a carbon tax is considered to be a 'first best' policy with respect to addressing carbon emissions because it is a Pigouvian tax that directly puts a price on the negative externalities.

However, a carbon tax can be regressive, meaning that it imposes higher relative costs on poorer households than rich households (Poterba 1991). These impacts depend on how the tax revenue is used (Williams et al. 2015). To address these distributional concerns, some policies will return the tax revenue in the form of a dividend to households on an income basis. Under a tax and dividend policy, lower-income households receive a higher proportion of the tax revenue than the high-income households, which can help reduce inequity from the policy. Williams et al. (2015) found that the regressive nature of the tax can be greatly improved by using the revenue for lump-sum rebates for poorer households.

While a carbon tax can be efficient if priced at the social cost of carbon, it can be difficult to estimate this metric, and therefore the tax may not capture the true cost of the damages (Marron and Toder 2014). Marron and Toder (2014) also discuss how determining the social cost of carbon depends on a number of subjective factors – namely, the difference between global and local impacts, and therefore its value varies significantly by national assessments. Another critique of a carbon tax is that by setting the price, the quantity of emission reductions is unknown, so a policymaker will not be guaranteed that the policy will achieve a certain target.

Despite numerous failed attempts in the US at the national and state levels, carbon taxes have been implemented all over the world, including several European nations, Chile, Japan and the Canadian province of British Columbia (BC). BC's carbon tax, a frequently studied case that was implemented in 2008, has been successful in many ways despite its modest stringency, including reducing carbon emissions while also keeping pace with Canada's economic growth (Murray and Rivers 2015). Yamazaki (2017) also found that BC's carbon tax was actually associated with slight employment growth overall due to an increase in employment in the clean energy sector. Also, by using a tax and dividend approach, the BC carbon tax is found to be progressive and minimizes impact on low-income households (Beck et al. 2015).

2.1.2   Cap and trade

A cap-and-trade policy is similar to the carbon tax but uses a quantity-based rather than price-based approach to reduce emissions. In a cap-and-trade programme, a policymaker will set a cap for carbon emissions from the electricity sector, which will restrict pollution from generators. To determine which generators can emit under the cap, policymakers will either freely distribute or auction off emission allowances. A firm must possess an allowance in order to emit carbon dioxide.

Generators that are covered by the programme must not exceed the cap in aggregate, but they are free to trade among themselves for the right to pollute. Both allowance trading and allowance auctioning should theoretically lead to the lowest-cost procurement for allowances since prices in both scenarios are set competitively. For electricity markets with retail competition, there is theoretically no difference in overall programme cost between free allowance allocation based on a fixed metric with trading or auctions with trading. However, if a utility operates in a vertically integrated electricity market with cost-of-service rate regulation, then electricity price impacts would be higher if allowances are auctioned rather than freely distributed since utilities cannot recover costs without an explicit expense (Burtraw and Palmer 2008).

A cap-and-trade policy has numerous design features that enable lawmakers to shape the policy. The stringency of the policy can be strengthened by reducing the cap, and most policies include a downward trajectory for the cap over a number of years. Similarly, there are mechanisms available for controlling both costs and the level of emission reductions. A cost containment reserve (CCR) is a price ceiling for allowances that is triggered in the event that the allowance price becomes too high, in which case policymakers will introduce more allowances into the market. Allowance markets can also impose a price floor below which no allowances will be sold and thus if the allowance price falls that low, it acts more like a tax. Additional price steps can be added in between the two extremes at which some quantity of allowances is withdrawn (released) from (in) the market to allow for an adequate balance of environmental and costs benefits when demand for allowances is less (more) than expected (Burtraw et al. 2017). A policy can also include allowance banking, which allows firms to keep allowances for compliance in future years, so improving the flexibility of the policy.

Cap-and-trade programmes are also quite popular and have been implemented in Europe and parts of the US, among others. The European Union currently operates the largest carbon cap-and-trade programme in the world with 31 participating nations and covers both power stations and industrial plants. North America has two regional carbon cap-and-trade programmes, the Regional Greenhouse Gas Initiative (RGGI), a cap-and-trade programme in the Northeastern US that covers the electricity sector only, and the Western Climate Initiative, a cap-and-trade programme that includes California and Quebec and covers economy-wide emissions.

Assessment of these programmes is mixed with respect to emission reductions and programme design. The European Union Emission Trading System (EU ETS) has been criticized for not being flexible enough to respond to changing market conditions like the 2008 financial crisis, which resulted in allowance price collapses and little emission reductions from the policy (Laing et al. 2013). Flexibility of the policy has since improved because the EU ETS recently implemented a market stability reserve (MSR) to prevent allowance prices from dipping too low or too high (Perino 2018). The EU ETS was also limited in effectiveness by the presence of other complementary policies, like renewables support policies, which crowded out the cap's role in driving emission reductions. The result of overlapping support for renewable energy is not to increase total abatement, which is determined by the cap, but rather to interfere in the market for abatement effort, driving down allowance prices and increasing the overall costs of abatement (Böhringer and Rosendahl 2010, Fischer and Preonas 2010, Schmalensee and Stavins 2017). We discuss these issues further in Section 5.

RGGI has also faced similar issues regarding low allowance prices in the wake of the 2008 financial crisis but the programme implemented an emissions containment reserve in 2016 that limits the likelihood of very low prices going forward. Murray and Maniloff (2015) show that falling emissions within the RGGI region relative to other parts of the country are attributable to the policy.

Regional cap-and-trade policies also face challenges with respect to emissions leakage, which refers to an increase in emissions in jurisdictions not subject to the cap, which can limit the effectiveness of the policy. RGGI, for example, has resulted in an increase in emissions in states that border RGGI (Fell and Maniloff 2018).

2.1.3   Comparison

A carbon tax and a cap-and-trade system offer similar economic incentives for decarbonization but have some important practical and institutional differences (Pollitt 2019). A cap-and-trade programme can provide more certainty of a quantity of carbon reductions, which a carbon tax cannot. However, cap-and-trade can be more administratively costly than a carbon tax due to administrative requirements like allowance tracking and allocation and compliance monitoring (Goulder and Schein 2013). A carbon tax also has the benefit of price stability, since allowance prices can vary significantly under a cap-and-trade scheme unless additional policy measures are taken, such as the auction reserve prices in California or the MSR in the EU ETS.

Both a carbon tax and a quantity system have the potential to raise revenue for the government, depending on how the allowances are distributed under a cap-and-trade system. Taxes may be earmarked for special projects or rebated (for example, as dividend checks to households, as in Canada). Allowances may be auctioned and the revenues used in the same way as the revenues of a carbon tax, or they may be distributed freely (as is the case for energy-intensive industries in the EU ETS). In practice, the default allocation of allowances under cap-and-trade systems is typically to the covered firms, while the default allocation of carbon tax revenues is to the government, for subsequent recycling

(Avi-Yonah and Uhlmann 2009). However, that need not be the case; in fact, in the EU and in the state-run programmes in the US, the electricity sector must purchase all of its allowances at auction or in the market. Either way, the impacts of these policies can depend on how the collected revenue is used. Popular uses are to reduce the impact of such programmes on low-income households or to reinvest the funds into programmes that help reduce the cost of the programmes, such as research in clean energy or improving existing technologies.

A recent strain of research is interested in whether price or quantity-based policies are more conducive to fostering international agreements on emissions reductions that increase ambition and promote price harmonization and cost-effective abatement. Given that more is known about the global carbon budget than the prices needed to stay within it, quantities are typically more intuitive as national targets. Prices can then be equalized across countries through linking or joint implementation, and the allocation of the targets can serve as a compensation mechanism as well. However, from a negotiation perspective, national governments tend to prefer more lenient targets for themselves, to improve the terms of their carbon trade, which collectively tends to depress carbon prices (Cramton et al. 2017). By contrast, negotiating over a minimum common carbon price should encourage national governments to accept more stringency (Weitzman 2014). Evaluating compliance is likely easier with quantity targets. Comparing carbon prices requires considering exchange rates, coverage and adjustments in other policies (for example, energy taxes). Given the multiplicity of policies in use, the evaluation of a minimum carbon price would entail some comparison of effective carbon prices that do not result from carbon taxes (see Gollier and Tirole 2015 for a comparison of prices versus quantity mechanisms in an international context).

2.2   Tradable Standards

Tradable standards come in several forms, some more technology-neutral than others. A tradable performance standard (TPS) is a market-based, technology-inclusive standard intended to reduce emissions from the power sector. A traditional TPS would set an average emissions intensity standard for all generation; other versions modify this format to differentiate performance standards or benchmarks according to the generation technology. A related form of tradable standards are portfolio standards, which intend to ensure a minimum market share of a given class of clean technologies, as opposed to ensuring a maximum emissions rate. We discuss these versions of tradable standards from the more broad-based to the more technology specific.

In considering these policies, one should keep in mind all the different margins for obtaining emissions reductions from the power sector, including (1) improving the efficiency with which given fuels are used; (2) substituting dirtier with cleaner fuels; (3) substituting generation technologies; and (4) reducing electricity demand. A large body of literature indicates that policies that provide incentives along multiple margins can be substantially more cost-effective than policies just targeting specific margins (see, for example, Fischer and Newell 2008, Fischer, Preonas and Newell, 2017, Paul, Palmer and Woerman 2015). However, even less cost-effective measures can still produce substantial increases in social welfare, given the benefits of reducing the burdens of air pollution and climate change (Paul et al. 2015).

2.2.1   Emissions intensity standard

The purest form of TPS is an emissions intensity standard that intends to limit the average emissions *rate* of an industry. A performance benchmark is set, which effectively allocates credits per unit of generation. Producers with emissions rates below the benchmark can sell credits equal to that shortfall times their generation. Producers with emissions rates above the benchmark must buy credits to cover their total excess emissions. Allowing the market to determine price enables competition and helps ensure that the standard is met at the lowest possible cost. If the performance standard is challenging to meet collectively, the market for credits will produce a positive price for emissions credits.

From an incentive standpoint, a TPS effectively combines a price on emissions – since additional emissions create an additional compliance requirement – with a subsidy to output – since additional generation creates an additional allocation of credits. That combination ensures that there is an incentive to reduce the emissions intensity of generation, on average, but reducing emissions by reducing output is discouraged by the implicit subsidy. The result is lower electricity prices and higher emissions than with a carbon tax of the same price. Alternatively, to meet the same emissions target as with a cap-and-trade system, the carbon price will need to be higher with a TPS (Fischer and Fox 2007, Fischer and Newell 2008).

There can be some benefits to limiting carbon cost pass-through to electricity prices. One is if markets are already distorted by labour taxes, keeping product prices from rising limits further erosion of the real wage and exacerbation of the labour market distortions (Fischer and Fox 2007, Goulder, Parry and Burtraw 1997). Another is limiting the range and heterogeneity of impacts on consumers, particularly lower-income ones (Fischer and Pizer 2019). Political economy pressures often point toward standards over straight carbon pricing, as polls consistently reveal greater public acceptance of the former over the latter (for example, Newport 2018). Finally, performance standards – even tradable ones – can often be implemented under existing regulatory authority (at least in the US), while a carbon tax or cap-and-trade system can require new legislation.

We observe several variations of emissions intensity standards in practice. Many deviate from the traditional design of a common benchmark to all generators and instead offer different benchmarks according to different technologies. For example, the Chinese national emissions trading scheme awards higher benchmarks for more emissions-intensive sources (Goulder et al. 2020). While it may seem practical to give each source a similar reduction *rate* target, the effect in a tradable credit system is to price all emissions the same and subsidize the output of higher-emitting sources more. The result is an additional efficiency loss from the benchmarking, since not only is conservation discouraged, but so is fuel-switching, which is typically the most cost-effective means for reducing emissions in the electricity sector. In Canada, the output-based performance standard (OBPS) in the federal backstop policy begins with differentiated benchmarks for coal and gas but transitions to a single benchmark in ten years. Furthermore, non-emitting sources are excluded, meaning they do not receive extra support (although they may be covered by other technology-specific policies, as listed below).

2.2.2   Clean energy standard

A clean energy standard (CES) is similar to a differentiated emissions intensity standard but is structured similarly to a portfolio standard (a policy commonly used in the US for renewable energy, as discussed in the next subsection). Rather than comply with an emissions performance standard, a utility is required to procure a certain *percentage* of its electricity from 'clean' resources. These resources may include both carbon-free resources – not only new renewables, but also hydropower, nuclear, or fossil plants fitted with carbon capture – and some sources that are relatively clean but not fossil-free, like natural gas combined-cycle plants, occasionally with partial credit. To meet the standard, utilities must either procure clean power directly or purchase clean energy certificates. The minimum standard increases over time, which spurs investment in credit-eligible clean sources of generation.

Under a CES, a clean plant is given clean energy credits for each megawatt-hour (MWh) of zero-carbon power produced that utilities can purchase to comply with the standard. Which power plants will be credited and how many credits are earned can vary depending on policy specifics. For example, some policies compare the carbon content of the fuel to a baseline, like coal, and award credits according to how much 'cleaner' that fuel is relative to the baseline. Under this construct, natural gas, for example, may earn 0.5 credits per MWh, while renewables will earn a full one credit per MWh for power generated. The crediting of emitting generators may be fixed by technology type, or it may depend on its emissions rate relative to a benchmark, but credits are always denominated in MWh even when the extent of partial crediting depends on source-specific emission rates. This system allows the clean energy standard to incentivize marginal emission reductions within the subset of generators that can earn partial credit.

Like TPS, clean energy credits are traded, which determines the credit price and quantity procured. A subtle distinction lies in terms of the market incentives. Recall that with a TPS, emissions are priced, and all electricity output is subsidized. By contrast, with a CES, clean output is subsidized – since additional clean generation creates additional credits – while all electricity output is taxed – since additional electricity creates an additional portfolio compliance requirement. In both cases, dirty sources face a net tax and clean sources a net subsidy. Unlike a TPS, however, the CES does not target emissions directly: sources in dirty categories cannot reduce their net penalty by reducing their emissions intensity. Furthermore, a CES often excludes certain sources, making them ineligible to earn any credits. Because it lacks direct incentives to reduce the emissions intensity of given types of sources, the effectiveness of the CES relies fully on inducing changes in the generation mix, and the incentives to switch between fossil-fuel sources ultimately depend on the relative crediting.

While a CES is typically less efficient at reducing carbon emissions relative to a carbon price or cap-and-trade scheme (Blanford, Merrick and Young 2014, Paul et al. 2015), the efficiency and cost-effectiveness of the policy can vary by its design. Paul et al. (2015) show that a CES can become much more efficient by crediting generators based on emission rates rather than technologies. This method accounts for heterogeneity in the fossil fleet with respect to emission rates and encourages marginal abatement. Mignone et al. (2012) also argues that crediting existing generators (like nuclear and hydro) can be more cost-effective than not crediting the existing fleet; however, this decision could lead to a transfer of wealth from consumers to producers and result in a regressive policy. The study argues that these impacts could be mitigated if policymakers can distinguish between which generators require the credit to continue operating.

In summary, being less direct, a CES is generally less efficient than a well-designed TPS. However, by being more comprehensive in its compliance options and technology coverage, a well-designed CES can be more cost-effective than a traditional renewable portfolio standard, which we discuss next.

2.2.3   Renewable portfolio standards

A renewable portfolio standard (RPS) is a quota and market-based policy instrument used to encourage renewable energy. Countries or states with an RPS usually mandate that a certain percentage of a utility's electricity sales come from renewable resources (the definition of which can vary by policy). A renewable energy project within the RPS territory qualifies to produce a renewable energy credit (REC), which is generated per MWh of power produced. A utility is able to meet these obligations by either generating renewable energy or by purchasing RECs from a qualified facility.

An RPS is thus like a CES, but with credits restricted only to the pre-defined renewable sources. In that sense, an RPS provides a subsidy to renewable energy – since additional renewable output generates credits – paid for by an implicit tax on electricity – since additional generation creates an additional portfolio requirement.

In an REC market, policy requirements determine credit demand and supply reflects the number of renewable projects in the market. If the standard increases and demand for RECs increases, then the prices tend to rise, while an increase in the supply of renewables drives down the REC price. The net effect of the renewable supply subsidy and implicit electricity tax may be to raise or lower electricity prices (Fischer 2010). RPSs are commonly used in the US at the state level. As of 2018, 29 US states plus the District of Columbia had mandatory RPS policies, while an additional eight had voluntary renewable energy goals.

As of 2015, over 150 nations had some kind of renewable energy target, including both mandatory standards and voluntary goals (Kieffer and Couture 2015). While not as common, some countries have adopted an RPS similar to those used in the US. The UK, for example, has a target that 15 per cent of electricity consumption comes from renewables by 2020 (UK Department of Energy & Climate Change [UK DECC] 2010). Other nations, like South Africa and Brazil, require a certain installed capacity of renewables rather than a percentage of power generated.

More narrowly defined policies are generally less cost-effective methods for reducing emissions relative to directly placing a price on carbon pollution. Marcantonini and Valero (2017) found the abatement costs implicit in Italian renewable energy policies were one or two orders of magnitude higher than prevailing EU ETS prices: around 165 €/tCO$_2$ for wind and around 1000 €/tCO$_2$ for solar. Marcantonini and Ellerman (2015) find similar, though somewhat less extreme, results for Germany. Johnson (2014) found that RPS policies in the US cost at least 11 US$/ton of CO$_2$ abated versus 3 US$/ton under the RGGI, a regional carbon cap-and-trade programme mentioned earlier in this chapter. Under the latter, assuming no other imperfections or barriers, the market solves for the most efficient (and lowest-cost) option to reduce carbon emissions rather than requiring the use of certain technologies with the intent that they may reduce emissions but by an unknown amount.

Being more technologically specific, RPS is also less cost-effective than a TPS (Fischer and Newell 2008, Fischer, Preonas and Newell 2017). However, it can be an effective tool to address technology-related market failures. Fischer and Newell (2008) argue that an RPS is more effective at encouraging both learning by doing and research and development (R&D) than direct R&D subsidies or emission performance standards. Rivers and Jaccard (2006) similarly argue that market-based policies like an RPS are more cost-effective at addressing learning failures relative to a command-and-control policy.

3.   TECHNOLOGY-SPECIFIC MECHANISMS

Many climate-oriented policies in the electricity sector differentiate even further among technologies. Many target renewable energy technologies directly; others focus on nuclear or coal-fired generation.

3.1   Targeting Renewables

Policies that mandate or encourage the deployment of renewable energy sources serve as an indirect method to phase out fossil fuels and decarbonize the electricity sector. The RPS was one method, but these policies can come in many forms, including subsidies such as feed-in tariffs, tax credits and regulatory aids, among others. In addition to deployment policies, governments also intervene upstream in the market with preferential policies for manufacturers of renewable energy technologies.

   Many of these policies have as objectives not only expanding renewable generation capacity but also spurring technological innovation. Deployment incentives can help overcome barriers and lower costs through scale economies, network effects and learning by doing (Nemet 2006). The interested reader may also look at Chapter 12 in this handbook for additional discussion. Recently, there has been some interesting debate as to the relative role of upstream versus downstream interventions (Fischer, Greaker and Rosendahl 2017, Gerarden 2018, Nemet 2019).

3.1.1   Renewable subsidies
Low adoption of renewable technologies is related to market failures of both environmental pollution and technology (Jaffe, Newell and Stavins 2005). Historically, renewable technologies have been more expensive and less technologically advanced relative to other energy sources and have thus not been viable substitutes. Subsidies for renewables can help overcome these barriers to adoption. Subsidizing renewables is often viewed as a way to address the technology market failure through learning by doing, and therefore they could be necessary in addition to a carbon price to achieve the optimal investment in the technologies (Lehmann 2009, Reichenbach and Requate 2012). By overcoming learning and R&D market failures, subsidies for renewables can significantly reduce the compliance costs of an emissions price policy (Fischer and Newell 2008).

Feed-in tariffs   Feed-in tariffs (FiTs) encourage renewables through a price-based incentive structure. Owners of a renewable project (typically wind or solar, depending on the programme) qualify for the programme and are guaranteed to earn a set price per kWh of energy produced for a certain number of years. Historically, FiTs have set high rates to encourage participation.

   FiTs are very common globally and were present in 111 national, state and provincial jurisdictions by 2018 (REN21 2019). Germany was one of the first European countries to establish an FiT in 1991 as part of its *Energiewende*, or energy transition, which aims to reduce GHG emissions by 55 per cent relative to 1990 levels by 2030. Since 1991, the policy has been revised multiple times, with the most recent revisions establishing auctions to determine the level of the support to be awarded, a policy move that is expected to lower the cost of the programme by introducing competition. The new auctions set quantity demanded for the bid round and choose the lowest-cost bids to meet that demand, and the participants receive their exact bids for 20 years (Anatolitis and Welisch 2017).

Studies have shown that FiTs can be very effective at encouraging renewable generation (Behrens et al. 2016, Dijkgraaf, Van Dorp and Maasland 2018, Haas et al. 2011). However, the cost of the programme can be very high depending on how rates are set. Spain, for example, implemented an FiT programme by Royal Decree with very lucrative rates for solar energy, which led to a boom in solar photovoltaics (PV) deployment in 2008 (Del Río and Mir-Artigues 2014). However, the subsidy payments totalled over €2.6 billion per year as of 2009. Consequently, the Spanish government was forced to halt the programme in 2012 to allow the utilities to recover from their debts and halt the accumulation of more. The collapse of Spain's FiT serves as a lesson for programme design for other nations to set rates that still encourage participation but are also reasonable and have the ability to contain costs. In Germany, the FiTs in support of the energy transition have led to some of the highest consumer electricity prices in Europe, due to the surcharges needed to cover the subsidies (Agency for the Cooperation of Energy Regulators and Council of European Energy Regulators [ACER/CEER] 2019).

Both FiTs and RPS can be effective mechanisms at encouraging deployment of renewables (Dong 2012). However, both empirical and theoretical studies have shown that while an FiT can be relatively more impactful than an RPS in terms of renewables deployment (Lipp 2007, Sun and Nie 2015), an RPS is normally more economically efficient in reducing carbon emissions and leads to higher social welfare relative to an FiT (Sun and Nie 2015, Tamas, Shrestha and Zhou 2010).

FiTs are generally considered to be an effective policy for addressing technology market failures and overcoming learning barriers to renewable technology adoption. Falconett and Nagasaka (2010) find that an FiT can be the best policy to lower costs and increase profitability for specific renewable technologies. However, Del Río (2012) finds that there is a trade-off between high FiT support that leads to learning and the cost to consumers, and that the balance can be difficult to strike due to uncertainty, as evidenced by Spain's policy developments. Lehmann (2009) finds that if designed well, an FiT coupled with a carbon tax can serve as a first-best policy to address carbon externalities, technology market failures and learning barriers together.

Tax credits   Tax credits can be used to promote renewable energy by either reducing the upfront capital costs or costs of production. In the US, there are two federal tax credits available for renewable projects: the investment tax credit (ITC) and the production tax credit (PTC). The ITC offers an upfront tax credit of the total investment value, while the PTC provides a per kWh production credit for the first ten years of the project's operation. Renewables in the US have relied heavily on these policies to lower project costs and attract investors. Since the costs of renewable technologies have fallen considerably in the last decade, the ITC and PTC are set to phase-down in the coming years, with the

PTC falling to zero after 2019 and the ITC phasing down from 30 per cent prior to 2019 to 10 per cent by 2022.

Tax credits of this nature are not considered to be very cost-effective at reducing carbon emissions. Palmer and Burtraw (2005) compared a renewable energy PTC to an RPS and found that the RPS was more cost-effective at promoting renewables and at reducing carbon emissions because an RPS may raise electricity prices, consequently leading to a reduction in electricity demand, while a tax credit will likely do the opposite. Murray et al. (2014) similarly found that investment and PTCs have led to a very small reduction in overall GHG emissions. While they may not be very effective at reducing emissions, these policies are considered to have been essential in supporting the financing that has underpinned the deployment of renewables in the US (Mai et al. 2016).

3.1.2   Regulatory aids

Policymakers and grid operators use other forms of regulation to assist renewables as well. These include priority dispatch and net metering.

Priority dispatch   Priority dispatch guarantees that renewables can sell their power into wholesale markets whenever it is produced. This mechanism allows renewable energy projects to take full advantage of their production capabilities since production is contingent on the renewable resource, such as solar radiation or wind, and can vary significantly throughout the course of the day. This mechanism has been popular in the EU since FiT participants are typically guaranteed dispatch of their generation units.

Priority dispatch can be economic and relatively non-disruptive to the operation of the electricity market since renewable energy plants have often zero marginal costs and are therefore usually dispatched first in energy markets regardless (see Chapters 15 and 16 in this handbook). However, studies argue that while priority dispatch has helped the growth of renewables in the EU, it can sometimes lead to negative electricity prices and local congestions during times when production exceeds demand (Newbery et al. 2018, Oggioni, Murphy and Smeers, 2014). If grid operators are not allowed to curtail renewable production during these times, not curtailing production leads to high market inefficiency and thus decreased social welfare (Andor et al. 2010).

Net metering   Net metering is a similar construct to an FiT in that it allows renewable generation owners who are also electricity consumers to sell electricity back to the grid. Unlike an FiT that requires a separate meter for the renewable energy production, customers with net metering use one bi-directional meter that allows them to sell only their excess renewable energy back to the grid, typically at the retail rate of electricity. This policy allows customers to take advantage of their system's production even if they are not able to use it directly. Since electricity must be used at the time it is generated, customers would otherwise have to install storage capacity to take advantage of all generation from their system, which is possible but can be expensive. Projects that can participate are typically capped in size, and in some areas the aggregate net metering programme for the utility can also be capped.

While it can be an effective method of encouraging rooftop solar, net metering has been criticized because it allows participants to be credited for non-generation charges, such as distribution and transmission costs, that are part of a utility's fixed costs but largely recovered from consumers in per kWh prices. Consequently, a utility will normally have to recover these fixed costs from the rest of their customers who do not have solar, thus causing a cross-subsidy between those with solar and those without (Comello and Reichelstein 2017, Eid et al. 2014). For this reason, net metering can create problems of inequity as more households participate.

3.1.3   Subsidies to technology producers

Subsidies to the manufacturers of renewable energy technologies – like wind turbines or solar panels – come in many forms as well. In many countries, supporting these technologies has been viewed as a kind of industrial policy. The Danish wind industry success story began in the mid-1970s with concerted government support for R&D in renewable energy, funded by electricity taxes, followed by support for the construction and operation of wind turbines; gradually, the capital incentives switched to deployment incentives and mandates (International Renewable Energy Agency [IRENA] 2013).

Many capital and investment subsidies continue to this day. Most ITCs are subsidies to deployment projects. However, some incentives target manufacturers directly, including tax breaks, low-cost financing, loan guarantees, public funding of demonstration projects and other benefits. In the US, an advanced energy manufacturing tax credit (MTC) has awarded tax credits to establishing or expanding domestic manufacturing facilities that support clean energy development. Many individual states offer manufacturers tax incentives specific to renewable energy.

Producer subsidies have grown to the extent that they have become a subject of controversy in international trade. Designating solar manufacturing a 'strategic industry', the Chinese federal government has allegedly spent as much as US$47 billion in tax incentives to help build it (the global industry is valued at about US$100 billion; Fialka 2016). Studies by the European Commission and the US International Trade Commission have argued that such large Chinese subsidies to domestic PV producers constitute illegal aid under World Trade Organization rules.

While downstream subsidies to deployment are less likely to run afoul of trade rules, upstream subsidies to manufacturers may have greater spillover benefits. Expanding demand for renewables in the EU means that more of the global supply will be drawn to relatively clean regions that already have emissions policies, putting upward price pressure on those technologies in global markets and potentially diverting them from markets in developing countries lacking such policies. By contrast, upstream subsidies to manufacturers drive down technology costs for everyone, including in regions without carbon pricing. With China's concerted expansion of solar PV production capacity, global solar panel prices dropped by 80 per cent from 2008 to 2013 (Fialka 2016). Downstream incentives can spur innovation, learning by doing and scale economies (Newbery 2017) but can result in inefficient distribution of technologies globally if the policies are not coordinated (Gerarden 2018; Nemet 2019). Upstream incentives are thus more robust for avoiding emissions leakage in an international context and may also better address issues of knowledge spillovers and imperfect competition relevant for new-technology industries (Fischer, Greaker and Rosendahl 2017). In fact, when scale economies are important, subsidies for renewable energy technologies – particularly upstream – can potentially achieve more global emissions reductions in the power sector at lower costs than carbon pricing limited to a few principal economies (Fischer 2016).

3.1.4 Energy storage targets

One approach to better integrating the intermittent generation of renewable sources into the grid is to encourage the pairing of renewable projects with energy storage. During times of high renewable production, renewables can charge batteries that can then be discharged during periods of low renewable energy production and high electricity demand. Some studies suggest that energy storage could be necessary to accommodate a high penetration of renewables on the grid (Denholm and Margolis 2016).

A few US states, including California, Massachusetts, New York and Oregon, have set targets for energy storage procurement that vary by target type (generation or capacity) and by year. These targets are typically in addition to an existing RPS.

Go, Munoz and Watson (2016) found that energy storage can improve the economics of high penetration of renewable energy by deferring transmission and distribution investments. However, other studies have found that zero or low-carbon dispatchable plants (like nuclear or natural gas) serve as a more economic back-up for renewable power than energy storage (Safaei and Keith 2015). Linn and Shih (2019) also find that decreases in storage costs will not necessarily lead to lower emissions, though emission reductions are more likely with falling storage costs if a carbon price is in place. Consistent with economic theory, interfering with the market through mandates could increase costs of achieving the same outcome of improved renewable integration and reduced emissions.

3.2 Targeting Nuclear

3.2.1 Subsidies

Nuclear power has historically provided a large portion of carbon-free baseload generation in the US and abroad. However, in the wake of the shale gas boom, many nuclear plants in the US have retired earlier than anticipated due to competition from cheap natural gas (Clemmer et al. 2018). In the hope of retaining a large portion of this carbon-free generation, some US states have chosen to keep struggling nuclear plants online with subsidies called zero-emission credits (ZECs).

While economists typically use the term 'credit' to describe a quantity-based instrument in which the price varies, ZECs are actually a price-based instrument. ZECs offer nuclear plants a fixed subsidy payment per MWh of carbon-free energy produced. New York, Illinois and New Jersey, the three states with ZEC programmes, vary with respect to specific ZEC values. Unlike RECs, ZECs are not determined through a market but rather based on a pre-determined fixed price that changes on an annual or biannual basis.

Roth and Jaramillo (2017) find that preserving the existing US nuclear fleet through subsidies can be cost-effective since the required subsidies are lower than the social cost of carbon. In the absence of a more efficient carbon price, subsidizing nuclear plants can be a cheaper way to encourage zero-carbon generation than RPS and other renewable policies (Haratyk 2017). However, since the ZECs are not determined in a market, economic efficiency could be improved by using a market-based approach to keeping nuclear plants online, such as implementing a clean energy standard that would expand an RPS to include zero-emission nuclear power. A clean energy standard would allow for credit trading that would likely improve economic efficiency while achieving the same emission reduction target (Krupnick et al. 2010).

3.2.2 Phase-outs

Nuclear disasters like Fukushima (2011) and Chernobyl (1986) have prompted many nations, such as Germany and Switzerland, to take the opposite stance and phase out nuclear power altogether due to safety concerns. A nuclear phase-out in these nations could, however, cause electricity prices to rise considerably and CO_2 emissions to rise as gas plants replace nuclear power (Glomsrød et al. 2015).

3.3 Targeting Coal

Decarbonization of the electricity sector is typically understood to require a complete elimination of coal-fired generation. Coal has the highest carbon emission rate of any fuel used for electricity generation and produces nearly twice the amount of CO_2 per metric million British thermal units (MMBtu) as natural gas (US Energy Information Administration [US EIA] 2019). Without carbon capture and storage, coal will likely be unable to participate in a low-carbon future. In addition to its high CO_2 intensity, coal also contributes significantly to local air pollution. The production and burning of coal emit sulphur dioxide, nitrogen oxides, mercury and particulate matter, all of which have negative impacts on the environment and human health.

Consequently, several nations and subnational regions have chosen to eliminate coal through policy mandates as a method to promote decarbonization of the electricity sector. These policies typically either require the long-term phase-out of coal-fired generation or the prohibition of the construction of new coal plants. Under the latter policy, existing coal plants continue to operate and coal is eventually phased out when the last existing coal plant retires. The timeline of such an approach is therefore more uncertain compared to a mandated phase-out.

The Canadian province of Ontario was one of the first regions in the world to successfully eliminate coal completely using a generation phase-out approach. In 2007, the province enacted legislation (Ontario Regulation 496/07) that required the region's four remaining coal-fired power plants to stop burning coal by 31 December 2014. These plants would have been allowed to remain open if they were able to use an alternative fuel. As of 2014, all of the coal plants had closed and two re-opened in 2015 as biomass plants (Ontario Government 2019). Following in its province's footsteps, Canada announced in December 2018 plans to phase out coal generation throughout the entire nation by 2030.

In the wake of the 2015 Paris Agreement, many nations joined the Powering Past Coal Alliance, an organization dedicated to phasing out coal generation in developed nations by the year 2030. As of 2018, 30 nations had become members and committed to eliminating coal usage before 2030. Most of the participating countries are from the EU.

While the US has not committed to a coal phase-out, some states have taken action. Oregon was the first state to commit to eliminating coal with the Clean Electricity and Coal Transition Act (SB 1547) of 2016 that required the state's large utilities stop using coal for electricity generation by 1 January 2030. Other states have adopted policies that ban the new construction of coal plants or impose strict emissions standards on new plants without explicitly banning coal generation. California, for example, enacted emission performance standards legislation in 2006 (SB 1368) that requires that any new baseload generation under a long-term contract (applicable to both newly constructed and newly renewed contracts for existing projects) emit less than 1000 lb of CO_2 per MWh. Similarly, the UK announced in 2009 that no new coal plants would be allowed to be built after 2025 unless the plants were able to capture 100 per cent of the carbon emissions. The UK is on track to remove all remaining coal-fired plants by 2025 with no new plants planned.

Coal phase-outs can be effective at reducing emissions, as evidenced by Ontario's 17 per cent reduction in CO_2 emissions after its coal phase-out, albeit at the price of an additional CA\$5 billion per year in electricity bills (Harris, Beck and Gerasimchuk 2015). As command-and-control regulation, mandated coal phase-outs are generally considered to be very costly policies for decarbonization since they do not allow the market to decide which units to retire to achieve emission reduction targets. Heinrichs and Markewitz (2017), using a hypothetical coal phase-out in Germany by 2040 as an example, argue that a technology-neutral policy could achieve the same emissions reduction target as a coal phase-out but for much lower costs.

The costs of a phase-out, however, will ultimately depend on market forces. Since 2014 when Ontario shut down its last remaining coal plant, low natural gas prices have driven the retirement of coal plants in the market even without a policy, which would likely make a coal phase-out going forward less costly. Regardless, market-based policies, such as carbon pricing or cap-and-trade schemes, are likely cheaper options available to achieve the same result. On the other hand, the forced retirement in Ontario has proved to be a very durable emissions reduction policy, contrary to its cap-and-trade programme from which the province withdrew after a change in government.

4. INCENTIVIZING ENERGY EFFICIENCY

Consumers do not actually enjoy energy, but rather the services that energy provides, like light, heating and cooling, or transportation. Reducing energy consumption, either through conservation behaviour (reduced use of energy services) or through investments in more efficient energy-using products and buildings, which provide more services per energy used, in turn can avoid the carbon emissions associated with producing that energy. A 2010 report from McKinsey & Company (2010) finds that energy efficiency has the potential to reduce global GHG emissions by about 40 per cent. Encouraging energy efficiency and conservation is typically considered to be one of the lowest-cost options for decarbonization because many energy saving investments appear to save both utilities and consumers money, resulting in a net positive return. An oft-cited study by McKinsey & Company (2009) finds that 30 per cent of the measures available to keep the world below a 2°C warming threshold appear to be net-positive-return investments in energy efficiency.

Despite this apparent value, society tends to underinvest in energy efficiency and conservation, and can require policy to encourage higher levels of adoption. The policy interventions frequently used to promote energy efficiency usually target reduction of energy usage through incentives for equipment replacement or encouragement to conserve energy.

4.1 Subsidies

Energy efficiency subsidies are incentives for efficient electricity-using equipment typically in the form of tax credits, rebates or subsidized loans (Gillingham and Palmer 2014). Energy-efficient appliances and equipment can be more expensive than other models, and these high upfront costs can deter customers from purchasing them even if they promise to deliver total cost savings as a result of energy savings over the product's lifetime. Subsidies help address this issue by lowering the upfront expenditure to encourage the purchase of products that will use less energy and therefore have fewer use-related emissions.

Subsidies of this nature have received mixed reviews in terms of effectiveness and efficiency. Some studies find that rate-payer-funded subsidies for energy-efficient equipment can yield energy and monetary savings for both the customer and the utility that outweigh the costs of the programme (Alberini and Towe 2015, Arimura et al. 2012). Alberini and Bigano (2015) found that the Italian households in their study were more likely to replace their heating system as the subsidy increased, indicating that subsidies were an effective mechanism for encouraging energy efficiency uptake. However, the study finds that the subsidies were typically not cost-effective at reducing carbon emissions since the cost per ton of CO_2 abated exceeded the social cost of carbon under 10 per cent savings scenarios. Higher realized energy savings of 40 per cent were considered more cost-effective, but these results were less likely.

Energy efficiency subsidies are typically considered to be 'second-best' policies for reducing carbon since a direct tax on the pollution associated with energy use would be more efficient. Consequently, these subsidies can result in economic efficiency losses, particularly in the absence of a market failure separate from the carbon externality that contributes to underinvestment in efficiency (Gillingham and Palmer 2014).

Subsidies are typically a set amount for everyone and therefore do not account for heterogeneity across different consumer types, and this can create issues with respect to free riding. The free-rider problem refers to consumers who take advantage of the subsidy but would have purchased the equipment without it, thus indicating that a market failure related to uptake may not exist. Rivers and Shiell (2016) found that a Canadian programme that offered subsidies for home heating efficiency improvements resulted in a 70 per cent rate of free riding, meaning that 70 per cent of programme participants would have made the improvement without the incentive. As a result, the programme was far costlier than it needed to be to achieve the same level of energy reductions.

Another issue with subsidies is that they may amplify the rebound effect associated with energy efficiency improvements by making the investment even cheaper. Since energy-efficient appliances are cheaper to operate, they can therefore lead to consumers using more energy services than they would with a less efficient appliance. Consequently, the increase in energy usage due to the rebound effect offsets some of the energy savings expected from the investment, thus leading to lower than expected energy savings. Alberini, Towe and Gans (2016) found that the rebound effect was intensified by the presence of subsidies, and that as the size of the subsidy decreased, the amount of energy reduced by the replacement heater increased, indicating an inverse relationship. Chitnis et al. (2014) modelled requirements for UK households to install energy-efficient lighting and home insulation and also found that households that had received a subsidy for the equipment showed a significantly higher estimated rebound effect (in terms of GHG emissions) versus households that had not received a subsidy.

4.2   Information and Labelling

Asymmetric information between a seller and a buyer is sometimes considered to be one explanation for the low uptake of energy efficiency products that would save customers money and reduce carbon emissions. To correct for this, some energy efficiency programmes use information campaigns or require labels that include relevant information on energy savings and associated cost savings. Information labelling can be a low-cost method for encouraging energy efficiency uptake.

Information labelling has been used all over the world for many years in Europe, Asia and North and South America (World Energy Council 2008). Examples of labelling interventions are the EnergyGuide labels required in the US that display information on annual estimated operating costs and energy usage relative to other technologies, the energy efficiency grade labels required in the EU that display annual energy usage with a given grade, and the energy labels in Japan that include a grade, annual energy savings and annual cost savings. Newell and Siikamäki (2014) found that that providing cost savings information can significantly increase energy efficiency adoption. Additionally, Davis, Fuchs and Gertler (2014) found that information that is more specifically tailored to the consumer can further improve the uptake of energy efficiency, in this case being energy cost savings specific to a state.

Other studies have also found that non-price messaging can be also impactful for energy efficiency uptake. Asensio and Delmas (2015) found that information messaging that focused on health and environmental impacts of electricity usage actually resulted in higher energy savings than messaging focused on individual monetary savings.

4.3   Nudges

Nudges are a form of targeted information policies intended to address behavioural failures associated with inattention or misinformation regarding energy efficiency. Nudges allow consumers to make their own choices but attempt to point them in the direction of making the energy-efficient choice (Gillingham and Palmer 2014). Nudges can use interventions such as social pressure or purposeful ordering of options. One frequently used nudge is a chart on a customer's utility bill that compares their energy usage with that of their neighbours. Such an approach attempts to use social pressure to subtly convince customers to reduce their energy usage. Nudges have been shown to yield energy consumption reductions of about 1 or 2 per cent (Allcott 2011, Ayres, Raseman and Shih 2013) but results can vary substantially by demographic group (Costa and Kahn 2013).

Since neighbour comparison nudges typically only require adding information to a customer's bill, they are low cost and have the potential to be very cost-effective at reducing energy usage and thus reducing electricity-related emissions. The frequency and duration of the treatment can also impact energy savings. Ayres et al. (2013) found that monthly treatments showed higher energy savings than quarterly treatments, while

Allcott and Rogers (2014) found that longer-duration programmes improved energy savings and therefore cost-effectiveness of the programme.

Allcott and Rogers (2014) also argue that social nudge programmes (in particular, the OPower home energy report programme) can be cost-effective, and that their savings are actually underestimated on occasions because they do not take into account the long-term behavioural changes from the programme. For example, the study found that utility assumptions regarding programme cost savings were actually half of what the true savings of the programme were due to long-term behavioural adjustments as a result of the programme. Nonetheless, savings from these programmes still seem fairly small, typically around 1 or 2 per cent (Allcott and Rogers 2014, Ayres et al. 2013).

However, utility nudge programmes can also have self-selection bias. Allcott (2015) found that many utilities that were early adopters of nudge programmes were located in environmentally conscious areas, which led to higher energy reductions by the area's energy users. The programmes also initially targeted subpopulations with high energy use. Consequently, Allcott found that the effectiveness of the programme was reduced as it expanded to more utilities and was targeted toward more customers.

4.4   Energy Efficiency Equipment Standards

Governments also have the option to mandate that end-use technologies meet certain energy efficiency requirements rather than leaving the decision up to consumers. These requirements include minimum efficiency standards for appliances and equipment and building codes.

Appliance standards are typically not considered to be efficient policies for reducing carbon emissions; minimum standards are blunt instruments, only affecting the tail end of low-performing appliances, and they do not internalize the cost of using the appliances. However, they are simple, politically popular, and therefore widely implemented around the world (Gillingham and Palmer 2014). As of 2018, over 80 countries had implemented minimum energy performance standards on electric products (International Energy Agency [IEA] 2018). In one of the few attempts to assess aggregate energy savings from the collection of policies targeted at energy use in buildings, Gillingham, Newell and Palmer (2006) find that savings from appliance standards accounted for roughly 29 per cent of the energy savings and carbon emissions reductions obtained in 2000 from the collection of government energy efficiency policies directed at energy use in buildings.

A majority of US states have commercial and residential building codes for energy efficiency, though the standards differ in stringency from state to state (US Department of Energy [US DOE] 2018). A few empirical studies have shown that these building codes have successfully reduced energy consumption in buildings, albeit by a wide range (Aroonruengsawat, Auffhammer and Sanstad 2012, Jacobsen and Kotchen 2013, Papineau 2017). The cost-effectiveness of building codes specifically has not been studied extensively, though Papineau (2017) found that commercial building codes in the US cost about 7.7 cents per kWh saved in 2009, which was 2.5 cents below the retail electricity rate but above many estimates of the cost of utility energy efficiency programmes (Arimura et al. 2012, Gillingham, Keyes and Palmer 2018).

4.5 Energy Efficiency Resource Standards and White Certificates

A larger-scale approach to encouraging energy efficiency is through public policy that requires energy utilities to encourage their customers to reduce energy consumption (or energy consumption growth) through efficiency investment. These policies, often termed energy efficiency resource standards (EERS), typically require that electricity and/or gas utilities achieve a certain target energy savings rate relative to total energy sales. To meet the target, utilities can either conserve energy or purchase white certificates that represent a credit per unit of energy (typically MWh) *not* produced.

White certificates, similar to RECs (or green certificates), are tradable, and therefore their prices are determined in a market setting. A market-based energy efficiency mandate that allows for the use of white certificates therefore has the potential to improve economic efficiency by allowing the market to set the lowest possible cost for compliance.

Studies have found that this tends to be the case. Giraudet, Bodineau and Finon (2012) actually found that white certificate programmes can be net positive where the programme's benefits in terms of climate and energy savings outweigh the programme's costs. A few nations, including Italy, France and the UK, and several US states, have implemented white certificate programmes. A review of the existing European programmes has shown that energy efficiency mandates with white certificates can be cost-effective at reducing energy use and have co-benefits related to health and environmental impacts (Rosenow and Bayer 2017).

However, the effectiveness of an EERS on reducing carbon emissions will depend on the fuel intensity of the technologies it displaces (Brennan and Palmer 2013). If the energy not used would have come from clean or low-carbon energy sources, then there are little or no marginal climate benefits to reducing that energy consumption.

5. POLICY INTERACTIONS

The electricity market is by its nature replete with many distortions and market failures, meaning it will not yield efficient allocations of electricity production, taking into account the full range of societal impacts, without policy interventions. The problems include not only the questions of distortions to competition discussed elsewhere in this handbook, but also damages to the environment and human health, knowledge spillovers from technological innovation, and behavioural failures on the part of electricity consumers.

As a general rule, correcting market failures requires one intervention for each problem (Tinbergen 1952). That means that using multiple policies for clean energy promotion can be useful. For example, an emissions price is needed to address environmental damages; incentives for energy efficiency are needed to address challenges that lead to underinvestment; and additional support for renewable energy can promote broader benefits from innovation and scale economies that individual firms would not realize on their own (Fischer, Preonas and Newell 2017). However, one must also bear in mind how policies interact with each other (Fischer and Preonas 2010).

Toward that end, it is useful to distinguish between fixed-price policies, like most taxes and subsidies, and flexible-price policies, like tradable credit programmes, in which the market determines the price. Under fixed-price policies, adding some other intervention will not change the price but will affect the outcome. For example, with a carbon tax, support for renewable energy will displace more fossil generation and reduce emissions. By contrast, under tradable credit programmes, any overlapping policy will influence the market price, rather than the objective of the mandate.

For example, when CO_2 emissions are already fixed by a cap-and-trade policy, supplementary policies to support renewable energy will result in zero incremental reduction of carbon emissions. Instead, the price of emission allowances falls to allow other sources to expand and meet the cap. In fact, these supplementary policies tend to increase the overall costs of reducing emissions, while disproportionately lowering the compliance costs for the dirtiest fossil-fuel producers. That means that the renewable energy subsidies will tend to support coal-fired generation, to the detriment of gas-fired, because they benefit more from lower allowance prices (Böhringer and Rosendahl 2010).

As another example, an RPS requires a certain percentage of electricity generation to come from renewables; if that requirement is binding, that also means that a certain share of the market must come from non-renewable energy. As a result, additional subsidies that make the mandate easier to meet also drive down credit prices, making fossil sources more competitive and allowing both sources – and emissions – to expand. Additional taxes on fossil energy sources, on the other hand, reduce the overall supply of electricity, decreasing demand for renewable credits.

These consequences may or may not be intended by policymakers. For example, an emissions cap may reflect a science-based quantity threshold to respect – such as a maximum concentration of a local air pollutant beyond which health impacts rise steeply – and the corresponding price is a secondary concern. In this case, falling emissions prices from overlapping policies do not undermine the primary goal and there may even be political benefits to low prices (even if they mask higher costs from the complementary policies). For other pollutants, the relationship between additional pollution and additional damages may be clearer, meaning that the efficient policy is to target a price that reflects those social costs. For CO_2, although the long-run goal is to limit cumulative emissions, there is recognition that decisions about emissions are made over many years and across many countries, bringing more attention toward targeting the social cost of carbon. In these cases, overlapping policies can mean that the resulting prices in the tradable credit systems no longer align with the intended marginal benefits of reducing carbon or promoting renewable energy.

Thus, some consideration should be given to whether and how the primary policy may need to be adjusted in response to a secondary policy. For example, the collapse in EU ETS allowance prices coincided with the overlapping targets and policies for renewable energy and energy efficiency, requiring an overhaul and reduction in allowances and creation of an MSR. Fixed-price policies can be more transparent in how they interact with other policies and more robust in maintaining their original incentives. Policy designs that introduce more price certainty into a quantity-based method could also help to preserve those incentives and mitigate some of the policy offsetting interactions between cap-and-trade policies and other technology-focused policies to encourage clean electricity.

6.   CONCLUSION

The electricity sector is a major source of local and global pollutants in countries around the world. As concerns about climate change mount, a growing number of countries as well as subnational jurisdictions are adopting a range of different policies to address electricity sector GHG emissions. The most efficient of those policies place a price on CO_2 emissions across the sector, providing important incentives for cleaner generation and lower consumption. Other policies focus on aspects of production, either encouraging growing investment in clean generation or specifically targeting high-emitting technologies like coal boilers for elimination. The efficiency of these approaches depends on aspects of design and, particularly, on the role of incentives or market mechanisms in encouraging compliance. Energy efficiency policies have played a role in the electricity sector for several decades, justified by an apparent private energy efficiency gap, but they have seen newfound interest as climate concerns take centre stage. These policies have likely contributed in important ways to the flattening of electricity demand growth in the developed world and will continue to play an important role. Generally, none of these policies occurs in isolation, in part due to multiple market failures associated with electricity production and technology development that may deserve policy intervention. Overlapping policy goals inevitably raise the potential for important and too often unanticipated policy interactions that must be kept in mind as new policies to reduce emissions from the electricity sector are designed and adopted.

REFERENCES

Agency for the Cooperation of Energy Regulators and Council of European Energy Regulators (ACER/CEER) (2019), *Annual Report on the Results of Monitoring the Internal Electricity and Natural Gas Markets in 2018*.

Alberini, A. and A. Bigano (2015), 'How effective are energy-efficiency incentive programs? Evidence from Italian homeowners', *Energy Economics*, **52** (S1), S76–S85.

Alberini, A. and C. Towe (2015), 'Information v. energy efficiency incentives: evidence from residential electricity consumption in Maryland', *Energy Economics*, **52** (S1), S30–S40.

Alberini, A., C. Towe and W. Gans (2016), 'Free riding, upsizing, and energy efficiency incentives in Maryland homes', *The Energy Journal*, **37** (1), 259–90.

Allcott, H. (2011), 'Social norms and energy conservation', *Journal of Public Economics*, **95** (9–10), 1082–95.

Allcott, H. (2015), 'Site selection bias in program evaluation', *The Quarterly Journal of Economics*, **130** (3), 1117–65.

Allcott, H. and T. Rogers (2014), 'The short-run and long-run effects of behavioral interventions: experimental evidence from energy conservation', *American Economic Review*, **104** (10), 3003–37.

Anatolitis, V. and M. Welisch (2017), 'Putting renewable energy auctions into action – an agent-based model of onshore wind power auctions in Germany', *Energy Policy*, **110**, 394–402.

Andor, M., K. Flinkerbusch and M. Janssen et al. (2010), 'Rethinking feed-in tariffs and priority dispatch for renewables', Foundation for Research on Market Design and Energy Trading, accessed 16 July 2021 at https://hepg.hks.harvard.edu/files/hepg/files/rethinking_feed-in_tariffs.pdf.

Arimura, T. H., S. Li, R. G. Newell and K. Palmer (2012), 'Cost-effectiveness of electricity energy efficiency programs', *The Energy Journal*, **33** (2), 63–99.

Aroonruengsawat, A., M. Auffhammer and A. H. Sanstad (2012), 'The impact of state level building codes on residential electricity consumption', *The Energy Journal*, **33** (1), 31–52.

Asensio, O. I. and M. A. Delmas (2015), 'Nonprice incentives and energy conservation', *Proceedings of the National Academy of Sciences*, **112** (6), E510–E515.

Avi-Yonah, R. S. and D. M. Uhlmann (2009), 'Combating global climate change: why a carbon tax is a better response to global warming than cap and trade', *Stanford Environmental Law Journal*, **28** (1), 3–50.

Ayres, I., S. Raseman and A. Shih (2013), 'Evidence from two large field experiments that peer comparison feedback can reduce residential energy usage', *The Journal of Law, Economics, and Organization*, **29** (5), 992–1022.

Beck, M., N. Rivers, R. Wigle and H. Yonezawa (2015), 'Carbon tax and revenue recycling: impacts on households in British Columbia', *Resource and Energy Economics*, **41**, 40–69.

Behrens, P., J. F. Rodrigues, T. Brás and C. Silva (2016), 'Environmental, economic, and social impacts of feed-in tariffs: a Portuguese perspective 2000–2010', *Applied Energy*, **173**, 309–19.

Blanford, G. J., J. H. Merrick and D. Young (2014), 'A clean energy standard analysis with the US-REGEN model', *The Energy Journal*, **35** (Special Issue), 137–64.

Böhringer, C. and K. E. Rosendahl (2010), 'Green promotes the dirtiest: on the interaction between black and green quotas in energy markets', *Journal of Regulatory Economics*, **37** (3), 316–25.

Brennan, T. J. and K. L. Palmer (2013), 'Energy efficiency resource standards: economics and policy', *Utilities Policy*, **25**, 58–68.

Burtraw, D. and K. Palmer (2008), 'Compensation rules for climate policy in the electricity sector', *Journal of Policy Analysis and Management*, **27** (4), 819–47.

Burtraw, D., C. Holt and K. Palmer et al. (2017), *Expanding the Toolkit: The Potential Role for an Emissions Containment Reserve in RGGI*, Resources for the Future report, August, accessed 16 July 2021 at https://media.rff.org/documents/RFF-Rpt-RGGI_ECR.pdf.

Chitnis, M., S. Sorrell and A. Druckman et al. (2014), 'Who rebounds most? Estimating direct and indirect rebound effects for different UK socioeconomic groups', *Ecological Economics*, **106**, 12–32.

Clemmer, S., J. Richardson, S. Sattler and D. Lochbaum (2018), *The Nuclear Power Dilemma: Declining Profits, Plant Closures, and the Threat of Rising Carbon Emissions*, Union of Concerned Scientists, November, accessed 16 July 2021 at https://www.ucsusa.org/sites/default/files/attach/2018/11/Nuclear-Power-Dilemma-full-report.pdf.

Comello, S. and S. Reichelstein (2017), 'Cost competitiveness of residential solar PV: the impact of net metering restrictions', *Renewable and Sustainable Energy Reviews*, **75**, 46–57.

Costa, D. L. and M. E. Kahn (2013), 'Energy conservation "nudges" and environmentalist ideology: evidence from a randomized residential electricity field experiment', *Journal of the European Economic Association*, **11** (3), 680–702.

Cramton, P., D. J. C. MacKay, A. Ockenfels and S. Stoft (2017), *Global Carbon Pricing: The Path to Climate Cooperation*, Cambridge, MA: MIT Press.

Davis, L. W., A. Fuchs and P. Gertler (2014), 'Cash for coolers: evaluating a large-scale appliance replacement program in Mexico', *American Economic Journal: Economic Policy*, **6** (4), 207–38.

Del Río, P. (2012), 'The dynamic efficiency of feed-in tariffs: the impact of different design elements', *Energy Policy*, **41**, 139–51.

Del Río, P. and P. Mir-Artigues (2014), *A Cautionary Tale: Spain's Solar PV Investment Bubble*, International Institute for Sustainable Development, February, accessed 16 July 2021 at https://www.iisd.org/gsi/sites/default/files/rens_ct_spain.pdf.

Denholm, P. and R. Margolis (2016), *Energy Storage Requirements for Achieving 50% Solar Photovoltaic Energy Penetration in California*, NREL/TP-6A20-66595, Golden, CO: National Renewable Energy Lab.

Dijkgraaf, E., T. P. van Dorp and E. Maasland (2018), 'On the effectiveness of feed-in tariffs in the development of solar photovoltaics', *The Energy Journal*, **39** (1), 81–100.

Dong, C. G. (2012), 'Feed-in tariff vs. renewable portfolio standard: an empirical test of their relative effectiveness in promoting wind capacity development', *Energy Policy*, **42**, 476–85.

Eid, C., J. R. Guillén, P. F. Marín and R. Hakvoort (2014), 'The economic effect of electricity net-metering with solar PV: consequences for network cost recovery, cross subsidies and policy objectives', *Energy Policy*, **75**, 244–54.

Falconett, I. and K. Nagasaka (2010), 'Comparative analysis of support mechanisms for renewable energy technologies using probability distributions', *Renewable Energy*, **35** (6), 1135–44.

Fell, H. and P. Maniloff (2018), 'Leakage in regional environmental policy: the case of the regional greenhouse gas initiative', *Journal of Environmental Economics and Management*, **87**, 1–23.

Fialka, J. (2016), 'Why China is dominating the solar industry', *Scientific American*, 19 December, accessed 16 July 202 at https://www.scientificamerican.com/article/why-china-is-dominating-the-solar-industry/.

Fischer, C. (2010), 'Renewable portfolio standards: when do they lower energy prices?', *The Energy Journal*, **31** (1), 101–19.

Fischer, C. (2016), 'Strategic subsidies for green goods', *RFF Discussion Paper 16-12*, Resources for the Future.

Fischer, C. and A. K. Fox (2007), 'Output-based allocation of emissions permits for mitigating tax and trade interactions', *Land Economics*, **83** (4), 575–99.

Fischer, C. and R. G. Newell (2008), 'Environmental and technology policies for climate mitigation', *Journal of Environmental Economics and Management*, **55** (2), 142–62.

Fischer, C. and W. A. Pizer (2019), 'Horizontal equity effects in energy regulation', *Journal of the Association of Environmental and Resource Economists*, **6** (S1), S209–S237.

Fischer, C. and L. Preonas (2010), 'Combining policies for renewable energy: is the whole less than the sum of its parts?', *International Review of Energy and Resource Economics*, **4** (1), 51–92.

Fischer, C., M. Greaker and K. E. Rosendahl (2017), 'Robust policies against emission leakage: the case for upstream subsidies', *Journal of Environmental Economics and Management*, **84**, 44–61.

Fischer, C., L. Preonas and R. G. Newell (2017), 'Environmental and technology policy options in the electricity sector: are we deploying too many?', *Journal of the Association of Environmental and Resource Economists*, **4** (4), 959–84.

Gerarden, T. D. (2018), 'Demanding innovation: the impact of consumer subsidies on solar panel production costs', *Discussion Paper 18-77*, Harvard Environmental Economics Program, May, accessed 16 July 2021 at https://heep.hks.harvard.edu/files/heep/files/gerarden_dp_77.pdf.

Gillingham, K. and K. Palmer (2014), 'Bridging the energy efficiency gap: policy insights from economic theory and empirical evidence', *Review of Environmental Economics and Policy*, **8** (1), 18–38.

Gillingham, K., A. Keyes and K. Palmer (2018), 'Advances in evaluating energy efficiency policies and programs', *Annual Review of Resource Economics*, **10**, 511–32.

Gillingham, K., R. Newell and K. Palmer (2006), 'Energy efficiency policies: a retrospective examination', *Annual Review of Environment and Resources*, **31**, 161–92.

Giraudet, L. G., L. Bodineau and D. Finon (2012), 'The costs and benefits of white certificates schemes', *Energy Efficiency*, **5** (2), 179–99.

Glomsrød, S., T. Wei, T. Mideksa and B. H. Samset (2015), 'Energy market impacts of nuclear power phase-out policies', *Mitigation and Adaptation Strategies for Global Change*, **20** (8), 1511–27.

Go, R. S., F. D. Munoz and J. P. Watson (2016), 'Assessing the economic value of co-optimized grid-scale energy storage investments in supporting high renewable portfolio standards', *Applied Energy*, **183**, 902–13.

Gollier, C. and J. Tirole (2015), 'Negotiating effective institutions against climate change', *Economics of Energy & Environmental Policy*, **4** (2), 5–28.

Goulder, L. H. and A. R. Schein (2013), 'Carbon taxes versus cap and trade: a critical review', *Climate Change Economics*, **4** (3), Article 1350010.

Goulder, L., X. Long, J. Liu and R. Morgenstern (2020), 'China's unconventional nationwide CO_2 emissions trading system: the wide-ranging impacts of an implicit output subsidy', *RFF Working Paper 20-02*, Resources for the Future.

Goulder, L. H., I. W. Parry and D. Burtraw (1997), 'Revenue-raising versus other approaches to environmental protection: the critical significance of pre-existing tax distortions', *RAND Journal of Economics*, **28** (4), 708–31.

Haas, R., G. Resch and C. Panzer et al. (2011), 'Efficiency and effectiveness of promotion systems for electricity generation from renewable energy sources – lessons from EU countries', *Energy*, **36** (4), 2186–93.

Haratyk, G. (2017), 'Early nuclear retirements in deregulated US markets: causes, implications and policy options', *Energy Policy*, **110**, 150–66.

Harris, M., M. Beck and I. Gerasimchuk (2015), *The End of Coal: Ontario's Coal Phase-out*, International Institute for Sustainable Development, June, accessed 16 July 2021 at https://www.greengrowthknowledge.org/sites/default/files/downloads/resource/End-of-coal-ontario-coal-phase-out_IISD.pdf.

Heinrichs, H. U. and P. Markewitz (2017), 'Long-term impacts of a coal phase-out in Germany as part of a greenhouse gas mitigation strategy', *Applied Energy*, **192**, 234–46.

Intergovernmental Panel on Climate Change (IPCC) (2014), *Climate Change 2014: Mitigation of Climate Change*, contribution of Working Group III to the Fifth Assessment Report of the Intergovernmental Panel on Climate Change, Cambridge, UK: Cambridge University Press.

International Energy Agency (IEA) (2018), *Energy Efficiency 2018: Analysis and Outlooks to 2040*, October, accessed 5 July 2021 at https://webstore.iea.org/download/direct/2369?fileName=Market_Report_Series_Energy_Efficiency_2018.pdf.

International Renewable Energy Agency (IRENA) (2013), *30 Years of Policies for Wind Energy: Lessons from 12 Wind Energy Markets*, January, accessed 16 July 2021 at https://www.irena.org/-/media/Files/IRENA/Agency/Publication/2013/GWEC_WindReport_All_web-display.pdf.

Jacobsen, G. D. and M. J. Kotchen (2013), 'Are building codes effective at saving energy? Evidence from residential billing data in Florida', *Review of Economics and Statistics*, **95** (1), 34–49.

Jaffe, A. B., R. G. Newell and R. N. Stavins (2005), 'A tale of two market failures: technology and environmental policy', *Ecological Economics*, **54** (2–3), 164–74.

Johnson, E. P. (2014), 'The cost of carbon dioxide abatement from state renewable portfolio standards', *Resource and Energy Economics*, **36** (2), 332–50.

Kieffer, G. and T. D. Couture (2015), *Renewable Energy Target Setting*, International Renewable Energy Agency, June, accessed 12 July 2021 at https://www.irena.org/-/media/Files/IRENA/Agency/Publication/2015/IRENA_RE_Target_Setting_2015.pdf.

Krupnick, A. J., I. W. Parry and M. Walls et al. (2010), *Toward a New National Energy Policy: Assessing the Options*, Resources for the Future and National Energy Policy Institute, November, accessed 16 July 2021 at https://media.rff.org/documents/RFF-Rpt-NEPI20Tech20Manual_Final.pdf.

Laing, T., M. Sato, M. Grubb and C. Comberti (2013), 'Assessing the effectiveness of the EU Emissions Trading System', *Working Paper No. 126*, Centre for Climate Change Economics and Policy.

Lehmann, P. (2009), 'Climate policies with pollution externalities and learning spillovers', *UFZ-Discussion Paper No. 10/2009*, Helmholtz Centre for Environmental Research.

Linn, J. and J. S. Shih (2019), 'Do lower electricity storage costs reduce greenhouse gas emissions?', *Journal of Environmental Economics and Management*, **96**, 130–58.

Lipp, J. (2007), 'Lessons for effective renewable electricity policy from Denmark, Germany and the United Kingdom', *Energy Policy*, **35** (11), 5481–95.

Mai, T., W. Cole and E. Lantz et al. (2016), *Impacts of Federal Tax Credit Extensions on Renewable Deployment and Power Sector Emissions*, No. NREL/TP-6A20-65571, Golden, CO: National Renewable Energy Laboratory (NREL).

Marcantonini, C. and A. D. Ellerman (2015), 'The implicit carbon price of renewable energy incentives in Germany', *The Energy Journal*, **36** (4), 205–39.

Marcantonini, C. and V. Valero (2017), 'Renewable energy and CO2 abatement in Italy', *Energy Policy*, **106**, 600–613.

Marron, D. B. and E. J. Toder (2014), 'Tax policy issues in designing a carbon tax', *American Economic Review*, **104** (5), 563–8.

McKinsey & Company (2009), *Pathways to a Low-carbon Economy: Version 2 of the Global Greenhouse Gas Abatement Curve*, accessed 16 July 2021 at https://www.mckinsey.com/~/media/McKinsey/Business%20Functions/Sustainability/Our%20Insights/Pathways%20to%20a%20low%20carbon%20economy/Pathways%20to%20a%20low%20carbon%20economy.pdf.

McKinsey & Company (2010), *Energy Efficiency: A Compelling Global Resource*, McKinsey Sustainability & Resource Productivity, accessed 16 July 2021 at https://ecocloud360.com/wp-content/uploads/2015/02/A_Compelling_Global_Resource.pdf.

Mignone, B. K., T. Alfstad and A. Bergman et al. (2012), 'Cost-effectiveness and economic incidence of a clean energy standard', *Economics of Energy & Environmental Policy*, **1** (3), 59–86.

Murray, B. C. and P. T. Maniloff (2015), 'Why have greenhouse emissions in RGGI states declined? An econometric attribution to economic, energy market, and policy factors', *Energy Economics*, **51**, 581–9.

Murray, B. and N. Rivers (2015), 'British Columbia's revenue-neutral carbon tax: a revie of the latest "grand experiment" in environmental policy', *Energy Policy*, **86**, 674–83.

Murray, B. C., M. L. Cropper, F. C. de la Chesnaye and J. M. Reilly (2014), 'How effective are US renewable energy subsidies in cutting greenhouse gases?', *American Economic Review*, **104** (5), 569–74.

Nemet, G.F. (2006), 'Beyond the learning curve: factors influencing cost reductions in photovoltaics', *Energy Policy*, **34** (17), 3218–32.

Nemet, G. F. (2019), *How Solar Energy Became Cheap: A Model for Low-Carbon Innovation*, Abingdon, UK: Routledge.

Newbery, D. M. (2017), 'How to judge whether supporting solar PV is justified', *EPRG Working Paper 1706*, Energy Policy Working Group, University of Cambridge, accessed 16 July 2021 at http://www.eprg.group.cam.ac.uk/wp-content/uploads/2017/03/1706-Text.pdf.

Newbery, D., M. G. Pollitt, R. A. Ritz and W. Strielkowski (2018), 'Market design for a high-renewables European electricity system', *Renewable and Sustainable Energy Reviews*, **91**, 695–707.

Newell, R. G. and J. Siikamäki (2014), 'Nudging energy efficiency behavior: the role of information labels', *Journal of the Association of Environmental and Resource Economists*, **1** (4), 555–98.

Newport, F. (2018), 'Americans want government to do more on environment', *Gallup News*, 29 March, accessed 28 October 2020 at https://news.gallup.com/poll/232007/americans-want-government-more-environment.aspx.

Oggioni, G., F. H. Murphy and Y. Smeers (2014), 'Evaluating the impacts of priority dispatch in the European electricity market', *Energy Economics*, 42, 183–200.

Ontario Government (2019), 'The end of coal', accessed 11 June 2019 at https://www.ontario.ca/page/end-coal.

Palmer, K. and D. Burtraw (2005), 'Cost-effectiveness of renewable electricity policies', *Energy Economics*, **27** (6), 873–94.

Papineau, M. (2017), 'Setting the standard? A framework for evaluating the cost-effectiveness of building energy standards', *Energy Economics*, **64**, 63–76.

Paul, A., K. Palmer and M. Woerman (2015), 'Incentives, margins, and cost effectiveness in comprehensive climate policy for the power sector', *Climate Change Economics*, **6** (4), Article 1550016.

Perino, G. (2018), 'New EU ETS Phase 4 rules temporarily puncture waterbed', *Nature Climate Change*, **8** (4), 262–4.

Pollitt, M. G. (2019), 'A global carbon market?', *Frontiers of Engineering Management*, **6** (1), 5–18.

Poterba, J. M. (1991), 'Tax policy to combat global warming: on designing a carbon tax', *NBER Working Paper No. 3649*, National Bureau of Economic Research.

Reichenbach, J. and T. Requate (2012), 'Subsidies for renewable energies in the presence of learning effects and market power', *Resource and Energy Economics*, **34** (2), 236–54.

REN21 (2019), *Renewables 2019 Global Status Report*, Paris: REN21 Secretariat.

Rivers, N. and M. Jaccard (2006), 'Choice of environmental policy in the presence of learning by doing', *Energy Economics*, **28** (2), 223–42.

Rivers, N. and M. L. Shiell (2016), 'Free-riding on energy efficiency subsidies: the case of natural gas furnaces in Canada', *Energy Journal*, **37** (4), 239–66.

Rosenow, J. and E. Bayer (2017), 'Costs and benefits of Energy Efficiency Obligations: a review of European programmes', *Energy Policy*, **107**, 53–62.

Roth, M. B. and P. Jaramillo (2017), 'Going nuclear for climate mitigation: an analysis of the cost effectiveness of preserving existing US nuclear power plants as a carbon avoidance strategy', *Energy*, **131**, 67–77.

Safaei, H. and D. W. Keith (2015), 'How much bulk energy storage is needed to decarbonize electricity?', *Energy & Environmental Science*, **8** (12), 3409–17.

Schmalensee, R. and R. N. Stavins (2017), 'The design of environmental markets: what have we learned from experience with cap and trade?', *Oxford Review of Economic Policy*, **33** (4), 572–88.

Stewart, R. B. and J. B. Wiener (2003), *Reconstructing Climate Policy: Beyond Kyoto*, Washington, DC: American Enterprise Institute Press.

Sun, P. and P. Y. Nie (2015), 'A comparative study of feed-in tariff and renewable portfolio standard policy in renewable energy industry', *Renewable Energy*, **74**, 255–62.

Tamas, M. M., S. B. Shrestha and H. Zhou (2010), 'Feed-in tariff and tradable green certificate in oligopoly', *Energy Policy*, **38** (8), 4040–47.

Tinbergen, J. (1952), *On the Theory of Economic Policy*, Amsterdam: North-Holland.

UK Department of Energy & Climate Change (2010), *National Renewable Energy Action Plan for the United Kingdom: Article 4 of the Renewable Energy Directive 2009/28/EC*, accessed 11 June 2019 at https://assets.publishing.service.gov.uk/government/uploads/system/uploads/attachment_data/file/47871/25-nat-ren-energy-action-plan.pdf.

US Department of Energy (US DOE) (2018), 'Status of state energy code adoption', accessed 16 April 2019 at https://www.energycodes.gov/status-state-energy-code-adoption.

US Energy Information Administration (US EIA) (2019), 'How much carbon dioxide is produced when different fuels are burned?', *FAQs*, accessed 4 June 2019 at https://www.eia.gov/tools/faqs/faq.php?id=73&t=11.

Weitzman, M. L. (2014), 'Can negotiating a uniform carbon price help to internalize the global warming externality?', *Journal of the Association of Environmental and Resource Economists*, **1** (1–2), 29–49.

Williams, R. C., H. Gordon and D. Burtraw et al. (2015), 'The initial incidence of a carbon tax across income groups', *National Tax Journal*, **68** (1), 195–214.

World Bank Group (2019), *State and Trends of Carbon Pricing 2019*, June, accessed 16 July 2021 at https://openknowledge.worldbank.org/handle/10986/31755.

World Energy Council (2008), *Energy Efficiency Policies around the World: Review and Evaluation*, accessed 16 July 2021 at https://www.worldenergy.org/assets/downloads/PUB_Energy_Efficiency_-Policies_Around_the_World_Review_and_Evaluation_Exec_Summary_2008_WEC.pdf.

Yamazaki, A. (2017), 'Jobs and climate policy: evidence from British Columbia's revenue-neutral carbon tax', *Journal of Environmental Economics and Management*, **83**, 197–216

15. Shifting supply as well as demand: the new economics of electricity with high renewables

Richard Green[*]

1. INTRODUCTION

Since the very beginnings of the industry, the demand for electricity has varied over time and the power system has been built and operated to meet that demand. Most power stations have been dispatchable, such that they followed instructions from the system operator to ensure that generation and demand were in constant balance. Every generator on the system would be rotating at the same speed, and this frequency would fall rapidly if generation fell short of demand. Once the frequency becomes too low, equipment will automatically disconnect to protect itself and there will be a cascading blackout.

Chapter 3 has shown how to choose the optimal mix of power stations and how to calculate the marginal cost of electricity at each point in time. Many countries have introduced wholesale markets for electricity in which the price of power should be close to its marginal cost as long as there is sufficient competition between different generating companies or regulatory measures to control their behaviour. When demand is low, so is the wholesale price, since only the most efficient stations, or those burning particularly cheap fuels, are required. Higher demands imply higher prices, since less efficient stations, or more expensive fuels, must be used as well. At peak times, when demand at these prices would exceed the available generating capacity, the price should rise until demand falls back to the level of available capacity. Chapter 3 shows that the price would then be equal to the marginal value of electricity; it could also be seen as equal to the marginal (variable) cost of generating plus the marginal opportunity cost of not having enough capacity. Chapter 3 has shown how wholesale market prices set in this way should be able to provide enough revenue for every generator, as long as the industry has the right capacity mix and prices are allowed to rise enough at peak times. Chapter 4 describes what this requires in practice, and the country studies in Chapters 6–11 show how well it has worked since liberalization policies were adopted in the 1990s.

This traditional paradigm features a supply curve that does not change very much from day to day – the available plants and the merit order that ranks them from the cheapest to the most expensive (and hence rarely used) tend to be quite stable. Of course, plants break down and are then repaired, fuel prices rise and fall at different rates, and generators are commissioned and retired, but these changes generally have less short-run impact on prices than the regular daily and seasonal variations in demand.

This chapter asks how far this paradigm must change in the light of efforts to decarbonize the power system by investing in renewable generators. Table 15.1 gives key statistics for the main types of generation, listing four main types of renewables: biomass, hydro, solar and wind power. Note the dramatic rise in wind and (especially) solar generation (from a low base), and the slow growth in nuclear power output. Hydroelectricity is the third most important generation type, growing almost in line with the overall demand for

Table 15.1   World electricity generation, 2019

		2019 Generation (TWh)	2019 Share (%)	Compound Average Growth Rate, 2009–19 (%)
Fossil fuelled	Coal	9 824	36.4	1.9
	Gas	6 298	23.3	3.5
	Oil	825	3.1	–1.8
Nuclear		2 796	10.4	0.4
Renewable	Biomass	652	2.4	6.7
	Hydro	4 222	15.6	2.6
	Solar	724	2.7	42.5
	Wind	1 430	5.3	17.9
Other		234	0.9	7.3
Total		27 005	100.0	2.9

Source: BP (2020).

power. Coal remains by far the most important fuel source, even though its share is slowly declining, and that of gas slowly increasing.

In many ways, biomass generators are similar to thermal generators burning fossil fuels; their marginal costs are dominated by fuel costs and they can be dispatched in response to system operator requirements. Hydro generators are also dispatchable, but their marginal costs are essentially the opportunity cost of using water in one period rather than saving it for a later one. That opportunity cost depends on how much water the generator is storing, which can vary significantly from year to year with rainfall and snowfall in the generator's catchment area. Prices in a dry year will be higher than when the reservoirs are full.

Solar photovoltaic (PV) and wind generators are non-dispatchable in the sense that they can only generate when the sun is shining or the wind is blowing, and this changes over time. Once a power system contains a significant proportion of these generators, the supply curve will be shifting as well as the demand curve. Because their marginal costs are very low, wind and solar output will tend to displace the output from higher-cost plants, depressing prices in the hours when they are available. Their fixed costs have also been falling rapidly, and in some countries, they now have a lower levelized cost of electricity than coal or gas generation.

This is not sufficient to make them the best option for new generation. Joskow (2011) points out that the levelized cost of electricity is inappropriate, either for comparing intermittent technologies with different output patterns or for assessing them against conventional plants. The next section of this chapter extends the analysis of Chapter 3 to show how the output from renewable generators should be valued, given its impact on the supply and demand for electricity. It shows how the screening curve analysis of capacity choices can be modified to take account of variable-output renewable generators.

The longer the distance between two renewable generators, the more likely they are to have dissimilar outputs. Section 3 discusses electricity transmission and its potential for smoothing the variability of wind and solar generation. While economists have written many pieces on transmission, the detailed operational challenges of keeping the power system stable are more often left to engineers. The growth of renewable generation makes some of those challenges harder, as described in Section 4.

Many of those operational challenges are eased in systems with large amounts of electricity storage, which is the subject of Section 5. Electricity prices are now based on opportunity costs since hydroelectric generators face the choice between using water now and saving it for future output. The analysis can be extended to the case where stored energy does not come from rain and snow, but from charging a battery or pumping water uphill. Section 6 considers how large amounts of renewable energy will change the operational and financial risks facing electricity companies. The chapter ends with a brief conclusion. Wholesale electricity markets should be able to cope with increased amounts of renewable electricity generation but may have to adapt their rules; possible adaptations are the subject of the next chapter in this handbook.

2. ADDING RENEWABLE GENERATORS TO THE SUPPLY CURVE

Figure 15.1 shows the merit-order supply curve introduced in Chapter 3. In panel (a), there are three types of generators with different marginal costs, shown by the thick stepped line. Four representative demand curves suggest that while some consumers respond to wholesale prices, the elasticity of demand to prices is very low. In particular, the amount that can be generated is less than the highest level of demand (D_1) would be if the price were equal to the marginal cost just before the capacity constraint became binding (equal to P_2). A noticeably higher price (P_1) is needed to reduce demand to the level that can be supplied. At the other times, the price (P_2, P_3 and P_4) is equal to a

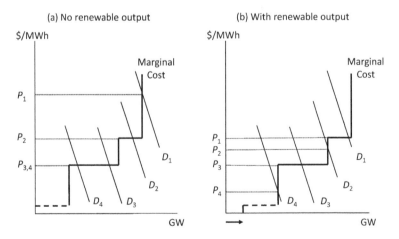

Source: Author's variant of a well-known figure.

Figure 15.1   *Supply and demand in a simple electricity market: (a) no renewable output; (b) with renewable output*

generator's marginal cost. As Chapter 3 explains, with the right capacity mix, every generator should in theory be able to recover its costs from this kind of pricing system, as long as peak prices are allowed to rise to levels that recover the costs of the peaking generators. These are stations with high variable costs (so that it is uneconomic to run them for long periods) but low fixed costs. They might be relatively cheap open-cycle gas turbines or older stations with fully depreciated capital costs.

Other generators have higher fixed costs but are cheaper to run, and if they can run for enough hours per year, it is better to use these than to deploy additional peaking stations. The load-duration curve of Figure 15.2 has vertical dashed lines at two such crossover points. The left-hand line shows where the costs of peaking plants and (so-called) mid-merit plants are equal, while mid-merit and baseload plants have the same costs at the right-hand line. The thick curved line shows the demand in each hour of the year, ranked in order of decreasing demand. Assume that the Hth-highest demand is for L gigawatts (GW). If plants could be turned on and off in perfect merit order of increasing costs, then the generator placed at L GW in the merit order (with the Lth-lowest costs) would run for H hours a year. If H is to the left of the first vertical line, then generator L should be a peaking plant; if H is to the right of the second vertical line, it should be baseload. The thick horizontal dashed lines show how the total amount of capacity should be divided between the three types of our example.

Because biomass generators have essentially the same cost structure as fossil-fuelled plants, they can easily be added to this analysis. Wind and solar generators are different because their output depends not on their (negligible) variable costs but on the weather. Panel (b) of Figure 15.1 shows how the supply curve shifts to the right when these variable renewable stations are generating. Even the peak demand can now be met in full at a price equal to the marginal cost of the peaking generators, and P_2 and P_4 have also fallen. The average electricity price is clearly going to be lower. This has become known as the merit-order effect (Sáenz de Miera, del Río González and Vizcaíno 2008, Senfuß, Ragwitz and Genoese 2008).

The merit-order effect is not unique to renewable generation. Adding production capacity to any industry is likely to reduce prices and profit margins. The particular issues with variable renewable generators are that their zero marginal costs almost guarantee that they will displace other stations' output whenever they are available, and that their entry has usually depended on government policy (as described in Chapter 14) rather than on market conditions. Boom-and-bust cycles of market-driven entry can drive prices below average long-run costs (Chapter 6 shows that a wave of gas-fired investment in the 1990s was followed by a steep fall in wholesale prices around the turn of the millennium in England and Wales), but are self-limiting in a way that the widespread adoption of renewable power targets need not be.

Even so, Figure 15.2 suggests that the capacity of other generators can adjust to the large-scale entry of variable renewables. The thin curved line shows how the load-duration curve faced by the remaining power stations will change. Note that the highest levels of demand are almost as great as when there was no renewable capacity. There will be some hours of high demand with very little renewable output, and so the total amount of dispatchable capacity required will not change by much. At the other end of the curve, there are likely to be some hours with low (overall) demand and very high levels of renewable output, and so the minimum demand for dispatchable capacity falls

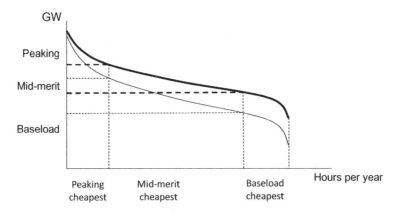

Source: Author's variant of a well-known figure.

Figure 15.2   Load duration and capacity choice

significantly. The middle of the net load-duration curve (showing the demand net of variable renewable output) contains some hours with high demands and high levels of renewable output and others with lower demand but little output from variable renewable generators.

Given time, the capacity mix should change. With the mix implied by the thick horizontal lines in Figure 15.2 (which was suitable for the original, gross load-duration curve), baseload and mid-merit stations would be setting the price for too many hours of the year, and would be unable to recover their fixed costs (the number of hours is not shown in the figure, but occurs where the lower of the thick horizontal dashed lines crosses the thin net load-duration curve, roughly halfway along its length). If there was less baseload capacity, there would be more hours with higher prices set by mid-merit and peaking stations, allowing the baseload stations to recover their full costs. The thin dashed horizontal lines show the new levels of capacity. There will inevitably be less baseload capacity and more peaking capacity; in this example there is also more mid-merit capacity, but that result depends on the shape of the load-duration curves. That shape could change, of course, if demand becomes more flexible or is shifted in time by storage (discussed later in this chapter).

Green and Léautier (2015) show that as long as the lowest net demand still allows (some) baseload plants to operate throughout the year, the time-weighted average price in the long-run equilibrium does not depend on the amount of renewable capacity. The cost of operating a baseload station throughout the year has not changed (given the simple assumptions of this model) and so the average price it must receive in equilibrium does not change either. Whether the demand-weighted average price paid by consumers changes depends on the timing of renewable output. If that output is concentrated in periods with above-average gross demands, then large amounts of electricity consumption will benefit from the merit-order effect and the demand-weighted price will tend to fall. But if wind output is greater at night and away from the months of highest demand, as it is in summer-peaking Texas (Cullen 2013), then the demand-weighted price might rise. This is because the price reductions from wind power are concentrated in hours with little demand, while higher-demand hours see increases as the plant mix shifts towards stations with higher variable costs.

The relative price received by a generator depends on the correlation between its output and net demand. The output of dispatchable generators responds to shifts in demand and so is positively correlated with prices; all except baseload generators can expect to earn more than the time-weighted average price. Whether wind or solar generators' availabilities are positively or negatively correlated with the gross demand for electricity, their output shifts the supply curve to the right and hence reduces the market price in the hours when they actually generate. Unless its output is uncorrelated with that of existing plants, adding more capacity will strengthen this effect (Twomey and Neuhoff 2010). Hirth (2013) refers to the value factor as the ratio between the average price that a renewable generator would receive (hypothetically, as few get all of their revenues from the wholesale market) and the time-weighted average wholesale price.

Figure 15.3, inspired by Bushnell and Novan (2018), shows how solar PV output has affected market prices in California across a typical day. The top pair of lines show that overnight demand was similar in 2012 and 2016, although demand in the middle of the day was slightly lower in the later year. Prices in the real-time market were noticeably lower at the times when solar output (shown at the bottom of the graph) was typically high. Bushnell and Novan estimate that each gigawatt-hour (GWh) of solar output (spread across a day) reduced the price at midday by 0.39 dollars per megawatt-hour

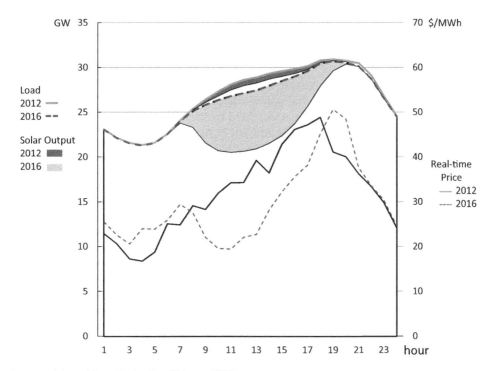

Source: Adapted from Bushnell and Novan (2018).

Figure 15.3   Load, PV output and prices in California

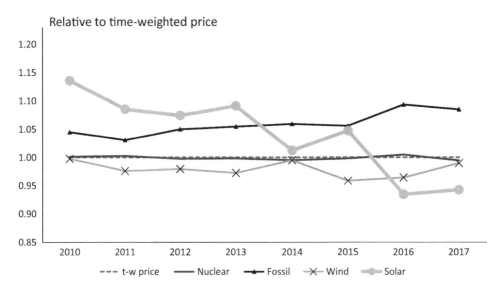

Source: Author's calculations from Elexon data.

Figure 15.4   Annualized relative prices by plant type (Great Britain)

($/MWh). Since California's average daily solar output rose from 5.5 GWh in 2012 to 57.8 GWh in 2016, this would have depressed prices by 20.40 $/MWh. The actual average price at midday in 2016 was 22.05 $/MWh. Bushnell and Novan compare estimates of 2016 market prices with 10 GW of PV capacity (the actual number rose from just below to just over this level during the year) to a counterfactual with just 2 GW. Expanding PV capacity in this way reduced the wholesale market value per MWh by 52 per cent.

Figure 15.4 shows the relative prices weighted by the output of different types of generators in Great Britain between 2010 and 2017. At the start of the period, solar PV output is the most valuable per MWh, since it is concentrated in the daytime hours of higher demand and prices. But, just as in California, the concentrated output tends to depress prices in those hours, and it is unusual for a PV panel to produce much power at times when others are not also generating. By 2016, with 12 GW of PV capacity on the system, this meant that the prices at times of high PV output had been depressed so much that the average value of PV output was lower than the time-weighted average price of electricity.

Wind output is more dispersed over time and less correlated between (distant) locations. This increases the chance that a station can produce a significant amount of output at times when the price has not been driven down by other wind farms. Chyong, Pollitt and Cruise (2019) predict that the 10 per cent of German wind capacity that is offshore will benefit from this effect by receiving a higher price than onshore farms across a range of scenarios for 2025; the correlation between hour-by-hour offshore and onshore load factors is 0.79 (Staffell and Pfenninger 2016) and the (much larger) onshore output will have more impact on price patterns. British wind farms also produce above-average quantities during the winter months when prices are generally higher. Despite this, Britain has enough wind capacity to significantly depress prices on windy days, and the average value of wind output is always below the time-weighted average price. In contrast, Figure 15.4 shows that nuclear stations have always received close to the time-weighted price (since they try to generate continuously). Fossil-fuelled stations have to receive more than the time-weighted average price as a matter of mathematical logic, and the differential has been growing. They generate an increasing proportion of their output at the times when the demand curve is shifted to the right and the supply curve is at the left-hand end of its range.

As Chapter 12 has shown, the levelized cost of electricity (LCOE) from wind and solar generators has fallen dramatically over time. In many countries, the LCOE of domestic PV is now well below consumer electricity prices, and some wind and solar projects have offered prices that are less than time-weighted wholesale prices. This is not quite enough to make those projects economic without considering externalities if they have a value factor of less than one. Green and Léautier (2015) write of a race between technology developers to reduce the LCOE and the falling value factor as more renewable capacity is added.

The comparison between domestic PV costs (typically higher than for larger schemes) and consumer prices artificially favours PV when the latter contain significant per-kWh charges to help recover the fixed costs of the network. The PV owner who pays for less power from the grid reduces their contribution towards these costs, but rarely reduces the actual network costs. Prices must rise to recover those costs from a smaller volume of grid-supplied electricity, increasing the incentive to self-supply. Describing this as the 'utility death spiral' exaggerates the proportion of load that will be reduced in this way, but the phenomenon certainly raises distributional issues (Simshauser 2016, and Chapter 9 of this handbook), since it tends to be the better-off customers who install solar panels and hence reduce their allocated share of grid costs. Making things worse, the need for the network to cope with new power flows may increase distribution network costs. We consider transmission issues in the next section.

3.   TRANSMITTING RENEWABLE ELECTRICITY

The electricity industry started as a collection of small local systems, because the technology for transmitting power over long distances did not exist. But once the option was available, there were many advantages to developing a high-voltage transmission grid. Aggregating demands over large areas made it possible to build larger power stations with economies of scale. The diversity of demand increased, raising the system load factor (the average demand as a proportion of the peak demand). It was possible to build power stations near their fuel sources. For hydro stations, this is, of course, essential, while it is advantageous for coal-fired stations as they burn a fuel that is heavy and expensive to transport. In contrast, it can be cheaper to move gas than electricity, suggesting that gas-fired stations (which are smaller and generally less polluting than coal-fired plants) can be closer to load centres.

Like coal, biomass is expensive to transport over land, suggesting that stations should be sited in crop-growing regions (or near ports). PV panels produce most electricity if sited in places with high solar insolation – relatively close to the equator and without too much cloud cover or atmospheric dust. Even within a medium-sized country, there can be noticeable differences in expected output. A wind turbine near Hamburg in the north of Germany would produce twice as much as one near Munich in the south, with load factors of 32 per cent and 16 per cent, respectively. A solar panel, on the other hand, would generate a tenth more in the south (Pfenninger and Staffell 2016; Staffell and Pfenninger 2016).

The output from wind generators is a function of the wind speed cubed. This magnifies the impact of differences in the local wind resource and increases the benefit of building tall turbines – the wind speed increases with the height above ground. Complex terrain is likely to reduce wind speeds, which is not a problem in the open sea. This helps explain why offshore turbines (at least in Europe) have higher load factors than those on land, although in terms of LCOE, this has been offset (so far) by higher capital costs. On land, some of the best load factors are found well away from major load centres and transmission is needed to bring the electricity to consumers.

Unfortunately, transmission lines typically take much longer to build than renewable generators. The issue need not be with the physical construction period, but in the amount of consultation with communities along the route before permission to build can be granted. This means that it is not uncommon to find a region with more renewable generators than the grid could accommodate. At times of high potential output, some must be rejected. As described in Chapter 4, this may happen automatically in markets based on locational marginal prices (LMPs), because the excess of generation behind a transmission constraint pushes down the area's LMPs. In countries that set prices to apply over wider zones (or nationwide), it may be necessary to instruct the generator to disconnect or to 'constrain it off'. In this case the system operator must offer compensation. The details depend on the market design (for example, whether the generator has already committed to sell the power and must now buy it back at a low price) and on any subsidy regime in place. Generators that receive a subsidy for every MWh actually generated are likely to want compensation equal to that subsidy for each MWh they are instructed not to generate.

The LMP system has the advantage of sending clearer price signals in response to changing conditions on the grid. As the proportion of renewable electricity generators with variable output increases, conditions are likely to change more, magnifying this advantage. In countries that currently have zonal or national prices, the problem with any change to an existing market rule is that it will generally create winners and losers. If the losers are electricity companies, they will be aware of this and will fight the change.

There are many transmission lines between countries, often called interconnectors. These allow renewable energy to be pooled over much larger areas, reducing the (relative) variability in output (Grams et al. 2017). Denmark generated 48 per cent of its electricity from wind in 2017, helped by its ability to export power when output was high. In hours with less wind production, the country imported electricity. Not all cross-border flows are desirable, however. Germany's neighbours have faced significant loop flows when renewable electricity generated in the north of that country flows south along all available routes, respecting Kirchhoff's laws rather than national boundaries (Agency for the Cooperation of European Regulators [ACER] 2015). In an attempt to resolve the problem, ACER imposed a limit on flows between Germany and Austria. This reduced loop flows but created a separate price zone, raising prices for Austrian consumers.

In the longer term, it would be possible to build renewable generators in high-resource areas specifically to export power along international transmission lines. The DESERTEC Foundation has advocated bringing solar power from North Africa to Europe through high voltage direct current cables. Green et al. (2016) use an engineering model to assess the consequences of a coordinated deployment of renewable generators across Europe, compared to national plans that sited many plants in areas with relatively poor resources. The same level of aggregate output could be achieved while spending €19 billion a year less in capacity costs. This would be offset by additional transmission lines that cost €3 billion a year and higher operating costs of €1 billion a year. Renewable output would be more variable, since the capacity was concentrated in fewer areas, and this changed the load factors of the conventional stations. Cheaper baseload stations generated less and peaking generators more. The overall estimated saving was €15 billion a year, about 5 per cent of annual costs.

While there were overall cost savings, some countries saw cost increases. The data used for the simulation implied that renewable generation was more expensive than conventional power, and so countries that hosted a larger number of wind and solar generators would be paying more. Income from net exports of electricity would not offset this. An international system of renewable electricity certificates might redistribute the costs in an acceptable manner, but the negotiations would be complex.

4.   OPERATIONAL CHALLENGES FROM RENEWABLE POWER

Economists are familiar with the way that electricity prices change over time and with the idea that the value of power depends on its location. Less consideration has been given to the operational challenges of keeping the system stable. While generation must equal demand at all times, most power stations take time to start and are limited in the speed with which they can ramp or change their output level. Since technical problems with a generator or a transmission line can lead to the sudden loss of a large infeed, this creates a problem. The solution is for the system operators to ensure that enough spare capacity is available and be able to change output in time to respond to almost all the plausible problems that might occur.

The first response to an imbalance must be almost immediate, and the typical answer is to keep a number of generators part-loaded, able to increase output automatically if the system frequency falls. This is only a short-term solution, however, and so other generators must be kept in reserve, able to provide power within a few minutes (often already online and hence described as 'spinning reserve', although some fast-starting plants can also provide non-spinning reserve). As they do so, the generators that provided the initial response can be de-loaded again so they are ready in case there is another problem. A third wave of generators will also start up, so that, in due course, the second wave of stations can back down, ready for the next problem. These 'replacement reserve' stations are slower, perhaps allowed 30 minutes or longer to reach their contracted output levels. The details of the hierarchy (and the names given to each level) vary from market to market, but the principle is that by the time the replacement reserve stations are operating fully, the stations with faster response times have returned to their stand-by status.

System operators should schedule generators in such a way that the system remains stable after any single fault – this is known as N-1 operation. Typically, a system will also be resilient to many possible pairs of faults, but it would be very expensive to ensure that it could withstand every possible combination of problems. The system should be built to an N-2 standard so that it can be run in N-1, whichever (single) component is out of service for maintenance, but fully N-2 operation is rare. After all, it is unlikely that a second fault will occur before the system has recovered from the first one and the risk of not being able to cope with this is acceptable. Nonetheless, southern Sweden and eastern Denmark suffered a blackout in September 2003 when a transmission fault occurred too soon after a problem at a nuclear power station, and so system operators only aim to be resilient to 'almost all' plausible problems.

System operators have decades of experience in responding to unanticipated demand changes and plant failures, but once the level of wind or solar capacity is large enough, weather-related variations can also prove significant. Nonetheless, the studies surveyed by Heptonstall, Gross and Steiner (2017) mostly found that the need for additional reserves added 5 £/MWh or less to the cost of wind or solar electricity, as long as its share was no more than 30 per cent of annual generation. If the share rose to 50 per cent, the additional cost of reserves varied between 15 £/MWh and 45 £/MWh, depending on how flexible the plants making up the rest of the system were. They point out that 'it is important to emphasise that high cost outliers often make assumptions designed to test extreme conditions, such as a particularly inflexible system' (ibid., p. 2), suggesting that most systems will experience lower costs than these.

The rise of variable renewable generators raises two particular problems for system operators. First, solar panels and most wind generators have no inertia. Traditional power stations have turbines that are connected directly to a generator, and those turbine generators have significant mass. They are 'synchronous' generators as they rotate at the system frequency. If there is a problem, their rotational inertia means that it will take time for them to slow down, just as a heavy bowling ball would not be deflected by a small obstacle in its path. The less inertia the system has, the faster its frequency would fall in the event of a problem, and the less time there is for the shortfall to be made up. Historically, this was not an issue, as generators naturally had more inertia than was needed, but if wind turbines are connected to the system via power electronics rather than directly, inertia is no longer provided automatically. Ireland is a small system with a high proportion of wind power (24 per cent of output in 2017) and the system operator has to limit the proportion of non-synchronous generation (Royal Academy of Engineering [RAEng] 2014). These include wind turbines or solar panels and the direct current interconnectors to Great Britain. As the system operator has gained experience, the levels of wind power that can be accepted have increased. Heptonstall et al. (2017) have suggested that for most systems, high shares of wind output will become manageable with very fast-acting reserves and wind turbine power electronics altered to provide 'synthetic inertia'. Eirgrid and the System Operator for Northern Ireland (SONI) have bought 310 MW of fast-frequency response services able to respond fully within two seconds of a frequency change (Eirgrid and SONI 2018). They have also required loads and generators to be more resilient to the rate of change of frequency, reducing the risk that self-disconnection in response to an initial problem creates a system collapse.

The second particular issue is that renewable stations can sometimes produce 'free' electricity at a time when this is unhelpful. When demand is relatively low or renewable output particularly high, system operators need to avoid pushing thermal power stations below their minimum operating limits. Rapidly cooling and heating a turbine would reduce its life due to thermal stress, and the cost of this makes it more economic to reduce the output of some wind farms. Their marginal costs are zero, but the marginal generation cost of a thermal generator that otherwise faces the cost of shutting down is negative. The Irish system operator had to constrain off around 3 per cent of the available wind generation in 2018 to avoid pushing thermal stations below their operating limits (Eirgrid 2019). Affected generators are often compensated with out-of-market payments, but the issue helps explain why electricity markets with high proportions of renewable generation are increasingly seeing negative prices, particularly in the real-time or balancing markets that adjust the output of available generators to the actual demand.

When demand is less than expected, or wind and solar output higher, it may be possible to turn down some power stations at relatively low cost, or the price may become negative, as described above. In either case, the real-time price is less than the day-ahead price, while it is likely to be much higher when more output is required and only the most flexible generators can provide it. These generators often have high costs, and they normally face little competition. Hirth (2015) suggests that electricity should be thought of as a three-dimensional product, with a price that varies according to time of delivery, location and lead time. Day-ahead markets schedule plants well in advance so that cheaper, less flexible stations can be deployed. Their prices accordingly vary much less than those in real-time markets. The standard deviation of real-time prices in Great Britain (measured over a year) is typically almost double that of day-ahead prices for the same period. The two markets have similar average prices, however, due to the constraints of arbitrage. If prices in the day-ahead market were consistently expected to be significantly lower than in the real-time market, arbitrageurs would increase demand in the earlier market, bringing expected prices back into balance.

Figure 15.3 shows that the growth of solar generation in California has created a sharp increase in the demand on other plants in the afternoon, as solar output declines while overall demand rises, part of the pattern known as the 'duck curve'. Bushnell and Novan (2018) have shown that this leads to a change in the type of plant required at those times, with higher-cost gas turbines replacing lower cost plants. Late afternoon prices are actually higher, other things being equal, on days with more solar generation. Wind generation is more evenly spread through the day and does not lead to a predictable price increase at particular times but can still cause individual ramping events and price rises.

This creates an opportunity for demand response. Some demands can be shifted for a few hours with little cost, such as pre-heating water or pre-cooling an air-conditioned house. Improved information and communications technology could allow devices to communicate with the electricity system and to anticipate ramping events. Bringing consumption forward would help fill in the trough in net demand and reduce the size of the peak. One problem with demand response is that in most cases, the gain from an individual response would be small (a few cents) and unlikely to motivate a manual intervention. Automated systems would get round this but might face consumer resistance. Richter and Pollitt (2018) surveyed consumers and found that most would want to retain a share of the potential savings, which left little remaining for intermediaries' costs and profits.

5. ELECTRICITY STORAGE

In most commodity markets, storage can help to offset fluctuations in output or demand. Most industries hold some of their product in inventory as a natural feature of their production and distribution systems. Electricity cannot be held in this kind of 'automatic' inventory, but most fuels can be stored. For hydro generators with reservoirs, the fuel comes in the form of water and the generator must decide when to release it. The opportunity cost of generation now is not the price of the coal or gas that must be burned, but the revenue that must be given up since some water is no longer available for future generation. If water is plentiful, this opportunity cost will be low, but at times of scarcity it can be very high and will stay high until the next rainfall or snowfall replenishes the reservoirs.

Figure 15.5 presents the problem in a two-period diagram due to Førsund (2007). The left-hand part of the diagram shows a conventional downwards-sloping demand curve (D_1) for the first period, measured from the normal (left-hand) vertical axis – the price is determined by the level of generation in that period and hence the amount of water released. The total amount of water available for use in the two periods is given by the length of the horizontal axis, with the inflow in the first period shown by the thicker horizontal arrow pointing to the right. We use GWh on this axis to emphasize that we are considering a stock of energy rather than a flow of power in GW. The second period has a smaller inflow, given by the thin arrow pointing left from the right-hand vertical axis. The demand curve in the second period (D_2) is also measured from that axis, and therefore slopes in the opposite direction to D_1. If possible, electricity consumers' utility would be maximized by storing so much energy from period 1 to period 2 that prices (and hence marginal utilities) were equalized (with no discounting between periods). If the storage capacity of the reservoirs is limited, as shown by the dashed vertical lines, this is not possible. More water must be released in the first period, relative to demand, than in

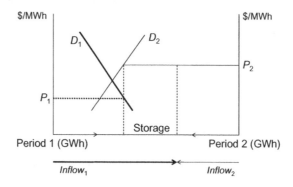

Source: Førsund (2007).

Figure 15.5 Economics of hydroelectricity

the second, and so its price is lower. The difference between the two prices gives the marginal value of expanding reservoir capacity.

It is unusual for a hydroelectric scheme to have so much water that it can generate at full capacity throughout the year. To obtain enough energy storage capacity (MWh), a pure hydro system will need so many generators that its installed power capacity (MW) is well above the maximum demand. This makes the kind of price spikes seen in thermal systems unusual. Prices do rise and fall over the day, since the amount of water each power station can store is different. When demand is low, it can be met from generators with a lot of storage, which have relatively low water values. As demand rises, other generators with less storage and a higher water value must also be called on. Nonetheless, the variation over the day and the year is typically lower than in a thermal system. Hydro-based systems can have a lot of price variation between wet and dry years, however, and droughts can call for electricity rationing, as in Brazil in 2014–17.

Figure 15.5 shows a system with hydro generators alone, as was the case in Norway for many years, but it is (relatively) straightforward to add thermal power stations to the analysis. The optimal generation plan then equalizes the price of electricity and the marginal cost of thermal power within each period; as far as possible, water is released to equalize prices across periods. Green and Vasilakos (2012) added intermittent generation from wind power, thus representing the combined Nordic system. Denmark would export power to its neighbours (or reduce its imports) when the wind was stronger than normal (for the time of day and month), so that they could reduce the amount of water they used at those times. When the wind was below average levels, Norway and Sweden would generate more, and Denmark would import. Effectively, Denmark was storing excess wind power in the form of water and paying about 6 per cent of the value of its production for each MWh stored. Longer-term patterns in Denmark's trade depended on the level of precipitation to the north. If water levels were low, prices in Norway and Sweden would be high, and Denmark would produce more power from its thermal stations, exporting the excess.

The analysis can be adapted for the case of rechargeable storage, such as pumped storage hydro or batteries (which convert electrical to chemical energy and back again). In Figure 15.6, the distance between the axes is not a fixed quantity of water available but the overall level of demand, divided between two periods as before. Each period has thermal generation with its own marginal cost curve. The thick period 1 curve (MC_1) slopes up to the right from the left-hand axis, while MC_2 slopes to the left from the right-hand axis. Demand in period 2 is so much higher than in period 1 that if all the energy were generated in the relevant period, as shown by the thick vertical dashed line, the price then (above P_2) would be far higher than in period 1 (when it would be below P_1).

Again, storage can shift energy from period 1 to period 2. The price in period 1 rises to the marginal cost of the additional generation, while output and the price fall in period 2. Note that the total generation across the two periods has to rise, as it is inevitable that some of the energy input to storage is lost in charging or discharging. Lithium-ion batteries had an average cycle efficiency of 86 per cent in 2015, while pumped storage stations averaged 78 per cent (Schmidt et al. 2019). The thin dashed vertical line showing the increase in period 1 output has moved a greater distance than the short line above it that indicates the reduction in period 2.

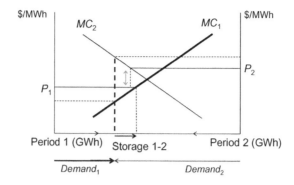

Source: Author.

Figure 15.6   Economics of chargeable storage

There are now two constraints on the amount of energy stored. As with the lossless hydro system of Figure 15.5, there is a physical limit on the amount of energy that the battery or upper hydro reservoir can hold. There is also an economic limit – the ratio of P_1/P_2 must be less than the efficiency of the charge–discharge cycle. If a 75 per cent efficient system is to sell 3 MWh of energy for 40 $/MWh, it must pay no more than $120 for the 4 MWh it needs to buy. This implies a maximum price of 30 $/MWh (note that it is a maximum price, not an average, since if the last MWh cost more than $30, the storage operator would do better to limit its sales to 2.25 MWh). The double-headed vertical arrow in Figure 15.6 is to show the need for P_2 to exceed P_1, although the constraint is on the price ratio rather than their absolute difference.

This kind of arbitrage is the easiest activity to model, but far from the best use of storage. Strbac et al. (2017) show that when storage is optimally used for a mix of activities, only a few per cent of its value comes from pure energy arbitrage – that is, moving bulk energy over time – at least for the first units to be deployed able to meet the (sometimes quite limited) demands for the highest-value services. In their simulation, five times as much value comes from short-term charging and discharging to help balance fluctuations in demand and generation. Even more comes from providing reserve, standing by in case another generator has a sudden fault. Batteries can respond very fast, so fast that this helps compensate for the reduction in inertia as wind and PV panels replace synchronous turbine generators. Furthermore, their opportunity cost of providing reserve is usually low. When a generator reduces output to provide reserve, it forever gives up the opportunity to sell some energy at a price that would usually exceed its marginal costs. The owner will want some compensation for the lost profits, and reserve providers are usually paid an availability charge (plus an exercise charge per MWh if they are needed). However, since reserve capacity that is not called upon does not discharge energy, a storage unit preserves its ability to sell energy in the following period. The opportunity cost of standing by is thus the difference in prices between the two periods, which may even be negative.

Depending on their location, storage units may also be able to relieve congestion on the transmission or distribution grids. If a constraint binds for only a few hours, the storage unit can be charged while the constraint is not binding and then discharged to reduce the amount of power that needs to flow over the congested line. Finally, storage units can also provide dispatchable capacity to help when this is scarce, although the calculations needed to compare energy-limited short-term storage units with a dispatchable power station are complex (Edwards et al. 2017). The system operator must estimate the amount of energy the storage unit will hold at times when the available dispatchable generation is low relative to the demand on it (after taking account of variable wind and solar output). If a shortage is expected to last for three hours and the unit would only hold two hours of charge, its contribution to reducing the unserved load during that event would only be two-thirds of its nameplate capacity.

In most regions of the world, there are significant inter-seasonal differences in the amount of energy that wind and solar power can supply, and in the level of electricity demand. The right mix of wind and solar power may reduce these differences, but it remains the case that very large amounts of inter-seasonal storage would be required to balance the variations. Newbery (2018) shows how large these variations are compared to the amounts of storage available from hydro systems. At present, the capacity available in batteries is a tiny proportion of that in hydro reservoirs. There is no question that energy storage can help to even out intra-daily variations in electricity supply and demand, and to provide reserve to deal with short-term fluctuations. A truly massive expansion would be needed to cope with inter-seasonal variations, however.

6.   RISK AND RENEWABLE ENERGY

We have already discussed some of the risks and uncertainties faced by power systems. Extreme conditions cause the risk of outages, particularly if they coincide with plant failures. While most hour-to-hour variations in demand are unlikely to affect a generator's annual profits by an important amount, high prices in a relatively small number of peak hours are needed if generators in an 'energy only' market are to recover their full costs, as described above and in Chapter 3. A year with mild weather may see demand and hence prices fail to reach the levels needed to compensate generators; a harsh winter or hot summer can be very profitable for generators.

Over a longer period, the level of economic growth and the links between this growth, the demand for energy services, and the amount of electricity needed to provide them will affect the size of the market. Energy efficiency reduces the amount of electricity needed per lumen of lighting, for example, although the rebound effect may increase the number of lumens chosen. Demand for electricity is likely to rise as consumers adopt electric vehicles, but the rate at which they will do so is highly uncertain. If demand changes faster than the stock of power stations can adapt, wholesale prices will respond, providing a signal for entry or exit. Exit can be rapid once generators are sure conditions have changed but planning and building even gas-fired power stations takes two or three years.

The relative profitability of different generators depends on their fuel prices and, in many places, on the price of carbon. Roques et al. (2006) show that this is a particular risk for nuclear (and renewable) generators with a high proportion of fixed costs, compared to the fossil-fuelled stations that set the wholesale price of electricity at their marginal cost. Long-term contracts at a fixed price can make fixed-cost generators such as (most) renewables much more attractive to a risk-averse investor, even if they offer no more than the expected market price (Green 2008). The greater the price risks that renewable generators are exposed to, the higher their cost of capital.

Adding significant amounts of renewable generation to the power system introduces the additional risk of variations in its availability. For hydro generators with significant amounts of storage, this typically implies that a wet year will have low prices, while a dry year will have high prices and perhaps the risk of rationing, as already discussed. Biomass generators may face higher or lower fuel prices depending on the state of the harvest. For wind and solar generators, the variability is hour-to-hour and day-to-day as well as year-to-year.

As described above, systems with significant amounts of wind and solar generation will have a much steeper residual load-duration curve of demand less wind and solar output. More peaking capacity will be required, expected to generate for relatively short periods, and fewer baseload stations. This increase in the variability of (net) demand might be expected to lead to an increase in price variability. Pollitt and Chyong (2018) model a 50 per cent expansion and a doubling of renewable capacity in Europe and show modest increases in the coefficient of variation of prices in most regions. That model is based on a single year of data, but inter-year variations in renewable output can be significant. Staffell and Pfenninger (2016) estimate that the annual capacity factor for onshore wind across Great Britain would have varied between 24 per cent in 2010 and 34 per cent in 1990, holding capacity constant at recent levels. The inter-annual variability in solar output is smaller, but 2003 would have seen a capacity factor of 11.1 per cent, and 1992 one of 10.3 per cent (Pfenninger and Staffell, 2016).

Nonetheless, the overall effect is smaller than might be expected. Green and Vasilakos (2011) calculated long-run equilibria for Great Britain in a model that used 12 years of wind capacity factors and demand shapes (adjusted to the same underlying demand). They compared the outcomes with no wind capacity and with 30 GW after conventional capacity had adjusted to long-run equilibrium values, as shown in Figure 15.2. They find that the standard deviation of prices over the entire period rises by less than 10 per cent, comparing the case with no wind and with 30 GW of capacity. The range of annual generator profits, comparing the worst year to the best, would increase by between 20 and 40 per cent. Note that these calculations are based on economic profits after deducting the return on capital; the variation in accounting profits would be smaller.

In a long-run market equilibrium, there will be more peaking capacity with relatively short and uncertain annual running hours. Since these stations face particular risks, this may reinforce the argument for a capacity market or other mechanism to ensure an adequate plant margin – issues that were discussed in Chapters 4 and 6–11 and will be returned to in Chapter 16. If risks are not mitigated, the cost of capital will rise. Appropriate risk-reduction measures will reduce both the average cost of electricity to customers and its inter-year variation.

7.   CONCLUSIONS

Over the last 30 years, wholesale electricity markets have spread into many countries around the world. Over the last ten, the share of wind and solar generation has risen dramatically. Their falling costs make further expansion almost inevitable. A rising share of output with zero marginal costs presents a dramatic challenge to markets where prices are normally linked to (positive) marginal fuel costs. How can conventional generators recover their costs if there are many hours in which a surplus of renewable electricity drives prices to zero?

One possible answer is to distinguish between shifts in electricity supply and electricity demand. Conventional plants that are needed when demand is high will be able to charge higher prices at these times. Provided that excess capacity is reduced (which may be painful for investors and employees), stations that are needed would be able to cover their costs. Renewable output shifts the supply curve and depresses prices, and a large number of very low prices would cut the revenue available to new projects. This could limit the attractiveness of market-driven entry, although it does not rule out generators receiving higher policy-mandated prices.

Another answer is to remember that renewable generation includes biomass stations with similar cost structures to conventional plants, and storage hydro where the marginal cost of electricity is an opportunity cost. These can be used to raise the share of renewable output without the same problems of short-run variability as wind and solar power. Other forms of electricity storage can also absorb excess power, although huge volumes would be required to offset seasonal variations in solar or wind generation.

Electricity transmission is a further way to find value for renewable power when there is a local surplus. It works best when systems with uncorrelated net demands can be connected; unfortunately, this may often mean long distances and hence high costs. Alternatively, the need to keep the system electrically stable will require continued generation from conventional stations, and revenues will shift from energy to ancillary services such as balancing and reserve.

Experience to date, and the analysis of this chapter, both suggest that wholesale markets will be able to operate with an increasing share of variable renewable generators. Nonetheless, some market designs may need to change in response to the operating challenges that they bring. The need for such changes, and the options available, are the subject of the next chapter.

NOTE

*   I would like to thank the editors and David Newbery for helpful comments. The chapter was written while enjoying the hospitality of the Isaac Newton Institute for Mathematical Sciences, University of Cambridge, UK during the programme on the Mathematics of Energy Systems, supported by EPSRC Grant No. EP/R014604/1.

REFERENCES

Agency for the Cooperation of Energy Regulators (ACER) (2015), *ACER Opinion 09-2015 on the Compliance of NRAs' Decisions Approving Methods of Cross-border Capacity Allocation in the CEE region*, accessed 28 March 2019 at https://acer.europa.eu/Official_documents/Acts_of_the_Agency/Opinions/Opinions/ACER%20Opinion%2009-2015.pdf.

BP (2020), *BP Statistical Review of World Energy*, accessed 6 July 2021 at https://www.bp.com/en/global/corporate/energy-economics/statistical-review-of-world-energy.html.

Bushnell, J. and K. Novan (2018), 'Setting with the sun: the impacts of renewable energy on wholesale power markets', *NBER Working Paper No. 24980*, National Bureau of Economic Research, accessed 6 July 2021 at http://www.nber.org/papers/w24980.

Chyong, K., M. G. Pollitt and R. Cruise (2019), 'Can wholesale electricity prices support "subsidy-free" generation investment in Europe?', *EPRG Working Paper No. 1919*, Energy Policy Research Group, University of Cambridge, accessed 6 July 2021 at https://www.eprg.group.cam.ac.uk/eprg-working-paper-1919/.

Cullen, J. (2013), 'Measuring the environmental benefits of wind-generated electricity', *American Economic Journal: Economic Policy*, **5** (4), 107–33.

Edwards, G., S. Sheehy, C. Dent and M. C. M. Troffaes (2017), 'Assessing the contribution of nightly rechargeable grid-scale storage to generation capacity adequacy', *Sustainable Energy, Grids and Networks*, **12**, 69–81.

Eirgrid (2019), 'All-Island quarterly wind dispatch down report 2018 Q4', accessed 29 March 2019 at http://www.eirgridgroup.com/site-files/library/EirGrid/2018-Qtr4-Wind-Dispatch-Down-Report.pdf.

Eirgrid and SONI (2018), 'DS3 System Services Regulated Arrangements', accessed 5 April 2019 at http://www.eirgridgroup.com/site-files/library/EirGrid/Procurement-SummaryPh2.pdf.

Førsund, F. R. (2007), *Hydropower Economics*, New York: Springer.

Grams, C. M., R. Beerli and S. Pfenninger et al. (2017), 'Balancing Europe's wind power output through spatial deployment informed by weather regimes', *Nature Climate Change*, **7**, 557–62.

Green, R. J. (2008), 'Carbon tax or carbon permits: the impact on generators' risks', *Energy Journal*, **29** (3), 67–89.

Green, R. J. and T.-O. Léautier (2015), 'Do costs fall faster than revenues? Dynamics of renewables entry into electricity markets', *TSE Working Paper No. 15-591*, accessed 6 July 2021 at http://www.tse-fr.eu/sites/default/files/TSE/documents/doc/wp/2015/wp_tse_591.pdf.

Green, R. J. and N. Vasilakos (2011), 'The long-run impact of wind power on electricity prices and generating capacity', *Discussion Paper 11-09*, Department of Economics, University of Birmingham.

Green, R. J. and N. Vasilakos (2012), 'Storing wind for a rainy day: what kind of electricity does Denmark export?', *The Energy Journal*, **33** (3), 1–22.

Green, R. J., D. Pudjianto, I. Staffell and G. Strbac (2016), 'Market design for long-distance trade in renewable electricity', *The Energy Journal*, **37** (Special Issue), 5–22.

Heptonstall, P., R. Gross and F. Steiner (2017), *The Costs and Impacts of Intermittency: 2016 Update*, London, UK Energy Research Centre, accessed 5 April 2019 at http://www.ukerc.ac.uk/programmes/technology-and-policy-assessment/the-intermittency-report.html.

Hirth, L. (2013), 'The market value of variable renewables: the effect of solar wind power variability on their relative price', *Energy Economics*, **38** (7), 218–36.

Hirth, L. (2015), 'The optimal share of variable renewables: how the variability of wind and solar power affects their welfare-optimal deployment', *The Energy Journal*, **36** (1), 149–84.

Joskow, P. L. (2011), 'Comparing the cost of intermittent and dispatchable electricity generation technologies', *American Economic Review Papers and Proceedings*, **100** (3), 238–41.

Newbery, D. M. (2018), 'Shifting demand and supply over time and space to manage intermittent generation: the economics of electrical storage', *Energy Policy*, **113**, 711–20.

Pfenninger, S. and I. Staffell (2016), 'Long-term patterns of European PV output using 30 years of validated hourly reanalysis and satellite data', *Energy*, **144**, 1251–65.

Pollitt, M. G. and C. K. Chyong (2018), *Europe's Electricity Market Design: 2030 and Beyond*, Centre on Regulation in Europe (CERRE), accessed 5 April 2019 at https://www.cerre.eu/sites/cerre/files/181206_CERRE_MarketDesign_FinalReport.pdf.

Richter, L. L. and Pollitt, M. G. (2018), 'Which smart electricity service contracts will consumers accept? The demand for compensation in a platform market', *Energy Economics*, **72**, 436–50.

Roques, F. A., W. J. Nuttall and D. M. Newbery et al. (2006), 'Nuclear power: a hedge against uncertain gas and carbon prices?', *The Energy Journal*, **27** (4), 1–23.

Royal Academy of Engineering (RAEng) (2014), *Wind Energy: Implications of Large-scale Deployment on the GB Energy System*, accessed 29 March 2019 at https://www.raeng.org.uk/publications/reports/wind-energy-implications-of-large-scale-deployment.

Sáenz de Miera G., P. del Río González and I. Vizcaíno (2008), 'Analysing the impact of renewable electricity support schemes on power prices: the case of wind electricity in Spain', *Energy Policy*, **36** (9), 3345–59.

Schmidt, O., S. Melchior, A. Hawkes and I. Staffell (2019), 'Projecting the future levelized cost of electricity storage technologies', *Joule*, **3** (1), 81–100.

Sensfuß, F., M. Ragwitz and M. Genoese (2008), 'The merit-order effect: a detailed analysis of the price effect of renewable electricity generation on spot market prices in Germany', *Energy Policy*, **36** (8), 3076–84.

Simshauser, P. (2016), 'Distribution network prices and solar PV: resolving rate instability and wealth transfers through demand tariffs', *Energy Economics*, **54**, 108–22.

Staffell, I. and S. Pfenninger (2016), 'Using bias-corrected reanalysis to simulate current and future wind power output', *Energy*, **114**, 1224–39.

Strbac, G., M. Aunedi and I. Konstantelos et al. (2017), 'Opportunities for energy storage: assessing whole-system economic benefits of energy storage in future electricity systems', *IEEE Power and Energy Magazine*, September/October, 32–41.

Twomey, P. and K. Neuhoff (2010), 'Wind power and market power in competitive markets', *Energy Policy*, **37** (7), 3198–210.

16. The future design of the electricity market
*Michael G. Pollitt**

1. INTRODUCTION

This chapter will explore some of the issues in the future design of the electricity market, building on Chapter 15 in this handbook. In doing so, it will assume that the market design will have to cope with increasing amounts of intermittent renewable electricity generation, driven both by concerns about fossil fuel emissions, the relatively low costs of renewable electricity generation production and the increasingly flexible nature of electricity demand characterized by electric vehicles (EVs), electric heating and electrical energy storage.

We have in mind developments in three major electricity markets: Europe, the US and China. Collectively, these represent more than 58 per cent of world electricity consumption in 2016 (International Energy Agency [IEA] 2018). In Europe, the 2030 energy and climate goals suggest that 55 per cent of electricity will be coming from renewable energy sources (RES) by that date (see Newbery et al. 2018). In the US, individual states such as California, New York and the New England states have similarly ambitious plans for the addition of renewable energy to their electricity grids.[1] In China, ambitious targets for the reduction of local air pollution and decarbonization imply a large increase in the share of renewable (and nuclear) electricity generation.[2]

What each of these sets of markets share in common is that they currently have electricity systems based on fossil fuels. For the US and Europe, they have market designs for wholesale electricity markets that were designed with fossil fuel generation in mind. Chapter 2 discusses the evolution of this traditional model of the electricity market and Chapter 4 details the current state of learning on existing wholesale electricity markets of this type. These chapters draw heavily on the extensive experience of wholesale electricity markets in the US. As China (see Chapter 21) attempts to introduce comprehensive electricity markets for the first time, it is a matter of current debate as to which market design to introduce, with many provinces in the process of introducing a combination of spot markets based on the PJM Interconnection and contract markets based on European power exchanges.

In what follows we will begin by discussing why market design for electricity markets is so difficult (Section 2). In Section 3, we will then go on to compare the PJM market design (described in detail in Chapter 7) based on centralized markets run by an ISO with the European market design based on self-dispatch (described in Chapter 11). We also will discuss how intermittent renewables and flexible demand are stress testing the current market designs. We proceed with a discussion of the concerns of regulators in Section 4 and how this relates to market design, emphasizing how regulators have multiple policy objectives, which include a desire to limit high (and low) prices and price discrimination. In Section 5, we examine the nature of the firm and market choices and how these are directly relevant to future market design. Here we point out that electricity economists emphasize flexible market arrangements that maximize welfare, while electrical engineers tend to favour mechanistic pricing arrangements. These later arrangements often favour producer interests (who can better understand how to game them). In Section 6, we conclude with a discussion of potential new market arrangements that are radically different from the current market design, drawing out ideas from the management of the Internet, and hybrid arrangements that combine elements of the current designs with radically different arrangements.

2. WHY MARKET DESIGN FOR ELECTRICITY MARKETS IS SO DIFFICULT

The economic 'optimization' of the electricity system – which lies at the heart of the 'design' of the market – is a genuinely hard problem (Biggar and Hesamzadah 2014). This is because the nature of the electricity supply industry is complex (see Joskow 1996 for a discussion). It involves generation, transmission, distribution and retailing, activities that can be competitive or monopolistic. It involves assets that are long-lived and where investments are often large and lumpy. Governments and their regulators are concerned to limit prices and price fluctuations, which restricts the use of time- and space-varying price signals that might otherwise be a good way to manage the system. In addition, there are legitimate societal concerns about quality of service, environmental impacts and the promotion of particular technologies (such as renewables, nuclear, smart meters and EVs) that must be taken into account by market designers.

Looking forward, optimizing the electricity system is complicated by the uncertain future for electrification of transport and heating. The further extension of the use of electricity to transport and heating presents challenges and opportunities. This is true in the US and Europe where electricity demand in terms of annual energy consumption (terawatt-hours [TWh]) and in terms of peak consumption (gigawatts [GW] peak) have been flat since 2007–08, and in China where electricity demand has been rising sharply (at 8.5 per cent per year from 2004 to 2019).[3] Transport electrification (see Chapter 18) offers the possibility of the significant expansion of customer-owned battery capacity at the same time as slightly increasing electricity demand over a period of 20 or so years (as fossil fuel vehicles are substituted by new EVs).

It is interesting to think about some numbers. If all 30 million cars in the UK were to be fully electric and use 3000 kilowatt-hours (kWh) of power per year this would increase annual electricity demand by 90 TWh or 30 per cent of 2018 demand.[4] However, with batteries capable of delivering say 3 kW each back to the grid, this would be 90 GW (the entire current generation capacity), and with available storage of 10 kWh each, this would be enough electricity to power the grid for almost a day.[5] However, charging the cars up would need to be managed in a smart way, especially to prevent overloading of parts of the distribution grid.

Heating electrification has been largely achieved in some countries, such as Norway,[6] but is more challenging and presents less opportunity than electrification of transport. Heating demand can be several times that of electricity demand at the peak time (in the late afternoon of a winter day). Providing the extra ramping capacity to enable the electricity system to cope with this would be a severe challenge to the current electricity system, as would the fact that the heating capacity would be highly seasonal.[7]

As previous chapters have discussed (notably in Chapters 3 and 4), the product, electricity, has particular characteristics with market design implications. It cannot be easily stored, and supply and demand must be balanced in real time at every node on the electricity system. While energy content, kWh, is its main component, electricity requires frequency regulation, voltage control, constraint management and reserve capacity as additional elements that must be supplied simultaneously with energy (see National Grid 2017 for a discussion of these services). Energy supply and demand must be balanced in real time and cannot rely solely on day-ahead markets. This gives rise to the phenomenon of energy markets that are yearly, monthly, day-ahead and real time, working together with procurement markets for non-energy ancillary services: frequency regulation, voltage control, constraint management and reserve markets. And this is just to discuss 'wholesale' electricity markets. Retail electricity markets are about selling electricity to final customers and involve retailers packaging wholesale energy of the required quality with transmission and distribution service, metering and billing.

Thus, when we simply state 'market design for electricity markets', we must explain which of the many markets for electricity we are talking about. In this chapter, we largely focus on wholesale energy markets.

Optimizing the electricity system to supply customers at least quality-adjusted cost is a complex problem involving trading off the cost of energy, ancillary services, network and retailing costs over both the short and the long run. However, even this is not quite enough. Customers do not consume electricity, they consume energy services from devices that use electricity, thus part of the global optimization of the provision of energy services includes the investments in energy service equipment that customers make. An electricity system that does not take into account the implications of market design for customer energy investment is not likely to be optimal. Thus, for example, future electricity market design cannot assume that consumers will buy electrical equipment that will facilitate certain types of energy service products or that they will buy them immediately. As Platchkov and Pollitt (2011) discuss, consumers have strong financial incentives to buy more energy-efficient lightbulbs and gas boilers but very weak incentives to buy consumer electronics on the basis of their electricity consumption.

In judging a current market design or in evaluating a future market design we need to consider its efficacy across multiple scales and timeframes. Does the market design encourage co-optimization of the use of generation and network assets? Does it encourage optimal future investment in generation and networks? It is not enough that a market design prices one dimension of cost variability (such as marginal grid losses in a locational marginal pricing, LMP, scheme) and completely ignores many others.[8] Indeed, a market design that does this can easily fall foul of the theory of second best (Lipsey and Lancaster 1956) and produce worse outcomes than in the absence of such prices. The reason that market designs vary so much across the world is because different jurisdictions take a different view on which timescale they want to focus on. Both the European and PJM models for wholesale markets are implemented on systems that have experienced a contraction of demand over the last ten or more years. This has focussed attention on the efficient use of the current assets. China's slowness in adopting either of these two models is explained at least in part by its focus on meeting rapidly growing demand for electricity that has prioritized financing rapid growth in investment in generation to facilitate general economic growth. Existing wholesale electricity markets have been great for promoting operational efficiency; they have been rather less good at supporting desirable investments in low-carbon generation or network expansion, which has required additional forms of subsidy and policy support.

3. TWO EXISTING MARKET DESIGNS AND THEIR ABILITY TO COPE WITH RISING RENEWABLE ENERGY SOURCES

As discussed in Chapters 2 through 11, there are basically two competing market designs that seem to have emerged as the dominant designs for wholesale electricity markets – the PJM (and Texas) model and the European market design (in the British and Nordic markets).

Variants of the PJM model have been adopted – over time – across all of the organized independent system operator/regional transmission organization (ISO/RTO) markets of the US (in Texas, New England, New York and California) and in the Australian National Electricity Market (NEM) discussed in Chapter 9. The European model has been largely adopted across the single European electricity market area (see Pollitt 2019 for a review of progress, and Chapter 11 in this handbook).

The PJM model is characterized by centralized control of the market by the ISO. As discussed in Chapter 7, PJM is an ISO and runs the day-ahead and real-time markets for energy. It also operates markets for frequency control and reserves, most notably the capacity market. It uses day-ahead prices to generate five minute nodal prices on the day, which represent the prices that generators get paid from the money going through the compulsory gross power pool. These prices are used to manage constraints. Voltage support providers are paid cost-based prices. Customers are not directly exposed to individual nodal prices, only the average nodal price. Financial markets allow generators (and customers) to hedge their position. There are markets for financial transmission rights (FTRs) that give generators a certain amount of access to transmission capacity that allows them to sell out of a constrained node. Financial markets for longer-term power can be used to hedge exposure to spot energy prices. Nodal prices (which can vary at thousands of nodes in PJM) give rise to the need to heavily regulate price bids at some nodes and impose maximum bid prices on certain generators at these nodes. The centralized dispatch model has the advantage of coordinating bids and dispatch and reducing the risk of miscalculation by generators and loads of their relative costs. The nodal pricing system provides strong signals for congestion management and reflects network conditions in real time. However, it is unclear how linked nodal prices really are to actual investments in the transmission system to provide more capacity in PJM.

The European model (for example, in Great Britain) is usually fundamentally different. European markets work on the basis of self-dispatch with centralized balancing markets. This means that generators and retailers notify the system operator which plants they want to run and their expected demand. Typically, they can alter their expected physical positions up to until one hour ahead of real time (European Network of Transmission System Operators for Electricity [ENTSO-E] 2018). In real time, system operators (SOs) then push up or down generators or loads according to bids in the balancing energy market (see Pollitt and Dale 2018 for a description of the British balancing market). Generators and retailers have incentives to minimize balancing energy because generators on average receive less than they would in day-ahead markets and retailers pay more. This is because even if the market is equally likely to be short or long overall, retailers are more likely to be buying on the short days and generators more likely to be selling on the long days because this is what is determining balancing position.

Power can be traded day-ahead (or longer ahead) through competitive power exchanges. Across Europe the day-ahead power price is resolved through a market algorithm – EUPHEMIA – which links all power exchanges and results in a single area-wide price in the absence of cross-border transmission constraints. Power exchanges operate wide zonal pricing areas, usually at the level of an individual country. Internal network constraints are handled by a combination of zonal transmission charging and constraint management payments whereby generators (and active loads) are constrained on and off according to local transmission constraints. The self-dispatch model has the advantage of internalizing all generator and load costs into the self-dispatch notified position (avoiding the need for mechanistic translations of bid components into the dispatch algorithm as in PJM), while the constraint management regime can be part of the incentive regulation regime of the transmission company (as in Great Britain), which can be given strong incentives to reduce constraints by making more transmission capacity available. However, the system does not provide good real-time signals to manage congestion to the market participants, although the transmission company (and distribution companies at lower voltages) could decide to sign contracts to do this.

PJM's extensive use of nodal prices partly reflects the fact that it has proved difficult to get the state-level regulators of the US's relatively small power grids to agree to upgrade their networks, especially when power flows across the network may relate to supply and demand outside their service territories. PJM covers 14 states, many of which are small and with poorly resourced regulatory agencies. This has encouraged sophisticated price signals to make better use of the existing networks in the face of the difficulty of altering quantities of network capacity. The alternative is to fix the prices and alter the quantities optimally, something that seems to have happened better in Europe.

Rising intermittent renewables stress test both of these current market designs, though we should point out that the PJM system, where renewables were only 6 per cent of production in 2018, has not been stressed by renewables to the same extent that many European grids have (renewables were over 30 per cent of electricity production for the EU-28 by 2018). They do so in ways discussed in Chapter 15 of this handbook. The PJM system could give rise to much greater nodal variation in prices and requirements to coordinate investment in the network more closely with the nodal price signals arising from the intermittent nature of renewables. The European system could increase constraint costs, though they have less impact on the wide area zonal prices and also require better coordination of the network investment with the renewables investment.

Renewables are more difficult to forecast than conventional generation and hence increase the reliance on real-time markets. This reduces the need to coordinate system operation with day-ahead markets and increases the value of physical notification. Hence, moving all markets towards real time is important for the short-run management of the system. However, the problem remains of how reliable the real-time market prices are for signalling long-run investments in both generation and networks with both of the current market designs.

Pollitt and Anaya (2019) discuss the impact of rising amounts of RES on the demand for non-energy ancillary services. Current market designs are often quite sophisticated with respect to energy, but often much less so with respect to non-energy ancillary services. Frequency regulation, voltage control, constraint management and reserves could become much more important parts of the wholesale energy markets and hence will need to become more sophisticated market arrangements, which are co-optimized with energy and network investments.

In Great Britain, there were 30 non-energy ancillary services products in 2016 (Pollitt and Anaya 2019). These are currently being rationalized. Many of them were procured at fixed prices or under bilateral contracts. Many have restrictive rules that mean they cannot be supplied simultaneously with each other and that bidding across multiple markets is restricted in ways that could be rationalized (Greve et al. 2018). This might have been acceptable in the days when these services were supplied by conventional generators as by-products from a reserved part of their output; however, this is not an optimal arrangement when distributed energy resources (DERs), such as batteries or distributed generation, can supply several of these products simultaneously as a key part of a value stack business model (Ruz and Pollitt 2016, Sidhu, Pollitt and Anaya 2018). An interesting development is the increasing use by the distribution system operator (DSO) of competitive mechanisms to manage constraints and voltage control within the distribution system (sometimes in coordination with the with the transmission system operator (TSO)). An interesting case of this is the Power Potential Project in the UK (Anaya and Pollitt 2018), where a local distribution company is procuring reactive power, on behalf of the TSO, to provide voltage control at four nodes on the DSO–TSO boundary.

In PJM, some use is being made of co-optimization in the provision of some non-energy ancillary services such as frequency regulation. However, voltage control remains a fixed price service not subject to market testing (ibid.). While nodal pricing is used for constraint management, it is only generators and not loads that are exposed to nodal pricing, meaning that the market is not two-sided. Some other US states such as New York and California, with PJM-style market designs, are experiencing European levels of renewables penetration.[9] These states have begun to look at how non-energy ancillary services can be procured not only by the transmission-level ISO but also by the DSO – hence, New York's Reforming the Energy Vision (REV) initiative and California's Demand Reduction Auction Mechanism (DRAM), both of which seek to facilitate the acquisition of response services from within the distribution system.

These developments suggest that market design is not just about wide-area energy markets but increasingly about local procurement of voltage and constraint management services.

4. THE NATURE OF REGULATION IN ELECTRICITY MARKETS

It is quite fashionable to suggest that the future of the electricity market involves more use of time-of-day and locational price signals than we see today (following Schweppe et al. 1988).[10] This is because the nature of intermittent renewables and flexible demand will mean that there is more value in signalling underlying system costs more clearly – the idea being that these sorts of price signals will be more necessary in a world where consumers can vary when and where they charge their storage devices and EVs, where power market investors can choose where to place their DERs and where network companies will be under pressure to decentralize their operations and to outsource network functions wherever possible (see, for example, Electric Power Research Institute [EPRI] 2015 and MIT Energy Initiative 2016).

The actual use of price signals within the electricity system is informative. PJM and other organized markets in the US make use of locational spot market price signals to inform generators on network constraints. However, in general, they are not used to provide signals to loads. This shows the impact of regulatory intervention: regulators (and their stakeholders – that is, retailers and customers) are quite happy for sophisticated and often diversified generators to be exposed to locational and time-varying spot prices; they are not happy for customers (many of whom are only at one location) to be exposed to these.

Electricity is a heavily price-regulated product. In all the jurisdictions I am aware of, the average price of network services is regulated and regulators are against the fragmentation of retail pricing. In particular, they do not like the creation of 'confusopolies' of price offerings with multiple price components, where all but the most sophisticated consumers are unsure of how their bill is calculated. In the majority of the world, the final price paid by residential (and small non-residential) users is subject to a default tariff or provided at a regulated price. Even in the EU with the most sophisticated electricity market reform programme in the world, half of all member states still have a default regulated electricity tariff for households, openly in contravention of agreed EU-wide policy (Pollitt 2019). In almost all wholesale markets there is a maximum price cap (which can be quite large). In the Guangdong (China's largest province) spot market pilot – for a market significantly larger than Germany – there is a minimum and a maximum bid price cap (70 yuan [US$10.1] per MWh and 400 yuan [US$58] per MWh). Many other aspects of pricing in most jurisdictions are regulated, including the distribution of payments for ancillary services and the maximum bids that can be submitted under nodal pricing at certain regularly congested nodes.

Thus, the idea that every customer and every generator will be exposed to a real-time, nodal two-sided price equivalent to the shadow value of consumption and generation to the system is not something that happens now and is unlikely to happen in the future (see Pollitt 2016 for a discussion of the concerns of regulators). Attempts to increase the scope of time of use and locational pricing have not been successful (as with smart metering in the Pacific Gas & Electric service area in California). Similarly attempts to introduce more cost reflectivity into charging for grid use, where these unwind an historic pricing settlement, have also proved difficult (for example, the many attempts to move away from net metering of solar photovoltaics [PV] and charge for export grid use from residential PV). The idea that those with their own storage facility or EV will be able to substantially reduce their unit electricity bill, relative to poor consumers without those devices is something that is likely to produce a negative regulatory reaction (as has happened in Australia following substantial redistribution effects around network distribution charges due to the rise of PV; see Pollitt 2018). It is also by no means clear that rising customer-owned distributed generation will be particularly willing to be exposed to locational- and time-varying prices for the electricity that they produce, potentially undermining the existing use of locational pricing in the organized markets of the US.

Related to the idea that the future could be characterized by more use of market prices with finer time and space resolution is the idea that electricity might be traded directly between a producer and a consumer using blockchain-based technologies that bypass conventional settlement processes run by transmission-level SOs (see Kiesling 2016 for a discussion of the sharing economy in electricity, and also Chapter 17 in this handbook). This possibility arises from the falling platform costs of running a settlement system and the ability to have a distributed settlement ledger to verify transactions have taken place.

As Küfeoğlu et al. (2019) discuss, this is an interesting development that poses challenges to conventional regulation. Fully bilateral trading makes price monitoring and market power assessment more difficult. It also raises the issue of whether these platforms will genuinely be efficient and provide lower prices to consumers and higher prices to producers. As with Airbnb and Uber, the issue is whether these could be vehicles for avoiding environmental taxes, contributions to network fixed costs and financial regulation (by settling in cryptocurrencies and not in central bank money), and have quality issues associated with them, let alone whether the platforms themselves will eventually become monopolists taking large rents for their owners. The likelihood would seem to be that falling platform costs will facilitate the extension of existing trading platforms to include smaller DERs, rather than allow the bypassing of existing markets and settlement systems. Indeed, many of the new platform firms in electricity are working with existing utilities.

These examples of regulatory constraints on smarter pricing arise because electricity regulators do not simply have the minimization of total system costs as their only regulatory objective. They also have to take due account of poverty (and perceived fairness) concerns – also part of the Bonbright (1961) principles of good regulation – the promotion of renewable energy supply (RES), decarbonization objectives, quality of service and network security. In many countries, there is a desire to maintain access to electricity on equal terms for all (not just residential users but also for business users). This is an important principle that may have the effect of promoting wider and more inclusive economic development, which has social welfare benefits beyond the electricity sector (even though it could in theory be better achieved by direct subsidy).

Against this view of the future is the idea that if basic electricity demand – for essential household appliances – becomes a less significant part of household expenditure, then households might be more willing to accept locational- and time-varying prices. This might well be true, and to some extent this phenomenon has been observed in telecoms where the basic telephone service has been less subject to regulation over time as discretionary use of the telecoms network has increased and essential service has become a less financially significant part of bill.

Similarly, electrification of transport moves the use of electricity into an area that is already characterized by time- and space-varying prices, with gasoline prices being perhaps the most visible real-time price in the whole economy. By contrast, however, electrification of heating extends the use of electricity into an area where there are more concerns about the provision of basic service – even more basic than electricity – as this is directly related to human health and where often more money is spent per household on heating than on power.

This discussion raises the important issue of whether regulators (and the politicians behind them) will favour the increased exposure of consumers to fluctuating market prices or whether there will continue to be limits on price variation and non-price solutions to the management of the electricity system.

5.   THE NATURE OF THE FIRM AND MARKET CHOICES

Markets are one way of organizing production in market-based economic systems. The alternative is organize production through the firm (Coase 1937). Spot markets are an extreme form of market organization; long-term contracts are closer to in-house production (Richardson 1972). The choice between the firm and the market as alternative forms of economic organization is driven by efficiency considerations and the need to economize on transaction costs (the costs of negotiating and agreeing prices and quality).

Coase emphasized the optimal size of the firm as being the point of equilibrium between the cost of in-house transaction and organizing the same activity through the market, as some point transaction costs rose within the firm and made market organization cheaper. In-house production has the advantage of potentially avoiding formal contracting costs, while market organization allows the competitive provision of standardized inputs. Internal production makes use of incomplete contracting with labour and capital and the presence of hierarchy in decision making, while markets rely on formal complete contracts that exactly specify the product, quality, delivery date and so on.

Williamson (1975) distinguished between the fact that external production was, in theory, always cheaper due to the ability to aggregate demands, but that the extra transaction costs of assuring the quality of external production might mean that the total cost could be more or less expensive than in-house production. This is important when it comes to the future design of electricity markets, because often the interesting questions are the extent to which the electricity system should be organized around spot markets and spot market pricing as opposed to via vertical integration and long-term contracting. Joskow (1996) points out that the key governance question in electricity systems is how to unlock the benefits of competition that arise from vertical and horizontal separation without losing the undoubted benefits of vertical coordination that arise within integrated firms.

Traditionally, the electricity industry was organized around integrated companies that were heavily vertically integrated, often covering generation, transmission, distribution and retailing (for example, EdF in France and Duke Energy in the US). Some countries had centralized generation and transmission (for example, the UK, Austria and New Zealand), with smaller regional or municipal distribution and retail companies. Since liberalization began in the early 1990s there has been a worldwide movement to create wholesale power markets based on generation companies that compete with each other and have no interests in network assets (as we see in Chapters 2 through 11). More recently, wholesale power markets have been increasingly supplemented by markets for non-energy ancillary services and for the provision of network capacity services, such as use of batteries to avoid network reinforcement expenditure. This movement can be seen as the increasing use of market arrangements in the electricity sector and a move away from internal firm organization towards more spot-type markets. Future market design rests on whether the future electricity system will favour more or less formal use of markets and the nature of the markets that it might favour.

(Spot) markets work best when the product being procured via the market is standardized and provided competitively. They work better the bigger they are (that is, the greater the area they cover), as this increases competition and better covers the fixed costs of running the market. They also work best when the market is likely to be long-lived and hence historic spot prices are likely to give rise to good long-term price signals that can determine future prices and longer-term financial hedging contracts that are important for guiding investment.

Large firms work best in dealing with complex multi-level optimization problems that are actually quite difficult to write down (think of how difficult it would be to write down Apple's optimization problem over the years ex post, let alone ex ante). Firms have to make decisions that relate to present and future products, and past and future investments. They have to match their actions with available resources and respond to the legitimate views of their managers as to future prospects. Firms have to bet on the future (for example, on what future demand will be and the nature of it). Inside the firm is a 'planned' system as opposed to the 'market-based' system that exists outside of the firm. A key idea in Coase (1937) is that the capitalist firm is a planned system and that ebb and flow of market shares and vertical integration within the market reflect the changing nature of the optimal scope of planning versus market competition.

An essential feature of what happens inside the firm is that relationships and the nature of decision making is not fixed. The firm can choose to push decision making down its internal hierarchy and can also decide to follow a fixed rule around certain activities. Thus, the firm can decide to follow a market-based procurement process or it can keep (or take back) activities in-house. The decision to take activities back in-house might be done on discovery that the market was providing poor quality or that a monopoly supplier was beginning to exercise market power. Inside the firm, formal optimization or procurement rules can guide decision making but do not have to rule it. Firms can decide to drop suppliers and procurement processes or to change IT providers. Of course, firms can make mistakes and catastrophically fail to predict the future (for example, Kodak failing to appreciate the advent of the digital camera or Nokia failing to anticipate the rise of the smartphone).

The nature of decision making within the firm is to be contrasted with market-based arrangements. These have to be formal and follow well-publicized rules. This is especially true of the organized markets run by SOs in the US and in Europe. The introduction of a spot market for energy or a market for frequency response specifies a level of optimization and the nature of the algorithms used to determine supply, demand and price, which are quite difficult to change. Changing the operation of the market to allow co-optimization or the package procurement of multiple services at the same time is quite difficult and hard to even experiment around.

Thus, though these market arrangements are potentially very competitive, they are also difficult to change. Indeed, this is one of the reasons they have not been extended to include DERs in the distribution system. In-house arrangements to manage voltage and local constraints in the distribution system may be more efficient because they are flexible and do not require formal recourse to the market. Local energy markets are even more problematic because of the largely arbitrary boundaries that they would introduce and the fact that once introduced they become difficult to change, even though some might be successful and some would not prove viable.[11]

Whether the future will favour the flexibility of in-house production or the competitiveness of the use of the market remains to be seen. However, it is important to recognize that a move to self-consumption with own storage is a move towards in-house production, while more use of wide-area markets with nodal pricing would be a move towards more use of markets.

Engineers often see the future of the power system as being about more use of market prices that are explicitly communicated to all consumers and all generators (Burger et al. 2019, Schweppe et al. 1988). Indeed, some views of the Internet of energy foresee pricing to devices, not just customers (this is an extreme version of the transactive energy future as exemplified by the Pacific Northwest Smart Grid Demonstration project in the US).

It is important for economists to point out just how extreme a view of the use of a spot market in either of the above ways would be. Most products are subject to simple pricing and customers expect the providers of the products to manage their own internal costs of provision to different customers. Only certain types of price discrimination are acceptable and worth doing in conditions where simple advertising messages, corporate trust and perceived fairness in pricing are important considerations for corporate pricing policy. That is not to say that some providers of services to the electricity system cannot be exposed to time- and space-varying prices, but that ability to expose all parties to these sorts of prices is limited. Engineers also fail to take seriously the reality of market power and the linkages between markets. As discussed at length in Chapters 3 and 4, market power is pervasive in the electricity system and was one of the original reasons for introduction of regulation. Market power increases with market fragmentation. Market power can be handled in different ways, but one way of handling it is to bring production in-house and regulate the overall activity. Another is to have wide area markets with suppression of nodal pricing. There is also no reason to assume that unregulated markets for related activities (energy, non-energy ancillary services and network investments) will cumulatively add up to a social optimum, according to the theory of the second best. It is only under extreme conditions that the general equilibrium will be overall efficient.

As Joskow (1996, p. 381) argues, the task of regulators of the electricity sector is to achieve 'a favourable trade off' between short-run and long-run costs and benefits in conditions where some coordination is necessary (at the level of short-run system operation and in lumpy transmission investments) and where the benefits of competition are often long term. One might add to this the rather mixed record on long-term benefits in some competitive electricity markets (the recent experiences of California and Australia being the most obvious) and new generation observation that coordination has been required for whole classes of new-generation technologies.

6.   A NEW MARKET DESIGN?

One issue for the future market design is whether rising distributed generation and flexible demand mean that markets are zonal, local or nodal, rather than national (or even regional). Will there be more energy markets of a PJM type in the future, with more use of markets for non-energy ancillary services?

It is highly likely that there will be more DER participation within existing markets. Falling platform costs and increases in distributed generation and storage suggest that the trend to more DER participation in energy and non-energy ancillary service markets must increase. This will require minor, conceptually speaking, changes to existing markets to lower participation thresholds and allow greater roles for aggregators of small DERs.[12] It will increase distribution utility interaction with transmission-level SOs to coordinate local procurement with area-wide transmission-level markets. This is at the same time that there will be greater pressure to integrate markets over a wider area to manage intermittent energy resources with large negative correlations over long distances, as we have seen with the single European electricity market. The electricity system will be more integrated at lower voltages and over wider areas at high voltages. We will likely see a period of much experimentation with smaller-scale markets for ancillary services and with integration of different types of electricity product to facilitate the new business models of DERs and their aggregators who can play at multiple scales and across multiple timeframes.

One suspects that a truly nodal or fully distributed pricing system is not sustainable in a smart world, partly because of the computational complexity involved.[13] Rather like the Internet, the greater likelihood is that capacity should be expanded to reduce nodal (actual or virtual) price differences and that any rationing that does occur should be on a non-price basis for residential and small non-residential users. As Burger et al. (2019) note for the US in 2016, only 9.7 per cent of customers with smart meters have chosen a 'dynamic tariff', rising to only 26.9 per cent of industrial customers, with only a small fraction of these on 'real-time' (that is, hourly) pricing.[14]

This gives rise to a new potential market design that is based on non-price rationing of the available intermittent generation to loads in priority order. This would exploit the ability of smart meter-enabled systems to communicate with individual devices to switch them on and off. A fully flexible system would have every device prioritized and supplied on the basis of customer-specified priority. Thus, lighting and TV might have the highest priority, with cooker and kettle next, followed by washing machine and dishwasher, and the EV last. Customers might be able to override contracted priorities for a fee or choose more or less items in higher priorities for higher or lower fees. This sort of market design whereby demand was rationed by priority order would move the emphasis from price flexibility to quantity flexibility. This is what happens with the Internet, whereby users can pay for the size of their connection but packet speeds are reduced for everyone when the Internet is congested at peak times, rather than rationed by price via charging more at the peak times to maintain packet speeds. This would be a true Internet of Energy, even though it would – no doubt – be complex to set up. One could imagine China, with its relative lack of experience with market pricing of energy, being strongly attracted to this sort of market design for both technological and distributional reasons.

Another advantage of more flexible demand is that it both levels up the price intermittent renewables receive relative to dispatchable plants and levels down the prices that consumers have to pay during periods of low generation of intermittent electricity. This raises the likelihood that wide area markets could support subsidy-free renewables sooner by improving the relative economics of intermittent generation. It would also encourage investment in fully distributed storage. In the future, individual devices (such as TVs or lighting systems) could be increasingly equipped with batteries as the price of batteries falls and the potential for device-specific interruption increases.

Of course, the likelihood is that some sort of new hybrid market design might develop. This would make use of some price-based elements, particularly towards non-energy ancillary services, and of non-price based rationing. One could imagine the default contracts being rationing contracts and these would exist on the basis of public desire for zero-carbon energy systems. Retailers or energy communities (such as exist in California or the EU) might provide power on this basis to their own customers, acting as intermediaries between price-based charging and quantity-based rationing. Equally, we might imagine that households would have two contracts – one for basic service and one for EV charging. Thus, there might be sophisticated price-based control of EV charging at home alongside much less sophisticated contracts for the rest of home energy. This might be particularly the case given that consumption at home is not primarily determined by the bill payer, while, currently, the individual who makes the choice of provision of fuel to the vehicle is the one who pays the fuel bill.

We know a lot about how individuals consume and choose to pay for energy already: they prefer to pay a fixed amount per month (where they can afford to do this) for household energy and prefer simple tariff structures (Oseni and Pollitt 2017). They also have high expectations of energy regulators with respect to transparency of information, price fluctuations and quality of service. Those preferences are likely to change slowly (if at all) and will influence the nature of the future market design that regulators approve. We also know that consumers are concerned about fairness and the achievement of environmental targets and that they like renewables and EVs as technologies, and hence support policies that encourage their adoption (see, for example Oseni et al. 2013). We also know that consumers have adopted new practices with respect to charging up mobile ICT devices (for example, leaving them plugged in at night). There may hence be some scope for behaviour change that facilitates smart charging of EVs. Thus, a world where targeted use of price signals may help facilitate better matching of intermittent supply with flexible demand is possible. However, a world with extensive sophisticated use of price signals for most electricity customers does not seem in keeping with past experience.

NOTES

*   With thanks to my fellow editors, Paul Joskow and Jean-Michel Glachant, for constructive comments.
1.   California, New York and Connecticut have 50 per cent, 70 per cent and 48 per cent targets, respectively, for the share of renewable electricity by 2030 (see, for example, https://www.eia.gov/todayinenergy/detail.php?id=38492, accessed 10 July 2021).
2.   China's National Energy Administration (NEA) has recently proposed an increase in the share of total renewable and nuclear electricity to 40 per cent by 2030 (see https://www.reuters.com/article/us-china-climatechange-renewables-iduskbn2aa0ba, accessed 10 July 2021).
3.   See BP (2020).
4.   30 million × 3000 kWh = 90 TWh; current UK electricity demand = circa 300 TWh. See Küfeoğlu and Pollitt (2019) and Newbery and Strbac (2016).
5.   30 million × 10 kWh = 0.9 TWh. Daily electricity demand in the UK = 300 TWh/365 = 0.82 TWh.
6.   Seventy-three per cent of households in Norway have electric heating (see https://www.swecourbaninsight.com/urban-energy/race-to-electrification-norway-in-a-pole-position/, accessed 10 July 2021).

7. See Samson (2015), who shows that for the UK, peak heating demand is six times higher than peak electricity demand.
8. For a detailed discussion of optimality of PJM's optimization, see Synapse Energy Economics (2006).
9. In 2019, 29 per cent of New York's electricity generation came from renewable electricity, while that share was 43 per cent for California in 2018 (source: Energy Information Administration). It is important to point out, however, that renewables can be dispatchable (hydro, geothermal, biomass and methane from waste plants).
10. See for example, https://es.catapult.org.uk/reports/rethinking-electricity-markets-the-case-for-emr-2/?download=true, accessed 10 July 2021.
11. Burger et al. (2019, p. 67) note problems with decentralized markets.
12. Burger et al. (2019) discuss the system architecture issues of whether this involves increasing the role of the current SOs (balancing authorities) or the current DSOs (distribution network operators [DNOs]/SOs).
13. This is in line with the Kristov, De Martini and Taft's (2016) view that neither the total TSO nor total DSO is computationally possible.
14. And one assumes that almost no smaller customers are on real-time *and* location (that is, nodal) varying tariffs.

REFERENCES

Anaya, K. and M. G. Pollitt (2018), *Reactive Power Management and Procurement Mechanisms: Lessons for the Power Potential Project*, report for National Grid, 11 June.
Biggar, D. R. and M. R. Hesamzadah (2014), *The Economics of Electricity Markets*, Chichester, UK: John Wiley & Sons.
Bonbright, J. C. (1961), *Principles of Public Utility Rates*, New York: Columbia University Press.
BP (2020), *Statistical Review of World Energy 2020*, London: BP.
Burger, S. P., J. D. Jenkins, C. Batlle and I. J. Pérez-Arriaga (2019), 'Restructuring revisited part 2: coordination in electricity distribution systems', *The Energy Journal*, **40** (3), 55–76.
Coase, R. H. (1937), 'The theory of the firm', *Economica*, **4** (16), 386–405.
Electric Power Research Institute (EPRI) (2015), *The Integrated Grid – A Benefit–Cost Framework*, Palo Alto, CA: EPRI.
European Network of Transmission System Operators for Electricity (ENTSO-E) (2018), *Electricity Balancing in Europe*, Brussels: ENTSO-E.
Greve, T., F. Teng, M. G. Pollitt and G. Strbac (2018), 'A system operator's utility function for the frequency response market', *Applied Energy*, **231**, 562–9.
International Energy Agency (IEA) (2018), *Electricity Information 2018 Overview*, Paris: IEA.
Joskow, P. L. (1996), 'Introducing competition into regulated network industries: from hierarchies to markets in electricity', *Industrial and Corporate Change*, **5** (2), 341–82.
Kiesling, L. (2016), 'An "Uber for electricity": institutional theory for a platform model in an historically regulated industry', mimeo.
Kristov, L., P. De Martini and J. Taft (2016), 'Two visions of a transactive electric system', *IEEE Power & Energy Magazine*, **14** (3), 63–9.
Küfeoğlu, S. and M. G. Pollitt (2019), 'The impact of PVs and EVs on domestic electricity network charges: a case study from Great Britain', *Energy Policy*, **127**, 412–24.
Küfeoğlu, S., G. Liu, K. Anaya and M. G. Pollitt (2019), 'Digitalisation and new business models in energy sector', *EPRG Working Paper No. 1920*, Energy Policy Research Group, University of Cambridge.
Lipsey, R. G. and K. Lancaster (1956), 'The general theory of second best', *The Review of Economic Studies*, **24** (1), 11–32.
MIT Energy Initiative (2016), *Utility of the Future*, Cambridge, MA: MIT.
National Grid (2017), *System Needs and Product Strategy*, Warwick, UK: National Grid.
Newbery, D. and G. Strbac (2016), 'What is needed for battery electric vehicles to become socially cost competitive?', *Economics of Transportation*, **5**, 1–11.
Newbery, D., M. G. Pollitt, R. Ritz and W. Strielkowski (2018), 'Market design for a high-renewables European electricity system', *Renewable and Sustainable Energy Reviews*, **91**, 695–707.
Oseni, M. and M. G. Pollitt (2017), 'The prospects for smart energy prices: observations from 50 years of residential pricing for fixed line telecoms and electricity', *Renewable and Sustainable Energy Reviews*, **70**, 150–60.
Oseni, M. O., M. G. Pollitt and D. M. Reiner et al. (2013), '2013 EPRG public opinion survey: smart energy – attitudes and behaviours', *EPRG Working Paper No. 1327*, Energy Policy Research Group, University of Cambridge.

Platchkov, L. M. and M. G. Pollitt (2011), 'The economics of energy (and electricity) demand', in T. Jamasb and M. G. Pollitt (eds), *The Future of Electricity Demand: Customers, Citizens and Loads*, Cambridge, UK: Cambridge University Press, pp. 17–47.

Pollitt, M. (2016), 'The future of electricity network regulation: the policy perspective', in M. Finger and C. Jaag (eds), *The Routledge Companion to Network Industries*, Abingdon, UK: Routledge, pp. 169–82.

Pollitt, M. (2018), 'Electricity network charging in the presence of distributed energy resources: principles, problems and solutions', *Economics of Energy and Environmental Policy*, 7 (1), 89–103.

Pollitt, M. (2019), 'The single market in electricity: an economic assessment', *Review of Industrial Organization*, **55** (1), 63–87.

Pollitt, M. and K. Anaya (2019), 'Competition in markets for ancillary services? The implications of rising distributed generation', *EPRG Working Paper No. 1928*, Energy Policy Research Group, University of Cambridge.

Pollitt, M. and L. Dale (2018), 'Restructuring the Chinese electricity supply sector – how industrial electricity prices are determined in a liberalized power market: lessons from Great Britain', *EPRG Working Paper No.1839*, Energy Policy Research Group, University of Cambridge.

Richardson, G. B. (1972), 'The organisation of industry', *The Economic Journal*, **82** (327), 883–96.

Ruz, F. C. and M. G. Pollitt (2016), 'Overcoming barriers to electrical energy storage: comparing California and Europe', *Competition and Regulation in Network Industries*, **17** (2), 123–50.

Samson, R. (2015), 'The challenges of decarbonising space and water heating', UKERC Summer School presentation.

Schweppe, F. C., M. C. Caramanis, R. D. Tabors and R. E. Bohn (1988), *Spot Pricing of Electricity*, New York: Springer.

Sidhu, A., M. G. Pollitt and K. Anaya (2018), 'A social cost benefit analysis of grid-scale electrical energy storage projects: a case study', *Applied Energy*, **212**, 881–94.

Synapse Energy Economics (2006), *LMP Electricity Markets: Market Operations, Market Power, and Value for Consumers*, report prepared for the American Public Power Association.

Williamson, O. E. (1975), *Markets and Hierarchies: Analysis and Antitrust Implications*, New York: Free Press.

17. New business models in the electricity sector
*Jean-Michel Glachant**

1. INTRODUCTION

A new wave of deep changes is beginning to shake the electricity sector as we enter the third decade of the twenty-first century. Having an earlier wave in the last decade of the twentieth century, we already know that it can happen. In the 1990s, it was the combined cycle gas turbine (CCGT) and the open wholesale market – a new type of asset to generate electricity and a new framework to price and trade electricity between 'wholesale size' units. Today, key trends are represented, on the one hand by windmills and solar PV panels, and on the other hand by a deepening digitalization of price and trade electricity between 'retail size' units. Of course, these new trends are only beginning, and they will not present the same characteristics or occur at the same pace in different electricity sectors around the world. It will depend on what the former wave of change in electricity already did or did not do; whether wholesale and retail markets are open to entry and competition; whether vertically integrated companies and/or national governments control investments, technology choices, siting of new assets, tariffs and support schemes; and whether market and grid operations are ruled by a government administration, the industry itself or an independent body and so on.

Various chapters in this handbook explore concrete cases around the world, both in developed and developing countries. What the present chapter will concentrate on are new changes emerging in western countries that have already been implementing the open wholesale market model for 20 or 30 years. These new changes appear both on a large scale – such as the 'greening of electricity' – and on a smaller scale – such as the deepening digitalization of 'retail-size' units. While still being relatively new, post-2010, these changes are already significant enough to be of great interest, not only for the future of those electricity sectors that have been liberalized, but also for those that are not – or not yet – market based.[1]

In a market-based industry, business models are key – as propellers for investments, for technology choices, for the definition of the characteristics of the products and for the siting and operation of the asset base. The business model literature identifies up to nine possible components of sophisticated business strategies (Osterwalder, Pigneur and Clark 2010). A simpler and still robust version can be built with only two pairs of components of business model differentiation: first can be the type of assets that are engaged and the revenue streams they can secure; second can be the definition of particular characteristics for the new products put on sale and the selection of customers especially targeted for that sale. This simple and basic framework of two models works well with the empirical evidence available until 2020. On the one hand, the greening of electricity is strongly characterized by the kind of assets it requires to generate power, as well as the types of revenue streams that allow it to grow. On the other hand, the ongoing digitalization of retail-size units is deepening because new products and new characteristics are invented to attract targeted customers. In between – that is, between the greening of electricity and the deepening digitalization of retail-size units – we find the regulated grids, both transmission and distribution networks that must react to these changes, undertaken upstream and downstream, while being regulated businesses with limited space for autonomous strategic initiatives. Hence, the three sections of this chapter: first, new assets and special revenue streams for the greening of electricity; second, new services for targeted customers; and third, between new assets and new services – the case of regulated grids.

2. NEW ASSETS AND SPECIAL REVENUE STREAMS FOR THE GREENING OF ELECTRICITY

The energy contained in renewable resources like wind and solar is not owned by anyone and can be directly extracted by the generating units. It does not have to be harvested, concentrated or refined, transported, stored and conditioned for injection into the electricity generating process. For this reason, wind and solar units look, at first sight, like hydropower plants – they are mainly made of fixed costs paid upfront. However, water can be stored and then released by its owner at its 'opportunity cost', while the recovery of wind and solar upfront costs is left at the mercy of its non-dispatchable generation. Chapter 2 by Schmalensee and Chapter 15 by Green in this handbook explain in detail how wholesale markets and their pricing mechanisms work with or without a significant amount of renewables. It suffices here, in this chapter, to remember that wind and solar would not have taken off in market-based systems without particular types of revenue streams, guaranteeing the recovery of their expensive upfront investments.[2]

Various revenue models have been devised to incentivize investments in renewables. They are mainly regulated schemes, pushed by public authorities. The most well known are: (1) *feed-in tariffs*, typical of the EU, where renewable energy source (RES) generation is guaranteed a fixed price for each unit of output, irrespective of its economic value for the whole electricity system; (2) *feed-in premia*, where a fixed premium is added to the volatile market prices that express the fluctuating economic value of electricity at different times; and (3) *renewable portfolio standards*, typical of the US, which oblige a generator or supplier to incorporate a certain share of RES on average in their output. Another scheme is very common for small-scale generating units, such as, for instance, roof-top photovoltaics (PV) – so-called 'net metering', which works in practice as a 'retail feed-in' by proportionally reducing the total bill (for energy, grid and taxes alike) paid by the prosumer (that is, a consumer that self-generates [part of] of the electricity they consume by typically installing rooftop solar) after each volumetric unit of renewables generated at home, with a significant impact on the recovery of network and policy costs and redistributive effects among network users. Such a process, where new assets introducing a new generation technology are receiving special revenue streams guaranteeing their financial success, is very consequential for the other generation assets that can sell only to the residual demand (that is, demand being not primarily covered by the renewables). As a result, the business models of conventional generators are perturbed and can be fully destroyed (Joskow 2019a).

Another key aspect of the same issue is that the economic value of renewables tends to go down when their penetration rate in the generation mix goes up, because the increasing RES generation output does not necessarily follow demand and scarcity – the so-called cannibalization effect. In 2012, the economic value of electricity generated by the solar PV units installed in California was on average 125 per cent of the electricity wholesale price. In 2018, that value was down to 79 per cent.[3] In Texas, where PV penetration was less pronounced, it was still 127 per cent (Bolinger and Seel 2018). With this in mind, new utility-scale onshore wind is already cheaper (by mid-2020), as with some utility-scale solar, than generating with fuels on a levelized cost basis and, when guaranteed access to demand irrespective of their intermittency, is able to beat the competing conventional technologies[4] – in many countries the intermittency is dealt with at the system level and not directly by the RES generator. A few cases of 'subsidy-free' projects were therefore seen in Spain, Italy, Portugal and so on.[5] And in a few advanced cases, such as in the US, solar at utility scale plus storage can also beat the cost of a new CCGT and enter the portfolio of tools that regulatory authorities allow to be employed for system management (California, Arizona, Hawaii and so on). Still in the US, the levelized cost for the best onshore wind farms in 2018 was already down to $29 per megawatt-hour ($/MWh), $7 lower than that for coal plants.[6]

Pure market-based renewables also appear, built on bilateral contracts linking a big consumer with a brand that benefits from green labelling (such as Facebook for 2650 MW, AT&T for 820 MW, Walmart for 670 MW, and then Google, Apple, Amazon, Microsoft, Ikea and so on) or even skilled people from heavy industry that know how to position such a contract into their large portfolio of energy supply (such as the EU leader in aluminium, NorskHydro for 667 MW and its competitor Alcoa for 524 MW). These corporate power purchase agreements (PPAs) are still small compared with the whole volume of RES investments, but might have a promising future in jurisdictions where electricity retailers have renewables obligations.[7] Indeed, corporate PPAs have been the fastest-growing segment for utility renewables sales in the US.[8] Moreover, a new type of corporate PPA emerged: groups of smaller off-takers led by bigger and more experienced partners – the 'anchor tenants'. Depending on the size of a typical generating asset and on the particular skills needed for its siting and operation, at least four types of new renewables businesses must be distinguished.

2.1   Onshore Wind for All, Or for a Few

The typical size of a single modern onshore windmill (from 500 kilowatts [kW] to 2 MW) is small, in 2020, compared with traditional fossil fuel power units (×100 MW for a CCGT to 1800 MW for a nuclear reactor like the EPR), and it costs less than $1 million per MW for a typical 2 MW turbine, plus $500 000 to $1 million to install (BNEF 2018). Entities able to invest $2–3 million dollars are numerous, while those with the skills needed to site and operate – such as consultancy – are low by nature. If a guaranteed revenue stream is set, investment flows. Local communities and cooperatives too can enter such a landscape, even by targeting the smaller windmill size.

However, when the revenue stream is changed from a feed-in tariff to a feed-in premium with auctioning, players increasingly become pure professionals, able to manage the market pricing uncertainties as well as to decrease the input costs by bargaining with vendors, by increasing the size of each turbine, and by building wind parks of several units.[9] This shift to professional players according to the type of revenue stream offered is underlined by the successful entry into the US of green subsidiaries of European utilities such as EDP Renováveis (the fourth company in the world for wind capacity at the beginning of 2020, with 5300 MW in the US – nearly half of its world fleet) or Enel Green Power (4400 MW wind and 230 MW solar in the US). The highest category of renewables units, the giant onshore wind farms (such as in the US, India or China), ranges from 500 MW to more than 1 GW, entailing investments in the order of billions of dollars for each project.

2.2 Offshore Wind for the Champions League

Offshore wind is attractive because its load factor (around 50 per cent, sometimes up to 60 or 70 per cent) is able to increase two to three times higher than onshore (Brittany in France 19 per cent, Great Britain 25 per cent), which could partially solve the problem of intermittency of generation.[10] The wind farm size targeted is also larger – the latest project in the UK at the beginning of the 2020s goes above 1 GW. The five latest farms projected in the Netherlands for 2019–26 are mainly 700 MW, and one giant stands at 4000 MW. These Dutch investments are estimated at €1.6–1.9 million per MW, ending with a typical €1.2 billion for a 700 MW park.

However, it is not only size that is a barrier to smaller investors. The other substantial barrier is because the success of offshore requires high skills for siting and building. Only a handful of companies really master those skills at world level, explaining why, for example, the Danish Ørsted was number one in the UK as well as in Taiwan. At the very beginning of the 2020s, US investors had not entered the offshore wind sector in a major way (only 30 MW of total capacity), although the US Department of Energy estimated a potential of 22 GW by 2030 and 86 GW by 2050. Similarly, Chinese companies have concentrated on onshore parks and have already entered the EU on this basis, not yet mastering offshore wind skills, although this will happen in the 2020s. In this particular segment – international offshore renewables – the Swiss bank UBS was predicting, in 2018, the emergence after 2020 of a few highly skilled and easily financed 'world majors' in offshore wind,[11] such as Ørsted, or the European oil and gas companies[12] or, later, a Chinese company – possibly Three Gorges – which has already tried to take control of the Portuguese EDP and its green branch.[13] Following this new trend, European utilities like Enel and Iberdrola announced in 2020 target portfolios of 100 GW or more renewable assets at the 2030 horizon; European oil and gas majors like Shell or Total announced targets in excess of 10GW, such as 35GW in 2025 for French Total. Public authorities contributed to strengthen the move, with both UK and EU competing in autumn 2020 to set ambitious targets for their respective offshore wind fleets: UK at 40GW in 2030 and 100GW in 2050; EU at 60 GW in 2030 and 300 GW in 2050 (1 GW of offshore wind is worth €2–3 billion).[14]

2.3 PV at Utility Scale

In the US, like at world level, utility scale dominates solar generation, with about 60 per cent of the total capacity. The whole of the US entered the 2020s with about 2500 utility-scale PV facilities, most with a capacity smaller than 5 MW, but around two-thirds of their total capacity is from facilities larger than 50 MW (US Energy Information Administration [EIA] 2019). More than 500 new utility-scale projects have been finalized in 2018, a typical one being 30–40 MW for an investment of $60–80 million. The two best deciles of investments were 10 per cent cheaper than the median and the unique absolute best under half of that (Bolinger and Seel 2018).

At the world level, the International Energy Agency (IEA) long-term outlook foresees a continued growth for solar.[15] On a case by case basis, in open bidding for countries with good sun resources, several utility-scale solar offers are already well below $30 per MWh – one at $21 in Chile (well known for the quality of its solar resources), 300 MW in Portugal (won in an auction by a South Korean firm) at $13.4 per MWh, followed by 600 MW at $10, also in Portugal. However, according to BNEF specialists, it is hard to know what is due to lowering intrinsic costs or to aggressive bidding. Because of the relatively low skills needed to enter the solar busines (the highest practical skill is the cleaning of the PV panels), contrary to offshore wind, new entrepreneurs may bid aggressively to get a foot-hold, hoping to make their living later. However, because of this low barrier to entry, it is not obvious when margins will stabilize in future auction rounds.[16] As a consequence, the 'major' international players are not necessarily those with a large installed base in their home market. For example, the two French companies EDF and ENGIE have proven global ability to attract bank financing and to convince developers that the park really will be built after having won the call, despite small home markets for intermittent renewables generation (Wood Mackenzie 2019a). Similarly, Shanghai Electric led the gigantic 950 MW project of concentrated solar in Dubai for $4.4 billion.

2.4   Rooftop PV Prosumers

According to the Lazard (2018) cost of energy review, prosumer costs for solar were still high before 2020 in the US: $160–267 per MWh for residential, $81–170 for commercial – compared with $36–46 for utility scale. The continuous expansion of prosumers in the western world and their large PV market share at world level (around 40 per cent of world's total installed capacity) are therefore the result of favourable incentives, arising mainly from the rules and the tariffs used to bill western final consumers that work as pure 'retail feed-in' tariffs when the bill tariff is based on net metering. In California, for example, this effect is amplified by the local regulation of domestic tariffs – the use of categories of prices that increase when the volume of electricity consumed is higher. This works as an additional incentive for the wealthier to defect by investing in rooftop PV. In Australia, on the contrary, the mass market for rooftop PV is said to be flooded by the middle class population willing to invest to escape high bills (€125–200 a month) driven by high demand for air conditioning,[17] triggering costly grid reinforcement (Sioshansi 2017, 2019).

3.   NEW SERVICES FOR TARGETED CUSTOMERS

Electricity has long been known as a heavy industry – that is, where you have to invest a lot and at such a scale to do business. A typical extreme is the EDF investment in a British nuclear power plant at Hinkley Point – $7.67 million per MW of capacity was committed in 2019. Even with a government-guaranteed price, the annual turnover per MW will be – at best – in the range of $700 000, putting the investment/turnover ratio at 11 to 1. Add to this the size of a single unit, here 3260 MW, it is $25 billion for the whole plant. Such numbers explain why, in this case, there is a link between the type of assets engaged and the possible revenue streams at the core of the business model.

Opposite to this extreme is a typical twenty-first-century new trend – the 'asset-light' industry (Haskel and Westlake 2018), typical of the 'new economy' in a digital era. Here the core of any business model is to identify particular product characteristics that can attract certain targeted customers by creating 'value for the customer'. The accuracy of any 'asset-light/new product characteristics' strategy will be revealed by the targeted customers themselves, as only they are able to validate the particular value offered. Of course, consumers need time to discover novelties and to adapt to them, but if the capital engaged to attract those targeted is not too high, the confirmation of the business sustainability of new offers may have to wait, up to a decade, as demonstrated in the tech industry by the rise of the very first 'digital platforms' (Choudary 2015).

Where then, can new services be conceived to create value within the electricity sector more deeply in its demand side? The first path is to bridge activation of demand and the already existing wholesale trade. Traditionally, demand was able to react to differentiated wholesale signals only if tariffs of suppliers had a time-of-use component. The proper idea of demand selling its activation at the wholesale level was confined to big interruptible customers. It is this older landscape that 'retail aggregation' changes. Via super-smart metering and activation, retail flexibility can re-enter the wholesale trade as an offer made to balance the whole power system.

The second path of change on the retail side addresses another type of trade, typical of a 'platform economy' – the direct trade between small units, bypassing the control that utilities, as large generators or suppliers, have exercised to trade electricity in open markets since the 1990s. This can go down to very direct 'peer-to-peer' (P2P), like with automatic trading supported by blockchains.

The third path is a departure from the unilateral control that electricity grids and their system operators have always kept over exchange schemes using their network infrastructures as an unavoidable 'delivery loop' for electricity products. Now comes the creation of 'behind-the-meter' (BTM) smart management systems. As soon as many consumption units (within the demand side of electricity systems) can directly coordinate their own self-generation, their own storage and their various devices consumption profiles, grids lose their unilateral control loop (Sioshansi 2017, 2019). And smart consumption units can act as autonomous 'mini-systems' or 'mini-grids' ('micro-grids', if you prefer this image, as closer to 'microeconomics'). It can be a fleet of electrical cars, or a 'zero-net-consumption' building, or a world of smart homes or premises equipped with digital assistants and interactive devices connected via the 'Internet of Things' (IoT).

In sum, there are three emerging business models: (1) aggregation, re-entering retail into wholesale; (2) peer-to-peer, bypassing utilities as intermediaries; and (3) autonomous territories, behind the meter.

3.1   Aggregation: Re-entering Retail into Wholesale

The building of open electricity wholesale markets was the big innovation of the 1990s, raising questions of how retail would be linked to their 8760 hourly or 17 520 semi-hourly wholesale pricing units. A first response was the use of a proxy (the 'profiles'), creating a two-step settlement in the wholesale market (a first step, based on the proxies, the second occurring later with availability of accurate numbers). A more comprehensive response was a one-step full bridge with 'smart metering', twinning each individual consumption in real time with the proper wholesale equilibrium short timeframe. 'Dynamic pricing', in the meaning of full exposure of an individual consumer to each hourly or semi-hourly wholesale price, can then appear. It gained a certain amount of consumer interest in the Nordic countries. However, as explained by the Nordic Council of Ministers (2017), other conditions must be met to fully re-enter retail activation into the wholesale. First, the wholesale time pricing must be shared by consumption units in the very same time-frame to permit a rational retail response. Second, the consumption devices must be controllable and monitored within the same timeframe. And then, third, ICTs must ensure fully interactive communications in two directions (from wholesale to retail and the other way around). Furthermore, rules in both electricity system operation (at distribution and transmission level) and wholesale market operation must be adapted to welcome consumption variations as offers taken into account in the wholesale and the system equilibrium.[18]

This is exactly where aggregators appear, as intermediaries reducing the transaction costs on both sides – on the wholesale side, the cost of dealing with units too small and heterogeneous, and, on the retail side, the cost of understanding, adapting and reacting to the actual wholesale process. Finally, aggregators work like 'reverse retailers' – instead of fractioning the wholesale output to feed consumption units on the retail side, like retailers typically do, aggregators enlarge their grouping of consumption units output to the wholesale side.

On this wholesale side, transmission system operators (TSOs) may also have to buy downward adjustments from aggregators. Another trade can also be made at a local level if distribution system operators (DSOs) and aggregators arrange it in a suitable framework. The work of 'value creation' by an aggregator is therefore to 'build' a portfolio of consumption units, of actionable consumption devices, and of certified ICT tools to better answer the particular needs and special operational requirements of the wholesale or local buying counterparts. These needs and requirements vary considerably from one market to the other, as well as from one system operator to the other, making the concrete job of an aggregator very 'condition specific'. For example, a TSO can impose a particular type of communication tool to guarantee the control of a consumption unit, with a related expense of up to €6000 for each unit control box; such a requirement excludes, by definition, the direct participation of small and medium consumers. On the other hand, other TSOs may allow cheaper communication such as via DSL. If consumption devices themselves were going to be standardized (electric vehicles, heat pumps, fridges and so on), the size of the aggregation business potential could dramatically increase. The same is also valid for the market rules. As long as flexibility is not very accurately priced in wholesale markets, the business potential for aggregators is limited.

The landscape of aggregation companies is still remarkably diverse. Some are subsidiaries of big electric utilities, such as Enel X. Others are typical start-ups to be sold later to 'deep-pocket' players, sometimes from outside the electricity sector, such as Shell buying Limejump, for example. A few independent aggregators continue to grow in the EU, such as Next Kraftwerke, already managing more than 7000 units and 6 GW in 2020, which makes the average unit under its control at 857 kW. In the US, as in the EU, independent aggregators are the most numerous and still have the largest market share – so far (European Network of Transmission System Operators for Electricity [ENTSO-E] 2019, Monitoring Analytics 2019).

3.2   Peer-to-peer Bypassing Utilities as Intermediaries

Having understood what an aggregator does (reducing transaction costs to open trade for a new type of product with targeted customers), we must only go a step further to find the next business model. Aggregators build private portfolios of clients, harvested within a formal contract that gives aggregators an exclusive franchise on the final product reselling. Here, the 'platforms' business model acts very differently.

To reduce the costs of transacting, platforms openly define particular products' characteristics and implement the corresponding automatized rules for operation and interaction to create a proper 'club' of trade, while letting the two sides of their market platform (both the sellers and the buyers) match directly, at their own initiative but within the particular framework set by the platform. We have already seen that the aggregator was substituting their intermediation to any direct link between the upstream and the downstream. On the contrary, the platform re-establishes a direct link. This link, however, stays framed by the precise characteristics defined by the platform for the product and its trade process, including delivery and settlement. This said, many different platforms can appear and live their own lives, as each is free to define its own products and trade characteristics to attract a particular type of user.

At the beginning of the 2020s was a platform from where a British distribution network operator (DNO) was buying local ancillary services to solve congestion and to postpone physical investments in the grid. On another platform, German prosumers were selling certified local renewables to neighbouring consumers. Others shared local storage, charging electrical cars and so on. All these platforms can work in an open environment, targeting particular customers within open crowds. They can also voluntarily restrict themselves to a particular audience, even to a really closed milieu, as in the new European legal notion of 'energy communities'. Restricting access is a simple means to define particular groups of 'targeted customers'. Since the cost of establishing a platform business is mainly represented by software development, customer enrolment, database and process management, the initial size of a new business can be quite small.

Another way of simplifying trade in well-defined audiences, or within established communities, is to automatize this trade with blockchain algorithms. While blockchain trade within large anonymous crowds (as with cryptocurrencies) is quite complex and expensive, it can become much easier and cheaper within 'energy clubs' with conditions for entry. Before the 2020s, a Mexican regulator was considering using blockchain for self-registered prosumers (identified by a smartphone scan of their PV panel barcode) to manage the green certificates attached to their generation.

Both 'simple' platforms and advanced blockchain groups can bypass utilities as intermediaries and implement new types of 'peer-to-peer' exchange. However, other cases also reveal an active role for some utilities, such as Axpo and its partner Wüppertal Stadtwerke (in Germany) and Piclo and UK Power Networks (in the UK). The growing number of prosumers and 'prosumagers' (that is, prosumers endowed with their own storage units) feeds the process and nurtures the hopes of many start-ups (Burger et al. 2020, Sioshansi 2019).

3.3 Autonomous Territories 'Behind the Meter'

The last type of new business model to be encountered in the retail domain is another step ahead. Aggregators link the wholesale level with activated retail units. Peer-to-peer recreates direct interactions between the individual ultimate buyers and sellers. What else can be done, differently but in a similar vein, that could make business sense? It is to organize autonomous economic zones beyond the traditional electricity system – that is, 'behind the meter' (Glachant 2019). As soon as individual units, on the consumption side, can programme and coordinate their own generation, own storage and the various load profiles of their various consumption devices they become something entirely new – 'autonomous electrical territories'. They behave as sub-nodal systems from the point of view of the entire traditional electricity system, and as mini-grids from the point of view of the incumbent distribution grid. Aggregators and, to a large extent, peer-to-peer trade, still need the traditional grids as their unavoidable 'delivery loop', which is a significant constraint and a real limit to their creativity and business models.[19] The new territories created 'behind the meter' bypass the traditional electricity system, including its grids and the energy regulator. It is a gigantic 'free zone', open to many innovations and experiments, while not having to beg for any 'regulatory sandbox' from any energy authority.

A first candidate here could be the management of fleets of electrical cars. As electrical cars managed in a fleet can easily choose where to connect to the grid and what to do when connected (withdrawing or injecting – then storing, how much and how frequently, at what speed and so on), they can easily behave like an autonomous electricity system 'on wheels', surrounding the 'site specificity' of the fixed networks of cables and substations owned by the distribution companies. A simple estimate of a car battery, in 2030, at 60 kWh puts a 1000-car fleet at 60 MWh full charge, and the annual EU battery market for new cars, in say 2040, would be close to 1 TWh, with 900 GWh/year. With a single car battery at 120 kWh, the former numbers double, and almost 2 TWh of battery storage could enter the total EU car fleet every year.

A second obvious candidate is the 'zero-net-consumption' building, with an EU-wide regulation soon becoming mandatory, as in California, for all new buildings. Each new building will have to generate, to store if economical, and to manage its various internal loads to be regulation compliant. It is clearly a case for a kind of mini-grid and sub-nodal electricity system.

Another candidate is the future individual 'smart home' or 'smart premise', where digital assistants, fed by local sensors and obeying a wide artificial intelligence operating system, will dialogue with local interactive devices connected to the 'Internet of Things'. This is another vision of another species of mini-grids and sub-nodal systems.

4.   BETWEEN NEW ASSETS AND NEW SERVICES: THE CASE OF REGULATED GRIDS

There are two ways of looking at new business models for the regulated grids, emerging from the greening of energy and the digitalization of trade for retail units. One way is more prudent and pragmatic, looking only at potentially strong business innovations still rooted in the three decades of practice established since the creation of open markets. Most of this belongs to the wide potential of incentive regulation for grids, which is another branch of electricity market reforms that this handbook does not fully address.[20] New promise developed in the US by Paul Joskow in this regard deserves a tribute. The other way is more of a vision, a set of intuitions, while here or there, in the EU, Australia, Texas or California, there are signs of such transfiguration.[21]

4.1   The New Forward-looking Pragmatism

Both the pragmatism and the vision can actually be linked because of the powerful capability of the incentive regulation toolbox. Incentive regulation of grids covers both the regulation of the assets as infrastructure fixed costs, and the regulation of the services being delivered from this asset base during the operation of the system. For a long time, Paul Joskow has advocated that quality of service (interruption, level of reliability), losses and congestion management should typically submit to 'performance-based regulation' (Glachant et al. 2012, Joskow 2014) because the measurement of the outcome can easily be used as a metric. Joskow goes another step forward, this time for the basic infrastructure regulation, in his inspiring working paper on 'Competition for electric transmission projects in the US' (Joskow 2019b). The full monopoly of existing transmission incumbents on the design and implementation of new transmission investments has no rational basis. It is more of a habit than a clever regulatory choice, and the US has implemented and tested a new regime: the 'competitive transmission procurement model'.[22] The US hosts two typical institutions: a quite strong federal energy regulator, FERC, which the EU, for example, does not have, and many independent system operators (ISOs) not owning or maintaining the transmission assets but nevertheless operating the whole electricity system. In such a landscape, a new incentive process for new transmission investments can be built, where any developer can submit a proposal (comprising both a technical proposal and a standard revenue contract, or with an open and innovative revenue contract). The ISO could do a first screening of all the proposals submitted, with the federal regulator taking the final decision and bypassing the many local regulators (called 'state regulators' in the US). As about 16 cases of open submission of transmission investment projects have already occurred in the US before 2020, Joskow's proposal is already deeply rooted in the existing avant garde of practice. Of course, in the EU, we immediately think about the many offshore grids that European energy transition requires, and that could benefit from this innovative extension of incentive regulation. Unfortunately, the European institutional landscape is not yet very favourable (Glachant 2021, Meeus and Glachant 2018), as its 'local' energy regulators and TSOs are still well entrenched in their national monopoly of rights and authority. Offshore transmission links offer more opportunities.

4.2 The New Vision

Being placed between the new assets deployed upstream for greening electricity and the particular services conceived downstream for specially targeted customers, the grids (transmission or distribution) might enjoy a formidable business position, such as Amazon combining both a physical delivery loop and a digital space for trade. But how could this happen if these grids are so tightly regulated? Everything is regulated for these grids – their investments, their technology choices, their entry into new businesses, their definition of product characteristics and of categories of targeted customers, and each related price – either by the energy regulator or by the energy ministry behind it, if not by parliament, the competition authority[23] or the courts.

This does not mean that the grids do not act and do not play any role, But it does mean that this role, even when fully appropriate, is more reactive than proactive. The grids allow the 'upstream assets' to move and the 'blossoming downstream services' to strike first. Of course, there are exceptions where the grids are chosen, or accepted, by the relevant authorities as 'champions' for this or that particular change or challenge, but these are usually exceptions.

Therefore, the grids' own new business models are deeply heterogeneous and subject to many future new transformations or revisions because they intimately depend on both the business models chosen by other independent players (the grid users, upstream or downstream) and the reactions of many authorities to this newly created landscape.

While such conditions do not favour a simple and coherent view of the renewal of the business models for electricity grids, there is nevertheless a kind of underlying general logic at work. It will be made clearer in four steps: first, building grid assets in reaction to investments in offshore green generators – the influence of the grid/generators' incentive framework; second, acknowledging the loop between onshore grid owners' revenue streams and onshore active users' own incentives to invest; third, building an efficient loop between the business models for grid users and for grid companies; and fourth, slow-moving and fragmented decision-making.

4.2.1 Building grid assets in reaction to investments in offshore green generators – the influence of the grid/generators' incentive framework

As the offshore grid case will exemplify, the relation between the amount of new green assets that are being connected to the grid and the amount of assets the grid companies must invest in reaction is far from being a purely technical datum, as one might have thought. The case of offshore grids is interesting to examine because no offshore grid existed anywhere before the deployment of green assets, apart from international interconnectors transmitting power from onshore generation assets. New offshore grids are a case of pure assets grid reaction to investment decisions taken by green generators.

At the beginning of the 2020s, the offshore wind industry (that is, wind turbine manufacturers, wind park developers and builders, grid developers and builders, and park operators) was still dominated at world level by Europeans ('first-mover advantage'), and sea parks by two countries – the UK, with more than 8 GW, and Germany, with less than 6 GW. Comparing these two countries is therefore of interest, if not a 'natural experiment' (Meeus and Schittekatte 2018).

The British framework for offshore grid development and building is typical of the new Revenues = Incentives + Innovation + Outputs (RIIO) regulatory framework implemented from around 2009 onwards. It is centred on the incentives given to the players intervening offshore. It assumes that the offshore generators are strongly innovative and strongly interested in the success of the design, building and operation of the offshore grids connecting their farms to the onshore grid. Therefore, offshore generators are allowed to lead the initial stage of the offshore grid development – that is, its design and building – if they want to. If they do not, they can externalize these early tasks to a third party (called an OFTO, offshore transmission owner). Regardless, when the offshore grid assets are built offshore, generators are asked to auction them off to an OFTO, selected via this auction. Therefore, offshore green generators in the UK are fully responsible for the practicalities and costs of their connection to the shore.[24]

The German framework is different, but it did change. Until 2013, the offshore green generator was free to settle in priority sea areas defined by the federal maritime agency (BSH) and the federal energy regulator (BNetzA). The coastal onshore TSO was obligated to connect any wind farm located in the sea. Starting in 2013, the German TSOs were collectively producing a ten-year offshore development plan (O-NEP), updated every year and submitted to the energy regulator. From 2017, the federal maritime agency and the federal energy regulator produce a jointly centralized sea parks and offshore grid 'Area Development Plan', which defines the generation sites, the capacity of offshore farms, the timing of the auctioning, the location of offshore grid converters and substations, and the connection cable routes. The green generators are still kept aside from this process, while they also do not pay for offshore grids, since they benefit from super-shallow connection charges. Both offshore and onshore grids costs are borne by the TSOs and socialized among all the electricity network users.

A comparative study, performed by the leading economic team at the federal research institute DIW in Germany, weighs up both approaches (Girard et al. 2019). The study finds the German regime 40 per cent more expensive than the British, after correction for connection lengths, technologies, environmental requirements and financing conditions, ending with a €10 surcharge per MWh.[25] The study does not believe that the 2017 new regime will put an end to this gap and values the total excess costs from 2013 to 2030 at more than €8 billion. The study designates the non-involvement of the offshore green generators into the design and building of the offshore grids, and the absence of any other open competitive process to substitute for that policy choice, as a strategic error in the German incentive framework.[26]

4.2.2   Acknowledging the loop between onshore grid owners' revenue streams and onshore active users' own incentives

The fact that in the offshore case, the amount of grid assets to be invested is not fully determined by technology and engineering, but substantially influenced (up to + 40 per cent) by the incentive regulatory framework being used, is not a particular exception that escapes the economic logic linking investors in green assets and investors in grid assets. It is also verified when linking the onshore grid revenue streams, as defined by the regulated grid tariffs, and the incentives given to individually active grid users (the individual 'prosumers') investing in their own set of individually owned assets.

When individual grid users face new technologies permitting small units of investments, allowing them to become self-producers ('prosumers') and operators of their own unit of storage ('prosumagers'), what they mostly look at is the change that their investments will trigger for their own individual electricity bill. It is exactly what Florence School of Regulation researcher, Tim Schittekatte, investigated with a new modelling approach, taking into account the fact that, while many grid users are not willing to invest on their own (they are 'passive' users), some actually will (they are 'active' users). And these active users take changes in their bill as a key parameter to make their own investment decisions (Schittekatte 2019).

First, let us assume that all grid costs are sunk, and that grid tariffs are only used to allocate these costs among grid users. The introduction of new technologies permitting individual grid users to invest in units of generation and storage as small as their own individual consumption needs, creates a reaction function to individual bill changes permitted within the currently applied grid tariff. This reaction function creates both equity and efficiency concerns – equity concerns because the sunk costs that active users bypass must be recovered from the remaining passive users; efficiency concerns because individual investors add new costs (at the level of the whole system) when leaving the grid billing because of 'low enough' unitarian costs of new individual investments (for their own generation and storage) with regard to the expected bill changes (be they volumetric or capacity based).[27]

Second, let us now assume – on the contrary – that demand can evolve, that grid use, and costs, can grow. What active prosumers invest can be used positively by the grid in a forward-looking tariff setting, as long as 'fairness' is not too big an issue for the designers of the grid tariffs. However, if tariff designers want to push fairness in protection of passive grid users, against the reduction of active grid users' contribution to total costs, the future-oriented efficiency is lost. There is no magic, simultaneously cost-reflecting tariff for all, future-oriented for the active, and fair for the passive.[28]

Third, let us now go more deeply into individual storage investments permitted by capacity-based and volumetric tariffs. According to Schittekatte (2019, p. 86):

> When grid costs are sunk, all network tariff design options will over-incentivise battery options at the expense of overall welfare. In contrast, when many future grid costs are to be made, the considered network tariff design options will mostly under-incentivise battery adoption, and potential welfare gains are missed out. Besides, the network tariff design, also time-varying energy prices do improve the business case of storage. However, some unwanted interactions between the network tariff design and time-varying energy prices are possible.

In our previous examination of offshore grids, the role allocated to the green generator in the incentive scheme for grid building influenced variations in the amount of assets invested in the offshore grid, in reaction to the given amount of green assets. In our current examination of onshore grids, the incentives sent by the onshore grid revenue stream framework to the prosumers, via changes in the electricity bill, influence variations in the amount of investments undertaken by these prosumers and change the total amount of assets put into the whole electricity system to deliver the same amount of energy consumption.[29]

4.2.3   Building an efficient loop between the business models for grid users and for grid companies

Knowing that business models for grid users and business models for grid companies interact, a normative question emerges: what would be an efficient loop to put in place between these two worlds? There are already two approaches to address that question: a conceptual vision, such as the RIIO framework introduced by the British regulator Ofgem in 2009; and a new techno-economic model, as described in the *Utility of the Future* report published by the MIT Energy Initiative in 2016.

As already seen with the offshore case, the new British regulatory framework – established in the 2010s – considers the incentive framework as key to the success of grid regulation. It is also the message conveyed by the conceptual RIIO formula 'Revenues = Incentives + Innovation + Outputs' (see Rious and Rossetto 2018 for more details).

Incentives target both capital expenditures and operational expenditures in an open 'menu of contracts' where companies reveal their own core choices (such as choosing to design and build the grid, or to externalize this, as in the offshore case). Outputs can be availability, energy losses or environmental impact and so on. Innovation is a bit fuzzier and covers alternative blueprints and candies for tests, pilots or beauty contests. Joskow added a stronger 'competitive transmission procurement model'.

The MIT Energy Initiative (2016) research, *Utility of the Future*, fits well in the RIIO conceptual world and is also centred on the rebuilding of 'incentives'. In that research, the distribution grid stands between many new business models of 'asset/revenues' and 'services/customers' and must stay neutral with regard to all of them, be they wind, solar, heat pump, storage, peer-to-peer, retail-to-wholesale and so on. The distribution utility of the future should not look at 'behind-the-meter' usages' own characteristics to discriminate among them, and must treat all injections and all withdrawals equally, as long as they are equal from the point of view of the grid. This 'equal treatment' then calls for finer granularity, both spatial and temporal, to obtain an efficient 'distribution nodal price system', taking each connection point to the distribution grid as a unit of calculation, and the smallest unit of time of distribution operation as a unit of time for settlement. Therefore, two simple principles must guide tariffs setting. The first applies to grid users: peak-coincident capacity charges – reflecting users' contribution to incremental costs incurred – and scarcity-coincident generating capacity charges. The second applies to grid owners: forward-looking multi-year revenue trajectories with profit-sharing mechanisms. Beyond this core of 'right incentives', this MIT Energy Initiative (2016) research is also open to the 'outputs' and the 'innovation' add-ons foreseen in the RIIO framework. However, the survey published three years later by MIT researchers (Burger et al. 2019a, 2019b) showed that the full implementation of this vision had not yet begun. The institutional and computational difficulties being identified caused some to doubt it, as also expressed in Chapters 8 and 16 of this handbook.

4.2.4   Slow-moving and fragmented decision-making

The need for a comprehensive reaction to the new business models to be introduced into the electricity sector has been acknowledged for several years. The New York Public Utility Commission's new conceptual framework for the transformation of distribution grids into open platforms dates back to April 2014, while the MIT Energy Initiative (2016) proposal in *Utility of the Future* is from December 2016. The European utility industry launched its own manifesto for 'distribution grids transformation into plat-forms' in 2019 (Colle et al. 2019). The Council of European Energy Regulators (CEER) programmed a three-year regulatory regime review led by 'digitalization and dynamic regulation' for 2019–21 (CEER 2019). However, in practical terms, the move is slow. The biggest contribution we know of is from Ofgem, which did react to offshore grids with two implementable regimes in 2009 and 2014.

The move is slow because many conditions must be met to make it work. On the grid side, the MIT Energy Initiative (2016) report and subsequent papers made clear that utilities must have accurate data on each grid user and on the grid itself, an extensive smart grid/smart metering infrastructure with two-way ICT, a significant accumulated database, and the right and comprehensive engineering model of the distribution grids with responsive algorithms, plus a favourable property rights framework and incentive alignment (Burger et al. 2019a, 2019b). This will result in a proper new revolution, as big as the past building of open wholesale markets 30 years ago. Will it ever happen?[30]

On the grid users' side, the Nordic Council of Ministers' (2017) report also made it clear that calculating 'right' prices is not enough. Grid users must be able to react to pricing: with real-time access to the prices, devices able to be actioned by price signals, and a certified settlement and billing process duly acknowledging the activation. Researchers at Comillas University in Madrid have even shown that sending waves of price signals to active individual users does not guarantee that these grid users will be able to coordinate their reactions to the signals and prevent the creation of other grid problems. Therefore, there are new 'coordination tools' to be defined and tested to make that new 'distribution platforms plus active prosumers' revolution coherently work, both in short-term and long-term horizons (Abdelmotteleb et al. 2019).

Even forgetting the fairness issue, which complicates the agenda for many regulators who are hyper-sensitive to public opinion (Burger et al. 2019c), the building of a new framework is made difficult by the need for grid users to have several things changed in their proper realm (that is, behind the meter). Active grid users tend to be wealthier and prone to change their liability for grid charges by investing money into it. Passive grid users include many poor and low-income people who just live their lives with their current revenues and cannot invest to avoid future charges. Many grid users also do not own their homes and depend on their landlords to take 'activation investment' decisions. If numerous grid users cannot, or do not want to, invest in the activation of their consumption and stay highly inflexible to refined price signals, any shift to a strongly incentivizing price system would act mainly as a highly redistributive fixed tax increase (Fredriksson and Zachmann 2018).

Nevertheless, even when restricting the decision-making area to the professionals, fragmentation is still an obvious key factor when it comes to the implementation of a reform change where no key player can act alone in the common interest of the whole system, corresponding to the normative interests of the society as a whole.[31]

Activating flexibility is identified by many regulators and regulated companies as a core tool to build less grid assets, and to end the costly 'fit and forget' doctrine of grid assets investments. But research at the Florence School of Regulation shows that even the 'simple' implementation of new trade schemes to incentivize flexibility delivery is deeply dependent on who takes part in the decision process, be they a really independent plat-form allying with six different distribution grids; or two competing established wholesale exchanges allying either with a TSO and a DSO or only with DSOs; or four leading DSOs grouping with their national TSO in a single coordination mechanism. All these different initiatives have defined different product standards, different links with the sequence of wholesale markets, and different rules for reservation payments (Schittekatte and Meeus 2020). Even within each of the two core groups of players (the TSOs and the DSOs) one finds different needs, different approaches, different skills and different innovation profiles.

5.   CONCLUSION

The electricity sector is facing, again, a wave of radical changes, as big or potentially bigger than the invention of open markets in the 1990s. Some of these changes can be seen from a business model angle, as any market-based industry always needs adequate frameworks to feed investments, to choose technology and product characteristics, and to steer operation.

At least two kinds of business model are at work in this new revolution. The first, favoured by investors in green electricity, is to secure ex ante high fixed costs by generating assets with long-term guaranteed revenue streams. Be they professional investors or individual prosumers, identifying and securing ex ante long-term revenue streams is key to taking such an irreversible investment decision, and to obtain banking or financial investors' support. The still small, but fast-growing segment of purely private contracting, via corporate PPAs, exhibits the same logic of ex ante long-term revenue guarantee. The second model, rooted in an era of 'asset-light' and digitalization, links particularly defined product characteristics to specially targeted customers. Innovators push the novelties they defined, hoping that customers will react and welcome them. Many areas at the outset of the 2020s are opened or opening soon, such as aggregators (linking retail units to wholesale trade); digital platforms (bypassing intermediaries and permitting direct trade); other peer-to-peer exchange chains (as with blockchains); and fleets of consumption units (self-managed as mini-grids or off-grid). Many of these initiatives are still being piloted or tested in regulatory sandboxes. Their business scalability and sustainability in most cases has still, as of early 2020, to be demonstrated.

Between these two models, the grid companies – both transmission and distribution – will have to find their way. For most of them, it will not be today. In France, for example, one finds less than 50 000 prosumers and no giant offshore wind park at the beginning of the 2020s. However, over time, appropriate new business models for the grids will be invented or tested. It cannot make sense to remunerate TSOs with a guaranteed return on the amount of steel and concrete put into their balance sheets for much longer, or to back DSOs for the 'fit-and-forget' expansion of their network capacity. Furthermore, the network owners and the network users must be brought into interactive loops of key performance indicators, incentives, coordination and commitments, with regard to the way electricity is injected, withdrawn or stored, and the grids planned and used, right up to changing the way all the players (including all grid users, all electricity consumers) invest in their own portfolio of assets, be they connected or off-grid. New incentive regulation and coordination tools must be invented and inserted into a multi-level operation and investment framework, to allow smarter interactions between the grid users and the grid owners, via their new digital interface, or via intermediaries, at all levels – transmission, distribution, behind the meter and off-grid.

NOTES

* I thank Paul Joskow and Michael Pollitt for their review and advice. I thank Nicolò Rossetto, Piero dos Reis and Golnoush Soroush, from Florence School of Regulation, for their assistance. They helped me with collecting the literature, reviewing it, finding facts and figures on wind and solar and a careful reading of the chapter. I am, of course, the only one responsible for interpretation and errors.
1. Pérez-Arriaga et al. show in Chapter 20 of this handbook the role of renewables and digital technologies in the electrification of countries whose electricity industry has not yet been restructured.
2. To my knowledge, CCGT presents the opposite characteristic – with a business model that can quite easily enter into the operation of an open wholesale market because it can link well with its short-run marginal pricing mechanism.
3. Another key aspect, as underlined by Joskow (2019a), is that increased renewable penetration can raise the frequency of scarcity pricing or the need for capacity payments. Hence, the system value of renewables should not just reflect short-run energy prices but rather a long-run equilibrium that satisfies a balanced budget constraint.
4. Joskow (2011) explains why the levelized cost of electricity cannot be taken as an appropriate metric to compare technologies generating at different times, with different dispatching and flexibility capabilities.
5. In the summer of 2020, a Portuguese solar auction obtained 600 megawatts (MW) of utility-scale solar at €10 per MWh.
6. This value ignores the costs of managing intermittency (Lazard 2018).
7. Bloomberg NEF (BNEF) weights them at 13.4 gigawatts (GW) in 2018 (up from 6.1 GW in 2017) – ending with a cumulated total of more than 35 GW worldwide (BNEF 2019), compared with almost 1200 GW of total non-hydro RES installed capacity accounted for by the International Renewable Energy Agency (IRENA 2019) for the same year.
8. Accounting in 2018 for about 22 per cent of all new wind and solar procurement contracts in the US (Wood Mackenzie 2019b).
9. The average size of new projects in the US in 2017–18 was 85 MW, hence in the hundred million dollar range (Federal Energy Regulatory Commission [FERC] 2018).
10. However, while bigger scale and higher average efficiency for offshore wind means that the minimum output may be higher on average than onshore, it does not mean that offshore wind has less variance than onshore.
11. The latest trend in European renewables policy, after the choice in 2020 of an ambitious European common target of a roughly 55 per cent reduction of greenhouse gas (GHG) emissions for 2030, and a 'net zero' target for 2050, is to look for 60 GW of offshore wind at horizon 2030 and 250–450 GW in 2050.
12. European oil and gas companies have entered this segment with high ambitions. French Total, British BP and Shell and Nordic Equinor are each building company portfolios of renewable generation (solar and wind) of 15–25 GW.
13. Before the Portuguese entered a deep 'green' alliance with the French utility ENGIE in 2019.
14. See European Commission (2020).
15. IEA (2019) foresees 8300 terawatt-hours (TWh) of wind and 7200 TWh of solar in the year 2040, exceeding hydropower (6950 TWh).
16. Logically, they must at some point, as per the basic economics of auctions.
17. The seasonality of the solar PV capacity factor works in favour of its use for air conditioning – the US EIA finds that summer median capacity is roughly double that of the winter median.
18. An active demand side increases in importance with a larger penetration of wind and solar to control system costs and meet reliability standards. See Chapter 8 on Texas in this handbook.
19. See MIT Energy Initiative (2016) and its follow-up papers: Burger et al. (2019a and 2019b).
20. See Peréz-Arriaga (2013) for a worldwide overview and Meeus and Glachant (2018) for an EU update.
21. See Chapter 13 by Sioshansi and Chapter 8 on Texas by Baldick et al. in in this handbook.
22. Electricity reform in Argentina provided another innovative approach to transmission expansion, based on votes by transmission users and then put out to competitive tender. See Littlechild and Sherk (2008).
23. In the US, the federal competition authority (Department of Justice) has a tradition of not intervening in the electricity sector to ensure implementation of its anti-trust policy, leaving this to the federal energy

regulator (FERC). In the EU, it is the opposite: the federal competition authority (DG Competition) has a tradition of regularly intervening in the electricity sector to implement its anti-trust policy or to accelerate the implementation of EU energy and climate policy.

24. An overview of Britain's independent energy regulator Ofgem's incentive regulation for old and new business cases is given in Meeus and Glachant (2018) – in particular, in Chapters 1, 5 and 6.
25. The gross difference was over 100 per cent, with €19 more in Germany than the €16/MWh in the UK.
26. This result comes very close to Joskow's (2019b) core argument: not using an incentive regulation framework to design or build new transmission assets in a market-based power system is rationally a mistake.
27. Schittekatte (2019), Chapter 2. This case is similar to the German or the Californian cases.
28. Schittekatte (2019), Chapter 3. This case is more similar to the Australian case.
29. This is what Schmalensee in Chapter 2 of this handbook and Joskow (2019a, 2019b) list as inefficiencies brought about by the current green push in the US, particularly in California.
30. Again, see Chapter 8 in this handbook.
31. See Glachant (2018) or Glachant (2021) for a review of the typical EU regulatory gaps and roadblocks. See also Meeus and Hadush (2018) and Burger et al. (2019a, 2019b) for TSO–DSO coordination issues.

REFERENCES

Abdelmotteleb, I., T. Gómez and J. P. C. Ávila (2019), 'New distribution network charges for new integrated network services', in F. Sioshansi (ed.), *Consumer, Prosumer, Prosumager: How Service Innovations Will Disrupt the Utility Business Model*, London: Elsevier/Academic Press, pp. 189–208.

Bloomberg NEF (BNEF) (2018), '2H 2017 Wind Turbine Price Index', 9 May, accessed 13 July 2021 at https://about.bnef.com/blog/2h-2017-wind-turbine-price-index/.

Bloomberg NEF (BNEF) (2019), 'Corporate clean energy buying surged to new record in 2018', 28 January, accessed 13 July 2021 at https://about.bnef.com/blog/corporate-clean-energy-buying-surged-new-record-2018/.

Bolinger, M. and J. Seel (2018), *Utility-Scale Solar: Empirical Trends in Project Technology, Cost, Performance, and PPA Pricing in the United States – 2018 Edition*, Lawrence Berkeley National Laboratory, Electricity Markets and Policy Group, September, accessed 13 July 2021 at https://eta-publications.lbl.gov/sites/default/files/lbnl_utility_scale_solar_2018_edition_report.pdf.

Burger, C., A. Froggatt, C. Mitchell and J. Weinmann (2020), *Decentralised Energy: A Global Game Changer*, London: Ubiquity Press.

Burger, S. P., J. D. Jenkins, C. Battle and I. Pérez-Arriaga (2019a), 'Restructuring revisited part 1: competition in electricity distribution systems', *The Energy Journal*, **40** (3), 31–54.

Burger, S. P., J. D. Jenkins, C. Battle and I. J. Pérez-Arriaga (2019b), 'Restructuring revisited part 2: coordination in electricity distribution systems', *The Energy Journal*, **40** (3), 55–76.

Burger, S., I. Schneider, A. Botterud and I. Pérez-Arriaga (2019c), 'Fair, equitable, and efficient tariffs in the presence of DERs', in F. Sioshansi (ed.), *Consumers, Prosumers, Prosumagers: How Service Innovations Will Disrupt the Utility Business Model*, London: Elsevier/Academic Press, pp. 155–88.

Choudary, S. P. (2015), *Platform Scale: How an Emerging Business Model Helps Startups Build Large Empires with Minimum Investment*, Platform Thinking Labs.

Colle, S., P. Micallef, A. Legg and A. Horstead (2019), 'Where does change start if the future is already decided? DSOs must keep pace with the new ways to generate, distribute and consume energy and become catalysts of change', *EY.com*, January, accessed 13 July 2021 at https://www.ey.com/en_gl/power-utilities/where-does-change-start-if-the-future-is-already-decided.

Council of European Energy Regulators (CEER) (2019), *Annual Report 2018*, Brussels: CEER.

European Commission (2020), *Communication from the Commission to the European Parliament, the Council, the European Economic and Social Committee and the Committee of the Regions: An EU Strategy to Harness the Potential of Offshore Renewable Energy for a Climate Neutral Future*, COM(2020) 741 final, 19 November, accessed 13 July 2021 at https://ec.europa.eu/energy/sites/ener/files/offshore_renewable_energy_strategy.pdf.

European Network of Transmission System Operators for Electricity (ENTSO-E) (2019), *Power Facts Europe 2019*, January, accessed 13 July 2021 at https://docstore.entsoe.eu/Documents/Publications/ENTSO-E%20general%20publications/ENTSO-E_PowerFacts_2019.pdf.

Federal Energy Regulatory Commission (FERC) (2018), *Energy Infrastructure Update for July 2018*.

Fredriksson, G. and G. Zachmann (2018), 'The distributional effects of climate policies', in S. Nies (ed.), *The European Energy Transition: Actors, Factors, Sectors*, Deventer, the Netherlands: Clayes & Casteels, pp. 75–91.

Girard, Y., C. Kemfert, F. Neumann and J. Stoll (2019), *Marktdesign für eine effiziente Netzanbindung von Offshore-Windenergie: Politikberatung kompakt*, *136*, DIW Berlin, accessed 13 July 2021 at https://www.diw. de/documents/publikationen/73/diw_01.c.618644.de/diwkompakt_2019-136.pdf.

Glachant, J.-M. (2018), 'TSO-TSO seams issues', in L. Meeus and J.-M. Glachant (eds), *Electricity Network Regulation in the EU: The Challenges Ahead for Transmission and Distribution*, Cheltenham, UK and Northampton, MA, USA: Edward Elgar Publishing, pp. 57–76.

Glachant, J.-M. (2019), 'Foreword', in F. Sioshansi (ed.), *Consumer, Prosumer, Prosumager: How Service Innovations Will Disrupt the Utility Business Model*, London: Elsevier/Academic Press, pp. xxvii–xxxiv.

Glachant, J.-M. (2021), 'Building a single market with no single regulator: the case of the European electricity market', in E. Brousseau, J.-M. Glachant and J. Sgard (eds), *The Oxford Handbook of Institutions of International Economic Governance and Market Regulation*, Oxford: Oxford University Press.

Glachant J.-M., H. Khalfallah and Y. Perez et al. (2012), 'Implementing incentive regulation and regulatory alignment with resource bounded regulators', *RSCAS Working Paper 2012/31*, EUI.

Haskel, J. and S. Westlake (2018), *Capitalism Without Capital*, Princeton, NJ: Princeton University Press.

International Energy Agency (IEA) (2018), *World Energy Outlook 2018*, Paris: IEA.

International Energy Agency (IEA) (2019), *World Energy Outlook 2019*, Paris: IEA.

International Renewable Energy Agency (IRENA) (2019), *Renewable Capacity Statistics 2018*, Abu Dhabi: IRENA.

Joskow, P. L. (2011), 'Comparing the costs of intermittent and dispatchable electricity generating technologies', *American Economic Review*, **101** (3), 238–41.

Joskow, P. L. (2014), 'Incentive regulation and its application to electricity networks', *Review of Network Economics*, **7** (4), 547–60.

Joskow, P. L. (2019a), 'Challenges for wholesale electricity markets with intermittent renewable generation at scale: the US experience', *MIT-CEEPR Working Paper 2019-001*, January.

Joskow, P. L. (2019b), 'Competition for electric transmission projects in the US: FERC Order 1000', *MIT-CEEPR Working Paper 2019-004*, March.

Lazard (2018), *Lazard's Levelized Cost of Energy Analysis – Version 12.0*, November.

Littlechild, S. and C. Sherk (2008), 'Transmission expansion in Argentina: a review of performance', *Energy Economics*, **30** (4), 1462–90.

Meeus, L. and J.-M. Glachant (2018), *Electricity Network Regulation in the EU: The Challenges Ahead for Transmission and Distribution*, Cheltenham, UK and Northampton, MA, USA: Edward Elgar Publishing.

Meeus, L. and S. Y. Hadush (2018), 'DSO–TSO seams issues', in L. Meeus and J.-M. Glachant (eds), *Electricity Network Regulation in the EU: The Challenges Ahead for Transmission and Distribution*, Cheltenham, UK and Northampton, MA, USA: Edward Elgar Publishing, pp. 77–102.

Meeus, L. and T. Schittekatte (2018), 'New grey areas at the frontiers of European power grids', in L. Meeus and J.-M. Glachant (eds), *Electricity Network Regulation in the EU: The Challenges Ahead for Transmission and Distribution*, Cheltenham, UK and Northampton, MA, USA: Edward Elgar Publishing, pp. 130–54.

MIT Energy Initiative (2016), *Utility of the Future*, Cambridge, MA: MIT.

Monitoring Analytics (2019), *PJM State of the Market – 2018*, PJM, March, accessed 13 July 2021 at https://www.monitoringanalytics.com/reports/PJM_State_of_the_Market/2018.shtml.

Nordic Council of Ministers (2017), *Flexible Demand for Electricity & Power: Barriers & Opportunities*, Copenhagen: Nordic Council of Ministers, Nordic Energy Research.

Osterwalder, A., Y. Pigneur and T. Clark (2010), *Business Model Generation: A Handbook for Visionaries, Game Changers, and Challengers*, Hoboken, NJ: John Wiley & Sons.

Pérez-Arriaga, I. (ed.) (2013), *Regulation of the Power Sector*, London: Springer.

Rious, V. and N. Rossetto (2018), 'The British reference model', in L. Meeus and J.-M. Glachant (eds), *Electricity Network Regulation in the EU: The Challenges Ahead for Transmission and Distribution*, Cheltenham, UK and Northampton, MA, USA: Edward Elgar Publishing, pp. 3–27.

Schittekatte, T. (2019), 'Distribution network tariff design and active consumers: a regulatory impact analysis', PhD thesis, Paris Saclay, accessed 13 July 2021 at http://www.theses.fr/2019SACLS054.

Schittekatte, T. and L. Meeus (2020), 'Flexibility markets: Q&A with project pioneers', *Utilities Policy*, **63**, Article 101017.

Sioshansi, F. P. (ed.) (2017), *Innovation and Disruption at the Grid's Edge: How Distributed Energy Resources Are Disrupting the Utility Business Model*, London: Elsevier/Academic Press.

Sioshansi, F. P. (ed.) (2019), *Consumer, Prosumer, Prosumager: How Service Innovations Will Disrupt the Utility Business Model*, London: Elsevier/Academic Press.

US Energy Information Administration (EIA) (2019), 'Most U.S. utility-scale solar photovoltaic power plants are 5 megawatts or smaller', *Today in Energy*, 7 February, accessed 13 July 2021 at https://www.eia.gov/today inenergy/detail.php?id=38272.

Wood Mackenzie (2019a), '10 trends shaping the global solar market in 2019', 21 January, accessed 13 July 2021 at https://www.woodmac.com/news/editorial/10-trends-shaping-the-global-solar-market-in-2019/.

Wood Mackenzie (2019b), 'US wind and solar markets: technology giants top list in bumper year for corporate procurement', 1 February, accessed 13 July 2021 at https://www.woodmac.com/news/editorial/us-renewables-technology-giants-top-of-the-list-in-a-bumper-year-for-corporate-procurement/.

18. Electrifying transport: issues and opportunities
Bentley C. Clinton, Christopher R. Knittel
and Konstantinos Metaxoglou

1. INTRODUCTION

The stock of electric vehicles (EVs) worldwide increased by 65 per cent between 2017 and 2018 to approximately 5 million (International Energy Agency [IEA] 2019b). While this is a small percentage of the global stock of more than 1 billion passenger vehicles, increasing adoption rates and model availability signal the potential for EVs to become a significant component of future transport markets. An expanding EV fleet represents a potentially large transition in energy demand from the established liquid transport fuel supply network to the electricity system. The IEA estimates this transition could reduce oil demand by 2.5 to 4.3 million barrels per day and increase electricity demand by 640 to 1110 terawatt-hours (TWh) (IEA 2019a).

This transition is motivated in part by increasing pressure for policy makers to deeply decarbonize both the electricity and transport sectors – a response to warnings from atmospheric scientists that 45 per cent reductions in 2010 carbon dioxide (CO_2) levels by 2030 and net-zero carbon emissions by 2050 are necessary to maintain global average temperature increases below 1.5°C (Intergovernmental Panel on Climate Change [IPCC] 2018). In this chapter, we examine the challenges and implications of decarbonizing the transport sector.

Decarbonizing transport is generally regarded as a more difficult undertaking than decarbonizing the electricity sector. Decarbonization of the electricity sector can be achieved via a deployment of a variety of technologies. These technologies represent a range of approaches, including nuclear fission and renewables such as wind turbines and solar photovoltaics. Advances in demand response and energy storage are important decarbonization tools in the electric power sector as well. Fewer options are available for transport. In most of our discussion in this chapter, we will focus on understanding the role electrification will play in one segment of global transport: the light-duty vehicle (LDV) sector. This sector is typically defined to include passenger automobiles and light trucks. Two leading candidates exist for a decarbonized LDV fleet: battery electric vehicles (BEVs) and hydrogen fuel cell electric vehicles (FCEVs). Each of these technologies has its own set of advantages and disadvantages. Our focus is on BEVs, as they are seen by many to have a leg up on FCEVs because of recent progress in lithium-ion battery technology. Although FCEVs may affect the demand for electricity (for example, through the production of hydrogen for fuel cells), BEVs also provide the most direct – and potentially substantial – demand for electricity in the coming decades.

EVs have several advantages over traditional internal combustion engine vehicles (ICEVs).[1] The biggest advantage is that, provided the electric grid is decarbonized, EVs can serve to decarbonize the LDV sector. Other advantages exist, however. Electric motors are highly efficient. Synchronous motors with permanent magnets, such as those used by Nissan, BMW and Chevrolet EVs, have peak efficiencies in excess of 95 per cent (Doppelbauer and Winzer 2017).[2] In contrast, internal combustion engines (ICEs) average only 20 per cent efficiency and have a peak efficiency of roughly 40 per cent (Roberts, Brooks and Shipway 2014). Electric motors also have higher torque through-out their power cycle. This increases the utility of driving EVs through performance and towing ability. The use of electric motors and the lack of a traditional gasoline engine in BEVs also means these vehicles do not require the costly maintenance that accompanies high-temperature combustion and cylinder friction (for example, BEVs avoid engine lubrication, fuel system wear and the associated servicing). In many cases, battery place-ment in EVs lowers the centre of gravity of vehicles, directly improving handling characteristics.

EVs have several drawbacks, as well. Despite large reductions in the cost of batteries in recent years, EVs remain more expensive than ICEVs. Because of the cost, energy density and added weight of batteries compared to liquid fuel systems, EVs also have more limited range compared to ICEVs. These range limits increase the frequency of recharging and may create 'range anxiety' among drivers. While financial incentives and infrastructure build-outs exist in part to allay these concerns, range anxiety, battery cost and infrastructure are primary concerns of prospective BEV buyers (Egbue and Long 2012).

In what follows, we expand on these advantages and disadvantages and explore the opportunities and challenges of the LDV fleet electrification, highlighting the major impediments to large-scale EV adoption and discussing technological trends and policy interventions aimed at overcoming these barriers. We first discuss the current state of the LDV sector, taking stock of the number of vehicles worldwide and describing the broader LDV ecosystem. We pay particular attention to fuel markets and refuelling infrastruc-ture. Having discussed the system we seek to decarbonize, we turn to EVs. We compare vehicle cost factors and investigate the break-even cost relationship between oil and battery prices. We include a discussion of policy interventions and their effectiveness. We then quantify the energy demand effects for a range of LDV electrification scenarios before turning to the emissions and fuel taxation implications of this transition. We con-clude with some thoughts on electrification in other transport sector contexts – heavy-duty freight transport – and the role EVs may have in ride sharing and autonomous vehicle networks.

2.   THE EXISTING LIGHT-DUTY VEHICLE ECOSYSTEM

2.1   Vehicles on the Road

As of 2015, there were roughly 950 million passenger cars in use worldwide. There are three striking observations regarding the growth and spatial distribution of LDVs (Figure 18.1). First, the number of vehicles in use increased by 45 per cent between 2005 and 2015. This increase occurred despite the Great Recession in the late 2000s. The negative effects of the most recent financial crisis were dwarfed by long-run global LDV growth trends. Second, the stock of passenger cars is concentrated in a few regions. The

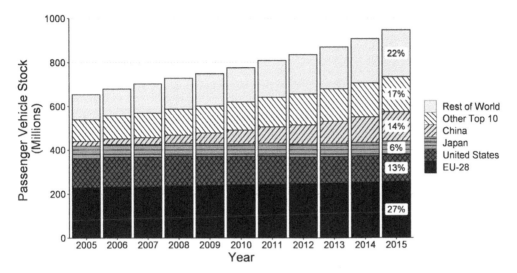

Source: The figure is constructed using data from the International Organization of Motor Vehicle Manufacturers (OICA) Vehicles in Use database, accessed November 2019 at http://www.oica.net/category/vehicles-in-use/.

Figure 18.1   Global count of passenger cars in use

European Union (EU), US, Japan and China represent more than half the total vehicle stock worldwide. Third, while other regions have seen some modest growth in the vehicle market, the demand for passenger cars in China is the main driver behind the market growth during this time. Most of this global vehicle stock is powered by ICEs, burning either gasoline or diesel to create the mechanical power to move the vehicle and its contents (ExxonMobil 2019). The efficiency with which these vehicles convert fuel inputs to kinetic output dictates total energy use in the sector.

The efficiency of ICEVs has come a long way since the days of Karl Benz and Henry Ford. Knittel (2011) finds that the efficiency of the modern-day car increases by roughly 2.4 per cent per year. This is a combination of efficiency improvements in engine and in other parts of the drivetrain. The efficiency of modern-day gasoline engines is roughly 30–35 per cent (Edwards et al. 2011). That is, modern-day gasoline engines, operating at ideal conditions, convert 30–35 per cent of the British thermal units (BTUs) they consume into work. The rest of the BTUs escape as heat. In practice, the average efficiency of ICEVs, accounting for all other energy losses, is closer to 20 per cent (US Department of Energy [US DOE] 2019). Although diesel engines are roughly 20 per cent more efficient than gasoline engines, their average efficiency is approximately 40 per cent (Edwards et al. 2011, Universal Technical Institute [UTI] 2019).

Vehicle efficiency is evaluated in terms of miles per gallon (MPG, in the US) or litres per kilometre (in most other countries). Figure 18.2 shows fuel efficiency trends and targets as calculated in Yang and Bandivadekar (2017). The EU and Japan are leaders in fuel efficiency, while North America lags behind. Overall, LDV efficiency is gradually increasing. Many regions have exhibited substantial fuel efficiency improvements since 2005 regardless of their initial efficiency level. The EU and US, for example, have seen

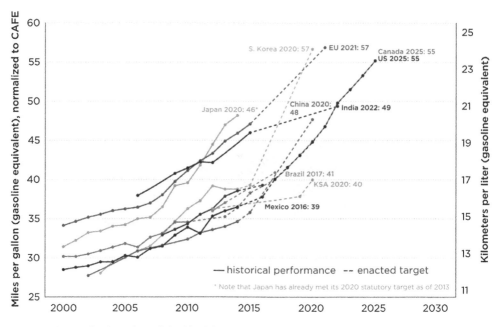

Notes: KSA = Kingdom of Saudi Arabia; CAFE = Corporate Average Fuel Economy (US vehicle efficiency standard). For additional information on normalizing fuel efficiency, please see Kühlwein, German and Bandivadekar (2014).

Source: Reproduced from Yang and Bandivadekar (2017), Figure 4.

Figure 18.2   Historical fleet fuel efficiency and current standards for passenger cars (MPG normalized to United States test cycles)

improvements of approximately 20–30 per cent. To maintain this course and meet increasing regulatory stringency, automakers must continue to find and implement fuel-saving technologies in their LDV model offerings.

These efficiency measures are important factors in the discussion of vehicle electrification. Decarbonization is a key motivator for policies that promote the electrification of transport, and vehicle fuel efficiency plays a central role in determining the decarbonization benefits of an electrified vehicle fleet. In addition to fuel economy, the climate change benefits of electrification depend on vehicle usage patterns and the CO_2 emissions associated with the electricity grid. Holding fixed grid emissions intensity and total vehicle miles travelled, the climate change benefits of electrification will be largest in the Americas. As we show later in this chapter, many other regions also stand to benefit from a transition to EVs.

2.2   Fuel Price Levels and Trends

Behind depreciation costs, refuelling makes up a significant portion of total vehicle ownership costs (Palmer et al. 2018). For mainstream ICEVs, the principal driver of refuelling costs is the price of fuel. Globally, most ICEVs are gasoline and diesel powered. Market penetrations of diesel-fuelled ICEVs vary greatly by country. For example, diesel vehicles represented only 1 per cent of the passenger car fleet in the United States in 2015, compared to 52 per cent in the EU-28 states (Yang and Bandivadekar 2017). While there are some signs that this level is set to decline, including changing diesel taxation policy and proposals to ban diesel vehicles from urban areas in some European countries, the level of existing diesel vehicle stock suggests that drivers may still consider a diesel option when selecting new car purchases (Tietge 2018).

Figure 18.3 shows real gasoline prices ($/litre) at the pump for various countries between 1998 and 2016. In panel (a), we plot prices in Canada, Australia and in Asia. In panel (b), we plot US prices along with prices in Europe. The price spread between diesel and gasoline is reported in panels (c) and (d). Gasoline prices in Asia and Europe are consistently higher than prices in other regions. The majority of spatial heterogeneity in prices can be attributed to spatial variation in fuel tax rates. For example, tax levels in Spain are the lowest within the group of EU countries shown, but higher than those in the US and Canada (Organisation for Economic Co-operation and Development [OECD] 2018, Wappelhorst, Mock and Yang 2018). Moreover, price spreads between gasoline and diesel vary widely by country. Prices in the US consistently favour gasoline as the less expensive fuel option, while the opposite is true for many European countries in the figure. In the EU countries in particular, this is likely due to lower fuel tax rates on diesel than gasoline (OECD 2019). Finally, with respect to trends, gasoline prices in European countries tend to follow similar price patterns, while trends for other areas vary considerably. With the exception of Korea and India – where price increases occurred prior to 2006 – global gasoline prices increase prior to 2012 before declining through 2016. The trends for both gasoline and diesel generally follow global crude oil price patterns.[3]

As vehicle electrification expands, electricity price trends are expected to affect fuel prices in the transport sector. Figure 18.4 shows a gradual increase in electricity prices over the past decade for European countries and steady prices in the US, Korea and Canada. To facilitate a uniform comparison across fuels, Figure 18.5 shows travel-distance-adjusted prices for a number of countries in 2016.[4] EVs are the least expensive option in all countries, followed by diesel. As we note later in this chapter, diesel vehicles and EVs are both more fuel efficient than gasoline-powered ICEVs. The price discrepancies and efficiency levels combined produce the striking heterogeneity across fuel types. Assessed strictly on a marginal fuel cost basis, EVs hold clear advantages over existing ICEV technologies.

2.3   Vehicle Miles Travelled

Where fuel prices determine the marginal cost of LDV energy consumption, the quantity of energy consumed is determined primarily by LDV use. One key measure of LDV use is the number of vehicle miles travelled (VMTs). While availability of VMT information varies by country, Figure 18.6a clearly shows the stark contrast between VMT levels in the US compared to other regions. More relevant to consideration of future trends for energy use in the transport sector are global trends in vehicle use. Figure 18.6b shows a modest increase in VMT levels for most OECD countries, with some large markets, notably Japan, seeing a VMT decrease in recent years. These growth patterns are driven in part by macroeconomic factors, regional transport network capacities and evolving

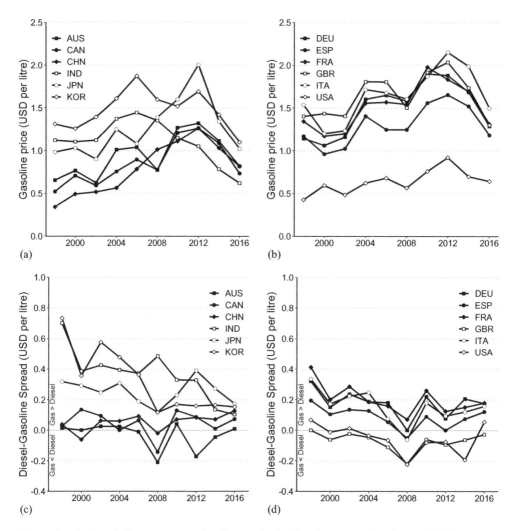

Notes: Panels (a) and (b) report pump prices for gasoline in $/litre by country. Panels (c) and (d) display the spread between pump prices of retail gasoline and diesel (negative spreads denote that gasoline is less expensive than diesel). The prices are expressed in real 2010 dollars, adjusted based on the Consumer Price Index.

Source: Price levels and spreads are reported biennially and are based on data from the World Bank World Development Indicators, accessed November 2019 at https://datacatalog.worldbank.org/dataset/world-development-indicators.

Figure 18.3 *Transportation fuel price trends*

consumer mobility needs. In the US, for example, Leard, Linn and Munnings (2019) attribute a portion of VMT growth to changes in household-level socioeconomic factors. Since the Great Recession, growth in vehicle travel has remained relatively flat, and is predicted to remain at a rate of approximately 1 per cent annually (US Department of Transportation [US DOT] 2019).

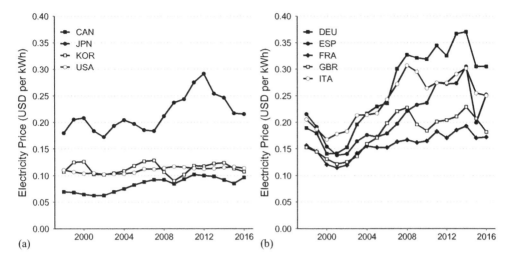

Notes: We report tax-inclusive household electricity price in US dollars ($) per kilowatt-hour (kWh). The prices are expressed in real terms, adjusted based on the Consumer Price Index (2010 base year).

Sources: Electricity prices from 'End-use prices: economic indicators (Edition 2018)', IEA Energy Prices and Taxes Statistics (database), accessed November 2019 at https://doi.org/10.1787/d087d8da-en.

Figure 18.4   Household electricity prices

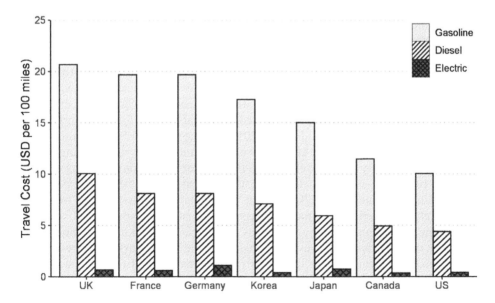

Notes: Travel cost based on standardized fuel efficiency levels across countries: gasoline (26.7 MPG), diesel (56.0 MPG) and electric (0.3 kWh/mile). Fuel prices differ by country and are based on 2016 levels.

Sources: See sources for Figure 18.3 (gasoline and diesel) and Figure 18.4 (electricity).

Figure 18.5   Normalized travel cost comparison

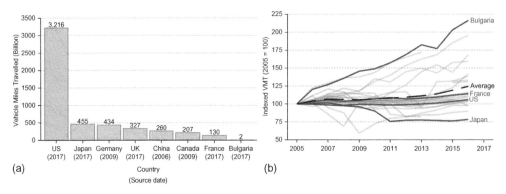

Note: Panel (a) shows VMT levels for selected countries. Panel (b) shows VMT trends for OECD countries.

Source: The OECD data are from the 'Total Road Motor Vehicle Traffic' database, accessed 19 April 2020 at https://stats.oecd.org/.

Figure 18.6   Trends in vehicle miles travelled for OECD countries

The steady VMT levels observed in the US are present in other markets as well. Although some predict an end to slow and steady VMT growth rates (IHS Markit 2017), future growth trends are uncertain and depend on a multitude of factors. Crucially, as global vehicle use trends evolve and national economies grow, annual, individual travel distances may approach saturation levels (Ecola et al. 2014). The current trends in VMTs and predictions related to these potential upper bounds for individual mobility illustrate the challenges of employing altered vehicle use behaviour as a lever for reducing emissions from the transport sector.[5]

Another important consideration regarding LDV use – one that is unique to the transition to EVs – is the presence of consumer 'range anxiety', the concern about insufficient electrical energy stored for EV trips. Several studies on consumer perceptions of EVs cite range anxiety as a barrier to adoption or a concern that is more prevalent in EVs than ICEVs (Daziano 2013, Franke and Krems 2013, Franke et al. 2012). Data from the US DOE (2018) show average daily VMT ranges of 30–50 miles. Analysis of driving patterns in the US and Germany indicates that more than 90 per cent of daily driving distances are within 100 miles – a range less than the capacity limits of most existing EV models (Gnann, Plötz and Kley 2012). Hence, for the majority of trips, VMT limitations are more likely perceived than a product of technical constraints. Nonetheless, the failure to address the perception of range anxiety may hinder wider adoption of EV models. One reason these range anxiety concerns are *de minimis* in the ICEV market is the wide availability of refuelling locations. We turn to this component of the LDV ecosystem in the next section.

2.4   Refuelling Stations

ICEV refuelling relies on a wide network of supply infrastructure that covers fuel refining, blending and distribution. After fuel blendstocks and additives are combined, trucks deliver liquid motor fuels to fuelling stations that store the finished fuel in underground tanks until it is pumped into vehicles. Although gasoline and diesel have an advantage of being relatively energy dense, battery technology is improving and narrowing this gap (Vijayagopal et al. 2016). Near-term favourability of liquid fuels also stems from the fact that the infrastructure for their distribution and storage in the transport sector is more mature than that of electricity. In contrast, while EV energy distribution is similarly well-developed, as it relies on the existing electric grid, the final retail stage of EV fuelling is less developed.

Table 18.1 demonstrates the heterogeneity of public EV charging infrastructure relative to a number of market metrics across countries. For example, the ratio of EVs to public EV charge locations is between five (Germany and Korea) and 16 (US). To put the relative maturity of liquid transport fuel retailing and electric charging into context, we also include a calculation of EV chargers to gasoline stations. The emphasis that Norway and China place on EV deployment – multiple charge points for every gasoline station – stands out among the countries listed in this table.

Norway is a special case worth noting, and the density of charge points illustrates why. The 11 charge points per 100 km of road network is due in part to a 2015 push to install fast-charging stations every 50 km on main roads in the country (Lorentzen et al. 2017). While Norway's high level of EV adoption is a result of numerous factors that include incentives, high ICEV taxation rates and resident travel preferences, the robust charging infrastructure plays a role in supporting and sustaining the country's place as a leader in the EV space. The availability of charging infrastructure in Norway has not yet had a significant effect on total electricity demand in the country, and full electrification is likely to have a minimal impact on energy demand overall (IEA 2018b). At the distribution level, however, urban areas with high population density and popular, more remote travel destinations experienced some distribution disturbances (IEA 2018b, Klingenberg 2017).

While public EV charging availability lags behind that of ICEV refuelling in many areas, the number of EV charging locations is increasing. Table 18.2 shows the recent expansion of EV charging stations in several European countries, the US and China, highlighting non-trivial build-outs of EV charging infrastructure. Whether this trend of new installations will continue is likely to play a key role in sustaining EV market development. In the US, Li et al. (2017) demonstrate significant feedback effects between EV adoption and investments in public EV charging infrastructure. The authors' estimates suggest that a 10 per cent increase in public chargers produces an 8 per cent increase in adoptions, and a 10 per cent increase in adoptions results in a 6 per cent increase in public supply points. These findings lead the authors to posit policy focused on infrastructure, rather than adoption, could produce greater overall consumer uptake of EVs. These estimates are based on observations in urban areas of the US between 2011 and 2013 and therefore represent an early period of EV availability in the US. Many consumers purchasing EVs during that period are likely to be early adopters who are less price sensitive than the general car-buying population. The extent to which these estimates scale and their applicability in other market contexts is an area that would benefit from additional empirical research.

EV owners have the capability to charge their vehicles using electrical connections at home or at their place of work, unlike ICEV owners that rely nearly exclusively on public refuelling infrastructure. Another relevant consideration when assessing the future of

Table 18.1   Relative coverage of electric vehicle fuelling infrastructure

	Charge Points (CP)			EVs			CP per 100 km of Road Network	EVs per CP	Ratio of CP to Fuel Stations
	Fast	Slow	Total	BEVs	PHEVs	Total			
Canada	673	5 168	5 841	23 620	22 330	45 950	0.6	7.9	0.5
China	83 395	130 508	213 903	951 190	276 580	1 227 770	4.4	5.7	2.1
France	1 571	14 407	15 978	92 950	25 820	118 770	1.7	7.4	1.4
Germany	2 076	22 213	24 289	59 090	50 470	109 560	3.8	4.5	1.7
Japan	7 372	21 507	28 879	104 490	100 860	205 350	2.4	7.1	0.8
Korea	2 531	3 081	5 612	24 070	1 840	25 910	5.1	4.6	0.5
Norway	2 058	8 292	10 350	116 129	60 181	176 310	11	17	6.6
UK	2 037	11 497	13 534	45 010	88 660	133 670	3.4	9.9	1.6
US	6 267	39 601	45 868	401 550	360 510	762 060	0.7	16.6	0.4

Notes: PHEVs = plug-in hybrid electric vehicles. The table shows the number of normal (3.7–22 kW) and fast power (AC 43kW chargers, DC chargers, inductive and Tesla superchargers) publicly accessible charging points.

Sources: The data on BEVs and PHEVs and electric charging stock are from the European Alternative Fuel Observatory (accessed 28 June 2019) and the IEA Global EV Outlook (accessed 2 July 2019). All other data are from https://www.gocompare.com, accessed 2 July 2019.

Table 18.2   Stock of electric vehicle fuelling infrastructure

Year	EU	France	Germany	Italy	UK	Spain	US	China
2012	13 350	809	1 518	1 351	2 840	406	13 392	17 900
2013	23 541	1 802	2 447	1 356	5 691	891	19 410	21 200
2014	34 448	1 834	2 941	1 363	7 912	918	25 602	23 000
2015	59 200	10 665	5 571	1 749	9 837	1 663	30 945	49 600
2016	119 615	20 439	25 240	2 741	14 256	4 974	42 029	140 000
2017	126 503	22 011	25 373	2 885	16 553	5 089	50 627	213 900
2018	143 589	24 850	27 459	3 562	19 076	5 209	61 067	299 800

Sources: For Europe, we report the total number of normal and fast public charging points from the European Alternative Fuel Observatory. For the US, we report electric fuelling stations from the Alternative Fuel Data Center of the Department of Energy. For China, we report the number of public and dedicated fleet EV charging posts from Figure 5 in Hove and Sandalow (2019).

LDV fuelling infrastructure is therefore the necessity for public fuel supply and the effect that EV expansion will have on existing retail fuelling station owners. Already, areas such as the UK have seen significant declines in gasoline and diesel fuelling locations (Campbell 2018). This is a result of increased vehicle fuel efficiencies and will accelerate with fuel demand reductions that accompany broader EV adoption. A recent study by the Boston Consulting Group indicates many fuel retailers could struggle to be profitable within the next two decades. As the traditional network of retailers confronts this challenging landscape, opportunity exists for new business models tailored to the needs of EV drivers (Rubeis et al. 2019). Beyond these implications for existing fossil fuel retailers and the liquid fuel distribution market, we also must consider the relative benefits of home and workplace charging of EVs in the context of both consumer value of refuelling time and in considering the grid-based consequences of a fully electrified vehicle fleet. We turn to these and other challenges in the next section.

3.   CHALLENGES

The decision to purchase an EV is one of purchasing a durable good: it involves an intertemporal trade-off between upfront (purchase price) and operating costs and the lifetime benefits of the vehicle. Both the costs and benefits of vehicle ownership, in general, are multidimensional. That is, vehicles are differentiated products that vary in terms of their performance and size, among other dimensions. The private costs of owning the vehicle include the upfront costs, maintenance costs, costs of refuelling in terms of both fuel and time, and associated costs of the complementary products. There are also external costs in terms of emissions and congestion.

In this section, we discuss the likely impediments to large-scale EV adoption. We begin by discussing the lifetime costs associated with owning EVs and ICEVs. In general, EVs have higher upfront costs, but lower future costs of ownership through a lower cost per mile and lower maintenance costs. These lower per-mile and maintenance costs are potentially counterbalanced by higher time costs associated with refuelling and higher disposal costs. We discuss some efforts to overcome the higher upfront costs of EVs through policies that provide EV buyers with subsidies or other benefits. We then turn to the challenges associated with complementary products. For EVs, the challenges pertain to costs attributed to the recharging network – both the physical recharging infrastructure and the associated electricity grid-level costs – that an expanded recharging network will require.

3.1   Vehicle Costs

The biggest challenge to large-scale EV adoption is the price of batteries. Batteries represent a significant portion of the retail price premium of EVs over their ICEV counterparts. Current estimates suggest that the cost of batteries at the system level is roughly $160 per kWh (BloombergNEF 2019, Kapoor, MacDuffie and Wilde 2020).[6] To put this number in perspective, the Tesla Model S requires 0.3 kWh per mile. For an average daily-trip distance of approximately 60 miles, this vehicle requires a battery of 18 kWh to operate on a single charge per day, on average.[7] At battery costs of $160 per kWh, the battery for such a vehicle would cost $2880. Producing an EV with a range similar to that of an ICEV would be significantly more costly. The median range for ICEVs available in the US is approximately 400 miles (EVAdoption 2018). An EV with this range would require a 120 kWh battery for a cost of $19 200 at current prices. This cost is similar to the average price of a mid-size ICEV. In the remainder of this section, we assess the cost competitiveness of EVs by estimating price parity between ICEVs and EVs based on battery costs and oil price levels.

We undertake a series of calculations. We first build on the analysis in Covert, Greenstone and Knittel (2016). They calculate the break-even price for oil for a range of battery costs.[8] Such an analysis requires several assumptions. An interactive tool that calculates results presented in this section is available on our website for those who would like to vary these assumptions.[9] We then extend the analysis by Covert et al. (2016) in a number of ways.

Our break-even analysis requires assumptions on the mapping from oil prices to gasoline prices, the annual travel distance, the desired range, the discount rates, the efficiency levels of ICEVs and EVs and the price of electricity. As in Covert et al. (2016), we assume that the vehicle travels 15 000 miles annually and the owner would like an EV range of 250 miles. We compare an EV that uses 0.3 kWh per mile to an ICEV that gets 30 MPG of gasoline. As such, we are comparing, effectively, two medium-sized sedans such as the Tesla Model S and the Honda Accord.[10] We use a discount rate of 5 per cent. To map oil prices to gasoline prices in the US, we use monthly data on US gasoline prices and Brent Crude prices and estimate a log–log relationship between the two series. Our gasoline prices include state and federal taxes. The federal gasoline tax is approximately 18 cents per gallon. The average state-level tax is roughly 30 cents per gallon (US Energy Information Administration [US EIA] 2019).[11] Finally, we assume an electricity price of 12.4 cents per kWh, which is the average residential retail price in the US in January 2017 (US EIA 2017).

Figure 18.7a plots the results of this exercise. The estimated line of cost parity is represented by the solid back line. Points below the line represent oil price and battery price pairs where ICEVs are less expensive to operate than EVs. The opposite relationship holds for points above the line. To a first order, the relationship is close to a 1:1 mapping

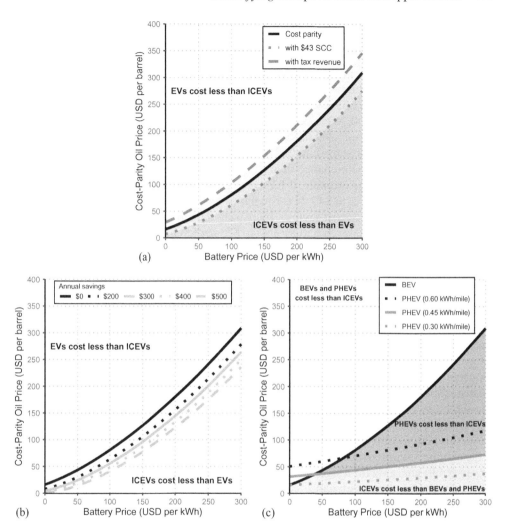

Notes: Panel (a) presents results of an analysis of the EV battery/oil price–cost parity frontier. Panel (b) includes results of alternative scenarios based on specified savings thresholds. Panel (c) incorporates assumptions for plug-in hybrid electric vehicles (PHEVs). Prices in 2018 dollars. In panel (a), a social cost of carbon of $43 in 2007 dollars equates to approximately $51 in real 2018 terms (US Environmental Protection Agency [US EPA] 2016). Dotted lines in panel (c) represent PHEV cost parity results for alternative PHEV electric efficiency levels. For additional detail, see Section 3.1.

Figure 18.7   Electric vehicle battery/oil price–cost parity analysis

between oil prices and battery costs. This does not bode well for EVs. For example, at the time of writing, the price of Brent Crude is roughly $40 per barrel with NYMEX futures out to 2026 approaching $50 per barrel. At an oil price of $40 per barrel, battery prices must be roughly $44 per kWh for EVs and ICEVs to be at cost parity. At battery costs of $160, the price of oil needs to be approximately $140 per barrel, which exceeds the peak oil prices over the past decade. These results can be used to evaluate existing battery cost goals and projections. Consider, for example, the US DOE goal of $125 per kWh by 2022. At parity, oil would need to be priced at approximately $100 per barrel.

We extend this analysis in several directions. We start with assumptions that make EVs more attractive. One advantage of EVs is that they have fewer moving parts, do not require as many system fluids and, due to regenerative braking, may have longer-lasting brake systems. Hence EVs have lower maintenance costs than similar ICEVs (Union of Concerned Scientists 2018). We repeat our calculations for four levels of annual maintenance savings, ranging from $200 to $500 in Figure 18.7b. We include the cost parity line of Figure 18.7a (that is, assumed annual savings of $0). At current oil prices of $40 per barrel, $100 of annual maintenance savings reduce the break-even cost of batteries by roughly $10 per kWh. For example, if EVs save $200 per year in maintenance costs, the break-even cost of batteries at $40 oil is roughly $65 per kWh, compared to $45 per kWh if there are no maintenance cost savings. Increasing the annual maintenance cost savings to $300 increases the break-even battery cost to $75 per kWh. With large savings in maintenance costs, cost parity is attainable at the US DOE's target of $125 per kWh. With maintenance savings of $700 per year, the break-even oil price is $43 per barrel at the US DOE's target.

In some cases, the higher frequency and longer wait times associated with EV recharging counterbalance the maintenance savings associated with EVs. In our second series of calculations, we compute back-of-the-envelope costs associated with the longer wait times, ignoring the more frequent recharging. Such a calculation requires two inputs: the value of time and the share of charges that take place outside of home. The latter is important because charging at home likely reduces the lost value of time. We calculate the lost value of time for values ranging from $5 per hour to $100 per hour and the outside-the-home charging share between zero and 100 per cent. We assume that it takes 30 minutes to charge the EV, while it takes five minutes to refuel the ICEV. Table 18.3 shows this new set of calculations. We emphasize values in the table that are comparable to the assumed maintenance cost savings discussed above. In instances where EV owners rely on public charging for a significant portion of refuelling events, the lost value of time can easily exceed the maintenance cost savings even at relatively low time valuation. The table also demonstrates scenarios in which EV charging is less costly on a value-of-time basis, especially in instances of infrequent public charging. Based on current trends in EV refuelling – with EV owners commonly relying on home charging more than 80 per cent of the time – EV time costs are unlikely to be significant and may represent an additional benefit rather than a cost.

These calculations are biased toward EVs because they ignore the revenue generated from gasoline taxes. That is, they implicitly assume that these revenues will not be collected from EVs. There are two ways to think about this issue. On the one hand, one could argue that these taxes reflect the relative social cost of the fuels. In the US context, this is not exactly true because the state-level taxes do not vary based on the external costs associated with electricity production. However, the average federal- plus state-level gasoline tax is close to implied social cost of carbon of roughly $50 per ton. Therefore, one could argue that it is unnecessary to adjust the EV calculations for this revenue shortfall.[12] On the other hand, in the US, gasoline tax revenues largely go toward road maintenance. From this standpoint, it is possible, if not likely, that in an EV regime, electricity prices would be taxed to cover this revenue shortfall.[13] If we adjust the electricity prices

Table 18.3   Estimates of lost value of time resulting from electric vehicle charge duration

Value of Time ($/hour)	Share of Charges Away from Home																				
	0	0.05	0.10	0.15	0.20	0.25	0.30	0.35	0.40	0.45	0.50	0.55	0.60	0.65	0.70	0.75	0.80	0.85	0.90	0.95	1.00
5	-21	-15	-8	-2	4	10	17	23	29	35	42	48	54	60	67	73	79	85	92	98	104
10	-42	-29	-17	-4	8	21	33	46	58	71	83	96	108	121	133	146	158	171	183	196	208
15	-62	-44	-25	-6	13	31	50	69	88	106	125	144	163	181	200	219	238	256	275	294	312
20	-83	-58	-33	-8	17	42	67	92	117	142	167	192	217	242	267	292	317	342	367	392	417
25	-104	-73	-42	-10	21	52	83	115	146	177	208	240	271	302	333	365	396	427	458	490	521
30	-125	-87	-50	-12	25	63	100	138	175	212	250	288	325	362	400	438	475	513	550	588	625
35	-146	-102	-58	-15	29	73	117	160	204	248	292	335	379	423	467	510	554	598	642	685	729
40	-167	-117	-67	-17	33	83	133	183	233	283	333	383	433	483	533	583	633	683	733	783	833
45	-187	-131	-75	-19	38	94	150	206	262	319	375	431	488	544	600	656	712	769	825	881	938
50	-208	-146	-83	-21	42	104	167	229	292	354	417	479	542	604	667	729	792	854	917	979	1042
55	-229	-160	-92	-23	46	115	183	252	321	390	458	527	596	665	733	802	871	940	1008	1077	1146
60	-250	-175	-100	-25	50	125	200	275	350	425	500	575	650	725	800	875	950	1025	1100	1175	1250
65	-271	-190	-108	-27	54	135	217	298	379	460	542	623	704	785	867	948	1029	1110	1192	1273	1354
70	-292	-204	-117	-29	58	146	233	321	408	496	583	671	758	846	933	1021	1108	1196	1283	1371	1458
75	-312	-219	-125	-31	63	156	250	344	438	531	625	719	813	906	1000	1094	1188	1281	1375	1469	1562
80	-333	-233	-133	-33	67	167	267	367	467	567	667	767	867	967	1067	1167	1267	1367	1467	1567	1667
85	-354	-248	-142	-35	71	177	283	390	496	602	708	815	921	1027	1133	1240	1346	1452	1558	1665	1771
90	-375	-262	-150	-37	75	188	300	413	525	638	750	863	975	1088	1200	1312	1425	1538	1650	1762	1875
95	-396	-277	-158	-40	79	198	317	435	554	673	792	910	1029	1148	1267	1385	1504	1623	1742	1860	1979
100	-417	-292	-167	-42	83	208	333	458	583	708	833	958	1083	1208	1333	1458	1583	1708	1833	1958	2083

Notes: The table shading is based on savings thresholds as discussed in the main text. All reported dollar values are in nominal terms. The lost value of time assumes 15 000 annual VMTs, 50 refuelling events per year, and refuelling times of 30 minutes (EV) and five minutes (ICEV).

in our calculations such that the same amount of taxes is collected, this adds a little over 5 cents per kWh to the price and increases the break-even oil price from $103 per barrel at the DOE target to $127 per barrel.[14] Alternatively, one may annualize the tax revenues, making them comparable to the maintenance savings discussed above. When computed this way, annual tax revenues are roughly $240 per year.

Figure 18.7a also includes results for a scenario in which gasoline is taxed at levels that internalize the social cost of carbon (SCC in the figure legend); this is represented by the dotted line on the figure. Because this additional tax increases the cost of gasoline, a given battery price requires a lower oil price for cost parity. Put another way, there is a slice of oil–battery price pairs where EVs are now less expensive to operate than ICEVs than under the baseline scenario. As expected, this has the opposite effect of the tax scenario discussed above. The fuel for EVs is more expensive and there is a larger region of prices under which the ICEV operating costs are lower than the EV costs.

We implement a similar cost parity calculation for PHEVs. This calculation adds a level of complexity as PHEVs are able to operate on both liquid fuel and electricity. We allow for 'dual-fuel' operation and account for smaller battery sizes, lower efficiencies when propelled by electricity and higher internal combustion engine efficiencies observed in today's PHEVs. We allocate a portion of travel distance to electric energy only and the remaining travel to an ICE mode. The resulting parity line, along with the BEV parity line, is shown in Figure 18.7c. PHEVs require lower oil prices at parity, which is due in large part to the smaller battery sizes in PHEVs and the resulting lower vehicle fixed costs. Using PHEV battery range along with electric and gasoline mode efficiencies equal to the average for US PHEV models in 2019, at today's battery cost of $160 per kWh, parity requires oil prices of roughly $50 per barrel. These prices are below crude prices observed prior to the April 2020 price declines. At the US DOE battery price target of $125 per kWh, break-even oil prices are approximately $47 per barrel – similar to futures prices in 2025 at the time of writing. When calculated using BloombergNEF's forecast of $100 per kWh batteries in 2023, the corresponding break-even oil price is $44 per barrel. This estimate is below current oil futures prices for 2023.

The figure also illustrates points at which BEVs can be more cost effective than PHEVs and ICEVs. While these points occur at very low battery price levels, it is worth noting that such an inflection point exists at around $38 per kWh and $36 per barrel of oil. The fact that BEVs become more cost effective at low battery prices suggests that PHEVs can facilitate the transition from ICEVs to BEVs. In the presence of additional market failures, such as research and development or learning-by-doing spillovers, policy makers can incentivize the adoption of PHEVs while battery costs are above this 'switch point', allowing for technology to advance either through technological progress or learning by doing. As battery costs continue to fall, policy makers can shift their attention to BEVs. We caution, however, that this inflection point is sensitive to assumptions about EV, ICEV and PHEV efficiencies and predictions about future trade-offs and PHEV-to-EV switching points would benefit from additional work to understand the interactions in efficiency gains across powertrain types.

As a last step to our extension of the Covert et al. (2016) analysis, we examine the sensitivity of our BEV results to a set of key input parameters. Figure 18.8 presents battery price parity levels corresponding to specified ranges of (1) gasoline price; (2) ICEV efficiencies (in MPG); (3) oil prices ($/barrel); and (4) gasoline tax levels ($/gallon). The main

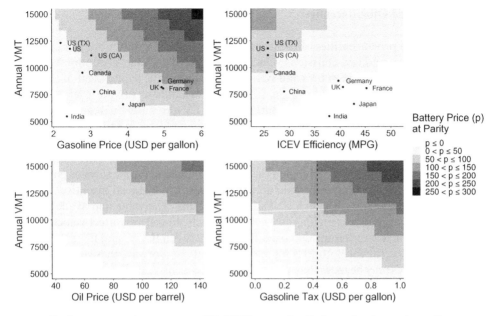

Notes: Shading represents battery costs at EV–ICEV cost parity. Each panel varies one input (for example, gasoline price) relative to annual VMT levels and leaves all other values at their baseline levels, as outlined in Section 3.1. For example, in the upper left panel, holding all inputs fixed, an increase in gasoline price produces higher break-even battery prices. Gasoline tax levels are additional taxes above existing rates, as gasoline prices for the fuel price regression analysis are tax inclusive. The baseline tax level assumes the full value of tax revenues go to transport-related funding. The vertical line in the gasoline tax plot (lower right) represents a social cost of carbon of $0.43, and hence can be used to recentre calculations with carbon tax revenue (that is, all values to the right of this vertical line contribute to transport expenditures).

Figure 18.8   Battery price–cost parity sensitivities

message of these calculations is that a decline in ICEV cost components requires larger reductions in EV battery prices. For example, lower gasoline prices, more fuel-efficient ICEVs, lower oil prices and lower gasoline taxes require significant battery price reductions beyond current levels to achieve an ICEV-EV cost parity.

While our analysis indicates that cost parity for PHEVs may be on the horizon in the US, parity levels for BEVs remain out of reach at current price levels. Battery costs for BEVs have a long way to go to achieve cost parity. As noted, battery costs have fallen dramatically over the past decade; continued battery price declines coupled with steady oil price levels may produce vehicle price parity in the near future. Several papers have estimated learning-by-doing models of battery production and extrapolated these out in time. See, for example, Nykvist and Nilsson (2015), Schmidt et al. (2017), Kittner, Lill and Kammen (2017) and Berckmans et al. (2017). These papers estimate learning rates of roughly 8–10 per cent, implying an 8–10 per cent drop in costs for every doubling of past production. At these learning rates, battery costs will fall below $100 per kWh by 2030 (MIT Energy Initiative 2019).[15]

3.2 Financial and Other Incentives

Many public and private entities offer incentives to promote EV adoption. For example, incentives for zero- and low-emissions vehicles are coupled with fuel economy standards to bridge the cost gap between EVs and ICEVs and promote the deployment of charging infrastructure. Incentives offered at the national, subnational and private levels represent notable portions of a consumer's initial outlays for an EV purchase. Fuel economy standards and mandates for clean vehicle production are driving forces in expanding the availability of more efficient and electrified LDV options.

IEA (2019a) summarizes EV-related policies for various countries. This summary is reproduced here as Table 18.4. All regions in the table implement some form of targets for both vehicles and recharging infrastructure. Most also offer financial incentives to prospective EV consumers to offset vehicle and charger costs. The value and availability of these incentives varies across regions and vehicle models. In general, direct vehicle incentives do not completely overcome the cost differential between ICEVs and EVs; Yang et al. (2016) show this is true for both PHEVs and BEVs only in Norway. In Sweden, Canada and Germany, EVs may be more than 50 per cent more expensive than comparable ICEVs.

An extensive body of literature investigates the effectiveness of EV incentives in stimulating new EV adoptions.[16] In general, subsidies play an important role in EV purchase decisions. In a survey of California EV owners, respondents indicated that federal and state incentives played a significant role in their ultimate EV purchase decision (Jenn et al. 2020). In the EU, a survey of public and private sector experts across five countries indicated that tax incentives and vehicle purchase subsidies had the potential for a strong, positive impact on EV adoption (Santos and Davies 2019). Sierzchula et al. (2014)

Table 18.4 Electric vehicle policy landscape for selected countries

			Canada	China	EU	India	Japan	US
Vehicles	Regulations	ZEV mandate	✓*	✓				✓*
		Fuel economy standards	✓	✓	✓	✓	✓	✓
	Incentives	Fiscal incentives	✓	✓	✓	✓		✓
	Targets		✓	✓	✓	✓	✓	✓*
Chargers	Regulations	Hardware standards**	✓	✓	✓	✓	✓	✓
		Building regulations	✓*	✓*	✓	✓		✓*
	Incentives	Fiscal incentives	✓	✓	✓		✓	✓*
	Targets		✓	✓	✓	✓	✓	✓*
Industrial policies	Subsidies		✓	✓			✓	

Notes: ✓ indicates that the policy is set at national level; ✓* denotes policies that are implemented at a state/province/local level only; ** indicates that standards for chargers are a fundamental prerequisite for the development of EV supply equipment. All regions have developed standards for chargers. Some (China, EU, India) are mandating specific standards as a minimum requirement; others (Canada, Japan, United States) are not. Building regulations refer to an obligation to install chargers (or conduits to facilitate their future installation) in new and renovated buildings. Incentives for chargers include direct investment and purchase incentives for both public and private charging. ZEV = zero-emissions vehicles.

Source: Reproduced from IEA (2019a), *Global EV Outlook 2019*, Table 1. All rights reserved.

estimate the effect of EV adoption incentives on passenger vehicle fleet electrification. The authors examine a cross-section of 20 countries in 2012 and find a significant, positive relationship between EV incentives and EV market shares. Though the magnitude of this effect varies across countries in the study, their findings lend support to the general perception of EV subsidy effectiveness.[17]

Compared to one-time financial incentives, measuring the effectiveness of recurring and non-monetary incentives is more challenging, due in part to the difficulty in assigning consumer value to these offerings. In the US, Jin, Searle and Lutsey (2014) monetize benefits such as carpool lane access and parking privileges and find positive correlation between incentives and EV adoptions. A review study by Hardman et al. (2018) demonstrates the potential for a wide variety of incentives that include the incentives above along with infrastructure investment, and toll, licensing and other fee waivers, to actively promote EV adoption. Individually, each of these incentives can reduce the barriers to broader EV adoption. In some cases, multiple incentives (for example, financial incentives and infrastructure advancement) exhibit complementarities in promoting adoption (Li et al. 2017).

The approach to EV promotion in Norway deserves particular attention in a discussion of incentive structure and effectiveness. Norway has made a concerted effort to target EV price competitiveness with ICEVs. This is aided by the country's taxation structure. Since 2001, EVs in Norway are exempt from purchase/import taxes, the 25 per cent VAT on vehicle purchases and are charged no annual road tax (EV Norway 2020). Additional taxes levied at the time of vehicle purchase are a function of vehicle weight and emissions, which produces significant tax penalties for gasoline and diesel vehicles. Combined, these measures ensure price competitiveness of EVs over ICEV models (Haugneland et al. 2017). The comprehensive package of incentives and other interventions that bolster EVs play an important role in driving the successes observed in the Norwegian EV market (Bjerkan, Nørbech and Nordtømme 2016, Zhang et al. 2016).

An important future consideration for market participants is the sustainability of the EV market in the absence of these incentives. Subsidies or tax incentives valued at a few thousand dollars per vehicle represent a significant outlay of funds, especially in the context of higher levels of EV demand. Other concerns, such as the implementation of incentive programmes as a transfer from taxpayers to EV adopters, highlight the importance of evaluating incentive effectiveness and optimal phase-out (Egbue, Long and Samaranayake 2017). Many existing EV incentive structures include phase-outs based on temporal or aggregate sales thresholds.

One alternative to incentive offerings at the time of vehicle purchase is to emphasize total cost of vehicle ownership (TCO) to EV buyers. The EV TCO exhibits a negative relationship with overall EV market share in EU member states (that is, lower EV TCO corresponds to higher EV market share) (Lévay, Drossinos and Thiel 2017). Providing this information to consumers for consideration when purchasing a vehicle may influence their ultimate vehicle purchase. Dumortier et al. (2015) present survey respondents with TCO information for ICEV and EV models and find higher rankings for EVs in the presence of this information. It is interesting to note that this finding does not require EVs to be strictly less expensive than ICEVs; the results generally hold when EV and ICEV models were of similar TCO. An information-based intervention such as this is likely to be less costly than direct financial incentives, though its effectiveness on a broad scale remains an open question.

3.3 Vehicle Variety

While pricing is perhaps the paramount factor in consumers' decision making, manufacturers must also provide potential buyers with a mix of vehicle offerings that adequately cover the range of consumer preferences. Compared to ICEVs, the number of available BEV and PHEV models is limited. Table 18.5 shows the number of ICEV, BEV and PHEV models marketed in the US for 2011–19. Although there is notable increase in the number of both BEVs and PHEVs, EVs only account for about 5 per cent of total vehicle models offered in the US. IEA (2019a) reports similar data for China, Europe and the US. The number of available PHEV models ranges from 30 to 40 in these countries. The number of BEV models differs dramatically. There are 19 BEV models offered in the US, 40 in Europe and 122 in China.

Although available models do span vehicle segments, the majority of the BEVs and PHEVs offered today occupy the small and medium car segment. The decision to design and build vehicles in this segment is not surprising, as models of this type are typically of lower weight and therefore more efficient and less expensive than larger vehicles. However, concentrating offerings in this vehicle class leaves some untapped segments of vehicle buyers. In the US and Europe, there is a growing interest in crossovers and sport utility vehicles (SUVs) among consumers. This trend is expected to continue, likely at the expense of the market share of small and medium cars (Cozzi and Petropoulos 2019).

Although the trends in overall vehicle model offerings signal a growing sector, it will be necessary to overcome challenges inherent in porting EV powertrains to larger vehicle model segments to continue moving the electrified vehicle fleet to the mainstream. Higher weights, available all-wheel-drive systems and less advantageous aerodynamics of these vehicles often require larger and more expensive battery and drive systems. While this

Table 18.5 Number of vehicle models in the US

Year	ICEVs	EVs			EVs as % of Vehicles
		BEVs	PHEVs	Total	
2019	1255	36	31	67	5.1
2018	1287	24	34	58	4.3
2017	1245	30	19	49	3.8
2016	1214	31	18	49	3.9
2015	1255	18	12	30	2.3
2014	1201	15	10	25	2.0
2013	1167	15	2	17	1.4
2012	1143	7	3	10	0.9
2011	1133	4	1	5	0.4

Note: The rightmost column indicates the percentage of all vehicle models that electric vehicles (BEVs and PHEVs) account for.

Source: The numbers reported are based on the authors' calculations using data from https://fueleconomy.gov/, accessed 20 January 2020.

clearly presents a challenge to manufacturers, the crossover and SUV segment has seen the greatest increase in the number of model offerings in China, the US and the EU (IEA 2019a). Current product announcement schedules from leading vehicle manufacturers indicate that this emphasis will continue in the near term as the portfolio of available EV models expands (Automotive News 2018).

3.4 Electricity Grid Issues

Beyond consumer cost and vehicle performance concerns, broad EV adoption presents unique challenges to the energy supply network. Electrification of the vehicle fleet has the potential to generate a significant increase in aggregate electricity demand and alter intra-day load patterns. To maintain consistent supply, grid operators must address these challenges in the context of an evolving power system. In this section, we quantify aggregate electricity demand consequences of an electrified LDV sector. We also assess intra-day grid effects based on a set of vehicle charging scenarios. Both exercises illustrate the energy supply-side challenges of large-scale EV adoption.

To estimate aggregate EV energy demand, we combine data on electricity consumption, vehicles and VMT across multiple systems. We compute the total energy demanded assuming all existing VMTs were associated with EVs. The resulting total EV energy demand is compared to current annual system energy demand by country. Results of these calculations are presented in Table 18.6. Based on these values and assumptions, the scale of energy consumption effects from the move to an electrified vehicle fleet range from 9 per cent (in France, which has a relatively low level of annual VMT) to over 30 per cent (in the UK, where existing electricity consumption is relatively low compared to other nations). Given the current state of EV adoption – where EVs make up less than 1 per cent of many national LDV fleets – these loads in aggregate are not likely to challenge the existing fleet of electric power plants. That said, the long-term planning horizon for power plant construction and accelerating EV adoption trends in some areas suggest the value of more detailed insights with regard to these effects of LDV electrification. The costs required for electricity suppliers to meet these levels of energy demand will depend crucially on their need and ability to expand generating capacity to address demand

Table 18.6 Electricity grid implications

	Year	VMT (Million)	EV kWh Per Mile	EV kWh (Million)	System kWh (Million)	% of System-wide Total
Canada	2009	206 562	0.3	61 969	508 601	12.2
France	2017	129 693	0.3	38 908	415 300	9.4
Germany	2009	434 401	0.3	130 320	549 100	23.7
Japan	2017	454 932	0.3	136 480	960 000	14.2
UK	2017	327 104	0.3	98 131	309 000	31.8
US	2017	3 216 084	0.3	964 825	3 844 220	25.1

Sources: Miles are total road motor vehicle traffic from the OECD. The data for electricity consumption are from the EIA International Energy Statistics. The efficiency (kWh/mile) is average combined from https:// fueleconomy.gov/ for 2017 (accessed 20 January 2020).

changes, their accuracy in properly predicting the growth rates of EV stock, and on the cost trajectories of input fuels for power generation. With respect to the first of these three elements, the aggregate annual demand is likely less important than the effect EVs have on intraday load patterns.

While a rigorous analysis of grid implications accounting for existing load patterns, distribution grid topology and localized consumer adoption trends is beyond the scope of this chapter, we estimate regional grid consequences of EV adoption for a range of EV penetration scenarios in the US (California Independent System Operator [CAISO], PJM in the mid-Atlantic region and Electric Reliability Council of Texas [ERCOT] in Texas), the EU, China and Japan. We compute approximate energy demand based on total EV stock and fixed levels of annual VMT and vehicle energy efficiency. To estimate effects on an hourly scale, we approximate load due to EV charging using representative EV charging profiles developed by the US DOE's National Renewable Energy Laboratory and published as part of the US DOE's EVI-Pro simulation tool (Wood et al. 2017). We modify these profiles to produce four illustrative scenarios for EV charging: (1) uniform charging across all hours; (2) a base profile directly from the EVI-Pro tool; (3) charging without the availability of workplace charging networks; and (4) charging in the evening only.[18] The results of this exercise are presented in Table 18.7.

In all regions, current levels of EVs remain a small fraction of existing vehicle stock. Estimates of total generation and capacity requirements suggest that current EV penetration levels are of limited magnitude at a grid-wide scale; only in California do energy and power demands reach 0.5 per cent of existing levels. An increase in adoption rates, however, will make EV loads major players in dictating capacity expansion and grid operation patterns. EV adoptions at scale, whether split between BEVs and PHEVs or as part of a fully electrified fleet, produce a wide range of aggregate grid implications. In large systems, such as that in China, high levels of EV adoption only represent 6–7 per cent of current energy demand and 5–6 per cent of current system capacity. These requirements are in stark contrast to grids such as that in California, where penetrations of this size represent over 50 per cent of current energy generation and approximately 35 per cent of existing capacity. While it is unlikely that fleet electrification on this scale will be realized in the near term, these calculations illustrate the magnitude of the electrification task at hand.

In a scenario similar to that of the current state of the market in Norway, where roughly 7 per cent of the total passenger vehicle stock is BEVs and 4 per cent is PHEVs, total energy demand reaches single-digit percentages of existing energy demand and system-level capacities across the regions studied. Current annual energy demand from EVs in CAISO (1.05 TWh) is equivalent to the annual generation of one 250 MW natural gas combined cycle plant.[19] Adoption levels similar to those in Norway increase energy demand to levels that require eight such plants. Beyond concerns of total energy demand, grid operators must contend with the timing of EV charging events. The presence of homogeneous travel patterns, especially in urban commuting zones, means that coincident EV charging events contribute to system peak load levels.[20]

The loads calculated here are for EV charging alone and do not account for other sources of load or load growth. If these peak loads were to occur in the late afternoon hours, concurrent with evening load ramps, capacity margins are likely to be significantly diminished in high EV penetration scenarios. Figure 18.9 displays these charging

Table 18.7 *Energy and capacity effects of electric vehicles*

	CAISO (US)		PJM (US)		ERCOT (US)		EU-28		China		Japan	
	Level	%	Level	%	Level	%	Level	%	Level	%	Level	%
Vehicle stock (thousands)												
Total	29 652		55 631		18 905		267 834		189 303		62 026	
BEVs	204	0.7	43	0.1	12	0.1	536	0.2	1 767	0.9	131	0.2
PHEVs	136	0.5	38	0.1	10	0.1	268	0.1	539	0.3	124	0.2
Energy (GWh)												
Annual generation	193 078		803 064		379 643		3 070 057		6 266 000		935 000	
Current EV share	1 046	0.5	247	0.03	75	0.02	1 679	0.1	5 123	0.1	457	0.05
7% BEV, 4% PHEV	10 131	5.2	19 153	2.4	7 136	1.9	61 157	2	44 992	0.7	12 548	1.3
30% BEV, 70% PHEV	85 422	44.2	161 486	20.1	60 164	15.8	515 637	16.8	379 341	6.1	105 794	11.3
100% BEV	99 328	51.4	187 775	23.4	69 958	18.4	599 578	19.5	441 095	7	123 016	13.2
Power (MW)												
System capacity	70 341		204 289		107 609		1 010 998		1 794 000		313 000	
Current EV share	262	0.4	62	0.03	19	0.02	421	0.04	1 285	0.1	115	0.04
7% BEV, 4% PHEV	2 541	3.6	4 803	2.4	1 789	1.7	15 337	1.5	11 283	0.6	3 147	1.0
30% BEV, 70% PHEV	21 422	30.5	40 498	19.8	15 088	14	129 311	12.8	95 131	5.3	26 531	8.5
100% BEV	24 909	35.4	47 090	23.1	17 544	16.3	150 362	14.9	110 618	6.2	30 850	9.9

Notes and sources: The values in percentage columns are percentages of section headings (for example, BEVs are a percentage of total vehicle stock). The calculations assume energy intensities of 0.3 kWh/mile (BEV) and 0.4 kWh/mile (PHEV), and a PHEV electric mile factor of 0.6 (Smart, Bradley and Salisbury 2014). Annual VMT levels vary by region; US regions are vehicle-stock weighted VMT averages across states. The EV shares of 7% (BEV) and 4% (PHEV) represent approximate shares in Norway in 2018 (from total vehicle inventory data: https://ofv.no/kjoretoybestanden/; accessed 21 January 2021). Due to vehicle mile accounting and aggregate generation source differences, totals may not exactly match Table 18.6. The charging profiles for hourly max load are scaled from the charging profile of the US DOE's EVI-Pro market simulation. The US regional vehicle stock is estimated based on region-wide population levels and state-level per capita EV ownership in 2017. Annual US generation and system capacity are from SNL Financial. The EU-28 vehicle stock for 2018 is from the ACEA Vehicles in Use database. Annual generation and capacity from Eurostat. The vehicle stock for China is from the *China Statistical Yearbook 2019*. The vehicle stock for Japan is from the Motor Vehicle Statistics of Japan (2019).

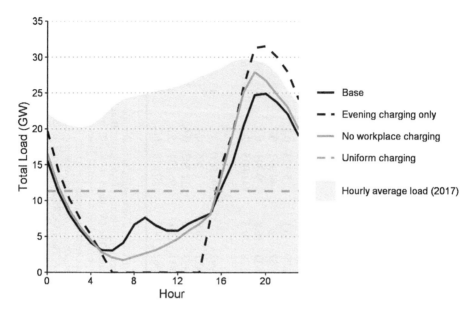

Notes: Black lines represent aggregate energy for charging profiles derived from CAISO 100 per cent EV penetration scenario. The average hourly load (grey line) is 2017 annual average load by hour computed from CAISO hourly data. The charging scenarios are based on DOE's EVI-Pro charging simulation. See Figure 18.A1 in the Appendix for charging profiles and derivation.

Figure 18.9   Estimated load profiles and average hourly demand (CAISO)

profiles along with the current load profile within CAISO. The evening ramp of EV charging is predicted to coincide with the current evening increase in system-wide energy demand. Current analysis of summer capacity margins in the CAISO indicates median capacity margins of approximately 36 per cent (CAISO 2019). Applying this value to the reported system operating capacity of 70 GW indicates median capacity margin levels of 25 GW. Although near-term EV adoption levels are not likely to approach these limits, capacity constraints are likely to become binding in scenarios with high levels of EV adoption. This result is similar in PJM, where current reserve margins are approximately 40 GW (PJM 2019), and in ERCOT, where they are approximately 12 GW (ERCOT 2019).

Given that mechanisms exist to shift EV charging, implementation of these mechanisms would diminish the computed peak load levels. One such mechanism allows consumers or aggregators to delay or schedule charging events and alter charging durations. In the case of the Netherlands, Refa and Hubbers (2019) found peak shifting of approximately four hours, no longer coinciding with the evening load period. The authors estimate an increase in this shifted peak demand of approximately 13 per cent and an increase in aggregate demand of approximately 23 per cent over the patterns for typical charging behaviour. The peak energy increases mean that our estimates may be on the lower end of the spectrum if the results of the Netherlands study hold in other settings. Additional work in this space is necessary as EV penetrations increase and aggregation pilots such as those studied by Refa and Hubbers are implemented in varied settings. Importantly, load shifting to avoid coincident peaks between EV loads and non-EV loads has the potential to reduce capacity requirements and avoid possible price spikes and marginal emissions rate increases due to steep evening ramp events. We turn to implications for emissions in the next section.

4.   IMPLICATIONS

Challenges like vehicle costs, meeting consumer demands and ensuring sufficient electricity supply infrastructure are of primary interest when considering the potential for high levels of LDV fleet electrification. Next, we outline two important implications of such a shift in transport fuel choice. A primary motivator for a transition to an electrified vehicle fleet is the decreased reliance on fossil fuel sources and the corresponding emissions benefits. Here, we estimate differences in average CO_2 emissions levels across fuels and across regions. We then summarize existing work that measures these implications through both simulation modelling and empirical estimates. Subsequently, we turn to the tax revenue effects of EVs and estimate the magnitude of forgone tax revenues for the current electrified fleet and compare alternative means to raise equivalent revenue from EVs.

4.1 CO_2 Emissions

The emissions benefits of LDV fleet electrification depend primarily on two items: (1) how electricity is generated; and (2) what types of vehicles EVs displace. Specifically, emissions benefits of a switch to EVs are determined in large part by the carbon intensities of the aforementioned factors.[21] Figure 18.10 presents annual carbon intensities of electricity generation in grams of CO_2 per kWh for a number of national electricity grids, illustrating the regional heterogeneity in these intensities. To better represent the relative emissions levels of ICEVs and energy generation, we also compute emissions intensities for vehicle categories: the LDV fleet average in each individual country, a compact car, a hybrid electricity vehicle (HEV), and a PHEV. Each of these values is based on the emissions coefficient for gasoline – 19.6 lb of CO_2 per gallon (US EIA 2016) – and the assumed MPG value for each respective vehicle category as described in the figure note. With the exception of India, average grid carbon intensities are lower than the LDV fleet average. While this figure is illustrative, it should be noted that because values in this figure are system-wide averages, they do not represent the complete system dynamics of EV charging. Specifically, realized emissions benefits will depend on the time at which the EV is drawing power from the grid and on the marginal, rather than the average, emissions intensity.[22]

A wealth of studies explores the implications that carbon intensity of grid infrastructure has on CO_2 abatement potential in the transport sector. Woo, Choi and Ahn (2017) conduct a comprehensive well-to-wheels comparison of EVs and ICEVs in 70 countries. The authors aggregate emissions levels for a set of representative vehicle models. Based on median grid-level emissions factors through 2016, EVs produce lower emissions levels than gasoline or diesel ICEVs for most model types studied. This result does not consistently hold for the set of subcompact models tested, likely a result of the fuel

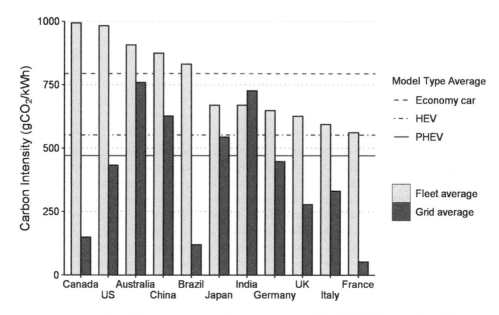

Notes and sources: The grid-level average emissions rates are from IEA (2018a). The light-duty (LD) fleet average emissions for each country are based on average fleet fuel economy in Table 18A.2. The vehicle-level carbon intensities are computed based on the following fuel economies (representative vehicle): economy car, 32 MPG (Toyota Corolla/Honda Civic average); HEV, 46 MPG (Toyota Prius C), PHEV, 54 MPG (Toyota Prius Prime). Vehicle calculations assume 19.6 lb CO_2 per gallon of gasoline (US EIA 2016).

Figure 18.10   Relative carbon intensities of light-duty vehicle and electricity sectors

efficiency levels of subcompact vehicles. Interestingly, repeating the calculation with maximum emissions intensities leads to mixed results, with EVs producing higher levels of emissions than ICEVs under this assumption. This again illustrates the importance of understanding the timing of vehicle charging and corresponding power system operation.

Work by Jochem, Babrowski and Fichtner (2015) reinforces this conclusion with a study of EV charging and emissions consequences in Germany. The authors employ an energy system model and estimate EV emissions levels in a hypothetical market with 6 million EVs, or approximately 15 per cent vehicle market share. Emissions are higher with marginal electricity mix in the presence of EV loads than their counterparts assuming average emissions rates in the system. This result holds only in the case of uncontrolled charging (that is, vehicles charge immediately when connected to the grid). Controlled charging (that is, vehicle charging can be optimally scheduled) produces a 30 per cent reduction in emissions levels.

Graff Zivin, Kotchen and Mansur (2014) use data from various US regions to demonstrate the difference between average and marginal emissions rates and the importance of accounting for the time of day during which an EV is charged. The authors estimate marginal intensities as much as 44 per cent under, and 54 per cent over, the computed average emissions intensity. Based on marginal rates for each hour of the day and different parts of the country, the ratio of intraday maximum-to-minimum marginal emissions rates is as high as 2.4. That is, depending on when an EV is plugged in, its marginal contribution to

CO_2 emissions could be 2.4 times higher than if the EV were plugged in during the lowest carbon-intensity hour. Holland et al. (2016) couple the analysis of Graff Zivin et al. (2014) with a model of emissions damages and calculate the optimal subsidy (tax) for forgone emissions benefits (costs) of EVs. The heterogeneity of grid infrastructure carries through to this result, indicating a spatially differentiated optimal intervention regime for consumers to fully internalize costs of emissions from LDV use.

While these studies offer valuable insights into the link between marginal energy demand and marginal emissions, it is important to note the limitations of such studies in drawing conclusions about long-run implications of EVs. With the exception of the Jochem et al. (2015) study, the analyses mentioned here are based on observed generation data and therefore measure grid effects only within the bounds of the study data. They therefore provide general clues about potential carbon implications only in so much as the future grid represents current grid conditions. While this may be a reasonable assumption in the near term, expansion of renewable sources (for example, solar and wind), unit retirements (for example, coal), or development of grid-level storage capacity are likely to alter these results. In the presence of a trend toward decarbonization in the electricity system, long-run grid emissions factors have the potential to produce significant emissions reductions (Hawkes 2014).

It is also important to understand the substitution patterns of EV purchases when evaluating the comparative emissions benefits of EVs. The emissions benefits of EVs are much higher if they replace a fuel-inefficient vehicle (usually an older, larger, more powerful ICEV) than a more efficient vehicle (that is, a newer, smaller, less powerful ICEV). Xing, Leard and Li (2019) find that households purchasing EVs also prefer more fuel-efficient vehicles. Hence, the counterfactual to an EV purchase is more accurately specified by an efficient ICEV or hybrid. Revisiting Figure 18.10, this finding suggests other grids, such as those in Australia and China, may require additional grid decarbonization efforts to bring EV emissions levels below those of existing ICEV options.

4.2 Tax Revenues

A primary consequence of the increased reliance on electric powertrains in the LDV fleet is declining demand for conventional transport fuels. In many regions, excise taxes on fuels are important revenue sources for funding transport infrastructure. As this revenue stream decreases, national and subnational entities will need to revisit these revenue-raising instruments.

We follow Davis and Sallee (2019) to estimate forgone fuel tax revenue due to EVs for a number of countries. Davis and Sallee estimate annual forgone fuel tax revenues as a function of fuel excise taxes, travel distances, ICEV efficiency and the total stock of EVs in the US. Using existing national excise tax levels for gasoline and country-wide averages of vehicle fleet attributes, we provide estimates of forgone annual tax revenue. The results of our calculations are presented in the first panel of Table 18.8. Revenue shortfalls from EVs are largest in the US, where low fuel tax levels are offset by low ICEV efficiency, high annual VMTs and a relatively large number of EVs. Canada's revenue value is much lower than any of the other countries in the table, though the similarity of market characteristics with the US indicates this number would likely rise in line with that of the US as EV penetration increased.

Table 18.8   Tax revenue effects of an electrified vehicle fleet

(a) Forgone Revenue Levels for Current Fleet					
	Excise tax ($/gallon)	Total EVs	Avg. Annual VMT	Fleet Avg. MPG	Forgone Tax Revenue (million $/year)
Canada	0.74	45 950	9 548	25.6	12.7
France	2.77	118 770	8 076	45.2	58.8
Germany	2.79	109 560	8 766	39.2	68.4
Japan	1.91	205 350	6 611	37.9	68.3
UK	2.82	133 670	8 188	40.6	76.1
US	0.56	762 060	11 112	25.8	182.0

(b) Alternative Revenue Generation Options					
	Equiv. Elec. Excise Tax ($/kWh)*			Residential Electricity Prices ($/kWh)	Equivalent Annual Fee ($)	Existing Ownership Tax ($/year)
	0.3	0.2	0.1			
Canada	0.10	0.15	0.29	0.10	277.33	62.77
France	0.20	0.31	0.61	0.17	495.32	0.00
Germany	0.24	0.36	0.71	0.31	624.14	30.51
Japan	0.17	0.25	0.50	0.22	332.40	324.32
UK	0.23	0.35	0.70	0.18	569.68	140.57
US	0.07	0.11	0.21	0.11	238.88	44.57

Notes and sources: *Subheadings for this column grouping represent assumed EV efficiencies in kWh/mile. Equivalent excise tax rates assume taxes levied on electricity for EV use only. Existing gasoline excise tax rates ($/gallon in 2017 dollars) are from OECD (2018). The number of EVs is the stock of BEVs and PHEVs from IEA (2017). The data on VMT are from the ODYSSEE-MURE project (Europe) for 2015, US DOT (2017) for the US, Figure 11 in the Summary Report of the 2009 Canadian Vehicle Survey for Canada, and Japan 2050 Low Carbon Navigator for Japan in 2010. The data on fuel efficiency (MPG) are from Global Fuel Economy Initiative (GFEI) (2017).

There are a variety of methods for recovering these lost revenues. Here, we explore two: a per-kWh excise tax on electricity for EV charging and an annual fee for EV drivers.[23] Both have precedent in the ICEV market in the form of the aforementioned gasoline excise tax and existing annual fees for ICEV owners – often called ownership or circulation taxes. Calculated per-kWh taxes and annual fees are presented in panel (b) of Table 18.8. The table also shows current residential electricity taxes and ICEV annual ownership fees. These estimates reveal two important insights. First, imposing an additional energy charge on EV drivers to recoup ICEV fuel tax revenue would effectively double EV charging rates. Research in the fossil-fuelled transport space indicates that vehicle efficiency, annual travel distance and individual trip elasticities are relatively low (Antweiler and Gulati 2019, Dong et al. 2012, Litman 2019). Coupled with the fact that EV refuelling costs per mile are well below that of ICEVs, more work is necessary to understand the effect a change of this magnitude might have on EV adoption and driving behaviour of EV owners. Alternatively, spreading this charge over all electricity consumption would greatly reduce the per-kWh rate necessary to raise revenues and could take advantage of relative inelasticity of electricity consumption. However, such a move would require proper accounting of the distributional consequences of increased electricity taxation for a full assessment of the relative costs and benefits. Second, regarding the imposition of an annual EV use fee, the full value of the fee is significant when compared to existing ownership tax rates. In fact, the smallest estimated change is in Japan, where annual fees would double from approximately $300 to $600. These results suggest that policy prescriptions for addressing revenue shortfalls from fossil fuel displacement in the transportation sector should be regarded with caution, especially as EVs currently face concerns about cost competitiveness with ICEVs.

The results of our calculations require a set of simplifying assumptions that have implications for the level of displaced excise tax revenues and level of alternative revenue generation methods. The three primary determinants of these values are the existing excise taxes, the efficiencies of ICEVs and those of EVs. Taken individually, higher excise taxes and lower ICEV efficiencies (MPG) both contribute to higher equivalent annual fees. Additional per-kWh charges are also affected by the efficiency level of EVs. Specifically, higher EV efficiencies (kWh/mile) require higher equivalent electricity excise tax levels. As an example of the magnitude of these effects, we include three EV efficiency levels in Table 18.8 panel (b); efficiency improvements from 0.3 kWh/mile to 0.1 kWh/mile results in a tripling of the equivalent excise tax rates.

5. THE NEXT FRONTIERS FOR ELECTRIFICATION

The LDV sector is not the only segment of transport with its eye toward an electrified future. Commercial trucking, rail, ship and airborne operators are all weighing the costs and benefits of switching fuel sources. To reach climate goals outlined by IPCC (2018), all these sectors must undergo dramatic efforts to reduce carbon consumption and electrification is an important route to this end. There is an expansive, and rapidly growing, body of literature that addresses the full spectrum of transport sector electrification. In this section, we discuss the electrification opportunities that are most closely related to our preceding discussion of LDV electrification: electrification of medium- and heavy-duty vehicles, and EV implications for ride-hailing services and autonomous vehicles (AVs).

5.1 Medium- and Heavy-duty Transportation

LDVs represent one segment of the global on-road vehicle market. Oil consumption by LDVs represents approximately 60 per cent of transport energy use in the US and approximately 50 per cent worldwide (IPCC 2014, US EIA 2020). In what follows, we discuss the prospects for electrification of the medium- and heavy-duty sectors. We split our discussion into medium-duty trucks and delivery vehicles, heavy-duty trucks (for example, Class 8 trucks), and buses. The US Federal Highway Administration classifies medium-duty vehicles as having a gross vehicle weight between 10 000 and 26 000 pounds (Classes 3 through 6), while heavy-duty vehicles exceed 26 000 pounds (Classes 7 and 8).[24] For comparison, a large walk-in delivery truck, similar to those that UPS and FedEx use for home delivery in the US, would be at the low end of medium-duty vehicles, a school bus would typically be at the high end of medium-duty vehicles, a city-transit bus tends to be at the low end of the heavy duty spectrum, while the '18 wheeler' tractors we typically think of would be Class 8 trucks (US DOE, 2011).

Electric versions of medium- and heavy-duty vehicles currently exist and are being inserted into company fleets. For example, UPS recently ordered 950 EV delivery trucks, above their initial order of 50 for testing purposes.[25] China has put into the market over 400 000 electric transit buses.[26]

One characteristic of the markets in which medium- and heavy-duty vehicles operate that might make electrification more attractive compared to the light-duty market is that these larger vehicles tend to operate more. For example, the average Class 8 truck drives nearly 70 000 miles per year, and the average transit bus drives 35 000 miles per year.[27] This increases the relative importance of the lower operating costs associated with EVs as well as any maintenance benefits that might also exist.

A second characteristic of the medium- and heavy-duty sector that lends itself to electrification is that many of the vehicles operate over set routes, thus saving on recharging infrastructure needs. For example, medium-duty delivery vehicles that support last-mile service operate out of central hubs on regular schedules or heavy-duty vehicles that predominantly operate across interstate highways. Operators of these vehicles could centralize infrastructure investments and charge vehicle batteries between daily shifts or establish charging infrastructure along the highway system. Buses travelling on established routes and out of a network of depots have similar advantages. Electrification of long-haul, heavy-duty freight transport will require extensive work to ensure sufficient geographic distribution and local charging capacity. Regardless of use, all modes of commercial trucking will have significant consequences for the electricity grid when deployed at scale. To illustrate the implications of commercial truck charging, consider first the relative energy quantities required for electric trucks. Commercial truck models currently proposed or in production include battery capacities of 200 to 300 kWh, approximately five times the capacity of typical LDVs.[28] Daily energy demand of 3 MWh for a fleet of ten vehicles translates to a power demand of up to 1.5 MW for simultaneous DC fast charging.[29] In the case of overnight charging, these charge events may be coordinated to lessen the aggregate power requirements, but long-haul trucking – which represents 74 per cent of the commercial trucking sector with respect to ton-miles – may require new approaches to incentivize temporal and geographic distribution of charging events.[30]

As with the LDV sector, range requirements for the heavy-duty, and to a lesser extent medium-duty, sector are a major hurdle. The typical Class 8 truck has a fuel capacity of 200–300 gallons (Truckload Indexes 2020). A recent survey of fuel economy finds a median fuel economy of 6.5 MPG, implying a range of 1300–1950 miles. In principle, this is overkill, or option value for when the truck is towing heavy loads, as drivers are constrained to drive only 11 hours per day; at 60 MPH and average fuel consumption, this would require roughly 100 gallons of fuel.[31] For electric buses, the required battery capacity is likely to be much lower.

The battery capacity required for a range of roughly 660 miles per day is somewhat controversial. Tesla has announced that the Tesla Semi will consume less than 2 kWh per mile, fully loaded, prompting some scepticism by those in the industry.[32] However, calculations based on theory suggest the claims are feasible, if not likely (MacKenzie 2018,

Sripad and Viswanathan 2017). Taking the mean consumption value from Sripad and Viswanathan (2017) of 1.9 kWh per mile, a Class 8 truck with a 660-mile range would require, roughly, a 1250 kWh battery. At battery costs of $200 ($100) per kWh, the cost of the battery exceeds $250 000 ($125 000). At both of these battery cost levels, the total battery cost is greater than the average price of a Class 8 truck,[33] but, of course, there are significant fuel-cost savings. While we do not perform similar cost-parity calculations as above for the LDV market, we provide a simple comparison at current prices. At the time of writing, the average price of diesel in the US is $3.07 per gallon. Assuming a truck is driven 70 000 miles per year, the annual fuel savings from an EV Class 8 truck would be over $16 500. Over a ten-year period, using a discount rate of 5 per cent, the fuel savings alone exceed $130 000, just under the battery cost at $200 per kWh and well under the $100 kWh figure.[34]

We can perform similar calculations for electric buses. The average transit bus gets roughly 3.3 MPG,[35] while the 'E-bus' version requires roughly 2.5 kWh per mile.[36] At $3.07 a gallon for diesel fuel and 12.2 cents per kWh for electricity, the E-bus saves roughly 87 cents per mile driven. If a bus were to be driven the average annual of 35 000 miles, the annual savings would be over $30 000. Sizing the battery to be able to travel roughly 100 miles per day would require 250 kWh of energy. At battery costs of $200 ($100) per kWh battery, the battery would cost $50 000 ($25 000), implying a payback period of just over (just under) a year. In practice, E-bus companies appear to be using batteries much larger than 250 kWh. For example, Proterra offers transit buses with battery capacities of 440 and 660 kWh. The battery cost of these models would be $88 000 and $132 000 at a battery cost of $200 per kWh, respectively. Even at these capacity levels, the payback period is short. These calculations only account for the battery costs. A number of sources suggest that the added upfront costs for an electric bus is $300 000.[37] These might reflect other costs associated with making an electric bus or market power that may subside as the industry thickens. Here, the payback period would be ten years, and discounting the fuel savings would obviously imply that the EV bus is more expensive over a ten-year period.

These simple calculations ignore a number of important factors. In favour of EVs, we are not accounting for maintenance savings, crediting for cheaper drivetrain costs, and, of course, external costs associated with diesel consumption. In favour of the ICEs, we are not accounting for the recharging infrastructure costs associated with EVs, which, given the size of the batteries and desired recharging times, are likely to be substantial. We also do not include estimates of differences in vehicle payload attributable to the weight and volume of vehicle batteries.[38] Although more real-world data are needed for a comprehensive estimate of these savings, an analysis of the New York City bus fleet estimates total lifetime savings for electric buses over diesel-powered buses of approximately $168 000, or 12.5 per cent (Aber 2016).

In all, these numbers suggest that at battery costs of $100 per kWh, electrification of the medium- and heavy-duty sectors has real potential; perhaps, more potential than in the LDV sector.

5.2   Ride Sharing and Autonomous Vehicles

Two emerging trends in the transport space are (1) the expanded availability of ride-sharing services provided by transport network companies (TNCs); and (2) the development, testing and preliminary deployment of autonomous vehicles (AVs). TNCs compete with traditional ride-hailing services and convert consumer LDVs to dual-use vehicles (that is, used for both personal and ride-hailing trips). AVs allocate a portion of driving tasks to the vehicles' computerized systems. As a result, both TNCs and AVs have the potential to alter traditional use patterns for LDVs and represent sources of disruption for transport markets in the future.

AVs and TNCs interact with an electrified LDV fleet in multiple ways. Efforts to reduce congestion and emissions in city centres pose opportunities for a combined transition that includes TNC services and vehicle electrification. In the US, legislation in California (SB 1014) will require TNC operators to transition to zero-emission vehicles. This legislation is aimed at meeting California's state-wide ZEV targets and at decreasing per-passenger-mile GHG emissions in the state. Elsewhere, London is implementing plans to mandate all private hire vehicles to be 'zero emission capable' by 2023, and Shenzhen, China, where the city's bus fleet is already fully electrified, has now made EVs the only vehicles eligible for ride-hailing licences.

Compared to typical drivers, TNC drivers tend to have higher average daily driving distances. Coupled with increased vehicle stock from TNC EV mandates, these two factors combined drive up local electricity demand, which may affect electricity supply infrastructure and, at sufficiently high levels, electricity pricing. Further, TNC drivers are more likely to rely on fast charging to minimize time when they are ineligible to pick up new fares. An increased reliance on fast charging creates larger peak power demands than an equivalent frequency of charge events using lower voltage chargers and also has implications for battery life and vehicle resale value.

With respect to electrified vehicle technology, AVs draw a significantly higher electric load than traditional vehicle systems. This fact has implications for the battery size – and, hence, vehicle cost and maximum range – of the AV. As these are key attributes that consumers weigh when considering an EV purchase, AVs will need to overcome these hurdles to make electric AVs an attractive purchase option. That said, AV technology will also allow users to send vehicles off to charge independently when their energy storage levels are low. This has advantages in allowing more centralized charging locations, reducing costs for infrastructure installation.

The most significant parameter to consider for both innovations, however, is the effect each will have on total VMT. AVs and TNCs alike may increase the number of deadhead trips (driver-only trips for TNCs and passenger-free trips for AVs), which in turn can increase congestion and contribute to greater energy use (Taiebat, Stolper and Xu 2019, Wadud, Mackenzie and Leiby 2016). These concerns could be reduced with implementation of centralized ownership models and optimized driving, passenger load and charging activities. Additionally, the extent to which these new transport approaches allow for right-sizing of vehicles (that is, more efficiently matching vehicle size and capacity with vehicle trip usage) represent opportunities for energy demand reductions.

Recent work by MIT researchers hypothesizes that AVs are likely to be prohibitively expensive in their early availability and considers a business case for so-called robotaxis, where AVs are owned by firms and hired out for consumer use (MIT Energy Initiative 2019). Should this scenario become reality, it is likely well suited for EV deployment, as electrification infrastructure and flexible vehicle scheduling could be centralized. This model would also make revenue collection for infrastructure costs easier and more direct, as aggregate vehicle travel distances could be more easily tracked without raising individual privacy concerns. Last, with regard to carbon intensity considerations, an AV taxi fleet represent a potential avenue to reducing LDV emissions (Greenblatt and Saxena 2015). Each of these innovations represents a potentially significant disruption to the existing transportation paradigm. A simultaneous push for electrification is likely to play a role in dictating their future trajectories. The relationship among these innovations is not likely to be unidirectional and additional simulation and empirical analysis are necessary to understand the interactions between and among the transport infrastructure and use cases of the future.

6.   CONCLUSION

Electric drivetrains are emerging again as viable options in many segments of the transport sector. This is motivated in part by a move to reduce reliance on fossil fuels and decrease the emissions consequences of energy use. While calls for full electrification of the vehicle fleet are widespread, a transition of this magnitude is a significant undertaking and is not likely to happen rapidly. In this chapter, we set out to provide context for a discussion of the future of electrified transportation and to consider the challenges and issues on the road ahead. As we assess the likely future trajectory of transport electrification, three important observations merit consideration.

First, the barriers to full electrification are non-trivial. Areas such as Norway, China and the state of California in the US offer valuable case studies in overcoming early hurdles in building a market for EVs. At the time of this writing, no nation has demonstrated a shift to an electrified vehicle fleet without significant policy intervention. This may change with continued technological progress, manufacturing improvements and future movements in fuel prices. However, in the near term, we anticipate the push for a fully electrified vehicle fleet to remain an aspirational goal in the absence of intervention. As these interventions are likely to come with significant economic costs, rigorous and targeted analysis of policy effectiveness and efficiency is needed.

Second, any move to increase the role electricity plays in transport networks is likely to produce benefits in the form of carbon emissions reductions, especially in the presence of routines for optimized vehicle charging. The linking of transport emissions and emissions from electricity generation will require careful planning and analysis to fully account for marginal vehicle emissions. This consolidation of energy supply sources will also amplify the need for continued decarbonization progress for electricity suppliers.

Finally, the nature of current infrastructure and transport support mechanisms requires scrutiny. As these elements of the transport system grew in a world of ICEVs, some attributes are not currently designed to accommodate an electrified fleet. Strategic thinking must guide investments that influence how, when and where EV drivers refuel their vehicles. Moreover, existing structures for public funding of transport-related expenditures need to be revisited and updated accordingly.

Although fleet electrification is likely to be a gradual process, there are important near-term considerations. On a per-mile basis, electricity is significantly less expensive than either gasoline or diesel as a result of differences in fuel prices and vehicle energy efficiencies. This illustrates that one of the main economic barriers to broader EV adoption is the additional fixed cost of an EV, specifically the battery cost. As our cost parity calculation demonstrates, significant battery cost reductions are necessary if oil prices remain at or near current levels. This is further complicated by the ongoing debate around the achievable lower bound to battery costs based on technological limits and the markets for battery manufacturing inputs. Our analysis indicates that PHEV–ICEV cost parity is potentially achievable in the near term. As PHEVs compare favourably to BEVs with respect to obstacles for consumer adoption (for example, shorter battery charge times, extended ranges, optional charging), they represent a potential off-ramp from the current ICEV-dominated vehicle fleet.

Meeting climate goals set forth by the IPCC requires sweeping changes to existing markets. These changes in the transport sector likely manifest in a move toward sector-wide electrification, at least in the horizon laid out by the IPCC. Such a move poses challenges, but near-term opportunities exist to move toward a low-carbon, electrified future. Ultimately, the feasibility of such a future will require a break from the status quo on the part of all transport sector participants on both the supply and demand sides of the market.

NOTES

1. For the discussion that follows, we use the term EVs to refer to electric vehicles that rely on stored electric power. In many cases, our current EV metrics combine fully electric (battery electric vehicles, or BEVs) and plug-in hybrid electric vehicles (PHEVs) that have a gasoline engine on board but can also be plugged directly into the grid for charging.
2. When comparing efficiencies, one would also want to account for inefficiencies upstream. If the marginal power plant is a combined cycle gas turbine power plant, which is roughly 60 per cent efficient, the efficiency of the EV would be roughly 48 per cent. Oil refineries are roughly 90 per cent efficient, bringing the efficiency of the internal combustion engine (ICE) vehicles to 18 per cent.
3. Currently, IEA models predict flat to moderate growth in oil prices to 2040, contingent on policy scenario assumptions (IEA 2019b).
4. In line with this section's discussion, this figure illustrates differences in fuel prices alone. For ease of comparison, we hold vehicle efficiencies fixed by vehicle type, across countries.
5. For a summary of the literature on the inelasticity of VMTs, see Knittel (2012).
6. Except where otherwise noted, prices are in real 2018 US dollars.
7. This travel distance is equal to the 85th percentile of daily driving for conventional vehicles in the United States (Li, Liu and Jia 2019). We use the US as a reference point to maintain consistency with the other inputs of our calculation. While we are not aware of a systematic study of travel ranges at the country level outside of the US, Plötz, Jakobsson and Sprei et al. (2017) study data from four locations (Germany, Western Sweden, Winnipeg, Canada, Seattle, US) and indicate values may be slightly lower in some other regions.
8. In line with Covert et al. (2016), analysis here relies on data and assumptions for the US and is based on our analysis of the US oil–gas price relationship and existing fuel tax levels. Outside the US context, we refer the reader to Newbery and Strbac (2016) for an exploration of cost parity calculations for the UK. Newbery and Strbac make a noteworthy effort to account for the full social costs across delivered energy source options in their model.
9. See http://ceepr.mit.edu/research/projects/WP-2020-010-tool, accessed 23 July 2021.
10. Honda offers two engines for the 2019 Honda Accord four-door. The combined fuel economy for the 1.5L Turbo is 33 MPG, while the combined fuel economy for the 2.0L Turbo is 27 MPG. For details, see fueleconomy.gov, accessed 23 July 2021.

11. Gasoline tax revenues typically fund road infrastructure. We return to this point in Section 4.2.
12. Tax rates elsewhere, especially in the EU, are higher than those in the US. This produces tax levels above the implied social cost of carbon. Accounting for this cost differential, and recognizing other potential externality costs (for example, damages from local emissions, especially in heavily populated areas), suggests that cost adjustments in other contexts may be necessary.
13. Alternatively, policy makers could adopt mileage taxes. This would have the same effect of increasing the costs of operating an EV relative to the costs assumed above.
14. See Figure 18.7a for tax-adjusted values across the computed battery price range.
15. These estimates are based on what MIT Energy Initiative (2019) calls a one-stage learning model. Effectively, the log of costs is regressed on the log of cumulative production, generating the learning rate. These models imply that battery costs will fall to below $100 per kWh by 2030 bringing them nearly to cost parity with an associated oil price of $80 per barrel. It is important to note that this calculation holds constant ICEV technology, which as noted above improves by roughly 2.4 per cent per year. If we account for these improvements, the 30 MPG comparison vehicle will instead have a fuel economy of 39 MPG by 2030, leading to a cost-parity oil price of $124 per barrel in our base case.
16. For a comprehensive review of existing studies, see Münzel et al. (2019).
17. Existing work finds similar results for national (Tal and Nicholas 2016, Tietge et al. 2016) and subnational policies (Clinton and Steinberg 2019, DeShazo, Sheldon and Carson 2017, Mersky et al. 2016).
18. Illustrations of these charging profile scenarios are included in Figure 18A.1 in the Appendix.
19. We assume an average annual capacity factor of 0.6 per cent. Source: https://www.eia.gov/todayinenergy/detail.php?id=25652, accessed 28 January 2020.
20. These base scenarios assume charging coincides with evening demand peaks based on observed vehicle charging behaviour and assumptions of the EVI-Pro model. Similar metrics for the various load scenarios are included in Table 18A.1 in the Appendix.
21. For the remainder of this section we focus on emissions for BEVs. Assessment of marginal PHEV emissions is complicated by the fuel-switching nature of PHEVs. As BEVs rely solely on electricity for power, the marginal emissions factor of the electricity grid plays a more significant role in determining the emissions from BEVs than PHEVs. For a discussion of BEV and PHEV emissions effects, see, for example, McLaren et al. (2016).
22. The average carbon intensity is defined to be total emissions from power generation divided by aggregate energy production. Marginal carbon intensity metrics instead measure the change in emissions intensity for an additional unit of power demand. As it is this additional demand that alters system power flows and subsequently modifies emissions levels, it is more accurate to focus on marginal emissions levels when considering the effect of charging additional EVs.
23. In our hypothetical example, the per-kWh tax is levied for electricity for EVs only and would therefore require separate metering for vehicle charging. For the purposes of this calculation, we assume zero cost and full compliance with this requirement.
24. See https://afdc.energy.gov/data/10380, accessed 23 July 2021.
25. See https://www.trucks.com/2018/06/14/ups-order-950-workhorse-electric-delivery-trucks/, accessed 23 July 2021.
26. See https://www.wired.com/story/electric-buses-havent-taken-over-world/, accessed 23 July 2021.
27. See https://afdc.energy.gov/data/10309, accessed 23 July 2021.
28. See https://theicct.org/blog/staff/benchmarking-growth-zero-emissions-trucking, accessed 23 July 2021; Renault Zoe, 41 kWh; Nissan Leaf 40 kWh.
29. See https://www.volvogroup.com/en-en/news/2018/apr/news-2879838.html, accessed 23 July 2021.
30. Long-haul trucking is defined as trips over 250 miles. Trucking sector ton-miles distribution is based on US observations and calculated from data provided by the US Bureau of Transportation Statistics, 'Value, tonnage, and ton-miles of freight by distance band', accessed 20 January 2020 at https://www.bts.gov/browse-statistical-products-and-data/freight-facts-and-figures/value-tonnage-and-ton-miles-freight.
31. Long-haul truckers often idle at night to provide electricity to the cabin. This consumes roughly 1 gallon of fuel per hour.
32. See, for example, https://www.electrek.co/2018/02/21/tesla-semi-defies-laws-physic-daimlers/, accessed 22 July 2021.
33. In the US, the average selling price of a new Class 8 truck was $117 426 in 2018 (American Truck Dealers 2018).
34. While Class 8 trucks are often on the road for longer than ten years, we would not expect the battery to last beyond ten years and therefore perform the calculation over this time interval. The typical ICE-based Class 8 truck engine is rebuilt twice within timeframe (US EPA 1995).
35. See, for example, https://afdc.energy.gov/data/, accessed 23 July 2021.
36. See Zhou et al. (2016), Gallet, Massier and Hamacher (2018) and https://www.proterra.com/vehicles/catalyst-electric-bus/range/, accessed 23 July 2021.

37. See Blynn (2018) and https://www.forbes.com/sites/sebastianblanco/2018/08/31/84-million-electric-buses, accessed 23 July 2021.
38. For example, estimates from Couch et al. (2019) suggest currently available electric Class 8 trucks weigh more than 7000 lb more than typical diesel vehicles. The authors point out that increases in tractor curb weight decrease maximum payload limits by a 2:1 ratio, indicating that payload capacity penalties for EVs could be substantial.

REFERENCES

Aber, J. (2016), *Electric Bus Analysis for New York City Transit*, Columbia University and NYC Transit report, accessed 17 January 2020 at http://www.columbia.edu/~ja3041/Electric%20Bus%20Analysis%20for%20 NYC%20Transit%20by%20J%20Aber%20Columbia%20University%20-%20May%202016.pdf.
American Truck Dealers (2018), *Annual Financial Profile of America's Franchised New-Truck Dealerships 2018*, accessed 13 February 2020 at https://www.nada.org/WorkArea/DownloadAsset.aspx?id=2147484 6413.
Antweiler, W. and S. Gulati (2019), *Estimating the Fuel-tax Elasticity of Vehicle Miles Travelled from Aggregate Data*, University of British Columbia white paper, accessed 31 January 2020 at https://pdfs.semanticscholar. org/1f7d/d76565994448b29ed1845bb55a68d7c17125.pdf.
Automotive News (2018), 'Nearly 100 electrified models slated to arrive through 2022', 1 October, accessed January 2020 at https://www.autonews.com/article/20181001/OEM04/181009990/nearly-100-electrified-models-slated-to-arrive-through-2022.
Berckmans, G., M. Messagie and J. Smekens et al. (2017), 'Cost projection of state of the art lithium-ion batteries for electric vehicles up to 2030', *Energies*, **10** (9), 1314.
Bjerkan, K. Y., T. E. Nørbech and M. E. Nordtømme (2016), 'Incentives for promoting battery electric vehicle (BEV) adoption in Norway', *Transportation Research Part D: Transport and Environment*, **43**, 169–80.
BloombergNEF (2019), 'Battery pack prices fall as market ramps up with market average at $156/kWh in 2019', 3 December, accessed January 2020 at https://about.bnef.com/blog/battery-pack-prices-fall-as-market-ramps-up-with-market-average-at-156-kwh-in-2019/.
Blynn, K. (2018), 'Accelerating bus electrification: enabling a sustainable transition to low carbon transportation systems', Master's thesis, MIT.
California Independent System Operator (CAISO) (2019), *2019 Summer Loads and Resources Assessment*, accessed 29 January 2020 at http://www.caiso.com/Documents/Briefing-2019-SummerLoads-Resources-Assessment-Report-May2019.pdf.
Campbell, P. (2018), 'Electric cars pave way to end of filling stations', *Financial Times*, 11 February, accessed February 2020 at https://www.ft.com/content/d9aee562-0838-11e8-9650-9c0ad2d7c5b5.
Clinton, B. C. and D. C. Steinberg (2019), 'Providing the spark: impact of financial incentives on battery electric vehicle adoption', *Journal of Environmental Economics and Management*, **98**, Article 102255.
Couch, P., J. Leonard and E. Johnstone et al. (2019), *2018 Feasibility Assessment for Drayage Trucks*, Clean Transportation and Energy Consultants, accessed 13 February 2020 at https://www.gladstein.org/gna_whitepapers/2018-feasibility-assessment-for-drayage-trucks.
Covert, T., M. Greenstone and C. R. Knittel (2016), 'Will we ever stop using fossil fuels?', *Journal of Economic Perspectives*, **30** (1), 117–38.
Cozzi, L. and A. Petropoulos (2019), Growing preference for SUVs challenges emissions reductions in passenger car market, IEA, 15 October, accessed October 2019 at https://www.iea.org/commentaries/growing-preference-for-suvs-challenges-emissions-reductions-in-passenger-car-market.
Davis, L. W. and J. M. Sallee (2019), 'Should electric vehicle drivers pay a mileage tax?', *NBER Working Paper No. 26072*, National Bureau of Economic Research.
Daziano, R. A. (2013), 'Conditional-logit Bayes estimators for consumer valuation of electric vehicle driving range', *Resource and Energy Economics*, **35** (3), 429–50.
DeShazo, J. R., T. L. Sheldon and R. T. Carson (2017), 'Designing policy incentives for cleaner technologies: lessons from California's plug-in electric vehicle rebate program', *Journal of Environmental Economics and Management*, **84**, 18–43.
Dong, J., D. Davidson, F. Southworth and T. Reuscher (2012), *Analysis of Automobile Travel Demand Elasticities with Respect To Travel Cost*, Oak Ridge National Laboratory, accessed 14 February 2020 at https://www.fhwa.dot.gov/policyinformation/pubs/hpl-15-014/TCElasticities.pdf.
Doppelbauer, M. and P. Winzer (2017), 'A lighter motor for tomorrow's electric car', *IEEE Spectrum*, **54** (7), 26–31.

Dumortier, J., S. Siddiki and S. Carley et al. (2015), 'Effects of providing total cost of ownership information on consumers' intent to purchase a hybrid or plug-in electric vehicle', *Transportation Research Part A: Policy and Practice*, **72**, 71–86.

Ecola, L., C. Rohr and J. Zmud et al. (2014), *The Future of Driving in Developing Countries*, Rand Corporation Institute for Mobility Research, accessed 5 November 2019 at https://www.rand.org/pubs/research_reports/RR636.html.

Edwards, K. D., R. M. Wagner and T. E. Briggs et al. (2011), 'Defining engine efficiency limits', paper presented at 17th DEER Conference, Oak Ridge National Laboratory Detroit, MI, accessed 14 February 2020 at https://www.energy.gov/sites/prod/files/2014/03/f8/deer11_edwards.pdf.

Egbue, O. and S. Long (2012), 'Barriers to widespread adoption of electric vehicles: an analysis of consumer attitudes and perceptions', *Energy Policy*, **48**, 717–29.

Egbue, O., S. Long and V. A. Samaranayake (2017), 'Mass deployment of sustainable transportation: evaluation of factors that influence electric vehicle adoption', *Clean Technologies and Environmental Policy*, **19** (7), 1927–39.

ERCOT (2019), *Report on the Capacity, Demand and Reserves in the ERCOT Region, 2020–2029*, accessed 29 January 2020 at http://www.ercot.com/content/wcm/lists/167023/CapacityDemandandReserveReport-Dec2019.pdf.

EVAdoption (2018), 'Statistics of the week: comparing vehicle ranges for gas, BEV and PHEV models', 27 January, accessed November 2019 at https://evadoption.com/statistics-of-the-week-comparing-vehicle-ranges-for-gas-bevs-and-phevs/.

EV Norway (2020), 'Norwegian EV policy', accessed January 2020 at https://elbil.no/english/norwegian-ev-policy/.

ExxonMobil (2019), *2019 Outlook for Energy: A Perspective to 2040*, accessed 10 January 2020 at https://corporate.exxonmobil.com/-/media/Global/Files/outlook-for-energy/2019-Outlook-for-Energy_v4.pdf.

Franke, T. and J. F. Krems (2013), 'What drives range preferences in electric vehicle users?', *Transport Policy*, **30**, 56–62.

Franke, T., I. Neumann and F. Bühler et al. (2012), 'Experiencing range in an electric vehicle: understanding psychological barriers', *Applied Psychology*, **61** (3), 368–91.

Gallet, M., T. Massier and T. Hamacher (2018), 'Estimation of the energy demand of electric buses based on real-world data for large-scale public transport networks', *Applied Energy*, **230**, 344–56.

Global Fuel Economy Initiative (GFEI) (2014), 'International comparison of light-duty vehicle fuel economy: evolution over 8 years from 2005 to 2013', *Working Paper 11*, accessed 19 June 2019 at https://www.globalfueleconomy.org/data-and-research/publications/gfei-working-paper-11.

Global Fuel Economy Initiative (GFEI) (2017), 'International comparison of light-duty vehicle fuel economy 2005–2015', *Working Paper 15*, accessed 19 June 2019 at https://www.globalfueleconomy.org/data-and-research/publications/gfei-working-paper-15.

Gnann, T., P. Plötz and F. Kley (2012), 'Vehicle charging infrastructure demand for the introduction of plug-in electric vehicles in Germany and the US', paper presented at the 26th Electric Vehicle Symposium (EVS26), Los Angeles, California.

Graff Zivin, J. S., M. J. Kotchen and E. T. Mansur (2014), 'Spatial and temporal heterogeneity of marginal emissions: implications for electric cars and other electricity-shifting policies', *Journal of Economic Behavior & Organization*, **107**, 248–68.

Greenblatt, J. B. and S. Saxena (2015), 'Autonomous taxis could greatly reduce greenhouse-gas emissions of US light-duty vehicles', *Nature Climate Change*, **5** (9), 860–63.

Hardman, S., A. Jenn and G. Tal et al. (2018), 'A review of consumer preferences of and interactions with electric vehicle charging infrastructure', *Transportation Research Part D: Transport and Environment*, **62**, 508–23.

Haugneland, P., E. Lorentzen, C. Bu and E. Hauge (2017), 'Put a price on carbon to fund EV incentives – Norwegian EV policy success', paper presented at the 30th Electric Vehicle Symposium (EVS30), Stuttgart, Germany, accessed 18 January 2020 at https://elbil.no/wp-content/uploads/2016/08/EVS30-Norwegian-EV-policy-paper.pdf.

Hawkes, A. D. (2014), 'Long-run marginal CO_2 emissions factors in national electricity systems', *Applied Energy*, **125**, 197–205.

Holland, S. P., E. T. Mansur, N. Z. Muller and A. J. Yates (2016), 'Are there environmental benefits from driving electric vehicles? The importance of local factors', *American Economic Review*, **106** (12), 3700–29.

Hove, A. and D. Sandalow (2019), *Electric Vehicle Charging in China and the United States*, Columbia SIPA Center on Global Energy Policy, accessed 31 January 2020 at https://energypolicy.columbia.edu/sites/default/files/file-uploads/EV_ChargingChina-CGEP_Report_Final.pdf.

IHS Markit (2017), 'The future of cars 2040', accessed December 2019 at http://www.businesswire.com/news/home/20171113006466/en/.

Intergovernmental Panel on Climate Change (IPCC) (2014), 'Transport', in IPCC, *Climate Change 2014: Mitigation of Climate Change. Contribution of Working Group III to the Fifth Assessment Report of the Intergovernmental Panel on Climate Change*, Cambridge, UK and New York: Cambridge University Press.

Intergovernmental Panel on Climate Change (IPCC) (2018), 'Global warming of 1.5°C', in IPCC, *An IPCC Special Report on the Impacts of Global Warming of 1.5°C Above Pre-Industrial Levels and Related Global Greenhouse Gas Emission Pathways, in the Context of Strengthening the Global Response to the Threat of Climate Change, Sustainable Development, and Efforts to Eradicate Poverty*, accessed 31 January 2020 at https://www.ipcc.ch/sr15.

International Energy Agency (IEA) (2017), *Global EV Outlook 2017: Two Million and Counting*, Paris: IEA.

International Energy Agency (IEA) (2018a), *CO_2 Emissions from Fuel Combustion 2018*, Paris: IEA.

International Energy Agency (IEA) (2018b), *Nordic EV Outlook 2018: Insights from Leaders in Electric Mobility*, Paris: IEA.

International Energy Agency (IEA) (2019a), *Global EV Outlook 2019: Scaling-up the Transition to Electric Mobility*, Paris: IEA.

International Energy Agency (IEA) (2019b), *World Energy Outlook 2019*, Paris: IEA.

Jenn, A., J. H. Lee, S. Hardman and G. Tal (2020), 'An in-depth examination of electric vehicle incentives: consumer heterogeneity and changing response over time', *Transportation Research Part A: Policy and Practice*, **132**, 97–109.

Jin, L., S. Searle and N. Lutsey (2014), *Evaluation of State-level U.S. Electric Vehicle Incentives*, International Council on Clean Transportation white paper, accessed 17 January 2020 at https://theicct.org/sites/default/files/publications/ICCT_state-EV-incentives_20141030_0.pdf.

Jochem, P., S. Babrowski and W. Fichtner (2015), 'Assessing CO_2 emissions of electric vehicles in Germany in 2030', *Transportation Research Part A: Policy and Practice*, **78**, 68–83.

Kapoor, R., J. MacDuffie and D. Wilde (2020), 'Analysis shows continued industry-wide decline in electric vehicle battery costs', February, Mack Institute for Innovation Management, accessed March 2020 at https://mackinstitute.wharton.upenn.edu/2020/electric-vehicle-battery-costs-decline/.

Kittner, N., F. Lill and D. M. Kammen (2017), 'Energy storage deployment and innovation for the clean energy transition', *Nature Energy*, **2** (9), Article 17125.

Klingenberg, M. (2017), 'Nettet overbelastes, lamper blinker og sikringer ryker: el- bilen pekes ut som synde-bukk', [The grid is overloaded, lamps flash and fuses light up: electric car is designated as scapegoat], 4 October, accessed February 2020 at https://www.tu.no/artikler/nettet-overbelastes-lamper-blinker-og-sikringer-ryker-elbilen-pekes-ut-som-syndebukk/408789?utm_source=newsletter-2017-10-04.

Knittel, C. R. (2011), 'Automobiles on steroids: product attribute trade-offs and technological progress in the automobile sector', *American Economic Review*, **101** (7), 3368–99.

Knittel, C. R. (2012), 'Reducing petroleum consumption from transportation', *Journal of Economic Perspectives*, **26** (1), 93–118.

Kühlwein, J., J. German, and A. Bandivadekar (2014), *Development of Test Cycle Conversion Factors Among Worldwide Light-Duty Vehicle CO_2 Emission Standards*, White Paper, International Council on Clean Transportation, accessed 22 July 2021 at https://theicct.org/sites/default/files/publications/ICCT_LDV-test-cycle-conversion-factors_sept2014.pdf.

Leard, B., J. Linn and C. Munnings (2019), 'Explaining the evolution of passenger vehicle miles traveled in the United States', *The Energy Journal*, **40** (1), 25–54.

Lévay, P. Z., Y. Drossinos and C. Thiel (2017), 'The effect of fiscal incentives on market penetration of electric vehicles: a pairwise comparison of total cost of ownership', *Energy Policy*, **105**, 524–33.

Li, S., L. Tong, J. Xing and Y. Zhou (2017), 'The market for electric vehicles: indirect network effects and policy design', *Journal of the Association of Environmental and Resource Economists*, **4** (1), 89–133.

Li, X., C. Liu and J. Jia (2019), 'Ownership and usage analysis of alternative fuel vehicles in the United States with the 2017 National Household Travel Survey data', *Sustainability*, **11** (8), 2262.

Litman, T. (2019), *Understanding Transport Demand and Elasticities: How Prices and Other Factors Affect Travel Behavior*, Victoria Transport Policy Institute, accessed 31 January 2020 at https://www.vtpi.org/elasticities.pdf.

Lorentzen, E., P. Haugneland, C. Bu and E. Hauge (2017), 'Charging infrastructure experiences in Norway – the worlds most advanced EV market', paper presented at the 30th Electric Vehicle Symposium (EVS30), Stuttgart, Germany, accessed 18 January 2020 at https://elbil.no/wp-content/uploads/2016/08/EVS30-Charging-infrastrucure-experiences-in-Norway-paper.pdf.

MacKenzie, D. (2018), 'Does the Tesla Semi defy the laws of physics?', 26 February, University of Washington, accessed December 2019 at https://sites.uw.edu/stlab/2018/02/26/does-the-tesla-semi-defy-the-laws-of-physics/.

McLaren, J., J. Miller and E. O'Shaughnessy et al. (2016), 'CO_2 emissions associated with electric vehicle charging: the impact of electricity generation mix, charging infrastructure availability and vehicle type', *The Electricity Journal*, **29** (5), 72–88.

Mersky, A. C., F. Sprei, C. Samaras and Z. Qian (2016), 'Effectiveness of incentives on electric vehicle adoption in Norway', *Transportation Research Part D: Transport and Environment*, **46** (July), 56–68.

MIT Energy Initiative (2019), *Insights into Future Mobility*, accessed 19 November 2019 at http://energy.mit.edu/insightsintofuturemobility.

Münzel, C., P. Plötz, F. Sprei and T. Gnann (2019), 'How large is the effect of financial incentives on electric vehicle sales? A global review and European analysis', *Energy Economics*, **84**, Article 104493.

Newbery, D. and G. Strbac (2016), 'What is needed for battery electric vehicles to become socially cost competitive?', *Economics of Transportation*, **5**, 1–11.

Nykvist, B. and M. Nilsson (2015), 'Rapidly falling costs of battery packs for electric vehicles', *Nature Climate Change*, **5** (4), 329–32.

Organisation for Economic Co-operation and Development (OECD) (2018), 'Selected excise duties in OECD countries', in OECD, *Consumption Tax Trends 2018: VAT/GST and Excise Rates, Trends and Policy Issues*, Paris: OECD Publishing.

Organisation for Economic Co-operation and Development (OECD) (2019), *Taxing Energy Use 2019: Using Taxes for Climate Action*, Paris: OECD Publishing.

Palmer, K., J. E. Tate, Z. Wadud and J. Nellthorp (2018), 'Total cost of ownership and market share for hybrid and electric vehicles in the UK, US and Japan', *Applied Energy*, **209**, 108–19.

PJM (2019), *Summer 2019 PJM Reliability Assessment*, accessed 29 January 2020 at http://www.puc.state.pa.us/Electric/pdf/Reliability/Summer_Reliability_2019-PJM.pdf.

Plötz, P., N. Jakobsson and F. Sprei (2017), 'On the distribution of individual daily driving distances', *Transportation Research Part B: Methodological*, **101**, 213–27.

Refa, N. and N. Hubbers (2019), 'Impact of smart charging on EVs charging behaviour assessed from real charging events', paper presented at the 32nd Electric Vehicle Symposium (EVS32), Lyon, France, accessed 21 January 2020 at https://www.researchgate.net/publication/333262496_Impact_of_Smart_Charging_on_EVs_Charging_Behaviour_Assessed_from_Real_Charging_Events.

Roberts, A., R. Brooks and P. Shipway (2014), 'Internal combustion engine cold-start efficiency: a review of the problem, causes and potential solutions', *Energy Conversion and Management*, **82**, 327–50.

Rubeis, M., S. Groves, T. Portera and G. Bonaccorsi (2019), 'Is there a future for service stations?', Boston Consulting Group (BCG), 12 July, accessed February 2020 at https://www.bcg.com/publications/2019/service-stations-future.aspx.

Santos, G. and H. Davies (2019), 'Incentives for quick penetration of electric vehicles in five European countries: perceptions from experts and stakeholders', *Transportation Research Part A: Policy and Practice*, **137**, 326–42.

Schmidt, O., A. Hawkes, A. Gambhir and I. Staffell (2017), 'The future cost of electrical energy storage based on experience rates', *Nature Energy*, **2** (8), Article 17110.

Sierzchula, W., S. Bakker, K. Maat and B. van Wee (2014), 'The influence of financial incentives and other socio-economic factors on electric vehicle adoption', *Energy Policy*, **68**, 183–94.

Smart, J., T. Bradley and S. Salisbury (2014), 'Actual versus estimated utility factor of a large set of privately owned Chevrolet volts', *SAE International Journal of Alternative Powertrains*, **3** (1), 30–35.

Sripad, S. and V. Viswanathan (2017), 'Performance metrics required of next-generation batteries to make a practical electric semi truck', *ACS Energy Letters*, **2** (7), 1669–73.

Taiebat, M., S. Stolper and M. Xu (2019), 'Forecasting the impact of connected and automated vehicles on energy use: a microeconomic study of induced travel and energy rebound', *Applied Energy*, **247**, 297–308.

Tal, G. and M. Nicholas (2016), 'Exploring the impact of the federal tax credit on the plug-in vehicle market', *Transportation Research Record*, **2572** (1), 95–102.

Tietge, U. (2018), '2017 year in review: European diesel down, electric vehicles on the rise', 24 January, International Council on Clean Transportation, accessed October 2019 at https://theicct.org/blog/staff/2017-year-review-european-diesel-down-electric-vehicles-rise.

Tietge, U., P. Mock, N. Lutsey and A. Campestrini (2016), *Comparison of Leading Electric Vehicle Policy and Deployment in Europe*, International Council on Clean Transportation white paper, accessed 30 January 2020 at https://theicct.org/sites/default/files/publications/ICCT_EVpolicies-Europe-201605.pdf.

Truckload Indexes (2020), 'How many gallons does it take to fill up a big rig?', 3 January, accessed January 2020 at https://www.truckloadindexes.com/data-commentary/how-many-gallons-does-it-take-to-fill-up-a-big-rig.

Union of Concerned Scientists (2018), 'Electric vehicle batteries: materials, cost, lifespan', 9 March 2018, accessed 23 July 2021 at https://www.ucsusa.org/resources/ev-batteries.

Universal Technical Institute (UTI) (2019), 'Gas vs. diesel engines: what's the difference?', 29 August, accessed January 2020 at https://www.uti.edu/blog/Diesel/gas-vs-diesel-engines.

US Department of Energy (US DOE) (2011), 'Fact #707: December 26, 2011 illustration of truck classes' accessed 22 July 2021 at https://www.energy.gov/eere/vehicles/fact-707-december-26-2011-illustration-truck-classes.

US Department of Energy (US DOE) (2018), 'FOTW #1047, September 17, 2018: daily vehicle miles traveled varies with the number of household vehicles', accessed November 2019 at https://www.energy.gov/eere/vehicles/articles/fotw-1047-september-17-2018-daily-vehicle-miles-traveled-varies-number.

US Department of Energy (US DOE) (2019), 'Where the energy goes: gasoline vehicles', accessed January 2020 at https://fueleconomy.gov/feg/atv.shtml.

US Department of Transportation (US DOT) (2017), 'Table 2: average annual vehicle-miles of travel per vehicle and average age: 2009 NHTS', Bureau of Transportation Statistics, accessed December 2019 at https://www.bts.gov/archive/publications/bts_fact_sheets/oct_2015/table_02.

US Department of Transportation (US DOT) (2019), 'Forecasts of vehicle miles traveled, Spring 2019', US Department of Transport, accessed October 2019 at https://www.fhwa.dot.gov/policyinformation/tables/vmt/vmt_forecast_sum.cfm.

US Energy Information Administration (US EIA) (2016), 'Carbon dioxide emissions coefficients', accessed November 2019 at https://www.eia.gov/environment/emissions/co2_vol_mass.php.

US Energy Information Administration (US EIA) (2017), *Electric Power Monthly: March 2017*, US Energy Information Agency, accessed 30 January 2020 at https://www.eia.gov/electricity/monthly/archive/march2017.pdf.

US Energy Information Administration (US EIA) (2019), 'FAQ: How much tax do we pay on a gallon of gasoline and on a gallon of diesel fuel?', accessed October 2019 at https://www.eia.gov/tools/faqs/faq.php?id=10&t=10.

US Energy Information Administration (US EIA) (2020), *Annual Energy Outlook 2020 with Projections to 2050*, US Energy Information Agency, accessed 31 January 2020 at https://www.eia.gov/outlooks/aeo/pdf/AEO2020%20Full%20Report.pdf.

US Environmental Protection Agency (US EPA) (1995), *Heavy-Duty Engine Rebuilding Practices*, EPA-420-R-95-104, accessed 12 February 2020 at https://nepis.epa.gov/Exe/ZyPURL.cgi?Dockey=P100UN50.txt.

US Environmental Protection Agency (US EPA) (2016), *Technical Update of the Social Cost of Carbon for Regulatory Impact Analysis*, Interagency Working Group on Social Cost of Greenhouse Gases, accessed 12 February 2020 at https://www.epa.gov/sites/default/files/2016-12/documents/sc_co2_tsd_august_2016.pdf.

Vijayagopal, R., K. Gallagher, D. Lee and A. Rousseau (2016), 'Comparing the powertrain energy densities of electric and gasoline vehicles', *SAE Technical Paper 2016-01-0903*.

Wadud, Z., D. MacKenzie and P. Leiby (2016), 'Help or hindrance? The travel, energy and carbon impacts of highly automated vehicles', *Transportation Research Part A: Policy and Practice*, **86**, 1–18.

Wappelhorst, S., P. Mock and Z. Yang (2018), *Using Vehicle Taxation Policy to Lower Transport Emissions: An Overview for Passenger Cars in Europe*, International Council on Clean Transportation, accessed 14 January 2020 at https://theicct.org/sites/default/files/publications/EU_vehicle_taxation_Report_20181214_0.pdf.

Woo, J. R., H. Choi and J. Ahn (2017), 'Well-to-wheel analysis of greenhouse gas emissions for electric vehicles based on electricity generation mix: a global perspective', *Transportation Research Part D: Transport and Environment*, **51**, 340–50.

Wood, E., C. Rames and M. Muratori et al. (2017), *National Plug-In Electric Vehicle Infrastructure Analysis*, US Department of Energy, Office of Energy Efficiency and Renewable Energy.

Xing, J., B. Leard and S. Li (2019), 'What does an electric vehicle replace?', *NBER Working Paper No. 25771*, National Bureau of Economic Research.

Yang, Z. and A. Bandivadekar (2017), *2017 Global Update: Light-Duty Vehicle Greenhouse Gas and Fuel Economy Standards*, International Council on Clean Transportation, accessed 6 November 2019 at https://theicct.org/sites/default/files/publications/2017-Global-LDV-Standards-Update_ICCT-Report_23062017_vF.pdf.

Yang, Z., P. Slowik, N. Lutsey and S. Searle (2016), *Principles for Effective Electric Vehicle Incentive Design*, International Council on Clean Transportation white paper, accessed 14 February 2020 at https://theicct.org/sites/default/files/publications/ICCT_IZEV-incentives-comp_201606.pdf.

Zhang, Y., Z. Qian, F. Sprei and B. Li (2016), 'The impact of car specifications, prices and incentives for battery electric vehicles in Norway: choices of heterogeneous consumers', *Transportation Research Part C: Emerging Technologies*, **69**, 386–401.

Zhou, B., Y. Wu and B. Zhou et al. (2016), 'Real-world performance of battery electric buses and their life-cycle benefits with respect to energy consumption and carbon dioxide emissions', *Energy*, **96**, 603–13.

APPENDIX

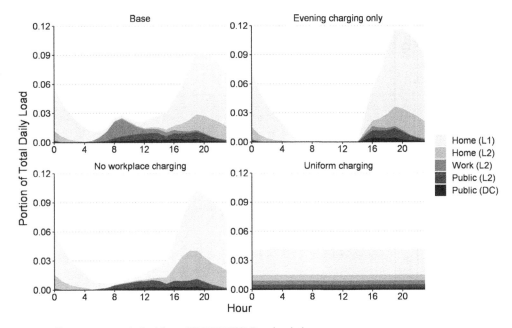

Note: Charge patterns derived from US DOE EVI-Pro simulations.

Sources: Wood et al. (2017) and authors' calculations. EVI-pro tool available at https://maps.nrel.gov/cec/, accessed 27 August 2019.

Figure 18A.1 Vehicle charging scenarios

Table 18A.1 Projected electric vehicle loads by charging scenario

	CAISO (US)		PJM (US)		ERCOT (US)		EU-28		China		Japan	
	MW	%	MW	%	MW	%	MW	%	MW	%	MW	%
Scenario: Current EV share												
Base case	262	0.4	62	0.03	19	0.02	421	0.04	1 285	0.1	115	0.04
Uniform	119	0.2	28	0.01	9	0.01	192	0.02	585	0.03	52	0.02
No workplace	294	0.4	69	0.03	21	0.02	471	0.05	1 438	0.1	128	0.04
Evening only	332	0.5	78	0.04	24	0.02	533	0.1	1 627	0.1	145	0.05
Scenario: 7% BEV 4% PHEV												
Base case	2 541	3.6	4 803	2.4	1 789	1.7	15 337	1.5	11 283	0.6	3 147	1
Uniform	1 157	1.6	2 186	1.1	815	0.8	6 981	0.7	5 136	0.3	1 432	0.5
No workplace	2 845	4	5 378	2.6	2 004	1.9	17 173	1.7	12 634	0.7	3 523	1.1
Evening only	3 217	4.6	6 082	3	2 266	2.1	19 421	1.9	14 288	0.8	3 985	1.3
Scenario: 30% BEV 70% PHEV												
Base case	21 422	30.5	40 498	19.8	15 088	14	129 311	12.8	95 131	5.3	26 531	8.5
Uniform	9 751	13.9	18 435	9	6 868	6.4	58 863	5.8	43 304	2.4	12 077	3.9
No workplace	23 987	34.1	45 345	22.2	16 894	15.7	144 791	14.3	106 519	5.9	29 707	9.5
Evening only	27 127	38.6	51 282	25.1	19 106	17.8	163 746	16.2	120 464	6.7	33 596	10.7
Scenario: 100% BEV												
Base case	24 909	35.4	47 090	23.1	17 544	16.3	150 362	14.9	110 618	6.2	30 850	9.9
Uniform	11 339	16.1	21 435	10.5	7 986	7.4	68 445	6.8	50 353	2.8	14 043	4.5
No workplace	27 891	39.7	52 727	25.8	19 644	18.3	168 362	16.7	123 860	6.9	34 543	11
Evening only	31 543	44.8	59 630	29.2	22 216	20.6	190 402	18.8	140 074	7.8	39 065	12.5

Notes: Percentage values are per cent of system capacity. The data sources and assumptions, including system capacity, are described in Table 18.7. The charging profiles for hourly maximum load are scaled from the charging profile of the US DOE's EVI-Pro market simulation. See Figure 18A.1 for source information and profile illustrations.

Table 18A.2   *Trends in new light-duty vehicle fuel economy (MPG)*

	2012	2013	2014	2015	Mean
France	45.2	47.0	43.6	45.2	45.3
Italy	42.8	44.4	41.3	42.8	42.8
Japan	45.2	48.0	39.9	37.9	42.8
UK	42.0	43.6	39.9	40.6	41.5
Germany	39.9	41.3	38.6	39.2	39.7
India	41.3	41.3	37.9	37.9	39.6
Brazil	33.6	34.1	29.8	30.5	32.0
China	30.9	31.4	28.3	29.0	29.9
Australia	28.3	29.4	27.7	28.0	28.4
Canada	27.0	27.4	25.6	25.6	26.4
US	25.6	26.1	25.8	25.8	25.8

Note: Reported values are average fuel economy for new LDVs and are normalized to the Worldwide Harmonized Light Vehicles Test Cycle.

Sources: The data for 2012–13 are from GFEI (2014); the data for 2014–15 are from GFEI (2017).

19. Electrification of residential and commercial heating

Mathilde Fajardy and David M. Reiner

1. INTRODUCTION

Heating and cooling involve multiple applications across various sectors and usually refer to temperature management of space, water and processes in residential and commercial buildings and across industry. The diversity of applications makes accounting for cooling – and especially heating-related energy demand and emissions across various sectors – challenging. Even extracting consistent data on heat-related energy demand and emissions can be very laborious, since national statistics will often aggregate at the sector (for example, buildings, industry) or sub-sector (residential, commercial, given industry) level, or simply lump heat and electricity together.

By any accounting, numbers for global heating and cooling energy demand and associated CO_2 emissions are staggering. In 2017, total heating demand accounted for 58 800 terrawatt-hours (TWh) of energy demand (half of total energy demand) and 12.6 gigatons of CO_2 ($GtCO_2$) of emissions (International Energy Agency [IEA] 2018a, 2019f), as shown in Figure 19.1. So far, demand for cooling is only responsible for 1900 TWh (1.7 per cent of total energy demand) and 1.1 $GtCO_2$ (3.4 per cent of global emissions), but has increased by 150 per cent in less than 20 years (IEA 2019a, 2019b).

Process, space and water heating is still largely dominated by direct combustion of fossil fuels (apart from traditional biomass, which is considered neutral from a carbon accounting perspective). This can be explained by the high energy density of these fuels and their ability to meet a variable heat demand. Thus, only 7 per cent of total heat demand is electrified (IEA 2018a), mostly in buildings, and less than 6 per cent is supplied by district heating, while 85 per cent is via direct combustion of fossil fuels (2017 values, IEA 2019f). Although 7 per cent is the global average, electrification rates vary greatly across the world, depending on availability and cost of electricity or its competitors. Figure 19.2 provides total and per capita residential heating demand by source in selected regions. For example, UK residential heating is 85 per cent reliant on natural gas, encouraged by gas reserves in the North Sea. In Sweden, however, solid biomass boilers meet 17 per cent of residential heating demand, and district heating make up 51 per cent of heating demand, of which 87 per cent is sourced from biofuels and wastes (IEA 2019c) owing to the high availability of bio-feedstock and established bioenergy supply chains. In regions that boast high availability of low-cost electricity, often based on hydroelectric power, such as Norway or Quebec, electrification of residential heat reaches 56–65 per cent (2017 values; European Commission 2019b, Natural Resources Canada 2019). Otherwise, high penetration rates are only found in countries with low heat demand, such as Albania or Malta, which highlights the difficulty of electrifying heat, since variability of heat demand poses significant load balancing challenges (European Commission, 2019b).

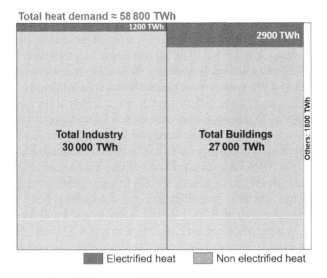

Source: Authors based on IEA (2018a, 2019a, 2019b).

Figure 19.1   Total and electrified heat demand per sector

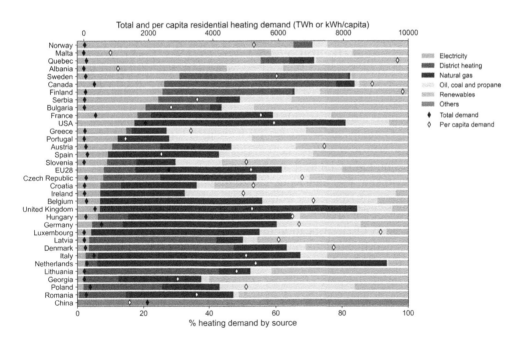

Sources: Authors based on Building Energy Research Center (BERC) (2018), Energy Information Administration (EIA) (2019), European Commission (2019b), Natural Resources Canada (2019).

Figure 19.2   Total and per capita residential heating by source in a selection of countries and provinces

While most climate policies have focused on decarbonizing the power sector, the heat sector has remained virtually untouched. In 2017, only 10 per cent of heat was generated from renewable sources (IEA 2018a). The largest share of renewable heat comes from bioenergy, mainly for industrial applications, followed by renewable electricity, mainly in buildings. Only 1100 TWh comes from renewable electricity (ibid.).

Electrification of heating enables the move from a highly dispersed CO_2 emissions model to a model where CO_2 emissions are centralized around electricity production and hence easier to abate. As current heating needs are largely met by fossil fuels and traditional biomass, it also means that supply is still subject to the availability and cost of these resources. In 2018, the USA, Russia and the Middle East were responsible for over 60 per cent of global natural gas production (IEA 2019f). From an energy security perspective, electrification enables diversification by decoupling heat sinks from heat sources. The integration of renewables, modern biomass and/or abated fossil-fuel electricity (for example, using carbon capture and storage or CCS) could provide more flexibility and make the overall energy system more resilient than the incumbent one.

Pathways to electrify heat in the residential and commercial sectors have been explored at the global (IEA 2019a, Knobloch et al. 2019), European (Connolly et al. 2014, Heinen et al. 2018) and national levels, in particular in the US (Paige et al. 2017, White and Rhodes 2019), and the UK (Cooper et al. 2016, Element Energy and E4Tech 2018, Strbac et al. 2018, Zhang et al. 2018).

The Paris Agreement's commitment to limit global temperature increase to 'well below 2°C' has been translated into regional, national and subnational initiatives to reach net zero greenhouse gas emissions by 2050 or earlier at the city (New York), state (California) and country (UK, France, Sweden, Finland, Norway and New Zealand) levels. These pledges have resulted in a renewed interest in further exploring deep decarbonization pathways for the heat sector.

The industrial sector is also responsible for a large fraction of heat demand and associated CO_2 emissions. Globally, about 30 000 TWh are used for space and process heating in industrial sites, and only about 10 per cent of this heat supply is renewable (2017 values, IEA 2018a). As a result, industrial heat was responsible for roughly 10 per cent of global CO_2 emissions (Friedmann, Fan and Tang, 2019). In the European context, a full electrification scenario of the industrial sector would increase total electricity demand in industry by more than a factor of ten, from 125 TWh to 1713 TWh (Lechtenböhmer et al. 2016). The challenges and costs of electrification of heat in industry are, however, much more context and industry dependent than in the building sector. Addressing the role of electrification in industrial heating requires detailed assessments of the different uses of heat across different industries in a given regional context. Given the scarcity of such surveys, and the high diversity of heat end-uses in industry, relatively few studies have looked at electrification of industrial heat (Beyond Zero Emissions 2018, Friedmann et al. 2019, Lechtenböhmer et al. 2016, Luh et al. 2019, Paige et al. 2017). For the purpose of this study, we chose to focus on the electrification of residential and commercial heating.

This chapter gathers evidence from global and country-level studies to explore the potential for electrification of heating in the buildings sector. The remainder of this chapter is structured as follows. Section 2 summarizes current heat supply and CO_2 emissions; Section 3 presents the different technology options to decarbonize heating; Section 4 provides an overview of the challenges and opportunities of electrification;

Section 5 discusses global and regional outlooks for the role of electrification of heat in the future; and Section 6 concludes.

As data related to energy demand and CO_2 emissions from heating is not straightforward to obtain or compare across countries, for the sake of consistency, most of the data we present is derived from various IEA publications.

2.   CURRENT ENERGY DEMAND, SUPPLY AND CO_2 EMISSIONS

First, it is helpful to understand how energy demand in buildings is distributed across different end-uses, and how this demand has evolved in the recent past. Figure 19.3 shows the evolution of the energy demand from the buildings sector by energy service, as well as total floor area and building energy intensity over the past two decades. Despite efficiency improvements to curb energy use in buildings, the 2000–2017 period has seen a 22 per cent increase in building energy demand. A key driver of this trend is the increase in floor area. While appliance efficiency and building envelope[1] improvements have enabled a 28 per cent drop in building energy intensity, global floor area has increased at a faster rate of 65 per cent over this period. This global increase in floor area is mainly driven by China, which has added 30 billion m^2 since 2000, roughly doubling its total to 58 billion m^2 by 2017, equivalent to 25 per cent of global floor area (IEA 2019a).

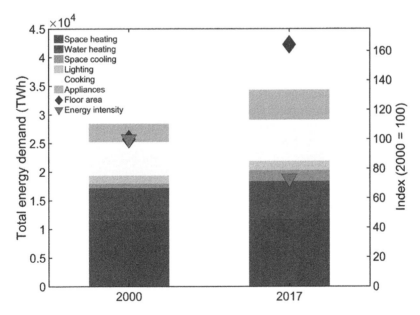

Source: Authors based on IEA (2019a).

Figure 19.3   *Energy demand in the buildings sector per end-use (y-axis LHS) and total floor area and energy intensity relative to 2000 (y-axis RHS), between 2000 and 2017*

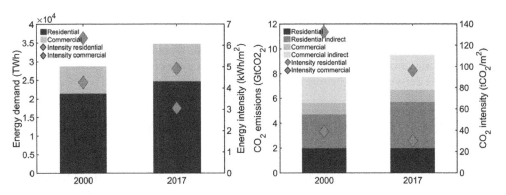

Note: Demand and emissions are displayed as stacked bars and measured on the LHS y-axis, while the intensities are displayed as diamonds and measured on the RHS y-axis.

Source: Authors based on IEA (2019a).

Figure 19.4   *Energy demand and energy intensity (left), and CO_2 emissions and CO_2 intensity (right) of residential and commercial buildings between 2000 and 2017*

Direct use of coal, oil or natural gas is responsible for 37 per cent of building energy demand (IEA 2018a), which results in the buildings sector reaching about 3 $GtCO_2$ in 2017 or 10 per cent of global emissions (IEA 2019a). It can be observed from Figure 19.4 that these direct emissions have remained constant over the past two decades. When accounting for indirect emissions associated with electricity generation, however, CO_2 emissions have increased from 7.7 $GtCO_2$ in 2000 to 9.5 $GtCO_2$ in 2017, which mirrors the increasing demand trend for new energy services. Accounting for indirect emissions from electricity also explains differences in emissions between the residential and commercial sectors. The commercial sector uses much more electricity (46 per cent, resulting in 43 per cent of indirect emissions), while the residential sector uses a significant amount of traditional biomass (30 per cent – that is, 8300 TWh), which is considered 'carbon neutral'. While carbon intensity has decreased, it has only declined by 7 per cent between 2000 and 2017 (from 540 kilograms of CO_2 per megawatt-hour [$kgCO_2$/MWh] to 490 $kgCO_2$/MWh) compared to the 59 per cent electricity demand increase in the buildings sector in the same period.

2.1   Space and Water Heating

Globally, space and water heating account for 53 per cent of building energy demand (IEA 2019a). Space heating is the largest contributor to energy demand and accounts for a third of total energy demand. The transition to more efficient technologies (for example, from conventional boilers to condensing boilers) and building-efficiency improvements, have kept demand for space and water heating relatively constant despite an increasing building floor area (IEA 2019b). Figure 19.5 illustrates trends in efficiency improvements in space and water heating in selected regions, between 2000 and 2017. In contrast with the more rapid increase in demand for cooling and electricity services, water heating and space heating only increased by 1 per cent and 18 per cent respectively between 2000 and 2017.

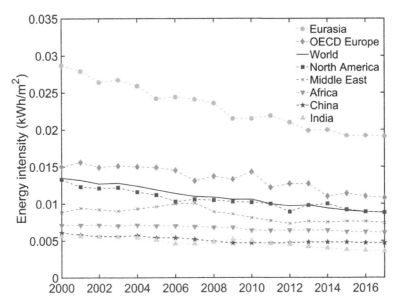

Source: Authors based on IEA (2019b).

Figure 19.5 *Energy performance improvement of space and water heating between 2000 and 2018*

Space and water heating is still overwhelmingly dominated by fossil fuels. Their use is mainly in conventional boilers, while electricity is typically used in conventional resistance heating, which are quite inefficient systems. In 2017, fossil-fuel-based and conventional heating equipment accounted for over 80 per cent of heating equipment sales. Excluding traditional use of biomass, water heating is mainly fuelled by fossil fuels and conventional electric boilers (IEA 2019b).

Geographically, the main contributors to this heating demand are the US, EU, Russia and China (IEA 2019a). Table 19.1 gathers residential heat demand data for China,

Table 19.1 *Residential space and water heating demand per region in 2017*

Region	Demand (TWh)	Note and References
Russia	970	Centralized and decentralized heating demand in Russia from 2009 (Nekrasov, Voronina and Semikashev 2012)
China	1960	Urban residential space and water heating demand and northern urban district heat demand from 2016 (BERC 2018)
USA	1910	2017 total residential space and water heating demand (EIA 2019)
Canada	330	2017 total residential space and water heating demand (Natural Resources Canada 2019)
EU	2670	2017 total residential space and water heating demand (European Commission 2019b)

Source: Authors.

North America (Canada and the USA), Russia and the EU. Assuming a total global residential water and heat demand of 11 100 TWh (40 exajoules [EJ]) (Gi et al. 2018), these four regions make up 70 per cent of total residential heating demand. Total heating demand per capita, however, varies greatly from one region to another as a function of building efficiency and level of development. While residential heating demand per capita is over 8800 kWh in Canada and Finland, it falls to 5000 kWh in Poland and the Netherlands, and to 1400 kWh in China (BERC 2018, European Commission 2019b, Natural Resources Canada 2019).

These same regions are also leading the drive for alternatives to fossil-based heating, including solar thermal technologies (China), high-efficiency heat pump water heaters (Japan, US, Europe) and hydrogen fuel cells (Japan) (IEA 2019b).

2.2   Space Cooling

A second driver of building energy demand is the increasing ownership of appliances and demand for new services (65 per cent increase between 2000 and 2017), especially space cooling (150 per cent increase between 2000 and 2017; see Figure 19.3) (IEA 2019a). Many drivers can explain these shifts, including population growth (World Bank 2019) and floor area, but also increase in temperatures (IEA 2018b), urbanization (Mohajerani, Bakaric and Jeffrey-Bailey 2017) and income level (Cayla, Maizi and Marchand 2011) (as described in Box 19.1). In 2017, space cooling represented only 6 per cent of energy use in the buildings sector but is currently the fastest increasing component. Ownership of air conditioning (AC) units is highest in Japan (90 per cent) and in the USA (90 per cent) (IEA 2018b). The China AC market has become one of the largest in the world, currently accounting for one-third of global AC sales, leading to dramatic increases in AC ownership from 15 per cent of households in 2000 to 60 per cent in 2017. The take-up of AC units has been slower in India, Southeast Asia and Africa but is expected to accelerate in the next decade. Brazil, India, Indonesia and Mexico are rapidly catching up (IEA 2019d). For example, AC ownership in India has doubled from 2 per cent of households in 2010 to 4 per cent in 2016 (IEA 2018b). Penetration rate, of course, does not necessarily imply high consumption since this will depend on the number of air-conditioned rooms and usage patterns such as the temperature and the hours used. In Japan, for example, despite having one of the highest penetration rates, space cooling only makes up some 5 per cent of household energy use, compared to Saudi Arabia where AC accounts for over 70 per cent of household electricity use (Enerdata 2019).

BOX 19.1   INCREASING DEMAND FOR COOLING AND BROADER ENERGY SERVICES

Demand for energy services has risen dramatically since 2000, which can be explained by the following factors:

● *Demography:* world population grew by 23 per cent between 2000 and 2017, with developing and emerging economies such as Sub-Saharan Africa and South Asia propelling the trend, 58 per cent and 29 per cent respectively (World Bank 2019).

- *Climate:* increases in air temperature and humidity levels over prolonged periods of time have driven up sales of cooling units around the world. Global air-conditioning unit sales increased by 16 per cent between 2017 and 2018 alone, after a particularly hot summer where many cities around the world reached record-breaking temperatures for an extended period of time (IEA 2018b).
- *Income level and development:* research suggests a high correlation between household energy demand and income (Cayla et al. 2011). In Singapore, where the average annual humidity is over 80 per cent, 99 per cent of households are equipped with AC. By comparison, in India, where summer temperatures can reach over 50°C, only 4 per cent of households own an AC (IEA 2018b). As income level increases in emerging economies, appliance ownership and energy consumption ramp up.
- *Urbanization:* The world's population is moving out of rural areas into cities. The proportion of the population living in urban environments has increased from 47 per cent to 55 per cent from 2000 to 2017 (World Bank 2019). Demand for energy services has been observed to be higher in urban areas, especially for cooling. This is partly due to higher income and urban populations living more energy-intensive lifestyles, partly due to higher temperatures in urban environments. This 'heat island effect' is mainly caused by the increasing density of heat-absorbing material (for example, asphalt on roads and pavements and dark rooftops) and the reduced amount of natural vegetation (Mohajerani et al. 2017). For AC units that release hot air, the heat island effect generates a vicious circle where cooling demand further drives up cooling demand.

Electricity consumption for space cooling increased twofold globally between 2000 and 2018, over fivefold in India, and eightfold in China (IEA 2018b). The increase between 2017 and 2018 alone is particularly notable – AC sales rose by 16 per cent (Figure 19.6), which can be explained by record-breaking and prolonged heatwaves that hit Europe, Korea, Japan and China in the summers of 2017 and 2018. Since increases in cooling demand have mostly occurred in emerging economies with a high carbon intensity in the power sector, notably China, CO_2 emissions from cooling have tripled since 1990, reaching 1.1 $GtCO_2$ in 2018 and have been rising much more rapidly than cooling demand overall (ibid.). Unlike heating, cooling demand may be better matched with growing

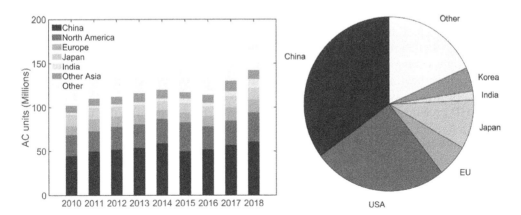

Source: Authors based on IEA (2018b, 2019b).

Figure 19.6   Total AC sales (left) and AC installed capacity in 2016 (right)

reliance on renewables in the power sector, particularly solar photovoltaics (PV). In principle at least, the path is more straightforward, but, to date, rapid growth in cooling demand continues to outstrip electricity decarbonization.

3.   TECHNOLOGY OPTIONS TO DECARBONIZE HEATING AND COOLING DEMAND IN BUILDINGS

While market-ready renewable heating solutions exist, renewable heat only represents 10 per cent of current heat supply (IEA 2018a). Alternatives to the current fossil-fuel-dominated heating system include heat pumps, solar thermal, biomass boilers, district heating and cooling networks, and substituting natural gas with 'greener gas' such as hydrogen and biomethane.

Between 2010 and 2017, fossil fuel equipment as a share of total sales dropped slightly from 62 per cent to 59 per cent as sales of alternatives expanded, conventional electric equipment increased from 20 to 22 per cent, heat pumps increased from 2 per cent to 3 per cent and renewables from 4 per cent to 6 per cent. District heating, on the other hand, has dropped slightly from 11 per cent to 10 per cent of total sales. Heat pump sales increased consistently by around 5 per cent per year over 2010–17 and by 10 per cent between 2017 and 2018 (IEA 2019b). While this suggests the transition to lower-carbon heating and cooling is underway, a much faster transition is required to meet decarbonization ambitions.

3.1   Household- and District-level Heat Pumps

When exploring electrification of the heating sector, household- or district-level HPs remain the main technology pathway.

3.1.1   Basic principles
Heat pumps (HPs) use a refrigerant (typically R-22 and R-410A in the residential sector) to exchange heat between a heat source – air, water, soil – and a heat sink – air or water. Air-source HPs (ASHPs), which derive heat from the outside air, and ground-source HPs (GSHPs), which exchange heat with the soil via underground pipes, are the typical configurations (Staffell et al. 2012). In terms of sinks, air-to-air systems provide space heating by directly warming and circulating the inside air of a property, while air-to-water can provide space heating by circulating hot water around the home via radiators or an underfloor heating system. The hot water can also be stored in a tank for direct use.

An HP exchanges heat between the cold source and the hot sink by circulating a working fluid in a thermodynamic cycle. The fluid evaporates in a heat exchanger in contact with the outside heat source (air, water or ground), to collect an amount of heat Q_C. It is then brought to a higher pressure in a compressor. This is the part of the process that requires work (W), from electricity. The fluid then condenses in a heat exchanger when in contact with the inside heat sink (air or water), thus delivering heat Q_H to the sink (Figure 19.7).

The efficiency of an HP is measured by its coefficient of performance (COP), which is defined by the amount of heat generated and the amount of work required to compress the fluid. Unlike boilers that are at most 90–95 per cent efficient using advanced

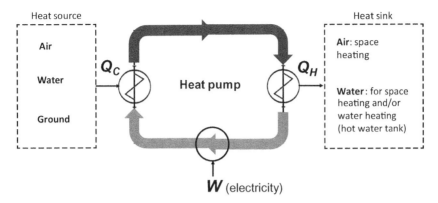

Source: Authors.

Figure 19.7   Basic principle of a heat pump

technologies (for example, condensing boilers), HPs typically have an efficiency that is much greater than 100 per cent. This coefficient will be very dependent on the temperature of the heat sink, hence can be variable throughout the year (ibid.). Typically, the COP of HPs is around 3.0, but will drop by 0.6 to 1 for every 10°C difference between indoor and outdoor temperatures (ibid.). Consequently, while a COP of 4.0 or 5.0 can be obtained in milder climates (Mediterranean, Central and Southern China), COP can drop to 2.0 in colder climates such as Canada (IEA 2019b). These values are, however, still twice as high as conventional resistive heating.

GSHPs are more resilient to changing outside air temperatures since soils maintain a fairly constant temperature profile throughout the year. However, GSHPs require significant space outdoors as pipes need to be buried underground, leading to higher capital costs, while an ASHP is a more compact system, which can be accommodated in a 2 m² surface area. Where feasible, geothermal HPs can provide a cheaper alternative to ASHPs, due to significantly lower operating costs.

3.1.2   Current sales and outlook
Current HP capacity is still very low, having been installed in some 18 million households, which accounts for only 5 per cent of heating equipment sales in 2017 and meeting 3 per cent of global heating needs (IEA 2019b). Like any electrification pathway, decarbonization of the electricity grid is a prerequisite if HPs are to successfully decarbonize the heating sector. However, because of the much higher efficiency of HP systems (300–400 per cent), they could already supply 90 per cent of space heating demand with a lower carbon footprint than condensing gas boilers (IEA 2019a).

Adoption rates of HPs are currently higher in moderate climates (US and Western Europe account for 50 per cent of sales) (IEA 2019d; see also Figure 19.8). This can be partly explained by the increasing sales of reversible units, which are also used for cooling (European Heat Pump Association [EHPA] 2019). The highest adoption rates are, however, in the Nordic countries of Sweden, Finland and Norway as well as Estonia, with total HP penetration rates between 23 per cent (Estonia) and 42 per cent (Norway) (EHPA 2019, IEA 2019b).

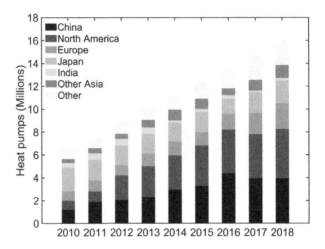

Source: Authors based on IEA (2019d).

Figure 19.8   Heat pump sales between 2010 and 2018 in different regions

Governmental subsidies can play a large role in technology adoption. HP water heater sales have tripled since 2010, mainly driven by China, which introduced subsidies to replace coal boilers with air-to-water HPs (Shuxue et al. 2019, Zhao et al. 2017). Since 2016, growth in HP sales has been largely driven by Europe and Japan, due to generous incentives – for example, HPs are covered in the UK's renewable electricity portfolio (Department of Energy & Climate Change 2014) – which have led EU sales to quadruple since 2010.

In pathways going out to 2050, HPs become the dominant technology, with approximately 1 billion households worldwide equipped with an HP, operating at a COP of 4.0 on average (IEA 2019a). Reaching this level of deployment would, of course, require significant increases in current levels of uptake.

3.2   Alternative Pathways to Decarbonization of Heating and Cooling

Aside from electrification, other pathways have been explored to decarbonize heating. These include district heating, solar energy, hydrogen, bioenergy and significant efficiency improvements in gas appliances.

3.2.1   District heating
District heating typically involves co-generation plants based on fossil fuel or biomass combustion producing both heat and electricity, but other sources include geothermal, solar nuclear energy or HPs. Waste-to-energy (such as in Dublin) also can provide an important source. The heat is then distributed by a network of pipes, which are laid out over a scale ranging from a few homes to an entire city (such as Stockholm or Bucharest). Often, district heating can be at the scale of a large commercial facility or an institution with a complex of buildings such as universities, hospitals or government buildings. By co-producing heat and electricity, these systems can achieve greater efficiencies and lower carbon emissions.

Today, district heating only provides 10 per cent of global heat demand, but constitutes a major source of heating in selected regions (Denmark 44 per cent, Sweden 51 per cent, Russia 42 per cent, China 10 per cent) (European Commission 2019b, IEA 2019a). Future opportunities in this space include fourth-generation low-temperature high-efficiency heat networks supplied by large-scale HPs (Lund et al., 2014, Werner, 2017) but the deployment of these networks is highly dependent on urban configuration, availability and proximity of energy supply and building improvements (IEA 2019b).

To date, 89 per cent of district heat is supplied by fossil energy, resulting in an average carbon intensity of 300 gCO_2/kWh (IEA 2019a). This share is as high as 91 per cent in Russia and 99 per cent in China, where coal supplies much of the heat. However, examples in Europe, such as in Sweden and Denmark, demonstrate the possibility of using lower carbon sources in district heating (two-thirds of energy supply is renewable in the Swedish district heating system and almost 60 per cent in Denmark) (ibid.).

The biggest challenge for district heating is the large-scale infrastructure required and the need for wholesale systemic change, which explains the current low level of uptake. There have been various approaches to encouraging uptake of district heating. In many cases, institutions such as hospitals or government buildings have adopted district heating schemes. In other cases, large urban centres have shifted to district heating. For example, Denmark introduced a zoning system whereby connection to the heat or natural gas network was mandatory in those areas while banning HPs, while HPs were subsidized outside these regions (Hanna, Parish and Gross 2016).

3.2.2 Solar energy for heating and cooling
Since first deployed in 2005, solar thermal heat capacity has expanded to 470 gigawatts-thermal (GWth), nearly as much as solar PV capacity, mostly driven by deployment in China (IEA 2018a) as well as regions with high water heating needs (relative to heating) and high solar irradiance. This increase has also been driven by the implementation of sustainable cooling policies to limit cooling demand. However, as of 2018, solar thermal still only meets just over 2 per cent of space and water heat demand, which means that the sector would need a 10 per cent per year increase by 2030 to meet 8 per cent of the buildings sector's heat demand (IEA 2018a, 2019a). To date, the fastest-growing technology is solar PV with storage (through chilled water/ice), with increasing sales in the Mediterranean, Middle East and Australia. Innovations in this space include flexible solar AC units (which adjust their capacity to the solar electricity available), as well as liquid desiccant evaporative cooling, which relies on cooling liquids. This simultaneously dehumidifies and cools the air and is particularly useful in humid and hot areas (IEA 2018b and 2019b).

3.2.3 More efficient gas appliances
Most straightforward would be switching to condensing gas boilers, which are 95–100 per cent efficient and provide a more efficient alternative to conventional boilers. In dense areas, district heating and cooling systems can substitute for gas-based equipment, although this involves considerable investment in infrastructure. If substitution is not possible, switching all remaining conventional gas boilers to gas hybrid HPs and condensing boilers would be required to curb natural gas demand and reduce CO_2 emissions from heating. Policies imposing minimum efficiency requirements on gas appliances, like the

Canadian 100 per cent efficiency space heating regulation by 2030, will be required to phase out low-efficiency gas systems. These minimum efficiency requirements need to ramp up to 150 per cent by 2050 for all heating appliances (IEA 2019a). Options to repurpose the gas grid to 'greener gas' such as hydrogen and biomethane are explored at the local level, but more R&D and demonstration projects are required to support the deployment of these solutions beyond the local level.

3.2.4   Hydrogen

Hydrogen is a versatile and potentially carbon-free fuel, which can be used in diverse applications including transport and heating. The first barrier to the roll-out of hydrogen though is the difficulty of producing low-carbon hydrogen at competitive costs with natural gas. When produced from fossil fuels (via steam methane reformation – SMR, coal gasification or partial oil oxidation), which currently makes up 96 per cent of the world's hydrogen production (Committee on Climate Change [CCC] 2018b), the carbon intensity of hydrogen – in this case also known as 'grey hydrogen' – can range from 205 to 600 grams of CO_2 per kilowatt-hour (gCO_2/kWh) depending on the assumptions (Sustainable Gas Institute 2017).[2] One option to reduce the carbon intensity of hydrogen is to combine steam methane reforming with CCS, the so-called 'blue hydrogen', which can result in carbon intensity as low as 20 gCO_2/kWh (ibid.). When produced from water electrolysis using carbon-free electricity, the hydrogen produced is zero carbon, also known as 'green hydrogen'. If combined with decentralized renewable generation (for example, wind or solar farm), this pathway also has the potential to use curtailed electricity from renewables, by storing it in the form of gas ('power-to-gas'). Costs of hydrogen by electrolysis are widely seen as higher than via SMR (IEA 2019e, Mulder, Perey and Moraga 2019), although there are claims that at least in certain niches, green hydrogen may start to become competitive over the coming decade (Glenk and Reichelstein 2019).

Another major barrier to the hydrogen economy is the infrastructure required to store, transport and deliver hydrogen to consumers. In countries with an extensive natural gas network, a key opportunity around the hydrogen economy is the possibility to reuse the natural gas distribution networks, thereby avoiding the cost of decommissioning under strong decarbonization policies. Current regulation in Europe only allows a share of 5 per cent (volumetric) of hydrogen in the natural gas distribution networks, due to concerns over pipe permeability, embrittlement and operation of existing gas end-use appliances. While full decarbonization would require the replacement of 100 per cent of natural gas by hydrogen, current trials such as the GHRYD project in Northern France that started in 2017 are exploring the injection of greater volumes (up to 20 per cent) of hydrogen in the gas grid (ENGIE 2019). The UK's £25 million Hy4Heat project, planned for 2020, will explore the feasibility of natural gas grid conversion to hydrogen in the UK.

Another pathway under investigation is domestic fuel cells for onsite electricity generation. The leading market for this option is Japan with its ENE-Farm hydrogen fuel cell installations surpassing 300 000 units in 2019 (Klippenstein 2019). By contrast, in Europe, the ene.field project has demonstrated domestic electricity generation with hydrogen fuel cells micro-combined heat and power (CHP) at a much smaller scale, having installed 1000 units across ten countries since 2012 (European Commission 2019a).

3.2.5 Solid biomass and biomethane

A final set of renewable options for space heating is bioenergy in the form of domestic solid biomass boilers or biomethane injection into the natural gas grid. Currently, 30 per cent of domestic heat is still supplied by traditional biomass. Traditional biomass used in stoves and heaters is often sourced unsustainably, burned inefficiently and has been linked with numerous health problems (Goldemberg and Coelho 2004). In comparison, modern biomass such as wood pellets in stoves only constitutes 5 per cent of current heat provision in homes (IEA 2018a). Domestic boilers need relatively high-grade biomass pellets to operate efficiently (CCC 2018a). While modern biomass is theoretically a carbon-neutral renewable resource, whether the large-scale logistics of producing, upgrading and transporting biomass pellets around the world is indeed sustainable remains controversial. Land use change and potential deforestation, biodiversity loss, soil depletion or water use are additional concerns likely to constrain the amount of biomass that can be sustainably sourced (Creutzig et al. 2015).

Other bioenergy applications such as converting agricultural residues and municipal solid wastes to biomethane that can be injected into the gas grid allow for the scope for bio-feedstock to be broadened and make use of what would otherwise be waste products, while continuing to use existing infrastructure. In France, for example, 44 biomethane injection stations injected 406 gigawatt-hours (GWh) of biomethane into the gas grid in 2017, which suggests rapid progress since the first pilot station in 2011 (Gaz Réseau Distribution France 2017).

4. CHALLENGES AND OPPORTUNITIES OF ELECTRIFICATION OF HEAT IN BUILDINGS

Electrification of residential and commercial heating can pose significant challenges to the design and operation of the electricity system. Sources of flexibility, both on the consumer and infrastructure side, will be key to alleviating these potential impacts.

4.1 Impact on Electricity Demand

A first set of challenges involves the impact of heat electrification on the electricity demand curve, which directly affects the power system's operation, as well as generation and transmission capacity requirements.

4.1.1 Winter and summer peaks

There has been increased attention to the relationship between temperature and electricity demand (Cassarino, Sharp and Barrett 2018, Thornton, Hoskins and Scaife 2016). The sensitivity of the electricity system towards variation in heat demand is called thermo-sensitivity. The thermo-sensitivity of an electricity system is measured by the rate at which electricity demand increases per °C of temperature decrease. For example, in France, where electricity provides 18 per cent of residential heat demand (European Commission 2019b), the thermo-sensitivity of the system reaches 2400 MW/°C (or 0.04 kW/°C/capita) when temperatures fall below 1°C, which is significantly higher than in the UK (800 MW/°C or 0.01 kW/°C/capita) where only 8 per cent of residential heating is electrified (Réseau de Transport d'Electricité [RTE] 2018). This suggests that electrification of heat would increase the power system's exposure to fluctuations in heat demand.

Additionally, in cold climates, the electricity profile is very different from the heat demand profile. Figure 19.9 shows the 2015 hourly profile of residential heat and total electricity demand in the UK (Charitopoulos, Chyong and Reiner 2019).[3] While demand for electricity remains relatively constant throughout the year, heat demand is highly seasonal, with a fourfold variation between average summer and winter demand. Linking electricity to heat could therefore completely reshape the electricity demand profile, adding seasonality. Finally, the scale of peak demand and the rate at which the heat sector reaches these peaks is much greater than in a traditional power system. Reducing peak demand is particularly important, as it is typically met by 'peaking' fossil-based generation units (usually gas plants) and constitutes one of the largest challenges and sources of uncertainties to the electrification of heating (Chaudry et al. 2015, Eyre and Baruah 2015, Watson, Lomas and Buswell 2019).

Increased electrification of heating, combined with lower HP efficiency on colder days, could drastically impact peak demand in winter. In the IEA Faster Transition Scenario to 2050,[4] HPs make up 30 per cent of the global heating equipment capacity by 2050, but this value increases to 45 per cent in the EU (IEA 2019a). A 50 per cent share of heating capacity by HPs would increase peak load by 60 per cent in the UK (Cooper et al. 2016). In 2050, a peak day in January could require 68 GW for heating – that is, 12 per cent of daily peak – or 69 GW in the morning – that is, 18 per cent of morning peak (Renaldi, Kiprakis and Friedrich 2017).

Rapid increase in energy services including cooling demand is also putting increasing strain on power systems. In 2017, cooling accounted for 15 per cent of peak electricity demand on average, and up to 50 per cent in some cities in China and India in summer (IEA 2018b).

In the IEA Faster Transition Scenario, higher cooling and electrified heating demand is likely to increase peak demand. In China, where 1.1 billion AC units are expected to be

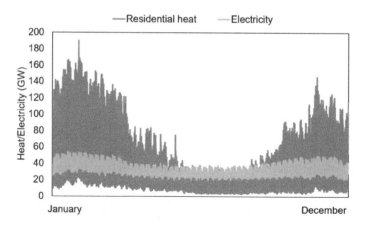

Source: Authors based on Charitopoulos et al. (2019).

Figure 19.9   2015 total electricity and residential heat demand profiles in the UK

owned by Chinese households by 2050, the evening peak could be one and a half times higher than the daily load (IEA 2019a).

4.1.2 Sources of flexibility

Hot water storage provides an opportunity to reduce the impact of electrification of heating demand, as well as secure heating supply at colder hours. For example, in the UK, combining HPs with hot water storage could help shift 15 per cent of the peak heating load to off-peak hours (Renaldi et al. 2017). For gas-connected homes, another option to secure the heat supply under cold conditions is by pairing an HP with continued use of natural gas, through the use of hybrid HPs (Zhang et al. 2018). Finally, another way to add flexibility to the system is to couple larger HPs with district heating or cooling networks. District-level HPs typically have a higher coefficient of performance (EHPA 2017) and can enable more flexible operations using the thermal inertia and flexibility provided by the heat networks (Schweiger et al. 2017).

4.1.3 Connected appliances and smart metering

To avoid electrification of heat having a large impact on both average and peak electricity demand, smart appliances combined with heat storage could: (1) reduce overall energy consumption through better management of overall household energy demand; and (2) shift peak demand by producing heat off peak. In particular, smart meters can help regulate load as a function of weather patterns. The pairing with storage capacity to shift the cooling load to off-peak hours, possibly when solar PV generation is available, is an example. These demand-side management options need to be facilitated with new tariff structures, such as (dynamic) off-peak electricity pricing, with the support of smart meters using time-of-use tariffs (Eid et al. 2016, Karlsen, Hamdy and Attia 2020). For example, in the US, a 55 per cent decrease in cooling demand during peak hours was achieved following the implementation of a 'rush hour reward' scheme (Buildings Performance Institute Europe [BPIE] 2016).

In the case of heating, the potential for load shifting and peak reduction is highly dependent on the system's energy efficiency and the thermal storage available (Arteconi and Polonara 2018). Schemes to shift electric heating load are being explored in the context of all-electric houses in Norway (Karlsen et al. 2020). However, flexible operation of heating systems will be enormously challenging on a cold winter's day, particularly without the use of flexible heating systems such as hybrid HPs.

Another critical element in any effort to manage demand is the growing deployment of smart meters, which has driven down costs. Roughly 800 million smart meters were installed as of 2017, 500 million in China alone, resulting in a 75 per cent drop in smart meter costs relative to 2010 (IEA 2019a). Furthermore, digitalization and access to this data could also boost innovation and research to better tailor solutions to consumers.

4.2 Outlook for Future Demand

Demand for cooling and other energy services has increased dramatically since 2000. From 2020 to 2050, population is expected to grow by about 30 per cent, and up to 50 per cent in the Middle East, one of the regions of highest demand for cooling (World Bank 2019). The urbanization rate is likely to reach 66 per cent and the number of cooling degree days is expected to grow by 25 per cent on average by 2050, with up to 37 per cent growth in regions like Mexico (IEA 2018b).

Despite continued improvements in efficiency, electrification of space heating and an increase in cooling needs could lead to an increase in power demand by 25 per cent, especially in developing economies with high cooling needs. Global electricity demand for space cooling alone could increase by up to 35 per cent (IEA 2019a). In the next decade, ten AC units could be sold every second, so addressing AC performance is of paramount importance (IEA 2018b).

Aside from changing how heat is supplied, demand-side response solutions are key to lowering heat demand in buildings and enabling greater heat electrification without imposing a strain on electricity systems.

4.2.1 Building envelope performance
One of the key levers of demand-side response is improving building envelope performance (Reyna and Chester 2017). Improvements to building envelopes need to be tailored to climate zones and those identified as the main levers for improving building efficiency in each zone are:

- hot climates: building orientation, wall-to-window ratios, green roofs, reflective contours and connected blinds/shutters;
- cold climates: ventilation with heat recovery, thermographic measurements and advanced insulation (multiple-pane windows, foam spray, reduction of thermal bridges);
- mixed climates: improved thermal inertia, smarter ventilation and low emissivity windows.

In all climates, these improvements need to be accompanied by better energy management through sensors, consumption and storage based on energy prices or incentives.

Building codes have an important role to play. Gillingham, Keyes and Palmer (2018) describe some of the debates over the effect of residential building codes. For example, Jacobsen and Kotchen (2013) find that when Florida tightened its code, electricity and natural gas consumption both fell (by 4 per cent and 6 per cent, respectively) and that effects were more pronounced on the hottest and coldest days. By contrast, for California, Levinson (2016) finds that houses built after the state's strict residential code was established consumed 10–15 per cent less electricity and 25 per cent less gas than those built before the codes, although the reductions were similar to those seen in states with much less stringent codes.

In any case, currently, codes only cover just over half of total floor area (IEA 2019b), which equates to 38 per cent of energy use and half of CO_2 emissions. Moreover, two-thirds of new buildings are put up in countries that have not implemented clear guidelines. While building codes extended to 54 countries by 2017, including China, India and Turkey, the stringency of these policies is not increasing as fast as floor area and energy demand (IEA 2019a). In the IEA clean energy transition outlook, renovation rates of existing building stock need to double by 2050 (ibid.). As global floor area is expected to increase by 80 per cent, building efficiency policies need to be carefully designed and implemented to ensure maximum coverage of new buildings to avoid lock-in effects.

Furthermore, in poorly ventilated dwellings, there is a concern that some building efficiency improvement measures, such as increased insulation, can lead to reduced indoor air quality (Derbez et al. 2018). Building efficiency measures will therefore have to be implemented in a way that does not lead to unintended consequences for occupant health. The design of combined air ventilation and cleaner systems, such as clean-air heat pumps (CAHPs; Sheng, Fang and Nie 2017), suggest that there is a rising interest in tackling indoor air quality and heating efficiency in a combined way.

At the global level, investments are needed to support innovation required to deliver on this rapid transition to a low-carbon heating system and policies will be needed to support such investments. In the IEA projection, which is consistent with a 2°C target (and which still does not assume full decarbonization of the heat sector), energy investments in buildings increase from \$4.9 trillion in 2017 to \$5.4 trillion by 2050 and are mainly directed towards improving building envelopes. The early timing of these investments is particularly important, to avoid (1) lock-in effects – for example, the possibility of having new inefficient buildings with lifetimes as long as 50 years; and (2) increased renovation and energy costs from delaying improvements – for example, a ten-year delay could incur \$2.5 trillion in extra spending (IEA 2019a).

4.2.2   Increasing AC efficiency

Appliance efficiency improvements are also needed to balance the increasing electricity demand for cooling and other services. The average seasonal energy efficiency ratio (SEER), which measures the energy performance of AC units, has steadily improved from 2.4–2.7 in 1990, to 3.8–4.2 in 2018.[5] However, the potential of AC unit efficiency improvement remains largely untapped, as average values remain much lower than appliances available on the market. On average, most AC units sold have a SEER of 2.0–8.0 below that of the best available units on the market. In the United States, the best available SEER on the market is more than three times that of the average SEER (Figure 19.10). In China, one of the fastest growing markets, the average SEER is 4.4, although units with a SEER reaching 8.3 are available at comparable prices (Figure 19.10). Using currently available high performance AC units could therefore already curb cooling energy demand by half.

Setting minimum energy performance (MEP) for appliances is another lever for policy makers. MEPs are by far the most used policy tool, covering 40 per cent of cooling, heating and appliances energy demand. However, the best covered appliances (for example, lighting), do not coincide with the greatest source of emissions (for example, space heating) (IEA 2019a), which suggests the potential for improvements.

Globally, 1.5 billion households have access to cooling, and demand is expected to grow substantially as rising incomes and temperatures drive ownership of AC and, importantly, utilization. Even under the most optimistic scenarios, the ambition is simply to limit projected increases in electricity consumption via significant improvements in appliance efficiency and building envelopes. MEP policies are required to encourage the adoption of high efficiency ACs that are already available on the market and phase out the lower efficiency range. Further improvements to existing designs (for example, using solid or liquid desiccants to reduce latent heat of water vaporization) will be required to reach the twofold efficiency increase target. In developed economies, efficiency improvements actually outbalance increase in electricity demand, resulting in a slight decrease in electricity consumption.

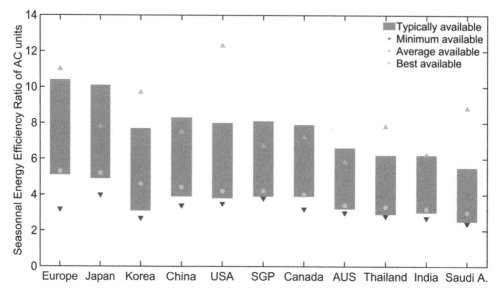

Source: Authors based on IEA (2019b).

Figure 19.10 *SEER of minimum, average, best and the range of typically available AC units in different regions (SGP = Singapore; Saudi A. = Saudi Arabia; AUS = Australia)*

4.3 Impact on Infrastructure and Total Energy System Cost

Electrification of heating comes at a cost, both to the householder – from an investment and operating cost perspective – and to the overall system. Systems integration costs typically arise from generation and transmission capacity deployment to meet the higher electricity demand and potential infrastructure decommissioning cost.

4.3.1 Total system cost

From a whole system perspective, the cost of transitioning from the incumbent heating system to a lower carbon one also includes infrastructure, capacity and decommissioning costs. For example, when comparing the total system costs of electrification, hydrogen and hybrid pathways to decarbonize heating in the UK, Strbac et al. (2018) found that annual costs were in a range of $109 billion and $123 billion/yr,[6] assuming 2050 emissions targets in the heating sector of 10 or 30 megatons of CO_2 per year ($MtCO_2$/yr), where the hybrid pathway was lowest cost and hydrogen the highest. If a zero-emission target was pursued by 2050, the hybrid and electrification pathways only increase costs by a further 5 per cent, while the cost of the hydrogen pathway increases by some 35 per cent, past $162 billion/yr, owing to the higher cost of producing zero-carbon hydrogen from electrolysis. By contrast, in a separate UK study, the electrification pathway was found to be twice as expensive as the hydrogen pathway, which suggests the high dependence of these findings on infrastructure cost (for example, CCS, gas grid conversion and grid reinforcement cost) and technology performance (for example, CO_2 capture efficiency of CCS plants) (Element Energy and E4Tech 2018). Other factors such as hourly heat demand and technology cost assumptions are also highly influential in these assessments. More systems level studies are required to quantify the overall cost to the energy system of electrifying domestic and commercial heating.

4.3.2 Impact on the natural gas infrastructure

Globally, 30 per cent of domestic heat is supplied by natural gas, and up to 85 per cent in natural gas-dominated heating systems such as the UK (Department for Business Energy & Industrial Strategy 2018). Under high electrification scenarios, the gas network could become underutilized, leading to these networks becoming stranded assets, thereby incurring significant decommissioning costs. At the UK scale, electrification of residential heat demand causes an 18 per cent reduction in annual gas supply in the distribution network due to a shift from natural gas boilers to HPs (Qadrdan et al. 2019).

In the IEA Faster Transmission Scenario, regions with extensive natural gas networks (for example, North America, Western Europe and Eurasia) do not decommission their existing gas networks and natural gas still supplies 15 per cent of space and water heating demand in 2050 (IEA 2019a). This scenario, however, does not consider full decarbonization of the heat sector. One major concern has been that an increase in the decarbonization targets for the heat sector could lead to a drop in natural gas demand, thereby forcing natural gas grid operators into decommissioning the gas grid (Frontier Economics 2016). Substituting natural gas with greener gas (for example, hydrogen or biomethane) at the distribution level is one option to avoid costs associated with decommissioning the gas grid, while complying with heat decarbonization targets (Sustainable Gas Institute 2017).

4.3.3 CO_2 removal to allow for less stringent decarbonization targets

National level studies of full heat decarbonization showed that the total system cost of a decarbonization pathway could increase dramatically with the stringency of the decarbonization target by 2050 (Element Energy and E4Tech 2018, Strbac et al. 2018). It is still unclear whether (1) more stringent targets will drive electrification further and reduce or even phase out reliance on natural gas networks; or (2) emissions from the building and industrial sectors that are expensive to mitigate will be offset with the deployment of CO_2 removal methods. Future whole systems studies of electrification of heating need to explore the optimal level of decarbonization and the role of these CO_2 removal methods.

4.3.4 The value of lost load

Total system cost is also highly related to the security criteria adopted for the electricity grid. The optimal level of security that is required to supply the electricity peak demand is very dependent on households' value of lost load, or VoLL, which measures the cost of disrupting power supply for consumers and is often incorporated into standards established by the regulator (see Box 19.2 and Chapter 3 in this handbook). While the security of electricity supply is of paramount importance for commercial and industrial consumers to sustain their economic activity, the extent to which higher consumer flexibility, encouraged by an increased knowledge of consumption provided by smart-metering devices, could lower the VoLL is a further opportunity to explore in the context of reducing the impact of electrification of heat on electricity systems.

BOX 19.2   VALUE OF LOST LOAD IN THE RESIDENTIAL SECTOR

Since the economy is highly dependent on electricity, disruptions in power supply can impose significant costs. Conversely, designing an electricity system with a high level of security typically involves adding power generation capacity and lowering the overall capacity factor of the system, which is equally costly to the economy. The point at which the marginal damages (from an interruption in electricity supply) equals the marginal cost of maintaining the security of the supply is the optimal level of security of the system and provides a measure of the VoLL (Cambridge Economic Policy Associates [CEPA] 2018, Röpke 2013, Schröder and Kuckshinrichs 2015).

VoLL can vary widely dependent on the sector, the type of service provided by electricity and the level of consumption. Given its role in regulatory efforts, it is crucial to quantify VoLL across different sectors of the economy in different regions (CEPA 2018, London Economics 2013). While VoLL for industrial and commercial activities can be calculated using added value metrics as proxies (London Economics 2013), quantifying VoLL in the residential sector is not as straightforward.

First, VoLL is closely linked to consumer willingness-to-pay (WTP) for a reliable electricity supply or willingness-to-accept (WTA) a power outage, which is often expressed as a monetary value over a period of time (e.g., one hour or eight hours). Consumer preference is therefore central to determining VoLL.

An additional challenge is related to the conflicting driving forces between consumption and VoLL. On the one hand, the electrification of residential heating, by increasing reliance on electricity at the household level, could put additional pressure on VoLL by resulting in a higher WTP/WTA. For example, a survey in the UK showed that VoLL was higher in the UK for all-electric households as compared to gas households (ibid.). On the other hand, an increase in consumption theoretically lowers VoLL, which is sometimes expressed as monetary value per unit of consumption (CEPA 2018).

The extent to which electrification of heating will impact VoLL in the residential sector therefore remains very uncertain.

4.4   The Power Sector Is Decarbonizing, But Not Fast Enough

As observed in Figure 19.4, 70 per cent of emissions from buildings come from indirect emissions associated with electricity generation (IEA 2019a). The electricity sector is going through a rapid decarbonization in many countries. For example, since 2010, the carbon intensity of electricity in the UK has dropped from 450 to 280 gCO_2/kWh (European Commission 2019b). In many other economies, including leading emerging markets, however, the carbon intensity of electricity is not decreasing as fast as demand for electricity is increasing. Between 2010 and 2017, the average carbon intensity of electricity decreased from 1000 gCO_2/kWh to 750 gCO_2/kWh in China, and from 1200 gCO_2/kWh to 1000 gCO_2/kWh in India, but sectoral emissions continue to increase (IEA 2018b). Efforts to fully decarbonize the electricity grid will be pivotal in delivering a low-carbon heating system through electrification.

On the other hand, building floor area is expected to almost double (+ 96 per cent) between today and 2050, reaching 460 billion m^2 by mid-century. Even assuming optimistic energy intensity improvements, this increase will likely drive up building energy demand. Out of the 230 billion m^2 of new floor area, 85 per cent will be built in emerging economies, most of which have yet to decarbonize their power sector. Over the next decade alone, 77 billion m^2 of new floor area will be built, primarily in countries like Brazil, India or Indonesia, where potential high demand for cooling will be critical (IEA 2019a).

4.5 Consumer Preferences and Technology Adoption

Because heating sources are highly dispersed, decarbonization of heat will largely rely on households' willingness to switch away from fossil-based heating systems to new, more efficient and renewable heating systems (Michelsen and Madlener 2012). This could mean connecting to a district heating and cooling network or installing an HP. While adopting more energy-efficient technologies could provide energy savings, research suggests that households do not necessarily act rationally when it comes to technology adoption, and that other factors such as thermal comfort play an important role in the final choice to adopt a new technology. Depending on tenancy type (owner/tenant), environment (urban/rural) or income level, households might have different technology adoption rates. Constraints on technology adoption can also involve space considerations (for a ground source HP, for example) or building density (connection to a district heating network will be unlikely in a rural environment) (Cayla et al. 2011, Li, Keppo and Strachan 2018, Michelsen and Madlener 2012). Accounting for this heterogeneity in household structure and preferences will likely be crucial when designing policies to encourage the uptake of low-carbon and efficient heating and cooling technologies. In particular, there are potential issues associated with how consumers process information, actual behaviour versus engineering models, including rebound effect, split responsibility between bill payers, residents and those making the investments, and changes in thermal comfort.

There have been relatively few empirical or experimental studies of consumer purchasing or switching behaviour regarding heating and cooling equipment. One area where there has been attention is on the role of information. Ramos et al. (2015) review many of the informational barriers and proposed policy solutions associated with residential energy efficiency, of which a number of specific studies address heating and cooling. Allcott and Sweeney (2016) found that providing information on efficiency of conventional hot water heaters did not in itself increase the purchase of more energy-efficient units, but a combination of large rebates plus information did increase the market share of more efficient heaters. Moreover, salespeople only targeted energy efficiency information at consumers who expressed interest in the subject, but did not discuss it with the disinterested majority. Bollinger and Hartmann (2019) found that information alone could reduce demand over the long term, but to change short-term elasticity, automation technology would also be needed.

There have been a number of studies that question many of the more optimistic predictions of techno-economic modelling, which echoes the literature seeking to describe the energy efficiency 'gap' (Gerarden, Newell and Stavins 2017). In consumer surveys, respondents typically overestimate the energy costs associated with low-usage goods (for example, computers or mobile phones) and underestimate the energy costs of high-usage goods (for example, water heaters) (Attari et al. 2010). Relatedly, real-world implementation may not match claimed savings. For example, ex ante engineering estimates overstated actual conservation by 13 per cent in an experiment providing households with insulation and heat, ventilation and air conditioning (HVAC) appliances (Dubin, Miedema and Chandran 1986). Even more glaring, a programme to replace inefficient air conditioners in Mexico actually led to increased electricity consumption, in stark contrast to engineering predictions of significant energy savings (Davis, Fuchs and Gertler 2014).

Another challenge is that the outcomes of home energy retrofits are difficult for home-owners to observe – Giraudet, Houde and Maher (2018) identify a moral hazard whereby contractors take advantage of the relative lack of knowledge regarding the quality of energy efficiency measures being implemented leading to lower energy savings, particularly for work conducted on Fridays. This subject is further explored in Chapter 15 in this handbook.

Other important considerations include ascertaining whether interventions can be demonstrated as effective, whether they can lead to any appreciable effect or even lead to a rebound effect. Alberini, Gans and Towe (2016) found that those who replaced their HPs but who did not receive any incentive to do so reduced their electricity usage by 16 per cent, while those who did receive an incentive actually did not reduce their electricity usage. Furthermore, the larger the rebate a household received, the less the household reduced energy usage. Davis et al. (2014) also employ matching to evaluate a programme in Mexico that subsidized replacement of refrigerators and air-conditioning units and find that although refrigerator replacements reduced electricity consumption by 8 per cent on average annually, air-conditioning replacements actually increased electricity consumption, again consistent with a rebound effect. Rivers and Shiell (2016) examine Canadian subsidies for natural gas furnace retrofits and find strong evidence for free riding – they estimate that in the long run, more than 80 per cent of subsidy recipients would have eventually purchased identical furnaces without a subsidy.

Another major challenge is the tension between ownership, tenancy and bill payers. Gillingham, Harding and Rapson (2012) find that tenants who pay for their own household energy are 16 per cent more likely to change their temperature setting at night. Furthermore, owner-occupied homes are 13–20 per cent more likely to have additional insulation. Myers (2019) finds that landlords responsible for energy bills are more likely to convert from less efficient oil heat to more efficient natural gas heat compared with landlords who do not pay for energy, despite the availability of significant cost savings.

One might also expect that environmental attitudes might be correlated with choice of heating or cooling technology and that 'greener' consumers might be most likely to be early adopters of low-carbon heating or cooling systems. Curtis, McCoy and Aravena (2018) find that environmental attitudes have no impact on fuel or technology choice and the main determinant of home heating fuel and technology choice is simply proximity to the gas grid. Similarly, although Lange, Moro and Traynor (2014) find a negative correlation between heating expenditures and environmental behaviours, they did not identify any relationship between environmental attitudes or perceptions and heating expenditures.

Finally, thermal comfort can also be a key deterrent to switch to HPs as a heating system. The use of HPs requires a good level of insulation to operate, as space heating will be typically slower than with a conventional gas-powered central heating system. In households connected to the gas grid, hybrid HPs that can be operated with both electricity and natural gas represent a good opportunity to secure heat supply during colder spells (Zhang et al. 2018).

The use of HPs could however increase thermal comfort during the warm seasons, as they can also be used for cooling. One of the key drivers of HP sales is interest in reversible HPs, which can be used for both heating and cooling driven by demand for space cooling. In the US, mini-split ductless HPs are on the rise (Weorpel 2018) owing to a higher SEER and low operating temperature for heating. Of course, improved thermal comfort also means greater energy use in summers. In temperate climate zones, where there had previously been little AC, energy would be increasingly devoted to cooling that would otherwise not have taken place with the existing infrastructure.

Aside from incentives to adopt new heating technologies, one other important consideration is the willingness of jurisdictions to impose outright bans on further use of gas for heating. For example, the UK has mandated that new homes should not have a gas connection by 2025 (Harrabin 2019) and in late 2020, the city of San Francisco banned natural gas in all new residential construction from mid-2021 (Dineen 2020). The Netherlands has mandated that all homes will move away from natural gas by 2050, but a large number of municipalities including Rotterdam, Amsterdam and Utrecht have agreed on near-term measures to increase the number of 'gasless neighbourhoods' in the coming years by disconnecting public housing, not permitting gas in new buildings and encouraging district heating and other options such as electric or hybrid HPs (Van den Ende 2017).

4.6   Demand Elasticity to Energy Prices and Energy Poverty

Another key impact of, and potential limitation to, electrification (and decarbonization) of heating is the incurred cost to the household. Fuel poverty is generally defined as the inability to heat own's home at a correct standard owing to a combination of factors, including household income, energy efficiency of the dwelling and energy prices (Charlier and Kahouli 2018). It is a major issue across the world, including in advanced economies. In the United Kingdom, 3000 people died in 2018 because of fuel poverty (Chapman 2018). In Canada, 1 million households are affected by energy poverty, during both winter cold and summer heatwaves (Tardy and Lee 2019).

Switching to a more efficient heating system typically requires an upfront investment, which could have implications for household energy spending. Micro-CHP fuel cells typically represent the highest investment from the householder's perspective. Capital costs range from $17 000 to 23 000 per unit in Japan, to $37 000 per unit in Europe (Dodds et al. 2015). Heat pumps also represent a substantial investment, with capital and installation costs ranging between $6700 and $15 300 for an air-source HP, and $12 000 to $26 700 for an GSHP (carbonConnect 2019, Department for Business Energy & Industrial Strategy 2018, Renewable Energy Hub 2019). Modern biomass boilers can cost between $9300 and $20 000, depending on the degree of sophistication (carbonConnect 2019, Renewable Energy Hub 2019). Hydrogen boilers are expected to cost the same as conventional gas boilers, anywhere between $700 and $4000 per unit depending on the size, but installation and pipeline conversion work could cost as much as $1300 to $5500 (carbonConnect 2019, CCC 2018b, Strbac et al. 2018). All the proposed alternatives are therefore likely to represent a significant upfront cost for residential or commercial consumers when compared to current natural gas boilers (capital costs between $700 and $3300 depending on the size for condensing boilers) or conventional electric systems (electric storage heaters typically cost $300–600 per panel) (carbonConnect 2019).

Owing to a higher energy efficiency, operating costs of alternative heating systems are expected to be lower than for fossil fuel boilers or conventional electric heaters (Honoré 2018). However, annual costs and potential savings are largely dependent on energy costs – natural gas, electricity, biomass, hydrogen – and on the incumbent system. In many countries that rely on natural gas for heating, the average price of natural gas is typically lower than the price of electricity (European Commission 2019b). Concerning the conversion to a 'greener gas', the cost of hydrogen fuel is currently prohibitive. Estimates of the cost of hydrogen from electrolysis can vary from over \$24/MWh (Sustainable Gas Institute 2017) to as low as \$10/MWh with best available technology (Mathis and Thornhill 2019), which is still twice the cost of natural gas. Hydrogen from steam methane reformation with CCS can cost as low as \$7/MWh, but only assuming a pre-existing CCS infrastructure (Sustainable Gas Institute 2017).

Energy savings generated when retrofitting a heating system to a more efficient one are also very variable. In a comparative assessment of residential heating technologies for a semi-detached house in Quebec, ASHPs are found to generate savings relative to a conventional electric heater when electricity prices reach \$44/MWh, while GSHPs need an electricity price of \$95/MWh to break even (Pedinotti-Castelle et al. 2019). The scale and variation in the electricity price profile in time can also impact the competitiveness of heating technologies. When considering variable electricity price profiles, HPs are only competitive with gas boilers and electric heaters for a large household and a short-run electricity price regime (average price of \$27/MWh), but HPs and micro-CHPs are never competitive at higher electricity prices (average price of \$96/MWh), regardless of the household size (Vijay and Hawkes 2017). Rebates and tariffs can be instrumental to the adoption of these technologies. The eligibility of HPs for the Renewable Heat Incentive (RHI) in the UK (Department of Energy & Climate Change 2014) or for local incentives in China (Zhao et al. 2017) are examples of such policies.

Finally, the introduction of more stringent decarbonization policies to decarbonize the electricity grid could also lead to an increase in electricity prices. Many studies have attempted to quantify the short-term and long-term price elasticity of energy demand (see Labandeira, Labeaga and López-Otero et al. 2017 for a meta-analysis). There have been a number of studies of residential demand (for example, Charlier and Kahouli 2018, Risch and Salmon 2017) to better inform the design of energy policies. Price elasticities of heating demand in particular are generally found to be influenced by income level, household type and total household expenditures (Schulte and Heindl 2017). A study on the elasticity of heating demand in Germany showed that the energy demand of lower-income consumers was much less elastic than that of higher-income consumers (ibid.). This highlights household energy as a necessary good and suggests that higher energy prices resulting from policies incentivizing demand reduction could disproportionally impact lower-income households (He and Reiner 2016). National and local policies such as the state-mandated heating prices in Quebec, via the control over hydropower generation (Tardy and Lee 2019), or the Energy Voucher in France allocated to the poorest 15 per cent of households (Charlier and Kahouli 2018), are required to ensure that electrification of heating (or decarbonization more generally) does not decrease the overall welfare of vulnerable heating consumers.

5.   OUTLOOK FOR THE ELECTRIFICATION OF HEAT

The role of electrification in future decarbonization pathways has been examined in the context of meeting both global 1.5°C and 2°C targets by the end of the century (IEA

2019a, Knobloch et al. 2019) and regional economy-wide 80 per cent to 100 per cent emissions reduction targets by mid-century (Connolly et al. 2014, Element Energy and E4Tech 2018, Honoré 2018, National Grid 2019a, Strbac et al. 2018, White and Rhodes 2019).

5.1   Global Outlook

In the IEA Faster Transition Scenario to 2050, which is consistent with a 2°C target, the buildings sector undergoes the most rapid economy-wide decarbonization, as direct and indirect CO_2 emissions drop from 9.5 gigatons of CO_2 ($GtCO_2$) in 2017 to 1.2 $GtCO_2$ in 2050 (IEA 2019a). Energy demand for services that are already electrified (for example, cooling) grows substantially in emerging economies, as level of development, increasing income and rising temperatures drive ownership of AC and other appliances. Deep efficiency improvements to appliances and building envelopes are required just to limit the global increase in electricity consumption to 30 per cent. This is achieved through a 50 per cent increase in AC unit performance by 2030, and a twofold increase by 2050. In developed economies, efficiency improvements actually outstrip the projected increase in electricity demand, resulting in a slight decrease in electricity consumption. Residential heating demand is primarily met with bioenergy and solar thermal, which reaches 3 billion households by 2030 and represents 85 per cent of the installed heating capacity by 2050. Heat pumps go through a rapid scale up, growing from 3 per cent of installed capacity to 30 per cent by 2050. To dampen the impacts that this growth might have on the electricity grid, the efficiency of HPs also needs to increase, to reach a COP of 3.5 in cold climates, 5.0 in temperate climates and 8.0–9.0 in climates where reversible HPs are used for both heating and cooling. Even in this ambitious scenario, natural gas still plays a role in the heating system, supplying 15 per cent of space and water heating demand by 2050 (ibid.).

5.2   Regional Outlooks

At the regional level, decarbonization pathways are highly dependent on technology performance and cost assumptions, as well as on existing heat supply and regulations to either discourage heat or actively promote alternatives. At the EU level, a decarbonization study assessing the impact of an economy-wide 80 per cent reduction target suggests the high potential of heating networks fuelled by HPs to decarbonize EU heating demand (Connolly et al. 2014). In the Northeast US, a scenario consistent with a 40 per cent emissions reduction target by 2030, projects electrification to meet 23 per cent of total heating demand (through air and ground source HPs), thereby increasing the electricity peak demand by 15 per cent and the heavy reliance on natural gas through the shift of oil boilers towards gas boilers (National Grid 2019a). The study does not, however, provide a clear pathway to meet the 80 per cent reduction target by 2050, nor does it discuss the feasibility of replacing natural gas by a low-carbon alternative. In the UK, two studies have recently compared electrification, hydrogen and hybrid pathways under different decarbonization targets (Element Energy and E4Tech 2018, Strbac et al. 2018), with significantly different results (see Section 4.3), which suggests the high dependence of these findings on infrastructure cost (for example, CCS, gas grid conversion and grid reinforcement cost) and technology performance (for example, CO_2 capture efficiency of CCS plants). Other factors such as hourly heat demand and technology cost assumptions are also highly influential in these assessments.

5.3   The Impact of More Stringent Emissions Reduction Targets

As net zero targets by 2050 are being legislated around the world, future pathways are expected to cover scenarios consistent with a 100 per cent economy-wide decarbonization target by mid-century. Most previous decarbonization outlooks to 2050 had explored the implications of a 80–85 per cent emissions reduction target (Connolly et al. 2014, Element Energy and E4Tech 2018, Honoré 2018, IEA 2019a). Full decarbonization of the heating sector would involve drastic changes in the structure and operation of the energy system.

National-level studies of full heat decarbonization showed that the total system cost of a decarbonization pathway could increase dramatically with the stringency of the decarbonization target by 2050 (see Section 4.3) (Element Energy and E4Tech 2018, Strbac et al. 2018), although the CCC (2019) report on net zero for the UK government notes that the total cost of meeting the 80 per cent target as assessed in 2008 was identical to the total cost of meeting 100 per cent reduction (1–2 per cent of GDP). Absent further analysis, it is unclear whether (1) more stringent targets will drive electrification further, shifting away from a reliance on natural gas networks, with implications for the security of the electricity supply; or (2) emissions from the building and industrial sectors that are expensive to mitigate will be offset with the deployment of CO_2 removal methods (for example, the UK relying on bioenergy with CCS to offset remaining emissions, see CCC 2019) or via international offsets. Future whole systems studies of the electrification of heating will need to explore the optimal level of decarbonization and the role of these CO_2 removal methods.

6.   CONCLUSIONS

This chapter explored the present role and future opportunities and challenges for electrification of heating in buildings. Electricity is expected to play an ever-larger role in emerging countries, owing to a booming demand for cooling and other energy services. High-efficiency HPs are projected to reach much higher level of deployment, complemented by biomass boilers, solar thermal, and a switch to high-efficiency gas boilers and/or hybrid HPs.

Despite scattered incentives for market-ready renewable and more efficient heating systems, the heating sector remains heavily fossil-fuel dominated. Key barriers to electrification of heating include (1) the impact of annual and peak electricity demand; (2) the simultaneous increasing demand for electricity services such as cooling; and (3) the potential financial and social impacts of increased cost of heating.

Policies such as building codes, appliance efficiency labels and incentives for the adoption of low-carbon or more efficient heating and cooling systems are key to enabling decarbonization of heating and cooling through electrification, but empirical evidence to date is still quite weak although existing evidence points to the severe challenges of rapid adoption of new technologies in the buildings sector.

The three innovation and policy levers of electrification of heating and cooling in the buildings sector are (1) setting minimum efficiency requirements for cooling and heating equipment; (2) exploiting synergies between heating/cooling equipment and storage, smart metering and district networks to enhance flexibility and reduce impact on peak demand; and (3) implementing policy measures to improve building envelopes. Table 19.2 summarizes the key innovation, investment and policy challenges and opportunities in decarbonizing heating and cooling in the buildings sector.

Finally, most previous heating decarbonization outlooks to 2050 do not achieve net zero emissions, although this may begin to change as more large economies such as the

Table 19.2   Opportunities in electrifying heating in buildings and associated challenges

Issue	Possible Opportunities	Associated Challenges
Increasing demand for electricity driven by cooling demand	Building performance improvement	Actual performance does not meet technical expectations
	Coincidence of solar PV peak and high cooling demand	Potential mismatch between rate of PV and AC uptake
	Improving appliance efficiency (via standards)	Uneven evidence over savings associated with building codes
	Voluntary schemes (for example, label technology performance; use same metric to facilitate like-for-like comparison)	Questions over how to overcome informational barriers and consumer interest in energy savings
Impact on existing infrastructure (for example, gas network) and total system cost	Improving efficiency of gas appliances	Technology lock-in to continued use of natural gas
	Hybrid HPs that avoid need for radical shift and stranded costs and deliver better performance	Incomplete shift away from natural gas resulting in significant residual emissions
	CO_2 removal (CDR) to offset residual emissions	Concerns over possible mitigation deterrent effect
	Revise VoLL to reflect changing views of security of supply and need for capacity expansion	VoLL is built into regulations and utility investment decisions so may be slow to change
	Repurpose gas grid with greener gas (hydrogen, biomethane or carbon-neutral synthetic fuels)	Potential competition between electrification and greener gas routes
Increased electricity peak demand	Encourage synergies with other alternative technologies (distributed solar PV, district heating, thermal storage)	Difficulty of coordinating timing of deployment different build-out rates
	Enhance flexibility with thermal storage	Minimal evidence on willingness of consumers to respond
	Shift peak demand to off-peak hours with smart meters and dynamic electricity pricing	Slow uptake of time of use pricing even in jurisdictions that have deployed smart meters

Table 19.2 *Continued*

Issue	Possible Opportunities	Associated Challenges
Technology adoption	Household level incentives for the purchase and operation of renewable heating technologies	Success strongly dependent on how consumers process information, split responsibility over bills and investments
	Market based measures/economy of scale to reduce the cost of new systems	Questions over actual behaviour versus engineering models, rebound effect, effectiveness of incentives
	Reversible HPs for thermal comfort in winter and summer	Greater energy use in summers and energy devoted to cooling that would otherwise not have taken place

UK and France have begun to adopt legally binding net zero targets. Full decarbonization of the heating sector involves drastic changes in the structure and operation of the energy system. The role of CO_2 removal methods to offset residual emissions from heating needs to be explored to determine the optimal level of electrification (and decarbonization) for residential heating system, in order to maintain reliability and affordability of heating.

NOTES

1. The physical separation of the interior and exterior of a building to facilitate climate control and protect the indoor environment.
2. Accounting for the lifecycle emissions of coal and natural gas supply.
3. Heat demand profile only includes dwellings connected to the gas grid, which represents 71 per cent of UK dwellings (National Grid 2019b).
4. The Faster Transition scenario envisions an ambitious transformation of the energy sector, with energy-related emissions peaking in 2020 and reducing by 75 per cent in 2050.
5. The SEER values collected from the IEA are calculated as the ratio of cooling energy output in kWh, to energy input in kWh. By contrast, SEER values in the US are typically three times higher as they are calculated as the ratio of cooling energy output in British thermal units (BTU), to energy input in kWh.
6. All cost data are presented in 2018 US dollars. British pound (GBP) and Canadian dollar (CAD) figures were converted using conversion rates of USD1 = 0.75 GBP (2018 exchange rate) and USD1 = 1.379 CAD (2016 exchange rate). US GDP deflators were used to convert cost data to 2018 dollars (World Bank 2019).

REFERENCES

Alberini, A., W. Gans and C. Towe (2016), 'Free riding, upsizing, and energy efficiency incentives in Maryland homes', *The Energy Journal*, **37** (1), 259–90.
Allcott, H. and R. L. Sweeney (2016), 'The role of sales agents in information disclosure: evidence from a field experiment', *Management Science*, **63** (1), 21–39.
Arteconi, A. and F. Polonara (2018), 'Assessing the demand side management potential and the energy flexibility of heat pumps in buildings', *Energies*, **11** (7), 1–19.
Attari, S. Z., M. L. DeKay, C. I. Davidson and W. Bruine de Bruin (2010), 'Public perceptions of energy consumption and savings', *Proceedings of the National Academy of Sciences*, **107** (37), 16054–9.
Beyond Zero Emissions (2018), *Zero Carbon Industry Plan: Electrifying Industry*, accessed 23 July 2021 at https://apo.org.au/sites/default/files/resource-files/2018-12/apo-nid270186.pdf.

Bollinger, B. K. and W. R. Hartmann (2019) 'Information vs. automation and implications for dynamic pricing', *Management Science*, **66** (1), 290–314.

Building Energy Research Center (BERC) (2018), *China Building Energy Use 2018*, accessed 23 July 2021 at https://www.researchgate.net/publication/337160052_China_Building_Energy_Use_2018.

Buildings Performance Institute Europe BPIE (2016), *Smart Buildings in a Decarbonised Energy System 10 Principles to Deliver Real Benefits for Europe's Citizens*, accessed 23 July 2021 at http://bpie.eu/wp-content/uploads/2016/11/BPIE-10-principles-final.pdf.

Cambridge Economic Policy Associates CEPA (2018), *Study on the Estimation of the Value of Lost Load of Electricity Supply in Europe*, accessed 23 July 2021 at https://extranet.acer.europa.eu/Events/Workshop-on-the-estimation-of-the-cost-of-disruption-of-gas-supply-CoDG-and-the-value-of-lost-load-in-power-supply-systems-VoLL-in-Europe/Documents/CEPAPresentation_VoLLWorkshop.pdf.

carbonConnect (2019), 'Supporting material 1: comparison of different types of low carbon heating from a householder perspective', accessed 23 July 2021 at https://www.policyconnect.org.uk/sites/default/files/migrate/cc/supporting_material_1-_tables_of_different_low_carbon_heating_options_0.pdf

Cassarino, T. G., E. Sharp and M. Barrett (2018), 'The impact of social and weather drivers on the historical electricity demand in Europe', *Applied Energy*, **229**, 176–85.

Cayla, J. M., N. Maizi and C. Marchand (2011), 'The role of income in energy consumption behaviour: evidence from French households data', *Energy Policy*, **39** (12), 7874–83.

Chapman, P. (2018), 'Fuel poverty crisis: 3,000 Britons dying each year because they can't heat their homes, study shows', *The Independent*, 22 February, accessed 23 July 2021 at https://www.independent.co.uk/news/business/news/cold-weather-uk-winter-deaths-europe-polar-vortex-a8224276.html.

Charitopoulos, V., C. K. Chyong and D. Reiner (2019), 'Modelling & optimisation of decarbonisation pathways for UK heat sector', paper presented at the EPRG & CEEPR International Energy Policy Conference, 'The Good Fight Against GHG Emissions', London, 2–3 September, accessed 23 July 2021 at https://www.eprg.group.cam.ac.uk/wp-content/uploads/2019/09/V.-Charitopoulos_2019.pdf.

Charlier, D. and S. Kahouli (2018), 'From residential energy demand to fuel poverty: income-induced non-linearities in the reactions of households to energy price fluctuations', *FAERE Working Paper No. 11*.

Chaudry, M., M. Abeysekera and S. H. R. Hosseini et al. (2015), 'Uncertainties in decarbonising heat in the UK', *Energy Policy*, **87**, 623–40.

Committee on Climate Change (CCC) (2018a), *Biomass in a Low-carbon Economy*, November, accessed 23 July 2021 at https://www.theccc.org.uk/wp-content/uploads/2018/11/Biomass-in-a-low-carbon-economy-CCC-2018.pdf.

Committee on Climate Change (CCC) (2018b), *Hydrogen in a Low-carbon Economy*, November, accessed 23 July 2021 at https://www.theccc.org.uk/wp-content/uploads/2018/11/Hydrogen-in-a-low-carbon-economy.pdf.

Committee on Climate Change CCC (2019), *Net Zero: The UK's Contribution to Stopping Global Warming*, May, accessed 23 July 2021 at https://www.theccc.org.uk/publication/net-zero-the-uks-contribution-to-stopping-global-warming/.

Connolly, D., H. Lund and B. V. Mathiesen et al. (2014), 'Heat roadmap Europe: combining district heating with heat savings to decarbonise the EU energy system', *Energy Policy*, **65**, 475–89.

Cooper, S. J. G., G. P. Hammond, M. C. McManus and D. Pudjianto (2016), 'Detailed simulation of electrical demands due to nationwide adoption of heat pumps, taking account of renewable generation and mitigation', *IET Renewable Power Generation*, **10** (3), 380–87.

Creutzig, F., N. H. Ravindranath and G. Berndes et al. (2015), 'Bioenergy and climate change mitigation: an assessment', *GCB Bioenergy*, **7** (5), 916–44.

Curtis, J., D. McCoy and C. Aravena (2018), 'Heating system upgrades: the role of knowledge, socio-demographics, building attributes and energy infrastructure', *Energy Policy*, **120**, 183–96.

Davis, L. W., A. Fuchs and P. Gertler (2014), 'Cash for coolers: evaluating a large-scale appliance replacement program in Mexico', *American Economic Journal: Economic Policy*, **6** (4), 207–38.

Department for Business Energy & Industrial Strategy (2018), *Clean Growth – Transforming Heating: Overview of Current Evidence*, accessed 23 July 2021 at https://assets.publishing.service.gov.uk/government/uploads/system/uploads/attachment_data/file/766109/decarbonising-heating.pdf.

Department of Energy & Climate Change (2014), 'The Renewable Heat Incentive (RHI) scheme', Appendix 6 in Department of Energy & Climate Change, *2010 to 2015 Government Policy: Low Carbon Technologies*, policy paper, accessed 23 July 2021 at https://www.gov.uk/government/publications/2010-to-2015-government-policy-low-carbon-technologies/2010-to-2015-government-policy-low-carbon-technologies#appendix-6-renewable-heat-incentive-rhi.

Derbez, M., G. Wyart and E. Le Ponner et al. (2018), 'Indoor air quality in energy-efficient dwellings: levels and sources of pollutants', *Indoor Air*, **28** (2), 318–38.

Dineen, J. K. (2020), 'No more natural gas in new San Francisco buildings starting next year', *San Francisco Chronicle*, 12 November.

Dodds, P. E., I. Staffell and A. D. Hawkes et al. (2015), 'Hydrogen and fuel cell technologies for heating: a review', *International Journal of Hydrogen Energy*, **40** (5), 2065–83.

Dubin, J. A., A. K. Miedema and R. V. Chandran (1986), 'Price effects of energy-efficient technologies: a study of residential demand for heating and cooling', *RAND Journal of Economics*, **17** (3), 310–25.

Eid, C., E. Koliou and M. Valles et al. (2016), 'Time-based pricing and electricity demand response: existing barriers and next steps', *Utilities Policy*, **40**, 15–25.

Element Energy and E4Tech (2018), *Cost Analysis of Future Heat Infrastructure Options*, report for National Infrastructure Commission March 2018, accessed 23 July 2021 at https://nic.org.uk/app/uploads/Element-Energy-and-E4techCost-analysis-of-future-heat-infrastructure-Final.pdf.

Enerdata (2019), 'The future of air conditioning', 26 September, accessed 23 July 2021 at https://www.enerdata.net/publications/executive-briefing/the-future-air-conditioning-global-demand.html.

Energy Information Administration (EIA) (2019), *Annual Energy Outlook 2019*, accessed 23 July 2021 at https://www.eia.gov/outlooks/aeo/data/browser/#/?id=2-AEO2019&sourcekey=0.

ENGIE (2019), 'The GHRYD demonstration project', accessed 23 July 2021 at https://www.engie.com/en/businesses/gas/hydrogen/power-to-gas/the-grhyd-demonstration-project/.

European Commission (2019a), 'Ene.field', accessed 23 July 2021 at http://enefield.eu/.

European Commission (2019b), *EUROSTAT*, accessed 23 July 2021 at https://ec.europa.eu/eurostat/data/database.

European Heat Pump Association (EHPA) (2017), *Large Scale Heat Pumps in Europe*, accessed 23 July 2021 at https://www.ehpa.org/fileadmin/red/03._Media/03.02_Studies_and_reports/Large_heat_pumps_in_Europe_MDN_II_final4_small.pdf.

European Heat Pump Association (EHPA) (2019), 'Market data', accessed 23 July 2021 at https://www.ehpa.org/market-data/.

Eyre, N. and P. Baruah (2015), 'Uncertainties in future energy demand in UK residential heating', *Energy Policy*, **87**, 641–53.

Friedmann, S. J., Z. Fan and K. Tang (2019), *Low-Carbon Heat Solutions for Heavy Industry: Sources, Options, and Costs Today*, Center for Global Energy Policy, Columbia University, 7 October, accessed 23 July 2021 at https://energypolicy.columbia.edu/research/report/low-carbon-heat-solutions-heavy-industry-sources-options-and-costs-today.

Frontier Economics (2016), *Future Regulation of the UK Gas Grid: Impacts and Institutional Implications of UK Gas Grid Future Scenarios – A Report for the CCC*, accessed 23 July 2021 at https://www.theccc.org.uk/wp-content/uploads/2016/10/Future-Regulationof-the-Gas-Grid.pdf.

Gaz Réseau Distribution France (2017), Renewable Gas French Panorama 2017, accessed at https://www.syndicat-energies-renouvelables.fr/wp-content/uploads/basedoc/ser-overviewrenewablegas2017-project05.pdf.

Gerarden, T. D., R. G. Newell and R. N. Stavins (2017), 'Assessing the energy efficiency gap', *Journal of Economic Literature*, **55** (4), 1486–525.

Gi, K., F. Sano and A. Hayashi et al. (2018), 'A global analysis of residential heating and cooling service demand and cost-effective energy consumption under different climate change scenarios up to 2050', *Mitigation and Adaptation Strategies for Global Change*, **23** (1), 51–79.

Gillingham, K., M. Harding and D. Rapson (2012), 'Split incentives in residential energy consumption', *The Energy Journal*, **33** (2), 37–62.

Gillingham, K., A. Keyes and K. Palmer (2018), 'Advances in evaluating energy efficiency policies and programs', *Annual Review of Resource Economics*, **10** (1), 511–32.

Giraudet, L. G., S. Houde and J. Maher (2018), 'Moral hazard and the energy efficiency gap: theory and evidence', *Journal of the Association of Environmental and Resource Economists*, **5** (4), 755–90.

Glenk, G. and S. Reichelstein (2019), 'Economics of converting renewable power to hydrogen', *Nature Energy*, **4**, 216–22.

Goldemberg, J. and S. T. Coelho (2004), 'Renewable energy – traditional biomass vs. modern biomass', *Energy Policy*, **32** (6), 711–14.

Hanna, R., B. Parrish and R. Gross (2016), *Best Practice in Heat Decarbonisation Policy: A Review of the International Experience of Policies to Promote the Uptake of Low-carbon Heat Supply*, UKERC Technology and Policy Assessment.

Harrabin, R. (2019), 'Gas heating ban for new homes from 2025', *BBC News*, 13 March, accessed 23 July 2021 at https://www.bbc.co.uk/news/science-environment-47559920.

He, X. and D. M. Reiner (2016), 'Electricity demand and basic needs: empirical evidence from China's households', *Energy Policy*, **90**, 212–21.

Heinen, S., P. Mancarella, C. O'Dwyer and M. O'Malley (2018), 'Heat electrification: the latest research in Europe', *IEEE Power and Energy Magazine*, **16** (4), 69–78.

Honoré, A. (2018), 'Decarbonisation of heat in Europe: implications for natural gas demand', *OIES Paper NG 130*, Oxford Institute for Energy Studies, accessed 23 July 2021 at https://ora.ox.ac.uk/objects/uuid:c808f872-16de-4d88-8190-5c17abcae0bd.

International Energy Agency (IEA) (2018a), *Renewables 2018: Analysis and Forecasts to 2023*, accessed 23 July 2021 at https://www.iea.org/reports/renewables-2018.

International Energy Agency (IEA) (2018b), *The Future of Cooling: Opportunities for Efficient Air Conditioning*, accessed 23 July 2021 at https://www.iea.org/reports/the-future-of-cooling.

International Energy Agency (IEA) (2019a), *Perspectives for the Clean Energy Transition: The Critical Role of Buildings*, accessed 23 July 2021 at https://www.iea.org/reports/the-critical-role-of-buildings.

International Energy Agency (IEA) (2019b), 'Tracking clean energy progress', accessed 23 July 2021 at https://www.iea.org/tcep/.

International Energy Agency (IEA) (2019c), *World Energy Balances – Overview*, accessed 23 July 2021 at https://webstore.iea.org/world-energy-balances-2019.

International Energy Agency (IEA) (2019d), *World Energy Investment 2019*, accessed 23 July 2021 at https://webstore.iea.org/world-energy-investment-2019.

International Energy Agency (IEA) (2019e), *The Future of Hydrogen: Seizing Today's Opportunities*, accessed 23 July 2021 at https://www.iea.org/reports/the-future-of-hydrogen.

International Energy Agency (IEA) (2019f), 'Data and statistics', accessed 23 July 2021 at https://www.iea.org/statistics/.

Jacobsen, G. D. and M. J. Kotchen (2013), 'Are building codes effective at saving energy? Evidence from residential billing data in Florida', *Review of Economics and Statistics*, **95**, 34–49.

Karlsen, S. S., M. Hamdy and S. Attia (2020), 'Methodology to assess business models of dynamic pricing tariffs in all-electric houses', *Energy and Buildings*, **207**, Article 109586.

Klippenstein, M. (2019), 'FCW exclusive: Tokyo Fuel Cell Expo 2019 – 300,000 Ene-Farms', *FuelCellsWork.com*, 18 April, accessed 23 July 2021 at https://fuelcellsworks.com/news/fcw-exclusive-tokyo-fuel-cell-expo-2019-300000-ene-farms/.

Knobloch, F., H. Pollitt and U. Chewpreecha et al. (2019), 'Simulating the deep decarbonisation of residential heating for limiting global warming to 1.5°C', *Energy Efficiency*, **12** (2), 521–50.

Labandeira, X., J. M. Labeaga and X. López-Otero (2017), 'A meta-analysis on the price elasticity of energy demand', *Energy Policy*, **102**, 549–68.

Lange, I., M. Moro and L. Traynor (2014), 'Green hypocrisy? Environmental attitudes and residential space heating expenditure', *Ecological Economics*, **107**, 76–83.

Lechtenböhmer, S., L. J. Nilsson, M. Åhman and C. Schneider (2016), 'Decarbonising the energy intensive basic materials industry through electrification – implications for future EU electricity demand', *Energy*, **115**, 1623–31.

Levinson, A. (2016) 'How much energy do building energy codes save? Evidence from California houses', *American Economic Review*, **106** (10), 2867–94.

Li, P. H., I. Keppo and N. Strachan, N. (2018), 'Incorporating homeowners' preferences of heating technologies in the UK TIMES model', *Energy*, **148**, 716–27.

London Economics (2013), *The Value of Lost Load (VoLL) for Electricity in Great Britain: Final Report for OFGEM and DECC*, July 2013, accessed 23 July 2021 at https://www.gov.uk/government/uploads/system/uploads/attachment_data/file/224028/value_lost_load_electricty_gb.pdf.

Luh, S., S. Budinis and S. Giarola et al. (2019), 'Long-term development of the industrial sector – case study about electrification, fuel switching, and CCS in the USA', *Computers & Chemical Engineering*, **133**, Article 106602.

Lund, H., S. Werner and R. Wiltshire et al. (2014) '4th Generation District Heating (4GDH): integrating smart thermal grids into future sustainable energy systems', *Energy*, **68**, 1–11.

Mathis, W. and J. Thornhill, J. (2019), 'Hydrogen's plunging price boosts role as climate solution', *Bloomberg.com*, 21 August, accessed 23 July 2021 at https://www.bloomberg.com/news/articles/2019-08-21/cost-of-hydrogen-from-renewables-to-plummet-next-decade-bnef.

Michelsen, C. C. and R. Madlener (2012), 'Homeowners' preferences for adopting innovative residential heating systems: a discrete choice analysis for Germany', *Energy Economics*, **34** (5), 1271–83.

Mohajerani, A., J. Bakaric and T. Jeffrey-Bailey (2017), 'The urban heat island effect, its causes, and mitigation, with reference to the thermal properties of asphalt concrete', *Journal of Environmental Management*, **197**, 522–38.

Mulder, M., P. Perey and J. L. Moraga (2019), 'Outlook for a Dutch hydrogen market: economic conditions and scenarios', *University of Groningen Policy Paper No. 5*, accessed 23 July 2021 at https://www.rug.nl/ceer/blog/ceer_policypaper_5_web.pdf.

Myers, E. (2019), 'Are home buyers inattentive? Evidence from capitalization of energy costs', *American Economic Journal: Economic Policy*, **11** (2), 165–88.

National Grid (2019a), *Northeast 80×50 Pathway*, white paper, accessed 23 July 2021 at https://www.nationalgridus.com/News/Assets/80x50-White-Paper-FINAL.pdf.

National Grid (2019b), 'The non-gas map', accessed 23 July 2021 at https://www.nongasmap.org.uk/.

Natural Resources Canada (2019), 'National Energy Use Database (NEUD)', accessed 23 July 2021 at http://oee.nrcan.gc.ca/corporate/statistics/neud/dpa/data_e/publications.cfm?attr=0#b.

Nekrasov, A. S., S. A. Voronina and V. V. Semikashev (2012), 'Problems of residential heat supply in Russia', *Studies on Russian Economic Development*, **23** (2), 128–34.

Paige, J., C. McMillan and D. Stenberg et al. (2017), *Electrification Futures Study: End-use Electric Technology Cost and Performance Projections Through 2050*, accessed 23 July 2021 at https://www.nrel.gov/docs/fy18osti/70485.pdf.

Pedinotti-Castelle, M., M. F. Astudillo, P.-O. Pineau and B. Amor (2019), 'Is the environmental opportunity of retrofitting the residential sector worth the life cycle cost? A consequential assessment of a typical house in Quebec', *Renewable and Sustainable Energy Reviews*, **101**, 428–39.

Qadrdan, M., R. Fazeli and N. Jenkins et al. (2019), 'Gas and electricity supply implications of decarbonising heat sector in GB', *Energy*, **169**, 50–60.

Ramos, A., A. Gago, X. Labandeira and P. Linares (2015), 'The role of information for energy efficiency in the residential sector', *Energy Economics*, **52** (S1), S17–S29.

Renaldi, R., A. Kiprakis and D. Friedrich (2017), 'An optimisation framework for thermal energy storage integration in a residential heat pump heating system', *Applied Energy*, **186**, 520–29.

Renewable Energy Hub (2019), 'A guide to heat pump prices in 2019', accessed 23 July 2021 at https://www.renewableenergyhub.co.uk/main/heat-pumps-information/a-guide-to-heat-pump-prices-in-2019/.

Réseau de Transport d'Electricité (RTE) (2018), *Bilan Electrique 2018*, accessed 23 July 2021 at https://bilan-electrique-2020.rte-france.com/wp-content/uploads/2019/02/BE-PDF-2018v3.pdf.

Reyna, J. L. and M. V. Chester (2017), 'Energy efficiency to reduce residential electricity and natural gas use under climate change', *Nature Communications*, **8** (2017), 1–12.

Risch, A. and C. Salmon (2017), 'What matters in residential energy consumption: evidence from France', *International Journal of Global Energy Issues*, **40** (1/2), 101–37.

Rivers, N. and M. L. Shiell (2016), 'Free riding on energy efficiency subsidies: the case of natural gas furnaces in Canada', *The Energy Journal*, **37**(4), 239–66.

Röpke, L. (2013), 'The development of renewable energies and supply security: a trade-off analysis', *Energy Policy*, **61**, 1011–21.

Schröder, T. and W. Kuckshinrichs (2015), 'Value of lost load: an efficient economic indicator for power supply security? A literature review', *Frontiers in Energy Research*, **3**, 1–12.

Schulte, I. and P. Heindl (2017), 'Price and income elasticities of residential energy demand in Germany', *Energy Policy*, **102**, 512–28.

Schweiger, G., J. Rantzer, K. Ericsson and P. Lauenburg (2017), 'The potential of power-to-heat in Swedish district heating systems', *Energy*, **137**, 661–9.

Sheng, Y., L. Fang and J. Nie (2017), 'Experimental analysis of indoor air quality improvement achieved by using a clean-air heat pump (CAHP) air-cleaner in a ventilation system', *Building and Environment*, **122**, 343–53.

Shuxue, X., W. Yueyue, N. Jianhui and M. Guoyuan (2019), '"Coal-to-electricity" project is ongoing in north China', *Energy*, **191**, Article 116525.

Staffell, I., D. Brett, N. Brandon and A. Hawkes (2012), 'A review of domestic heat pumps', *Energy and Environmental Science*, **5** (11), 9291–306.

Strbac, G., D. Pudjianto and R. Sansom et al. (2018), *Analysis of Alternative UK Heat Decarbonisation Pathways*, Imperial College London, accessed 23 July 2021 at https://www.theccc.org.uk/wp-content/uploads/2018/06/Imperial-College-2018-Analysis-of-Alternative-UK-Heat-Decarbonisation-Pathways.pdf.

Sustainable Gas Institute (2017), *A Greener Gas Grid: What Are the Options?* July 2017, accessed 23 July 2021 at https://www.sustainablegasinstitute.org/a-greener-gas-grid/.

Tardy, F. and B. Lee (2019), 'Building related energy poverty in developed countries – past, present, and future from a Canadian perspective', *Energy and Buildings*, **194**, 46–61.

Thornton, H. E., B. J. Hoskins and A. A. Scaife (2016), 'The role of temperature in the variability and extremes of electricity and gas demand in Great Britain', *Environmental Research Letters*, **11** (11), Article 114015.

Van den Ende, E. (2017), 'A revolution: the Netherlands kisses gas goodbye – but will it help the climate?', *Energy Post*, 7 June, accessed 23 July 2021 at https://energypost.eu/a-revolution-the-netherlands-kisses-gas-goodbye-but-will-it-help-the-climate/.

Vijay, A. and A. Hawkes (2017), 'The techno-economics of small-scale residential heating in low carbon futures', *Energies*, **10** (11), 1915.

Watson, S. D., K. J. Lomas and R. A. Buswell (2019), 'Decarbonising domestic heating: what is the peak GB demand?', *Energy Policy*, **126**, 533–44.

Weorpel, H. (2018), 'Mini-split heat pumps are one of the fastest growing HVAC sectors', *ACHR News*, 28 May 2018, accessed 23 July 2021 at https://www.achrnews.com/articles/137150-mini-split-heat-pumps-are-one-of-the-fastest-growing-hvac-sectors.

Werner, S. (2017), 'International review of district heating and cooling', *Energy*, **137**, 617–31.

White, P. R. and J. D. Rhodes (2019), *Electrification of Heating in the Texas Residential Sector*, report prepared for Pecan Street by Ideasmiths LLC, accessed 23 July 2021 at https://www.pecanstreet.org/electrictexas/.

World Bank (2019), *World Development Indicators*, accessed 23 July 2021 at https://datacatalog.worldbank.org/dataset/world-development-indicators.

Zhang, X., G. Strbac, F. Teng and P. Djapic (2018), 'Economic assessment of alternative heat decarbonisation strategies through coordinated operation with electricity system – UK case study', *Applied Energy*, **222**, 79–91.

Zhao, H., Y. Gao and Z. Song (2017), 'Strategic outlook of heat pump development in China', in *Proceedings of the 12th IEA Heat Pump Conference 2017*, 1–5.

20. Harnessing the power of integration to achieve universal electricity access: the case for the integrated distribution framework[*]

Ignacio J. Pérez-Arriaga, Divyam Nagpal, Grégoire Jacquot and Robert Stoner

1. INTRODUCTION

This chapter examines the economic, technical and regulatory factors underlying the present state of affairs in the developing world, where hundreds of millions of people – 789 million at last estimation in 2018[1] – live without access to electricity,[2] and billions more have poor-quality or unreliable supply. It then proposes an approach to accelerate the electrification process. The implications of limited access for socio-economic development are alarming. Access to affordable, reliable and sustainable energy is imperative to support income-generating activities, reduce drudgery and improve productivity, while also facilitating the delivery of public services such as healthcare and education. Ending poverty is largely contingent upon ending energy poverty.

Yet, electricity access expansion has seen slow progress and prospects for improvement remain limited. Most people without electricity live in what we shall term 'low-access countries', which largely coincide with the less developed countries (United Nations Conference on Trade and Development [UNCTAD] 2017). While the global population without access to electricity decreased from 1.2 billion in 2010 to about 789 million in 2018, most of the progress has been made in Central and Southern Asia (International Energy Agency [IEA] et al. 2020). Sub-Saharan Africa (SSA) has remained the region with the largest access deficit with more than half the population lacking access to electricity. A small fraction of the unelectrified population live in areas with difficult physical access, or are isolated for other social, economic or political reasons in countries like Indonesia, Peru or Colombia that have more than 95 per cent electrification rates.[3] Experience has shown that the electrification of the remaining 5 or 10 per cent can sometimes prove particularly difficult. India, which achieved full village-level electrification during 2019, is now striving to reach universal household-level access while also improving reliability of supply (Council on Energy, Environment and Water [CEEW] 2020).

A century of electrification projects has led to widely different outcomes in developing countries. Centralized electrification programmes, launched on a massive scale from the 1960s by state-owned utilities, led to significant success and quasi-universal energy access in densely populated developing countries in Latin America and Asia, where financing capacity could cope with the necessary investment for grid extension at the national scale. Most African countries, sparsely populated and characterized by limited ability to pay of rural communities, have been unable to finance capital-intensive electrification programmes, leading to limited progress in electricity access to date. The sub-par cost recovery for national utilities has led to cycles of repeated bankruptcy and bailouts, resulting in limited capacity to maintain existing infrastructure and *a fortiori* to extend infrastructure to underserved populations. Furthermore, the emergence of distributed renewables and digital technologies, massively deployed by the private sector since the late 2000s, has led to competing and uncoordinated public and private sector-driven electrification initiatives.

The electrification of the remaining populations, especially in the last mile, will become progressively more difficult, requiring substantially greater efforts and the use of all available electrification approaches. While access expansion in rural areas has grown at a slower than needed pace, it has remained almost constant in urban areas. Over 100 million people unserved live in urban areas and maintaining the urban access rate is going to be more challenging with the global urbanization trend (IEA et al. 2020). By 2030, the target year for reaching universal access under Sustainable Development Goal 7 (SDG 7), an estimated 620 million people will still remain without access, not accounting for the impact of COVID-19 on electrification efforts. Nine out of ten will live in SSA where the population is expected to double to roughly 2 billion by 2050 (World Bank 2019).

The incumbent power companies of many developing countries have not been able to deliver access, or an acceptable level of service (Hosier et al. 2017, Kojima and Trimble 2016, Maithani and Gupta 2015, Mukherjee 2014, Pargal and Ghosh-Banerjee 2014, World Bank 2017, and Chapter 22 by Foster et al. in this handbook). A narrow definition of access based on the setting up of distribution infrastructure and connection often fails to capture the quality, reliability, sufficiency and inclusiveness of electricity services received and consumed by different end-users in rural areas. In India, where a programme to provide electricity connections to every village and home was completed in 2019, unreliable supply of power remains a key challenge (Center for Strategic and International Studies [CSIS] 2019). The gap in the provision of electricity services has provided an opportunity for the private sector to develop mini-grids in already 'electrified' areas. The recent launch of the Tata Power collaboration with The Rockefeller Foundation to develop 10 000 mini-grids through 2026 is a key example of addressing the wide gap that often exists between connections and electricity services (Tata Power 2019).

To improve the understanding and reporting of the different facts of electricity access, the Energy Sector Management Assistance Program (ESMAP) has developed a multi-tier framework (MTF) that captures several attributes, including reliability, capacity, service hours, quality of supply and affordability (Bhatia and Angelou 2015). The MTF is being applied to several low-access countries to report progress on delivering electricity access, as reported in the annual *Tracking SDG 7: The Energy Progress Report* (e.g., IEA et al. 2020).

The failure to deliver electricity access has a number of well-identified causes, which must be examined in the broader context of the regulatory reforms that have taken place in the world for more than two decades. The situation in emerging economies, in SSA, Southeast Asia and some parts of Latin America, is very different from the standard model that is prevalent in most of Europe and the Americas, and Australia (Joskow 2006). In the few developing countries that have fully unbundled their utilities, private-sector participation has concentrated on independent power producers (IPPs), and wholesale and retail competition are generally absent. Instead, 'hybrid power markets' have developed (Eberhard and Godinho 2017, Gratwick and Eberhard 2008, Vagliasindi and Besant-Jones 2013), where incumbent state-owned utilities have retained dominant market positions and IPPs are introduced on the margin. A few countries have allowed the introduction of private capital and management in the distribution business, either via outright privatization, public–private partnerships (PPPs) or diverse types of franchises (Hosier et al. 2017, Jacquot et al. 2019, Mukherjee 2014). In general terms, the following key challenges in these power systems have been identified:

- The performance and financial viability of utilities needs substantial improvement. Inefficiencies in investment and operations, poor governance, limited cost recovery and few incentives for cost reduction lead to deterioration or collapse of services.
- Poor quality of service results in an adverse relationship between the utility and its customers, which incites illegal connections and unpaid bills, as well as a permissive attitude of the utilities and authorities. Politicians make use of subsidized tariffs to gain votes, leading customers to believe that they have right to inexpensive or even free electricity, often effectuated via lax or unenforced collection policies.
- Capacity expansion and electrification need financing; any existing public resources must leverage private investment under reasonably attractive conditions. Also, there is generally no clear assignment of responsibilities for planning, procurement and contracting.

Reaching universal access by 2030 and ensuring adequacy, affordability and reliability of electricity services will require tailored efforts across a wide variety of contexts where the electrification challenge persists. These range from the geographically large, but sparsely populated rural Congo, to dispersed islands of Indonesia, to remote clusters of population in the mountains of Peru or in the Amazon rainforest, to peri-urban and urban centres in Nigeria, and to rural households with unreliable grid connections in India. The 'economics of electricity' has a different meaning in these situations. The economic, technical, social and political challenge is to provide electricity for all in such a way that the supply of power can enable economic growth and human development. A rapid acceleration of progress in many countries will be needed. This requires thinking creatively and at scale about policies, regulation, delivery models and financing solutions that can rapidly mobilize substantial amounts of public and private capital, and align government and industry incentives towards an efficient, integrated electrification approach that taps into all available solutions – on-grid and off-grid.

Other chapters of this book describe and evaluate the situation of the power sector in different parts of the world. Special mention is deserved by Chapter 22 on Africa for its in-depth analysis of the difficult situation of the power sector in most SSA countries, with direct impact on the lack of access problem. The present chapter takes this description and analysis as the starting point but looks beyond Africa to other low-access countries, focuses on the distribution segment, and proposes a framework to define business models and regulatory approaches to turn electrification at distribution level into a financially viable proposition. The leitmotiv of the chapter is the value of integration: integration of all the electrification modes to reach the end customer, of connection and electricity services, of public and private participation, and of national power systems into regional power pools. And the focus is on distribution, as the bottleneck that impedes the flow of investment to supply the underserved population in most low-access countries.

This chapter is divided into four sections. In this introductory section, we briefly describe the status of electrification, the investment gap and the value of adopting an integrated approach. The second section reviews the core activities related to bulk supply – large-scale generation, transmission and power pools – while the third addresses distribution and retail (on-grid and off-grid). The fourth and most important section introduces the integrated distribution framework (IDF), which provides a pathway for expanding electricity access rapidly through all available solutions and ensuring that no one is left behind, while also strengthening the viability of the distribution sector.

1.1   Investment Gaps and Opportunity at Hand

The estimated volume of annual investment that would be needed to achieve universal residential access to even a modest level of electricity by 2030 is $41 billion. In comparison, investment commitments towards residential electricity access in 2018 across all segments of the power sector totalled over $16 billion, mostly focused on the generation segment (Sustainable Energy for All [SEforALL] and Climate Policy Initiative 2020). In SSA, the region with the largest access deficit, power investment grew 8 per cent in 2018 and has increased by 80 per cent since 2010. This growth, although insufficient to keep pace with investment needs, has all come from expanded generation, over 65 per cent of which was in renewables. Spending on grid infrastructure – which is critical for electrifying a large part of the population without access and connecting new generation – has stagnated (IEA 2019).

According to the latest UN estimations, SSA will double its present population of about 1 billion by 2050 – with 47 per cent of electrification in 2018. It is imperative to 'think big' to address the sheer magnitude of the electrification challenge. Given the perennial scarcity of public financing in most developing countries, substantial private investments will need to be mobilized to bridge the investment gap at every segment of the power supply chain, from power pools, utility-scale generation, transmission, distribution, retail and off-grid solutions.

While it is important to look at the classical power sector segments to tackle investment bottlenecks, it is equally crucial to acknowledge and leverage new technologies that present an opportunity to address the electrification challenge differently. Rapidly declining costs of renewables, battery technologies and energy-efficient appliances are making decentralized renewable energy systems increasingly affordable, and often competitive with grid extension in rural and dispersed communities. A recent ESMAP study of 53 operational mini-grids in Africa and Asia found that supply costs for mini-grids were highly competitive with those of grid extension – whose cost critically depends on demand level and dispersion, and distance to the existing grid – ranging from around $1000 or less per household or business, to just over $2100 (ESMAP 2019). At least 154 million people were estimated to have benefitted from electricity services from off-grid renewable energy technologies through 2017, mostly in SSA and South Asia – a seven-fold increase over 2011 (International Renewable Energy Agency [IRENA] 2018a). These solutions can be rapidly deployed, tailored to local resources and are capable of providing a wide range of electricity services from basic lighting and mobile charging to community-systems catering to diverse consumptive and productive loads. Decentralized systems can also be attractive in areas with grid access but unreliable power supply.

1.2   Value of Integration: Adopting a Holistic View of the Electrification Challenge

The opportunity to combine the three dominant modes of electrification – grid extension, mini-grid and stand-alone solutions – increases the number of possible pathways available to attain universal electricity access. Yet, these three modes of electrification have generally been deployed in developing countries in an uncoordinated manner and with the involvement of different entities, which has tended to lead to unhealthy competition rather than complementarity between electrification initiatives.

The first level of integration that will be critical for the success of any inclusive electrification plan is to harness the synergies between the three modes of electrification. Several electrification planning studies show that the mix of electrification modes in the lowest-cost plan strongly depends on some critical factors, such as the layout, capacity and reliability of the existing grid, the expected demand level, the topography, the cost of the components, the target reliability for off-grid solutions and the local price of diesel (Ciller et al. 2019).[4]

Furthermore, the integration of electricity supply with end-uses across sectors that support income-generating activities and delivery of public services will help to increase the socio-economic impacts from energy access. Integration of national power systems at a regional level and public and private investment will additionally provide the instruments to accelerate the pace of the electricity access expansion. The value of integration across these different aspects remains critical in designing an electricity access pathway that provides access to all in a timely manner.

Electrification involves a variety of activities, a range of different technologies and business approaches, and diverse actors. In many low-access countries, this process has not sufficiently started or deepened, leaving hundreds of millions of people without access to electricity, and still more with poor or unreliable service even if they are nominally connected to the national grid. To understand why progress on electrification has been slow, there is a need to examine every segment of the power sector that contributes to delivering electric energy to the very last mile to identify the barriers and devise the measures to overcome them. Investment gaps remain a common challenge, but the reasons and solutions vary for each segment, necessitating a system-level perspective. The focus of the review undertaken in the next two sections covering bulk supply (Section 2) and distribution (on-grid and off-grid) (Section 3), and of the measures that are proposed (Section 4), is to develop the conditions to attract public and (mostly) private investment in the most critical areas, in sufficient amounts to address the electrification challenge in its true dimension, compliant with the financial limitations of each country, and as efficiently as possible.

2.   THE BULK POWER SYSTEM

Traditionally, most investments in the electricity supply chain have taken place at bulk power system level – more than 90 per cent in large generation and over 6 per cent in transmission and distribution network (SEforALL and Climate Policy Initiative 2020). Low-access countries, and those in SSA in particular, have largely underinvested in each one of these three segments, but the reasons for it and the possible measures to encourage new investment are different in each case. This section analyses the situation and perspectives for centralized generation and the transmission network, as well as the impact of integration of power systems into regional power pools.

2.1 Large On-grid Generation

Regions with large, underserved populations have historically demonstrated low levels of investment in generation capacity. In SSA, excluding South Africa, the 1990s saw power capacity remain stagnant throughout the decade and only recently have capacity additions accelerated. Independent power producers (IPPs) are now the fastest-growing source of investment in generation capacity in more than 30 countries in SSA, with 270 existing projects larger than 5 megawatts (MW). Together these projects total more than 27 gigawatts (GW) of new capacity and represent about $52 billions of investment (Eberhard et al. 2017).[5]

This is a welcome shift from public utilities in low-access countries traditionally being the main sources of investment in new generation capacity. As the health of public utilities has deteriorated and along with it their capacity to mobilize the necessary new investment in infrastructure has declined, a number of countries have initiated structural power sector reforms. A starting point for many of these reforms has been the introduction of private-sector investment in the generation segment (African Development Bank and Association of Power Utilities of Africa [AfDB and APUA] 2019, Eberhard et al. 2017, and Chapter 22 in this handbook). In India, the share of privately owned generation capacity has steadily grown from 21 per cent in 2010 to 46 per cent in 2018 (Central Electricity Authority [CEA] 2021, Ministry of Power, Government of India 2011).

Despite these encouraging trends, larger private investments must be mobilized and these investments should be spread more evenly among countries to address the needs of countries with the largest access deficits, especially in SSA. In 2017, about two-thirds of total financing in the electricity sector was concentrated in India and Bangladesh, with Africa-focused investments remaining remarkably low (SEforALL and Climate Policy Initiative 2020). Public financing, through government budgets and development finance institutions (DFIs), will continue to have an important if not critical role to play to catalyse private investments as well as direct financing to ensure no one is left behind.

To mobilize further investment in the generation segment of the power sector, and thereby allow for improved service quality in the distribution sector, barriers need to be identified and addressed. Many of these barriers are well understood and can be broadly classified as follows:

- *Power sector structure and governance.* For many low-access countries, private-sector participation is only beginning to emerge. With the exception of a handful of cross-border projects, IPPs within SSA are currently structured on a bilateral basis (that is, with a single buyer and seller) and they are negotiated on a project-by-project basis. The transition from a traditional integrated monopoly utility structure to a partial or complete unbundling is still underway, although many countries have created conditions in the generation segment to encourage IPPs (AfDB and APUA 2019). The traditional model involving long-term PPAs has worked so far; however, as typically implemented, it has several shortcomings, including the bankability of off-takers and the limited ability of governments to back-stop with guarantees.

- *Regulatory framework.* A lack of clarity about the 'rules of the game' within the power sector is a source of substantial risk for private-sector investments. Relevant rules for investors include those that relate to tariff-setting processes, evacuation of power at the point of connection to the grid, and settlement of accounts or costs associated with third-party wheeling, which allows privately owned generation entities to sell power via the national transmission network to third-party users, including distribution companies and large commercial or industrial customers.

- *Regional integration and economies of scale.* Another factor that may impede the construction of power plants of sufficient size to achieve economies of scale or large hydropower plants to exploit existing untapped hydrological resources, is the lack of regional power system integration.

- *Financial risks.* Although each of the challenges listed here will be reflected in perceived financing risks for power projects, a fundamental investment risk relates to the creditworthiness of the off-taker (often a distribution company in dire financial straits). Other financial risks are related to contracts (for example, the structure and bankability of long-term contracts or PPAs, or the structure of contracts for land acquisition), political stability, legal security, corruption and currency fluctuations (Eberhard et al. 2016). Mechanisms for mitigating these risks include the aggregation of producers and off-takers in portfolios (Africa GreenCo 2017), the use of standardized project documents and reliance on local currency lending facilities, among other measures.

- *Macro-economic conditions.* At the country level, several factors influence the attractiveness of the overall investment climate. These include fiscal space for large-scale public investment, macroeconomic policies, legal systems that allow for arbitration and enforcement of contracts (such as power purchase agreements), investment-grade rating and previous experience with private investment (Eberhard et al. 2017).

- These barriers to private investment in generation are less connected to the nature of the generation business than they are related to external causes of risk. Known solutions to these barriers exist but their implementation depends on the context of the country.

2.1.1 Recommendations

Planning and policies Both solicited and unsolicited frameworks should be considered for IPP projects. Therefore, programmes for IPPs' development must be created at the government level, based on an integrative approach to identify the potential projects to be developed, technologies to be used, minimum or maximum sizes and location of projects under solicited and unsolicited proposals. Pipelines of projects must be defined at government level, based on sound integrated planning and policy, which would define clear objectives, target and provide a long-term view and direction to the private sector.

Legal and regulatory framework Well-designed, robust and bankable PPAs are critical for establishing secure, long-term revenue streams for IPPs, allowing the service of debt and providing risk-equivalent returns to investors, thus reducing risks and facilitating financing under more favourable conditions.[6] PPAs should address aspects such as the distribution of responsibilities between stakeholders, the quantity and price of power to be procured, capacity charges, tariff indexing and escalation, the denomination of the settlement currency (local or foreign) and arbitration for dispute resolution (Nehme 2013). Contract structures, including PPP agreement, must clearly define the allocation of risks and rewards (Rademeyer 2016). They should also be standardized to facilitate the negotiation and development process for IPPs. Contractual provisions must be understandable for both private-sector companies and local authorities and adapted to local context. Finally, there should be legal and regulatory certainty, backed by a certain level of political stability, for the development of such projects.

Competitive procurement procedures   Integrity and transparency of the procurement process must be protected. Early-stage preparation could be completed or supported by the government to set the stage for private-sector involvement for solicited projects. The work to be done upfront and the respective roles of government institutions and the private sector in the preparation phase must therefore be clearly defined and reflected in the regulatory framework. Auctions are increasingly common in public procurement for IPP projects and, when well designed, can be successful tools for price discovery. Licensing processes for unsolicited projects should be streamlined and consistent with different institutions' procedures and requirements.

Coordination   Coordination between institutions should be strengthened to avoid overlaps in licensing procedures (for example, environmental protection agencies, or entities in charge of providing land or water permits). More transparent information sharing systems and more efficient guidance should be provided to private players willing to develop unsolicited projects. This can be achieved notably through the establishment of independent authorities or agencies acting as one-stop-shop institutions.

Financing and risk mitigation   The attractiveness of the generation sector to investors relies heavily on creditworthy power purchasers. Even as structural reforms are being implemented to improve the technical and financial performance of distribution companies or utilities, concurrent measures are needed to mitigate risks for IPPs. If the off-taker is a utility with a poor credit rating, a sovereign guarantee aimed at shifting investment risk to the government may be provided, depending on the state's own fiscal position (ibid.). Alternative models to address off-taker risks are emerging, such as de-risking tools embedded within a broader portfolio of risk mitigation instruments on offer from DFIs and multilateral development banks (MDBs), or specific investment vehicles such as the Green Climate Fund and the Climate Investment Fund. The approach of Africa GreenCo (Africa GreenCo 2017) is to act as an intermediary off-taker, buying renewable electricity from small to medium IPPs through take-or-pay PPAs and on-selling to utilities and private off-takers through long-term contracts. Furthermore, MDBs and DFIs have introduced a wide range of risk-mitigation instruments and insurance products to address country- and project-level risks and catalyse private-sector investment in the sector.

At a macroeconomic level, given the limits on available public financing, new instruments are being designed to leverage additional private capital and develop a financing ecosystem that is sustainable over the long term. An instrument that has received attention is the use of blended concessional funds with funds from DFIs and other entities investing on commercial terms to improve the financial viability of projects and unlock private financing. Other mechanisms for mitigating risks include aggregation of producers and off-takers in investors' portfolios and development of local currency lending facilities.

The level of risk aversion, notably of green climate or renewable funds, DFIs or MDBs should be reconsidered or reviewed to support renewable projects (notably through longer tenures), aimed at increasing access with socio-economic impacts. There should be more risk capital available for such projects and activities. In addition to political risk coverage, there should be innovative guarantees designed to address targeted risks to mobilize private-sector investment. Finally, de-risking tools are also to be defined and designed to support investments when off-takers are private.

2.2   Transmission

Transmission accounts for a relatively small portion of the total cost[7] of the entire traditional power sector supply chain, but it is essential to connect low-cost, large-scale sources of electricity generation with important load-bearing distribution centres in cities and large industrial or commercial loads. By enabling efficient dispatch at the national and regional levels, robust transmission networks facilitate the development of generation with large economies of scale in resource-rich areas to serve distant loads. These networks also reduce the operating and capacity reserves needed to ensure the security of supply and support the integration of renewables into the power system. New transmission investments are strongly dependent on the siting, capacity and technology characteristics of new generation plants, and also on the volume and location of new demand connected to the distribution grid. Upgrading and building new transmission infrastructure is an essential part of the overall expansion of the power sector.

The existing African transmission system (defined as lines with a voltage equal or above 100 kilovolts – kV), with a total length of less than 113 000 km (World Bank 2017), is the major bottleneck for further energy system integration and cross-border trade, as indicated by the Programme for Infrastructure Development in Africa (PIDA). SSA has a combined transmission network smaller than that of Brazil. Nine SSA countries have no lines rated above 100 kV (World Bank 2017). On a per capita basis, Africa has fewer kilometres of transmission lines than any other region of the world, despite having a much larger landmass and more dispersed population. As with generation, substantial investment in transmission infrastructure will be needed to tap into low-cost energy resources and deliver electricity services at competitive rates.

Nevertheless, transmission investment in SSA has lagged for several reasons:

- *Barriers to private investment.* Transmission has not benefited from the same influx of private investment as generation in African countries. This is especially true in SSA, where only a handful of governments have introduced regulations that accept some form of private participation. Most countries finance transmission investments directly from utility revenues or from the government budget, which creates a major constraint on network expansion. Others rely on concessionary financing from DFIs, and in some cases grants from donor countries. Bilateral investments, mainly from state-backed enterprises from China, are also growing to bridge the financing gap in infrastructure projects, as also noted in Chapter 21 in this handbook. Weak private investment in transmission in African countries results from the absence of enabling policy, gaps in regulation (for example, relating to construction agreements, cost-sharing arrangements, payment guarantees and right-of-way permits) and unmitigated country-specific risk.

- *Regulatory risks.* Another risk factor, and one that is highly country dependent, stems from flaws or uncertainties in the regulation of transmission activity, including challenges associated with reaching agreements for construction, obtaining permits for necessary rights-of-way, enforcing sound rules for cost-sharing among different agents (this is particularly important for cross-border transmission lines), and providing payment guarantees. Another barrier is the lengthy procedures for negotiation and construction of transmission networks (in some cases in Africa, ten years).
- *Non-specific country-dependent risks.* As previously described for generation investments, this set of risks includes macroeconomic conditions, political stability, legal security and currency convertibility.

2.2.1 Recommendations

The private sector could play a major role in scaling up transmission capacity in Africa. Again, the lack of investment in this segment of the power sector should not be attributed to any intrinsic difficulty with creating a viable transmission business model in developing and low-access countries, since a sound model can be defined in a standard way as an independent infrastructure project that is mostly financed by private capital. Many countries in Latin America and Asia have successfully introduced private-sector participation in transmission financing and have succeeded in obtaining important investments at attractive costs. The approach is similar to the concept of IPPs in generation, which has already yielded good results in SSA.

There are four typical models for private-sector participation in transmission (World Bank 2017): (1) complete privatization; (2) concession for the entire network for a period of time (for example, 20 years); (3) independent power transmission (IPT) – that is, a concession for one or few lines; and (4) merchant lines. The most appropriate model for private-sector participation depends on the local context, but IPT tenders are seen as offering a promising model for both national and regional-level investments, as shown in numerous experiences.

IPTs have already performed well in several developing countries and are relatively straightforward to accommodate within the legal framework. Among other things, legislation, licences and other legal instruments can be made to provide for multiple transmission providers. Also, concessional finance, in wide use for generation IPPs, can be adapted to the IPT case.

Regarding governance and ownership model, the IPT model can utilize different PPP structures, most commonly build–own–operate–transfer and build–own–operate (ibid.). A key challenge for implementing the IPT model in SSA is the financial weakness of the power sector, which currently inhibits the recovery of transmission costs needed to provide the required returns to private investors. One option to address this challenge is to use revenue escrow arrangements to ring-fence consumer payments. Where escrow arrangements are deemed insufficient to make a project bankable, governments may also have to use government and multilateral guarantees to back payment obligations to IPTs.

Further, under a project finance structure, a government guarantee on payment can be linked to a small increase in electricity tariffs designed to provide for cost recovery, irrespective of the government's other debt-servicing burdens and expenditures. This protects the return on investment for private investors and can be used both for national internal transmission and interconnectors.

Coordinated planning for transmission infrastructure development is needed to identify investments that satisfy regional needs rather than the needs of each country alone. For transmission projects of regional scope, the costs of designing and implementing a project tend to be high and the benefits are often distributed among multiple agents spread across multiple countries. Some sound cost-allocation method that is agreed upon at a regional level is needed to guarantee cost recovery for network investments. Project sponsors could negotiate payments among potential beneficiaries, but this is not ideal as it would tend to limit the types of projects being developed to only those with a large cost–benefit ratio and a small number of easily identified beneficiaries.

2.3   Power Pools and System Operation

Regional power pools and cross-border electricity trading is beneficial for low-access countries for several reasons. They allow national power markets to access electricity supply that reduces wholesale costs, strengthens the security of supply and meets rapidly growing domestic demand growth. Access to regional markets is particularly attractive for investors in power capacity, allowing economies of scale that can help to reduce costs. Meanwhile, better coordination of generation dispatch can also reduce supply costs and improve system reliability.

Regional power pools are particularly relevant in the context of SSA. The size of the national power system in at least 20 countries in this region is below the efficient level of output for a single power plant, thus posing challenges for attracting private investments (PIDA 2012). Fourteen countries have power systems less than 100 MW each, while total installed capacity in 27 nations is under 500 MW (Eberhard 2019). At the same time, some countries in the region have surplus power capacity now (or in pipeline), and sufficient hydro and other renewable and non-renewable resources to meet domestic demand and export excess power.

A recent study estimates total investment needs of nearly $9 billion in regional interconnectors from 2018 to 2030 to support a least-cost power investment and expansion plan across the continent. Such an investment in integration and power trading could allow annual cost reduction of $3.4 billion in generating costs, especially beneficial for smaller, isolated national power systems (Multiconsult 2018).

Many low-access countries have well-established cross-border bilateral power trading arrangements and may be members of power pools. Four power pools have been established in SSA – the most advanced, the Southern Africa Power Pool, was launched in 1995. Concrete steps are being taken in other regions to transition from bilateral trade agreements to market-based trading platforms for electricity (an example is the ASEAN Power Grid in Southeast Asia). Countries that are rich in hydropower resources, such as

Lao PDR and Myanmar, are net exporters of electricity and sell power under bilateral contracts to their neighbours (IRENA 2018b).

In South Asia, bilateral trade in electricity is on the rise. For example, India exports electricity to Nepal, Bangladesh and Myanmar, and imports electricity from Bhutan. India recently became a net exporter. In March 2019, the Central Electricity Regulatory Commission (CERC) introduced updated regulations to facilitate further cross-border trade in electricity (CERC 2019). The CERC reportedly also favours setting up a regional market for power trading across South Asian countries (Mishra 2019), consistent with the 2014 South Asian Association for Regional Cooperation (SAARC) Framework Agreement for Energy Cooperation.

The Central America Regional Electricity Market (MER) is an example of a more mature system for facilitating regional electricity trade among developing countries, which was founded on a regional transmission infrastructure project called SIEPAC.[8] Legal, institutional and technical mechanisms were established to facilitate coordinated planning and operation and to promote private-sector investment in the region's electricity system (Organisation for Economic Co-operation and Development [OECD] 2017). MER countries undertook basic power sector reforms and created domestic regulatory bodies and regional institutions – such as a regional system operator and a regional regulatory agency – to support regional power trading (IDB 2019, Vaidya et al. 2019).

Despite the progress across regions, investment in regional integration is frequently hampered by the lack of institutional strength and flaws in the market rules and transmission regulation under which they operate (Oseni and Pollitt 2015, Rose 2017, United Nations Economic Commission for Africa [UNECA] 2017). From a governance perspective, the most salient issue is that existing power pools[9] generally lack executive powers in the two key regional institutions: the regional system operator and the regional regulator. This undermines regional transmission planning and results in poor regulatory harmonization.

Several regulatory weaknesses are common to most power pools that serve developing countries:

- Sound rules are often lacking that could strike the fine balance between pooling together generation resources to efficiently meet regional demand and coordinating the expansion of generation and interconnected network capacity, while also preserving the autonomy and sovereignty of participating countries. In particular, the current treatment of physical bilateral contracts results in significant efficiency losses, lack of flexibility in power system operation and lack of liquidity in incipient regional wholesale markets.
- The asymmetric allocation of benefits from trade among the agents in exporting and importing countries, together with the influence of existing vested interests, reduces the incentives needed to justify investments in interconnection infrastructure. For instance, 'energy champions' such as Ethiopia may have limited incentives to pioneer the development of a regional power pool as opposed to seeking bilateral contracts (Medinilla, Byiers and Karaki, 2019).
- Regulatory mechanisms that could mitigate some persistent risk factors in long-term contracts among parties to a multinational power pool are missing. This includes mechanisms for hedging price differences between countries, intervening

in scarcity situations and managing uncertainty in the determination of transmission charges.

- Poorly designed or uncertain transmission charges act as barriers to raising the substantial investments needed to support transmission network infrastructure.[10] The lack of a sound, commonly agreed procedure for allocating transmission costs and, consequently, the risk of not receiving adequate compensation can deter investors in cross-border transmission lines. Insufficient transmission capacity also generally impedes the development of large hydro, solar and wind resources.

2.3.1 Recommendations

Proven solutions to address the identified regulatory and governance issues exist based on the experiences of other power pools and regional markets. Combining experience from the implementation of the EU Internal Electricity Market (IEM), Central America's MER, the Indian and Australian National Electricity Markets, among others, with necessary adaptations to reflect the conditions of power pools in emerging economies could have significant value. Rules such as 'beneficiary pays' (applied to cost allocation for investments in cross-border transmission infrastructure) or 'transmission charges must not depend on commercial transactions' have been successfully implemented in some power pools and have universal validity.

Region-wide regulation is necessary to mitigate persistent risk factors in long-term contracts among parties to multinational power pools. This requires regional regulators with adequate capacity and executive powers. As an example, the 1996 Framework Treaty for Central America's MER established two strong regional institutions: CRIE the regional regulator and EOR the regional system operator. CRIE is tasked with enforcing the legal and regulatory framework, driving the development and consolidation of the MER, assuring the transparency and adequate functioning of the regional market and promoting competition among market agents. EOR proposes code approvals and modifications to CRIE; assures that the regional dispatch is performed using economic criteria and with adequate levels of reliability, security and quality; conducts commercial transactions among market agents; supplies information on the evolution of the market; and prepares non-binding plans for regional generation and transmission expansion. The six countries involved in MER worked jointly with private investors to create a mixed public–private company that built and owns the main regional transmission interconnection.

The context for implementing such solutions varies from region to region, depending on such factors as the status and maturity of national power systems, synergies between demand and generation profiles, government incentives to pursue regional integration, the existence of regional platforms that could be leveraged to promote cooperation on electricity issues, and access to financing for infrastructure development.

3. DISTRIBUTION: ON- AND OFF-GRID

Distribution is the critical link between bulk supply and end consumers. The objective of distribution is to provide reliable, affordable electricity services to every customer, as well as to invest in new infrastructure to expand access to unserved areas. In most cases, 'distribution' refers to both the network infrastructure activity that connects the consumers to the main grid from which most of the power is drawn (that is, the strict physical distribution activity), and also the retail activity that involves procuring the power at wholesale level so that it can be delivered to the end consumers at regulated retail tariffs. Electricity distribution is usually considered to be the weakest link in the entire value chain of the power sector in low-access countries, with important implications both upstream and downstream.

In virtually all low-access countries, the collected revenues from the tariffs fall short of recovering supply costs (Kojima and Trimble 2016). Decades of unviable operations have driven many distribution companies to a situation that severely limits their ability to invest adequately in existing and new assets necessary for expanding electricity access. Further, the weak financial situation has impaired their creditworthiness as off-takers for new private investments in generation and transmission. Although in some countries distribution has been unbundled as a separate company, in many others it continues to be one of the business areas of a vertically integrated utility, jointly with generation and transmission (Küfeoğlu, Pollitt and Anaya 2018).

The traditional grid-based electrification model is being disrupted by technological advancements and innovations in financing and delivery models of distributed and off-grid solutions. Rapid cost reduction and improved reliability are allowing distributed renewable energy technologies, both grid-connected and off-grid, to be adequate alternatives to centralized power infrastructure for end-users, offering new opportunities to accelerate progress towards universal access.

This section addresses the question of distribution in light of the structural viability challenges it encounters, and the new opportunities presented by distributed generation. First, the current situation and the challenges faced by the three electrification modes – grid extension, mini-grids and stand-alone systems – are described. Then, an approach – the integrated distribution framework (IDF) – that integrates these three modes, as well as public and private agents, and also electricity supply with the services that it provides, is proposed to address most of the difficulties encountered in distribution.

3.1   Distribution by Grid Extension

Distribution by grid extension in low-access countries is bundled with retail and is frequently vertically integrated with generation and transmission, with all these activities being led by a fully publicly owned utility. Some of these countries have allowed private-sector involvement in some or all segments, like Cameroon, Nigeria, Uganda or Ghana in Africa (AfDB and APUA 2019). India, which has made enormous progress in electrification through grid extension during the last few years, has introduced distribution franchises run by private companies, although mostly in urban areas. Meanwhile, some countries also have a cooperative model for managing distribution, including in Bangladesh and the Philippines.

In low-access countries, distribution companies typically struggle to provide reliable service to their present customers and make slow progress towards full electrification. The stubbornness of the problem has financial, technological and social roots. The insufficiency of politically influenced tariffs is typically at the root of this challenging puzzle. In SSA, electricity tariffs support a financially viable electricity sector in only two countries (the Seychelles and Uganda) out of 49, while in 19 countries the tariffs only cover the operating expenditures. Several countries lose in excess of $0.25 per kilowatt-hour (kWh) sold (Trimble et al. 2016). This inhibits cost recovery and results in a dire financial situation for many distribution companies, which then lack the resources needed to invest in and maintain their facilities. Thus, non-cost-reflective tariffs, combined with low operational efficiency, often lead to poor quality of service, customer defection and a vicious circle of theft and unpaid bills that further erodes revenues. The ripple effects of a financially weak distribution sector can be felt throughout the sector. The vertically integrated utilities or distribution companies have become unreliable off-takers, thus eroding the confidence of investors in centralized generation and transmission. Governments, therefore, must periodically bail out the publicly owned distribution companies at a high cost, leaving the root cause of the problem untouched.

Defecting commercial and industrial (C&I) customers investing in captive generation solutions, including diesel generators and distributed solar, represent a considerable loss of revenue to the distributor and can cause prices to rise for the remaining customers. Their loss can also mean the loss of an important source of cross-subsidies for residential consumers. In Nigeria, for instance, an estimated 86 per cent of the commercial or industrial companies own or share a diesel generator that provides nearly half of their total electricity demand, resulting in a high average cost of electricity supply (GIZ 2015).

Grid extension in rural areas presents additional challenges. Supplying geographically dispersed low-level rural loads is much more expensive per connection and per kWh than electrification in urban areas. These per-unit costs increase as electrification goes deeper into more isolated areas, far from the existing grid. If the regulated revenue requirement for the distribution companies were cost reflective, the corresponding tariffs for all end customers would have to increase whenever new rural customers become connected, since charging a cost-reflective local tariff in rural areas is politically fraught and unaffordable for often poor customers. In reality, in the vast majority of low-access countries, tariffs are set well below costs and are equalized for each category of customers, regardless of their geographic location, or whether they are rural or urban. Thus, extending access automatically results in a deficit in the remuneration of distribution companies. The more customers are connected, the higher are the economic losses of distribution.

It can be concluded that a subsidy is needed for any distribution company that expands electricity access if governments and regulatory authorities are not able to offset the additional cost of electrification through tariffs. Distribution of electricity in rural areas with dispersed and low demand has never been economically viable in any developed or developing country without subsidies under diverse formats, ranging from tariff cross-subsidization to direct payments to the incumbent distribution companies or territorial concessions under mutually agreed conditions. This applies both for on- and off-grid solutions. The challenge of making rural electrification attractive to private investors – a necessity now to accelerate progress – is harder than for other segments of the electricity supply chain.

Contrary to the situation for centralized generation and transmission, where problems and solutions have been identified and multiple success stories exist, distribution in rural areas still presents a major challenge from a regulatory and business model perspective. Utility-driven electrification approaches have been successful in contexts where substantial public expertise and financial support were available and/or where the utility's financial condition was not dire and the socio-economic profile of consumers was relatively more affluent (for example, in Morocco).

Different delivery models have been tested to catalyse private-sector participation and investment in electrification, including through zonal concessions (for example, in Senegal) and transformation of existing mini-grids into small power distributors when the grid arrives (for example, in Cambodia). However, most of these initiatives have been implemented with little or no utility involvement, which risks creating conflict in the future as the grid expands into areas that are being served by private-sector entities. The success of some distribution franchises in India – which have typically involved long-term territorial concessions based on public–private partnerships – is very encouraging, although these franchises have so far been limited to mostly urban areas.

Distribution companies could make use of the three modes of electrification – grid extension, mini-grid and standalone solutions – to efficiently attain universal access. The optimum share of each electrification solution in a national strategy will depend on context-specific factors, including cost of electricity service delivery, existing infrastructure, population density and existence of anchor productive loads.[11] However, so far, fragmented approaches, in which grid and off-grid solutions are pursued in silos by independent agents with limited institutional interaction and planning, have predominated. Despite its criticality to reaching full electrification, open questions remain about the format of the most promising business models, the need for enabling regulations and how to achieve financial viability of distribution service providers (Pérez-Arriaga 2017).

3.2   Mini-grids[12]

Mini-grids can be defined in general terms as micro-utilities with generation and distribution assets providing electricity services in areas unserved by the national grid. Such solutions could also be deployed in grid-connected urban settings for the purposes of resilience and/or affordability of supply. Sometimes they can also be connected to the national grid but intentionally isolated and act as back-up generation and distribution options. Mini-grids supply power to a range of possible consumers such as households, local businesses and anchor loads such as telecommunication towers, mines and agriculture units.

Around 19 000 mini-grids are currently providing electricity to an estimated 50 million people worldwide and may reach up to 490 million by 2030 due to maturing regulatory frameworks, reducing costs and the use of advanced digital monitoring systems (ESMAP 2019). In practice, mini-grids are typically owned and operated by private developers,[13] in most cases without any formal agreement with the local distribution company. They are usually subject to little or no regulation, at least until they reach a significant size, as measured by generation capacity (for example, 100–500 kW). To secure long-term revenue streams, many mini-grid operators seek contracts with large (anchor) customers.

All other things being equal, the cost per kWh of the mini-grid service in an isolated rural area is generally higher than the typically subsidized tariff of the incumbent utility, but often lower than the per kWh cost of delivered power obtained by grid extension. Depending on the current expenditures on energy, the financial resources of rural households may be too low to enable them to pay for either the connection costs or consumption that will underpin income-generation activities and support socio-economic development. In most rural areas, low ability to pay and unpredictable revenue streams strongly limit large-scale private investments in the sector.

This situation could be mitigated by public financing assistance in the form of up-front grants or on-going tariff subsidies; however, laws and regulations that would ensure the payment of such subsidies are typically not present. Where they are, mini-grid developers face the considerable risk that the subsidies will not be honoured for the lifetime of a project, which may reach about 25 years. To limit risks, profitability expectations are defined in the short/medium term, forcing mini-grid developers to quickly recover their costs, thereby limiting the affordability of the service. Recently though, new subsidy design instruments are being proposed and implemented, such as results/performance-based grants in Nigeria, that reduce risks associated with ongoing subsidies, while also providing incentives for private operators to expand rural access by linking magnitude of performance grants with the number and nature of verifiable connections.

In a dynamic electrification scenario involving multiple institutional stakeholders at the national level, a fundamental risk faced by mini-grids is that of main-grid encroachment in area of service. Arrival of the main grid and its offer of subsidized, yet often unreliable, electricity present a risk for the mini-grid operators. Without some form of assurance from the government or utility, such as an exclusive licence, sufficient guaranteed subsidies, or at least a secured payment for the residual value of the network assets and the power injected into the grid, mini-grid developers are typically hesitant to invest in areas likely to be connected to the grid within a foreseeable time horizon. Sound regulations must therefore provide a stable and reliable framework for mini-grid operators in the event of grid arrival either offering a clear computation of compensation or grid interconnection. The emergence of a number of low-cost innovative information and communication technologies, such as smart meters, electronic load controllers and remote monitoring systems, enables for later connection to the main grid when feasible (ibid.).

While the economic case for mini-grids may be strong, their large-scale development will rely on the timely adoption of a supportive regulatory framework and the availability of affordable financing underpinned by a sound business model, which will typically need subsidies. Within the portfolio of electrification solutions, mini-grids are generally the least-cost solution for providing electricity to populations that are too expensive for the main grid to reach in a timely manner and have sufficient demand and population density to justify centralized generation and a local network. Solar home systems remain better suited to remote areas with lower population density and levels of demand.

3.3 Stand-alone Systems

Stand-alone systems are typically designed to provide electricity services to a single entity of consumption whether households, farms, businesses or industries in rural areas. Stand-alone solar solutions, in particular, have been rapidly deployed and are offered in different sizes providing various electricity services, ranging from solar lanterns to solar lighting and mobile charging, and larger solar home systems (SHSs) capable of powering multiple lighting points, mobile charging and appliances (for example, television, fans). Solar systems coupled directly with productive end-use appliances, such as irrigation pumps, agro-processing equipment and pottery wheels, are also increasingly available and deployed.

Stand-alone solar systems have been deployed for decades now through a wide range of delivery and financing models. Bangladesh stands out as a key SHS market where over 4 million systems have been deployed, providing electricity services to over 12 per cent of the population (Infrastructure Development Company, Ltd [IDCOL] 2019). Key success factors for the programme have been the existence of a microfinance ecosystem, the design of tailored financing schemes for end-users, a focus on long-term sustainability and market development and, importantly, the existence of a sector 'champion' in the form of IDCOL (IRENA 2018a).

Within less than a decade, the emergence of a new generation of prepaid SHSs has propelled privately owned stand-alone solar solutions to the forefront of universal energy access initiatives. New business models provide financing for stand-alone solar systems using the so-called 'pay-as-you-go' (PAYG) system. Attracted by supportive regulations, mature solar technologies and mobile money markets in the late 2000s, a handful of East African start-ups developed a new generation of SHS providing remote rural markets with sustainable, affordable and safe electricity on market terms. Usually limited to basic lighting and phone charging, the use of these kits is prepaid by mobile payments allowing companies to significantly reduce the costs associated with bill recovery in remote rural areas, and payments are made on a PAYG basis conciliating affordability and profitability. Remote controllers block the system once the prepayment balance is spent out, which creates strong incentives for rural populations to prepay on time. Last, system durability is ensured through a technical warranty and after-sale service covering the whole repayment period, a key factor in establishing a trust relationship between private companies and local populations (Alstone et al. 2015).

This sector is in the hands of private companies that generally operate independently of the incumbent distribution companies, regulatory authorities or government planners. Some of these companies are fully integrated, with in-house design, manufacturing, distribution, customer management and training, while others procure systems from third parties and focus on distribution and consumer services. These companies raise funds on international debt and equity markets and are subject to strong profitability constraints.

To satisfy their investors and cope with high costs of capital, PAYG companies have long focused their activities on wealthier customers in the most densely populated urban and rural regions of some of the most populated SSA countries (for example, Kenya, Rwanda and Tanzania) where local regulations are most favourable. Stand-alone solar solutions remain, in practice, out of reach for nearly half of the rural populations of these countries. Innovative and inclusive financing schemes involving public funding could greatly increase the effective addressable market of the PAYG solar sector.

The dramatic diffusion of stand-alone solar systems since the late 2000s demonstrates its potential to contribute to energy access. PAYG solar companies have quickly overshadowed the efforts of non-governmental organizations (NGOs) and microfinance institutions (MFIs), but also of local utilities, which have found themselves unable to compete with the dramatic growth of venture-backed private companies operating on market terms. Within less than a decade, digitally financed off-grid solar has transitioned from pilot scale to a diverse and substantial sub-sector of the global off-grid energy market. As of 2018, more than 3000 PAYG SHSs were sold every day in SSA by nearly 30 companies in nearly complete independence from public supervision or any national electrification plans (GOGLA 2017). The number of PAYG SHSs sold in Kenya was about to reach 300 000 kits per year (ibid.), which is commensurate with the number of new rural households to be connected to the national grid. However, after years of growth, a number of the larger PAYG companies operating in SSA are facing unprecedented operational and financial challenges as they expand their activities to complex markets; consolidation of the industry into a smaller number of efficiently managed firms with strong business models and relationships with larger private utilities seems likely.

Beyond stand-alone solar systems, household bio-digesters have also been widely deployed in parts of SSA and South/Southeast Asia. These utilize locally available feedstock (for example, agricultural residues, food waste, livestock waste) to generate renewable cooking fuels, electricity and organic farm fertilizers. In Viet Nam, for instance, over 250 000 domestic biogas digesters have been deployed, benefitting over 1.2 million people (IRENA 2018b).

There is now broad consensus that off-grid solutions hold the potential to successfully address peri-urban and rural contexts characterized by a limited, sparse demand and a limited ability to pay – factors increasing the cost of grid-based electrification and affecting the economic feasibility of traditional energy access approaches (Debeugny, Gromard and Jacquot 2017). The question is – how do we harness on-grid, mini-grids and stand-alone solutions in the most effective and efficient manner to deliver electricity access in the fastest time possible?

4.   THE INTEGRATED DISTRIBUTION FRAMEWORK (IDF)

Universal electricity access cannot be achieved without an in-depth rethinking of electrification strategy at the distribution level. The strategy needs to result in viable business models for all stakeholders – utilities, mini-grid developers and operators, stand-alone system providers, and market development actors (for example, skills institutes) – to attract investments at the scale needed to achieve universal access. Importantly, the vision of the electrification strategy and the distribution sector should be compatible with a sound vision of the future power sector of the country. Responding to this challenge would require adherence to a minimum set of key principles when rethinking electrification:

- *A commitment to universal access that leaves no one behind.* This requires permanence of supply and the existence of a utility-like entity with ultimate responsibility for providing access in a defined territory.
- *Efficient and coordinated integration of on- and off-grid solutions* (i.e., grid extensions, mini-grids and standalone systems). This requires integrated planning at the distribution level and appropriate business models that take a comprehensive view of all types of consumers in a defined service territory.
- *A financially viable business model for distribution.* This will typically require some form of distribution concession to provide legal security and ensure the participation of external and mostly private investors, as well as subsidies for viability gap funding.
- *A focus on development* to ensure that electrification produces broad socio-economic benefits. This principle links expanded access to the delivery of critical public services (e.g., health, education) and to multiple economically beneficial end-uses.

This section defines the IDF that can help us design electrification approaches that meet the key requirements discussed above (that is, universality, mix of delivery modes, financially viable distribution and focus on development). The electrification approaches we identify must also be able to address the two major challenges of the distribution segment: they must provide a viable business model and be consistent with a reasonable vision of the future power sector.

4.1 Key Features of the IDF

The IDF concept has the versatility to be adapted to the diverse circumstances of the many developing countries that face access challenges, with modifications suited to different power sector structures and regulatory regimes. The IDF has been presented in various forums and discussed with experts (https://www.endenergypoverty.org/2020-report). A pilot implementation is currently being designed for deployment in a small territory of Nigeria.[14] The IDF has the following key features:

- For any geographical area there must be an entity with the explicit comprehensive obligation of universal electricity supply, by an appropriate mix of electrification modes, and with a vocation and capability of permanence. This requirement is closely related to the vision of the future structure of the power sector, since the entity that is allocated these responsibilities must play a fundamental role in it. This entity does not necessarily have to supply all customers and may partner with other entities (for example, SHS or mini-grid companies), but it would have the role of a default and last-resort supplier, ensuring the agreed level of service.
- The necessary managerial, financial and operational changes in the incumbent distributor will be achieved by some form of partnership with an external entity. In most cases, the most adequate form of partnership would adopt the format of a concession with a private-sector entity, with some financial guarantee support from a development financial institution, and the explicit agreement of government and regulatory authorities to create the appropriate legal and regulatory conditions, with the possible involvement of capable local companies, mini-grid developers and vendors of stand-alone systems (Jacquot et al. 2019). Other options are possible under the IDF umbrella. In the end, each country will need a tailor-made design.
- The remuneration scheme should recognize the different nature of the 'physical network assets and operation' (that is, strict distribution network activity or 'carriage') and the 'consumer interaction' (that is, the retail activity or 'content') components of the traditional distribution company.
- Consumer engagement is a critical component of the IDF, which brings a change of public perception and customer mindset with respect to the electricity supplier. A satisfactory quality of service is a necessary condition for any attempt to introduce cost-reflective tariffs and address unpaid bills and illegal connections.
- The economic viability of rural distribution in developing countries cannot be and has never been attained in any developed or developing country without some sort of subsidies. There are multiple strategies for reducing the amount of subsidies required: large-scale planning to find the least-cost mode of electrification; consumer satisfaction and advanced metering leading to drastic reduction of illegal

connections and unpaid bills; tariff cross-subsidization of lower-income house-holds by other loads that can absorb some price increases, such as high-consumption residential, commercial and industrial (C&I) customers; bringing back to the grid those C&I customers that defected because of poor reliability or excessive cross-subsidization; standardization in supply equipment and demand appliances with an emphasis on efficiency; and the creation of activities around electricity access to stimulate consumptive and productive demand, and reducing per-unit supply cost.

The key idea underpinning the IDF is that developing countries are unlikely to reach universal energy access without seeking integration at different levels. At the very heart of the IDF is integration that needs to take place at different levels for the success of electrification efforts. First, the integration between the three modes of electrification – grid extension, mini-grids and stand-alone systems. Second, the integration of the incumbent – typically publicly owned – utility with an external entity. Third, the integration between electricity supply and end-uses, which is critical for maximizing the economic and social impact of access. This requires a cross-sector view and an in-depth understanding of energy needs – power, heating/cooling and transport – in sectors critical for economic growth and human development (for example, health and education). Finally, the fourth level of integration focuses on the coordination between distribution planning and transmission and large generation planning, since the majority of the energy being distributed continues to be supplied from the bulk power system.

4.1.1 Integration of electrification modes

A key feature of the IDF is that the three modes of electrification – on-grid, mini-grids and stand-alone systems – are seen in an integrated manner and placed on a level playing field. So far, the three solutions have been developed in a largely uncoordinated manner with different entities involved, leading to competition rather than complementarity. This serves neither business interests nor the interests of consumers – and ultimately may result in inefficient infrastructure investment, poor service standards, sub-optimal resource utilization and, importantly, people being left behind.

Comprehensive integrated planning using advanced geographic information system (GIS) technologies can find the least-cost mix of electricity delivery modes; an IDF-compatible entity would make sure that the plan is implemented effectively, and dedicated policies and regulations would address any issues arising from the interaction between on- and off-grid solutions, as well as tariff-setting.

Morocco's universal rural electrification programme is an example where some of these principles were successfully followed. Key features of the programme included the use of all modes of electrification – on-grid, mini-grid and standalone systems – and coordination by the state-owned utility (ONEE). While grid extension and some mini-grids were developed by ONEE, well-defined territorial concessions were devised for private companies to install and maintain solar systems in remote areas (Choukri, Naddami and Hayani 2017). The utility-led programme raised access rates from 15 per cent to 95 per cent in less than 15 years (Islamic Development Bank 2013) and was also able to leverage substantial public financing from DFIs. Several conditions specific to Morocco facilitated these positive outcomes: the ability of the utility to exploit cross-subsidization between urban and rural consumers, favourable macro-economic development indicators, as well as the presence of a financially and technically sound utility.

At the end of the day, electrification cannot be perceived as a static process, but rather as a dynamic one. Mini-grids and stand-alone systems will play a critical role in expanding energy access in the short to medium term, while grid-based solutions will probably pick up in the longer term. Off-grid solutions have the potential to unlock latent community demand for electricity and to improve the understanding of consumption patterns and willingness to pay, thus justifying investments in larger systems or grid extension. Local communities could be active stakeholders in certain contexts, partnering with the IDF concessionaire and the private sector to own, operate and maintain decentralized energy systems in their unserved areas.

4.1.2   Integration with services

It is now widely accepted that access to modern energy is an important catalyst for economic growth and human development. A purely supply-side perspective on access – that is, number of connections, MW or kWh generated – often risks missing out on providing electricity services for end-uses that can have a transformative impact on advancing socio-economic development. To effectively sustain the accelerated expansion of rural electrification, there is a high urgency to test business models linking energy access with productive sectors (for example, agri-processing, assembling and manufacturing, service sector)[15] to increase their level of productivity, to support job creation and to achieve improvements in education, health and overall human well-being.[16]

Sufficiency, affordability and reliability of power supply are crucial for supporting end-uses, especially those related to income generation. Compared to on-grid based electrification, these considerations can more effectively be integrated and managed into the design of off-grid systems, such as mini-grids, in terms of sizing and identification of anchor productive loads (for example, agri-processing equipment and irrigation pumps). Moreover, the integration of productive end-uses strengthens off-grid business models by boosting local demand, increasing consumers' ability to pay, diversifies off-taker risk and improves capacity utilization. With advancements in energy-efficient appliances, a growing portfolio of productive end-use technologies (for example, milling machines, welding equipment or pottery wheels) are now available that can be powered by low-wattage off-grid solutions.

Linking electricity supply with public services, such as education and healthcare, can also have a positive impact on the well-being of the rural populations and a long-term impact on human capital development. In the health sector, for instance, off-grid technologies, often solar-based, are delivering reliable, affordable and sustainable energy to power medical devices and support the provision of basic amenities (for example, light, communications and water). About one in four health facilities in 11 countries in SSA has no access to electricity, and most facilities that do have access have an unreliable supply. Some African countries are already embracing solar energy – in Sierra Leone, 36 per cent of all health facilities and 43 per cent of hospitals use solar energy in combination with other electricity sources. In Liberia, more public sector primary health clinics use photovoltaic (PV) solar systems than generators. Meanwhile, in Uganda, 15 per cent of hospitals use PV-based systems to complement electrical grid access (World Health Organization [WHO] 2019).

To achieve effective linkages between electricity supply and different end-uses, several additional measures are needed. To support new income-generating activities and strengthen existing ones, capacity building is often required to develop skills and improve market access for products/services. Access to financing for formal and informal enterprises in rural areas is a crucial enabler to invest in new equipment and meet other enterprise development needs (for example, working capital). Utilities and private-sector practitioners may have limited capacity to develop the ecosystem for productive end-uses. Partnerships with local NGOs and community-based organizations, as well as local financing institutions can play a crucial role in providing the necessary support. DFI-sponsored electrification programmes equally are encouraged to ring-fence financing for additional efforts needed to link electricity supply with various end-uses.

4.1.3   Integration with regional and national planning

Distribution planning must be coordinated with transmission and large generation planning – even with regional or multinational power sector planning – since most of the energy being distributed is supplied from the bulk power system. Transmission planning is of essence here, since adequate transmission capacity is necessary to allow cross-border trade and regional generation plants. Currently, there are no computer models capable of dealing jointly with the distribution and bulk power system segments at the necessary level of detail, and some kind of iterative procedure is necessary to coordinate the distribution power requirements with the installation of transmission and large generation infrastructure.

4.2   Implementing the IDF Approach

The concept of IDF is highly flexible and can be adapted to the diverse circumstances of low-access countries with their range of power sector structures and regulatory regimes. In countries with vertically integrated utilities, for instance, distribution unbundling is not necessary to implement the IDF, since only a clear definition of the rights and obligations of the concession is needed, along with agreement about the method of remuneration. Although there is yet to be an example of a jurisdiction that has combined all the defining features of the IDF, each feature has been implemented successfully somewhere, providing a rich base of experience from which to draw lessons.

Financial viability is the key challenge of the IDF approach. The road to viability for distribution companies and to universal electrification will vary from country to country and is likely to involve different models for partnering with the private sector. Each approach will require a tailored portfolio of financing solutions that range from direct subsidies to address the viability gap for rural distribution to blended finance that allows different types of capital (that is, commercial, concessional, grants) to help bring private investors, including institutional investors, into the distribution sector. Depending on the appropriate mix of electrification modes, the target groups for financing will also vary, covering distribution companies, mini-grid and stand-alone projects and enterprises, as well as end-users with requirements for financing systems, productive appliances or connection fees.

Rural electrification needs subsidies because the electrification of dispersed, low-level loads is much more expensive than electrification in urban areas. A subsidy for any distribution entity is needed that expands access if governments and regulatory authorities are not able to apply tariffs that reflect the actual costs. Subsidies can adopt different formats, ranging from tariff cross-subsidization to direct payments to the incumbent distribution company or territorial concessions under mutually agreed conditions. This applies both for on- and off-grid solutions. And this makes distributors particularly dependent on legal security in their country.

In practice, these subsidies must be provided by the governments, and any potential investor in the distribution company will require guarantees that they will be delivered in the right amount and at the right time, which would require the cooperation of some DFI. Experience so far has shown that these guarantees are not easily obtained. These guarantees are not possible if the sovereign debt of the country has hit some limits that credit rating institutions consider unacceptable. Also, as indicated above, the situation is even more difficult for privatized distribution companies.

The financial challenge of the IDF can only be solved if there is an agreement of the major stakeholders in implementing this kind of approach: the national government, the regulatory authority, the distribution company and the off-grid developers, the investors and the DFI providing some form of financial guarantee. Other challenges – political and social acceptability, or any necessary regulatory reforms – are deemed to be manageable.

5. CONCLUSION

Achieving universal access to electricity is widely recognized as a key imperative for catalysing socio-economic development and meeting many of the Sustainable Development Goals by 2030. It is not merely a technological challenge but also has social, economic, political and ethical dimensions. The current trend in electricity access expansion illustrates that the number of people without electricity access is estimated to only reduce from 840 million in 2017 to about 650 million in 2030. It is evident that to reach universal access, a different strategy is needed. One that is capable of mobilizing the required large amounts of public and (mostly) private investments, one that synergistically taps into all available electrification solutions (on-grid and off-grid) and, importantly, one that is compatible with a broader vision of the power sector that ensures efficiency and long-term viability.

The distribution sector remains the key point of failure of electrification. Unviable distribution business models have hindered rural electrification efforts and there is no clear solution available. Incumbent distributors devote most of their efforts to grid extension, struggling with deteriorating assets and quality of service, theft and unpaid bills, poor reputation among consumers and financial survival. Holistic solutions are needed that can advance electrification based on the underlying principles of inclusivity, integration and permanence, while also facilitating external partnerships in the distribution sector, in particular with the private sector, to improve financial viability.

To this end, the IDF approach is presented in this chapter as a solution. The IDF is based on a small number of design criteria – an entity with the obligation of supply, use of different electrification approaches and delivery models, external partnerships through franchisees or independent micro-utilities, and consumer orientation. It leaves ample room for adaptation to the specific characteristics of each country. Although there is yet to be an example of a jurisdiction that has combined all the defining features of the IDF, each feature has been implemented successfully *somewhere*, providing a rich base of experience from which to draw lessons. Crucial for the implementation of the IDF will be sound regulations that support a viable business model for all stakeholders – utilities, private micro-utilities, off-grid product distributors – and enhance their ability to attract private investment.

NOTES

*   The research work that has allowed our team at the MIT/Comillas Universal Energy Access Lab to write this chapter has been made possible by support from the MIT-Tata Center for Technology and Design, the Shell Foundation, Iberdrola Foundation, Enel Foundation, Rockefeller Foundation and the World Bank.

1.   Based on International Energy Agency (IEA) et al. (2020).
2.   For the purpose of this chapter, access is defined as access that does not limit the supply of electricity that customers are willing to use and to pay for, at the applicable price. Beyond connection counts, meaningful access should be measured across several attributes, including reliability, capacity, service hours, quality of supply, affordability and safety. The Energy Sector Management Assistance Program (ESMAP) has developed a comprehensive and complex MTF to measure energy access across such attributes (Bhatia and Angelou 2015).
3.   3.7 per cent of the population of Latin America – about 24 million people – did not have access to electricity in 2018, and 1.7 per cent in Indonesia – about 4.5 million. Source: https://www.iea.org/energyaccess/, accessed 23 July 2021.
4.   See the MIT/IIT-Comillas Universal Energy Access Lab website: http://universalaccess.mit.edu/#/main, accessed 23 July 2021.
5.   Over 42 per cent of new capacity additions through IPPs during the last decade has been for solar photovoltaics (PV), and over 37 per cent for other renewables, including wind, hydro, biomass and geothermal generation. Auctions (international competitive bidding programmes) are now a well-established trend to guarantee lowest prices for new renewable energy projects.
6.   Ideally, a 'bankable' PPA would provide for a long-term agreement with a creditworthy off-taker over a time horizon that allows debt servicing and provides for risk-equivalent returns for investors.
7.   Generally equivalent to 10 per cent of total cost of electricity supply.
8.   MER currently supplies around 4.5 per cent of regional energy demand, with Guatemala as the main exporter (67 per cent of total sales) and El Salvador as the lead importer (88 per cent of total purchases). Energy exchanges totalled 2656 gigawatt-hours (GWh) in 2018, compared to 700 GWh in 2013 when MER began operations. Data from IDB (2019).
9.   We resist using the term 'regional market' and we typically opt for 'power pools' or an equivalent proxy when the basic conditions for a wholesale market are not met.
10. Multiconsult (2018) estimates total investment needs of $8.9 billion in regional interconnectors from 2018 to 2030 to support a least-cost power investment and expansion plan across the African continent.
11. Anchor loads refer to sources of electricity demand, often related to institutions (for example, schools, clinics) and income-generating activities (for example, irrigation pumps, agro-processing equipment), that are stable and predictable and provide generators/distributors with a sustained source of revenue, thus reducing reliance on residential consumers that usually consume less and have limited willingness-to-pay.
12. In this chapter, we shall use the term 'mini-grids' regardless of system size; it refers to any power grid operating independently from large-size centralized grids.
13. Community ownership in mini-grids is also seen commonly in South and Southeast Asia.
14. See Konexa, accessed 23 July 2021 at https://www.powerforall.org/news-media/articles/konexa-seeding-integrated-utility-future.
15. See for details https://www.ruralelec.org/publications/productive-use-renewable-energy-africa, accessed 23 July 2021.
16. Several case studies of productive end-use examples can be found here: http://www.ruralelec.org/project-case-studies, accessed 23 July 2021.

REFERENCES

Africa GreenCo (2017), *Africa GreenCo Feasibility Study*, The Rockefeller Foundation, accessed 23 July 2021 at https://www.rockefellerfoundation.org/wp-content/uploads/Africa-GreenCo-Feasibility-Study-2017.pdf.

African Development Bank and Association of Power Utilities of Africa (AfDB and APUA) (2019), *Revisiting Reforms in the Power Sector in Africa*, Africa, accessed 23 July 2021 at www.gsb.uct.ac.za/files/Final_Report_Revisiting_Power_Reforms.pdf.

Alstone, P., D. Gershenson and N. Turman-Bryant et al. (2015), *Off-Grid Power and Connectivity, Pay-as-you-go Financing and Digital Supply Chains for Pico-Solar*, Lighting Global and IFC, May, accessed 23 July 2021 at https://www.lightingglobal.org/wp-content/uploads/2015/05/Off_Grid_Power_and_Connectivity_PAYG_May_2015.pdf.

Bhatia, M. and N. Angelou (2015), *Technical Report, 008/15: Beyond Connections: Energy Access Redefined*, Energy Sector Management Assistance Program (ESMAP), accessed 23 July 2021 at https://openknowledge.worldbank.org/handle/10986/24368.

Center for Strategic and International Studies (CSIS) (2019), *Engaging with India's Electrification Agenda*, Washington, DC: CSIS.

Central Electricity Authority (CEA) (2021), *Executive Summary on Power Sector: May 2021*, accessed 17 July 2021 at https://cea.nic.in/wp-content/uploads/executive/2021/05/Executive_Summary_May_2021-3.pdf.

Central Electricity Regulatory Commission (CERC) (2019), *Central Electricity Regulatory Commission (Cross Border Trade of Electricity) Regulations, 2019*, accessed 17 July 2021 at https://cercind.gov.in/2019/regulation/CBTE-Regulations2019.pdf.

Choukri, K., A. Naddami and S. Hayani (2017), 'Renewable energy in emergent countries: lessons from energy transition in Morocco', *Energy, Sustainability and Society*, **7**, Article 25.

Ciller, P., D. Ellman and C. R. Vergara Ramírez et al. (2019), 'Optimal electrification planning incorporating on- and off-grid technologies: the Reference Electrification Model (REM)', *Proceedings of the IEEE*, **107** (9), 1872–905.

Council on Energy, Environment and Water (CEEW) (2020), *State of Electricity Access in India: Insights from the India Residential Energy Survey (IRES 2020)*, accessed 23 July 2021 at www.ceew.in/publications/state-electricity-access-india.

Debeugny, C., C. de Gromard and G. Jacquot (2017), 'L'électrification complète de l'Afrique est-elle possible d'ici 2030?', *Afrique Contemporaine*, No. 261–262, 139–53.

Eberhard, A. (2019), 'Bulk power supply in Africa: challenges, constraints and opportunities', presentation at the Bellagio Launch of the Global Commission to End Energy Poverty, 9 September.

Eberhard, A. and C. Godinho (2017), 'A review and exploration of the status, context and political economy of power sector reforms in Sub-Saharan Africa, South Asia and Latin America', *EEG State-of-Knowledge Paper Series No. 2.1*, accessed 23 July 2021 at https://cloudfront.escholarship.org/dist/prd/content/qt11k4210h/qt11k4210h.pdf.

Eberhard, A., K. Gratwick, E. Morella and P. Antmann (2016), *Independent Power Projects in Sub-Saharan Africa: Lessons from Five Key Countries*, Washington, DC: World Bank.

Eberhard, A., K. Gratwick, E. Morella and P. Antmann (2017), 'Independent power projects in Sub-Saharan Africa: investment trends and policy lessons', *Energy Policy*, **108**, 390–424.

Energy Sector Management Assistant Program (ESMAP) (2019), *Mini Grids for Half a Billion People: Market Outlook and Handbook for Decision Makers*, Washington, DC: World Bank.

GIZ (2015), *The Nigerian Energy Sector: An Overview with a Special Emphasis on Renewable Energy, Energy Efficiency and Rural Electrification*, accessed 23 July 2021 at www.giz.de/en/downloads/giz2015-en-nigerian-energy-sector.pdf.

GOGLA (2017), *Providing Energy Access through Off-Grid Solar: Guidance for Governments*, Utrecht: GOGLA.

Gratwick, K. N. and A. Eberhard (2008), 'Demise of the standard model for power sector reform and the emergence of hybrid power markets', *Energy Policy*, **36** (10), 3948–60.

Hosier, R., M. Bazilian and T. Lemondzhava et al. (2017), *Rural Electrification Concessions in Africa: What Does Experience Tell Us?*, World Bank, accessed 23 July 2021 at https://openknowledge.worldbank.org/handle/10986/27476.

Infrastructure Development Company, Ltd (IDCOL) (2019), 'IDCOL solar home system program', accessed 23 July 2021 at http://idcol.org/home/solar.

International Development Bank (IDB) (2019), *The IDB Group in the Central American Isthmus and the Dominican Republic: Activities Report 2018*, Washington, DC: IDB.

International Energy Agency (IEA) (2019), *World Energy Investment 2019*, Paris: IEA.

International Energy Agency (IEA), International Renewable Energy Agency (IRENA), United Nations Statistics Division (UNSD), World Bank and World Health Organization (WHO) (2020), *Tracking SDG 7: The Energy Progress Report*, Washington, DC: IBRD and World Bank.

International Renewable Energy Agency (IRENA) (2018a), *Off-grid Renewable Energy Solutions: Global and Regional Status and Trends*, Abu Dhabi: IRENA.

International Renewable Energy Agency (IRENA) (2018b), *Renewable Energy Market Analysis: Southeast Asia*, Abu Dhabi: IRENA.

Islamic Development Bank (2013), 'From darkness to light: rural electricity in Morocco', *ISDB Success Stories No. 11*, May.

Jacquot, G., I. Pérez-Arriaga, R. Stoner and D. Nagpal (2019), 'Assessing the potential of electrification concessions for universal energy access: towards integrated distribution frameworks', *MIT Energy Initiative Working Paper*, September, accessed 23 July 2021 at http://energy.mit.edu/publication/assessing-the-potential-of-electrification-concessions-for-universal-energy-access/.

Joskow, P. L. (2006), 'Introduction to electricity sector liberalization: lessons learned from cross-country studies', in F. Sioshansi and W. Pfaffenberger (eds), *Electricity Market Reform. An International Perspective*, Amsterdam: Elsevier, pp. 1–32.

Kojima, M. and C. Trimble (2016), *Making Power Affordable for Africa and Viable for Its Utilities*, World Bank, accessed 23 July 2021 at https://openknowledge.worldbank.org/handle/10986/25091.

Küfeoğlu, S., M. G. Pollitt and K. Anaya (2018), 'Electric power distribution in the world: today and tomorrow', *EPRG Working Paper 1826*, Energy Policy Research Group, University of Cambridge, accessed at https://www.eprg.group.cam.ac.uk/wp-content/uploads/2018/08/1826-Text.pdf.

Maithani, P. C. and D. Gupta (2015), *Achieving Universal Energy Access in India. Challenges and the Way Forward*, New Delhi: SAGE.

Medinilla, A., B. Byiers and K. Karaki (2019), 'African power pools: regional energy, national power', *Discussion Paper No. 244*, ecdpm, accessed 23 July 2021 at https://ecdpm.org/wp-content/uploads/DP-244-African-Power-Pools-1.pdf.

Ministry of Power, Government of India (2011), *Annual Report 2010–11*, accessed 23 July 2021 at https://powermin.nic.in/sites/default/files/uploads/Annual_Report_2010-11_English.pdf.

Mishra, T. (2019), 'CERC mulls regional power market for South Asia', *BusinessLine*, 12 March, accessed 23 July 2021 at www.thehindubusinessline.com/economy/policy/cerc-mulls-regional-power-market-for-south-asia/article26514471.ece.

Mukherjee, M. (2014), *Private Participation in the Indian Power Sector: Lessons from Two Decades of Experience*, World Bank, accessed 23 July 2021 at https://openknowledge.worldbank.org/handle/10986/20410.

Multiconsult (2018), *Roadmap to the New Deal on Energy for Africa: An Analysis of Optimal Expansion and Investment Requirements*, report to the AfDB, accessed 23 July 2021 at https://africa-energy-portal.org/sites/default/files/2018-10/lu313516crr2.pdf.

Nehme, B. (2013), 'PPAs and tariff design', presentation at the Renewable Energy Training Program, accessed 23 July 2021 at https://esmap.org/sites/default/files/esmap-files/ESMAP%20IFC%20Re%20Training%20World%20Bank%20Nehme.pdf.

Organisation for Economic Co-operation and Development (OECD) (2017), '139 CS – Energy integration: the Central American experience in designing and implementing the Regional Electricity Market', accessed 23 July 2021 at www.oecd.org/aidfortrade/casestories/casestories-2017/CS-139-SIECA-Integraci%C3%B3n-Energ%C3%A9tica-La-experiencia-de-Centroam%C3%A9rica-en-el-dise%C3%B1o-e-implementaci%C3%B3n-del-Mercado-El%C3%A9ctrico-Regional-English-Translation.pdf.

Oseni, M. and M. G. Pollitt, M. (2015), 'Institutional arrangements for the promotion of regional integration of electricity markets: international experience', *Policy Research Working Paper No. 6947*, World Bank, June.

Pargal, S. and S. Ghosh-Banerjee (2014), *More Power to India: The Challenge of Distribution: India Power Sector Diagnostic Review*, World Bank, June, accessed 23 July 2021 at http://documents.worldbank.org/curated/en/693951468044085739/India-power-sector-diagnostic-review-main-report.

Pérez-Arriaga, J. I. (2017), 'New regulatory and business model approaches to achieving universal electricity access', *Papeles de Energía*, **3**, 37–71.

Programme for Infrastructure Development in Africa (PIDA) (2012), *Interconnecting, Integrating and Transforming a Continent*, accessed 23 July 2021 at www.afdb.org/fileadmin/uploads/afdb/Documents/Project-and-Operations/PIDA%20note%20English%20for%20web%200208.pdf.

Rademeyer, G. (2016), 'How can Independent Power Producer (IPP) investments be accelerated on the African continent?', Norton Rose Fulbright, 17 June, accessed 23 July 2021 at https://www.insideafricalaw.com/publications/how-can-independent-power-producer-ipp-investments-be-accelerated-on-the-african-continent.

Rose, A. (2017), 'Improving the performance of regional electricity markets in developing countries: the case of the Southern African Power', PhD thesis, Massachusetts Institute of Technology, School of Engineering, Institute for Data, Systems, and Society.

Sustainable Energy for All (SEforALL) and Climate Policy Initiative (CPI) (2020), *Energizing Finance: Understanding the Landscape 2020*, Energizing Finance Research Series.

Tata Power (2019), 'Tata Power and The Rockefeller Foundation announce breakthrough enterprise to empower millions of Indians with renewable microgrid electricity, media release, 4 November, accessed 23 July 2021 at https://www.tatapower.com/media/PressReleaseDetails/1715/tata-power-and-the-rockefeller-foundation-announce-breakthrough-enterprise-to-empower-million-of-indians-with-renewable-microgrid-electricity.

Trimble, C., M. Kojima, I. Perez Arroyo and F. Mohammadzadeh (2016), 'Financial viability of electricity sectors in Sub-Saharan Africa: quasi-fiscal deficits and hidden costs', *Policy Research Working Paper No. 7788*, World Bank, August.

United Nations Conference on Trade and Development (UNCTAD) (2017), *The Least Developed Countries Report 2017*, Geneva: UNCTAD.

United Nations Economic Commission for Africa (UNECA) (2017), *Effective Regulatory Systems for Service Delivery and Structural Transformation in Africa: Infrastructure Development and the Case of Power Pools*, Addis Ababa: UNECA.

Vagliasindi, M. and J. Besant-Jones (2013), *Power Market Structure Revisiting Policy Options*, World Bank, March, accessed 23 July 2021 at https://openknowledge.worldbank.org/handle/10986/13115.

Vaidya, R. A., N. Yadav and N. Rai et al. (2019), 'Electricity trade and cooperation in the BBIN region: lessons from global experience', *International Journal of Water Resources Development*, **37** (3), 439–65.

World Bank (2017), *Linking Up: Public–Private Partnerships in Power Transmission in Africa*, Washington, DC: World Bank.

World Bank (2019), 'World's population will continue to grow and will reach nearly 10 billion by 2050', 8 July, accessed 23 July 2021 at https://blogs.worldbank.org/opendata/worlds-population-will-continue-grow-and-will-reach-nearly-10-billion-2050.

World Health Organization (WHO) (2019), *Harnessing Africa's Untapped Solar Energy Potential for Health*, accessed 23 July 2021 at www.who.int/bulletin/volumes/92/2/14-020214/en/.

21. Reforming China's electricity industry: national aspiration, bureaucratic empires, local interests
Xu Yi-chong

1. INTRODUCTION

The development of the electricity industry in China in the past four decades raises several paradoxes. The industry has delivered unprecedented progress in terms of providing reliable electricity supply and universal access to electricity, including to the most remote and harsh areas in China, while it is said to be among the most inefficient and wasteful industries in the world. It has the world's largest renewable sources of power production, while it also hosts the most highly polluting coal-fired generating capacities in the world. The industry has produced world-class technology innovation in supercritical thermal power plants, nuclear power plants and high-voltage transmission networks, although it is said to be suffering from low efficiency and poor quality control. The power industry was one of the first reformers in China and in the world that lowered entry barriers in generation and in providing services in some places in the mid-1980s. The industry was unbundled, albeit not completely, in 2002 before its counterparts in most other countries, including many Organisation for Economic Co-operation and Development (OECD) countries. After nearly four decades of constant change and reform, the industry is still considered state owned and monopolized even though it has become more entrepreneurial than ever before. While the Chinese Communist Party (CCP) has tightened its control over party discipline, appointment of senior managers and their behaviour, the central government still has great difficulty in getting the industry and provinces to adopt and implement a set of coherent policies to manage the three pressing challenges: competition, technology innovation and climate change.

The root of these contradictions is first and foremost political; technical complexities of electricity only contribute difficulties for government decision-makers to lead, rather than follow, the reform and restructuring of the industry. Moreover, like the electricity development elsewhere in the world, the industry started with small-scale generation stations supplying electricity locally, primarily to industry, and thus neither industry nor government are given a blank sheet with infinite opportunities to change the system. Finally, the difficulties in making changes must be multiplied by the size and diversity of the country.

There are comprehensive studies on the development and change of the electricity industry in general, analysing every aspect of the industry – from economic, technical and political, on generation, transmission and distribution (T&D) and retailing services, from thermal, hydro, nuclear to renewable sources of generation. All have contributed to our understanding of the complexity of the development and reform of the Chinese electricity industry. This chapter focuses on *politics*, rather than economics or technical complexities, especially on the way that politics has shaped and constrained the development and reform of the Chinese electricity industry in the past four decades. It starts with a discussion of the initial reform measures in the first two decades (1984–2002) that were driven by necessity and players other than those in the electricity industry – provinces, large enterprises and multilateral institutions and international consultants. It is followed by the discussion of the reforms in 2002–15, driven predominantly by the newly incorporated state-owned power-generating companies and the two grid corporations. The chapter then assesses the reforms proposed by the central government in 2015 and the difficulties in implementing them. The last section of this chapter discusses the overseas activities of the Chinese power companies and their implication for global electricity developments.

What is the nature of the electricity industry in China? How has it got to where it is now? What is the prospect that the industry will deliver economical, efficient and clean electricity services to meet demand from the modern economy? Understanding the history of its development is important to identify the problems and thereby potential solutions.

Electricity development in a country is conditioned by its natural endowments (coal, hydro, natural gas or petroleum). Coal is the main natural energy resource in China, followed by hydro resources (Table 21.1). In 1980, electricity was generated primarily by coal-fired thermal power plants.

In recent years, renewables (other than hydro) expanded much faster than thermal and hydro installed capacities, and the share of thermal generation capacity dropped to 62 per cent of the total. Wind resources share a similar feature with coal and hydro as they are all located in concentrated areas: coal is mainly in the west and northwest parts of China; hydro is predominantly in the southwest part of China; and wind is in northwest region too. Coastal regions are much more densely populated and have had faster economic development, but, in general, they lack natural energy endowment. Uneven allocation of natural resources has been one of the key challenges in Chinese energy development. Figure 21.1 illustrates the regional distribution installed capacity.

One major challenge is the overcapacity of thermal generation and its stranded assets. China has built the largest power generation fleet in the world, with 1777 GW in 2017. The average annual growth rate rose steadily at 7.6 per cent in the 1980s, 8.9 per cent in the 1990s, 11.4 per cent in 2000–09 and 9.3 per cent in 2010–17. Over two-thirds of the country's generation capacity was built in 2007–17 alone. Most provinces have had an overcapacity in generation and in some places available capacity reached nearly double peak demand. In Inner Mongolia, for instance, an available capacity of 75 GW is more than triple a peak demand of 20 GW and in Sichuan an available capacity of 51 GW is

Table 21.1   Installed generation capacity and generation in China by source (1980)

Total Installed Capacity (GW)	Thermal	Hydro	Total Generation (TWh)	Thermal	Hydro
66	46	20	301	243	58.4

Note: GW = gigawatts; TWh = terawatt-hours.

Source: Xu (2002), p. 57.

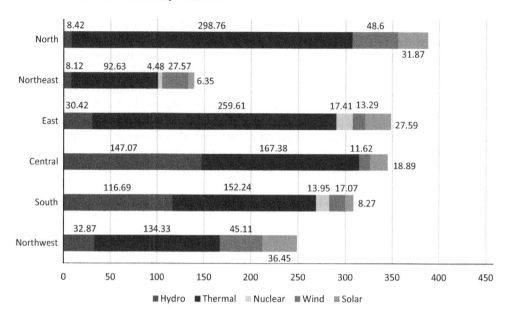

Source: China Electricity Council (CEC) (2018).

Figure 21.1   Distribution of installed generation capacity by region and source (2017)

more than double a peak demand of 23 GW. Even in resource-poor coastal provinces, such as Fujian and Zhejiang, the overcapacity problem was serious by 2017. The four provinces where peak demand remains higher than the available capacity, Shanghai, Guangdong, Beijing and Hebei, are all adjacent to provinces with overcapacity.

After 1949, electricity was developed primarily to serve industry (Smil 1976, 1988) and up to the mid-1990s, over 85 per cent of electricity was consumed by the industrial sector (around 60 per cent by heavy industries alone). This consumption pattern has been changing, but only slowly. In 2017, industry remained the largest electricity consumer (70.6 per cent, down from 71.3 per cent in 2016). In the first three decades of reform, much more investment went into generation than T&D. By the end of the 1990s, more than a dozen T&D networks remained operating independently with little or no connection with their neighbouring provinces and regions. The consequence of these fragmented T&D networks was inefficient allocation of resources: some provinces had over-supplies while their neighbouring provinces endured power shortages. The problem was quite serious until the State Grid Corporation of China (SGCC) and the China Southern Grid Limited (CSG) started building interconnected works in the first decade of the twenty-first century. With the construction of high-voltage transmission systems after 2004, the amount of electricity transmitted across provinces steadily increased (Figure 21.2).

The question whether China should construct one interconnected T&D network, or six regional synchronized T&D networks (as in continental North America with three independent grids: Eastern Interconnection, Western Interconnection and Electric Reliability Council of Texas), or networks based on provinces, was debated extensively. With a similar geographical size as the United States, China does not have a formal federalist

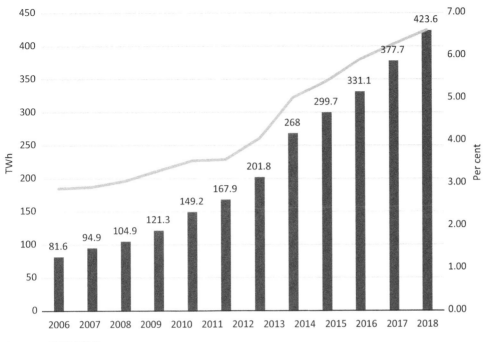

Source: CEC (2018).

Figure 21.2 Cross-province electricity supply and percentage of total electricity supply

system. 'The state – especially its absolutist features and highly centralized political and fiscal regime – figures prominently in the formation of property rights, contract enforcement and incentives' (Brandt, Ma and Rawski 2014, p. 60; see also Cai 2014, Chung 2016). The tension between a unitary rule and centrifugal forces of regions and groups is the key feature of the economic reform and development in China and electricity development was often the result of heavy bargaining between the centre and provinces. No discussion of electricity development in China makes any sense until this tension is taken seriously.

The need for reform has been the theme of the government policies since 1978 and reforms inevitably produce winners and losers. The process has been bitterly contested among 'powerful' players, whether vertically between the central and provincial government, or horizontally among different ministries. Undoubtedly, the balance of influence has shifted in favour of economic players (firms, regardless of their ownership). Their size, role in economy, control of information and technical expertise gave power companies unprecedented influence in shaping policies. This may be the unintended, yet inevitable, consequence of reforms. The fast pace of economic growth and changes in China has not been accompanied by adequate changes in the existing political, administrative and regulatory structure to address the rising influence of the 'market players' who have the intrinsic desire to 'privatize' benefits and 'socialize' losses – a phenomenon that has little to do with the ideology of the communist regime. By 2013, when a new government took over, everyone – from foreign observers, multilateral institutions, foreign and domestic companies and the government itself – was talking about the 'interest groups' or 'special interests' that had stalled the reform process (Naughton 2013). Yet, while most see themselves as the victims of the interest-group politics, few admit they are the special interests who enjoy favourable positions. In the electricity industry, there is enough blame going around, from the policies of central government, especially the National Development and Reform Commission (NDRC), a macroeconomic agency, and the National Energy Administration (NEA), to the protectionist policies of provinces, and to central state-owned power generation and grid corporations, the private captive power plants (plants generating electricity for their designated self-consumption), and even to large and small end-users. It is important to understand how different interests played out throughout the process to be able to explain all the paradoxical developments in the Chinese electricity industry and the difficulties confronting the recent round of reforms.

2.   THE FIRST TWO DECADES

Modern society cannot function without an adequate and reliable electricity supply, so little wonder the close correlation between electricity consumption and economic and social development (International Energy Agency [IEA] 2010). Electricity development in China mirrors this correlation. From 1949 to 1980, following Lenin's dictate: 'Communism equals Soviet power plus electrification', the CCP gave priority to the development of the country's electricity industry, which enjoyed favourable allocation of resources: privileged government budget allocation and other supports. A few large projects were constructed, with Soviet support, such as San Men Xia (三门峡) and Liu Jia Xia (刘家峡) hydro projects (Xu 2002, 2004, Zhang 1998). The average annual growth rate in electricity generation from 1949 to 1979 was about 12 per cent, higher than national economic growth rate. Despite these efforts, electricity development was far behind the world average level. China's electricity consumption per capita (259 kilowatt-hours [kWh]) in 1981 was lower than that of Ghana in 1968 (300 kWh). With over a quarter of the world population, electricity generation in China accounted for only 2.8 per cent of the world total. Severe power shortages were the main impediment to the economic reform launched by the CCP at the end of the 1970s.

The electricity industry was centrally controlled and managed as part of the planned economy. All property was state owned, and government allocated resources – human, financial and material – according to its five-year and annual plans. The Ministry of Electric Power (MOEP) controlled resource allocation, construction project planning, approval and management through an extensive and elaborate matrix system, as discussed by Lieberthal and Oksenberg (1988). Meanwhile, the lack of national or even regional electricity networks meant the industry operated in a decentralized fashion. There were three connected centres: one around Beijing, Tianjin and Tangshan, one around Shanghai, and another around Guangzhou. Beyond these centres were 30 fragmented grids in provinces, supported by predominantly 110 kilovolt (kV) and 220 kV lines. Provincial power bureaus accountable to both MOEP and provincial governments managed the vertically integrated power sector. This combination of centralization and decentralization explains two features of China's electricity industry: (1) an uneven development across provinces and between urban and rural areas because almost all resources, allocated by the central government through MOEP, went to municipal centres, leaving millions of people without access to electricity (Peng and Pan 2006, Smil 1988); and (2) organizational changes at the national level had little impact on the actual operation of the industry.

In 1983, Li Peng, the minister of electric power at the time, was made a vice-premier of the State Council – China's equivalent of a cabinet. Electricity development was immediately identified as one of the policy priorities. Yet, neither the central government nor the provinces had financial resources to build enough power plants. Without consciously heralding a fundamental reform, the State Council proposed to allow players other than MOEP to build small-size thermal, hydro, wind or geothermal power plants based on the principle of 'self-construct, self-manage, and self-use' (自建，自管，自用) (Li 2005). This proposal to lower entry barriers to allow local governments and large enterprises to invest in electricity generation was adopted as a formal policy in 1984, supported by two specific measures: (1) the policy of 'who invests, who benefits'; and (2) the 'dual pricing' system that would allow electricity generated from new power plants to be calculated at the cost of investment with a margin of profits (Shao et al. 1997, World Bank 1993). The central government continued to allocate resources for large power projects and set power tariffs for the old power plants (Sinton and Fridley 2000, Xu 2002). The policy of lowering entry barriers was not designed to reform or restructure the industry, nor intended to introduce competition or encourage efficiency. It was adopted, as was often the case with government policies, to deal with immediate problems, particularly power shortages that were bottlenecks for economic growth and reform. The policy nonetheless had significant impacts (both positive and negative) on the industry, on the relationship between central and local government, and on the public as well.

Electricity generation quickly expanded as enterprises (state owned, private or town/village owned) and provincial and local governments started investing in power generation. The central government also brought in multilateral financial institutions (for example, the World Bank and the Asian Development Bank) and foreign governments (for example, through their aid agencies or export–import banks) to form joint ventures to develop power generation facilities. From 1980 to 2000, total installed generation capacity expanded from 66 GW to 316 GW and electricity consumption quadrupled, from 259 TWh to 1081 TWh, with an average annual growth of over 9.5 per cent, in line with GDP growth. In over a decade, the share of centrally invested installed generation capacity had declined from 85 per cent in 1981 to 49.4 per cent in mid-1990s. The rest was split between those 'self-financed' (25.4 per cent) and those of 'other sources' (24.1 per cent) (Blackman and Wu 1999). Independent power producers (IPPs) emerged and expanded, driven in part by demands and in part by the higher price they were able to charge. In 1996, the policy of 'who invests, who benefits' was formally incorporated into the Electricity Law. The Electricity Law recognized the legal position of IPPs in China. Article 7 states: 'Electric power construction enterprises, production enterprises and network operation enterprises shall operate autonomously [and] be responsible for their own profits and losses'. Article 13 acknowledges: 'Investors in electric power shall enjoy legal rights and interests over the electricity generated from their investment' (MOEP 1997, p. 3; see also Lange and Howson 1997). Opening investment in power generation to sources other than state budget was novel in the world, as at that time the electricity industry in most countries remained publicly owned and vertically and horizontally integrated (Andrews-Speed 2004, Berrah, Ranjit and Zhao 2001, Hunt 2002, Joskow 1998, Joskow and Schmalensee 1983, Newbery 1995, 1999, Pollitt 1995).

In the 1990s, as restructuring of the electricity industry took place initially in Chile and spread to New Zealand, Australia and the UK (Bacon 1995, Besant-Jones 2006, Gilbert and Kahn 1996), international consultants were brought to China by the World Bank to advise on electricity reforms and Chinese officials were sent overseas to learn the reform experience in other countries. MOEP eventually adopted a three-pronged reform for China: corporatize the traditional power bureaus, commercialize their operation and legalize their management. It rejected the advice to privatize and completely unbundle the vertically and horizontally integrated electricity sector, as suggested by the World Bank and international consultants (Shao et al. 1997, World Bank 1993, 1994). Commercialization and corporatization of the electricity industry was confirmed by the adoption of the Electricity Law. The process speeded up in 1997–98, focusing on separation of government and business functions. Of course, the adoption of the Electricity Law did not lead to an immediate clarification of ownership. It took another decade or so gradually to sort out the entangled ownership of power enterprises, predominantly between the central and provincial governments. The significance of this development, however, was that at least there was a law the industry could follow, which did not exist for other energy sectors at the time.

In the late 1990s, commercialization and corporatization in the electricity industry was centrally planned and implemented by MOEP, which itself had to change. In December 1996, the State Council created the State Power Corporation of China (SPCC), which existed in parallel with MOEP for over a year, during which time MOEP gradually transferred its assets and business functions in the electricity industry to SPCC, while retaining government functions. One key issue at the time was to sort out disputes over the ownership of those generation plants co-funded by various sources after 1984 and decide the relationship and responsibilities of the central and provincial governments. As part of the general government reorganization in March 1998, the ministry was abolished and its government functions, predominantly project approval and price setting, were transferred to the electricity department of the State Planning Commission.

SPCC was created as a state-owned corporation, but it initially acted more as a government agency than a corporation. SPCC retained the MOEP's organizational structure and its organizational culture. Its 'management team' did not change in composition or behaviour, the minister and vice-ministers simply changed their titles to chief executives and deputies of SPCC. Nor did the State Council and other government agencies treat SPCC as a corporation. SPCC continued carrying out many functions of the ministry: appointing managers and supervisors, sending representatives to its newly corporatized subsidiaries, determining their operational guidelines, developing long-term strategies for the industry, conducting feasibility studies for potential projects, and tapping into funds from other sources to expand the industry. SPCC was also expected to continue carrying out social and political responsibilities without clearly defined financial accountability. At the same time, it was asked to restructure itself and to push forward ownership and structural reform of the electricity industry. In late 1998, the 'management' of SPCC adopted a four-stage reform plan (Box 21.1).

The purpose of reforming the electricity industry in the second half of the 1990s was two-fold, in line with the general reform ongoing in the country: (1) to separate

---

BOX 21.1   SPCC'S FOUR-STAGE REFORM PLAN

Phase I (Jan 1997–March 1998)   Establishment of SPCC, abolition of MOEP, separation of govern-
ment and business functions.
Phase II (1998–2000)   Commercialization, corporatization, gradual separation of generation from
T&D, pilot programmes introducing competition in generation (Shanghai, Zhejiang, Shandong,
Liaoning, Jilin and Heilongjiang).
Phase III (2001–10)   National interconnection of grids, unbundling generation from T&D, introduc-
tion of competition in generation, creation of electricity markets.
Phase IV (2010–ongoing)   Separation of distribution and retailing from transmission, creation of
grid companies.

Sources: SPCC (1999); *China Electricity Yearbook*, various years.

---

government and business functions; and (2) to start building large industrial groups
(Chow 1997). The reform was aimed more at changing the behaviour of production units
than the top governing structure of the industry.

Even though the industry remained state owned and vertically integrated at the end of
the 1990s, both objectives were achieved to a large extent and power companies were
expected to operate on a commercial basis rather than relying on centrally allocated
resources. SPCC took over all production functions – power generation, T&D, retail
services, power plant construction and some equipment manufacturers. It inherited personnel from the ministry, brought personnel from the provincial power departments
under its umbrella and consolidated the industry. In addition, SPCC inherited many
other 'businesses', such as running universities, hospitals, construction units and research
institutes. As 'a sprawling, heterogeneous and multi-layered organization', consisting of
more than 10 000 entities (Andrews-Speed and Dow 2000, p. 338), SPCC had difficulties
in operating as a coherent state-owned enterprise (SOE). It may have been in better shape
than many other sectors, but SPCC was still dogged by inefficiency, redundant workforce, triangular debts, high losses with non-production units, and continuing disputes
over the unresolved ownership of many new power plants.

The Asian Financial Crisis in 1997 provided an opportunity for SPCC to impose some
operational standards on its very diverse units and centralize the management. In 1999,
the central government adopted twin-scheme programmes: to improve T&D infrastructure in urban areas and retrofit that in rural areas. These programmes were designed to
stimulate the economy and to build an infrastructure that would make it possible for
power markets to work with interconnections. SPCC was asked to implement the programmes and it grabbed the opportunity (IEA 2006, Liu 2013, Xu 2002). When the
central government allocated direct credits to the programmes, banks, both commercial
and policy banks, such as China Development Bank and Agricultural Development Bank
of China, were reluctant to lend until they were guaranteed repayment. With over 30 per
cent line losses – that is, quantity of energy lost during transmission and distribution –
and serious triangular debt payment problems, many local electricity departments or
companies operated at losses and could not secure loans from banks (Cull and Xu 2003,
Yeung 2009). Lending based on ownership, size and sector all favoured SPCC. When

SPCC 'borrowed' to carry out the T&D retrofitting programmes, it reorganized five regional subsidiaries, and brought under its umbrella those provinces that had independent or unconnected grids – Shandong, Tibet, Xinjiang and four southern provinces. It placed those power bureaus that were traditionally locally controlled under the management of its regional or provincial subsidiaries. Meanwhile, as a condition of the retrofitting programmes, SPCC insisted on standardizing and centralizing the management of local operators. It also took a series of 'market' measures 'to incorporate the subsidiary provincial power companies, to implement a limited separation of generating assets from T&D, and to embark on experimental "market" trials in a number of provinces' (Andrews-Speed 2009, p. 234). By 2000, the issue was no longer how to make a new corporation work, but how to settle the differences between the newly created corporations and traditional government planning agencies, and between SPCC and provincial governments.

SPCC existed for only five years, during which time heated debate was going on among the very top decision-makers in the country and among the industry itself. One core issue at the debate was how to organize the industry. There was a general acceptance that generation should be separated from T&D and indeed, half the country's generation capacity was in the hands of 'others' – that is, provincial or local power companies (40 per cent) and private enterprises or IPPs (10 per cent). The general idea was that the coming reform should be province-based and SPCC started pilot programmes of separating generation from T&D in several provinces. Provinces would 'regulate' their generation in terms of how much and how fast generation capacity should be expanded and what sources of generation they would develop – thermal, hydro or nuclear. SPCC would manage the remaining 50 per cent of the generation capacity and more importantly would develop the country's transmission networks. On this last issue, the debate was on whether China should build one or several integrated transmission networks. The industry insiders insisted that the interconnected T&D would promote better utilization of resources and efficiency.

Before this debate could even go anywhere, provinces turned the policy of province-based reform into protectionist policies (Xu 2017). Several major disputes grabbed the political headlines of the day as well as attention of top decision-makers as provinces turned recently gained autonomy against their neighbours; they were more interested in investing in their 'own' power generation plants than utilizing the generation capacity in their neighbouring provinces. The dispute over the Ertan hydro project, financed jointly by the World Bank and several donor countries, was an example that drew national attention. Those provinces that could potentially benefit from the project insisted on building their own generation capacities rather than utilizing the 'clean electricity' from Sichuan where the Ertan hydro project was located because its electricity was much more expensive. As one of the key players, SPCC as a 'corporation' was in no position to resolve the issue when provincial governments were fighting for their own economic interests. The provincial protectionist policies catalysed the coming restructuring of the industry.

A major driving force behind the unbundling push in 2002 was bureaucratic bickering. The central government needed SPCC to push forward the reform policy of 'pulling the plug on socialism' – ending lifetime employment, free housing, free healthcare, and a variety of other non-wage benefits, and especially free credits for SOEs, while managing the reform's inevitable toll on political stability and economic growth (Steinfeld 1998).

When it was in charge of conducting corporatization of its subordinate units and when it developed long-term strategies and medium and short-term plans for the industry (Andrews-Speed and Dow 2000), SPCC was seen to step into the turf of the two powerful comprehensive macroeconomic planners: the State Development and Planning Commission (SDPC, renamed from the State Planning Commission in 1998) and the State Economic and Trade Commission (SETC). Even though created as a corporation, SPCC was placed under the State Council, not SETC or SDPC. Indeed, SPCC was at the same bureaucratic rank as SDPC and SETC. Bureaucratic bickering and 'covert' competition became the main driving force behind the dismantling of SPCC. SETC joined forces with SDPC and multilateral institutions, especially the World Bank, whose officials in China worked closely with the Ministry of Finance, to push for unbundling SPCC.

After more than two years of heated debates among the very top decision-makers in the central government, the State Council released its Electricity Reform Plan in December 2002, known as Document 5. The document spelt out the objective of electricity reform: 'to break up the monopoly, introduce competition, improve efficiency, reduce costs, improve the pricing mechanism, optimize the allocation of resources, promote electricity development, construct and strengthen national unified transmission networks, and build a governance structure under the supervision of an independent regulatory agency to ensure open and fair competition and orderly development of the electricity market system' (State Council 2002). These objectives were by and large justified by the rationale of the textbook model of electricity reform elsewhere: 'to develop a competitive, market-based, power sector, as a means to ensure an efficient and reliable power supply' (IEA 2006, p. 15) and 'to encourage the long-term development of the power sector' (State Council 2002).

Once the decision was made by the State Council, the debate on unbundling suddenly ended and people seemed to have endorsed the reform. The contentious issues were over the division of assets, functions, authorities and personnel. The Electricity Reform Leading Small Group set up some principal guidelines, but with very few details. One such detail was to divide SPCC into 11 pieces. Over the following 18 months between December 2002 and July 2004, SPCC remained in charge of this separation while effectively dismembering itself. Eleven SOEs emerged from SPCC. Among them were two grid companies: State Grid Corporation of China (SGCC 国网) and China Southern Power Grid Co. Ltd (CSG 南网); five generation companies (Table 21.2): Huaneng (华能), Datang (大唐) Guodian (国电), Huadian (华电) and China Power Investment Corp (CPI 中电投); and four power service companies: China Power Engineering Consulting Group (中国电力工程顾问集团公司), China Hydropower Engineering Consulting Group (中国水电工程顾问集团公司), China Water Resources and Hydropower Construction Group (中国水利水电建设集团公司) and China Gezhouba Group (中国葛洲坝集团公司).

Generation capacity in much of the country was carefully distributed among the five power companies, based on the principle that no one would have the monopoly. In each of the five geographical regions – Northeast, North, Northwest, Central and East China – generation capacity was carefully divided too (Figure 21.3). Each of the five generation companies was allocated about 20 per cent of the market share (about 30 GW), with thermal and hydro capacities relatively even distributed (Andrews-Speed 2009, IEA 2006). The rationale behind this arrangement was to prevent monopoly and encourage competition so that a market system could be eventually introduced. Power generation

Table 21.2   Distribution of generation capacity between the five major generation companies (2003)

Five Major Generation Firms	Installed Capacity (GW)	Power Components			Assets
		Hydro (%)	Thermal (%)	Nuclear (%)	RMB (Billion)
Huaneng	38.0	18	82		126.5
Datang	32.5	21	79		71.6
Huadian	31.3	19	81		71.2
Guodian	30.8	15	85		73.3
China Power Inv.	30.2	26	70	3.8	76.9

Sources: Andrews-Speed (2009), Xu (2017).

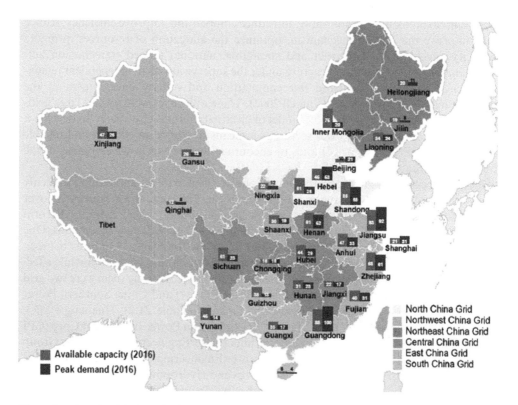

Note: Based on the global standard, we assumed available load factor of hydropower at 50 per cent, pumped hydro at 100 per cent, coal and gas at 90 per cent, nuclear at 80 per cent, wind at 10 per cent, solar at 30 per cent and biomass at 70 per cent.

Sources: Bloomberg New Energy Finance and CEC.

Figure 21.3   Available capacity versus peak demand by province, 2016 (GW)

plants nonetheless differed significantly in size, quality and performance. The old ones might not have a financial burden from their initial investment but would have carried a heavy financial responsibility for their retired employees and other associated costs. Some new ones were large and efficient, but the financial burden to service the borrowing for their investment was heavy. Some small ones were required by the government to be closed. Who should get what was up for grabs. One senior manager of a hydro company in Yunnan recalled years later: 'we were asked to be part of the Southern Grid, another subsidiary was given to Guodian, and some others were allocated to other power companies. There was no logic to it, but there were consequences' (Xu 2017, p. 71).

Over T&D, difficult and awkward negotiations between the central and Guangdong governments led to the creation of the China Southern Grid Company (CSG) as one of the 11 central SOEs. Yet it took another two years to negotiate the details. CSG did not register until 18 June 2004. During this period, several steps were undertaken. SPCC's Southern Power Company was transferred to SGCC; it was then merged with the Guangdong Power Company and the newly created Hainan Power Company, and on this basis, the CSG was created (Box 21.2). The Guangdong provincial government owned 70.4 per cent of stakes in the new CSG, the SGCC 26.4 per cent and Hainan 3.2 per cent. SGCC transferred its stake to CSG in 2007.

The electricity sector in West Inner Mongolia is owned and managed separately by the government of the Inner Mongolia Autonomous Region, so is its T&D system that is not part of SGCC. Tibet was placed as a custodian unit of SGCC.

The entangled asset relationships and difficult negotiations left an uneasy relation between the central and Guangdong government, between the State-owned Assets Supervision and Administration Commission of the State Council (SASAC) as the nominal owner of all central SOEs and its provincial branch in Guangdong and some other provinces, and between SGCC and CSG. For instance, even though CSG was 100 per cent state-owned and placed under SASAC, some insisted that CSG should not be given the responsibility to manage cross-province, cross-region power dispatch or infrastructure development for fear that the protectionist policies of Guangdong would impede the major projects of 'wiring electricity from west to east'. SGCC was asked to 'manage' the CSG's assets and accounts on behalf of the State Council because, after all, the central government, initially via the MOEP and then SPCC, owned a quarter of the stakes of CSG. This pleased those who repeatedly argued that the grid should not be

---

BOX 21.2   PRESENCE OF SGCC AND CSG IN THE CHINESE PROVINCES

SGCC
> Northeast: Heilongjiang, Jilin, Liaoning, east Inner Mongolia
> North: Beijing, Tianjin, Hebei, Shanxi, Shandong
> East: Shanghai, Zhejiang, Anhui, Jiangsu, Fujian
> Central: Jiangxi, Henan, Hubei, Hunan, Chongqing, Sichuan
> Northwest: Shaanxi, Gansu, Qinghai, Ningxia, Xinjiang

CSG
> South: Guangdong, Guangxi, Yunnan, Guizhou, Hainan

separated under different jurisdictions and the country needed well-interconnected T&D systems. This arrangement placed SGCC in a difficult position of 'managing' CSG. In practice, it never did, and this formal arrangement ended in 2013 when CSG became an independent entity, operating the T&D network of five southern provinces.

With the unbundling, SPCC's 2 million employees were relocated with their enterprises to the newly restructured 11 SOEs, while the top echelon made their own choices on whether they would like to work in one of the generation, grid or service companies or work at the newly established State Electricity Regulatory Commission. Despite the heated and difficult debate that has occurred for over three years, the actual unbundling met little resistance. As a senior official of SGCC who had been with the MOE, SPCC and SGCC, commented years later:

> Of course, there was little resistance. Have a look at how many senior positions were created. Low-level civil servants in some of our departments at the MOEP suddenly became senior managers of power companies, with their pay and benefits 10 or even 20 times those of civil servants. Meanwhile, their jobs did not change much. (Xu 2017, pp. 73–4)

3.   A DECADE OF EXPANSION

The decision to unbundle the electricity industry in 2002 was criticized by many inside and outside China. Many were disappointed because the restructuring was 'incomplete', as all 11 new power companies remained state owned and China showed no intention of privatizing its utilities. In addition, the restructuring created a single-buyer model as generation was separated from T&D, but the grid companies owned and operated T&D and retailing services (IEA 2006). In the following decade, both the positive and negative consequences of the 2002 restructuring emerged.

First, the changes created a juggernaut in expansion in generation capacity and T&D capacity. The total installed generation capacities grew from 356 GW in 2002 to 1257 GW (353 per cent) in 2013 and electricity production expanded from 1647 TWh to 5350 TWh (325 per cent) respectively. During the same period, SGCC completed two ultra-high-voltage (UHV) 1000 kV AC systems and four ±800 kV DC transmission systems (Liu 2014, 2015).

Second, this expansion was driven by the rising demand for electricity as well as the desire of all power companies to expand in size, assets and operation. For instance, the assets of Huaneng more than doubled in a decade and it turned around from a loss of RMB5.8 billion in 2008 to a net profit of RMB14 billion in 2012. SGCC significantly increased its profit, from RMB5.97 billion in 2003 to RMB70.56 billion (1182 per cent) in 2013, a little less than the combined total profits of the five largest generation companies (RMB74 billion). SGCC joined the top 50 of the Fortune Global 500 in 2004 (46), stayed there and moved up the ladder to number seven in 2011 and number two in 2016.

Third, all 11 state-owned power companies improved their corporate governance in the sense that they reported publicly regularly on their performance, and they were assessed by their nominal owner – the State-owned Asset Supervision and Administration Commission (SASAC). They operated much more like corporations than the puppets of the CCP or government (Yeh and Lewis 2004, Zhang 2015).

One major failure of the 2002 restructuring was what was known a decade later as the failure of 'top-level design' of economic structure in general and electricity industry specifically. That is, while economic players were given the authority and autonomy to act as market players, they operated in an environment where bureaucratic rivalries had prevented the establishment of an adequate regulatory regime. One major component of the 2002 restructuring was the creation of the State Electricity Regulatory Commission (SERC). Having realized the importance of a regulatory agency for creating a competitive electricity industry, central decision-makers did agree to grant this new agency ministerial status so that it could 'regulate' large SOEs and have an equal standing with other government agencies. Unfortunately, SERC was powerless and toothless when the NDRC refused to give up two key regulatory functions: project approval and price setting.

When 11 central SOEs were accountable to various different institutions, there were plenty of opportunities for them to play one against another and were consequently, in practice, regulated by none (Lin and Milhaupt 2013). Their senior managers were appointed jointly by the CCP personnel department and the State Council; they were evaluated by SASAC in terms of their performance; their investment and price were decided by NDRC; overall planning was supposed to be done by the NEA; and their technical standards were regulated by SERC. On any of these issue areas, power companies had to negotiate with provinces too. The complex and entangled institutional framework created ample room for those able and willing senior managers to act as entrepreneurs rather than obedient order-takers or what Joseph Schumpeter called 'managers'. They quickly turned the situation of fragmented and rival bureaucratic institutions to their advantage and started building their own empires. In the following decade, these large SOEs drove the expansion of the electricity industry in China (Brandt and Rawski 2019, Xu 2017). Meanwhile, the two key regulatory functions retained by NDRC offered abundant rent-seeking opportunities for its officials and its two departments on projects and pricing became fertile ground for corruption (Andrews-Speed 2012).

4. REFORM PLANS LAUNCHED IN 2015

In March 2015, the State Council and the Central Committee of the CCP issued a joint document on *Opinions on Further Deepening the Reform of Power Sector*, known as Document 9 (State Council 2015; IEA 2018). It was issued as a suggestion rather than as legislation or a 'decision' primarily because there was no agreement on what would need to be reformed and how to do so. NDRC and NEA in 2014 held extensive discussions and consultations with the industry and experts. The industry was facing a series of challenges at the time, such as overcapacity in generation, high debt–asset ratios of the five major power-generating companies, increasing renewable generation capacities accompanied by worsening curtailment, several serious corruption cases involving NDRC and NEA high-ranking officials, including NEA's minister in 2011–13, and general social and political complaints about large central SOEs, including the two grid companies (Pollitt, Yang and Chen 2017, 2018). The causes of these challenges varied significantly, so would their solutions. There was no agreement among bureaucracies and the industry on the priorities; nor was there agreement on the nature of the problems – were they ownership, structure (incompletely unbundled), control of pricing or lack of competition. Whether and how to further reform the industry was in question too. In addition, any reform proposal would have to fit the broad agenda of the new government that had taken office in March 2013.

Document 9 emphasized the broad agenda of the party and government rather than the specific challenges facing the industry per se – that is, to shift the economic development model away from its dependence on investment, cheap labour, cheap resources and exports; to tackle the corruption problems among party and government officials who had taken advantage of the rent-seeking opportunities that had emerged from the last round of reforms; and to deal with the issues of large central SOEs that had generated genuine concerns due to their dominant positions in the economy and the political jealousies among party and government officials who had been financially much worse-off than those working at central SOEs. None of these were industry-specific problems. Document 9 thus outlined a set of broad objectives:

- to provide better power sector planning to address the issue of coal generation overcapacity and expansion and siting of renewable generation;
- to restructure regulation of, and business models for, China's grid companies by reforming the tariff systems;
- to reform the traditional dispatch system of administratively allocating an entitlement of annual hours of production to each generator; and
- to create a new structure of wholesale markets.

The document was immediately interpreted differently by the different players. Some saw this as a step to dismantle the monopoly of the grid companies as the document did suggest peeling off the profitable retailing services from the grid companies. Others saw the reform as an opportunity to reduce the rent-seeking opportunities of the party and government officials who controlled project approvals and price setting by introducing market-pricing systems. Some emphasized that the reform was designed to introduce mixed ownership in central SOEs to change their behaviour and improve their profitability; and others saw opportunities to enter the segments of the electricity industry. With such a broad jumble of disparate agenda, it was difficult to see how the reform could be implemented. The central government, more specifically NDRC, then spent the following nine to ten months in 2015 working out nine separate documents to clarify the specifics of the reform and rolled out more detailed measures and regulations in 2016–18. These documents aimed to guide the electricity industry towards a more market-oriented system, but they also reflected the nature of reform – an evolution rather than revolution in building 'a combination of the old planned system together with the new market-based system' (IEA 2018, p. 29). They address several specific issues:

- long-term planning and investment – to encourage non-fossil generation capacity expansion (nuclear, wind, solar and other renewable sources of generation), integration of renewables into the current electricity generation and consumption;
- power trading via mid- and long-term contracts (intra-provincial, interprovincial and interregional trading) and gradual development in power markets;

- direct power purchasing – to reduce the power cost for local industries and commercial consumers by bypassing the fixed on-grid and retail prices benchmarked by government;
- generation rights trading – to improve efficiency and to reduce pollution by allowing generation rights to be traded from small and highly polluting coal-fired generators to large or supercritical generation units;
- dispatch rules – to improve the existing dispatching rules to encourage conservation and competition; and
- power price reforms.

With a broad agenda and ill-defined specifics, the central government adopted a local experiment strategy – that is, provincial and local governments would work out their own reform plans and then voluntarily apply for approval of their reform pilot programmes. This round of reform turned out to be much more difficult than the previous ones. It was not only the resistance of the players involved, as the literature suggests. More importantly, the reform would require new thinking and new design of the structure and institutions of the industry. Since the early 1990s when the World Bank brought to China international consultants to design the reform, policy makers, experts and the industry itself in China have been aware of various models adopted by countries around the world and their successes and failures. Few in China, especially in the electricity industry, were so naive that they believed that overnight change would be possible, or that one market model could be adopted throughout the country. Even though much of the discussion among experts outside China and some generalists in China was on the types of market model China should adopt – the one used in Australia, in PJM in the United States, or the one implemented in the EU, the recognition among policy makers and the industry itself has always been that no two regions have adopted exactly the same market design. They knew that even in the United States, the electricity industry in some regions remains vertically integrated – take, for instance, the southeast where companies like Duke own and operate generation, T&D and retailing services, while other states like California or Texas adopted different electricity market models (Pollitt and Dale 2018). China had to try its own way to move towards market competition (Feng 2017, 2019, Shi 2018, Zhang 2018). How to do so remains a debated question.

The two principles of the 2015 round of reform were 'letting go the two ends [generation and retailing services], regulating the middle [T&D])' (管住中间，放开两头), and allowing private investors to enter distribution and retailing services. This would involve separating T&D tariffs from retailing ones – T&D tariffs would be set by government, based on the principle of investment cost plus a profit margin, while retailing price would be decided by competition among retailing service providers and negotiation between large users and generators on the amount of electricity supplies. It is easy to have a separate pricing scheme on paper; it is extremely difficult to make this a political reality, in part because, historically, there were differences in power pricing according to the types of end-users and regions, but pricing for all segments was bundled together. Back in 1999–2001, SPCC had a trial run of creating a sort of power market in the northeast three provinces and Zhejiang, with an aim to introduce competition and build a market-based power sector. The trial allowed large end-users to negotiate with generation companies on the amount of electricity supplies and their price. All experiments halted in 2002, in part because of the unbundling of the industry, in part because of the severe power short-ages, and, more importantly, because of local protectionist policies. Pricing electricity remains a key issue: 'Power infrastructures raise local employment, tax revenue source, and manufacturing business' (IEA 2018, p. 25). Provincial and local governments would pressure local large end-users to sign electricity 'purchasing' contracts with their local power generators, even though they might be small, inefficient and high polluting. One immediate consequence of this is the reduction in the utilization rate of large supercritical power generators (that is, larger than 600 MW), which are often owned by the five national power generation companies. In 2016, on average, thermal power generators ran 4186 hours a year, while supercritical ones operated only 3796 hours a year (10 per cent less than the average), a historical low (CEC 2017). The same pattern continued the year after – the small-size generators operated at 20–25 per cent above the national average, while large ones (larger than 600 MW) operated at 20–25 per cent below the national average (CEC 2018). Separate pricing for grid and off-grid electricity remained nominal because those who controlled distribution networks tended to be the subsidiaries of the grid companies at provincial or county levels.

Creating separate and independent electricity retailing service providers is the key component of this round of reform. The progress is not only slow but confusing because there did not seem to be a good understanding of what the reform would require. Document 9 and other associated documents outlined a plan of creating retail companies based on the principle of permitting private investment into the segment. The rationale was that if consumers could choose from whom they would purchase electricity and at what price, there could be competition. The documents also stated that various investors could bid for retailing services and provincial governments would seek the approval from NDRC to create trials. Between 2016 and December 2018, with 320 experiment projects approved, only 49 received licences to operate across the country (about 15 per cent of the total) and only a few of these licensed ones were in operation (Fan, Li and Han 2019). Also, when the two grid companies were asked to give up their retailing service segments, they were able to request and receive approvals from local governments to take over the retailing service with a few symbolic partners. For instance, in 2018, within the SGCC's own service areas, 256 trial projects were approved, involving 87 retailing service firms, 47 of which were led by SGCC itself (Yu 2019). It remains to be seen how these new enti-ties would work as NDRC and NEA continue reviewing and even withdrawing the licence for some of them well into the second half of 2019.

Several issues emerged in the recent reform process. One is the division of responsibility. What is considered retailing service? What are retailing companies responsible for? Does retailing service cover only meters and lines to consumers? If power lines and power poles are included, what is the cut-off capacity? In most developed countries, there are laws and rules that define what core interconnected long-distance transmission networks are and who regulates them and what distribution lines are. In Australia, for instance, retailing services cover power lines of 240 V up to 66 kV, and anything above 66 kV is the respon-sibility of transmission grid companies. With a clear understanding, the division of cover-age between T&D and retailing services is often considered as a non-issue. In China, however, it is a hotly debated issue. Historically, the grid companies invested, built and operated not only interconnected cross-province, cross-region T&D networks, but also built, operated and managed local distribution networks and provided distribution and retailing service cables to end-users. At the end of the 1990s, SPCC took over the operation of many local distribution systems too under the programmes of upgrading urban and rural systems, even though NDRC in one of the supporting documents specified that new retail service companies (often called distributors) would cover the network below 110 kV for residential consumers and network of up to 220 kV for industries. The two national grid companies, provincial governments and local power companies, which may or may not be the subsidiaries of the two grid companies, are fighting over the division of networks (Fan et al. 2019, Zhang 2018). Without a clearly defined boundary between T&D and low-voltage distribution networks and services, price reform remains a pending issue.

However, even if an agreement can be reached on the division of responsibility of different segments, reform would require a proper assessment of the assets. So far, SGCC and CSG have invested in all high- and low-voltage transmission networks. Provincial governments would like to take over the infrastructure but are unwilling to pay for the investment. More importantly, the proposed retailing service projects were all in well-connected areas with well-established infrastructure and concentrated end-users. Few want to go to places where demand is dispersed and connections are not quite in place – a typical problem of public utility. These issues may not have anything to do with either the state ownership or pricing system. A market system could not be even discussed until they are sorted out.

In addition, one idea was that the reform should promote competition by introducing private investors to generation and retailing segments. Generation was open to other sources of investment back in the mid-1980s. For the retailing service providers, a more common form was to combine investment from a grid subsidiary, a financial platform created by provincial government, and one or two private investors. Struggle for control became one impediment for reform. For instance, when a province put one retailing project up for bidding, over a dozen potential providers showed interest. Only seven eventually managed to be formed and put in their bid. On the day of bidding, only three appeared. There were many similar cases, but competition for control over the new retailing company's ownership was one main reason – the grid companies did not want to retreat from the retailing services as they were the profitable segments that make up the rising investment costs in interconnected transmission networks; provinces would like to avoid paying for add-on costs of using inter-provincial networks and to protect and expand their local industries and employment; and private investors would not join unless they were guaranteed a say over the new companies. This is not a question the current reform is able to address.

Most importantly, one key component in Document 9 was to reduce the direct role of planning agencies in deciding projects and pricing. For the electricity industry, this cannot not be done until a regulatory regime is put in place. SERC was abolished in 2013 and its limited regulatory functions were given to NEA, which is no more than a little brother of NDRC. In March 2018, the National People's Congress, the Chinese national legislature, approved a new round of government reorganization. NDRC nonetheless remained unscathed. NDRC continues to be 'responsible for issuing and implementing industrial plans, policies, pricing and energy sector regulation' (IEA 2018, p. 19). It was in the driver's seat in designing and implementing the current reform as its economic system department designed the reform formula; its pricing department continues setting up the benchmark price for electricity as well as other energy sources, such as coal and petroleum; and other departments are deeply involved in decision making in the industry. The resistance of NDRC to give up its authority and control over investment and pricing was the main reason for the powerless and toothless SERC.

Of course, there are many specific issues in the reform plan of 2015. The critical one is the role of government, and more specifically the role of NDRC, in the economy in general and the electricity industry specifically. As a macroeconomic planner, NDRC and its predecessors have always been the pre-eminent player in national decision making. Its control over project approval and price setting for critical inputs gave it a special role but has also created fertile ground for corruption. Anti-corruption and streamlining bureaucratic measures are two objectives of the current government. Yet it has not changed the role of NDRC. Any talk about adopting various models of market systems in the electricity industry is pointless as long as NDRC refuses to give up its power and authority to control investment and price setting. An electricity market needs an independent third-party agency to do the research and overall industry projection, and an independent agency to regulate investment and pricing, rather than direct political intervention.

Given the slow implementation of the reform launched in 2015, all serious challenges facing the industry remain in place: overcapacity, low utilization rate of generation power plants, high debt–asset ratios, serious curtailment of renewables, and protectionist policies by the provinces.

Let us consider the challenge of overcapacity. Demand for electricity in the country slowed down from the annual growth rate of 15 per cent in 2010 to zero in 2015, while installed generation capacity continued to grow on average at 10 per cent, a rate higher than GDP growth (Figure 21.4).

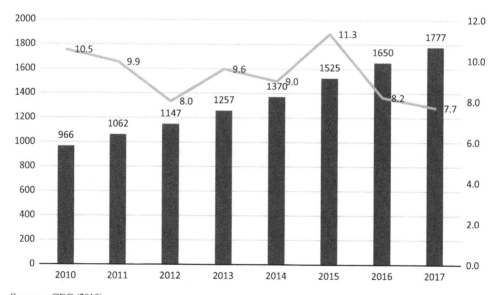

Source: CEC (2018).

Figure 21.4   Total installed generation capacity (GW) and annual growth rate (%) between 2010 and 2017

Overcapacity is a problem in all sources of generation. Along Yalong River (also called Nyag Chu) in Sichuan, for instance, seven large hydro stations with a potential capacity of 7.5–10 GW were under construction in 2018 and electricity was supposed to be exported to Jiangxi via a high-voltage DC line. Electricity consumption per capita in Jiangxi was only half of the national average, but the provincial government refused to accept electricity from Sichuan. Without this DC line to export electricity, all seven hydro stations would operate at a loss the day they were completed. SGCC had already planned for the project and NDRC and NEA issued many documents indicating that there would be a high-voltage DC line for these large hydro projects. The provincial government in Jiangxi meanwhile asked for approval for several coal-fired thermal power plants with a total capacity of 8.46 GW, labelling them as poverty-alleviation projects. This dispute was not settled in early 2019. It represents only one example of the difficulty in reaching any agreement among provinces – in great contrast to the common narrative about China telling that everyone obeys when the party decides (Zhou and Lu 2017).

To deal with the problem of overcapacity, the government did impose some mandatory measures. For instance, the total investment in power generation in 2016 declined by 13.4 per cent as NDRC cancelled the previously approved projects with a total capacity of 12.4 GW. In 2017, investment in hydro and solar went up, but that in thermal was down by 23.4 per cent. Also, investment in new nuclear and wind capacity was down by 9.9 and 26.5 per cent, respectively (CEC 2017, 2018).

Overcapacity directly affected the performance of the major power generation companies. In 2016, their total profit was down by 42.6 per cent from the previous year and their average debt–asset ratio went up to 82 per cent. In 2017, the losses of the five major generation companies totalled RMB 13.2 billion. The irony was that some small power producers running small and often less efficient power plants managed to make profits, thanks to the support of local governments. For some power generators, the more electricity they generate, the more losses they endure primarily because of the competition from renewable sources – a common phenomenon in the electricity industry globally, regardless of the ownership.

Let us now turn to renewable curtailment. Curtailment is an unplanned reduction of renewable energy generation output to the grid, whether due to technical or non-technical limitations. Even though renewable electricity penetration in China remains at a low level (about 5 per cent of total electricity generation), the country's wind and solar curtailment is the worst in the world. China's annual average wind curtailment in 2016 exceeded 17 per cent and wind curtailment rate was about 40 per cent in Qinghai and Xinjiang, 30 per cent in Jilin, 21 per cent in Inner Mongolia and about 10 per cent in other major wind-producing provinces. Xinjiang and Qinghai also suffered from over 30 per cent of the curtailment in solar production. One obvious reason for such high curtailment rates is the uneven allocation of resources and economic activities. This nonetheless was a well-known issue before the capacities were developed in the first place.

In 2017, the wind curtailment remained at 12 per cent (42 TWh), while solar curtailment was 6 per cent. There is a great variation in the utilization rate of wind power in the country and in some provinces, curtailment is much worse than the national average. For example, the total installed generation capacity in Inner Mongolia, a province with population of 24.7 million, was 120 per cent of that in the UK, a country with a population of 66 million. Inner Mongolia has been building thermal as well as wind capacity even though there is little demand from its neighbouring provinces. In Gansu, the curtailment problem is worse than that in Inner Mongolia. The province has the largest installed wind generation capacity and the lowest utilization rate (13.5 per cent). With the SGCC's ultra-high-voltage transmission projects, wind power would be transported to Hubei and Hunan where there is demand. Yet, the condition for the latter to 'import' wind power from Gansu was that the wind power cannot be priced higher than the hydro power from the Three Gorges Project. The consequence was that Gansu sold its wind power to other provinces at much lower price than it was sold in the province (Yan, Tan and Zhao 2019). Meanwhile the provincial government encouraged local firms to invest in coal-fired thermal power plants to send cheap electricity to its few energy-intensive industries. In sum, irrational planning and allocation of resources are usually behind the curtailment of renewables.

If curtailment of wind and solar power could be explained by their nature of intermittency, there is no technical or even economic reason to waste hydro power. Yet, according to some calculation, the total waste of 'clean' electricity can be as high as 110 TWh each year, and in 2016 alone the wasted hydro power in Sichuan and Yunnan amounted to half the annual electricity consumption in Beijing. Again, it is the politics rather than technology or market design that should resolve all these issues (Su 2018).

Finally, let us turn to ownership. Introducing mixed ownership to the existing SOEs in generation, T&D and auxiliary segments was part of the general reform of economic restructuring. There was little concrete idea how the policy of mixed ownership reform could be introduced in the electricity industry as the objective was not to privatize, but to introduce private capital into the large SOEs to improve their performance. The challenge was that all major central SOEs in the electricity industry had expanded significantly in size and in operation in 2002–15. In 2018, several of them were on the global Fortune 500 list: State Grid (2), China Southern Grid (110), PowerChina (82), Huaneng (289) and Datang (489). The question then became how to reform these unicorns that had become political power houses themselves. If not to privatize them, who would be willing to invest in these companies that were so large that the potential investment could hardly make any difference in changing the behaviour of these giant companies? This indeed was the reason little private investment was injected into these companies. Furthermore, some of their healthy subsidiaries had already been listed in the two Chinese stock markets and enjoyed a great degree of autonomy in their operation anyway.

5.   INTERNATIONALIZATION

The electricity industry has historically been considered not only a public service but also a domestic matter. Public utilities in general were not open for foreign investment until the early 1990s when saturated markets in some developed countries drove some utility companies to invest overseas. They were behind the privatization and restructuring of the electricity industry at home and abroad and were beneficiaries of the conditionalities imposed by multilateral financial institutions, such as the International Monetary Fund and the World Bank. Opening up to foreign investment in the generation segment in the electricity industry did not lead to the same development in T&D until the early 2000s when, for instance, the European Commission 'ordered' EU countries to adopt a strict separation of transmission from generation and mandated regulated third-party access in 2003. Even then, foreign investment was mainly among OECD countries and by and large from passive equity investors, which did not get involved in direct operations of the energy companies.

The Chinese government formulated its 'going out' policy in the early 1990s: 'to open wider to the outside world, we should encourage enterprises to expand their investments abroad and their transnational operations', Jiang Zemin declared in 1992 (Shambaugh 2013). This, however, was just confirmation and legitimization of what the petroleum company – China National Petroleum Corp (CNPC) – had proposed and done. The chief executive of CNPC, the former minister of the petroleum industry before the ministry merged with the rest of the energy sectors in 1988, argued that CNPC had to adopt a strategy of 'walking on two legs' to address its serious debt problems, caused by a combination of domestic factors. Its strategy was 'deepening reforms in the domestic petroleum sector by attracting foreign capital, technology, and management experience on the one hand, and actively "going out" to engage in overseas E&P [exploration and production] activities on the other hand' (Kong 2010, p. 41). Even after 'going out' was adopted as official policy, Chinese outward investment did not take place on a large scale until the SOE restructuring a decade later. Chinese firms were too small and fragmented to compete on global markets (Nolan 2001a, 2001b). At the initial stage, most outward foreign direct investment from China concentrated on resource sectors. SGCC did not join the 'going out' game until much later, partly because it became an independent entity much later than others, such as CNPC and Huaneng, but also because worldwide the electricity industry was still considered to be a domestic industry with limited foreign investment, especially in T&D.

In the late 1980s and especially in the 1990s when the domestic electricity market in developed countries was saturated, a few utilities ventured out to invest in generation as IPPs. They invested in developing countries as joint ventures or sole investors, often with guaranteed rates of return provided by host governments, and/or with reform promises as conditions demanded by multilateral financial institutions such as the World Bank, the European Bank for Reconstruction and Development and regional development banks (Bacon and Besant-Jones 2002, Besant-Jones 2006, Xu 2004). This was how the Chinese electricity industry developed in the late 1980s and 1990s, when the government decided to open the generation sector to investment other than that of the state and the World Bank helped bring in foreign investment, which delivered not only needed capital but also technologies and managerial skills (Andrews-Speed 2004, Xu 2002).

After 2003, foreign investment in generation as IPPs in China began to retreat. Freed coal prices and controlled power tariffs made these IPPs unprofitable and unsustainable (Andrews-Speed 2009). Meanwhile, Chinese generation companies, facing similar squeezes, started investing in overseas markets as a way to compensate for their domestic losses. Huaneng, for example, acquired a 50 per cent stake in OzGen, a power company operating in Queensland, Australia, in 2003, and then expanded to the electricity distribution business in Victoria, Australia. In 2008, Huaneng acquired Temasek's Tuas Power for 4235 billion Singapore dollars, which allowed Huaneng to control 25 per cent of the market in Singapore. Compared to Chinese investment in resources, Huaneng, and later other power generation companies, drew little international attention. If China investing in overseas resource industries is contentious because it represents 'the mercantilist case of the go-out strategies [that] reflects China's sense of weakness and vulnerability regarding reliable access to energy supplies' (Lieberthal and Herberg 2006, p. 14), investment in power generation is often considered positively by host countries as it brings necessary investment and occasionally technologies too.

Investing in T&D was a relatively new phenomenon and investing as an active operator was even rarer because transmission around the world is a publicly owned and highly regulated activity. In the early 2000s, SGCC was an unknown entity outside China. Some of its subsidiaries had taken on a few engineering, procurement and construction (EPC) projects around the world, but SGCC did not take major international initiatives until an opportunity in the Philippines emerged in 2006. Its management decided to grab the opportunity of overseas expansion, but also made a conscious decision that it would invest only in its own business – that is, electricity T&D.

By investing in the Philippines, the management of SGCC was well aware of the difficulties and risks. It took the decision as a trial run. SGCC's investment started its operation in 2009 and experienced ups and downs in the following decade. By the time SGCC entered Brazil in 2010, it had learned a lot from its experience in the Philippines. The management decided that: (1) it would need to have the controlling stakes in any overseas project (in the Philippines, in the end SGCC had only 40 per cent with regard to its local partners); and (2), more importantly, it would have to adapt to local conditions and indeed 'indigenize' its operation in Brazil. This was important because SGCC was in Brazil *not* for 'a quick short-term return', but rather as part of its long-term development strategy. SGCC went to Brazil with an ambitious goal – to build its brand name with the UHV technologies, to take its technology and experience to other places and to help Chinese electric equipment manufacturing industries open new markets. The joint venture with SGCC holding the majority stake won the bid to construct and operate a high-voltage transmission system for the Belo Monte hydro station in northern Brazil.

Given that only a few countries permit foreign companies to own and operate their national grid, SGCC decided to invest as an equity investor in countries whose economy was struggling in the aftermath of the global financial crisis (2008–09). It took advantage of the Global Financial Crisis, the associated vulnerability of some grid companies, the austerity policies that forced some governments to sell off some state assets, and the limited number of willing global investors. It entered the T&D market as equity investor in Australia, Portugal and Italy. By 2019, it had invested US$21 billion as a direct investor or as an equity investor and its overseas assets had reached US$60 billion. In recent years, SGCC also bid on large international projects, such as constructing a 500 kV transmission project in Egypt and a few other projects in Africa. The accumulated earning from EPC projects was US$43 billion by 2019. SGCC's management argued about a decade ago that 'our overseas projects gave us more profits than we received in China' (Xu 2017).

SGCC was particularly active in participating in setting international standards with its high-voltage projects in China. Its management consistently argued that the evolution toward a twenty-first-century grid is under way, and in this process, whoever controls the technologies and their standards controls the future. Thus, it is a global competition and SGCC wanted to be at the same starting point as other global majors in both power grid operations as seen in the GO 15 – the world's largest power grid operators – and in transmission technology innovation as in Siemens and ABB. It leveraged its high-voltage projects to compete with its global peers. As one senior official at SGCC explained:

> We live in a globalized economic environment. We cannot survive and have sustainable development unless we know how to take advantage of the resources available globally, identify our niche, and find our space. Meanwhile, our global competitiveness also indicates the competitiveness of China in this globalized economy. National economic competition is competition among corporations and competition among large states is competition among their multinational corporations. Consequently, whether for the interests of SGCC or the interests of China, we cannot take comfort just staying at home. (Wang 2014)

The most audacious idea proposed by SGCC was the global energy interconnection. In 2015, at the Edison Electric Institute, UN Secretary-General Ban Ki-moon launched the SGCC's CEO's book, *Global Energy Interconnection*. The central idea behind the proposal to build cross-region interconnections with high-voltage transmission lines and smart grid technologies might be too ambitious for many and even dangerous for some. It placed the Chinese firm in a strong position on the global stage to develop an alternative solution to ensure safe, clean, efficient and sustainable energy development. This won the endorsement of the International Energy Agency too.

6. CONCLUSION

Reform and restructuring of the electricity industry have been a continuous process in the past four decades. The industry has provided universal access to electricity, system reliability and security. Competition has never been so tense. Yet this study of the evolution, operation and expansion of the Chinese electricity industry shows that an emphasis on the ownership structure or the industry structure is by itself unable to explain either the behaviour of electricity enterprises – public and private alike – or their changing relationship with government. Neither can the evaluation of various electricity market models explain why 'best practice' was not adopted in China. In China, industry insiders, experts and government officials in charge are quite aware of the various models adopted by other countries. There were frequent overseas trips and communications with people in the policy community. Lack of knowledge is not necessarily the main impediment for restructuring and reform. It is politics – the competing views of what should change, how specific changes should take place and whose interests should be protected – that has constrained governments. Ministries, government agencies, conglomerate SOEs, provinces and local governments all have constituencies to protect, interests to push and their own future to chart. These competing interests put their own future, not any national model, at the core of their actions and they could not be overcome by simple diktat. Since all the key senior officials are members of the CCP, these contests are continuing within party ranks and among different components of government, rather than a case of party against technocrats. Every step must be negotiated. This explanation may seem to contradict the image of an authoritarian system, but it is the political reality in China.

To understand why it works in its current form, with all the apparent inconsistencies and inefficiencies, we need to understand its history and development, which created expectations, standard practices and interests. Political and institutional inertia has made electricity reform extremely difficult. Meanwhile, China is concerned with its own standing; its firms desire to be part of the future so that they can survive and expand. They are involved in overseas expansion, in participating in international standard setting, and in developing the nirvana of a high-voltage interconnected electricity grid and other massive technological changes. China's electricity future will be determined in part by technology, by its ability to participate in world markets, but its own progress will be shaped by its local conditions, by local interests as they provide services to the world's largest market. This overseas ambition may in turn become a major driving force for electricity reforms towards a more market-based electricity system.

REFERENCES

Andrews-Speed, P. (2004), *Energy Policy and Regulation in the People's Republic of China*, The Hague: Kluwer Law International.

Andrews-Speed, P. (2009), 'Power sector reform', in *OECD Reviews of Regulatory Reform China: Defining the Boundary between the Market and the State*, Paris: OECD Publishing, pp. 229–66.

Andrews-Speed, P. (2012), *The Governance of Energy in China*, New York: Palgrave Macmillan.

Andrews-Speed, P. and S. Dow (2000), 'Reform of China's electric power industry', *Energy Policy*, **28** (5), 335–47.

Bacon, R. W. (1995), 'Privatization and reform in the global electricity supply industry', *Annual Review of Energy and the Environment*, **20**, 119–43.

Bacon, R.W. and J. E. Besant-Jones (2002), 'Global electricity power reform: privatization and liberalization of the electric power industry in developing countries', *Energy and Mining Board Discussion Paper No. 2*, June, World Bank.

Berrah, N., L. Ranjit and J. Zhao (2001), 'Fostering competition in China's power markets', *World Bank Discussion Paper No. 416*, March.

Besant-Jones, J. E. (2006), *Reforming Power Markets in Developing Countries*, Washington, DC: The World Bank.

Blackman, A and X. Wu (1999), 'Foreign direct investment in China's power sector', *Energy Policy*, **27** (12), 695–711.

Brandt, L., D. Ma and T. G. Rawski (2014), 'From divergence to convergence', *Journal of Economic Literature*, **52** (1), 45–123.

Brandt, L. and T. G. Rawski (eds) (2019), *Policy, Regulation, and Innovation in China's Electricity and Telecom Industries*, New York: Cambridge University Press.

Cai, Y. (2014), 'Managing groups in China', *Political Science Quarterly*, **129** (1), 107–31.

China Electricity Council (CEC) (2017), *Annual Report of Electricity Development Report* [中国电力行业年度发展报告], Beijing: CEC.

China Electricity Council (CEC) (2018), *Annual Report of Electricity Development Report* [中国电力行业年度发展报], Beijing: CEC.

China Electricity Yearbook [中国电力年] (1998, 1999, 2000, 2001), Beijing: China Electric Power Press.

Chow, D.C.K. (1997), 'An analysis of the political economy of China's enterprise conglomerates', *Law and Policy in International Business*, **28** (2), 383–433.

Chung, J. H. (2016), *Centrifugal Empire: Central–Local Relations in China*, New York: Columbia University Press.

Cull, R. and L. Xu (2003), 'Who gets credit?', *Journal of Development Economics*, **71** (2), 533–9.

Fan, P., R. Li and P. Han (2019), 'How to manage the difficulties in electricity reform' [增量配电改革难题如何破解], *China Energy News*, 21 January.

Feng, Y. (2017), 'Understanding Chinese electricity reform and marketization' [理解中国电力体制改革的市场化与制度背景], *Finance and Economics Think Tank*, **1** (5), accessed 13 July 2021 at http://www.escn.com.cn/news/show-443459.html.

Feng, Y. (2019), 'Constructing a competitive electricity market' [构建适应竞争性电力市场的增量配电体制科学推进增量配电改革], *Chinese Social Science Today*, accessed 13 July 2021 at http://shupeidian.bjx.com.cn/html/20190220/963946.shtml.

Gilbert, R. J. and E. Kahn (eds) (1996), *International Comparisons of Electricity Regulation*, New York: Cambridge University Press.

Hunt, S. (2002), *Making Competition Work in Electricity*, New York: John Wiley & Sons.

International Energy Agency (IEA) (2006), *China's Power Sector Reforms*, Paris: IEA.
International Energy Agency (IEA) (2010), *Energy Poverty*, Paris: IEA.
International Energy Agency (IEA) (2018), *Power Sector Reform in China*, Paris: IEA.
Joskow, P. L. (1998), 'Electricity sectors in transition', *The Electricity Journal*, **19** (2), 25–51.
Joskow, P. L. and R. Schmalensee (1983), *Markets for Power: An Analysis of Electric Utility Deregulation*, Cambridge, MA: MIT Press.
Kong, B. (2010), *China's International Petroleum Policy*, Santa Barbara, CA: ABC-CLIO.
Lange, J. E. and N. C. Howson (1997), 'Generating a regulatory framework', *China Business Review*, **23** (5), 22–8.
Li, P. (2005), *Li Peng's Diary: Electricity as Priority* [电力要先行] Beijing: China Electric Power Press.
Lieberthal, K. and M. Herberg (2006), 'China's search for energy security – implications for U.S. policy', *NBR Analysis*, **17** (1).
Lieberthal, K. G. and M. Oksenberg (1988), *Policy Making in China: Leaders, Structures, and Processes*, Princeton, NJ: Princeton University Press.
Lin, L. W. and C. J. Milhaupt (2013), 'We are the (national) champions', *Stanford Law Review*, **65** (4), 697–760.
Liu, J. (2013), *Manoeuvring an Ocean Liner: Review and Prospect of the 18 Years of Electricity Reform*, Beijing: Orient Publishing [in Chinese].
Liu, Z. (2014), *Ultra-High Voltage AC/DC Grids*, Waltham, MA: Elsevier/Academic Press.
Liu, Z. (2015), *Global Energy Interconnection*, Waltham, MA: Elsevier/Academic Press.
Ministry of Electric Power (MOEP) (1997), *Electricity Law of the People's Republic of China*, Beijing: China Electric Power Press.
Naughton, B. (2013), 'The narrow road to reform', *China Leadership Monitor*, Issue 42 (Fall).
Newbery, D. M. (1995), 'Power markets and market power', *The Energy Journal*, **16** (3), 39–66.
Newbery, D. M. (1999), *Privatization, Restructuring, and Regulation of Network Utilities*, Cambridge, MA: MIT Press.
Nolan, P. (2001a), *China and the Global Economy: National Champions, Industrial Policy and the Big Business Revolution*, New York: Palgrave Macmillan.
Nolan, P. (2001b), *China and the Global Business Revolution*, New York: Palgrave Macmillan.
Peng, W. and J. Pan (2006), 'Rural electrification in China: history and institution', *China & World Economy*, **14** (1), 71–84.
Pollitt, M. G. (1995), *Ownership and Performance in Electric Utilities*, Oxford: Oxford University Press.
Pollitt, M. G. and L. Dale (2018), 'Restructuring the Chinese electricity supply sector – how industrial electricity prices are determined in a liberalized power market: lessons from Great Britain', *EPRG Working Paper No. 1839*, Energy Policy Research Group, University of Cambridge, 13 July 2021 in Chinese at https://www.eprg.group.cam.ac.uk/wp-content/uploads/2018/11/1839-Text_ChineseV.pdf.
Pollitt, M. G., C. H. Yang and H. Chen (2017), 'Reforming the Chinese electricity supply sector', *EPRG Working Paper No. 1704*, Energy Policy Research Group, University of Cambridge, accessed in Chinese 13 July 2021 at http://www.eprg.group.cam.ac.uk/wp-content/uploads/2017/03/1704_-Chinese-Version.pdf.
Pollitt, M. G., C. H. Yang and H. Chen (2018), 'Restructuring the Chinese electricity supply sector', *EPRG Working Paper No. 1807*, Energy Policy Research Group, University of Cambridge, accessed in Chinese at https://www.eprg.group.cam.ac.uk/wp-content/uploads/2018/02/1807-Chinese-version.pdf.
Shambaugh, D. (2013), *China Goes Global: The Partial Power*, New York: Oxford University Press.
Shao, S., L. Zhengyong and N. Berrah et al. (1997), 'China: power sector regulation in a socialist market economy', *World Bank Discussion Paper No. 361*.
Shi, Y. (2018), 'Electricity reform: from planning to market' [电力改革：从'计划'到'市场'], *CEC Media*, 30 November, accessed 13 July 2021 at http://www.energynews.com.cn/show-55-16054-1.html.
Sinton, J. E. and D. G. Fridley (2000), 'What goes up: recent trends in China's energy consumption', *Energy Policy*, **28** (10), 671–87.
Smil, V. (1976), *China's Energy: Achievements, Problems, Prospects*, New York: Praeger Publishers.
Smil, V. (1988), *Energy in China's Modernization: Advances and Limitations*, New York: M.E. Sharpe.
SPCC (1999), *Market Economy and Electricity Planning and Investment* [市场经济与电力计划投资工作], Beijing: China Electric Power Press.
State Council (2002), *Plan for Electricity Structural Reform* [Document No. 5].
State Council (2015), *Opinions on Further Deepening the Reform of Power System* [关于进一步深化电力体制改革的若干意见] [Document No. 9].
Steinfeld, E. S. (1998), *Forging Reform in China: The Fate of State-owned Industry*, New York: Cambridge University Press.
Su, N. (2018), 'Waste in hydroelectricity' [300亿度四川水电面临"投产即遭弃"], *China Energy News*, 8 January.
Wang, X. (2014), 'SGCC: overseas adventure around the globe' [国家电网：全球布局出海扬帆], *China Energy News*, 4 August.

World Bank (1993), *Strategic Options for Power Reform in China*, ESMAP Report No. 156/93, Washington, DC: World Bank.

World Bank (1994), *China Power Sector Reform: Toward Competition and Improved Performance*, Report No. 12929-CHA, 15 September, Washington, DC: World Bank.

Xu, Y. (2002), *Powering China: Reforming the Electric Power Industry in China*, Aldershot, UK: Ashgate.

Xu, Y. (2004), *Electricity Reform in China, India and Russia: The World Bank Template and the Politics of Power*, Cheltenham, UK and Northampton, MA, USA: Edward Elgar Publishing.

Xu, Y. (2017), *Sinews of Power: The Politics of the State Grid Corporation of China*, Oxford: Oxford University Press.

Yan, X. J., X. Tan and Q. L. Zhao (2019), 'Gansu: how to reform its resources-based economy' [甘肃：能源资源型地区如何转型], *China Energy News*, 4 March.

Yeh, E. T. and J. I. Lewis (2004), 'State power and the logic of reform in China's electricity sector', *Pacific Affairs*, **77** (3), 437–65.

Yeung, G. (2009), 'How banks in China make lending decisions', *Journal of Contemporary China*, **18** (59), 285–302.

Yu, T. (2019), 'Ten questions on energy industry in 2019' [十问 2019 年能源行业], *Energy Review*, No. 2.

Zhang, Y. (2018), 'Dilemma and future of power distribution reform' [棋至中局 论增量配电的困境与未来], *Energy Review*, 26 November, accessed in Chinese 13 July 2021 at http://shupeidian.bjx.com.cn/html/20181126/944344-2.shtml.

Zhang, Y.-F. (2015), 'The regulatory framework and sustainable development of China's electricity sector', *The China Quarterly*, **222**, 475–98.

Zhang, Z.-X. (1998), *The Economics of Energy Policy in China: Implications for Global Climate Change*, Cheltenham, UK and Northampton, MA, USA: Edward Elgar Publishing.

Zhou, Y. and S. Lu (2017), *China's Renewables Curtailment and Coal Assets Risk Map*, Bloomberg New Energy Finance, October, 13 July 2021 at https://data.bloomberglp.com/bnef/sites/14/2017/10/Chinas-Renewable-Curtailment-and-Coal-Assets-Risk-Map-FINAL_2.pdf.

22. The evolution of electricity sectors in Africa: ongoing obstacles and emerging opportunities to reach universal targets
Vivien Foster, Anton Eberhard and Gabrielle Dyson

1. INTRODUCTION

Africa stands out from the rest of the world in its struggles to develop the power sector. Notably, in Sub-Saharan Africa, over half the population still lack electricity access (World Bank and Sustainable Energy for All 2019). In contrast, average electrification rates across low- and middle-income countries of South Asia, Latin America, the Caribbean, the Middle East and North Africa are over twice as high. Still, electricity demand outstrips supply in many African countries, which endure periodic power cuts and poor reliability (Farquharson, Jaramillo and Samaras 2018). Average population growth of 3 per cent year-on-year since 2000, combined with high economic growth, nurtures the rising demand but per capita consumption remains low (World Bank 2018a, 2018b). Average consumption in South Asia was 46 per cent higher than in Sub-Saharan Africa in 2014, even with a greater share of poor and remote populations enjoying electricity connections in Asia (Organisation for Economic Co-operation and Development and International Energy Agency [OECD/IEA] 2014). High levels of inequality continue to create an uneven distribution of the benefits of economic growth, keeping electricity connections out of reach for the majority of poor households.

Inadequate electricity supply is a 'wicked problem' in Africa (Rittel and Webber 1973). Causes vary from insufficient generating capacity and poor maintenance of existing generation plants, to underdeveloped transmission and distribution infrastructure, compounded by unreliable contracts for cross-border electricity trade and environmental changes impacting hydropower potential. Underlying these technical shortcomings, governance challenges – corruption, lack of rule of law, political instability, and lack of transparency and accountability – are rife, contributing to the contested political economies that surround the power sector. Chronic power supply crises have hobbled the economic development of African countries, extending socio-economic inequalities and grievances among populations disappointed by the outcomes of post-independence governments (Kojima and Trimble 2016).

Poor utility performance and lack of capacity form a core pillar of the access and supply deficiencies experienced in most African countries. Utilities are plagued with perennial financial deficits, unable to cover their costs through electricity sales (Trimble et al. 2016). Only two countries in Sub-Saharan Africa fully recover their cost of service through their revenues – the Seychelles and Uganda (Trimble et al., 2016). Most countries resign themselves to providing longstanding – and often inadequate – public subsidies to the power company to keep it afloat, entrenching the company's dependency on bailouts and exacerbating national dependency on foreign loans. At the same time, technical and non-technical losses remain high.

Most Sub-Saharan African countries share a number of objectives to solve the electricity supply challenge. These can be boiled down to:

- achieving universal energy access as a catalyst for economic development and well-being in society;
- improving the quality and affordability of electricity supply;
- meeting growing electricity demand and consumption in line with economic and population growth;
- ensuring least-cost, efficient power sector expansion and infrastructure maintenance to underpin quality of service for consumers;
- bringing utilities' technical and financial operations and governance up to standard, notably by reducing line losses and improving bill collections;
- reducing inefficient, costly public subsidies to build a viable, sustainable financial future for utilities;
- adopting innovative supply models and technologies that can offer services to remote, poor and underserved populations; and
- promoting regional cross-border trade to enable economies of scale.

A new global power sector reform model took root in developing countries in the 1990s (Foster et al. 2017, Urpelainen and Yang 2019). Development finance institutions (DFIs) encouraged developing countries to pursue reforms to the structure, regulation, competition and ownership of the power sector. These reforms targeted strategic sectors of the economy through separation of powers and functions, and introducing market-based incentives to attract private financing (African Development Bank [AfDB] and Associations of Power Utilities of Africa [APUA] 2019, Foster et al. 2017).[1] Many African countries accepted structural adjustment packages and reform recommendations, but none implemented power sector reforms as extensively as in other regions, such as Latin America and Eastern Europe. Recent analyses show that these changes have brought mixed results, sometimes reducing corruption in the sector, and often increasing investment, but utility performance remains disappointing (Imam, Llorca and Jamasb 2018). Major funders and stakeholders in the African power sector are re-examining the implementation of these reforms to understand their effects on governance and performance in the power sector.

Today, realizing sustainable reforms in the power sector creates a particular bind for African policy-makers, planners and operators, as the dynamics of the electricity supply industry are being upended. Customers are gaining ever-greater roles in controlling their engagement with the power system, with the help of new technologies and actors in the power sector, as explored elsewhere in this handbook.[2] The playing field is shifting for incumbent utilities and regulatory regimes. Changing climate patterns and natural resource availability add major external forces and uncertainties for power sector economics, policies and planning to reckon with (Cervigni et al. 2015).

The electricity sector has a central role to underpin and catalyse green growth strategies. African power sectors need to adopt creative approaches to respond to rapid global innovation in energy technologies and markets, by identifying what types of reforms and implementation strategies will be useful and necessary to unlock the desired transformation. Countries must define context-specific models for future reforms, ensuring local ownership to embrace solutions that will work to meet countries' needs. These localized approaches are critical to mitigate negative ideas or apprehension about reforms, which often centre around losing sovereignty or control. While this chapter presents selected energy data and projections for all of Africa, the focus of the analysis and discussion is on Sub-Saharan Africa, where the need for electrification and investment in power infrastructure at all levels is most severe. North African countries and South Africa represent outliers among African countries, with quasi-universal levels of electricity access through traditional grids.

This chapter explores the current state of affairs in electricity systems across the (sub) continent in Section 2, including through investment trends in generation, utility-scale renewable energy plants, procurement and planning frameworks, and the transmission subsector. Next, Section 3 considers African countries' progress and difficulties in achieving universal electricity access. Section 4 examines data on utility performance and the record of structural reforms on the continent. Section 5 offers a view of how technological innovations and economic trends are likely to interact with the tenuous power sectors typical of African countries.

2.   IS AFRICA ANY CLOSER TO MEETING ITS POWER NEEDS?

Supply shortages continue widespread in the face of growing demand and chronic mismanagement, even following decades of reforms to liberalize the sector and increase investment in generation capacity and networks (IEA 2019, Streatfeild 2018). As well as the lack of capital for expanding and maintaining infrastructure, the endemic deficits are symptoms of poor utility management and planning deficiencies. In addition, energy resources on the continent are unevenly distributed, and demand in many individual countries – though rising constantly – has previously been too low to capture economies of scale for new projects. Highly variable spatial distribution of production and demand heightens the need for regional power trade mechanisms.

Inexorable demand growth compounds these power supply challenges as countries expand electricity access, unlocking latent or as yet untapped demand among the 600 million people who today lack an electricity connection. An AfDB-funded study projects that across the continent, demand will grow by over 70 per cent in the decade to 2030, through a combination of increased economic activity (GDP growth) and the effects of unprecedented access expansion (Multiconsult 2018). East Africa leads the trend, with demand projected to grow by 10 per cent annually to 2030, more than doubling within the decade. The cost of addressing Africa's upcoming power supply needs is estimated to range from US$29 billion to US$39 billion annually until 2025, varying depending on objectives for decarbonizing the sector, as well as on progress and investment achieved to bolster regional trade.

Section 2.1 reviews the evolving investment trends in generation that are accelerating to meet growing demand. Section 2.2 considers the growing importance of variable renewable energy as preferred technologies for utility-scale grid investments, while the evolution of procurement and planning approaches is described in Section 2.3. The stagnating and underinvested transmission landscape is briefly discussed in Section 2.4.

2.1   New Capacity: Independent and Chinese Finance

The past decade has witnessed a surge in new capacity additions in response to these deficits. These investments are spurred by two pools of capital (Figure 22.1): private investment in independent power projects (IPPs) and Chinese-funded projects, the fastest-growing sources of investment in the region's power sector (Gratwick, Morella and Antmann 2017).

China will fund over 17 gigawatts (GW) of (primarily utility-scale) generation projects in Africa from 2010 to 2020, worth about US$36 billion (IEA 2016). In the previous decade, until 2010, Chinese funding accounted for about 4 GW and close to US$7 billion in power project investments on the continent (ibid.). These investments represent 30 per cent of capacity additions in Sub-Saharan Africa. Focused in areas of high economic growth and new markets, East and Southern Africa each receive about a third of the share of Chinese investments (by capacity volume). West Africa receives a further quarter of the share, while only 8 per cent is directed to Central Africa. Chinese funding is frequently linked to Chinese engineering, procurement and construction (EPC) contractors who control the largest share in new power sector development in Africa, far outpacing representatives of other countries (ibid.). Most greenfield hydropower plants are built by Chinese firms, typically financed through sovereign loans guaranteed by African governments. Chinese commercial loan and equity financing is also growing as commercial banks enter the market, with some Chinese projects already operating as IPPs.

Transmission and distribution sectors on the continent have also benefited from growing Chinese investment. In the decade to 2020, Chinese contractors are projected to build over 28 000 km of power grids, encompassing cross-border interconnectors,

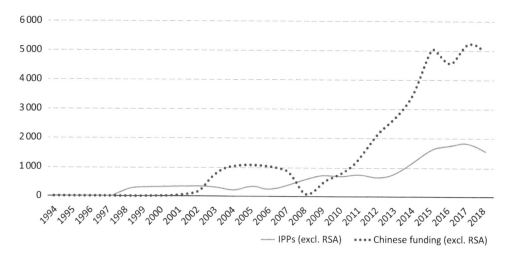

Source: Gratwick, Morella and Antmann (2017).

Figure 22.1   Private IPP and Chinese funding for power projects in Sub-Saharan Africa (US$ millions, five-year rolling average, excluding South Africa [RSA])

national transmission and local urban and rural distribution networks (ibid.). These investments are critical in extending and strengthening the backbone of African countries' power systems, which have fewer transmission lines per capita than any other world region. These are essential to creating pathways for regional power trade, contributing to stabilizing grids, and thereby encouraging least-cost generation expansion, as well as enabling a transition to variable renewables.

The private sector is fuelling a second fastest-growing source of funding for power projects in Africa. Many countries have introduced reforms to allow private participation from IPPs, thereby engaging with sources of capital that would otherwise be unavailable (Eberhard et al. 2016). At utility scale (greater than 5 megawatt [MW] generating capacity), 270 IPP arrangements are operating or under construction in Africa, funded largely by the private sector and DFIs through build-own-operate (BOO) arrangements (ibid.). These represent about US$51.7 billion in investments and 27.1 GW of installed generation capacity (Figure 22.2).

A 'single buyer' model, which allows the utility to procure from privately owned power generation, is the most prevalent structure in African countries, creating space for IPPs

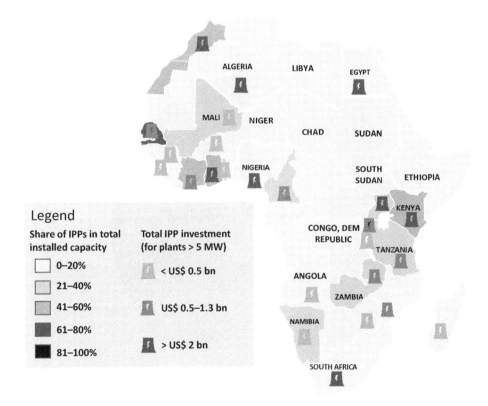

Source: Authors' elaboration based on AfDB and APUA (2019).

Figure 22.2   IPPs in Africa: share of total installed capacity (%) and investments per country (US$)

to enter the market. In addition to allowing private plants to sell to the utility, some countries have adopted third-party wheeling rules to allow independent generators to sell power via the transmission grid, for a fee, to third-party users (including independent distribution companies, or large industrial and commercial customers). But this model also introduces risks for future market development, including rigidity in power dispatching owing to inflexible take-or-pay arrangements with IPPs, and public exposure due to widespread sovereign guarantees for IPP investments.

2.2   Renewable Energy Generation at Utility Scale

Breakthroughs in prices of solar and wind energy in the past decade have spurred African countries to take advantage of these technologies. In response, privately financed IPP projects are accelerating renewable energy additions on the grid. Since 2008, IPP additions have overwhelmingly favoured renewable energy sources: 83 per cent of projects that have reached financial close were for renewable energy technologies. Notably, over 60 per cent of IPP capacity has invested in solar photovoltaics (PV) and wind, followed by 10 per cent for hydroelectric capacity. The converse therefore also holds: less than a fifth of IPP investments in Africa in the past decade were based on thermal or fossil fuel sources (Figure 22.3).

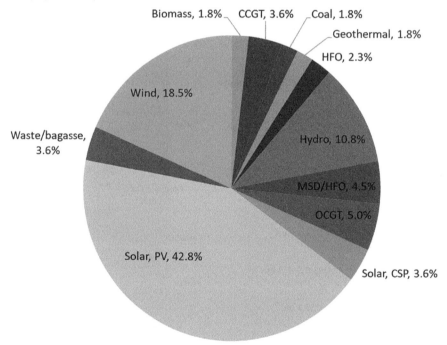

Note: CCGT = combined cycle gas turbines; HFO = heavy fuel oil; MSD/HFO = medium-speed diesel/heavy fuel oil; OCGT = open cycle gas turbine; CSP = concentrated solar power.

Sources: AfDB and APUA (2019).

Figure 22.3   IPP additions by capacity and technology type since 2008

Investing in renewable energy offers Africa a head start on the transition to green growth pathways and decarbonizing the energy sector, with comparatively fewer existing thermal assets to amortize. Building renewable generation capacity also strengthens countries' energy security by reducing reliance on fuel imports. But grid integration of variable renewable energy poses particular challenges in the African context, where small systems combined with poor maintenance and primitive supervisory control and data acquisition (SCADA) systems can reach breaking points with relatively little renewable investment. At the same time, small power systems are under pressure to grow quickly to meet future demand, opening up opportunities to invest in suitable flexible resources to complement the variability of solar and wind energy.

2.3 Procurement Processes and Planning Frameworks

Procurement processes continue to evolve in the continent. Despite the continued prevalence of unsolicited proposals and direct negotiations for new projects, countries are turning in growing numbers to competitive methods to ensure least-cost generation expansion. State-owned utilities or government off-takers in at least 30 countries have pursued competitive tenders or auctions to procure new power contracts (Table 22.1), with increasingly positive results (AfDB and APUA 2019, Kruger, Stritzke and Trotter 2019).

Power purchase agreements (PPAs) for new solar PV projects have recently been signed for as little as 2.9 US cents per kilowatt-hour (¢/kWh) in Egypt and 4.3 US¢/kWh in Senegal. The results of a solar PV auction in Zambia, announced in April 2019, set a new record for Sub-Saharan Africa: 3.99 US¢/kWh. These are impressive improvements on previous PPA prices achieved through feed-in tariffs, direct negotiations or unsolicited bids, where prices upwards of 20 to 30 US¢/kWh were the norm until 2016 (Kruger,

Table 22.1   Progress of competitive procurements for IPPs in African countries

Procurement Announced	Auction Winner(s) Announced; Financing in Progress	Auctioned Project(s) Reached Financial Close
Algeria	Burkina Faso	Cabo Verde
Benin	Chad	Egypt
Botswana	Côte d'Ivoire	Mali
Gambia	Ethiopia	Mauritius
Guinea-Bissau	Ghana	Morocco
Kenya	Malawi	Namibia
Madagascar		South Africa
Niger		Uganda
Nigeria		Zambia
Rwanda		
Senegal		
Seychelles		
Tanzania		
Togo		
Tunisia		

Source: Eberhard et al. (2016).

Eberhard and Swartz 2018). As well as the changing global economy of renewable energy, these examples reflect particular conditions of the tender, including the financial viability of the off-taker (which is often bolstered by a sovereign guarantee or escrow account); the country's track record of competitive tenders (successive rounds tend to attract significantly lower prices); the level of assistance offered to bidders (such as free land or pre-feasibility assessments); and the country's overall governance and investment environment (Eberhard and Gratwick 2011). The quality of governance in a country – taking into account levels of corruption, political stability, rule of law, regulatory environment and public accountability – is also a determining factor for the degree of private sector participation (PSP) and investment in the power sector (AfDB and APUA 2019).

Some countries adopt procurement requirements to mitigate the perceived risk of foreign influence and control via private sector investment in the power sector. For example, a threshold for local participation or ownership ('local content requirements') might be stipulated, typically in the context of procurement processes such as competitive auctions or feed-in-tariff regimes (OECD 2015). South Africa's flagship auction programme, REIPPP, incorporates several locally specific socio-economic factors and minimum requirements, which participating developers must comply with to out-perform competitors. In addition to the generation technology and price of power, proposals under the REIPPP are rated according to the local content of the proposed installation (defined in terms of the capital costs and costs of services for construction of the facility), estimated job creation under the proposed development, the share of local ownership of the facility and measures for local community development, among other factors (International Renewable Energy Agency [IRENA] and Clean Energy Ministerial [CEM] 2014).

Questions of planning and procurement frameworks have too often been an afterthought in efforts to reform and improve the power sector, dwarfed by other policy and regulatory concerns. Around the world, power system designers and technocrats have in many ways operated under an implicit assumption that creating wholesale power markets would obviate the need for detailed sector planning and integrated procurement frameworks for generation and transmission (Rudnick and Velasquez 2018). But in less-developed contexts, markets alone have not delivered adequate investment capacity, requiring additional measures to incentivize investments (ibid.). Even countries with wholesale power markets such as in Latin America have found it necessary to use supply auctions for long-term contracts based on indicative generation plans. In the context of small, less-developed power systems with tentative liberalization reforms and vertically integrated utilities, as in the vast majority of African countries, competitive wholesale power markets remain a distant and impractical dream. Power planning, as far as it exists, remains centralized, and procurement is conducted by state-owned utilities or the line ministry.

For states that seek to obtain external funding for new generation projects, sound planning and procurement frameworks tend to serve as prerequisites, directing investment prospectuses and guiding decision-making. Sector planning can only be effective when married with a procurement framework that launches timely, competitive, cost-effective and transparent processes. Countries lacking such a coherent framework end up suffering inadequate generation reserves and insufficient transmission capacities. However, the questions of planning and procurement – essential for building security of supply – were broadly neglected in the 1990s' paradigm for power sector reforms (Malgas and

Eberhard 2011). While most African countries have drawn up a generation and transmission master plan, implementing these plans is seldom mandatory. Too often, they gather dust on an energy ministry's shelf. In Tanzania, for instance, master plans are developed by the Ministry of Energy with inputs from sector experts and adopted as policy with appropriate solemnity, but subsequent decision-making neglects to follow the investment roadmap and projections outlined in the document. This leaves the country in tenuous supply situations with inadequate reserves (Godinho and Eberhard 2018).

2.4   Transmission Needs to Underpin Regional Energy Integration

Thanks to the increase in investment in generation projects in recent years, several countries expect, for the first time in decades, to face a supply surplus soon. In East Africa, a regional overcapacity of 2689 MW is anticipated in at least five countries by 2022, echoed by emerging surplus in other parts of the continent, such as Ghana (United States Agency for International Development [USAID] and Power Africa 2018). A resurgent interest in cross-border interconnection projects to enhance regional integration will help address this surplus and solve some countries' power deficits, supported by DFIs and overseas financing, including Chinese, as previously mentioned.

The transmission sub-sector in Africa has not benefited from the same influx of private investment as generation. Only a handful of Sub-Saharan countries have some form of private participation in transmission. This reflects a widely held view that the natural monopoly of transmission should remain in public ownership. Private participation in transmission can occur through long-term concession arrangements, *affermage* or lease, private management contracts, or full privatization programmes. Nigeria – with a separate transmission company following the most complete unbundling experience on the continent – has added 8000 km of transmission lines since 2010 (AfDB and APUA 2019). Other countries, notably Uganda, Mali and Cameroon, have put in place private concessions, which among other things serve to draw capital funding into the transmission network. Ghanaian utility ECG also recently entered a concession agreement. More common among francophone countries (including Gabon and Côte d'Ivoire) is introducing PSP in transmission through long-term *affermage* contracts with a vertically integrated utility, where investors agree to operate and maintain the transmission lines, but are not obliged to finance transmission assets (Africa Intelligence 2019). Zambia offers the sole example of having privately owned transmission, indefinitely, through the Copperbelt Energy Corporation (an electricity company originally created to serve the mining industry in the north of the country).

Sub-Saharan Africa still has a combined transmission network smaller than that of the country of Brazil (Global Transmission Report 2018).[3] Investment in transmission is essential to connect low-cost, large-scale sources of electricity generation with major load-bearing distribution centres in cities and towns. But per capita, Africa has fewer kilometres of transmission lines than any other region – despite having much larger land mass and dispersed population, which would logically imply a need for more transmission capacity than otherwise (World Bank Group 2017). Transmission investments are still mostly financed either directly from utility revenues or from the government budget, which poses a major constraint on expanding the network, or from concessionary finance from DFIs or even grants from donor countries.

Ongoing efforts for regional electricity interconnections remain an important tool for supporting optimal system performance on the continent, even as distributed energy resources and decentralized grids begin to adopt a leading role in the power system (Programme for Infrastructure Development in Africa [PIDA] 2010). Power pools and other cross-border trading mechanisms offer parties opportunities to optimize their power costs, protect against fuel price shocks and be relieved in case of generation short-fall (Olmos and Pérez-Arriaga 2013; Oseni and Pollitt 2014). African countries with small power systems stand to gain the most from additional transmission interconnections to create economies of scale and enhance their energy security. And for larger systems, the opportunities for electricity trade are especially interesting in the context of geographically varied energy resources. While some countries such as Nigeria and Ghana benefit from ample gas reserves, others have built or planned large hydropower reservoirs, or need to draw on flexible resources to balance downtime from variable renewable plants.

To underpin optimal, least-cost power system expansion and universal electricity access across Africa by 2030, additional transmission interconnectors are needed, but these would relatively rapidly pay for themselves by allowing countries to tap into lower-cost sources of energy across borders. An early study put the incremental investments of regional cross-border interconnection across Africa at US$5 billion generating annual savings of US$2.7 billion, which represents an economic rate of return of around 27 per cent (Eberhard et al. 2011). More recent work finds that needed interconnections would represent investment of US$8.9 billion, leading to annual cost savings of US$3.4 billion (Multiconsult 2018). Such incremental costs are modest relative to the overall grid investment needs for the same period estimated at US$500 billion. The savings represent the benefits expected from both displacing costly liquid fuels as well as creating revenue for power plants that would otherwise be idle at certain times of day. These benefits are disproportionately concentrated in small and isolated systems that are able to substitute inefficient oil-fired domestic power generation with more cost-effective electricity imports. In addition, regional integration provides larger balancing areas that favour the integration of variable renewable energy. For instance, IRENA estimates that enhancing regional integration of investments and operations in Southern and Western Africa would allow renewable penetration to reach 46 per cent and 52 per cent by 2030, respectively (Rose et al. 2019).

All African regions have set up regional power pool institutions since the Southern African Power Pool (SAPP) was created in 1995, offering avenues for regional-level planning and cross-national policy-making in power. The West African and East African Power Pools (WAPP and EAPP, respectively) are in advanced stages of implementation, while the North African equivalent – Comité Maghrébin de l'Electricité (COMELEC) – and Central African Power Pool are still in early stages of planning.[4] SAPP has been operating for over 25 years, with sufficient experience to inform its design of regional trading platforms and market rules. Even so, trade and regulatory reforms to allow adopting common rules and enforcement mechanisms remain insufficient, especially in neighbouring power pools. Beyond core planning and technical needs such as market trading mechanisms, infrastructure and regulations, chronic political uncertainty and unstable relationships among African countries are not conducive to fomenting the trust needed to sustain cross-border markets (AfDB and APUA 2019). Security of payments remains a critical challenge to upholding cross-border systems. Parties to power pools must establish a solid foundation of trust to allow national and regional institutions to coordinate in creating common policies, regulations and enforcement mechanisms. Questions of national sovereignty, energy security and irregular payments can complicate and unravel the trust-based relationships underlying power trade, leaving countries wary of relying on a foreign or third party to provide their basic energy security.

The share of electricity traded in Africa's more developed power pools is already significant by global standards. As of 2017/18 the WAPP was trading somewhat under 10 per cent of regional electricity consumption, while the SAPP saw a surge in trading activity from 10 per cent up to 24 per cent of regional electricity consumption (SAPP 2019). Nevertheless, volumes of cross-border power trade still fall short of the levels that would be desirable according to economic analysis, and lag behind the targets set by the power pools themselves.

Despite such challenges, several examples highlight successful multinational or bilateral cooperation efforts to plan cost-effective, cross-border generation and transmission on the continent, including initiatives like the Manantali Dam managed by the tripartite Mali-Mauritania-Senegal Société de gestion de l'énergie de Manantali. Also in West Africa, Togo and Benin have shared a power generation and transmission company, the Communauté électrique du Bénin (CEB), for half a century. The CEB was recently put under temporary administration with a schedule of payment for its debts to Nigerian, Ghanaian and Ivoirian suppliers, due to high arrears (Energies Media with Xinhua 2018). The company is now being restructured to act as transmission system operator for the two countries' shared transmission grid, and to run the system's incumbent hydro and gas facilities (CEB 2019).

Power pools suffer from funding deficits leading to insufficient transmission investment and maintenance to support the desired capacity of trade. Regional generation capacity shortfalls, market design flaws and weak regulatory frameworks exacerbate these challenges. While the installed capacity from private IPP generation projects in Sub-Saharan Africa is doubling in capacity every five years since the early 1990s, investment in transmission and distribution infrastructure lagged significantly in the same period (Castellano et al. 2015). Outright privatization is not a clear solution for enhancing investment and maintenance of transmission assets in the context of small power systems (World Bank Group 2017). DFIs are especially active in funding transmission interconnections, and many of these are implemented by Chinese contractors (IEA 2016). Active projects include several in East Africa (Ethiopia–Kenya, Djibouti–Ethiopia, Kenya–Tanzania, Tanzania–Zambia); Southern Africa (Zambia–Malawi); and West Africa (Togo–Benin, CLSG, NorthCore, OMVG and OMVS) (Olingo 2018a, 2018b).[5] In fact, the full regional grid for the 14 countries of the WAPP is expected to be completed by the early 2020s. Further projects have been identified across the continent, including four major transmission corridor projects that would serve to transport low-cost hydropower energy from large-scale projects to buyers across the continent: spanning West, Central and North Africa, with a North–South bridge to connect to the SAPP (PIDA 2010).

Despite promising developments – such as increasing attention towards power sector regulation and management, as well as growing investment in generation capacity, renewable energy investment and regional interconnections – Africa still faces a monumental challenge of providing 'sustainable energy for all'. The following section presents some of the dynamics and actors at play in the field of electrification, as well as the various approaches that states are adopting to tackle the problem.

3.   HAS AFRICA REACHED A TURNING POINT ON THE PATH TO UNIVERSAL ACCESS?

With an access rate of 44 per cent in 2017, Sub-Saharan Africa remains the region with the largest electrification deficit globally: some 573 million people live without electricity (Figure 22.4) (IEA, IRENA and UN et al. 2018). In fact, Sub-Saharan Africa is home to 15 of the 20 countries worldwide with the largest unelectrified populations, including Democratic Republic of Congo, Ethiopia and Nigeria, each with unserved populations of 50–100 million. Furthermore, Sub-Saharan Africa contains the world's 20 least electrified countries, with access rates ranging from 10 to 40 per cent. For many years, Sub-Saharan Africa's efforts on electrification struggled to keep pace with demographic growth. However, since 2015, the region has significantly accelerated its rate of electrification and has managed to outpace population expansion. Nevertheless, Sub-Saharan Africa's absolute unelectrified population is projected to remain at around 580 million by the year 2030, which is similar to today's level, albeit in the context of a much higher regional population. If so, Sub-Saharan Africa would account for 95 per cent of the unelectrified population globally in 2030 (IEA 2018).

Africa's low rate of electrification reflects challenges both on the supply side and the demand side. Supply-side barriers include low urbanization rates and overall population density combined with rapid demographic growth, which increase the investment cost associated with service provision, even as the sector institutions suffer from weak

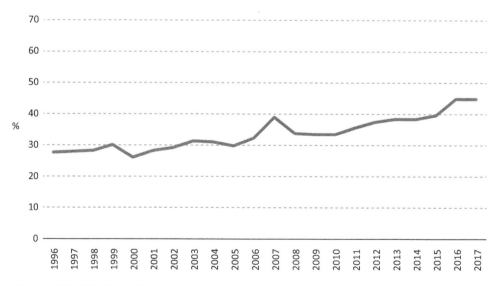

Sources: World Bank and Sustainable Energy for All (2019).

Figure 22.4   Electricity access in Sub-Saharan Africa, %

financial performance. Demand-side barriers are more significant than has previously been appreciated (Blimpo and Cosgrove-Davies 2019). Across Africa, only around 60 per cent of the population that live under an electricity grid actually choose to make a connection. This rate of service uptake varies hugely from as low as 20 per cent in low-income environments, such as Malawi, to around 90 per cent in upper middle-income environments, such as South Africa. Simulations conducted for ten African countries suggest that national electrification rates could be doubled, if only all households living close to the grid were able to make a connection. Factors behind the low uptake of electricity service include high connection charges, unreliable quality of service and absence of complementary economic factors, such as finance, infrastructure and appliances.

While electrification rates are certainly low, even those with grid connections suffer significantly from poor reliability and quality of service. Many African countries are affected by regular and extensive outages, while voltage surges on the grid can damage or destroy electric appliances. A new framework aims to measure electricity access in a more meaningful way by integrating multiple dimensions of the service experience into a single multi-tier metric ranging from Tier 0 (no access) to Tier 5 (continuous high-quality supply) (Bhatia and Angelou 2015). Recent survey-based research shows that most households with electricity connections in countries such as Ethiopia and Rwanda experience access only at Tier 3 level. Households with Tier 3 access must live with one or more serious supply issues, such as load limits of 200 watts, voltage surges, more than two interruptions daily, or service hours constrained to eight hours during the day or three hours in the evening (Koo et al. 2018, Padam et al. 2018).

The United Nation's Sustainable Development Goal 7.1 – which calls for universal access to affordable, reliable, modern and sustainable energy by 2030 – has galvanized national governments as well as the global community in support of intensified electrification efforts. New initiatives have emerged such as the United Nation's Sustainable Energy for All and the AfDB's New Deal on Energy for Africa. As of 2018, 24 African countries had adopted national electrification targets and produced electrification masterplans, often applying a spatial methodology that delimits the economic frontier between grid and off-grid electrification. The experience of countries that have electrified successfully worldwide underscores the importance of strong parallel programmes covering both grid and off-grid electrification. Chapter 20 discusses one such complementary approach through the synergistic proposal of an 'integrated distribution framework'.

Progress on grid electrification calls for a strong utility with the capacity to implement grid extension projects, but also with the customer focus needed to address the significant demand-side barriers to service uptake. Electrification poses commercial and financial challenges, since given low tariffs and relatively modest consumption, new connections may actually be loss-making from the utility's perspective. Hence, the importance of driving electrification through clearly articulated policy targets and supportive finance. The World Bank's Regulatory Indicators for Sustainable Energy (RISE) found that half of African countries met less than half the enabling conditions for grid electrification, in particular due to the lack of funding support for electrification or for consumer connections. Figure 22.5a and b shows the RISE scores for electricity access in 2010 and 2017, respectively, and Figure 22.6 presents countries' RISE scores for regulatory frameworks to enable electricity access – none scoring above 70 on a 100-point scale (ESMAP 2018).[6] In some countries, the utility's efforts are complemented by rural electrification agencies

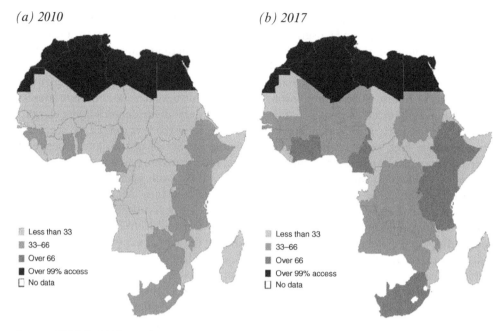

Source: ESMAP (2018).

Figure 22.5   RISE electricity access scores for (a) 2010 and (b) 2017, Africa

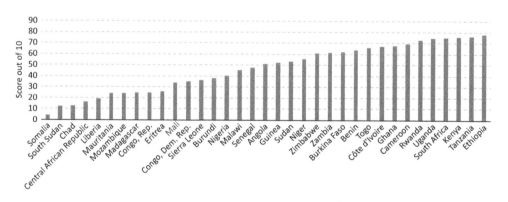

Source: ESMAP (2020).

Figure 22.6   Regulatory frameworks for access, Sub-Saharan Africa, 2017

that may act as a conduit for donor finance and typically have responsibility for construct-ing grid extension projects that are subsequently transferred to the utility for operations. Such agencies have played an important role in countries such as Tanzania and Senegal but have not been so central in other successful cases such as Ghana and Kenya.

Affordability represents a key barrier to grid electrification, despite widespread subsidies.[7] Even as household incomes are among the lowest in the world, the cost of

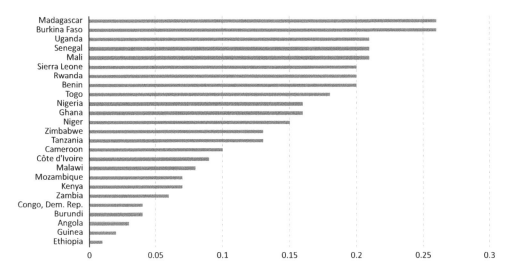

Source: Banerjee et al. (2017).

Figure 22.7   Average residential tariffs, 2015 (US$/kWh)

power paradoxically remains higher than elsewhere, and still does not allow utilities to operate sustainably (Kojima and Trimble 2016). Despite prevalent cross-subsidies from commercial and industrial customers, residential tariffs in 12 countries exceed US$0.15 per kWh (Figure 22.7), yet are insufficient to cover utility operating and capital costs. As a result, affordability is typically an issue for countries with GDP per capita of under US$1000 per year due to average residential monthly bills in the range of US$5–15 (Figure 22.8). Moreover, the prevalent increasing block tariff structures counter-productively penalizes poor users that share electricity connections, by increasing the volume of power consumed per connection, and thereby the cost per unit (Kojima et al. 2016). Of even greater concern, however, are connection charges that are often prohibitively high for residential customers: half of the African countries for which data was collected by ESMAP 2018 have connection charges over US$100.[8]

The rapid decline in the cost of solar energy in recent years offers considerable promise for progress on off-grid electrification, particularly in isolated rural areas that have proved difficult to reach through the grid. Recent studies show that mini-grids and individual solar systems have appeared in every country surveyed (AfDB and APUA 2019). Off-grid systems in nine African countries now offer such services to over 1 per cent of households (IRENA 2018). The East Africa region has been relatively rapid in promoting the rollout of solar energy. Solar electrification (of at least Tier 1 or above) already reaches 3 per cent of the population in Ethiopia, Kenya and Tanzania and as much as 6 per cent in Rwanda; and these shares approximately double if lower capacity solar lighting also known as solar lanterns (equivalent to Tier 0) is also considered. Considering the rural population alone, solar energy accounts for two-thirds of rural access in Ethiopia and Rwanda and one-third in Kenya. These developments reflect a relatively well-developed enabling environment for off-grid electrification in East Africa. However, across Africa, barely half of the enabling policies are in place. Nevertheless, the 2017 score

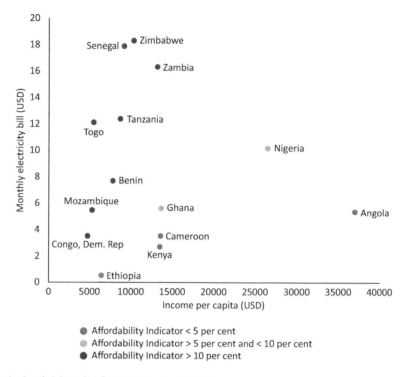

Source: Authors' elaboration from Kojima et al. (2016).

Figure 22.8   *Affordability of electricity: income per capita vs monthly electricity bill*

has doubled since 2010, indicating growing attention by governments in the region to the off-grid policy space (ESMAP 2018). In particular, a significant percentage of countries have adopted duty exemptions for solar home systems (SHS) and created regulatory frameworks for quality certification of solar panels.

In addition to SHS, mini-grids have also become increasingly cost-competitive (IRENA 2018). These localized electricity networks – increasingly harnessing small modular renewable generation technologies – connect several customers in a community or village, often using locally available renewable resources such as solar PV, biomass or small hydropower plants (Alstone, Gershenson and Kammen 2015). While small, localized networks have higher unit capital costs, they offer the opportunity to provide high-quality electricity to communities that would otherwise have to wait years to receive a connection to the main grid. In contrast to individual solutions such as SHS, even relatively small mini-grids (under 30 kW) can offer power not only for basic household uses but also for productive uses such as small commercial and industrial applications, supporting local development through economic activity as well as other essential needs (Lee and Callaway 2018). They can develop and operate on a community-owned, privately owned, or publicly owned basis, depending on local policies, regulatory settings and available financing models.

Tanzania has emerged as a regional leader in mini-grid development. Since 2005, the Rural Energy Agency (REA) developed policies and projects to encourage small power producers (SPPs) to invest and provide electricity services to rural communities, targeting areas where extending the national grid would be costly and slow (Odarno et al. 2017). Since the adoption of its innovative mini-grid policy and regulatory framework in 2008, the number of mini-grids in the country has doubled and the rural electricity access rate has increased eightfold. Over 110 mini-grid systems – owned by private business, local communities, the national utility (TANESCO) or non-profit organizations – now operate and sell electricity to rural customers, mostly operating with renewable technologies, including biomass, solar PV, small hydro and hybrid systems (renewable sources with back-up diesel generators). The national regulator, EWURA, adopted specific light-handed regulatory requirements for mini-grids, exempting developers from licensing requirements as well as tariff reviews for projects under 100 kW capacity. This encouraged independent operators to participate and invest in what is otherwise a relatively new, unproven business model. REA also offered special performance grants for mini-grid developers (through a donor-supported facility).

Finally, while many African countries are making slow progress, a handful of countries have recently accelerated their pace of electrification, driving the overall improvement at the continental level and demonstrating what can be possible (Figure 22.9). These include Kenya, Mali, Rwanda, South Sudan, Sudan, Tanzania and Zambia, which have all been electrifying well above two percentage points of their population each year since 2010.

Of these, Kenya has been by far the most impressive electrifying more than six percentage points of the population each year, more than tripling the access rate in less than a decade from 22 per cent in 2010 to 75 per cent in 2018. This is the fastest pace of progress

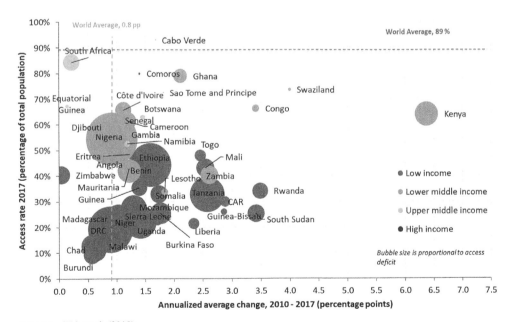

Source: IEA et al. (2018).

Figure 22.9 *Sub-Saharan Africa: change in access rate vs current access*

observed anywhere in the developing world over this time frame. Kenya's electrification programme worked in parallel on both grid and off-grid electrification, and was guided by ambitious and high-profile government electrification targets. The rapid expansion of grid electrification was driven primarily by the national distribution utility, KPLC, leveraging strong technical capacity and substantial public funding from both national government and international donors. Nevertheless, the utility's finances suffered as a result of the rapid scale-up of investment. The government's strategy was based on grid densification, promoting uptake of electricity by consumers already living close to the grid, with a particular focus on peri-urban areas. In addition, Kenya has offered a strong enabling environment for private-sector-led off-grid electrification based on SHS, leveraging its well-developed mobile money market.

While it is a widely held view that electrification leads to welfare gains, in practice, it is not easy to quantify the positive impact of electrification. Benefits from electrification can be both direct and indirect. Direct benefits include the immediate monetary savings from replacing sources of lighting like kerosene and battery-powered torches (which are much more expensive on a per unit basis) with electricity. Indirect benefits include higher productivity of household-based micro-enterprises due to longer work hours or the ability to use electrical appliances leading to increased income generation (Vernet et al. 2019). There can also be non-monetary indirect benefits, such as longer homework hours for students leading to improved educational outcomes (Khandker, Barnes and Samad, 2013, Khandker et al. 2009).

A multitude of studies have shown overall important positive impacts of electrification, albeit of varying magnitude. Growing evidence shows that other factors, such as access to markets, access to other infrastructure, access to finance, and reliability of service, influence electrification impacts. Furthermore, electrification is a long-term process. Impact evaluation studies from countries that have now achieved universal access (such as Vietnam) show that not all households connect at the same time. From the time the community gets electricity, it may take years before all houses receive a connection. Households' electricity consumption grows gradually until a plateau, along with any economic benefit they might perceive from electricity access (in the case of Vietnam, consumption levels out in about nine years from the electrification year; see Khandker et al. 2009). Long-term studies are essential to capture all the benefits of electrification. These confirm that electrification has proven highly cost effective in contexts such as Vietnam, where the benefits accrued to participants exceed the costs of electrification (US$500 per connection) by over 400 per cent. In Bangladesh, benefits exceed cost by more than 150 per cent (Khandker, Barnes and Samad 2012). On the other hand, studies examining more immediate impacts of electricity on poverty sometimes reveal more modest results. A recent randomized control trial over three years in Kenya found that mass rural household electrification does not improve social welfare in Kenya, but attributes this partly to relatively high costs due to deficiencies in the operating efficiency of sector institutions (Lee, Miguel and Wolfram 2020).

The struggles of electrification programmes and policies illustrates the pivotal role played by utilities in Africa's power sector. The following section provides further detail on the state of Africa's utilities and the impact of diverse strategies to turn around sector performance.

4. WHERE DOES AFRICA STAND ON THE LINGERING CHALLENGES OF UTILITY PERFORMANCE AND STRUCTURAL REFORM?

Post-independence African governments have depended heavily on external donor funding for development. In the 1990s, overseas development assistance often came in the form of structural adjustment packages (Gore et al. 2019). Since then, countries across the continent have faced a suite of power sector reform recommendations based on the Washington consensus aimed at:

- establishing independent regulation and committing to principles of cost-reflective electricity tariffs (to protect the financial sustainability of utilities);
- restructuring the national monopoly power companies through vertical and horizontal unbundling of generation, transmission and distribution services;
- commercializing sector practices and corporatizing utility management, with a view to transitioning towards PSP in power generation and distribution;
- opening up the sector to competition, through the creation of an independent system and market operator (ISO) and the eventual creation of a wholesale power market (AfDB and APUA 2019).

As has been noted (Figure 22.10), to date, no country in Africa has fully adopted the 1990s' consensus model for power sector reforms (Foster et al. 2017). In fact, the median African country adopted only 30 per cent of the 1990s' reform model, only nine African countries implemented more than 50 per cent, and only two countries (Nigeria and Uganda) followed around 80 per cent of the model prescriptions. By far the most popular reform measure was the creation of a regulatory agency, which has been done in 77 per cent of African countries (Figure 22.11). Over 60 per cent of countries in the continent have introduced the private sector into power generation through IPPs, but only 35 per cent have allowed PSP in power distribution.[9] A minority of countries have undertaken vertical unbundling of the national state-owned utility; while horizontal full unbundling has taken place only in Nigeria. Finally, not a single country on the African continent has implemented a wholesale power market, even if third-party access to the grid is permitted in some cases (Kapika and Eberhard 2013).

Establishing an independent regulator is typically one of the first steps taken in power sector reforms in Africa (Rodríguez Pardina and Schiro 2018). Over two-thirds of countries have established a regulatory agency separate from the government's energy ministry, and momentum continues with four countries (Botswana, Liberia, Morocco and Mozambique) creating such agencies since 2017 (Kapika and Eberhard 2013). Only a handful of (small) power sectors still lack a regulator, notably Sierra Leone and Equatorial Guinea. Indeed, in many African countries, the creation of a regulator may be the only reform that is ever adopted. The vast majority of African regulators oversee state-owned utilities (as opposed to the private utilities originally envisaged by the 1990s reform model). This detail is important as many of the tools of utility regulation are designed to harness the profit motive of privatized utilities through the introduction of incentive schemes.

Objective evaluations of regulatory performance suggest that Africa's regulatory agencies fall significantly short of the theoretical ideal. The AfDB published an Electricity

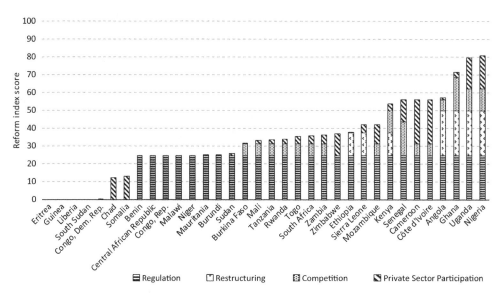

Note: The Global Power Sector Reform Index, created for the Rethinking Power Sector Reform project, gives each country a score on an interval of 0 to 100 on each dimension of power sector reform: restructuring, regulation, PSP and competition.

Source: Foster et al. (2017).

Figure 22.10   Power sector reforms in Africa, 2015

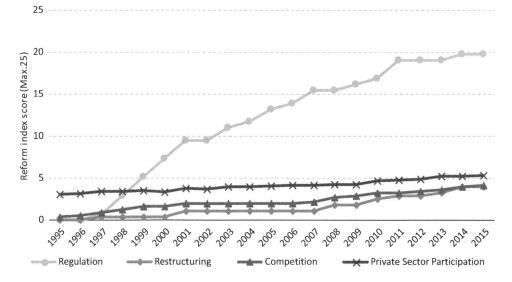

Source: Foster et al. (2017).

Figure 22.11   Evolution of components of power sector reforms in Africa, 1995–2015

Regulatory Index for 15 countries in 2018, covering: (1) regulatory governance; (2) regulatory substance; and (3) regulatory outcomes (AfDB 2018). Most countries assessed received a moderate ('well developed') score, while only two (Uganda and Namibia) revealed a high level of regulatory quality. Results show that independence from government and other political or vested interests is not a reality for most regulators in Africa, neither in the sense of financial matters (the provenance of regulatory funding) nor for operations and decision-making (the appointment process for regulatory commissioners and rules preventing commissioners working for utilities following their term). Regulators commonly derive their funding from levies on regulated entities, sometimes also including licensing fees, though a large portion still rely on the government budget (in whole or in part) to fund their regulatory activities; in addition, many regulators rely on government approval for the regulatory budget, further entangling government and regulatory interests. Only two of the electricity regulators surveyed have best practice rules prohibiting financial ties to ensure the independence of regulatory commissioners from the regulated utilities.

In addition, the World Bank has conducted an in-depth evaluation of regulatory performance in four African countries (Kenya, Senegal, Tanzania and Uganda) (Foster and Rana 2019). Again, the evaluation focuses on the quality of regulatory governance (comprising accountability and autonomy) and regulatory substance (encompassing tariff-setting, quality of service and market entry). For all aspects of regulation, the study contrasts the countries' performance *de jure* (in terms of the regulatory framework on paper) and *de facto* (what actually happens in practice) and finds a major divergence between the two. This divergence is particularly marked when it comes to the regulator's decision-making power over tariffs and to the practice of quality-of-service regulation. Of the four countries considered, Uganda's regulatory framework performs relatively well, but nonetheless remains only about halfway towards international best practice.

One of the central motivations for establishing a regulatory agency is to provide an independent and objective basis for determining tariffs that better align with the cost-of-service provision. However, despite the proliferation of regulatory agencies in Africa, lack of regulatory independence hampers much progress towards setting cost-reflective tariffs. According to the AfDB's Electricity Regulatory Index, fewer than 10 per cent of utilities surveyed have tariffs that are cost reflective for the residential sector, and only 20 per cent for the non-residential sector. A 2016 World Bank study reveals the median level of under-pricing of electricity was US\$0.04/kWh in Sub-Saharan Africa, compared to the median tariff of US\$0.15/kWh (Trimble et al. 2016). Only 32 per cent of the countries applied residential tariffs high enough to cover operating costs, while barely 5 per cent covered full capital costs. This under-pricing of electricity services is one of the main contributors to the sizeable quasi-fiscal deficit associated with Africa's power utilities, which takes a median value of just over 1 per cent of GDP (Figure 22.12) (Kojima and Trimble 2016). The remainder is attributable to system losses and under-collection of revenues, which remain a major issue in some countries, and make cost recovery even harder to achieve.

When it comes to sector restructuring, only ten African countries are known to have partially or completely unbundled the electricity sector, typically by separating the monopoly utility into distinct generation, transmission and distribution companies (sometimes only separating generation or distribution from the other segments). The

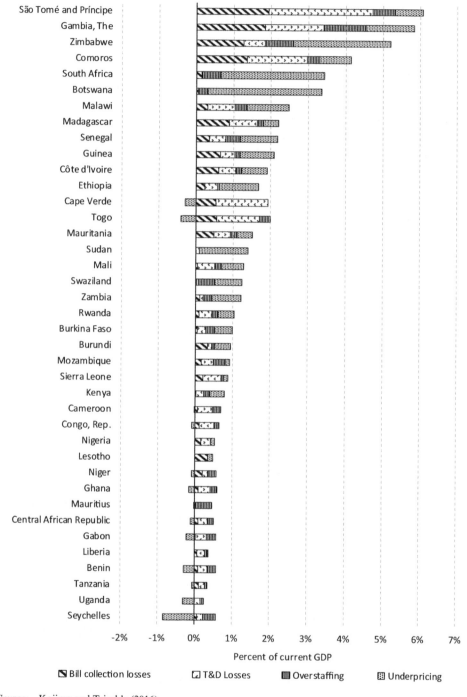

Figure 22.12   Quasi-fiscal deficits in Sub-Saharan Africa

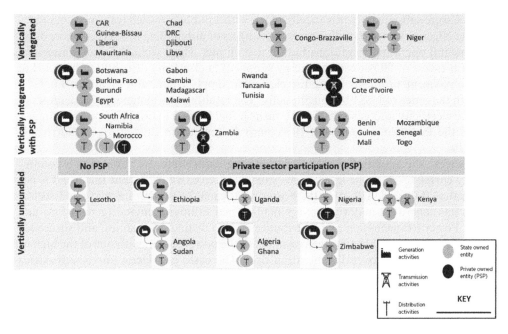

Source: AfDB and APUA (2019).

Figure 22.13 Structure of electricity sectors and private participation in 43 African countries

remaining power systems have maintained integrated utility companies with various forms of additional state-owned and private participation in the sector, making the single buyer model by far the most prevalent structural model across the African continent. Figure 22.13 shows the variety of sector structures and modes of private participation (through majority ownership or concession) in 43 countries on the continent (AfDB and APUA 2019).

Many of Africa's national power systems are too small for full unbundling to be practicable (Besant-Jones 2006). As many as 32 countries have an installed capacity of under 1 GW.[10] Even among the five largest national power systems on the continent (in the 5–50 GW range), unbundling is comparatively rare. In Egypt and Morocco, for instance, generation, transmission and distribution are separated for operational purposes, but the companies remain under common state ownership through a holding company structure. In South Africa, the continent's largest power utility, Eskom, has long operated as a single vertically integrated national utility (albeit with significant municipal participation in the distribution segment). However, the possibility of vertical unbundling is now being considered in South Africa,[11] with a view to creating an independent grid company and transmission system operator, or independent system operator, so as to remove any conflict of interest between Eskom's generation and single buyer roles (Eberhard and Godinho 2018).

The only fully unbundled power sector in Africa is Nigeria, where the former national utility was restructured in 2005 to create six generation and 11 distribution companies (all of which were subsequently privatized), along with a publicly owned transmission operator. The Nigerian experience illustrates the dangers of unbundling in a sector where other fundamental operating conditions have not been met. Huge technical and commercial losses (in excess of 50 per cent of energy supplied) in electricity distribution have led to chronic payment problems along the electricity supply chain, and created a financial deficit in the order of US$1 billion annually. The resulting unwillingness of generators to produce electricity and gas suppliers to furnish fuel has led to crippling power outages, despite the fact that around half the country's generation capacity is paradoxically lying idle.

In general, the extent of liberalization and regulatory reforms pursued in a country broadly correlates with the level of investments received via IPPs, but this trend is not universal (AfDB and APUA 2019, Foster and Rana 2019). With a mid-sized sector, Kenya has separated majority government-owned utilities KenGen (generation) and Kenya Power (transmission and distribution)[12] into distinct companies, and succeeded in attracting considerable private investment in the power sector, with one of the highest shares of IPPs in the overall generation fleet. The cases of Algeria and South Africa reveal additional conditions that stimulate private investments, even when central aspects of the power sector have not been subject to reforms and retain traditional operational structures. Effective and accountable generation planning in those countries has proven indispensable to show the country has laid the groundwork to anticipate generation needs for a defined period (Eberhard et al. 2016). Boosting investor confidence and mitigating risks are also critical. Ensuring 'bankable' contracts with a financially viable utility off-taker, offering risk guarantees to support PPAs, fostering stable and predictable political environments and designing clear, efficient tender processes all support these goals.

Most of Africa's national power utilities are state-owned (AfDB and APUA 2019). Weak corporate governance – particularly with regard to human resource practices and measures to promote financial discipline – goes some way towards explaining the poor performance of African power utilities (Foster and Rana 2019). Many utilities still perform significantly below international benchmark levels in terms of system losses and revenue collection (Figure 22.14). Weighted average losses for Sub-Saharan African countries are as high as 23 per cent (excluding South Africa, which has an outsized capacity and good technical performance compared to the rest of the continent). A well-performing utility is considered to have at most 10 per cent of system losses (ibid.). Bill collection losses – measuring electricity that is billed but not paid for – range from insignificantly small in nine countries to over a quarter of billable revenue in six countries. Meanwhile, quality of service remains highly unsatisfactory, giving little reason for customers to accept paying higher tariffs (Figure 22.15).

While IPPs are quite prevalent (as noted above), relatively few African countries have explored PSP in the distribution segment (Bacon 2018). This is in part due to the absence of suitable enabling conditions, such as cost recovery pricing, good operational information systems and a predictable regulatory framework. It also reflects significant political opposition to PSP, whether from labour unions anticipating job losses, customers fearing tariff hikes, or political parties unwilling to forgo an important channel of patronage.

In view of these considerations, around a dozen African countries have experimented with management contracts, which are the most limited form of PSP, entailing delegation

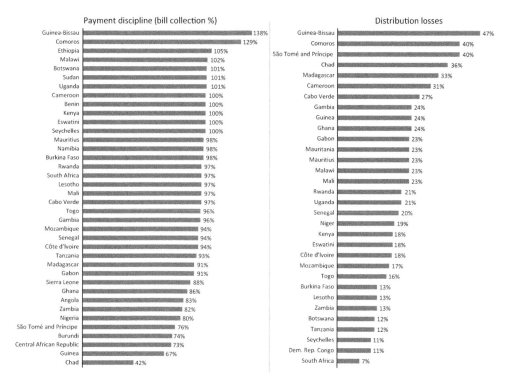

Note: The figure depicts average bill collection and average distribution losses at country level for 2012–18.

Source: World Bank staff.

Figure 22.14 Key performance indicators for utilities in Sub-Saharan Africa, 2012–18

of power utility management typically to a foreign operator for a period of two to three years in return for a management fee. However, in practice, even these relatively simple arrangements have been difficult, with some 30 per cent resulting in premature cancellation (Public–Private Infrastructure Advisory Facility [PPIAF] 2016). Challenges have included attracting and retaining suitable managerial talent as well as significant tensions with local staff over differential remuneration, skills transfer to local staff and control of the enterprise. Most critically, management contracts have often lacked the prior foundation of a clear performance improvement plan with associated targets and incentives, making it difficult to channel the efforts of contractors whose remuneration takes the form of a fixed service fee.

A handful of countries have adopted deeper forms of PSP in power distribution, including a long-term lease contract in Côte d'Ivoire, concessions in Cameroon and Uganda, as well as outright divestiture in Nigeria. The UMEME concession in Uganda illustrates the complexity of such arrangements. By the end of its first decade, UMEME had achieved 100 per cent revenue collection and halved the level of system losses from 34 to 17 per cent, and is one of the few utilities in Africa with full capital cost recovery. Nevertheless, these gains took some years to materialize as the concession was affected by drought conditions leading to contract renegotiation, and insufficient attention was

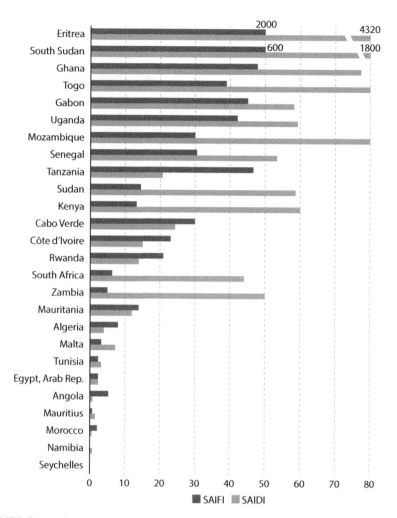

Note: SAIDI (System Average Interruption Duration Index) measures the average total duration of outages (hours/year) while SAIFI (System Average Interruption Frequency Index) measures the average frequency of outages (number/year).

Source: World Bank (2018c).

Figure 22.15   Quality of service in Africa, SAIDI and SAIFI, 2018

paid initially to the country's very low electrification rate. The repeated significant tariff hikes needed to meet full cost recovery, under contractual conditions that guaranteed a 20 per cent return on investment to the concessionaire, prompted public discontent and led to repeated parliamentary enquiries.

Concessions in Africa sometimes provoke suspicion of profiteering by the private investor, or of outright privatization, with the associated fears and accusations of ceding public control of essential assets to foreign firms. On occasion, this has led to the reversal or non-renewal of concession and private management contracts, as in the case of Senegal, which terminated the concession for SENELEC after only two years in 2001, or the case of SEEG in Gabon in 2018 (Reuters 2018). Overall, arrangements for PSP in power distribution in Africa have proved to be relatively risky, with cancellation rates exceeding 20 per cent (or about ten times higher than in other parts of the developing world). An alternative means of introducing private sector discipline into a majority publicly owned company is the one adopted in Kenya, where the national distribution utility, KPLC, floated a 49 per cent stake on the Nairobi stock exchange.

5. WHAT ARE THE IMPLICATIONS OF CURRENT TECHNOLOGICAL DISRUPTIONS FOR AFRICA'S POWER SECTOR?

A raft of new actors and technologies in the electricity playing field (explored in Chapters 12 and 13 of this handbook) are bringing unprecedented disruptions to African power sectors. These offer a hopeful, albeit daunting, outlook for the continent to meet its energy needs (Zinaman et al. 2015). Accelerated innovations in power technologies, services and markets, correlated with a sea change in the global energy mix, are upending relative prices and market shares, and the location and patterns of energy production and use (Carvallo et al. 2017). New capacity additions from increasingly economical variable renewable energy are being followed by similar trends in energy storage costs and technological innovation (BloombergNEF 2018). The geometric architecture of power grids in space will transform as countries integrate increasing quantities of variable renewable energy generation plants and mini-grid projects (Buljan 2018). Smart grids will emerge from a new landscape of traditional electricity networks interspersed with mini-grids, community grids and distributed individual generation systems (De Martini and Kristov 2015). These trends will unlock a need for new grid management approaches and rules, including for utility business models (Alstone et al. 2015). Traditional regulatory models also face new challenges in the rise of distributed energy resources, including mini-grids and off-grid electricity providers in under-electrified areas (Tenenbaum et al. 2014). These transformations are being swept along with increasing digitalization, the arrival of proactive, self-generating consumers (so-called prosumers), and the electrification of transport and electric vehicles (Jairaj et al. 2016).

Developing countries are experiencing the impacts of these innovations very differently from industrialized countries (ibid.). In industrialized countries, developed wholesale and retail power markets are struggling to adjust to growing shares of competitive renewable energy, witnessing zero or even negative pricing phenomena, while stranded power assets are becoming commonplace. Alternative utility models are emerging, causing incumbent service providers to fear a so-called utility death spiral, with declining sales and increased grid defections (Laws et al. 2017). But alongside generally low levels of electricity access and consumption, African countries for the most part lack the wholesale and retail power markets that exist in more developed systems. As a result, African countries will not experience the same power market challenges.

Recent technological disruptions ought not represent solely a source of apprehension for African countries. Many can take hold of opportunities presented by new and increasingly established technologies by 'leapfrogging' to alternative decentralized models according to their context. Along the way, they can circumvent the shortcomings of traditional utilities and wholesale markets. However, their small size also means their power systems are more susceptible to market disruptions, with the potential to rapidly change and be reshaped by innovative, disruptive technologies. These require us to draw several lessons or implications, which we briefly outline along the following dimensions: institutional implications relating to system governance and operating structure, technical implications relating to renewable integration, policy, financial and institutional implications for electrification planning and procurement, business implications for utilities, and deeper sectoral implications of decentralizing power system ownership and operation.

Larger African power systems are more likely to benefit from technological change once they create an ISO, which would untangle state-owned generation from the transmission and market operator. African ISOs are likely to remain under public ownership, given the strategic status of the power grid and electricity access issues in national development discourse and plans. But they will need to develop the capacity to respond to new markets and supply models, manage increasingly complex energy demand and production patterns, and engage in real-time power trade. System flexibility, reliability, strength and quality all require an operator to execute dispatch and plan grid extension, including for possible interconnections with decentralized systems and mini-grids. Restructuring system operations could also mitigate possible tensions between incumbent state-owned generators and the need to integrate new technologies and markets (for example, the need to run auctions for flexible and distributed resources, such as batteries, to complement cheap variable solar and wind energy technologies) (MIT Energy Initiative 2016). A system operator's role in planning, procurement, contracting and dispatch expands as new energy technologies take an increasing share of power markets. Well-designed and skilled ISOs can build channels for regional interconnections to achieve economies of scale and can manage contracts for new variable renewable energy alongside flexible balancing resources, forging a path to least-cost low-carbon networks.

Integrating variable renewable energy will be particularly challenging given the relatively small scale and fragmented topography of Africa's power grids. With typically small power systems, a relatively modest amount of investment in renewable energy can lead to a high share of variable generation on the grid. This compounds with often poor maintenance of grids and primitive SCADA systems, which may lack the technical capacity to manage variability (Mkhwanazi 2018). These stresses provoked by renewable energy generation can have significant implications for quality of supply in smaller power systems, where the construction of a single large solar farm can instantaneously boost the renewable energy share of electricity generation to double digits. For example, the Senegalese utility, SENELEC, conducted capacity building to prepare to respond to the technical challenges of adding variable renewable energy to a small existing power fleet, after government policy targeted an integration of 30 per cent renewable energy on the grid (Ba 2018, Gesellschaft für Internationale Zusammenarbeit [GIZ] 2014). In this sense, battery storage technologies, whether grid-located or coupled with variable renewable energy generation, will be particularly important in enabling the integration process in Africa, also due to the recent decline in cost (IRENA 2017). Storage technologies provide not only bulk energy services for integrating renewable energy through arbitrage, but also ancillary services such as spinning reserve, voltage support and regulation, as well as transmission and distribution infrastructure services.

The rapidly declining costs of off-grid electrification combined with the proliferation of new business models will have an even greater impact in Africa than other world regions, given the magnitude of its electrification challenge. The economic frontier between areas suited for grid electrification versus off-grid electrification is continually shifting in favour of the latter, as new decentralized technologies offer the promise of substantially accelerating the pace of electrification in the continent. In 2017 in Sub-Saharan Africa, over 10 million households (equivalent to 50 million people) already received electricity supply exclusively through privately owned distributed renewable generation systems (Power for All 2017). An explosion of new business models propose to develop SHS and mini-grids in remote regions at affordable costs. Such approaches combine affordable decentralized renewable energy technologies with battery storage systems, smart meters and efficient appliances. Remote parts of the continent will be able to access 24-hour supply, powered by small-scale renewable energy on a mini-grid. Mobile money linked with mobile telephony and pay-as-you-go contracts are now wide-spread, particularly in East Africa. These actors collaborate and sometimes compete with decentralized electrification operators. Industries and mines are also investing in their own mini-grids or self-generation with renewables, while residential energy communities are emerging, linked by embedded grids. Peer-to-peer electricity distribution and payment systems could use distributed ledgers or blockchain technology for accounting purposes, even between neighbours (John 2018).[13]

On the utility side, disruptive technology also poses an existential threat to conventional business models in Africa, no less than in other regions. Many African utilities provide unreliable electricity service at relatively high costs (inflated by rampant inefficiency and widespread cross-subsidies), which makes them more vulnerable to grid defection by non-residential and high-end residential customers turning to rooftop solar PV generation. Such customers account for the bulk of service revenues and their conversion to prosumers could further undermine weak sector finances. At the same time, technology offers opportunities for improving utility performance. Investing in advanced metering infrastructure and bill and data collection would allow African utilities to significantly reduce technical and non-technical losses to improve operational efficiency and shave peak demand. New low-cost mobile applications also offer utilities real-time data from customers, allowing a proliferation of electricity supply service companies to respond rapidly to clients' needs. Utilities and system designers have recognized a need to overhaul traditional business models to enable power supply companies to deal with these shifts (MIT Energy Initiative 2016).

Distributed generation resources offer African countries an opportunity to transition directly to decentralized systems, especially in contexts where centralized monopoly utilities remain under-capacitated, inefficient and unable to meet demand. Grid infrastructure remains essential in balancing and wheeling services for distributed generation. Some of the standard market reforms advanced in the context of dominant utilities may be redundant in such a context, which calls for new power market arrangements that can attract investment in difficult economic environments tailored to distributed energy resources. Full wholesale and retail power markets, the norm in OECD countries, could become superfluous, as services such as installation and maintenance of individual renewable energy systems or mini-grids can be ensured by a number of smaller electricity service companies. Telecom companies are also moving in this space to offer off-grid solar kits to mobile phone customers. These different actors playing new roles in the system offer an opportunity for African countries to embrace these technology, business, market and regulatory innovations, which offer the potential to accelerate to a more resilient and sustainable electricity future.

6.   CONCLUDING REMARKS

Africa remains a global outlier in terms of inadequate investment in power generating capacity and networks, low levels of electricity reliability, access and consumption, poor utility performance and incomplete regulatory and market reforms. But these relative disadvantages can also afford African countries greater agility to react to sweeping innovations bringing low-cost, disruptive energy technologies, services and markets spread across the globe. With vast needs and fast-growing power sectors, Africa has the potential to adopt and adapt these innovations with relatively lower sunk costs and fewer stranded assets. The right response can catalyse significant progress in delivering adequate, reliable and clean electricity to power economic growth and to improve the welfare of its populations.

NOTES

1. See http://esmap.org/rethinking_power_sector_reform, accessed March 2019.
2. The reader may refer in particular to Chapters 12, 13, 15 and 17.
3. Brazil's transmission lines extend over 137 000 km, compared to 112 000 km in Sub-Saharan Africa.
4. SAPP was the first true power pool founded in 1995, with 16 members representing 13 countries. WAPP followed in 2000 with 14 countries, EAPP with seven, and the proposed Central African Power Pool has ten. The COMELEC, or North African Power Pool, comprises five countries in North Africa.
5. CLSG: WAPP interconnector (Côte d'Ivoire–Liberia–Sierra Leone–Guinea) (https://www.transcoclsg. org/project-presentaton/, accessed 11 July 2021); NorthCore: 330 kV WAPP Project: Nigeria–Niger–Burkina Faso–Bénin (http://pipes.ecowapp.org/en/project/implementation/330-kv-wapp-northcore-interconnection-project-nigeria-niger-burkina-faso, accessed 11 July 2021). OMVG (Gambia River Basin Development Organisation): Gambia–Senegal; OMVS (Senegal River Basin Development Organisation): Guinea–Mali–Mauritania–Senegal.
6. The RISE Electricity Access score for each country considers: (1) the existence, monitoring and scope of officially approved electrification plans; (2) the existence of a framework for electrification through the grid, mini-grids and standalone systems; (3) the affordability of electricity; and (4) utility performance and governance.
7. For a wider sample of countries there is a slight correlation between tariffs and access (as tariffs increase access falls). Surprisingly for Sub-Saharan countries, this correlation reverses. However, not much should be read into this as current access would actually be impacted by tariffs in years past. Since we do not have panel data for tariffs, this analysis could not be carried out.
8. Based on 2017 data from ESMAP (2018).
9. Based on World Bank Private Participation in Infrastructure (PPI) database (2019).
10. Based on IEA data for 2016.
11. President Ramaphosa announced the intention to split Eskom into three entities in his State of the Nation Address in South Africa's Parliament on 7 February 2019.
12. Kenya Power and Lighting Company, also commonly referred to as KPLC. A separate company, KETRACO, houses new transmission investments.
13. Blockchain, an online communication protocol that eliminates intermediaries, allows companies or individuals to create an auditable encrypted ledger that can record energy consumption and credit histories. These secure ledgers can facilitate energy trading between households.

REFERENCES

Africa Intelligence (2019), 'GABON: Veolia's SEEG ejection: Libreville picks arbitrator at last', 15 January, accessed 11 July 2021 at https://www.africaintelligence.com/aem/consultants/2019/01/15/veolia-s-seeg-ejection-libreville-picks-arbitrator-at-last,108340285-bre.

African Development Bank (AfDB) (2018), *Electricity Regulatory Index for Africa 2018*, Abidjan: AfDB.

African Development Bank (AfDB) and Associations of Power Utilities of Africa (APUA) (2019), *Revisiting Reforms in the Power Sector in Africa: Report to African Development Bank*, accessed 11 July 2021 at https://africa-energy-portal.org/sites/default/files/2019-09/Revisiting%20Power%20Sector%20Reforms%20in%20Africa%20v03.pdf.

Alstone, P., D. Gershenson and D. M. Kammen (2015), 'Decentralized energy systems for clean electricity access', *Nature Climate Change*, **5** (4), 305–14.

Ba, A. S. (2018), 'The energy policy of the republic of Senegal – evaluation and perspectives', *HAL Papers*, accessed 11 July 2021 at https://hal.archives-ouvertes.fr/hal-01956187/document.

Bacon, R. (2018), 'Taking stock of the impact of power utility reform in developing countries: a literature review', *Policy Research Working Paper No. 8469*, World Bank, May.

Banerjee, S. G., F. A. Moreno and J. E. Sinton et al. (2017), *Regulatory Indicators for Sustainable Energy: A Global Scorecard for Policy Makers*, Washington, DC: World Bank, accessed 11 July 2021 at http://documents.worldbank.org/curated/en/538181487106403375/Regulatory-indicators-for-sustainable-energy-a-global-scorecard-for-policy-makers.

Besant-Jones, J. E. (2006), 'Reforming power markets in developing countries: what have we learned?', *Energy and Mining Board Discussion Paper No. 19*, World Bank, September.

Bhatia, M. and N. Angelou (2015), *Beyond Connections: Energy Access Redefined*, ESMAP Technical Report 008/15, Washington, DC: World Bank.

Blimpo, M. P. and M. Cosgrove-Davies (2019), *Electricity Access in Sub-Saharan Africa: Uptake, Reliability, and Complementary Factors for Economic Impact*, Washington, DC: World Bank.

BloombergNEF (2018), *New Energy Outlook 2018*.

Buljan, A. (2018), 'Offshore wind and meshed offshore grid(s) to benefit energy security in EU', *OffshoreWIND.biz*, 19 October, accessed 11 July 2021 at https://www.offshorewind.biz/2018/10/19/offshore-wind-and-meshed-offshore-grids-to-benefit-energy-security-in-eu/.

Carvallo, J.-P., B. J. Shaw, N. I. Avila and D. M. Kammen (2017), 'Sustainable low-carbon expansion for the power sector of an emerging economy: the case of Kenya', *Environmental Science & Technology*, **51** (17), 10232–42.

Castellano, A., A. Kendall, M. Nikomarov and T. Swemmer (2015), *Brighter Africa: The Growth Potential of the Sub-Saharan Electricity Sector*, McKinsey & Company, February.

Cervigni, R., R. Liden, J. Neumann and K. Strzepek (2015), *Enhancing the Climate Resilience of Africa's Infrastructure: The Power and Water Sectors*, Washington, DC: World Bank.

Communauté électrique du Bénin (CEB) (2019), 'Clients de la CEB'.

De Martini, P. and L. Kristov (2015), *Distribution Systems in a High Distributed Energy Resources Future: Planning, Market Design, Operation and Oversight*, Report No. 2: October, LBNL-100397, Future Electric Utility Regulation, Lawrence Berkeley National Laboratory.

Eberhard, A. and C. Godinho (2018), 'Decarbonization and power market reform in developing countries: the case of South Africa', *Oxford Energy Forum*, **114**, 54–7.

Eberhard, A. and K. Gratwick (2011), 'IPPs in Sub-Saharan Africa: determinants of success', *Energy Policy*, **39** (9), 5541–9.

Eberhard, A., K. Gratwick, E. Morella and P. Antmann (2016), *Independent Power Projects in Sub-Saharan Africa: Lessons from Five Key Countries (Directions in Development – Energy and Mining)*, Washington, DC: World Bank.

Eberhard, A., K. Gratwick, E. Morella and P. Antmann (2017), 'Independent Power Projects in Sub-Saharan Africa: Investment Trends and Policy Lessons', *Energy Policy*, **108**, September, pp. 390–424.

Eberhard, A., O. Rosnes, M. Shkaratan and H. Vennemo (2011), *Africa's Power Infrastructure: Investment, Integration, Efficiency (Directions in Development – Infrastructure)*, Washington, DC: World Bank.

Energies Media with Xinhua (2018), 'La Communauté électrique du Bénin sous administration provisoire dès le 1er janvier 2019', 30 November, accessed 11 July 2021 at https://energies-media.com/togo-benin-ceb-administration-provisoire-1-janv-2019.

Energy Sector Management Assistance Program (ESMAP) (2018), *Regulatory Indicators for Sustainable Energy*, Washington, DC: World Bank.

Energy Sector Management Assistance Program (ESMAP) (2020), 'RISE – Regulatory Indicators for Sustainable Energy', accessed https://rise.esmap.org/.

Farquharson, D. V., P. Jaramillo and C. Samaras (2018), 'Sustainability implications of electricity outages in Sub-Saharan Africa', *Nature Sustainability*, 1 (10), 589–97.

Foster, V. and A. Rana (2019), *Rethinking Power Sector Reform in the Developing World*, Washington, DC: World Bank.

Foster, V., E. Portale and D. Bedrosyan et al. (2018), *Policy Matters: Regulatory Indicators for Sustainable Energy*, Washington, DC: World Bank, accessed 11 July 2021 at http://documents.worldbank.org/curated/en/553071544206394642/Policy-Matters-Regulatory-Indicators-for-Sustainable-Energy.

Foster, V., S. Witte, S. G. Banerjee and A. Moreno (2017), 'Charting the diffusion of power sector reforms across the developing world', *Policy Research Working Paper No. 8235*, November, World Bank.

Gesellschaft für Internationale Zusammenarbeit (GIZ) (2014), *Analysis of System Stability in Developing and Emerging Countries*, accessed 11 July 2021 at https://energypedia.info/images/a/a5/BMZ_Format_V3_GIZ_2013_EN_Power_System_Stability_in_Senegal.pdf.

Global Transmission Report (2018), 'Update on Brazilian power sector: key highlights of 2017', 8 January, accessed 11 July 2021 at https://www.globaltransmission.info/archive.php?id=32000.

Godinho, C. and A. Eberhard (2018), 'Power sector reform and regulation in Tanzania', in *Tanzania Institutional Diagnostic*, Economic Development & Institutions, Oxford Policy Management Ltd/Department for International Development.

Gore, C. D., J. N. Brass, E. Baldwin and L. M. MacLean (2019), 'Political autonomy and resistance in electricity sector liberalization in Africa', *World Development*, 120, 193–209.

Imam, M. I., M. Llorca and T. Jamasb (2018), 'Power sector reform and corruption: evidence from Sub-Saharan Africa', *EPRG Cambridge Economics Working Paper 1801*, Energy Research Policy Group, University of Cambridge.

International Energy Agency (IEA) (2016), *Boosting the Power Sector in Sub-Saharan Africa: China's Involvement*, Paris: IEA.

International Energy Agency (IEA) (2018), *World Energy Outlook 2018*, Paris: IEA.

International Energy Agency (IEA) (2019), *Africa Energy Outlook 2019: World Energy Outlook Special Report*, accessed 11 July 2021 at https://www.iea.org/reports/africa-energy-outlook-2019.

International Energy Agency (IEA), International Renewable Energy Agency (IRENA), UN, World Bank Group and World Health Organization (WHO) (2018), *Tracking SDG7: The Energy Progress Report 2018*, Washington, DC: World Bank.

International Renewable Energy Agency (IRENA) (2017), *Electricity Storage and Renewables: Costs and Markets to 2030*, Abu Dhabi: IRENA.

International Renewable Energy Agency (IRENA) (2018), 'Off-grid renewable energy solutions: global and regional status and trends', July, IRENA brief.

International Renewable Energy Agency (IRENA) and Clean Energy Ministerial (CEM) (2014), *The Socio-Economic Benefits of Large-Scale Solar and Wind: An EconValue Report*, May.

Jairaj, B., S. Martin and J. Ryor et al. (2016), *The Future Electricity Grid: Key Questions and Considerations for Developing Countries*, Washington, DC: World Resources Institute.

John, N. (2018), 'Blockchain can revolutionise the energy industry in Africa', World Economic Forum, 29 November, accessed 11 July 2021 at https://www.weforum.org/agenda/2018/11/blockchain-will-change-the-face-of-renewable-energy-in-africa-here-s-how.

Kapika, J. and A. Eberhard (2013), *Power-Sector Reform and Regulation in Africa: Lessons from Kenya, Tanzania, Uganda, Zambia, Namibia and Ghana*, Cape Town: Human Sciences Research Council Press.

Khandker, S. R., D. F. Barnes and H. A. Samad (2012), 'The welfare impacts of rural electrification in Bangladesh', *The Energy Journal*, 33 (1), 187–206.

Khandker, S. R., D. F. Barnes and H. A. Samad (2013), 'Welfare impacts of rural electrification: a panel data analysis from Vietnam', *Economic Development and Cultural Change*, 61 (3), 659–92.

Khandker, S. R., D. F. Barnes, H. A. Samad and N. H. Minh (2009), 'Welfare impacts of rural electrification: evidence from Vietnam', *Policy Research Working Paper No. 5057*, September, World Bank.

Kojima, M. and C. Trimble (2016), *Making Power Affordable for Africa and Viable for Its Utilities*, Washington, DC: World Bank.

Kojima, M., X. Zhou and, J. J. Han et al. (2016), 'Who uses electricity in Sub-Saharan Africa? Findings from household surveys', *Policy Research Working Paper No. 7889*, August, World Bank.

Koo, B. B., D. Rynsakova and E. Portale et al. (2018), *Rwanda – Beyond Connections: Energy Access Diagnostic Report Based on the Multi-Tier Framework*, Washington, DC: World Bank.

Kruger, W., A. Eberhard and K. Swartz (2018), *Renewable Energy Auctions: A Global Overview*, Report 1: Energy and Economic Growth Research Programme (W01 and W05), PO Number: PO00022908, accessed 11 July 2021 at http://www.gsb.uct.ac.za/files/EEG_GlobalAuctionsReport.pdf.

Kruger, W., S. Stritzke and P. A. Trotter (2019), 'De-risking solar auctions in Sub-Saharan Africa – a comparison of site selection strategies in South Africa and Zambia', *Renewable and Sustainable Energy Reviews*, 104, 429–38.

Laws, N. D., B. P. Epps and S. O. Peterson et al. (2017), 'On the utility death spiral and the impact of utility rate structures on the adoption of residential solar photovoltaics and energy storage', *Applied Energy*, **185**, 627–41.

Lee, J. T. and D. S. Callaway (2018), 'The cost of reliability in decentralized solar power systems in Sub-Saharan Africa', *Nature Energy*, **3** (11), 960–68.

Lee, K., E. Miguel and C. Wolfram (2020), 'Experimental evidence on the economics of rural electrification', *Journal of Political Economy*, **128** (4), 1523–65.

Malgas, I. and A. Eberhard (2011), 'Hybrid power markets in Africa: generation planning, procurement and contracting challenges', *Energy Policy*, **39** (6), 3191–8.

MIT Energy Initiative (MIT) (2016), *Utility of the Future*, Cambridge, MA: MIT.

Mkhwanazi, M. (2018), 'Utility automation and control – it's not your daddy's SCADA', *ESI Africa*, 5 March, accessed 11 July 2021 at www.esi-africa.com/industry-sectors/business-and-markets/utility-automation-control-not-daddys-scada.

Multiconsult (2018), *Roadmap to the New Deal on Energy for Africa: An analysis of Optimal Expansion and Investment Requirements*, report to the AfDB, June, accessed 11 July 2021 at https://africa-energy-portal.org/sites/default/files/2018-10/lu313516crr2.pdf.

Odarno, L., E. Sawe and M. Swai et al. (2017), *Accelerating Mini-grid Deployment in Sub-Saharan Africa: Lessons from Tanzania*, Washington, DC: World Resources Institute.

Olingo, A. (2018a), 'Boost for East Africa Power Pool project as Dar, Nairobi Secure $600m', *The East African*, 2 July, accessed 11 July 2021 at www.theeastafrican.co.ke/business/Boost-for-East-Africa-power-pool-project/2560-4642124-tgp4b6/index.html.

Olingo, A. (2018b), 'Phase One of regional power pool project set for completion by mid-2019', *The East African*, 6 August, accessed 11 July 2021 at www.theeastafrican.co.ke/business/Phase-One-of-regional-power-pool-project-set-for-completion/2560-4699790-g706gj/index.html.

Olmos, L. and I. J. Pérez-Arriaga (2013), 'Regional markets', in I. J. Pérez-Arriaga (ed.), *Regulation of the Power Sector*, London: Springer, pp. 501–38.

Organisation for Economic Co-operation and Development (OECD) (2015), *Overcoming Barriers to International Investment in Clean Energy, Green Finance and Investment*, Paris: OECD Publishing.

Organisation for Economic Co-operation and Development and International Energy Agency (OECD/IEA) (2014), 'Electric power consumption (kWh per capita)', accessed 11 July 2021 at https://data.worldbank.org/indicator/EG.USE.ELEC.KH.PC.

Oseni, M. O. and M. G. Pollitt (2014), 'Institutional arrangements for the promotion of regional integration of electricity markets: international experience', *Policy Research Working Paper No. 6947*, World Bank, June.

Padam, G., D. Rysankova and E. Portale et al. (2018), *Ethiopia – Beyond Connections: Energy Access Diagnostic Report Based on the Multi-Tier Framework*, Washington, DC: World Bank.

Power for All (2017), *Decentralized Renewables: From Promise to Progress*, March, accessed 11 July 2021 at https://www.powerforall.org/resources/reports/decentralized-renewables-promise-progress.

Programme for Infrastructure Development in Africa (PIDA) (2010), *Interconnecting, Integrating and Transforming a Continent*, accessed 11 July 2021 at https://www.afdb.org/fileadmin/uploads/afdb/Documents/Project-and-Operations/PIDA note English for web 0208.pdf.

Public–Private Infrastructure Advisory Facility (PPIAF) (2016), 'PPIAF Database – Multi-Donor Technical Assistance Facility', accessed 11 July 2021 at https://ppiaf.org/.

Reuters (2018), 'Gabon accuses France's Veolia of polluting amid concession dispute', 27 February, accessed 11 July 2021 at www.reuters.com/article/us-gabon-veolia-environ/gabon-accuses-frances-veolia-of-polluting-amid-concession-dispute-idUSKCN1GB2OO.

Rittel, H. W. J. and M. M. Webber (1973), 'Dilemmas in a general theory of planning', *Policy Sciences*, **4** (2), 155–69.

Rodríguez Pardina, M. and J. Schiro (2018), 'Taking stock of economic regulation of power utilities in the developing world: a literature review', *Policy Research Working Paper No. 8461*, World Bank, May.

Rose, A., I. Pérez-Arriaga, R. Stoner and R. de Neufville (2019), 'Harnessing Africa's energy resources through regional infrastructure projects', in N. Gil, A. Strafford and I. Musonda (eds), *Duality by Design – The Global Race to Build Africa's Infrastructure*, Cambridge, UK: Cambridge University Press.

Rudnick, H. and C. Velasquez (2018), 'Taking stock of wholesale power markets in developing countries: a literature review', *Policy Research Working Paper No. 8519*, World Bank, July.

Southern Africa Power Pool (SAPP) (2019), *Annual Report: Accelerating Development of Energy Projects to Optimise Electricity Trading*.

Streatfeild, J. (2018), 'Low electricity supply in SSA: causes, implications, and potential remedies', *Journal of International Commerce and Economics*, June 2018, accessed 11 July 2021 at https://www.usitc.gov/publications/332/journals/low_electricity_supply_in_ssa_final.pdf.

Tenenbaum, B., C. Greacen, T. Siyambalapitiya and J. Knuckles (2014), *From the Bottom Up: How Small Power Producers and Mini-Grids Can Deliver Electrification and Renewable Energy in Africa (Directions in Development – Energy and Mining)*, Washington, DC: World Bank.

Trimble, C., M. Kojima, I. Perez-Arroyo and F. Mohammadzadeh (2016), 'Financial viability of electricity sectors in Sub-Saharan Africa: quasi-fiscal deficits and hidden costs', *Policy Research Working Paper No. 7788*, World Bank, August.

United States Agency for International Development (USAID) and Power Africa (2018), *Power Africa Transmission Roadmap – A Practical Approach to Unlock Electricity Trade*, Washington, DC: Power Africa/ USAID, November, accessed 11 July 2021 at https://www.usaid.gov/sites/default/files/documents/1860/PA_ Transmission_Roadmap_508.pdf.

Urpelainen, J. and J. Yang (2019), 'Global patterns of power sector reform, 1982–2013', *Energy Strategy Reviews*, **23**, 152–62.

Vernet, A., J. N. O. Khayesi and V. George et al. (2019), 'How does energy matter? Rural electrification, entrepreneurship, and community development in Kenya', *Energy Policy*, **126** (March), 88–98.

World Bank (2018a), 'GDP growth (annual %)', accessed 11 July 2021 at https://data.worldbank.org/indicator/ NY.GDP.MKTP.KD.ZG.

World Bank (2018b), 'Population, total', accessed at https://data.worldbank.org/indicator/SP.POP.TOTL.

World Bank (2018c), *Doing Business 2018 – Reforming to Create Jobs*, Washington, DC: World Bank.

World Bank Group (2017), *Linking Up: Public–Private Partnerships in Power Transmission in Africa*, Washington, DC: World Bank.

World Bank and Sustainable Energy for All (2019), 'Access to electricity (% of population)', SE4ALL Global Tracking Framework, accessed 11 July 2021 at https://data.worldbank.org/indicator/EG.ELC.ACCS.ZS.

Zinaman, O., M. Miller and A. Adil et al. (2015), *Power Systems of the Future – A 21st Century Power Partnership Thought Leadership Report*, Technical Report NREL/TP-6A20-62611, National Renewable Energy Laboratory, February, accessed 11 July 2021 at https://www.nrel.gov/docs/fy15osti/62611.pdf.

Index

Printed and bound by CPI Group (UK) Ltd, Croydon, CR0 4YY

16/04/2025

14658390-0005